Customers in the UK, Europe & Rest of World

Tests, Scales and Questionnaires Online

The Practitioner's Guide to Measuring Outcomes after Acquired Brain Impairment

The majority of the tests, scales and questionnaires in this book are available online. Visit **www.compendium-of-scales.com/contents.htm** to see which tests, scales and questionnaires are available online.

For a one-off payment of $150 (plus local sales tax), you can gain online access to the majority of tests, scales and questionnaires featured in the book as downloadable PDFs on a password-protected website. To order, please tear out and fill in this voucher and return it to us at the address below. Please send the original voucher; photocopies are not valid.

This subscription will be valid for the lifetime of the book, and at least until January 1st 2015. Psychology Press cannot guarantee the availability of *Tests, Scales and Questionnaires Online* indefinitely.

Customer Details

Please give me access to *Tests, Scales and Questionnaires Online: The Practitioner's Guide to Measuring Outcomes after Acquired Brain Impairment*, 978-1-84872-060-2.

Name

Institution

Address

City

County Postal Code

Country

Email

Phone

Fax

Method of Payment

Tests, Scales and Questionnaires Online: The Practitioner's Guide to Measuring Outcomes after Acquired Brain Impairment, 978-1-84872-060-2: £100.00+VAT

☐ Please invoice me for £

☐ I enclose a chequе for £

UK/Europe/Rest of World customers: cheques should be drawn on a UK bank and should be made payable to **Taylor & Francis Informa Ltd.**

☐ Please charge my credit/debit card (delete as appropriate) with £

Card type ☐ VISA ☐ MasterCard ☐ AMERICAN EXPRESS ☐ Maestro

Card number

Expiration Date

Start Date

Issue No.

3-Digit Security Code

Signature

Date

Credit Card Address (if different from above)

Customers in the EU: VAT Registration Number

Please return your order to Julie Norton, Psychology Press, 27 Church Road, Hove, BN3 2FA, UK.
Email: customer.services.psychology@psypress.co.uk. Tel: +44 (0) 207 017 7747. Fax: +44 (0) 207 017 6717.

☐ Please tick here if you do not wish to join the Psychology Press mailing list. ☐ Please tick here if you do not wish to receive special offers and updates by email.

Customers in the USA & Canada

Tests, Scales and Questionnaires Online

The Practitioner's Guide to Measuring Outcomes after Acquired Brain Impairment

The majority of the tests, scales and questionnaires in this book are available online. Visit **www.compendium-of-scales.com/contents.htm** to see which tests, scales and questionnaires are available online.

For a one-off payment of $150 (plus local sales tax), you can gain online access to the majority of tests, scales and questionnaires featured in the book as downloadable PDFs on a password-protected website. To order, please tear out and fill in this voucher and return it to us at the address below. Please send the original voucher; photocopies are not valid.

This subscription will be valid for the lifetime of the book, and at least until January 1st 2015. Psychology Press cannot guarantee the availability of *Tests, Scales and Questionnaires Online* indefinitely.

Customer Details

Please give me access to *Tests, Scales and Questionnaires Online: The Practitioner's Guide to Measuring Outcomes after Acquired Brain Impairment*, 978-1-84872-060-2.

Name

Institution

Address

City

State/Province Zip Code

Country

Email

Phone

Fax

Method of Payment

Tests, Scales and Questionnaires Online: The Practitioner's Guide to Measuring Outcomes after Acquired Brain Impairment, 978-1-84872-060-2: $150.00

Residents of AZ, CA, CO, CT, FL, GA, KY, MA, MD, MO, NJ, NY, PA, TN, TX and VA please add local sales tax. Canadian residents please add 6% GST.

Total payable: $

☐ Please invoice me for $

☐ I enclose a check/money order for $

US/Canada customers: checks and money orders should be in US dollars and should be made out to Taylor & Francis.

☐ Please charge my credit/debit card (delete as appropriate) with $

Card type ☐ VISA ☐ MasterCard ☐ AMERICAN EXPRESS

Card number

Expiration Date

Start Date

Issue No.

3-Digit Security Code

Signature

Date

Credit Card Address (if different from above)

Please return your order to Kevin Williams, Psychology Press, 270 Madison Ave 4th Fl, New York NY 10016.

☐ Please tick here if you do not wish to join the Psychology Press mailing list. ☐ Please tick here if you do not wish to receive special offers and updates by email.

A Compendium of Tests, Scales and Questionnaires

This Compendium is a comprehensive reference manual containing an extensive selection of instruments developed to measure signs and symptoms commonly encountered in neurological conditions, both progressive and non-progressive. It provides a repository of established instruments, as well as newly developed scales, and covers all aspects of the functional consequences of acquired brain impairment.

In particular, the text provides a detailed review of approximately 150 specialist instruments for the assessment of people with neurological conditions such as dementia, multiple sclerosis, stroke and traumatic brain injury. Part A presents scales examining body functions, including consciousness and orientation; general and specific cognitive functions; regulation of behaviour, thought, and emotion; and motor-sensory functions. Part B reviews scales of daily living activities and community participation. Part C focuses on contextual factors, specifically environmental issues, and Part D contains multidimensional and quality of life instruments.

Each instrument is described as a stand-alone report using a uniform format. A brief history of the instrument's development is provided, along with a description of item content and administration/scoring procedures. Psychometric properties are reviewed and a critical commentary is provided. Key references are cited and in most cases the actual scale is included, giving the reader easy access to the instrument. The structure of the book directly maps onto the taxonomy of the influential *International Classification of Functioning, Disability and Health* (World Health Organization, 2001), enabling linkage of clinical concepts across health conditions.

The Compendium will be a valuable reference for clinicians, researchers, educators, and graduate students, and a practical resource for those involved in the assessment of people with brain impairment.

Dr Robyn Tate is a clinical psychologist and neuropsychologist with more than 30 years of clinical and research experience. Her primary field of expertise is traumatic brain injury. She is currently Professor in the Rehabilitation Studies Unit, Sydney Medical School, University of Sydney, Australia where, in addition to her own clinical and research work, she is involved in the teaching and research supervision of post-graduate medical and psychology students.

A Compendium of Tests, Scales and Questionnaires

The Practitioner's Guide to Measuring Outcomes after Acquired Brain Impairment

Robyn L. Tate

with contribution by
Ian D. Cameron

HOVE AND NEW YORK

First published 2010
by Psychology Press
27 Church Road, Hove, East Sussex BN3 2FA

Simultaneously published in the USA and Canada
by Psychology Press
711 Third Avenue, New York NY 10017

Reprinted 2011

Psychology Press is an imprint of the Taylor & Francis Group, an Informa business

Typeset in Times by RefineCatch Ltd, Bungay, Suffolk
Printed and bound in Great Britain by TJ International Ltd, Padstow, Cornwall
Cover design by Andy Ward

British Library Cataloguing in Publication Data
A catalogue record for this book is available from the British Library

Library of Congress Cataloging-in-Publication Data
Tate, Robyn L.
A compendium of tests, scales, and questionnaires : the practitioner's guide to measuring outcomes after acquired brain impairment / Robyn L. Tate.
p. ; cm.
Includes bibliographical references and indexes.
ISBN 978–1–84169–561–7 (hardcover)
1. Neuropsychological tests. I. Title.
[DNLM: 1. Brain Diseases—diagnosis. 2. Neuropsychological Tests. WL 141 T217c 2010]
RC386.6.N48T38 2010
616.8'0475—dc22 2009011393

ISBN 978-1-84169-561-7

To my father, Kevin Roy Tate (1925–2001) and
my husband, Michael Perdices with gratitude

Contents

Figures

Tables

Foreword

This invaluable compendium fills in what has been a serious gap between clinicians' and clinical researchers' need to know screening tests and rating scales and their ready access to this information. The inspiration and the exceptionally useful contents of the book come from Dr Tate's own clinical and research work with patients whose bad luck, bad genes, or bad judgment left them with mental, behavioral, and/or physical impairments that need to be fixed or at least evaluated. This book reflects her wide-range, close and intensive clinical and research experiences and the knowledge she has gained about these patients and their needs.

Most of us working with patients whose impairments have limited their activities, their abilities or their enjoyment of life have wished we knew where to find the appropriate instruments to document these problems, follow a patient's course, plan appropriate treatment, or explain to patient and family just what the patient can and cannot do, what may help or hinder the patient's progress. Dr Tate has realized our wish in this most comprehensive, well-detailed, and thoughtfully evaluated compendium. The immediate availability of these scales and screening tests, questionnaires and inventories, will help practitioners develop and communicate the multidimensional understanding of their patients that best practices – whether clinical or for research purposes – require.

Although Dr Tate's work has been primarily in rehabilitation settings and, most specifically, with neurobehaviorally impaired patients, this compilation of behavioral, physical, and social measures will serve workers in all clinical sciences. Many of the sections of *A Compendium of Tests, Scales and Questionnaires* also have much more general applicability to every area of clinical practice and research. For example, geriatricians should find scales and inventories that are useful for monitoring their patients in Part B: Activities and Participation, which present information about "Scales assessing activities of daily living" (Chapter 7) and "Scales assessing participation and social role" (Chapter 8). And, regardless of the nature of their patients' infirmities, physical and occupational therapists will be able to make good use of the chapter written by Dr Ian Cameron, "Scales of sensory, ingestion and motor functions," which can be applicable to both their patients and their research.

Thank you, Dr Tate, for gathering and publishing for us what we've all needed and never got around to doing for ourselves.

Muriel Deutsch Lezak
Oregon Health Sciences University and
Veterans Administration Hospital
Portland, Oregon, USA

Preface

In one way or another, throughout my entire career I have grappled with the advantages and limitations of instruments to assess people with acquired brain impairment. When I began working as a clinical psychologist in the 1970s there was a relative dearth of assessment instruments suitable for various applications for people with acquired brain impairment. My initial appointment coincided with publication of the first edition of Muriel Lezak's *Neuropsychological Assessment* (now in its 4th edition), but unfortunately I did not learn about this invaluable resource until later. At the time, the assessment instruments at my disposal seemed insufficient to shed much light on the type of ecological prognostic questions I was expected to answer about the patients on the neurology, geriatric and rehabilitation wards of Lidcombe Hospital in Sydney. In order to achieve greater veridicality in my cognitive evaluations, I therefore developed my own comprehensive screening test, fondly referred to by my colleagues at that time as the TMFT (Tate Mental Function Test). I abandoned work on the TMFT when I discovered both Muriel Lezak's *Neuropsychological Assessment* and Kevin Walsh of Melbourne University, who kindly sent me a prepublication copy of his *Neuropsychology. A Clinical Approach*. In later years I continued revisiting instrument development to address what I saw as gaps in methods to examine psychosocial reintegration after traumatic brain injury, and to measure the even more nebulous construct of care and support needs.

In the 1970s, then, suitable instruments to assess the variety of domains of functioning pertinent to people with acquired brain impairment were limited in number, scope and relevance. Decades later the situation is at the other end of the spectrum, with the result that the clinician and researcher can be overwhelmed by the sheer volume of available tools. Such a quantum demands a comprehensive guide for the reader in the selection of the best instrument for the task at hand. The present work had its origins in a survey of the literature to identify assessment instruments to measure disability after traumatic brain injury, conducted for the Motor Accidents Authority of New South Wales by myself and Ian Cameron, assisted by Cheryl Soo. That nascent work was broadened in depth, scope and complexity for the present volume, and additionally included other neurological conditions apart from traumatic brain injury, as well as other areas of functioning apart from activity limitations.

The driving aim of this compendium has been to bring order to an increasingly diverse and complex field and to synthesize an accumulating body of knowledge so that the reader has an easy, one-step reference point for selecting and evaluating both established and newly developed screening tests, rating scales and questionnaires. A broad selection of approximately 150 instruments and their derivatives is included, which together provide a comprehensive overview of the functional consequences of all aspects of acquired brain impairment: consciousness, cognition, behaviour, motor-sensory functions, activities of daily living, social functioning and environmental factors. Additional features include a description of the instrument that is written as a stand-alone report. Each entry includes a brief history of the development of the instrument, item description, administration and scoring procedures, psychometric properties, a critical commentary and key references. Appendices are provided to enable the reader to make quick comparisons among the content of scales of activity and participation from both conceptual and clinical perspectives.

In collecting and collating the candidate measures, the objective has been to produce a compendium of assessment instruments that spans the gamut of functioning, ranging from specific disorders of consciousness and cognition through to broad constructs of community participation. The structure of the book directly maps onto the taxonomy of the influential *International Classification of Functioning Disability and Health* (ICF), which updates and revises the older nomenclature of impairments, disabilities and handicaps. Accordingly, instruments are classified in four sections corresponding to Body Functions (formerly impairments; 5 chapters), Activities/Participation (formerly disabilities and handicaps; 2 chapters), and Contextual Factors (1 chapter). A final chapter contains multidimensional and quality of life scales that do not neatly fall within the above boundaries.

This book is written for health professionals who work with people with acquired brain impairment and is intended for clinicians, researchers, educators and advanced student trainees from a range of fields including medicine, psychology and the rehabilitation professions. The instruments included are those that are suitable for administration by generic health professionals, and tests that require special equipment or specialist training are excluded.

It goes without saying that no single volume can meet all needs and suit all purposes. In particular, publishing a book on cognitive screening tests and rating scales is not tantamount to recommending their use over detailed neuropsychological or other evaluations. With few exceptions, while the developers of all the cognitive screening tests which I reviewed for this book emphasized the limitations of such instruments for diagnostic and rehabilitation planning purposes, they agreed with me that there is a place for cognitive screening tests in acquired brain impairment, arguments that are dealt with in Chapters 1 and 3. Moreover, the present volume is best regarded as a resource, rather than a test manual. Even though the scales featured in this book are cognitive screening tests and rating scales, they vary greatly in complexity of administration and scoring procedures. For the more involved instruments, the reader will need to consult the specific test manual or original publication.

One major problem that presented itself was that of selection. Many hundreds of instruments were reviewed and considered for inclusion, and it was necessary to make decisions regarding selection of one particular instrument over another. Such decisions were not made easily and a set of criteria was established for instrument selection (see Chapter 1). Unfortunately, a number of measures with sound clinical application and good psychometric properties had to be omitted in the interests of space. An additional guiding principle for inclusion was to provide a broad array of the state of play, rather than an exhaustive coverage of a narrow field. Similarly, space dictated a word limit for each of the instruments described, and the reader is advised that this volume is intended to provide the salient psychometric properties of the instruments, rather than a detailed review of every published study. Although care was taken to identify pertinent psychometric literature, some relevant references may have been missed. The intent of including information on the psychometric properties is to enable the reader to appreciate the calibre of the scale and its suitability for various applications. Wherever possible and practical the actual scale has been included.

In reviewing instruments for this compendium, I have been acutely aware of my responsibilities to the authors whose work I am critiquing. I have endeavoured to provide a fair, balanced and informative evaluation of instruments included in the book and trust I have done justice to the authors' work. Having been at the coalface of instrument development myself, I understand only too well the time and effort that go into producing a good measure. I have learnt an immeasurable amount from my detailed study of the work of other investigators during the preparation of this book, and I am full of admiration for the expertise of many researchers whose measures I am privileged to include in this volume.

This compendium has benefited from the input of many people at various stages of its development. A multidisciplinary group of expert clinicians and clinical researchers initially gave feedback on the proposed structure of the book and the format of the entries on specific scales, and I thank Adeline Hodgkinson, Annie McCluskey, Anne Moseley, Grahame Simpson, Barbara Strettles, Leanne Togher and Mary-Clare Waugh for their suggestions. It seemed that an important and innovative angle would be to classify and unify the instruments within the conceptual framework of the ICF. A good idea – but many challenges were confronted in applying the ICF to the area of acquired brain impairment. In this daunting endeavour, helpful discussions were held with Ian Cameron, and I received advice from Ros Madden and Catherine Sykes from the

Australian Institute of Health and Welfare, Canberra, Australia, and from Alarcos Cieza from the ICF Research branch of the WHO Collaborating Center at Ludwig-Maximilian University, Munich, Germany. It was clear that if the book were to provide the breadth of evaluation relevant for people with acquired brain impairment vis-à-vis the ICF, then a necessary inclusion would be instruments to measure sensory and motor functions. Chapter 6, written by Ian Cameron, provides an essential balance to the remainder of the compendium.

When some of the entries on instruments were at draft stage, a group of graduate neuropsychology students from Macquarie University in Sydney provided helpful responses, which then guided a revised format of the entries to increase their relevance for an advanced student readership. Colleagues have provided valued feedback on pertinent chapters and special thanks are due to Ian Cameron (Chapters 1, 2, 3 and 7), Catherine Skyes (Chapter 1), Grahame Simpson (Chapter 5), Lisa Harvey and Cheryl Soo (Chapter 6), and Jennifer Fleming (Chapter 7). Ian Cameron and Grahame Simpson reviewed various additional entries on individual instruments as well. Particular thanks are due to Michael Perdices, who made a detailed and meticulous review of 9 of the 10 chapters of the book (Chapters 1–5 and 7–10), thereby also providing a comparative evaluation of the compendium as a whole. Additionally, Michael used his creativity and computer expertise to construct the wonderful "ICF trees" that appear throughout the volume.

The support and encouragement from my workplace and colleagues at the Rehabilitation Studies Unit were fundamental to the completion of this work and are appreciated. I acknowledge with gratitude the library resources of the University of Sydney and the Royal Rehabilitation Centre Sydney, as well as the invaluable help of Judith Allen and Michelle Lee. Research and administrative assistance was gratefully received at various stages over the years from James Banks, Lara Leibbrandt and Danielle Debono, along with voluntary work from Hanna Brackenreg and Shruti Venkayesh. Special thanks are due to Michelle Genders for research and administrative support over the past 18 months; her professionalism and good humour made the final stages of this book so much easier for me.

I am especially grateful to those authors and their publishers who gave permission to include their instruments, which serves to increase the usefulness of the compendium. The scales compiled in this book have been drawn from a variety of sources including scientific journals, websites and personal communication with authors. In some instances the instrument, as originally presented in a journal, was suitable for direct administration; but in other cases information was limited to item content listed in a table or appendix, or embedded in the text. This necessitated a reformatting of many scales in order that they could be readily administered, as well as providing consistency of presentation across the book. In all cases where instruments have been reformatted from the original presentation, I have endeavoured to retain the spirit of the scale. Extensive efforts were made to trace the original source of the material and obtain permission for its use from copyright holders, and if omissions have occurred the author and publisher would be pleased to receive information in order to make corrections for future editions. I also acknowledge the support of my publishers, Psychology Press, especially Rebekah Edmondson and Michael Forster; along with consultant Sharon Rubin who assisted in the permissions process. It has been a pleasure to work with the production team at Psychology Press under the expert direction of Dawn Harris, Senior Production Editor.

During the course of writing this book, I have been most fortunate in having had a supportive and steadfast band of family, friends, colleagues and graduate students, too numerous to name individually but who have cheered me along from the sidelines. The cheerleader has been my husband who, by every thought and deed, has ensured that I reached the finish line (alive and in reasonable shape). Thank you, Michael; thank you, all.

RLT
Sydney, Australia
March, 2010

1 Introduction

Assessment after acquired brain impairment (ABI) or any other health condition is conducted for at least three main reasons: diagnosis, prognosis and evaluation (Dekker, Dallmeijer, & Lankhorst, 2005; Kirshner & Guyatt, 1985). This compendium provides a resource of assessment instruments for these purposes and the measures are described in the following nine chapters. The present introductory chapter contains three sections. First, a background to the book is provided, including the methodology used in the selection and description of the instruments. The second section describes the *International Classification of Functioning, Disability and Health* (ICF; WHO, 2001), which is the conceptual framework underlying the structure and organization of the compendium. Challenges that were encountered in placing instruments developed for ABI into the ICF framework are addressed in the final section of the chapter. The following nine chapters are grouped into four parts, which correspond in an approximate way to components of the ICF: Part A – Body Functions; Part B – Activities and Participation; Part C – Contextual Factors, specifically Environmental Factors; and Part D presents multidimensional scales – that is, instruments containing a disparate set of items crossing multiple ICF components and domains.

Background and methodology

Purpose

This compendium is intended primarily for health professionals who work with people experiencing (or at risk of) ABI. Users will include clinical practitioners in diagnostic, rehabilitation and community settings, as well as clinical researchers, educators and advanced student trainees. The main objective is to present a range of tests, scales and questionnaires suitable for administration by generic health professionals, as well as by specialists including clinical and neuropsychologists, medical practitioners, nurses, occupational therapists, physiotherapists, speech pathologists, and social workers. There is a vast array of such measures, and the observations made in 1969 by Lawton and Brody, whose instrumental activities of daily living scale continues to be widely used today, still apply: "The present state of the trade seems to be one in which each investigator or practitioner feels an inner compulsion to make his own scale and to cry that other existent scales cannot possibly fit his own setting" (p. 179). Indeed, recent years have seen an explosion of published tests, scales and questionnaires. More than one quarter of the instruments included in this compendium were published in the last 10 years.

Good assessment is fundamental to evidence-based clinical practice. The advantage of using standardized assessment instruments is that they provide a systematic and often objective means of evaluating level of functioning. This may be an end in itself, as in differential diagnosis, or it may provide a baseline against which future change (either improvement or deterioration) can be measured. Sometimes the need will be for prediction of the natural history and course of the condition; other times the baseline will be used to measure the effect of a therapeutic intervention. Prigatano and Pliskin (2003) and others observed that there is an increasing pressure to justify services – the best measures will yield the most valid results. Additionally, results from assessments can be used in clinical practice to describe levels of functioning from various perspectives, identify areas of need, ascertain the differential contribution of a range of factors, inform treatment planning and decisions, help people to make practical decisions, and educate families and people with ABI as well as other professionals.

As shown in the ICF model in the next section, a person's level of functioning can be assessed from a variety of perspectives (e.g., body system, functional activities, social role and participation, environmental milieu), and in turn, level of functioning is a consequence of interaction among such factors. The assessment instruments presented in this volume examine functioning from each of these various perspectives, and best practice suggests that comprehensive evaluation of an individual requires evaluation of each domain. Hall (1992) and Wade (2003) proffer a series of questions that clinicians and researchers can pose to refine the process of selecting measures. Even so, they still can be placed in the situation of not knowing what measures are available. Moreover, Jette and Haley (2005) point to the tension between the need for comprehensive and clinically sensitive outcome instruments and the demands from the field for measures that are feasible in busy clinical settings. A resource manual such as the present one can provide guidance in these respects.

A number of other compendia of assessment instruments for clinical populations is available. Some cover a range of health conditions, not only neurological disorders (e.g., Bowling, 1997; Cole, Finch, Gowland, & Mayo, 1995; Cushman & Scherer, 1995; McDowell, 2006; Sederer & Dickey, 1996). These generally include generic as well as condition-specific instruments. It is recognized that both types of assessment measures have advantages and disadvantages. Yet, the large and increasing number of instruments developed specifically to measure neurological and neuropsychological function are testimony to the limitations and short-comings that clinicians and researchers have found in the application of generic instruments to people with neurological conditions (Kersten, Mullee, Smith, McLellan, & George, 1999).

Indeed, the sheer volume of assessment measures developed specifically for the investigation of ABI demands a dedicated compendium. Such resources are available for specialized neuropsychological tests (e.g., Lezak, Howieson, & Loring, 2004; Mitrushina, Boone, & D'Elia, 1999; Strauss, Sherman, & Spreen, 2006). Compendia of assessment instruments that are suitable for administration by generic health professionals are also available, some of which focus on specific areas such as cognitive screening (e.g., Shulman & Feinstein, 2006; Strub & Black, 2000) and others address a range of functional areas (e.g., Herndon, 1997; Wade, 1992). In the years since these latter books were published, however, a multitude of new measures has appeared in the literature.

An important development, also since the publications of Herndon (1997) and Wade (1992), has been the introduction of the ICF. This is "a globally agreed framework and classification to define the spectrum of problems in functioning" (Geyh et al., 2004a, p. 137), which is likely to exert an increasing influence on clinical and research practice. Üstün, Chatterji, and Kostanjsek (2004) liken the ICF to the Rosetta Stone, enabling linkage of data across health conditions and interventions. Systematic reviews, such as that of Geyh et al. (2004b) examining assessment instruments used in clinical trials of interventions for stroke, showed how concepts can be successfully linked to the ICF. Eighty-three different ICF categories were measured in at least 10% of trials, and more than 100 additional ICF categories for less frequently measured concepts. The present volume draws on the ICF framework to classify instruments for ABI.

Methodology

A range of methods was used to identify and select instruments for inclusion in this compendium. The literature was examined using various procedures. Searches of the electronic databases, Medline and PsycINFO, were used to identify scales in cognate areas of ICF domains and categories pertinent to ABI (e.g., delirium, memory questionnaires, community participation). Additionally, searches were conducted of websites, along with hand-searching of reference lists, review papers, books, journals, as well as recommendations from colleagues and the author's personal reference collection.

Candidate instruments were examined to identify those meeting the following five selection criteria for inclusion in the book:

1 An empirical study of the instrument, using an ABI population (or one at risk of ABI, e.g., older adults investigated for dementia), was published in a scientific, peer-reviewed journal.
2 Information was available on the psychometric properties of the instrument.
3 The instrument was suitable for administration by a generic health professional and was not restricted to a particular discipline (e.g., specialist neuropsychological tests).
4 Administration and/or scoring procedures did not require specialized equipment, although some commonly available and portable stimulus materials were deemed acceptable (e.g., pen and paper, stopwatch, torch, picture cards, common objects).
5 The instrument was in current clinical and/or research use and available in the English language.

For reasons of space, it was not possible to include all pertinent measures identified. The guiding principle for the final selection was to provide a representative array of instruments across broad ranges of functioning, at the expense of exhaustive coverage of a narrow area. For some areas (e.g., general cognitive screening, self-care functions) there are large numbers of scales, but the item content and structure of many instruments are very similar, thereby raising the question of the value of a detailed inclusion of all scales in these areas. Consequently, instruments selected for inclusion in this volume are those with adequate psychometric properties, as well as those representing industry standards, in frequent use, or having special features.

The principle of a broad coverage of functional areas extended to including special-purpose instruments that are not necessarily in wide circulation (e.g., scales to assess minimally conscious states, establish mental competence), as well as those with special features (such as evaluation of neglected groups, e.g., people in advanced stages of dementia, patient/client-centred approaches). An effort was made to cover the spectrum of ABI, including progressive conditions (such as Alzheimer's disease and other dementias), as well as non-progressive conditions (such as stroke, traumatic brain injury). Appendix A lists the clinical conditions for which the included instruments were originally developed and with which they are currently used.

Inevitably, there are omissions. Sometimes these will be author-related, and in particular the scope of the book did not allow inclusion of scales examining psychological well-being. Many such scales, however, are instruments developed for other populations that have been applied to ABI groups, and the decision was taken to focus largely on those scales specifically developed for the ABI population rather than instruments that are available in other compendia. Another area not covered is that of so-called carer-burden. The reason for its omission relates to the conceptual framework of the ICF used as the structure for this book, which explicitly excludes the providers of support (i.e., caregivers) – see the introduction to Chapter 9 for discussion of this point. Furthermore, some neurological conditions (e.g., dementia, traumatic brain injury) contain a much larger number of published instruments than other conditions (e.g., neurotoxicity, cerebral neoplasms) and the scales featured in this book reflect this imbalance. In other situations, the apparent omissions reflect the state of the field – for instance, there is a dearth of instruments suitable for the assessment of children with ABI.

Structure of the entries on instruments

In order to facilitate use of this compendium, each entry describing an instrument is written as a stand-alone report and follows the same format. The structure of the entries has been informed by the characteristics delineated by Andresen (2000). A particularly appealing aspect of her set of 11 characteristics is the blend of clinical considerations (viz. administrative and respondent burdens, availability of alternative forms, cultural/language adaptations, normative/comparative data), along with the conceptual underpinnings of the instrument and the strength of its measurement properties (viz. conceptual characteristics, measurement model, instrument bias, reliability, validity, responsiveness). These characteristics and criteria, which appear in various configurations in many psychometric texts, provide the "gold standard" against which instruments can be evaluated and compared.

By the same token, it is also recognized that various psychometric or clinimetric criteria may differ in relevance according to the purpose of the instrument (Kirshner & Guyatt, 1985). Responsiveness, for example, is more important for instruments whose purpose is evaluative rather than diagnostic (Guyatt, Walter, & Norman, 1987); internal consistency may be compromised in those diagnostic or prognostic instruments that, perhaps in the interests of minimizing respondent burden, intentionally select a small set of items that make separate and distinctive contributions to the scale; knowledge of practice effects is particularly relevant for cognitive tests and they need to be taken into account in subsequent administrations of the instrument, and so forth.

The intention of the standardized presentation of each entry is to provide the reader with practical information, including item description, administration and scoring procedures. Wherever possible and feasible, items from instruments that are in the public domain are reproduced, using a standardized format to lend consistency of presentation of the scales across the book. In so doing, however, this compendium is not intended to be a replacement for the test manual, and users are advised to consult the original source. Information is also provided to assist the reader to determine the calibre of the scale in terms of the manner of its initial development and psychometric properties. The entries do not provide an exhaustive coverage of all the published psychometric studies on an instrument. Rather, the aim has been to strike a balance between detail and breadth of coverage, such that the reader gains an overall flavour of the characteristics of the instrument. Every effort was made to identify pertinent psychometric information, but some relevant references may have been missed. Each entry concludes with a brief commentary, regarding the strengths and limitations of the instrument. A selection of key references, with a psychometric focus, is also included.

Terminology and definitions

The screening tests, rating scales and questionnaires included in this compendium are largely based on behavioural observation, but they differ according to the way in which (a) information is collected and (b) responses are coded. Classification of the types of instruments is operationally defined as follows:

- *Objective tests or performance-based scales:* Those instruments that objectively measure observable performance. In most cases, the veracity of the response can be readily ascertained by an objective criterion (e.g., "repeat these numbers after me: 5, 8, 3"; "open your eyes"). Responses may be scored using a variety of procedures. Sometimes a continuous score range is used, such as the number of words correctly recalled or the time taken to complete a task. For other tests, the clinician elicits a behavioural response that is then classified into a hierarchy according to predetermined criteria; for example, whether the eyes open spontaneously, after verbal request, in response to noxious stimuli, not at all. Other instruments in this category measure the presence or other objectively verifiable characteristic of natural observations.

- *Rating scales:* Those instruments where the response involves a judgement, generally using a rating scale describing intensity, frequency or other characteristic (e.g., "how much pain do you experience?", "how often do you forget things?", "how well do you get along with other people?"). Responses for many rating scales use a Likert-type rating scale, for example, a 5-point scale from "not at all" to "a lot". Ratings can be made by a clinician, using behavioural observation, clinical judgement or direct questioning. Ratings can also be made by an informant (such as a relative, friend, caregiver) or can be self-ratings by the person with/at risk of ABI.
- *Questionnaires/interviews:* Those instruments using open-ended questions in which the respondent is free to give an individualized response (e.g., "when did you have your injury?", "what duties did your work entail?", "what problems do you experience?").

A uniform set of terms is generally used throughout the book, and on occasion these may depart from terms that authors of an instrument have used. For instance, there is considerable variability in the way in which authors describe sources of information provided by proxies (e.g., relative, family member, significant other, caregiver, informant). In the present volume, the term "informant" is frequently used to refer to all proxy respondents who are not clinicians. Similarly, a report provided by the person with ABI (who may be a patient, client, resident, participant, or respondent, depending on the setting) is generally referred to as "self" report. Following on from Wade and Halligan (2003) the person with/at risk of ABI is also often referred to as a patient, this being "the most appropriate word for someone who is in contact with and using health care systems . . . The word *client* suggests a different relationship, not the type usually found in health professional relationships" (p. 350). An exception to this principle is terminology used by authors to refer to various cognitive constructs and processes. For example, in the area of memory authors use different labels to refer to very similar processes (e.g., short-term, recent, anterograde, episodic) and in these instances the terminology used by the authors to describe/classify items from their instruments is retained. Variation also occurs in definitions of measurement properties of instruments. For example, the internal consistency of an instrument is conceptualized by some authors as a component of reliability and by others as an aspect of validity. A standard set of definitions for common psychometric properties, consistent with those used by Hinderer and Hinderer (2005), has been adopted for this book (see Table 1.1), and these may vary from terms used by the authors. Additionally, Appendix B presents a list of abbreviations used in this compendium.

Diagnostic tests, a number of which are described in Chapters 2 to 6 in Part A, need to provide information on diagnostic accuracy. This can be done by using a criterion-referenced measure or normative data. The former compares the new test against accepted standards, procedures or criteria (such as a diagnosis). Commonly used statistics to judge diagnostic accuracy include likelihood ratios, defined as "the odds that a given level of a diagnostic test would be predicted in a patient with (as opposed to one without) the target disorder" (Sackett, Haynes, Guyatt, & Tugwell, 1991, p. 120) and sensitivity/specificity. Cut-off scores to indicate the presence/absence of the condition are established, often using receiver operating characteristic (ROC) curves, and investigators usually report on the levels of sensitivity, specificity and/or likelihood ratios obtained using the cut-off scores.

Generally, there is a trade-off between sensitivity and specificity, and different situations will dictate the desirability of one over another: screening tests often require high sensitivity to maximize detection of real cases, whereas other situations may demand high specificity to screen out non-cases (e.g., clinical situations depending on the base rate of the condition, clinical trials and other types of research studies). Different cut-off scores on a single test may be established to differentiate diagnostic conditions (e.g., dementia vs no dementia; Alzheimer's disease vs frontotemporal dementia). In the tables appearing for relevant entries, where practical the convention is used of referring to cut-off scores as follows: "x/y" where x and y refer to scores either side of the cut-off (e.g., present/absent, or vice versa according to the direction of the scores). This bypasses the misunderstanding that can arise when "score x" is stipulated as the cut-off (i.e., is score x, the cut-off itself, to be classified as present or absent?). Related concepts to sensitivity and specificity, which are reported less commonly but arguably are more clinically useful, are the positive and negative predictive values. These characteristics of diagnostic tests, described by Sackett, Straus, Richardson, Rosenberg, and Haynes (2000), among others, are easily calculated using Table 1.2.

Table 1.1 Psychometric properties frequently examined by scales included in this book

Term	*Definition*
Validity	The extent to which the test measures what it was designed to measure (i.e., *what* the test measures)
Types of validity:	
Content	The test provides a representative sampling of the domain of behaviours. Methods use evidence provided for development procedures of the test and use of expert judges
Criterion	Extent to which the test measures (is correlated with) a specific criterion
(a) Concurrent	The criterion is obtained at the same time as the test is administered
(b) Predictive	The criterion is obtained at some time after the test is administered
Construct	Extent to which the test measures a theoretical construct or trait. Methods use factor analysis, multitrait–multimethod matrix
Internal consistency	Homogeneity of items within a test, a statistical test of content sampling
Convergent and Divergent	The test is correlated with similar constructs, and the test is *not* correlated with dissimilar constructs
Discriminant	The test discriminates between groups with different characteristics pertinent to the test
Reliability	Reproducibility or consistency of scores obtained on the test (i.e., *how well* the test measures what it measures)
Types of reliability:	
Alternate form	An alternate (or parallel) form of the test with comparable item content, response format and scoring procedures. Important for instruments subject to practice effects (e.g., cognitive tests)
Inter-rater	Extent of agreement between scores of two (or more) independent examiners of a single test administration or behavioural observation
Test–retest	Also referred to as intra-rater reliability or temporal stability. Refers to the stability of test scores over time. The interval should be sufficiently long to counteract effects of memory of the previous administration, but short enough to ensure clinical change does not occur. Deyo, Diehr, and Patrick (1991) suggest a 1–2 week interval
Responsiveness	Sensitivity to detect true changes occurring in the individual, as opposed to random fluctuations (error) against which the test should be impervious (see test–retest reliability)

Table 1.2 Determining sensitivity, specificity, positive predictive value and negative predictive value of a test

		Target disorder		
		Positive	*Negative*	
Test result	Positive	a	b	a+b
	Negative	c	d	c+d
		a+c	b+d	

- Sensitivity: Proportion of people with the target disorder who have a positive test result (a/(a+c))
- Specificity: Proportion of people without the target disorder who have a negative test result (d/(b+d))
- Positive predictive value: Proportion of people with a positive test result who have the target disorder (a/(a+b))
- Negative predictive value: Proportion of people with a negative test result who are free of the target disorder (d/(c+d))

Studies published in the older literature often used Pearson (r) or Spearman (r_s) correlation coefficients to examine aspects of an instrument's reliability, or used percentage agreement in the case of dichotomous data. Current practice recommends the use of the more conservative intra-class correlation coefficient (ICC) for continuous data because it takes into account not only the rank order of the association between data points but also score differences. Similarly, the kappa statistic, which takes account of chance level of agreement, is recommended for dichotomous classifications; weighted kappa, used for ordinal data, adjusts for the magnitude of the disagreements. The criteria of Cicchetti (1994, 2001), presented in Table 1.3 are used to describe the clinical or practical significance of (i) the ICC and kappa statistic, (ii) Cronbach coefficient alpha, which is commonly used to determine the internal consistency of a test, and (iii) diagnostic accuracy for sensitivity, specificity, positive and negative predictive values. As noted earlier, however, the importance of coefficients for Cronbach alpha and the levels of sensitivity/specificity may vary according to the purpose of the instrument and its particular applications. If Pearson coefficients are used for reliability analyses, then high values are required and the range $r = .80$ to $r = .90$ is recommended (Anastasi & Urbina, 1997).

Table 1.3 Descriptive terms corresponding to coefficients for intra-class correlation (ICC), kappa, Cronbach coefficient alpha, sensitivity, specificity, positive and negative predictive values (after Cicchetti, 1994, 2001)

Level of clinical significance	*ICC and kappa*	*Cronbach coefficient alpha*	*Sensitivity, specificity, positive and negative predictive values*
	Coefficient	*Coefficient*	*Diagnostic accuracy (%)*
Excellent	≥.75	≥.90	90–100
Good	.6–.74	.8–.89	80–89
Fair	.4–.59	.7–.79	70–79
Poor	<.4	<.7	<70

In the assessment of inter-rater reliability, Andresen's (2000) criteria include patient-proxy reliability (i.e., the degree to which proxy or informant responses are similar to those of the respective patients). A number of instruments presented in this book have information available on patient-proxy reliability, but the coefficients are often relatively low, in the order of $r = .4$ to $r = .5$. Emphasis has not been placed on this type of reliability because when the patient is a person with ABI, the resulting coefficient may not so much measure the reliability of the instrument, but rather be confounded by compromised cognitive functioning, particularly if the patient experiences significant impairments in memory, insight and judgement. In this context it is more meaningful to report inter-rater reliability between different clinicians or different informants and, when available, such information has been provided.

When reporting coefficients for the individual instruments described in Chapters 2 to 10, results are generally recorded for the total score (where applicable and information is available), as well as the range for subscales/items (where applicable/available). Often the range of coefficients for the subscales/items is wide. The reader is assisted to make an overall determination of the number of subscales/items with good (e.g., ICC/$k \geq .6$) or poor (e.g., ICC/$k < .4$) coefficients by use of the following summary notation. A scale with 10 items, for example, may have the following profile entered into the "psychometric box" for test–retest reliability: "Total score $k = .7$, item range $k = .2$–.9 ($k \geq .6$ for 5/10 items; $k < .4$ for 2/10 items)", which means that kappa coefficients for 5 out of 10 items were .6 or higher, coefficients for 2 out of 10 items were less than .4, and thus, by implication, for the remaining 3 out of 10 items kappa coefficients were between .4 and .59.

Effect sizes are a common means of measuring the responsiveness of an instrument. The rule of thumb for interpreting the strength of the effect size varies according to the type of analysis, but for comparisons of mean scores Cohen (1988) suggested that $d = .8$ is large, $d = .5$ is medium, and $d = .2$ is small. These thresholds to classify effect sizes have not gone unchallenged, however, with some authors suggesting that lower values are significant for health status measures (Kazis, Anderson, & Meenan, 1989) and other authors arguing that higher values are required for treatment studies (Beeson & Robey, 2006). At the individual level, it is helpful to know whether or not the change that occurs (either improvement or deterioration) is beyond that which can be attributed to measurement error of the test (i.e., a statistically reliable change); and further, whether such a change is also clinically significant (i.e., that the patient's classification changes from dysfunctional to functional or vice versa). Few studies, however, report on these features. A number of procedures are available to calculate the reliable change index, and Perdices (2005) has provided a review of formulae.

All instruments presented in this book are quantitative and use numbers to summarize responses. A feature of scores yielded by many of these instruments is that the unit of measurement is at the ordinal level (see Cicchetti et al., 2006, for an interesting critical re-evaluation of levels of measurement). That is, there is a rank order or hierarchy of measurement units within an item (e.g., each item rated on a 5-point scale reflecting an increasing degree of disability). With ordinal data (unlike interval and ratio levels of measurement), it cannot be assumed that the intervals between the units are equivalent (e.g., that the degree of disability between response categories 2 and 3 is the same degree of disability as between response categories 3 and 4). Yet it is very common for developers of test instruments to transgress this assumption and sum scores from the items to form subscale scores, aggregate subscale scores to form a total score, and conduct statistical analysis on the data as if the units of measurement represent interval data. In other words, ordinal data are often treated in a manner that is appropriate only for interval and ratio levels of measurement. In a strict sense, "because the intervals on an ordinal scale are either not known or are unequal, mathematical manipulations such as addition, subtraction, multiplication, or division of ordinal numbers are not meaningful" (Domholdt, 2005, p. 246). Some authors of instruments acknowledge the licence they take in aggregating scores, and the consequent caution needed to interpret results. Increasingly, however, scaling procedures, such as Rasch analysis, are being applied to instruments to develop an equal-interval measure from raw scores (see Bond & Fox, 2007; Tesio, 2003). The routine application of such procedures in test development is a welcome advance in improving measuring instruments in the field of ABI.

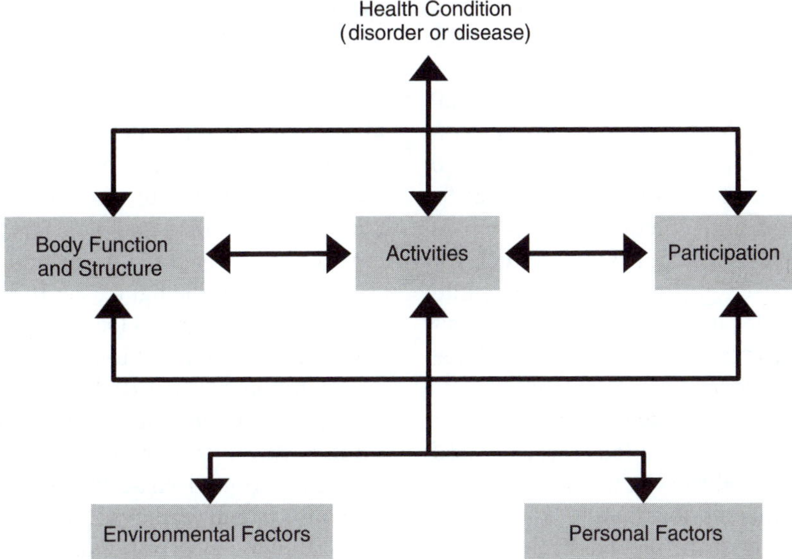

Figure 1.1 International classification of functioning, disability and health (reproduced from World Health Organization (2001). *International Classification of Functioning, Disability and Health* (Chapter 1, Section 5, Model of functioning and disability, p. 18, Fig. 1). Geneva: World Health Organization. Reprinted by permission of WHO Press).

The International Classification of Functioning, Disability and Health (ICF)

Organization of this compendium draws on the ICF taxonomy. The ICF is depicted graphically in Figure 1.1. A more specific tabular overview of the ICF is presented in Figure 1.2, which also shows correspondence between ICF domains and the chapters covered in this book. Appendix C (Tate & Perdices, 2008) provides a graphical representation of an "ICF tree" containing the categories and codes for selected Body Functions, Activities/ Participation and Environmental Factors components nested within the above domains.

The aim of the ICF is "to provide a unified and standard language and framework for the description of health and health-related states" (WHO, 2001, p. 3). It is therefore in the interests of clinicians and researchers in the area of ABI, as well as in other fields, that the instruments they use to measure health and health-related states conform to such a standard. Stineman, Lollar, and Üstün (2005) report that the ICF has been accepted by 191 counties, and "is fast becoming the world standard for describing health and disabilities" (p. 1099). Challenges that were encountered in placing instruments developed for assessment of ABI within the ICF framework are discussed in the following section.

Origins and uses of the ICF

The ICF is a revision of the *International Classification of Impairments, Disabilities and Handicaps* (ICIDH; WHO, 1980). Development of the original ICIDH is described in detail in the 1980 publication and Bickenbach, Chatterji, Badley, and Üstün (1999) provide an informative review of issues necessitating the revision. The ICF retains a number of elements of the ICIDH, building on, updating and refining the terminology for impairments and disablement. It also differs from the ICIDH in significant ways; in particular, the inclusion of contextual factors and the use of neutral language (e.g., "participation" replaces "handicap") allow positive experiences to be described. In so doing, the ICF has more fully integrated medical and social models to adopt a "biopsychosocial" approach; in a rehabilitation context it "will engender expansion of the restorative rehabilitative paradigm to include empowerment" (Stineman et al., 2005, p. 1104).

The primary reference for the ICF (WHO, 2001) essentially comprises a listing of approximately 1500 alphanumeric codes describing various aspects of functioning. *The ICF Australian User Guide* (Australian Institute of Health and Welfare [AIHW], 2003) is intended to complement the ICF, and it provides information regarding the revision process, instructions in its use and its practical applications. Similar, but briefer overviews can be found in de Kleijn-de Vrankrijker (2003), Stucki, Cieza, and Melvin (2007), Stucki and Melvin (2007) and Üstün, Chatterji, Bickenbach, Kostanjsek, and Schneider (2003). Other descriptions of the ICF (e.g., Peterson, 2005) and critical reviews of its strengths and weaknesses (Wade and Halligan, 2003) have appeared, along with progress towards the development of a procedural manual to facilitate use of the ICF in health care settings in the USA (Reed et al., 2005). Discussions of the application of the ICF to clinical practice, education and research are also available

(Bruyère, van Looy, & Peterson, 2005; Stucki, 2007; Stucki & Grimby, 2007; Stucki, Reinhardt, & Grimby, 2007; Wade, 2005).

The WHO (2001) enumerates a range of potential applications of the ICF: for statistical purposes; as a research tool; for clinical practice in vocational and needs assessment, matching treatments with specific conditions, rehabilitation and outcome evaluation; in the planning and design of social policy; as a vehicle for education in curriculum design, raising awareness and taking social action. Ideally, it provides a scientific basis to learn about and research health and health-related states and provides a uniform coding system, thereby enabling comparison of data. It is recommended that for specialist services, such as rehabilitation, geriatrics and mental health, coding is conducted at the more detailed fourth-level category, whereas for surveys and health outcome evaluation coding at the second-level category is appropriate.

Components of the ICF

The ICF classifies health and health-related states; the health conditions (i.e., diseases, disorders, injuries, etc.) to which they relate are classified in the complementary WHO taxonomy, the *International Statistical Classification of Diseases and Related Health Problems*, 10th revision (ICD-10; WHO, 1992). The specific sections within components of the ICF are defined as follows (WHO, 2001, p. 10):

- *Body functions*: Physiological functions of body systems (including psychological functions).
- *Body structures*: Anatomical parts of the body, such as organs, limbs and their components.
- *Activity*: The execution of a task or action by an individual.
- *Participation*: Involvement in a life situation.
- *Environmental factors*: Physical, social and attitudinal environments in which people live and conduct their lives.

These sections (along with another, not yet classified, *Personal Factors*) work in an interactive and recursive fashion (see Figure 1.1), for example, Environmental Factors (e.g., distracting stimuli or ground texture) can interact with Body Functions (attention or balance respectively).

Structure of the ICF

A nested, hierarchical structure, described as stem–branch–leaf, is used in the ICF. It comprises parts, components, domains (also referred to as the first level of classification), blocks (which are "provided as a convenience to the user and, strictly speaking, are not part of the structure of the classification and normally will not be used for coding purposes"; WHO, 2001, p. 220) and categories (second, third and fourth levels of classification). This detailed organizational structure results in a very large number of categories. Therefore, a schematic summary of the ICF is depicted in Figure 1.2 adapted from Tate and Perdices (2008) to enable the reader to quickly grasp the overall structure of the ICF.

As shown in the figure, the ICF comprises two parts: (i) Functioning and Disability, and (ii) Contextual Factors. Within Functioning and Disability, there are two components: (a) Body (Functions and Structures) and (b) Activities and Participation. The component "Body" has eight domains for each of Functions and Structures, organized according to the body system (e.g., nervous system, cardiovascular system); each domain of Body Function corresponds to one of Body Structure. The component "Activities and Participation" contains a single set of nine domains, addressing both individual and social aspects of functioning (e.g., mobility, interpersonal interactions and relationships). Unlike the ICIDH, there is no recommended partitioning to distinguish domains *within* the Activities and Participation component. In fact, the ICF suggests any of four separate options for their differentiation, which "if users so wish [they can apply] in their own operational ways" (WHO, 2001, p. 16; see pp. 224–237 for options). This recommendation to use any one of a variety of methods of partitioning the Activities/Participation component is less than satisfactory in that it serves to create confusion among users and is not in keeping with the principle of promoting a unified framework.

Within the second part of the ICF, Contextual Factors, there are also two components: (a) Environmental Factors and (b) Personal Factors. The "Environmental Factors" component contains five domains, referring to physical, social and attitudinal environments. The second component, "Personal Factors", is not yet classified within the ICF "because of the large social and cultural variance associated with them" (WHO, 2001, p. 8). According to the ICF, Personal Factors comprise the following: "gender, race, age, other health conditions, fitness, lifestyle, habits, upbringing, coping styles, social background, education, profession, past and current experience (past life events and concurrent events), overall behaviour pattern and character style, individual psychological assets and other characteristics" (p. 17).

Some degree of variability occurs at the domain and category levels of the ICF. Domains may or may not have blocks (e.g., there are none in the Body Structures and Environmental Factors components), but all domains contain categories. Categories are subdivided. The domain of Mental functions, for instance, contains

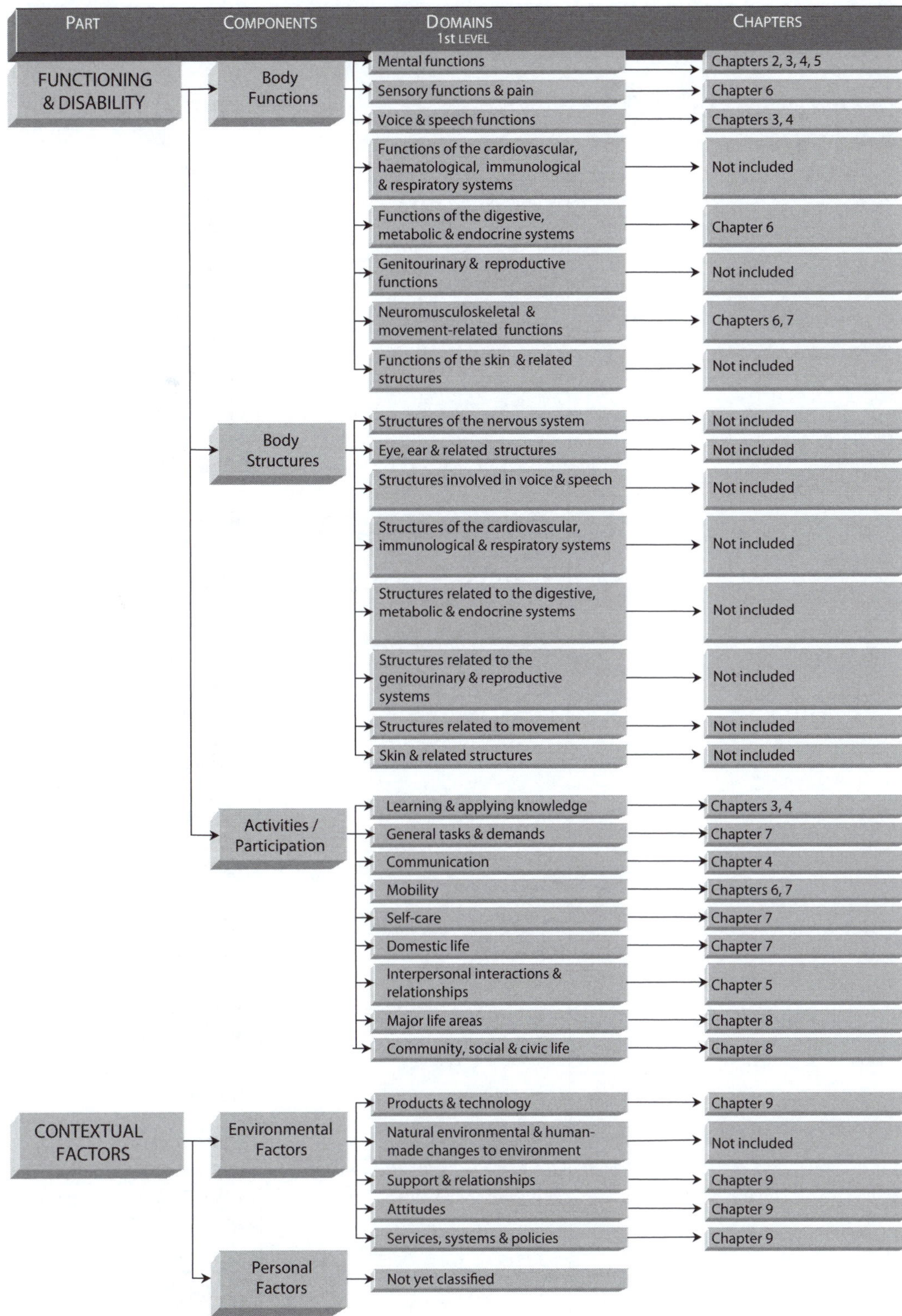

Figure 1.2 Overview of the International Classification of Functioning, Disability and Health, and chapters in which instruments mapping to ICF domains are located.

two blocks, one of which has 8 categories and the second block contains 14 categories. Each of these 22 categories is further subdivided. Figure 1.3 depicts the full ICF listing for the block, Global mental functions, which is subdivided to at least the third level (orientation to person is subdivided to the fourth level).

The ICF recognizes both positive and negative aspects of the components. For Body Functions, Body

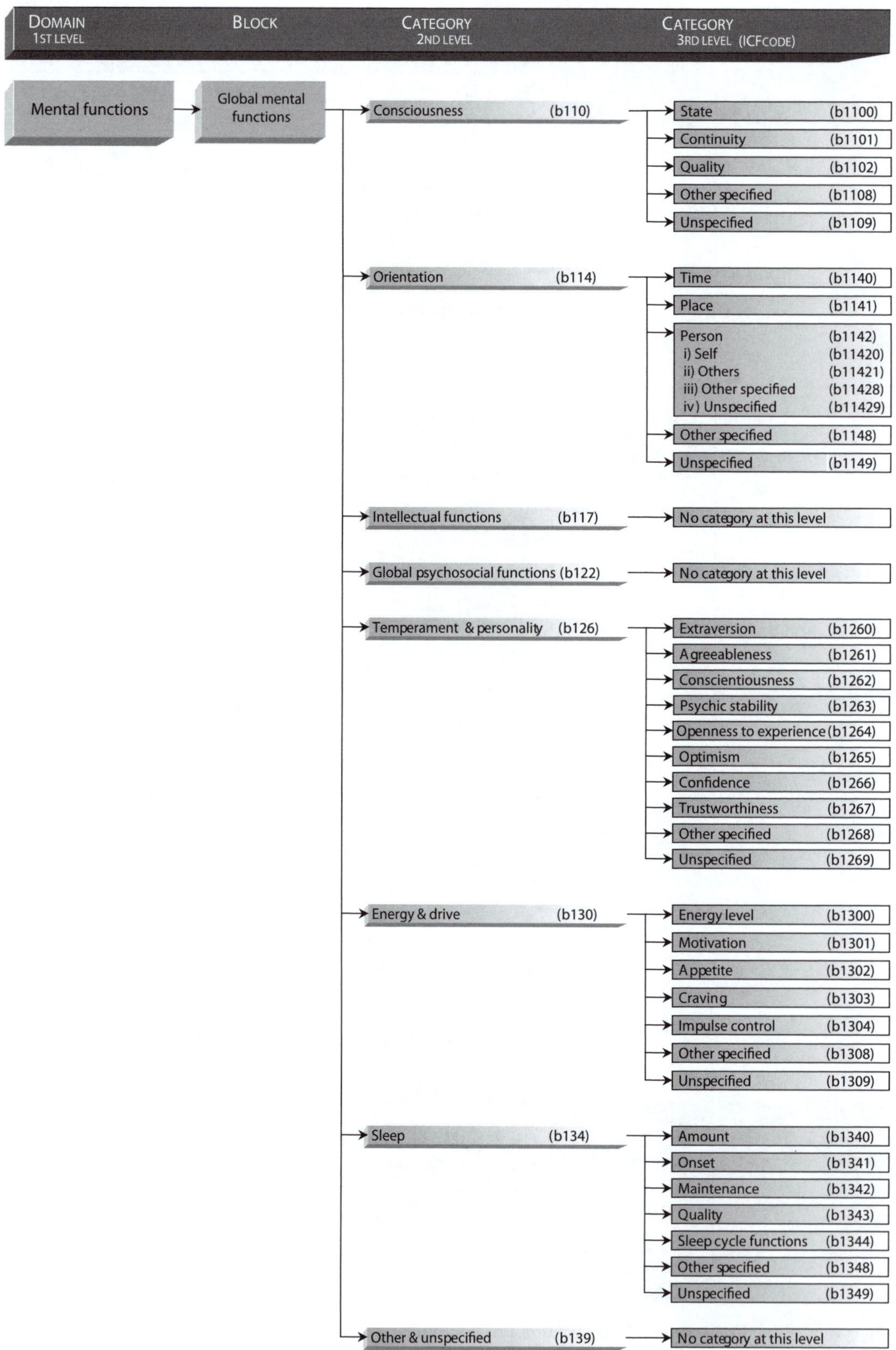

Figure 1.3 Full listing of the ICF block of Global mental functions.

Structures, Activities and Participation, the positive aspect is labelled *functioning*, as defined above. The negative aspects are labelled *impairments* for Body Functions and Body Structures, and *limitations* and *restrictions* for Activities and Participation respectively. The term *disability* is used as an umbrella term to refer to impairment, activity limitation and participation restriction. For Environmental Factors, positive aspects are labelled *facilitators* and negative aspects *barriers* or *hindrances*.

Codes and qualifiers used in the ICF

As noted, each of the ICF categories is assigned a code, using alphanumeric notation: commencing with "b" for body functions, "s" for body structures, "d" for domain (referring to domains of the Activities and Participation component, which alternatively can be referred to as "a" and "p" respectively if the user so desires) and "e" for environment. For example, as shown in Figure 1.3, the code b1142 is classified to the fourth level and refers to "orientation to person", which lies within b114 second-level "orientation function", within the block of Global mental functions, within the domain of Mental functions (b110–b139), within the component of Body Functions. In total, there are 1424 codes at the third and fourth category level (WHO, 2001, p. 220). The category codes are fully enumerated in the 2001 WHO publication (see also Appendix C for codes attached to the Body Functions and Activities/Participation components that are addressed in this volume).

The ICF also advises the use of at least one qualifier, without which "the codes have no inherent meaning" (WHO, 2001, p. 222). The qualifiers are numeric descriptors that appear following a point after the code. The first qualifier is generic, referring to extent or severity; Body Structures additionally use second and third qualifiers to designate the nature of the impairment (e.g., partial absence) and location of impairment (e.g., left side) respectively. Two codes are used for Activity Limitation and Participation Restriction, which refer to the environments in which the measurements occur. The first code refers to *performance* (i.e., what a person actually does in the current or usual environment, including use of aids and personal assistance) and the second refers to *capacity* (i.e., the person's ability or highest level of functioning occurring in a standardized environment, such as a testing area, typically reflecting their "true ability which is not enhanced by an assistive device or personal assistance"; p. 230). Identifying the gap between performance and capacity "provides a useful guide as to what can be done to the environment of the individual to improve performance" (WHO, 2001, p. 15). Environmental Factors uses the same set of numeric qualifiers as impairments to describe the extent of the barriers with a – sign preceding the qualifier; facilitators use the same set of codes with a + sign preceding the qualifier.

The first qualifiers for impairments, the performance and capacity qualifiers for Activity Limitation/Participation Restriction, and environmental factors, all of which refer to the *extent* of the problem, are tabulated in Table 1.4; coding for other qualifiers is listed in Annex 2 of the ICF publication (WHO, 2001). Taking the above example of disorientation to person, a severe impairment would be coded b1142.3. Stineman et al. (2005) and Tate and Perdices (2008) provide worked examples of the application of the ICF and their codes in clinical practice.

Table 1.4 First qualifiers for ICF codes

Code	*Definition*	*Percentage*
.0 – no problems	none, absent, negligible . . .	0–4
.1 – mild problem	slight, low . . .	5–24
.2 – moderate problem	medium, fair . . .	25–49
.3 – severe problem	high extreme . . .	50–95
.4 – complete problem	total . . .	96–100
.8 – not specified		
.9 – not applicable		

Adapted from World Health Organization (2001). *International classification of functioning, disability and health*. Geneva: World Health Organization.

Further development of the ICF

It is recognized that the ICF is an evolving classification, and the 2001 reference publication points to further developmental work that is required. There is also discussion in the literature regarding the practical application of the ICF. For example, it has been tailored for specific purposes, one of these being the development of "core sets" of ICF categories pertinent to various health conditions (see special issues of the *Journal of Rehabilitation Medicine* (Supplement 44, 2004) and *Disability and Rehabilitation* (Issue 7/8, 2005)), the ICF checklist for use in clinical practice, and the availability of a procedural manual (AIHW, 2003). Further developmental work is being conducted on the use and reliability of the codes (see Cieza et al., 2002; Cieza, Geyh, Chatterji, Kostanjsek, Üstün, & Stucki, 2005; Granlund, Eriksson, & Ylvén, 2004; Okochi, Utsunomiya, & Takahashi, 2005), along with empirical studies on the factor structure of the Activities/Participation component (Jette, Haley, & Kooyoomjian, 2003). Development of the Personal Factors component is specifically identified as an area of future work, and this is particularly relevant for the area of ABI in terms of an apparent overlap with some of the categories from the Mental functions domain (see below).

Placing measuring instruments for ABI within the ICF taxonomy

Challenges

A number of challenges were encountered in attempting

to place instruments designed for assessing ABI into the ICF taxonomy. One insurmountable difficulty is that many instruments currently used in clinical and research practice were developed prior to the introduction of the ICF. Thus, the structure of such instruments reflects the clinical manifestation of impairments and/or disablement in people with ABI, rather than adhering in an a priori way to a taxonomic structure.

As a consequence, a large number of instruments included in this book, even those addressing a very specific area of functioning, such as motor function, contain an admixture of items crossing Body Functions and Activities/Participation components (e.g., domains of Neuromusculoskeletal and movement-related functions vs Mobility respectively). The crossing of ICF components as well as domains also occurs in the Global psychosocial functions category (Mental functions domain of the Body Functions component) versus the Interpersonal interactions and relationships domain (Activities/Participation component). A third relevant area where admixtures occur is the speech/language/communication area. Within the Body Functions component is the Voice and speech domain and the Language category (Mental functions domain). In turn, these can be contrasted with the Communication domain within the Activities/Participation component.

Reed et al. (2005) have also commented on overlapping ICF codes between ICF components. By way of example they contrast the Body Function, Expression of written language, with the Activity, Writing. They note that "these items cannot be distinguished clinically and would be assessed using the same tests or procedures. That is, expression of written language cannot be assessed except by writing" (p. 126). At a conceptual level, however, it is recognized that a distinction *can* be drawn between the linguistic and motor components of writing and, indeed, in clinical practice the impairment of one and/or the other can be readily distinguished. But a writing sample is needed for this purpose, and hence, in this instance, application of the appropriate code/s is difficult. Stineman et al. (2005) raise similar issues with respect to the Body Function "seeing" versus the Activity "watching"; and "hearing" versus "listening".

The complexities of accurate code assignment, along with the admixture of item content of ABI scales across various ICF components and domains, has implications for the way in which instruments are described and classified in the present volume. In other cases, the ICF does not cover particular constructs that are pertinent to health conditions. In their systematic review of outcome measures used in clinical trials of interventions for depressive disorders, Brockow et al. (2004) found that the ICF did not include a number of "personal concepts" contained in measures used by researchers (e.g., locus of control, life satisfaction, self-esteem).

Other challenges centred on the level of agreement between current conceptualizations of ABI versus the ICF constructs and terminology. For example, although Personal Factors are defined as the particular background of an individual's life and living, and "comprise features of the individual that *are not* part of a health condition or health states" (WHO, 2001, p. 17; emphasis added), in a number of neurological conditions some personal factors that represent cognitive/psychological constructs can, in fact, be "impaired" as a direct consequence of the health condition (e.g., executive functions regulating problem-focused or emotion-focused coping strategies in frontal systems dysfunction; the store of knowledge in semantic dementia). In the area of ABI, the Body Structure relevant to the health condition (viz. the brain) is itself responsible for these personal factors. Thus it is difficult to conceptualize the Personal Factors as merely contextual – rather, they are integral to Body Functions. A proposed method of distinguishing between the two is that if one of the constructs from the Personal Factors component is impaired (e.g., coping skills as a result of executive impairment with frontal systems dysfunction), then it should be classified and coded as an impairment (in this case, of Mental functions); not as a Personal Factor. In this sense, because Personal Factors are not part of functioning, they cannot be impaired, limited or restricted; age and race being clear examples of this principle (personal communication, A. Cieza, 18 May 2008).

Notwithstanding the laudable objective of the ICF to establish a *lingua franca*, important differences in terminology used in the ICF and current nomenclature in the area of ABI were encountered. This was particularly notable in the domain of Mental functions. For example, the term "executive functioning", appearing in the second edition of Lezak's (1983) seminal reference work, has been standard usage in the field of neuropsychology for decades, replacing the older term "higher cognitive functioning" that is currently used in the ICF. Similarly, neuropsychologists refer to "self-awareness" (see Prigatano & Schacter, 1991) rather than the ICF terminology, "experience of self". Where discrepancies occur, preference has been given to current ABI terminology.

Moreover, it can be appreciated from Figure 1.3 that a large number of specific areas of function are addressed at the category level of the ICF, and Appendix C provides the specific detail for five domains of the Body Functions component, nine domains of the Activities/Participation component and four domains of Environmental Factors that are addressed in this volume. Some scales included in this compendium focus on the degree of detail at the ICF category level. This was commonly the case for scales of mental functions, where individual tests are available for virtually all of the second-level categories described (e.g., consciousness, orientation, attention, memory, etc.). By contrast, it is uncommon for scales addressing the Activities/Participation component to have this degree of specificity; rather scales of Activities/Participation generally adopt a broader selection of items, at the level of domain (first level); for example, self-care, domestic life (although there are some instances of specific scales addressing categories of the self-care domain, e.g., the Nottingham Stroke Dressing Assessment of Walker and Lincoln, 1990, 1991). Consequently, there is some variation in detail among scales in different chapters of this book.

Decisions

The foregoing considerations necessitated a slight reconfiguration of the ICF terminology and structure for this compendium in order to increase its relevance to ABI, particularly for the Mental functions domain. The decisions are summarized below and the rationale is provided in the relevant chapters. At the outset, it is recognized that overlap occurs between some Body Functions (as defined in the ICF) and Health Conditions (as defined in ICD-10). For example, delirium is classified within the ICF Mental functions domain (Consciousness category, b110), as well as within ICD-10 Chapter V: Mental, Behavioural Disorders (F05: delirium, not induced by alcohol and other psychoactive substances). Similarly, temperament and personality functions are classified within the ICF Body (Mental functions) domain (Temperament and personality category, b126), as well as within ICD-10 Chapter V: Mental, Behavioural Disorders (F07: personality and behavioural disorders due to brain disease, damage and dysfunction). A number of scales presented in this volume, particularly those examining Mental functions, have as their aim a diagnosis (e.g., delirium, fronto-temporal dementia). In this sense, they are arguably more properly considered assessments of the health condition per se (see ICD), as opposed to a consequence or component of that health condition. Nonetheless, because the categories that these instruments examine appear within the ICF nomenclature, they have been included in this compendium.

The guiding principle in organizing this volume was to place the ABI instruments in ICF domains that best represented the item content and made clinical sense – a model of best-fit, if you will. Consequently, in the interests of providing a simple and logical structure to this compendium, all instruments assessing a conceptually similar construct (e.g., speech/language/communication; movement-related/mobility function) are placed together. Additionally, some arbitrary decisions were made in reference to the grouping of sets of scales within the ICF structure. Thus, all scales in the speech/language/communication area appear within the Specific mental functions block (Mental functions domain) even though it could be argued that they are more properly placed within the Activities/Participation component (Communication domain). The reason that they have been grouped within the Body Functions component (Specific Mental Functions block) is because they assess a specific cognitive function (as do attention, memory, etc.). Figure 1.2 indicates the chapters that address those ICF domains represented by instruments included in this book.

More specifically, in Part A, Chapters 2 to 6 describe instruments assessing Mental functions, Sensory functions and pain, Voice and speech, Neuromusculoskeletal and movement-related functions, as well as the Ingestion category from the Digestive, metabolic and endocrine domain. Within the ICF taxonomy, these five domains fall within the component of Body Functions (see Figure 1.2). Although the Body Functions component comprises an additional three domains (Cardiovascular, haematological, immunological and respiratory; Genitourinary and reproductive; and Skin and related structures), these have less direct relevance to ABI. In keeping with common clinical practice in ABI, the instruments in Part A are grouped into two sections: (i) Mental functions (Chapters 2 to 5) and (ii) Sensory, ingestion and motor functions (Chapter 6). The imbalance in the number of chapters reflects the quantity of standardized instruments in the respective areas of functioning; the tradition of psychology (i.e., mental functions) being grounded in functional measurement. The specific chapters primarily addressing ICF domains and categories are described below.

Mental functions

The seven specific second-level categories of the block of Global mental functions are reconfigured for Chapters 2 to 5 in order to facilitate an integration of the ICF with current clinical conceptualizations of ABI. For reasons explained in the introduction to Chapter 2, the first two ICF categories of the Global mental functions block (Consciousness and Orientation) are combined. Intellectual functions is relabelled with the more commonly used term in ABI parlance, Cognitive, and entitled General cognitive functions (Chapter 3) to distinguish it from Specific cognitive functions (Chapter 4). Scales in Chapter 3 often include items that are pertinent to other categories of Mental functions. As explained in the introduction to Chapter 5, Global psychosocial functions, Temperament and personality functions and Energy and drive functions (as well as three categories from Specific mental functions and the Interpersonal interactions and relationships domain from Activities/Participation) are combined. Scales of Sleep functions, the final category of Global mental functions, are not considered in this volume.

The second block, Specific mental functions, contains 11 specific second-level categories (see Appendix C) and a number of representative tests are described in Chapter 4, Specific cognitive functions. Instruments included in Chapter 4 address the following ICF categories: (i) Attention, (ii) Memory, (iii) Higher-level cognitive (relabelled with the more commonly used term, Executive), (iv) Language (including the Voice and speech domain from Body Functions, as well as the Communication domain from Activities/Participation), and (v) Experience of self and time (relabelled with the more commonly used term, Self-awareness). At the item level, scales in Chapter 4 (and Chapter 3) overlap with the Learning and applying knowledge domain from Activities/Participation. Instruments assessing (vi) Emotional functions and (vii) Thought functions, are covered in Chapter 5 on scales assessing the Regulation of behaviour, thought and emotion. Specific instruments assessing (viii) Psychomotor, (ix) Perceptual, (x) Calculation, and (xi) Sequencing complex movements are not covered. Items reflecting some these Specific mental functions categories are occasionally included in multidimensional scales (see Chapter 10).

Sensory, ingestion and motor functions

Tests and scales described in Chapter 6 map to at least three ICF domains from the Body Functions component: mainly (i) Sensory and pain, (ii) Functions of the digestive, metabolic and endocrine systems, and (iii) Neuromusculoskeletal and movement-related functions, as well as the Mobility domain from the Activities/Participation component. A number of performance-based measures that are suitable for use by generic health professionals are available. These have the advantage of providing a standardized and objective evaluation. Additionally, rating scales and self-report measures of sensory-motor functions also contribute to evaluation, and for some Body Functions are arguably the best methods of assessment, the obvious example being pain. As noted earlier in this chapter, there is often an admixture of motor function items between Body Functions and Activities/Participation components. All tests and scales that exclusively assess motor function, as distinct from multiple Activities/Participation domains including Mobility, are included in Chapter 6.

In Part B, Chapters 7 and 8 present scales relating to Activities and Participation. Within the ICF taxonomy, the Activities and Participation component contains nine domains (see Figure 1.2). Scales from three of the nine domains (General tasks and demands, Self-care, and Domestic life) are presented in Chapter 7 (Activities of daily living). As noted in the preceding paragraph, scales exclusively addressing the Mobility domain are presented in Part A, Chapter 6 (Sensory, ingestion and motor scales). It is not uncommon, however, for scales of basic activities of daily living to focus on self-care *and* mobility, and in these cases, where self-care items predominate, the scale is more appropriately placed in Chapter 7 rather than Chapter 6. A further two Activities/Participation domains (Major life areas and Community, social and civic life) are addressed in Chapter 8 (Participation and social role). The arbitrary demarcation of scales in Chapters 7 and 8 is acknowledged and the problem of admixtures of items across multiple domains in the Activities/Participation component means that there is not always a neat separation between the item content of scales located in Chapters 7 and 8. Multidimensional scales, which often include items at the Activities/Participation level, as well as the Body Function level, are presented in Chapter 10. Finally, instruments sampling the remaining three Activities/Participation domains (Learning and applying knowledge, Communication, and Interpersonal interactions and relationships) are dealt with in Chapters 3 to 5 in Part A, in the interests of locating conceptually similar scales together.

As noted, with few exceptions, scales for ABI classified in the Activities/Participation component do not address specific ICF categories in isolation. Rather, the approach is more global, and ABI scales of Activities/Participation tend to be spread across the nine domains. In order to enable the reader to quickly grasp the sampling of ICF domains within each instrument and compare the content of instruments, Appendix D provides a comparative checklist for the scales featuring in Chapters 7, 8 and 10, identifying the number of items in each scale that address the ICF domains within the Activities/Participation component. Additionally, Appendix E provides a comparative checklist of the item content of scales assessing functional activities of daily living from a clinical perspective.

Part C examines the single component of Contextual Factors currently classified in the ICF, Environmental Factors (Chapter 9). The importance of incorporating contextual factors into the ICF cannot be overstated. Its presence serves to remind clinicians and researchers that people with ABI (or other health conditions) are not defined by that health condition, but rather live in a physical, social and attitudinal environment that can exert a dramatic (positive or negative) influence on their functioning. The five domains comprising the component of Environmental Factors represent a diverse range. In some domains, notably Support and relationships, a number of instruments are available, but few have been developed for or used with the ABI group. In other domains pertinent to the physical environment, specific scales are just starting to appear in the literature.

Part D (Chapter 10) is the final chapter of the compendium, containing scales that cannot be classified neatly within specific components of the ICF. They are described as multidimensional scales because they provide a sampling of disparate items from both the Body Functions and Activities/Participation components and their domains. A small selection of generic scales assessing so-called health-related quality of life is also included in Chapter 10.

Cautionary statements

It is recognized that for each of the components and domains of the ICF there are specialists who are trained to provide detailed and comprehensive evaluations of respective functions and their disorders: for example, clinical and neuropsychologists in Mental functions; physicians in Sensory and other body systems; speech pathologists in Voice and speech, Language, and Communication; physiotherapists in Neuromusculoskeletal and movement-related functions; occupational therapists, social workers and other allied health professionals in various domains of Activities and Participation and Environmental Factors. In particular, the tests of Mental functions described in this volume are essentially cognitive screening tests, and while these serve a useful purpose in many situations, they are not a substitute for a detailed neuropsychological or language assessment by a specialist clinician. Johnston, Keith, and Hinderer (1992, p. S13) recommend that:

> screening tests should be used cautiously for diagnostic, placement, or treatment planning . . . Screening tests are most effectively used to indicate the need for more extensive testing and treatment of specific problem areas. Flexibility and professional judgment are essential to the use of measures in professional practice.

Thus, while the instruments contained in this volume are recommended as suitable for administration by generic health professionals, it is expected that the administrator will adhere to standards of test administration and best clinical practice, as recommended by professional colleges and organizations (see Johnston et al. for discussion of measurement standards and responsibilities that are applicable to both test developers and test users).

An obvious caveat applies to the administration of rating scales, questionnaires and interviews. Responses on these instruments involve the person's perceptions. In situations where an actual, objective evaluation is desired, the veracity of responses on rating scales from people with ABI may be compromised when significant cognitive impairments, particularly in memory, judgement and/or awareness, are present. A score may well be produced, but the validity of that score needs to be evaluated. Even visual analogue rating scales (both vertical and horizontal) have been shown to be an unreliable method of measurement of some functions for people with stroke (Price, Curless, & Rodgers, 1999). For these reasons, rating scales are often completed by a proxy-respondent, generally a family member who has close contact with the person and knew them well prior to the onset of their ABI. Yet, this method, wherein the informant's responses are used as a "gold standard", can introduce another set of problems, because informants may over-estimate or under-estimate level of functioning for a variety of reasons (Kertesz, Nadkarni, Davidson, & Thomas, 2000; McKinlay & Brooks, 1984; Prigatano, Altman, & O'Brien, 1990). A number of the scales presented in this volume have data collected from three sources: patient, family member and clinician, and there are advantages and disadvantages to each. Who should do the rating? Wilson, Alderman, Burgess, Emslie, and Evans (1996) intimate that judicious selection of the family member is probably the best source, whereas Bennett, Ong, and Ponsford (2005) conclude that the treating clinician provides the most accurate evaluation.

On a final note, tests and scales are developed for different purposes, and that which is suitable for one application will be unsuited to another purpose. Hall, Bushnik, Lakisic-Kazazic, Wright, and Cantagallo (2001, p. 368) observed that "using a measure at the wrong phase of recovery may . . . jeopardize the validity of an otherwise valid scale". Accordingly, the selection of instruments featured in this volume is intended to present the reader with a representation of a variety of methods, procedures and formats, while at the same time enabling a reliable and valid evaluation of functioning. Responsibility for the selection and use of a particular instrument as suitable for a given purpose, however, rests with the clinician or researcher.

References

Anastasi, A., & Urbina, S. (1997). *Psychological testing* (7th ed.). Englewood Cliffs, NJ: Prentice Hall International, Inc.

Andresen, E. M. (2000). Criteria for assessing the tools of disability outcomes research. *Archives of Physical Medicine and Rehabilitation*, *81*(Suppl. 2), S15–S20.

Australian Institute of Health and Welfare. (2003). *ICF Australian user guide. Version 1.0*. Canberra: Australian Institute of Health and Welfare.

Beeson, P. M., & Robey, R. R. (2006). Evaluating single-subject treatment research: Lessons learned from aphasia literature. *Neuropsychology Review*, *16*(4), 161–169.

Bennett, P. C., Ong, B., & Ponsford, J. (2005). Assessment of executive dysfunction following traumatic brain injury: Comparison of the BADS with other clinical neuropsychological measures. *Journal of the International Neuropsychological Society*, *11*(5), 606–613.

Bickenbach, J. E., Chatterji, S., Badley, E. M., & Üstün, T. B. (1999). Models of disablement, universalism and the international classification of impairments, disabilities and handicaps. *Social Science and Medicine*, *48*(9), 1173–1187.

Bond, T. G., & Fox, C. M. (2007). *Applying the Rasch model. Fundamental measurement in the human sciences* (2nd ed.). Mahwah, NJ: Lawrence Erlbaum Associates, Inc.

Bowling, A. (1997). *Measuring health: A review of quality of life measurement scales*. (2nd ed.). Buckingham & Philadelphia: Open University Press.

Brockow, T. T., Wohlfahrt, K., Hillert, A., Geyh, S., Weigl, M., Franke, T., et al. (2004). Identifying the concepts contained in outcome measures of clinical trials on depressive disorders using the *International Classification of Functioning, Disability and Health* as a reference. *Journal of Rehabilitation Medicine*, *Suppl. 44*, 49–55.

Bruyère, S. M., van Looy, S. A., & Peterson, D. B. (2005). The *International Classification of Functioning, Disability and Health*: Contemporary literature overview. *Rehabilitation Psychology*, *50*(2), 113–121.

Cicchetti, D. V. (1994). Guidelines, criteria, and rules of thumb for evaluating normed and standardized assessment instruments in psychology. *Psychological Assessment*, *6*(4), 284–290.

Cicchetti, D. V. (2001). The precision of reliability and validity estimates re-visited: Distinguishing between clinical and statistical significance of sample size requirements. *Journal of Clinical and Experimental Neuropsychology*, *23*(5), 695–700.

Cicchetti, D., Bronen, R., Spencer, S., Haut, S., Berg, A., Oliver, P., et al. (2006). Rating scales, scales of measurement, issues of reliability: Resolving some critical issues for clinicians and researchers. *The Journal of Nervous and Mental Disease*, *194*(8), 557–564.

Cieza, A., Brockow, T., Ewert, T., Amman, E., Kollerits, B., Chatterji, S., et al. (2002). Linking health-status measurements to the *International Classification of Functioning, Disability and Health. Journal of Rehabilitation Medicine*, *34*(5), 205–210.

Cieza, A., Geyh, S., Chatterji, S., Kostanjsek, N., Üstün, B., & Stucki, G. (2005). ICF linking rules: An update based on lessons learned. *Journal of Rehabilitation Medicine*, *37*(4), 212–218.

Cohen, J. (1988). *Statistical power analysis for the behavioral sciences*. Hillsdale, NJ: Lawrence Erlbaum Associates, Inc.

Cole, B., Finch, E., Gowland, C., & Mayo, N. (1995). *Physical rehabilitation outcome measures*. Baltimore: Williams & Wilkins.

Cushman, L. A., & Scherer, M. J. (Eds.). (1995). *Psychological assessment in medical rehabilitation*. Washington, DC: American Psychological Association.

de Kleijn-deVrankrijker, M. W. (2003). The long way from the *International Classification of Impairments, Disabilities and Handicaps* (ICIDH) to the *International Classification of Functioning, Disability and Health* (ICF). *Disability and Rehabilitation*, *25*(11–12), 561–564.

Dekker, J., Dallmeijer, A. J., & Lankhorst, G. J. (2005). Clinimetrics in rehabilitation medicine: Current issues in developing and applying measurement instruments. *Journal of Rehabilitation Medicine*, *37*(4), 193–201.

Deyo, R. A., Diehr, P., & Patrick, D. L. (1991). Reproducibility and responsiveness of health status measures. Statistics and strategies for evaluation. *Controlled Clinical Trials*, *12*(S4), 142S–158S.

Domholdt, E. (2005). *Rehabilitation research. Principles and applications* (3rd ed.). St Louis, MO: Elsevier Saunders.

Geyh, S., Cieza, A., Schouten, J., Dickson, H., Frommelt, P., Omar, Z., et al. (2004a). ICF core sets for stroke. *Journal of Rehabilitation Medicine*, *Suppl. 44*, 135–141.

Geyh, S., Kurt, T., Brockow, T., Cieza, A., Ewert, T., Omar, Z., et al. (2004b). Identifying the concepts contained in outcome measures of clinical trials on stroke using the *International Classification of Functioning, Disability and Health* as a reference. *Journal of Rehabilitation Medicine*, *S44*, 56–62.

Granlund, M., Eriksson, L., & Ylvén, R. (2004). Utility of *International Classification of Functioning, Disability and Health*'s participation dimension in assigning ICF codes to items from extant rating instruments. *Journal of Rehabilitation Medicine*, *36*(3), 130–137.

Guyatt, G., Walter, S., & Norman, G. (1987). Measuring change over time: Assessing the usefulness of evaluative instruments. *Journal of Chronic Disease*, *40*, 171–178.

Hall, K. M. (1992). Overview of function assessment scales in brain injury rehabilitation. *NeuroRehabilitation*, *2*(4), 98–113.

Hall, K. M., Bushnik, T., Lakisic-Kazazic, B., Wright, J., & Cantagallo, A. (2001). Assessing traumatic brain injury outcome measures for long-term follow-up of community-based individuals. *Archives of Physical Medicine and Rehabilitation*, *82*(3), 367–374.

Herndon, R. M. (Ed.). (1997). *Handbook of neurologic rating scales*. New York: Demos Vermande.

Hinderer, S. R., & Hinderer, K. A. (2005). Principles and applications of measurement methods. In J. A. DeLisa, B. M. Gans, N. E. Walsh, W. L. Bockenek, W. R. Frontera, S. R. Geiringer, et al. (Eds.), *Physical medicine and rehabilitation: Principles and practice* (4th ed., pp. 1139–1162). Philadelphia: Lippincott, Williams & Wilkins.

Jette, A. M., & Hayley, S. M. (2005). Contemporary measurement techniques for rehabilitation outcomes assessment. *Journal of Rehabilitation Medicine*, *37*(6), 339–345.

Jette, A. M., Haley, S. M., & Kooyoomjian, J. T. (2003). Are the ICF Activity and Participation dimensions distinct? *Journal of Rehabilitation Medicine*, *35*(3), 145–149.

Johnston, M. V., Keith, R. A., & Hinderer, S. R. (1992). Measurement standards for interdisciplinary medical rehabilitation. *Archives of Physical Medicine and Rehabilitation*, *73*(S12), S3–S23.

Kazis, L. E., Anderson, J. J., & Meenan, R. F. (1989). Effect sizes for interpreting changes in health status. *Medical Care*, *27*(S3), S178–S189.

Kersten, P., Mullee, M. A., Smith, J. A. E., McLellan, L., & George, S. (1999). Generic health status measures are unsuitable for measuring health status in severely disabled people. *Clinical Rehabilitation*, *13*(3), 219–228.

Kertesz, A., Nadkarni, N., Davidson, W., & Thomas, A. (2000). The Frontal Behavioral Inventory in the differential diagnosis of frontotemporal dementia. *Journal of the International Neuropsychological Society*, *6*(4), 460–468.

Kirshner, B., & Guyatt, G. (1985). A methodological framework for assessing health indices. *Journal of Chronic Disease*, *38*(1), 27–36.

Lawton, M. P., & Brody, E. M. (1969). Assessment of older people: Self-maintaining and instrumental activities of daily living. *Gerontologist*, *9*(3), 179–186.

Lezak, M. D. (1983). *Neuropsychological assessment* (2nd ed.). New York: Oxford University Press.

Lezak, M. D., Howieson, D. B., & Loring, D. W. (2004). *Neuropsychological assessment* (4th ed.). Oxford: Oxford University Press.

McDowell, I. (2006). *Measuring health: A guide to rating scales and questionnaires*. (3rd ed.). New York: Oxford University Press.

McKinlay, W. W., & Brooks, D. N. (1984). Methodological problems in assessing psychosocial recovery following severe head injury. *Journal of Clinical Neuropsychology*, *6*(1), 87–99.

Mitrushina, M. N., Boone, K. B., & D'Elia, L. F. (1999). *Handbook of normative data for neuropsychological assessment*. New York: Oxford University Press.

Okochi, J., Utsunomiya, S., & Takahashi, T. (2005). Health measurement using the ICF: Test–retest reliability study of ICF codes and qualifiers in geriatric care. *Health and Quality of Life Outcomes*, *3*, 46.

Perdices, M. (2005). How do you know whether your patient is getting better (or worse)? A user's guide. *Brain Impairment*, *6*(3), 219–226.

Peterson, D. B. (2005). *International Classification of Functioning, Disability and Health*: An introduction for rehabilitation psychologists. *Rehabilitation Psychology*, *50*(2), 105–112.

Price, C. I. M., Curless, R. H., & Rodgers, H. (1999). Can stroke patients use visual analogue scales? *Stroke*, *30*(7), 1357–1361.

Prigatano, G., P., Altman, I., M., & O'Brien, K. P. (1990). Behavioural limitations that traumatic-brain-injured patients tend to underestimate. *The Clinical Neuropsychologist*, *4*(2), 163–176.

Prigatano, G. P., & Pliskin, N. H. (2003). *Clinical neuropsychology and cost outcome research: A beginning*. New York: Psychology Press.

Prigatano, G. P., & Schacter, D. L. (Eds.). (1991). *Awareness of deficit after brain injury: Clinical and theoretical issues*. New York: Oxford University Press.

Reed, G. M., Lux, J. B., Bufka, L. F., Trask, C., Peterson, D. B., Stark, S., et al. (2005). Operationalizing the *International Classification of Functioning, Disability and Health* in clinical settings. *Rehabilitation Psychology*, *50*(2), 122–131.

Sackett, D. L., Haynes, R. B., Guyatt, G. H., & Tugwell, P. (1991). *Clinical epidemiology: A basic science for clinical medicine* (2nd ed.) Boston: Little, Brown & Company.

Sackett, D. L., Straus, S. E., Richardson, W. S., Rosenberg, W., & Haynes, R. B. (2000). *Evidence based medicine: How to practise and teach EBM* (2nd ed.). Edinburgh: Churchill Livingstone.

Sederer, L. I., & Dickey, B. (Eds.). (1996). *Outcomes assessment in clinical practice*. Baltimore: Williams & Wilkins.

Shulman, K., & Feinstein, A. (2006). *Quick cognitive screening for clinicians: Mini-mental, clock drawing and other brief tests*. Abingdon, UK: Martin Dunitz.

Strauss, E., Sherman, E. M. S., & Spreen, O. (2006). *A compendium of neuropsychological tests. Administration, norms and commentary* (3rd ed.). New York: Oxford University Press.

Stineman, M. G., Lollar, D. J., & Üstün, T. B. (2005). The *International Classification of Functioning, Disability, and Health*: ICF empowering rehabilitation through an operational bio-psycho-social model. In J. A. DeLisa, B. M. Gans, N. E. Walsh, W. L. Bockenek, W. R. Frontera, S. R. Geiringer, et al. (Eds.), *Physical medicine and rehabilitation: Principles and practice* (4th ed., pp. 1099–1108). Philadelphia: Lippincott, Williams & Wilkins.

Strub, R. L., & Black, F. W. (2000). *The mental status examination in neurology*. (4th ed.). Philadelphia: F. A. Davis Company.

Stucki, G. (2007). Developing human functioning and rehabilitation research. Part I: Academic training programs. *Journal of Rehabilitation Medicine*, *39*(4), 323–333.

Stucki, G., Cieza, A., & Melvin, J. (2007). The *International Classification of Functioning, Disability and Health*: A unifying model for the conceptual description of the rehabilitation strategy. *Journal of Rehabilitation Medicine*, *39*(4), 279–285.

Stucki, G., & Grimby, G. (2007). Organizing human functioning and rehabilitation research into distinct scientific fields. Part I: Developing a comprehensive structure from cell to society. *Journal of Rehabilitation Medicine*, *39*(4), 293–298.

Stucki, G., & Melvin, J. (2007). The *International Classification of Functioning, Disability and Health*: A unifying model for the conceptual description of physical and rehabilitation medicine. *Journal of Rehabilitation Medicine*, *39*(4), 286–292.

Stucki, G., Reinhardt, J. D., & Grimby, G. (2007). Organizing human functioning and rehabilitation research into distinct scientific fields. Part II: Conceptual descriptions and domains for research. *Journal of Rehabilitation Medicine*, *39*(4), 299–307.

Tate, R. L., & Perdices, M. (2008). Facilitating use of the *International Classification of Functioning, Disability and Health* in acquired brain impairment. *Brain Impairment*, *9*(3), 282–292.

Tesio, L. (2003). Measuring behaviours and perceptions: Rasch analysis as a tool for rehabilitation research. *Journal of Rehabilitation Medicine*, *35*(3), 105–115.

Üstün, T. B., Chatterji, S., Bickenbach, J., Kostanjsek, N., & Schneider, M. (2003). The *International Classification of Functioning, Disability and Health*: A new tool for understanding disability and health. *Disability and Rehabilitation*, *25*(11–12), 565–571.

Üstün, B., Chatterji, S., & Kostanjsek, N. (2004). Comments from WHO for *Journal of Rehabilitation Medicine* supplement on ICF core sets. *Journal of Rehabilitation Medicine, Suppl. 44*, 7–8.

Wade, D. T. (1992). *Measurement in neurological rehabilitation*. New York: Oxford University Press.

Wade, D. T. (2003). Outcome measures for clinical rehabilitation trials: Impairment, function, quality of life or value? *American Journal of Physical Medicine and Rehabilitation, 82*(10), S26–S31.

Wade, D. T. (2005). Applying the WHO ICF framework to the rehabilitation of patients with cognitive deficits. In P.W. Halligan & D. T. Wade (Eds.), *Effectiveness of rehabilitation for cognitive deficits* (pp. 31–42). Oxford: Oxford University Press.

Wade, D. T., & Halligan, P. (2003). New wine in old bottles: The WHO ICF as an explanatory model of human behaviour. *Clinical Rehabilitation, 17*(4), 349–354.

Walker, M. F., & Lincoln, N. B. (1990). Reacquisition of dressing skills after stroke. *International Disability Studies, 12*, 41–43.

Walker, M. F., & Lincoln, N. B. (1991). Factors influencing dressing performance after stroke. *Journal of Neurology, Neurosurgery, and Psychiatry, 54*, 699–701.

Wilson, B. A., Alderman, N., Burgess, P. W., Emslie, H., & Evans, J. J. (1996). *Behavioural assessment of the dysexecutive syndrome*. Bury St Edmunds, UK: Thames Valley Test Company.

World Health Organization. (1980). *International classification of impairments, disabilities, and handicaps*. Geneva: World Health Organization.

World Health Organization. (1992). *The international statistical classification of diseases and related health problems, 10th revision, Australian modification (ICD-10-AM)*. Sydney: National Centre for Health Classification in Health.

World Health Organization. (2001). *International classification of functioning, disability and health*. Geneva: World Health Organization.

Part A

Body Functions

Part A of this compendium contains five chapters that focus on the domains of most relevance to acquired brain impairment (ABI) within the Body Functions component of the World Health Organization (WHO, 2001) *International Classification of Functioning, Disability and Health* (ICF; see Figure 2.1 below and Appendix C): consciousness and orientation (Chapter 2); general cognitive functions (Chapter 3); specific cognitive functions (Chapter 4); regulation of behaviour, thought and emotion (Chapter 5); and sensory, ingestion and motor functions (Chapter 6).

2 Scales of consciousness and orientation

Instruments presented in Chapter 2 map to the component, domain and categories of the *International Classification of Functioning, Disability and Health* (ICF; WHO, 2001) as depicted in Figure 2.1.

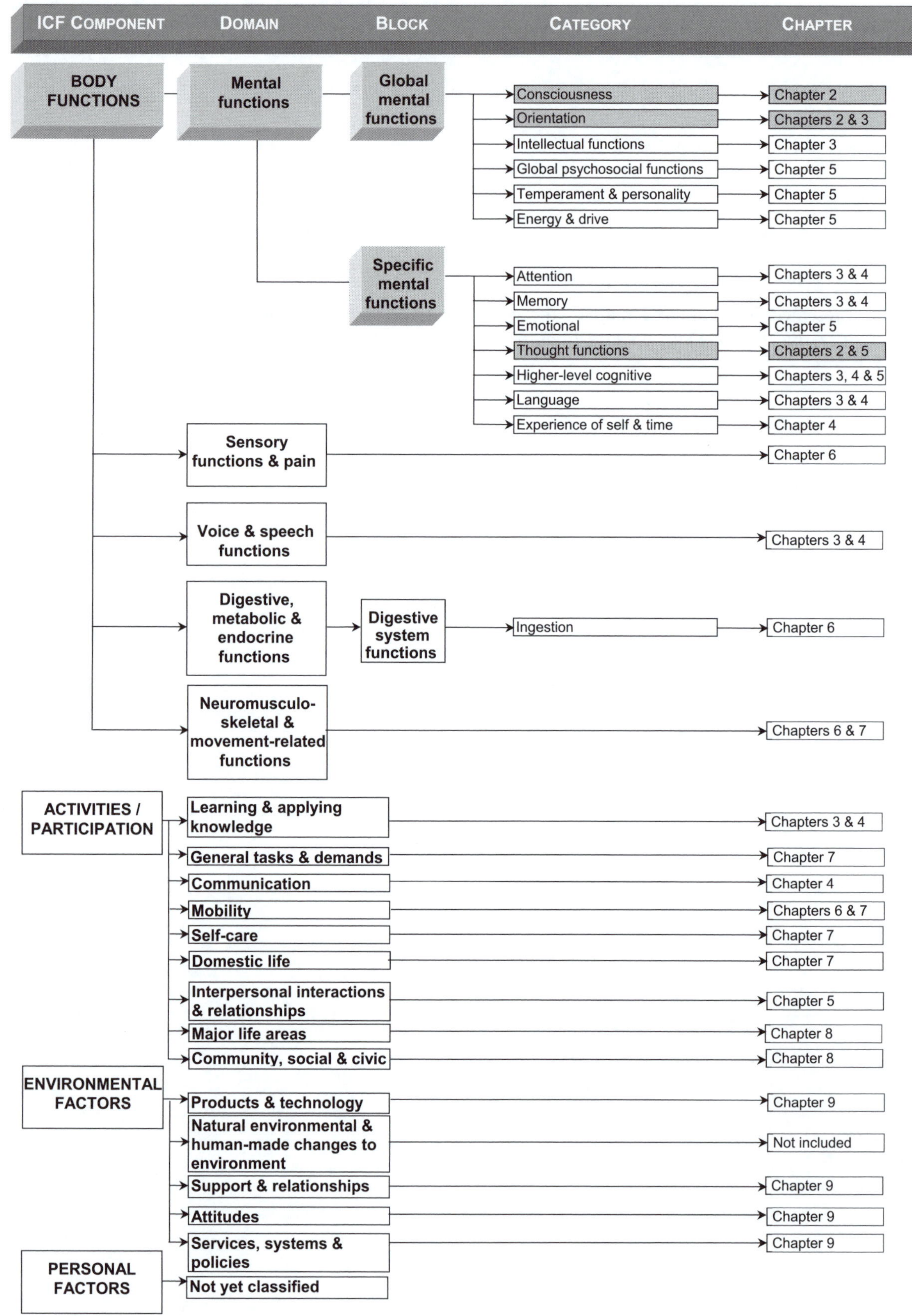

Figure 2.1 Instruments included in the compendium in relation to the ICF taxonomy – the highlighted component, domain and categories appear in this chapter. *Note:* The Figure presents a partial listing of five out of the eight Body Function domains and does not include any of the Body Structure domains. Categories for Mental functions also represent a partial listing and categories for the remaining domains are not listed. Refer to Appendix C for further detail on the ICF taxonomy.

Introduction

The ICF taxonomy draws a distinction between consciousness and orientation, which are the first two categories appearing within the block of Global mental functions (see Figure 2.1 and Appendix C). Within the ABI context, the constructs of consciousness and orientation represent altered states of consciousness, in contrast to other categories within Global mental functions. In recognition of this distinction, the present chapter groups together 17 scales, along with a number of their derivatives, measuring altered states of consciousness and orientation (some multidimensional scales, described in Chapter 10, also include items pertinent to this chapter). Within this grouping, natural divisions occur, and these form the structure of Chapter 2: coma and minimally consciousness states, delirium, and post-traumatic amnesia.

Section 1: Scales measuring coma, vegetative and minimally conscious states

Publication of the Glasgow Coma Scale (GCS; Teasdale & Jennett, 1974) heralded a standardized approach to measuring coma based on the quantification of systematic observations of behavioural responses. Along with this, in the decades since the GCS was published improved medical technology has enabled the survival of people who would have otherwise died (see Coleman, 2005). Some of these survivors can remain for many months in the vegetative state (VS) and minimally conscious state (MCS) with extremely impaired levels of awareness and responsiveness. An increasing number of scales has been developed to detect fine gradations of change in these patients, and a selection of these is described. Consensus-based diagnostic criteria to differentiate coma, VS and MCS (Giacino et al., 2002; Multi-Society Task Force on PVS, 1994; Teasdale & Jennett, 1974; further refined in Giacino, Kalmar & Whyte, 2004) are summarized in Table 2.1.

Section 2: Scales measuring delirium

The ICF classifies delirium within the category of consciousness; specifically, quality of consciousness. Some of the symptomatology characteristic of delirium also involves disturbance of thought function. Established criteria to diagnose delirium (*Diagnostic and Statistical Manual of Mental Disorders*, 4th ed., DSM-IV; American Psychiatric Association, 1994) are tabulated in summary form in Table 2.2.

Most delirium scales have been developed for people with a variety of medical conditions, often the older population. Many scales assessing delirium were identified in literature review. A number of these were considered to provide a valid evaluation of delirium, but were similar in item content to more widely used scales and hence were omitted in favour of the more established instruments. The five delirium scales selected for inclusion are those with sound psychometric properties, in current use in clinical/research settings, and considered to be industry standards or to have special features.

Table 2.1 Behavioural features distinguishing coma, the vegetative state and the minimally conscious state

Presence of coma	Requires absence of: i. eye opening ii. verbalization or mouthing words iii. response to commands iv. intentional movement
Emergence from coma	Requires presence of: i. periods of eye opening ii. return of autonomic functions, e.g., sleep–wake cycles, roving eye movements (without tracking ability)
Emergence from the vegetative state	Requires the presence of: i. reproducible movement to command ii. visual fixation iii. motor localization to noxious stimuli iv. intelligible verbalization *and* v. intentional (even if non-functional) communication
Emergence from the minimally conscious state	Requires the presence of all of the above, as well as: i. functional object use *and/or* ii. accurate, functional communication

Table 2.2 DSM-IV criteria for diagnosis of delirium

A	A disturbance of consciousness (i.e., reduced clarity of awareness of the environment) with reduced ability to focus, sustain, or shift attention
B	A change of cognition (such as memory deficit) or the development of a perceptual disturbance that is not better accounted for by a pre-existing, established, and evolving dementia
C	Develops over a short period (usually hours to days) and tends to fluctuate during the course of the day
D	Evidence from the history, physical examination or laboratory findings that the disturbance is caused by direct physiological consequences of a general medical condition.

Acknowledgement: *Diagnostic and Statistical Manual of Mental Disorders*, 4th ed. (1994), reproduced by permission of the American Psychiatric Association.

Section 3: Scales measuring orientation and post-traumatic amnesia (PTA)

At the upper level of altered states of consciousness are disturbances of orientation. Following emergence from coma after traumatic brain injury, a period of PTA usually occurs in which disorientation is a central (but not the sole) feature. PTA is defined as "an interval during which the patient is confused, amnesic for ongoing events and likely to evidence behavioral disturbance" (Levin, O'Donnell, & Grossman, 1979, p. 675). The importance of the duration of PTA is that it is a commonly used index of the severity of the initial injury and is one of the best predictors of recovery and outcome. Injury severity classifications using duration of PTA were described by Russell and Smith (1961) and later expanded by Jennett and Teasdale (1981), as summarized in Table 2.3.

Table 2.3 Traditional classifications of injury severity

Duration of PTA	*Traditional PTA severity classification (Jennett & Teasdale, 1981; Russell & Smith, 1961)*
< 5 mins	very mild
5–60 mins	mild
1–24 hours	moderate
1–7 days	severe
1–4 weeks	very severe
> 1 month	extremely severe

The WHO Collaborating Centre Task Force on Mild Traumatic Brain Injury (Carroll, Cassidy, Holm, Kraus, & Coronado, 2004) has revised the definition of mild injury to include all PTA durations up to 24 hours (thereby subsuming the category of moderate injury). The above groupings refer to PTA durations in isolation from other variables, and additional criteria that Carroll et al. use to define mild traumatic brain injury include GCS scores from 13 to 15 taken 30 minutes after injury, or loss of consciousness for 30 minutes, and/or other transient neurological abnormalities. Presence of skull fracture, intracranial lesions requiring neurosurgery, or persisting focal neurological deficits indicate more severe injury. Using GCS scores to classify injury severity, by convention, GCS scores from 3 to 8 indicate a severe injury, from 9 to 12 correspond to a moderate injury, and as noted above scores from 13 to 15 denote a mild injury. Von Holst and Cassidy (2004) observe, however, that in individual cases the GCS and PTA criteria may not be compatible (e.g., GCS score indicating mild injury and PTA score indicating severe injury). The rule of thumb takes the more severe classification for grading purposes. A range of methods and instruments are available to measure depth and duration of PTA, and five measures featuring prominently in the literature are described in this chapter. Orientation items feature in each of these scales, and additionally are often found as components of general cognitive screening tests, reviewed in Chapter 3.

References

American Psychiatric Association. (1994). *Diagnostic and statistical manual of mental disorders* (4th ed.). Washington, DC: APA.

Carroll, L. J., Cassidy, J. D., Holm, L., Kraus, J., & Coronado, V. G. (2004). Methodological issues and research recommendations for mild traumatic brain injury: The WHO Collaborating Centre Task Force on mild traumatic brain injury. *Journal of Rehabilitation Medicine, Suppl. 43*, 113–125.

Coleman, M. R. (Ed.). (2005). The assessment and rehabilitation of vegetative and minimally conscious patients. *Neuropsychological Rehabilitation, 15*(3/4), 161–162.

Giacino, J. T., Ashwal, S., Childs, N., Cranford, R., Jennett, B., Katz, D. I., et al. (2002). The minimally conscious state: Definition and diagnostic criteria. *Neurology, 58*(3), 349–353.

Giacino, J. T., Kalmar, K., & Whyte, J. (2004). The JFK Coma Recovery Scale-Revised: Measurement characteristics and diagnostic utility. *Archives of Physical Medicine and Rehabilitation, 85*, 2020–2029,

Jennett, B., & Teasdale, G. (1981). *Management of head injuries*. Philadelphia: F. A. Davis Company.

Levin, H. S., O'Donnell, V. M., & Grossman, R. G. (1979). The Galveston Orientation and Amnesia Test. A practical scale to assess cognition after head injury. *The Journal of Nervous and Mental Disease, 167*(11), 675–684.

Russell, W. R., & Smith, A. (1961). Post-traumatic amnesia in closed head injury. *Archives of Neurology, 5*, 16–29.

Teasdale, G., & Jennett, B. (1974). Assessment of coma and impaired consciousness: A practical scale. *The Lancet, 2*(7873), 81–84.

The Multi-Society Task Force on PVS (1994). Medical aspects of the persistent vegetative state (1). *The New England Journal of Medicine, 330*(21), 1499–1508.

Von Holst, H., & Cassidy, J. D. (2004). Mandate of the WHO Collaborating Centre Task Force on Mild Traumatic Brain Injury. *Journal of Rehabilitation Medicine, Suppl. 43*, 8–10.

World Health Organization. (2001). *International classification of functioning, disability and health*. Geneva: World Health Organization.

SECTION 1
Scales measuring coma, vegetative and minimally conscious states

Coma/Near Coma (C/NC) Scale

Rappaport, Dougherty, and Kelting (1992)

Source

The recording form for the C/NC is provided in Rappaport et al. (1992) and materials are also available on the website of the Center for Outcome Measurement in Brain Injury (http://www.tbims.org/combi/cnc/index.html). The recording form and a description of the C/NC levels appear below.

Purpose

The C/NC is an objective, clinician-administered test providing quantification of level of consciousness for patients with ABI in vegetative and minimally conscious states. It was developed so that "early microchanges in clinical status, which may be predictive of further progress, are not overlooked" (Rappaport et al., 1992, p. 628). The authors regard the C/NC as an expansion of the lower levels of the Disability Rating Scale (DRS; Rappaport, Hall, Hopkins, Belleza, & Cope, 1982; described in Chapter 10), and appropriate for those patients scoring ≥ 21 on the DRS (i.e., vegetative state). Rappaport (2005) also describes the clinical utility of the C/NC as providing a systematic method of charting changes in the patient, and a rationale for selecting and supporting long-term rehabilitation.

Item description

The 11 items of the C/NC examine response to simple commands and sensory stimulation, and document the presence of primitive reflexes. Specifically, the items comprise: auditory response (1 item), response to command (1 item), visual response (2 items), threat (1 item), olfactory (1 item), tactile response (2 items), pain (2 items) and vocalization (1 item).

Scale development

Limited information is available on the development of the C/NC, but Rappaport et al. (1992) describe it being revised a number of times following pilot testing. Scores from the C/NC are classified into one of five levels, but no information is provided on the procedures used to establish these levels.

Administration procedures, response format and scoring

Stimulus materials (bell, torch and ammonia sample) are required for administration. The C/NC is described as providing an easy and quick assessment, and the authors reported that administration was learned easily. Training on 5 to 10 patients is recommended for new raters and even after training, two independent clinicians should be used to ensure reliability. The authors suggest that for patients scoring ≥ 21 on the DRS, the C/NC is administered twice per day for 3 days, then weekly for 3 weeks, then every 2 weeks thereafter while DRS scores continue to be 21 or higher. If DRS scores fall below 21, the C/NC can be administered monthly, in combination with the DRS.

Responses to all items are rated on a 3-point scale: 0 (equivalent of maximal response), 2 (partial response), 4 (no response). A total score is obtained by summing scores for the 11 items, and dividing the score by the total number of items to obtain the average C/NC score. Average scores are then converted to levels: 0 (no coma), 1 (near coma), 2 (moderate coma), 3 (marked coma), 4 (extreme coma) using the descriptive categories of the scale (see below).

Psychometric properties

Information on the measurement properties of the C/NC is available from a number of sources. In the initial study, Rappaport et al. (1992) recruited 20 inpatients (age $M = 33.7$ years, range 12–70) from an inpatient rehabilitation unit in California, USA. Cause of injury was mainly road traffic crash and the initial C/NC administration occurred 8.9 months post-trauma ($SD = 10.59$, range 1–48). Patients were followed for 16 weeks. Two trained raters observed the patient simultaneously and made ratings independently. A consensus score was used to validate the C/NC against the DRS and evoked potential responses (EPR). Information on temporal stability is available from Pilon and Sullivan (1996) who studied 12 patients (age $M = 50$ years, $SD = 15.26$; 2–27 years post-trauma) from a skilled nursing care facility in Montreal, Canada. Data on responsiveness are also available from a case series reported by Talbot and Whitaker (1994) in the course of their intervention study on sensory stimulation. The seven participants had been in an "altered state of consciousness" for more than 1 month. No statistical analyses were conducted on the data, but the individual scores were presented in the report for each subject, and analysis was conducted on these by the author to determine responsiveness. Psychometric properties of the C/NC, taken from Rappaport et al. (1992) unless otherwise stated, are shown in Box 2.1.

Box 2.1

Validity:	Criterion: *Concurrent:* with DRS: $r_s = .69$ – with EPR: $r_s = .52$ Construct: *Internal consistency:* Cronbach alpha: .43, .65, .65 for scores at 1, 8 and 16 weeks respectively after initial testing
Reliability:	Inter-rater: $r = .97–.98$ Test–retest: Pilon & Sullivan: 2 weeks: ICC = .89
Responsiveness:	Initial C/NC score $M = 2.35$ ($SD = 0.60$) vs 16 weeks later $M = 1.52$ ($SD = 1.28$); $d = 1.38$ Talbot & Whitaker: Significant improvement in scores before ($M = 2.72$, $SD = 0.55$) vs after ($M = 1.01$, $SD = 1.01$) a sensory stimulation programme; $z = -2.37$, $p < .02$, $d = 3.11$

Comment

A number of scales developed for people with severely altered states of consciousness provide a detailed, and thence necessarily time-consuming, evaluation of level of functioning. An advantage of the C/NC is its brevity (O'Dell, Jasin, Lyons, Stivers, & Meszaros, 1996), although this, together with item diversity, may be at the expense of internal consistency. Only a small research literature is available on the C/NC, but it has demonstrated very good inter-rater reliability, is stable yet responsive to changes in the patient when these occur, and shows evidence of concurrent validity. A drawback of the instrument is that the nomenclature of the C/NC does not correspond to more recent diagnostic criteria for vegetative and minimally conscious states as recommended by expert groups (e.g., Giacino et al., 2002).

Key references

Giacino, J. T., Ashwal, S., Childs, N., Cranford, R., Jennett, B., Katz, D. I., et al. (2002). The minimally conscious state: Definition and diagnostic criteria. *Neurology*, *58*(3), 349–353.

Giacino, J. T., Kalmar, K., & Whyte, J. (2004). The JFK Coma Recovery Scale-Revised: Measurement characteristics and diagnostic utility. *Archives of Physical Medicine and Rehabilitation*, *85*, 2020–2029.

O'Dell, M. W., Jasin, P., Lyons, N., Stivers, M., & Meszaros, F. (1996). Standardized assessment instruments for minimally-responsive, brain-injured patients. *NeuroRehabilitation*, *6*, 45–55.

Pilon, M., & Sullivan, S. J. (1996). Motor profile of patients in minimally responsive and persistent vegetative states. *Brain Injury*, *10*(6), 421–437.

Rappaport, M. (2005). The Disability Rating and Coma/Near Coma scales in evaluating severe head injury. *Neuropsychological Rehabilitation*, *15*(3–4), 442–453.

Rappaport, M., Dougherty, A. M., & Kelting, D. L. (1992). Evaluation of coma and vegetative states. *Archives of Physical Medicine and Rehabilitation*, *73*(7), 628–634.

Rappaport, M., Hall, K. M., Hopkins, K., Belleza, T., & Cope, D. N. (1982). Disability rating scale for severe head trauma: Coma to community. *Archives of Physical Medicine and Rehabilitation*, *63*(3), 118–123.

Talbot, L. R., & Whitaker, H. A. (1994). Brain-injured persons in an altered state of consciousness: Measures and intervention strategies. *Brain Injury*, *8*(8), 689–699.

Coma/Near Coma Scale – Recording Form

Rappaport, Dougherty, and Kelting (1992)

Name:	**Administered by:**	**Date:**

Instructions: For patients with a Disability Rating (DR) score ≥ 21, i.e., vegetative state or greater. Complete twice a day for 3 days, then weekly for 3 weeks; every 2 weeks thereafter if DR score ≥ 21. If DR < 21 follow monthly with DR scores.

Whether or not patient appears receptive to speech, speak encouragingly and supportively for about 30 seconds to help establish awareness that another person is present and advise patient you will be asking him/her to make a simple response. Then request the patient try to make the same response with brief priming before 2nd, 3rd and subsequent trials. Make sure patient is not sleeping.

Parameter	Stimulus	No. of trials	Response measures	Score	Criteria	Date: / Time: / Assessor:					
AUDITORY*	1. Bell ringing 5 s at 10 s intervals	3^	Eye opening or orientation towards sound	0 2 4	≥ 3 times 1 or 2 times No response						
COMMAND RESPONSIVITY with priming	2. Request patient to open or close eyes, mouth, move finger, hand or leg	3	Response to command	0 2 4	Responds to command 2 or 3 times Tentative or inconsistent 1 time No response						
VISUAL^^ with priming Must be able to open eyes; if not score 4 for each stimulus situation (items 3, 4, 5) and check here ☐	3. Light flashes (1/s × 5) in front; slightly left, right and up and down each trial	5	Fixation or avoidance	0 2 4	Sustained fixation or avoidance 3 times Partial fixation 1 or 2 times None						
	4. Tell patient "Look at me" move face 20 inches away from side to side	5	Fixation and tracking	0 2 4	Sustained tracking (at least 3 times) Partial tracking 1 or 2 times No tracking						
THREAT	5. Quickly move hand forward to within 1–3 inches of eyes	3	Eye blink	0 2 4	3 blinks 1 or 2 blinks No blinks						
OLFACTORY (block tracheostomy 3–5 seconds if present)	6. Ammonia capsule/ bottle 1 inch under nose for about 2 seconds	3	Withdrawal or other response linked to stimulus	0 2 4	Responds 2 or 3 times quickly (≤3 s) Slow partial withdrawal; grimacing 1 time No withdrawal or grimacing						
TACTILE	7. Shoulder tap – Tap shoulder briskly 3 times without speaking to patient: each side	3^	Head or eye orientation or shoulder movement to tap	0 2 4	Orients toward tap 2 or 3 times Partially orients 1 time No orienting or response						
	8. Nasal swab (each nostril: entrance only – do not penetrate deeply)	3^	Withdrawal or eye blink or mouth twitch	0 2 4	Clear, quick (within 2 s) 2 or 3 times Delayed or partial response 1 time No response						
PAIN (Allow up to 10 s for response) If spinal cord injury check here ☐ and go to stimulus 10	9. Firm pinch finger tip: pressure of wood of pencil across nail; each side	3^	See score criteria	0 2 4	Withdrawal 2 or 3 times General agitation/non specific movement 1 time No response						
	10. Robust ear pinch/pull × 3; each side	3^	Withdrawal or other response linked to stimulus	0 2 4	Responds 2 or 3 times General agitation/non-specific movement 1 time No response						
VOCALIZATION ^^ (Assuming no tracheostomy) If tracheostomy present do not score but check here ☐	11. None (score best response)	–	See score criteria	0 2 4	Spontaneous words Non-verbal vocalization (moan, groan) No sounds						

COMMENTS: (Include important changes in physical condition such as infection, pneumonia, hydrocephalus, seizures, further trauma, etc.)

Total C/NC Score (add scores): A						
Number of items scored: B						
Average C/NC score (A/B): C						
Coma/Near Coma Level (0–4): D						

* If possible use brain stem auditory evoked response (BAER) test at 80 db nHL to establish ability to hear in at least one ear.
^ Each side up to 3 times if needed.
^^ Consult with nursing staff on arousability; do not judge solely on performance during testing. If patient is sleeping, repeat the assessment later.

Levels of the Coma/Near Coma Scale

Rappaport, Dougherty, and Kelting (1992)

Level	Score	Description
0	**0.00–0.89 No coma**	Patients are consistently and readily responsive to at least three (of 10) sensory stimulation tests and show consistent responsivity to simple commands. This category overlaps and phases into the lower levels of the extremely severe disability category of the DRS (DRS scores 17 to 19).
1	**0.90–2.00 Near coma**	Patients are consistently responsive to stimulation presented to two (of 10) sensory modalities, or they are inconsistently or partially responsive to simple commands. This category overlaps and phases into the upper levels of the extremely severe disabled and lower levels of the vegetative state categories of the DRS (DRS scores 20 to 21 and 22 to 23, respectively).
2	**2.01–2.89 Moderate coma**	Patients are inconsistently responsive to stimulation presented to two or three (of 10) sensory modalities, but they are not responsive to simple commands. Patients may vocalize (in the absence of tracheostomy) with moans, groans and grunts, but no recognizable words. This category overlaps and phases into the upper levels of the vegetative state and lower levels of the extreme vegetative state categories of the DRS (DRS scores of 24 to 26, respectively).
3	**2.90–3.49 Marked coma**	Patients are inconsistently responsive to stimulation presented to one (of 10) sensory modalities, and they are not responsive to simple commands. No vocalization (without tracheostomy). This category overlaps and phases into the middle levels of the extreme vegetative category of the DRS (DRS score 27 to 28).
4	**3.50–4.00 Extreme coma**	There is no responsivity to any of the sensory stimulation tests (of 10), no response to simple commands, and no vocalization (without tracheostomy). This category overlaps and phases into upper level of the extreme vegetative state category of the DRS (DRS score of 29).

Acknowledgement: Reprinted from Coma/Near Coma Scale (CNCS); Rappaport, M., Dougherty, A. M., & Kelting, D. L. (1992). Evaluation of coma and vegetative states. *Archives of Physical Medicine and Rehabilitation, 73*(7), 628–634, reprinted with permission from the American Congress of Rehabilitation Medicine and the American Academy of Physical Medicine and Rehabilitation and Elsevier.

Comprehensive Level of Consciousness Scale (CLOCS)

Stanczak et al. (1984)

Source

Detailed instructions and scoring procedures for the CLOCS are provided in Stanczak et al. (1984) and are reproduced below.

Purpose

The CLOCS is an objective, clinician-administered test, designed to measure a range of behaviours associated with impaired consciousness. It has been used with acute neurosurgical patients, mainly with traumatic brain injury (TBI) and stroke, as well as patients with neoplasms, hypoxia, drug overdose, hydrocephalus and cerebral infection.

Item description

The eight scales of the CLOCS examine posture, movement, responsiveness and communication, as well as four scales for eye and pupillary responses. Each of the eight scales contains between five and nine operationally defined levels, representing a hierarchy of responsiveness.

Scale development

Development of the CLOCS was in response to perceived limitations of the Glasgow Coma Scale (GCS). The authors identified a need to develop an instrument examining a wider range of behaviours than the GCS and one that was more sensitive to subtle changes in the patient. No information is provided in Stanczak et al. (1984), however, regarding scale development in terms of the item selection process or response format.

Administration procedures, response format and scoring

A torch to examine pupillary responses is the only equipment required to administer the CLOCS. In the initial validation study, the CLOCS was administered by a team of neurosurgical residents and neuropsychology doctoral candidates. It is described as being suitable for administration by technical and "paraprofessional" staff members. Administration time for experienced users is brief (3–5 mins).

Scores with a variable range are assigned to each of the levels within the eight scales. The level allocated, and corresponding score, is that which best represents the patient's functioning. The total score ranges from 0 to 48, with higher scores indicating a better level of functioning.

Psychometric properties

The validation sample for the CLOCS comprised 101 consecutive patients (mainly TBI) recruited from the neurosurgical service of the Baptist Memorial Hospital, in Memphis, Tennessee, USA (Stanczak et al., 1984). All patients (age $M = 44.75$ years, range 5–92) had a GCS score ≤ 13 ($M = 6.10$, $SD = 3.16$) and were within $M = 19.1$ hours ($SD = 17.3$) of symptom onset. They were assessed with the CLOCS and GCS every 12 hours for the first week and at less frequent intervals until any of the following occurred: GCS scores ≥ 13 on two consecutive occasions, discharge or death. Inter-rater reliability was established using three pairs of raters who jointly conducted (but independently scored) 20 evaluations. Temporal stability compared results of the initial assessment and re-evaluation after 12 hours. Validation included evaluations of a global assessment of consciousness by nurses using a 7-point scale from "coma depasse" to "alert and oriented". Predictive validity used the initial CLOCS score against an adapted nine-level version of the Glasgow Outcome Scale (GOS) made at discharge/death. A subsequent report (Johnston, Thomas, & Stanczak, 1996) used a subset of 43 out of the 101 patients from the Stanczak et al. study who had computerized tomography (CT) or electroencephalography (EEG) within 1 hour of CLOCS observation. Ratings from CT/EEG were converted to a 9-point Likert scale (from 0 = no change to 8 = profound change) by a rater who was blind to the CLOCS score. Results from Stanczak et al., unless otherwise stated, are shown in Box 2.2.

Box 2.2

Validity:	Criterion:
	Concurrent: with nurses' global ratings: $r = .71$
	Johnston et al.: with GCS: $r = .90$
	– with CT/EEG: $r = -.49$
	Predictive: initial CLOCS with GOS at discharge/death: $r = .58$
	Johnston et al.: in multiple regression analysis, CLOCS score was a significant individual contributor to prediction of outcome, after CT/EEG score, the final model accounting for 33% of the variance
	Construct:
	Internal consistency: Cronbach alpha: .86
Reliability:	Inter-rater: Median: $r = .96$
	Test–retest: 12 hours: $r_s = .89$
Responsiveness:	No information available

Comment

The CLOCS provides a reliable and valid measure of level of consciousness. Its very good psychometric properties are further enhanced with the exclusion of Scale 2 (Eye Position at Rest), and the authors recommend this scale be deleted for research studies. In comparing the CLOCS with the GCS, Stanczak et al. (1984) found that it had greater internal consistency and test–retest reliability, but comparable validity. Its very high correlation with the GCS ($r = .90$) also indicates that there is a great deal of overlap between the two instruments. One possible drawback of the CLOCS is the absence of cut-off scores for severity gradings, which has proved useful with other instruments such as the GCS for classifying patients and research participants into broad groupings for descriptive purposes (e.g., mild, moderate, severe degrees of injury). On the other hand, a particular strength of the CLOCS is the wide score range (0–48), which enables it to detect small changes in level of consciousness although a formal responsiveness study has not been reported.

Key references

Johnston, M. D., Thomas, L., & Stanczak, D. E. (1996). Construct validity of the Comprehensive Level of Consciousness Scale: A comparison of behavioral and neurodiagnostic measures. *Archives of Clinical Neuropsychology*, *11*(8), 703–711.

Stanczak, D. E., White, J. G., Gouvier, W., D., Moehle, K. A., Daniel, M., Novack, T., et al. (1984). Assessment of level of consciousness following severe neurological insult. A comparison of the psychometric qualities of the Glasgow Coma Scale and the Comprehensive Level of Consciousness Scale. *Journal of Neurosurgery*, *60*(5), 955–960.

Comprehensive Level of Consciousness Scale

Stanczak et al. (1984)

Name: **Assessor:** **Date:**

SCALE 1: POSTURE

Instructions: Prior to any stimulation, observe the patient's posture and record the number of the most appropriate description.

4 Posture is under volitional control and is normally flexible
3 Normal periodic postural changes as in sleep
2 Asterixis, cerea flexibilitas, or rigid extension
1 No abnormal posture; muscle tonus is normal
0 No abnormal posture but muscle tonus is completely flaccid

SCALE 2: EYE POSITION AT REST

Instructions: Observe the patient's resting eye position and degree of conjugate movement of eyes. Record the number of the most appropriate description.

6 Midposition and conjugate
5 Full conjugate deviation
4 Resting deviation of the eyes below the horizontal meridian *OR* resting vertical, dysconjugate gaze
3 Conjugate ocular deviation in which the eyes cannot be brought back past the midline
2 Unilateral inward or outward deviation
1 Eyes converge
0 Skew deviation

SCALE 3: SPONTANEOUS EYE-OPENING

Instructions: Prior to any stimulation, observe the patient for spontaneous eye-openings. If none, try to elicit eye-openings by presenting the following *verbal stimuli* in order: 1) speaking the patient's name, and 2) shouting the patient's name. If these mild stimuli fail, the following *moderate stimuli* should be applied: 1) shaking the patient lightly, 2) repeated light slapping of the medial aspect of the patient's arms, and 3) shaking the patient vigorously taking care not to dislodge any life support systems or to exacerbate any injuries. If the mild and moderate stimuli fail to elicit eye-opening, the following *noxious stimuli* should be applied: 1) rubbing the sternum vigorously with your thumb, 2) pressing on the nailbeds of fingers of both the patient's hands, and 3) squeezing the webbed tissue between the thumb and index finger on both the patient's hands. Stimulation is terminated when a recordable response is elicited. If none of these procedures elicits eye-opening assign a score of zero for this scale.

4 Volitional control of eye-opening
3 Eye-opening in response to mild (verbal) stimuli
2 Eye-opening only in response to moderate stimuli
1 Eye-opening only in response to noxious stimuli
0 No spontaneous or elicited eye-opening

SCALE 4: GENERAL MOTOR FUNCTIONING

Instructions: Prior to any stimulation, observe the patient's spontaneous movements. If no spontaneous movements are observed, a knowledgeable informant should be questioned to determine if spontaneous movements have been observed during the previous 6-hour period. Record the number of the most appropriate description of the patient's BEST performance.

6 Normal spontaneous movements within the limits of the patient's physical abilities
5 Psychomotor excitation *OR* marked torpor
4 Any of the following: yawning, sneezing, spontaneous swallowing, hiccoughing, sucking, or gnawing on lower lip, rhythmic tongue protrusions, kissing movements, and/or chewing movements
3 Polishing movements by the hand on the thigh, abdomen, or chest, *OR* stirring motions and scratching of the skin or bed, *OR* flexion and extension of the toes and/or ankles, *OR* fine picking movements of the fingers
2 Multifocal or rhythmic myoclonus or spasms of the extremities
1 Athetoid or ballistic movements of the fingers, wrists, elbows, toes, ankles, or knees, *AND/OR* torsions of the shoulders, hips, spine, neck, or face, *OR* periodic seizure activity
0 No spontaneous motor movements

SCALE 5: ABNORMAL OCULAR MOVEMENTS

Instructions: Observe the patient's ocular movements and record the number of the most appropriate description.

6 None
5 Slow, random horizontal movements that may vary from conjugate to dysconjugate
4 Refractory nystagmus
3 Convergence nystagmus
2 Ocular bobbing *OR* nystagmoid jerking of either eye in a lateral, vertical, or rotational direction
1 Slow, irregular eye movements that are bilateral and sometimes reciprocal such that one eye may move downward and outward while the other moves upward and inward
0 Complete absence of ocular motility

SCALE 6: PUPILLARY LIGHT REFLEXES

Instructions: Pupillary reactivity to a strong light source should be noted, and the number of the most appropriate description should be recorded.

7 Normal direct and consensual light reflexes
6 Unilateral absence of direct light reflex
5 Unilateral absence of direct and consensual light reflexes
4 Bilateral absence of direct and consensual light reflexes
3 Hippus
2 Pontine (pinpoint) pupils
1 Eyes at midposition, 4–5 mm in diameter, and fixed to all stimuli *OR* pupils may be slightly irregular and/or slightly unequal
0 Wide pupillary dilation and fixed to all stimuli *OR* bilaterally small (pinpoint) pupils which are fixed to all stimuli

SCALE 7: GENERAL REPONSIVENESS

Instructions: The following definitions are appropriate to this scale: *Arousal*: any intelligible verbalization and/or eye-opening coupled with the apparently volitional establishment of reliable eye-contact with the examiner; concomitant motor activity may or may not be observed. *Mild stimulation*, *moderate stimulation*, and *noxious stimulation*: same as in Scale 3. Record the number of the description which most adequately reflects the patient's response.

8 The person is fully aroused and alert or, if asleep, arouses and attends to the examiner following only mild or moderate stimulation. The arousal outlasts the duration of the stimulus
7 The person is aroused by mild or moderate stimulation but, upon cessation of stimulation, returns to his/her former state *OR* the patient displays marked psychomotor agitation shortly after the stimulus onset
6 The patient is aroused only by noxious stimulation
5 In response to noxious stimulation, the patient displays a purposeful, coordinated withdrawal and/or a typical facial grimace. There is no arousal
4 In response to noxious stimulation, the patients display a gross, disorganized withdrawal. There is no facial grimace or arousal
3 In response to noxious stimulation, the patient displays only a feeble, disorganized withdrawal *OR* flexion. There is no arousal or facial grimace
2 Any decorticate rigidity
1 Any decerebrate rigidity
0 Total absence of discernible motor activity even in response to noxious stimulation

SCALE 8: BEST COMMUNICATIVE EFFORT

Instructions: Observe the patient's communicative efforts and record the number of the description that most accurately reflects the patient's BEST response. Additional information regarding communicative efforts during the previous 6-hour period may be solicited from a knowledgeable informant.

7 Normal communication is possible through speech, writing, gesturing, etc.
6 Profuse spontaneous or elicited verbalizations (signs/gestures). The communication is intelligible but may be bizarre, jargonistic, and/or perseverative
5 The patient responds to verbal, written, or signalled instructions with spontaneous but unintelligible or poorly articulated verbalizations (sign/gestures) or in a coded manner such as eye-blinking, finger-tapping, or hand-squeezing. If intubated, the person responds appropriately to commands
4 The patient spontaneously vocalizes, verbalizes, makes signs, or gestures but gives no indication that he /she comprehends any form of receptive language
3 The patient visually tracks an object passed through his/her visual field and/or turns his/her head towards the examiner as if wishing to communicate *OR* the patient generates spontaneous moaning or muttering coupled with reliable eye contact or searching behaviours
2 Spontaneous, random muttering or moaning only
1 Muttering or moaning in response to noxious stimulation
0 No elicited or spontaneous vocalizations, searching behaviours, or eye-contact

GLOSSARY

ASTERIXIS: intermittent lapses of an assumed posture
ATHETOID: slow, sinuous, writhing movements
BALLISTIC: violent, flinging movements
CEREA FLEXIBILITAS: waxy flexibility commonly seen in catatonia
CONVERGENCE NYSTAGMUS: slow, drifting ocular divergence followed by a quick convergent jerk; may be interspersed with refractory nystagmus
DECEREBRATE RIGIDITY: extended, adducted (drawn towards the median plane), and internally rotated upper limbs; bilaterally extended and plantar-flexed lower limbs; opisthotonos (head and heels bent backward and the body bowed forward) and/or jaw-clenching may be observed
DECORTICATE RIGIDITY: upper limbs are flexed at the elbows, wrists, and fingers, and are adducted (drawn towards the median plane) at the shoulders; the lower limbs are extended, plantar-flexed, and internally rotated
HIPPUS: eyes at midposition, 5–6 mm in diameter, round, and regular but spontaneously fluctuate in size and may show abnormal exaggeration of rhythmic contraction and dilation independent of changes in illumination
NYSTAGMUS: involuntary, rapid movement of the eyeball
OCULAR BOBBING: conjugate, brisk, downward eye movements followed by a slower return to the primary position in a kind of bobbing action
REFRACTORY NYSTAGMUS: irregular jerks of the eye backward into the orbit
SKEW DEVIATION: one eye looking upward while the other looks downward
TORPOR: sluggishness, motor retardation
TORSION: twisting

Acknowledgement: Reprinted from Stanczak, D. E. et al. (1984). Assessment of level of consciousness following severe neurological insult. *Journal of Neurosurgery, 60*, 955–960, Figure 1, p. 956, reprinted by permission of the American Association of Neurological Surgeons.
www.thejns-net.org

Glasgow Coma Scale (GCS)

Teasdale and Jennett (1974)

Source

The GCS was originally described in Teasdale and Jennett (1974). The typical recording chart appears in Jennett and Teasdale (1981), is available on the Internet Stroke Center website (http://www.strokecenter.org), and is also reproduced below.

Purpose

The GCS is an objective, clinician-administered test, designed to assess depth and duration of impaired consciousness and coma arising from any medical condition. These include neurological conditions (such as cerebral infections, stroke and traumatic brain injury, TBI), as well as non-neurological conditions that may result in altered levels of consciousness (e.g., diabetic ketosis, drug overdose, renal failure). The aim was to develop a bedside examination that could be repeated throughout a 24-hour period to monitor change in level of consciousness.

Item description

The GCS examines hierarchical levels of functioning in three domains: Eye opening, Verbal response and Motor response. There are four levels of Eye opening, ranging from the lowest level, no eye opening, not even in response to pain, through to the highest level, spontaneous eye opening. Five levels of Verbal response range from no verbal response, not even incomprehensible sounds, through to oriented to person, place and time for year, season and month. Six levels of Motor response range from no motor response, not even in response to pain, through to obeying commands, such as "squeeze my hand".

Scale development

Development of the GCS arose in an effort to improve methods of assessment of impaired consciousness available at that time, many of which used unstructured observations and descriptive labels (e.g., stupor, torpor, obtunded) that did not have clear behavioural descriptors allowing reliable assessment. Limited information is available regarding the developmental process of the GCS, but the three components selected for the GCS (eye opening, verbal and motor responses) feature commonly in reports of impaired consciousness. Levels of response were independently evaluated in each component and graded in rank order of the degree of dysfunction (four for Eye opening, five for Verbal and six for Motor). The Motor domain initially contained five levels, but was subsequently increased to six by subdividing flexion to take account of withdrawal versus abnormal flexion (Teasdale & Jennett, 1976).

Teasdale and Jennett (1974) initially resisted a definition of "either consciousness or coma in absolute terms" (p. 82), although they used an operational definition of coma as "a patient who showed no eye opening, who did not obey commands, nor give any comprehensible verbal response" (Jennett & Teasdale, 1977, p. 880). Early investigations into the GCS focused on analysis of these three components separately, but Jennett and Teasdale (1977) also recognized that a summed score could provide a useful index of overall responsiveness of the patient. Based on analysis of GCS scores from 700 patients in the International Data Bank (Jennett & Teasdale, 1977), later increased to 1000 patients, they further defined the presence of coma in relation to a summed GCS score (Jennett & Teasdale, 1981, p. 81):

> In the range from 3 to 15 there is not a point that discriminates absolutely between patients in coma (by our definition) and those who are more responsive than this. However, all combinations that sum to 7 or less define coma, as do . . . 90 percent of all observations summing to 8 or less, and none of those that add up to 9 or more.

By convention, total GCS scores can be classified into severity groupings (mild, moderate and severe), but no information is available regarding the methodology of this determination (see Teasdale, 1995).

Administration procedures, response format and scoring

No special materials are required to administer the GCS. The authors aimed to develop a scale that did not require special training for the clinician, but even so, clinicians need to be experienced in assessing altered states of consciousness to ensure reliability, as the results of Rowley and Fielding (1991) demonstrated. Time to administer the GCS is very quick – a matter of a few minutes. Factors impeding administration (e.g., eye swelling, intubation, splints) are recorded. When responses are variable (e.g., differences between limb movements) the best response is recorded.

The total GCS score ranges from 3 to 15, and scores for the domains can also be reported separately in notation form: for example, E4+V1+M3 referring to scores for Eye opening, Verbal response and Motor response respectively. Total scores can also be converted to injury severity groupings: mild (GCS scores 13–15), moderate (scores 9–12), and severe (scores ≤ 8).

Psychometric properties

In spite of the large literature on the GCS, relatively little information is available on its psychometric properties. Earlier studies by the test developers focused on examining specific psychometric features, such as inter-rater reliability (Teasdale, Knill-Jones, & Van der Sande, 1978). Although results were positive, more specific questions posed by subsequent research groups, have tempered the earlier findings. For example, Rowley and Fielding (1991) examined inter-rater reliability of the GCS with four groups of nurses with varying degrees of training and experience in using the GCS. Experienced/trained nurses had higher inter-rater reliability (r = .87–1.0) for all components than student nurses without training or experience on neurosurgical wards (r = .76–1.0). Discrepancies were particularly noted in scoring the more difficult mid-range patients where agreement was substantially lower (8–14%) than at the extremes (97%).

Predictive validity of the GCS was also the subject of a number of early studies. Jennett, Teasdale, Braakman, Minderhoud, and Knill-Jones (1976) examined prediction on Glasgow Outcome Scale (GOS) at 6 months post-trauma from GCS data collected in the acute stages after TBI in patients recruited from the Institute of Neurological Sciences, Glasgow, UK (n = 428) and two centres in the Netherlands (n = 172). It is noted, however, that Teasdale and Jennett (1976) had already placed caveats on the predictive validity of the GCS, recommending that the GCS score should be used in combination with other variables, such as age and brainstem function, and they further asserted that "impaired consciousness alone . . . is not enough to make accurate prediction in individual patients" (Jennett & Teasdale, 1977, p. 881). The low to moderate correlation coefficients between GCS scores in isolation and outcome measures such as the Functional Independence Measure have been subsequently confirmed by independent research groups (e.g., Zafonte, Hammond, Mann, Wood, Black, & Millis, 1996).

There is considerable evidence to support the construct validity of the GCS. Outcome studies in which participants have been stratified according to the three GCS severity bands have demonstrated the differential outcomes for those whose initial injuries were mild, moderate or severe. Thornhill, Teasdale, Murray, McEwan, and Roy (2000), for example, followed up 549 patients with head injury admitted to five general hospitals in Glasgow in a 12-month period (66% mild with GCS 13–15, 18% moderate with GCS 9–12, 13% severe with GCS ≤ 8, 3% unclassified).

In the course of validating other instruments, psychometric data are also furnished for the GCS, and concurrent validity has been demonstrated by Majerus, Van der Linden, and Shiel (2000) with the Wessex Head Injury Matrix (WHIM), by Wijdicks, Bamlet, Maramattom, Manno, and McClelland (2005) with the Full Outline of UnResponsiveness (FOUR) score and so forth. A comprehensive psychometric study in a single sample was conducted by Stanczak et al. (1984) to validate the Comprehensive Level of Consciousness Scale (CLOCS; also described in this chapter). The sample comprised 101 consecutive admissions to the neurosurgical service of the Baptist Memorial Hospital, Memphis, Tennessee, USA. Patients were aged M = 44.8 years (SD = 24.5, range 5–92), mainly with TBI and stroke, and assessed within hours of symptom onset. All had GCS scores of 13 or less. Inter-rater reliability was determined using three pairs of independent raters making 20 joint evaluations. Temporal stability was established by comparing initial evaluation with reassessment 12 hours later. Concurrent validity was examined with nurses' ratings on a global 7-point scale to assess level of consciousness from "coma depasse" to "alert and oriented". Predictive validity was examined with initial GCS scores and a 9-level version of the Glasgow Outcome Scale at discharge/death. Results of the Stanczak et al. study, except where otherwise stated, are shown in Box 2.3.

Box 2.3

Validity:	Criterion: *Concurrent:* with nurses' ratings: $r = .68$ Majerus et al.: with initial WHIM: $r = .83$, with final WHIM: $r = .95$ Wijdicks et al.: with FOUR: $r_s = .92$ *Predictive:* initial GCS with GOS at discharge/death: $r = .56$ Jennett et al.: GCS in first 24 hours with death/persistent vegetative state vs survival 97% accuracy – GCS in first 3 days with death/persistent vegetative state vs severe disability vs moderate disability/good recovery 97% accuracy Construct: *Internal consistency:* Cronbach alpha: .69 *Discriminant:* Thornhill et al.: at 12 month follow-up, – 42% of severe vs 22% of mild and 28% of moderate had problems with activities of daily living inside the home – 67% of severe vs 34% of mild and 38% of moderate had such problems outside the home – 82% of severe vs 58% of mild and 66% of moderate experienced physical problems – 76% of severe vs 43% of mild and 49% of moderate experienced cognitive problems; all $p < .01$
Reliability:	Inter-rater: Median: $r = .95$ Test–retest: 12 hours: $r_s = .85$
Responsiveness:	No information available

Derivatives of the GCS

The GCS is very widely used and has spawned a number of other applications, two of which are described below.

Paediatric Glasgow Coma Scale (PGCS); Simpson and Reilly (1982)

As noted by Jennett and Teasdale (1977), there are several reasons other than coma why patients may not speak, and they highlighted the special case of children. Simpson and Reilly (1982) amended the GCS for children. They described motor and verbal responses in relation to developmental stages from babies < 6 months of age to age 5 years and a subsequent publication provided validity data (Simpson, Cockington, Hanieh, Raftos, & Reilly, 1991). Their descriptions are shown in Box 2.4.

The British Paediatric Neurological Association (2001) (http://www.bpna.org.uk; accessed 27 April, 2008) further revised the verbal response category for children younger than 5 years as follows:

V5. Alert, babbles, coos, words or sentences to usual ability
V4. Less than usual ability, irritable cry
V3. Cries to pain
V2. Moans to pain
V1. No vocal response to pain

Glasgow Coma Scale – Extended (GCS-E); Nell, Yates, and Kruger (2000)

An extension to the GCS was published by Nell et al. (2000) known as the GCS-E. The aim of the GCS-E is to capture variations within the mild injury group, that is, those scoring 13 to 15 on the GCS. A coded set of "behavioural landmarks", which estimates the duration of post-traumatic amnesia, is added to the GCS score. The 8-point Amnesia Scale is reproduced below. The authors note that when the GCS score is 12 or less, it is seldom possible to use the Amnesia Scale, but other procedures are available and suited to this purpose (see Section 3 of this chapter for a selection of instruments to measure post-traumatic amnesia). Scores 0 to 7 derived from the Amnesia Scale of the GCS-E can be used as an "optional diagnostic variable" by entering the score after a colon placed after the GCS score. Thus a person scoring 13 on the GCS who also has an amnesia of approximately 1 hour would be coded as 13:5. The GCS-E uses a training manual, which includes a proficiency test.

Comment

The GCS established a landmark in the evaluation of patients with altered states of consciousness. Some reports, however, have raised concerns about the psychometric properties of the GCS (see the systematic review of Prasad, 1996). A number of these issues are easily addressed (e.g., training for novice examiners to

Box 2.4

Age	*Best verbal response*	*Age*	*Best motor response*	*Age*	*Maximum score*
0–6 mths	Cries (score 2)	0–6 mths	Flexion (score 3)	0–6 mths	9
> 6–12 mths	Noises (score 3)	6 mths – 2 yrs	Localizes pain, but does not obey (score 4)	> 6–12 mths	11
1–5 yrs	Words (score 4)	> 2 yrs	Obeys commands	> 1–2 yrs > 2–5 yrs	12 13
> 5 yrs	Oriented (aware that in hospital – score 5)			> 5 yrs	14

improve inter-rater reliability), and others (e.g., low internal consistency) may be expected given that the GCS comprises only three disparate components that are evaluated independently. An important limitation is the incomplete assessment that results when patients are intubated, paralysed or sedated. In terms of predictive validity, the GCS was developed for emergency medicine, where arguably the critical prediction is one of survival and level of function early post-trauma, which the GCS does well. Other measures are probably better suited as predictors of detailed functional outcomes in rehabilitation samples. Notwithstanding criticisms of the GCS, as Nell et al. (2000) note: "The benefits of international acceptance, familiarity, ease of use, and a high degree of inter-rater reliability weigh the balance heavily against the introduction of alternative methods of assessing level of consciousness" (p. 614).

Key references

Jennett, B., & Teasdale, G. (1977). Aspects of coma after severe head injury. *The Lancet*, *1*(8017), 878–881.

Jennett, B., & Teasdale, G. (1981). *Management of head injuries*. Philadelphia: F. A. Davis Company.

Jennett, B., Teasdale, G., Braakman, R., Minderhoud, J., & Knill-Jones, R. (1976). Predicting outcome in individual patients after severe head injury. *The Lancet*, *1*(7968), 1031–1034.

Majerus, S., Van der Linden, M., & Shiel, A. (2000). Wessex Head Injury Matrix and Glasgow Coma Scale/Glasgow-Liège Coma Scale: A validation and comparison study. *Neuropsychological Rehabilitation*, *10*(2), 167–184.

Nell, V., Yates, D. W., & Kruger, J. (2000). An Extended Glasgow Coma Scale (GCS-E) with enhanced sensitivity to mild brain injury. *Archives of Physical Medicine and Rehabilitation*, *81*(5), 614–617.

Prasad, K. (1996). The Glasgow Coma Scale: A critical appraisal of its clinimetric properties. *Journal of Clinical Epidemiology*, *49*(7), 755–763.

Rowley, G., & Fielding, K. (1991). Reliability and accuracy of the Glasgow Coma Scale with experienced and inexperienced users. *The Lancet*, *337*(8740), 535–538.

Simpson, D. A., Cockington, R. A., Hanieh, A., Raftos, J., & Reilly, P. L. (1991). Head injuries in infants and young children: The value of the Pediatric Coma Scale. *Child's Nervous System*, *7*, 183–190.

Simpson, D., & Reilly, P. (1982). (Letter) Paediatric coma scale. *The Lancet*, *2*(8295), 450.

Stanczak, D. E., White, J. G., Gouview, W., D., Moehle, K. A., Daniel, M., Novack, T., et al. (1984). Assessment of level of consciousness following severe neurological insult. A comparison of the psychometric qualities of the Glasgow Coma Scale and the Comprehensive Level of Consciousness Scale. *Journal of Neurosurgery*, *60*(5), 955–960.

Teasdale, G. (1995). Head injury. *Journal of Neurology, Neurosurgery, and Psychiatry*, *58*, 526–539.

Teasdale, G., & Jennett, B. (1974). Assessment of coma and impaired consciousness. A practical scale. *The Lancet*, *2*(7873), 81–84.

Teasdale, G., & Jennett, B. (1976). Assessment and prognosis of coma after head injury. *Acta Neurochirurgica*, *34*(1–4), 45–55.

Teasdale, G., Knill-Jones, R., & Van der Sande, J. (1978). Observer variability in assessing impaired consciousness and coma. *Journal of Neurology, Neurosurgery, and Psychiatry*, *41*(7), 603–610.

Thornhill, S., Teasdale, G. M., Murray, G. D., McEwan, J., & Roy, C. W. (2000). Disability in young people and adults one year after head injury: Prospective cohort study. *British Medical Journal*, *320*, 1631–1635.

Wijdicks, E. F. M., Bamlet, W. R., Maramattom, B. V., Manno, E. M., & McClelland, R. L. (2005). Validation of a new coma scale: The FOUR score. *Annals of Neurology*, *58*, 585–593.

Zafonte, R. D., Hammond, F. M., Mann, N. R., Wood, D. L., Black, K. L., & Millis, S. R. (1996). Relationship between Glasgow Coma Scale and functional outcome. *American Journal of Physical Medicine and Rehabilitation*, *75*(5), 364–369.

Summary score sheet for the Glasgow Coma Scale

Teasdale and Jennett (1974)

Name:

	Date:							
	Time:							
	Assessor:							
EYE OPENING	Spontaneous 4							
	To speech 3							
	To pain 2							
	None 1							
BEST VERBAL RESPONSE	Oriented 5							
	Confused 4							
	Inappropriate words 3							
	Incomprehensible sounds 2							
	None 1							
BEST MOTOR RESPONSE	Obeys commands 6							
	Localizes pain 5							
	Withdraws 4							
	Flexion to pain 3							
	Extension to pain 2							
	None 1							
	TOTAL SCORE:							

Acknowledgement: Adapted from Teasdale, G., & Jennett, B. (1974). Assessment of coma and impaired consciousness: A practical scale. *The Lancet*, *304*(7872), 81–84, figure from p. 83, reprinted by permission of *The Lancet*, and Jennett, B. (1976). Assessment and prognosis of coma after head injury. *Acta Neurochirurgica*, *34*(1–4), 45–55, reprinted by permission of Springer-Verlag.

Items of the Amnesia Scale for Glasgow Coma Scale – Extended

Nell, Yates, and Kruger (2000)

Name:	Assessor:	Date:

7	No amnesia: client can remember impact, can remember falling and striking a solid surface, etc.
6	Amnesia for 30 minutes or less: client regained consciousness while still in vehicle, in street at scene of incident, etc.
5	Amnesia of ½ hour to 3 hours: remembers being loaded into ambulance, in ambulance on way to hospital, arriving at emergency room, admission to ward, etc.
4	Amnesia of 3 to 24 hours: determine duration by content of the first memory, which will be for an event in the ward or other hospital procedure
3	Amnesia of 1 to 7 days
2	Amnesia of 8 to 30 days
1	Amnesia of 31 to 90 days
0	Amnesia greater than 3 months
X	Cannot be scored, e.g., can speak but responses are inappropriate or unintelligible, cannot speak because unconscious, intubated, facial fractures, etc.

Acknowledgement: From Nell, V., Yates, D. W., & Kruger, J. (2000). An extended Glasgow Coma Scale (GCS-E) with enhanced sensitivity to mild brain injury. *Archives of Physical Medicine and Rehabilitation*, *81*(5), 614–617, Table 1, p. 615, reprinted with permission of the American Congress of Rehabilitation Medicine and the American Academy of Physical Medicine and Rehabilitation and Elsevier.

JFK Coma Recovery Scale – Revised (CRS-R)

Giacino and Kalmar (2004)

Source

An appendix to Giacino, Kalmar, and Whyte (2005) provides the Response Profile to the JFK CRS-R, which is also reproduced below. The actual scale items, manual and other information are available on the website of the Center for Outcome Measurement in Brain Injury (http://www.tbims.org/combi/crs/index.html).

Purpose

Both the original CRS (Giacino, Kezmarsky, DeLuca, & Cicerone, 1991) and the revised scale provide an objective, clinician-administered test of behavioural and cognitive responses of patients in coma, the vegetative state (VS) and minimally conscious state (MCS). The CRS/CRS-R was designed for patients with ABI with Rancho Los Amigos Levels of Cognitive Functioning Scale (LCFS) from Level I (no response) to Level IV (confused, agitated). Development of the scale was conducted with patients with anoxia, stroke, traumatic brain injury (TBI) and tumour. The CRS-R is intended for diagnosis, rehabilitation and longer-term planning, and monitoring patient progress and treatment effectiveness.

Item description

The CRS-R comprises six subscales: Auditory, Visual, Motor, Oromotor/verbal, Communication, and Arousal. Within each subscale there is a hierarchy of levels, representing increasing complexity of responses. The responses are elicited with standardized instructions. The lowest level responses within a subscale represent reflex activity and the highest represent "cognitively mediated behaviors". For example, items in the Auditory subscale range from the lowest item (no response, not even auditory startle after presentation of a loud noise above patient's head and out of view) to the highest (passing all four trials of the request to look at one of two simultaneously presented common objects).

Scale development

Development of the original CRS was in response to a number of limitations of traditional instruments used at that time to measure recovery of consciousness. Prominent among the limitations were poor prognostic utility beyond the acute phase of recovery and insensitivity to subtle changes in functioning. Item development for the CRS used an initial pool of 41 items generated by a multidisciplinary group with expertise in acute brain injury rehabilitation. Six items considered difficult to score were eliminated, leaving 35 items. The scale was subsequently revised to improve its clinical utility and psychometric properties, as well as to incorporate criteria of the Aspen Neurobehavioral Conference Workgroup (Giacino et al., 2002).

Administration procedures, response format and scoring

Test materials (everyday objects such as comb, ball, mirror) are required for administration of the CRS-R. Standardized test procedures for administration are described in the manual. Alternative items are provided for a range of response modalities, thereby allowing examination of a domain, even if the patient cannot respond within a particular modality (e.g., presence of a tracheostomy tube preventing speech). Administration time is 20 to 25 minutes, and new examiners are trained with a standard training protocol.

Operationally defined criteria describe various levels of response complexity within each of the subscales, and each level is assigned a score. The total score ranges from 0 to 23, revised from 0 to 24 in Giacino et al. (2005) (level 3 for Orientation in the Communication Scale has been excluded – Personal communication: J. T. Giancino, 27 May, 2006). Higher scores reflect better performance.

Scores can be converted to a classification of VS, MCS or emergence from MCS using the Response Profile. Five domains are used for this purpose, with the following algorithm: *Emergence from VS* requires achievement of, at minimum, *all* of the following: (i) reproducible movement to command, (ii) visual fixation,

(iii) motor localization to noxious stimuli, (iv) intelligible verbalization and (v) intentional (even if non-functional) communication. *Emergence from MCS* requires additional criteria: *either* (i) functional object use *and/or* (ii) accurate, functional communication.

Psychometric properties

A sample of 80 patients (age $M = 38.86$ years, $SD = 13.18$) recruited from a specialized Coma Intervention Program within an inpatient rehabilitation centre in the USA was examined (Giacino et al., 2005). A subset of 20 out of the 80 patients was studied prospectively for the reliability study, and data from the remaining 60 patients were drawn from an existing database and combined with the prospective group in a validation study. Cause of ABI was mainly stroke or TBI, and time post-onset was approximately 2 months. Inter-rater and test–retest reliability were examined with separate and independent examinations of the patients by two raters. The CRS-R demonstrated an even spread of scores across the range, without floor or ceiling effects. Establishing the diagnostic accuracy of the CRS-R (VS, MCS and emergence from MCS (MCS+)) was hampered by the absence of an independent criterion. Correspondence with Disability Rating Scale (DRS) classifications, however, was 87.5%. Giacino et al. (2005) argued that the CRS-R was more sensitive than the DRS in that 10 out of 80 cases were classified as MCS on the CRS-R, but VS on the DRS. In each case, visual pursuit was intact, a defining feature of emergence from VS, but this domain is not examined on the DRS. Data on responsiveness, using the CRS, come from the case series of Passler and Riggs (2001) who treated five patients in VS with bromocriptine. CRS scores improved substantially over a 3-month treatment period, and the authors noted that the CRS was "able to document even subtle changes" (p. 314), with a large effect size. Results from Giacino et al. (2005), except where otherwise stated, are shown in Box 2.5.

Box 2.5

Validity:	Criterion: *Concurrent:* with DRS: $r_s = -.90$ – with original CRS: $r_s = .97$
	Predictive: Giacino & Croll, 1991 (cited in Kalmar & Giacino, 2005): scores on original CRS subscales (Motor, Communication and Auditory) at 1–3 months predicted DRS outcome at 12 months
	Construct:
	Internal consistency: Cronbach alpha: Total score: .83
	Discriminant: able to distinguish among diagnostic categories (VS $n = 5$, MCS $n = 13$, MCS+ $n = 2$, with good inter-rater and test–retest reliability – see below)
Reliability:	Inter-rater: Total score: $r_s = .84$
	– Diagnostic agreement for VS vs MCS vs MCS+: $k = .60$ – Subscale range for VS vs MCS: $k = .58–.88$ (with $k \geq .75$ for 4/5 subscales)
	Test–retest: 36 hours: Total score: $r_s = .94$
	– Diagnostic agreement for VS vs MCS vs MCS+: $k = .82$ – Subscale range for VS vs MCS: $k = .23–1.0$ (with $k \geq .6$ for 4/5 scales, $< .4$ for 1/5 – Oromotor/Verbal $k = .23$)
Responsiveness:	Passler & Riggs: initial CRS score $M = 8.2$ ($SD = 4.5$) vs highest score with treatment $M = 20.2$ ($SD = 4.6$); $d = 2.7$

Comment

The CRS-R is a carefully developed instrument, which incorporates revisions in line with recent diagnostic recommendations of the Aspen Workgroup on the MCS. Giacino et al. (2005) and Kalmar and Giacino (2005) express reservations about psychometric properties of individual subscales of the CRS-R and suggest that such scores should be used with caution until further data are available. Yet in comparison with other similar scales, psychometric properties of the CRS-R fare very well – although the Visual subscale had moderate inter-rater reliability and the Oromotor/verbal subscale showed poor temporal stability, reliability was otherwise good to excellent. An appealing feature of the CRS-R is its diagnostic capacity in distinguishing among VS, MCS, and emergence from MCS. This facility gives the CRS-R an advantage over other scales that do not have this feature. Giacino and Kalmar (2004) point to the "alarming" rates of misdiagnoses of disorders of consciousness, the most common error being diagnosis of VS in patients who function at a higher level, and in this regard the CRS-R has the capacity to improve diagnostic accuracy.

Key references

Giacino, J. T., Ashwal, S., Childs, N., Cranford, R., Jennett, B., Katz, D. I., et al. (2002). The minimally conscious state: Definition and diagnostic criteria. *Neurology*, *58*(3), 349–353.

Giacino, J. T., & Kalmar, K. (2004). *CRS-R Coma Recovery Scale-Revised: Administration and scoring guidelines*. Edison, NJ: Center for Head Injuries, JFK Johnson Rehabilitation Institution.

Giacino, J. T., Kalmar, K., & Whyte, J. (2005). The JFK Coma Recovery Scale-Revised: Measurement characteristics and diagnostic utility. *Archives of Physical Medicine and Rehabilitation*, *85*(12), 2020–2029.

Giacino, J. T., Kezmarsky, M. A., DeLuca, J., & Cicerone, K. D. (1991). Monitoring rate of recovery to predict outcome in minimally responsive patients. *Archives of Physical Medicine and Rehabilitation*, *72*(11), 897–901.

Kalmar, K., & Giacino, J. T. (2005). The JFK Coma Recovery Scale-Revised. *Neuropsychological Rehabilitation*, *15*(3/4), 454–460.

Passler, M. A., & Riggs, R. V. (2001). Positive outcomes in traumatic brain injury – vegetative state: Patients treated with bromocriptine. *Archives of Physical Medicine and Rehabilitation*, *82*(3), 311–315.

Profile for the JFK Coma Recovery Scale – Revised

Giacino and Kalmar (2005)

Name:

SCORE	Date: / Assessor:									
	Date:									
	Assessor:									
	AUDITORY FUNCTION SCALE									
4	Consistent movement to command *									
3	Reproducible movement to command *									
2	Localization to sound									
1	Auditory startle									
0	None									
	VISUAL FUNCTION SCALE									
5	Object recognition *									
4	Object localization: reaching *									
3	Visual pursuit *									
2	Fixation *									
1	Visual startle									
0	None									
	MOTOR FUNCTION SCALE									
6	Functional object use †									
5	Automatic motor response*									
4	Object manipulation *									
3	Localization to noxious stimulation *									
3	Flexion withdrawal									
1	Abnormal posturing									
0	None/flaccid									
	OROMOTOR/ VERBAL FUNCTION SCALE									
3	Intelligible verbalization *									
2	Vocalization/oral movement									
1	Oral reflexive movement									
0	None									
	COMMUNICATION SCALE[1]									
2	Functional: accurate †									
1	Non-functional: intentional *									
0	None									
	AROUSAL SCALE									
3	Attention									
2	Eye opening without stimulation									
1	Eye opening with stimulation									
0	Unarousable									
	TOTAL SCORE									

* Denotes MCS

† Denotes emergence from MCS

1. Communication Scale: score 3 (oriented) appears in Giacino et al. (2005) but is omitted from the Profile because it is no longer part of the scoring system (Personal communication: J. T. Giacino, 27 May, 2006).

Acknowledgement: From Giacino, J. T., Kalmar, K., & Whyte, J. (2005). The JFK Coma Recovery Scale – Revised: Measurement characteristics and diagnostic utility. *Archives of Physical Medicine and Rehabilitation*, *85*(12), 2020–2029, reprinted with permission of the American Congress of Rehabilitation Medicine and the American Academy of Physical Medicine and Rehabilitation and Elsevier.

Rancho Los Amigos Levels of Cognitive Functioning Scale (LCFS)

Hagen, Malkmus, and Durham (1972)

Source

The LCFS, also referred to as the Rancho Los Amigos Scale, is available in Appendix C of Hagen, Malkmus, Durham, and Bowman (1979). Additionally, the LCFS appears on the website of the Center for Outcome Measurement in Brain Injury (http://www.tbims.org/combi/lcfs/index.html), and is reproduced below.

Purpose

The LCFS is a clinician rating scale, using clinical observations to judge and classify level of cognitive functioning in overall terms. It was designed for people with traumatic brain injury (TBI), focusing on the post-acute stage until emergence from post-traumatic amnesia.

Item description

The eight hierarchical categories of the LCFS are as follows: I: no response; II: generalized response; III: localized response; IV: confused, agitated response; V: confused, inappropriate, non-agitated response; VI: confused, appropriate response; VII: automatic, appropriate response; VIII: purposeful, appropriate response. Each level is accompanied by a detailed behavioural description (see below).

Scale development

Limited information is available on the development of the LCFS. According to Flannery (1995), Malkmus, Booth, and Kodimer (1980; cited in Flannery, 1995) ascribed development of the LCFS to the observations made by their interdisciplinary team of 1000 patients during recovery from TBI. The structure and content of the LCFS were (Flannery, 1995, p. 47):

> based on the assumption that observation of the type, nature and quality of the patient's behavioural responses can be used to estimate the cognitive level at which the patient is functioning. Furthermore, it was theorized that, if recovery was possible, cognitive functioning would be regained following a definable and predictable pattern.

Administration procedures, response format and scoring

There is no administration of the LCFS per se; rather the clinician classifies the patient into the category of best fit, based on behavioural observations and knowledge of the patient. Completion of the LCFS itself is thus very quick. The LCFS yields a classification at one of eight levels.

Psychometric properties

Gouvier, Blanton, LaPorte, and Nepomuceno (1987) published the first psychometric report on the LCFS, comparing it with the Disability Rating Scale (DRS). They examined 40 patients (age $M = 24.8$ years, range 5–69) with TBI admitted to an acute rehabilitation centre in Birmingham, Alabama, USA. Ratings were made 4 days per week until discharge, with pairs of three raters making independent ratings on the 4th day of each week. Test–retest reliability was determined by summing all scores for the odd days and comparing those with the sum of scores for the even days. Validation instruments were administered at discharge and comprised the Stover-Zeiger Scale (SZS), Glasgow Outcome Scale (GOS), and a 10-category expanded GOS (E-GOS). Talbot and Whitaker (1994) used the LCFS to examine the effect of sensory stimulation in a case series of seven patients (aged 19–55 years) who had been in an "altered state of consciousness" for more than 1 month. The individual scores presented in the report for each patient enable an assessment of responsiveness of the LCFS, and statistical analysis was conducted on the data by the author. Box 2.6 presents a summary of the findings from Gouvier et al., except where otherwise indicated.

Box 2.6

Validity:	Criterion: *Concurrent:* Discharge LCFS with SZS: $r_s = .73$ – with GOS: $r_s = .76$ – with E-GOS: $r_s = .79$
	Predictive: Initial LCFS with discharge SZS: $r_s = .59$ – with discharge GOS: $r_s = .57$ – with discharge E-GOS: $r_s = .68$
Reliability:	Inter-rater: Mean $r_s = .89$ (rater range .87–.94)
	Test–retest: 1 day: $r_s = .82$
Responsiveness:	Talbot & Whitaker: Pre-treatment LCFS $M = 2.29$ ($SD = 0.49$) vs post-treatment $M = 4.43$ ($SD = 0.98$); $z = -2.46$, $p < .02$, $d = 4.37$

Derivatives of the LCFS: Levels of Cognitive Functioning Assessment Scale (LCFAS); Flannery (1995)

Flannery (1995) used the LCFS to develop the slightly differently named LCFAS, using the first five LCFS levels. The narrative descriptions of the LCFS levels were converted to a list of 41 behavioural descriptors. The clinician uses the checklist of items to endorse those observed in the patient and "visual inspection" is used to determine the category in which most behaviours are endorsed. This method resulted in very good inter-rater reliability ($k = 1.0$ with neuropsychology experts, $k = .84$ with student nurses) and 2-week test–retest reliability ($k = .86$ with student nurses).

Comment

Although the LCFS provides a quick overall summation of the patient's level of cognitive functioning and is commonly used as a benchmark, it has a number of limitations. Horn, Sheil, McLellan, Campbell, Watson, and Wilson (1993) point to the problem that a patient may fluctuate between levels simultaneously, depending on environmental factors (e.g., Level IV: confused, agitated vs Level V: confused, non-agitated). Another drawback of the LCFS is that it has a limited number of response categories, and as such, the scale is not suited to measuring very small gradations of change in the patient, even though it is responsive to changes on a broader scale. Furthermore, Gouvier et al. (1987) were critical of the psychometric properties of the LCFS which were lower than the DRS on all counts. They concluded that it "makes it difficult to endorse the continued use of the LCFS when a superior evaluation instrument is so readily available" (p. 96). Even so, the LFCS has survived this criticism, and 14 years later was described as having "almost universal acceptance in the United States because of its simplicity and clinical utility" (Hall, Bushnik, Lakisic-Kazazic, Wright, & Cantagallo, 2001, p. 369).

Key references

Flannery, J. (1995). Cognitive assessment in the acute care setting: Reliability and validity of the Levels of Cognitive Functioning Assessment Scale (LOCFAS). *Journal of Nursing Measurement*, *3*(1), 43–58.

Gouvier, W. D., Blanton, P. D., LaPorte, K. K., & Nepomuceno, C. (1987). Reliability and validity of the Disability Rating Scale and the Levels of Cognitive Functioning Scale in monitoring recovery from severe head injury. *Archives of Physical Medicine and Rehabilitation*, *68*(2), 94–97.

Hagen, C., Malkmus, D., & Durham, M. S. (1972). *Rancho Los Amigos Levels of Cognitive Functioning Scale*. Downey, CA: Rancho Los Amigos Hospital.

Hagen, C., Malkmus, D., Durham, M. S., & Bowman, K. (1979). In Professional Staff Association of Rancho Los Amigos Hospital. *Rehabilitation of the head injured adult: Comprehensive physical management*. Downey, CA: Rancho Los Amigos Hospital.

Hall, K. M., Bushnik, T., Lakisic-Kazazic, B., Wright, J., & Cantagallo, A. (2001). Assessing traumatic brain injury outcome measures for long-term follow-up of community-based individuals. *Archives of Physical Medicine and Rehabilitation*, *82*(3), 367–374.

Horn, S., Sheil, A., McLellan, L., Campbell, M., Watson, M., & Wilson, B. (1993). A review of behavioural assessment scales for monitoring recovery in and after coma with pilot data on a new scale of visual awareness. *Neuropsychological Rehabilitation*, *3*(2), 121–137.

Talbot, L. R., & Whitaker, H. A. (1994). Brain-injured persons in an altered state of consciousness: Measures and intervention strategies. *Brain Injury*, *8*(8), 689–699.

Rancho Los Amigos Levels of Cognitive Functioning Scale

Hagen, Malkmus, and Durham (1972)

I. NO RESPONSE

Patient appears to be in a deep sleep and is completely unresponsive to any stimuli presented to him.

II. GENERALIZED RESPONSE

Patient reacts inconsistently and non-purposefully to stimuli in a non-specific manner.

Responses are limited in nature and are often the same regardless of stimulus presented. Responses may be physiological changes, gross body movements and/or vocalization. Often the earliest response is to deep pain. Responses are likely to be delayed.

III. LOCALIZED RESPONSE

Patient reacts specifically but inconsistently to stimuli.

Responses are directly related to the type of stimulus presented as in turning head toward a sound, focusing on an object presented. The patient may withdraw an extremity and/or vocalize when presented with painful stimulus. He may follow simple commands in an inconsistent, delayed manner, such as closing his eyes, squeezing or extending an extremity. Once external stimuli are removed, he may lie quietly. He may also show a vague awareness of self and body by responding to discomfort by pulling at nasogastric tube or catheter or resisting restraints. He may show a bias toward responding to some persons (especially family, friends) but not to others.

IV. CONFUSED-AGITATED

Patient is in a heightened state of activity with severely decreased ability to process information.

He is detached from the present and responds primarily to his own internal confusion. Behaviour is frequently bizarre and non-purposeful relative to his immediate environment. He may cry out or scream out of proportion to stimuli even after removal, may show aggressive behaviour, attempt to remove restraints or tubes or crawl out of bed in a purposeful manner. He does not, however, discriminate among persons or objects and is unable to cooperate directly with treatment efforts. Verbalization is frequently incoherent and/or inappropriate to the environment. Confabulation may be present; he may be euphoric or hostile. Thus gross attention to environment is very short and selective attention is often nonexistent. Being unaware of present events, patient lacks short-term recall and may be reacting to past events. He is unable to perform self-care (feeding, dressing) without maximum assistance. If not disabled physically, he may perform motor activities as sitting, reaching and ambulating, but as part of his agitated state and not as a purposeful act or on request necessarily.

V. CONFUSED, INAPPROPRIATE, NON-AGITATED

Patient appears alert and is able to respond to simple commands fairly consistently.

However, with increased complexity of commands or lack of any external structure, responses are non-purposeful, random, or at best fragmented towards any desired goal. He may show agitated behaviour, but not on an internal basis (as in Level IV) but rather as a result of external stimuli, and usually out of proportion to the stimulus. He has gross attention to the environment, but is highly distractible and lacks ability to focus attention to a specific task without frequent redirection back to it. With structure, he may be able to converse on a social-automatic level for short periods of time. Verbalization is often inappropriate; confabulation may be triggered by present events. His memory is severely impaired, with confusion of past and present in his reaction to ongoing activity. Patient lacks initiation of functional tasks and often shows inappropriate use of objects without external direction. He may be able to perform previously learned tasks when structured for him, but is unable to learn new information. He responds best to self, body, comfort and often family members. The patient can usually perform self-care activities with assistance and may accomplish feeding with maximum supervision. Management on the ward is often a problem if the patient is physically mobile, as he may wander off either randomly or with vague intention of "going home".

VI. CONFUSED-APPROPRIATE

Patient shows goal-directed behaviour, but is dependent on external input for direction.

Response to discomfort is appropriate and he is able to tolerate unpleasant stimuli (such as NG tube) when need is explained. He follows simple directions consistently and shows carry-over for tasks he has relearned (as self-care). He is at least supervised with old learning; unable to be maximally assisted for new learning with little or no carry-over. Responses may be incorrect because of memory problems, but they are appropriate to the situation. They may be delayed and he shows decreased ability to process information with little or no anticipation or prediction of events. Past memories show more depth and detail than recent memory. The patient may show beginning immediate awareness of situation by realizing he does not know an answer. He no longer wanders and is inconsistently orientated to time and place. Selective attention to tasks may be impaired especially with difficult tasks and in unstructured settings, but is now functional for common daily activities (30 minutes with structure). He may show a vague recognition of some staff, has increased awareness of self, family and basic needs (such as food), again in an appropriate manner as in contrast to Level V.

VII. AUTOMATIC-APPROPRIATE

Patient appears appropriate and orientated within hospital and home settings, goes through daily routine automatically, but frequently robot-like, with minimal to absent confusion, but has shallow recall of what he has been doing.

He shows increased awareness of self, body, family, foods, people and interaction in the environment. He has superficial awareness of, but lacks insight into his condition, decreased judgement and problem-solving and lacks realistic plans for his future. He shows carry-over for new learning, but at a decreased rate. He requires at least minimal supervision for learning and for safety purposes. He is independent in self-care activities and supervised in home and community skills for safety. With structure he is able to initiate tasks such as social or recreational activities in which he now has interest. His judgement remains impaired; such that he is unable to drive a car. Pre-vocational or avocational evaluation and counselling may be indicated.

VIII. PURPOSEFUL AND APPROPRIATE

Patient is alert and orientated, is able to recall and integrate past and recent events and is aware of and responsive to his culture.

He shows carry-over for new learning if acceptable to him and his life role, and needs no supervision once activities are learned. Within his physical capabilities, he is independent in home and community skills, including driving. Vocational rehabilitation, to determine ability to return as a contributor to society (perhaps in a new capacity), in indicated. He may continue to show decreased ability, relative to pre-morbid abilities, in abstract reasoning, tolerance for stress, judgement in emergencies or unusual circumstances. His social, emotional and intellectual capacities may continue to be at a decreased level for him, but functional for society.

Acknowledgement: From Hagen, C. et al. (1979). *Rehabilitation of the head injured adult: Comprehensive physical management*, pp. 87–89, by permission of Professional Staff Association Rancho Los Amigos Hospital.

Wessex Head Injury Matrix (WHIM)

Shiel, Wilson, McLellan, Horn, and Watson (2000b)

Source

The WHIM is commercially available from Pearson (http://www.pearson-uk.com).

Purpose

The WHIM is an objective, clinician-administered test, with the aims of (i) monitoring the patient's recovery from the time of coma until emergence from post-traumatic amnesia and (ii) facilitating realistic goal-planning for rehabilitation. It was designed for people with traumatic brain injury (TBI), particularly those described as "slow-to-recover", who experience prolonged periods with reduced levels of consciousness. The WHIM has also been used with other neurological groups, including stroke (Majerus, Van der Linden, & Shiel, 2000).

Item description

The 62-item WHIM is a hierarchically organized test, with items rank-ordered in terms of their sequence of recovery. Three types of behaviours are examined: spontaneous behaviours (e.g., random eye movements), responses to naturally occurring stimuli (e.g., tracks source of a sound), and responses to presentation of standard stimuli (e.g., performs physical movement in response to verbal request). Four broad groups of behaviours within the hierarchy have a demonstrated sequential order of recovery: basic responses are the first group of behaviours to show recovery (e.g., "eyes open briefly"), purposeful actions and beginnings of social interaction appear next (e.g., "makes eye contact" after name is called, "shows selective response to preferred people"), that group is followed by attention and cognitive organization (e.g., "choose an object when requested", "is momentarily distracted by external stimulus but can return to task"), and the final group of behaviours to emerge is orientation and continuous memory (e.g., "can say what part of day it is", "remembers something from the day before"). An example of the item content for the attention and organizing group of items is provided in Table 2.4. Each item is operationally defined.

Table 2.4 WHIM: Items from the attention and cognitive organization group

Item	*Descriptor*
30	Seeks eye contact
31	Monosyllabic or single words in response to questions
32	Looks at, and apparently explores, pictures, magazine, TV, etc.
33	Switches gaze from one person to another, spontaneously
34	Speech is fluent but rambling. Lots of words but meaning hard to discern
35	Looks for object that has been shown and then removed from line of vision
36	Can attend to task, TV, etc., but concentration is vulnerable
37	Monosyllabic or single words to express mood or need
38	Is momentarily distracted by external stimulus but can return to task
39	Can find a specific playing card from a selection of four
40	Smiles
41	Uses writing, typing or other communication aid, but is hard to understand
42	Can say what part of day it is
43	Brief phrases
44	Points with eyes
45	Initiates conversation
46	Vocalizes to attract attention

Acknowledgement: From Shiel, A. et al. (2000a). Wessex Head Injury Matrix (WHIM) main scale: A preliminary report on a scale to assess and monitor recovery after severe head injury. *Clinical Rehabilitation*, *14*(4), 408–416, by permission of Sage Publications Ltd.

Scale development

An early literature review by Horn, Shiel, McLellan, Campbell, Watson, and Wilson (1993) on assessment scales suitable for monitoring recovery during and after coma, heralded work that was being conducted on the WHIM. A detailed description of the developmental process is described in Shiel, Horn, Wilson, Watson, Campbell, and McLellan (2000a). At the outset, the authors aimed not to make assumptions about either the patterns of recovery or those behaviours that might contribute to it. Instead, they undertook the "laborious task" of determining the actual behaviours occurring during coma. A sample of 88 patients with TBI (age $M = 30$ years, range 14–67; coma duration median = 6 days; duration of PTA median = 30 days) recruited from two hospitals in the UK had daily observations of between 15 minutes and several hours. Additionally, video recordings of up to 24 hours were made in order to sample behaviour throughout the diurnal cycle. A set of "simple stimuli" was also used to elicit behavioural response to stimulation. Almost 150 behaviours that were observed were initially categorized into 10 subscales. The categories were later abandoned, largely because of overlap across a number of subscales. Duplicated items were excluded, resulting in a 58-item scale; some adjustment of item content subsequently occurred, with the final version comprising 62 items. The authors developed operational definitions for each item, the definitions were then reviewed by their larger research team, and thereafter refined in further prospective pilot testing with patients. Date of first emergence of each of the behaviours was recorded and used to calculate the rank order of recovery of behaviours using a paired-preference technique. This item ordering technique is described in detail in Horn, Shiel, McLellan, Campbell, Watson, and Wilson (1993) and Watson, Horn, Wilson, Shiel, and McLellan (1997). The sequence of recovery was largely replicated in an independent sample using a 66-item version of the WHIM (Majerus et al., 2000).

Administration procedures, response format and scoring

The WHIM requires simple test materials comprising everyday items (e.g., a coin, key, playing cards, magazine pictures). The observation period may range from 5 minutes to several hours. Administration starts at Item 1 and continues until the occurrence of 10 consecutive failures. The test manual advises that the WHIM is designed to be used by all qualified members of a multidisciplinary team caring for patients who are in coma. Training of the clinician is required in order to ensure reliable administration. In the reliability studies, the authors developed a 2-hour training session, including video demonstration. Behaviours can be recorded by clinicians either working individually or in pairs, and the latter procedure is recommended for clinicians unfamiliar with the scale.

Responses to items that meet the operational criteria are endorsed. The WHIM score is the rank number of the highest behaviour successfully passed in the 62-item sequence. Shiel et al. (2000a) note that in individual patients the order of recovery of the individual WHIM items is not absolute.

Psychometric properties

Reliability of the WHIM was examined by Shiel et al. (2000a) with an independent sample of 25 patients (age median = 36 years; coma median = 7 days) with TBI recruited from the same hospitals as the sample used for development of the scale. Inter-rater reliability was established with two novice raters who underwent brief training. Another inter-rater reliability study was conducted providing raters with a more detailed, 2-hour training session, including video demonstrations. Validation of the WHIM was reported by Majerus et al. (2000) using a 66-item version of the WHIM in 23 patients (age $M = 50$ years, range 16–75; coma $M = 12.7$ days, range 1–136), mostly with stroke or TBI, recruited from a regional hospital in Liège, Belgium. They were first examined $M = 6$ days (range 0–18) after onset of coma. Reliability was also studied in videotaped behaviours of five patients at various stages of recovery, using two experienced intensive-care nurses who received a 4-hour training package. Test–retest reliability was examined using data from the first session and a second session 1 day later. At 4 years post-trauma, Shiel and Wilson (2005) re-examined 38 of the original 88 patients who had participated in the development of the scale. They identified 14 WHIM behaviours as potential predictor variables and compared the time post-trauma when each behaviour recovered for the subgroup that remained in a minimally conscious state (MCS) at follow-up ($n = 8$) versus those who could participate in testing ($n = 30$). Responsiveness of the WHIM has not been reported in a formal sense, but graphed data from case studies in Shiel et al. (2000b) show marked improvement of scores over time. Results of the foregoing studies are shown in Box 2.7.

Comment

The WHIM is a carefully developed instrument that represents a different approach to measuring recovery of cognitive functioning in patients with an altered level of consciousness. The authors intentionally avoided allocating scores to different levels of response that are then tallied to form either a total and/or subscale scores. Rather, the 62-item scale is rank ordered in terms of the demonstrated sequences of behaviours emerging during coma and its aftermath. Although the authors intended to develop a scale that focused on "what the subject does or does not do, rather than upon clinical diagnostic features" (Sheil et al., 2000a, p. 410), it would be useful to be able to establish when patients have exited from the vegetative and minimally conscious states, particularly

Box 2.7

Validity:	Criterion: *Concurrent:* Majerus et al.: initial WHIM with Glasgow Coma Scale (GCS): $r = .83$ – final WHIM with GCS: $r = .95$ *Predictive:* Shiel & Wilson: 7 WHIM behaviours recovered significantly later in MCS vs non-MCS groups (eyes open, attention held by a dominant stimulus, obeys command to verbal request, watches someone move in line of vision, looks at person giving attention, turns head to look at person talking, focus on person talking)
Reliability:	Inter-rater: Shiel et al. (2000a): novice raters: $k = .25–.84$ – with 2-hour training package: mean $k = .86$ (range $k = .62–1.00$) Majerus et al.: $r_s = .93$; individual items mean $k = .84$ (range $k = –.1–1.00$; grouped results reported as follows: $k \geq .8$ for 73% of items, $k = .4–.73$ for 20%, $k = –.1–.07$ for 7% of items) Test–retest: Shiel et al. (2000a): ~ 2 hour: novice raters: $k = –.66–.12$ – with 2-hour training package: mean $k = .74$ (range $k = .22–1.00$) Majerus et al.: > 1 day: $r_s = .98$
Responsiveness:	No information available

given the conclusions of Majerus et al. (2000) that the WHIM is sensitive to subtle changes in these groups of patients. Considerable efforts have been made to ensure adequate inter-rater reliability of the WHIM, and with the training package the overall reliability is excellent. At the item level, however, a number of items remain poor. A particular strength of the WHIM is the hierarchy of behaviours, which has direct application to individual patient goal-setting and rehabilitation programming.

Key references

Horn, S., Sheil, A., McLellan, L., Campbell, M., Watson, M., & Wilson, B. (1993). A review of behavioural assessment scales for monitoring recovery in and after coma with pilot data on a new scale of visual awareness. *Neuropsychological Rehabilitation*, *3*(2), 121–137.

Majerus, S., Van der Linden, M, & Shiel, A. (2000). Wessex Head Injury Matrix and Glasgow/Glasgow-Liège Coma Scale: A validation and comparison study. *Neuropsychological Rehabilitation*, *10*(2), 167–184.

Sheil, A., Horn, S. A., Wilson, B. A., Watson, M. J., Campbell, M. J., & McLellan, D. L. (2000a). The Wessex Head Injury Matrix (WHIM) main scale: A preliminary report on a scale to assess and monitor patient recovery after severe head injury. *Clinical Rehabilitation*, *14*(4), 408–416.

Shiel, A., & Wilson, B. A. (2005). Can behaviours observed in the early stages of recovery after traumatic brain injury predict poor outcome? *Neuropsychological Rehabilitation*, *15*(3/4), 494–502.

Shiel, A., Wilson, B. A., McLellan, L., Horn, S., & Watson, M. (2000b). *WHIM. The Wessex Head Injury Matrix – Manual.* London: Harcourt Assessment.

Watson, M. J., Horn, S., Wilson, B. A., Shiel, A., & McLellan, L. (1997). The application of a paired comparison technique to identify sequence of recovery after severe head injury. *Neuropsychological Rehabilitation*, *7*(4), 441–458.

Western Neuro Sensory Stimulation Profile (WNSSP)

Ansell, Keenan, and de la Rocha (1989)

Source

The WNSSP is commercially available from Western Neuro Care Center, Tustin, California, USA (http://www.tustinrehab.com).

Purpose

The WNSSP is an objective, clinician-administered test that provides a detailed and standardized assessment of cognitive function in patients with traumatic brain injury (TBI), who are classified on the Rancho Los Amigos Levels of Cognitive Functioning Scale (LCFS) from Level II (generalized, non-purposeful responses) to the early stages of Level V (confused, inappropriate, non-agitated). The WNSSP is designed to evaluate cognitive status, monitor progress and predict improvement in this patient group, which includes patients in the vegetative state (VS) and minimally conscious state (MCS).

Item description

The WNSSP comprises 33 items classified into six subscales: Arousal/attention (4 items), Auditory comprehension (6 items), Visual comprehension (5 items), Visual tracking (7 items), Object manipulation (3 items), and Expressive communication (3 items). An additional 5 items are used to document other responses: auditory response to sound and speech (2 items), olfactory response to smell (1 item), and tactile response to touch (2 items). Each item contains a variable number of levels that are organized hierarchically. For example, in the Arousal/attention subscale the four items address: (i) arousability (4 levels, ranging from a low of "requires repeated presentation of two or more stimuli" to a high of "already awake"), (ii) wakefulness (3 levels, from awake without being re-aroused for "10 minutes or less" to "21 minutes or more"), (iii) eye contact (3 levels, from "eyes closed" to "eyes focused on the examiner 50% or more" of the session), and (iv) attention to task (2 levels, either "attends less than 50% of the time" or "attends 50% or more of the time").

Scale development

Development of the WNSSP was based on "extensive observation of patients' responses to a variety of stimuli" (Ansell et al., 1989, p. 2) which served as a basis for item selection. It was developed within the paradigm of sensory stimulation, such as used at the Rancho Los Amigos Hospital in the 1970s. Response levels for the WNSSP were organized hierarchically, but no information is available regarding the developmental procedures for defining the response levels. Ansell (1993) suggested that a score in the range 65 to 75 indicated that the patient is "rehabilitation ready", although no information was provided about the methods used to derive this range.

Administration procedures, response format and scoring

Stimulus materials (everyday items, such as a comb, teaspoon) are required for administration. The test manual advises the need for a skilled clinician who "must be an astute observer of behaviour" and able to elicit responses in patients with poor responsiveness. Preparation of the raters for the reliability analyses involved them studying and practising administration procedures, discussing scoring discrepancies and conducting 10 administrations (Ansell et al., 1989). Administration time is 20 to 40 minutes. The manual suggests that clinicians spend 15 to 30 minutes prior to assessment observing the patient "at rest" to familiarize themselves with his/her repertoire of behaviours in the natural environment.

Response format for the items varies from dichotomous scoring (1 item from the Arousal/attention subscale) to a 6-point rating scale (e.g., Auditory comprehension). The total score ranges from 0 to 113, with higher scores indicating better levels of functioning.

Psychometric properties

The validation sample comprised 57 consecutive patients with TBI recruited from the Western Neuro

Care Center, Tustin, California, USA (Ansell & Keenan, 1989; Ansell et al., 1989). Average age was 29 years (range 14–72), at an average of 8 months post-trauma (range 1–43), with initial WNSSP assessment occurring within 10 days of admission. Examinations were conducted fortnightly until any of the following occurred: (i) Level V on the LCFS, (ii) scored > 80/113 on the WNSSP on two consecutive test occasions, or (iii) discharge/death. Inter-rater reliability used three raters who simultaneously examined (but independently scored) 23 patients. Examination of predictive validity was reported by Ansell (1993) who examined 116 patients, 55 of whom reached a "rehabilitation ready" criterion (operationalized for that study as WNSSP scores ≥ 72/113) within 2 to 48 months post-trauma. Data on responsiveness are available from Lammi, Smith, Tate, and Taylor (2005) who administered the WNSSP to 18 people in the MCS at rehabilitation admission and at follow-up between 2 and 5 years post-trauma, as well as from Smith, Taylor, Lammi, and Tate (2001) who assessed a subset of 12 patients on four occasions during the course of rehabilitation admission. Results from Ansell et al., except where otherwise stated, are shown in Box 2.8.

Comment

The WNSSP was one of the first published instruments to provide a detailed and objective method to measure small gradations of change in a range of domains of cognition in patients with very low levels of functioning. An increasing number of specialized instruments is available for this purpose, but comparative studies are rare. In a single case study, Canedo, Grix, and Nicoletti (2002) compared five such scales. They were critical of the WNSSP in comparison with other instruments, in part because they found the scoring system difficult to quantify, an issue that has been raised by other investigators (Smith et al., 2001). O'Dell, Jasin, Lyons, Stivers, and Meszaros (1996) also raised concerns about floor effects of the WNSSP in comparison with some other scales. Additionally, the clinical utility of the WNSSP would be enhanced if its scores could be mapped to VS and MCS diagnoses, using established criteria (Giacino et al., 2002).

Box 2.8

Validity:	Criterion: *Concurrent:* with LCFS: $r = .73$ *Predictive:* Ansell: initial WNSSP score was significantly higher for the group that subsequently became "rehabilitation ready" $M = 23.53$ ($SD = 13.15$) vs not "rehabilitation ready" $M = 14.02$ ($SD = 10.83$); $t = -4.28$, $p < .001$ – logistic regression analysis: visual tracking predicted "rehabilitation ready" status; auditory comprehension predicted speed of improvement Construct: *Internal consistency:* Cronbach alpha: .95 (subscale range .35 – .94; with < .8 for 2/6 subscales – arousal/attention, expressive communication) *Discriminant:* LCFS Level II $M = 11.28$ ($SD = 7.39$) vs Level III $M = 40.32$ ($SD = 15.50$); $p < .05$ – Level IV $M = 50.78$ ($SD = 28.37$) vs Level V $M = 85.09$ ($SD = 24.77$); $p < .05$
Reliability:	Inter-rater: Mean $k = .70$ (item range $k = .43 – .96$; with $k > .6$ for 23/33 items) Test–retest: No information available
Responsiveness:	Lammi et al.: Initial WNSSP $M = 35.56$ ($SD = 22.43$) vs 2–5 year follow-up $M = 101.67$ ($SD = 23.88$); $d = 2.95$ Smith et al.: Initial WNSSP $M = 28.25$ ($SD = 26.66$) vs Time 4 $M = 41.47$ ($SD = 27.20$); $d = 0.50$

Key references

Ansell, B. J. (1993). Slow-to-recover patients: Improvement to rehabilitation readiness. *Journal of Head Trauma Rehabilitation*, *8*(3), 88–98.

Ansell, B. J., & Keenan, J. E. (1989). The Western Neuro Sensory Stimulation Profile: A tool for assessing slow-to-recover head-injured patients. *Archives of Physical Medicine and Rehabilitation*, *70*(2), 104–108.

Ansell, B. J., Keenan, J. E., & de la Rocha, O. (1989). *Western*

Neuro Sensory Stimulation Profile. Tustin, CA: Western Neuro Care Centre.

Canedo, A., Grix, M. C., & Nicoletti, J. (2002). An analysis of assessment instruments for the minimally responsive patient (MRP): Clinical observations. *Brain Injury*, *16*(5), 453–461.

Giacino, J. T., Ashwal, S., Childs, N., Cranford, R., Jennett, B., Katz, D. I., et al. (2002). The minimally conscious state: Definition and diagnostic criteria. *Neurology*, *58*(3), 349–353.

Lammi, M. H., Smith, V. H., Tate, R. L., & Taylor, C. M. (2005). The minimally conscious state and recovery potential: A follow-up study 2 to 5 years after traumatic brain injury. *Archives of Physical Medicine and Rehabilitation*, *86*, 746–754.

O'Dell, M. W., Jasin, P., Lyons, N., Stivers, M., & Meszaros, F. (1996). Standardised assessment instruments for minimally responsive, brain-injured patients. *NeuroRehabilitation*, *6*, 45–55.

Smith, V. H., Taylor, C. M., Lammi, M. H., & Tate, R. L. (2001). Recovery profiles of cognitive-sensory modalities in patients in the minimally conscious state following traumatic brain injury. *Brain Impairment*, *2*(1), 29–38.

SECTION 2
Scales measuring delirium

Cognitive Test for Delirium (CTD)

Hart, Levenson, Sessler, Best, Schwartz, and Rutherford (1996)

Source

Items for the CTD and the recording form can be found in the Appendix to Hart et al. (1996). An abbreviated version of the CTD has also been published (Hart, Best, Sessler, & Levenson, 1997).

Purpose

The CTD is an objective, clinician-administered test developed to identify patients in an intensive care setting with delirium. Most, though not all, will be older adults hospitalized for medical problems. The CTD has also been used with younger people with traumatic brain injury (TBI; Kennedy, Nakase-Thompson, Nick, & Sherer, 2003; Nakase-Thompson, Sherer, Yablon, Nick, & Trzepacz, 2004). A special feature of its design allows responses to be made exclusively in the non-verbal mode.

Item description

Five cognitive domains are sampled in the CTD, which also incorporates some items from other commercially available cognitive tests: Orientation (3 items: month, time of day, name of place), Attention (2 items: forward and backward visual memory span), Incidental and recognition memory (2 items: recall of 5 pictures), Comprehension (6 items: 4 items requiring yes/no response, e.g., "Will a stone float on water?"; 2 items identifying the odd item from a set of 4 items, e.g., "arm, house, foot, nose") and Vigilance (2 items: auditory cancellation task). Two alternate forms are available for the memory, comprehension and vigilance items. The abbreviated version of the CTD examines two domains: Visual attention span and Memory (picture recognition).

Scale development

Item development drew on existing instruments, but limited information is provided on the rationale for selection of the specific scales. Items drawn or adapted from other standardized cognitive tests include the Visual Memory Span subtest from the Wechsler Memory Scale – Revised (WMS-R) for attention, and the Auditory Comprehension, Part D, Complex Ideational Material from the Boston Diagnostic Aphasia Examination for comprehension. These instruments, which are commercially available, are described in Lezak, Howieson, and Loring (2004). Other items for the Orientation, Vigilance and Memory subtests are commonly found in cognitive screening tests. Receiver operating characteristic (ROC) curves were used to derive a cut-off score. Stepwise discriminant analysis conducted on data from the original validation sample was used to derive an abbreviated CTD (Hart et al., 1997). The visual attention span and picture recognition memory items were discriminating and able to differentiate among four clinical groups, including a delirium group. ROC analysis indicated that the most discriminating cut-off score for the abbreviated version was 10/11 (95% sensitivity; 99% specificity). The abbreviated version correlated highly with the full version ($r = .91$).

Administration procedures, response format and scoring

Test materials required for administration include the sets of pictures (available in the Appendix to Hart et al., 1996) and the Visual Memory Span materials from the WMS-R. The examiner needs to construct stimulus materials for the multiple choice orientation items, anchored to the current date. Visual stimuli are enlarged (1.5 cm high for print and 3.5 cm for pictures). Instructions for administration are incorporated into the recording form. In the validation study the CTD was administered by a psychologist trained in test administration procedures. Administration time is 10 to 15 minutes, but the abbreviated version requires only a few minutes.

A unique feature of the CTD is the response format, which was developed to take account of the special needs of people in intensive care, who may be intubated, functionally illiterate or have restricted movement. All responses can be made in the non-verbal mode, using pointing for multiple choice responses (orientation and memory items), head movement to indicate yes/no response (comprehension items), and hand movement (attention and vigilance items).

Responses to the CTD are scored for accuracy, usually 1 point for each correct response. Raw scores for each subtest are then converted, using formulae described in the scoring procedures. For this purpose, the recording and scoring forms have a good format and are easy to follow. The resulting score range is 0 to 6 for each subtest. The total score ranges from 0 to 30, with higher scores indicating better performance. Scores can also be used to diagnose delirium, using a cut-off score of 18/19.

Psychometric properties

Reliability and validity of the CTD were examined in 103 patients in four clinical groups: delirium ($n = 22$), dementia ($n = 26$), depression ($n = 30$) and schizophrenia ($n = 25$) recruited from Medical College of Virginia Hospitals, Richmond, Virginia, USA (Hart et al., 1996). Equivalence of the two alternate forms was examined in the dementia sample, using a counterbalanced order of administration. There were no differences between the parallel forms or administration order and the two forms were very highly inter-correlated (ICC = .90). For the validation study, criteria from the *Diagnostic and Statistical Manual for Mental Disorders* 3rd ed. – Revised (DSM-III-R) were used to diagnose delirium, which was made by a psychiatrist after a clinical interview, mental status examination and medical record review. Other validation instruments were the Mini-Mental State Examination (MMSE) and the Mattis Dementia Rating Scale (MDRS). The cut-off score of 18/19, identified by ROC analyses, yielded 100% sensitivity and 95% specificity in differentiating delirium from other conditions. The authors noted that although the CTD did not reliably distinguish delirium from severe dementia, the latter is commonly accompanied by a degree of confusion. Data on responsiveness are available from the case series of Mittal et al. (2004) who treated 10 patients with risperidone.

In its application to the TBI group, Kennedy et al. (2003) analysed ROC curves and recommended a higher cut-off score (21/22) for optimal diagnosis (sensitivity 71%, specificity 72%). In this clinical group, the lower cut-off score recommended for the CTD (18/19) increased specificity (75%), but at the cost of sensitivity (62%). They also examined the underlying factor structure using principal components analysis. A single factor was extracted, accounting for 79% of the variance, suggesting that the CTD was unidimensional. Nakase-Thompson et al. (2004) examined 85 patients admitted for rehabilitation after TBI, 69% of whom met DSM-IV criteria for delirium. Results from Hart et al. (1996), unless otherwise stated, are shown in Box 2.9.

Box 2.9

Validity:	Criterion: *Concurrent:* Delirium group: with MMSE: $r = .82$ Dementia group: with MMSE: $r = .81$ – with MDRS: $r = .76$
	Construct: *Internal consistency:* Cronbach alpha: Delirium group: .87
	Factor analysis: Kennedy et al.: a single factor
	Discriminant: Delirium group $M = 9.5$ ($SD = 5.0$) vs dementia $M = 24.5$ ($SD = 1.9$), depression $M = 28.8$ ($SD = 1.9$), schizophrenia $M = 27.9$ ($SD = 2.2$); $p < .05$ – Differential diagnosis between delirium vs other conditions using cut-off score 18/19: sensitivity 100%, specificity 95%
	Nakase-Thompson et al.: patients in delirium median = 11 vs patients not in delirium median = 28; $p < .001$
	Kennedy et al.: Differential diagnosis between delirium vs no delirium in patients with TBI using cut-off score 21/22: sensitivity 71%, specificity 72%
Reliability:	Inter-rater: No information available
	Test–retest: No information available
Responsiveness:	Mittal et al.: significant improvement with risperidone: Day 1 $M = 7.1$ ($SD = 2.0$) vs Day 6 $M = 16.9$ ($SD = 3.0$); $p < .01$, $d = 4.9$

Comment

Although a number of symptom rating scales for delirium are available, one of the strengths of the CTD is that it makes an objective evaluation of cognitive symptoms, using a standardized set of items, with alternate forms and empirical data to support cut-off scores. Another advantage is the response format in the non-verbal mode, allowing administration to patients with speech limitations. The CTD does, however, require the patient's active cooperation. In their study of advanced cancer patients using a different delirium measure, Lawlor, Nekolaichuk, Gagnon, Mancini, Pereira, and Bruera (2000) found that 21% were unable to participate in initial testing. They thus recommended the need for instruments that are "at least partially observational" in this population. Moreover, although the CTD provides a good evaluation of the cognitive symptomatology of delirium, in isolation it has limitations as a delirium measure because it does not consider other cardinal symptoms necessary for a diagnosis of delirium, such as sudden onset with fluctuating course. Thus it may have wider application as a more general cognitive screening test.

Key references

Hart, R. P., Best, A. M., Sessler, C. N., & Levenson, J. L. (1997). Abbreviated Cognitive Test for Delirium. *Journal of Psychosomatic Research*, *43*(4), 417–423.

Hart, R. P., Levenson, J. L., Sessler, C. N., Best, A. M., Schwartz, S. M., & Rutherford, L. E. (1996). Validation of a Cognitive Test for Delirium in medical ICU patients. *Psychosomatics*, *37*(6), 533–546.

Kennedy, R. E., Nakase-Thompson, R., Nick, T. G., & Sherer, M. (2003). Use of the Cognitive Test for Delirium in patients with traumatic brain injury. *Psychosomatics*, *44*(4), 283–289.

Lawlor, P. G., Nekolaichuk, C., Gagnon, B., Mancini, I. L., Pereira, J. L., & Bruera, E. D. (2000). Clinical utility, factor analysis, and further validation of the Memorial Delirium Assessment Scale in patients with advanced cancer. *Cancer*, *88*(12), 2859–2867.

Lezak, M. D., Howieson, D. B., & Loring, D. W. (2004). *Neuropsychological assessment* (4th ed.). Oxford: Oxford University Press.

Mittal, D., Jimerson, N. A., Neely, E. P., Johnson, W. D., Kennedy, R. E., Torres, R. A., et al. (2004). Risperidone in the treatment of delirium: Results from a prospective open-label trial. *Journal of Clinical Psychiatry*, *65*(5), 662–667.

Nakase-Thompson, R., Sherer, M., Yablon, S. A., Nick, T. G., & Trzepacz, P. T. (2004). Acute confusion following traumatic brain injury. *Brain Injury*, *18*(2), 131–142.

Confusion Assessment Method (CAM)

Inouye, van Dyck, Alessi, Balkin, Siegal, and Horwitz (1990)

Source

Description of the CAM and supporting interview procedures, along with operational definitions of the four CAM diagnostic features and scoring algorithm, are available in appendices in Inouye et al. (1990), and are reproduced below. A derivative of the CAM, CAM-ICU (Ely et al., 2001) is also briefly described below.

Purpose

The CAM is a clinician rating scale that uses information from patient history, clinical observations and objective cognitive tests to diagnose delirium in older adults. It was developed in order to provide a quick, accurate and standardized method that could be used by non-psychiatrists.

Item description

The CAM is a nine-item scale addressing specific clinical features commonly observed in delirium. The nine items are as follows (with the four items used in the algorithm to diagnose delirium asterisked): acute onset and fluctuating course*, inattention*, disorganized thinking*, altered level of consciousness*, disorientation, memory impairment, perceptual disturbance, psychomotor activity (psychomotor agitation, psychomotor retardation), and sleep–wake cycle.

Scale development

Development of the CAM, described in Inouye et al. (1990), drew on criteria from the *Diagnostic and Statistical Manual of Mental Disorders* – 3rd ed. – Revised (DSM-III-R). Important clinical features indicative of delirium were identified and defined using non-technical language. A literature review and expert panel were used to identify diagnostically important clinical features. The algorithm was developed using the expert panel, who recommended that the last five of the nine items not be included because of their lack of specificity to delirium.

Administration procedures, response format and scoring

Test materials are required for the patient assessment component of the CAM (Mini-Mental State Examination, MMSE, described in Chapter 3; and Digit Span, DS). The CAM is completed by the clinician following informant interview, patient assessment and chart review. The authors advise that some training is required for optimal use of the CAM. Following collection of the necessary background information, completion time for the CAM record form itself is less than 5 minutes.

Items are endorsed if they are present, or the response that best represents the patient's presentation is selected. The following algorithm for diagnosing delirium is used: *both* feature 1 (acute onset and fluctuating course) *and* feature 2 (inattention) are present, as well as *either* feature 3 (disorganized thinking) *or* feature 4 (altered level of consciousness).

Psychometric properties

An expert panel completed a detailed, standardized critique of the extent to which the CAM addressed general concepts and specific features of delirium, as well as the utility of the algorithm. The CAM was regarded as having high face validity, although concern was expressed regarding the diagnostic specificity in distinguishing between dementia and delirium. Measurement properties of the CAM were examined by Inouye et al. (1990) in studies at a number of sites in the USA, using two samples of elderly hospitalized patients ($n = 30$ and $n = 26$; age range 65–98 years). Patients were a mixed group; some had diagnoses of suspected delirium, confusion, dementia, depression; others had normal mental status; others were observed by nurses to exhibit abnormal thinking or behaviour. Inter-rater reliability used data from 10 patients and validating instruments comprised the MMSE, story recall, DS, and the Visual Analogue Scale for Confusion (VASC). Diagnostic accuracy against psychiatrist diagnosis using DSM-IV criteria yielded 100% sensitivity and 95% specificity.

Inouye, Leo-Summers, Zhang, Bogardus, Leslie, and Agostini (2005) conducted a prospective, validation study with 919 general medical patients to compare standard interview-derived CAM classifications with a potentially quicker method, using medical chart review. A high rate of false negatives (26%) occurred because of lack of documentation of delirium symptoms in the medical record, and thus the authors did not recommend this procedure for individual patient management. No direct information is available on the responsiveness of the CAM, but it has been used as the gold standard criterion when assessing the responsiveness of other instruments (e.g., O'Keefe, Mulkerrin, Nayeem, Varughese, & Pillay, 2005). Results from Inouye et al. (1990) are shown in Box 2.10.

Box 2.10

Validity:	Content: Formally assessed (see above) Criterion: *Concurrent:* with MMSE: $k = .64$ –with story recall: $k = .59$ –with DS: $k = .66$ –with VASC: $k = .82$ *Discriminant:* Differential diagnosis between delirium vs no delirium using DSM-IV criteria: sensitivity 100%, specificity 95%
Reliability:	Inter-rater: on classifying presence/absence of delirium: $k = 1.00$ –for classifying all 9 clinical features: $k = .67$ –for classifying 4 diagnostic features: $k = .81$ (range: $k = .56–1.00$) Test–retest: No information available
Responsiveness:	No information available

Derivatives of the CAM: CAM-ICU; Ely et al. (2001)

An adapted version of the interview procedures suitable for non-verbal patients in intensive care units, referred to as CAM-ICU, was developed by Ely et al. (2001), and is available in appendices to their article. The CAM-ICU uses the same four diagnostic features of the CAM, but the MMSE and DS test for patient assessment are replaced by an "attention screening examination", comprising the picture recognition-memory task from the Cognitive Test for Delirium (CTD; also described in this chapter) and a vigilance task similar to that used in the CTD. Psychometric properties of the CAM-ICU were examined with 38 patients. Inter-rater agreement using three raters was excellent ($k = .79–.95$). Comparison against independent diagnosis using DSM-IV criteria made by delirium experts yielded 95% to 100% sensitivity and 89% to 93% specificity.

Comment

Given the careful development, high inter-rater reliability, sensitivity and specificity of the CAM, the authors have achieved their aim of producing a quick, accurate and standardized instrument to assess delirium. It also affords an evaluation of the presence of symptoms commonly associated with delirium, although other scales described in this section additionally examine severity of such symptoms. The CAM is widely used, has been employed to establish the prevalence of delirium (Kiely, Bergman, Murphy, Jones, Orav, Marcantonio, 2003), and is regarded as a good screening instrument. Inouye et al. (1990) recommend that diagnosis using the CAM should be confirmed with further evaluation, a point also raised by Jackson (2003). Like some other highly regarded delirium measures described in this section, the CAM does not have a standardized set of items for administration. For classificatory purposes, however, the detailed operational criteria appear to suffice, as demonstrated by the good to excellent inter-rater reliability.

Key references

Ely, E. W., Margolin, R., Francis, J., May, L., Truman, B., Dittus, R., et al. (2001). Evaluation of delirium in critically ill patients: Validation of the Confusion Assessment Method for the Intensive Care Unit (CAM-ICU). *Critical Care Medicine*, *29*(7), 1370–1379.

Inouye, S. K., Leo-Summers, L., Zhang, Y., Bogardus, S. T., Leslie, D. L., & Agostini, J. V. (2005). A chart-based method for identification of delirium: Validation compared with interviewer ratings using the Confusion Assessment Method. *Journal of the American Geriatrics Society*, *53*, 312–318.

Inouye, S. K., van Dyck, C. H., Alessi, C. A., Balkin, S., Siegal, A. P., & Horwitz, R. I. (1990). Clarifying confusion: The Confusion Assessment Method. A new method for detection of delirium. *Annals of Internal Medicine*, *113*, 941–948.

Jackson, J. C. (2003). [Letter] The Confusion Assessment Method (CAM). *International Journal of Geriatric Psychiatry*, *18*, 557.

Kiely, D. K., Bergman, M. A., Murphy, K. M., Jones, R. N., Orav, E. J., & Marcantonio, E. R. (2003). Delirium among newly admitted postacute facility patients: Prevalence, symptoms, and severity. *The Journal of Gerontology*, *58A*(5), 441–445.

O'Keefe, S. T., Mulkerrin, E. C., Nayeem, K., Varughese, M. & Pillay, I. (2005). Use of serial Mini-Mental State Examinations to diagnose and monitor delirium in elderly hospital patients. *Journal of the American Geriatrics Society*, *53*, 867–870.

Confusion Assessment Method

Inouye, van Dyck, Alessi, Balkin, Siegal, and Horwitz (1990)

Name: **Assessor:** **Date:**

Yes/No

1. ACUTE ONSET
Is there evidence of an acute change in mental status from the patient's baseline? ______

2. INATTENTION*
a) Did the patient have difficulty focusing attention, for example, being easily distractible, or having difficulty keeping track of what was being said? ______

____Not present at any time during interview
____Present at some time during interview, but in mild form
____Present at some time during interview, in marked form
____Uncertain

b) (If present or abnormal) Did this behaviour fluctuate during the interview, that is, tend to come and go or increase and decrease in severity?

____Yes
____No
____Uncertain
____Not applicable.

c) (If present or abnormal) Please describe this behaviour:

3. DISORGANIZED THINKING
Was the patient's thinking disorganized or incoherent, such as rambling or irrelevant conversation, unclear or illogical flow of ideas, or unpredictable switching from subject to subject? ______

4. ALTERED LEVEL OF CONSCIOUSNESS
Overall, how would you rate this patient's level of consciousness? ______

____Alert (normal)
____Vigilant (hyperalert, overly sensitive to environmental stimuli, startled very easily)
____Lethargic (drowsy, easily aroused)
____Stupor (difficult to arouse)
____Coma (unarousable)
____Uncertain

5. DISORIENTATION
Was the patient disoriented at any time during the interview, such as thinking that he or she was somewhere other than the hospital, using the wrong bed, or misjudging the time of day? ______

6. MEMORY IMPAIRMENT
Did the patient demonstrate any memory problems during the interview, such as inability to remember events in the hospital or difficulty remembering instructions? ______

7. PERCEPTUAL DISTURBANCES
Did the patient have any evidence of perceptual disturbance, for example, hallucinations, illusions, or misinterpretations (such as thinking something was moving when it was not)? ______

8. PSYCHOMOTOR ACTIVITY:

Part 1: PSYCHOMOTOR AGITATION
At any time during the interview, did the patient have an unusually increased level of motor activity, such as restlessness, picking at bedclothes, tapping fingers, or making frequent sudden changes of position? ______

Part 2: PSYCHOMOTOR RETARDATION
At any time during the interview, did the patient have an unusually decreased level of motor activity, such as sluggishness, staring into space, staying in one position for a long time, or moving very slowly? ______

9. ALTERED SLEEP–WAKE CYCLE
Did the patient have evidence of disturbance of the sleep–wake cycle, such as excessive daytime sleepiness with insomnia at night? ______

* The questions listed under this topic (Inattention) were repeated for each topic where applicable.

Confusion Assessment Method – Diagnostic Algorithm

Inouye, van Dyck, Alessi, Balkin, Siegal, and Horwitz (1990)

Feature	Definition
1. Acute onset and fluctuating course	This feature is usually obtained from a family member or nurse and is shown by positive responses to the following questions: Is there evidence of an acute change in mental status from the patient's baseline? Did the (abnormal) behaviour fluctuate during the day, that is, tend to come and go, or increase and decrease in severity?
2. Inattention	This feature is shown by positive response to the following question: Did the patient have difficulty focusing attention, for example, being easily distractible, or having difficulty keeping track of what was being said?
3. Disorganized thinking	This feature is shown by a positive response to the following question: Was the patient's thinking disorganized or incoherent, such as rambling or irrelevant conversation, unclear or illogical flow of ideas, or unpredictable switching from subject to subject?
4. Altered level of consciousness	This feature is shown by any answer other than "alert" to the following question: Overall, how would you rate this patient's level of consciousness? (alert [normal], vigilant [hyperalert], lethargic [drowsy, easily aroused], stupor [difficult to arouse], or coma [unarousable])

Diagnosis of delirium by CAM requires the presence of features 1 and 2 and either 3 or 4.

Acknowledgement: From Inouye, S. K., van Dyck, C. H., Alessi, C. A., Balkin, S., Siegal, A. P., & Horwitz, R. I. (1990). Clarifying confusion: The Confusion Assessment Method: A new method for detection of delirium. *Annals of Internal Medicine*, *113*(12), 941–948, Appendix Tables 1 & 2 with permission of Dr Sharon Inouye.

Confusion Assessment Protocol (CAP)

Sherer, Nakase-Thompson, Yablon, and Gontkovsky (2005)

Source

Instruments incorporated into the CAP are described in Sherer et al. (2005) and scoring criteria are provided in an appendix. Information about the CAP, including the recording form, is also available from the website of the Center for Outcome Measurement in Brain Injury (COMBI; http://www.tbims.org/combi/cap/index.html).

Purpose

The CAP is an amalgam of previously published clinician rating scales and objective tests, some of which are commercially available. It is designed for patients with TBI to measure the post-traumatic confusional state (PTCS). The specific aim of the CAP is to delineate different patterns of confusion symptoms and to chart differential rates of their recovery.

Item description

Seven "key symptoms" are examined in the CAP: cognitive impairment, disorientation, restlessness, symptom fluctuation, psychotic-type symptoms, sleep disturbance, daytime arousal. Cognitive impairment is documented with objective clinician-administered tests: the four-item attention task from the Toronto Test of Acute Recovery from TBI (TOTART), together with three tasks from the Cognitive Test for Delirium (CTD; also described in this chapter) using the vigilance, five-item picture recognition memory and four-item comprehension items. Disorientation is measured with the Galveston Orientation and Amnesia Test (GOAT – described in Section 3 of this chapter). Clinician ratings are used to assess restlessness using the Agitated Behavior Scale (ABS – described in Chapter 5), symptom fluctuation and psychotic-type symptoms are drawn from the Delirium Rating Scale – Revised (also described in this chapter), and sleep disturbance and daytime arousal are measured with the checklist of criteria from the *Diagnostic and Statistical Manual of Mental Disorders* – 4th ed. (DSM-IV).

Scale development

Development of the CAP arose in response to increasing recognition that in TBI the acute period of recovery following emergence from coma represents a more generalized confusional state as opposed to an encapsulated disturbance of orientation and memory that is targeted in traditional tests of post-traumatic amnesia (PTA). The conceptual basis of the CAP drew on the work of Stuss et al. (1999), and the particular scales selected for inclusion in the CAP were identified by literature review.

The challenge in developing the CAP was to amalgamate the scores from the seven sets of disparate measures into a common metric. The authors did this by dividing a sample of 62 patients with TBI who, within 3 days of admission to an inpatient rehabilitation unit, were assessed as either meeting ($n = 40$, 64%) or not meeting ($n = 22$, 36%) DSM-IV diagnostic criteria for delirium. Scores on the instruments from these two groups were compared, and the item content and scoring procedures were selected to maximize separation between the groups.

Administration procedures, response format and scoring

Test equipment from the CTD is required to administer the CAP. Administration time is reported as approximately 30 minutes for most patients, although additional time is needed to obtain background information to rate the ABS and complete the DSM-IV checklist. Although the COMBI website advises that no formal training or test materials are required, reliable assessment of the confused patient with clinical ratings does require expertise and novice assessors need training.

Responses to items on the CAP are given weighted scores, and cut-off scores for each of the seven domains are used to indicate presence of "one symptom of post-traumatic confusion". PTCS is deemed to be present if at least 4 out of 7 symptoms are present, or 3 out of 7 symptoms including disorientation.

Psychometric properties

The CAP was validated on the sample of 93 patients recruited from the participating centres of the TBI Model Systems research programme in the USA who were assessed within one day of admission to rehabilitation (Sherer et al., 2005). The validation sample was independent of the initial sample of 62 patients used to develop the CAP. Diagnostic accuracy of the CAP was examined in relation to independent classification of delirium according to DSM-IV criteria. Results from Sherer et al. are shown in Box 2.11.

Box 2.11

Validity:	Criterion: *Concurrent:* with PTCS diagnosis using DSM-IV: $k = .84$ (agreement 93.5%) *Predictive:* initial CAP with discharge Disability Rating Scale: PTCS patients at admission $M = 8.5$ ($SD = 3.6$) vs no PTCS $M = 6.1$ ($SD = 2.4$); $p < .01$ – with length of rehabilitation admission: PTCS patients $M = 22.3$ ($SD = 11.1$) vs no PTCS $M = 17.1$ ($SD = 9.8$); $p < .05$ Construct: *Discriminant:* with time (days) to follow commands PTCS patients $M = 13.4$ ($SD = 14.2$) vs no PTCS $M = 4.9$ ($SD = 8.1$); $p < .01$ – Differential diagnosis between delirium vs no delirium using DSM-IV criteria: sensitivity 91.5%, specificity 100%
Reliability:	Inter-rater: No information available Test–retest: No information available
Responsiveness:	No information available

Comment

The CAP represents a promising instrument for the assessment of patients with TBI in the post-acute period after emergence from coma. As the authors acknowledge, further work on its measurement properties, especially reliability, is required. Given that the CAP uses pre-existing instruments with demonstrated good reliability, however, the results of such studies are expected to be positive. Yet, the base rate for altered states of consciousness, including PTCS, at admission to TBI rehabilitation units is high (Nakase-Thompson, Sherer, Yablon, Nick, & Trzepacz, 2004; Tate, Perdices, Pfaff, & Jurjevic, 2001) and the clinical challenge is to determine the point at which the patient is no longer confused. This necessitates the repeated administration of instruments. Thus, although the CAP has the potential to fill a gap not currently met by traditional tests of PTA in that it provides a comprehensive evaluation of the disparate symptomatology accompanying the post-acute recovery after TBI, its clinical utility for daily administration may be hampered by administration time.

Key references

Nakase-Thompson, R., Sherer, M., Yablon, S. A., Nick, T. G., & Trzepacz, P. T. (2004). Acute confusion following traumatic brain injury. *Brain Injury*, *18*(2), 131–142.

Sherer, M., Nakase-Thompson, R., Yablon, S. A., & Gontkovsky, S. T. (2005). Multidimensional assessment of acute confusion after traumatic brain injury. *Archives of Physical Medicine and Rehabilitation*, *86*(5), 896–904.

Stuss, D. T., Binns, M. A., Carruth, F. G., Levine, B., Brandys, C. E., Moulton, R. J., et al. (1999). The acute period of recovery from traumatic brain injury: Posttraumatic amnesia or posttraumatic confusional state? *Journal of Neurosurgery*, *90*(4), 635–643.

Tate, R., L., Perdices, M., Pfaff, A., & Jurjevic, L. (2001). Predicting duration of posttraumatic amnesia (PTA) from early PTA measurements. *Journal of Head Trauma Rehabilitation*, *16*(6), 525–542.

Delirium Rating Scale – Revised – 98 (DRS-R-98)

Trzepacz (1998)

Source

A detailed appendix in Trzepacz, Mittal, Torres, Kanary, Norton, and Jimerson (2001) contains the DRS-R-98, which is reproduced below.

Purpose

The DRS-R-98 is a clinician rating scale, using information derived from medical history, laboratory tests, family and clinician reports, and patient assessment to assess the breadth and severity of symptoms characterizing delirium or other confusional states in adults. It was developed for use by psychiatrists, but clinicians with appropriate backgrounds (e.g., other physicians, nurses, psychologists) can use it after training.

Item description

The 16-item DRS-R-98 contains 13 items examining symptom severity: sleep–wake cycle, perceptual disturbances and hallucinations, delusions, lability of affect, language, thought process abnormalities, motor agitation, motor retardation, orientation, attention, short-term memory, long-term memory, visuospatial ability. The remaining three "diagnostic" items are temporal onset of symptoms, fluctuation of symptom severity, and presence of physical disorder. Detailed behavioural descriptors are attached to each point of the rating scale.

Scale development

Development of DRS-R-98 drew on the structure of the original 10-item DRS (Trzepacz, Baker, & Greenhouse, 1988), although the DRS-R-98 "differs substantially" from the DRS in item content. Limited information is available regarding scale development of the original DRS, but item selection was based on literature describing delirium and criteria of the *Diagnostic and Statistical Manual of Mental Disorders* – 3rd ed. (DSM-III). Receiver operating characteristic (ROC) curves were used to identify the optimal cut-off scores to indicate the presence of delirium and significant symptom severity.

Administration procedures, response format and scoring

No special equipment is required to administer the DRS-R-98, but its completion requires knowledge of the patient and draws on all available information, including patient assessment, family and nursing reports, medical history, laboratory tests. A 24-hour time frame is recommended as the basis for rating DRS-R-98 items because of fluctuating symptoms; the bare minimum being a 2-hour period. It is suggested that the 13-item symptom severity scale can be administered at repeated intervals to chart progress. Appropriate training is required to administer the DRS-R-98; examiners need to be sufficiently skilled in the assessment of confused patients to make differential diagnoses between delusions versus confabulation, language impairment versus thought process abnormalities, and so forth.

All 13 symptom severity items are rated on a 4-point scale, generally corresponding to 0 (no impairment), 1 (mild), 2 (moderate), 3 (severe disturbance), with additional operational descriptions individually tailored for each item. Use of clinical judgement is encouraged, and the clinician is advised to use an intermediate score (0.5-point interval) if a decision cannot be made between two choices. The three diagnostic items are rated on a 3- or 4-point scale. The total score (symptom severity + diagnostic items) ranges from 0 to 46, with higher scores indicating a greater degree of confusion. The symptom severity score ranges from 0 to 39, with higher scores indicating greater symptom severity. Cut-off scores, set at > 17.75 (total) and > 15.25 (severity), indicate the presence of delirium and significant symptom severity respectively.

Psychometric properties

Trzepacz et al. (2001) assessed the measurement properties of DRS-R-98 in 68 patients from five diagnostic groups: delirium ($n = 24$), dementia ($n = 13$), depression ($n = 12$), schizophrenia ($n = 9$), and other psychiatric conditions ($n = 10$). Samples were recruited from inpatient units of hospitals in Mississippi, USA. Diagnosis of delirium was made by a physician, using DSM-IV criteria and pertinent clinical information. DRS-R-98 ratings over a 24-hour period were made by psychiatrists trained in the instruments, using information from all available sources, but remaining blind to diagnosis. Inter-rater reliability was established using independent ratings following a single interview with each of 26 patients. The DRS-R-98 was validated against other instruments including the original DRS and the Cognitive Test for Delirium (CTD). The cut-off scores of > 17.75 for total and > 15.25 for severity scores yielded 92% sensitivity for both scores and 95% and 93% respectively for specificity. When the delirium group was compared with the dementia only group, sensitivity remained high, but specificity was lower at 85% and 77% for total and severity scores respectively. Mittal et al. (2004) treated 10 medical patients in delirium using risperidone. The DRS-R was responsive to changes occurring in the patients from this case series. A summary of findings from Trzepacz et al., except where otherwise stated, is shown in Box 2.12.

Comment

The original DRS was widely used and translated into many languages and a synthesis of the research studies is reported by Trzepacz (1999). The revised version retains the excellent psychometric properties, provides a comprehensive and detailed evaluation of those clinical features pertinent to delirium, and as such is regarded as a "gold standard" of delirium assessment measures. Although there is no set battery for the cognitive items, specific examples are provided of suggested items, which are operationalized on the score sheet. This procedure is effective as demonstrated by the excellent inter-rater reliability. Nonetheless, the authors advise that "it may be useful for a given clinician to standardize the questions used routinely in his/her practice" (Trzepacz et al., 2001, p. 238).

Box 2.12

Validity:	Criterion: *Concurrent:* with DRS: $r = .83$ (Total score), $r = .80$ (Severity score) – with CTD: $r = -.62$ (Total score), $r = -.63$ (Severity score) Construct: *Internal consistency:* Cronbach alpha: Delirium group: .90 (Total score), .87 (Severity score) *Discriminant:* Total score: Delirium group $M = 26.9$ ($SD = 6.7$) vs dementia $M = 13.9$ ($SD = 4.2$), depression $M = 7.0$ ($SD = 3.5$), schizophrenia $M = 7.7$ ($SD = 4.3$), other psychiatric $M = 8.9$ ($SD = 4.3$); $F = 47.9, p < .001$ – Severity score: Delirium group $M = 21.3$ ($SD = 6.3$) vs dementia $M = 12.4$ ($SD = 3.5$), depression $M = 5.9$ ($SD = 3.3$), schizophrenia $M = 7.1$ ($SD = 4.0$), other psychiatric $M = 6.4$ ($SD = 2.2$); $F = 35.0$, $p < .001$
Reliability:	Inter-rater: ICC = .98 (Total score), ICC = .99 (Severity score) Test–retest: No information available
Responsiveness:	DRS-R: significant improvement in severity scores of 6 patients when in delirium $M = 21.5$ ($SD = 5.6$) vs post-treatment $M = 5.2$ ($SD = 3.5$); $t = 7.13, p < .001, d = 2.9$ Mittal et al.: DRS: significant improvement between pre-treatment (Day 1) $M = 25.2$ ($SD = 0.9$) vs Day 6 $M = 11.3$ ($SD = 1.5$); $d = 15.44$

Key references

Mittal, D., Jimerson, N. A., Neely, E. P., Johnson, W. D., Kennedy, R. E., Torres, R. A., et al. (2004). Risperidone in the treatment of delirium: Results from a prospective open-label trial. *Journal of Clinical Psychiatry*, *65*(5), 662–667.

Trzepacz, P. T. (1998). The Delirium Rating Scale – Revised – 98. In P. T. Trzepacz, D. Mittal, R. Torres, K. Kanary, J. Norton, & N. Jimerson (2001). Validation of the Delirium Rating Scale-Revised-98: Comparison with the Delirium Rating Scale and the Cognitive Test for Delirium. *Journal of Neuropsychiatry and Clinical Neurosciences*, *13*(2), 229–242.

Trzepacz, P. T. (1999). The Delirium Rating Scale: Its use in consultation-liaison research. *Psychosomatics*, *40*(3), 193–205.

Trzepacz, P. T., Baker, R. W., & Greenhouse, J. (1988). A symptom rating scale for delirium. *Psychiatry Research*, *23*, 89–97.

Trzepacz, P. T., Mittal, D., Torres, R., Kanary, K., Norton, J., & Jimerson, N. (2001). Validation of the Delirium Rating Scale-Revised-98: Comparison with the Delirium Rating Scale and the Cognitive Test for Delirium. *Journal of Neuropsychiatry and Clinical Neurosciences*, *13*(2), 229–242.

Delirium Rating Scale - Revised - 98

(Trzepacz, 1998)

General instructions

The Delirium Rating Scale – Revised – 98 (DRS-R-98) is a 16-item clinician-rated scale with two sections and a score sheet. The 13-item severity section can be scored separately from the 3-item diagnostic section; their sum constitutes the total scale score. The severity section functions as a separate scale for repeated measures at short intervals within an episode of delirium. The total score can be scored initially to enhance differential diagnosis by capturing characteristic features of delirium, such as acute onset and fluctuation of symptom severity. Concomitant use of diagnostic criteria such as from the *International Classification of Disease (ICD)-10 Research Manual* or versions of the *Diagnostic and Statistical Manual* (DSM) will enhance its ability to measure delirium when demented patients are involved because the DRS-R-98 is mostly a severity scale.

All items are anchored by text descriptions as guides for rating along a continuum from normal to severely impaired. Severity items are rated from 0 to 3 points and diagnostic items from 0 to either 2 or 3 points. The scoresheet offers space to circle item ratings and to optionally note characteristics of symptoms (e.g., type of hallucination) or the condition of patients during the rating (e.g., restrained).

Though designed to be rated by psychiatrists, other physicians, nurses, and psychologists can use it if they have appropriate clinical training in evaluating psychiatric phenomenology in medically ill patients. It can be used in research or comprehensive clinical evaluations. It does require enough clinical expertise to distinguish, for example, language problems from thought process abnormalities or delusions from confabulation. Even with sufficient clinical expertise, at times it may be difficult to make certain distinctions and more than one item may need to be rated to reflect that presentation (e.g., Wernicke's aphasia and severe loose associations).

The DRS-R-98 can be used in conjunction with the Delirium Rating Scale (DRS) for certain research purposes because they differ substantially in description of items. For example, the DRS may be more helpful for patients emerging from stupor.

The DRS-R-98 measures symptoms without regard to cause. Thus, pre-existing conditions may add points, for example dysphasia will affect the language item. However, longitudinal ratings will clarify effects of pre-existing conditions after the delirium has cleared. The inclusion of mentally retarded and cognitive disorder not otherwise specified subjects during the validation study suggests that delirium can still be reliably assessed in the presence of such confounds.

All sources of available information are used to rate the patient – family, visitors, hospital staff, doctors, medical chart and so on. Even a hospital roommate can contribute information. During interviews for such collateral information, ensure that terms used are mutually understood before accepting others' interpretation of symptoms.

Any time frame can be chosen for the DRS-R-98. Time frames greater than 24 hours are probably not necessary as this coincides with circadian rhythms and their possible disruptions. Shorter periods (e.g., 4 to 12 hours) may be helpful for intervention assessment – either for clinical or research purposes – though the fluctuating nature of symptom severity may need to be considered when interpreting the scores. Choosing periods less than 2 hours risks not adequately capturing some items (e.g., hallucinations, sleep–wake cycle disturbance) that occur intermittently. In such circumstances, a researcher may wish to use a smaller subset of items to monitor the patient, though such a subscale has not been validated.

Some items are rated based on examinations and history, while others incorporate formal testing (e.g., cognitive and language items). It may be useful for a given clinician to standardize the questions used routinely in his/her practice, for example, asking months of the year backwards for attention, clockface or puzzle pieces for visuospatial ability, and particular items for confrontational naming. Adjunctive use of the Cognitive Test for Delirium (CTD) or some of its items offers the advantage of not needing the patient to write or speak. Evaluation of general information included in the long-term memory item should be geared appropriately to the educational and cultural background of the patient.

When both interview behaviour and formally elicited responses are used, the relative contribution of each needs to be weighed by the clinician and a scoring judgement needs to be made. For example, on the attention item a patient has difficulty with reciting months of the year backwards but attends fairly well during the interview, or on long-term memory a patient recalls personal remote information accurately, but cannot recall well on formal testing of three words after 15 minutes.

Despite text descriptions for each item rating, the rater may need to exercise judgement in scoring. At times an intermediate rating with a 0.5 point interval may be needed (e.g., 2.5 points) if the rater cannot decide between two choices. Also, the time frame chosen may affect how to weigh the presence of certain symptoms. For example, a patient who has periods of intense hyperactivity and hypoactivity in a 24-hour period would be rated as "3" on both items #7 and 8. If this same patient is rated for a shorter interval that only involved hyperactivity, then item #7 would be rated as "3" and item #8 would be rated as "0".

In cases where an item cannot be rated at all, the rater should make a notation on the score sheet and decide later how to handle that item's scoring. If used for research, a statistical consultant may have to advise. If used clinically, altering the denominator of the maximum possible score may be acceptable.

Delirium Rating Scale – Revised – 98

(Trzepacz, 1998)

Name:	**Assessor:**	**Date:**

This is a revision of the Delirium Rating Scale (Trzepacz et al., 1988). It is used for initial assessment and repeated measurements of delirium symptom severity. The sum of the 13 item scores provides a severity score. All available sources of information are used to rate the items (nurses, family, chart) in addition to examination of the patient. For serial repeated ratings of delirium severity, reasonable time frames should be chosen between ratings to document meaningful changes because delirium symptom severity can fluctuate without interventions.

1. SLEEP–WAKE CYCLE DISTURBANCE

Instructions: Rate sleep–wake pattern using all sources of information, including from family, caregivers, nurses' reports, and patient. Try to distinguish sleep from resting with eyes closed.

0 Not present
1 Mild sleep continuity disturbance at night or occasional drowsiness during the day
2 Moderate disorganization of sleep–wake cycle (e.g., falling asleep during conversations, napping during the day or several brief awakenings during the night with confusion/behavioural changes or very little night-time sleep)
3 Severe disruption of sleep–wake cycle (e.g., day-night reveral of sleep–wake cycle or severe circadian fragmentation with multiple periods of sleep and wakefulness or severe sleeplessness)

2. PERCEPTUAL DISTURBANCES AND HALLUCINATIONS

Instructions: Illusions and hallucinations can be of any sensory modality. Misperceptions are "simple" if they are uncomplicated, such as a sound, noise, colour, spot or flashes and "complex" if they are multidimensional, such as voices, music, people, animals, or scenes. Rate if reported by patient or caregiver, or inferred by observation.

0 Not present
1 Mild perceptual disturbances (e.g., feelings of derealization or depersonalization; or patient may not be able to discriminate dreams from reality)
2 Illusions present
3 Hallucinations present

3. DELUSIONS

Instructions: Delusions can be of any type, but are most often persecutory. Rate if reported by patient, family or caregiver. Rate as delusional if ideas are unlikely to be true yet are believed by the patient who cannot be dissuaded by logic. Delusional ideas cannot be explained otherwise by the patient's usual cultural or religious background.

0 Not present
1 Mildly suspicious, hypervigilant, or preoccupied
2 Unusual or overvalued ideation that does not reach delusional proportions or could be plausible
3 Delusional

4. LABILITY OF AFFECT

Instructions: Rate the patient's affect as the outward presentation of emotions and not as a description of what the patient feels.

0 Not present
1 Affect somewhat altered or incongruent to situation; changes over the course of hours; emotions are mostly under self-control
2 Affect is often inappropriate to the situation and intermittently changes over the course of minutes; emotions are not consistently under self-control, though they respond to redirection by others
3 Severe and consistent disinhibition of emotions; affect changes rapidly, is inappropriate to context, and does not respond to redirection by others

5. LANGUAGE

Instructions: Rate abnormalities of spoken, written or sign language that cannot be otherwise attributed to dialect or stuttering. Assess fluency, grammar, comprehension, semantic content and naming. Test comprehension and naming non-verbally if necessary by having patient follow commands or point.

0 Normal language
1 Mild impairment including word-finding difficulty or problems with naming or fluency
2 Moderate impairment including comprehension difficulties or deficits in meaningful communication (semantic content)
3 Severe impairment including nonsensical semantic content, word salad, muteness, or severely reduced comprehension

6. THOUGHT PROCESS ABNORMALITIES

Instructions: Rate abnormalities of thinking processes based on verbal or written output. If a patient does not speak or write, do not rate this item.

0 Normal thought processes
1 Tangential or circumstantial
2 Associations loosely connected occasionally, but largely comprehensible
3 Associations loosely connected most of the time

7. MOTOR AGITATION

Instructions: Rate by observation, including from other sources of observation such as by visitors, family and clinical staff. Do not include dyskinesia, tics or chorea.

0 No restlessness or agitation
1 Mild restlessness of gross motor movements or mild fidgetiness
2 Moderate motor agitation including dramatic movements of the extremities, pacing, fidgeting, removing intravenous lines, etc.
3 Severe motor agitation, such as combativeness or a need for restraints or seclusion

8. MOTOR RETARDATION

Instructions: Rate movements by direct observation or from other sources of observation such as family, visitors, or clinical staff. Do not rate components of retardation that are caused by Parkinsonian symptoms. Do not rate drowsiness or sleep.

0 No slowness of voluntary movements
1 Mildly reduced frequency, spontaneity or speed of motor movements, to the degree that may interfere somewhat with the assessment
2 Moderately reduced frequency, spontaneity or speed of motor movements to the degree that it interferes with participation in activities or self-care
3 Severe motor retardation with few spontaneous movements

9. ORIENTATION

Instructions: Patients who cannot speak can be given visual or auditory presentation of multiple choice answers. Allow patient to be wrong by up to 7 days instead of 2 days for patients hospitalized more than 3 weeks. Disorientation to person means not recognizing familiar persons and may be intact even if the person has naming difficulty but recognizes the person. Disorientation to person is most severe when one doesn't know one's identity and is rare. Disorientation to person usually occurs after disorientation to time and/or place.

0 Oriented to person, place and time
1 Disorientated to time (e.g., by more than 2 days or wrong month or wrong year) or to place (e.g., name of building, city, state) but not both
2 Disorientated to time and place
3 Disorientated to person

10. ATTENTION

Instructions: Patients with sensory deficits or who are intubated or whose hand movements are constrained should be tested using an alternative modality besides writing. Attention can be assessed during the interview (e.g., verbal perseverations, distractibility, and difficulty with set shifting) and/or through use of specific tests, e.g., digit span.

0 Alert and attentive
1 Mildly distractible or mild difficulty sustaining attention, but able to refocus with cueing. On formal testing makes only minor errors and is not significantly slow in responses
2 Moderate inattention with difficulty focusing and sustaining attention. On formal testing, makes numerous errors and either requires prodding to focus or finish the task
3 Severe difficulty focusing and/or sustaining attention, with many incorrect or incomplete responses or inability to follow instructions. Distractible by other noises or events in the environment

11. SHORT-TERM MEMORY

Instructions: Defined as recall of information (e.g., 3 items presented either verbally or visually) after a delay of about 2 to 3 minutes. When formally tested, information must be registered adequately before recall is tested. The number of trials to register as well as effect of cueing can be noted on scoresheet. Patient should not be allowed to rehearse during the delay period and should be distracted during that time. Patient may speak or non-verbally communicate to the examiner the identity of the correct items. Short-term deficits noticed during the course of the interview can be used also.

0 Short-term memory intact
1 Recalls 2/3 items; may be able to recall third item after category cueing
2 Recalls 1/3 items; may be able to recall other items after category cueing
3 Recalls 0/3 items

12. LONG-TERM MEMORY

Instructions: Can be assessed formally or through interviewing for recall of past personal (e.g., past medical history or information or experiences that can be corroborated from another source) or general information that is culturally relevant. When formally tested, use a verbal and/or visual modality for 3 items that are adequately registered and recalled after at least 5 minutes. The patient should not be allowed to rehearse during the delay period during formal testing. Make allowances for patients with less than 8 years of education or who are mentally retarded regarding general information questions. Rating the severity of deficits may involve a judgement about all the ways long-term memory is assessed, including recent and/or remote long-term memory ability informally tested during the interview as well as any formal testing of recent long-term memory using 3 items.

0 No significant long-term memory deficits
1 Recalls 2/3 items and/or has minor difficulty recalling details of other long-term information
2 Recalls 1/3 items and/or has moderate difficulty recalling other long-term information
3 Recalls 0/3 items and/or has severe difficulty recalling other long-term information

13. VISUOSPATIAL ABILITY

Instructions: Assess informally and formally. Consider patient's difficulty navigating one's way around living areas or environment (e.g., getting lost). Test formally by drawing or copying a design, by arranging puzzle pieces, or by drawing a map and identifying major cities, etc. Take into account any visual impairments that may affect performance.

0 No impairment
1 Mild impairment such that overall design and most details or pieces are correct; and/or little difficulty navigating in his/her surroundings
2 Moderate impairment with distorted appreciation of overall design and/or several errors of details or pieces; and/or needing repeated redirection to keep from getting lost in a newer environment despite no trouble locating familiar objects in immediate environment
3 Severe impairment on formal testing; and/or repeated wandering or getting lost in environment

DRS-R-98 OPTIONAL DIAGNOSTIC ITEMS

These three items can be used to assist in the differentiation of delirium from other disorders for diagnostic and research purposes. They are added to the severity score for the total scale score, but are NOT included in the severity score.

14. TEMPORAL ONSET OF SYMPTOMS

Instructions: Rate the acuteness of onset of the initial symptoms of the disorder or episode being currently assessed, not their total duration. Distinguish the onset of symptoms attributable to delirium when it occurs concurrently with a different pre-existing psychiatric disorder. For example, if a patient with major depression is rated during a delirium episode resulting from an overdose, then rate the onset of the delirium symptoms.

0 No significant change from usual or longstanding baseline behaviour
1 Gradual onset of symptoms, occurring over a period of several weeks to a month
2 Acute change in behaviour or personality occurring over days to a week
3 Abrupt change in behaviour occurring over a period of several hours to a day

15. FLUCTUATION OF SYMPTOM SEVERITY

Instructions: Rate the waxing and waning of an individual or cluster of symptoms(s) over the time frame being rated. Usually applies to cognition, affect, intensity of hallucinations, thought disorder, language disturbance. Take into consideration that perceptual disturbances usually occur intermittently, but might cluster in period of greater intensity when other symptoms fluctuate in severity.

0 No symptom fluctuation
1 Symptom intensity fluctuates in severity over hours
2 Symptom intensity fluctuates in severity over minutes

16. PHYSICAL DISORDER

Instructions: Rate the degree to which a physiological, medical or pharmacological problem can be specifically attributed to have caused the symptoms being assessed. Many patients have such problems but they may or may not have causal relationship to symptoms being rated.

0 Not present or active
1 Presence of any physical disorder that might affect mental state
2 Drug, infection, metabolic disorder, CNS lesion or other medical problem that specifically can be implicated in causing the altered behaviour or mental state

---

Acknowledgement: From Trzepacz, P. T. et al. (2001). Validation of the Delirium Rating Scale – Revised – 98: Comparison with the Delirium Rating Scale and the Cognitive Test for Delirium. *Journal of Neuropsychiatry and Clinical Neurosciences*, *13*(2), 229–242, Table 2, p. 232 & Scale and instructions, p. 238, reprinted with permission of the American Psychiatric Association.

Memorial Delirium Assessment Scale (MDAS)

Breitbart, Rosenfeld, Roth, Smith, Cohen, and Passik (1997)

Source

Instructions and items for the MDAS are provided in Breitbart et al. (1997), and also appear below.

Purpose

The MDAS is a clinician rating scale, integrating "behavioral observations and objective cognitive testing" (Breitbart et al., 1997, p. 129). It was specifically designed to measure the severity of delirium symptoms (as opposed to diagnosis of delirium) in clinical intervention trials. The MDAS was developed with patients with advanced cancer, with the aim of it being suitable for repeated administration within the same day.

Item description

The 10-item MDAS covers arousal (1 item), level of consciousness (1 item), psychomotor activity (1 item), and a range of cognitive functions: orientation (1 item), attention and verbal memory (3 items), disturbances of thought and perception (3 items).

Scale development

Scale development is briefly described in Breitbart et al. (1997). A potential item pool was drawn up by two of the authors, selected to be consistent with criteria of the *Diagnostic and Statistical Manual of Mental Disorders* (DSM-IV) and the *International Classification of Diseases* (ICD-9). These items were reviewed by a group of experienced psychiatrists for item content as well as ease of administration and rating procedures. A range of possible cut-off scores to determine emergence from delirium was examined to identify the optimal score.

Administration procedures, response format and scoring

No special equipment or test materials are required to administer the MDAS. It requires approximately 10 minutes to complete, but additional time is necessary to collect background information, review medical charts and so forth. No specific training is recommended for clinicians to use the MDAS, although other instruments measuring delirium recommend tuition for clinicians.

Scoring uses a 4-point rating scale, generally corresponding to 0 (no symptoms), 1 (mild), 2 (moderate), 3 (severe), with each response category being further operationally defined for each item. For items that cannot be administered, the authors suggest that a total score can be prorated using the remaining items, although recommended practice is that the MDAS is completed in its entirety. The total score ranges from 0 to 30, with higher scores indicating more severe symptomatology. A cut-off score of 12/13 differentiates patients with moderate and severe delirium from patients with dementia.

Psychometric properties

Two initial studies were conducted to establish the psychometric properties of the MDAS with patients with advanced degrees of cancer recruited from the Memorial Sloan-Kettering Cancer Center, New York, USA (Breitbart et al., 1997). In Study 1, 33 patients (age $M = 56.1$ years) were simultaneously evaluated by two psychiatrists using the MDAS. Diagnosis had been established independently within the preceding 24 hours as delirium ($n = 17$), non-delirium cognitive disorders ($n = 8$) and psychiatric disorders ($n = 8$). The optimal cut-off score was 13, which had 71% sensitivity and 94% specificity. Lawlor, Watanabe, Walker, and Bruera (1998) questioned the cut-off score of 12/13. They reported that they had diagnosed delirium, using DSM-IV criteria, in patients with MDAS scores as low as 7. Their concerns are substantiated in that only 1 of the 23 patients in the Breitbart et al. (1997) study with mild delirium was identified with the MDAS. In a subsequent study, Lawlor, Nekolaichuk, Gagnon, Mancini, Pereira, and Bruera (2000) determined the optimal cut-off score was 6/7 (97% sensitivity; 95% specificity), whereas the cut-off of 12/13 only yielded 51% sensitivity. As Lawlor et al. (2000) noted, however, the sample characteristics of the two studies differed; moreover, Lawlor et al.

aimed to diagnose the *presence* of delirium, whereas Breitbart et al. (1997) aimed to distinguish *between* delirium and dementia.

Concurrent validity of the MDAS was examined by Breitbart et al. (1997) in Study 2, in which 51 patients (age $M = 57.8$ years, range 27–88) were examined. All patients met DSM-IV criteria for delirium. Validation instruments included the Delirium Rating Scale (DRS) and Mini-Mental State Examination (MMSE). The underlying factor structure was examined by Lawlor et al. (2000) with 56 patients with delirium from advanced cancer. Two factors were extracted accounting for 43% of the variance: global cognitive and neurobehavioural. Data on responsiveness are available from Moryl, Kogan, Comfort, and Obbens (2005) who treated 20 cancer patients with uncontrolled pain and delirium using an opioid rotation strategy. Results from Breitbart et al., except where otherwise stated, are shown in Box 2.13.

Box 2.13

Validity:	Criterion: *Concurrent:* with DRS: $r = .88$ – with MMSE: $r = -.91$ – MDAS scores predicted global rating of delirium ($R^2 = .79$)
	Construct: *Internal consistency:* Cronbach alpha: .91
	Factor analysis: Lawlor et al. (2000): 2 factors: Global cognitive (6 items), Neurobehavioural (4 items)
	Discriminant: Delirium group $M = 16.94$ ($SD = 7.64$) vs non-delirium cognitive disorders $M = 8.50$ ($SD = 2.78$) and psychiatric disorders $M = 5.38$ ($SD = 4.17$); $F = 10.49, p < .001$ – Differential diagnosis between delirium vs dementia using 12/13: sensitivity 71%, specificity 94% (but also see text)
Reliability:	Inter-rater: ICC = .92 (item range ICC = .64–.99)
	Test–retest: No information available
Responsiveness:	Moryl et al.: MDAS prior to treatment rotation $M = 23.6$ vs 3 days later $M = 10.6$ (*SD* not reported)

Comment

Like other delirium scales described in this section, the MDAS has good psychometric properties, although its sensitivity in distinguishing between delirium and dementia, at 71%, is not as high as other delirium scales. Additionally, it is insensitive to milder degrees of delirium. An advantage of the structure of the MDAS is that it is a stand-alone instrument, with objective cognitive items incorporated into the scale, thereby avoiding the need for administration of an independent cognitive screening test as occurs with some other delirium measures. A set battery of items is not included in the MDAS for some domains (e.g., Digit span) and the clinician thus needs to be knowledgeable about the kinds of stimuli that should be selected and conversant with appropriate administration procedures. In spite of some limitations, the MDAS affords a reliable and valid evaluation of delirium symptom severity, and in their systematic review, de Rooij, Schuurmans, van der Mast, and Levi (2005) identified the MDAS as having the capacity to evaluate delirium subtypes (psychomotor varieties).

Key references

Breitbart, W., Rosenfeld, B., Roth, A., Smith, M. J., Cohen, K., & Passik, S. (1997). The Memorial Delirium Assessment Scale. *Journal of Pain and Symptom Management*, *13*(3), 128–137.

de Rooij, S. E., Schuurmans, M. J., van der Mast, R. C., & Levi., M. (2005). Clinical subtypes of delirium and their relevance for daily clinical practice: A systematic review. *International Journal of Geriatric Psychiatry*, *20*(7), 609–615.

Lawlor, P. G., Nekolaichuk, C., Gagnon, B., Mancini, I. L., Pereira, J. L., & Bruera, E. D. (2000). Clinical utility, factor analysis, and further validation of the Memorial Delirium Assessment Scale in patients with advanced cancer. *Cancer*, *88*(12), 2859–2867.

Lawlor, P. G., Watanabe, S., Walker, P., & Bruera, E. (1998). [Letter] Memorial Delirium Assessment Scale and commentary. *Journal of Pain and Symptom Management*, *15*(2), 73–74.

Moryl, N., Kogan, M., Comfort, C., & Obbens, E. (2005). Methadone in the treatment of pain and terminal delirium in advanced cancer patients. *Palliative and Supportive Care*, *3*; 311–317.

Memorial Delirium Assessment Scale

Breitbart, Rosenfeld, Roth, Smith, Cohen, and Passik (1997)

Name:	Assessor:	Date:

General instructions:
Rate the severity of the following symptoms of delirium based on current interaction with patient or assessment of his/her behaviour or experience over past several hours (as indicated in each time).

1. REDUCED LEVEL OF CONSCIOUSNESS (AWARENESS)

Instructions: Rate the patient's current awareness of and interaction with the environment (interviewer, other people/objects in the room; for example, ask patients to describe their surroundings).

0 None: patient spontaneously fully aware of environment and interacts appropriately
1 Mild: patient is unaware of some elements in the environment, or not spontaneously interacting appropriately with the interviewer; becomes fully aware and appropriately interactive when prodded strongly; interview is prolonged but not seriously disrupted
2 Moderate: patient is unaware of some or all elements in the environment, or not spontaneously interacting with the interviewer; becomes incompletely aware and inappropriately interactive when prodded strongly; interview is prolonged but not seriously disrupted
3 Severe: patient is unaware of all elements in the environment with no spontaneous interaction or awareness of the interviewer, so that the interview is difficult-to-impossible, even with maximal prodding

2. DISORIENTATION

Instructions: Rate current state by asking the following 10 orientation items: date, month, day, year, season, floor, name of hospital, city, state, and country.

0 None: patient knows 9–10 items
1 Mild: patient knows 7–8 items
2 Moderate: patient knows 5–6 items
3 Severe: patient knows no more than 4 items

3. SHORT-TERM MEMORY IMPAIRMENT

Instructions: Rate current state by using repetition and delayed recall of 3 words (patient must immediately repeat and recall words 5 minutes later after an intervening task. Use alternate sets of 3 words for successive evaluations; for example, apple, table, tomorrow; sky, cigar, justice).

0 None: all 3 words repeated and recalled
1 Mild: all 3 repeated, patient fails to recall 1
2 Moderate: all 3 repeated, patient fails to recall 2 or 3
3 Severe: patient fails to repeat 1 or more words

4. IMPAIRED DIGIT SPAN

Instructions: Rate current performance by asking patient to repeat first 3, 4 then 5 digits forward and then 3, then 4 backwards; continue to the next step only if patient succeeds at the previous one.

0 None: patient can do at least 5 numbers forward and 4 backward
1 Mild: patient can do at least 5 numbers forward, 3 backward
2 Moderate: patient can do 4–5 numbers forward, cannot do 3 backward
3 Severe: patient can do no more than 3 numbers forward

5. REDUCED ABILITY TO MAINTAIN AND SHIFT ATTENTION

Instructions: As indicated during the interview by questions needing to be rephrased and/or repeated because patient's attention wanders, patient loses track, patient is distracted by outside stimuli or over-absorbed in a task.

0 None: none of the above; patient maintains and shifts attention normally
1 Mild: above attentional problems occur once or twice without prolonging the interview
2 Moderate: above attentional problems occur often, prolonging the interview without seriously disrupting it
3 Severe: above attentional problems occur constantly, disrupting and making the interview difficult-to-impossible

6. DISORGANIZED THINKING

Instructions: As indicated during the interview by rambling, irrelevant, or incoherent speech, or by tangential, circumstantial or faulty reasoning. Ask patient a somewhat complex question (for example, "Describe your current medical condition").

- 0 None: patient's speech is coherent and goal-directed
- 1 Mild: patient's speech is slightly difficult to follow; responses to questions are slightly off target but not so much as to prolong the interview
- 2 Moderate: disorganized thoughts or speech are clearly present, such that interview is prolonged but not disrupted
- 3 Severe: examination is very difficult or impossible as a result of disorganized thinking or speech

7. PERCEPTUAL DISTURBANCE

Instructions: Misperceptions, illusions, hallucinations inferred from inappropriate behaviour during the interview or admitted by patient, as well as those elicited from nurse/family/chart accounts of the past several hours or of the time since last examination:

- 0 None: no misperception, illusions or hallucinations
- 1 Mild: misperceptions or illusions related to sleep, fleeting hallucinations on 1–2 occasions without inappropriate behaviour
- 2 Moderate: hallucinations or frequent illusions on several occasions with minimal inappropriate behaviour that does not disrupt the interview
- 3 Severe: frequent or intense illusions or hallucinations with persistent inappropriate behaviour that disrupts the interview or interferes with medical care

8. DELUSIONS

Instructions: Rate delusions inferred from inappropriate behaviour during the interview or admitted by the patient, as well as delusions elicited from nurse/family/chart accounts of the past several hours or of the time since the previous examination:

- 0 None: no evidence of misinterpretation or delusions
- 1 Mild: misinterpretations or suspiciousness without clear delusional ideas and inappropriate behaviour
- 2 Moderate: delusions admitted by the patient or evidenced by his/her behaviour that do not or only marginally disrupt the interview or interfere with medical care
- 3 Severe: persistent and/or intense delusions resulting in inappropriate behaviour, disrupting the interview or seriously interfering with medical care

9. DECREASED OR INCREASED PSYCHOMOTOR ACTIVITY

Instructions: Rate activity over past several hours, as well as activity during the interview, by circling: (a) hypoactive, (b) hyperactive or (c) elements of both present.

- 0 None: normal psychomotor activity
- 1 a b c Mild: hypoactivity is barely noticeable, expressed as slightly slowing of movement. Hyperactivity is barely noticeable or appears as simple restlessness
- 2 a b c Moderate: hypoactivity is undeniable, with marked reduction in a number of movements or marked slowness of movement; patient rarely spontaneously moves or speaks. Hyperactivity is undeniable, patient moves almost constantly; in both cases, exam is prolonged as a consequence
- 3 a b c Severe: hypoactivity is severe; patient does not move or speak without prodding or is catatonic. Hyperactivity is severe; patient is constantly moving, overreacts to stimuli, requires surveillance and/or restraint; getting through the exam is difficult or impossible

10. SLEEP–WAKE CYCLE DISTURBANCE (DISORDER OF AROUSAL):

Instructions: Rate patient's ability to either sleep or stay awake at the appropriate times. Utilize direct observation during the interview, as well as reports from nurses, family, patient, or charts describing sleep–wake cycle disturbance over the past several hours or since last examination. Use observations of the previous night for morning evaluations only.

- 0 None: at night, sleeps well; during the day, has no trouble staying awake
- 1 Mild: mild deviation from appropriate sleepfulness and wakefulness states: at night, difficulty falling asleep or transient night awakenings, needs medication to sleep well; during the day, reports periods of drowsiness or, during the interview, is drowsy but can easily fully awaken him/herself
- 2 Moderate: moderate deviations from appropriate sleepfulness and wakefulness states: at night, repeated and prolonged night awakening; during the day, reports of frequent and prolonged napping or, during the interview, can only be roused to complete wakefulness by strong stimuli
- 3 Severe: severe deviations from appropriate sleepfulness and wakefulness states: at night sleeplessness; during the day, patient spends most of the time sleeping or, during the interview, cannot be roused to full wakefulness by any stimuli

---

Acknowledgement: From Breitbart, W. et al. (1997). The Memorial Delirium Assessment Scale (MDAS). *Journal of Pain and Symptom Management*, *13*(3), 128–137, reprinted by permission of The U.S. Cancer Pain Relief Committee and Elsevier.

SECTION 3
Scales measuring orientation and post-traumatic amnesia

Galveston Orientation and Amnesia Test (GOAT)

Levin, O'Donnell, and Grossman (1979)

Source

Items comprising the GOAT, along with scoring instructions, are available in Levin et al. (1979), and are reproduced below. Additionally, a children's version of the GOAT (Children's Orientation and Amnesia Test, COAT) has been published (Ewing-Cobbs, Levin, Fletcher, Miner, & Eisenberg, 1990) and is briefly described below.

Purpose

The GOAT is an objective, clinician-administered test designed to measure duration of post-traumatic amnesia (PTA) in patients with traumatic brain injury (TBI). It was the first published instrument to offer a standardized and prospective procedure for this purpose. The authors aimed to develop a brief, practical and reliable scale that could be administered at the bedside or in the emergency room by clinicians from a range of disciplines.

Item description

Levin et al. (1979) describe the GOAT as a 10-item scale, although a number of items have multiple components, making 14 questions in total (and an additional two items probe for further details). The majority of items focus on orientation: autobiographical details (3 items), place (2 items), and time (5 items). The remaining four items sample historical memories to enable an estimation of the duration of retrograde and anterograde amnesia.

Scale development

Development of the GOAT was conducted in a careful and systematic manner, including a review of brief cognitive screening tests of the day. Item selection was based on the original literature of the 1930s describing features characterizing PTA, as well as the authors' clinical observations of patients during the post-acute recovery period. Orientation items were trialled on medical inpatients without neurological conditions. The GOAT was standardized on a sample of 50 patients with mild TBI recruited from the Neurosurgery Service of the University of Texas Medical Branch at Galveston, USA. They were tested close to the time of discharge from hospital to ensure that maximal recovery had occurred (Levin et al., 1979). Weighted error points were developed for scoring purposes, but no information is available regarding the procedures that were used to determine the weightings. Cut-off scores to designate emergence from PTA were determined from the distribution of scores of the mild TBI sample: 92% scored > 75/100 and the remaining 8% scored > 65/100. These respective scores were used to identify patients who had emerged from PTA or were in the borderline-abnormal range.

Administration procedures, response format and scoring

No special materials are required to administer the GOAT, although for scoring purposes the examiner needs to verify information proffered by the patient from consulting the medical record or an informant. Formal training is not required and administration time is brief, usually a few minutes. Levin et al. (1979) advise that the GOAT should be administered on at least a daily basis and suggest that it can be incorporated into the medical rounds or recording of vital signs. Jain, Layton, and Murray (2000) have published a variant of the administration procedures suitable for testing patients with aphasia.

GOAT responses are scored in terms of weighted error points, which are subtracted from 100. Emergence from PTA is defined as consistent scores (i.e., at least two consecutive days) greater than 75/100. In the original publication (Levin et al., 1979), duration of PTA was taken as the period between emergence from coma until the patient reached criterion on the GOAT. However, universal practice now adopts the easier method of calculating PTA duration from the time of the injury.

Psychometric properties

Initial reliability and validity studies of the GOAT were reported by Levin et al. (1979), with TBI patients recruited from the same neurosurgery service as the standardization sample. Inter-rater reliability was established with two raters assessing 13 patients who had a range of injury severity levels: each examiner administered the GOAT to half the patients while the other observed. The GOAT was validated with 52 inpatients who had varying degrees of injury severity. Validation instruments comprised components of the Glasgow Coma Scale (GCS), mass lesion identified by computer tomography (CT) scans, and Glasgow Outcome Scale data (GOS; $n = 32$) collected at least 6 months post-trauma.

Rasch analysis of the GOAT was conducted by Bode, Heinemann, and Semik (2000), using data from 77 patients recruited from six inpatients rehabilitation units in the USA. Initially, the GOAT was found to have acceptable levels of person separation and item separation. Some misfit of items occurred, suggesting that not all items measured the same construct. Further calibrations improved the structure of the GOAT, resulting in a hierarchical item structure (with person and item separations both > 2.0, which the authors reported as corresponding to a reliability of .80) and dichotomous scoring using three strata of PTA (autobiographical items, orientation to place and time, and memory items). Results from Levin et al. (1979), except where otherwise indicated, are shown in Box 2.14.

Box 2.14

Validity:	Criterion: *Concurrent:* using PTA duration of > 14 days, and GCS subscales at admission: – with spontaneous eye opening: $\chi^2 = 21.09, p < .001$ – with motor response: $\chi^2 = 18.98, p < .001$ – with verbal response: $\chi^2 = 19.53, p < .001$
	Predictive: with GOS at > 6 months, a greater proportion of those with moderate and severe disability (15/16) had GOAT duration > 14 days than those with good recovery (2/16); $\chi^2 = 18.0, p < .001$
	Construct: *Discriminant:* with CT scan, a greater proportion of those with evidence of bilateral mass lesion/diffuse injury had GOAT duration > 14 days; Fisher exact: $p < .02$
	Rasch analysis: Bode et al.: Calibration 3 – person separation 2.03, item separation 8.35, no misfitting items
Reliability:	Inter-rater: Kendall $r = .99$
	Test–retest: No information available
Responsiveness:	No information available

Derivatives of the GOAT: Children's Orientation and Amnesia Test (COAT); Ewing-Cobbs et al. (1990)

The COAT (see below), designed for children aged 3 to 15 years, takes 5 to 10 minutes to administer. It is described as a 16-item test, but a number of items contain multiple questions. Three areas are sampled: General orientation, Temporal orientation and Memory. There is some overlap with GOAT items, but the General orientation and Memory items are age-appropriate. Development of the COAT proceeded in two stages. Following item selection, the COAT (with the exception of the temporal orientation items in children younger than 8 years) was examined in 146 healthy children aged 3 to 15 years. Unlike the GOAT, error points are not used for the COAT. Normative data, using different sets of questions for different age groups, are provided in Ewing-Cobbs et al. (and reproduced below). Normal performance is defined as a score on two consecutive days that is within 2 standard deviations of the age-corrected mean score. The COAT was then validated in 37 children and adolescents with TBI. They were divided into three groups according to PTA duration (≤ 7 days, 8–14 days, > 14 days). Significant group differences were found for GCS scores at hospital admission (and correlation was also significant: $r = -.61$), along with Glasgow Outcome Scale classifications at 12 months post-trauma ($\chi^2 = 12.04$, $p < .02$). Inter-rater reliability was established in a subset of 11 children (reported as $\alpha = 0.98$).

Comment

Introduction of the GOAT marked a milestone in the assessment of the acutely confused patient after TBI. Until that time, duration of PTA was estimated clinically, usually by questioning the patient retrospectively *after* emerging from PTA regarding the time when continuous day-to-day memories first returned. The GOAT is regarded as the standard against which other PTA tests are compared, although it is not without its limitations, which have resulted in development of other scales. Even so, the GOAT remains the most systematically and thoroughly developed of all PTA scales published to date, it has good psychometric properties, and is widely used. The alternative scoring version produced by the Rasch analysis (Bode et al., 2000) simplifies the administration and scoring procedures thereby making the GOAT a more user-friendly instrument.

Key references

Bode, R. K., Heinemann, A. W., & Semik, P. (2000). Measurement properties of the Galveston Orientation and Amnesia Test (GOAT) and improvement patterns during inpatient rehabilitation. *Journal of Head Trauma Rehabilitation, 15*(1), 637–655.

Ewing-Cobbs, L., Levin, H. S., Fletcher, J. M., Miner, M. E., & Eisenberg, H. M. (1990). The Children's Orientation and Amnesia Test: Relationship to severity of acute head injury and to recovery of memory. *Neurosurgery*, *27*(5), 683–691.

Jain, N., Layton, B. S., & Murray, P. K. (2000). Are aphasic patients who fail the GOAT in PTA? A modified Galveston Orientation and Amnesia Test for persons with aphasia. *The Clinical Neuropsychologist*, *14*(1), 13–17.

Levin, H. S., O'Donnell, V. M., & Grossman, R. G. (1979). The Galveston Orientation and Amnesia Test. A practical scale to assess cognition after head injury. *The Journal of Nervous and Mental Disease*, *167*(11), 675–684.

Galveston Orientation and Amnesia Test

Levin, O'Donnell, and Grossman (1979)

Name:	**Assessor:**	**Date:**

	Error points
1. What is your name? ______	└─┴─┘
When were you born? ______	└─┴─┘
Where do you live? ______	└─┴─┘
2. Where are you now (town/city)? ______	└─┴─┘
Where are you now (hospital)? ______	└─┴─┘
(Unnecessary to state name of hospital)	
3. On what date were you admitted to this hospital? ______	└─┴─┘
How did you get here? ______	└─┴─┘
4. What is the first event you can remember *after* the injury? ______	└─┴─┘
Can you describe it in detail (e.g., date, time, companions)? ______	└─┴─┘
5. What is the first event you can remember *before* the accident? ______	└─┴─┘
Can you describe it in detail (e.g., date, time, companions)? ______	└─┴─┘
6. What time is it now? ______	└─┴─┘
7. What day of the week is it? ______	└─┴─┘
8. What day of the month is it? ______	└─┴─┘
9. What is the month? ______	└─┴─┘
10. What is the year? ______	└─┴─┘
TOTAL ERROR POINTS	└─┴─┴─┘
TOTAL GOAT SCORE (100-total error points)	└─┴─┴─┘

Acknowledgement: From Levin, H. S., O'Donnell, V. M., & Grossman, R. G. (1979). The Galveston Orientation and Amnesia Test. A practical scale to assess cognition after head injury. *Journal of Nervous and Mental Disease*, *167*(11), 675–684, Figure 1 and Appendix 1, reproduced by permission of Wolters Kluwer and the author.

Galveston Orientation and Amnesia Test – Scoring Instructions

Levin, O'Donnell, and Grossman (1979)

Question 1: Assign 2 error points if patient fails to state first and last names correctly; 4 points if patient fails to state date of birth correctly; 4 points are scored if patient fails to state the town of his residence (street address is unnecessary). A maximum of 10 error points could be scored and entered in the two columns on the extreme right of the test form.

Question 2: If the patient is unable to state the town he is in at time of assessment, 5 points are scored; 5 additional points are deducted if the patient fails to state that he is in the hospital, although mentioning the name of the hospital is unnecessary.

Question 3: Five error points are given if the patient is unable to recall the date of admission; 5 additional points are deducted if the patient fails to describe accurately the mode of transportation to the hospital.

Question 4: Five error points are given when the patient is unable to recall the first event after injury (e.g., waking up in hospital room); patients who cannot recall an event after the injury would have 5 additional error points deducted because of failure to present details of such an event. Those patients who describe a verifiable or at least plausible post-traumatic event, but are unable to provide details, would accrue 5 error points on this question.

Question 5: Criteria for scoring responses are similar to those used in question 4; 5 error points are deducted for vague recall of an event prior to the injury (e.g., driving a car shortly before the accident), whereas 5 additional points are deducted for total failure to recall any retrograde event.

Question 6: Score 1 error point for each half hour that the patient's response deviates from the correct time, up to a maximum of –5.

Question 7: Assign 1 error point for each day that the patient's response is removed from the correct day of the week.

Question 8: Score 1 error point for each day of the month that the patient's response deviates from the correct date, to a maximum of –5.

Question 9: Five error points are deducted for each month that the patient's response is removed from the correct month, to a maximum of –15.

Question 10: Ten error points are deducted for each year that the patient's response deviates from the correct one, to a maximum of –30.

Computation of GOAT score
Enter the total error points accrued for the 10 items in the lower right hand corner of the test form. The GOAT score equals 100 minus total error points.

Acknowledgement: From Levin, H. S., O'Donnell, V. M., & Grossman, R. G. (1979). The Galveston Orientation and Amnesia Test. A practical scale to assess cognition after head injury. *Journal of Nervous and Mental Disease*, *167*(11), 683–684, Scoring instructions reproduced by permission of Wolters Kluwer and the authors.

Children's Orientation and Amnesia Test

Ewing-Cobbs, Levin, Fletcher, Miner, and Eisenberg (1990)

Name: **Assessor:** **Date:**

SCORE

GENERAL ORIENTATION

1. What is your name? First: (2) ____ Last: (3) ____ ____(5)
2. How old are you? (3) ____ When is your birthday? Month: (1) ____ Day: (1) ____ ____(5)
3. Where do you live? City: (3) ____ State: (2) ____ ____(5)
4. What is your father's name? (5) ____ What is your mother's name? (5) ____ ____(10)
5. What school do you go to? (3) ____ What grade are you in? (2) ____ ____(5)
6. Where are you now? (5) ____ ____(5)

   May rephrase question: Are you at home now? Are you in the hospital? If rephrased, child must correctly answer both questions to receive credit

7. Is it day time or night-time? (5) ____ ____(5)

GENERAL ORIENTATION TOTAL ____(40)

TEMPORAL ORIENTATION

Instructions: Administer if age 8 to 15 years

8. What time is it now? (5) ____ ____(5)

   Scoring: 5 = Correct; 4 = < 1 hour off; 3 = 1 hour off; 2 = > 1 hour off; 1 = 2 hours off

9. What day of the week is it? (5) ____ ____(5)

   Scoring: 5 = Correct; 4 = 1 off; 3 = 2 off; 2 = 3 off; 1 = 4 off

10. What day of the month is it? (5) ____ ____(5)

    Scoring: 5 = Correct; 4 = 1 off; 3 = 2 off; 2 = 3 off; 1 = 4 off

11. What is the month? (10) ____ ____(10)

    Scoring: 10 = Correct; 7 = 1 off; 4 = 2 off; 1 = 3 off

12. What is the year? (15) ____ ____(15)

    Scoring: 15 = Correct; 10 = 1 off; 5 = 2 off; 1 = 3 off

TEMPORAL ORIENTATION TOTAL ____(40)

MEMORY

13. Say these numbers after me in the same order ____(14)

    Instructions: Discontinue when the child fails both series of digits at any length. Score 2 points if both digit series are correctly repeated; score 1 point if only 1 is correct.

3	5	____	35296	81493	____
58	42	____	539418	724856	____
643	926	____	8129365	4739128	____
7216	3279	____			

14. How many fingers am I holding up? Two fingers (2) ____ Three fingers (3) ____ 10 fingers (5) ____ ____(10)
15. Who is on *Sesame Street*? (10) ____ ____(10)

    Instructions: Can substitute other major television show

16. What is my name? (10) ____ ____(10)

MEMORY TOTAL ____(44)

OVERALL TOTAL ____(124)

Acknowledgement: From Ewing-Cobbs, L. et al. (1990). The Children's Orientation and Amnesia Test: Relationship to severity of acute head injury and to recovery of memory. *Neurosurgery*, *27*(5), 683–691, Figure 1, p. 684, reproduced by permission of Wolters Kluwer Health.

Normative data for the COAT

Age (year)	N	Total score[1]	
		Mean	SD
3	16	46.8	12.6
4	26	59.4	8.5
5	25	61.6	6.3
6	12	64.1	8.5
7	10	68.3	6.1
8	17	114.8	5.6
9	8	113.3	7.4
10	14	117.6	5.7
11	10	116.4	4.1
12–15	8	119.8	1.5

[1] For ages 3 to 7 years the total score is based on the general orientation (Questions 1–7) and memory (Questions 13–16) items. The total score for children aged 8 to 15 years is based on Questions 1 to 16.

Acknowledgement: From Ewing-Cobbs, L. et al. (1990). The Children's Orientation and Amnesia Test: Relationship to severity of acute head injury and to recovery of memory. *Neurosurgery*, *27*(5), 683–691. Table 1, p. 685, reproduced by permission of Wolters Kluwer Health.

Orientation Group Monitoring System (OGMS)

Corrigan, Arnett, Houck, and Jackson (1985)

Source

Procedures used in the OGMS are described in Corrigan et al. (1985) and summaries appear throughout this entry.

Purpose

The OGMS represents a unique method for determining duration of post-traumatic amnesia (PTA). It is a procedure that uses clinical observations in the context of a daily therapeutic group to judge whether specified behaviours indicative of PTA have resolved. The OGMS was developed for patients with traumatic brain injury (TBI), but it is also appropriate for patients with other neurological conditions, such as stroke and hypoxia. Corrigan et al. (1985) advise that the OGMS is not suited to patients functioning at less than Level IV on the Rancho Los Amigos Levels of Cognitive Functioning Scale (LCFS; i.e., patients who, at maximum, are only able to react specifically but inconsistently to stimuli, although they may follow simple commands for motor action, viz. LCFS III).

Item description

There are no items per se for the OGMS; rather specific goals are set in seven domains (see Tables 2.5 and 2.6): 1: orientation to time, 2: orientation to place, 3: identities of staff and group members, 4: ability to attend to group activities, 5: associative learning, 6: ability to repeat significant events from the previous day, and 7: ability to accurately utilize environmental cues and scheduling aids. Performance is monitored and rated in a 30-minute therapy group conducted 5 days each week. Specific objectives are incorporated into the group session on specific days, such that within the period of 1 week all seven domains are covered (Table 2.5).

Scale development

Development of the underlying structure for the OGMS drew on the content of reality orientation groups developed for older people, and also applied in rehabilitation settings for people with TBI. The group therapy context becomes the clinical vehicle by which to evaluate the patient's level of functioning. As such, the specific activities used in the daily therapy groups are selected to ensure "a broad sampling of content . . . to keep activities fresh and varied" (Corrigan et al., 1985, p. 626). Behavioural domains for the OGMS were selected and criterion levels established by psychology and occupational therapy staff working within the rehabilitation unit. The minimum percentage for each domain was selected as representing the levels of performance necessary for activities of daily living

Table 2.5 OGMS: An example of a week's group activities, along with domains addressed by each activity

Day	*Activity*	*Domains*	*Day*	*Activity*	*Domains*
Monday	Mark calendars	1	Wednesday	Mark calendars	1
	Group introductions	3		Elicit general fund of information	4
	Recall weekend	6, 4		Elicit knowledge of facility and location	2
	Present/recall current events	4	Thursday	Mark calendars	1
Tuesday	Mark calendars	1		Free recall tasks	5, 4
	Therapists' identities	3		Sequential recall tasks	5, 4
	Test knowledge of schedule	7, 4	Friday	Mark calendars	1
				Games	4

Acknowledgement: From Corrigan, J. D. et al. (1985). Reality orientation for brain injured patients: Group treatment and monitoring of recovery. *Archives of Physical Medicine and Rehabilitation*, *66*(9), 626–630, Table 2, reprinted with permission of the American Congress of Rehabilitation Medicine and the American Academy of Physical Medicine and Rehabilitation and Elsevier.

Table 2.6 OGMS: Operational criteria for successful performance in the seven OGMS domains

Domain	*Description*
1	Patient is oriented to the day, date, and year 80% of the time over a 2-week period (time orientation aids such as calendars and clocks may be used).
2	Patient can correctly identify the name of the institution, city, state and location of the group treatment room 100% of the time over a 2-week period.
3	Patient can identify without aids other group members and therapists 80% of the time over a 2-week period.
4	Patient is able to attend to group activities sufficiently to allow an appropriate response 70% of the time over a 2-week period.
5	Patient is able to repeat five paired associations 100% of the time over a 2-week period.
6	Patient correctly reports significant events of the previous day or weekend, with or without verbal cues, 100% of the time over a 2-week period.
7	Patient is able to use planning and scheduling aids to correctly report daily activities 100% of the time over a 2-week period.

Acknowledgement: From Corrigan, J. D. et al. (1985). Reality orientation for brain injured patients: Group treatment and monitoring of recovery. *Archives of Physical Medicine and Rehabilitation*, *66*(9), 626–630, Table 1, reprinted with permission of the American Congress of Rehabilitation Medicine and the American Academy of Physical Medicine and Rehabilitation and Elsevier.

(Table 2.6). A cut-off score (≥ 2.8/3) was established to indicate when the patient had emerged from PTA (Corrigan & Jackson, 1984), later revised by Mysiw, Corrigan, Carpenter, and Chock (1990) as > 2.75/3 for 2 consecutive weeks. No information is provided in the publications regarding the method by which the cut-off score was determined. Corrigan et al. (1985) note that patients at Rancho LCFS VI (confused, appropriate responses) score between 2.2 and 2.6 on the OGMS, and those at Level VII (automatic, appropriate responses) "have difficulty scoring above 2.85" (p. 629).

Administration procedures, response format and scoring

In the rehabilitation unit, the 30-minute therapy session is conducted at 9 am each weekday in a group room. Group members need to attend at least three sessions per week in order to sample a sufficient number of behaviours in the domains to enable a valid rating. Mysiw, Bogner, Arnett, Clinchot, and Corrigan (1996) recommend the ideal group size is less than 10 patients, and they provide detailed description of the types of activities that can be included to assess the seven domains. Groups are conducted by two staff members, one of whom leads the group and the other records responses of the patients. Each patient is rated on every stimulus item ("rating event") as these occur throughout the session. A simple recording form is used for this purpose. No special training is advocated for the clinician to complete the OGMS.

Each item is rated on a 3-point scale: 1 (failure), 2 (questionable), 3 (correct). Scores are then aggregated into a weekly average score (range 1–3). For example, in Table 2.5 there are 19 "rating events". The total score for a patient who attends all sessions would range from 19 to 57. If such a hypothesized patient scored 2 for 10 rating events and 3 for the remaining 9 events, the total score would be 47. The total score is divided by 19, to arrive at the weekly average (which would be 2.47 in the case of the hypothesized patient). Scores > 2.75/3 for 2 consecutive weeks are taken to indicate emergence from PTA (and hence the hypothesized patient would be classified as still in PTA).

Psychometric properties

Corrigan and colleagues conducted a series of psychometric studies with patients recruited from a TBI rehabilitation service in Columbus, Ohio, USA. Inter-rater reliability of the OGMS was reported in Corrigan et al. (1985), but no methodological details are provided. Corrigan and Mysiw (1988) established concurrent validity of the OGMS with the Mini-Mental State Examination (MMSE). Mysiw et al. (1990) compared the OGMS with Galveston Orientation and Amnesia Test (GOAT) in 21 patients with TBI (age $M = 25.5$ years, range 16–55; coma duration $M = 11$ days, $SD = 14$). Jackson, Mysiw, and Corrigan (1989) examined responsiveness in 42 patients (86% TBI, $n = 33$ within 12 months post-onset). Based on retrospective examination of their files, they identified a cut-off score of ≥ 0.23 as indicative of significant change. A total of 248 observations from the 42 patients revealed 27 instances with a significant decrement. In 25 out of 27 instances the decline in scores was accompanied by documented medical problem, including adverse drug effect ($n = 13$), hydrocephalus, chronic subdural haematoma and infections. Results of these studies are shown in Box 2.15.

Comment

The OGMS provides a comprehensive and sensitive method for measuring PTA duration that differs from the standard approaches in that ratings are made in the context of a group therapy setting. As the authors observe, the advantages are that the 2.5 hours per week of structured observation provide a large sample of behaviour relative to that which standard PTA tests use. Additionally, the structure of the OGMS captures the variety of behaviours characterizing PTA. The OGMS

Box 2.15

Validity:	Criterion: *Concurrent:* Corrigan & Mysiw: with MMSE: $r = .87$ Mysiw et al. (1990): with GOAT: 71% (15/21) agreement that patients emerged from PTA in the same week ($n = 12$) or not at all ($n = 3$)
Reliability:	Inter-rater: Corrigan et al.: $r = .875$ Test–retest: No information available
Responsiveness:	Jackson et al.: on 25/27 occasions when a significant decrement in score occurred, an acute medical problem was responsible

also lends itself more readily than other PTA assessment instruments to clinical recommendations about the patient's improvement, lack of change or deterioration. In this regard, the responsiveness of the OGMS is an important feature. As a measure of PTA per se, however, the OGMS is, as the authors acknowledge, "cumbersome and time-consuming". Moreover, weekly aggregate scores mean that it does not have the facility to document PTA durations of less than 2 weeks. The OGMS may thus be seen as a hybrid instrument, combining a screening instrument with the introduction of cognitive rehabilitation procedures, suitable for patients with very severe degrees of TBI.

Key references

Corrigan, J. D., Arnett, J. A., Houck, L. J., & Jackson, R. D. (1985). Reality orientation for brain injured patients: Group treatment and monitoring of recovery. *Archives of Physical Medicine and Rehabilitation*, *66*(9), 626–630.

Corrigan, J. D., & Jackson, R. D. (1984). (Abstract) Prospective system for monitoring length of post-traumatic amnesia. *Archives of Physical Medicine and Rehabilitation*, *65*, 652.

Corrigan, J. D., & Mysiw, W. J. (1988). Agitation following traumatic head injury: Equivocal evidence for a discrete stage of cognitive recovery. *Archives of Physical Medicine and Rehabilitation*, *69*(7), 487–492.

Jackson, R. D., Mysiw, W. J., & Corrigan, J. D. (1989). Orientation Group Monitoring System: An indicator for reversible impairments in cognition during posttraumatic amnesia. *Archives of Physical Medicine and Rehabilitation*, *70*(1), 33–36.

Mysiw, W. J., Bogner, J. A., Arnett, J. A., Clinchot, D. M., & Corrigan, J. D. (1996). The Orientation Group Monitoring System for measuring duration of posttraumatic amnesia and assessing therapeutic interventions. *Journal of Head Trauma Rehabilitation*, *11*(6), 1–8.

Mysiw, W. J., Corrigan, J. D., Carpenter, D., & Chock, S. K. L. (1990). Prospective assessment of posttraumatic amnesia: A comparison of the GOAT and the OGMS. *Journal of Head Trauma Rehabilitation*, *5*(1), 65–72.

Orientation Log (O-Log)

Jackson, Novack, and Dowler (1998)

Source

Items and scoring criteria for the O-Log appear in Jackson et al. (1998) and are also available from the website of the Center for Outcome Measurement in Brain Injury (http://www.tbims.org/combi/olog/index.html). O-Log items are reproduced below.

Purpose

The O-Log is an objective, clinician-administered test developed to provide a brief bedside assessment of orientation. It was designed for evaluating degrees of confusion in people with traumatic brain injury (TBI), as well as patients receiving rehabilitation for other neurological conditions including hypoxia, infections, stroke and tumour. It is intended that the O-Log be used serially, to chart progress over time.

Item description

The O-Log consists of 10 items examining orientation in three domains: place (3 items), time (5 items), and "situation" (i.e., examining awareness of circumstances; 2 items).

Scale development

Development of the O-Log arose in response to some of the perceived problems of the Galveston Orientation and Amnesia Test (GOAT), including repeated administration of the amnesia items and scoring procedures not taking into account partially correct responses. Additionally, the authors noted the need for a screening test that was suitable for all patients eligible for admission to neurorehabilitation units, not only those with TBI. Limited information is provided in Jackson et al. (1998) regarding specific item selection, but the authors excluded items examining orientation to person because they represent over-learned biographical information and are generally impervious to impairment in the types of neurological disorders seen in rehabilitation units. There is considerable overlap in item content with the GOAT, with 7 out of the 10 O-Log items also included in the GOAT. Novack, Dowler, Bush, Glen, and Schneider (2000) used the GOAT to calibrate emergence from confusion on the O-Log and determine cut-off scores.

Administration procedures, response format and scoring

Although no special test materials are required for administration of the O-Log, it is necessary to construct multiple-choice responses for each of the items. Jackson et al. (1998) describe this process as "embedding the correct response among three choices ('Are we in Huntsville, Birmingham, or Mobile?')" (p. 718). The authors advise that these should not be presented in the same order each time. No formal training of the clinician is required to administer the O-Log. Clear guidelines are provided for administration, recording and scoring. Administration time is very brief, a matter of minutes.

Each item is rated on a 4-point scale: 0 (incorrect/inappropriate/no response), 1 (correct response with multiple choice or phonemic cuing), 2 (correct response with logical cuing), 3 (correct response without cue or prompt). Jackson et al. (1998) provide an example of logical cueing: "That was yesterday, so today must be . . ." (p. 718). The total score ranges from 0 to 30. Two consecutive scores ≥ 25/30 indicate a non-impaired performance.

Psychometric properties

The measurement properties of the O-Log were examined in three samples of inpatients recruited from a rehabilitation centre at Birmingham, Alabama, USA. Reliability was evaluated by Jackson et al. (1998) with 15 patients (age $M = 42.2$ years, range 16–85), mostly with stroke or TBI. Inter-rater reliability was examined with two raters who completed the O-Log independently, but simultaneously observed the assessment conducted by one of the raters. Novack et al. (2000) examined validity of the O-Log in 68 patients (age $M = 39.8$ years, range 16–88; 78% with moderate/severe TBI). Validation instruments comprised the GOAT, Glasgow Coma Scale (GCS), and Functional Independence Measure (FIM). The O-Log and GOAT were administered simultaneously five times per week, yielding 554 sets of scores. The data were used to establish cut-off scores for the O-Log by examining O-Log scores that corresponded to GOAT scores > 75/100. Dowler, Bush, Novack, and Jackson (2000) studied predictive validity in 60 inpatients (age $M = 31.3$ years, range 16–69; 55% with GCS scores ≤ 8). O-Log scores were collected soon after admission ($M = 20$ days post-trauma). Validation instruments comprised the FIM, Community Integration Questionnaire (CIQ) and Disability Rating Scale (DRS) at 6 months and 12 months post-trauma, as well as neuropsychological test scores at 6 months in a subset ($n = 41/60$). Results of the above studies are shown in Box 2.16.

Box 2.16

Validity:	Criterion: *Concurrent:* Novack et al.: with GOAT: $r = .90$ – minimum O-Log with GCS: $r = .43$ – minimum O-Log with FIM admission: $r = .78$
	Predictive: Dowler et al.: minimum O-Log score with 8/11 neuropsychological measures at 6 months: range $r = .28–.38$ – with 12-month CIQ: $r = .40$ – with 12-month DRS: $r = .30$
	Novack et al.: minimum O-Log with discharge FIM: $r = .58$
	Construct: *Internal consistency:* Jackson et al.: Cronbach alpha: Total score: .92 (place .81, time .87, situation .83)
Reliability:	Inter-rater: Jackson et al.: Total score: $r_s = .99$ (item range: $r = .85–1.00$)
	Test–retest: No information available
Responsiveness:	No information available

Comment

Although the authors do not claim that the O-Log is a measure of post-traumatic amnesia (PTA), Jackson et al. (1998) do state that in patients with TBI the O-Log can replace the GOAT, thereby implying that it can be used as such. Presence of disorientation is a useful surrogate marker of confusion, but the O-Log has restrictions for use as a measure of PTA. At the minimum, the dual domains of orientation and memory need to be assessed, given the substantial dissociations that can occur between resolution of disorientation and amnesia after TBI (Tate et al., 2006). Moreover, inclusion of items examining orientation to person would have resulted in the O-Log having a broader applicability to discriminate at very low levels of functioning. On the other hand, Rasch analysis of the GOAT (Bode, Heinemann, & Semik, 2000) clearly demonstrated that items examining orientation to person are the easiest to pass, and this vindicates the authors' decision to omit them in the interests of producing a quick and sensitive test suitable for use in neurorehabilitation units. A special feature of the O-Log is the scoring system, whereby credit is given for partially correct responses after cueing or multiple-choice response. There is a place for a simple measure of orientation, and the O-Log is a good candidate, having very good psychometric properties, and being quick and easy to administer.

Key references

Bode, R. K., Heinemann, A. W., & Semik, P. (2000). Measurement properties of the Galveston Orientation and Amnesia Test (GOAT) and improvement patterns during inpatient rehabilitation. *Journal of Head Trauma Rehabilitation, 15*(1), 637–655.

Dowler, R. N., Bush, B. A., Novack, T. A., & Jackson, W. T. (2000). Cognitive orientation in rehabilitation and neuropsychological outcome after traumatic brain injury. *Brain Injury, 14*(2), 117–123.

Jackson, W. T., Novack, T. A., & Dowler, R. N. (1998). Effective serial measurement of cognitive orientation in rehabilitation: The Orientation Log. *Archives of Physical Medicine and Rehabilitation, 79*(6), 718–720.

Novack, T. A., Dowler, R. N., Bush, B. A., Glen, T., & Schneider, J. J. (2000). Validity of the Orientation Log, relative to the Galveston Orientation and Amnesia Test. *Journal of Head Trauma Rehabilitation, 15*(3), 957–961.

Tate, R. L., Pfaff, A., Baguley, I. J., Marosszeky, J. E., Gurka, J. A., Hodgkinson, A. E., et al. (2006). A multicentre, randomized trial examining the effect of test procedures measuring emergence from post-traumatic amnesia. *Journal of Neurology, Neurosurgery, and Psychiatry, 77*, 841–849.

Summary score sheet for the Orientation Log

Jackson, Novack, and Dowler (1998)

Name:

Date:									
Time:									
Assessor:									
1. City									
2. Kind of place									
3. Name of hospital									
4. Month									
5. Date									
6. Year									
7. Day of week									
8. Clock time									
9. Etiology/event									
10. Pathology/deficits									
TOTAL SCORE									
30									
25									
20									
15									
10									
5									
0									

Acknowledgement: From Jackson, W. T. et al. (1998). Effective serial measurement of cognitive orientation in rehabilitation: The Orientation Log. *Archives of Physical Medicine and Rehabilitation*, *79*(6), 718–720, Figure 1, p. 719, reprinted by permission of Elsevier.

Post-traumatic Amnesia Questionnaire (PTAQ)

McMillan, Jongen, and Greenwood (1996)

Source

Interview questions for the PTAQ are available in an appendix to McMillan et al. (1996) and are also reproduced below.

Purpose

The PTAQ is essentially an interview procedure, designed to enable the duration of post-traumatic amnesia (PTA) to be measured retrospectively using a standardized method. It was developed for people with traumatic brain injury (TBI). In situations where no record of PTA duration is available, it can be estimated retrospectively after the patient has emerged from PTA by the use of interview techniques, such as the PTAQ.

Item description

The PTAQ comprises a combination of factual information questions and semi-structured interview with the patient/client. The focus of the five sections of the PTAQ is to establish temporal landmarks and a variable number of items, tailored to the individual's circumstances, are required for this purpose. Dates of specific events include the following: injury, stages of hospitalization, hospital discharge, and special events, particularly those occurring in the vicinity of the PTA period, such as birthdays. The fifth and final section involves interview where the patient/client is questioned about his/her memory for these events.

Scale development

Development of the PTAQ derived from the early literature describing characteristic features of PTA and methods of its determination using historical data (Russell, 1932; Russell & Nathan, 1946). Emergence from PTA was taken to be the point at which continuous, day-to-day memories return. In addition to measuring the precise number of days of PTA, McMillan et al. (1996) used bands of PTA duration, representing levels of severity of injury. This can circumvent two problems when using retrospective methods: the occurrence of islands of memories, which can be mistaken for the resolution of PTA; and that the types of events signalling the return of ongoing memories often represent non-specific events or those that are not easily tied to an identifiable day (e.g., "My first memories are of the nurse standing beside my bed asking me questions"). McMillan et al. examined PTA bands > 1 day, using a range of methods of groupings reported in the literature, including the most commonly used configuration of bands, described in Table 2.7 below.

Administration procedures, response format and scoring

Following compilation of the temporal landmarks from the medical record or other reliable source, the patient/client is interviewed to establish when his/her memories for events became reliable. It is recommended that inexperienced clinicians are trained in administration of the PTAQ. No information is provided regarding administration time, but the procedure is straightforward and in most circumstances could be completed within 10 minutes, although this does not include time required to collect the background data.

There is no scoring of the PTAQ per se; rather the clinician/researcher uses the information to establish the number of days between the injury and return of continuous day-to-day memories. This interval is the duration of PTA, which can then be converted to a band or classification representing severity of injury (see Table 2.7), using traditional criteria (Jennett & Teasdale, 1981; Russell & Smith, 1961). McMillan et al. (1996) focused on severe injuries (i.e., PTA duration > 1 day), but theoretically PTA duration <24 hours can be determined with retrospective methods, as was done by King, Crawford, Wenden, Moss, Wade, and Caldwell (1997).

Psychometric properties

As part of another study, McMillan et al. (1996) recruited a consecutive series of patients with severe TBI from hospitals in London, UK and used data from the

Table 2.7 Traditional severity groupings of PTA

Duration of PTA	*Severity classification*[a] *(Jennett & Teasdale, 1981; Russell & Smith, 1961)*
< 5 mins	very mild
5–60 mins	mild
1–24 hours	moderate
1–7 days	severe
1–4 weeks	very severe
> 1 month	extremely severe

[a] These groupings refer to PTA durations in isolation from other variables (see introduction to this chapter for further detail on injury severity groupings). The definition of mild injury has been revised by the WHO Collaborating Task Force on Mild Traumatic Brain Injury (Carroll, Cassidy, Holm, Kraus, & Coronado, 2004), now defined as up to 24 hours, thereby incorporating the category of moderate injury.

series to examine the validity of the PTAQ. The patients were assessed prospectively with the Galveston Orientation and Amnesia Test (GOAT) and a sample of 79 out of 125 were followed up between 3.5 and 6 years later. Age at injury ranged from 16 to 58 years ($M = 29.2$) and 78% scored ≤ 8 on the Glasgow Coma Scale (GCS), indicating a severe TBI. At follow-up, they were interviewed with the PTAQ by phone by an interviewer who was blind to GOAT results. There was no significant difference in duration of PTA as measured by the PTAQ ($M = 38.9$ days, $SD = 50.8$, median = 15.0) versus the GOAT ($M = 34.3$ days, $SD = 41.7$, median = 20.0). Other data on psychosocial outcomes collected as part of the larger study were used to examine the predictive validity of the PTAQ. Results are shown in Box 2.17.

Box 2.17

Validity:	Criterion: *Concurrent:* with GOAT: $r_s = .87$ – with GCS: $r_s = .48$ – with days of coma: $r_s = .65$ *Predictive:* with months of work since injury: $r_s = -.38$ – with hours of attendant care at follow-up: $r_s = .34$ – with emotional problems at follow-up: $r = .32$
Reliability:	Inter-rater: No information available Test–retest: No information available
Responsiveness:	Not applicable

Comment

The widely held view that prospective measurement of PTA is more accurate than retrospective rating was not supported by the results of the validation study by McMillan et al. (1996). It is acknowledged, however, that retrospective methods do not afford the precision that can be achieved with a prospective measure – McMillan et al. were able to determine the exact day of emergence from PTA in 84% (66/79). For a variety of reasons, there are situations where PTA is not measured prospectively with instruments such as those described in this volume, or if it is, clinicians/researchers may not have access to the information. The PTAQ thus fills an important gap in providing a standardized and valid method of estimating PTA duration in situations where such information is not available. Two drawbacks of the PTAQ are the lack of reliability data and validity data for PTA duration < 1 day. Both these issues have been satisfactorily addressed by King et al. (1997) using an alternative instrument, the Rivermead Post-traumatic Amnesia Protocol.

Key references

Carroll, L. J., Cassidy, J. D., Holm, L., Kraus, J., & Coronado, V. G. (2004). Methodological issues and research recommendations for mild traumatic brain injury: The WHO Collaborating Centre Task Force on mild traumatic brain injury. *Journal of Rehabilitation Medicine*, *Suppl. 43*; 113–125.

Jennett, B., & Teasdale, G. (1981). *Management of head injuries*. Philadelphia: F. A. Davis Company.

King, N. S., Crawford, S., Wenden, F. J., Moss, N. E. G., Wade, D. T., & Caldwell, F. E. (1997). Measurement of post-traumatic amnesia: How reliable is it? *Journal of Neurology, Neurosurgery and Psychiatry*, *62*, 38–42.

McMillan, T. M., Jongen, E. L. M. M., & Greenwood, R. J. (1996). Assessment of post-traumatic amnesia after severe closed head injury: Retrospective or prospective? *Journal of Neurology, Neurosurgery and Psychiatry*, *60*, 422–427.

Russell, W. R. (1932). Cerebral involvement in head injury. A study based on the examination of two hundred cases. *Brain*, *55*, 549–603.

Russell, W. R., & Nathan, P. W. (1946). Traumatic amnesia. *Brain*, *69*, 280–301.

Russell, W. R., & Smith, A. (1961). Post-traumatic amnesia in closed head injury. *Archives of Neurology*, *5*, 16–29.

Post-traumatic Amnesia Questionnaire

McMillan, Jongen, and Greenwood (1996)

Name: **Assessor:** **Date:**

Questions 1, 2, 3, 4: to be filled in before the interview

Questions 4, 5 and final PTA: to be completed in the interview

1	Date of injury:				
2	Accident and Emergency:			Hospital	
	Intensive Care Unit:			Hospital	
	From:	to			days
	NSU:			Hospital	
	From:	to			days
	DGH:			Hospital	
	Rehabilitation Unit:			Hospital	
	From:	to			days
3	Date of discharge (going home)				
4	Special Events			Birthday	

5 Do you remember:

i. Being taken to hospital?

ii. Being in casualty?

iii. Being in intensive care unit?

iv. Being on the ward NSU/DGH/rehab?

v. Being taken to another hospital?

vi. Going home from hospital?

vii. Special event (birthday/Christmas)?

PTA duration = **hours** **days** **months**

Acknowledgement: From McMillan, T. et al. (1996). Assessment of post-traumatic amnesia after severe closed head injury: Retrospective or prospective? *Journal of Neurology, Neurosurgery and Psychiatry*, *60*, 422–427, Appendix 2, p. 426, by permission of the British Medical Journal and Rightslink.

Westmead Post-traumatic Amnesia Scale (WPTAS)

Shores, Marosszeky, Sandanam, and Batchelor (1986)

Source

The WPTAS is described in Shores et al. (1986) and the recording form is reproduced below. A test manual has been published (Marosszeky, Ryan, Shores, Batchelor, & Marosszeky, 1998) and is available at the following website http://www.psy.mq.edu.au/PTA. Test materials are available from the authors (Department of Rehabilitation Medicine, Westmead Hospital, Westmead, NSW, 2145, Australia). Other PTA scales similar to the WPTAS, including a revised version of the WPTAS suitable for mild injury, are briefly described below.

Purpose

The WPTAS is an objective, clinician-administered test, designed for the prospective assessment of recovery from post-traumatic amnesia (PTA) after traumatic brain injury (TBI). The authors aimed to develop a simple, standardized procedure suitable for routine use in hospitals.

Item description

The WPTAS comprises 12 items, covering the domains of orientation and memory. The seven orientation items assess orientation to person (2 items), time (4 items) and place (1 item). The five memory items examine 24-hour recognition of the examiner's face, recall of his/her name, and recall of three pictures of common objects.

Scale development

In developing the WPTAS, Shores et al. (1986) aimed to improve on the Galveston Orientation and Amnesia Test (GOAT). The authors were concerned that the scoring procedures for the GOAT meant that patients who were unable to answer the memory items could still obtain GOAT scores in the normal range. They therefore used procedures described by Fortuny, Briggs, Newcombe, Ratcliffe, and Thomas (1980) in Oxford, UK to examine anterograde memory. The WPTAS was formed by combining an adaptation of the Fortuny et al. memory items with a number of orientation items, but the selection process of the orientation items is not described. Emergence from PTA was deemed to have occurred on the first occasion of three consecutive (daily) scores of 12/12, but no information was provided regarding procedures used to establish this criterion.

Administration procedures, response format and scoring

Test materials (pictures of common everyday objects and a picture of the examiner's face) are required for administration of the WPTAS. Administration time is brief, a matter of minutes. The manual advises that a range of clinicians (occupational therapists, nurses) can administer the WPTAS provided that they are familiar with administration requirements. Responses for five of the orientation items use free recall, but either free recall or recognition memory is acceptable for two of the orientation items (time of day and place) and the five memory items. When the patient first obtains the maximum score (12/12), variations in administration procedures are required, with which the clinician needs to be thoroughly familiar (refer to test manual).

Each item is awarded 1 point for a correct response. The total score for the first day of PTA testing (consisting of the orientation items alone because recall of the memory items can only occur from the second day of PTA testing) ranges from 0 to 7, and for subsequent days, from 0 to 12. Traditionally, PTA is deemed to have resolved on the first of three consecutive days on which the score of 12/12 is obtained. A revised criterion for very severely injured patients has been recommended, whereby the end of PTA is signalled by the *first* occasion on which 12/12 is scored (Tate et al., 2006).

Psychometric properties

Information on the psychometric properties of the WPTAS comes from a number of sources. All samples comprised patients with TBI, mostly younger than 50 years of age, who were recruited from inpatient rehabilitation units in Australia. In the initial study, Shores et al.

(1986) validated the WPTAS using the Selective Reminding Test (SRT) with three groups of 20 patients (in PTA, emerged from PTA and orthopaedic controls). A TBI sample ($n = 22$) was used to determine predictive validity of the WPTAS using linear regression analysis (Shores, 1989). Inter-rater reliability was examined in 10 patients by two raters who simultaneously examined but independently scored the WPTAS (Geffen, Bishop, Connell, & Hopkins, 1994). The results of these studies are shown in Box 2.18.

Box 2.18

Validity:	Criterion: *Predictive*: Shores: PTA duration, as measured by the WPTAS, predicted verbal learning and non-verbal problem solving at 2 years post-trauma
	Construct: *Discriminant:* Shores et al. (1986): SRT scores significantly lower for TBI patients in PTA vs TBI patients not in PTA vs controls ($p < .01$) – descriptive data not reported
Reliability:	Inter-rater: Geffen et al.: Total score: $r = .99$ (item range: $r = .72$–1.00)
	Test–retest: No information available
Responsiveness:	No information available

Derivatives of the Oxford procedure/WPTAS: (i) Child version

Marosszeky, Batchelor, Shores, Marosszeky, Klein-Boonschate, and Fahey (1993) standardized the WPTAS on 90 children recruited from medical and surgical wards Westmead Hospital, Sydney, Australia, who were aged 6 to 16 years without a history of TBI or other neurological/psychiatric conditions or academic difficulties. Item content was identical to the adult version, but some variation in administration procedures was used. They reported that the adult version of the scale was suitable for children older than 7 years, but not for children aged 6 to 7 years or younger. Rocca, Wallen, and Batchelor (2008) examined the WPTAS in 46 healthy children aged 4 to 5 years and found that a six-item version, which also included adapted administration procedures, was developmentally appropriate. The six-item scale was examined in an independent sample of 59 healthy children, aged 4 to 6 years, where 93% achieved 6/6 on 4 consecutive days of testing.

(ii) Adult version for mild TBI

A modification of the WPTAS was published by Ponsford et al. (2004). One limitation of the WPTAS is that it is only suitable for assessing patients with PTA > 1 day because of the requirement for 24-hour recall of the memory items. Ponsford et al. used a 1-hour recall of the memory items thereby enabling the determination of duration of PTA in patients with TBI of mild and moderate degrees. Additionally, they found that 2 of the 12 items were poor discriminators between TBI and control groups, and suggested that these items (day of the week and examiner's name) be excluded. Internal consistency of the resulting 10-item version using Cronbach alpha coefficients was .76 to .85 on Trials 1 to 3.

Shores et al. (2008) have conducted further work on application of the WPTAS to the mild TBI group, resulting in a revised version, referred to as the R-WPTAS. They amalgamated the 10 items recommended by Ponsford et al. (2004) together with the verbal response component of the Glasgow Coma Scale (GCS). As with the Ponsford et al. modification, recall of the picture items occurred on an hourly basis. The total score range on Trial 1 is 0 to 9, and for subsequent trials is 0 to 12, with criterion for emergence set at the first occasion of scoring 12/12. In their validation study of 82 patients with mild TBI and 88 control patients admitted to the emergency department, the R-WPTAS was found to be more sensitive than the GCS in identifying impairment.

(iii) Other PTA scales

A number of other PTA scales similar to the WPTAS are also available, derived either from the Fortuny et al. (1980) descriptions (e.g., Modified Oxford PTA Scale, MOPTAS) or the WPTAS itself (e.g., Julia Farr Services PTA Scale, JFSPTAS). The MOPTAS (Pfaff & Tate, 2004) is also a 12-item PTA scale, very similar to the WPTAS. It comprises eight orientation items and four memory items. The procedure for administering the memory items differs from the WPTAS and adheres more strictly to the original descriptions of Fortuny et al. (1980). The 11-item JFSPTAS (Forrester & Geffen, 1995) uses the picture-memory items of the WPTAS but different orientation items. It also differs in administration procedures, with administration of the memory items commencing after the patient passes the orientation items. Scoring procedures are also more refined, differentiating among free recall, cued recall, recognition and failure. Examination of the psychometric properties of the JFSPTAS indicates the scale is reliable and valid.

Comment

The WPTAS is widely used in rehabilitation units in Australia. Limited information is available regarding the developmental phases of the WPTAS, however, and recent research findings have highlighted weaknesses in the structure of the scale indicating that further work is warranted regarding item content (Ponsford et al., 2004) and the criterion to establish emergence from PTA (Ponsford et al., 2004; Tate et al., 2006). At a clinical level, however, a distinct advantage of the WPTAS is its simple and objective method of measuring return of continuous memories. It also has good inter-rater reliability and clinical utility in its brevity and administrative ease. An earlier drawback of the original scale was its limitation is measuring PTA durations < 1 day, and in this regard the revised procedures (Ponsford et al., 2004; Shores et al., 2008) are a welcome development.

Key references

Forrester, G., & Geffen, G. (1995). *Julia Farr Services Post-traumatic Amnesia Scales manual.* South Australia: Julia Farr Foundation Inc.

Fortuny, L., Briggs, M., Newcombe, F., Ratcliffe, G., & Thomas, C. (1980). Measuring the duration of post traumatic amnesia. *Journal of Neurology, Neurosurgery, and Psychiatry*, *43*(5), 377–379.

Geffen, G., Bishop, K., Connell, J., & Hopkins, P. (1994). Inter-rater reliability of the Westmead Post-Traumatic Amnesia (PTA) Scale. *Australian Occupational Therapy Journal*, *41*(1), 31–36.

Marosszeky, N. E. V., Batchelor, J., Shores, E., A., Marosszeky, J. E., Klein-Boonschate, M., & Fahey, P. P. (1993). The performance of hospitalized, non head-injured children on the Westmead PTA Scale. *The Clinical Neuropsychologist*, *7*(1), 85–95.

Marosszeky, N. E. V., Ryan, L., Shores, E. A., Batchelor, J., & Marosszeky, J. E. (1998). *The PTA Protocol: Guidelines for using the Westmead Post-traumatic Anmesia (PTA) Scale.* Sydney: Department of Rehabilitation Medicine, Westmead Hospital and Department of Psychology, Macquarie University.

Pfaff, A., & Tate, R. L. (2004). *Manual for the Modified Oxford Post-traumatic Amnesia Scale (MOPTAS)*. Sydney: Liverpool Hospital, Injury Rehabilitation Unit: Unpublished manuscript.

Ponsford, J., Facem, P. C., Willmott, C., Rothwell, A., Kelly, A.-M., Nelms, R., et al. (2004). Use of the Westmead PTA Scale to monitor recovery of memory after mild head injury. *Brain Injury*, *18*(6), 603–614.

Rocca, A., Wallen, M., & Batchelor, J. (2008). The Westmead Post-traumatic Amnesia Scale for Children (WPTAS-C) aged 4 and 5 years old. *Brain Impairment*, *9*(1), 14–21.

Shores, E. A. (1989). [Letter] Comparison of the Westmead PTA Scale and Glasgow Coma Scale as predictors of neuropsychological outcome following extremely severe blunt head injury. *Journal of Neurology, Neurosurgery, and Psychiatry*, *52*, 126–127.

Shores, E. A., Lammél, A., Hullick, C., Sheedy, J., Flynn, M., Levick, W., et al. (2008). The diagnostic accuracy of the Revised Westmead PTA Scale as an adjunct to the Glasgow Coma Scale in the early identification of cognitive impairment in patients with mild traumatic brain injury. *Journal of Neurology, Neurosurgery, and Psychiatry*, *79*, 1100–1106.

Shores, E. A., Marosszeky, J. E., Sandanam, J., & Batchelor, J. (1986). Preliminary validation of a clinical scale for measuring the duration of post-traumatic amnesia. *The Medical Journal of Australia*, *144*(11), 569–572.

Tate, R. L., Pfaff, A., Baguley, I. J., Marosszeky, J. E., Gurka, J. A., Hodgkinson, A. E., et al. (2006). A multicentre, randomized trial examining the effect of test procedures measuring emergence from post-traumatic amnesia. *Journal of Neurology, Neurosurgery, and Psychiatry*, *77*, 841–849.

Summary score sheet for the Westmead Post-traumatic Amnesia Scale

Shores, Marosszeky, Sandanam, and Batchelor (1986)

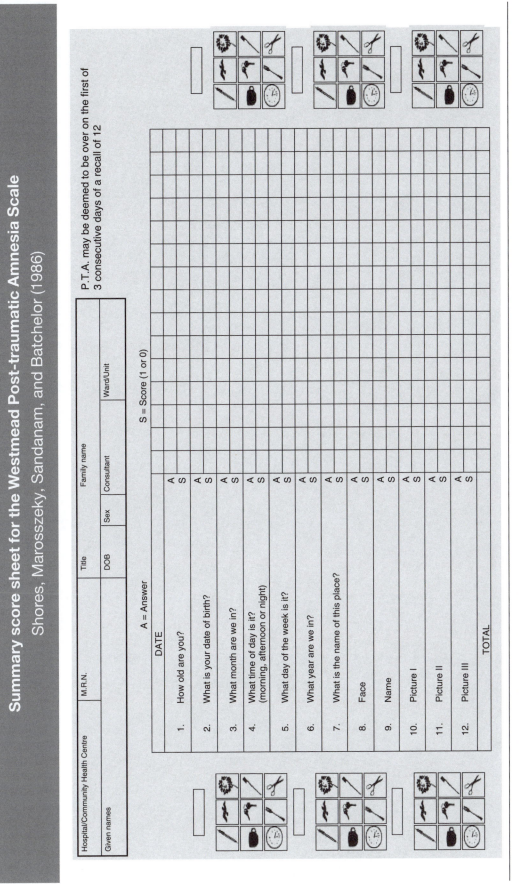

Hospital/Community Health Centre	M.R.N.	Title		Family name	
Given names		DOB	Sex	Consultant	Ward/Unit

P.T.A. may be deemed to be over on the first of 3 consecutive days of a recall of 12

A = Answer S = Score (1 or 0)

DATE																	
1.	How old are you?	A															
		S															
2.	What is your date of birth?	A															
		S															
3.	What month are we in?	A															
		S															
4.	What time of day is it? (morning, afternoon or night)	A															
		S															
5.	What day of the week is it?	A															
		S															
6.	What year are we in?	A															
		S															
7.	What is the name of this place?	A															
		S															
8.	Face	A															
		S															
9.	Name	A															
		S															
10.	Picture I	A															
		S															
11.	Picture II	A															
		S															
12.	Picture III	A															
		S															
TOTAL																	

Acknowledgement: Scale provided by Dr Shores, reproduced with permission of the author.

3 Scales of general cognitive functions

Instruments presented in Chapter 3 map to the components, domains and categories of the *International Classification of Functioning, Disability and Health* (ICF; WHO, 2001) as depicted in Figure 3.1.

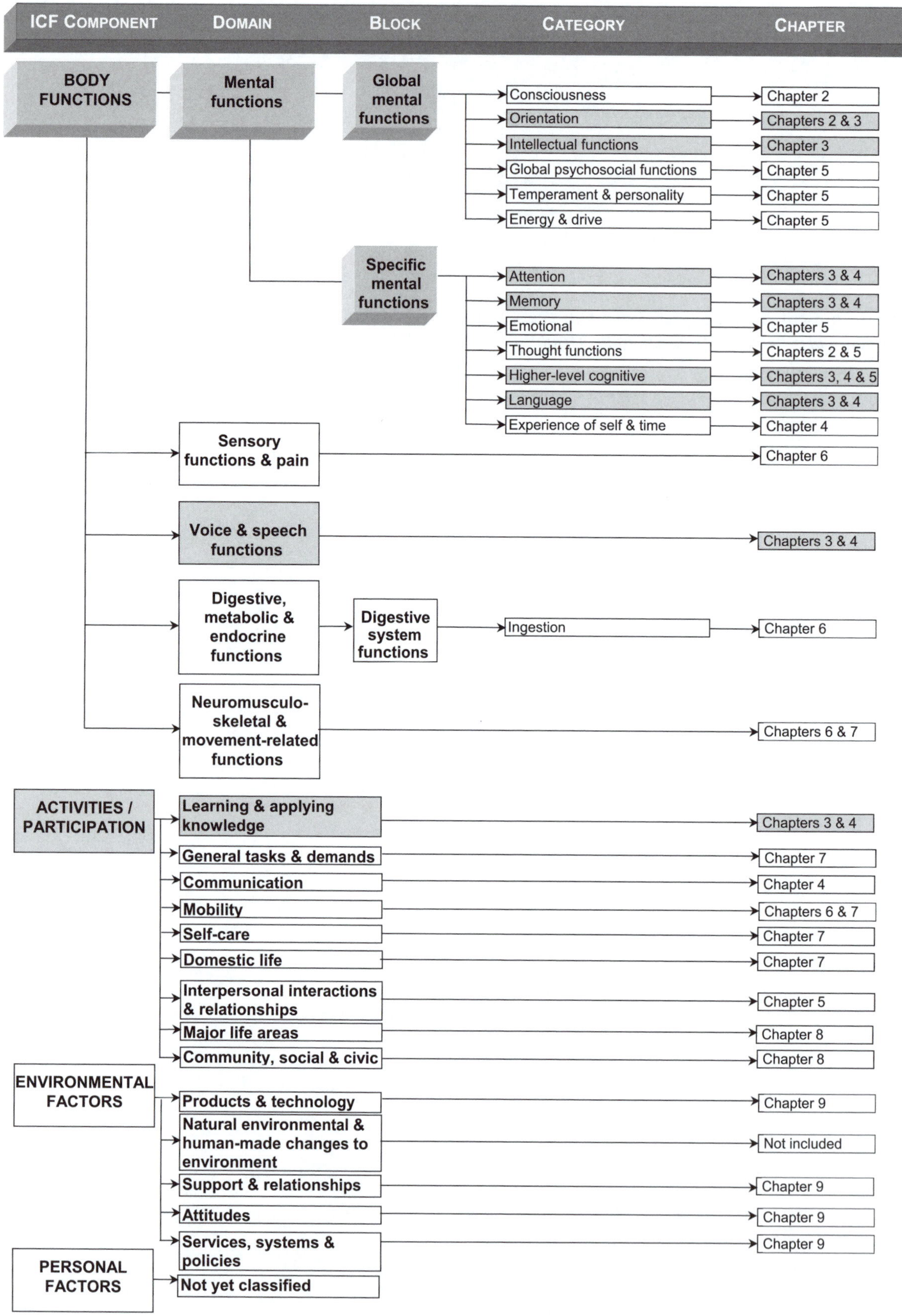

Figure 3.1 Instruments included in the compendium in relation to the ICF taxonomy – the highlighted components, domains and categories appear in this chapter. *Note:* the Figure presents a partial listing of five out of the eight Body Function domains and does not include any of the Body Structure domains. Categories for Mental functions also represent a partial listing and categories for the remaining domains are not listed. Refer to Appendix C for further detail on the ICF taxonomy.

Introduction

The third category within the ICF block of Global mental functions is Intellectual functions (see Figure 3.1 and Appendix C). A large volume of objective tests and rating scales of cognitive functions has been developed for people with acquired brain impairment (ABI). In keeping with the ICF distinction between global mental functions versus specific mental functions (such as attention, memory, etc.), those instruments that examine multiple areas of cognitive functioning are described in this chapter; tests that focus on one specific cognitive function are described in Chapter 4, and multidimensional scales addressing cognition along with other areas of function are described in Chapter 10. Excluded from this book as a whole, are tests that are not suitable for administration by generic health professionals, such as neuropsychological tests requiring formal training (see Lezak, Howieson, & Loring, 2004; Mitrushina, Boone, & D'Elia, 1999; Strauss, Sherman, & Spreen, 2006) or those requiring special apparatus, such as computers, reaction time or other administration/ recording equipment.

That leaves cognitive screening tests, which are described in the present chapter. Developers of such screening tools readily acknowledge their limitations; specifically, that they "cannot be substituted for diagnostic evaluation based on multiple sources of information and thoughtful clinical judgement" (Borson, Scanlan, Brush, Vitaliano, & Dokmak, 2000, p. 1026). Many are also subject to age, education and cultural biases (Parker & Philp, 2004); others do not have adequate normative or comparison data to allow for accurate interpretation or diagnosis. Nonetheless, the psychometrically stronger instruments *do* have a place in both clinical and research settings, particularly in situations where time is of the essence. In some circumstances, patient characteristics may dictate the need for brief examination; for example, depending on the referral question, a detailed neuropsychological evaluation may be neither necessary nor appropriate for people with very low levels of cognitive functioning. Alternatively, situations may arise where cognitive assessment competes with other types of data collection; for example, in population-based surveys or routine evaluation as part of general medical practice. Indeed, Boustani, Peterson, Hanson, Harris, and Lohr (2003) cite evidence indicating that more than 50% of people with dementia attending general practitioners never receive that diagnosis, largely because routine history and physical examinations are not suitable for diagnosing dementia. A cognitive screening test would facilitate that process.

A common focus of cognitive screening tests is the identification/diagnosis of people with cognitive impairment, and for this purpose cut-off scores or normative data are required. In the course of standardizing such measures, investigators generally recruit populations with a diagnosis of dementia, and examine the capacity of the test to distinguish between people with versus those without dementia diagnosis or, in other instances, distinguish among dementia subtypes. Independent criteria to define dementia are usually used for this purpose and many scales presented in this and other chapters make reference to these criteria. The *Diagnostic and Statistical Manual of Mental Disorders* – 4th ed. (DSM-IV; American Psychiatric Association, 1994) presents criteria for the diagnosis of Alzheimer's disease (AD), as well as vascular dementia. More specific criteria for AD come from the National Institutes of Neurological and Communicable Disorders and Stroke (NINCDS) and the Alzheimer's Disease and Related Disorders Association (ADRDA; McKhann, Drachman, Folstein, Katzman, Price, & Stadlan, 1984). The National Institute of Neurological Disorders and Stroke (NINDS) and the Association Internationale pour la Recherche et l'Enseignement en Neurosciences (AIREN) have published specific criteria for vascular dementia (Román et al., 1993). Consensus criteria for the more recently described (and controversial) diagnostic category, mild cognitive impairment, are also available (Petersen, 2004; Petersen et al., 2001; Winblad et al., 2004). Additionally, some researchers use severity gradings of dementia, frequently determined by the staging procedure of the Clinical Dementia Rating scale (CDR; Hughes, Berg, Danziger, Coben, & Martin, 1982) or the Global Deterioration Scale (GDS; Reisberg, Ferris, de Leon, & Crook, 1982), both of which are described in detail in Chapter 10 on multidimensional scales. A comparative summary of the criteria for these dementia diagnoses is summarized in Table 3.1. The essential defining features of two classifications from the NINCDS/ADRDA criteria (Definite and Probable AD) are tabulated below, but the reader is referred to McKhann et al. for a complete listing of inclusion and exclusion criteria, as well as a description of Possible AD.

Criteria for the other main dementia subtype, frontotemporal dementia, were published by the Lund and Manchester Groups (Brun et al., 1994). These criteria were subsequently refined by Neary et al. (1998) and three variants described: behavioural variant, progressive non-fluent aphasia and semantic dementia. Each variant was accompanied by core and supportive diagnostic features:

- The core features for the behavioural variant comprise: (i) insidious onset and gradual progression, (ii) early decline in social interpersonal conduct, (iii) early impairment in regulation of personal conduct,

Table 3.1 Diagnostic criteria for Alzheimer's disease, vascular dementia and mild cognitive impairment

DSM-IV: Dementia of the Alzheimer type	*NINCDS/ADRDA: Alzheimer's disease*	*DSM-IV: Vascular dementia*	*NINDS/AIREN: Vascular dementia*	*International Working Group on mild cognitive impairment*
A. Development of multiple cognitive deficits: 1. memory impairment, *and* 2. aphasia, apraxia, agnosia or executive impairment B. Each impairment has a significant impact on social or occupational functioning, and represents a significant decline from a previous level C. A gradual onset and progressive decline D. The impairments are not due to other CNS condition or substance-induced condition E. The impairments do not occur exclusively during the course of delirium F. The impairments are not better accounted for by another AXIS I disorder (e.g., Major Depressive Disorder)	*For Definite and Probable Alzheimer's disease:* *Definite* Alzheimer's disease: 1. clinical criteria for probable Alzheimer's disease 2. histopathological evidence obtained from biopsy or autopsy *Probable* Alzheimer's disease: dementia established by clinical examination, documented by an established cognitive screening test and confirmed by neuropsychological tests, as: 1. deficits in two or more areas 2. progressive worsening of memory and other cognitive functions 3. no disturbance of consciousness 4. onset between ages 40–90, most often after age 65 5. absence of systemic disorders or other brain diseases that could account for the progressive deficits	A. Development of multiple cognitive deficits: 1. memory impairment, *and* 2. aphasia, apraxia, agnosia or executive impairment B. Each impairment has a significant impact on social or occupational functioning, and represents a significant decline from a previous level C. Presence of focal neurological signs and symptoms (e.g., weakness of an extremity) or laboratory evidence of cerebrovascular disease (e.g., multiple infarcts) that are judged to be aetiologically related D. The impairments do not occur exclusively during the course of delirium	1. Presence of dementia, using ICD-10NA definition: a decline in memory and intellectual abilities causing impaired functioning in daily living. Deficits to be present in at least two of the following cognitive areas (in addition to memory): orientation, attention, language-verbal skills, visuospatial abilities, calculations, executive functions, motor control, praxis, abstraction or judgement 2. evidence of cerebrovascular disease, demonstrated by any of history, clinical examination or brain imaging 3. the two disorders (dementia and cerebrovascular disease) must be reasonably related	1. Not normal, not demented (does not meet DSM-IV/ICD 10 criteria for dementia) 2. Cognitive decline: – self and/or informant report and – impairment on objective cognitive tasks and/or – evidence of decline over time on objective cognitive tasks 3. Preserved basic activities of daily living and minimal impairment in complex instrumental functions

Acknowledgements: *Diagnostic and Statistical Manual of Mental Disorders* (4th ed.) (1994), reproduced by permission of the American Psychiatric Association; McKhann, G. et al. (1984). Clinical diagnosis of Alzheimer's disease. *Neurology*, *34*, 939–944, Table 1, p. 940, reproduced by permission of Wolters Kluwer; Román, G. C. et al. (1993). Vascular dementia: Diagnostic criteria for research studies. *Neurology*, *43*(2), 250–260, material from p. 257; Winblad, B. et al. (2004). Mild cognitive impairment – beyond controversies, towards consensus. *Journal of Internal Medicine*, *256*(3), 240–246, Figure 2, p. 243, used with permission of Wiley-Blackwell.

(iv) early emotional blunting, and (v) early loss of insight.

- For progressive non-fluent aphasia, the core features comprise: (i) insidious onset and gradual progression, and (ii) non-fluent spontaneous speech with at least one of the following: a) agrammatism, b) phonemic paraphasias or c) anomia.
- Core features for semantic dementia comprise: (i) insidious onset and gradual progression, (ii) language disorder characterized by: a) progressive, fluent, empty spontaneous speech, b) loss of word meaning, manifest by impaired naming *and* comprehension, c) semantic paraphasia *and/or*, (iii) perceptual disorder characterized by: a) prosopagnosia *and/or*, b) associative agnosia, (iv) preserved perceptual matching and drawing reproduction, (v) preserved single word repetition, (vi) preserved ability to read aloud and write to dictation orthographically regular words.

Progressive non-fluent aphasia and semantic dementia are now generally combined under the single rubric of Primary Progressive Aphasia (Rascovsky et al., 2007). A number of instruments in the present chapter, as well as in Chapters 4 and 5, assess features associated with the frontotemporal dementias.

A multitude of cognitive screening tests are available (see reviews by Brodaty, Low, Gibson, & Burns, 2006; Lorentz, Scanlan, & Borson, 2002; Shulman & Feinstein, 2006; Stuss, Meiran, Guzman, Lafleche, & Willmer, 1996), starting with those that can be administered in 1 minute or less. The earliest standardized cognitive screening instrument that continues to be widely used is the Blessed Information-Memory-Concentration Test, published in 1968 (Blessed, Tomlinson, & Roth, 1968). It has had various revisions, adaptations and name changes over the years, but its content and structure have had an enduring effect on virtually all cognitive screening tests published since that time. Another early test, the Mini-Mental State Examination (MMSE; Folstein, Folstein, & McHugh, 1975), remains the most widely used cognitive screening test in clinical practice and research, with thousands of citations in the literature.

In the time since the Blessed and Folstein tests were published, a diverse range of cognitive screening tests addressing an array of issues has been developed. The present chapter contains a sample of these instruments, many of which have been published in recent years. The scales selected for inclusion comprise the standard cognitive screening tests, rating scales and informant-based questionnaires, as well as tools developed for specialized purposes and populations. The latter group includes instruments suitable for telephone administration; those that aim to distinguish among different subtypes of dementia; assess people from culturally, linguistically and educationally diverse backgrounds; determine competency to consent to medical treatments; and examine people with very low levels of cognitive functioning who score at the floor on other screening instruments such as the MMSE.

The measures featured in this chapter are relatively brief tests, all having average administration times of 20 minutes or less. A number of batteries that form an intermediate position between brief cognitive screening tests and detailed neuropsychological examinations are not included. With clinical populations, such tests generally take 30 minutes or more to administer and some require discipline-specific qualifications for administration. Representative instruments, such as the Alzheimer Disease Assessment Scale (also known as ADAS-Cog; Rosen, Mohs, & Davis, 1984), Cambridge Cognitive Examination (CAMCOG; Huppert, Brayne, Gill, Paykel, & Beardsall, 1995), Consortium to Establish a Registry for Alzheimer's Disease (CERAD) Battery (Morris et al., 1989), Mattis Dementia Rating Scale (Jurica, Leitten, & Mattis, 2001; Mattis, 1988), and the Neurobehavioural Cognitive Status Examination (also known as Cognistat; Kiernan, Mueller, Langston, & Van Dyke, 1987), are reviewed in Lezak et al. (2004).

References

American Psychiatric Association (1994). *Diagnostic and statistical manual of mental disorders* (4th ed.). Washington, DC: APA.

Blessed, G., Tomlinson, B. E., & Roth, M. (1968). The association between quantitative measures of dementia and of senile change in cerebral grey matter of elderly subjects. *British Journal of Psychiatry*, *114*(512), 797–811.

Borson, S., Scanlan, J., Brush, M., Vitaliano, P., & Dokmak, A. (2000). The Mini-Cog: A cognitive "vital signs" measure for dementia screening in multi-lingual elderly. *International Journal of Geriatric Psychiatry*, *15*(11), 1021–1027.

Boustani, M., Peterson, B., Hanson, L., Harris, R., & Lohr, K. N. (2003). Screening for dementia in primary care: A summary of the evidence for the US Preventative Services Task Force. *Annals of Internal Medicine*, *138*(11), 927–937.

Brodaty, H., Low, L.-F., Gibson, L., & Burns, K. (2006). What is the best dementia screening instrument for general practitioners to use? *American Journal of Geriatric Psychiatry*, *14*(5), 391–400.

Brun, A., Englund, B., Gustafson, L., Passant, U., Mann, D. M. A., Neary, D., et al. (1994). Clinical and neuropathological criteria for frontotemporal dementia. *Journal of Neurology, Neurosurgery, and Psychiatry*, *57*, 416–418.

Folstein, M. F., Folstein, S. E., & McHugh, P. R. (1975). "Mini-Mental State". A practical method for grading the cognitive state of patients for the clinician. *Journal of Psychiatric Research*, *12*(3), 189–198.

Hughes, C. P., Berg, L., Danziger, W. L., Coben, L. A., & Martin, R. L. (1982). A new clinical scale for the staging of dementia. *British Journal of Psychiatry*, *140*, 566–572.

Huppert, F. A., Brayne, C., Gill, C., Paykel, E. S., & Beardsall, L. (1995). CAMCOG – a concise neuropsychological test to assist dementia diagnosis: Socio-demographic determinants in an elderly population sample. *British Journal of Clinical Psychology*, *34*(Pt 4), 529–541.

Jurica, P. J., Leitten, C. L., & Mattis, S. (2001). *DRS-2. Dementia Rating Scale – 2. Professional manual.* Lutz, FL: Psychological Assessment Resources, Inc.

Kiernan, R. J., Mueller, J., Langston, J. W., & Van Dyke, C. (1987). The Neurobehavioral Cognitive Status Examination: A brief but differentiated approach to cognitive assessment. *Annals of Internal Medicine*, *107*(4), 481–485.

Lezak, M. D., Howieson, D. B., & Loring, D. W. (2004). *Neuropsychological assessment* (4th ed.). Oxford: Oxford University Press.

Lorentz, W. J., Scanlan, J. M., & Borson, S. (2002). Brief screening tests for dementia. *Canadian Journal of Psychiatry*, *47*(8), 723–732.

Mattis, S. (1988). *Dementia Rating Scale. Professional manual.* Lutz, FL: Psychological Assessment Resources, Inc.

McKhann, G., Drachman, D., Folstein, M., Katzman, R., Price, D., & Stadlan, E. M. (1984). Clinical diagnosis of Alzheimer's disease: Report of the NINCDS-ADRDA Work Group under the auspices of Department of Health and Human Services Task Force on Alzheimer's Disease. *Neurology*, *34*, 939–944.

Mitrushina, M. N., Boone, K. B., & D'Elia, L. F. (1999). *Handbook of normative data for neuropsychological assessment*. New York: Oxford University Press.

Morris, J. C., Heyman, A., Mohs, R. C., Hughes, J. P., van Belle, G., Fillenbaum, G., et al. (1989). The Consortium to Establish a Registry for Alzheimer's Disease (CERAD). Part I. Clinical and neuropsychological assessment of Alzheimer's disease. *Neurology*, *39*(9), 1159–1165.

Neary, D., Snowden, J. S., Gustafson, L., Passant, U., Stuss, D., Black, S., et al. (1998). Frontotemporal lobar degeneration. A consensus on clinical diagnostic criteria. *Neurology*, *51*, 1546–1554.

Parker, C., & Philp, I. (2004). Screening for cognitive impairment among older people in black and minority ethnic groups. *Age and Ageing*, *33*, 447–452.

Petersen, R. C. (2004). Mild cognitive impairment as a diagnostic entity. *Journal of Internal Medicine*, *256*, 183–194.

Petersen, R. C., Doody, R., Kurz, A., Mohs, R. C., Morris, J. C., Rabins, P. V., et al. (2001). Current concepts in mild cognitive impairment. *Archives of Neurology*, *58*, 1985–1992.

Rascovsky, K., Hodges, J. R., Kipps, C. M., Johnson, J. K., Seeley, W. W., Mendez, M. F., et al. (2007). Diagnostic criteria for the behavioural variant of frontotemporal dementia (bvFTD): Current limitations and future directions. *Alzheimer Disease and Associated Disorders*, *21*, S14–S18.

Reisberg, B., Ferris, S. H., de Leon, M. J., & Crook, T. (1982). The Global Deterioration Scale for assessment of primary degenerative dementia. *American Journal of Psychiatry*, *139*(9), 1136–1139.

Román, G. C., Tatemichi, T. K., Erkinjuntti, T., Cummings, J. L., Masdeu, J. C., Garcia, J. H., et al. (1993). Vascular dementia: Diagnostic criteria for research studies. Report of the NINDS-AIREN International Workshop. *Neurology*, *43*(2), 250–260.

Rosen, W. G., Mohs, R. C., & Davis, K. L. (1984). A new rating scale for Alzheimer's disease. *American Journal of Psychiatry*, *141*(11), 1356–1364.

Shulman, K., & Feinstein, A. (2006). *Quick cognitive screening for clinicians: Mini-mental, clock drawing and other brief tests* (2nd ed.). London: Martin Dunitz.

Strauss, E, Sherman, E.M.S., & Spreen, O. (2006). *A compendium of neuropsychological tests. Administration, norms and commentary* (3rd ed.). New York: Oxford University Press.

Stuss, D. T., Meiran, N., Guzman, D. A., Lafleche, G., & Willmer, J. (1996). Do long tests yield a more accurate diagnosis of dementia than short tests? A comparison of 5 neuropsychological tests. *Archives of Neurology*, *53*(10), 1033–1039.

Winblad, B., Palmer, K., Kivipelto, M., Jelic, V., Fratiglioni, L., Wahlund, L. O., et al. (2004). Mild cognitive impairment – beyond controversies, towards consensus: Report of the International Working Group on Mild Cognitive Impairment. *Journal of Internal Medicine*, *256*(3), 240–246.

World Health Organization. (2001). *International classification of functioning, disability and health*. Geneva: World Health Organization.

Addenbrooke's Cognitive Examination – Revised (ACE-R)

Mioshi, Dawson, Mitchell, Arnold, and Hodges (2006)

Source

Items for the ACE-R are described in Mioshi et al. (2006). The ACE-R is available from Dr Hodges (Prince of Wales Medical Research Institute, University of New South Wales, Sydney, 2052, Australia; email: j.hodges@unsw.edu.au), can be downloaded from the following website (http://www.ftdrg.org/research/test-downloads/ace-r) and is reproduced below.

Purpose

The ACE-R is an objective, clinician-administered test with two aims: (i) the reliable detection of the early stages of dementia, and (ii) differentiation among dementia subtypes, specifically, Alzheimer's disease (AD) versus frontotemporal dementia (FTD). It has also been examined in dementia subgroups with predominantly subcortical pathology, including corticobasal degeneration, multiple system atrophy, progressive supranuclear palsy (Bak, Rogers, Crawford, Hearn, Mathuranath, & Hodges, 2005), as well as mild cognitive impairment (MCI; Mioshi et al., 2006; Ahmed, Mitchell, Arnold, Nestor, & Hodges, 2008).

Item description

The ACE-R incorporates the Mini-Mental State Examination (MMSE; also described in this chapter). It comprises five subtests: Attention/orientation (13 items), largely taken from the MMSE. Memory assesses both episodic memory (3 items) and semantic knowledge (names of 4 prominent political figures). Fluency (2 items) examines both letter and category (animal) fluency. The Language subtest samples five domains: comprehension, repetition, confrontation naming of line drawings, reading irregular words, and writing is examined with the MMSE item. The final subtest, Visuospatial, consists of copying the MMSE overlapping pentagons and a cube, constructing a clock face, dot counting and identifying fragmented letters.

Scale development

Development of the original ACE (Mathuranath, Nestor, Berrios, Rakowicz & Hodges, 2000) arose in response to the need for a cognitive screening test to distinguish among dementia subtypes, as well as to detect subtle impairments. None of the existing screening instruments were suitable and more comprehensive batteries required test equipment and examiners with specialized training. Limited information is provided in Mathuranath et al. regarding item selection for and development of the ACE, however items are those commonly used in language and neuropsychological test batteries in the examination for AD and FTD. Subsequently, slightly revised item content and scoring procedures were conducted to increase sensitivity and improve administration (Mioshi et al., 2006). The revisions for the ACE-R "underwent numerous cycles of interactive modification after piloting in various patients" (Mioshi et al., 2006, p. 1079).

Administration procedures, response format and scoring

The authors do not make any recommendations regarding formal training for the clinician to administer the ACE-R. Administration instructions are clearly specified on the recording form and no special equipment is required. Administration and scoring time averages 16 minutes (range 12–20 mins; Mioshi et al., 2006).

Correct responses are generally awarded 1 point for all subtests except Fluency, which uses a scaled scoring system. Detailed scoring guidelines are available from the website (http://www.ftdrg.org/research/test-down loads/ace-r). The sum of subtest scores provides the total ACE-R score (range 0–100), with higher scores indicating better cognitive functioning. A MMSE score can also be derived from the ACE/ACE-R. Cut-off scores, set at 2 standard deviations below the mean score of the control group, can be used to classify impairment; the ACE-R recommends separate cut-off scores for three age bands: 85/86 for 50–59 years; 84/85 for 60–69 years; 83/84 for 70–75 years. Mioshi et al. (2006) also report cut-off scores for the five ACE-R subtests stratified by age band, as well as likelihood ratios for probability of dementia at different ACE-R cut-off scores.

Additionally, using a ratio of (i) Verbal fluency plus Language, divided by (ii) Orientation plus Memory of name and address delayed recall (VLOM), diagnoses of AD and FTD can be made. In the initial standardization study (Mathuranath et al., 2000) a VLOM ratio of > 3.2 optimally differentiated AD from non-AD and a VLOM ratio of < 2.2 optimally differentiated FTD from non-FTD. These cut-off scores and results were replicated with the ACE-R (Mioshi et al., 2006), as shown in Data box 3.1.

Psychometric properties

Two samples were initially used to standardize the ACE (Mathuranath et al., 2000). The clinic sample comprised 139 patients recruited from the Cambridge Memory Clinic in Cambridge, UK and the control group consisted of 127 healthy age- and education-matched community volunteers and patients from non-neurological clinics (age $M = 64.4$ years, $SD = 9.3$; education $M = 11.3$ years, $SD = 2.6$). Using established criteria (National Institute of Neurological and Communicative Disorders and Stroke/Alzheimer's Disease and Related Disorders Association, *Diagnostic and Statistical Manual of Mental Disorders* 4th ed. [DSM-IV] and Clinical Dementia Rating, CDR), the clinic sample was classified into dementia ($n = 115$; age $M = 66.6$ years, $SD = 8.9$; education $M = 11.1$ years, $SD = 2.6$) and non-dementia ($n = 24$; age $M = 63.8$ years, $SD = 7.0$; education $M = 12.7$ years, $SD = 3.6$) subgroups. Diagnostic categories in the dementia sample comprised AD ($n = 69$), vascular dementia (VaD, $n = 14$), FTD ($n = 29$) and other neurological groups ($n = 27$). Cut-off scores were confirmed using receiver operating characteristic (ROC) analysis. Using a cut-off score of 87/88, sensitivity/specificity of the ACE in detecting dementia versus non-dementia was 93%/71%. A total of 82% with CDR < 1 (i.e., mild dementia) scored below the cut-off.

Mioshi et al. (2006) validated the ACE-R in 241 participants in three groups: dementia (AD $n = 67$, FTD $n = 55$, dementia with Lewy bodies $n = 20$), MCI ($n = 36$) and a healthy control group ($n = 63$). Descriptive data are shown in Data box 3.1. The ACE-R was validated using the CDR scale. Significant differences were found between clinical and control groups providing evidence for discriminant validity. Bak et al. (2005) examined the sensitivity of the ACE to detect three groups with subcortical pathology, as well as a group with AD, and to distinguish these from healthy controls. They also examined the MMSE and Mattis Dementia Rating Scale (MDRS). The ACE was comparable to the more detailed MDRS and superior to the MMSE in discriminating the patient groups from controls. ROC curves indicated that sensitivity approached 80%.

Data from Kipps, Nestor, Dawson, Mitchell, and Hodges (2008) provide information on the responsiveness of the ACE. It was administered on at least two occasions at least 6 months apart to 50 people with documented FTD. Retrospective inspection of ACE scores showed significant decline in the subset who had died with confirmed FTD pathology ($n = 16$) and those with abnormalities in their initial scans ($n = 12$) in comparison with those whose scans were no different to controls ($n = 22$) and healthy controls ($n = 10$). Results for the ACE (Mathuranath et al., 2000) and ACE-R (Mioshi et al., 2006) samples, except where otherwise indicated, are shown in Box 3.1.

Data box 3.1 Descriptive data from the ACE-R standardization sample (Mioshi et al., 2006)

	Age ***M (SD)***	**Education** ***M (SD)***	**ACE-R** ***M (SD)***	**Cut-off score**	**Sensitivity / Specificity**
Control ($n = 63$)	64.4 (5.7)	12.7 (2.1)	93.7 (4.3)	87/88	Dementia vs non-dementia: 94% / 89%
MCI ($n = 36$):	68.8 (9.0)	12.8 (3.4)	84.2 (7.3)		
Dementia ($n = 142$)	65.7 (8.0)	11.9 (2.7)	65.4 (15.9)	VLOM ratio:	
				> 3.2 →	AD vs non-AD 74% / 85%
				< 2.2 →	FTD vs non-FTD 58% / 95%
ACE-R subtest:	Attention / Orientation	Memory	Fluency	Language	Visuospatial
(maximum score):	(18)	(26)	(14)	(26)	(16)
Control	17.7 (0.5)	23.4 (2.7)	11.9 (1.7)	25.1 (1.5)	15.7 (0.7)
MCI	17.2 (1.0)	17.8 (4.7)	10.1 (2.4)	23.9 (1.6)	14.9 (2.0)
Dementia	14.4 (3.2)	12.4 (5.8)	6.0 (3.5)	20.0 (5.6)	12.6 (3.5)

Adapted table from Mioshi, E. et al. (2006). The Addenbrooke's Cognitive Examination Revisited (ACE-R): A brief cognitive test battery for dementia screening. *International Journal of Geriatric Psychiatry*, *21*, 1078–1085, Table 1, reproduced by permission of Wiley-Blackwell Journal Publishers.

Box 3.1

Validity:	Criterion: *Concurrent:* ACE: with clinical diagnosis (DSM-IV): $k = .62$ with neuropsychological tests: – ACE name and address recall with Logical Memory: $k = .69$ – ACE naming of line drawings with Graded Naming Test: $k = .41$ – ACE visuospatial subtest with copy of the Rey Complex Figure: $k = .53$
	ACE-R: with CDR: $r = -.32$
	Construct: *Internal consistency*: Cronbach alpha: ACE: .78; ACE-R: .80
	Convergent/Divergent: ACE: AD group scored significantly more poorly than FTD group on Memory ($M = 16.5$, $SD = 7.4$ vs $M = 22.3$, $SD = 7.2$; $p = .002$); conversely, FTD group scored significantly more poorly than AD group on Language ($M = 21.8$, $SD = 5.5$ vs $M = 25.0$, $SD = 4.0$; $p = .003$)
	Discriminant: ACE-R: Dementia group scored significantly more poorly than controls on all subtests ($p < .001$) – descriptive data in Data box 3.1 – Dementia group scored significantly more poorly than MCI on all subtests ($p < .001$) – descriptive data in Data box 3.1 – MCI group scored significantly more poorly than controls on Memory ($p < .001$), Fluency ($p < .001$), Language ($p < .005$) – descriptive data in Data box 3.1
	ACE: Differential diagnosis: between dementia vs non-dementia using cut-off score of 87/88: sensitivity 93%, specificity 71%; ACE-R: sensitivity 94%, specificity 89%
Reliability:	Inter-rater: No information available
	Test–retest: No information available *Practice effects:* ACE: Kipps et al.: Healthy controls ($n = 10$) over $M = 74.7$ months: initial test: $M = 96.1$ ($SD = 2.8$) vs final test $M = 93.8$ ($SD = 4.1$); $M = -2.3$
Responsiveness:	ACE: Kipps et al.: FTD (with pathology confirmed) over $M = 15.9$ months: initial test: $M = 73.6$ ($SD = 17.4$) vs final test $M = 52.9$ ($SD = 21.2$); $d = 1.2$; – FTD (with abnormal initial scans) over $M = 19.9$ months: initial test: $M = 72.1$ ($SD = 15.3$) vs final test $M = 57.3$ ($SD = 25.4$); $d = 0.97$

Comment

The ACE/ACE-R represents one of the new generation of cognitive screening tests. It has demonstrated validity in detecting mild degrees of dementia and in differentiating dementia subtypes and is responsive to changes over time in groups with evidence of FTD, showing large effect sizes. Bak and colleagues (2005) point to the increasing gap between cognitive screening tests and the differential diagnostic capacity of a more detailed neuropsychological examination. In this respect the ACE-R is a promising instrument, a particular strength being its sampling of language functions. Although the number of items suggests a lengthy test, the choice of items is well balanced: they yield maximal information and the test can still be administered within 15 to 20 minutes. Psychometrically, there is mounting evidence indicating that the ACE-R has very sound measurement properties. Moreover, the ACE-R has substantially improved specificity over the ACE, and the provision of likelihood ratios accompanying a range of ACE-R scores is advantageous.

Key references

Ahmed, S., Mitchell, J., Arnold, R., Nestor, P. J., & Hodges, J. R. (2008). Predicting rapid clinical progression in amnestic mild cognitive impairment. *Dementia and Geriatric Cognitive Disorders*, *25*(2): 170–177.

Bak, T. H., Rogers, T. T., Crawford, L. M., Hearn, V. C., Mathuranath, P. S., & Hodges, J. R. (2005). Cognitive bedside assessment in atypical Parkinsonian syndromes. *Journal of Neurology, Neurosurgery and Psychiatry*, *76*(3), 420–422.

Kipps, C. M., Nestor, P. J., Dawson, C. E., Mitchell, J., & Hodges, J. R. (2008). Measuring progression in frontotemporal dementia: Implications for therapeutic interventions. *Neurology*, *70*(22), 2046–2052.

Mathuranath, P. S., Nestor, P. J., Berrios, G. E., Rakowicz, W., & Hodges, J. R. (2000). A brief cognitive test battery to differentiate Alzheimer's disease and frontotemporal dementia. *Neurology*, *55*(11), 1613–1620.

Mioshi, E., Dawson, K., Mitchell, J., Arnold, R., & Hodges, J. R. (2006). The Addenbrooke's Cognitive Examination Revised (ACE-R): A brief cognitive test battery for dementia screening. *International Journal of Geriatric Psychiatry*, *21*, 1078–1085.

Addenbrooke's Cognitive Examination – Revised

Mioshi, Dawson, Mitchell, Arnold, and Hodges (2006)

Name : Date of birth : Hospital no. : *Addressograph*	Date of testing: ..../........../.......... Tester's name: .... Age at leaving full-time education: .... Occupation: .... Handedness: ....

ORIENTATION

➤ Ask: What is the	Day	Date	Month	Year	Season	[Score 0–5]
➤ Ask: Which	Building	Floor	Town	County	Country	[Score 0–5]

REGISTRATION

[Score 0–3]

➤ Tell: "I'm going to give you three words and I'd like you to repeat after me: lemon, key, and ball." After subject repeats, say: "Try to remember them because I'm going to ask you later." Score only the first trial (repeat 3 times if necessary).

Register number of trials ....

ATTENTION & CONCENTRATION

[Score 0–5] (for the best performed task)

➤ Ask the subject: "Could you take 7 away from 100?" After the subject responds, ask him or her to take away another 7 to a total of 5 subtractions. If subject makes a mistake, carry on and check the subsequent answer (i.e., 93, 84, 77, 70, 63 – score 4)

Stop after five subtractions (93, 86, 79, 72, 65) ....

➤ Ask: "Could you please spell WORLD for me?" Then ask him/her to spell it backwards:

....

MEMORY – Recall

[Score 0–3]

➤ Ask: "Which 3 words did I ask you to repeat and remember?"

....

MEMORY – Anterograde Memory

[Score 0–7]

➤ Tell: "I'm going to give you a name and address and I'd like you to repeat after me. We'll be doing that 3 times, so you have a chance to learn it. I'll be asking you later."

Score only the third trial

	1st Trial	2nd Trial	3rd Trial
Harry Barnes	....	....	....
73 Orchard Close	....	....	....
Kingsbridge	....	....	....
Devon	....	....	....

MEMORY – Retrograde Memory

[Score 0–4]

➤ Name of current Prime Minister ....

➤ Name of the woman who was Prime Minister ....

➤ Name of the USA president ....

➤ Name of the USA president who was assassinated in the 1960s ....

ATTENTION & ORIENTATION

MEMORY

VERBAL FLUENCY – Letter "P" and animals

➢ **Letters**

Say: "I'm going to give you a letter of the alphabet and I'd like you to generate as many words as you can beginning with that letter, but not names of people or places. Are you ready? You've got a minute and the letter is P."

[Score 0–7]

total	correct
> 17	7
14–17	6
11–13	5
8–10	4
6–7	3
4–5	2
2–3	1
< 2	0

➢ **Animals**

Say: "Now can you name as many animals as possible, beginning with any letter?"

[Score 0–7]

total	correct
> 21	7
17–21	6
14–16	5
11–13	4
9–10	3
7–8	2
5–6	1
< 5	0

FLUENCY

LANGUAGE – Comprehension

➢ Show written instruction:

[Score 0–1]

Close your eyes

➢ 3 stage command:

"Take the paper in your right hand. Fold the paper in half. Put the paper on the floor."

[Score 0–3]

LANGUAGE – Writing

➢ Ask the subject to make up a sentence and write it in the space below.

Score 1 if sentence contains a subject and a verb (see guide for examples)

[Score 0–1]

LANGUAGE

LANGUAGE – Repetition

➢ Ask the subject to repeat: **"hippopotamus"**; **"eccentricity"**; **"unintelligible"**; **"statistician"**
Score 2 if all correct; 1 if 3 correct; 0 if 2 or less.

[Score 0–2]

➢ Ask the subject to repeat: **"Above, beyond and below"**

[Score 0–1]

➢ Ask the subject to repeat: **"No ifs, ands, or buts"**

[Score 0–1]

LANGUAGE – Naming

➢ Ask the subject to name the following pictures:

[Score 0–2]
pencil +
watch

[Score 0–10]

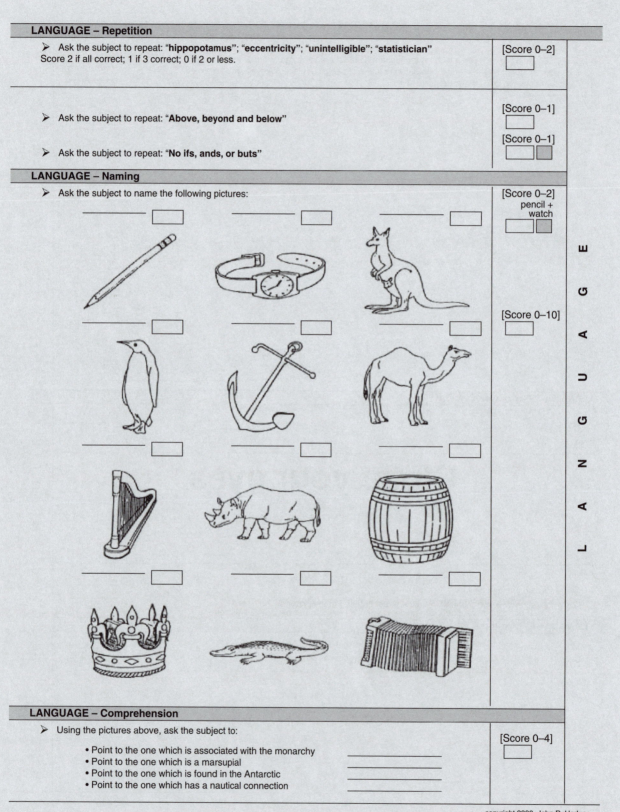

LANGUAGE – Comprehension

➢ Using the pictures above, ask the subject to:

- Point to the one which is associated with the monarchy
- Point to the one which is a marsupial
- Point to the one which is found in the Antarctic
- Point to the one which has a nautical connection

[Score 0–4]

L A N G U A G E

LANGUAGE – Reading		
➢ Ask the subject to read the following words. (Score 1 only if all correct) **sew** **pint** **soot** **dough** **height**	[Score 0–1]	LANGUAGE

VISUOSPATIAL ABILITIES		
➢ Overlapping pentagons. Ask the subject to copy this diagram:	[Score 0–1]	VISUOSPATIAL
➢ Wire cube. Ask the subject to copy this drawing (for scoring, see instructions guide):	[Score 0–2]	
➢ Clock: Ask the subject to draw a clock face with numbers and hands at ten past five. (For scoring see instruction guide: circle = 1, numbers = 2, hands = 2 if all correct)	[Score 0–5]	

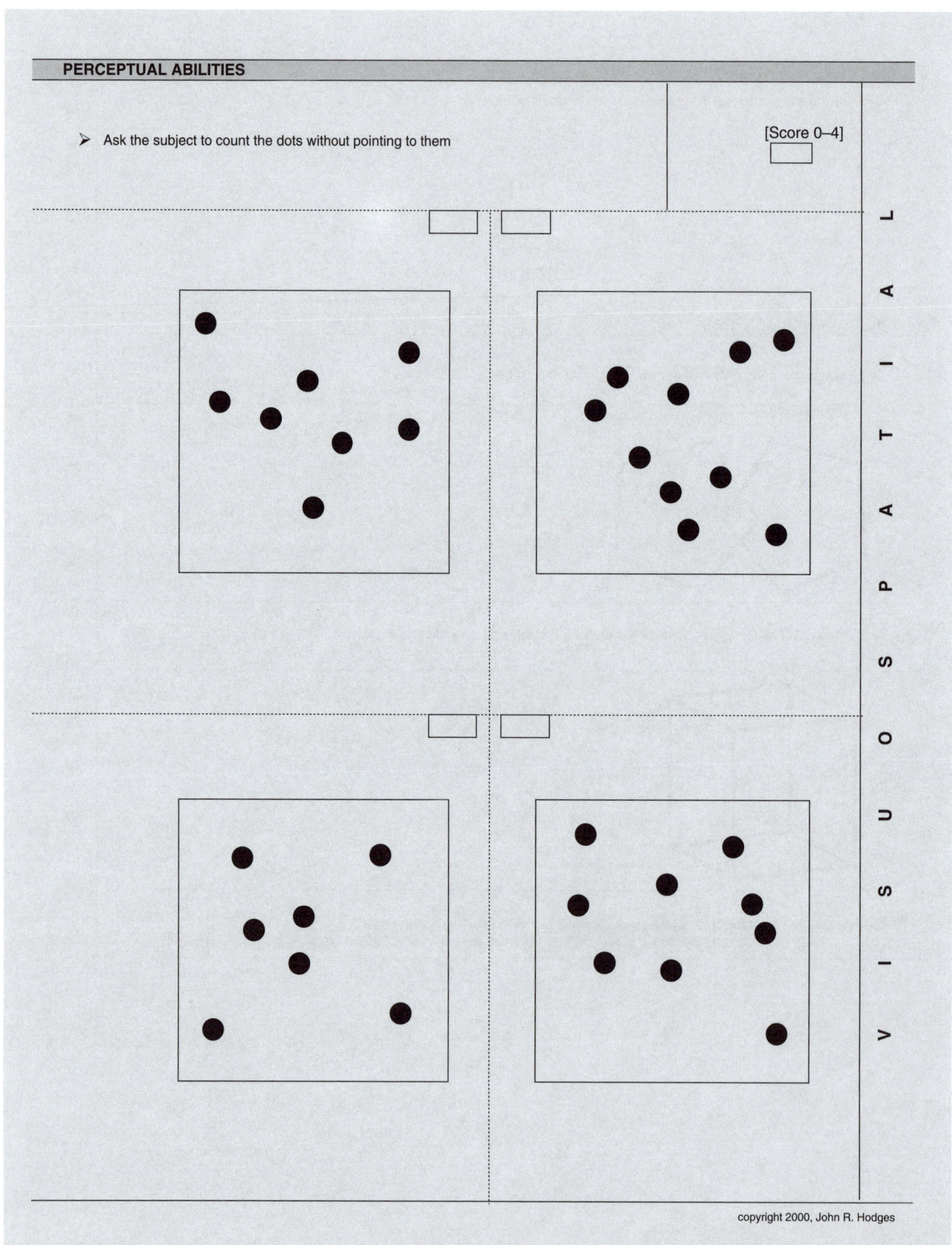
PERCEPTUAL ABILITIES

➢ Ask the subject to count the dots without pointing to them

[Score 0–4]

PERCEPTUAL ABILITIES

VISUOSPATIAL

➤ Ask the subject to identify the letters

[Score 0–4]

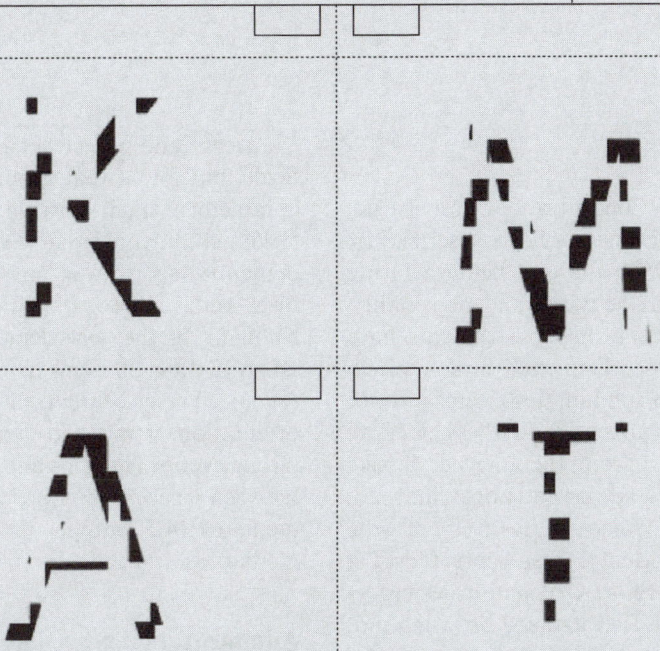

RECALL

MEMORY

➤ Ask: "Now tell me what you remember of that name and address we were repeating at the beginning."

Harry Barnes	....	[Score 0–7]
73 Orchard Close	....	
Kingsbridge	....	
Devon	....	

RECOGNITION

➤ This test should be done if subject failed to recall one or more items. If all items were recalled, skip the test and score 5. If only part is recalled start by ticking items recalled in the shadowed column on the right-hand side. Then test not recalled items by telling "OK, I'll give you some hints; was the name X, Y or Z?" and so on. Each recognized item scores one point, which is added to the point gained by recalling.

[Score 0–5]

Jerry Barnes		Harry Barnes		Harry Bradford		recalled	
37		73		76		recalled	
Orchard Place		Oak Close		Orchard Close		recalled	
Oakhampton		Kingsbridge		Dartington		recalled	
Devon		Dorset		Somerset		recalled	

General Scores

SCORE

MMSE	/30
ACE-R	/100

Subscores

Attention and Orientation	/18
Memory	/26
Fluency	/14
Language	/26
Visuospatial	/16

Normative values based on 63 controls aged 52–75 and 142 dementia patients aged 46–86

Cut-off < 88 gives 94% sensitivity and 89% specificity for dementia

Cut-off < 82 gives 84% sensitivity and 100% specificity for dementia

Acknowledgement: Addenbrooke's Cognitive Examination (ACE-R) from http//:pentorch.net/ACEfinal-v05-A1.pdf, reproduced by permission of John Hodges.

Blessed Information-Memory-Concentration Test (BIMCT)

Blessed, Tomlinson, and Roth (1968)

Source

The Information-Memory-Concentration Test is the second of two parts of the Dementia Scale described by Blessed and colleagues (1968); the first being a rating scale of changes in everyday activities and personality. By convention over the years, these instruments have become known as the Blessed Dementia Scales, which can be used separately or in combination. Items of both scales are available in an appendix to Blessed et al. (1968), can be downloaded from the Internet Stroke Center website (http://www.strokecenter.org) and are also reproduced below. Some derivatives of the BIMCT, the Abbreviated Mental Test Score (AMTS; Hodkinson, 1972) and the Short Orientation-Memory-Concentration Test (SOMCT; Katzman, Brown, Fuld, Peck, Schechter, & Schimmel, 1983), are also briefly described below.

Purpose

The BIMCT is an objective, clinician-administered test, designed to measure the extent of cognitive impairment. It has been used mainly in people with dementia. Application to other neurological groups has included multiple sclerosis, stroke, and traumatic brain injury (Wade & Vergis, 1999).

Item description

The 27-item BIMCT samples the domains of information, memory and concentration, although the 12-item information subtest is in reality an orientation test. The 12-item memory subtest examines autobiographical memories (7 items), semantic information (4 items), and episodic memory (5-minute recall of a name and address). The concentration subtest contains three items.

Scale development

Development of the BIMCT arose during the course of studies by this research group in which they had used standard cognitive tests, such as the Raven's Progressive Matrices and Wechsler-Bellevue Adult Intelligence Scale, but found that groups with dementia could only complete a small portion of the tests. Blessed et al. (1968) commented that "it was for this reason that the dementia score was introduced, together with the brief and simple tests which could be attempted even by many of the very demented patients" (p. 800). The BIMCT drew on items developed by Hopkins and Roth (1953). Their 20-item information test consisted of orientation items and items assessing knowledge of public events. Hopkins and Roth found good separation between people with affective disorders ($n = 20$; median = 14.5, range 6–20) and dementia ($n = 14$, median = 2, range 0–6).

Administration procedures, response format and scoring

Administration of the BIMCT is straightforward and can be completed within 10 minutes. No special materials are required, nor does the clinician need specific training to administer the test.

A number of scoring procedures have been used. In the original publication 1 or 2 points are awarded for each correct response. The total score ranges from 0 to 37, with higher scores indicating better cognitive functioning. Some researchers (e.g., Meiran, Stuss, Guzman, Lafleche & Willmer, 1996; Stern et al., 1992; Villardita & Lomeo, 1992) use error points (range generally 0–37), with higher scores indicating poorer performance.

Psychometric properties

Blessed et al. (1968) recruited patients from psychiatric, geriatric and general hospital wards in Newcastle upon Tyne, UK (descriptive data shown in Data box 3.2). They were classified into diagnostic groups using the criteria of Roth (1955). Data were presented on 60 cases with post-mortem examinations who were relatively free of cerebral infarctions. As expected, the dementia group had a significantly higher senile plaque count ($M = 20.85$, $SD = 12.17$) than other groups such as those

Data box 3.2 Descriptive data from the standardization sample (Blessed et al., 1968)

	Age M (SD)	Education	BIMCT M (SD)	Cut-off score	Sensitivity / Specificity
Physically sick (control; $n = 8$)	76.88 (6.08)	No information	31.8 (4.40)	No information	No information
Senile dementia ($n = 26$)	78.15 (8.17)		10.5 (9.15)		
Delirium ($n = 14$)	76.36 (8.26)		20.8 (8.28)		
Functional psychosis ($n = 12$)	73.17 (5.73)		27.1 (7.45)		

with functional psychosis ($M = 2.75$, $SD = 3.33$) or physically ill control patients ($M = 5.13$, $SD = 4.32$).

Box 3.2

Validity:	Criterion: *Concurrent:* Villardita & Lomeo: with MMSE: $r = -.80$ to $r = -.88$ *Predictive:* Blessed et al.: BIMCT score with mean senile plaque count at post-mortem: $r = -.59$ Construct: *Discriminant:* Blessed et al.: dementia group performed significantly more poorly ($M = 10.5$, $SD = 9.15$) than all other groups: delirium ($M = 20.8$, $SD = 8.28$), functional psychosis ($M = 27.1$, $SD = 7.45$) and physically ill controls ($M = 31.8$, $SD = 4.40$) – statistical result not reported
Reliability:	Inter-rater: No information available Test–retest: Villardita & Lomeo: 4 weeks: $r = .89$ *Practice effects*: Time 1 $M = 12.9$ ($SD = 6.53$) vs Time 2 $M = 13.09$ ($SD = 5.93$); $M = 0.29$ Telephone version: Kawas et al.: $r = .96$ *Practice effects:* no significant increase in score at retest: $M = -0.17$; $t = -0.46$, $p > .05$
Responsiveness:	Stern et al.: significant deterioration in scores over 6-month ($M = 2.2$ points, $SD = 3.2$) and 12-month ($M = 4.1$ points, $SD = 4.1$) retest intervals

Data on temporal stability are available from Villardita and Lomeo (1992) who examined 41 patients with probable AD initially and 4 weeks later. Kawas, Karagiozis, Resau, Corrada, and Brookmeyer (1995) examined the comparability of a telephone version of the BMICT in a sample of 84 people (70% of whom met criteria for dementia using the *Diagnostic and Statistical Manual of Mental Disorders* 3rd ed. – Revised (DSM-IIIR). A subset ($n = 35$) was re-examined, on average 20 days later. Concurrent validity with in-person administration ($n = 49$) was $r = .96$. Responsiveness data are available from Stern et al. (1992), who followed 111 patients with probable AD over a 6 to 96 month period, and examined them at 6-monthly intervals. The number of assessments was $M = 4.9$ ($SD = 3.0$). There were 251 pairs of ratings 6 months apart and 213 pairs of ratings 12 months apart. Results of these studies are shown in Box 3.2.

Derivatives of the BIMCT

There are briefer mental status tests, many of which have been derived from the BIMCT. Hodkinson's (1972) 26-item test was "closely based" on the BIMCT, and the subset of 10 items forming the Abbreviated Mental Test Score (AMTS) are indicated in the BIMCT Scale that follows. Another widely used version is the Short Orientation-Memory-Concentration Test, briefly described below.

Short Orientation-Memory-Concentration Test (SOMCT); Katzman, Brown, Fuld, Peck, Schechter, and Schimmel (1983)

The SOMCT is also known as the Short Blessed Test (Lorentz, Scanlan, & Borson, 2002). The six SOMCT items (3 for orientation to time, 1 for episodic memory, and 2 for concentration) are largely derived from stepwise linear regression analysis on BIMCT data from 322 people. SOMCT items are indicated in the BIMCT Scale that follows. Katzman et al. used error points with weights derived from multiple regression analysis that were applied to yield a total error score. The total score ranges from 0 to 28, with higher scores indicating more impaired performance. This score has been criticized by

Wade and Vergis (1999) as unwieldy. They retain the same weights, but invert the scoring system (range 0–28), so that higher scores represent better performance. A cut-off score 22/23 was used to identify cognitive impairment.

Katzman et al. found correlation with plaque counts in 38 post-mortem cases for the SOMCT ($r = .54$) was comparable to a 26-item version of the BIMCT ($r = .60$). Wade and Vergis examined convergent validity using paragraph recall of the Rivermead Behavioural Memory Test ($r = .68$ immediate recall, $r = .74$ delayed recall), and divergent validity in that no significant coefficient was obtained with the Barthel Index ($r = .23$). On retest 3 to 7 days later the score showed a statistically significant increment ($M = 1.79$). Inspection of the scatter plot indicated that increases of more than 6 points or declines of more than 2 points were clinically significant. Brooke and Bullock (1999) compared the SOMCT in 287 patients and controls, with 53% of the sample having dementia. The SOMCT correlated highly with the Mini-Mental State Examination (MMSE; $r = .91$) and was more sensitive to mild degrees of dementia than the MMSE. Meiran et al. (1996) provide detailed normative and comparison data from samples with Alzheimer's disease ($n = 163$), vascular dementia ($n = 76$) and healthy controls ($n = 145$) from which they derive descriptive data, percentile scores and likelihood ratios to assist in diagnosis.

Comment

The BIMCT holds the distinction of being the first brief, standardized cognitive screening test to be developed for people with dementia that is still commonly used in clinical and research practice. It can also boast being validated against the undisputed "gold standard" – post-mortem confirmation of dementia. Additionally, temporal stability is excellent. The BIMCT was specifically developed for people with severe degrees of cognitive impairment or those who experience difficulty in completing lengthy examinations. The short six-item version (SOMCT) can be completed in approximately 5 minutes, as can the telephone version of the original 27-item test. Normative/comparison data for diagnostic purposes are sparse, however, and the best data are only available for the SOMCT (Meiran et al., 1996). As with other cognitive screening tests containing a high proportion of linguistic content, the BMICT is subject to education bias and hence is not suitable for people from culturally, linguistically and educationally diverse backgrounds.

Key references

Blessed, G., Tomlinson, B. E., & Roth, M. (1968). The association between quantitative measures of dementia and of senile change in cerebral grey matter of elderly subjects. *British Journal of Psychiatry*, *114*(512), 797–811.

Brooke, P., & Bullock, R. (1999). Validation of a 6 item cognitive impairment test with a view to primary care usage. *International Journal of Geriatric Psychiatry*, *14*, 936–940.

Hodkinson, H. M. (1972). Evaluation of a mental test score for the assessment of mental impairment in the elderly. *Age and Ageing*, *1*(4), 233–238.

Hopkins, B., & Roth, M. (1953). Psychological test performance in patients over sixty. II. Paraphrenia, arteriosclerotic psychosis and acute confusion. *Journal of Mental Science*, *99*, 451–463.

Katzman, R., Brown, T., Fuld, P., Peck, A., Schechter, R., & Schimmel, H. (1983). Validation of a short Orientation-Memory-Concentration Test of cognitive impairment. *American Journal of Psychiatry*, *140*(6), 734–739.

Kawas, C., Karagiozis, H., Resau, L., Corrada, M., & Brookmeyer, R. (1995). Reliability of the Blessed Telephone Information-Memory-Concentration Test. *Journal of Geriatric Psychiatry and Neurology*, *8*(4), 238–242.

Lorentz, W. J., Scanlan, J. M., & Borson, S. (2002). Brief screening tests for dementia. *Canadian Journal of Psychiatry*, *47*(8), 723–733.

Meiran, N., Stuss, D. T., Guzman, D. A., Lafleche, G., & Willmer, J. (1996). Diagnosis of dementia: Methods for interpretation of scores of 5 neuropsychological tests. *Archives of Neurology*, *53*(10), 1043–1054.

Roth, M. (1955). The natural history of mental disorder in old age. *Journal of Mental Science*, *101*, 281–301.

Stern, R. G., Mohs, R. C., Bierer, L. M., Silverman, J. M., Schmeidler, J., Davidson, M., et al. (1992). Deterioration on the Blessed Test in Alzheimer's disease: Longitudinal data and their implications for clinical trials and identification of subtypes. *Psychiatry Research*, *42*(2), 101–110.

Villardita, C., & Lomeo, C. (1992). Alzheimer's disease: Correlational analysis of three screening tests and three behavioral scales. *Acta Neurologica Scandinavica*, *86*(6), 603–608.

Wade, D. T., & Vergis, E. (1999). The Short Orientation-Memory-Concentration Test: A study of its reliability and validity. *Clinical Rehabilitation*, *13*(2), 164–170.

Blessed Dementia Scales

Blessed, Tomlinson, and Roth (1968)

1. Behaviour Rating Scale

Name: **Administered by:** **Date:**

Instructions: Information obtained as far as possible from a relative in close and continual contact with the patient. Inquiries are directed towards defining changes in capacity, habits and personality. Allowance is made in scoring for physical disabilities that would restrict activities.

SCORE

EVERYDAY ACTIVITIES

Scoring for items 1–8:
0: able to do the activity; 0.5: there is difficulty; 1: unable to do the activity

1. Inability to perform household tasks ______
2. Inability to cope with small sums of money ______
3. Inability to remember short list of items, e.g., in shopping ______
4. Inability to find way about indoors ______
5. Inability to find way about familiar streets ______
6. Inability to interpret surroundings (e.g., to recognize whether in hospital, or at home; to discriminate between patients, doctors and nurses, relatives and hospital staff etc.) ______
7. Inability to recall recent events (e.g., recent outings, visits of relatives or friends to hospital etc.) ______
8. Tendency to dwell in the past ______

CHANGES IN HABITS

For items 9–11, circle the number that best applies

9. Eating
   - 0 Cleanly with proper utensils
   - 1 Messily with spoon only
   - 2 Simple solids, e.g., biscuits
   - 3 Has to be fed ______
10. Dressing
    - 0 Unaided
    - 1 Occasionally misplaced buttons, etc.
    - 2 Wrong sequence, commonly forgetting items
    - 3 Unable to dress ______
11. Continence
    - 0 Complete sphincter control
    - 1 Occasional wet beds
    - 2 Frequent wet beds
    - 3 Doubly incontinent ______

CHANGES IN PERSONALITY, INTERESTS, DRIVE

For items 12–22, score 0 if there has been no change in personality or if interests have been retained; otherwise score 1 for each area of change

Changes in personality:

12. Increased rigidity
13. Increased egocentricity ______
14. Impairment of regard for feelings of others ______
15. Coarsening of affect ______
16. Impairment of emotional control, e.g., increased petulance and irritability ______
17. Hilarity in inappropriate situations ______
18. Diminished emotional responsiveness ______
19. Sexual misdemeanour (appearing de novo in old age) ______

Interests:

20. Hobbies relinquished ______
21. Diminished initiative or growing apathy ______
22. Purposeless hyperactivity ______

TOTAL SCORE: ______

2. Information-Memory-Concentration Test

Name:	Administered by:	Date:

SCORE

INFORMATION

Scoring: Items 1–12: 1 point for each correct response (maximum 15 points)

1. Name ________ ____
2. Age[1] ________ ____
3. Time (hour)[1] ________ ____
4. Time of day ________ ____
5. Day of week ________ ____
6. Date ________ ____
7. Month[2] ________ ____
8. Season ________ ____
9. Year[1, 2] ________ ____
10. Place: Name ________ ____
 Street ________ ____
 Town ________ ____
11. Type of place[1] (e.g., home, hospital etc.) ________ ____
12. Recognition of two persons[1] (cleaner, doctor, nurse, patient, relative; any 2 available) ________ ____

MEMORY

Scoring: Items 13–19: 1 point for each correct response

Personal

13. Date of birth[1] ________ ____
14. Place of birth ________ ____
15. School attended ________ ____
16. Occupation ________ ____
17. Name of siblings / name of spouse ________ ____
18. Name of any town where patient worked ________ ____
19. Names of employers ________ ____

Non-personal

Scoring: Items 20–23: 1 point for each correct response; for items 20–21 score 0.5 points if correct within 3 years

20. Date of First World War[1] ________ ____
21. Date of Second World War ________ ____
22. Monarch[1] ________ ____
23. Prime Minister ________ ____
24. Five minute recall[1, 2]

Scoring: Item 24: 1 point for each correct element (subtotal 5 points)

Mr John Brown ________ ____
42 West Street ________
Gateshead ________

CONCENTRATION

Scoring: Items 25–27:
2 points for each correct response; 1 point for self-corrected errors; 0 points for uncorrected errors; (maximum 6 points)

25. Months of year backwards[2] ________ ____
26. Counting 1–20 ________ ____
27. Counting 20–1[1, 2] ________ ____

TOTAL SCORE: ____

[1] Denotes items for the Abbreviated Mental Test Score (AMTS)
[2] Denotes items for the Short Orientation, Memory and Concentration Test (SOMCT)

Capacity to Consent to Treatment Instrument (CCTI)

Marson, Ingram, Cody, and Harrell (1995b)

Source

The CCTI is described in Marson et al. (1995b) and the actual instrument can be purchased from Dr Marson (Department of Neurology, Clinical Neuropsychology Laboratory, The University of Alabama at Birmingham, Birmingham, Alabama, 35294–0017, USA).

Purpose

The CCTI is an objective, clinician-administered test, developed to assess the capacity to consent to medical treatments. Initially designed for people with Alzheimer's disease (AD), the CCTI has also been used in people with Parkinson's disease (Dymek, Atchison, Harrell, & Marson, 2001).

Item description

The CCTI comprises a set of questions about two vignettes, describing hypothetical medical problems and symptomatology. In each vignette (Vignette A about neoplasm and Vignette B about cardiac problems), two alternative treatments (including risks and benefits) are described. The questions about the vignettes relate to five legal standards (LS), which are hierarchically based: LS1: the capacity to make a decision (1 item), LS2: the decision is reasonable (1 item – applies only to Vignette A), LS3: demonstrate awareness about the consequences of the decision (2 items), LS4: provide rational reasons for the choice (1 item), and LS5: understand the situation and choices (9 items). An example of a question from LS4 in Vignette A is as follows: "You decided to have the brain surgery. Based only on the story, can you tell me all the reasons why you decided to have the brain surgery?"

Scale development

Marson et al. (1995b) observed that although determination of a person's competency is a legal matter, competency issues can arise in a hospital rather than a legal setting (e.g., regarding medical treatments, health research). In these situations, physicians and other health professionals need to make competency judgements, which can be particularly difficult in patients who have cognitive impairment. They further noted that methods of assessing competency are seldom incorporated into training curricula. Consequently, procedures to determine competency in clinical settings "have relied almost exclusively on subjective clinical impressions and brief mental status testing." (p. 950). The CCTI was therefore developed to provide a standardized approach to assessing competency in patients with AD, in terms of their capacity to consent to treatment under commonly established LS.

Four of the five LS used in the CCTI are "discrete, established standards or thresholds drawn from legal case law and psychiatric literature" (Dymek et al., 2001, p. 18). A fifth standard pertaining to "reasonable choice" (LS2 on the CCTI) was included to "better understand treatment preferences of neurologic patients". Two hypothetical vignettes were developed as a vehicle to objectively assess the patient's ability to demonstrate appropriate understanding of and decision making processes about the vignettes, and hence his or her competency. Having developed the vignettes, the medical content was reviewed by a neurologist with expertise in older people and dementia. The vignettes were written at the 5th and 6th grade levels, and although syntactic complexity was low, they contained a "moderate information load". The vignettes were examined psychometrically (see below).

Administration procedures, response format and scoring

The examiner reads the two vignettes to the patient, who is also given a written copy of the material. After each vignette the patient responds to the set questions. The examiner records the patient's responses on the record form. Administration time is 20 to 25 minutes.

The CCTI contains detailed scoring criteria for each item corresponding to the LS, as well as for each response level within the items. Mastery of the scoring procedures requires detailed study, and this is facilitated by operationalized criteria. Items are scored in terms of the quantity and accuracy of detail reported by the patient, with most responses scored on a 3-point scale: 0 (equivalent of no response/not correct), 1 (equivalent of an indirect response to the correct answer), 2 (equivalent of a direct and fully elaborated correct response). LS4 and 6 out of 9 items in LS5 have multiple correct responses. For example, item 6 in LS5 of Vignette A asks the following: "in the story, what were some of the benefits of having surgery on the brain tumour", and up to 10 benefits can be listed. The score for this item thus ranges from 0 to 20.

Scores for each of the five LS for Vignettes A and B are summed. The total scores for the five LS range as follows: LS1: 0 to 4, LS2: 0 to 1, LS3: 0 to 8, LS4: 0 to 48, LS5: 0 to 134. Higher scores indicate higher competency. Cut-off scores for classifying competency (which are intended as guidelines only and should not be substituted for clinical judgement) were derived from the control group established at 2 SD below the mean for LS 3 and 5. Scores lying on the cut-off itself are classified as "marginal" competence. For LS1, the control group performed perfectly, and the cut-off score was therefore set by the research group; for LS4, the cut-off score was set to eliminate all outliers in the control group. A system of error scores, based on a qualitative analysis of the responses, has also been developed (Marson, Annis, McInturff, Bartolucci, & Harrell, 1999).

Psychometric properties

Initial reliability and validity studies were reported in Marson et al. (1995b). Patients with AD (descriptive data shown in Data box 3.3), determined by established criteria, along with 15 people without brain impairment were recruited from the University at Birmingham AD Center Core, Birmingham, Alabama, USA. The AD group was subdivided on the basis of their score on the Mini-Mental State Examination (MMSE) into those with mild ($n = 15$, MMSE score > 19) and moderate ($n = 14$, MMSE score 11–19) dementia. Discriminant validity was established by comparing performance of the AD and control groups, as well as the mild and moderate AD subgroups. No group differences were found for LS1 or LS2, but significant differences among all groups ($p < .01$) were found for the remaining three LS.

Marson, Cody, Ingram, and Harrell (1995a) reported on concurrent validity of LS4 (capacity to provide rational reasons for the choice) with a large battery of neuropsychological tests (22 separate measures) in the above samples. These included MMSE; Dementia Rating Scale (DRS); word generativity using the letters C, F, and L; among others. The underlying factor structure of the CCTI was examined by Dymek, Marson, and Harrell (1999) in 82 people with probable/possible AD, focusing on LS 3, 4, and 5. A two-factor solution (Verbal reasoning and Verbal memory), accounting for 56% of the variance, provided the best fit for the data from 12 out of 13 items. A number of items were complex, loading on both factors. A detailed study of inter-rater reliability was reported by Marson, Earnst, Jamil, Bartolucci, and Harrell (2000) who assessed 31 participants (21 with mild and moderate AD and 10 healthy older people) who were videotaped performing the CCTI. Independent ratings were made by five physicians who were experienced in competency assessment. All combinations of rater-pairs ($n = 10$) were examined for the five LS, as well as their overall judgement of competency. Results from the above studies are shown in Box 3.3.

Data box 3.3 Descriptive data from the standardization sample (Marson et al., 1995b)

	Age *M* (*SD*)	Education *M* (*SD*)	CCTI *M* (*SD*)	Cut-off score	Sensitivity / Specificity
Control ($n = 15$):	67.9 (6.5)	14.1 (2.2)		LS 3 and 5 at > 2 SD below; 6.3 and 45.4 respectively (but see text)	No information
LS 1 (evidencing choice)			4.0 (0.0)		
LS 2 (reasonable choice)			0.9 (0.3)		
LS 3 (consequences)			8.7 (1.2)		
LS 4 (reasons for choice)			10.3 (3.8)		
LS 5 (understanding)			58.3 (6.6)		
Alzheimer's disease ($n = 29$):	71.0 (8.1)	12.5 (2.5)			
LS 1 (evidencing choice)			3.7 (0.7)		
LS 2 (reasonable choice)			0.9 (0.3)		
LS 3 (consequences)			6.5 (2.4)		
LS 4 (reasons for choice)			4.3 (3.6)		
LS 5 (understanding)			22.8 (11.0)		

Box 3.3

Validity:	Criterion: *Concurrent:* Marson et al. (1995a): AD: LS4 with MMSE: $r = .55$ – with DRS-Initiation/ Perseveration: $r = .60$ – with C,F,L: $r = .57$
	Construct: *Factor analysis:* Dymek et al. (1999): 2 factors: Verbal reasoning (8 items), Verbal memory (7 items)
	Discriminant: Marson et al. (1995b): LS3: AD $M = 6.5$ ($SD = 2.4$) vs controls $M = 8.7$ ($SD = 1.2$); $t = 4.0$, $p < .001$ – LS4: AD $M = 4.3$ ($SD = 3.6$) vs controls $M = 10.3$ ($SD = 3.8$); $t = 4.8$, $p < .001$ – LS5: AD $M = 22.8$ ($SD = 11.0$) vs controls $M = 58.3$ ($SD = 6.6$); $t = 13.4$, $p < .001$
Reliability:	Inter-rater: Marson et al. (2000): $k = .48$ (LS range: $k = .31$–$.57$, with $k < 0.4$ for 4/5 – LS1, LS2, LS3, LS4)
	Test–retest: No information available *Practice effects:* No information available
Responsiveness:	No information available

Comment

The CCTI is a practical and innovative method to assess competency to consent to treatment. Basic psychometric features have been examined, and it shows evidence of concurrent validity with neuropsychological tests of cognitive functioning and the capacity to distinguish among varying levels of cognitive functioning and impairment. A particular strength and singular advantage of the CCTI is the correspondence with established LS. Because the LS are hierarchically based, this enables the examiner to determine the level of breakdown in competency, referred to by Marson et al. (1995b) as legal thresholds. Scoring procedures for the CCTI are detailed, however, and the unfamiliar examiner needs to attain mastery by close study and reference to the scoring criteria. Inter-rater reliability is fair for overall judgement, but more variable for the individual LS. Marson et al. (1995b) place a caveat on their instrument, which "is intended to assist, but certainly not displace, the clinician. A single instrument and score can never take account of the variety of medical, legal, ethical, and other factors that inform a competency decision" (p. 953). Nonetheless, the CCTI is a valuable adjunct in competency evaluations.

Key references:

Dymek, M. P., Atchison, P., Harrell, L., & Marson, D. C. (2001). Competency to consent to medical treatment in cognitively impaired patients with Parkinson's disease. *Neurology*, *56*(1), 17–24.

Dymek, M. P., Marson, D. C., & Harrell, L. (1999). Factor structure of Capacity to Consent to Medical Treatment in patients with Alzheimer's disease: An exploratory study. *Journal of Forensic Neuropsychology*, *1(1)*, 27–48.

Marson, D. C., Annis, S. M., McInturff, B., Bartolucci, A., & Harrell, L. E. (1999). Error behaviors associated with loss of competency in Alzheimer's disease. *Neurology*, *53*(9), 1983–1992.

Marson, D. C., Cody, H. A., Ingram, K. K., & Harrell, L. E. (1995a). Neuropsychologic predictors of competency in Alzheimer's disease using a rational reasons legal standard. *Archives of Neurology*, *52*(10), 955–959.

Marson, D. C., Earnst, K. S., Jamil, F., Bartolucci, A., & Harrell, L. E. (2000). Consistency of physicians' legal standard and personal judgements of competency in patients with Alzheimer's disease. *Journal of the American Geriatrics Society*, *48*, 911–918.

Marson, D. C., Ingram, K. K., Cody, H. A., & Harrell, L. E. (1995b). Assessing the competency of patients with Alzheimer's disease under different legal standards. *Archives of Neurology*, *52*(10), 949–954.

Clifton Assessment Procedures for the Elderly (CAPE)

Pattie and Gilleard (1979)

Source

The CAPE is commercially available from Hodder and Stoughton (http://www.hodderstoughton.uk). An abbreviated version, referred to as the CAPE Survey Version (Pattie, 1981), is also briefly described below.

Purpose

The CAPE is a combination of an objective, clinician-administered test of cognition and a clinician rating scale of behaviours. It is designed to provide "a reasonably brief method for assessing the cognitive (mental) and behavioural competence of the elderly" (Pattie & Gilleard, 1979, p. 1). The authors suggest clinical applications include diagnosis and prognosis, patient selection and placement, and therapeutic evaluations. The CAPE is used with older people, often with dementia.

Item description

The CAPE consists of two scales: (i) the Cognitive Assessment Scale (CAS) and (ii) the Behaviour Rating Scale (BRS), which can be used separately or in combination. The CAS comprises three subtests: The Information/Orientation (I/O) subtest contains 12 items (including orientation items to person, time and place, as well as three general knowledge questions, such as "what are the colours of the British flag?"). The Mental Abilities Test examines four domains of "well-established skills": counting from 1 to 20, reciting the alphabet, reading 10 words ranked in increasing difficulty (from "free" to "precocious") and writing one's name. Finally, the Psychomotor Test assesses fine-motor and eye–hand coordination using the Gibson spiral, in which the patient draws a pathway around a spiral that covers an A4 page without touching the sides or obstacles in the course. The 18-item BRS samples a range of behaviours in four domains: physical disability (PD, 6 items), apathy (5 items), communication difficulties (2 items) and social disturbance (5 items).

Scale development

Development of the CAPE was based on a series of research studies conducted by the authors in the 1970s. Pattie and Gilleard (1975) noted that a number of psychogeriatric patients were not able to tolerate lengthy tests, and they aimed to construct a briefer scale. Items from the CAS were initially published in 1975 and those of the BRS, which was derived from the Stockton Geriatric Rating Scale, in 1977. Limited information is provided in the manual regarding the initial item selection process or establishment of the dependency grades.

Administration procedures, response format and scoring

The CAS is described as a short, psychological test, which can be administered with little training. Apart from a stop-watch and stimulus materials for the Psychomotor Test (Gibson Spiral), no equipment is required and the manual provides detailed administration instructions. The BRS can be completed by an informant who is familiar with the person's behaviour (e.g., clinician, relative, facility staff).

Scoring instructions for the CAS are clearly stipulated in the manual. Points are awarded for correctness of response, and bonus points are awarded for some timed responses. The total CAS score ranges from 0 to 35, with higher scores reflecting better functioning. Each BRS item is rated on a 3-point scale: 0 (equivalent of never/no problem), 1 (equivalent of some problem), 2 (equivalent of frequently/maximal assistance), with levels of response operationally defined for each item. Total BRS scores range from 0 to 36, with higher scores reflecting greater difficulty.

Individual scores for the CAS and BRS, as well as scores for the I/O subtest and Survey Version, can be converted to one of five "dependency grades" as shown in Data box 3.4. For example, a CAS score of 26 corresponds to Dependency Grade B, mild impairment; a BRS score of 14 corresponds to Dependency Grade D, marked impairment.

Data box 3.4

Dependency Grade	Description	CAS score	BRS score	CAS I/O score	Survey score (see below)
A	No impairment: independent elderly – comparable to those living without support in the community	30–35	0–3	11–12	10–12
B	Mild impairment: low dependency – likely to include those needing some support in the community, warden-supervised accommodation and the better residents in residential accommodation	24–29	4–7	9–10	6–9
C	Moderate impairment: medium dependency – people functioning at this level are likely to need residential care or considerable support and help if at home	16–23	8–12	6–8	2–5
D	Marked impairment: high dependency – it is within this category that there is the greatest overlap between those in social services accommodation and those in hospital care	9–15	13–17	3–5	1 to –3
E	Severe impairment: maximum dependency – this level is seen most often in psychogeriatric wards and the ones who remain in community homes/EMI hostels often present considerable problems to staff in terms of their demands on staff time	0–8	18+	0–2	< –3

Acknowledgement: Pattie, A. H. (1981). A survey version of the Clifton Assessment Procedures for the Elderly (CAPE). *British Journal of Clinical Psychology*, *20*(3), Appendix, pp. 177–178, reproduced with permission from the *British Journal of Clinical Psychology* © The British Psychological Society.

Psychometric properties

The manual for the CAPE (Pattie & Gilleard, 1979) draws together a series of early psychometric studies conducted on independent samples recruited from York, UK. Participants were aged ≥ 65 years with varying degrees of dependency, ranging from living independently in the community to nursing home residents. Normative data for subscales and total CAS and BRS scores are presented separately for nine such groups. Because CAS test–retest scores are stable, the authors recommended that absolute changes of ≥ 2 points are significant. Inter-correlation between the CAS and BRS in a range of samples is moderate (range $r = -.51$ to $-.72$), suggesting that the subscales measure overlapping abilities rather than a single dimension. Inter-subscale-total correlation coefficients, however, are high for CAS subscales (range $r = .84 - .87$), but more variable for BRS (range $r = .65 - .92$). Moran, Cockram, Walker, and McPherson (1990) studied predictive validity of the CAS by following 261 inpatients mainly with dementia over a 5-year period. The factor structure of the CAPE was examined by Pattie (1981), using seven subtests from CAS and BRS from four samples ($n = 400$, aged 60–98 years, with participants experiencing varying degrees of dependency). A single factor was extracted, accounting for 60% of variance, and the CAS and BRS subtests with the highest loadings were renamed "Survey Version". McPherson, Gamsu, Cockram, and Gormley (1986) reported an inter-rater reliability study on the Psychomotor Test (Gibson Spiral), using 100 protocols rated independently by four raters. The results for the CAS shown in Box 3.4 are reported in Pattie and Gilleard, except where otherwise stated.

Derivates of the CAPE: CAPE Survey Version; Pattie (1981)

The Survey Version of the CAPE was derived from the factor analysis described above. It comprises the I/O and PD scales, selected because they had the highest loadings on the first factor. The six PD items cover the following: requiring assistance with bathing/dressing and walking, incontinence, bed-bound, confusion, and disorderly appearance. A revised scoring system was developed: the total score ranges from +12 (zero errors on the I/O scale and zero on the PD scale) to –12 (zero correct on I/O scale and maximum rating on the PD scale). One-week test–retest reliability on the total score was $r = .91$; although practice effects for I/O were small ($M = 6.2$, $SD = 3.8$ vs $M = 6.3$, $SD = 4.2$), 37% showed a different dependency grade (McPherson & Tregaskis, 1985). Significant group differences were found among six groups with varying levels of dependency ($F = 76.5$, $p < .001$), as well as for I/O and PD subscales (McPherson, Gamsu, Kiemle, Ritchie, Stanley, & Tregaskis, 1985). The I/O scale is commonly used in isolation. Receiver operating characteristic (ROC) analysis of data from 438 people identified optimal cut-off scores on the I/O scale of 11/12 for mild dementia (sensitivity/specificity values not provided; area under curve 0.896, $SE = .014$) and 8/9 for moderate dementia (area under curve 0.979, $SE = .003$; Jagger, Clarke, & Anderson, 1992). Predictive validity for

Box 3.4

Validity:	Criterion:
	Concurrent: $n = 33$ acute psychogeriatric patients, CAS I/O with Wechsler Memory Scale: $r=.90$
	Predictive: $n = 34$ people (aged > 60 years) admitted to acute psychiatric wards, scores of CAS significantly differentiated those with "satisfactory" ($M = 27.4$, $SD = 3.3$), "intermediate" ($M = 24.4$, $SD = 6.6$) and "unsatisfactory" ($M = 22.3$, $SD = 7.4$) living situations 2 years later
	Moran et al.: survival at 48 months using baseline CAS scores: scores of survivors ($M = 19.4$, $SD = 9.1$) were significantly higher than non-survivors ($M = 14.7$, $SD = 7.7$)
	Construct: *Internal consistency*: McPherson et al. (1985): significant item-total correlation coefficients ($r = .46 - .83$) for 11/12 items from I/O scale
	Factor analysis: 1 factor
Reliability:	Inter-rater: McPherson et al. (1986): Scoring errors on the Psychomotor Test compared 4 raters with 100 protocols: ICC = .98, but it was noted that agreement on 600 pairs of scores was 58%
	Test–retest: 3–4 days, $n = 38$ hospital admissions on CAS: $r = .87$ (I/O), $r = .89$ (Mental Abilities), $r = .79$ (Psychomotor Test) *Practice effects*: Time 1 vs Time 2: I/O ($M = 8.2$, $SD = 3.1$ vs $M = 8.1$, $SD = 3.4$), Mental Abilities ($M = 8.3$, $SD = 2.4$ vs $M = 8.2$, $SD = 2.5$), Psychomotor Test ($M = 7.6$, $SD = 3.7$ vs $M = 7.8$, $SD = 4.2$)
	– 6 months: $n = 29$ community dwelling older people, $r = .84$ (I/O), $r = .74$ (Mental Abilities), $r = .69$ (Psychomotor Test). Practice effects also minimal.
Responsiveness:	No information available on CAPE as a whole

mortality over 8 years was demonstrated for the I/O scale (Clarke et al., 1996).

Comment

The CAPE is one of the first generation of briefer test batteries specifically designed to screen for cognitive and behavioural impairments in older people. Particular strengths are the co-norming of cognitive (CAS) and behavioural (BRS) scales and predictive validity. The CAPE continues to be widely used in clinical practice and was found to be one of the six most frequently used instruments with psychogeriatric patients in England and Northern Ireland (Reilly, Challis, Burns, & Hughes, 2004). Although the CAS is limited in item content in that it does not sample episodic memory or executive abilities, Jagger et al. (1992) found that the I/O subtest alone performed as well as the Mini-Mental State Examination in detecting moderate to severe degrees of dementia. They also reported that both tests are subject to a number of biases, including social class and education. A special feature of the CAPE, which may account for its popularity among clinicians, is the translation of test scores to "dependency grades" for competence in everyday living. In this sense, the CAPE meets the acid test put by Bell and Gilleard (1986) which "demands that our assessments tell us something we do not already know, or predict something we cannot already predict" (p. 195).

Key references

Bell, J. S., & Gilleard, C. J. (1986). Psychometric prediction of psychogeriatric day care outcome. *British Journal of Clinical Psychology*, *25*(Pt 3), 195–200.

Clarke, D., Morgan, K., Lilley, J., Arie, T., Jones, R., Waite, J., et al. (1996). Dementia and "borderline dementia" in Britain: 8-year incidence and post-screening outcomes. *Psychological Medicine*, *26*(4), 829–836.

Jagger, C., Clarke, M., & Anderson, J. (1992). Screening for dementia – A comparison of two tests using receiver operating characteristic (ROC) analysis. *International Journal of Geriatric Psychiatry*, *7*(9), 659–665.

McPherson, F. M., Gamsu, C. V., Cockram, L. L., & Gormley, A. J. (1986). Inter-scorer agreement in scoring errors on the Pm (Maze) Test of the CAPE. *British Journal of Clinical Psychology*, *25*(3), 225–226.

McPherson, F. M., Gamsu, C. V., Kiemle, G., Ritchie, S. M., Stanley, A. M., & Tregaskis, D. (1985). The concurrent validity of the survey version of the Clifton Assessment Procedures for the Elderly (CAPE). *British Journal of Clinical Psychology*, *24*(Pt 2), 83–91.

McPherson, F. M., & Tregaskis, D. (1985). The short-term stability of the survey version of CAPE. *British Journal of Clinical Psychology*, *24*(Pt 3), 205–206.

Moran, S. M., Cockram, L. L., Walker, B., & McPherson, F. M. (1990). Prediction of survival by the Clifton Assessment Procedures for the Elderly (CAPE). *British Journal of Clinical Psychology*, *29*(2), 225–226.

Pattie, A. H. (1981). A survey version of the Clifton Assessment Procedures for the Elderly (CAPE). *British Journal of Clinical Psychology*, *20*(3), 173–178.

Pattie, A. H., & Gilleard, C. J. (1975). A brief psychogeriatric assessment schedule. Validation against psychiatric diagnosis and discharge from hospital. *British Journal of Psychiatry*, *127*, 489–493.

Pattie, A. H., & Gilleard, C. J. (1979). *Clifton Assessment Procedures for the Elderly (CAPE)*. Sevenoaks, UK: Hodder & Stoughton.

Reilly, S., Challis, D., Burns, A., & Hughes, J. (2004). The use of assessment scales in old age psychiatry services in England and Northern Ireland. *Aging and Mental Health*, *8*(3), 249–255.

Cognitive Abilities Screening Instrument (CASI)

Teng et al. (1994)

Source

Items and the recording form for the CASI appear in an appendix to Teng et al. (1994), along with the detailed scoring sheet. The administration form is reproduced below. A CASI-Short form is also described.

Purpose

The CASI is an objective, clinician-administered test, designed to measure cognitive impairment in people with dementia. Teng et al. (1994) suggest that in addition to a screening test, the CASI is suitable for monitoring the course of disease progression, as well as being able to provide a profile of impairment across a range of cognitive domains.

Item description

The 25 tasks of the CASI contain a variable number of items. It incorporates most items of the Mini-Mental State Examination (MMSE) which is also described in this chapter. The tasks sample nine cognitive domains: Attention (2 tasks), Concentration/mental manipulation (2 tasks), Orientation (4 tasks), Short-term memory (3 tasks), Long-term memory (5 tasks), Language (5 tasks: reading, writing and following a 3-stage command from MMSE, along with naming body parts and common objects), Visual construction (1 task), Generativity (1 task), and Abstraction/judgement (2 tasks). The four-item CASI-Short form uses repetition and first recall of three words, category generativity and temporal orientation items.

Scale development

Development of the CASI drew on existing screening tests, notably the MMSE, the Hasegawa Dementia Screening Scale, and the Modified MMSE (also known as the 3MS), the last two instruments being those previously developed by the authors. Items from the scales that had proved to have limitations were excluded (e.g., translation of the MMSE item, "no ifs, ands, or buts"). Teng and colleagues (1994) developed English and Japanese versions of the CASI during the course of three workshops. Pilot testing with healthy ($n = 235$) and dementia ($n = 208$) groups was conducted in Los Angeles and Seattle, USA for the English version and Osaka and Tokyo, Japan for the Japanese version. The four-item short form of the CASI was developed using those items most sensitive to dementia. In addition to English and Japanese, a Chinese version of the CASI has been used in epidemiological studies (Lin, Wang, Liu, Chen, Lee, & Liu, 2002).

Administration procedures, response format and scoring

Test materials include the recording form and everyday common objects (e.g., toothbrush, spoon). Teng et al. (1994) reported that typical administration time was 15 to 20 minutes ($M = 18.2$ mins for the dementia group and $M = 13.7$ for the control group). A manual of administration and scoring procedures is available for novice users of the CASI. Additionally, Teng et al. have produced a 1-hour videotape, demonstrating administration of the CASI to patients with different levels of functioning, as well as a 30-item competency test for training in administration and scoring the CASI.

Scoring procedures for the CASI are detailed and are described in the manual. Scoring takes into account accuracy of response and hence scores are awarded for correct or partially correct responses. Most domains have a maximum score of 10. The total score ranges from 0 to 100, with higher scores indicating better performance. The total score for the CASI-Short ranges from 0 to 33. A CASI-estimated score for the MMSE can also be derived from the CASI.

Various cut-off scores were derived from the standardization samples (Teng et al., 1994), and those of Graves, Teng, Larson, and White (1992) were derived from a sample of 88 healthy controls and 57 people with probable Alzheimer's disease (AD), using receiver operating characteristic (ROC) analysis. A cut-off score of 86/87 gave the best balance of sensitivity (97%) and specificity (92%) for distinguishing between healthy

Data box 3.5 Descriptive data from the Los Angeles sample in the standardization groups (Teng et al., 1994)

	Age *M* (*SD*)	Education *M* (*SD*)	CASI *M* (*SD*)	Cut-off score*	Sensitivity/Specificity*
Los Angeles sample:				86/87 →	Normal vs AD 97% / 92%
Control (*n* = 50)	70.0 (13.3)	12.7 (3.5)	88.9 (7.9)	89/90 →	Education 13+ years 100% / 93%
Dementia (*n* = 62)	74.2 (7.8)	12.1 (4.1)	54.3 (19.5)	84/85 →	Education 12 years 100% / 92% Education 0–11 years 94% / 100%

* Using data from Graves et al. (1992).

controls and AD. Because performance on cognitive tests shows significant correlation with years of education, Graves et al. provided other cut-off scores for various education levels (see Data box 3.5).

Normative data on 2524 older adults, stratified by age and education, are published by McCurry et al. (1999). Participants were recruited from a community-based prospective research study into ageing and dementia in Seattle, Washington, USA. They were aged $M = 75.3$ years (range 65–101) and had $M = 13.7$ years of education (range 3–21).

Psychometric properties

The CASI was standardized on four samples of residents in USA (two centres) and Japan (two centres), which had similar demographic features – descriptive data for the Los Angeles sample are shown in Data box 3.5 (Teng et al., 1994). CASI and CASI-Short scores were also very similar among the groups. Significant age and education biases were documented in all samples and these were also found by Lin et al. (2002) in their epidemiological study in Taiwan (see Box 3.5).

Box 3.5

Validity:	Construct: *Discriminant*: Graves et al.: Differential diagnosis between AD vs no dementia using a cut-off score of 86/87: sensitivity 97%, specificity 92%
Reliability:	Inter-rater: No information available
	Test–retest: No information available *Practice effects:* No information available
Responsiveness:	No information available

Comment

The CASI is a carefully developed instrument that utilizes the best items from established instruments and has been refined through pilot testing for its applicability to two cultures. As a screening test, it provides a good sampling of pertinent domains, a particular strength being the inclusion of items examining executive skills (abstraction, judgement and generativity), which are usually absent from such instruments. Although the CASI is lacking in psychometric detail, it is derived from instruments with known reliability and validity. Like many other cognitive screening tests, however, age and education biases are, as noted by Lin et al. (2002), "clear and unambiguous", highlighting the need for cut-off scores for different education groups in an attempt to reduce false-positive rates in people with limited formal education. These are available from Graves et al. (1992) and McCurry et al. (1999).

Key references

Graves, A. B., Teng, E. L., Larson, E. B., & White, L. R. (1992). Education in cross-cultural dementia screening: Applications to a new instrument. *Neuroepidemiology*, *11*, 107.

Lin, K.-N., Wang, P.-N., Liu, C.-Y., Chen, W.-T., Lee, Y.-C., & Liu, H.-C. (2002). Cutoff scores of the Cognitive Abilities Screening Instrument, Chinese version in screening of dementia. *Dementia and Geriatric Cognitive Disorders*, *14*(4), 176–182.

McCurry, S. M., Edland, S. D., Teri, L., Kukull, W. A., Bowen, J. D., McCormick, W. C., et al. (1999). The Cognitive Abilities Screening Instrument (CASI): Data from a cohort of 2524 cognitively intact elderly. *International Journal of Geriatric Psychiatry*, *14*(10), 882–888.

Teng, E. L., Hasegawa, K., Homma, A., Imai, Y., Larson, E., Graves, A., et al. (1994). The Cognitive Abilities Screening Instrument (CASI): A practical test for cross-cultural epidemiological studies of dementia. *International Psychogeriatrics*, *6*(1), 45–58.

Cognitive Abilities Screening Instrument

Teng et al. (1994)

Name ______________________________ ID No. ☐☐☐☐☐☐

Date (dd-mm-yy) ☐☐ ☐☐ ☐☐ Examiner ______________ ☐☐

SEX ☐ 1 = male ☐ 2 = female

EDUCATION (years of schooling completed) (code 99 = Unk/Refused) ☐☐

Testing start time (hr:mins) ____:____

Item	Score
1. WHERE WERE YOU BORN?	
City (Town/Village) [0 1]	
State/Prefecture [0 1]	BPL
add above 2 scores then circle the answer →	2 / 1 / 0
2. WHEN WERE YOU BORN?	BYR
Year — Accurate	2
Year — Missed by 1–3 years	1
Year — Missed by >3 years	0
Month [0 1]	
Date [0 1]	BDAY
add above 2 scores then circle the answer →	2 / 1 / 0
3. HOW OLD ARE YOU?	AGE
Accurate	2
Missed by 1–3 years	1
Missed by >3 years	0
4. HOW MANY MINUTES ARE THERE IN AN HOUR? or HOW MANY DAYS ARE THERE IN A YEAR? *(Score 2 if either question answered correctly)*	MNT 2 / 0
5. IN WHAT DIRECTION DOES THE SUN SET? *(If confused, may provide 4 choices)*	SUN 2 / 0

Item	Score
Select version #, then circle corresponding words in Question 8 and Question 22	VRS# 1 / 2 / 3
6. a. I AM GOING TO SAY 3 WORDS FOR YOU TO REMEMBER. REPEAT THEM AFTER I HAVE SAID ALL THREE	RGS1 3 / 2 / 1 / 0
☐ 1. SHIRT ____ BROWN ____ HONESTY ____	
☐ 2. SHOES ____ BLACK ____ MODESTY ____	
☐ 3. SOCKS ____ BLUE ____ CHARITY ____	
b. If participated can't answer the first time, elaborate and repeat up to a total of 3 times. Score last performance.	RGS2 3 / 2 / 1 / 0
7. I SHALL SAY SOME NUMBERS, AND YOU REPEAT WHAT I SAY BACKWARDS. FOR EXAMPLE, IF I SAY 1–2, YOU SAY 2–1. OK? REMEMBER: YOU REPEAT WHAT I SAY BACKWARDS.	
(Rate: 1 digit/second)	
1–2–3 (If unable, coach for 3–2–1, but score 0)	DBA 1 / 0
6–8–2	DBB 2 / 0
(If score is 0 in both DBA and DBB, score DBC 0) 3–5–2–9	DBC 2 / 0
8. WHAT THREE WORDS DID I ASK YOU TO REMEMBER EARLIER?	RC1A
Spontaneous recall	1.5
After: "one word was something to wear"	1
After "Was it SHOES, SHIRT, or SOCKS"?	0.5
Still incorrect	0
	RC1B
Spontaneous recall	1.5
After: "one word was a color"	1
After "Was it BLUE, BLACK, or BROWN"?	0.5
Still incorrect	0
	RC1B
Spontaneous recall	1.5
After: "one word was a good personal quality"	1
After "Was it HONESTY, CHARITY, or MODESTY"?	0.5
Still incorrect	0
Unless recall is perfect, give another reminder of the 3 words.	

(For the first error only: score 0, but provide the correct answer. If subject asks examiner to repeat answer from previous step, provide the answer but score 0 at that step.)

9. a. FROM 100, TAKE AWAY 3 = HOW MANY? (97) — SUB3A: 1 / 0

b. AND TAKE AWAY 3 FROM THAT EQUALS? (94) — SUB3B: 1 / 0

(If a. and b. are both scored 0, score part c. 0)

c. Repeat "AND TAKE AWAY 3 AGAIN EQUALS?" three more times. 1 point each (91 88 85) — SUB3C: 3 / 2 / 1 / 0

10. WHAT IS TODAY'S DATE?

[YEAR]	Accurate	YR 4
	Missed by 1 year	2
	Missed by 2–5 years	1
	Missed >= 6 years	0
[MONTH]	Accurate or within 5 days	MO 2
	Missed by 1 month	1
	Missed >= 2 months	0
[DATE]	(of the month) Accurate	DATE 3
	Missed 1 or 2 days	2
	Missed 3–5 days	1
	Missed >= 6 days	0

11. WHAT DAY OF THE WEEK IS TODAY? — DAY: Accurate 1; Inaccurate 0

12. WHAT SEASON ARE WE IN? *(may provide 4 choices if necessary)* — SSH: Accurate within 1 month 1; Missed by > 1 month 0

13. a. WHAT ______________ ARE WE IN?

State [0 2]

City/Town/Village [0 2]

add above 2 scores then circle the answer → SPA: 4 / 2 / 0

b. IS THIS PLACE A HOSPITAL (CLINIC). A STORE ( ), OR HOME? — SPB: 1 / 0

14. WHAT ANIMALS HAVE 4 LEGS? TELL ME AS MANY AS YOU CAN (30 sec.)

ANML — *number of correct answers:* 0 1 2 3 4 5 6 7 8 9 10

15. AN ORANGE AND A BANANA ARE BOTH FRUIT.
(pause for 2 sec. then ask:)
(coach for correct answer if needed for "a." only)

a. AN ARM AND A LEG ARE BOTH ...?

Body parts, limbs, extremities	2
Long, bend, muscles, bones, etc.	1
Incorrect, DK: tells difference	0

b. LAUGHING AND CRYING ARE BOTH ...?

Expressions of feelings/emotions	2
Other correct answer	1
Incorrect, DK: tells difference	0

c. EATING AND DRINKING ARE BOTH ...?

Necessary bodily functions	2
Other correct answer	1
Incorrect, DK: tells difference	0

add above 3 scores then circle the answer → SIM: 6 / 5 / 4 / 3 / 2 / 1 / 0

16. a. WHAT ACTIONS WOULD YOU TAKE IF YOU SAW YOUR NEIGHBOR'S HOUSE CATCHING FIRE?
(prompt "WHAT ELSE MIGHT YOU DO?" once only, if necessary)

No. of appropriate actions: 0 1 2

b. WHAT ACTIONS WOULD YOU TAKE IF YOU LOST A BORROWED UMBRELLA?
1 point for each category of actions:

- Inform/Apologize
- Replace/Compensate 0 1 2

c. WHAT WOULD YOU DO IF YOU FOUND AN ENVELOPE THAT WAS SEALED, ADDRESSED AND HAD A NEW STAMP?

Mail	2
Try to locate owner	1
Inappropriate action	0

add above 3 scores then circle the answer → JGMT: 6 / 5 / 4 / 3 / 2 / 1 / 0

17. a. REPEAT EXACTLY WHAT I SAY:
"HE WOULD LIKE TO GO HOME."

Correct	RPTA 2
1 or 2 missed or wrong words	1
>= 3 missed or wrong words	0

(for each part of 17b, score 1 only if repeated exactly as given)

b. NOW REPEAT ...

"THIS YELLOW CIRCLE [0 1]
IS HEAVIER THAN [0 1]
BLUE SQUARE" [0 1]

add above 3 scores then circle the answer → RPTB: 3 / 2 / 1 / 0

18. PLEASE DO THIS:
(Point to statement "RAISE YOUR HAND")

	READ
Raises hand without prompting	1.5
Raises hand after prompting	1
Reads correctly, but does not raise hand	0.5
Neither reads nor obeys	0

19. LET ME HAVE A SAMPLE OF YOUR HANDWRITING.
PLEASE WRITE:
(HE) WOULD LIKE TO GO HOME. (1 min.)
(may dictate 1 word at a time if necessary)

WRITE

0 0.5 1 1.5 2 2.5 2.5

20. PLEASE COPY THIS:
(show pentagons – 1 minute)

	Left Pentagon	Right Pentagon
5 approx. equal sides	4	4
5 but un-equal (> 2:1) sides	3	3
Any other enclosed figure	2	2
>= 2 lines but without closure	1	1
Less than 2 lines	0	0

	Intersection:
4-cornered	2
Not 4-cornered enclosure	1
No enclosure	0

add above 3 scores then circle the answer →

DRAW: 10 9 8 7 6 5 4 3 2 1 0

(note: for question 21, do not repeat any part of the command)
(use non-dominant hand)

21. TAKE THIS PAPER WITH YOUR

			CMD
L (R) HAND	[0	1]	3
FOLD IT IN HALF, AND	[0	1]	2
HAND IT BACK TO ME.	[0	1].	1
add above 3 scores then circle the answer →			0

22. WHAT THREE WORDS DID I ASK
YOU TO REMEMBER EARLIER?

	RC2A
Spontaneous recall	1.5
After: "one word was something to wear"	1
After was it SHOES, SHIRT, or SOCKS?"	0.5
Still incorrect	0

	RC2B
Spontaneous recall	1.5
After: "one word was a color"	1
After was it BLUE, BLACK, or BROWN?"	0.5
Still incorrect	0

	RC2C
Spontaneous recall	1.5
After: "one word was a good personal quality"	1
After was it HONESTY, CHARITY, or MODESTY?"	0.5
Still incorrect	0

23. WHAT DO WE CALL THIS PART OF THE FACE/BODY?
(2 sec. each)

			BODY
FOREHEAD	[0	.3]	1.5
CHIN	[0	.3]	1.2
SHOULDER	[0	.3]	0.9
ELBOW	[0	.3]	0.6
WRIST	[0	.3]	0.3
add above 5 scores then circle the answer →			0

24. WHAT IS THIS? *(show one at a time, any order OK)*

			OBJA
SPOON	[0	.3]	0.6
COIN	[0	.3]	0.3
add above 2 scores then circle the answer →			0

			OBJB
TOOTHBRUSH	[0	.3]	0.9
KEY	[0	.3]	0.6
COMB	[0	.3]	0.3
add above 3 scores then circle the answer →			0

(Total number of objects either named spontaneously or repeated correctly after coaching.)

RPNM: 0 1 2 3 4 5

25. REMEMBER THESE FIVE OBJECTS!
(Wait for 5 sec.: cover, then ask:)

WHAT 5 OBJECTS DID I JUST SHOW YOU?
(Any order is OK, circle the correct ones.)

SPOON COIN TOOTHBRUSH KEY COMB

0.5 points each →

RCOBJ: 3.0 2.4 1.8 1.2 0.6 0

Finish time (hr:min) ______:______ Duration (minutes) [ ][ ]

VALIDITY OF SCORE

Valid	1
Probably invalid: poor hearing	2
Probably invalid: poor eyesight	3
Probably invalid: impaired motor control	4
Probably invalid: language barrier	5
Probably invalid: impaired alertness or attentiveness	6
Probably invalid: significant physical or mental discomfort	7
Probably invalid: other reasons (specify):	8

RAISE YOUR HAND

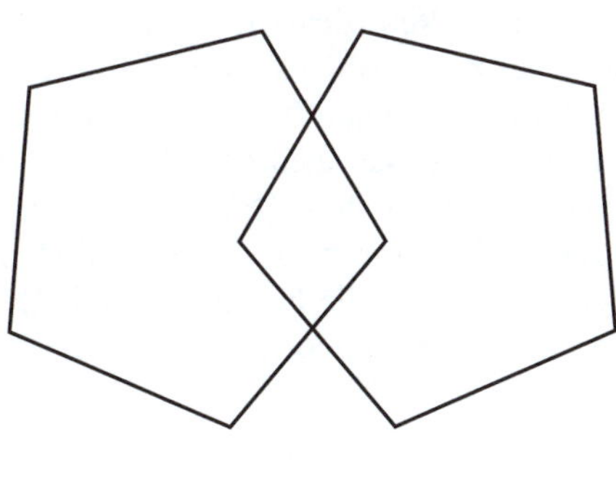

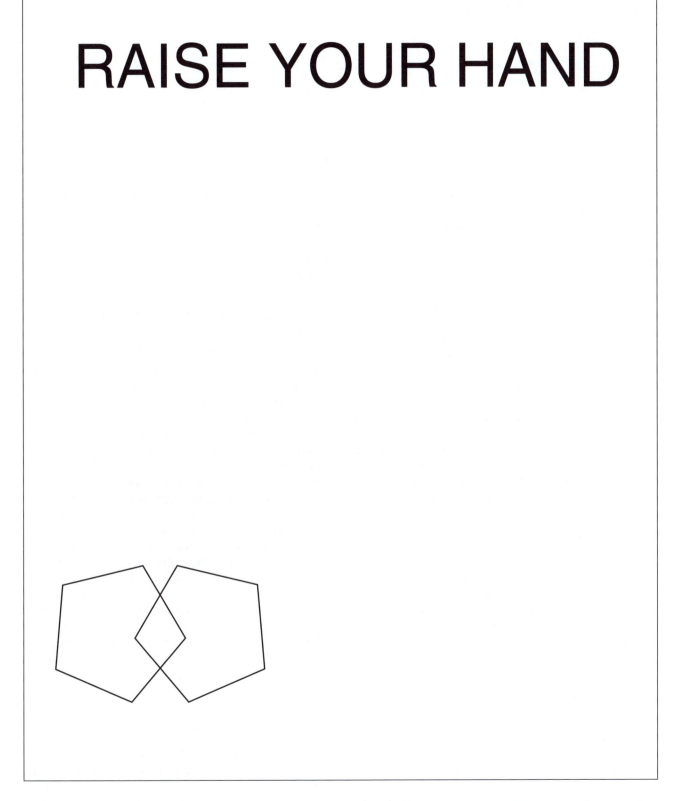

Acknowledgement: From Teng, E. L. et al. (1994). The Cognitive Abilities Screening Instrument (CASI): A practical test for cross-cultural epidemiological studies of dementia. *International Psychogeriatrics*, *6*(1), 45–58, Appendix 1, pp. 56–57, reproduced by permission of Cambridge University Press.

Cognitive Failures Questionnaire (CFQ)

Broadbent, Cooper, Fitzgerald, and Parkes (1982)

Source

Two versions of the CFQ, self and informant, each with different item content, are available in appendices to Broadbent et al. (1982), and are reproduced below.

Purpose

The CFQ is a self-rating scale, designed to measure "minor everyday slips or errors . . . [which] may involve perceptual failures, or failures of memory, or actions which are misdirected" (Broadbent et al., 1982, p. 1). It was intended to sample a broader range of cognitive processes than memory and to be used as an external validity measure beyond laboratory-based cognitive tests. The CFQ originates from the perspective of cognitive psychology, and was designed for the general population rather than as a clinical instrument. Even so, it has been used with specialized samples, including older people (Knight, McMahon, Green, & Skeaff, 2004; Rabbit & Abson, 1990) and people with traumatic brain injury (Hart, Whyte, Junghoon, & Vaccaro, 2005).

Item description

The self-version of the CFQ contains 25 items, sampling the areas of memory, perception and action. The eight-item informant version of the CFQ uses the same Likert rating scale, but comprises different, more generic items: absent-mindedness, lack of concentration, forgetfulness, failure to notice things, clumsiness, indecision, disorganization, and irritability.

Scale development

In developing the CFQ, the authors drew up a set of 25 items, based on their personal experiences of cognitive failures. An early version also included five items taken from the Lie Scale of the Eysenck Personality Questionnaire, included to determine "the willingness of the person to admit to damaging facts about themselves" (Broadbent et al., 1982, p. 4). These were subsequently discarded based on results of preliminary studies. Various response and scoring formats were trialled in different samples, six of which (total $n = 910$) are described in Broadbent et al. (1982). The informant version with different item content (see above) was developed to measure "those aspects of cognitive failures which are apparent to others; unfortunately some failures are likely to remain unknown to anybody except the person who suffers them" (p. 8).

Administration procedures, response format and scoring

The CFQ is designed for self-completion, and administration is quick and easy. Ratings are made from the perspective of cognitive failures that have occurred in the preceding 6 months.

Items on the self-version are rated on a 5-point scale: 0 (never), 1 (very rarely), 2 (occasionally), 3 (quite often), 4 (very often). The total scores ranges from 0 to 100, with higher scores indicating more frequent cognitive failures. The informant version uses the same 5-point scale, resulting in a score range from 0 to 32.

Normative data for an older sample are available in Knight et al. (2004). As part of a broader study, 270 community volunteers aged 65 years and older from the Dunedin area in New Zealand were administered the CFQ and other measures. The total CFQ score was $M = 32.10$ ($SD = 10.66$). There were no significant differences between the subset aged 65–74 years ($n = 161$, $M = 31.2$, $SD = 11.17$) versus ≥ 75 years ($n = 109$, $M = 33.42$, $SD = 9.75$), nor were there significant differences for sex, scores on the National Adult Reading Test, years of education, or scores on the Mini-Mental State Examination.

Psychometric properties

The samples referred to in Broadbent et al. (1982), totalling $n = 910$, came from different researchers in the UK, but limited methodological details are provided. Moreover, the studies were conducted at different stages of development of the CFQ, with the result that the data from the various samples are not comparable and cannot be pooled. Data on concurrent validity were cited from the results of studies by Reason, as well as Weeks. Not all results have provided support for concurrent validity, however: Weeks found no evidence of an association with standard intelligence tests (Mill Hill Vocabulary $r = -.16$ ($n = 128$), Ravens Progressive Matrices $r = -.15$ ($n = 51$)). Similarly, in a sample of 182 older people ($M = 81.1$ years), Moore et al. (2007) found low correlation with the Cognitive Assessment Screening Test – Revised (CAST-R; $r = -.12$), but higher correlation with the mental component of the Health Survey Short Form (SF36; $r = .49$). Knight et al. (2004) also found significant correlation with the Geriatric Depression Rating Scale ($r = .49$, $p < .001$). Broadbent et al. report work from Melhuish who, as part of a study on stress in middle management, administered the CFQ-informant version to a sample of 171 males and 82 females. The spouse of each participant also completed the CFQ with respect to the participant, providing information on participant-proxy agreement.

The underlying factor structure of the CFQ has been explored in a number of studies and a variable number of factors has been reported. That of Broadbent et al. (1982) was unidimensional, largely supported by Larson, Alderton, Neideffer, and Underhill (1997), using data from 2379 Navy personnel, who identified a two-factor solution (General Cognitive Failures and "a minor name-processing factor"). Other researchers have provided support for a multidimensional structure, however, including that reported by Wallace (2004) with 709 college students. Confirmatory factor analysis was used to examine the factor solutions of previous researchers using LISREL. The best fitting model was that previously reported by Wallace, Kass, and Stanny (2002) with 335 college students. Four factors were extracted, accounting for 54% of the variance: Memory, Distractibility, Blunders and Names. Results of studies reported in Broadbent et al. (1982), except where otherwise stated, are summarized in Box 3.6.

Box 3.6

Validity:	Criterion: *Concurrent:* Reason (cited in Broadbent): $n = 94$ students using self-report cognitive measures: $r = .59$ with a "forgetting scale", $r = .62$ with an "absent-mindedness questionnaire", $r = .57 - .58$ with "slips of action" scales;
	Broadbent: with Middlesex Hospital Questionnaire, a symptom inventory: multiple
	samples total score *tau* $= .22 - .54$ (all $p < .01$)
	Moore et al.: with CAST-R $r = -.12$, but $r = .49$ with SF36
	Construct: *Internal consistency:* Broadbent: Using an earlier 4-point scale, Cronbach alpha: .89
	Wallace: Cronbach alpha: .96
	Knight et al.: Cronbach alpha .89
	Factor structure: variable: Broadbent: 1 factor
	Wallace et al.: 4 factors: Memory (8 items), Distractibility (9 items), Blunders (7 items), Names (2 items)
Reliability:	Inter-rater: Not applicable for self-version; no information for informant version
	Test–retest: Weeks (cited in Broadbent): 21 weeks: $r = .82$ ($n = 57$) – 65 weeks: $r = .80$ ($n = 32$)
Responsiveness:	No information available

Comment

To date, the main application of the CFQ has been in cognitive psychology and its use in people with ABI has been limited. Part of the reason may be that, unlike objective cognitive tests, the CFQ shows no differences among age groups, even those as diverse as the second versus sixth decades of life (Kramer, Humphrey, Larish, Logan, & Strayer, 1994). Nor does it show any significant correlation with tests of intelligence, thereby not meeting one of the aims of it being used as an external validity measure of laboratory-based cognitive tests. By contrast, correlations with mood are relatively strong. It has been suggested that these patterns of results, which have been replicated in independent samples, may indicate that the CFQ is more closely related to non-cognitive processes, such as the willingness to disclose cognitive failures, than to cognitive impairments. Broadbent et al. (1982), however, comment that "there is some evidence that high scores do correspond to a true liability to make such failures rather than simply to report them" (p. 9). Nonetheless, in the area of ABI, the value of the CFQ may not be so much as a measure of cognitive impairments, as its application for other purposes, such as that of Hart et al. (2005) who used the CFQ to examine discrepancies between self and informant ratings as a measure of awareness of deficits. They considered it particularly advantageous because the CFQ addresses everyday cognitive lapses, rather than being a scale developed for a clinical population.

Key references

Broadbent, D. E., Cooper, P. F., Fitzgerald, P., & Parkes, K. R. (1982). The Cognitive Failures Questionnaire (CFQ) and its correlates. *British Journal of Clinical Psychology*, *21*(Pt 1), 1–16.

Hart, T., Whyte, J., Junghoon, K., & Vaccaro, M. (2005). Executive function and self-awareness of "real-world" behaviour and attention deficits following traumatic brain injury. *Journal of Head Trauma Rehabilitation*, *20*(4), 333–347.

Knight, R. G., McMahon, J., Green, T. J., & Skeaff, C. M. (2004). Some normative and psychometric data for the Geriatric Depression Scale and the Cognitive Failures Questionnaire from a sample of healthy older persons. *New Zealand Journal of Psychology*, *33*(3), 163–168.

Kramer, A. F., Humphrey, D. G., Larish, J. F., Logan, G. D., & Strayer, D. L. (1994). Aging and inhibition: Beyond a unitary view of inhibitory processing in attention. *Psychology and Aging*, *9*(4), 491–512.

Larson, G. E., Alderton, D. L., Neideffer, M., & Underhill, E. (1997). Further evidence on dimensionality and correlates of the Cognitive Failures Questionnaire. *British Journal of Psychology*, *88*, 29–38.

Moore, D. J., Sitzer, D., Depp, C. A., Montross, L. P., Reichstadt, J., Lebowitz, B. D., et al. (2007). Self-administered cognitive screening for a study of successful aging among community-dwelling seniors. A preliminary study. *International Journal of Geriatric Psychiatry*, *22*(4), 327–331.

Rabbit, P., & Abson, V. (1990). "Lost and found": Some logical and methodological limitations of self-report questionnaires as tools to study cognitive ageing. *British Journal of Psychology*, *81*, 1–16.

Wallace, J. C. (2004). Confirmatory factor analysis of the Cognitive Failures Questionnaire: Evidence for dimensionality and construct validity. *Personality and Individual Differences*, *37*, 307–324.

Wallace, J. C., Kass, S. J., & Stanny, C. J. (2002). The Cognitive Failures Questionnaire revisited: Dimensions and correlates. *The Journal of General Psychology*, *129*(3), 238–256.

Cognitive Failures Questionnaire – Self version

Broadbent, Cooper, Fitzgerald, and Parkes (1982)

Name:	**Administered by:**	**Date:**

Instructions: The following questions are about minor mistakes that everyone makes from time to time, but some of which happen more often than others. We want to know how often these things have happened to you in the last 6 months. Please write the appropriate number in the space provided.

Response key:
4 = Very often
3 = Quite often
2 = Occasionally
1 = Very rarely
0 = Never

		RESPONSE
1.	Do you read something and find you haven't been thinking about it and must read it again?	______
2.	Do you find you forget why you went from one part of the house to the other?	______
3.	Do you fail to notice signposts on the road?	______
4.	Do you find you confuse right and left when giving directions?	______
5.	Do you bump into people?	______
6.	Do you find you forget whether you've turned off a light or a fire or locked the door?	______
7.	Do you fail to listen to people's names when you are meeting them?	______
8.	Do you say something and realize afterwards that it might be taken as insulting?	______
9.	Do you fail to hear people speaking to you when you are doing something else?	______
10.	Do you lose your temper and regret it?	______
11.	Do you leave important letters unanswered for days?	______
12.	Do you find you forget which way to turn on a road you know well but rarely use?	______
13.	Do you fail to see what you want in a supermarket (although it's there)?	______
14.	Do you find yourself suddenly wondering whether you've used a word correctly?	______
15.	Do you have trouble making up your mind?	______
16.	Do you find you forget appointments?	______
17.	Do you forget where you put something like a newspaper or a book?	______
18.	Do you find you accidentally throw away the thing that you want and keep what you meant to throw away – as in the example of throwing away the matchbox and putting the used match in your pocket?	______
19.	Do you daydream when you ought to be listening to something?	______
20.	Do you find you forget people's names?	______
21.	Do you start doing one thing at home and get distracted into doing something else (unintentionally)?	______
22.	Do you find you can't quite remember something although it's "on the tip of your tongue"?	______
23.	Do you find you forget what you came to the shops to buy?	______
24.	Do you drop things?	______
25.	Do you find you can't think of anything to say?	______

TOTAL SCORE: ______

Acknowledgement: Broadbent, Donald E. et al. (1982). The Cognitive Failures Questionnaire (CFQ) and its correlates. *British Journal of Clinical Psychology*, *21*, 1–16, Appendix 1, p. 15, reproduced with permission from the *British Journal of Clinical Psychology*, © The British Psychological Society.

Cognitive Failures Questionnaire for Others

Broadbent, Cooper, Fitzgerald, and Parkes (1982)

Name: **Administered by:** **Date:**

Instructions: The questions given below are about mistakes and difficulties that everybody has from time to time. We want to know how often, in your opinion, your relative or partner has shown any of these troubles during the last 6 months. After each question please tick only one of the five possible answers. Please make sure you read them carefully because for some questions "very often" is on the left side of the page and "never" is on the right, but for other questions "never" is on the left and "very often" is on the right. During the last 6 months has your relative or partner seemed to be:

1 Absent-minded, that is making mistakes in what he/she is doing because he/she is thinking something else?

☐ Very often ☐ Quite often ☐ Occasionally ☐ Very rarely ☐ Never

2. Finding it difficult to concentrate on anything because his/her attention tends to wander from one thing to another?

☐ Never ☐ Very rarely ☐ Occasionally ☐ Quite often ☐ Very often

3. Forgetful, such as forgetting where he/she has put things, or about appointments, or about what he/she has done?

☐ Very often ☐ Quite often ☐ Occasionally ☐ Very rarely ☐ Never

4. Busy thinking about his/her own affairs and so not noticing what is going on around him/her?

☐ Never ☐ Very rarely ☐ Occasionally ☐ Quite often ☐ Very often

5. Clumsy, for example, dropping things or bumping into people?

☐ Very often ☐ Quite often ☐ Occasionally ☐ Very rarely ☐ Never

6. Having difficulty in making up his/her mind?

☐ Never ☐ Very rarely ☐ Occasionally ☐ Quite often ☐ Very often

7. Disorganized, that is, getting into a muddle when doing something because of lack of planning or concentration?

☐ Very often ☐ Quite often ☐ Occasionally ☐ Very rarely ☐ Never

8. Getting unduly cross about minor matters?

☐ Never ☐ Very rarely ☐ Occasionally ☐ Quite often ☐ Very often

TOTAL SCORE: ________

Coding: 0 = Never; 1 = Very rarely; 2 = Occasionally; 3 = Quite often; 4 = Very often

Acknowledgement: Broadbent, Donald E. et al. (1982). The Cognitive Failures Questionnaire (CFQ) and its correlates. *British Journal of Clinical Psychology*, *21*, 1–16. Appendix 2, p. 16, reproduced with permission from the *British Journal of Clinical Psychology*, © The British Psychological Society.

Cognitive Log (Cog-Log)

Alderson and Novack (2003)

Source

Items of the Cog-Log are available in an appendix to Alderson and Novack (2003) and are reproduced below. Information is also available from the website of the Center for Outcome Measurement in Brain Injury (http://www.tbims.org/combi/coglog/index.html).

Purpose

The Cog-Log is an objective, clinician-administered test designed to provide a brief bedside assessment of cognitive functioning in people with severe cognitive and behavioural impairments after ABI. It has been used with people with hypoxia, stroke and traumatic brain injury (TBI). The Cog-Log is intended to be administered at frequent intervals in order to chart progress during the early stages of rehabilitation and to provide an estimate of cognitive functioning. It is a companion measure to the Orientation Log (O-Log; Jackson, Novack, & Dowler, 1998; described in Chapter 2), and is most suitable for patients scoring ≥ 15/30 on the O-Log.

Item description

Five cognitive domains are sampled in the Cog-Log using 10 items: Orientation (3 items), Anterograde memory (2 items), Concentration (2 items), Praxis (1 item) and Executive (2 items) functions.

Scale development

The Cog-Log was developed to meet the need for an easily administered instrument that was suitable for serial administration in patients with severe impairments. Limited information is available on the item selection and development process, but the authors report that they drew on their clinical experience of the types of impairments frequently encountered at the post-acute stage and that exerted an influence on rehabilitation efforts.

Administration procedures, response format and scoring

Procedures for administering and scoring the Cog-Log are clear and easy to apply. Alderson and Novack (2003) administer the Cog-Log 3 to 5 times weekly, as part of the morning patient rounds. Seven alternate forms are used for the memory items (recall of a name and address) – one for each day of the week. Administration time is short; Alderson and Novack report 7 to 10 minutes for confused patients and 5 minutes for those performing well. No administration materials are required. In the validation study, the Cog-Log was administered by a neuropsychologist and a postdoctoral fellow.

Each item is scored on a 4-point scale (0–3). Correct spontaneous responses receive 3 points; 2 or 1 points are given for various degrees of accuracy that are operationally defined for each item (e.g., number of correct repetitions, amount of prompt provided by the examiner, number of errors). The total score ranges from 0 to 30, with higher scores indicating better cognitive functioning.

Normative data provided in Alderson and Novack (2003) and shown in Data box 3.6 were derived from a sample of 83 people without ABI, mainly students. Very high scores were obtained, suggesting that the Cog-Log can be used as a criterion- or domain-referenced test. Cog-Log scores were not predicted by demographic variables (age, sex and years of education). Stepwise discriminant analysis, using data from 164 people (82 with and without brain injury) identified a cut-off score of 25, with 88.4% of people correctly classified.

Psychometric properties

One hundred and fifty patients, mainly with TBI (80%), stroke and hypoxia, were recruited from an inpatient rehabilitation hospital in the USA (Alderson & Novack, 2003; descriptive data shown in Data box 3.6). Inter-rater reliability was determined by two raters who observed a single assessment conducted by one of the raters, but independently scored by both raters. Data

Data box 3.6 Descriptive data from the standardization sample (Alderson & Novack, 2003)

	Age *M* (*SD*)	Education *M* (*SD*)	Cog-Log *M* (*SD*)	Cut-off score	Sensitivity / Specificity
Control ($n = 83$)	27.73 (5.82)	14.0 (1.4)	28.0 (1.9)	24/25	No information
Clinical ($n = 150$): (a) TBI ($n = 120$) (b) Other neurological ($n = 30$)	45.0 (18.7)	73% with high school or less	15.7 (6.5) (initial testing)		

from 19 patients were used, totalling 75 observations. Stepwise multiple regression analyses were used to examine concurrent validity in a subset of 52 patients who were administered a short battery of neuropsychological tests after emergence from post-traumatic amnesia. Validating tests included Story Recall from the Wechsler Memory Scale – Revised (WMS-R), Rey Auditory Verbal Learning Test (RAVLT), Digit Span Backwards (DSB), Trail Making Test – Part B (TMT-B). Principal components analysis (PCA) was conducted on the Cog-Log scores of 150 patients with brain injury, revealing a single factor (percentage of variance not reported).

The Mini-Mental State Examination (MMSE), along with the O-Log, was used by Penna and Novack (2007) to further establish concurrent validity in a sample 45 inpatients of a neurorehabilitation unit. Predictive validity was examined in 50 patients with TBI recruited from an inpatient rehabilitation centre (Lee, LoGalbo, Baños, & Novack, 2004). They were aged $M = 35.2$ years ($SD = 14.9$), mostly with severe injury (57.8%). At 12 months post-trauma they were assessed neuropsychologically, addressing a broad range of domains (processing speed, attention, language, memory, executive and visuospatial). Results from Alderson and Novack (2003), except where otherwise stated, are shown in Box 3.7

Box 3.7

Validity:	Criterion: *Concurrent:* Cog-Log memory items predicted WMS-R, RAVLT, – Cog-Log attention predicted DSB, TMT-B Penna and Novack: with O-Log: $r = .75$ – with MMSE: $r = .75$ *Predictive:* Lee et al.: lowest Cog-Log score in rehabilitation predicted cognitive outcome in attention, executive and visuospatial functioning at 12 months post-trauma, accounting for 10–16% of the variance beyond demographic and injury severity variables Construct: *Internal consistency:* Cronbach alpha: .78 *Factor structure*: PCA extracted 1 factor
Reliability:	Inter-rater: individual items: range $r_s = .75–1.0$; 9/10 items $r_s > .92$ Test–retest: No information available *Practice effects:* No information available
Responsiveness:	No information available

Comment

As a very brief (10 mins or less) measure of cognitive function, designed for the serial assessment of patients with severe impairments in the early recovery phase from neurological conditions of acute onset, the Cog-Log is a promising instrument and fills a gap. It complements the O-Log developed by the same research group, and makes a suitable tool for monitoring progress during the transition phase when the patient is emerging from post-traumatic amnesia and early thereafter. As acknowledged by the authors, there are some limitations regarding item content (e.g., absence of items for language and visuospatial functions); additionally co-existing motor-sensory impairments may preclude administration of those items requiring motor response. Empirical data currently available indicate that the Cog-Log is not subject to age and education biases, but confirmation of this important feature will require examination with a more representative sample. Results of validation studies to date have been positive, but more specific psychometric information is required for responsiveness, temporal stability and practice effects, which are unknown. Further information on the sensitivity and specificity of the cut-off score would also be helpful.

Key references

Alderson, A. L., & Novack, T. A. (2003). Reliable serial measurement of cognitive processes in rehabilitation: The Cognitive Log. *Archives of Physical Medicine and Rehabilitation*, *84*(5), 668–672.

Jackson, W. T., Novack, T. A., & Dowler, R.N. (1998). Effective serial measurement of cognitive orientation in rehabilitation: The Orientation Log. *Archives of Physical Medicine and Rehabilitation*, *79*(6), 718–720.

Lee, D., LoGalbo, A., P., Baños, J. H., & Novack, T. A. (2004). Prediction of cognitive abilities 1 year following traumatic brain injury from inpatient rehabilitation cognitive screening. *Rehabilitation Psychology*, *49*(2), 167–171.

Penna, S., & Novack, T. A. (2007). Further validation of the Orientation and Cognitive Logs: Their relationship to the Mini-Mental State Examination. *Archives of Physical Medicine and Rehabilitation*, *88*(10), 1360–1361.

Cog-Log

Administration and Scoring Instructions

The Cognitive Log (C-Log) is designed to be quick quantitative measure of cognition for use at bedside with rehabilitation patients. It is intended for individuals who have achieved consistent accurate orientation, such as measured by the Orientation Log (O-Log). The C-Log can be used to document cognitive progress on a daily basis when time is short, such as when rounding on patients. All items are scored from 0 to 3 for a total possible score of 30, which can be graphed for quick reference.

Date, Time, and Hospital Name: These are components of orientation that may present problems for even those who otherwise are oriented. Scoring is similar to scoring on the O-Log, with 3 points given for a spontaneous correct response, 2 points for a correct response with a logical cue, and 1 point for a correct response to multiple choice.

Repeat Address: The person is asked to repeat one of the following addresses based on the day of the week. The person is informed that the address is not of anyone they know, but is presented simply as a test of memory. If repeated accurately three times, 3 points is assigned. Correct repetition on two occasions is awarded 2 points and 1 point is assigned for correct performance on one occasion. All subjects hear and repeat the address three times. After the repetition phase, advise the person that recall of the address will be expected later.

Monday—John Brown, 42 Market Street, Chicago
Tuesday—Tim Smith, 84 Center Ave., Cleveland
Wednesday—Sally Jones, 23 North Blvd., Seattle
Thursday—Bill Jackson, 16 Maple Court, Houston
Friday—Judy Wilson, 75 Ocean Ave., Baltimore
Saturday—Bob Taylor, 37 Main Street, Los Angeles
Sunday—Susan Anderson, 58 River Road, Atlanta

20–1: The person is asked to count backwards from 20 to 1. Performance without error is assigned 3 points, one error is awarded 2 points, and two errors 1 point. Errors are corrected as they occur.

Months Reversed: The person is asked to say the months in reverse order beginning with December. The examiner can prompt the person by saying "December, November" and errors should be corrected as they occur. Prompting by the examiner to continue after stopping should be counted as an error. Performance without error is assigned 3 points, one error is awarded 2 points, and two errors one point.

30 Second Test: Without the benefit of a time piece the person is asked to estimate when 30 seconds has passed with the examiner stating "Beginning now." If the person attempts to see a clock or watch the examiner should make an attempt to stop the behavior, but not to an extent that generates a confrontation. If the person insists on looking at a time piece the item is scored 0. Score 3 points for an estimation from 25–35 seconds, 2 points for a response from 20–24 or 36–40 seconds, and 1 point for an estimate that is from 15–19 or 41–45 seconds.

Fist-Edge-Palm: The examiner demonstrates the hand positions of fist, edge, and palm two times telling the person to "Watch what I do." The person is then asked to repeat the sequence (either hand can be used) until told to stop by the examiner. Three correct repetitions is assigned 3 points, two repetitions 2 points, and one repetition 1 point.

Go/No-Go: The examiner instructs the person to "Raise your finger when I say red and then put it down. Do nothing if I say green." One practice trial is allowed. The order of presentation thereafter is: red, green, red, red, green, green. Assign 3 points for correct response on each trial, 2 points for correct response on 4 or 5 trials, and 1 point if correct on 3 or fewer trial trials.

Address Recall: The person is asked to recall the address presented earlier. Give 3 points for full, accurate recall, 2 points for partial spontaneous recall, and one point if any further information is recalled after the name of the person is provided as a prompt.

Acknowledgement: Instructions kindly provided by Dr Novack.

Summary score sheet for the Cognitive Log

Alderson and Novack (2003)

Name:

Date									
Time									
1. Date									
2. Time									
3. Hospital name									
4. Immediate recall									
5. 20–1									
6. Months backwards									
7. Time estimation									
8. Fist-edge-palm									
9. Go/no-go									
10. Delayed recall									
TOTAL SCORE									
30									
25									
20									
15									
10									
5									
0									

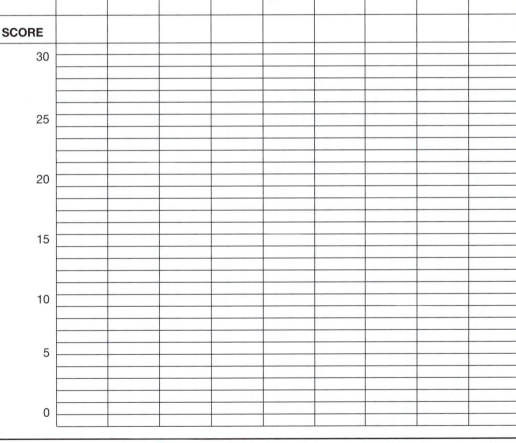

Acknowledgement: From Alderson, A. L., & Novack, T. A. (2003). Reliable serial measurement of cognitive processes in rehabilitation: The Cognitive Log. *Archives of Physical Medicine and Rehabilitation*, *84*(5), 668–672, reprinted with permission of the American Congress of Rehabilitation Medicine and the American Academy of Physical Medicine and Rehabilitation and Elsevier.

General Practitioner Assessment of Cognition (GPCOG)

Brodaty et al. (2002)

Source

Items of the GPCOG are available in an appendix to Brodaty et al. (2002) and are also reproduced below.

Purpose

The GPCOG is a combination of an objective, clinician-administered test and informant rating scale, which was developed to screen for dementia. It was primarily designed as a tool that would be taken up by frontline family physicians and general practitioners (GPs) to administer during the course of routine clinical examination.

Item description

There are two parts to the GPCOG. The Patient test comprises four items (orientation to time, clock drawing, report of a recent news event, and recall of a name and address). The Informant interview contains six items addressing historical information on the patient's everyday functioning for memory of events and conversations, word finding, managing money and medications, and use of transport.

Scale development

Development of the GPCOG arose in response to the dearth of cognitive screening tests that were acceptable to GPs as being suitable for routine administration. Previous research by Brodaty, Howarth, Mant, and Kurrle (1994) and others had shown that GPs found existing cognitive screening tests unsatisfactory and did not use them. The GPCOG was therefore designed with the following key features in mind: brief in content, easy to administer, perceived by GPs as an advance over existing instruments, and being reliable and valid. Item content for the GPCOG drew on three existing measures: the Cambridge Cognitive Examination (CAMCOG), Abbreviated Mental Test, and the Lawton and Brody Instrumental Activities of Daily Living Scale. Requirements for selection were sensitivity, non-redundancy and face validity for both patients and GPs. Initial testing occurred with 283 community dwelling older people recruited from general medical practices. Diagnosis of dementia was made using criteria of the *Diagnostic and Statistical Manual of Mental Disorders* – 4th ed. (DSM-IV) and was identified in 82 (29%) patients. Items were refined by eliminating those that were not discriminating, either in terms of the frequency of occurrence or based on the results of logistic regression analyses. Receiver operating characteristic (ROC) curves were constructed to determine optimal sensitivity and specificity. Participants and 49 out of 67 GPs anonymously responded to satisfaction surveys regarding their experience with the GPCOG.

Administration procedures, response format and scoring

The GPCOG is easy to administer and score. Clear and explicit administration and scoring instructions are included on the recording form. Administration time for the Patient test is an average of 3.3 minutes (range 2–5.8) and for the Informant interview is 1.2 minutes (range 0.5–2.5).

Correct responses for each item (or part item, as indicated on the scoring sheet) are awarded 1 point. The total score for the Patient test ranges from 0 to 9 and for the Informant interview ranges from 0 to 6, with higher scores indicating better performance.

Interpretation of scores uses the following two-stage algorithm, which is also depicted graphically below: if scores on the Patient test are 9 or < 5, the patient is assumed to be cognitively intact or impaired respectively. If Patient test scores are any of 5, 6, 7, or 8, then the Informant interview scores are used to determine impairment. In these cases, Informant scores of 3 or less will classify the patient as cognitively impaired (as shown in the GPCOG "impaired"/"not impaired" diagram).

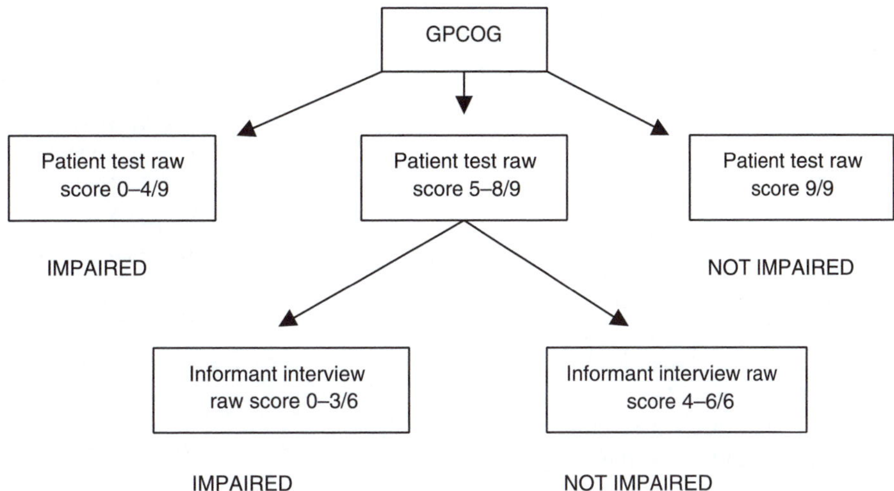

Brodaty, Kemp, and Low (2004) subsequently used a total score (range 0–15), calculated as follows, also depicted in the GPCOG "total score" diagram. If Patient test raw score is 9 (far right box), then award score = 15 for total; if Patient test raw score is 5 to 8 (middle box), then add the Informant interview raw score (i.e., 0–6, and hence possible total score range is 5–14); if Patient test raw score is < 5 (far left box), then that score remains as the total score.

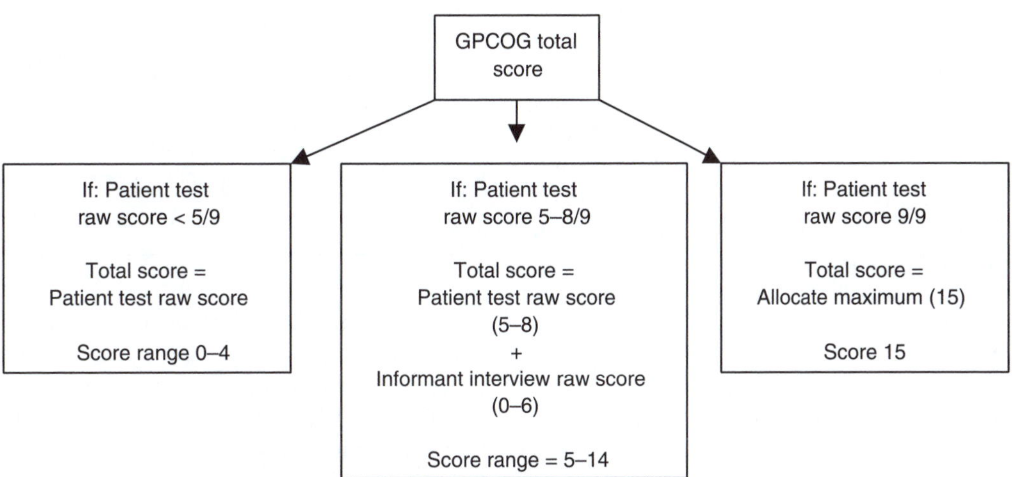

Psychometric properties

The standardization sample was used to establish psychometric properties of the GPCOG (Brodaty et al., 2002). A sample of 283 community dwelling older people (> 75 years of age, unless a memory problem was suspected in people > 50 years) was recruited from general medical practices in Sydney, Australia. Descriptive data are shown in Data box 3.7. Diagnosis of dementia

Data box 3.7 Descriptive data from the standardization sample (Brodaty et al., 2002)

	Age *M* (*SD*)	**Education**	**GPCOG**	**Cut-off score**	**Sensitivity / Specificity**
Non-dementia (*n* = 201)	79.1 (5.7)	No information	No information		Dementia vs non-dementia
Dementia (*n* = 82)	80.7 (6.8)			Patient: 7/8 → Informant: 4/5 → 2-stage algorithm →	82% / 70% 89% / 66% 85% / 86%

was made using DSM-IV criteria and was identified in 82 (29%) patients. Inter-rater reliability was examined in a subset of 37 patients. The GPCOG was readministered 5 weeks later to a subset of 71 patients (and 36 informants), along with an abridged version of the Cambridge Mental Disorder of the Elderly Examination (CAMDEX), from which was derived DSM-IV diagnosis, CAMCOG and Mini-Mental State Examination (MMSE) score. The best combination of scores to determine optimal sensitivity (85%) and specificity (86%) in the GPCOG was the two-stage clinical algorithm. Total misclassification rate was 14.2%. Using the cut-off score of < 24 for the MMSE, sensitivity (81%), specificity (76%), and misclassification rate (23.0%) were inferior to the GPCOG, but the area under the ROC curve was not significantly different from the GPCOG.

Brodaty et al. (2004) examined the influence of biographic variables on the GPCOG. Bivariate correlation coefficients were low; for example, GPCOG total score with patient's age $r = -.20$, education $r = .15$, Geriatric Depression Scale $r = -.16$, and the physical and mental health scales of the Medical Outcomes Study – Short Form Health Survey (SF-12) $r = -.08$ and $r = .01$ respectively. Results of logistic regression analysis with DSM-IV dementia diagnosis, patient age and education as predictors, found that only dementia diagnosis and age were significant individual predictors of GPCOG Patient test score. Correlation between Patient test and Informant interview scores was $r = .56$. Results from Brodaty et al. (2002), except where otherwise indicated, are shown in Box 3.8.

Box 3.8

Validity:	Concurrent: with MMSE: $r = .68$
	Construct: *Internal consistency:* Cronbach alpha: Patient test .84, Informant interview .80
	Discriminant: Differential diagnosis in classifying dementia vs no dementia using two-stage scoring algorithm: sensitivity 85%, specificity 86%
	Brodaty et al. (2004): Patients with vs without dementia had significantly lower scores for Patient test ($M = 4.22$, $SD = 2.89$ vs $M = 7.84$, $SD = 1.45$); $t = 10.72$, $p < .001$, and Informant interview ($M = 2.51$, $SD = 1.63$ vs $M = 4.73$, $SD = 1.43$); $t = 10.04$, $p < .001$
Reliability:	Inter-rater: Patient test: ICC = .75, Informant interview: ICC = .56
	Test–retest: 5 weeks: Patient test: ICC = .87, Informant interview: ICC = .84 *Practice effects:* No information available
Responsiveness:	No information available

Comment

The GPCOG fulfils the authors' original aims of producing a brief scale that is quick and easy to administer, reliable, valid and, within the context of a general medical practice, an advance over existing instruments. Average administration time is less than 4 minutes for patients and less than 2 minutes for informants. The structure of the instrument is such that it can blend seamlessly into routine history taking. Survey of GPs provided support for its high acceptance, with 88% reporting it was practical and economically viable; 98% said it was acceptable to patients. The GPCOG was also favourably received by most patients (76%). A special feature of the GPCOG is that it combines objective test results with informant report, which resulted in superior sensitivity and specificity than if either component was used in isolation. The GPCOG was carefully developed and has very good psychometric properties for such a short instrument, with high internal consistency, excellent temporal stability and inter-rater reliability for the patient test (but fair inter-rater reliability for the informant interview), demonstrated validity, and no evidence of education or mood biases. In systematic and other reviews of cognitive screening tests, the GPCOG was consistently identified as one of the few measures that met criteria for use in clinical practice (Brodaty, Low, Gibson, & Burns, 2006; Lorentz, Scanlan, & Borson, 2002).

Key references

Brodaty, H., Howarth, G. C., Mant, A., & Kurrle, S. E. (1994). General practice and dementia: A national survey of Australian GPs. *Medical Journal of Australia*, *160*(1), 10–14.

Brodaty, H., Kemp, N. M., & Low, L.-F. (2004). Characteristics of the GPCOG, a screening tool for cognitive impairment. *International Journal of Geriatric Psychiatry*, *19*(9), 870–874.

Brodaty, H., Low, L.-F., Gibson, L., & Burns, K. (2006). What is the best dementia screening instrument for general practitioners to use? *American Journal of Geriatric Psychiatry*, *14*(5), 391–400.

Brodaty, H., Pond, D., Kemp, N. M., Luscombe, G., Harding,

L., Berman, K., et al. (2002). The GPCOG: A new screening test for dementia designed for general practice. *Journal of American Geriatrics Society*, *50*(3), 530–534.

Lorentz, W. J., Scanlan, J. M., & Borson, S. (2002). Brief screening tests for dementia. *Canadian Journal of Psychiatry*, *47*(8), 723–733.

General Practitioner Assessment of Cognition

Brodaty et al. (2002)

Name:	**Administered by:**	**Date:**

PATIENT EXAMINATION

Instructions: Unless specified, each question should only be asked once

Name and address for subsequent recall test

1. I am going to give you a name and address. After I have said it, I want you to repeat it. Remember this name and address because I am going to ask you to tell it to me again in a few minutes: John Brown, 42 West Street, Kensington. (Allow a maximum of 4 attempts but do not score yet.)

	Correct	Incorrect
TIME ORIENTATION		
2. What is the date? (exact only) ____________	☐	☐
CLOCK DRAWING (visuospatial functioning) – use page with printed circle		
3. Please mark all the numbers to indicate the hours of a clock (correct spacing required)	☐	☐
4. Please mark in hands to show 10 minutes past eleven o'clock (11:10)	☐	☐
INFORMATION		
5. Can you tell me something that happened in the news recently? (recently = in the last week) ____________	☐	☐
RECALL		
6. What was the name and address I asked you to remember?		
John	☐	☐
Brown	☐	☐
42	☐	☐
West (St)	☐	☐
Kensington	☐	☐

TOTAL CORRECT: ________

SCORING GUIDELINES:

Clock drawing: For a correct response to question 3, the numbers 12, 3, 6, and 9 should be in the correct quadrants of the circle and the other numbers should be approximately correctly placed. For a correct response to question 4, the hands should be pointing to the 11 and the 2, but do not penalize if the respondent fails to distinguish the long and short hands.

Information: Respondents are not required to provide extensive details, as long as they demonstrate awareness of a recent news story. If a general answer is given, such as "war", "a lot of rain", ask for details – if unable to give details, the answer should be scored as incorrect.

General Practitioner Assessment of Cognition

Brodaty et al. (2002)

Name:	**Administered by:**	**Date:**

INFORMANT INTERVIEW

Ask the informant: “Compared to a few years ago,”

	RESPONSE			
	Yes	**No**	**Don’t Know**	**N/A**
1. Does the patient have more trouble remembering things that have happened recently?	☐	☐	☐	
2. Does he or she have more trouble recalling conversations a few days later?	☐	☐	☐	
3. When speaking, does the patient have more difficulty in finding the right word or tend to use the wrong words more often?	☐	☐	☐	
4. Is the patient less able to manage money and financial affairs (e.g., paying bills, budgeting)?	☐	☐	☐	☐
5. Is the patient less able to manage his or her medication independently?	☐	☐	☐	☐
6. Does the patient need more assistance with transport (either private or public)?	☐	☐	☐	☐

TOTAL (for “No” RESPONSE): ______

Acknowledgement: Brodaty, H. et al. (2002). The GPCOG: A new screening test for dementia designed for general practice. *Journal of the American Geriatrics Society*, *50*, 530–534, Appendix, p. 534, by permission of Wiley-Blackwell Publishers.

Hopkins Competency Assessment Test (HCAT)

Janofsky, McCarthy, and Folstein (1992)

Source

Stimulus materials for the HCAT are provided in Janofsky et al. (1992), and the essays, along with the questions, are reproduced below.

Purpose

The HCAT is an objective, clinician-administered test designed to provide a quantitative assessment of a patient's clinical competency for the specific purposes of making medical treatment decisions and writing advance directives. The authors note that the HCAT "does not determine legal competency but rather is used as an aid to the clinician in forming an opinion about clinical competency" (Janofsky et al., 1992, p. 132).

Item description

The HCAT comprises a short essay that describes informed consent and enduring power of attorney. The essay is reproduced at three reading levels. The patient is required to answer six standardized questions about the essay. Four of the six questions (2, 3, 4 and 6) consist of a single item, and the remaining two questions (1 and 5) contain four and two items respectively, making 10 items in all.

Scale development

Janofsky et al. (1992) report that development of the HCAT was based on the principle of informed consent for medical procedures; namely that the patient (i) understands what the intended medical procedure entails, (ii) is aware of the risks, advantages and alternatives, and (iii) knows that consent is voluntary. No specific details are provided regarding the procedures used to construct and refine the content of the essay. The decision to write the essay at the various reading levels was based on literature examining comprehension of written information and pilot testing of the essay with patients. A computer program based on the Flesch-Kincaid method was used for this purpose. The essay was written at the 13th grade, 8th grade and 6th grade reading levels and the six questions were written at the 6th grade level.

Administration procedures, response format and scoring

The patient is given the 13th grade essay in enlarged print (14 point) and asked to read it while at the same time the examiner also reads it aloud. This is followed by the questions and the patient's responses are recorded. For patients who score ≤ 7, the 8th grade essay is presented and the procedures repeated. Again, if the patient scores ≤ 7, the procedure is repeated with the 6th grade essay. Administration time is approximately 10 minutes. Training in HCAT administration is advisable, given that the rater for the psychometric studies (a medical student) received such training.

The 10 items from the six questions of the HCAT are each awarded 1 point. The total score ranges from 0 to 10, with higher scores reflecting better performance. The cut-off score of 3/4 identifies patients who are not clinically competent to give consent to medical procedures.

Psychometric properties

The validation sample comprised 41 patients recruited from medical ($n = 16$) and geriatric psychiatry ($n = 25$) wards of the Johns Hopkins Hospital, Baltimore, Maryland, USA (Janofsky et al., 1992). Twenty-nine patients (71%) had (unspecified) central nervous system deficits. Descriptive data are shown in Data box 3.8. A clinical competency examination performed by a forensic psychiatrist within 24 hours of the HCAT rating was used to calibrate the HCAT and 14 out of 41 patients were classified as incompetent. Janofsky et al. do not provide any specific descriptive data for HCAT scores for the two subgroups, although it is noted that all 14 patients classified as incompetent scored 3/10 or less on the HCAT, and all 27 competent patients scored 4/10 or higher. The Mini-Mental State Examination (MMSE)

Data box 3.8 Descriptive data from the standardization sample (Janofsky et al., 1992)

	Age *M* (*SD*)	**Education** *M* (*SD*)	**HCAT** *M* (*SD*)	**Cut-off score**	**Sensitivity / Specificity**
Patients ($n = 41$):	54.0 (18.9)	9.7 (4.2)		3/4	100% / 100%
Medical ($n = 16$)			5.75 (3.23)		
Psychiatric ($n = 25$)			5.04 (3.38)		

was also administered, but the authors did not report any results of statistical analysis. Comparisons using the MMSE data from the Janofsky et al. sample were subsequently reported by Silberfeld, Stephens, and O'Rourke (1994). Inter-rater reliability was initially examined by Janofsky et al. in a pilot group of 16 consecutive administrations of the HCAT by two trained raters. Inter-rater reliability was also evaluated by Barton, Mallick, Orr, and Janofsky (1996) in their study of 44 nursing home residents.

Using the cut-off score of 3/4, Janofsky et al. (1992) reported that both sensitivity and specificity of the HCAT were 100% against the formal clinical competency assessment of the forensic psychiatrist. In this respect, the HCAT was superior to the MMSE (using a cut-off score of 23/24, sensitivity and specificity were 74% and 100% respectively). A subsequent study by Holzer, Gansler, Moczynski, and Folstein (1997) did not replicate these unequivocally accurate results for the HCAT: data provided in their report indicated correct classification of incompetent patients was 81% and competent patients was 73%. Results of the above studies are shown in Box 3.9.

Comment

At the time the HCAT was developed there was no objective test to inform the health practitioner's opinion about a patient's capacity to consent to medical treatment; rather assessment required a specialized and time-consuming clinical competency evaluation. The HCAT filled this gap by providing a quick, standardized, sensitive and valid assessment. The HCAT is not without its critics, however, and concern has been raised over its focus on comprehension and its neglect of reasoning ability, an integral feature of competency (Lavin, 1992; Palmer, Nayak, Dunn, Appelbaum, & Jeste, 2002). These authors also commented on the risk level of various medical procedures, which the HCAT does not address – a patient may be competent to consent to having blood drawn, but not to amputation of a gangrenous limb. These issues highlight the complexity of assessing competency. Nonetheless, there is a place for brief tests such as the HCAT, as the study of Barton et al. (1996) graphically demonstrated. Using HCAT criteria, 45% (20/44) of nursing home residents were identified as clinically incompetent, but only 65% (13/20) had been so identified by nursing home staff. Yet none of even these 13 residents had (the legally required) surrogate decision makers appointed. Arguably, a quick and easy procedure such as the HCAT could be used to advantage in such settings. Janofsky and colleagues (1992) point to the greater classification accuracy of the HCAT over other cognitive screening tests, such as the MMSE, thus highlighting the need for context-specific instruments. They suggest that the method used for the HCAT would be suitable for the development of other needed instruments of clinical competency, such as for testamentary capacity.

Box 3.9

Validity:	Construct: *Discriminant:* Silberfeld et al.: HCAT-competent MMSE $M = 25.70$ ($SD = 4.50$) vs HCAT-not competent MMSE $M = 12.90$ ($SD = 7.50$); $t = -6.84$, $p < .001$
	Janofsky et al.: Differential diagnosis between competent vs not competent using a cut-off score of 3/4: sensitivity 100%, specificity 100%
	Holzer et al.: Differential diagnosis between competent vs not competent using a cut-off score of 3/4: sensitivity 73%, specificity 81%
Reliability:	Inter-rater: Janofsky et al.: $r = .95$
	Barton et al: $r_s = .96–.99$
	Test–retest: No information available *Practice effects:* No information available
Responsiveness:	No information available

Key references

Barton, C. D., Mallik, H. S., Orr, W. B., & Janofsky, J. S. (1996). Clinicians' judgement of capacity of nursing home patients to give informed consent. *Psychiatric Services*, *47*(9), 956–960.

Holzer, J. C., Gansler, D. A., Moczynski, N. P., & Folstein, M. F. (1997). Cognitive functions in the informed consent evaluation process: A pilot study. *The Journal of the American Academy of Psychiatry and the Law*, *25*(4), 531–540.

Janofsky, J. S., McCarthy, R. J., & Folstein, M. F. (1992). The Hopkins Competency Assessment Test: A brief method for evaluating patients' capacity to give informed consent. *Hospital and Community Psychiatry*, *43*(2), 132–136.

Lavin, M. (1992) [Letter to the Editor]. *Hospital and Community Psychiatry*, *43*(6), 646–647.

Palmer, B. W., Nayak, G. V., Dunn, L. B., Appelbaum, P. S., & Jeste, D. V. (2002). Treatment-related decision-making capacity in middle-aged and older patients with psychosis: A preliminary study using the MacCAT-T and HCAT. *American Journal of Geriatric Psychiatry*, *10*(2), 207–211.

Silberfeld, M., Stephens, D., & O'Rourke, K. (1994). Cognitive deficit and mental capacity evaluation. *Canadian Journal on Aging*, *13*(4), 539–549.

Hopkins Competency Assessment Test – Essays

Janofsky, McCarthy, and Folstein (1992)

13th grade

Before undergoing a medical procedure, a patient must be informed about the procedure. The patient must understand what the procedure is about, the risks of the procedure, the benefits of the procedure, and alternatives to the procedure. After learning about the procedure the patient then has the option of agreeing to go forth with the procedure or not.

Patients with chronic disease may lose the ability to understand the information necessary to make responsible decisions regarding their own health care. When that time comes they will not be able to consent to medical treatment and this power must then be delegated to someone else.

Patients can leave formal legal instructions regarding what they would want to have done in specific medical situations and who they would want to make such decisions if they become unable to make them themselves. Such instructions are called a durable power of attorney.

The durable power of attorney allows patients to designate who will make medical decisions for them and what limitations, if any, are placed on the decision-making authority.

8th grade

Before a patient has a medical procedure, he must be told about the procedure by the doctor. The patient must know what the procedure is and what could go wrong. The patient should also know what are the good things that could happen as a result of the procedure and what else could be done instead of the procedure. After the patient finds out about the procedure from his doctor the patient then can decide whether to have the procedure done or not.

Patients who are sick for a long time may not be able to understand what the doctor tells them about what might need to be done. When this happens some patients are not able to give permission to their doctors to have certain tests or procedures done. Then someone else has to make their decisions for them.

There are two things such patients can do. First, the patient can tell the doctor who he wants to make decisions for him if he is unable. Second, the patient can tell the doctor directly what he wants done if he becomes unable to make decisions himself. These instructions are called a durable power of attorney.

The durable power of attorney lets patients decide who will make medical decisions for them if they are unable. It also lets the patient decide what the patient himself wants to have done if he is unable to make decisions.

6th grade

Before a doctor can do something to a patient, he must tell the patient what he is going to do. The patient must know what the doctor is going to do, what could go wrong, what could go right, and what else the doctor could do instead. After the doctor tells the patient these things, the patient may agree to let the doctor go ahead. Or the patient can tell the doctor not to go ahead.

Some patients have been sick for a long time. After a while, their thinking might not be so good. At that time, the patient might not be able to think well enough to understand what his doctor says. When that time comes he will not be able to let the doctor know what he wants the doctor to do.

Well patients can tell their doctor what they want the doctor to do. Well patients can also tell their doctor which person they would like the doctor to talk with when the patient is not able to let the doctor know what he wants done himself. Such things need to be written down on paper. This paper is called a durable power of attorney.

The durable power of attorney lets patients say who will tell the doctor what to do if the patient can't tell the doctor himself. The durable power of attorney also lets a patient say now what he wants to have done and what he doesn't want to have done if he gets sick.

Hopkins Competency Assessment Test – Questions

Janofsky, McCarthy, and Folstein (1992)

Name:	**Administered by:**	**Date:**

QUESTIONS	**ANSWERS (1 point for each correct answer)**	**SCORE**
1. What are the four things a doctor must tell a patient before beginning a procedure?	What the doctor is going to do.	______
	What could go right.	______
	What could go wrong.	______
	What else the doctor could do instead.	______
2. True or false: After learning about the procedure, the patient can decide not to have the procedure done.	True.	______
3. What can sometimes happen to the thinking of a patient who has been sick for a long time?	After a while, the patient's thinking may not be as good as is it now.	______
4. Finish the sentence: A patient whose thinking gets bad may not be able to ______________	Tell the doctor what the patient wants done.	______
5. What two things should such patients tell their doctor and family, before their thinking gets bad?	Patients can write down who else the doctor can talk to in order to make medical decisions for them.	______
	Patients can write down what medical procedures they want to have done or not have done.	______
6. What are these instructions to doctors and family called?	They are called durable powers of attorney.	______
	TOTAL SCORE:	______

Acknowledgement: Janofsky, J. S. et al. (1992). Hopkins Competency Assessment Test: A brief method for evaluating patients' capacity to give informed consent. *Hospital and Community Psychiatry*, *43*(2), 132–136, data from Table 1, p. 133, and Table 2, p. 134, by permission of American Psychiatric Publishing, Inc.

Informant Questionnaire on Cognitive Decline in the Elderly (IQCODE)

Jorm and Korten (1988)

Source

Items of the IQCODE are available in Jorm and Korten (1988), and both the original and a short form in Jorm (1994). The scale is also reproduced below.

Purpose

The IQCODE is an informant rating scale that uses informant report to measure cognitive decline from the premorbid level. It is particularly useful in situations where the person is not able to participate in cognitive assessment (e.g., because of acute illness, poor co-operation) or for people with low levels of education and literacy. It has also been used with people with mild cognitive impairment (Isella, Villa, Russo, Regazzoni, Ferraresse, & Appollonio, 2006).

Item description

The 26-item IQCODE (and its 16-item short form) rates change over the previous 10 years in "intelligence and memory . . . on everyday cognitive tasks" (Jorm & Korten, 1988, p. 209). Memory items sample both acquisition of new information and retrieval of existing knowledge; the intelligence items draw on verbal skills, as well as reasoning ability.

Scale development

Development of the IQCODE had its origins in a 39-item interview used in a research study of 64 elderly volunteers, some of whom were living in the community as well as some in residential care (Jorm & Korten, 1988). Limited information is available regarding the initial item selection process, but in the original study 13 out of the 39 items were eliminated, either because they were difficult to rate ($n = 12$) or because of low item-total correlation ($n = 1$). A number of variants have been trialled, including those that used a 5-year time frame, or a flexible one. The 16-item short form reported by Jorm (1994) was developed using principal components analysis (PCA) on pooled data collected in four previous studies. The short form was cross-validated on two samples: a community sample ($n = 945$) and a nursing home sample ($n = 100$). The short form correlated $r = .98$ with the full version and had comparable validity when compared against diagnosis. On the basis of these results, Jorm (2004) argued that there was no reason not to use the short form, which was better than the full version in detecting early decline (but poorer in discriminating among "clearly demented patients").

Administration procedures, response format and scoring

The IQCODE is completed by an informant who has known the person for at least the preceding 10 years. It has been used in both face-to-face and telephone interview (Jorm, 2004). Administration time is approximately 10 minutes.

Items are rated on a 5-point scale: 1 (much improved), 2 (a bit improved), 3 (not much change), 4 (a bit worse), 5 (much worse). A total average score is usually used (range 1–5), with lower scores indicating improvement and higher scores indicating deterioration; a score of 3 represents "no change". Based on review of all published studies on the IQCODE, Jorm (2004) recommended a cut-off score for the short form of ≥ 3.44 to indicate significant cognitive decline, this score providing a "reasonable compromise" to balance sensitivity and specificity.

Normative data on the full version of the IQCODE are available for an Australian sample of 613 respondents from a pool of 4000 names on the Canberra electoral roll, with referents (i.e., the person rated by the informant) stratified in four age groups from 70 to 85+ years (Jorm & Jacomb, 1989). The pooled data from four studies were used to develop the short form (Jorm, 1994). Cut-off scores were established using receiver operating characteristic (ROC) analysis. On the short form, 3.31/3.38 classified significant decline in cognitive functioning (sensitivity 79%, specificity 82%), and 3.27/3.30 on the long form (sensitivity 79%, specificity 83%). Jorm (2004) cites a 1997 study by Harwood and colleagues, who examined 177 older medical inpatients and used a cut-off score of 3.44, finding 100% sensitivity and 86% specificity. Mackinnon and Mulligan (1998) combined the IQCODE (cut-off score > 4.0) with MMSE (cut-off score 23/24) and found sensitivity of 93% and specificity of 81%, which was an improvement on the IQCODE alone using a cut-off score of ≥ 3.6 (90% and 65% respectively).

Psychometric properties

Jorm and colleagues have conducted a large number of studies on the psychometric properties of the IQCODE, and these, along with those conducted by other groups, have been reviewed by Jorm (2004). The original study (Jorm & Korten, 1988) was conducted with 64 people, whose health status "varied enormously". Internal consistency was .96 and correlation with the Mini-Mental State Examination (MMSE) was $r = .74$. Psychometric properties of the IQCODE were reported in more detail in a subsequent paper, using two samples: 613 respondents in the general community and 260 members of the Alzheimer's Disease and Related Dementias Society (ADARDS; Jorm & Jacomb, 1989). Jorm et al. (1996) examined 144 older males (age $M = 72.9$ years, range 66–83) with a broad range of investigations, including assessment of basic and instrumental activities of daily living (ADL), neuropsychological tests and computerized tomography (CT). Many studies have made specific examination of the influence of education (both of informants and referents) and none have found any effect (Jorm, 2004). Some of the results collated by Jorm (2004), except where otherwise stated, are shown in Box 3.10.

Comment

The IQCODE is a thoroughly researched and widely used instrument that has been translated into many languages. It has good measurement properties (although responsiveness is questionable) and other features to recommend it. Foremost among these is that it does not depend on direct assessment and hence can be used to obtain information on patients who may not be able to participate in testing. Moreover, results of multiple studies have confirmed that it is independent of the influence of education, which confounds many objective tests. Additionally, it adopts the perspective of change from a previous level of functioning, thereby controlling for premorbid factors. As Jorm and Jacomb (1989) point out, this has the dual advantages of being able to avoid the danger "that individuals who have always been dull may be mistakenly diagnosed as demented, or conversely, that individuals who were pre-morbidly very bright may be classified as normal despite substantial cognitive decline" (p. 1015). Sensitivity and specificity

Box 3.10

Validity:	Criterion *Concurrent:* 15 studies with MMSE: median $r = -.61$ (range $-.37$ to $-.78$)
	Jorm et al. (1996): with basic and instrumental ADL: $r = -.47$ to $-.50$ – with 14/28 cognitive variables: $r > .30$ – with infarcts on CT: $r = .27 - .37$
	Predictive: Jorm & Jacomb: those institutionalized the following year had poorer scores at baseline ($M = 4.72$, $SD = 0.19$) vs those who remained in the community ($M = 4.44$, $SD = 0.41$); $t = 5.32$, $p < .001$. Scores were not, however, predictive of mortality
	Construct: *Internal consistency:* 7 studies: Cronbach alpha: .93 – .95
	Factor analysis: 5 studies: PCA revealed a single general factor accounting for 42–61% of the variance
	Discriminant: Jorm & Jacomb: General population $M = 3.37$ ($SD = 0.51$) vs ADARDS sample $M = 4.67$ ($SD = 0.51$); $t = 41.69$, $p < .001$
	Harwood et al.: Differential diagnosis between dementia vs no dementia using cut-off score of ≥ 3.44: sensitivity 100%, specificity 86%
Reliability:	Inter-rater: No information available
	Test–retest: 3 days: $r = .96$
	Jorm & Jacomb: 1 year: $r = .75$
Responsiveness:	Jorm & Jacomb: significant decline in scores occurred over 12 months in ADARDS sample: Time 1 $M = 4.67$ ($SD = 0.37$) vs Time 2 $M = 4.76$ ($SD = 0.34$); $t = 5.97$, $p < .001$, $d = .2$

analyses, however, have yielded variable results and Jorm (2004) suggests that using the IQCODE in conjunction with an objective, performance-based test may improve diagnostic accuracy, as demonstrated by Mackinnon and Mulligan (1998). A possible drawback of the IQCODE is that the informant needs to have known the patient for at least 10 years, which may be a restricting factor in some cases. Moreover, like other instruments providing informant-based data, accuracy of reporting is very much dependent on the informant, and Jorm (2004) suggests that further work is required in this area to understand characteristics of the best informants.

Key references

Jorm, A. F. (1994). A short form of the Informant Questionnaire on Cognitive Decline in the Elderly (IQCODE): Development and cross-validation. *Psychological Medicine*, *24*(1), 145–153.

Jorm, A. F. (2004). The Informant Questionnaire on Cognitive Decline in the Elderly (IQCODE): A review. *International Psychogeriatrics*, *16*(3), 275–293.

Jorm, A. F., Broe, G. A., Creasey, H., Sulway, M. R., Dent, O., Fairley, M. J., et al. (1996). Further data on the validity of the Informant Questionnaire on Cognitive Decline in the Elderly (IQCODE). *International Journal of Geriatric Psychiatry*, *11*(2), 131–139.

Jorm, A. F., & Jacomb, P. A. (1989). The Informant Questionnaire on Cognitive Decline the Elderly (IQCODE): Socio-demographic correlates, reliability, validity and some norms. *Psychological Medicine*, *19*(4), 1015–1022.

Jorm, A. F., & Korten, A. E. (1988). Assessment of cognitive decline in the elderly by informant interview. *British Journal of Psychiatry*, *152*, 209–213.

Isella, V., Villa, L., Russo, A., Regazzoni, R., Ferraresse, C., & Appollonio, I. M. (2006). Discriminative and predictive power of an informant report in mild cognitive impairment. *Journal of Neurology, Neurosurgery, and Psychiatry*, *77*(2), 166–171.

Mackinnon, A., & Mulligan, R. (1998). Combining cognitive testing and informant report to increase accuracy in screening for dementia. *The American Journal of Psychiatry*, *155*(11), 1529–1535.

Informant Questionnaire on Cognitive Decline in the Elderly

Jorm and Korten (1988); Jorm (1994)

Name: **Administered by:** **Date:**

Instructions: I want you to remember what your friend or relative was like 10 years ago and compare it with what he/she is like now. 10 years ago was in [insert year]. Below are situations where this person has to use his/her memory or intelligence and I want you to indicate whether he/she has improved, stayed the same, or got worse in that situation over the past 10 years. Note the importance of comparing his/her present performances with 10 years ago. So if 10 years ago he/she always forgot where he/she had left things lying around the house, and still does, then this would be considered "Hasn't changed much."

Response key:
1 = Much improved
2 = A bit improved
3 = Not much change
4 = A bit worse
5 = Much worse

	RESPONSE
1. Recognizing the faces of family and friends	______
2. Remembering the names of family and friends	______
3. Remembering things about family and friends, e.g., occupations, birthdays, addresses *	______
4. Remembering things that have happened recently *	______
5. Recalling conversations a few days later *	______
6. Forgetting what s/he wanted to say in the middle of a conversation	______
7. Remembering his/her address and telephone number *	______
8. Remembering what day and month it is *	______
9. Remembering where things are usually kept *	______
10. Remembering where to find things that have been put in a different place from usual *	______
11. Adjusting to any change in her/his day-to-day routine	______
12. Knowing how to work familiar machines around the house *	______
13. Learning how to use a new gadget or machine around the house *	______
14. Learning new things in general *	______
15. Remembering things that happened to him/her when s/he was young	______
16. Remembering things s/he learned when s/he was young	______
17. Understanding the meaning of unusual words	______
18. Understanding magazine or newspaper articles	______
19. Following a story in a book or on TV *	______
20. Composing a letter to friends or for business purposes	______
21. Knowing about important historical events of the past	______
22. Making decisions on everyday matters *	______
23. Handling money for shopping *	______
24. Handing financial matters, e.g., the pension, dealing with the bank *	______
25. Handling everyday arithmetic problems e.g., knowing how much food to buy, knowing how long between visits from family and friends*	______
26. Using his/her intelligence to understand what's going on and to reason things through *	______

TOTAL SCORE: ______

* Items used in the short form.

Adapted from Jorm, A. F., & Korten, A. E. (1988). Assessment of cognitive decline in the elderly by informant interview. *British Journal of Psychiatry*, *152*, 209–213.

Mini-Cog

Borson, Scanlan, Brush, Vitaliano, and Dokmak (2000)

Source

A description of the Mini-Cog is provided in various papers by Borson and colleagues and the scale is reproduced below.

Purpose

The Mini-Cog is an objective, clinician-administered test, developed to identify people in the general population with cognitive impairment. It was intentionally designed to be very brief and suitable for people with different linguistic, cultural and educational backgrounds.

Item description

The Mini-Cog has three components: repetition of three unrelated words, a clock-drawing task (CDT), and recall of the three words. The word recall and clock drawing tasks are used for scoring purposes.

Scale development

Development of the Mini-Cog had its origins in a brief, freehand version of the CDT, with simple scoring procedures based on criteria used by the Consortium to Establish a Registry for Alzheimer's Disease (CERAD; Morris et al., 1989). Borson et al. (1999) found the CDT superior to the Mini-Mental State Examination (MMSE) in predicting dementia in poorly educated, non-English speakers, but in a more general population it had limited sensitivity (82%). Additionally, the omission of memory items, a core symptom in dementia, prompted the authors to include the three-word learning task from the Cognitive Abilities Screening Instrument (CASI; Teng et al., 1994): shirt, brown, honesty. Three alternate forms of the words are available. Receiver operating characteristic (ROC) curves were used to confirm the scoring algorithm used in the Mini-Cog (Scanlan & Borson, 2001). The authors have used the Mini-Cog with a range of cultural groups, including Spanish, Asian-Pacific Islander, native-American, Asian-American and African-American (although all were resident in the USA).

Administration procedures, response format and scoring

No special equipment or formal training of the clinician is required for administration of the Mini-Cog. Instructions for the CDT are provided on the recording form. Repetition of instructions is acceptable and examinees are informed to draw a larger circle, if needed. No time limit is imposed, but administration time for the entire Mini-Cog is very brief: 3.7 minutes (+/– 2) for people with dementia and 2.5 minutes (+/– 1) for normal older people (Borson et al., 2000).

One point is awarded for each correctly recalled word. The CDT is scored as normal if all the numbers are present, in the correct sequence and position, and the hands readably display the requested time. Borson et al. (1999) provide an appendix with exemplars of clocks from normal to varying degrees of abnormality (see below). In the standard method of scoring the Mini-Cog, the algorithm first uses the 3-word recall, followed by the CDT for non-extreme 3-word recall scores (i.e., scores of 1 or 2), as shown in the Mini-Cog diagram on the next page.

In a subsequent publication, Borson, Scanlan, Watanabe, Tu, and Lessig (2005) reported an alternative continuous scoring method (descriptive data shown in Data box 3.9): responses for the CDT were scored using specific criteria, with scores ranging from 0 (abnormal) to 2 (normal). For word recall 1 point is awarded for each correct response (score range 0–3). The total score thus ranges from 0 to 5, with higher scores indicating better performance. An algorithm classifies scores of 0 to 2 as representing a high likelihood of cognitive impairment and scores of 3 to 5 as low likelihood.

Psychometric properties

The Mini-Cog was validated with 249 older adults recruited from a research centre in Seattle, Washington, USA (Borson et al., 2000). The group had diverse cultural and linguistic backgrounds and only half spoke

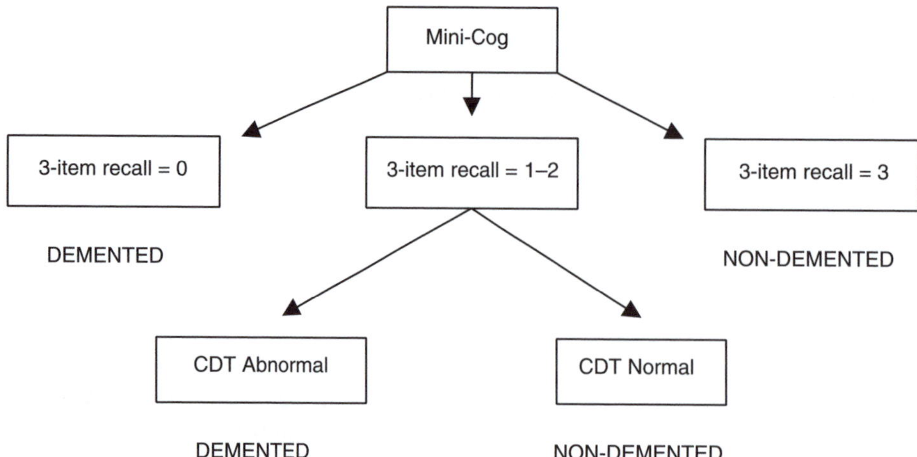

Acknowledgement: Borson, S. et al. (2000). *International Journal of Geriatric Psychiatry, 15*, Figure 1, p. 1024 © John Wiley and Sons Limited. Reproduced with permission.

Data box 3.9 Descriptive data for continuous scoring method (Borson et al., 2005)

	Age Mean	Education Mean	Mini-Cog *M* (*SD*)	Cut-off score	Sensitivity / Specificity
Control (n = 140)	73	11.5	3.9 (1.2)	2/3	77% / 83%
Mild cognitive impairment (n = 77)	74	10.4	2.5 (1.4)		
Dementia (n = 154)	78	8.5	1.2 (1.2)		

English as their primary language. An independent sample of 44 older adults was used to examine administration time of the test. Based on patient history provided by an informant using an adapted CERAD protocol and Clinical Dementia Rating (CDR) scale, participants were clinically classified as probable dementia ($n = 129$; age $M = 77.9$ years, $SD = 9.1$; education 9.8 years, $SD = 9.4$) or probable non-dementia ($n = 120$; age $M = 69.0$ years, $SD = 9.0$; education $M = 12.9$, $SD = 4.3$). Using the standard cut-off score for the MMSE (23/24) yielded 91% sensitivity and 92% specificity; those for the Mini-Cog algorithm were 99% and 93% respectively. Results of logistic regression analyses demonstrated that education and language biases exerted a very weak (and non-significant) influence on the predictive power of the Mini-Cog, in contrast to significant language biases for the MMSE. The diagnostic accuracy of the Mini-Cog was replicated in a second sample ($n = 371$, 62% classified with cognitive impairment), again purposely over-represented to sample cultural and educational diversity (Borson et al., 2005).

Sensitivity of a screening test in detecting dementia is directly linked to the base rate of cognitive impairment in a given sample and hence can be inflated in samples deliberately over-represented with specific cases. Therefore, Borson, Scanlan, Chen, and Ganguli (2003) also examined an unselected random sample of 1179 participants from an age-stratified sample of more than 17,000 older adults from 23 communities in Pennsylvania, USA. In keeping with population prevalence estimates, 6.4% of the sample was diagnosed with dementia using standard criteria. The Mini-Cog result was derived using retrospective data for the CDT drawn from the CERAD protocol, using adapted scoring procedures. As expected, sensitivity and specificity were lower than in the previously selected samples (76% and 89% respectively), and were comparable to the MMSE in this sample (71% and 94% respectively). In a community sample of 371 people, 231 of whom met criteria for cognitive impairment, Borson, Scanlan, Watanabe, Tu, and Lessig (2006) found that the Mini-Cog was more effective than primary care physicians in diagnosing cognitive impairment (84% vs 41% respectively). Results from the above studies are shown in Box 3.11.

Comment

The Mini-Cog has a number of special features. It can be administered in less than 5 minutes and is suitable for people from culturally and linguistically diverse backgrounds, as well as those with limited education. On these grounds alone, it is superior to many other cognitive screening tests that yield a high false positive rate in people with limited literacy skills. In their review of 13 cognitive screening tests with an administration time of

Box 3.11

Validity:	Construct: *Discriminant:* Borson et al. (2003): Differential diagnosis in an unselected random sample of the population classifying dementia vs no dementia using the algorithm: sensitivity 76%, specificity 89%; Borson et al. (2000): Differential diagnosis in samples purposely over-represented with people from educationally and culturally diverse backgrounds: sensitivity 99%, specificity 93%
Reliability:	Inter-rater: Borson et al. (2005, citing their own unpublished data), using score range 0–5: agreement > 95% with authors, 93% in an independent group; Borson et al. (1999): ICC = .97 for CDT Test–retest: No information available *Practice effects:* No information available
Responsiveness:	No information available

less than 10 minutes, the Mini-Cog met all eight criteria set by the authors (Lorentz, Scanlan, & Borson, 2002). Given the very favourable results of cross-cultural studies, the Mini-Cog holds promise for more universal application, pending results of future studies in countries outside the USA, especially non-Western cultures. More specific details on different aspects of the reliability of the Mini-Cog are warranted, and practice effects are unknown. Its sensitivity (76%) in an unselected population (while comparable to the MMSE) indicates that approximately 1 in 4 people in the general population with cognitive impairment will not be identified. In clinical settings, however, sensitivity of the Mini-Cog is very good and it was identified in a systematic review as one of the best measures for routine use in general practice (Brodaty, Low, Gibson, & Burns, 2006).

Key references

Borson, S., Brush, M., Gil, E., Scanlan, J., Vitaliano, P., Chen, J., et al. (1999). The Clock Drawing Test: Utility for dementia detection in multiethnic elders. *Journal of Gerontology*, *54A*(11), M534–M540.

Borson, S., Scanlan, J., Brush, M., Vitaliano, P., & Dokmak, A. (2000). The Mini-Cog: A cognitive "vital signs" measure for dementia screening in multi-lingual elderly. *International Journal of Geriatric Psychiatry*, *15*(11), 1021–1027.

Borson, S., Scanlan, J. M., Chen, P., & Ganguli, M. (2003). The Mini-Cog as a screen for dementia: Validation in a population-based sample. *Journal of the American Geriatrics Society*, *51*(10), 1451–1454.

Borson, S., Scanlan, J. M., Watanabe, J., Tu, S-P., & Lessig, M. (2005). Simplifying detection of cognitive impairment: Comparison of the Mini-Cog and Mini-Mental State Examination in a multiethnic sample. *Journal of the American Geriatrics Society*, *53*(5), 871–874.

Borson, S., Scanlan, J. M., Watanabe, J., Tu, S-P., & Lessig, M. (2006). Improving identification of cognitive impairment in primary care. *International Journal of Geriatric Psychiatry*, *21*(4), 349–355.

Brodaty, H., Low, L.-F., Gibson, L., & Burns, K. (2006). What is the best dementia screening instrument for general practitioners to use? *American Journal of Geriatric Psychiatry*, *14*(5), 391–400.

Lorentz, W. J., Scanlan, J. M., & Borson, S. (2002). Brief screening tests for dementia. *Canadian Journal of Psychiatry*, *47*(8), 723–733.

Morris, J. C., Heyman, A., Mohs, R. C., Hughes, J. P., van Belle, G., Fillenbaum, G., et al. (1989). The Consortium to Establish a Registry for Alzheimer's Disease (CERAD). Part I. Clinical and neuropsychological assessment of Alzheimer's disease. *Neurology*, *39*(9), 1159–1165.

Scanlan, J., & Borson, S. (2001). The Mini-Cog: Receiver operating characteristics with expert and naive raters. *International Journal of Geriatric Psychiatry*, *16*(2), 216–222.

Teng, E. L., Hasegawa, K., Homma, A., Imai, Y., Larson, E., Graves, A., et al. (1994). The Cognitive Abilities Screening Instrument (CASI): A practical test for cross-cultural epidemiological studies of dementia. *International Psychogeriatrics*, *6*(1), 45–58.

Mini-Cog

Borson, Scanlan, Brush, Vitaliano, and Dokmak (2000)

DATE ________ **ID** ____________________ **AGE** ________ **GENDER M F**

LOCATION ____________________ **TESTED BY** ________________

MINI-COG ™

1) **GET THE PATIENT'S ATTENTION, THEN SAY: "I am going top say three words that I want you to remember now and later. The words are**

Banana Sunrise Chair.

Please say them for me now." (Give the patient 3 tries to repeat the words. If unable after 3 tries, go to next item.) (Fold this page back at the TWO dotted lines BELOW to make a blank space and cover the memory words. Hand the patient a pencil/pen.)

2) **SAY ALL THE FOLLOWING PHRASES IN THE ORDER INDICATED: "Please draw a clock in the space below. Start by drawing a large circle."** (When this is done, say) **"Put all the numbers in the circle."** (When done, say) **"Now set the hands to show 11:10 (10 past 11)."** If subject has not finished clock drawing in 3 minutes, discontinue and ask for recall items.

---

3) **SAY: "What were the three words I asked you to remember?"**

________________ ________________ ________________

(Score 1 point for each) 3-Item Recall Score ☐

Score the clock (see other side for instructions): Normal clock 2 points; Abnormal clock 0 points. Clock Score ☐

Total Score = 3-item recall plus clock score ☐

0, 1 or 2 possible impairment; 3, 4, or 5 suggests no impairment

CLOCK SCORING

NORMAL CLOCK

A NORMAL CLOCK HAS ALL OF THE FOLLOWING ELEMENTS:

All numbers 1-12, each only once, are present in the correct order and direction (clockwise).

Two hands are present, one pointing to 11 and one pointing to 2.

ANY CLOCK MISSING ANY OF THESE ELEMENTS IS SCORED ABNORMAL. REFUSAL TO DRAW A CLOCK IS SCORED ABNORMAL.

SOME EXAMPLES OF ABNORMAL CLOCKS (THERE ARE MANY OTHER KINDS)

Abnormal Hands

Missing Number

Acknowledgement: Mini-Cog[tm] [Versions 7.0, 2.0, 2.1, 3.0] Copyright S. Borson. Reprinted with permission of the author, solely for clinical and teaching use. May not be modified or used for research without permission of the author (soob@u.washington.edu). All rights reserved.

Mini-Mental State Examination (MMSE)

Folstein, Folstein, and McHugh (1975)

Source

The MMSE is now commercially available through Psychological Assessment Resources (http://www.parinc.com). Items and instructions for administration are presented in the original article (Folstein et al., 1975), as well as the clinical guide (Folstein, Folstein, & Fanjiang, 2000), and are also available on the Internet Stroke Center website (http://www.strokecenter.org).

Purpose

The MMSE is an objective, clinician-administered test, intentionally designed to provide a brief, bedside assessment that is suitable for older people with delirium or dementia who may only be able to cooperate for short periods of time. It is the most commonly and widely used of all cognitive screening tests, both in clinical settings as well as in research studies, including population surveys. The MMSE is traditionally regarded as the standard reference against which all newly developed cognitive screening tests are measured.

Item description

Folstein et al. (1975) describe the MMSE as containing 11 questions. Basic cognitive processes are sampled in a range of domains: orientation for time (year, season, month, date, day), orientation for place (state, county, town, hospital, floor), registration and later recall of three unrelated words (apple, penny, table), attention (5 responses to serial 7s or spelling of "world" backwards), five aspects of language (confrontation naming, repetition, following a 3-stage command, reading a phrase, writing a sentence initiated by the patient), and construction (copy of overlapping pentagons).

Scale development

Development of the MMSE was driven by the need for a brief test that was easy to use in routine practice and could be administered serially. Limited information is provided on the item selection process, but Folstein et al. (1975) drew on "clinical tests of the sensorium" of the day. The MMSE was comprehensively examined in a number of samples, described below. No cut-off scores were suggested by Folstein et al., although they did note that no person with a primary diagnosis of neurosis or personality disorder or normal controls scored ≤ 20. By convention, however, because the lowest score of the normal control group was 24, a cut-off score 23/24 has been adopted. Sensitivity and specificity of this cut-off score to classify dementia versus no dementia in various groups are often around 80% (Folstein et al., 2000; Tombaugh & McIntyre, 1992).

Administration procedures, response format and scoring

Test materials required to administer the MMSE are designed to be easy to acquire and readily available (recording form, wrist watch, pencil). Instructions for administration are clear, including suggested interactions with the patient to maximize his or her performance. The clinical guide states that the MMSE "can be administered by anyone who has experience with (a) persons who have cognitive impairment and (b) the conventions of administration and scoring" (Folstein et al., 2000, p. 1). Administration time is brief, in the order of 5 to 10 minutes.

Scoring instructions for the MMSE and interpretation guidelines are fully explicated in the clinical guide. Each correct response is awarded 1 point. The total score ranges from 0 to 30, with higher scores indicating better performance. Traditionally, a cut-off score 23/24 is used to classify cognitive impairment. Additional cut-off scores have been recommended for a more fine-grained classification of degree of cognitive impairment: normal (27–30), mild (21–26), moderate (11–20), severe (0–10) cognitive impairment (Folstein et al. 2000).

Normative data, using T scores ($M = 50$, $SD = 10$) stratified by age and education, are available in an appendix to the clinical guide.

Data box 3.10 Descriptive data from the standardization sample (Folstein et al., 1975)

	Age Mean	Education	MMSE M (SD) range	Cut-off score	Sensitivity / Specificity
Control ($n = 63$)	73.9	No information	27.6 (1.7) 24–30	23/24	Multiple studies: approximately 80% for both (see text)
Dementia ($n = 29$)	80.8		9.6 (5.8) 0–22		
Depression with cognitive impairment ($n = 10$)	74.5		19.0 (6.6) 9–27		
Depression without cognitive impairment ($n = 30$)	49.8		25.1 (5.4) 8–30		

Psychometric properties

The initial validation study (Folstein et al., 1975) examined three samples (descriptive data shown in Data box 3.10). The main sample was a clinical group, comprising patients recruited from two hospitals in New York, USA, with (i) dementia ($n = 29$) and (ii) affective disorder, with ($n = 10$) and without ($n = 30$) cognitive impairment. A comparison group comprised 63 normal older people recruited from a senior citizen centre and a retirement apartment complex. A third clinical sample comprised a consecutive series of 137 patients. Responsiveness was examined in subset of patients from the first sample with affective (depressive) disorder and cognitive impairment ($n = 7$) who were retested after treatment. Validation was examined by using clinical diagnosis established by one of the authors who examined the patient's medical record, but remained blind to the MMSE score. Subsets of patient groups were used to examine test–retest reliability over 24 hours in 22 patients with depressive symptoms, and over 28 days in 23 patients with dementia, depression and schizophrenia. A group of 26 patients with dementia ($n = 7$) and various psychiatric conditions was also administered the Wechsler Adult Intelligence Scale (WAIS).

Data on predictive validity are available from Pedersen, Jørgensen, Nakayama, Raaschou, and Olsen (1996) who examined 541 patients with stroke with the MMSE 1 week post-onset. At discharge from rehabilitation they were assessed with the Barthel Index (BI). A large number of additional psychometric studies have been conducted on the MMSE, and results of these have been synthesized by Tombaugh and McIntyre (1992) and Folstein et al. (2000). A clinically important study is that of Hensel, Angermeyer and Riedel-Heller (2007). They determined the reliable change index for the MMSE from their study of 119 people without cognitive impairment at least 75 years of age who were examined six times at 1.5 yearly intervals. At least a 2 to 4 point change was required over a 1.5 year period to qualify as reliable. Results of Folstein et al. (1975), except where otherwise indicated, are shown in Box 3.12.

Derivatives of the MMSE

There are a number of derivatives of the MMSE. Some incorporate MMSE items into a more comprehensive battery of tests (two of which are described in this chapter: Addenbrooke's Cognitive Examination – Revised, ACE-R, and the Cognitive Abilities Screening Instrument, CASI), whereas others focus on reducing the item content even further. Generally the aim of the latter approach is to select those items that can most quickly identify people with moderate and severe degrees of dementia, one such scale being the Six-Item Screener.

Six-Item Screener (SIS); Callahan, Unverzagt, Hui, Perkins, and Hendrie (2002)

The SIS comprises the three-item recall (apple, table, penny) and three temporal orientation items (day of the week, month, and year) from the MMSE. The score used is the number of errors (range 0–6). Callahan et al. compared the SIS with the MMSE and other measures in an older community of African Americans ($n = 344$) and a clinical sample ($n = 651$; 16% African American). The SIS compared favourably with the MMSE. The authors provide tables of data for the community and clinical samples for both the SIS and MMSE, allowing the user to select various cut-off points depending on the balance of sensitivity/specificity desired. In the community sample, a cut-off score of 2/3 yielded 89% sensitivity and 88% specificity. Callahan and colleagues enumerate advantages of the SIS, including its comparable sensitivity and specificity to the MMSE, brevity (administration time 1–2 mins), lack of requirement for test materials, facility for telephone administration, and ease of scoring.

Box 3.12

Validity:	Criterion: *Concurrent:* with WAIS Verbal and Performance IQ: $r = .78$ and $r = .66$ respectively Folstein et al. (2000): with cognitive screening tests: $r = .78–.82$ *Predictive:* Pedersen et al.: admission MMSE with BI at rehabilitation discharge: $r = .39$ – Admission MMSE for patients discharged to independent living $M = 24.5$ vs patients discharged to nursing homes $M = 17.4$; $t = -5.82$, $p < .001$ Construct: *Internal consistency:* Cronbach alpha: Tombaugh & McIntyre (1992): 3 studies: range .68–.96; Folstein et al. (2000): 9 studies: range .31–.96; generally higher in clinical samples (0.56–.96 in 4 studies; < .8 for 2/4 studies) *Discriminant:* Dementia $M = 9.6$ ($SD = 5.8$) vs depression with cognitive impairment $M = 19.0$ ($SD = 6.6$) vs affective disorder without cognitive impairment $M = 25.1$ ($SD = 5.4$) vs normal controls $M = 27.6$ ($SD = 1.7$); each $p < .001$ Folstein et al. (2000): summarized 28 studies – significant differences and large effect sizes between normal vs dementia groups
Reliability:	Inter-rater: Folstein et al. (2000): 4 studies: $r = .83–.95$ Test–retest: 24 hour: $r = .89$ and $r = .83$ with 2 different examiners, – 28 days: $r = .99$ *Practice effects:* Time 1 $M = 19.3$ ($SD = 10.0$) vs Time 2 $M = 19.2$ ($SD = 9.2$); $M = -0.1$
Responsiveness:	36 days after treatment commencement: significant improvement in MMSE pre-treatment $M = 18.3$ ($SD = 5.0$) vs post-treatment $M = 23.4$ ($SD = 2.4$); Wilcoxon T = 1.0, $p < .025$, $d = 1.0$

Comment

In more than 30 years since publication of the MMSE it continues to be the most widely used cognitive screening test and has been translated into many languages. The reputation of the MMSE is deserved – for its day, the MMSE met an important need for a brief, bedside screening test and the initial report on its psychometric properties was both relatively comprehensive and impressive, demonstrating high reliability and evidence for validity. Subsequent studies have found floor and ceiling effects in specific populations. A drawback of the MMSE, common to many other cognitive screening tests, is its susceptibility to age, education, literacy, socioeconomic and cultural differences, along with its insensitivity to mild, severe and/or focal impairments. In view of these weaknesses, Tombaugh and McIntyre (1992) enumerate a series of recommendations regarding the clinical use of the MMSE. In particular, Folstein et al. (2000) emphasize that "the MMSE cannot be used as a diagnostic tool" (p. 1). In fairness to the MMSE, Tombaugh and McIntyre further note that "the MMSE, in its current form, is expected to provide too many different types of screening functions. It may be unrealistic to expect a single version of the test to meet all these demands" (p. 931).

Key references

Callahan, C. M., Unverzagt, F. W., Hui, S. L., Perkins, A. J., & Hendrie, H. C. (2002). Six-Item Screener to identify cognitive impairment among potential subjects for clinical research. *Medical Care*, *40*(9), 771–781.

Folstein, M. F., Folstein, S. E., & Fanjiang, G. (2000). *MMSE. Mini-Mental State Examination. Clinical guide*. Lutz, FL: Psychological Assessment Resources.

Folstein, M. F., Folstein, S. E., & McHugh, P. R. (1975). "Mini-Mental State". A practical method for grading the cognitive state of patients for the clinician. *Journal of Psychiatric Research*, *12*(3), 189–198.

Hensel, A., Angermeyer, M. C., & Riedel-Heller, S. G. (2007). Measuring cognitive change in older adults: Reliable change indices for the Mini-Mental State Examination. *Journal of Neurology, Neurosurgery, and Psychiatry*, *78(12)*, 1298–1303.

Pedersen, P. M., Jørgensen, H. S., Nakayama, H., Raaschou, H. O., & Olsen, T. S. (1996). General cognitive function in acute stroke: The Copenhagen Stroke Study. *Journal of Neurologic Rehabilitation*, *10*(3), 153–158.

Tombaugh, T. N., & McIntyre, N. J. (1992). The Mini-Mental State Examination: A comprehensive review. *Journal of the American Geriatrics Society*, *40*(9), 922–935.

Mini-Mental State Examination

Folstein, Folstein, and McHugh (1975)

Folstein, Folstein, and Fanjiang (2000)

Date of examination ______/______/______ Examiner ______________________

Name ______________________ Age ______ Years of School Completed ______

Instructions: Words in boldface type should be read aloud clearly and slowly to the examiner. Item substitutions appear in parentheses. Administration should be conducted privately and in the examinee's primary language. Circle 0 if the response is incorrect, or 1 if the response is correct. Begin by asking the following two questions:

Do you have any trouble with your memory? May I ask you some questions about your memory?

ORIENTATION TO TIME		RESPONSE	SCORE (circle one)	
What is the...	**year?**	______	0	1
	season?	______	0	1
	month of the year?	______	0	1
	day of the week?	______	0	1
	date?	______	0	1

ORIENTATION TO PLACE*

Where are we now? What is the...

state (province)**?**	______	0	1
county (or city/town)**?**	______	0	1
city/town (or part of city/neighborhood)**?**	______	0	1
building (name or type)**?**	______	0	1
floor of the building (room number or address)**?**	______	0	1

*Alternative place words that are appropriate for the setting and increasingly precise may be substituted and noted.

REGISTRATION*

Listen carefully. I am going to say three words. You say them back after I stop. Ready? Here they are...APPLE [*pause*]**, PENNY** [*pause*]**, TABLE** [*pause*]**. Now repeat those words back to me.** [Repeat up to five times, but score only the first trial]

APPLE	______	0	1
PENNY	______	0	1
TABLE	______	0	1

Now keep those words in mind. I am going to ask you to say them again in a few minutes.

*Alternative word sets (e.g., PONY, QUARTER, ORANGE) may be substituted and noted when retesting an examinee.

ATTENTION AND CALCULATION [Serial 7s]*

Now I'd like you to subtract 7 from 100. Then keep subtracting 7 from each answer until I tell you to stop.

What is 100 take away 7?	[93]	______	0	1
If needed say: **Keep going.**	[86]	______	0	1
If needed say: **Keep going.**	[79]	______	0	1
If needed say: **Keep going.**	[72]	______	0	1
If needed say: **Keep going.**	[65]	______	0	1

*Alternative item (WORLD backward) should only be administered if the examinee refuses to perform the Serial 7s task. ⟶

Substitute and score this item only if the examinee refuses to perform the Serial 7s Task

Spell WORLD forward, then backward.

Correct forward spelling if misspelled.
but only score the backward spelling.

____	____	____	____	____	____
(D = 1)	(L = 1)	(R = 1)	(O = 1)	(W = 1)	(0 to 5)

RECALL	RESPONSE	SCORE (circle one)	
What were those three words I asked you to remember? [*Do not offer any hints.*]			
APPLE	____________	0	1
PENNY	____________	0	1
TABLE	____________	0	1

NAMING*

What is this? [*Point to a pencil or pen.*]	____________	0	1
What is this? [*Point to a watch.*]	____________	0	1

*Alternate common objects (e.g., eyeglasses, chair, keys) may be substituted and noted.

REPETITION

Now I am going to ask you to repeat what I say. Ready "NO IFS, ANDS, OR BUTS." Now you say that.
[*Repeat up to 5 times, but score only the first trial.*]

NO IFS, ANDS, OR BUTS.	____________	0	1

Use the upper half of the next page (blank) for the Comprehension, Writing, and Drawing items that follow. Use the lower half of the page as a a stimulus form for the Reading ("CLOSE YOUR EYES") and the following page for Drawing (intersecting pentagons) items.

COMPREHENSION

Listen carefully because I am going to ask you to do something.
Take the paper in your right hand [*pause*]**, fold it in half** [*pause*]**, and put it on the floor (***or* **table).**

TAKE IT IN RIGHT HAND	____________	0	1
FOLD IN HALF	____________	0	1
PUT ON FLOOR (or TABLE)	____________	0	1

READING

Please read this and do what it says. [*Show examinee the words on the stimulus form.*]

CLOSE YOUR EYES	____________	0	1

WRITING

Please write a sentence. [*If examinee does not respond say:* **Write about the weather**.] 0 1

Place the blank piece of paper (unfolded) in front of the examinee and provide a pen or pencil. Score 1 point if the sentence is comprehensible and contains a subject and a verb. Ignore errors in grammar or spelling.

DRAWING

Please copy this design. [*Display the interesecting pentagons on the stimulus form.*] 0 1

Score 1 point if the drawing consists of two 5-sided figures that intersect to form a 4-sided figure.

Total Score = ________
(*Sum all item scores*) (30 points max.)

Assessment of level of consciousness.

Alert/ Responsive	Drowsy	Stuporous	Comatose/ Unresponsive

CLOSE YOUR EYES

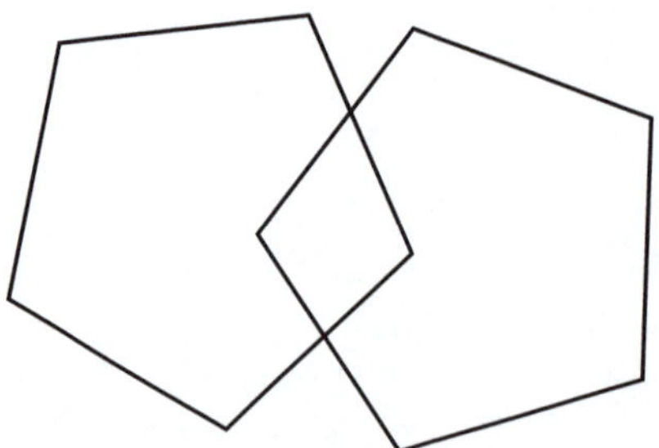

Acknowledgement: From Folstein, M. F. et al. (1975). "Mini-Mental State". A practical method for grading the cognitive state of patients for the clinician. *Journal of Psychiatric Research*, *12*(3), 189–198, and also from *Psychopharmacology Bulletin* (1988), *24*(4), reproduced by permission of Medworks Media and Psychological Assessment Resources.

Montreal Cognitive Assessment (MoCA)

Nasreddine et al. (2005)

Source

Items for the MoCA are described in Nasreddine et al. (2005). The recording form, along with administration and scoring instructions and normative data, can be downloaded from the following website: http://www.mocatest.org, and is reproduced below.

Purpose

The MoCA is an objective, clinician-administered test developed for older people as a screening tool to identify mild cognitive impairment (MCI). As Nasreddine et al. (2005) note, "MCI is an intermediate clinical state between normal cognitive aging and dementia, and it precedes and leads to dementia in many cases . . . The concept of MCI is new, evolving, and somewhat controversial" (p. 695). See also Petersen (2004) and Winblad et al. (2004) regarding diagnostic criteria for MCI, which are summarized in the introduction to this chapter. The MoCA was designed for use with people who perform in the normal range on other screening instruments, such as the Mini-Mental State Examination (MMSE), yet who complain of mild cognitive difficulties. The specific aim was to bring together a set of sensitive cognitive tests that could be administered quickly and easily.

Item description

Nasreddine et al. (2005) describe the MoCA as examining eight domains: Orientation (6 items for date, month, year, day of the week, place and city), Attention/calculation (4 items for digit span forwards and backwards, a short vigilance task, and serial 7s), Memory (5-min recall of five nouns), Executive/visuoconstructive (3 items for alternating trails, copy of a cube, and drawing of a clock), two aspects of Language (3 items for Confrontation naming and 2 items for Repetition), and two aspects of Executive/language (2 items for Similarities between pairs of words and 1 item for Letter fluency).

Scale development

Development of the MoCA, which occurred over a 5-year period, is described in Nasreddine et al. (2005). The item selection process focused on identifying "domains of impairment commonly encountered in MCI and best adapted to a screening test" (p. 696). A number of items are derived from standard neuropsychological tests (e.g., the initial sequence of Trail Making Test – Part B, the first letter (F) of the Controlled Oral Word Association Test), as well as tasks commonly used in mental status examinations (e.g., serial sevens, digit span, repetition, orientation items). An initial version of the MoCA was trialled on 46 people with MCI or Alzheimer's disease (AD), as well as 46 healthy community volunteers who performed in the normal range on neuropsychological evaluation. On the basis of the results, item content and scoring were adjusted to refine the instrument and improve its discrimination. The final version was examined with 234 people from three groups (see below). A cut-off score, derived on the basis of clinical diagnosis, was set at 25/26 (sensitivity 90%, specificity 87%), with positive and negative predictive values of 89% and 91% respectively.

Administration procedures, response format and scoring

The MoCA is suitable for patients who score ≥ 24/30 on the MMSE. The recording form, containing pictorial and other visual materials, is required to administer the MoCA. Although it is intended that the MoCA be used by "firstline physicians", administration procedures for this test are more detailed than the commonly used MMSE, and the examiner needs to be thoroughly familiar with the instructions for administration that accompany the test. Administration time is approximately 10 minutes.

Responses to items are awarded points according to operationally defined criteria, which are clearly specified in the scoring instructions. When the total score is less than 30, 1 point is added to the total score for

Data box 3.11 Descriptive data from the standardization sample (Nasreddine et al., 2005)

	Age M (SD)	Education M (SD)	MoCA M (SD)	Cut-off score	Sensitivity / Specificity
Controls (n = 90)	72.84 (7.03)	13.33 (3.40)	27.4 (2.2)	25/26	MCI vs Normal
Mild cognitive impairment (n = 94)	75.19 (6.27)	12.28 (4.32)	22.1 (3.1)		90% / 87%
Probable (mild) AD (n = 93)	76.72 (8.83)	10.03 (3.84)	16.2 (4.8)		AD vs Normal
					100% / 87%

respondents who have 12 or less years education. The total score ranges from 0 to 30, with higher scores indicating better degrees of functioning. A cut-off score of 25/26 is used to classify MCI.

Psychometric properties

The three groups of participants for the validation study were recruited from two hospital- and university-associated memory clinics in Montreal, Canada (Nasreddine et al., 2005; descriptive data shown in Data box 3.11). The groups comprised 93 people meeting established criteria for probable (mild) AD, using the *Diagnostic and Statistical Manual of Mental Disorders* – 4th ed. (DSM-IV), National Institutes of Neurological and Communicable Disorders and Stroke (NINCDS) and the Alzheimer's Disease and Related Disorders Association (ADRDA). Additional groups comprised 94 people with neurologist/geriatrician diagnosis of MCI after clinical review against established criteria, and 90 people who were free of complaint of memory or cognitive impairment and who performed normally on neuropsychological examination. Temporal stability was examined in a subset (n = 26 patients and controls) who were retested after M = 35 days (SD = 17.6). Education effects were found and corrected by adding one point to the total score (if < 30) for people with ≤ 12 years of education.

Clinical diagnosis was used to determine the best balance of sensitivity and specificity. Using the cut-off score 25/26, the MoCA was more sensitive in identifying MCI (90%) and AD (100%) than was the MMSE, using the same cut-off score (i.e., 25/26; 18% and 78% respectively). Specificity to exclude normal controls was, however, higher with the MMSE (100%) than the MoCA (87%). English and French versions of the MoCA were tested and their equivalence established. The high sensitivity of the MoCA relative to the MMSE was replicated by Smith, Gildeh, and Holmes (2007) in 23 people meeting criteria for MCI (83% vs 17%), but specificity of the MoCA was at chance, compared to 100% for the MMSE. A summary of findings from Nasreddine et al. is shown in Box 3.13.

Box 3.13

Validity:	Criterion: *Concurrent:* with MMSE: r = .87
	Construct: *Discriminant:* Normal M = 13.33 (SD = 3.40) vs MCI M = 12.28 (SD = 4.32) vs AD M = 10.03 (SD = 3.84); F = 232.91, p < .001 – Differential diagnosis between MCI vs normal using cut-off score of 25/26: sensitivity 90%, specificity 87%
	Internal consistency: Cronbach alpha: .83
Reliability:	Inter-rater: No information available
	Test–retest: M = 35 days: r = .92 *Practice effects:* M = .9 (SD = 2.5)
Responsiveness:	No information available

Comment

A common problem with many screening tests is that they are subject to ceiling effects, and consequently do not detect early stages of diseases or mild deficits. The MoCA overcomes this difficulty. Results of the initial study are promising and suggest that the MoCA will be a welcome addition to the new generation of cognitive screening tests. Conversely, a risk is that such a screening test will be subject to (in particular) education biases. The authors tested for this problem and made scoring adjustments accordingly. Psychometric properties indicate that the MoCA has good internal consistency, is a stable and valid instrument, and the item content has been selected and trialled to ensure the MoCA is sensitive. On the other hand, high sensitivity of a screening test is at the expense of specificity, and a significant proportion of the non-impaired participants (13%) were classified as impaired on the MoCA. Moreover, a UK sample showed comparable sensitivity, but specificity was low, at 50% (Smith et al., 2007). The MoCA is a newly developed instrument and it will be important to examine its application in other samples. The present specificity data, however, suggest that the MoCA should not be used as the sole diagnostic instrument, and results need to be confirmed with neuropsychological evaluation.

Key references

Nasreddine, Z. S., Phillips, N. A., Bédirian, V., Carbonneau, S., Whitehead, V., Collin, I., et al. (2005). The Montreal Cognitive Assessment, MoCA: A brief screening tool for mild cognitive impairment. *Journal of the American Geriatrics Society*, *53*(4), 695–699.

Petersen, R. C. (2004). Mild cognitive impairment as a diagnostic entity. *Journal of Internal Medicine*, *256*, 183–194.

Smith, T., Gildeh, N., & Holmes, C. (2007). The Montreal Cognitive Assessment: Validity and utility in a memory clinic setting. *Canadian Journal of Psychiatry*, *52*(5), 329–332.

Winblad, B., Palmer, K., Kivipelto, M., Jelic, V., Fratiglioni, L., Wahlund, L. O., et al. (2004). Mild cognitive impairment – Beyond controversies, towards consensus: Report of the International Working Group on Mild Cognitive Impairment. *Journal of Internal Medicine*, *256*(3), 240–246.

Montreal Cognitive Assessment (MoCA)

Nasreddine et al. (2005)

NAME : Date of birth : Sex :
DATE : Education :

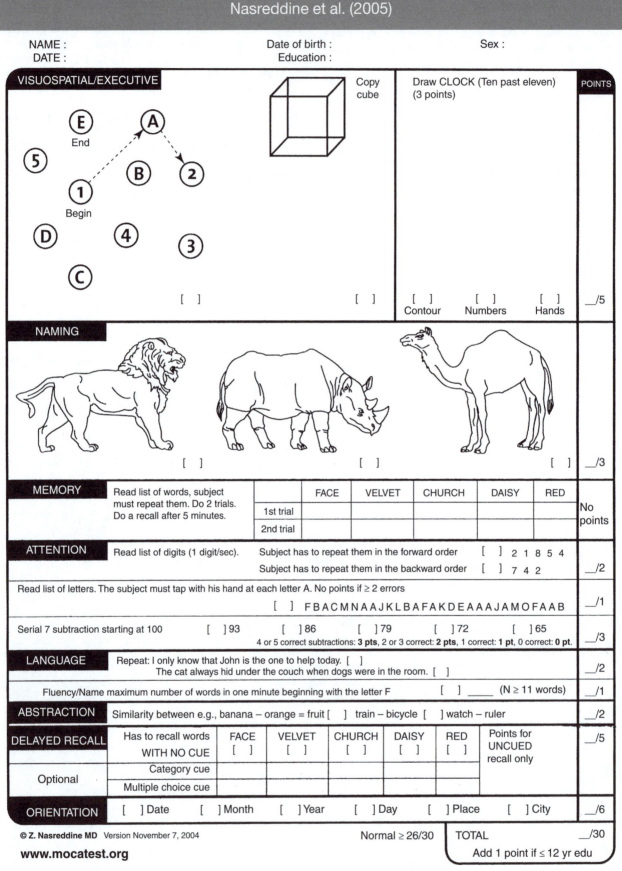

VISUOSPATIAL/EXECUTIVE			POINTS
(E) End, (A), (5), (B), (2), (1) Begin, (D), (4), (3), (C) [ ]	Copy cube [ ]	Draw CLOCK (Ten past eleven) (3 points) [ ] Contour [ ] Numbers [ ] Hands	__/5
NAMING [ ]	[ ]	[ ]	__/3

MEMORY	Read list of words, subject must repeat them. Do 2 trials. Do a recall after 5 minutes.		FACE	VELVET	CHURCH	DAISY	RED	No points
		1st trial						
		2nd trial						

ATTENTION Read list of digits (1 digit/sec). Subject has to repeat them in the forward order [ ] 2 1 8 5 4
Subject has to repeat them in the backward order [ ] 7 4 2 __/2

Read list of letters. The subject must tap with his hand at each letter A. No points if ≥ 2 errors
[ ] F B A C M N A A J K L B A F A K D E A A A J A M O F A A B __/1

Serial 7 subtraction starting at 100 [ ] 93 [ ] 86 [ ] 79 [ ] 72 [ ] 65
4 or 5 correct subtractions: **3 pts**, 2 or 3 correct: **2 pts**, 1 correct: **1 pt**, 0 correct: **0 pt**. __/3

LANGUAGE Repeat: I only know that John is the one to help today. [ ]
The cat always hid under the couch when dogs were in the room. [ ] __/2

Fluency/Name maximum number of words in one minute beginning with the letter F [ ] ____ (N ≥ 11 words) __/1

ABSTRACTION Similarity between e.g., banana – orange = fruit [ ] train – bicycle [ ] watch – ruler __/2

DELAYED RECALL	Has to recall words WITH NO CUE	FACE [ ]	VELVET [ ]	CHURCH [ ]	DAISY [ ]	RED [ ]	Points for UNCUED recall only	__/5
Optional	Category cue							
	Multiple choice cue							

ORIENTATION [ ] Date [ ] Month [ ] Year [ ] Day [ ] Place [ ] City __/6

 Version November 7, 2004 Normal ≥ 26/30 TOTAL __/30
Add 1 point if ≤ 12 yr edu

www.mocatest.org

Acknowledgement: MoCa test used by permission of the author © Ziad Nasreddine MD FRCP www.mocatest.org

Rowland Universal Dementia Assessment Scale (RUDAS)

Storey, Rowland, Conforti, and Dickson (2004)

Source

Items for the RUDAS are described in Storey et al. (2004). The recording form and administration guide are available from the following website (http://www.immigration.govt.nz) and appear in summary form below.

Purpose

The RUDAS is an objective, clinician-administered cognitive screening test. It was designed to be "a simple, portable method for detecting dementia that is valid across cultures" (Rowland, Basic, Storey, & Conforti, 2006, p. 2). The RUDAS has been used with dementia populations, including Alzheimer's disease and vascular dementia (Iype, Ajitha, Antony, Ajeeth, Job, & Shaji, 2006).

Item description

The authors describe the RUDAS as a six-item test, but one of the items contains a number of questions, and it is thus better described as a 10-item test covering six domains of function: Visuospatial orientation (5 items – body part identification), Praxis (1 item – alternating fist–palm), Visuoconstruction (1 item – copy of a cube), Judgement (1 item – crossing the road safely), Memory (1 item – recall 4 shopping items), and Language (1 item – animal generativity in 1 minute).

Scale development

Rowland et al. (2006) reported on the limitations of existing cognitive screening tests, such as the Mini-Mental State Exam (MMSE), in assessing people from culturally and linguistically diverse backgrounds, in that "many words cannot be easily translated and several concepts are less relevant to people from other cultures" (p. 2). Additionally, they noted that item content of the MMSE did not sample executive functions. As observed by Iype et al. (2006, p. 514), this is particularly problematic in developing countries where "people without dementia but with less education, illiterate and innumerate may be screened positive for dementia". The RUDAS was developed within a multicultural context, drawing on a geographic region in south-western Sydney, Australia, in which more than 80 languages are spoken and 40% of the population was born in a non-English speaking country.

The item development process for the RUDAS is described in Storey et al. (2004). Initially, two advisory groups with expertise in culture/health were established and generated a pool of 60 potential items, 42 of which met the following criteria: good construct validity, limited cultural and linguistic bias, endorsed by interpreters, and facilitating easy administration. The items were empirically examined in a group of 166 consecutive new referrals to a geriatric outpatient clinic at Liverpool Hospital, Sydney (age $M = 77.9$ years, $SD = 7.0$; 69% female; $M = 9$ years education; 25 language groups). Items were administered by a research psychologist (or interpreter, where appropriate) who was blind to patient medical history and dementia diagnosis using criteria of the *Diagnostic and Statistical Manual of Mental Disorders* – 4th ed. (DSM-IV) which was independently made by a geriatrician. Items with low correlation ($r_s < .35$) with diagnosis were excluded, and logistic regression analysis was used to identify the items that best predicted dementia. The final set of items was validated in a random sample of 90 older people living in the community, half of whom had a diagnosis of dementia. Scoring procedures for the RUDAS used a weighting process, based on the size of the standardized coefficients from the logistic regression analysis. Receiver operating characteristic (ROC) curve analysis was conducted, with the area under the curve of 0.95 and indicating that the most sensitive cut-off score was 22/23 (89% sensitivity, 98% specificity).

Administration procedures, response format and scoring

Rowland et al. (2006) report that the RUDAS is suitable for administration by both skilled and unskilled health

Data box 3.12 Descriptive data from the validation sample (Rowland et al., 2006)

	Age Mean (*SD*)	**Education Median**	**RUDAS Median (Q1–Q3)**	**Cut-off score**	**Sensitivity / Specificity**
Control (*n* = 48)	77.7 (8.6)	6.5	27 (25–28)	22/23	81% / 98%
Dementia (*n* = 63)	81.5 (7.5)	6.0	14 (4–21)		

care workers. The authors have developed a 40-minute training procedure, using a videotape. Administration time is 10 minutes.

Correct responses to the items are allocated a variable number of points, depending on accuracy. Explicit scoring criteria are available to distinguish partially correct responses/need for prompt from full and complete responses. The total score ranges from 0 to 30, with higher scores indicating better performance. A cut-off score of 22/23 is used to identify cognitive impairment.

Psychometric properties

Initial validation of the RUDAS was reported by Storey et al. (2004). A random sample of 90 people living in the community was examined, half of whom had a dementia diagnosis. An interpreter was used in 44% and 67% of those with and without dementia respectively. There were no group differences for age, sex or years of education. Inter-rater reliability was examined in the 90 participants by one of two examiners (determined by coin toss), while the other observed. The sample was re-examined 1 week later. In a subsequent study, Rowland et al. (2006) compared the RUDAS with the MMSE, using a random sample of 129 older people (*n* = 111 had either dementia or normal cognition – descriptive data shown in Data box 3.12) who were living in the community and drawn from all referrals to their aged-care team. They were stratified into six groups by language background (English speaking 34%, Asian, non-English speaking 31%, non-Asian, non-English speaking 35%) and cognitive status (with and without dementia – 48–50% in each of the language groups). Order of administration of the RUDAS and the MMSE was alternated randomly. Each test was administered independently by different assessors who were blind to dementia diagnosis, which was made by a geriatrician using DSM-IV criteria and the Clinical Dementia Rating (CDR) scale. Data on the Barthel Index (BI) and the Lawton and Brody instrumental activities of daily living scale (IADL) were also collected by the geriatrician. The area under the ROC curve was similar for the RUDAS (0.92) and MMSE (0.91), but different patterns of sensitivity (81% vs 93% respectively) and specificity (96% vs 79% respectively) emerged. Results of logistic regression analyses demonstrated that in contrast to the MMSE, the RUDAS was not influenced by preferred language, education or sex.

An independent research group in southern India (Iype et al., 2006) found that the RUDAS translated easily into Malaylam. Their sample comprised 58 people (age $M = 65.1$ years) meeting DSM-IV criteria for dementia and classified by the CDR as mild to moderate, along with an age-matched healthy control group (*n* = 58). The minority (38% dementia group, 35% control group) had more than 6 years of formal education. Sensitivity of the RUDAS and the MMSE was comparable (90% and 88% respectively), but specificity of the RUDAS (76%) was significantly higher than the MMSE (48%, $p < .001$). Iype et al. did find significant correlation between education and the RUDAS ($r_s = .45$), but it was lower than that of the MMSE ($r_s = .64$). Results of the above studies are shown in Box 3.14.

Box 3.14

Validity:	Criterion: *Concurrent:* Rowland et al.: with MMSE: $r_s = .85$
	Construct: *Discriminant:* Rowland et al.: control group scored significantly higher than dementia group (median = 27 vs 14 respectively); $p < .001$
	Rowland et al.: Differential diagnosis between dementia vs non-dementia using cut-off score of 22/23: sensitivity 81%, specificity 96%
Reliability:	Inter-rater: Storey et al.: ICC = .99
	Test–retest: Storey et al.: 1 week: ICC = .98 *Practice effects:* No information available
Responsiveness:	No information available

Comment

Information available to date suggests that the RUDAS meets its aim of being a culture-free cognitive screening test. It is readily translated into "at least 30 other languages, without the need to change the structure or the format of any item" (Storey et al., 2004, p. 27) and has been empirically tested in Asian, European and Indian languages. The RUDAS is not subject to demographic biases to the same extent as the MMSE. In other respects it also has very good psychometric properties, both in terms of criterion and construct validity and reliability. These features make the RUDAS an appealing screening instrument for people from culturally and linguistically diverse backgrounds.

Key references

Iype, T., Ajitha, B. K., Antony, P., Ajeeth, N. B., Job, S., & Shaji, K. S. (2006). Usefulness of the Rowland Universal Dementia Assessment Scale in South India. *Journal of Neurology, Neurosurgery, and Psychiatry*, *77*, 513–514.

Rowland, J. T., Basic, D., Storey, J. E., & Conforti, D. A. (2006). The Rowland Universal Dementia Assessment Scale (RUDAS) and the Folstein MMSE in a multicultural cohort of elderly persons. *International Psychogeriatrics*, *18(1)*, 1–10.

Storey, J. E., Rowland, J. T. J., Conforti, D. A., & Dickson, H. G. (2004). The Rowland Universal Dementia Assessment Scale (RUDAS): A multicultural cognitive assessment scale. *International Psychogeriatrics*, *16(1)*, 13–31.

Rowland Universal Dementia Assessment Scale

Storey, Rowland, Conforti, and Dickson (2004)

Name:	Administered by:	Date:

SCORE

1. MEMORY

I want you to imagine that we are going shopping. Here is a list of grocery items. I would like you to remember the following items that we need to get from the shop. When we get to the shop in about 5 minutes time I will ask you what it is that we have to buy. You must remember the list for me.

Tea, cooking oil, eggs, soap.

Please repeat this list for me

> Ask person to repeat the list 3 times. If person did not repeat all four items, repeat the list until the person has learned them and can repeat them, or up to a maximum of five times.

2. VISUOSPATIAL ORIENTATION

I am going to ask you to identify/show me different parts of the body.

> Scoring: Each correct response is awarded 1 point. Once the person correctly answers 5 parts of this question, do not continue as the maximum score is 5.

i. Show me your right foot ______________________ ______

ii. Show me your left hand ______________________

iii. With your right hand touch your left shoulder ______________

iv. With your left hand touch your right ear ________________

v. Which is (indicate/point to) my left knee ________________

vi. Which is (indicate/point to) my right elbow ______________

vii. With your right hand point to/indicate my left eye __________

viii. With your left hand point to/indicate my left foot __________

3. PRAXIS

I am going to show you an action/exercise with my hands. I want you to watch me and copy what I do. Copy me when I do this . . . (Demonstrate: put one hand in a fist, the other hand palm down on the table or your knees and then alternate simultaneously.) Now do it with me: I would like you to keep doing this action at this pace until I tell you to stop – approximately 10 seconds or 5 or 6 sequences. (Demonstrate at moderate walking pace.)

> Scoring:
> Normal = 2 points: very few if any errors; self-corrected, progressively better; good maintenance; only very slight lack of synchrony between hands
> Partially adequate = 1 point: noticeable errors with some attempt to self-correct; some attempt at maintenance; poor synchrony
> Failed = 0 points: cannot do the task; no maintenance; no attempt whatsoever

______

4. VISUOCONSTRUCTIVE DRAWING **SCORE**

Please draw this picture exactly as it looks to you (show cube below).

Scoring: 1 point for each "yes" answer:
1. Has person drawn a picture based on a square? ______
2. Do all internal lines appear in person's drawing? ______
3. Do all external lines appear in person's drawing? ______

5. JUDGEMENT

You are standing on the side of a busy street. There is no pedestrian crossing and no traffic lights. Tell me what you would do to get across to the other side of the street safely.

If person gives incomplete response that does not address both parts of the answer, use prompt: "Is there anything else you would do?" Record exactly what patient says and circle all parts of response that were prompted.

Scoring:
1. Did person indicate that they would look for traffic?
   2 points = YES; 1 point = YES PROMPTED; 0 points = NO
2. Did person make any additional safety proposals?
   2 points = YES; 1 point = YES PROMPTED; 0 points = NO ______

MEMORY RECALL

We have just arrived at the shop. Can you remember the list of groceries that we need to buy?

Prompt: If person cannot recall any of the list say "The first one was 'tea'."
Scoring: 2 points each for an item recalled that was not prompted – use only "tea" as a prompt.

Tea ______ Eggs ______ Cooking oil ______ Soap ______ ______

6. LANGUAGE

I am going to time you for 1 minute. In that 1 minute, I would like you to tell me the names of as many different animals as you can. We'll see how many different animals you can name in 1 minute.

Repeat instructions if necessary. Maximum score for this item is 8. If person names 8 new animals in less than 1 minute there is no need to continue. ______

1........ 4........ 7........

2........ 5........ 8........

3........ 6........

TOTAL SCORE: ______

Acknowledgement: The Rowland Universal Dementia Assessment Scale developed by Rowland, J., Storey, J., Conforti, D., and Dickson, H., with funding from NSW Health Australia, is reproduced by permission of the authors.

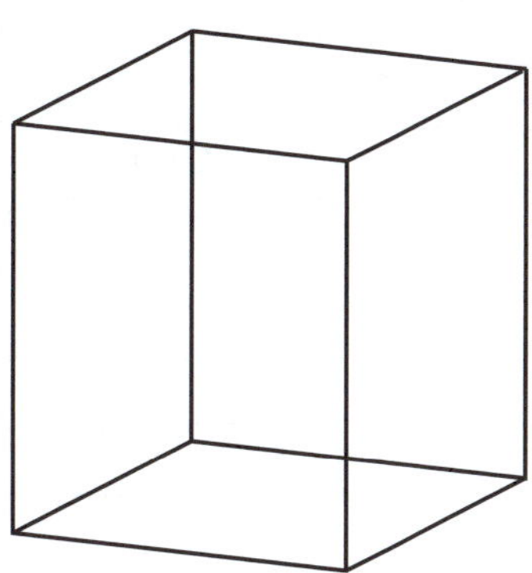

Severe Mini-Mental State Examination (SMMSE)

Harrell, Marson, Chatterjee, and Parrish (2000)

Source

Items for the SMMSE, along with administration and scoring instructions, appear in an appendix to Harrell et al. (2000), and the test is reproduced below.

Purpose

The SMMSE is an objective, clinician-administered test, designed specifically for patients in the later stages of progressive dementias, such as moderate and severe Alzheimer's disease (AD). It therefore aims to eliminate "floor" effects that are commonly encountered with other cognitive screening tests when used with this patient group.

Item description

The SMMSE uses 10 items to examine three cognitive domains: orientation to person (name and birthdate), language (following commands, repetition of 3 words, naming 3 objects, animal generativity, spelling a word, writing own name) and construction (copying a square and drawing a circle).

Scale development

Development of the SMMSE aimed to improve on the Mini-Mental State Examination (MMSE) when used with patients in the later stages of dementia. Although Harrell et al. (2000) stated that the SMMSE is modelled after the MMSE, there is little similarity between the two instruments, except for the score range. Item selection for the SMMSE focused on "cognitive functions that are still relatively preserved in severely impaired patients with [Alzheimer's disease]" (p. 169). There is thus a notable absence of items to examine memory. The language items that are selected draw on well-established skills (e.g., writing one's own name, spelling the word "CAT").

Administration procedures, response format and scoring

Administering and scoring the SMMSE is quick and easy. Administration time is less than 5 minutes. Items were intentionally selected to minimize the need for test equipment, and no special training is required for the clinician.

Points are awarded for each correct response, with points also awarded for partially correct answers. The total score ranges from 0 to 30, with higher scores indicating better degrees of functioning.

Psychometric properties

Harrell et al. (2000) standardized the SMMSE on a group of 182 patients (descriptive data shown in Data box 3.13) with physician-diagnosed probable AD (mild to severe), as determined by established criteria.

Data box 3.13 Descriptive data from the standardization sample (Harrell et al., 2000)

	Age *M* (*SD*)	Education *M* (*SD*)	SMMSE *M* (*SD*)	Cut-off score	Sensitivity / Specificity
Alzheimer's disease ($n = 182$):	73.3 (7.7)	11.9 (2.9)		No information	No information
with GDS scores ($n = 132$):					
GDS Level 4 ($n = 4$)			29.2 (0.9)		
GDS Level 5 ($n = 22$)			26.7 (2.6)		
GDS Level 6 ($n = 87$)			21.1 (4.7)		
GDS Level 7 ($n = 19$)			7.6 (5.7)		

Note: GDS = Global Deterioration Scale

Validation instruments comprised the MMSE, and a subset ($n = 132$) was additionally assessed on the Global Deterioration Scale (GDS) and Clinical Dementia Rating (CDR) scale.

Another subgroup of patients ($n = 59$) was examined on a second occasion $M = 155$ days ($SD = 70$) later. Inter-rater reliability was established with 19 patients independently scored by two raters, one of whom administered the test while the other observed. Of $n = 37$ scoring < 16 on the SMMSE, scores on the MMSE were restricted (< 4/30). The authors report that 53% scored > 10 on the SMMSE, even when scoring 0 on the MMSE. No significant correlation was found between education and SMMSE score. Results from Harrell et al. are shown in Box 3.15.

Box 3.15

Validity:	Criterion: *Concurrent:* with patients whose MMSE ≤ 5: $r = .61$ – with patients whose MMSE 5–9: $r = .51$ – with 37 patients whose SMMSE < 16: $r = .43$ with MMSE
	Construct:
	Discriminant: significant decrease in SMMSE score with GDS stages ($F = 68.5$, $p < .001$): – GDS stage 5 $M = 26.7$ ($SD = 2.6$) vs GDS stage 6 $M = 21.1$ ($SD = 4.7$); $p < .05$ – GDS stage 6 vs GDS stage 7 $M = 7.6$ ($SD = 5.7$); $p < .05$
	The same pattern of results occurred with CDR stages
Reliability:	Inter-rater: $r = .99$
	Test–retest: $M = 155$ days: $r = .75$
	Practice effects: Time 1 $M = 23.9$ ($SD = 5.2$) vs Time 2 $M = 21.8$ ($SD = 6.8$); $M = -2.1$
Responsiveness:	No information available

Comment

The SMMSE adopts a novel conceptual stance. With patients in advanced stages of progressive dementia, it is clear that the relevant clinical question is not "is the patient impaired?", but rather "what is still preserved?" As such, the SMMSE focuses on identifying the degree to which redundant, overlearned and well-established skills are still retained. This feature differentiates the SMMSE from many other cognitive screening instruments and turns around the usual approach adopted for cognitive screening from one of deficit measurement to one of ability testing. This approach can be used to advantage for planning patient programmes and developing strategies for management. The SMMSE is a reliable and valid test for patients with moderate and severe degrees of impairment and meets the authors' aim of not being subject to floor effects. It is thus a welcome addition to the field.

Key reference

Harrell, L. E., Marson, D., Chatterjee, A., & Parrish, J. A. (2000). The Severe Mini-Mental State Examination: A new neuropsychologic instrument for the bedside assessment of severely impaired patients with Alzheimer disease. *Alzheimer Disease and Associated Disorders*, *14*(3), 168–175.

Severe Mini-Mental State Examination

Harrell, Marson, Chatterjee, and Parrish (2000)

Name: **Administered by:** **Date:**

SCORE

1. **NAME**:
   First: ____________ Last: ____________

   Scoring: for each name 1 point if close; 3 for each if completely accurate ______

2. **BIRTHDAY**: ____________

   Scoring: 1 point if any elements correct; 2 points if completely accurate ______

3. **REPEAT THREE WORDS**:
   Bird____________ House____________ Umbrella____________

   Scoring: 1 point for each correct response ______

4. **FOLLOW SIMPLE DIRECTIONS**:
   Raise your hand____________ Close your eyes____________

   Scoring: 1 point for following command; 2 points for continuing to hold command (i.e., 5 seconds) until told to stop ______

5. **NAME SIMPLE OBJECTS**:
   Pen____________ Watch____________ Shoe____________

   Scoring: 1 point for each correctly named object ______

6. **DRAW CIRCLE FROM COMMAND**:

   Scoring: 1 point if correct ______

7. **COPY SQUARE**:

   Scoring: 1 point if correct ______

8. **WRITE NAME**:
   First____________ Last____________

   Scoring: for each name 1 point if close; 2 points if completely accurate ______

9. **ANIMAL GENERATION**: ____________

   Scoring: Number of animals in 1 minute:
   1 point for 1–2 Animals, 2 points for 3–4 Animals, 3 points for > 4 animals ______

10. **SPELL "CAT" FORWARD**:

    Scoring: 1 point for each letter given in correct order ______

TOTAL SCORE: ______

Acknowledgement: From Harrell, L. E. et al. (2000). The Severe Mini-Mental State Examination: A new neuropsychologic instrument for the bedside assessment of severely impaired patients with Alzheimer disease. *Alzheimer Disease and Associated Disorders*, *14*(3), 168–175, Appendix 1, p. 174, with permission of Lippincott, Williams & Wilkins and Wolters Kluwer.

Severe Mini-Mental State Examination – Scoring Rules

Harrell, Marson, Chatterjee, and Parrish (2000)

1. The patient is asked to state his or her first and last names. Three points are given for each correct answer. Women, if married, must give married name.
2. The patient is asked to state the month, day, and year of birth. Any order is acceptable. Two points if completely correct. One point for any of the three items.
3. The examiner tells the patient that he/she is going to say three words and then ask the patient to repeat them. The examiner then says "bird, house, umbrella", and asks the patient to repeat them. One point is given for each correctly named item.
4. The patient is asked to follow a direction (for 5 seconds). The first direction is "shut your eyes"; the second is "raise your hand" (either or both hands acceptable). Two points are given for each direction if the patient follows and continues the command until told to stop by the examiner. One point is given for each command if the patient follows the command but does not maintain it until told to stop by the examiner.
5. The examiner shows the patient three items, one at a time, and asks the patient to name them. A pen, a watch, and a shoe are then shown to the patient. One point is given for each correctly named item.
6. The patient is verbally asked to draw a circle. One point if the item drawn resembles a circle; i.e., it must be closed, may be somewhat elliptical, any size acceptable.
7. A copy of a square is presented to the patient, and he/she is asked to copy it. The examiner should not identify the square orally. One point is given if the copy has four sides that touch; rectangular-appearing squares are acceptable.
8. The patient is given a clean sheet of paper and a pen and is asked to write (printing or cursive acceptable) his or her first and last name. Two points are awarded for each item if totally correct and legible, one point if poorly legible or if letters are left out. Women must write their married last name.
9. The patient is asked to generate as many animals as he/she can think of in 1 minute. One point is given for up to two animals, two points for up to four animals, three points for more than four animals.
10. The patient is asked to spell the word "CAT". Letters must be in correct order. One point is given for each correct letter.

Acknowledgement: From Harrell, L. E. et al. (2000). The Severe Mini-Mental State Examination: A new neuropsychologic instrument for the bedside assessment of severely impaired patients with Alzheimer disease. *Alzheimer Disease and Associated Disorders*, *14*(3), 168–175, Appendix 2, pp. 174–175, with permission of Lippincott, Williams & Wilkins and Wolters Kluwer.

Telephone Interview for Cognitive Status (TICS)

Brandt and Folstein (2003)

Source

The TICS, originally published by Brandt, Spencer, and Folstein (1988), is now available commercially through Psychological Assessment Resources (http://www.parinc.com).

Purpose

The TICS is an objective, clinician-administered test designed to be administered via the telephone, "in situations where in-person cognitive screening is impossible or impractical" (Brandt & Folstein, 2003, p. 1). It was developed for people with dementia, but has also been used with other neurological groups, including amnestic mild cognitive impairment (Lines, McCarroll, Lipton, & Block, 2003), stroke (Barber & Stott, 2004), and traumatic brain injury (Dombovy & Olek, 1996), as well as in community surveys of older people (Brandt, Welsh, Breitner, Folstein, Helms, & Christian, 1993; Buckwalter, Crooks, & Petitti, 2002; de Jager, Budge, & Clarke, 2003). The TICS aims to evaluate global cognitive functioning, and "is not intended to diagnose any specific neurological or psychiatric disorder" (p. 9).

Item description

The TICS, as described in the test manual (Brandt & Folstein, 2003), comprises 11 items, although a number of items contain multiple questions. Six domains are sampled: Orientation (name, date, address), Attention (counting backwards from 20 to 1), Calculation (serial sevens), Language (including responsive naming, e.g., "What do people usually use to cut paper?", comprehension, e.g., "From what animal do we get wool?", repetition e.g., "no ifs, ands, or buts", reasoning, e.g., word opposites "east", and semantic knowledge, e.g., name of the president and vice-president), Praxis (tap 5 times on telephone receiver), and Memory (immediate recall of a 10-word list).

Scale development

Limited information is available regarding development of the TICS. Brandt and Folstein (2003) reported that the aim was to "survey the basic cognitive functions that are affected by dementia and delirium . . . Most [of the items] are variations of questions and mental challenges frequently used in the bedside mental status examination" (p. 13). An item assessing delayed recall of the word learning list was originally considered for inclusion in the TICS, but it was rejected on the basis that in pilot testing all participants with Alzheimer's disease (AD) failed the test (Brandt et al., 1988). It is retained in the slightly modified version (TICSm; Welsh, Breitner, & Magruder-Habib, 1993). Studies with the TICSm using the delayed recall of the word learning list did not result in increased discriminatory power, and Brandt and Folstein (2003) concluded that they "see no reason to prefer it to the original instrument" (p. 19).

Brandt et al. (1988) initially selected a cut-off score of 30/31 (3 standard deviations below the control group) to denote cognitive impairment. In a sample of people with mild cognitive impairment (MMSE score ≥ 20) sensitivity was 94% and specificity 100% (positive and negative predictive values 100% and 97% respectively). Welsh et al. (1993) examined two community samples ($n = 214$), recruited from retirement communities, with facilities ranging from independent apartment living to skilled nursing care They compared the TICSm and TICS, and on the basis of receiver operating characteristic (ROC) analyses recommended a slightly higher cut-off score (32/33) for the TICS to maximize sensitivity and specificity (values were not provided in the report). Using the original cut-off score (30/31) achieved 85% sensitivity and 83% specificity, which was considerably lower than in the standardization study of Brandt et al. (1988).

Administration procedures, response format and scoring

Administration and scoring of the TICS are straightforward. Administration time is brief, less than 10

Data box 3.14 Descriptive data from the standardization sample (Brandt et al., 1988)

	Age *M (SD)*	**Education** *M (SD)*	**TICS** *M (SD)*	**Cut-off score**	**Sensitivity / Specificity**
Control ($n = 33$)	67.06 (6.47)	15.0 (3.07)	35.79 (1.75)	30/31	94% / 100%
Probable Alzheimer's disease ($n = 100$)	71.42 (7.83)	13.07 (3.70)	13.20 (8.53)		

minutes. The test manual advises that the TICS should be administered by a qualified and credentialled professional who is familiar with the test, or a person who is trained and supervised by the professional. Given the mode of administration via a telephone, the need for clear pronunciation and articulation by the examiner is of obvious importance. Prior to testing, the examiner needs to speak with another person at the test location (e.g., family member) to ensure the test environment is suitable and the examinee is able to hear spoken language at a conversational volume.

Responses are recorded verbatim. Instructions for scoring are provided in the test manual, with a variable number of points awarded depending on the accuracy of response. The total score ranges from 0 to 41, with higher scores indicating better cognitive functioning.

Cut-off scores have been established to identify unequivocally normal performance (32/33), with scores in the range 26–32 being classified as ambiguous. Degrees of impaired performance are classified as follows: mild impairment is classified with scores of 21 to 25, and moderate to severe impairment with scores ≤ 20. The test manual describes these cut-off scores as "interpretative guidelines [which] must be used with caution and should not override professional judgement" (Brandt & Folstein, 2003, p. 9). A table in the test manual also enables a Mini-Mental State Examination (MMSE) score estimate to be derived from TICS data.

Normative data are provided in the test manual (Brandt & Folstein, 2003) derived from 6338 women, aged 60–89 years, with a professional background in nursing. The data are presented as *T* scores ($M = 50$, $SD = 10$), stratified by age group in three bands by decade.

Psychometric properties

Initial psychometric studies of the TICS (Brandt et al., 1988) were based on a sample of 100 people with probable AD (descriptive data shown in Data box 3.14), along with 33 healthy control participants. The MMSE was administered face-to-face and the TICS administered separately within 6 weeks of initial assessment. A subset ($n = 34$) of the dementia group had the TICS administered twice. No correlation was found with age (patients $r = .16$, controls $r = .04$) or education for controls ($r = -.01$), although education was statistically significant in the patient group ($r = .35$). In the subsequent study of 4302 twin pairs, the majority of whom did not have cognitive impairment, the TICSm score was correlated with years of education ($r = .43$; Brandt et al., 1993). Substantial evidence has been provided for the concurrent validity of the TICS in independent studies using the Revised-CAMCOG, including studies by Barber and Stott (2004) with a sample of 64 patients with stroke, and de Jager et al. (2003) with a sample of 120 older people living in the community.

The underlying factor structure of the TICS was examined by Brandt et al. (1993) using principal components analysis on 13 discriminating TICSm items in 4302 elderly twin pairs ($N = 8604$) from a national registry. Four components were extracted accounting for 46% of the variance: Memory, Language/attention, Recent memory, and Orientation. Lines et al. (2003) reported a similar factor structure using data from 6090 people with amnestic mild cognitive impairment. The TICSm factor structure identified by Buckwalter et al. (2002), in 3506 older women participating in a memory study, however, did not replicate previous studies. Results of Brandt et al. (1988), except where otherwise indicated, are shown in Box 3.16.

Comment

The availability of a standardized instrument that has the facility of not requiring face-to-face examination is advantageous. There are, however, limitations to this assessment procedure, as highlighted by Järvenpää et al. (2002): notably the inability to examine some cognitive domains (e.g., reading), as well as administrative concerns – older people often experience impairments in hearing ability (significant difficulty occurring in 9.6% of examinees in the Buckwalter et al. (2002) study), there can be difficulty in controlling the environment for distractions, and the examiner needs to ensure that prompts are not used (e.g., calendars to cue the examinee for orientation items). On the upside, an advantage of the TICS is its suitability for face-to-face administration for people with visual and motor impairments (Moylan et al., 2004). In their rehabilitation sample of elderly

Box 3.16

Validity:	Criterion: *Concurrent:* with MMSE: $r = .94$ Barber & Stott: with R-CAMCOG: $r = .86$ de Jager et al.: with R-CAMCOG: $r = .62$ Construct: *Internal consistency*: Buckwalter et al.: Cronbach alpha: .70 *Factor analysis*: Brandt et al. (1993): 4 components: Memory (2 items), Language/attention (6 items), Recent memory (2 items – names of political figures), Orientation (3 items) *Discriminant:* dementia group $M = 13.20$ ($SD = 8.53$) vs healthy controls $M = 35.79$ ($SD = 1.75$); $t = 15.07$, $p < .001$ – Differential diagnosis between dementia vs no dementia using cut-off score of 30/31: sensitivity 94%, specificity 100% Welsh et al.: Differential diagnosis between dementia vs no dementia using cut-off score of 30/31: sensitivity 85%, specificity 83%
Reliability:	Inter-rater: No information available Test–retest: 6 weeks: $r = .97$; ICC = .99 *Practice effects*: Time 1 $M = 12.0$ ($SD = 1.34$) vs Time 2 $M = 11.79$ ($SD = 1.27$); $M = -0.21$
Responsiveness:	No information available

people, Moylan et al. found that 95% could complete the TICS, but only 75% completed the MMSE. Additionally, as noted by Brandt and Folstein (2003), the TICS is suitable for people who are illiterate. It is also well received by examinees. Psychometric properties of the TICS are good, showing excellent temporal stability over a period of weeks, minimal practice effects, and evidence to support its validity.

Key references

Barber, M., & Stott, D., J. (2004). Validity of the Telephone Interview for Cognitive Status (TICS) in post-stroke subjects. *International Journal of Geriatric Psychiatry*, *19*(1), 75–79.

Brandt, J., & Folstein, M. F. (2003). TICS: Telephone Interview for Cognitive Status. Lutz, FL: Psychological Assessment Resources.

Brandt, J., Spencer, M., & Folstein, M. (1988). The Telephone Interview for Cognitive Status. *Neuropsychiatry, Neuropsychology and Behavioural Neurology*, *1*(2), 111–117.

Brandt, J., Welsh, K. A., Breitner, J. C. S., Folstein, M. F., Helms, M., & Christian, J. C. (1993). Hereditary influences on cognitive functioning in older men. A study of 4000 twin pairs. *Archives of Neurology*, *50*(6), 599–603.

Buckwalter, J. G., Crooks, V. C., & Petitti, D. B. (2002). A preliminary psychometric analysis of a computer assisted administration of the Telephone Interview of Cognitive Status-Modified. *Journal of Clinical and Experimental Neuropsychology*, *24*(2), 168–175.

de Jager, C. A., Budge, M. M., & Clarke, R. (2003). Utility of TICS-M for the assessment of cognitive function in older adults. *International Journal of Geriatric Psychiatry*, *18*(4), 318–324.

Dombovy, M. L., & Olek, A. C. (1996). Recovery and rehabilitation following traumatic brain injury. *Brain Injury*, *11*(5), 305–318.

Järvenpää, T., Rinne, J. O., Räihä, I., Koskenvuo, M., Löppönen, M., Hinkka, S., et al. (2002). Characteristics of two telephone screens for cognitive impairment. *Dementia and Geriatric Cognitive Disorders*, *13*(3), 149–155.

Lines, C. R., McCarroll, K. A., Lipton, R. B., & Block, G. A. (2003). Telephone screening for amnestic mild cognitive impairment. *Neurology*, *60*, 261–265.

Moylan, T., Das, K., Gibb, A., Hill, A., Kane, A., Lee, C., et al. (2004). Assessment of cognitive function in older hospital inpatients: Is the Telephone Interview for Cognitive Status (TICS-M) a useful alternative to the Mini Mental State Examination? *International Journal of Geriatric Psychiatry*, *19*(10), 1008–1009.

Welsh, K. A., Breitner, J. C. S., & Magruder-Habib, K. M. (1993). Detection of dementia in the elderly using telephone screening of cognitive status. *Neuropsychiatry, Neuropsychology, and Behavioural Neurology*, *6*(2), 103–110.

Test for Severe Impairment (TSI)

Albert and Cohen (1992)

Source

Items for the TSI appear in an appendix to Albert and Cohen (1992) and are reproduced below.

Purpose

The TSI is an objective, clinician-administered test designed for severely cognitively impaired patients with dementia. It was designed for people who "generally have minimal verbal skills remaining" (Albert & Cohen, 1992, p. 449) and results can be used as a marker of current functioning, against which to measure future change (either improvement in response to treatment or deterioration as a result of disease progression).

Item description

The 24-item TSI samples six domains of functioning, each domain containing four items: Motor performance, Language comprehension, Language production, Memory, General knowledge, and Conceptualization.

Scale development

Development of the TSI arose in response to the paucity of suitable measures to examine people with advanced dementia. Albert and Cohen (1992) sought to construct a test tailored to the needs of such a group, ensuring short administration time, sampling a broad range of cognitive functions yet having minimal demands on language, and using item content that would "extend the range of measurement downward" from traditional cognitive tests. The floor effects even of cognitive screening tests, such as the Mini-Mental State Examination (MMSE), for this patient group are well known. Albert and Cohen (1992) had originally planned for the TSI to give credit for attempt at the task, but this was abandoned after pilot testing. A procedure that approximates this intention has been developed by Appollonio et al. (2001; 2005), and is referred to as a modified TSI (mTSI).

Administration procedures, response format and scoring

Only a few simple test materials (common objects) are required for administration. The TSI is easy to administer and requires little time (approximately 10 mins). The modified version of the TSI (mTSI, Appollonio et al., 2001) uses a facilitating cue after an incorrect response, thereby enabling credit for partially correct responses.

For the TSI, 1 point is awarded for each correct response. The total score ranges from 0 to 24, with higher scores indicating better performance. For the mTSI, partial credit is given for a correct response following the facilitating cue to the previously incorrect response. For this version, each item is thus as follows: 0 (incorrect response, even after the facilitating cue), 1 (correct response after the facilitating cue), 2 (spontaneous correct response without the need for the facilitating cue). The total score for the mTSI ranges from 0 to 48.

Psychometric properties

The initial study was conducted with 40 residents (descriptive data shown in Data box 3.15) who were recruited from a chronic care facility in Boston, Massachusetts, USA (Albert & Cohen, 1992). All residents had dementia of various types, including Alzheimer's disease (AD), multi-infarct dementia and Parkinson's disease with dementia, and required nursing care for basic activities of daily living. They were selected for inclusion if their scores on the MMSE were ≤ 10 ($M = 6.4$, $SD = 3.2$, range 1–10). A subset ($n = 19$) was re-examined 2 weeks later. Albert and Cohen explored the underlying factor structure of the TSI using principal components analysis. Three components were extracted, accounting for 52% of the variance.

Psychometric properties of the TSI are also available from reports of other investigators. Jacobs et al. (1999) followed a group of 66 patients with AD over a period of 1.5 to 4.5 years, with at least three administrations of the TSI. They found that patients scoring very low on the MMSE (< 3) still showed a range of scores on the

Data box 3.15 Descriptive data from the standardization sample (Albert & Cohen, 1992)

	Age range	Education range	TSI M (SD)	Cut-off score	Sensitivity / Specificity
Dementia ($n = 40$)	72–98 years	5–16 years	14.6 (5.5)	No information	No information

TSI. Temporal stability was reported by Foldi, Majerovitz, Sheikh, and Rodriguez (1999, $n = 26$) and Appollonio et al. (2001, $n = 87$). Foldi et al. also compared the TSI with other instruments including the Mattis Dementia Rating Scale (MDRS). There was no significant correlation with age ($r = .05$) or education ($r = .21$) and these patterns of results have been replicated in an independent sample by Appollonio et al. (2001). The latter group also examined the mTSI in relation to Clinical Dementia Rating (CDR) scale.

Box 3.17

Validity:	Criterion *Concurrent:* Jacobs et al.: with MMSE: $r = .83$ Foldi et al.: with MDRS: $r = .88$ – as well as similar subscales between TSI and MDRS: memory ($r = .73$), conceptualization ($r = .71$), motor/construction ($r = .62$) *Predictive*: Jacobs et al.: in a longitudinal study of patients with AD the TSI (but not the MMSE) was a significant predictor of survival until death Construct: *Internal consistency:* Cronbach alpha: .91 *Factor structure*: 3 factors: Memory (5 items), Verbal production (7 items), Knowledge of body parts (3 items) *Discriminant:* Foldi et al.: differentiated between subgroups with MDRS scores ≥ 75 ($M = 22.73$) vs < 75 ($M = 14.14$); $t = -7.29, p < .001$ Appollonio et al. (2001): mTSI: differentiated between subgroups at CDR levels: CDR1 $M = 41.7$ ($SD = 2.2$) vs CDR2 $M = 40.9$ ($SD = 2.8$) vs CDR3 $M = 30.2$ ($SD = 5.1$) vs CDR4 $M = 5.0$ ($SD = 8.5$); $F = 125.4$, $p < .001$
Reliability:	Inter-rater: Appollonio et al. (2001): mTSI: $r = .94$ Test–retest: 2 weeks: total score: $r = .96$ (subscale range $r = .74–.97$) *Practice effects:* Time 1 $M = 14.6$ ($SD = 5.5$) vs Time 2 $M = 13.4$ ($SD = 5.9$); $M = -1.2$ Foldi et al.: 1 month: $r = .74$ Appollonio et al. (2001): mTSI: 1 month: $r = .77$
Responsiveness:	Jacobs et al.: annual rate of change −18.0 (+/− 1.8%) points; $t = 5.7, p < .001$

Results from Albert and Cohen for the TSI, except where otherwise stated, are shown in Box 3.17.

Comment

Few instruments are suitable for the examination of people in advanced stages of dementia. The TSI was one of the first cognitive screening tests to deal with the problem of floor effects occurring for this clinical group by developing item content that was appropriate and suitable while still retaining a breadth of coverage of cognitive domains. In this respect, the TSI has many special features, including short administration time (10 mins), low reliance on verbal responses (which means that the test can distinguish between patients who can make a meaningful but incorrect response and those for whom administration is not possible), limited age and education biases and excellent psychometric properties. Even so, the TSI does require the patient to be able to actively participate in test administration and Appollonio et al. (2005) found that only 67% of their sample of 130 people resident in nursing homes with dementia had rateable scores on the TSI. Nonetheless, for patients in the advanced stages of dementia who are conscious and able to cooperate with test administration, the TSI is an excellent choice. Moreover, the authors suggest the TSI can address the special needs of this patient group in terms of identifying areas of spared abilities that can then be used by staff to develop treatment plans and management strategies. This in itself is a very affirming approach to assessment.

Key references

Albert, M., & Cohen, C. (1992). The Test for Severe Impairment: An instrument for the assessment of patients with severe cognitive dysfunction. *Journal of American Geriatrics Society*, *40*(5), 449–453.

Appollonio, I., Gori, C., Riva, G. P., Spiga, D., Ferrari, A., Ferrarese, C., et al. (2001). Cognitive assessment of severe dementia: The test for severe impairment (TSI). *Archives of Gerontology and Geriatrics. Supplement*, *7*(S7), 25–31.

Appollonio, I., Gori, C., Riva, G., Spiga, D., Ferrari, A., Ferrarese, C., et al. (2005). Assessing early to late stage dementia: The TSI and BANS-S scales in the nursing home. *International Journal of Geriatric Psychiatry*, *20*(12), 1138–1145.

Foldi, N. S., Majerovitz, S. D., Sheikh, K., & Rodriguez, E. (1999). The Test for Severe Impairment: Validity with the Dementia Rating Scale and utility as a longitudinal measure. *The Clinical Neuropsychologist*, *13*(1), 22–29.

Jacobs, D. M., Albert, S. M., Sano, M., del Castillo-Castañeda, C., Paik, M. C., Marder, K., et al. (1999). Assessment of cognition in advanced AD: The Test for Severe Impairment. *Neurology*, *52*(8), 1689–1691.

Test for Severe Impairment

Albert and Cohen (1992)

Name:	**Administered by:**	**Date:**

Instructions: Write down all responses verbatim that are different from those on the sheet. If the patient does not hear a question or is distracted, you may repeat the questions up to three times in order to engage their attention. Award 1 point for each correct response.

MOTOR PERFORMANCE **SCORE**

Item 1: Materials: Comb. Instructions: Hand patient a comb

1. Show me how you would use this comb ______

Item 2: Materials: Pen and top. Instructions: Remove the top from the pen in full view of patient. Hand the pen and top to patient
Score correct if puts top on pen (not on bottom of pen)

2. Can you put the top on the pen? ______

Item 3: Materials: Pen and paper. Instructions: Hand patient the pen (without the top) and place paper on table in front of him/her.
Score correct if writes name correctly (first and last name legible)

3. Write your name ______

LANGUAGE – COMPREHENSION

4. Point to your ear ____________________ ______
5. Close your eyes ____________________ ______

Items 6 and 7: Materials: Coloured pens. Instructions: Red, Blue, Green: Place the three pens on the table spread out so that they have some space between them.

6. Show me the red pen ______
7. Show me the green pen ______

LANGUAGE – PRODUCTION

Item 8: Instructions: Point to your nose

8. What is this called? ____________________ ______

Items 9 and 10: Materials: Pens. red and green. Instructions: One at a time hold up a (red/green) pen in front of patient

9. What colour is this pen? _______ Correctly names red pen ______
10. What colour is this pen? _______ Correctly names green pen ______

Item 11: Materials: Key Instructions: Show key

11. What is this called? ____________________ ______

MEMORY – IMMEDIATE

Items 12 and 13: Materials: One large paperclip. Instructions: Place clip in your hand so patient can see. Hold hands out to patient

Watch carefully.

12. With hands open: Which hand is the clip in? ____________________ ______
13. With hands closed: Which hand is the clip in? ____________________ ______

Item 14: Instructions: Move hands behind back:

14. Watch carefully. Which hand/side is the clip in/on? _______ ______

GENERAL KNOWLEDGE **SCORE**

15. How many ears do I have? ______________ Correctly states two. ______

> Item 16: Instructions: Place hands in front of patient with fingers pointing up, palms towards patient. Scoring: Credit given even if there is no 1-to-1 correspondence between fingers and numbers. If patient only gives final answer, ask "can you count to 10 starting at '1'?"

16. Count my fingers and thumbs ______________ Correctly counts to 10 ______
17. How many weeks are in a year? ______________ Correctly states 52 ______

> Item 18: Instructions: Softly sing "Happy birthday". Score correct if sings most of the words

18. I'm going to sing a song. If you know the words, I want you to sing along with me. ______

CONCEPTUALIZATION

> Item 19: Materials: Two large paper clips, one pen. Instructions: Spread objects out on the table. Score correct if points to pen or states pen

19. Which one of these is different from the other two? ______________ ______

> Item 20: Materials: Two red pens, one green pen. Instructions: Place 1 red and 1 green pen spread out on the table. Hand patient the other red pen. Score correct if places the red pen next to the other red pen

20. Put this next to the pen that is the same colour ______________ ______

> Item 21: Materials: One large paperclip. Instructions: Place hands out in front of patient. Alternate clip between the open hands 4 times.

21. Watch me move the paperclip. Which hand will I put the paper clip in next? ______

> Item 22: Instructions: After patient responds, place clip in correct hand. If patient is incorrect say "I'd put the clip in this hand". Score correct if patient points to the correct hand

22. Which hand will I put it in next? ______________ ______

MEMORY – DELAYED

> Item 23: Materials: Present thread, key, paperclip. Instructions: Place objects spread out on table. Score correct if patient points to thread

23. Which one of these haven't we done something with while you were here with me? ______

____

MOTOR PERFORMANCE

> Item 24: Instructions: Extend hand and shake hands. Score 1 point if patient correctly shakes hands

24. Thank you for spending time with me ______

TOTAL SCORE ______

Acknowledgement: From Albert, M., & Cohen, C. (1992). The Test for Severe Impairment: An instrument for the assessment of patients with severe cognitive dysfunction. *Journal of American Geriatrics Society*, *40*(5), pp. 452–453, by permission of Wiley-Blackwell Publishers.

4 Scales of specific cognitive functions

Instruments presented in Chapter 4 map to the components, domains and categories of the *International Classification of Functioning, Disability and Health* (ICF; WHO, 2001) as depicted in Figure 4.1.

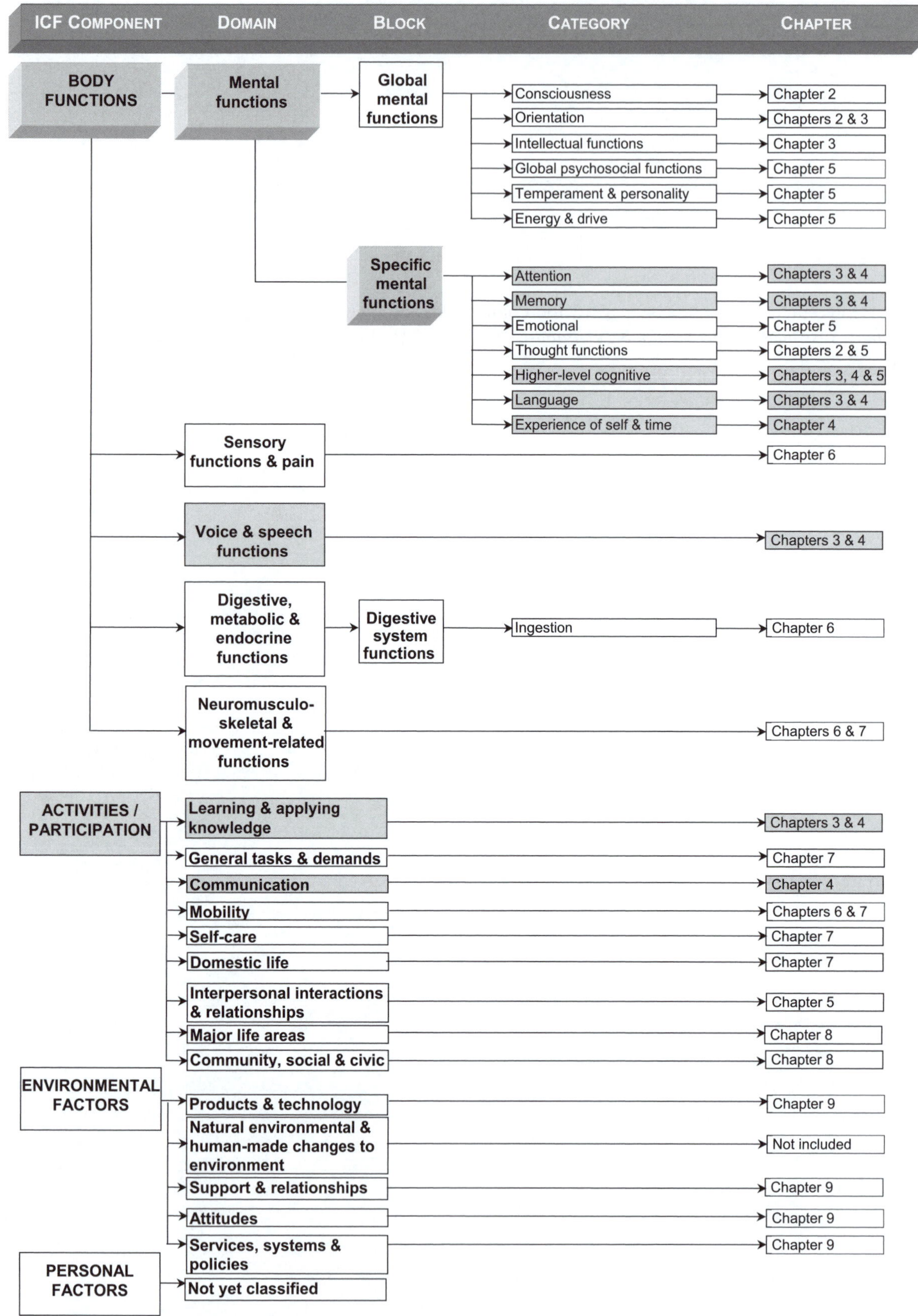

Figure 4.1 Instruments included in the compendium in relation to the ICF taxonomy – the highlighted components, domains and categories appear in this chapter. *Note:* the Figure presents a partial listing of five out of the eight Body Function domains and does not include any of the Body Structure domains. Categories for Mental functions also represent a partial listing and categories for the remaining domains are not listed. Refer to Appendix C for further detail on the ICF taxonomy.

Introduction

The second block within the ICF domain of Mental functions is Specific mental functions (see Figure 4.1 and Appendix C). This block contains a listing of 11 specific second-level categories (attention, memory, psychomotor, emotional, perceptual, thought functions, higher-cognitive, language, calculations, sequencing complex movements, and experience of self and time). Scales from five categories are included in this chapter (attention, memory, higher-cognitive, language, and experience of self and time), with functions addressing "high-cognitive" relabelled as "executive", and "experience of self and time" relabelled as "self-awareness". These changes in nomenclature have been made in keeping with the more commonly used terms in clinical practice and the research literature on acquired brain impairment (ABI); as is the term "cognitive" (rather than "mental") – hence the title of this chapter.

With respect to the remaining six categories of the Specific mental functions block, measures of emotional functions are reviewed in Chapter 5. Thought functions, as defined in the ICF, relate to pace, form, content and control of thought. Disturbances of thought function can occur as a consequence of ABI, particularly in the context of dementia. A number of scales of delirium (see Chapter 2) also include items to assess thought functions, as do a selection of items from scales in Chapter 5 and multidimensional scales in Chapter 10. Specific instruments to assess the remaining four categories (psychomotor, perceptual, calculations, and sequencing complex movements) are not included in this volume, although a number of cognitive screening tests sample these functions (see Chapter 3), as do multidimensional scales (see Chapter 10). All scales pertinent to language-related abilities are located in this chapter, thus including the Voice and speech domain of Body Functioning (although many measures from this domain are specialist instruments used by speech pathologists/speech and language therapists), along with the Communication domain of the Activities/Participation component. Similarly, all measures exclusively examining memory functions are located in this chapter, thereby overlapping with the Activities/Participation domain of Learning and applying knowledge. The 19 scales included in Chapter 4 are grouped into five sections: Section 1: Attention, Section 2: Executive, Section 3: Language, Section 4: Memory, and Section 5: Self-awareness.

Some of the instruments presented in this chapter to assess specific cognitive functions have affinity with items from scales presented in other chapters. The assessment of memory and language, in particular, features frequently in general cognitive screening tests (see Chapter 3). Virtually all of the instruments included in that chapter provide an objective evaluation of memory/language function using clinician-administered tests. There are few objective tests that are specifically devoted to memory alone, however, that are not specialist neuropsychological tests. Consequently, the majority of instruments of specific memory functions presented in the current chapter are rating scales and the reader who is interested in objective screening tests of memory should also consult Chapter 3. Similarly, the executive category overlaps with those scales in Chapter 3 that include items sampling executive functions (e.g., Cognitive Abilities Screening Instrument, Montreal Cognitive Assessment). A small number of executive scales presented in this chapter are objective, clinician-administered tests with a cognitive focus. Additionally, there is overlap with instruments presented in Chapter 5 on the regulation of behaviour, thought and emotion. Some scales presented in Chapter 5 provide either an objective evaluation of the regulation of behaviour that directly pertains to executive functions (e.g., Behavioral Dyscontrol Scale); other instruments (e.g., Behavior Rating Inventory of Executive Function, Frontal Systems Behavior Scale) include subscales specifically addressing the cognitive components of executive dysfunction. In recent years assessment of language in some neurological samples has incorporated a cognitive-linguistic approach (see McDonald & Togher, 2006) in order to capture non-aphasic communication disorders. Some language-specific scales are available (see La Trobe Communication Questionnaire in this chapter) and items from some scales in Chapter 5 are also sensitive to these types of impairments.

Although many of the instruments described in this chapter are rating scales, objective clinician-administered screening tests suitable for administration by generic health professionals have also been included where appropriate, as have clinician rating scales that are based on detailed behavioural observation of patients. Rating scales of cognitive functions proliferated in the early 1980s largely in response to researchers' concerns about the ecological validity of "laboratory-based tests". Their clinical and research role in persons with ABI remains controversial and the question posed by Sunderland, Harris, and Baddeley (1984) 25 years ago remains: "the major problem here is that of validity: can questionnaires, diaries or checklists provide an accurate account of the actual incidence of memory failures?" (p. 192). Although memory questionnaires, for example, can be useful as checklists of common memory problems, their potential use as screening tools for use in ABI populations is problematic. Indeed, Kinsella et al. (1996) comment "that it seems counter-intuitive to expect [people with traumatic brain injury], who have demonstrated memory deficits, to be able to recall previous memory failures" (p. 506).

One validity issue, raised in other chapters, pertains to the question of "who should do the rating?" The candidate respondents are the person with ABI, an informant or the clinician/researcher. There are advantages and disadvantages to each. With respect to cognition, however, some constructs can only be validly rated by the person themselves (e.g., "Do you put in effort when you want to memorize a funny story?"; "Do you read something and find you haven't been thinking about it and must read it again?"), but for people who experience significant impairments in memory, judgement and awareness the validity of their responses is jeopardized. Thus, while a test score may well be produced, the question arises as to the extent to which the score represents an accurate response. Relative-informants have the advantage that they knew the person before the brain impairment and hence they have a valuable comparison standard, yet it is recognized that relatives may not provide a totally objective frame of reference. Kertesz, Nadkarni, Davidson, and Thomas (2000) comment that, in relation to their Frontal Behavioral Inventory, "the accuracy and validity of the answers are, to a large extent, dependent on the caregiver. Some caregivers are not as perceptive as others and a few are very protective, minimizing the symptoms" (p. 466). Bennett, Ong, and Ponsford (2005) indicate that the clinician (who has knowledge of the patient) is in the best position, and certainly in their study the correlation coefficient between two clinicians ($r = .79$) was remarkably higher than those between informants and clinicians ($r = .42 - .45$).

Another set of issues pertinent to cognitive rating scales relates to the curious feature that rating scales of specific cognitive functions often show modest correlation with objective tests of the constructs they are supposed to measure, raising issues of construct validity. Correlation coefficients between, for example, cognitive questionnaires and objective, clinically based tests in neurological populations are often around $r = .50$, implying that more than 75% of the variance is accounted for by other factors. Coefficients can also be considerably lower, as reported by Randolph, Arnett, and Freske (2004) between self-ratings on the Memory Functioning Questionnaire and neuropsychological tests ($r = .04 - .27$) and by Bogod, Mateer, and MacDonald (2003) between informant ratings on the Dysexecutive Questionnaire and neuropsychological tests ($r = .14 - .27$). Parenthetically, when interpreting correlation coefficients it is noted that some researchers emphasize statistical significance, but in this context the more important issue is the magnitude of the coefficient, not its statistical significance, which is influenced by the size of the sample. With large sample sizes, it is not uncommon for correlation coefficients as low as $r = .2$ to be statistically significant, but the magnitude of such coefficients indicates that there is very little relationship between the two variables.

A specific area of concern with the construct validity of self-report cognitive rating scales is the limited evidence for their divergent validity. Some investigators have examined the relationship between cognitive questionnaires and mood state. A not uncommon finding is that the correlation coefficients between depressive symptomatology and cognitive questionnaires can be as high as, or exceed, those between the objective cognitive tests and the questionnaire. Hannon, Adams, Harrington, Fries-Dias, and Gipson (1995), for instance, reported a correlation coefficient of $r = -.41$ between the Prospective Memory Questionnaire and the Beck Depression Inventory, but coefficients as low as $r = .17$ between the memory questionnaire and objective memory tasks. These findings suggest that self-report cognitive questionnaires are not specific to cognition, but rather encompass much broader constructs, a factor that needs to be taken into account in the interpretation of results.

All these issues may suggest that cognitive rating scales are too flawed to serve their purpose, but this needs to be put into the wider perspective of other functional areas. It is perhaps understandable that correlation coefficients between the rating of an abstract construct such as cognition and objective cognitive tests may well be low, and it is reasonable to expect coefficients to be much higher between a tangible construct as basic self-care tasks (e.g., ability to eat independently, dress, walk) and physical assistance for such activities. Yet, in their study of 182 people with spinal cord injury ($n = 53$) or traumatic brain injury ($n = 129$), Heinemann et al. (1997) found only moderate correlation ($r = -.54$) between ratings on the Motor Scale of the Functional Independence Measure and actual minutes of nursing care.

In spite of the foregoing limitations, the use of rating scales of cognitive function with people with ABI has advantages: rating scales are able to address functioning in ecological terms to a degree of specificity and relevance that objective tests have not been able to match. They also provide the person's perspective of their functioning and can serve as a guide for remediation programmes. Thus, the place of rating scales of cognitive function in people with ABI is probably best seen as a supplement to, rather than a replacement of, the objective and detailed evaluation of a cognitive domain by a specialist clinician/researcher.

References

Bennett, P. C., Ong, B., & Ponsford, J. (2005). Measuring executive dysfunction in an acute rehabilitation setting.

Using the dysexecutive questionnaire (DEX). *Journal of the International Neuropsychological Society*, *11*, 376–385.

Bogod, N. M., Mateer, C. A., & MacDonald, S. W. S. (2003). Self-awareness after traumatic brain injury: A comparison of measures and their relationship to executive functions. *Journal of the International Neuropsychological Society*, *9*, 450–458.

Hannon, R., Adams, P., Harrington, S., Fries-Dias C., & Gipson, M. T. (1995). Effects of brain injury and age on prospective memory self-rating and performance. *Rehabilitation Psychology*, *40* (4), 289–298.

Heinemann, A. W., Kirk, P., Hastie, B. A., Semik, P., Hamilton, B. B., Linacre, J. M., et al. (1997). Relationships between disability measures and nursing effort during medical rehabilitation for patients with traumatic brain and spinal cord injury. *Archives of Physical Medicine and Rehabilitation*, *78*, 143–149.

Kertesz, A., Nadkarni, N., Davidson, W., & Thomas, A. (2000). The Frontal Behavioral Inventory in the differential diagnosis of frontotemporal dementia. *Journal of the International Neuropsychological Society*, *6*(4), 460–468.

Kinsella, G., Murtagh, D., Landry, A., Homfray, K., Hammond, M., O'Beirne, L., et al. (1996). Everyday memory following traumatic brain injury. *Brain Injury*, *10*(7), 499–507.

McDonald, S., & Togher, L. (2006). The new age of communication research: discourse, cognition and behaviour. *Brain Impairment*, *7* (3), 169–174.

Randolph, J. J., Arnett, P. A., & Freske, P. (2004). Metamemory in multiple sclerosis: Exploring affective and executive contributors. *Archives of Clinical Neuropsychology*, *19*, 259–279.

Sunderland, A., Harris, J. E., & Baddeley, A. D. (1984). *Assessing everyday memory after severe head injury*. In J. E. Harris and R. E. Morris (Eds.), *Everyday memory, actions and absent-mindedness* (pp. 191–206). London: Academic Press.

World Health Organization. (2001). *International classification of functioning, disability and health*. Geneva: World Health Organization.

SECTION 1
Scales measuring attention functions

Moss Attention Rating Scale (MARS)

Whyte, Hart, Bode, and Malec (2003) and Hart et al. (2006)

Source

The MARS is available from Drs Whyte and Hart (Moss Rehabilitation Research Institute, 60 E Township Line Road, Elkins Park, PA, 19027, USA; email: jwhyte@einstein.edu; thart@einstein.edu). The scale and scoring instructions appear in appendices to Whyte, Hart, Ellis, and Chervoneva (2008), and are also reproduced below.

Purpose

The MARS is an observational rating scale, designed for use by rehabilitation clinicians to assess a range of specific components of attention in the everyday environment. It was developed for people with traumatic brain injury (TBI).

Item description

The 22-item MARS contains three statistically derived factors: Restlessness/distractibility (5 items), Initiation (3 items), and Sustained/consistent attention (3 items). The remaining 11 items do not load on any factor, and are included to capture the multidimensional nature of attention and ensure items represent various difficulty levels.

Scale development

A systematic approach was adopted in developing the MARS (Whyte et al., 2003). The authors aimed to develop a scale that sampled components of attention: sustained attention and persistence, internal and external distractibility, arousal and alertness, orienting, working memory and attention span, shifting and dividing attention, initiation, performance consistency, ability to mobilize and direct attentional resources. A literature search was used "to identify key words and phrases that might characterize dimensions within the domain of attention" (p. 269). Thereafter a group of 11 experts generated information pertinent to attention and edited a preliminary list of items. The items were piloted on 10 patients, using clinician-raters from a range of therapy disciplines. Focus groups were subsequently held with the raters and problematic items were either eliminated or rephrased. This resulted in 53 items, 45 of which examined components of attention and the remaining 8 were "control" items. The rationale for including the latter group of control items that were not directly related to attention was to ensure the scale was specific to attentional problems, rather than general injury-severity factors. The 53 items were piloted with another sample of 20 inpatients. Inter-rater reliability of the majority of items was described as at least "moderately good" and confirmed in a subsequent study (Whyte et al., 2008).

Hart et al. (2006) subjected the 45 attention items to exploratory and confirmatory factor analysis, along with Rasch analysis, using data from 372 TBI rehabilitation inpatients from eight participating centres in the USA. Exploratory factor analysis extracted three factors (Restlessness/distractibility, Initiation, and Sustained/consistent attention) with loadings from 19 items, and confirmatory factor analysis yielded a three-factor model. These items were subject to Rasch analysis, demonstrating good separation, reliability and overall fit (details below). Calibrations were made to improve item fit and distribution, with some items deleted and others added. Finalization of item content was guided by clinical as well as statistical considerations, and resulted in the final 22-item version of the MARS.

Administration procedures, response format and scoring

In the initial research studies, experienced clinicians (the patients' treating therapists) made MARS ratings. The ratings were made after 2 or 3 "consecutive days of 'normal' observation and interaction in the clinical setting" (Whyte et al., 2003, p. 269). Following the

Data box 4.1 Descriptive data from the reliability sample (Whyte et al., 2008)

	Age *M* (*SD*)	Education *M* (*SD*)	MARS *M* (95% CI)	Cut-off score	Sensitivity / Specificity
TBI rehabilitation inpatients (*n* = 149)	43.3 (19.7)	12.1 (3.4)		No information	No information
Nursing			72.2 (68.4–76.0)		
Occupational Therapy			71.2 (68.1–74.4)		
Physical Therapy			70.2 (67.8–72.7)		
Speech & Language			71.9 (66.6–77.2)		

observation period, completion time for the MARS itself is quick and easy.

Items are rated on a 5-point scale: 1 (definitely false), 2 (false, for the most part), 3 (sometimes true, sometimes false), 4 (true, for the most part), 5 (definitely true). Approximately half of the items require reverse scoring. The total score ranges from 22 to 110, with higher scores indicating better attention. Normative data are not currently available to assist in interpretation of the scores. A conversion table is used to convert the MARS raw scores to Rasch logits (see later).

Psychometric properties

Hart et al. (2006) conducted Rasch analysis on the 22-item version, using the above sample of 372 TBI rehabilitation inpatients (age $M = 37.0$ years, range 16–90; injury severity – time to follow commands $M = 8.4$ days, $SD = 11.6$; assessed between days 3–17 post-trauma). A 3-day observation period was used to inform the ratings by the treating occupational and physical therapists (OT and PT respectively). Results of the Rasch analysis revealed no item misfit or distributional gaps. The total score showed good person and item separations. Rasch results for the individual factors were not as strong, but in each case the factors showed good item separation and reliability (with respective scores of 3.42 and 0.92 for Restlessness/distractibility, 3.42 and 0.92 for Initiation, and 7.06 and 0.98 for Sustained/consistent attention), although person separation and reliability were not as high (separation < 2.0; reliability 0.44–0.63). Inter-rater reliability and responsiveness were examined in a multicentre study, in a sample of 149 people (descriptive data shown in Data box 4.1) who were admitted for acute rehabilitation following moderate to severe TBI (Whyte et al., 2008). MARS ratings were made by PT, OT, speech and language pathologists and nurses (a total of 52 raters) after admission ($n = 142$; $M = 11.5$ days post-admission) and again towards the time of discharge ($n = 104$; in all but 3 cases, at least 7 days after initial ratings). Results of these studies are shown in Box 4.1.

Box 4.1

Validity:	Construct: *Factor analysis:* Hart et al.: 3 factors: Restlessness/distractibility (5 items), Initiation (3 items), Sustained/consistent attention (3 items) *Rasch analysis*: Hart et al.: Person separation: 2.60 (reliability 0.87), item separation: 8.04 (reliability 0.98), no misfitting items
Reliability:	Inter-rater: Whyte et al. (2008): initial ratings: – within the same disciplines: ICC = .59–.78 – among different disciplines: ICC = .64–.76 Test–retest: No information available
Responsiveness:	Whyte et al. (2008): significant change in score between initial and discharge ratings for all disciplines: Time 1 Mean range = 70.2–72.2 vs Time 2 Mean range = 79.1–85.3; change score Mean range = 7.8–13.1; each $p < .001$

Comment

The MARS has been developed and refined during the course of a number of empirical studies. The 22-item version avoids the administrative burden of the earlier longer 53-item version and is a good fit to a Rasch model, providing support for its construct validity. The MARS shows good to excellent inter-rater reliability among different therapy disciplines, and is responsive to change, all of which support its clinical utility. At this stage of its development, it would be helpful to have information on its temporal stability and concurrent validity, particularly with objective tests of attention.

Key references

Hart, T., Whyte, J., Millis, S., Bode, R., Malec, J., Nakase Richardson, R., et al. (2006). Dimensions of disordered attention in traumatic brain injury: Further validation of the Moss Attention Rating Scale. *Archives of Physical Medical and Rehabilitation*, *87*(5), 647–655.

Whyte, J., Hart, T., Bode, R. K., & Malec, J. F. (2003). The Moss Attention Rating Scale for traumatic brain injury: Initial psychometric assessment. *Archives of Physical Medical and Rehabilitation*, *84*, 268–276.

Whyte, J., Hart, T., Ellis, C. A., & Chervoneva, I. (2008). The Moss Attention Rating Scale for traumatic brain injury: Further explorations of reliability and sensitivity to change. *Archives of Physical Medical and Rehabilitation*, *89*, 966–973.

Moss Attention Rating Scale

Whyte, Hart, Bode, and Malec (2003)

Hart et al. (2006)

Name:	**Administered by:**	**Date:**

Instructions:

Using the number key below, please indicate to what degree each descriptor applies to the person you are rating. Please do not leave any items blank. If you are not sure how to answer, just make your best guess.

Response key:
1 = Definitely false
2 = False, for the most part
3 = Sometimes true, sometimes false
4 = True, for the most part
5 = Definitely true

		RESPONSE
1.	Is restless and fidgety when unoccupied	______
2.	Sustains conversation without interjecting irrelevant or off-topic comments	______
3.	Persists at a task or conversation for several minutes without stopping or "drifting off"	______
4.	Stops performing a task when given something else to do or to think about	______
5.	Misses materials needed for tasks even though they are within sight and reach	______
6.	Performance is best early in the day or after a rest	______
7.	Initiates communication with others	______
8.	Fails to return to a task after an interruption or unless prompted to do so	______
9.	Looks toward people approaching	______
10.	Persists with an activity or response after being told to stop	______
11.	Has no difficulty stopping one task or step in order to begin the next one	______
12.	Attends to nearby conversations rather than the current task or conversation	______
13.	Tends not to initiate tasks that are within his/her capabilities	______
14.	Speed or accuracy deteriorates over several minutes on a task, but improves after a break	______
15.	Performance of comparable activities is inconsistent from one day to the next	______
16.	Fails to notice situations affecting current performance, e.g., wheelchair hitting against table	______
17.	Perseverates on previous topics of conversation or previous actions	______
18.	Detects errors in his/her own performance	______
19.	Initiates activity (whether appropriate or not) without cueing	______
20.	Reacts to objects being directed toward him/her	______
21.	Performs better on tasks when directions are given slowly	______
22.	Begins to touch or manipulate nearby objects not related to task	______
	TOTAL SCORE:	______

Acknowledgement: From Whyte, J. et al. (2008). The Moss Attention Rating Scale for traumatic brain injury: Further explorations of reliability and sensitivity to change. *Archives of Physical Medicine and Rehabilitation*, *89*(5), 966–973, Appendix 1 used with permission of the American Congress of Rehabilitation Medicine and the American Academy of Physical Medicine and Rehabilitation and Elsevier Limited.

Moss Attention Rating Scale

Whyte, Hart, Ellis, and Chervoneva (2008)

Scoring instructions

The table shows the scoring procedure for the 22-item version of the MARS. The first column provides the item number from the original MARS instrument, and the second column provides the number corresponding to the current 22-item form. To score the MARS, first transform the scores for the items that are reverse worded (indicated by "6-X" in the column labelled "scoring direction"). Once these items are transformed, the item scores are summed to get a total MARS score. Specific items also contribute to factor scores as indicated by the next 3 columns. Because the number of contributing items varies by factor, means of these items (after score transformation) are used to calculate the factor scores.

Original item number	New item number	Item text	Scoring direction	Factor 1: Restless/ distraction	Factor 2: Initiation	Factor 3: Sustained/ consistent
1	1	Is restless or fidgety when unoccupied	6-X	X		
2	2	Sustains conversation without interjecting irrelevant or off-topic comments	X			
4	3	Persists at a task or conversation for several minutes without being stopped or "drifting off"	X			
6	4	Stops performing a task when given something else to do or to think about	6-X			
7	5	Misses materials needed for tasks even though they are within sight and reach	6-X			
8	6	Performance is best early in the day or after a rest	6-X			X
11	7	Initiates communication with others	X		X	
13	8	Fails to return to a task after an interruption unless prompted to do so	6-X			
16	9	Looks toward people approaching	X			
18	10	Persists with an activity or response after being told to stop	6-X	X		
27	11	Has no difficulty stopping one task or step in order to begin the next one	X			
28	12	Attends to nearby conversations rather than the current task or conversation	6-X	X		
33	13	Tends not to initiate tasks that are within his/her capabilities	6-X		X	
34	14	Speed or accuracy deteriorates over several minutes on a task, but improves after a break	6-X			X
38	15	Performance of comparable activities is inconsistent from one day to the next	6-X			X
39	16	Fails to notice situations affecting current performance, e.g., wheelchair hitting against table	6-X			
40	17	Perseverates on previous topics of conversation or previous actions	6-X	X		
43	18	Detects errors in his/her own performance	X			
45	19	Initiates activity (whether appropriate or not) without cueing	X		X	
46	20	Reacts to objects being directed toward him/her	X			
47	21	Performs better on tasks when directions are given slowly	6-X			
50	22	Begins to touch or manipulate nearby objects not related to task	6-X	X		
			Total: ____	**Mean:** ____	**Mean:** ____	**Mean:** ____

Acknowledgement: From Whyte, J. et al. (2008). The Moss Attention Rating Scale for traumatic brain injury: Further explorations of reliability and sensitivity to change. *Archives of Physical Medicine and Rehabilitation*, *89*(5), 966–973, Appendix 2 used with permission of the American Congress of Rehabilitation Medicine and the American Academy of Physical Medicine and Rehabilitation and Elsevier Limited.

Moss Attention Rating Scale

Conversion table: raw scores to logit-based scores

raw	logit	raw	logit	raw	logit	raw	logit
22	0						
23	10.89	45	40.74	67	49.86	89	59.4
24	17.19	46	41.23	68	50.24	90	59.95
25	20.89	47	41.7	69	50.63	91	60.53
26	23.54	48	42.17	70	51.02	92	61.13
27	25.6	49	42.62	71	51.41	93	61.75
28	27.3	50	43.06	72	51.8	94	62.41
29	28.75	51	43.5	73	52.19	95	63.1
30	30.01	52	43.93	74	52.59	96	63.83
31	31.13	53	44.35	75	52.99	97	64.6
32	32.15	54	44.76	76	53.4	98	65.43
33	33.07	55	45.17	77	53.81	99	66.32
34	33.93	56	45.58	78	54.23	100	67.28
35	34.72	57	45.98	79	54.65	101	68.34
36	35.46	58	46.38	80	55.08	102	69.51
37	36.16	59	46.77	81	55.52	103	70.82
38	36.82	60	47.16	82	55.96	104	72.32
39	37.45	61	47.55	83	56.42	105	74.08
40	38.06	62	47.94	84	56.88	106	76.2
41	38.63	63	48.32	85	57.36	107	78.91
42	39.19	64	48.71	86	57.85	108	82.69
43	39.72	65	49.09	87	58.35	109	89.06
44	40.24	66	49.48	88	58.87	110	100

Acknowledgement: Unpublished data kindly provided by Dr Whyte.

Rating Scale of Attentional Behaviour (RSAB)

Ponsford and Kinsella (1991)

Source

The items and recording form for the RSAB are available in Ponsford and Kinsella (1991) and are reproduced below.

Purpose

The RSAB is an observational rating scale designed for clinicians to assess attentional difficulties in the day-to-day therapy setting. It was developed for people with traumatic brain injury (TBI).

Item description

The RSAB comprises 14 items, with principal components analysis (PCA) identifying three components: Attention (e.g., difficulty concentrating, easily distracted, unable to pay attention to more than one thing at a time), Psychomotor retardation (e.g., seemed lethargic, slow in movement, stared into space for long period), and Ability to focus on a task (e.g., difficulty concentrating, restless, unable to stick at an activity for long).

Scale development

Development of the RSAB arose from the authors' work in evaluating a therapeutic intervention for attentional dysfunction in people with TBI. The aim was to develop an ecologically valid scale to "bridge the gap between theoretical constructs of attention and behaviours that are both observable and meaningful in a clinical setting" (Ponsford & Kinsella, 1991, p. 243). Selected items sampled specific types of attentional dysfunction described in the literature, including alertness, selective attention and sustained attention, but no information is provided regarding the item selection process.

Administration procedures, response format and scoring

Clinicians make ratings based on their observations of the patient during the course of their therapy sessions. The scale itself is brief and easy to complete.

Items are rated in terms of frequency on a 5-point scale: 0 (not at all), 1 (occasionally), 2 (sometimes), 3 (almost always), 4 (always). The total score ranges from 0 to 56, with higher scores indicating greater attentional problems. Mean scores were used in the reliability study, thereby anchoring the total score to the 5-point scale.

Psychometric properties

The initial standardization studies reported in Ponsford and Kinsella (1991) used data from 50 patients with TBI recruited from Bethesda Hospital, Melbourne, Australia (descriptive data shown in Data box 4.2). They had a duration of post-traumatic amnesia of 56 days (range 5–183), and were 189.4 days post-trauma

Data box 4.2 Descriptive data from the standardization sample (Ponsford & Kinsella, 1991)

	Age *M* (*SD*)	**Education**	**RSAB** *M* (*SD*)	**Cut-off score**	**Sensitivity / Specificity**
TBI rehabilitation inpatients ($n = 50$)	28.0 (12.4)	No information		No information	No information
Occupational Therapist 1			1.80 (0.75)		
Occupational Therapist 2			1.81 (0.75)		
Speech Pathologist 1			1.92 (0.91)		
Speech Pathologist 2			1.97 (0.92)		

(range 45–718). The patients were rated by their treating occupational therapist (OT) and speech pathologist (SP) at the end of a designated day (and again 3 days later to examine temporal stability) using observations from each clinician's therapy sessions with the patients. PCA was used to examine the underlying factor structure using the data from the same set of 50 patients rated by the two clinicians on two occasions. There was some variability among data sets, but three of the four PCAs contained three factors accounting for approximately 70% to 80% of the variance: Attention, Psychomotor retardation, and Ability to focus on task, although a number of items were complex, loading on multiple components. Concurrent validity of the RSAB was examined with a subset of the sample ($n = 38$) who was administered a battery of attentional measures, including the Stroop, simple and choice reaction time (RT), Symbol Digit Modalities Test (SDMT), and Paced Auditory Serial Addition Test (PASAT). Results are shown in Box 4.2.

Comment

The RSAB fulfils the authors' aims of developing a scale tapping into theoretical constructs, while at the same time producing a practical and clinically meaningful tool. Some measurement properties are very good: it has excellent internal consistency and temporal stability, and shows evidence of concurrent validity with objective cognitive measures of attention. Although the PCAs had small subject:variable ratios, the four analyses yielded an overall consistency in the underlying factor structure of the RSAB, suggesting the factor solution is reliable. The main psychometric drawback of the RSAB appears to be the low inter-rater reliability, but it is noted that the design of the study did not allow a precise evaluation of the RSAB in this respect, because the clinician-raters used different observational samples on which to base their ratings. As the authors note, this information itself is interesting and important, in terms of differences in perspective of the same patient by treating clinicians from various backgrounds.

Box 4.2

Validity:	Criterion: *Concurrent:* with subtests of Stroop: $r = -.33$ to $-.50$ – with RT: $r = .23–.38$ – with SDMT: $r = -.44$ to $-.53$ – with PASAT: $r = -.37$ to $-.55$
	Construct: *Internal consistency:* Cronbach alpha: OT & SP raters on 2 occasions: .92–.95
	Factor analysis: 4 PCAs: most consistent structure 3 components: Attention (~8 items), Psychomotor retardation (~6 items), Focus on task (~5 items)
Reliability:	Inter-rater: OT × SP: $r = .51–.56$ on 2 occasions
	Test–retest: 3 days: OT $r = .93$, SP $r = .91$
Responsiveness:	No information available

Key reference

Ponsford, J., & Kinsella, G. (1991). The use of a rating scale of attentional behaviour. *Neuropsychological Rehabilitation*, *1*(4), 241–257.

Rating Scale of Attentional Behaviour

Ponsford and Kinsella (1991)

Name:	**Administered by:**	**Date:**

Instructions: Could you please answer the following questions about. . . . [name] . . . by recording the number that most closely applies to their behaviour now.

Response key:
0 = Not at all
1 = Occasionally
2 = Sometimes
3 = Almost always
4 = Always

Has .... recently?	**RESPONSE**
1. Seemed lethargic (i.e., lacking energy)	________
2. Tired easily	________
3. Been slow in movement	________
4. Been slow to respond verbally	________
5. Performed slowly on mental tasks	________
6. Needed prompting to get on with things	________
7. Stared into space for long periods	________
8. Had difficulty concentrating	________
9. Been easily distracted	________
10. Been unable to pay attention to more than one thing at once	________
11. Made mistakes because he/she wasn't paying attention properly	________
12. Missed important details in what he/she was doing	________
13. Been restless	________
14. Been unable to stick to an activity for very long	________
TOTAL SCORE:	________

Acknowledgement: From Ponsford, J., & Kinsella, G. (1991). The use of a rating scale of attentional behaviour. *Neuropsychological Rehabilitation*, *1*(4), 241–257, Figure 1, p. 244 reproduced with permission of IOS Press.

SECTION 2
Scales assessing executive functions

Dysexecutive Questionnaire (DEX)

Burgess, Alderman, Wilson, Evans, and Emslie (1996)

Source

The DEX, which accompanies the Behavioural Assessment of the Dysexecutive Syndrome (BADS; Wilson, Alderman, Burgess, Emslie, and Evans, 1996), is commercially available from Pearson (http://www.pearson-uk.com).

Purpose

The DEX is a rating scale, using clinician, informant and/or self-ratings. It was designed to sample everyday problems commonly associated with frontal systems dysfunction. The DEX was used as a validation tool for the BADS, although it is not a formal part of the BADS in that its results do not contribute to the BADS score (Wilson et al., 1996; Wilson, Evans, Emslie, Alderman, & Burgess, 1998). The DEX can also be used as a measure of awareness, by calculating a discrepancy score between self and informant responses. The BADS (and DEX) were initially examined in people with dementia, encephalitis, stroke and traumatic brain injury (TBI). Published work with other neurological groups includes people with multiple sclerosis (Norris & Tate, 2000), and Parkinson's disease (PD; Mathias, 2003), as well as older people.

Item description

The DEX comprises 20 items sampling four domains: emotional (e.g., "I sometimes get overexcited about things and can be a bit 'over the top' at these times"), motivational (e.g., "I am lethargic, or unenthusiastic about things"), behavioural (e.g., "I tend to be restless and 'can't sit still' for any length of time") and cognitive (e.g., "I have trouble making decisions, or deciding what I want to do"). The DEX has two forms, Self and Informant, which contain the same items, but phrased as appropriate.

Scale development

Available information suggests that the DEX was developed at approximately the same time as the BADS, but independently from the latter instrument. The initial publication describing the DEX in detail is the BADS manual (Wilson et al., 1996). In addition to its role as a validation tool for the BADS, it was also anticipated that informants' ratings on the DEX would be used to supplement information provided by the BADS or other cognitive tests, thereby furnishing qualitative information about executive functioning in everyday terms. Limited information is available on the item selection process for the DEX, although Burgess, Alderman, Evans, Emslie, and Wilson (1998) describe it as aiming "to cover 20 of the most commonly reported symptoms of the dysexecutive (or 'frontal lobe') syndrome" (p. 548). Items were generated using the four broad areas identified by Stuss and Benson (1984, 1986): emotional, motivational, behavioural, and cognitive.

Administration procedures, response format and scoring

The DEX can be completed either (i) independently by a clinician or an informant who has good knowledge of the person or (ii) as a self-rating. Administration time is generally brief, but it can vary – the manual advises that "often people may need a little time to think about what each question means ... what may seem an obvious question to an experienced clinician may often seem quite confusing to a lay-person" (Wilson et al., 1996, p. 11).

All items are rated in terms of frequency on a 5-point scale: 0 (never), 1 (occasionally), 2 (sometimes), 3 (fairly often), 4 (very often). Scores are summed and the total scores range from 0 to 80, with higher scores indicating greater problems with executive functioning. The discrepancy score to measure awareness ranges from –80 to +80; scores in the positive direction indicate that the informant endorses greater frequency of problem than the patient, suggestive of the patient having problems with awareness.

Data box 4.3 Descriptive data from the initial sample reported in the BADS (Wilson et al., 1996)

	Age *M* (*SD*)	Education	BADS *M* (*SD*)	Cut-off score	Sensitivity/Specificity
Neurological outpatients ($n = 78$)	38.8 (15.7)	No information		No information	No information
Informant ratings			32.85 (15.98)		
Self-ratings			27.21 (14.48)		

Psychometric properties

The BADS manual (Wilson et al., 1996) focuses on the development and psychometric properties of the six BADS subtests and no reliability or validity data are provided for the DEX. A mixed neurological sample ($n = 78$) was used to validate the BADS against the DEX. The patient group (descriptive data shown in Data box 4.3) mostly comprised people with TBI (59%), but also included patients with encephalitis, dementia, and stroke. Burgess et al. (1998) examined the factor structure of the DEX in a mixed neurological group ($n = 96$) and also examined its concurrent validity against neuropsychological tests, encompassing both executive (e.g., Six Elements Test; SET, and Trail Making Test; TMT) and other cognitive domains, including memory (e.g., Rivermead Behavioural Memory Test; RBMT). The factor analysis, conducted on the DEX informant ratings, extracted five factors accounting for 67% of the variance: Inhibition, Intentionality (described as the inability to formulate and carry through goal-oriented plans), Executive memory, Positive affect, and Negative affect, the last two factors referring to emotional and personality changes. This factor structure bore some correspondence with an exploratory factor analysis reported in the manual.

Reliability data on the DEX are available from Bennett, Ong, and Ponsford (2005), who studied 64 people with TBI (age $M = 33$ years, range 17–73 years), mostly within 1 year post-trauma (75% were still hospitalized). Four types of raters were used: two clinicians (treating neuropsychologist [NP] and occupational therapist [OT]), a family member and self-ratings. The DEX was compared with a 65-item "extended DEX" developed by the authors, which showed very high correspondence with the DEX (e.g., for NP ratings $r = .98$). Information on the concurrent validity of the DEX with comparable rating scales (Neuropsychology Behavior and Affect Profile; NBAP, and Neurobehavioral Rating Scale – Revised; NRS-R) was reported by Mathias (2003). She studied 30 people with PD (age $M = 63.7$ years, $SD = 7.3$; years since diagnosis $M = 5.4$, $SD = 2.6$) and 30 health community volunteers with comparable age and years of education. Results of the above studies are shown in Box 4.3.

Box 4.3

Validity:	Criterion: *Concurrent:* Wilson et al. (1996): Informant: with BADS: $r = -.62$ (subtest range $r = .31 - .46$) – Informant–Self discrepancy with BADS: $r = -.40$ Burgess et al. (1998): Informant: with SET: $r = .40$ – with TMT-B: $r = .35$ Mathias: Informant: with NBAP: $r = .85$ – with NRS-R: $r = .89$ – Control: with NBAP: $r = .66$ – with NRS-R: $r = .84$ Other studies, however, report substantially lower coefficients (see text)
	Construct: *Internal consistency:* Bennett et al.: Cronbach alpha with 4 types of raters: .92–.95 *Factor analysis:* Burgess et al. (1998): 5 factors: Inhibition (7 items), Intentionality (5 items), Executive memory (3 items), Positive affect (3 items), Negative affect (2 items) *Convergent/divergent:* Burgess et al. (1998): higher correlation with similar constructs (DEX-Inhibition vs TMT-B: $r = .43$, DEX-Intentionality vs SET: $r = .46$), lower correlation with dissimilar constructs (e.g., Inhibition/Intentionality vs RBMT: both $r = .06$) *Discriminant:* Wilson et al. (1996): Informant $M = 32.85$ ($SD = 15.98$) vs Self $M = 27.21$ ($SD = 14.48$); $t = 2.85$, $p = .006$
Reliability:	Inter-rater: Bennett et al.: NP with OT: $r = .79$ Test–retest: No information available
Responsiveness:	No information available

Other studies of concurrent validity have not been as positive as the original studies. Bennett et al. (2005) reported low coefficients between the DEX and the BADS, both with informants ($r = .14$, subtest range $r = .03$ to $-.29$), and to a lesser extent with clinicians ($r = .37 - .39$, subtest range $r = -.09$ to $-.51$). Similar findings were reported by Norris and Tate (2000) using data from informants of a mixed neurological group of 36 people with TBI and multiple sclerosis and 37 healthy volunteers ($r = .28$, subtest range $r = .06$–$.38$). In 45 people with TBI, Bogod, Mateer, and MacDonald (2003) reported low coefficients between the DEX and other executive instruments including the Self-Ordered Pointing Test ($r = .22$), Go/No-Go test ($r = .27$), and Stroop ($r = .14$).

Comment

The DEX was one of the first standardized rating scales of executive symptomatology to be published that was developed specifically for people with acquired brain impairment. It is a brief test, with good inter-rater reliability and evidence of construct validity. It shows evidence of concurrent validity, with high correlation with other comparable self-report measures of executive functioning, such the NBAP. Although the initial validation studies showed moderately strong correlation coefficients between the DEX and other objective tests of executive functions, results from independent research groups have been lower, using both the BADS and other executive measures. Some researchers have also questioned the validity of the relative-informant responses, Bennett et al. (2005) reporting coefficients of $r = .42/.45$ between relative-informant and clinician ratings. This resonates with the recommendation of Wilson et al. (1996) to carefully consider the relative-informant who is best suited to complete the DEX.

Key references

Bennett, P. C., Ong, B., & Ponsford, J. (2005). Measuring executive dysfunction in an acute rehabilitation setting. Using the dysexecutive questionnaire (DEX). *Journal of the International Neuropsychological Society*, *11*, 376–385.

Bogod, N. M., Mateer, C. A., & MacDonald, S. W. S. (2003). Self-awareness after traumatic brain injury: A comparison of measures and their relationship to executive functions. *Journal of the International Neuropsychological Society*, *9*, 450–458.

Burgess, P. W., Alderman, N., Evans, J., Emslie, H., & Wilson, B. A. (1998). The ecological validity of tests of executive function. *Journal of the International Neuropsychological Society*, *4*, 547–558.

Burgess, P. W., Alderman, N., Wilson, B. A., Evans, J. J., & Emslie, H. (1996). The Dysexecutive Questionnaire. In B. A. Wilson, N. Alderman, P. W. Burgess, H. Emslie, & J. J. Evans. (1996). *BADS. Behavioural Assessment of the Dysexecutive Syndrome*. Bury St Edmunds, UK: Thames Valley Test Company.

Mathias, J. L. (2003). Neurobehavioral functioning of persons with Parkinson's disease. *Applied Neuropsychology*, *10*(2), 57–68.

Norris, G., & Tate, R., L. (2000). The Behavioural Assessment of the Dysexecutive Syndrome (BADS): Ecological, concurrent and construct validity. *Neuropsychological Rehabilitation*, *10*(1), 33–45.

Stuss, D. T., & Benson, D. F. (1984). Neuropsychological studies of the frontal lobes. *Psychological Bulletin*, *95*, 3–28.

Stuss, D. T., & Benson, D. F. (1986). *The frontal lobes*. New York: Raven Press.

Wilson, B. A., Alderman, N., Burgess, P. W., Emslie, H., & Evans, J. J. (1996). *BADS. Behavioural Assessment of the Dysexecutive Syndrome*. Bury St Edmunds, UK: Thames Valley Test Company.

Wilson, B. A., Evans, J. J., Emslie, H., Alderman, N., & Burgess, P. (1998). The development of an ecologically valid test for assessing patients with a dysexecutive syndrome. *Neuropsychological Rehabilitation*, *8*(3), 213–228.

Executive Interview (EXIT25)

Royall, Mahurin, and Gray (1992)

Source

A general description of items comprising the EXIT25 is contained in Royall et al. (1992), and a sample response is reproduced below. The test itself is available from Dr Royall (Department of Psychiatry, The University of Texas Health Center at San Antonio, 7703 Floyd Curl Drive, San Antonio, TX 78284–7792, USA; email: royall@utscsa.edu).

Purpose

The EXIT25 is a combination of an objective, clinician-administered test, along with behavioural observations. It was developed to provide a brief, clinically based, bedside screen of executive control functions. The aims of the EXIT25 are to identify the presence and severity of executive impairments, predict everyday problems in self-care and functional abilities, and predict problem behaviours resulting from executive dyscontrol (Royall et al., 1992). The EXIT25 was designed for people with dementia, but has also been used in general medical settings (Schillerstrom et al., 2005) and community surveys (Royall, Palmer, Chiodo, & Polk, 2004; 2005b).

Item description

The EXIT25 contains 25 items that target areas compromised by frontal systems dysfunction, which are manifest in motor signs, behavioural features, and cognitive regulation. Items are derived from other established test procedures of frontal systems dysfunction, including shortened variants of the Trail Making Test, verbal and design fluency, picture description, repetition of anomalous sentences (e.g., "tinkle, tinkle little star"), memory of three words ("apple, table, penny") after distraction, (spelling "cat" forwards and backwards), a Stroop-like interference task, go/no go task, two Luria hand sequences, reciting the months of the year backwards. Additionally, traditional neurological test procedures are incorporated (e.g., cogwheel rigidity, grasp reflex, motor impersistence, snout reflex, finger–nose accuracy, echopraxia, utilization behaviour, imitation) to examine frontal release signs, environmental dependency and so forth. All these tasks provide the opportunity for the examiner to observe the presence of pathognomonic behavioural features including perseveration, disinhibition, aspontaneity, intrusions.

Scale development

Development of the EXIT25 started with a pool of 50 items, generated from literature review and the authors' clinical experience with older people with dementia. Items were selected for acceptability to the examinee, and to facilitate bedside testing and unambiguous scoring. During a process of pilot testing, item content was refined by excluding items with low clinical utility and poor inter-correlation. The final set of 25 items has a fixed order of presentation, and standardized administration procedures. Cut-off scores were explored in the standardization sample, and were provisionally set at 15/16, at which no abnormal score on the Nursing Home Behavior Problem Scale (NHBPS) was found in the normal participants. In a subsequent publication, Royall, Rauch, Román, Cordes, and Polk (2001) cite data from a sample of 200 people, in which receiver operating characteristic (ROC) analysis yielded an area under the curve of 0.93 (sensitivity 93%; specificity 83%).

Administration procedures, response format and scoring

No special test materials are required for the EXIT25. Tasks are presented to the patient "in rapid succession and with minimal instruction, which allows little time for reflection and therefore may enhance any tendency of disinhibition or inappropriate responses" (Stockholm, Vogel, Gade, & Waldemar, 2005, p. 1578). Administration time is 15 minutes. Although designed for administration by non-psychiatric personnel, it is necessary for examiners to be trained in administration procedures for both the motor and the cognitive items.

Each item uses a 3-point response scale: 0 (equivalent of intact performance), 1 (a specific partial error or

Data box 4.4 Descriptive data from the standardization sample (Royall et al., 1992)

	Age *M* (*SD*)	Education *M* (*SD*)	EXIT *M* (*SD*)	Cut-off score	Sensitivity / Specificity *
Older adults (*n* = 40)				15/16	93% / 83%
Accommodation: Level 1	85.6 (6.1)	12.8 (2.6)	10.2 (3.7)		
Level 2			16.8 (7.3)		
Level 3	84.1 (7.0)	13.5 (3.3)	22.9 (7.2)		
Level 4			31.1 (5.5)		

* Using data cited in Royall et al. (2001).

equivocal response), 2 (specific incorrect response or failure to perform). The total score ranges from 0 to 50, with higher scores indicating greater impairment. The cut-off score is set at 15/16.

Psychometric properties

Royall et al. (1992) standandized the EXIT25 on a sample of 40 people (descriptive data shown in Data box 4.4), who were recruited from 537 residents in an extended care community in San Antonio, Texas, USA. The community had four levels of accommodation suited to the resident's level of dependency: 1: retirement apartments without services provided; 2: domestic services provided; 3: intermediate care nursing units; and 4: "Alzheimer's Care Units". Levels 1 and 2 were designated by the authors as non-institutionalized; Levels 3 and 4 as institutionalized. Ten residents were randomly selected from each of the four levels. Validation instruments included the Mini-Mental State Examination (MMSE), Trail Making Test (TMT), Wisconsin Card Sorting Test (WCST), Serial Addition Test (SAT) and NHBPS. Examiners were blind to EXIT25 scores. No significant correlation coefficients were found between EXIT25 scores and age, sex or education. Inter-rater reliability was examined in an independent sample (*n* = 30) from a range of accommodation levels who were tested independently by two physicians.

Data from the above study were also used to establish discriminant validity. In a subsequent study (Royall, Chiodo, & Polk, 2005a), a larger sample (*n* = 193) comprising residents from accommodation Levels 1 and 2, showed significant differences on EXIT25 scores. Discriminant validity was also examined by Stockholm et al. (2005) in a mild dementia sample (*n* = 33) compared with a healthy control group (*n* = 30). Royall et al. (2001) examined the association between magnetic resonance imaging (MRI) and EXIT25 scores in a consecutive series of 52 older people recruited from a dementia assessment clinic. Information on convergent and divergent validity was provided by comparing ratings of lesion severity made by a neuroradiologist (blind to EXIT25 scores). Leukoaerosis (abnormal T2-weighted hyperintensity) in different neuroanatomical regions was hypothesized to be related to EXIT25 scores (viz. frontal vs non-frontal regions).

Evidence for the ecological validity of the EXIT25 is provided by the authors and independent research groups. For example, Dymek, Atchison, Harrell, and Marson (2001) reported moderate correlation coefficients with the Capacity to Consent to Treatment Instrument (CCTI). Using the Older Americans Resources Scale (OARS), Royall et al. (2005b) also found moderate correlation with instrumental activities of daily living. The results from Royall et al. (1992), except where otherwise indicated, are shown in Box 4.4.

Comment

In the space of a brief, bedside test, the EXIT25 provides a reliable, sensitive, discriminating and valid measure of executive impairments as a whole. It is mainly used with the older population and is available in many languages. An aim of the EXIT25 was its prediction of functional independence, and there is evidence of its utility in this regard (but see also the systematic review of cognitive correlates of functional status by Royall et al., 2007). A special feature of the EXIT25 is that it targets pathogonomic signs of frontal systems dysfunction. By including motor signs (e.g., cogwheel rigidity, snout reflex) as well as behavioural features (e.g., utilization behaviour, echopraxia) it is able to discriminate within the lower levels of functioning. This is its main application, although the range of cognitive items (e.g., sequencing, generativity) means that it is also able to discriminate between healthy people and those with mild executive impairments (Stokholm et al., 2005). Traditional neuropsychological examinations, however, may be required to tease out executive impairments at the higher levels of planning, conceptual reasoning abilities and so forth. Moreover, Hooten, and Lyketsos (1998) examined ROC curves of the EXIT25, and found that it was not well

Box 4.4

Validity:	Criterion: *Concurrent:* with MMSE: $r = -.85$ – with TMT-Part A: $r = .73$, TMT-Part B: $r = .64$ – with WCST: $r = .52$ – with SAT errors: $r = .83$, time: $r = .82$ – EXIT25 scores > 15 with disruptive behaviour: $r = .79$ Royall et al. (2001): with MMSE: $r = .66$ Royall et al. (2005a): with OARS: $r = .48$ Dymek et al. (2001): with CCTI subtests: range $r = .53$ to $r = -.75$ Construct: *Internal consistency:* Cronbach alpha: .87 *Convergent/divergent:* Royall et al. (2001): significant differences in MRI severity ratings in related neuroanatomical sites (left frontal cortex $F = 5.89$, $p = .002$, right frontal cortex $F = 6.99$, $p < .02$), but no significant differences in MRI ratings in unrelated neuroanatomical sites (e.g., left posterior cortex $F = 3.86$, $p > .05$, right hippocampus $F = 0.09$, $p > .05$) *Discriminant:* Non-institutionalized $M = 14.2$ ($SD = 7.5$) vs institutionalized $M = 27.9$ ($SD = 7.6$); $t = 5.39$, $p < .001$, as well as differences at each of the 4 accommodation levels Royall et al. (2005a): accommodation Level 1 $M = 13.3$ ($SD = 5.4$) vs Level 2 $M = 15.3$ ($SD = 5.2$); $p = .01$ Royall et al. (2001): cite data for cut-off score of 15/16: sensitivity 93%, specificity 83% Stockholm et al.: Control $M = 8.4$ ($SD = 3.2$) vs mild dementia $M = 17.6$ ($SD = 4.6$); $p < .001$
Reliability:	Inter-rater: $r = .90$ Test–retest: No information available *Practice effects:* No information available
Responsiveness:	Royall et al. (2004): annual rate of change on EXIT25: 0.89 points (SE = 0.16) – Time 1 ($n = 547$) $M = 12.5$ ($SD = 4.64$), Time 2 ($n = 468$) $M = 13.70$ ($SD = 5.29$), Time 3 ($n = 137$) $M = 15.15$ ($SD = 6.77$)

suited to differentiating between dementia subtypes (Alzheimer's disease vs frontotemporal dementia), which they attributed to the specialized nature of the EXIT25 and executive impairments being present in both clinical groups.

Key references

Dymek, M. P., Atchison, P., Harrell, L., & Marson, D. C. (2001). Competency to consent to medical treatment in cognitively impaired patients with Parkinson's disease. *Neurology*, *56*, 17–24.

Hooten, W. M., & Lyketsos, C. G. (1998). Differentiating Alzheimer's disease and frontotemporal dementia: Receiver operating characteristic curve analysis of four rating scales. *Dementia and Geriatric Cognitive Disorders*, *9*, 164–174.

Royall, D. R., Chiodo, L. K., & Polk, M. J. (2005a). An empiric approach to level of care determinations: The importance of executive measures. *Journal of Gerontology*, *60A*(8), 1059–1064.

Royall, D. R., Lauterbach, E. C., Kaufer, D., Malloy, P., Coburn, K. L., Black, K. J., et al. (2007). The cognitive correlates of functional status: A review from the Committee on Research of the American Neuropsychiatric Association. *Journal of Neuropsychiatry and Clinical Neurosciences*, *19*(3), 249–265.

Royall, D. R., Mahurin, R. K., & Gray, K. F. (1992). Bedside assessment of the executive cognitive impairment: The Executive Interview. *Journal of the American Geriatrics Society*, *40*, 1221–1226.

Royall, D. R., Palmer, R., Chiodo, L. K., & Polk, M. J. (2004). Declining executive control in normal aging predicts change in functional status: The Freedom House Study. *Journal of the American Geriatrics Society*, *52*, 346–352.

Royall, D. R., Palmer, R., Chiodo, L. K., & Polk, M. J. (2005b). Normal rates of cognitive change in successful aging: The Freedom House Study. *Journal of the International Neuropsychological Society*, *11*, 899–909.

Royall, D. R., Rauch, R., Román, G. C., Cordes, J. A., & Polk, M. J. (2001). Frontal MRI findings associated with impairment on the Executive Interview (EXIT25). *Experimental Aging Research*, *27*, 293–308.

Schillerstrom, J. E., Horton, M. S., Schillerstrom, T. L.,

Joshi, K. G., Earthman, B. S., Velez, A. M., et al. (2005). Prevalence, course and risk factors for executive impairment in patients hospitalised on general medicine service. *Psychosomatics*, *46*(5), 411–417.

Stockholm, J., Vogel, A., Gade, A., & Waldemar, G. (2005). The Executive Interview as a screening test for executive dysfunction in patients with mild dementia. *Journal of the American Geriatrics Society*, *53*, 1577–1581.

Executive Interview

Royall, Mahurin, and Gray (1992)

Patient	1	2
Age/Sex	86/F	85/M
EXIT Score	2/50	24/50
Verbal Fluency (Spontaneous words generated in 60 s)	20	3
Design Fluency	"Look at these pictures. Each is made with only four (4) lines. I am going to give you one minute to draw as many DIFFERENT designs as you can. The only rules are that they must each be different and be drawn with four lines. Now go!"	
	Score: (0) → 10 or more unique drawings (no copies of examples) 1 → 5.9 unique drawings 2 → less than 5 unique drawings **Testing Observations** ☐ Perseveration ☐ Imitation Behavior ☐ Prompting Needed ☐ Frontal Release Signs ☐ Lack of Spontaneity ☐ Disinhibited Behaviors ☐ Utilization Behavior	**Score:** 0 → 10 or more unique drawings (no copies of examples) 1 → 5.9 unique drawings (2) → less than 5 unique drawings
Comments	(R) Shoulder fixed (L) Wrist broken	(R) Frontal hygroma MMSE = 29

Acknowledgement: From Royall, D. R. et al. (1992). Bedside assessment of the executive cognitive impairment: The Executive Interview. *Journal of the American Geriatrics Society*, *40*(2), 1221–1226, Figure 1, p. 1222 reprinted by permission of Wiley-Blackwell.

Frontal Assessment Battery (FAB)

Dubois, Slachevsky, Litvan, and Pillon (2000)

Source

Items for the FAB are available in an appendix to Dubois et al. (2000) and are reproduced below.

Purpose

The FAB is an objective, clinician-administered test. It aims to identify a dysexecutive syndrome, both for diagnostic and prognostic purposes (especially dementia subtypes), as well as the evaluation of its severity. The FAB was developed with various dementia groups, including patients with corticobasal degeneration, frontotemporal dementia (FTD), multiple system atrophy and progressive supranuclear palsy. It has also been used in people with Parkinson's disease (Paviour et al., 2005) and Alzheimer's disease (AD; Slachevsky, Villalpando, Sarazin, Hahn-Barma, Pillon, & Dubois, 2004).

Item description

The FAB contains 17 items/trials, in six subtests: Conceptualization (3 items), Mental flexibility (1 item), Motor programming (6 trials), Sensitivity to interference (3 trials), Inhibitory control (3 trials), and Environmental autonomy ("prehension behaviour"; 1 item).

Scale development

Development of the FAB arose in response to the difficulties in assessing executive function without recourse to a detailed and time-consuming neuropsychological evaluation. Dubois and colleagues (2000) aimed to develop a brief, bedside instrument that sampled the types of executive impairments manifest in several different neurological conditions. Items for the FAB drew on known functions mediated by the prefrontal cortex "for elaborating appropriate goal-directed behaviours and for adapting the subject's response to new or challenging situations" (p. 1621). Accordingly, the authors collated items from existing tests that examined the component processes of "conceptualization and abstract reasoning, mental flexibility, motor programming and executive control of action, resistance to interference, self-regulation, inhibitory control, and environmental autonomy" (p. 1621).

Administration procedures, response format and scoring

The FAB is administered in accordance with the test instructions that are clearly specified in the appendix to Dubois et al. (2000). A stop-watch is required for the verbal fluency task. Administration time is 10 minutes.

Responses for items within the six subtests are scored for correctness on a 4-point scale, ranging from 0 (the equivalent of none correct) to 3 (the equivalent of best response/no error). Criteria for each score vary according to the item and are individually operationalized. The total score ranges from 0 to 18, with higher scores indicating better performance. Using receiver operating characteristic (ROC) curve analysis, various cut-off points have been suggested: 12 to distinguish between FTD and early AD (sensitivity 77%, specificity 87%; Slachevsky et al., 2004); 14/15 to distinguish between progressive supranuclear palsy and multisystem atrophy or Parkinson's disease (sensitivity and specificity both 78%; Paviour et al., 2005).

Normative data are available from an Italian sample (Appollonio et al. 2005), using a sample of 364 healthy people aged 50 to 94 years.

Psychometric properties

Dubois et al. (2000) standardized the FAB on 42 people without brain impairment (descriptive data shown in Data box 4.5) and 121 patients recruited from Hôpital de la Salpêtrière, Paris, France, with mild ($n = 30$), moderate ($n = 21$) or severe ($n = 23$) dementia of various types (corticobasal degeneration, FTD, multiple system atrophy and progressive supranuclear palsy). Validating instruments included the Mattis Dementia Rating Scale (MDRS) and Wisconsin Card Sorting Test (WCST). Inter-rater reliability was established using two

Data box 4.5 Descriptive data from the standardization sample (Dubois et al., 2000)

	Age M (SD)	Education	FAB M (SD)	Cut-off score*	Sensitivity/Specificity*
Controls ($n = 42$)	58.0 (14.4)	No information	17.3 (0.8)	12	AD vs FTD 77% / 87%
Patients ($n = 121$)	64.4 (9.3)		10.3 (4.7)		
Parkinson's disease ($n = 24$)			15.9 (3.8)		
Multiple system atrophy ($n = 6$)			13.5 (4.0)		
Corticobasal degeneration ($n = 21$)			11.0 (3.7)		
Progressive supranuclear palsy ($n = 47$)			8.5 (3.4)		
Frontotemporal dementia ($n = 23$)			7.7 (4.2)		

* Using data from Slachevsky et al. (2004).

independent raters, one of whom administered the FAB. Iavarone et al. (2004) examined an Italian version of the FAB, using data from 236 healthy controls and 28 people with AD or FTD. Inter-rater reliability and temporal stability were evaluated in randomly selected subsets of the control group ($n = 26$ and $n = 31$ respectively). The underlying structure was investigated using principal components analysis (PCA), in which one factor, accounting for 59% of the variance, was extracted.

At this stage, evidence for discriminant validity, *among* clinical samples, is equivocal. Using established criteria, Slachevsky et al. (2004) examined 26 patients with FTD and 64 patients with probable AD and found significant group differences. By contrast, results from Lipton, Ohman, Womack, Hynan, Ninman, and Lacritz (2005) with 23 patients with FTD and 31 with probable AD, also diagnosed using established criteria, found no group differences for the total score, although significant differences were found on two subtests (Mental flexibility, $p < .001$; Motor programming, $p < .05$). Castiglioni et al. (2006) also found no differences between AD ($n = 38$) and FTD ($n = 20$) groups. Results from Dubois et al., except where otherwise indicated, are shown in Box 4.5.

Comment

As a screening test of executive functions, the FAB has advantages. It is brief and Dubois et al. (2000) report that it is easy to administer and well accepted by patients. Psychometrically, it has excellent inter-rater reliability and shows evidence of concurrent validity with comparable instruments, although empirical evidence regarding its capacity to discriminate among dementia subgroups is equivocal at this stage. Results of validation studies in other cultural groups, including Japanese, have shown good psychometric properties (Nakaaki et al., 2007).

Box 4.5

Validity:	Criterion: *Concurrent:* with MDRS: $r = .82$ – with WCST-categories: $r = .77$ – with WCST-perseverative errors: $r = .68$
	Construct: *Internal consistency:* Cronbach alpha: .78
	Factor analysis: Iavarone et al.: PCA: 1 component
	Discriminant: Patients $M = 10.3$ ($SD = 4.7$) vs control $M = 17.3$ ($SD = 0.8$); $F = 17.24$, $p < .001$
	Slachevsky et al.: FTD $M = 7.6$ ($SD = 4.2$) vs AD $M = 12.6$ ($SD = 3.7$); $p < .001$ cut-off score of 12: sensitivity 77%, specificity 87%
Reliability:	Inter-rater: $k = .87$
	Iavarone et al.: $k = .79$
	Test–retest: Iavarone et al.: (interval not specified): $k = .87$ *Practice effects*: No information available
	Responsiveness: No information available

Key references

Appollonio, I., Leone, M., Isella, V., Piamarta, F., Consoli, T., Villa, M. L., et al. (2005). The Frontal Assessment Battery (FAB): Normative values in an Italian population sample. *Neurological Sciences*, *26*(2), 108–116.

Castiglioni, S., Pelati, O., Zuffi, M., Somalvico, F., Marino, L., Tentorio, T., et al. (2006). The Frontal Assessment Battery does not differentiate frontotemporal dementia from Alzheimer's disease. *Dementia and Geriatric Cognitive Disorders*, *22*, 125–131.

Dubois, B., Slachevsky, A., Litvan, I., & Pillon, B. (2000). The FAB. A frontal assessment battery at bedside. *Neurology*, *55*(11), 1621–1626.

Iavarone, A., Ronga, B., Pellegrino, L., Loré, E., Vitaliano, S., Galeone, F., et al. (2004). The Frontal Assessment Battery (FAB): Normative data from an Italian sample and performances of patients with Alzheimer's disease and frontotemporal dementia. *Functional Neurology*, *19*(3), 191–195.

Lipton, A. M., Ohman, K. A., Womack, K. B., Hynan, L. S., Ninman, E. T., & Lacritz, L. H. (2005). Subscores of the FAB differentiate frontotemporal lobar degeneration from AD. *Neurology*, *65*, 726–731.

Nakaaki, S., Murata, Y., Sato, J., Shinagawa, Y., Matsui, T., Tatsumi, H., et al. (2007). Reliability and validity of the Japanese version of the Frontal Assessment Battery in patients with the frontal variant of frontotemporal dementia. *Psychiatry and Clinical Neurosciences*, *61*(1), 78–83.

Paviour, D. C., Winterburn, D., Simmonds, S., Burgess, G., Wilkinson, L., Fox, N. C., et al. (2005). Can the frontal assessment battery (FAB) differentiate bradykinetic rigid syndromes? Relation of the FAB to frontal neuropsychological testing. *Neurocase*, *11*, 274–282.

Slachevsky, A., Villalpando, J. M., Sarazin, M., Hahn-Barma, V., Pillon, B., & Dubois, B. (2004). Frontal Assessment Battery and differential diagnosis of frontotemporal dementia and Alzheimer disease. *Archives of Neurology*, *61*(7), 1104–1107.

Frontal Assessment Battery

Dubois, Slachevsky, Litvan, and Pillon (2000)

Name: **Administered by:** **Date:**

1. SIMILARITIES (CONCEPTUALIZATION) **SCORE**

In what way are they alike?

A banana and an orange:____

Administration note: In the event of total failure: "they are not alike" or partial failure: "both have peel", help the patient by saying: "both a banana and an orange are . . ."; but credit 0 for the item; do not help the patient for the two following items

A table and a chair:____

A tulip, a rose and a daisy:____

Scoring: Only category responses [fruits, furniture, flowers] are considered correct
3 = 3 correct, 2 = 2 correct, 1 = 1 correct, 0 = 0 correct ______

2. LEXICON FLUENCY (MENTAL FLEXIBILITY)

Say as many words as you can beginning with the letter "S", any words except surnames or proper nouns

Administration note: If the patient gives no response during the first 5 seconds say: "for instance, snake". If the patient pauses 10 seconds, stimulate him by saying: "any word beginning with the letter 'S' ". The time allowed is 60 seconds.

____

____

____

____

____

Scoring: Word repetitions or variations [shoe, shoemaker], surnames or proper nouns are not counted as correct responses.
3 = more than 9 words, 2 = 6–9 words, 1 = 3–5 words, 0 = less than 3 words ______

3. MOTOR SERIES (PROGRAMMING)

Look carefully at what I'm doing

Instructions: The examiner, seated in front of the patient, performs alone three times with his left hand the series of Luria "fist–edge–palm". "Now with your right hand do the same series, first with me, then alone." The examiner performs the series three times with the patient, then says to him/her: "Now, do it on your own."

____

____

____

Scoring:
3 = performs 6 correct consecutive series alone, 2 = performs at least 3 correct consecutive series alone, 1 = patient fails alone, but performs 3 correct consecutive series with the examiner, 0 = patient cannot perform 3 correct consecutive series even with the examiner ______

4. CONFLICTING INSTRUCTIONS (SENSITIVITY TO INTERFERENCE) **SCORE**

Tap twice when I tap once

Instructions: To be sure that the patient has understood the instruction, a series of three trials is run: 1–1–1. "Tap once when I tap twice." To be sure that the patient has understood the instruction, a series of three trials is run: 2–2–2. The examiner performs the following series: 1–1–2–1–2–2–2–1–1–2.

Scoring:
3 = no errors, 2 = one or two errors, 1 = more than two errors, 0 = patient taps like the examiner at least four consecutive times ______

5. GO–NO GO (INHIBITORY CONTROL)

Tap once when I tap once

Instructions: To be sure that the patient has understood the instruction, a series of three trials is run: 1–1–1. "Do not tap when I tap twice." To be sure that the patient has understood the instruction, a series of three trials is run: 2–2–2. The examiner performs the following series: 1–1–2–1–2–2–2–1–1–2.

Scoring:
3 = no errors, 2 = one or two errors, 1 = more than two errors, 0 = patient taps like the examiner at least four consecutive times ______

6. PREHENSION BEHAVIOUR (ENVIRONMENTAL AUTONOMY)

"Do not take my hands".

Instructions: The examiner is seated in front of the patient. Place the patient's hands palms up on his/her knees. Without saying anything or looking at the patient, the examiner brings his/her hands close to the patient's hands and touches the palms of both the patient's hands to see if he/she will spontaneously take them. If the patient takes the hands, the examiner will try again after asking him/her: "Now, do not take my hands."

Scoring:
3 = patient does not take the examiner's hands, 2 = patient hesitates and asks what he/she has to do, 1 = patient takes the hands without hesitation, 0 = patient takes the examiner's hand even after he/she has been told not to do so ______

TOTAL SCORE: ______

Acknowledgement: From Dubois, B. et al. (2000). The FAB: A frontal assessment battery at bedside. *Neurology*, *55*(11), 1621–1626, Appendix, pp. 1624–1625, with permission of Lippincott Williams & Wilkins and Wolters Kluwer.

Problem Solving Inventory (PSI)

Heppner and Petersen (1982)

Source

The PSI, published by Heppner (1988), is commercially available from Consulting Psychologists Press (http://www.cpp.com).

Purpose

The PSI is a self-rating scale, designed to measure "an individual's perceptions of his or her own problem-solving behaviours and attitudes" (Heppner, 1988, p. 1). It was developed for the general population, but has also been used with people with stroke and traumatic brain injury (TBI; Rath, Langenbahn, Simon, Sherr, Fletcher, & Diller, 2004; Rath, Simon, Langenbahn, Sherr, & Diller, 2000).

Item description

The PSI contains 35 items, with 32 items contributing to a total score. Three factors have been derived from PSI items: (i) Problem-solving confidence has 11 items, such as "When faced with a novel situation, I have confidence that I can handle problems that may arise"; (ii) Approach-avoidance style contains 16 items, such as "When making a decision, I weigh the consequences of each alternative and compare them against each other"; and (iii) Personal control comprises five items, such as "Even though I work on a problem, sometimes I feel like I am groping or wandering and am not getting down to the real issue". PSI items are written at the 9th grade reading level, and an adolescent version is available with items written at the 4th grade reading level.

Scale development

Development of the PSI drew on the social problem-solving model of D'Zurilla and Goldfried (1971). The components of this five-stage model comprise general orientation, problem definition and formulation, generation of alternative solutions, decision making, and verification. Problems are defined as "personal problems that many people experience, such as depression, inability to get along with friends, or deciding whether to get a divorce" (Heppner, Witty, & Dixon, 2004, p. 352). This definition is intentionally generic rather than specific in order that the respondent can adapt "the problems" to his or her own circumstances. In turn, applied problem solving is defined as a "highly complex, often intermittent, goal-directed sequence of cognitive, affective, and behavioural operations for adapting to what are often stressful internal and external demands" (Heppner et al., 2004, p. 346). Heppner (1988) reported that 35 items were selected from an initial pool of 50 items generated by Heppner and Petersen (1982) as indicators of the stages of the D'Zurilla and Goldfried model. Principal components analysis was applied to data from 150 students. A three-factor model was extracted, in which 32 items had significant loadings. An overview of the research conducted with the PSI over the past two decades is provided in Heppner et al. (2004).

Administration procedures, response format and scoring

The PSI is a pen and paper self-report scale, but Heppner (1988) advises that it should be administered and interpreted by a professional with expertise in testing and knowledge of the problem-solving literature. Administration time is 10 to 15 minutes.

Responses to the PSI are recorded using a 6-point scale: 1 (strongly agree), 2 (moderately agree), 3 (slightly agree), 4 (slightly disagree), 5 (moderately disagree), 6 (strongly disagree). The total score, which is used more frequently than factor scores, ranges from 32 to 192. Lower scores "are generally considered more functional" (Heppner et al., 2004) – the caveat being that perception of problem-solving skill does not necessarily correspond with actual competence, an issue that is pertinent for people who may experience impaired awareness as a result of acquired brain impairment (ABI).

Psychometric properties

The PSI has been the subject of more than 120 empirical studies with different populations and cultures. The seminal results are summarized in Heppner et al. (2004).

Data box 4.6 Descriptive data from the standardization sample (Heppner & Petersen, 1982)

	Age Mean	Education	PSI M (SD)	Cut-off score	Sensitivity / Specificity
College students ($n = 150$)	19.2	No information		No information	No information
Total score Item: M (SD)			91.50 (20.65) 2.86 (0.58)		
Factor 1: Problem-solving confidence Item: M (SD)			24.47 (7.53) 2.44 (0.33)		
Factor 2: Approach-avoidance style Item: M (SD)			46.21 (11.51) 2.88 (0.47)		
Factor 3: Personal control Item: M (SD)			18.40 (5.06) 3.68 (0.44)		

They observed the availability of a "wealth of data" supporting the construct validity of the PSI. Their initial study (Heppner & Petersen, 1982; descriptive data shown in Data box 4.6) identified 10 factors accounting for 65% of the variance, and on the basis of the scree test three factors were selected: Problem-solving confidence, Approach-avoidance style and Personal control. It is noted, however, that the subject:variable ratio of that study (3:1) was very low, raising questions about the reliability of the factor structure. Heppner et al. (2004, p. 351) commented that their factors "did not support the existence of the five stages [of the model, but rather] underlying dimensions across stages": self-assurance, problem-solving style and emotional/behavioural control in solving problems, respectively. The factors have been correlated with students' reports of their own skills and satisfaction with them.

Rath's group in New York, USA is the only research group to date that has made detailed study of the PSI in relation to ABI. In an early study, Rath et al. (2000) compared the PSI and other measures, including the Wisconsin Card Sorting Test (WCST), in two samples: 44 people with stroke and TBI (age $M = 43.7$ years, $SD = 11.0$) who were at least 1 year post-ABI (range 1–17.6 years) and a second study comprising 34 people with ABI (age $M = 44.8$ years, $SD = 13.8$) participating in a 6-month treatment programme. Rath and colleagues have replicated effects of the PSI in other studies. Further evidence for responsiveness was provided in the clinical trial of Rath, Simon, Langenbahn, Sherr, and Diller (2003) who compared an innovative problem-solving therapy with conventional treatment in 60 people with TBI. Rath et al. (2004) compared 61 people with TBI and 58 healthy people on a range of executive measures. No significant correlation coefficients were found with objective tests (e.g., WCST), but significant associations were found with other self-report inventories, such as the authors' Problem Solving Questionnaire (PSQ). Results summarized in Heppner et al. (2004), except where otherwise stated, are shown in Box 4.6.

Box 4.6

Validity:	Criterion: *Concurrent:* Rath et al. (2004): with PSQ subscales: $r = -.54$–$.71$ (but with WCST: $r = .04$) Construct: *Internal consistency:* Cronbach alpha: Total: high .80s (Factors: Problem-solving confidence and Approach-avoidance style low to mid .80s, Personal control low 0.70s) *Factor analysis:* 3 factors: Problem-solving confidence (11 items), Approach-avoidance style (16 items), Personal control (5 items) *Discriminant*: independent judges differentiated people with high vs low PSI scores Rath et al. (2000): ABI $M = 97.66$ ($SD = 36.14$) vs control $M = 73.26$ ($SD = 19.09$); $t = 4.46$, $p < .001$
Reliability:	Inter-rater: Not applicable Test–retest: 2 weeks to 2 years: range $r = .81$ (3 weeks and 4 months) to $r = .60$ (2 years)
Responsiveness:	Rath et al. (2000): Pre-treatment $M = 103.34$ ($SD = 39.03$) vs post-treatment $M = 90.69$ ($SD = 32.43$); $t = 2.12$, $p < .05$, $d = .32$ Rath, Hennessy, & Diller (2003): Innovative treatment ($d = .69$) vs conventional treatment ($p > .05$; descriptive data not reported)

Comment

In terms of the problem-solving literature, D'Zurilla and Maydeu-Olivares (1995) draw a distinction between process measures and outcome measures; the former assess "attitudes, skills and abilities that enable a person to find effective or adaptive solutions to specific, everyday problems" (D'Zurilla, Chang, Nottingham, & Faccini, 1998, p. 1092), whereas the latter assess actual competence. The PSI is an example of a process measure. It does not assess skill or competence at problem solving (and its concurrent validity with objective measures of executive function is generally poor), but rather the person's perceptions of their problem-solving skills. Within this context, the PSI has good psychometric properties, with high internal consistency for the total score, good stability, and evidence of construct validity and responsiveness (although effect sizes are variable). In its application to individuals with ABI, Rath et al. (2000) note that "the PSI's virtue is that it elicits the individual's acknowledgement of functional difficulties within a model that provides a framework for guiding remedial efforts" (p. 731), although this is predicated on the person having insight into such difficulties.

Key references

D'Zurilla, T. J., Chang, E. C., Nottingham, E. J., & Faccini, L. (1998). Social problem-solving deficits and hopelessness, depression, and suicidal risk in college students and psychiatric inpatients. *Journal of Clinical Psychology*, *54*(8), 1091–1107.

D'Zurilla, T. J., & Goldfried, M. (1971). Problem solving and behaviour modification. *Journal of Abnormal Psychology*, *78*, 107–126.

D'Zurilla, T. J., & Maydeu-Olivares, A. (1995). Conceptual and methodological issues in social problem-solving assessment. *Behavior Therapy*, *26*, 409–432.

Heppner, P. P. (1988). *The Problem Solving Inventory. Manual.* Palo Alto, CA: Consulting Psychologists Press.

Heppner, P. P., & Petersen, C. H. (1982). The development and implications of a personal Problem Solving Inventory. *Journal of Counseling Psychology*, *29*(1), 66–75.

Heppner, P. P., Witty, T. E., & Dixon, W. A. (2004). Problem-solving appraisal and human adjustment: A review of 20 years of research using the Problem Solving Inventory. *The Counseling Psychologist*, *32*(3), 344–428.

Rath, J. F., Hennessy, J. J., & Diller, L. (2003). Social problem solving and community integration in postacute rehabilitation outpatients with traumatic brain injury. *Rehabilitation Psychology*, *48*(3), 137–144.

Rath, J. F., Langenbahn, D. M., Simon D., Sherr, R. L., Fletcher, J., & Diller, L. (2004). The construct of problem solving in higher level neuropsychological assessment and rehabilitation. *Archives of Clinical Neuropsychology*, *19*, 613–635.

Rath, J. F., Simon, D., Langenbahn, D. M., Sherr, R. L., & Diller, L. (2000). Measurement of problem-solving deficits in adults with acquired brain damage. *Journal of Head Trauma Rehabilitation*, *15*(1), 724–733.

Rath, J. J., Simon, D., Langenbahn, D. M., Sherr, R. L., & Diller, L. (2003). Group treatment of problem-solving deficits in outpatients with traumatic brain injury: A randomised outcome study. *Neuropsychological Rehabilitation*, *13*(4), 461–488.

SECTION 3
Scales assessing language functions

Communicative Effectiveness Index (CETI)

Lomas, Pickard, Bester, Elbard, Finlayson, and Zoghaib (1989)

Source

Items from the CETI are available in an appendix to Lomas et al. (1989), and are also reproduced below.

Purpose

The CETI is an informant rating scale, designed to measure changes in functional communication (both language and non-language) in people with aphasia, predominantly after stroke. The aim was to develop an instrument to assess "the individual's overall ability to get his/her meaning across or understand someone else's meaning in daily-living situations, using any communication means at their disposal" (Lomas et al., 1989, p. 117). The authors' particular interest was to measure change between assessment occasions.

Item description

The CETI comprises 16 items representing different communication situations, such as giving "yes" and "no" answers appropriately, communicating emotions, understanding writing. It is designed to be rated by an informant who has current knowledge (via direct observation) of the person's communication performance in everyday situations.

Scale development

Development of the CETI was thorough, with great attention to detail. First, the investigators developed a set of criteria that the CETI should meet (e.g., assess both verbal and non-verbal communication, reflect patients' values, measure everyday performance, be simple and easy to administer, be responsive to change). The investigators then held a 4-hour meeting with a group of nine people with aphasia, who suggested communication situations for inclusion as items. The process was repeated with another (independent) group of five people, as a comparability check. A set of 51 unique item-situations was generated. Following this, an expert panel (five speech pathologists and three neuropsychologists) selected those item-situations meeting three predetermined criteria (that items were not redundant, assessed performance rather than potential, and were relevant to both institutional and community environments). The resulting 36 items were trialled on two small groups of people with aphasia mainly from stroke. Not all item-situations were applicable to all people, and in order to ensure generalizability of the item-situations, only those items were retained that were rated by 21 of the 22 informants on two occasions 6 weeks apart, resulting in the 16-item scale.

Administration procedures, response format and scoring

The CETI is designed for completion by an informant. It requires a brief training period with the informant to familiarize him or her with use of the visual analogue scale, and instructions on the type of communication performance (including non-verbal) that should be considered in completing the scale.

Responses to each item are made using a 10 cm visual analogue scale, from one end of the scale ("not at all able") to the other end ("as able as before the stroke"). In making ratings on subsequent occasions, informants are permitted to see their previous responses. Scoring the CETI is achieved by "laying a template marked with 1-mm divisions over the 10-cm VAS [visual analogue scale] and reading off a value between 1 and 100" (Lomas et al., 1989, p. 117). The total score is converted to a 100-point scale, by dividing the sum of the item-situations by the total number of situations. Higher scores represent better degrees of functional communication.

Psychometric properties

The two groups of participants on whom the CETI was trialled were also used to establish the psychometric

Data box 4.7 Descriptive data from the standardization sample (Lomas et al., 1989)

	Age **M (SD)**	**Education**	**CCTI** **M (SD)**	**Cut-off score**	**Sensitivity / Specificity**
Recovering group ($n = 11$)	65.4 (8.3)	No information	44.8 (12.7)	No information	No information
Stable group ($n = 11$)	57.0 (14.2)		68.0 (16.8)		

properties of the instrument (Lomas et al., 1989) – descriptive data shown in Data box 4.7. They were recruited from regional referral centres in Canada and each had a score the Western Aphasia Battery (WAB) < 93.8. The recovering group ($n = 11$; WAB score $M = 28.1$, $SD = 21.3$) was 6–10 weeks post-stroke and was reassessed on a second occasion 7 weeks later to determine responsiveness. The stable group ($n = 11$; WAB score $M = 60.0$, $SD = 26.4$) was ≥ 15 months post-stroke and was reassessed on two occasions 8 weeks apart to examine temporal stability. Inter-rater reliability was examined in a subset of 11 patients (6 recovering, 5 stable) with ratings from two informants per participant. Validity was evaluated in the combined group ($n = 22$), with the WAB, Speech Questionnaire (SQ) and global ratings of language and communication ability. No floor or ceiling effects were found on the CETI for either the recovering group or the stable group, with 2% scoring in the top 20% of the scale (although the sample sizes were very small).

Further psychometric information is available on the CETI from independent researchers. Additional data on responsiveness were provided by Aftonomos, Steele, Appelbaum, and Harris (2001) in their case series of 50 people with stroke, who participated in a community-based treatment programme and were assessed before and after aphasia therapy ($M = 37.8$ sessions). In a sample of 38 people with chronic aphasia, Code (2003) evaluated the relationship between severity of aphasia and number of hours spent out of the house "as an index of social and community activity". Psychometric examination of a Danish version of the CETI with $n = 68$ people at least 1 year after left hemisphere stroke (53 of the 68 were still aphasic) was reported by Pedersen, Vinter, and Olsen (2001), who also explored the underlying factor structure. Two factors were extracted: Verbal communication and Non-verbal communication, but the percentage of the variance accounted for by the factors was not reported. It is also noted that the subject:variable ratio was low (~4:1), indicating that the factor structure is likely to be unreliable. Results from the Lomas et al. study, except where otherwise indicated, are shown in Box 4.7.

Box 4.7

Validity:	Criterion: *Concurrent:* with WAB: $r = .61$ – with SQ: $r = .46$–$.47$ – with Global Ratings: $r = .79$
	Pedersen et al.: with WAB: $r = .76$
	Code: with number of hours spent out of the house: $r = .49$
	Construct: *Internal consistency:* Cronbach alpha: .90
	Pedersen et al.: Cronbach alpha: .96
	Factor structure: Pedersen et al.: 2 factors: Verbal communication (10 items), Non-verbal communication (6 items)
Reliability:	Inter-rater: ICC = .73 on change score
	Test–retest: 8 weeks: ICC = .94
	Pedersen et al.: 3 month: $r = .86$
Responsiveness:	Significant improvement over time: Time 1 $M = 44.8$ ($SD = 12.7$) vs Time 2 $M = 55.9$ ($SD = 12.6$); $F = 32.4$, $p < .002$, $d = .87$
	Aftonomos et al.: significant improvement after treatment: Pre-treatment $M = 43.2$ ($SD = 2.7$) vs post-treatment $M = 61.4$ ($SD = 2.8$); $t = 9.88$, $p < .001$, $d = 6.74$

Comment

The CETI is an impressive instrument to assess perceived communication ability in people with aphasia.

Meticulous attention was given to its development, incorporating a client-centred approach, as well as rigorous pilot testing. Its measurement properties have been thoroughly examined across all the important psychometric domains, giving the clinician and researcher confidence that the instrument is highly reliable and valid. The CETI provides an *overall* index of perceived functional communication from an observer's view, as was the authors' intention, but it is not suited for examining the specific components contributing to the overall level of function. The CETI is also subject to the ubiquitous limitations that come from having an informant complete the scale, but as Pedersen and colleagues (2001, p. 800) note:

> it is unlikely that we will ever develop a perfect instrument in any area of aphasia assessment. Trade-offs between different considerations are inevitable in aphasia assessment, and the balance of trade-offs for the CETI does not seem to imply an inordinately large proportion of problems.

Key references

Aftonomos, L. B., Steele, R. D., Appelbaum, J. S., & Harris, V. M. (2001). Relationships between impairment-level assessments and functional-level assessments in aphasia: Findings from LCC treatment programmes. *Aphasiology*, *15*(10/11), 951–964.

Code, C. (2003). The quality of life for people with chronic aphasia. *Neuropsychological Rehabilitation*, *13*(3), 379–390.

Lomas, J., Pickard, L., Bester, S., Elbard, H., Finlayson, A., & Zoghaib, C. (1989). The Communicative Effectiveness Index: Development and psychometric evaluation of a functional communication measure for adult aphasia. *Journal of Speech and Hearing Disorders*, *54*, 113–124.

Pedersen, P. M., Vinter, K., & Olsen, T. S. (2001). The Communicative Effectiveness Index: Psychometric properties of a Danish adaptation. *Aphasiology*, *15*(8), 787–802.

Communicative Effectiveness Index

Lomas, Pickard, Bester, Elbard, Finlayson, and Zoghaib (1989)

Name:	**Administered by:**	**Date:**

Please rate_____________'s ability at . . .

1. Getting somebody's attention

Not at all able ________________________________ As able as before the stroke

2. Getting involved in group conversations that are about him/her

Not at all able ________________________________ As able as before the stroke

3. Giving yes and no answers appropriately

Not at all able ________________________________ As able as before the stroke

4. Communicating his/her emotions

Not at all able ________________________________ As able as before the stroke

5. Indicating that he/she understands what is being said to him/her

Not at all able ________________________________ As able as before the stroke

6. Having coffee-time visits and conversations with friends and neighbours (around the beside or at home)

Not at all able ________________________________ As able as before the stroke

7. Having a one-to-one conversation with you

Not at all able ________________________________ As able as before the stroke

8. Saying the name of someone whose face is in front of him/her

Not at all able ________________________________ As able as before the stroke

9. Communicating physical problems such as aches and pains

Not at all able ________________________________ As able as before the stroke

10. Having a spontaneous conversation (i.e., starting the conversation and/or changing the subject)

Not at all able ________________________________ As able as before the stroke

11. Responding to or communicating anything (including yes or no) without words

Not at all able ________________________________ As able as before the stroke

12. Starting a conversation with people who are not close family

Not at all able ________________________________ As able as before the stroke

13. Understanding writing

Not at all able ________________________________ As able as before the stroke

14. Being part of the conversation when it is fast and there are a number of people involved

Not at all able ________________________________ As able as before the stroke

15. Participating in a conversation with strangers

Not at all able ________________________________ As able as before the stroke

16. Describing or discussing something in depth

Not at all able ________________________________ As able as before the stroke

TOTAL SCORE: ____

Acknowledgement: From Lomas, J. et al. (1989). The Communicative Effectiveness Index: Development and psychometric evaluation of a functional communication measure for adult aphasia. *Journal of Speech and Hearing Disorders*, *54*, 113–124.

Frenchay Aphasia Screening Test (FAST)

Enderby, Wood, and Wade (2006)

Source

The FAST was initially published by Enderby, Wood, Wade, and Langton Hewer (1987) and the second edition, published by Enderby et al. (2006), is available commercially through Wiley & Sons (http://www.wiley.com).

Purpose

The FAST is an objective, clinician-administered test, designed to provide "a short, simple and standardized method of identifying and gauging language deficit . . . to assist diagnostic accuracy and to give information upon which management decisions could be based" (Enderby & Crow, 1996, p. 238). The aim was to develop an instrument suitable for administration by non-specialist clinicians, including general practitioners and junior medical staff. The clinical group of interest is people with aphasia, predominantly from stroke, but the FAST has also been used with people with traumatic brain injury.

Item description

The 18-item FAST examines four language domains commonly disrupted in aphasia: Comprehension (10 items), Expression (2 items), Reading (5 items) and Writing (1 item). Comprehension is assessed using questions based on two stimulus cards; one depicting five shapes (rectangle, square, circle, half-circle and cone), the other depicting a river scene portraying a man walking a dog along the shore, with various watercraft on the river, some hills, trees and buildings on the opposite shore, and a bridge from which children are feeding ducks. The comprehension items have varying levels of grammatical complexity (e.g., "before pointing to a duck near the bridge, show me the middle hill"). The expression items examine verbal description of the river scene and animal fluency over 60 seconds. Reading is assessed with written instructions, using graded difficulty (e.g., "touch the bottom of the card and then the top of it"). Writing is examined from a written description of the river scene.

Scale development

Development of the FAST is described briefly in Enderby et al. (1987, 2006). The authors recognized the need for a short and easily administered screening test, and at the outset they acknowledged the limitations of the FAST. It was not intended to replace more detailed aphasia evaluations, nor to differentiate different aphasia subtypes. Item content focused on the major areas of language disorders in aphasia and the authors noted that disorders such as dysarthria and speech apraxia were not included. Preliminary trialling of the stimulus drawings to determine the ideal size and complexity was conducted, but no details are available regarding the item selection process. Cut-off scores were derived empirically from two standardization samples.

Administration procedures, response format and scoring

Two stimulus cards and a stop-watch are required for administration of the FAST. Formal training is not required for the clinician, and administration time is reported as between 3 and 10 minutes.

The FAST is easily scored. For some subtests (e.g., Comprehension) 1 point is awarded for each correct response, for other subtests (e.g., Expression) responses are coded according to the number of correct responses. Full scoring details are provided in the test manual. The total score ranges from 0 to 30, with higher scores indicating better performance. Each of the Comprehension and Expression subtests has a maximum of 10 points, and each of the Reading and Writing subtests has a maximum score of 5 points.

Descriptive data provided in the original publication (Enderby et al., 1987) and test manual (Enderby et al., 2006) are limited to frequency data. The control group comprised 123 people who were friends and relatives of people with stroke. Using the total score (maximum score of 30), two cut-off scores are recommended for different age groups: 26/27 for people aged 60 years or less and 24/25 for those aged older than 60 years. Cut-off scores can also be derived using the combined Comprehension/Expression subtests (maximum score of 20) for different age groups: 16/17, 15/16 and 14/15 for age groups 20–60 years, 61–70 years and > 70 years respectively. Using the stroke sample, a more conservative cut-off score of 23/24 for the total score (or 13/14 for the combined Comprehension/Expression subtests) can be used, which will increase specificity (see below). The authors note that "an abnormal score does not necessarily indicate aphasia and should be interpreted by someone with access to full clinical details" (Enderby et al., 1987, p. 169).

Psychometric properties

Measurement characteristics of the FAST are reported in Enderby et al. (1987, 2006) from the Frenchay Hospital, Bristol, UK. The FAST was initially validated against the Functional Communication Profile (FCP), using two aphasia samples: acute ($n = 14$; age $M = 67.6$ years, range 34–75 years; 3–32 days post-stroke) and long-term ($n = 12$, age $M = 67.8$ years; 1–3.5 years post-stroke). Another concurrent validation study was reported by Enderby and Crow (1996), who examined a consecutive series of 25 stroke patients between 3 and 6 weeks post-stroke. Validation instruments were the short version of the Minnesota Test for the Differential Diagnosis of Aphasia (MTDDA) and FCP. The sample exhibited a broad range of severity on FCP from severe ($n = 6$) to mild ($n = 3$). Inter-rater reliability was established on 17 aphasic patients (age $M = 68.2$ years, range 60–76) who attended a weekly speech therapy group (Enderby et al., 1987). Three raters were used, one of whom administered the FAST (raters were rotated), and all three made independent recording of the patient's responses. Temporal stability was examined in 30 people.

Cut-off scores were initially derived from the 123 healthy community volunteers recruited from local social clubs, in Bristol, UK, along with 50 patients with stroke (including 20 patients with aphasia) assessed 8 days post-stroke (range 1–36 days). Cut-off scores were set at (i) the score below which no healthy volunteer scored and (ii) the score above which no person with aphasia scored. Using the normative sample, although sensitivity was 100%, specificity was 53%. Specificity was improved by using cut-off scores derived from the aphasic sample (sensitivity 100%, specificity 77%) and the authors additionally recommended that testing did not occur within the first week of stroke. Use of the combined Comprehension/Expression subtests gave better specificity, both using the normative data (sensitivity 100%, specificity 77%) and the aphasia data (sensitivity 100%, specificity 90%). Some investigators use the Comprehension/Expression subtests in isolation (e.g., Al-Khawaja, Wade, & Collin, 1996; Rudd, Wolfe, Tilling, & Beech, 1997). Results from Enderby et al. (1987), except where otherwise stated, are shown in Box 4.8.

Box 4.8

Validity:	Criterion: *Concurrent:* with FCP: $r = .90$ (acute sample $r = .87$, long-term sample $r = .96$) Enderby & Crow: with FCP: $r = .73$ – with short MTDDA: $r = .91$ (subtests: Comprehension $r = .82$, Expression $r = .81$, Reading $r = .79$, Writing $r = .70$) Construct: *Discriminant:* Differential diagnosis between normal vs aphasia using total cut-off score of 23/24: sensitivity 100%, specificity 77% – Differential diagnosis between normal vs aphasia using Comprehension/Expression cut-off score of 13/14: sensitivity 100%, specificity 90%
Reliability:	Inter-rater: Kendall's coefficient of concordance: ≥ .97 total score and all subtests Test–retest: 24 days: Kendall's coefficient of concordance: .97; *Practice effects:* Time 1: $M = 16.4$ ($SD = 11.8$) vs Time 2: $M = 16.4$ ($SD = 12.1$); $M = 0$
Responsiveness:	No information available

Comment

The particular advantages of the FAST are the availability of an objective, practical and fast [sic] means to identify people in the community with language disturbance that may otherwise go undetected. Enderby et al. (1987) readily acknowledge limitations of the scope of item content of the FAST, but other tools are already available for the detailed analysis of aphasia. The FAST has excellent inter-rater reliability and temporal stability, practice effects are minimal, and it shows evidence of concurrent validity with established measures. Indeed, correlations are in the order of $r \geq .9$, thus raising questions of redundancy, but the distinctive feature of the FAST is as an objective tool to screen for language impairment. Classification accuracy is more equivocal using normative data, but specificity can be improved by using cut-off scores derived from the aphasia sample or the Comprehension/Expression subtests. Because people with confusion or visual defects (e.g., hemianopia or unilateral spatial neglect) can score poorly on the FAST for non-language-related reasons, the FAST score needs to be interpreted in the context of other clinical information.

Key references

Al-Khawaja, I., Wade, D. T., & Collin, C. F. (1996). Bedside screening for aphasia: A comparison of two methods. *Journal of Neurology*, *243*(2), 201–204.

Enderby, P., & Crow, E. (1996). Frenchay Aphasia Screening Test: Validity and comparability. *Disability and Rehabilitation*, *18*(5), 238–240.

Enderby, P., Wood, V., & Wade, D. (2006). *Frenchay Aphasia Screening Test* (2nd ed.). Chichester, UK: Wiley.

Enderby, P. M., Wood, V. A., Wade, D. T., & Langton Hewer, R. (1987). The Frenchay Aphasia Screening Test: A short, simple test for aphasia appropriate for non-specialists. *International Rehabilitation Medicine*, *8*, 166–170.

Rudd, A. G., Wolfe, C. D. A., Tilling, K., & Beech, R. (1997). Randomised controlled trial to evaluate early discharge scheme for patients with stroke. *British Medical Journal*, *315*(7115), 1039–1044.

La Trobe Communication Questionnaire (LCQ)

Douglas, O'Flaherty, and Snow (2000)

Source

Items for the LCQ are described in Douglas et al. (2000) and the scale is available from Dr Douglas (School of Human Communication Sciences, La Trobe University, Bundoora, 3056, Victoria, Australia; email: J.Douglas@latrobe.edu.au). The LCQ items are also reproduced below.

Purpose

The LCQ is a self-rating scale administered in the context of an interview, designed to measure perceived communicative ability after brain injury. It was intended for use with the traumatic brain injury (TBI) group, but Douglas, Bracy, and Snow (2007) suggest it is also suitable for other groups, including dementia and stroke. Development of the LCQ was conducted with healthy community volunteers, as well as people with TBI.

Item description

The LCQ comprises 30 items that cover six statistically derived components: Conversational tone, Effectiveness, Flow, Engagement, Partner sensitivity and Conversational attention/focus. Two forms are available: Form S (self-completion) and Form O ("close other" or informant) – the forms are identical in content, with variants in phrasing as appropriate. Clinicians use Form O. An additional response format includes assessment of change from a previous state (e.g., pre- vs post-trauma, pre- vs post-intervention).

Scale development

Development of the LCQ arose in response to the dearth of instruments specifically designed to measure perceived communication ability, in contrast to the many tools available to measure traditional language and speech processes. As Douglas et al. (2007) noted, "no single tool or procedure is likely to provide clinicians with an ecologically valid representation of a client's communication competence" (p. 31). Item selection for the LCQ was guided by two considerations: the theoretical basis characterizing normal communication using the models of Grice (1975) and Damico (1985), as well as the literature describing cognitive-communication deficits in people with TBI. Twenty items were selected to represent aspects of Damico's clinical discourse analysis (quantity, quality, relation, manner) and 10 items to examine typical cognitive-communication impairments occurring as a consequence of brain dysfunction, particularly executive impairments (e.g., tangentiality, disinhibition). Initially, items were piloted with 77 healthy volunteers (university students) and 35 of their informants. On the basis of interview feedback with the students and written feedback from the informants, nine items were modified to improve content and clarity. Wording of items was structured to avoid response bias.

Administration procedures, response format and scoring

Although the LCQ is designed for self-completion, and without the need for equipment, it is recommended that it be administered "interview-style" to people with TBI, so that assistance can be provided if necessary for recognizing reversed items (Douglas et al., 2007). Administration time with informants is approximately 15 minutes and interview format with people with TBI approximately 30 minutes.

Responses to each item are made on a 4-point scale in terms of frequency: 1 (never or rarely), 2 (sometimes), 3 (often), 4 (usually or always). Six items (11, 15, 19, 21, 23 and 28), designed to determine whether the LCQ is completed with a response bias, require reverse scoring. The total score ranges from 30 to 120, with higher scores indicating greater perceived frequency of communication difficulties.

Psychometric properties

Douglas et al. (2000) examined healthy community volunteers ($n = 147$ and 109 of their informants; descriptive

Data box 4.8 Descriptive data from the standardization sample (Douglas et al., 2000)

	Age *M* (*SD*)	**Education**	**LCQ** *M* (*SD*)	**Cut-off score**	**Sensitivity / Specificity**
Control group: Self-ratings (n = 147)	21.2 (range 16–39)	88% completed high school	52.47 (9.62)	No information	No information
Item *M* (*SD*)			1.75 (0.26)		
Informants (n = 109)	32.76		47.17 (9.93)		
Item *M* (*SD*)			1.57 (0.22)		

data shown in Data box 4.8) recruited from a wide range of educational institutions in Melbourne, Australia. The age group (16–39 years) was deliberately restricted in order to match the typical demographic profile of TBI. LCQ scores for males ($M = 55.44$, $SD = 9.74$) were significantly higher than for females ($M = 50.47$, $SD = 9.07$; $t = 3.11$, $p < .01$), but neither age nor education contributed significantly to perceived communication difficulties when tested with hierarchical regression analysis. Scores for self-ratings were also significantly higher ($M = 52.47$, $SD = 9.62$, range 31–78) than scores from informants ($M = 47.17$, $SD = 9.93$; range 30–77).

Measurement characteristics of the LCQ were examined in the above normative sample, as well as a clinical group with TBI recruited from rehabilitation and community disability services in Melbourne, Australia (Douglas et al, 2007). The 88 people with severe TBI (post-traumatic amnesia duration > 7 days) were aged $M = 32.26$ years ($SD = 12.12$) and were $M = 64.4$ months post-trauma ($SD = 70.45$). Temporal stability was examined in a subgroup ($n = 18$) who were more than 5 years post-trauma. Data on discriminant validity are available from Bracy and Douglas (2005) who examined 50 married couples in which the husband was injured more than 2.5 years previously: 25 with TBI and 25 with orthopaedic injury requiring hospitalization and surgery. The underlying factor structure of the LCQ was examined in the normative sample using self-ratings ($n = 147$). Principal components analysis extracted six components, accounting for 48.9% of the variance: Conversational tone, Effectiveness, Flow, Engagement, Partner/sensitivity, and Conversational focus. Temporal stability was also assessed in a subset (24 matched pairs) of the normative sample. Results from the normative sample (Douglas et al., 2000) and the TBI sample (Douglas et al., 2007) are shown in Box 4.9, except where otherwise stated.

Box 4.9

Validity:	Construct: *Internal consistency:* Cronbach alpha: Normative sample: Self .85, Informant .86 – TBI sample: Self .91, Informant .92 *Factor analysis*: 6 components: Conversational tone (5 items), Effectiveness (4 items), Flow (4 items), Engagement (4 items), Partner/sensitivity (4 items), Conversational focus (4 items) *Discriminant:* TBI sample: Informant: $M = 59.35$ ($SD = 14.94$) vs self $M = 54.94$ ($SD = 14.08$); $t = -2.12$, $p < .04$ Bracy & Douglas: TBI husbands $M = 59.88$ ($SD = 14.89$) vs orthopaedic husbands $M = 45.96$ ($SD = 8.87$); $t = 4.02$, $p < .0001$ – TBI wife-informants $M = 62.68$ ($SD = 15.47$) vs orthopaedic wife-informants $M = 39.6$ ($SD = 6.88$); $t = 6.82$, $p < .0001$
Reliability:	Inter-rater: No information available Test–retest: 8 weeks: Normative sample: Self $r = .76$, informant $r = .48$ – 2 weeks: TBI sample: Self $r = .81$, informant $r = .87$
Responsiveness:	No information available

Comment

Assessing communication competence, as opposed to the integrity of speech and language processes, is a difficult enterprise. Part of the reason relates to the wide range of communication competence observed in the normal population. Indeed, the LCQ informant ratings of the healthy volunteers in Douglas et al. (2000) spanned the entire range of the rating scale for 22 of the 30 items. These individual differences become the comparison standard against which it is necessary to determine whether communication competence has been compromised by the brain injury. Yet, only an informant who knew the person previously is in a position to make such a judgement. To date, there has not been a dedicated, standardized measure that is suitable for this purpose. The LCQ fills this gap and is a welcome addition to the field. It is well grounded theoretically and clinically, has demonstrated construct validity, high internal consistency and good temporal stability in the TBI sample. Information on criterion validity, particularly concurrent validity with other measures of communication, is not yet available. The provision of normative data enables interpretation of scores, but there are currently no normative data for people older than 40 years, thus limiting use of the LCQ with older age groups.

Key references

Bracy, C. A., & Douglas, J. M. (2005). Marital dyad perceptions of injured partners' communication following severe traumatic brain injury. *Brain Impairment*, *6*(1), 1–12.

Damico, J. S. (1985). Clinical discourse analysis: A functional approach to language assessment. In C. S. Simon (Ed.), *Communication skills and classroom success* (pp. 165–203). London: Taylor & Francis.

Douglas, J. M., Bracy, C. A., & Snow, P. C. (2007). Measuring perceived communicative ability after traumatic brain injury: Reliability and validity of the La Trobe Communication Questionnaire. *Journal of Head Trauma Rehabilitation*, *22*, 31–38.

Douglas, J., O'Flaherty, C. A., & Snow, P. C. (2000). Measuring perception of communicative ability: The development and evaluation of the La Trobe Communication Questionnaire. *Aphasiology*, *14*(3), 251–268.

Grice, H. P. (1975). Logic in conversation. In P. Cole and P. Morgan (Eds.), *Studies in syntax and semantics* (Vol. 3, pp. 41–58). New York: Academic Press.

La Trobe Communication Questionnaire

Douglas, O'Flaherty, and Snow (2000)

Self version

Name:	**Administered by:**	**Date:**

Instructions: The following questions ask you about aspects of your communication. For EVERY question please write the number that best answers the question. Make sure you consider all the communication situations you meet in your daily life, e.g., family, social, work, interviews, etc.

Response key:
1 = Never or rarely
2 = Sometimes
3 = Often
4 = Usually or always

When talking to others do you:	**RESPONSE**
1. Leave out important details?	______
2. Use a lot of vague or empty words such as "you know what I mean" instead of the right word?	______
3. Go over and over the same ground in conversation?	______
4. Switch to a different topic of conversation too quickly?	______
5. Need a long time to think before answering the other person?	______
6. Find it hard to look at the other speaker?	______
7. Have difficulty thinking of the particular word you want?	______
8. Speak too slowly?	______
9. Say or do things others might consider rude or embarrassing?	______
10. Hesitate, pause and/or repeat yourself?	______
11. Know when to talk and when to listen?	______
12. Get side-tracked by irrelevant parts of conversation?	______
13. Find it difficult to follow group conversations?	______
14. Need the other person to repeat what they said before being able to answer?	______
15. Give people information that is correct?	______
16. Make a few false starts before getting your message across?	______
17. Have trouble using your tone of voice to get the message across?	______
18. Have difficulty getting conversations started?	______
19. Keep track of the main details of conversations?	______
20. Give answers that are not connected to the questions asked?	______
21. Find it easy to change your speech style (e.g., tone of voice, choice of words) according to the situation you are in?	______
22. Speak too quickly?	______
23. Put ideas together in a logical way?	______
24. Allow people to assume the wrong impressions from your conversations?	______
25. Carry on talking about things for too long in conversations?	______
26. Have difficulty thinking of things to say to keep conversations going?	______
27. Answer without taking time to think about what the other person has said?	______
28. Give information that is completely accurate?	______
29. Lose track of the conversations in noisy places?	______
30. Have difficulty bringing conversations to a close?	______
TOTAL SCORE:	______

Acknowledgement: Adapted from Douglas, J. M. et al. (2000). Measuring perception of communicative ability: The development and evaluation of the La Trobe Communication Questionnaire. *Aphasiology*, *14*(3), 251–268, p. 257 reprinted by permission of Psychology Press. Scale provided by Dr. Douglas.

Mississippi Aphasia Screening Test (MAST)

Nakase-Thompson, Manning, Sherer, Yablon, Gontkovsky, and Vickery (2005)

Source

Items for the MAST are available from the website of the Center for Outcome Measurement in Brain Injury (COMBI; http://www.tbims.org/combi/mast/index.html), and also from Dr Nakase-Thompson (Department of Neuropsychology, Methodist Rehabilitation Center, 1350 East Woodrow Wilson Drive, Jackson, MI 39216, USA; email: nakase@aol.com). A sample of item content appears in an appendix in Nakase-Thompson et al. (2005) and the full scale is reproduced below.

Purpose

The MAST is an objective, clinician-administered test. It was designed as "a brief screening measure that could be administered at bedside or clinic appointments by a variety of health-care providers" (Nakase-Thompson et al., 2005, p. 690). It has been used in a range of neurological conditions, including dementia, encephalopathies, stroke, traumatic brain injury and tumour.

Item description

The 46-item MAST comprises nine subtests in two broad domains. The five Expressive subtests are Naming (5 items), Automatic speech (5 items), Repetition (5 items), Verbal fluency (1 item), and Writing/Spelling to dictation (5 items). Four Receptive subtests are Yes/No accuracy (10 items), Object recognition (5 items), Following verbal instructions (5 items), and Following reading instructions (5 items). The COMBI website (accessed 23 May 2008) advises that two alternate forms have been created for future research purposes.

Scale development

Development of the MAST was guided by a number of considerations, including the need for a scale suitable to assess people with severe language/communication impairment who may become frustrated or stressed by lengthy testing, as well as one that enables repeated evaluation to chart progress over time. The MAST was developed over a 2-year period by a multidisciplinary group of brain injury physicians, neuropsychologists and speech-language pathologists. Team members generated 15 to 30 items for each of the nine domains, and a preliminary version of the instrument was pilot tested. Finalisation of item content resulted in 1 to 10 items per subtest, but no details are provided regarding the item reduction process.

Administration procedures, response format and scoring

A few simple stimulus materials are required to administer the MAST, comprising a stop-watch, coloured photograph, written instructions and five common objects. Clear guidelines are provided on the COMBI website for the administration, recording and scoring of the MAST. No formal training of the clinician is recommended. Administration time is 5 to 15 minutes.

For most items, either 2 points are awarded for correct responses or 0 points for incorrect or partially correct responses. The Verbal fluency subtest uses coding to classify the number of words produced (0 = 0–4 words, 5 = 5–10 words, 10 => 10 words). Eight of the nine subtests has a maximum score of 10 points (Yes/No accuracy has a maximum of 20 points). Each of the Expressive and Receptive indexes has a maximum of 50 points, with the total score ranging from 0 to 100. Higher scores indicate better language functioning.

Psychometric properties

A preliminary report on concurrent validity of the MAST (Nakase-Thompson, Sherer, Yablon, Manning, Vickery, & Ng, 2003) examined a mixed neurological group of 33 patients, yielding 86 observations. The MAST was compared with other language tests, including the Boston Naming Test (BNT), Controlled Word Association Test (COWAT), and the Token Test (TT). Divergent validity was examined with the Mini-Mental State Examination (MMSE) and Agitated Behavior Scale (ABS).

Data box 4.9 Descriptive data from the standardization sample (Nakase-Thompson et al., 2005)

	Age *M* (*SD*)	**Education** *M* (*SD*)	**MAST** *M* (*SD*)	**Cut-off score**	**Sensitivity / Specificity**
Control group ($n = 36$)	46.6 (19.2)	13.8 (2.1)	95.9 (3.6)	No information	No information
Stroke: left hemisphere ($n = 38$)	61.7 (12.7)	12.2 (3.6)	47.2 (29.9)		
Stroke: right hemisphere ($n = 30$)	58.7 (15.7)	11.6 (2.3)	75.2 (29.1)		

Box 4.10

Validity:	Criterion: *Concurrent:* Nakase-Thompson et al. (2003): with BNT: $r = .89$ – with COWAT: $r = .57$ – with TT: $r = .79$
	Construct: *Convergent/divergent:* Nakase-Thompson et al. (2003): high correlation with similar constructs (MAST vs BNT $r = .89$, TT = .79), but no significant correlation with dissimilar constructs (MAST vs MMSE, ABS – coefficients not reported)
	Discriminant: Nakase-Thompson et al. (2005): left hemisphere group $M = 47.2$ ($SD = 29.9$) vs right hemisphere group $M = 75.2$ ($SD = 29.1$) vs controls $M = 95.9$ ($SD = 3.6$); $F = 29.9, p < .001, \eta^2 = .4$ (as well as statistical differences on both indexes and all subtests)
Reliability:	Inter-rater: No information available
	Test–retest: No information available *Practice effects:* No information available
Responsiveness:	No information available

Nakase-Thompson et al. (2005) examined the construct validity of the MAST in 68 people with unilateral stroke recruited from two hospitals in the USA, along with 36 healthy community volunteers (descriptive data shown in Data box 4.9). The patient group was < 60 days post-stroke, with 38 sustaining left hemisphere damage and 30 having right hemisphere damage, lesion laterality being confirmed by neuroimaging. Discriminant function analysis was used to determine classification accuracy; the total score correctly classified 71% (all control participants were correctly classified as were 65% of the left hemisphere group, but 50% of the right hemisphere group was classified as controls – and indeed they may not have had aphasia). Results of these studies are shown in Box 4.10.

Comment

The MAST provides a quick means by which to identify language impairments in patients with left (and right) hemisphere damage. It surveys the major domains of language function disrupted in aphasia and shows good diagnostic accuracy in differentiating people with left hemisphere lesions from healthy individuals. It will also be important to determine the diagnostic accuracy of the MAST with respect to aphasia per se (as opposed to laterality of lesion), and to provide information on cut-off scores to assist in diagnosis in the clinical context. A main aim of the MAST was to track recovery over time, but in order to determine the efficacy of the MAST in this respect, information on its temporal stability, practice effects and responsiveness is required. The MAST is a newly developed instrument that appears promising and the authors acknowledge that examination of other psychometric properties is warranted.

Key references

Nakase-Thompson, R., Manning, E., Sherer, M., Yablon, S. A., Gontkovsky, S. L. T., & Vickery, C. (2005). Brief assessment of severe language impairments: Initial validation of the Mississippi Aphasia Screening Test. *Brain Injury*, *19*(9), 685–691.

Nakase-Thompson, R., Sherer, M., Yablon, S. A., Manning, E., Vickery, C., & Ng, W. (2003). [Abstract] Assessment of language among neurorehabilitation admissions: Convergent and divergent validity of the MAST. *Journal of the International Neuropsychological Society*, *9*, 303.

Mississippi Aphasia Screening Test

Nakase-Thompson, Manning, Sherer, Yablon, Gontkovsky, and Vickery (2005)

Name: **Administered by:** **Date:**

Instructions: Say: *Now I am going to ask you to do a few things for me.*

NAMING **SCORE**

Instructions: Present object and say: *Tell me, what is this called?* For second and subsequent items, say: *And this?*
Scoring: 2 points are given for each item named correctly. If patient provides incorrect response such as a paraphasic error (word substitution), 0 points are given for that item.

1. Pen ________
2. Hand (point to both sides of your hand) ________
3. Thumb ________
4. Watch ________
5. Ceiling (also accept light) ________

AUTOMATIC SPEECH

Instructions: For items 3–5 say: *Now I am going to say something and I want you to finish it*
Scoring: 2 points are given for all items completed correctly. Items 1 and 2 must be completed without error in order to receive credit. If patient provides incorrect response or partially correct response, 0 points are given for that item.

1. Can you count to 10 for me ________
2. Recite the days of the week ________
3. Three strikes and you're . . . ________
4. I pledge allegiance to the . . . ________
5. The phone is off the . . . ________

REPETITION

Repeat these words

Instructions: *Now say* (present the first word). Record response and proceed with subsequent words
Scoring: 2 points are given for correct restatement of words and phrases. If the patient provides a word substitution or unintelligible response, 0 points are given for that item.

1. Pot ________
2. Carrot ________
3. Alphabet ________
4. Under the old wooden bridge ________
5. The silver moon hung in the dark sky ________

YES/NO RESPONSES

Instructions: *Now I am going to ask you some questions, and I want you to answer yes or no.* Present 10 items. If patient restates the phrase, repeat the statement and say: *Tell me just yes or no.* If patient gives a verbal and nonverbal response, score the verbal response. If the patient is nonverbal, establish a yes and no gesture and administer the subtest.
Scoring: 2 points are given for correct answers and 0 points are given for incorrect responses.

1. Is your name *Johnson* (change if last name is Johnson) ________
2. Is your name ______? (insert correct last name) ________
3. Do you live in *Rhode Island?* ________
4. Do you live in ______? *(insert correct state)* ________
5. Do you wear a glove on your foot? ________
6. Am I touching my eye (clinician touches his/her nose)? ________
7. Does Monday come before Tuesday? ________
8. Does summer come after spring? ________
9. Is a chicken bigger than a spider? ________
10. Do you put your shoe on before your sock? ________

OBJECT RECOGNITION IN A FIELD OF FIVE

I want to show you some things. Point to them as I call them out

SCORE

Instructions: Place stimuli in scrambled order in front of the patient. The first two items should be a watch and some keys. The last three items can include the following: paper, pen, photo (can use the Verbal Fluency stimulus photos), coin, name badge or cup. Say: *Point to the ___* (present stimulus in order on list)
Scoring: 2 points are given for each correct identification of an object named by the examiner.

1. Watch ______
2. Keys ______
3. ____________________ ______
4. ____________________ ______
5. ____________________ ______

FOLLOWING INSTRUCTIONS

Instructions: *Now I am going to ask you to do some things*
Scoring: 2 points are given for each correct execution of a verbal instruction presented. If any part of the instruction is not completed accurately, 0 points are given for that item.

1. Point to your nose ____________________ ______
2. Open your mouth ____________________ ______
3. With your left hand, point to your right eye ____________________ ______
4. Point to the floor, then point to your nose ____________________ ______
5. Before opening your mouth, touch your ear ____________________ ______

READING INSTRUCTIONS

Read this aloud and do what it says

Instructions: *Now I want you to read this card to yourself and do what it says* (present first card). *Again, read this one to yourself and do what it says* (present second card; keep going until all cards are presented) An alternative instruction is given for Item 3 if the person is unable to use their right upper extremity to complete the instruction. An alternative item 3 using the person's left upper extremity is available.
Scoring: 2 points are given for each correct execution of a written instruction presented. If any part of the instruction is not completed accurately, 0 points are given for that item.

1. Open your mouth ____________________ ______
2. Make a fist ____________________ ______
3. Point to the floor, then point to the ceiling ____________________ ______
4. With your right hand, point to your left knee ____________________ ______
5. Point to your left ear after you make a fist ____________________ ______

VERBAL FLUENCY DICTATION

Look at this picture for a while (pause). Now tell me everything that you can about this picture. Keep talking until I tell you to stop

Instructions: *I want you to look at this photo for 10 seconds.* (after exactly 10 seconds has elapsed say) *Now tell me everything you can about this picture; keep talking until I tell you to stop.* (Immediately begin timing responses for the next 10 seconds. Write all words that the patient says during the 10 second interval onto the recording sheet. Use a dash for unintelligible utterances). The 10 second duration that you record verbalizations begins immediately after you have finished stating the instructions. Any delay in patient response is included in the 10 seconds.
Scoring: Sum all intelligible words (relevant or irrelevant to the photo stimulus) given by the patient during the 10 second recording interval. Use the score conversion table below to obtain the subscale score:

Number of intelligible verbalizations: ______
Subscale score conversion:
0 points = 0–5 intelligible verbalizations
5 points = 5–10 intelligible verbalizations
10 points = 11+ intelligible verbalizations

____
____
____
____
____
____
____ ______

MAST page 3 of 3

WRITING/SPELLING **SCORE**

Instructions: Present a blank piece of paper and pen to the patient. Say: *Now I want you to write some words for me. Write* ______. (present the first word). *Now write* ______ (present second word and continue with the last three items)

Scoring: 2 points are given for each word correctly written. If there is an incorrect spelling of any word, a score of 0 is given for that item.

1. Sit ______
2. Twist ______
3. Airplane ______
4. Computer ______
5. Under the black bridge ______

Summary	Total: ______ / 100	Expressive: ______ / 50	Receptive: ______ /50
Optional[1]**:**			
Dysarthria: ______	Paraphasia: ______	Perseveration: ______	Oriented: ______

Expressive subtests:		Receptive subtests:	
Naming	______ / 10	Yes/no accuracy	______ / 20
Automatic speech	______ / 10	Object recognition	______ / 10
Repetition	______ / 10	Following instructions	______ / 10
Writing	______ / 10	Reading instructions	______ / 10
Verbal fluency	______ / 10		

[1] Optional ratings: indicate presence "+" or absence "–"

Acknowledgement: MAST reproduced by permission of Nakase-Thompson, R. (2004). *The Mississippi Aphasia Screening Test*. The Center for Outcome Measurement in Brain Injury, http://www.tbims.org/combi/mast

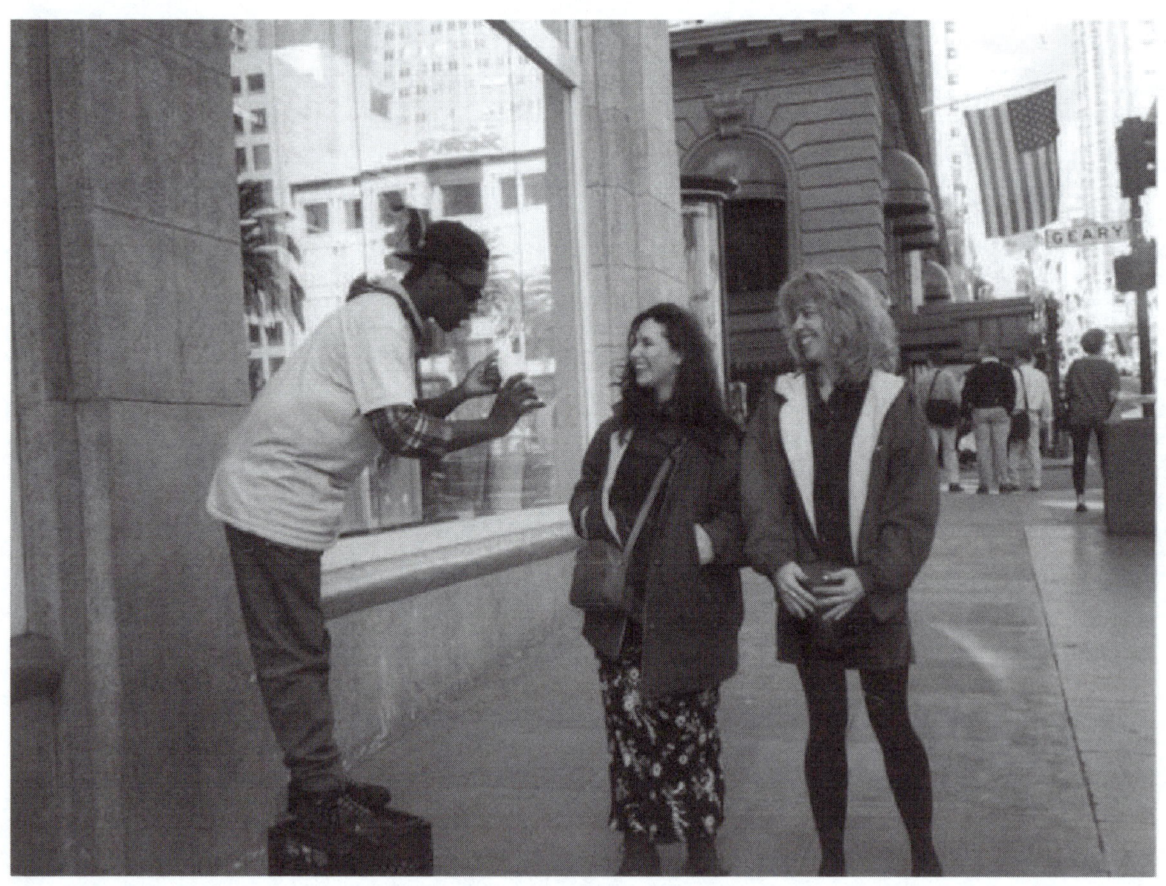

Colour photograph available from http://www.tbims.org/combi/mast

SECTION 4
Scales assessing memory functions

Comprehensive Assessment of Prospective Memory (CAPM)

Shum and Fleming (2008)

Source

Items for the three sections of the CAPM appear in the test manual (Shum & Fleming, 2008). Copies of the manual and record form are available from Dr Shum (School of Psychology, Griffith University, Nathan QLD, 4111, Australia; email: d.shum@griffith.edu.au). Items for Section A, Frequency Scale, also appear in Chau, Lee, Fleming, Roche, and Shum (2007) and items for Section C, Ways of Remembering Scale, in Roche, Moody, Szabo, Fleming, and Shum (2007). Items for Sections A and C are also reproduced below.

Purpose

The CAPM is a self-rating scale, designed to measure specific, everyday prospective memory lapses. Prospective memory refers to "the process or skills required to support the fulfilment of an intention to perform a specific action in the future" (Ellis & Kvavilashvili, 2000, p. S1) and is closely related to everyday functioning and independent living (Shum, Fleming, & Neulinger, 2002). The CAPM was originally developed for older people (Waugh, 1999), but has also been used with young people (Roche et al., 2007) and people with traumatic brain injury (TBI; Roche, Fleming, & Shum, 2002).

Item description

The CAPM comprises three sections. Section A contains 39 items examining perceived frequency of failure. It contains two statistically derived components: basic activities of daily living (BADL, 10 items), such as "leaving water taps on", and instrumental activities of daily living (IADL, 23 items), such as "forgetting to post a letter". The remaining six items did not load highly on either component. Section B uses the same 39 items from Section A to assess concern about the failures, also using the BADL (10 items) and IADL (23 items). Section C contains 15 items focusing on reasons associated with successes/failures. These items address encoding (9 items), retention interval (3 items), performance interval (2 items) and evaluation of outcome of intended actions (1 item). Self-rating and informant versions of the CAPM are available, which contain the same items, but phrased as appropriate.

Scale development

Development of the CAPM arose in an effort to provide a comprehensive evaluation of prospective memory, taking into account not only frequency of failures, but also level of concern about and reasons for such failures, using theoretical conceptualizations of prospective memory developed by Ellis (1996). For Sections A and B, items were constructed that were based on previous memory research and the authors' clinical experience about common memory difficulties reported by patients, their informants and health workers. For Section C, items were developed that covered all the stages of prospective remembering based on the model of Ellis, as well as items addressing other factors (e.g., motivation) that are related to prospective remembering. An exploratory principal components analysis on an initial version of the CAPM was conducted by Waugh (1999) with data from 527 healthy volunteers aged 17 to 91 years. Two components were extracted for Section A (Frequency Scale), accounting for 35% of the variance: BADL and IADL. Two components were also extracted for Section B (Concern Scale), accounting for 44% of the variance: Serious and Less serious consequences. Item content of the CAPM was subsequently revised to increase item meaningfulness for people with TBI and refined to improve readability (Chau et al., 2007).

Administration procedures, response format and scoring

The CAPM is designed for self-administration. The authors advise that completion time for people without brain impairment is approximately 20 to 25 minutes for the entire scale. For people with brain injury, it is recommended that the CAPM be administered in the context of a structured interview. In this case,

Data box 4.10 Descriptive data from the normative sample (Chau et al., 2007)

	Age *M* (*SD*)	**Education**	**CAPM Section A** *M* (*SD*)	**Cut-off score**	**Sensitivity / Specificity**
Control group ($n = 95$):	35.3 (13.4)	54% with >12 years		No information	No information
Total			1.82 (0.42)		
Basic Activities of Daily Living			1.43 (0.36)		
Instrumental Activities of Daily Living			2.02 (0.49)		

administration time for each of Sections A and B is 15 to 20 minutes and Section C approximately 5 to 10 minutes.

For Sections A and B, each item is rated on a 5-point scale: 1 (never), 2 (rarely), 3 (sometimes), 4 (often), 5 (very often/always). An optional rating category ('not applicable') is used as necessary, although respondents are encouraged to complete as many items as possible. Because of the 'not applicable' option, a variable number of items is completed. Thus, for scoring purposes, Chau et al. (2007) use the procedure of summing responses on the 1-to-5 scale and dividing the result by the number of items endorsed. The score is thus expressed as a mean score, ranging between 1 and 5. Higher scores indicate more frequent perceived prospective memory failures. Section B has the same score range, with higher scores indicating greater concern over prospective memory failures. Three scores can be derived for Sections A and B: BADL (10 items), IADL (23 items) and Total (all 39 items).

Responses to Section C items are rated on a 4-point scale: 1 (strongly disagree), 2 (disagree), 3 (agree), 4 (strongly agree). Items 8 and 10 are reverse scored. Although scores can be derived from Section C, information can also be used to inform the clinical process – to obtain an idea about reasons for failures, compare responses across items, between self and informant ratings and so forth.

Normative data are provided by Chau et al. (2007) ($n = 95$, descriptive data shown in Data box 4.10) stratified by age (15–30 and 31–60 years), sex and education (< 12 years and > 12 years). Mean scores for BADL ranged from $M = 1.23$ to 1.56 (*SD* range: 0.2–0.39) and for IADL from $M = 1.72$ to 2.17 (*SD* range: 0.38–0.53).

Psychometric properties

Measurement characteristics of the CAPM have been examined in a number of studies. The normative data set was used to determine internal consistency, along with temporal stability in a subset of 26 people (Chau et al., 2007). Roche et al. (2002) validated the CAPM in a sample of 33 people with TBI and a matched control group ($n = 29$), along with an informant for each group. The TBI group was recruited from a local hospital in Brisbane, Australia, and was aged $M = 29$ years ($SD = 10.8$), with duration of post-traumatic amnesia ranging from 9 to 185 days, and examined at $M = 58$ weeks post-trauma ($SD = 36$ weeks). Results from these studies are shown in Box 4.11.

Box 4.11

Validity:	Construct: *Internal consistency:* Chau et al.: Cronbach alpha: Total: .94 (BADL .74, IADL .92) *Factor analysis:* Waugh: Sections A & B: 2 components: BADL (10 items), IADL (23 items) *Discriminant:* Roche et al. (2002): Section A (Informants): BADL TBI $M = 1.65$ ($SD = 0.59$) vs Controls $M = 1.40$ ($SD = 0.36$); $t = 1.97$, $p < .05$ – IADL TBI $M = 2.25$ ($SD = 0.72$) vs Controls $M = 1.89$ ($SD = 0.49$); $t = 2.33$, $p < .05$
Reliability:	Inter-rater: Not applicable Test–retest: Chau et al.: 2 weeks: Total ICC = .76 (BADL ICC = .74, IADL ICC = .77)
Responsiveness:	No information available

Comment

A special feature of the CAPM is that it addresses not only frequency, but also other aspects of memory failures, such as concern about memory failures (Section B) and reasons for success/failures (Section C). These features have the potential to provide clinically useful information that is not possible to extract from objective test performance. Moreover, Roche et al. (2007) observe that "if clinicians were able to tap into the factors that trigger prospective memory breakdown, treatment could then, in turn, be more accurately targeted" (p. 318). At this stage, the CAPM shows promise in being an instrument with high internal consistency, excellent temporal stability and the capacity to discriminate between clinical and control groups, but the normative data currently published (for people between 15 and 60 years) will limit applicability of the CAPM to older age groups. Examination of criterion validity of the CAPM, particularly its correspondence with objective memory tests and other rating scales of prospective memory, is also needed.

Key references

Chau, L. T., Lee, J. B., Fleming, J., Roche, N., & Shum, D. (2007). Reliability and normative data for the Comprehensive Assessment of Prospective Memory (CAPM). *Neuropsychological Rehabilitation*, *17*(6), 707–722.

Ellis, J. A. (1996). Prospective memory or the realization of delayed intentions: A conceptual framework for research. In M. Brandimonte, G. O. Einstein, & M. A. McDaniel (Eds.), *Prospective memory: Theory and applications* (pp. 1–22). Mahwah, NJ: Lawrence Erlbaum Associates, Inc.

Ellis, J., & Kvavilashvili, L. (2000). Prospective memory in 2000: Past, present and future directions. *Applied Cognitive Psychology*, *14*, S1–S9.

Roche, N. L., Fleming, J. M., & Shum, D. H. K. (2002). Self-awareness of prospective memory failure in adults with traumatic brain injury. *Brain Injury*, *16*(11), 931–945.

Roche, N. L., Moody, A., Szabo, K., Fleming, J. M., & Shum, D. H. K. (2007). Prospective memory in adults with traumatic brain injury: An analysis of perceived reasons for remembering and forgetting. *Neuropsychological Rehabilitation*, *17*(3), 314–334.

Shum, D. H. K., & Fleming, J. M. (2008). *Comprehensive Assessment of Prospective Memory: Manual.* Brisbane: Applied Cognitive Neuroscience Research Centre.

Shum, D., Fleming, J., & Neulinger, K. (2002). Prospective memory and traumatic brain injury: A review. *Brain Impairment*, *3*(1), 1–16.

Waugh, N. (1999). *Self-report of the young, middle-aged, young-old and old-old individuals on prospective memory functioning*. Unpublished honours thesis, Griffith University, Australia.

Comprehensive Assessment of Prospective Memory
Section A: Frequency Scale

Shum and Fleming (2008)

Name: **Administered by:** **Date:**

Instructions:
This questionnaire is about memory lapses, which most people make from time to time. In the past month, how often have you been forgetting? Try to answer as many questions as you can without using the "Not Applicable" response

Response key:
1 = Never
2 = Rarely – once a month
3 = Occasionally – 2–3 times in a month
4 = Often – weekly
5 = Very often – daily

NA = not applicable –
if you have not had to do the task

RESPONSE

1. Forgetting to buy an item at the grocery store[I]
2. Forgetting an appointment with your doctor or therapist[I]
3. Leaving the iron on[I]
4. Forgetting to put the garbage bin out[I]
5. Forgetting a change in your daily routine (e.g., turning up to a regular appointment when the regular day has been changed)[I]
6. Not locking the door when leaving home[B]
7. Walking into a room and forgetting why you went there
8. Mistakenly following your old routine, when it has been changed (e.g., putting out rubbish at the wrong time when the collection has been changed)[I]
9. Forgetting to water pot plants or the garden[I]
10. Forgetting to pass on a message[I]
11. Forgetting to take tablets at a prescribed time[I]
12. Forgetting to take clothes off the line[I]
13. Forgetting to have a shower or bath[B]
14. Accidentally doing something twice by mistake (e.g., putting two lots of coffee in a cup)[B]
15. Forgetting to eat a meal[B]
16. Forgetting to get money from the bank/ATM[B]
17. Accidentally forgetting to put a piece of clothing on when you get dressed (e.g., forgetting to put your socks on)[B]
18. Forgetting to take your wallet or purse when you leave the house[B]
19. Having trouble remembering personal dates at the right time, such as someone's birthday or anniversary[I]
20. Accidentally forgetting a grooming activity (e.g., brushing your hair, shaving)[B]
21. Forgetting to make a telephone call you intended to make[I]
22. Forgetting to do cleaning chores[I]
23. Leaving water taps on[B]
24. Not remembering to bank a cheque
25. Leaving out an ingredient you planned to use while cooking or preparing a meal[I]
26. Accidentally forgetting to brush your teeth[B]
27. Arriving at a shop and forgetting what you planned to buy[I]
28. Forgetting to mention a point you intended to make during a conversation[I]
29. Forgetting to put petrol in your car
30. Not remembering to pay bills[I]
31. Checking whether or not you have already done something you had planned to do[I]
32. Forgetting to do the laundry[I]
33. Forgetting to meet a friend at a pre-arranged time[I]

34. Leaving the stove on ___
35. Forgetting to post a letter[I] ___
36. Not remembering to check the water levels/tyre pressure of your car[I] ___
37. Forgetting to check your calendar or diary[I] ___
38. Forgetting to turn the heater off ___
39. Forgetting to take you diary ___

BADL score = total score for BADL items ÷ total number of BADL items endorsed: ___
IADL score = total score for IADL items ÷ total number of IADL items endorsed: ___
TOTAL score = total score for all items ÷ total number of items endorsed: ___

[B] = BADL (Basic Activities of Daily Living) item.
[I] = IADL (Instrumental Activities of Daily Living) item.

Acknowledgement: CAPM Scale from Shum, D., & Fleming, J. (2008). *Comprehensive Assessment of Prospective Memory: Manual*. Brisbane: Applied Cognitive Neuroscience Centre, used by permission of the authors.

Comprehensive Assessment of Prospective Memory
Section C: Ways of Remembering Scale
Shum and Fleming (2008)

Name:	**Administered by:**	**Date:**

Instructions: In this section of the questionnaire, we are interested in finding out **how** people remember to do things in their everyday life. Please read each of the following statements carefully and indicate how much you agree or disagree with each statement. Write the number from 1 to 4, using the following scale:

Response key:
1 = Strongly disagree
2 = Disagree
3 = Agree
4 = Strongly agree

		RESPONSE
1.	When I forget to do something I had planned to do, it is usually not because I forgot what I had to do but because I forgot when I had to do it[a(i)]	______
2.	When I forget to do something I had planned to do, it is usually because I forgot what I actually had to do[a(i)]	______
3.	I frequently forget to do things that other people have asked me to do[a(ii)]	______
4.	I frequently forget to do things that I have planned to do[a(ii)]	______
5.	If something is very important to me I usually remember to do it[a(iii)]	______
6.	If something is very important for other people, I usually remember to do it[a(iii)]	______
7.	The more things (say two or three) I have to do, the more likely I will forget to do them[a(iv)]	______
8.	I rely on other people to remind me when I have to remember to do things[a(v)]	______
9.	I do not need to rely on aids such as a diary or to-do-list when I have to remember to do things[a(v)]	______
10.	If I have to do one thing in the immediate future (within the next half hour), I usually remember to do it[b]	______
11.	I tend to forget to do things if there is a long delay before they need to be done (e.g., if I plan to do a task in 3 weeks' time)[b]	______
12.	I tend to forget to do things if a lot of other activities take place before they need to be done[b]	______
13.	If I am engrossed in another task, I find it difficult to remember to do things[c]	______
14.	Sometimes even though I remember that something has to be done, I forget to do it if I'm interrupted (e.g., by a telephone call or by a person)[c]	______
15.	I do not usually need to check whether I have done something because I am confident of my own memory[d]	______

[a] = Formation and encoding of intentions: (i) what, that and when, (ii) self versus others initiation, (iii) motivation, (iv) complexity, (v) encoding.
[b] = Retention interval.
[c] = Performance interval and execution of intended actions.
[d] = Evaluation of outcome.

Acknowledgement: CAPM Scale from Shum, D., & Fleming, J. (2008). *Comprehensive Assessment of Prospective Memory: Manual*. Brisbane: Applied Cognitive Neuroscience Centre, used by permission of the authors.

Everyday Memory Questionnaire (EMQ)

Sunderland, Harris, and Baddeley (1983)

Source

There are a number of variants of the EMQ. The original 35-item version is reproduced in an appendix to Sunderland et al. (1983). Items for the more commonly used 28-item version are available in Sunderland, Harris, and Gleave (1984b) and are reproduced below. A 20-item version with a revised response format has been used (Tinson & Lincoln, 1987; Stewart, Sunderland, & Sluman, 1996) and adapted for interview format (Olsson, Wik, Östling, Johansson, & Andersson, 2006). Additionally, a children's version of the EMQ, called the Children's Memory Questionnaire (CMQ), has been developed by Drysdale, Shores, and Levick (2004) and is also briefly described below.

Purpose

The EMQ is a self-rating scale, designed to assess memory functioning in everyday life. It was originally developed for people with traumatic brain injury (TBI), but has also been used with other clinical populations, including Alzheimer's disease (Efklides, Yiultsi, Kangellidou, Kounti, Dina, & Tsolaki, 2002), multiple sclerosis (Lincoln et al., 2002), neurotoxicity (Koltai, Bowler, & Shore, 1996), stroke (Lincoln & Tinson, 1989; Sunderland, Stewart, & Sluman, 1996), and temporal lobectomy/amygdalo-hippocampectomy (Goldstein & Polkey, 1992).

Item description

Items of the EMQ sample a range of different types of potential memory failures in everyday situations, covering episodic memory for verbal and visuospatial material (e.g., "repeating to someone what you have just told them or asking them the same question twice", "getting lost or turning in the wrong direction on a journey, on a walk or in a building where you have often been before" respectively), as well as procedural memory (e.g., "having difficulty picking up a new skill. For example, finding it hard to learn a new game or to work some new gadget after you have practised once or twice") and prospective memory (e.g., "completely forgetting to do things you said you would do, and things you planned to do"). Informant and self-report versions are available, which contain the same items, but are phrased as appropriate.

Scale development

Development of the EMQ was driven by clinical needs. Sunderland and colleagues questioned the ecological validity of laboratory-based memory tests (such as list-learning) to evaluate the effectiveness of therapy programmes for memory disorders. Item selection for the EMQ was guided by three considerations: (i) cover a wide range of memory failures, (ii) occur in the course of daily life, and (iii) reflect prevalent memory failures after TBI (Sunderland et al., 1983). A 35-item EMQ was constructed sampling five domains: speech, reading and writing, faces and places, actions, and learning new things. It was examined with two clinical groups (TBI and orthopaedic), along with their relative-informants. The authors subsequently sought to improve the sensitivity of the scale to detect the types of memory problems experienced by people with TBI (Sunderland et al., 1984b). Item content was reworked: 16 of the 35 items that discriminated well between the clinical groups were retained, along with six items showing "floor" effects (and hence suitable to detect response bias), and six new items were added. The revised 28-item version was tested with two groups of 78 people with mild and severe TBI, along with their informants (Sunderland et al., 1984b).

Administration procedures, response format and scoring

The EMQ is designed for self-completion. Different authors have used various response formats for the EMQ. Sunderland et al. (1984b) originally proposed "an absolute frequency" 9-point scale, from A (not at all in the past 3 months) to I (more than once a day). The numerical notation for each item is 0 to 8, such that the total score ranges from 0 to 224, with higher scores

Data box 4.11 Descriptive data from the standardization sample for 28-item version (Sunderland et al., 1984b)*

	Age M (range)	Education	EMQ M (SD) (transformed scores: square root)	Cut-off score	Sensitivity / Specificity
Mild TBI ($n = 33$): Self-ratings	Males 33.4 (19–53) Females 35.3 (18–57)	No information	Males: 5.93 Females: 6.12	No information	No information
Informant ratings			Males: 4.20 Females: 4.92		
Severe TBI ($n = 50$) Self-ratings	Males 29.1 (19–64) Females 32.1 (18–61)		Males: 6.38 Females: 6.97		
Informant ratings			Males: 6.49 Females: 6.47		

* Transformed scores were used (square root): "The maximum possible score is 14.9, which would indicate that each form of memory failure happened more than once each day" (Sunderland et al., 1984b, p. 132).

indicating greater frequency of memory problems (Sunderland, Harris, & Baddeley, 1984a). A 5-point scale from "once or less in the last month/never" to "once or more a day" has also been used (Lincoln et al., 2002), and Efklides et al. (2002) used a simplified 4-point scale from 0 (never) to 3 (very often).

Psychometric properties

Sunderland et al. (1983, 1984a) reported on the 35-item version of the EMQ with 65 people with TBI (a "recent" group $n = 33$ examined $M = 11$ weeks after discharge and a "late" group $n = 32$ between 2 and 8 years post-trauma) and their relative-informants, along with 37 orthopaedic patients and their relative-informants. Age of the TBI participants, recruited from a regional hospital in Cambridge, UK, ranged from 16 to 69 years, with median durations of post-traumatic amnesia for the two groups of 14 and 16 days. Concurrent validity was examined with a selection of episodic memory and other cognitive tests. Examination of the revised 28-item version (descriptive data shown in Data box 4.11) largely replicated the results of the initial study (Sunderland et al., 1984a). The informant's EMQ (but not the self-rated version) was able to distinguish between mildly ($n = 30$) versus severely ($n = 50$) injured TBI patients.

Other groups have also examined other psychometric properties of the EMQ. Concurrent validity of the EMQ with a similar rating scale of everyday memory, the Subjective Memory Questionnaire (SMQ) was evaluated by Goldstein and Polkey (1992). Their sample comprised 81 patients with temporal lobectomy or amygdalo-hippocampectomy, along with 60 healthy controls. Construct validity of the EMQ was examined by Efklides et al. (2002), using a Greek version of the 28-item EMQ and the simplified 4-point rating scale, with 233 mainly older ($n = 148 > 60$ years), healthy community volunteers. Internal consistency of the EMQ was also calculated and temporal stability examined in a subset of 46 participants who were re-interviewed 3 months later. Principal components analysis on the total sample ($n = 223$) extracted seven components, accounting for 61.7% of the variance: Prospective/general memory, New learning and repetition, Forgetting changes in daily routine, Visuospatial memory, Semantic memory, Episodic and face memory, and Visual reconstruction. Results from the above studies, all of which use the 9-point scoring system unless otherwise indicated, are shown in Box 4.12.

Derivatives of the EMQ: Children's Memory Questionnaire (CMQ); Drysdale, Shores, and Levick (2004)

The CMQ was derived from both the 35-item and 28-item versions of the EMQ. Phrasing was slightly amended as appropriate for a child's version. Some items were omitted and others subdivided, resulting in a 34-item "school" version and a 29-item "clinic" version. Items appear in Drysdale et al. and are also reproduced below. The CMQ was administered to 261 children aged between 5 and 12 years; 226 of whom were recruited from four schools and 35 children, diagnosed with learning disorders and attention deficit hyperactivity disorder, recruited from a clinic. In the school group the CMQ showed very high internal consistency (Cronbach alpha .96) and excellent test–retest reliability in a subset of 30 children who were re-examined 3 to 4 weeks later

Box 4.12

Validity:	Criterion: *Concurrent*: Sunderland et al. (1984a): Informant EMQ with immediate recall of short story: $r = .72$ – Goldstein & Polkey: EMQ with SMQ: Informant: $r = -.51$, self: $r = -.53$
	Construct: *Internal consistency:* Cronbach alpha: Efklides et al. (4-point scale): .89
	Factor analysis: Efklides et al. (4-point scale): 7 factors: Prospective/general memory (7 items), New learning and repetition (6 items), Forgetting changes in daily routine (4 items), Visuospatial memory (4 items), Semantic memory (4 items), Episodic and face memory (4 items), Visual reconstruction (3 items)
	Discriminant: Sunderland et al. (1984a): Informant EMQ: mild TBI $M = 21$ vs severe TBI $M = 38$; $F = 4.77$, $p = .03$ – Goldstein & Polkey: patient groups scored more poorly than the control group: Self-ratings: patient $F = 5.32$, $p < .05$, informant ratings: $F = 10.0$, $p < .01$
Reliability:	Inter-rater: Not applicable
	Test–retest: Efklides et al. (4-point scale): 3 months $r = .85$
Responsiveness:	No information available

($r_s = .92$). Results from cognitive testing were significant for the 10-year age group (e.g., Verbal Learning delayed recall subtest of the Wide Range Assessment of Memory and Learning, $r = -.57$, $p < .01$), but were less reliable with the younger groups, and the authors concluded that the CMQ is appropriate to use with children 10 years of age or older. In the 29-item clinic version, total scores between the school and clinic samples were significantly different. Although a cut-off score was derived, the authors concluded that the sensitivity, specificity, positive and negative predictive power using the cut-off scores were too low to recommend the CMQ as a diagnostic instrument.

Comment

The EMQ is widely used as a self-report measure of perceived everyday memory functioning and a substantial amount of research has been conducted to understand the relationship between objective and self-reported memory functioning – a relationship that is not a simple one. Sunderland and colleagues were among the first to systematically raise the validity issues regarding self-ratings vis-à-vis informant ratings. Notwithstanding these challenges, at a psychometric level the EMQ holds up well in terms of good internal consistency (using a 4-point scale) and temporal stability. There is evidence for concurrent validity with other measures and the capacity to distinguish between groups. Although there is controversy over use of the EMQ as a diagnostic tool, a singular advantage is summarized by Lincoln and Tinson (1989): scales such as the EMQ "have clear advantages over conventional clinical memory tests for identifying problems that are occurring in daily life and ones which would be appropriate for treatment" (p. 65).

Key references

Drysdale, K., Shores, A., & Levick, W. (2004). Use of the Everyday Memory Questionnaire with children. *Child Neuropsychology*, *10*(2), 67–75.

Efklides, A., Yiultsi, E., Kangellidou, T., Kounti, F., Dina, F., & Tsolaki, M. (2002). Wechsler Memory Scale, Rivermead Behavioural Memory Test, and Everyday Memory Questionnaire in healthy adults and Alzheimer patients. *European Journal of Psychological Assessment*, *18*(1), 63–77.

Goldstein, L. H., & Polkey, C. E. (1992). Everyday memory after unilateral temporal lobectomy or amygdalo-hippocampectomy. *Cortex*, *28*, 189–201.

Koltai, D. C., Bowler, R. M., & Shore, M. D. (1996). The Rivermead Behavioural Memory Test and Wechsler Memory Scale-Revised: Relationship to everyday memory impairment. *Assessment*, *3*(4), 443–448.

Lincoln, N. B., Dent, A., Harding, J., Weyman, N., Nicholl, C., Blumhardt, L. D., et al. (2002). Evaluation of cognitive assessment and cognitive intervention for people with multiple sclerosis. *Journal of Neurology, Neurosurgery and Psychiatry*, *72*(1), 93–98.

Lincoln, N. B., & Tinson, D. J. (1989). The relation between subjective and objective memory impairment after stroke. *British Journal of Clinical Psychology*, *28*, 61–65.

Olsson, E., Wik, K., Östling, A.-K., Johansson, M., & Andersson, G. (2006). Everyday memory self-assessed by adult patients with acquired brain damage and their significant others. *Neuropsychological Rehabilitation*, *16*(3), 257–271.

Stewart, F. M., Sunderland, A., & Sluman, S. M. (1996). The nature and prevalence of memory disorder late after stroke. *British Journal of Clinical Psychology*, *35*, 369–379.

Sunderland, A., Harris, J. E., & Baddeley, A. D. (1983). Do laboratory tests predict everyday memory? A neuropsychological study. *Journal of Verbal Learning and Verbal Behaviour*, *22*, 341–357.

Sunderland, A., Harris, J. E., & Baddeley, A. D. (1984a). *Assessing everyday memory after severe head injury*. In J. E. Harris and R. E. Morris (Eds.), *Everyday memory, actions and absent-mindedness* (pp. 191–206). London: Academic Press.

Sunderland, A., Harris, J. E., & Gleave, J. (1984b). Memory failures in everyday life following severe head injury. *Journal of Clinical Neuropsychology*, *6*(2), 127–142.

Sunderland, A., Stewart, F. M., & Sluman, S. M. (1996). Adaptation to cognitive deficit? An exploration of apparent dissociations between everyday memory and test performance late after stroke. *British Journal of Clinical Psychology*, *35*, 463–476.

Tinson, D. J., & Lincoln, N. B. (1987). Subjective memory impairment after stroke. *International Disability Studies*, *9*, 6–9.

Everyday Memory Questionnaire

Sunderland, Harris, and Gleave (1984)

Name:	**Administered by:**	**Date:**

Response key:

0 = Not at all in the last 3 months
1 = About once in the last 3 months
2 = More than once in the last 3 months, but less than once a month
3 = About once a month
4 = More than once a month, but less than once a week
5 = About once a week
6 = More than once a week, but less than once a day
7 = About once a day
8 = More than once a day

		RESPONSE
1.	Forgetting where you have put something. Losing things around the house	______
2.	Failing to recognize places that you are told you have often been to before	______
3.	Finding a television story difficult to follow	______
4.	Not remembering a change in your daily routine, such as a change in the place where something is kept, or a change in the time something happens. Following your old routine by mistake	______
5.	Having to go back and check whether you have done something that you meant to do	______
6.	Forgetting when it was that something happened; for example, whether it was yesterday or last week	______
7.	Completely forgetting to take things with you, or leaving things behind and having to go back and fetch them	______
8.	Forgetting that you were told something yesterday or a few days ago, and maybe having to be reminded about it	______
9.	Starting to read something (a book or an article in a newspaper, or a magazine) without realizing you have already read it before	______
10.	Letting yourself ramble on to speak about unimportant or irrelevant things	______
11.	Failing to recognize, by sight, close relatives or friends that you meet frequently	______
12.	Having difficulty picking up a new skill. For example, finding it hard to learn a new game or to work some new gadget after you have practised once or twice	______
13.	Finding that a word is "on the tip of your tongue". You know what it is but cannot quite find it	______
14.	Completely forgetting to do things you said you would do, and things you planned to do	______
15.	Forgetting important details of what you did or what happened to you the day before	______
16.	When talking to someone, forgetting what you have just said. Maybe saying "What was I talking about?"	______
17.	When reading a newspaper or magazine being unable to follow the thread of a story; losing track of what it is about	______
18.	Forgetting to tell somebody something important. Perhaps forgetting to pass on a message or remind someone of something	______
19.	Forgetting important details about yourself, e.g., your birthdate or where you live	______
20.	Getting details of what someone has told you mixed up and confused	______
21.	Telling someone a story or joke that you have told them once already	______
22.	Forgetting details of things you do regularly, whether at home or at work. For example, forgetting details of what to do, or forgetting at what time to do it	______
23.	Finding the faces of famous people seen on television or in photographs, look unfamiliar	______
24.	Forgetting where things are normally kept or looking for them in the wrong place	______
25.	Getting lost or turning in the wrong direction on a journey, on a walk or in a building where you have OFTEN been before	______
26.	Getting lost or turning in the wrong direction on a journey, on a walk or in a building where you have ONLY BEEN ONCE OR TWICE before	______
27.	Doing some routine thing twice by mistake. For example, putting two lots of tea in the teapot, or going to brush/comb your hair when you have just done so	______
28.	Repeating to someone what you have just told them or asking them the same question twice	______
	TOTAL SCORE:	______

Acknowledgement: From Sunderland, A. et al. (1984). Memory failures in everyday life following severe head injury. *Journal of Clinical Neuropsychology*, *6*(2), 127–142, Appendix, pp. 140–142, with permission of Taylor & Francis.

Children's Memory Questionnaire

Drysdale, Shores, and Levick (2004)

Name:	**Administered by:**	**Date:**

Instructions:
Below is a list of problems children might experience with memory. Please rate how often your child experiences these problems by writing in the number for the description that best matches your child.

Response key:

1 = Never or almost never happens
2 = About once in 3 months
3 = About once a month
4 = About once in 1–2 weeks
5 = About once or twice a week
6 = About once a day
7 = More than once a day

		RESPONSE
1.	Forgets where she/he has put something	______
2.	Forgets where things are usually kept or looks for them in wrong place [a]	______
3.	Loses things	______
4.	Forgets to take things with him/her or leaves things behind and has to go back for them [a]	______
5.	Forgets to do a routine thing that she/he would normally do once or twice a day	______
6.	Forgets a change in the daily routine; such as a change in the place where something is kept, or in the time something happens	______
7.	Does some routine thing twice or more by mistake	______
8.	Forgets to do things she/he said she/he would or arranged to do	______
9.	Has to go back to check whether she/he has done something he/she meant to do	______
10.	Starts to do something, then seems to forget what she/he wanted to do	______
11.	Slow to pick up a new skill such as a game or working some new gadget	______
12.	Forgets when it was something happened, e.g., whether it was yesterday or last week [a]	______
13.	Forgets what she/he did yesterday or a few days ago, or gets the details of what happened mixed up or confused	______
14.	Forgets what she/he was told a few minutes ago	______
15.	Forgets what she/he was told a few days ago	______
16.	Forgets to tell someone something important such as passing on an important message	______
17.	Gets the details of what someone told him/her mixed up and confused	______
18.	Repeats something she/he has just said or says the same thing several times	______
19.	Seems to forget something she/he has just said	______
20.	Starts to say something, then forgets what it was she/he wanted to say	______
21.	Loses track of what someone is trying to tell him/her	______
22.	Tend to "ramble" about unimportant or irrelevant things	______
23.	A word seems to be "on the tip of the tongue" but she/he cannot quite find it	______
24.	Unknowingly tells someone a story or joke she/he has told that person before	______
25.	Finds television shows or movies (suitable for his/her age) difficult to follow	______
26.	Forgets the names of common things or uses the wrong names for them	______
27.	Forgets the names of friends or relatives she/he knows quite well or calls them the wrong name	______
28.	Forgets the name of someone she/he met for the first time recently	______
29.	Fails to recognize someone she/he met for the first time recently	______
30.	Fails to recognize by sight people, e.g., relatives or friends that she/he meets frequently [a]	______
31.	Fails to recognize well-known television characters or other famous people by sight	______
32.	Gets lost or turns in the wrong direction in places she/he has often been to before	______
33.	Gets lost in places she/he has only been once or twice before [a]	______
34.	Does not recognize places she/her has often been to before	______
	TOTAL SCORE:	______

Note: [a] Item not included in clinic or modified questionnaires.

Acknowledgement: From Drysdale, K., Shores, A., & Levick, W. (2004). Use of the everyday memory questionnaire with children. *Child Neuropsychology*, 10(2), 74–75, with permission of Taylor & Francis, www.tandf.co.uk/journals

Memory Compensation Questionnaire (MCQ)

Dixon and Bäckman (1992/1993)

Source

Items from the MCQ are available in an appendix to de Frias and Dixon (2005) and full administrative, recording and scoring details are available from Dr Dixon (Department of Psychology, University of Victoria, Victoria, BC V8W 3P5, Canada; email: rdixon@ualberta.ca).

Purpose

The MCQ is a self-rating scale, designed to evaluate "the variety and extent of means for compensating for memory losses and deficits" (Dixon, de Frias, & Bäckman, 2001, p. 653). It was originally developed to target normal cognitive ageing processes. It has also been used with clinical samples, including people with Alzheimer's disease (AD; Dixon, Hopp, Cohen, de Frias, & Bäckman, 2003) and younger people with memory disorders from various neurological conditions (Prigatano & Kime, 2003).

Item description

The 44-item MCQ has seven scales. Five scales relate to compensatory strategies, encompassing substitution (3 scales) and remediation (2 scales) mechanisms. The three substitution scales comprise use of external aids (External – 8 items, e.g., "Do you post notes on a board or other prominent place to help you remember things for the future (e.g., meetings or dates)?"), internal mnemonic strategies (Internal – 10 items, e.g., "Do you repeat telephone numbers to yourself to remember them well?"), and recruiting the assistance of other people (Reliance – 5 items, e.g., "When you want to remember an important appointment do you ask somebody else (e.g., spouse or friend) to remind you?"), whereas the two remediation scales involve increased use of time, for example to read information (Time – 5 items, e.g., "When you want to remember a story do you read it more than once?") and increased effort, for example concentration (Effort – 6 items, e.g., "Do you concentrate a lot to learn something you really want to remember?"). The final two scales examine general compensatory processes, specifically motivation to maintain compensatory use (Success – 5 items, e.g., "Is it important for you to remember things perfectly (as verbatim as possible)?") and awareness of changes over the preceding 5–10 years necessitating the use of compensatory techniques (Change – 5 items, e.g., "Do you use such aids for memory as notebooks or putting things in certain places more or less often today compared to 5–10 years ago?").

Scale development

Development of the MCQ occurred in the context of two large longitudinal studies of individual differences in older adults (Hultsch, Hertzog, Dixon, & Small, 1998). A number of scales of the MCQ are similar to the Metamemory in Adulthood (MIA) Questionnaire, previously developed by Dixon, Hultsch, and Hertzog (1988). The MCQ, however, is more focused in orientation, being developed within a model of compensatory mechanisms proposed by Dixon and Bäckman (1992/1993). The MIA was used in the longitudinal study, and the MCQ introduced in the second wave of testing. de Frias and Dixon (2005) note that "the construction of the MCQ was deliberately designed to focus on actual behaviours that could reflect memory compensations in older adults . . . [in whom] memory complaints are frequent and chronic – and some memory loss is normal" (p. 174). A large pool of items representing seven a priori dimensions of memory compensatory strategies was generated and reduced to 44 items, but procedures used to reduce the item pool were not described.

Administration procedures, response format and scoring

The MCQ is designed to be self-administered. Items are rated on a 5-point scale: 0 (never) to 4 (always). There is no recommended method of obtaining scores, but it is noted that Dixon et al. (2003) used a mean score for each of the scales, thereby anchoring the score back to the original descriptors, making scores directly

Data box 4.12 Descriptive data from longitudinal sample (Dixon et al., 2001)

	Age *M* (*SD*)	Education *M* (*SD*)	MCQ (total sample) *M* (*SE*)	Cut-off score	Sensitivity / Specificity
Sample 1 (*n* = 331):	71.45 (5.53)	Young-old: 14.42 (3.74)		No information	No information
External		to	3.26 (0.02)		
Internal		Old-old: 13.81 (3.33)	2.20 (0.03)		
Time			2.00 (0.03)		
Reliance			1.29 (0.03)		
Effort			2.55 (0.03)		

interpretable. Higher scores reflect greater use of compensatory strategies.

Psychometric properties

Initial psychometric studies were reported in Dixon et al. (2001). Data came from two independent longitudinal samples recruited in Victoria, Canada, comprising $n = 331$ and $n = 523$ healthy community volunteers (age $M = 71.45$ years, $SD = 5.53$ and $M = 68.26$ years, $SD = 7.31$ respectively, range 54 to 85 years). Convergent and divergent validity were examined with selected subtests of the MIA questionnaire, although the authors acknowledged that the two scales are not totally independent, in that they "share method variance and some content characteristics" (p. 657; descriptive data shown in Data box 4.12).

de Frias and Dixon (2005) conducted confirmatory factor analysis of the MCQ in an initial sample of 521 community volunteers drawn from the above longitudinal studies. They used the five strategy scales (comprising 34 items). The five-factor model of the MCQ strategies was accurately identified ($\chi^2 = 1424.44$, $p < .01$), although one item (#26) cross-loaded on another scale. The structure of the two general compensatory processes was also successfully identified ($\chi^2 = 82.54$, $p < .01$). In the course of their study of the five strategy scales comparing 85 healthy older people (control group) and 21 people with AD, who were evaluated on two occasions 6 months apart, Dixon et al. (2003) reported additional psychometric data on the MCQ. Results from Dixon et al. (2001), unless otherwise stated, are shown in Box 4.13.

Comment

The MCQ makes a unique contribution to the rating of memory functions. Most approaches focus on assessing the frequency and severity of memory failures; by contrast, Dixon and Bäckman take the perspective of examining adaptive behaviours to *prevent* memory

Box 4.13

Validity:	Construct: *Internal consistency:* Cronbach alpha: total score: .90–.91 (scale range: .65–.83; scales < .8 not specified)
	Dixon et al. (2003): Control: Cronbach alpha: .64–.82 (4/5 scales < .80 – External, Time, Reliance, Effort); – AD: .51–.88 (3/5 scales < .80; External, Time, Effort)
	Factor analysis: de Frias & Dixon: 5 factors, as per the MCQ strategy scales: External (8 items), Internal (10 items), Reliance (5 items), Time (4 items), Effort (7 items)
	Convergent/divergent: higher correlation with similar constructs (MCQ-External with MIA-External $r = .80$, MCQ-Internal with MIA-Internal $r = .67$), lower correlation with dissimilar constructs (MCQ-Reliance with MIA-External $r = .15$, MCQ-Success with MIA-External $r = .11$)
Reliability:	Inter-rater: Not applicable
	Test–retest: 3 years: total score: $r = .61–.78$ (descriptive data not reported)
	Dixon et al. (2003): 6 months: Control: 5 strategy scales $r = .41–.79$ – AD: $r = .29–.71$
Responsiveness:	Dixon et al. (2003): MCQ-Reliance AD: Time 1 $M = 1.77$ ($SD = 0.82$) vs Time 2 $M = 2.10$ ($SD = 1.15$); $d = .40$, but no such increase in Control: Time 1 $M = 1.72$ ($SD = 0.64$) vs Time 2 $M = 1.58$ ($SD = 0.66$); $d = .22$; $F = 5.82$, $p < .02$

failures. The importance of having a standardized measure of memory compensatory strategies is born out by the work of Wilson (1991) and Evans, Wilson, Needham, and Brentnall (2003). They found a significant difference in psychosocial independence for those young adults with memory disorders who used more than five memory aids versus those who used less. Users of the MCQ, however, will need to weigh up psychometric considerations – no information is available on its concurrent validity with similar measures and temporal stability is not high. The test–retest intervals were large, however (6 months and 3 years), and in an older population this may have been confounded by the occurrence of real changes.

Key references

de Frias, C. M., & Dixon, R. M. (2005). Confirmatory factor structure and measurement invariance of the Memory Compensation Questionnaire. *Psychological Assessment*, *17*(2), 168–178.

Dixon, R A., & Bäckman, L. (1992/1993). The concept of compensation in cognitive ageing: The case of prose processing in adulthood. *International Journal of Aging and Human Development*, *36*(3), 199–217.

Dixon, R. A., de Frias, C. M., & Bäckman, L. (2001). Characteristics of self-reported memory compensation in older adults. *Journal of Clinical and Experimental Neuropsychology*, *23*(5), 650–661.

Dixon, R. A., Hopp, G. A., Cohen, A.-L., de Frias, C. M., & Bäckman, L. (2003). Self-reported memory compensation: Similar patterns in Alzheimer's disease and very old adult samples. *Journal of Clinical and Experimental Neuropsychology*, *25*(3), 382–390.

Dixon, R. A., Hultsch, D. F., & Hertzog, C. (1988). The Metamemory in Adulthood Questionnaire. *Psychopharmacology Bulletin*, *24*(4), 671–688.

Evans, J. J., Wilson, B. A., Needham, P., & Brentnall, S. (2003). Who makes good use of memory aids? Results of a survey of people with acquired brain injury. *Journal of the International Neuropsychological Society*, *9*(6), 925–935.

Hultsch, D. F., Hertzog, C., Dixon, R. A., & Small, B. J. (1998). *Memory change in the aged*. Cambridge: Cambridge University Press.

Prigatano, G. P., & Kime, S. (2003). What do brain dysfunctional patients report following memory compensation training? *NeuroRehabilitation*, *18*, 47–55.

Wilson, B. A. (1991). Long-term prognosis of patients with severe memory disorders. *Neuropsychological Rehabilitation*, *1*(2), 117–134.

Memory Functioning Questionnaire (MFQ)

Gilewski and Zelinski (1988)

Source

Items for the MFQ are available in the appendix to Gilewski and Zelinski (1988) and are reproduced below. The authors have also derived a 10-item instrument from the MFQ, referred to as the Frequency of Forgetting Scale, which is described in Zelinski and Gilewski (2004).

Purpose

The MFQ is a self-rating scale, designed to provide a self-appraisal of everyday remembering and forgetting in adults. It was developed for the general population across all adult age groups (16–89 years) and has also been used with neurological populations, including multiple sclerosis (Randolph, Arnett, & Freske, 2004), traumatic brain injury (TBI; Kinsella et al., 1996), and people at risk for Alzheimer's disease (Small et al., 2001).

Item description

The 64-item MFQ comprises four statistically derived factors: Frequency of forgetting (33 items; 28 specific situations and 5 general performance items), Seriousness of forgetting (18 items describing specific situations), Retrospective functioning (5 comparison points with earlier life), and Mnemonic strategy use (8 specific mnemonics).

Scale development

Development of the MFQ derived from the 92-item, nine-scale Metamemory Questionnaire (MQ) developed by Zelinski, Gilewski, and Thompson (1980). The MQ aimed to include a wide range of specific situations, but the actual item selection process was not described. Data on the MQ from 778 healthy community volunteers aged 16 to 89 years were subject to principal components analysis (Gilewski, Zelinski, & Schaie, 1990). Four factors, accounting for 36.7% of the variance, were extracted (Frequency of forgetting, Seriousness of forgetting, Retrospective functioning, and Mnemonic strategy use) representing seven of the nine scales of the MQ. The 64 items loading on these factors were retained and relabelled the MFQ. The factor structure of the MFQ was comparable in younger (16–54 years) and older (55–89 years) age groups. Confirmation of the factor structure was established with an independent longitudinal sample ($n = 264$, aged 29–87 years), and the factor structure remained stable in this sample at retest 3 years later. A 10-item Frequency of Forgetting Scale was developed by Rasch analysis from the first (33-item) factor (Zelinski & Gilweski, 2004).

Administration procedures, response format and scoring

The MFQ is designed for self-completion. In spite of the MFQ being a shorter version of the original 92-item MQ, at 64 items it is still lengthy. For this reason, some researchers investigating clinical populations have used the first two scales, Frequency and Seriousness (51 items), representing some savings. The 10-item version creates less administrative burden, but its clinical application is yet untested.

For each item, ratings are made on a 7-point scale, with descriptors at ratings 1, 4 and 7, and these vary among item sets: 1 (major problem), 4 (some minor problems), 7 (no problems); 1 (much worse), 4 (same), 7 (much better); 1 (always), 4 (sometimes), 7 (never); 1 (very bad), 4 (fair), 7 (very good); 1 (very serious), 4 (somewhat serious), 7 (not serious). "Unit factor scores" are used, whereby scores on items loading on a factor are summed. Higher scores reflect higher levels of perceived memory functioning (i.e., fewer self-reported memory problems and less use of mnemonics). Interpretation is facilitated by dividing the total score by the number of items in each factor, thereby anchoring the score back to the original 7-point scale.

Normative data for the MFQ are available in Gilewski et al. (1990) for 778 adults aged between 16 and 89 years, stratified by decade.

Data box 4.13 Descriptive data from the validation sample (Zelinski et al., 1990)

	Age *M (SD)*	Education *M (SD)*	MFQ *M (SD)*	Cut-off score	Sensitivity / Specificity
Sample 1 (n = 198):	67.85 (6.89)	13.13 (2.71)		No information	No information
Frequency			158.13 (28.42)		
Seriousness			84.60 (21.53)		
Retrospective			17.04 (6.06)		
Mnemonic use			28.97 (11.56)		

Box 4.14

Validity:

Criterion:
Concurrent:
a) Normal samples: Zelinski et al. (1990): used hierarchical regression analyses: Sample 1: MFQ significantly predicted memory performance for word lists (but not prose recall) – Sample 2: MFQ significantly predicted Randt Test, MMSE, diary recordings, but not RBMT-PM

Kinsella et al.: Control: with RMBT-PM–Factor1: r = .43–.47, Factor 2: r = .17–.48, Factor 3: r = .31–.60, Factor 4: r = –.06 to –.09

b) Neurological samples – Kinsella et al.: TBI: with RAVLT: r = .02 to –.21 – with Rivermead-PM – Factor 1: r = .11–.38, Factor 2: r = .21–.37, Factor 3: r = .12–.47, Factor 4: r = .24–.31

Randolph et al.: with SRT: r = .04 to –.27 – with BDI: r = .32–.34

Small et al.: using multiple regression analysis predictors of MFQ performance included HDRS (HRSD), but not SRT

Construct:
Internal consistency: Gilewski et al.: Cronbach alpha: Factor 1: .94, Factor 2: .94, Factor 3: .89, Factor 4: .83

Factor structure: Gilewski et al.: 4 factors: Frequency of forgetting (33 items), Seriousness of forgetting (18 items), Retrospective functioning (5 items), Mnemonic strategy use (8 items)

Discriminant: Neurological samples – mixed evidence: Kinsella et al. found no difference in MFQ scores (Factors 1, 2, or 4) between TBI vs control groups (descriptive data not reported), even though the TBI group performed more poorly than controls on objective memory tests (e.g., RAVLT) M = 41.00 (SD = 10.24) vs M = 50.13 (SD = 9.06) respectively; t = 3.42, p < .01

Small et al.: found significant differences on 2/4 factors:
– Factor 3: mild group M = 13.9 (SD = 4.9) vs normative 50–59 age group M = 17.7 (SD = 4.6); t = 4.81, p < .001
– Factor 4: mild group M = 25.3 (SD = 9.3) vs normative 50–59 age group M = 30.5 (SD = 8.9); t = 3.43, p < .001

Reliability: Inter-rater: Not applicable

Test–retest: Gilewski et al.: Stability of the factor structure demonstrated over a 3-year period

Responsiveness: No information available

Psychometric properties

Zelinski, Gilweski, and Anthony-Bergstone (1990) reported data from two samples. The first examined concurrent validity of the MFQ in 198 older adults (55–85 years – descriptive data shown in Data box 4.13), recruited from a larger sample in the USA enrolled in a study on intelligence. Validation measures included objective memory test performance (recall of word list and a prose passage). The second sample recruited 89 community-dwelling adults over the age of 55 years, 53 of whom reported significant memory problems. Validation instruments included the Mini-Mental State Examination (MMSE), Randt Memory Test, Prospective Memory subtest from the Rivermead Behavioural Memory Test (RBMT-PM), and diary-recorded everyday memory failures.

Information on the psychometric properties of the MFQ in clinical samples is available from Kinsella et al. (1996) who examined 24 people with TBI (age $M = 32.5$ years, $SD = 13.6$) and 24 matched healthy volunteers. Clinical measures (e.g., Rey Auditory Verbal Learning Test, RAVLT, RMBT-PM) were used to examine concurrent validity. Randolph et al. (2004) examined 48 people with multiple sclerosis (age $M = 49.6$ years, $SD = 7.8$) and administered a range of tests including memory (e.g., verbal Selective Reminding Test, SRT) and mood (e.g., Beck Depression Inventory, BDI). Small et al. (2001) recruited 66 people with mild age-related memory complaints, but without dementia or major depression. They compared their sample with the normative data from Gilewski et al. (1990) and examined the influence of depression (Hamilton Depression Rating Scale, HDRS; also known as the Hamilton Rating Scale for Depression, HRSD) and objective memory test performance using the Bushke SRT. Results of the above studies are shown in Box 4.14.

Comment

The MFQ has been extensively examined and refined in healthy populations, including older people. Its four factors have good to excellent internal consistency, the factor structure shows temporal stability and the scale is suggested to be a "modest predictor" of memory test performance in healthy groups. Application of the MFQ to neurological groups has not been as positive or as straightforward, however. The MFQ is one of the few memory rating scales that has provided data on concurrent validity, but evidence currently available indicates that the correspondence between MFQ scores and objective memory testing is not high. Moreover depressed mood has a demonstrated influence on MFQ scores. Additionally, Kinsella et al. (1996) suggest that although people with TBI may have a general concept of memory functioning, they have difficulties in relating this retrospectively to specific instances.

Key references

Gilewski, M. J., & Zelinski, E. M. (1988). Memory Functioning Questionnaire (MFQ). *Psychopharmacology Bulletin, 24*(4), 665–670.

Gilewski, M. J., Zelinski, E. M., & Schaie, K. W. (1990). The Memory Functioning Questionnaire for assessment of memory complaints in adulthood and old age. *Psychology and Aging, 5*(4), 482–490.

Kinsella, G., Murtagh, D., Landry, A., Homfray, K., Hammond, M., O'Beirne, L., et al. (1996). Everyday memory following traumatic brain injury. *Brain Injury, 10*(7), 499–507.

Randolph, J. J., Arnett, P. A., & Freske, P. (2004). Metamemory in multiple sclerosis: Exploring affective and executive contributors. *Archives of Clinical Neuropsychology, 19*, 259–279.

Small, G. W., Chen, S. T., Komo, S., Ercoli, L., Miller, K., Siddarth, P., et al. (2001). Memory self-appraisal and depressive symptoms in people at genetic risk for Alzheimer's disease. *International Journal of Geriatric Psychiatry, 16*, 1071–1077.

Zelinski, E. M., & Gilewski, M. J. (2004). A 10-item Rasch modeled memory self-efficacy scale. *Aging and Mental Health, 8*(4), 293–306.

Zelinski, E. M., Gilewski, M. J., & Anthony-Bergstone, C. R. (1990). Memory Functioning Questionnaire: Concurrent validity with memory performance and self reported memory failures. *Psychology and Aging, 5*(3), 388–399.

Zelinski, E. M., Gilewski, M. J., & Thompson, L. W. (1980). Do laboratory tests relate to self-assessment of memory ability in the young and old? In L. W. Poon, J. L. Fozard, L. S. Cermak, D. Arenberg, & L. W. Thompson (Eds.), *New directions in memory and aging: Proceedings of the George A. Talland Memorial Conference* (pp. 519–544). Hillsdale, NJ: Lawrence Erlbaum Associates, Inc.

Memory Functioning Questionnaire

Gilewski and Zelinski (1988)

Name: **Administered by:** **Date:**

Instructions:
This is a questionnaire about how you remember information. There are no right or wrong answers. Circle a number between 1 and 7 that best reflects your judgement about your memory. Think carefully about your responses, and try to be as realistic as possible when you make them. Please answer all questions.

GENERAL RATING SCALE

1. How would you rate your memory in terms of the kinds of problems that you have?

1	2	3	4	5	6	7
Major problems			Some minor problems			No problems

Frequency of forgetting: Subtotal 1: __________

RETROSPECTIVE RATING SCALE **RESPONSE**

Using the following scale:

1	2	3	4	5	6	7
Much worse			Same			Much better

2. How is your memory compared to the way it was . . .
   a) 1 year ago? __________
   b) 5 years ago? __________
   c) 10 years ago? __________
   d) 20 years ago? __________
   e) when you were 18? __________

TOTAL RETROSPECTIVE FUNCTIONING SCORE: __________

FREQUENCY OF FORGETTING SCALE **RESPONSE**

Using the following scale:

1	2	3	4	5	6	7
Always			Sometimes			Never

3. How often do these present a problem for you?
   a) names __________
   b) faces __________
   c) appointments __________
   d) where you put things (e.g., keys) __________
   e) performing household chores __________
   f) directions to places __________
   g) phone numbers you've just checked __________
   h) phone numbers you use frequently __________
   i) things people tell you __________
   j) keeping up correspondence __________
   k) personal dates (e.g., birthdays) __________
   l) words __________
   m) going to the store and forgetting what you wanted to buy __________
   n) taking a test __________
   o) beginning to do something and forgetting what you were doing __________
   p) losing the thread of thought in conversation __________
   q) losing the thread of thought in public speaking __________
   r) knowing whether you already told someone something __________

Frequency of forgetting during reading: **RESPONSE**

Using the following scale:

1	2	3	4	5	6	7
Always			Sometimes			Never

4. As you are reading a novel, how often you have trouble remembering what you have read . . .
   a) in the opening chapters, once you have finished the book ________
   b) three or four chapters before the one you are currently reading ________
   c) the chapter before the one you are currently reading ________
   d) the paragraph just before the one you are currently reading ________
   e) the sentence before the one you are currently reading ________
5. When you are reading a newspaper or magazine article, how often do you have trouble remembering what you have read . . .
   a) in the opening paragraphs, once you have finished the article ________
   b) three or four photographs before the one you are currently reading ________
   c) the paragraph before the one you are currently reading ________
   d) three or four sentences before the one you are currently reading ________
   e) the sentence before the one you are currently reading ________

Frequency of forgetting: Subtotal 2 ________

Remembering past events: **RESPONSE**

Using the following scale:

1	2	3	4	5	6	7
Very bad			Fair			Very good

6. How well you remember things that occurred . . .
   a) last month is . . . ________
   b) between 6 months and 1 year ago is . . . ________
   c) between 1 and 5 years ago is . . . ________
   d) between 6 and 10 years ago is . . . ________

Frequency of forgetting: Subtotal 3 ________

TOTAL FREQUENCY OF FORGETTING SCORE (Subtotal 1 + 2 + 3): ________

SERIOUSNESS SCALE **RESPONSE**

Using the following response key:

1	2	3	4	5	6	7
Very serious			Somewhat serious			Not serious

7. When you actually forget in these situations, how serious a problem do you consider the memory failure to be?
   a) names ________
   b) faces ________
   c) appointments ________
   d) where you put things (e.g., keys) ________
   e) performing household chores ________
   f) directions to places ________
   g) phone numbers you have just checked ________
   h) phone numbers used frequently ________
   i) things people tell you ________
   j) keeping up correspondence ________
   k) personal dates (e.g., birthdays) ________
   l) words ________
   m) going to the store and forgetting what you wanted to buy ________
   n) taking a test ________
   o) beginning to do something and forgetting what you were doing ________
   p) losing the thread of thought in conversation ________
   q) losing the thread of thought in public speaking ________
   r) knowing whether you've already told someone something ________

TOTAL SERIOUSNESS SCORE: ________

MNEMONICS USAGE SCALE **RESPONSE**

Using the following scale:

1	2	3	4	5	6	7
Always			Sometimes			Never

8. How often do you use these techniques to remind yourself about things?
   a) keep an appointment book ______
   b) write yourself reminder notes ______
   c) make lists of things to do ______
   d) make grocery lists ______
   e) plan your daily schedule in advance ______
   f) mental repetition ______
   g) associations with other things ______
   h) keep things you need to do in a prominent place where you will notice them ______

TOTAL MNEMONIC USAGE SCORE: ______

Summary

Frequency of forgetting: ____ Seriousness of forgetting: ____ Retrospective functioning: ____ Mnemonic strategy: ____

Acknowledgement: From Gilewski, M. J., & Zelinski, E. M. (1988). Memory Functioning Questionnaire (MFQ). *Psychopharmacology Bulletin*, *24*(4), 665–670, reproduced by permission of Medworks Media and Psychological Assessment Resources.

Memory Impairment Screen (MIS)

Buschke et al. (1999)

Source

The MIS is described in Bushke et al. (1999) and the items and scale are available from Dr Buschke (Department of Neurology, Albert Einstein College of Medicine, Kennedy 912, Bronx, New York, 10461, USA).

Purpose

The MIS is an objective, clinician-administered test, designed to improve screening for dementia and Alzheimer's disease (AD). Buschke et al. (1999) aimed to develop an instrument that was sensitive to detection of the early stages of progressive dementias. They reasoned that because memory impairment is frequently the earliest sign of AD, a very brief test of memory would serve as a useful screening instrument. The MIS has also been used in patients with stroke (Riepe, Riss, Bittner, & Huber, 2004) and the utility of a telephone administration in patients with dementia has also been examined (Lipton et al., 2003).

Item description

The MIS entails the delayed recall (free and cued) of four words, each of which represent a different category (e.g. the word "potato" from the category "vegetable"). An alternate form of the MIS is also available. The four items are printed on an A4 page (8.5 inches × 11 inches) in 24-point, uppercase letters.

Scale development

Buschke et al. (1999) reported that development of the MIS evolved from their previous investigations into memory disorders in older people and clinical populations. It drew on a paradigm of controlled learning to maximize encoding specificity, which "requires the individual to search for and identify a to-be-remembered item in response to its category cue" (p. 232). This paradigm was used in the development of their Double Memory Test (DMT) and its forerunner, the multi-trial Free and Cued Recall Selective Reminding Test (FCSRT). The DMT has high sensitivity and specificity for mild dementia, but was not suitable as a screening tool because of its length. Standardization of the MIS used a sample of 483 community volunteers. A subset ($n = 50$) was diagnosed as having dementia using established criteria, with 39 of the 50 meeting criteria for AD (staging not specified). Receiver operating characteristic (ROC) curves were used to establish cut-off points for different base rates of dementia and AD (5%, 10%, 15% and 20%).

Administration procedures, response format and scoring

Only simple stimulus materials (page with words written in the specified format described above) are required for administration of the MIS, which does not require formal training of the clinician. The respondent is presented with the page and reads each item, the examiner then proffers a category whereupon the respondent identifies and names each item. The page is then removed, an interference activity of 2 to 3 minutes is introduced (counting from 1 to 20 and back, etc.), followed by free recall of the items. For items not retrieved by free recall, a cued-recall procedure is instituted in which the examiner proffers the category. Administration time is very brief (4 mins).

Two points are awarded for each correct response to free recall, and 1 point for those items retrieved following cued recall. The total score ranges from 0 to 8, with higher scores indicating better performance. The optimal cut-off score depends on the base rate of dementia and the decision-making process – for example, clinicians may require high sensitivity, whereas researchers may prefer high specificity (see below).

Normative data for the MIS are presented in Bushke et al. (1999) in terms of the probability of dementia given different cut-off scores. The probabilities were calculated according to Bayes theorem. Cut-off scores were also established using ROC curves: the area under the ROC curve for discriminating dementia was .94, and for discriminating AD was .97. The cut-off score of 4/5 had the highest sensitivity (80%), specificity (96%) and

Data box 4.14 Descriptive data from the standardization sample (Buschke et al., 1999)

	Age *M* (*SD*)	**Education** *M* (*SD*)	**MIS** *M* (*SD*)	**Cut-off score**	**Sensitivity / Specificity**
Control ($n = 433$)	79.3 (6.1)	12.2 (3.2)	7.2 (1.2)	4/5	80% / 96%
Dementia – including AD ($n = 50$)	81.4 (7.0)	11.0 (3.6)	2.5 (2.3)		
(AD only: $n = 39$)	81.1 (7.3)	11.3 (3.5)	2.1 (1.9)		

positive predictive value (> 69%) for all base rates except 5%.

The high sensitivity, specificity and positive predictive value were replicated by Kuslansky, Buschke, Katz, Sliwinski, and Lipton (2002) in a sample of 240 community-dwelling people aged 70 years or older.

Psychometric properties

The MIS was validated on the standardization sample (Bushke et al., 1999), which comprised 483 community volunteers (> 65 years of age – descriptive data shown in Data box 4.14) recruited from a longitudinal study into ageing and dementia, in New York, USA. Correspondence between alternate forms of the MIS, administered at the beginning and end of a neuropsychological assessment with 429 participants, was good (ICC = .69). The 16-item, multi-trial FCSRT was used to examine the concurrent validity of the MIS. The diagnostic accuracies of the MIS were superior to the three-word memory items from the Mini-Mental State Examination. Strong evidence for predictive validity comes from an autopsy study (Verghese et al., 2003). Ante-mortem MIS scores were examined in 21 people with AD markers identified at post-mortem (conducted within 24 hours of death). The median interval between final MIS scores and death was 15 months (range 1–52). When six non-AD cases were excluded, high correlation coefficients were found between final MIS score and AD pathology in the remaining 15 cases, which showed a range of severity of AD pathology. Data from these studies are shown in Box 4.15.

Comment

The MIS has many advantages: development was theoretically based, it has high sensitivity and specificity for detecting mild memory impairments, provides cut-off points for both dementia and AD at different base-rates, offers a reliable alternate form that can counteract practice effects with repeated administration, and has a very brief administration time. The validity of the MIS has been established, both criterion with other memory tests and post-mortem confirmation, as well as discriminant between groups with and without dementia. Reliability, however, remains largely unexamined. Internal consistency (Cronbach alpha .67) is likely to be compromised because of the small number of items ($n = 4$). Nonetheless, the MIS clearly works well as a screening tool to detect the early stages of AD and other progressive dementias.

Box 4.15

Validity:	Criterion: *Concurrent:* Buschke et al: using MIS cut-off score 4/5 with FCSRT: $k = .62$ *Predictive:* Verghese et al: with Braak stage (I-VI): $r = -.73$ – with hippocampal neurofibrillary tangle counts: $r = -.72$ – with hippocampal senile plaque counts: $r = -.74$ Construct: *Internal consistency:* Cronbach alpha: Buschke et al: .67 *Discriminant:* Buschke et al.: AD $M = 2.1$ ($SD = 1.9$) vs healthy controls $M = 7.2$ ($SD = 1.2$) – Dementia (including AD) $M = 2.5$ ($SD = 2.3$) vs healthy controls $M = 7.2$ ($SD = 1.2$) – Differential diagnosis in classifying dementia vs no dementia using cut-off score of 4/5: sensitivity 80%, specificity 96%
Reliability:	Inter-rater: No information available Test–retest: No information available *Practice effects:* No information available
Responsiveness:	No information available

Key references

Buschke, H., Kuslansky, G., Katz, M., Stewart, W. F., Sliwinski, M. J., Eckholdt, H. M., et al. (1999). Screening for dementia with the Memory Impairment Screen. *Neurology*, *52*(2), 231–238.

Kuslansky, G., Buschke, H., Katz, M., Sliwinski, M., & Lipton, R. B. (2002). Screening for Alzheimer's disease: The Memory Impairment Screen versus the conventional Three-Word Memory Test. *Journal of the American Geriatrics Society*, *50*, 1086–1091.

Lipton, R. B., Katz, M. J., Kuslansky, G., Sliwinski, M. J., Stewart, W. F., Verghese, J., et al. (2003). Screening for dementia by telephone using the Memory Impairment Screen. *Journal of the American Geriatrics Society*, *51*, 1382–1390.

Riepe, M. W., Riss, S., Bittner, D., & Huber, R. (2004). Screening for cognitive impairment in patients with acute stroke. *Dementia and Geriatric Cognitive Disorders*, *17*(1–2), 49–53.

Verghese, J., Buschke, H., Kuslansky, G., Katz, M. J., Weidenheim, K., Lipton, R. B., et al. (2003). [Letter] Antemortem Memory Impairment Screen performance is correlated with postmortem Alzheimer pathology. *Journal of the American Geriatrics Society*, *51*(7), 1043–1044.

Prospective and Retrospective Memory Questionnaire (PRMQ)

Smith, Della Sala, Logie, and Maylor (2000)

Source

Items for the PRMQ, along with administration instructions for various versions, are available in appendices to Smith et al. (2000). The informant version is reproduced below.

Purpose

The PRMQ is a rating scale, designed to assess the frequency of different types of memory failures. It was developed to determine the differential effects of normal ageing and Alzheimer's disease (AD) on various memory processes. For informants, the scale also includes an assessment of level of "frustration" caused by the memory failures.

Item description

The 16-item PRMQ contains two items representing each of eight categories: four items for prospective memory (both short-term and long-term, self-cued and environmentally cued) and four items for retrospective memory (both short-term and long-term, self-cued and environmentally cued). An additional four items comprise the informant-rated "frustration" component of the PRMQ: two items relate to the caregiver's own frustration for prospective and retrospective memory failures, and two items relate to the caregiver's perception of the frustration in these areas for the person with AD. Each version of the PRMQ for informant, patient, and healthy control contains identical items, but phrased as appropriate.

Scale development

Smith et al. (2000) observed the relative neglect of examination of prospective memory processes in older people, including those with AD. They argued for the importance of prospective memory (i.e., memory for intentions) in everyday living: "Remembering to do things at the right time is at least as important as being able to retrieve information about our past" (p. 312). Within the prospective memory paradigm, the authors were also interested in examining the different tasks described in the experimental literature. They posited that event-related tasks can be described as "environmentally cued" and time-based tasks as "self-cued". The 16 items were generated to represent each of eight categories in the configuration of prospective/retrospective versus short-term/long-term versus self-cued/environmentally cued (see the box below). A panel of eight experts in memory research were supplied with the 16 items and a description of each of the categories, and requested to sort the 16 items into the appropriate category. Agreement between the panel and the authors' intended configuration was 88%. One item was rephrased and agreement rose to 96%.

Data box 4.15 Configuration of items in the PRMQ

			Items
Prospective	Short-term	Self	1, 16
		Environment	3, 10
	Long-term	Self	5, 14
		Environment	7, 12
Retrospective	Short-term	Self	4, 11
		Environment	6, 13
	Long-term	Self	8, 15
		Environment	2, 9

Administration procedures, response format and scoring

The PRMQ is quick and easy to complete. Items are rated on a 5-point scale: 1 (never), 2 (rarely), 3 (sometimes), 4 (quite often), 5 (very often). Results for eight-item subscales can be derived for prospective or retrospective, short-term or long-term, self-cued or environmentally cued. Finer gradations can also be examined with combinations of the main categories, as shown in Data box 4.15. For the "frustration" component of the PRMQ, items are rated on a 4-point scale: 1 (not at all frustrating), 2 (slightly frustrating), 3 (quite frustrating), 4 (very frustrating).

Data box 4.16 Descriptive data from the standardization sample (Smith et al., 2000)

	Age M (SD)	Education M (SD)	PRMQ M range for categories	Cut-off score	Sensitivity / Specificity
Elderly control ($n = 242$)	72.7 (8.3)	13.0 (3.4)	1.91–3.00	No information	No information
Young control ($n = 164$)	44.2 (11.4)	14.0 (3.7)	1.78–2.86		
AD patients ($n = 155$)	74.0 (8.8)	12.1 (3.6)	4.41–4.67		
Informants ($n = 155$)	56.9 (13.2)	15.6 (3.6)	1.72–2.38		

In scoring the PRMQ, the authors used mean scores (range 1–5), thereby anchoring the score to the original rating scale, which not only assists in interpretation, but also provides a common metric for any combination of subscales. Higher scores represent greater frequency of memory failures. In reporting normative data for the PRMQ, Crawford, Smith, Maylor, Della Sala, and Logie (2003) and Crawford, Henry, Ward, and Blake (2006) used T scores ($M = 50$, $SD = 10$).

Normative data on the PRMQ are available from Crawford et al. (2003) for self-ratings ($n = 551$) and from Crawford et al. (2006) for proxy ratings ($n = 570$). The first (self-rating) sample was recruited from "a wide variety of sources in and around two UK cities" (p. 262), aged $M = 63.62$ years ($SD = 15.59$, range 17–94). No age effects were found with PRMQ scores ($r = .08$ on total score; $r = .08$ prospective items, $r = .07$ retrospective items). Crawford et al. (2003) reported descriptive data using a simple summation of scores: range 16 to 80 for the total score ($M = 38.88$, $SD = 9.15$) and 8 to 40 for each of the prospective ($M = 20.18$, $SD = 4.91$) and retrospective ($M = 18.69$, $SD = 4.98$) items. Tables of normative data are provided for total, prospective and retrospective scores, using T scores ($M = 50$, $SD = 10$), along with 95% confidence limits. A useful table of abnormality of differences between prospective and retrospective scores is also provided. Similar information is provided in the subsequent study (Crawford et al., 2006) on proxy-raters recruited from three UK centres (age of raters $M = 40.7$ years, $SD = 16.68$, range 18–87; age of referents $M = 42.6$ years, $SD = 17.02$, range 18–93), although unfortunately this sample is not related to the first sample, consequently limiting a direct comparison between self-ratings and proxy-ratings. Such information is available in the Smith et al. (2000) sample.

Psychometric properties

Samples recruited to examine the theoretical questions of interest to Smith et al. (2000) were carefully selected and some psychometric information is available. Pairs of patients with AD and their caregivers ($n = 155$ – descriptive data shown in Data box 4.16) were recruited from AD societies and memory clinics in the UK ($n = 40$ pairs), Italy ($n = 84$ pairs) and the USA ($n = 31$ pairs). Healthy control participants ($n = 406$, age range 17–93 years) were recruited from volunteer subject panels from the Universities of Aberdeen and Warwick, UK, as well as local clubs and societies. The control group was stratified by age into younger (< 60 years, $n = 164$) and older (≥ 60 years, $n = 242$) subgroups. Internal consistency was examined using the Spearman-Brown formula for split-half reliability of the two items from each of the eight categories.

Box 4.16

Validity:	Construct: *Internal consistency:* Smith et al.: $r_{SB} = .84$ Crawford et al. (2003): Self: Cronbach alpha: Total .89 (Prospective .84, Retrospective .80) Crawford et al. (2006): Informant: Cronbach alpha: Total .92 (Prospective .87, Retrospective .83) *Factor analysis:* Crawford et al. (2003): CFA – tripartite model with a General memory factor and 2 orthogonal specific factors (Prospective and Retrospective) *Discriminant:* Smith et al.: Significant group differences ($F = 561.52$), with mean scores across the 8 categories ranging as follows: AD: 4.41–4.67, informants: 1.72–2.38, older controls: 1.91–3.00, younger controls 1.78–2.86
Reliability:	Inter-rater: No information available Test–retest: No information available
Responsiveness:	No information available

Information on discriminant validity was provided by comparison across the four groups (AD, informants, older controls and younger controls). Crawford et al. (2003) examined the underlying structure of the PRMQ using confirmatory factor analysis (CFA). Ten models were tested, the best fitting model being a tripartite model containing a General memory factor (containing all 16 items) and two orthogonal specific factors (Prospective and Retrospective). Fit indexes for this model exceeded recommended levels: comparative fit index .95, root mean squared error of approximation .057. These results were replicated in a second independent sample using informant ratings (Crawford et al., 2006). Results of the above studies are shown in Box 4.16.

Comment

The PRMQ provides a brief yet efficient sampling of memory processes. As noted by Crawford et al. (2003) "it balances prospective and retrospective items, and measures these constructs systematically over a range of contexts" (p. 273). Moreover, its development was theoretically driven and content validity established empirically with an expert panel. Another of the strengths of the PRMQ is the large body of normative data provided by Crawford and colleagues, both for self-ratings and informant ratings, along with confidence intervals and data to determine abnormality of differences between prospective and retrospective ratings. These features will assist in clinical application of the PRMQ. Smith et al. (2000), however, raised concerns about ceiling effects in their AD group. No information was provided in that report on either the stage of AD or an independent objective evaluation of the severity of the memory impairment, and this aspect of the PRMQ, in particular, will require further examination in other clinical groups with memory impairment, as will its reliability and concurrent validity.

Key references

Crawford, J. R., Henry, J. D., Ward, A. L., & Blake, J. (2006). The Prospective and Retrospective Memory Questionnaire (PRMQ): Latent structure, normative data and discrepancy analysis for proxy-ratings. *British Journal of Clinical Psychology*, *45*, 83–104.

Crawford, J. R., Smith, G., Maylor, E. A., Della Sala, S., & Logie, R. H. (2003). The Prospective and Retrospective Memory Questionnaire (PRMQ): Normative data and latent structure in a large non-clinical sample. *Memory*, *11*(3), 261–275.

Smith, G., Della Sala, S., Logie, R. H., & Maylor, E. A. (2000). Prospective and retrospective memory in normal ageing and dementia: A questionnaire study. *Memory*, *8*(5), 311–321.

Prospective and Retrospective Memory Questionnaire
Informant version

Smith, Della Sala, Logie, and Maylor (2000)

Name:	**Administered by:**	**Date:**

Instructions: The following questions are about minor memory mistakes that everyone makes from time to time, but some of them happen more often than others. We would like you to tell us how often these things happen to the person you care for. Please indicate this by writing in the appropriate response. Please make sure you answer all of the questions even if they don't seem entirely applicable to your situation.

Response key:
1 = Never
2 = Rarely
3 = Sometimes
4 = Quite often
5 = Very often

	RESPONSE
1. Does s/he decide to do something in a few minutes time and then forget to do it?	______
2. Does s/he fail to recognize a place they have visited before?	______
3. Does s/he fail to do something s/he was supposed to do a few minutes later even though it is there in front of her/him, like take a pill or turn off the kettle?	______
4. Does s/he forget something s/he was told a few minutes before?	______
5. Does s/he forget appointments if s/he is not prompted by someone else or by a reminder such as a calendar or diary?	______
6. Does s/he fail to recognize a character in a radio or television show from scene to scene?	______
7. Does s/he forget to buy something they planned to buy, like a birthday card, even when they see the shop?	______
8. Does s/he fail to recall things that have happened to her/him in the last few days?	______
9. Does s/he repeat the same story to the same person on different occasions?	______
10. Does s/he intend to take something with her/him, before leaving a room or going out, but minutes later leave it behind, even though it's there in front of her/him?	______
11. Does s/he mislay something that s/he has just put down, like a magazine or glasses?	______
12. Does s/he fail to mention or give something to a visitor that s/he was asked to pass on?	______
13. Does s/he look at something without realizing s/he has seen it moments before?	______
14. If s/he tried to contact a friend or relative who was out, would s/he forget to try again later?	______
15. Does s/he forget what s/he watched on television the previous day?	______
16. Does s/he forget to tell someone something s/he had meant to mention a few minutes ago?	______
TOTAL SCORE:	______

Summary

	Total score: ______	Prospective: ______	Retrospective: ______
Short-term: ______	Long-term: ______	Self-cued: ______	Environmentally cued: ______

Acknowledgement: From Smith, G. et al. (2000). Prospective and retrospective memory in normal ageing and dementia: A questionnaire study. *Memory*, *8*(5), 311–321, Appendix A, p. 321, Appendix B, p. 321 (para 1), reproduced by permission of Taylor & Francis.

Prospective and Retrospective Memory Questionnaire
"Frustration component"
Smith, Della Sala, Logie, and Maylor (2000)

Name:	**Administered by:**	**Date:**

Instructions: Please rate how frustrating the memory problems are for you and the person for whom you care.

Response key:
1 = Not at all frustrating
2 = Slightly frustrating
3 = Quite frustrating
4 = Very frustrating

	RESPONSE
1. Do you find it frustrating that he/she forgets things from the past?	______
2. Do you find it frustrating that he/she forgets to do things?	______
3. Does he/she find it frustrating that he/she forgets things from the past?	______
4. Does he/she find it frustrating that he/she forgets to do things?	______

SECTION 5
Scales assessing self-awareness

Awareness Questionnaire (AQ)

Sherer, Bergloff, Boake, High, and Levin (1998)

Source

Items for the AQ are described in Sherer et al. (1998) and are reproduced below. Information about the AQ, including the recording form, is also available on the website of the Center for Outcome Measurement in Brain Injury (COMBI; http://www.tbims.org/combi/aq/index.html).

Purpose

The AQ is a rating scale, using clinician, informant and/or self-ratings. It was designed "to measure patient awareness of functioning in physical, cognitive and behavioural domains, as well as functioning in community activities" (Sherer et al., 1998, p. 64). The AQ was developed for people with traumatic brain injury (TBI), and has also been used with people with hypoxia, stroke and tumour (Wise, Ownsworth, & Fleming, 2005).

Item description

The AQ is a 17-item scale, with three statistically derived subscales: Cognitive (7 items), Behavioural/affective (6 items) and Motor-sensory (4 items). Sherer et al. (1998) advise that the AQ can be used in a number of ways to measure awareness, but the most common method is to use (at least) two sources of information, one of which is the patient's self-ratings; the other source is generally provided by an informant or clinician. The discrepancy between the patient's self-report and that of the informant/clinician is calculated. The discrepancy score thus represents the measure of awareness on the AQ. The materials on the COMBI website (accessed 4 August 2008) include a final item on the clinician form that provides a global rating of self-awareness.

Scale development

Item development for the AQ drew on the research literature and the authors' clinical experience (Sherer et al., 1998). Initially, a 46-item scale was developed, with 26 items focusing on self-awareness in general terms and 20 items targeting specific situations. On the basis of the authors' preliminary investigations, which found that the general items were more sensitive to impaired self-awareness than the specific items, 23 of the 26 general items were used to develop the final version of the AQ. Principal components analysis (PCA) yielded a three-component solution (see below), and the 17 items with significant loadings on the components were retained to form the AQ. Sherer, Hart, and Nick (2003) made a tentative suggestion for cut-off scores, derived from the probability of employment, although they advise the need for further validation.

Administration procedures, response format and scoring

The AQ is designed for self/informant-completion and no special materials are required. The respondents

Data box 4.17 Descriptive data from the validation sample (Sherer et al., 2003)

	Age Median	Education Median	AQ *M* (*SD*)	Cut-off score	Sensitivity / Specificity
TBI (*n* = 129)	33	12	48.5 (11.4)	19/20	No information
Informant			39.8 (11.1)		
Clinician			32.2 (5.9)		
Patient – informant			8.8 (15.7)		
Patient – clinician			16.4 (13.0)		

complete the AQ on the basis of their knowledge of change in the patient's functioning from the pre-injury level. The measure of self-awareness is the discrepancy between the self-rating and the comparison standard (informant, clinician). Administration time is approximately 10 minutes.

Items are rated on a 5-point scale: 1 (much worse [than before the injury]), 2 (a little worse), 3 (about the same), 4 (a little better), 5 (much better). The additional global rating is not included in the total score. Raw scores thus range from 17 to 85, and a score of 51 represents approximately the same level of functioning in comparison with the premorbid state. Discrepancy scores are obtained by subtracting the informant's score from the self-rating score and range from −68 to +68; Sherer et al. (2003) advise that negative scores are rare. Higher positive discrepancy scores indicate greater impairment of self-awareness. Suggested cut-off scores, subject to further validation before being applied in clinical decision making (Sherer et al., 2003), used the self-clinician discrepancy: < 20 = mild/no impairment, 20–29 = moderate impairment, > 29 = severe impairment. Some investigators (e.g., Hart, Sherer, Whyte, Polansky, & Novack, 2004) have used a mean score for each of the subtests, thereby anchoring the score back to the original rating scale, which assists in a direct interpretation of the score.

Psychometric properties

The first published psychometric study on the AQ examined its factor structure using data from 126 people with TBI and 75 family members recruited from a post-acute rehabilitation centre in the USA (Sherer et al., 1998). The participants were aged $M = 32.3$ years ($SD = 12.4$), $M = 10.2$ months post-trauma ($SD = 21.3$), and 68% had severe injury. The underlying factor structure of the initial item pool was examined and three components were extracted, accounting for 48.5% of the variance: Cognitive, Behavioural/affective and Motor-sensory. Concurrent and predictive validity of the AQ were examined by Sherer et al. (2003) in 129 people with TBI (descriptive data are shown in Data box 4.17; post-traumatic amnesia (PTA) duration median = 28 days, time post-trauma median = 35 days). The AQ, along with the Patient Competency Rating Scale (PCRS), was administered soon after emergence from PTA. Another study (Sherer, Hart, Whyte, Nick, & Yablon, 2005) compared results of computerized tomography (CT) and AQ ratings soon after emergence from PTA in 91 patients with TBI. In a direct comparison of different types of awareness measures, the AQ was compared with the Self-Awareness of Deficits Interview (SADI) in 38 people with TBI (Wise et al., 2005). Evidence for convergent and divergent validity was provided by Hart

Box 4.17

Validity:	Criterion: *Concurrent:* Sherer et al. (2003): with PCRS: Self: $r = .50$, Informant: $r = .62$, Clinician: $r = .69$
	Sherer et al. (2005): with number of lesions on CT: $r = .30$
	Wise et al.: with SADI: $r = .62$
	Predictive: Sherer et al. (2003): Self–Clinician discrepancy (but not Self–Informant discrepancy) predicted employability (using DRS) at rehabilitation discharge
	Construct: *Internal consistency:* Sherer et al. (1998): Cronbach alpha: Total score: .88 (both Self & Informant). Components for Self & Informant respectively: Cognitive: .80 for both; Behavioural/affective: .78, .80; Motor-sensory: .57, .68
	Factor analysis: Sherer et al. (1998): 3 components: Cognitive (7 items), Behavioural/affective (6 items), Motor-sensory (4 items)
	Convergent/divergent: Sherer et al. (2003): higher correlation with expected similar ratings (Clinician vs Informant: $r = .44$), but lower correlation with expected dissimilar ratings (Self vs Clinician: $r = -.06$, vs Informant: $r = .06$)
	Hart et al.: higher correlation with expected similar ratings (Clinician vs DRS: $r = -.46$, vs FIM $r = .35$); lower correlation with expected dissimilar ratings (Self vs DRS: $r = .13$, vs FIM: $r = -.08$)
	Discriminant: Sherer et al. (2003): Self $M = 48.5$ ($SD = 11.4$) vs Informant $M = 39.8$ ($SD = 11.1$) and Clinician $M = 32.2$ ($SD = 5.9$); $p < .001$
Reliability:	Inter-rater: No information available
	Test–retest: No information available
Responsiveness:	No information available

et al. (2004) with expected patterns of correlations between AQ ratings (Clinician and Self) and results of functional outcome measures (Disability Rating Scale, DRS and Functional Independence Measure, FIM). Results of these studies are shown in Box 4.17.

Comment

Substantial amounts of psychometric data are accumulating to validate the AQ. It has good internal consistency for the total score, shows evidence of concurrent validity with other awareness measures, and there is correlation with an external criterion (number of lesions on CT scan). Expected patterns of correlations and group differences provide evidence for construct validity. Information on its temporal stability and inter-rater reliability among different clinicians, however, is lacking. The AQ is easy to complete for clinicians who have knowledge of the patient, thereby providing a quick assessment. The response format using the pre-injury level of functioning as the comparison standard is a useful strategy for people in the early post-trauma stages, in that a direct comparison standard is available (i.e., the person themselves), as opposed to comparison with the 'average person' or need for normative data. This response format may, however, have limited applicability for a longer-term time-frame, where comparison with the premorbid level arguably has less relevance and may also introduce issues of accuracy of recall.

Key references

Hart, T., Sherer, M., Whyte, J., Polansky, M., & Novack, T. A. (2004). Awareness of behavioural, cognitive, and physical deficits in acute traumatic brain injury. *Archives of Physical Medicine and Rehabilitation*, *85*, 1450–1456.

Sherer, M., Bergloff, P., Boake, C., High, W., & Levin, E. (1998). The Awareness Questionnaire: Factor structure and internal consistency. *Brain Injury*, *12*(1), 63–68.

Sherer, M., Hart, T., & Nick, T. G. (2003). Measurement of impaired self-awareness after traumatic brain injury: A comparison of the Patient Competency Rating Scale and the Awareness Questionnaire. *Brain Injury*, *17*(1), 25–37.

Sherer, M., Hart, T., Whyte, J., Nick, T. G., & Yablon, S. A. (2005). Neuroanatomic basis of impaired self-awareness after traumatic brain injury. Findings from early computed tomography. *Journal of Head Trauma Rehabilitation*, *20*(4), 287–300.

Wise, K., Ownsworth, T., & Fleming, J. (2005). Convergent validity of self-awareness measures and their association with employment outcome in adults following acquired brain injury. *Brain Injury*, *19*(10), 765–775.

Awareness Questionnaire

Sherer, Bergloff, Boake, High, and Levin (1998)

Clinician Form

Name:	**Administered by:**	**Date:**

Response key:
1 = Much worse
2 = A little worse
3 = About the same
4 = A little better
5 = Much better

		RESPONSE
1.	How good is the patient's ability to live independently now as compared to before his/her injury?	________
2.	How good is the patient's ability to manage his/her money now as compared to before his/her injury?	________
3.	How well does the patient get along with people now as compared to before his/her injury?	________
4.	How well can the patient do on tests that measure thinking and memory skills now as compared to before his/her injury?	________
5.	How well can the patient do the things he/she wants to do in life now as compared to before his/her injury?	________
6.	How well is the patient able to see now as compared to before his/her injury?	________
7.	How well can the patient hear now as compared to before his/her injury?	________
8.	How well can the patient move his/her arms and legs now as compared to before his/her injury?	________
9.	How good is the patient's coordination now as compared to before his/her injury?	________
10.	How good is the patient at keeping up with time and date and where he/she is now as compared to before his/her injury?	________
11.	How well can the patient concentrate now as compared to before his/her injury?	________
12.	How well can the patient express his/her thoughts to others now as compared to before his/her injury?	________
13.	How good is the patient's memory for recent events now as compared to before his/her injury?	________
14.	How good is the patient at planning things now as compared to before his/her injury?	________
15.	How well organized is the patient now as compared to before his/her injury?	________
16.	How well can the patient keep his/her feelings in control now as compared to before his/her injury?	________
17.	How well adjusted emotionally is the patient now as compared to before his/her injury?	________

TOTAL SCORE: ________

18. To what extent is the patient's accurate self-awareness impaired by his/her brain injury?

1	2	3	4	5
completely	severely	moderately	minimally	not at all

Acknowledgement: Adapted from Sherer, M. et al. (1998). The Awareness Questionnaire: Factor structure and internal consistency. *Brain Injury*, *12*(1), 63–68, Table 1, p. 66, with permission of Taylor & Francis, www.tandf.co.uk/journals.

Patient Competency Rating Scale (PCRS)

Prigatano, Fordyce, Zeiner, Roueche, Pepping, and Wood (1986)

Source

Items for the PCRS are available in an appendix to Prigatano et al. (1986). The recording forms and other information on the PCRS are also available on the website of the Center for Outcome Measurement in Brain Injury (COMBI; http://www.tbims.org/combi/pcrs/index.html). Items from the PCRS are reproduced below. Borgaro and Prigatano (2003) developed a 13-item derivative (PCRS for neurorehabilitation, PCRS-NR) suitable for administration to rehabilitation inpatients.

Purpose

The PCRS was one of the first rating scales developed to assess self-awareness in people with traumatic brain injury (TBI). It uses the method of comparing self-ratings with a relative's report, which "provides one avenue for determining how realistic a patient is in evaluating his/her higher behavioral strengths and limitations" (Prigatano, Altman, & O'Brien, 1990, p. 164). The PCRS has been used mainly with people with stroke and TBI.

Item description

The PCRS comprises 30 items, spanning a range of everyday tasks and behaviours, which Leathem, Murphy, and Flett (1998) group into four face valid categories: activities of daily living (8 items), cognitive (8 items), emotional (7 items) and interpersonal (7 items) functioning. For each item the patient and an informant make a judgement about the person's level of competence.

Scale development

Development of the PCRS had its origins in the clinical neuropsychological rehabilitation programme conducted by Prigatano and colleagues at the Barrow Neurological Institute, Phoenix, Arizona, USA (Priganato et al., 1986). No information is reported regarding the item selection process. Summary details of an early study with the PCRS were reported by Prigatano (1987), in which he observed disparate ratings between patients and their relative-informants on nine items, with the patients making over-estimates of their competency in comparison with the informants on seven of the nine items.

Administration procedures, response format and scoring

An informant and patient independently complete the scale. The COMBI website advises that instructions are explained orally, and the examiner may read out the questions if necessary, and in that case the respondent is given a copy of the scale as a reminder of the response options. The informant's ratings provide the "gold standard" against which the patient's level of insight and awareness is measured. The PCRS can be completed in approximately 10 to 15 minutes by most people.

Items are rated on a 5-point scale: 1 (can't do), 2 (very difficult to do), 3 (can do with some difficulty), 4 (fairly easy to do), 5 (can do with ease). The total score ranges from 30 to 150, with higher scores indicating greater competency. In order to obtain an "awareness" score, it is necessary to calculate the discrepancy from an informant's responses. Fleming, Strong, and Ashton (1996) review three approaches to obtaining discrepancy scores for the PCRS: (i) a total score for both respondents is computed and the discrepancy between total scores calculated, (ii) the number of items on which a discrepancy occurs is tallied, and (iii) the magnitude of discrepancies on specific items is calculated and tallied. In each case, the higher the score, the poorer the patient's level of awareness. Fleming and colleagues recommend the last method as being the most sensitive because it captures both the magnitude of discrepancy, as well as the specific type of item. Nonetheless, the first method, using a simple discrepancy score derived from the total scores, is the most commonly used in the research literature.

Normative and comparison data are available in Leathem et al. (1998) who assessed 131 healthy volunteers, aged 16 to 70 years (109 of whom were university

Data box 4.18 Descriptive data from the validation sample (Prigatano, 1996)

	Age *M* (*SD*)	Education *M* (*SD*)	PCRS *M* (*SD*)	Cut-off score	Sensitivity / Specificity
Control (20)	38.3 (14.0)	13.1 (1.8)		No information	No information
Self-rating			105.3 (16.5)		
Informant rating			109.9 (17.9)		
TBI ($n = 31$)	25.8 (8.9)	13.0 (2.7)			
Self-rating			125.1 (13.3)		
Informant rating			119.0 (18.0)		
Right hemisphere ($n = 17$)	43.3 (13.7)	13.4 (2.4)			
Self-rating			115.9 (16.2)		
Informant rating			114.6 (22.8)		
Left hemisphere ($n = 18$)	37.1 (14.0)	13.2 (2.4)			
Self-rating			126.6 (13.1)		
Informant rating			121.1 (16.9)		

students), along with 53 people with TBI recruited from a university clinic in Palmerston North, New Zealand.

Psychometric properties

The initial psychometric study on the PCRS focused on temporal stability in 17 people with TBI (Prigatano et al., 1990). Information on other measurement properties

Box 4.18

Validity:

Criterion:
Concurrent: Prigatano (1996): with BNI Screen: TBI: $r = .51$, Control: $r = .66$

Sherer et al.: with AQ: Self: $r = .50$, Informant: $r = .62$, Clinician: $r = .69$

Fischer et al.: memory task with PCRS discrepancies: PCRS-Total: $r = .33$, PCRS-Social/emotional (10 items): $r = .34$

Construct:
Internal consistency: Cronbach alpha: Fleming et al. (1998): Self: .91, Informant: .93

Convergent/divergent: Prigatano (1996): TBI: hypothesized patterns of: self over-estimates on 10 emotional/social items (*M* discrepancy = 0.298) vs no discrepancies on 8 ADL items (*M* discrepancy = 0.005); $t = 5.08, p = .000$
– Control: as hypothesized no over-estimates on emotional/social vs ADL; $t = 0.77, p > .05$

Discriminant: Prigatano (1996): TBI $M = 125.1$ vs Controls $M = 105.3$; $t = 4.69$, $p < .001$

Leathem et al.: significant differences ($p < .001$) between

TBI and Control groups in all four domains. Using informant ratings:
– ADL: TBI $M = 3.99$ ($SD = 0.76$) vs Control $M = 4.73$ ($SD = 0.33$)
– Emotion TBI $M = 3.34$ ($SD = 0.79$) vs Control $M = 4.08$ ($SD = 0.59$)
– Interpersonal TBI $M = 3.45$ ($SD = 0.89$) vs Control $M = 4.20$ ($SD = 0.56$)
– Cognition TBI $M = 3.40$ ($SD = 0.79$) vs Control $M = 4.48$ ($SD = 0.44$)

Reliability:

Inter-rater: No information available

Test–retest: Prigatano et al. (1990): interval unspecified: Self: $r = .97$, Informant: $r = .92$

Fleming et al. (1998): 1 week: ICC = .85

Responsiveness: No information available

is available in subsequent publications. Prigatano (1996) examined the validity of the PCRS in 66 people with mixed neurological aetiology recruited from the Barrow Neurological Institute (BNI; descriptive data shown in Data box 4.18). Twenty "neuropsychological controls" (patients referred for neuropsychological assessment, but whose findings were negative) were also recruited and the groups were administered the BNI Screen, which is an objective neuropsychological examination. Prigatano compared informant and self-reports on 10 of the 30 PRCS items on which differences were expected (viz. social and emotional functioning), and 8 of the 30 items where differences were not expected (viz. activities of daily living, ADL). Fleming, Strong, and Ashton (1998) examined 55 people with TBI and 50 of their informants with the PCRS and other measures of awareness, including the Self-Awareness of Deficits Interview. A subset ($n = 20$) was re-examined 1 week later. In the course of validating the Awareness Questionnaire (AQ), Sherer, Hart, and Nick (2003) administered the PCRS to 129 people with TBI, providing data on concurrent validity. Similar data are reported by Fischer, Trexler, and Gauggel (2004) who compared self and clinician ratings on the PCRS in 24 people with stroke and TBI with 22 orthopaedic controls. An innovative component of that study was to have patients estimate their performance on two objective tests (motor and memory tasks), and compare these estimates with both actual performance as well as the awareness measure (discrepancy between Self and Clinician PCRS). Findings from the above studies are shown in Box 4.18.

Comment

The PCRS was the first standardized measure for assessing awareness in people with TBI and continues to be widely used. As Fleming et al. (1996) note, it is quick to administer, easy to interpret and covers functional ability, interpersonal skills and emotional status. The PCRS was developed within a clinical context and was not subject to the rigour of instrument development or initial psychometric analysis and refinement conducted for some more recently published instruments. Nonetheless, PCRS works well. Information on its psychometric properties is available from various sources, demonstrating excellent temporal stability and providing substantial evidence for its criterion and construct validity.

Key references

Borgaro, S. R., & Prigatano, G. P. (2003). Modification of the Patient Competency Rating Scale for use on an acute neurorehabilitation unit: The PCRS-NR. *Brain Injury*, *17*(10), 847–853.

Fischer, S., Trexler, L. E., & Gauggel, S. (2004). Awareness of activity limitations and prediction of performance in patients with brain injuries and orthopedic disorders. *Journal of the International Neuropsychological Society*, *10*, 190–199.

Fleming, J. M., Strong, J., & Ashton, R. (1996). Self-awareness of deficits in adults with traumatic brain injury: How best to measure? *Brain Injury*, *10*(1), 1–15.

Fleming, J. M., Strong, J., & Ashton, R. (1998). Cluster analysis of self-awareness levels in adults with traumatic brain injury and relationship to outcome. *Journal of Head Trauma Rehabilitation*, *13*(5), 39–51.

Leathem, J. M., Murphy, L. J., & Flett, R. A. (1998). Self- and informant-ratings on the Patient Competency Rating Scale in patients with traumatic brain injury. *Journal of Clinical and Experimental Neuropsychology*, *20*(5), 694–705.

Prigatano, G. P. (1987). Psychiatric aspects of head injury: Problem areas and suggested guidelines for research. In H. S. Levin, J. Grafman, & H. M. Eisenberg (Eds.), *Neurobehavioral recovery from head injury* (pp. 215–231). New York: Oxford University Press.

Prigatano, G. P. (1996). Behavioral limitations that TBI patients tend to underestimate: A replication and extension to patients with lateralized cerebral dysfunction. *The Clinical Neuropsychologist*, *10*(2), 191–201.

Prigatano, G. P., Altman, I. M., & O'Brien, K. P. (1990). Behavioural limitations that traumatic-brain-injured patients tend to underestimate. *The Clinical Neuropsychologist*, *4*(2), 163–176.

Prigatano, G. P., Fordyce, D. J., Zeiner, H. K., Roueche, J. R., Pepping, M., & Wood, B. C. (1986). *Neuropsychological rehabilitation after brain injury*. Baltimore: Johns Hopkins University Press.

Sherer, M., Hart, T., & Nick, T. G. (2003). Measurement of impaired self-awareness after traumatic brain injury: A comparison of the Patient Competency Rating Scale and the Awareness Questionnaire. *Brain Injury*, *17*(1), 25–37.

Patient Competency Rating Scale

Prigatano, Fordyce, Zeiner, Roueche, Pepping, and Wood (1986)

Patient Form

Name:	**Administered by:**	**Date:**

Instructions:

The following is a questionnaire that asks you to judge your ability to do a variety of very practical skills. Some of the questions may not apply directly to things you often do, but you are asked to complete each question as if it was something you "had to do". On each question, you should judge how easy or difficult a particular activity is for you and write the appropriate number in the space.

Response key:
1 = Can't do
2 = Very difficult to do
3 = Can do with some difficulty
4 = Fairly easy to do
5 = Can do with ease

How much of a problem do I have in	**RESPONSE**
1. preparing my own meals?	______
2. dressing myself?	______
3. taking care of my personal hygiene?	______
4. washing the dishes?	______
5. doing the laundry?	______
6. taking care of my finances?	______
7. keeping appointments on time?	______
8. starting conversation in a group?	______
9. staying involved in work activities even when bored or tired?	______
10. remembering what I had for dinner last night?	______
11. remembering the names of people I see often?	______
12. remembering my daily schedule?	______
13. remembering important things I must do?	______
14. driving a car if I had to?	______
15. getting help when I'm confused?	______
16. adjusting to unexpected changes?	______
17. handling arguments with people I know well?	______
18. accepting criticism from other people?	______
19. controlling crying?	______
20. acting appropriately when I'm around friends?	______
21. showing affection to people?	______
22. participating in group activities?	______
23. recognizing when something I say or do has upset someone else?	______
24. scheduling daily activities?	______
25. understanding new instructions?	______
26. consistently meeting my daily responsibilities?	______
27. controlling my temper when something upsets me?	______
28. keeping from being depressed?	______
29. keeping my emotions from affecting my ability to go about the day's activities?	______
30. controlling my laughter?	______
TOTAL SCORE:	______

Acknowledgement: From Prigatano, G.P. et al. (1986). *Neuropsychological Rehabilitation after Brain Injury*. Baltimore: Johns Hopkins University Press, reprinted with permission of the Johns Hopkins University Press.

Self-Awareness of Deficits Interview (SADI)

Fleming, Strong, and Ashton (1996)

Source

Questions for the SADI, along with scoring criteria, are available in an appendix to Fleming et al. (1996), and are reproduced below.

Purpose

The SADI is a semi-structured interview, designed for the clinician to assess both quantitative and qualitative aspects of the person's awareness of his or her deficits. It was originally developed for people with traumatic brain injury (TBI), but has been used with a number of other clinical populations, including hypoxia, stroke and tumour (Wise, Ownsworth, & Fleming, 2005).

Item description

There are three sections to the SADI. First, the interviewer questions the patient about knowledge of his or her own impairments, deficits and changes that have occurred since the injury. The second set of questions focus on awareness of the functional consequences of the impairments (e.g., their impact on work, social relationships). Finally, the interviewer evaluates the correspondence between the patient's level of functioning and his or her future plans, goals and expectations.

Scale development

Fleming and Strong (1995) examined a range of descriptions of self-awareness of deficits after acquired brain impairment (ABI) reported in the literature, and from this developed an integrated three-level model of awareness: (i) objective knowledge, (ii) subjective appreciation, and (iii) prognostications about the future. In formulating the structure of the SADI, Fleming et al. (1996) reviewed commonly used procedures to assess insight and awareness. Because of limitations in using self or informant ratings, they opted to construct a clinician-rated interview. A review of the types of questions used in structured interviews of people with insight disorders of neurological or psychiatric aetiology was used to guide item selection for the SADI. Responses to the structured interview questions were then scored by the interviewer according to a predetermined rating scale.

Administration procedures, response format and scoring

The SADI is administered as a semi-structured interview. The interviewer is encouraged to adapt or reword questions, as well as to prompt to elicit additional information "provided the essence of the questions remains unchanged" (Fleming et al., 1996, p. 8). Set prompts are provided. The SADI is a more difficult instrument to administer than a structured rating scale, and valid completion therefore requires that the clinician/researcher is sufficiently skilled in interview technique with people with TBI and is knowledgeable about effects of TBI. Administration time is approximately 20 to 30 minutes.

Each section of the SADI is scored on a 4-point scale: 0 (equivalent of response representing accurate knowledge, awareness of functional implications, and ability to set reasonably realistic goals), 1 (response indicates some problems/implications; goals somewhat unrealistic), 2 (response comparable to an acknowledgement of problems/implications, but minimizes them, and inability to set goals or they are unrealistic), 3 (response reflects no knowledge of deficits, acknowledgement of functional consequences, or realistic appraisal of the future level of functioning). The total score ranges from 0 to 9, with higher scores indicating greater unawareness.

Psychometric properties

A number of studies examining people with TBI have provided information on the reliability and validity of the SADI. Inter-rater reliability was examined by Fleming et al. (1996), using data from 25 people recruited from a large metropolitan hospital in Brisbane, Australia (age 15–65 years, post-traumatic amnesia duration > 24 hours, 3–9 months post-trauma). Five

Data box 4.19 Descriptive data from the temporal stability sample (Simmond & Fleming, 2003)

	Age M (SD)	Education M (SD)	SADI M (SD)	Cut-off score	Sensitivity / Specificity
TBI ($n = 20$)	34.8 (15.3)	11.6 (1.9)		No information	No information
Total score:			4.9 (2.86)		
Section 1:			1.4 (1.05)		
Section 2:			1.7 (1.03)		
Section 3:			1.8 (1.06)		

raters were trained and given written information on the participant regarding the injury, deficits and current level of functioning. They then made SADI ratings based on transcripts of the interviews. Data on temporal stability were published by Simmond and Fleming (2003), derived from 20 people interviewed on two occasions, 2 to 4 weeks apart (descriptive data shown in Data box 4.19).

Information on responsiveness is available in Fleming, Winnington, McGillivray, Tatarevic, and Ownsworth (2006), who examined 34 people (age $M = 26.4$ years, range 17–58) at discharge from rehabilitation and 2 months later. Concurrent validity with the Awareness Questionnaire (AQ) was evaluated by Wise et al. (2005) in a mixed neurological group ($n = 38$, age $M = 38.2$ years, range 19–58, at $M = 4.3$ months after onset, range 0.5–91). Bogod, Mateer, and MacDonald (2003) examined concurrent and construct validity in 40 people recruited from rehabilitation programmes and the local community in Victoria, Canada (age $M = 37.4$ years, range 22–66), with 19 sustaining mild to moderate degrees of injury and 21 having severe injuries. Discriminant function analysis (DFA) was used to predict injury-severity group membership. Concurrent validity was examined with another rating scale of awareness, the discrepancy score on the Dysexecutive Questionnaire (DEX), and objective tests of executive functions, including the Self-Ordered Pointing Test (SOPT), Go/No-Go test, and the Stroop. Results of these studies are shown in Box 4.19.

Box 4.19

Validity:	Criterion: *Concurrent:* Wise et al.: with AQ: SADI Total score: $r_s = .62$ (Sections 1: $r_s = .81$, 2: $r_s = .48$, 3: $r_s = .22$) Bogod et al.: with DEX: $r = .40$ – with SOPT: $r = .56$ – with Go/No-Go: $r = .48$ – with Stroop errors: $r = .40$ Construct: *Discriminant:* Bogod et al.: DFA significant ($\chi^2 = 9.42$, $p = .002$), correctly classified 72.5% (sensitivity 75%, specificity 71%); Mild/moderate $M = 2.68$ ($SD = 2.31$) vs Severe $M = 5.19$ ($SD = 2.48$)
Reliability:	Inter-rater: Fleming et al. (1996): Total score: ICC = .82 (Sections 1: ICC = .78, 2: ICC = .57, 3: ICC = .78) Test–retest: Simmond & Fleming: 2–4 weeks: Total score: ICC = .94 (Sections 1: ICC = .85, 2: ICC = .86, 3: ICC = .86)
Responsiveness:	Fleming et al. (2006): Pre-discharge: $M = 4.9$ ($SD = 2.2$) vs post-discharge: $M = 3.0$ ($SD = 2.6$); $z = -3.61$, $p < .01$, $d = .86$

Comment

The SADI has very good psychometric properties. The total score shows excellent inter-rater reliability and temporal stability over 2 to 4 weeks, yet it is sensitive to changes over time with a large effect size and is able to detect group differences. There is moderate concurrent validity with other rating scales of awareness and with objective tests of executive abilities. A number of instruments are currently available to measure awareness. A comparative strength of the SADI is that the clinician evaluates awareness in the context of an interview. This has two advantages in particular. First, the assessment goes beyond surface reporting from a set checklist of symptoms, thus providing an attempt to examine the underlying construct comprising different aspects of awareness. Additionally, it is not dependent on an informant, such as a family member, to provide the "gold standard" against which the self-rating is compared, an approach which has some short-comings. One possible drawback of the SADI may be its administration time which, at 20 to 30 minutes, is longer than checklist measures. By the same token, the types of questions comprising the SADI are those that would normally be asked during the course of an initial interview with the person in the clinical context.

Key references

Bogod, N. M., Mateer, C. A., & MacDonald, S. W. S. (2003). Self-awareness after traumatic brain injury: A comparison of measures and their relationship to executive functions. *Journal of the International Neuropsychological Society*, *9*, 450–458.

Fleming, J., & Strong, J. (1995). Self-awareness of deficits following acquired brain injury: Considerations for rehabilitation. *British Journal of Occupational Therapy*, *58*(2), 55–60.

Fleming, J. M., Strong, J., & Ashton, R. (1996). Self-awareness of deficits in adults with traumatic brain injury: How best to measure? *Brain Injury*, *10*(1), 1–15.

Fleming, J. M., Winnington, H. T., McGillivray, A. J., Tatarevic, B. A., & Ownsworth, T. L. (2006). The development of self-awareness and relationship to emotional functioning during early community reintegration after traumatic brain injury. *Brain Impairment*, *7*(2), 83–94.

Simmond, M., & Fleming, J. (2003). Reliability of the Self-Awareness of Deficits Interview for adults with traumatic brain injury. *Brain Injury*, *17*(4), 325–337.

Wise, K., Ownsworth, T., & Fleming, J. (2005). Convergent validity of self-awareness measures and their association with employment outcome in adults following acquired brain injury. *Brain Injury*, *19*(10), 765–775.

Self-Awareness of Deficits Interview

Fleming, Strong, and Ashton (1996)

Name: **Administered by:** **Date:**

SCORE

1. SELF-AWARENESS OF DEFICITS

Probing items:

- Are you any different now compared to what you were like before your accident?
- In what way?
- Do you feel that anything about you or abilities has changed?
- Do people who know you well notice that anything is different about you since the accident?
- What might they notice?
- What do you see as your problems, if any, resulting from your injury?
- What is the main thing you need to work on/would like to get better?

Prompts

Physical abilities (e.g., movement of arms and legs, balance, vision, endurance)?
Memory/confusion?
Concentration?
Problem-solving, decision-making, organizing and planning things?
Controlling behaviour?
Communication?
Getting along with other people?
Has your personality changed?
Are there any other problems that I haven't mentioned?

2. SELF-AWARENESS OF FUNCTIONAL IMPLICATIONS OF DEFICITS

Probing items:

- Does your head injury have any effect on your everyday life? In what way?

Prompts

Ability to live independently?
Managing finances?
Look after family/manage home?
Driving?
Work/study?
Leisure/social life?

Probing items:

- Are there any other areas of life that you feel have changed/may change?

3. ABILITY TO SET REALISTIC GOALS

Probing items:

- What do you hope to achieve in the next 6 months?
- Do you have any goals?
- What are they?
- In 6 months time, what do you think you will be doing?
- Where do you think you will be?
- Do you think your head injury will still be having an effect on your life in 6 months' time?

If yes: how? ______

If no: are you sure? ______

TOTAL SCORE: ______

Self-Awareness of Deficits Interview – Scoring Key
Fleming, Strong, and Ashton (1996)

1. SELF-AWARENESS OF DEFICITS

0 = Cognitive/psychological problems (where relevant) reported by the patient/client in response to general questioning, or readily acknowledged in response to specific questioning.

1 = Some cognitive/psychological problems reported, but others denied or minimized. Patient/client may have a tendency to focus on relatively minor physical changes (e.g., scars) and acknowledge cognitive/psychological problems only on specific questioning about deficits.

2 = Physical deficits only acknowledged; denies, minimizes or is unsure of cognitive/psychological changes. Patient/client may recognize problems that occurred at an earlier stage but denies existence of persisting deficits, or may state that other people think there are deficits, but he/she does not think so.

3 = No acknowledgement of deficits (other than obvious physical deficits) can be obtained, or patient/client will only acknowledge problems that have been imposed on him/her, e.g., not allowed to drive, not allowed to drink alcohol.

2. SELF-AWARENESS OF FUNCTIONAL IMPLICATIONS OF DEFICITS

0 = Patient/client accurately describes current functional status (in independent living, work/study, leisure, home management, driving), and specifies how his/her head injury problems limit function where relevant, and/or any compensatory measures adopted to overcome problems.

1 = Some functional implications reported following questions or examples of problems in independent living, work, driving, leisure, etc. Patient/client may not be sure of other likely functional problems, e.g., is unable to say because he/she has not tried an activity yet.

2 = Patient/client may acknowledge some functional implications of deficits but minimizes the importance of identified problems. Other likely functional implications may be actively denied by the patient/client.

3 = Little acknowledgement of functional consequences can be obtained; the patient/client will not acknowledge problems except that he/she is not allowed to perform certain tasks. He/she may actively ignore medical advice and may engage in risk-taking behaviours, e.g., drinking, driving.

3. ABILITY TO SET REALISTIC GOALS

0 = Patient/client sets reasonably realistic goals, and (where relevant) identifies that the head injury will probably continue to have an impact on some areas of functioning, i.e., goals for the future have been modified in some way since the injury.

1 = Patient/client sets goals that are somewhat unrealistic, or is unable to specify a goal, but recognizes that he/she may still have problems in some areas of function in the future, i.e., sees that goals for the future may need some modification, even if he/she had not yet done so.

2 = Patient/client sets unrealistic goals, or is unable to specify a goal, and does not know how he/she will be functioning in 6 months' time, but hopes he/she will return to pre-trauma, i.e., no modification of goals has occurred.

3 = Patient/client expects without uncertainty that in 6 months' time he/she will be functioning at pre-trauma level (or at a higher level).

Acknowledgement: From Fleming, J. et al. (1996). Self-awareness of deficits in adults with traumatic brain injury: How best to measure? *Brain Injury*, *10*(1), 1–15, Appendix, pp. 14–15, with permission of Taylor & Francis, www.tandf.co.uk/journals.

5 Scales assessing the regulation of behaviour, thought and emotion

Instruments presented in Chapter 5 map to the components, domains and categories of the *International Classification of Functioning, Disability and Health* (ICF; WHO, 2001) as depicted in Figure 5.1.

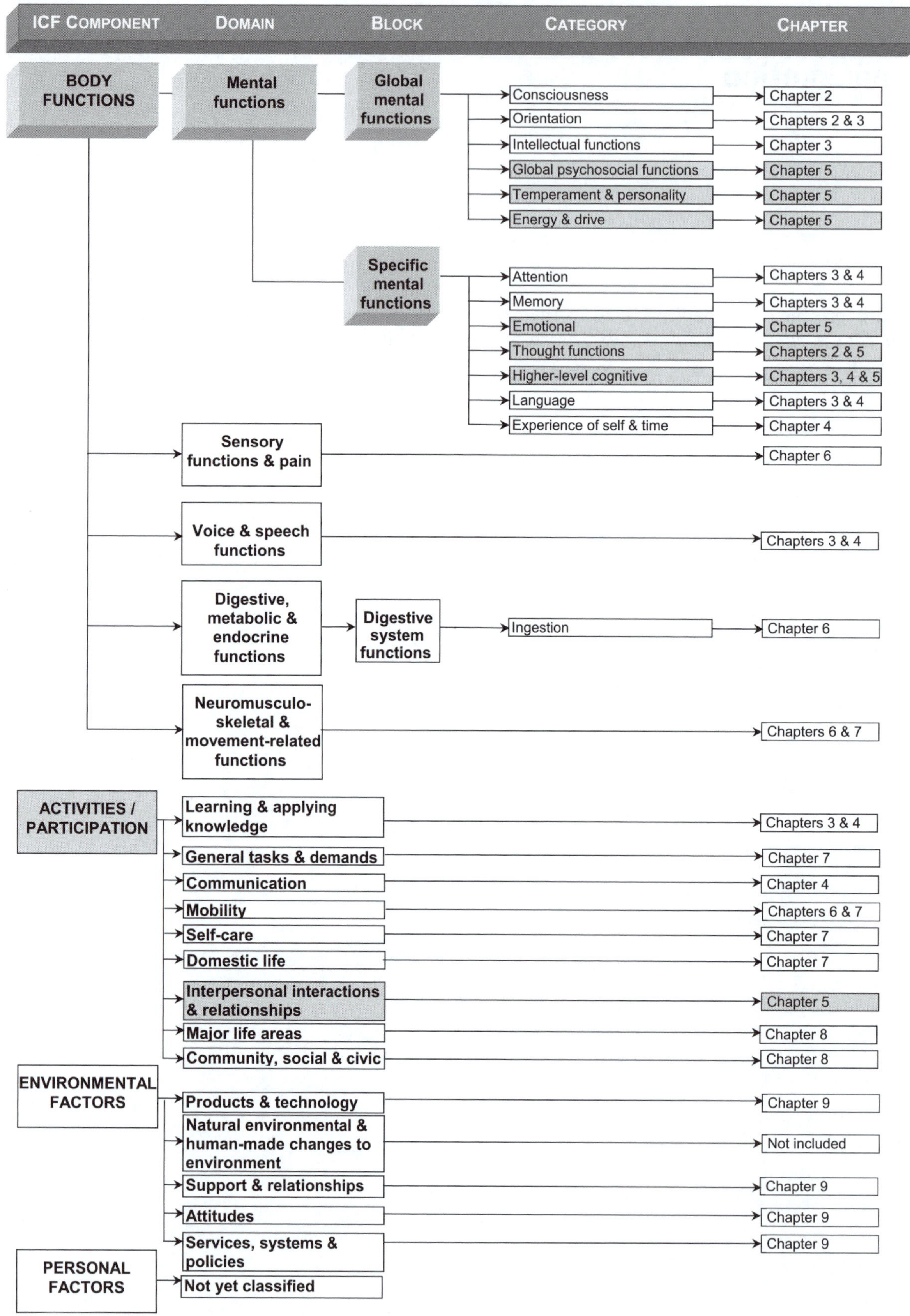

Figure 5.1 Instruments included in the compendium in relation to the ICF taxonomy – the highlighted components, domains and categories appear in this chapter. *Note:* the Figure presents a partial listing of five out of the eight Body Function domains and does not include any of the Body Structure domains. Categories for Mental functions also represent a partial listing and categories for the remaining domains are not listed. Refer to Appendix C for further detail on the ICF taxonomy.

Introduction

As depicted graphically in Figure 5.1 and Appendix C, this chapter brings together six ICF categories from two blocks of the Mental functions domain that are pertinent to the regulation of behaviour, thought and emotion: from the Global mental functions block these are the categories of (i) Global psychosocial, (ii) Temperament and personality, and (iii) Energy and drive; from the Specific mental functions block they are the categories of (i) Emotional, (ii) Thought and (iii) Higher-level cognitive. Additionally, the Interpersonal interactions and relationships domain from the Activities/Participation component is relevant to the topic of this chapter. At a conceptual level, there is overlap between on the one hand, the regulation of behaviour, thought and emotion, and on the other, the so-called higher cognitive functions (i.e., executive functions). Instruments that focus exclusively on the latter area are described in Chapter 4. Some multi-dimensional scales (see Chapter 10) also include items pertinent to this chapter.

Scales assessing the above ICF categories are combined into a single chapter because of the considerable overlap at a functional level. For example, within the Mental functions domain it is acknowledged that impairments in impulse control (Energy and drive category, e.g., "sudden, intense urges to do something") are theoretically distinct from impairments in agreeableness (Temperament and personality category, e.g., "being oppositional and defiant") and from regulation of emotion (Emotional functions category, e.g., "display of affect"). In practice, however, their differentiation in the individual person can be difficult, and chances are that in the arena of acquired brain impairment (ABI) if one of these impairment areas is present, the others will be present also. Moreover, usually a single scale will be used to assess multiple behavioural (e.g., impulse control), verbal (e.g., defiance), and/or emotional (i.e., affective) components of a particular construct.

Dysfunction of brain areas that are directly responsible for the initiation and control of behaviour, thought and emotion (e.g., prefrontal and temporal lobes, limbic system) occurs commonly in many neurological conditions. The instruments featured in this chapter address changes in behaviour, thought, and emotion that are a *direct* consequence of the ABI. Lishman (1973, 1987) was one of the first to draw a distinction between direct and indirect effects of ABI. Direct effects refer to the organic basis of alteration in functioning, whereas indirect effects are more varied. The latter group encompasses the individuals' reactions and responses to their impairments and their functional consequences, premorbid personality, mental constitution and so forth. The scope of this compendium did not permit the inclusion of scales developed to address the indirect, secondary consequences of ABI on the individual. One candidate area is that of psychological well-being, targeting areas such as anxiety, depression, self-esteem, stress and so forth. Parenthetically, although some of these emotional states can be a direct consequence of specific lesions, in the majority of cases they are secondary consequences of the brain impairment. A number of these emotional states are addressed within multidimensional scales included in Chapter 10, but the reader is referred to other compendia for specific scales of mood and psychological well-being (e.g., Bowling, 1997; McDowell, 2006; Wade, 1992).

The eight third-level categories of the ICF Temperament and personality category represent core personality features that are often included in personality inventories (e.g., NEO Personality Inventory; Costa & McCrae, 1992). As described in Chapter 1, the ICF uses neutral language, but this is one of the categories where it does enumerate the deficit counterparts and these are commonly observed after ABI – the so-called "characterological changes" (Lezak, 1978): for example, withdrawn, inhibited behaviours (see ICF third-level category: extraversion); oppositional, defiant (see agreeableness); unreliable, irresponsible (see conscientiousness); irritable, erratic (see psychic stability); inattentive, emotionally inexpressive (see openness to experience). Calls for the development of theoretically driven instruments to assess changes in personality after ABI have resulted in a new generation of scales published in the last 10 years or so that afford a pertinent and informative evaluation. It is anticipated that this previously impoverished area will continue to grow as new instruments are published (e.g., Andrewes, Kaye, Aitken, Parr, Bates, & Murphy, 2003; Obonsawin et al., 2007).

More than 60 scales were reviewed for this chapter and 16 instruments were selected for inclusion. An attempt was made to sample a broad spectrum of scales with respect to neurological condition, age group and symptomatology. The Behavior Rating Inventory of Executive Function (BRIEF) is one of the few scales developed specifically for children with ABI, which also includes a preschool version suitable for children as young as 2 years of age (Gioia, Espy, & Isquith, 2003), as well as an adult version (Roth, Isquith, & Gioia, 2005), with normative data up to 90 years. Thus assessment across the lifespan is possible with this scale. The instruments in this chapter also contain a variety of symptomatology. A number of instruments are diagnostic for frontotemporal dementias (see introduction to Chapter 3 for core diagnostic features); some scales in Chapter 3, as well as Section 2 of Chapter 4, are also appropriate for this purpose. Other scales evaluate the gamut of changes in behaviour, thought and emotion (e.g., BRIEF), in contrast to those that focus on specific areas, such as apathy, fatigue, agitation. For some applications, the choice of measure may be a general overview; in other cases a specific instrument may be indicated. Generally, there is a trade-off between overview versus detail and specificity.

In the past 15 to 20 years, major advances have been made in developing instruments to facilitate a standardized and systematic evaluation of impairments in behaviour, thought and emotion as a consequence of ABI (see Malloy & Grace, 2005 for a review). Nonetheless, the range and variety of instruments appropriate to evaluate these domains still lag behind the cognitive area and it would be advantageous for research efforts to extend to the further development of objective tests, such as the Behavioral Dyscontrol Scale (Grigsby and Kaye, 1996). Because of the paucity of such performance-based tests, most instruments presented in this chapter are rating scales. Sometimes the respondent will be a clinician, other times an informant or the person with ABI. The same validity issues apply as highlighted in Chapters 1 and 4 with respect to informant-based rating scales of specific cognitive functions, and the choice of respondent needs to be made judiciously.

References

Andrewes, D. G., Kaye, A., Aitken, S., Parr, C., Bates, L., & Murphy, M. (2003). The EDSQ: A new method of assessing emotional and social dysfunction in patients following brain surgery. *Journal of Clinical and Experimental Neuropsychology*, *25*(2), 173–189.

Bowling, A. (1997). *Measuring health: A review of quality of life measurement scales* (2nd ed.). Buckingham & Philadelphia: Open University Press.

Costa, P. T., & McCrae, R. R. (1992). *NEO PI-R. Professional manual. Revised NEO Personality Inventory (NEO PI-R) and NEO Five-factor Inventory (NEO-FFI)*. Odessa, FL: Psychological Assessment Resources, Inc.

Gioia, G. A., Espy, K. A., & Isquith, P. K. (2003). *BRIEF-P: Behavior Rating Inventory of Executive Function – Preschool version. Professional manual*. Odessa, FL: Psychological Assessment Resources, Inc.

Grigsby, J., & Kaye, K. (1996). *Behavioral Dyscontrol Scale: Manual* (2nd ed.). Denver, CO: University of Colorado Health Sciences Center.

Lezak, M. D. (1978). Living with the characterologically altered brain injured patient. *Journal of Clinical Psychiatry*, *39*(7), 592–598.

Lishman, W. A. (1973). The psychiatric sequelae of head injury: A review. *Psychological Medicine*, *3*(3), 304–318.

Lishman, W. A. (1987). *Organic psychiatry: The psychological consequences of cerebral disorder* (2nd ed.). Oxford: Blackwell Scientific Publications.

Malloy, P., & Grace, J. (2005). A review of rating scales for measuring behavior change due to frontal systems damage. *Cognitive and Behavioural Neurology*, *18*(1), 18–27.

McDowell, I. (2006). *Measuring health: A guide to rating scales and questionnaires* (3rd ed.). New York: Oxford University Press.

Obonsawin, M. C., Jefferis, S., Lowe, R., Crawford, J. R., Fernandes, J., Holland, L., et al. (2007). A model of personality change after traumatic brain injury and the development of the Brain Injury Personality Scale (BIPS). *Journal of Neurology, Neurosurgery, and Psychiatry*, *78*, 1239–1247.

Roth, R. M., Isquith, P. K., & Gioia, G. A. (2005). *BRIEF-A: Behavior Rating Inventory of Executive Function – Adult version*. Lutz, FL: Psychological Assessment Resources.

Wade, D. T. (1992). *Measurement in neurological rehabilitation*. Oxford: Oxford University Press.

World Health Organization. (2001). *International classification of functioning, disability and health*. Geneva: World Health Organization.

Agitated Behavior Scale (ABS)

Corrigan (1989)

Source

Items of the ABS are available in Corrigan (1989), as well as the website of the Center for Outcome Measurement in Brain Injury (http://www.tbims.org/combi/abs/index.html), and are also reproduced below.

Purpose

The ABS is an observational scale, designed for patients in the early stages of recovery from traumatic brain injury (TBI). It is intended to be used clinically to improve assessment, monitoring and management of patients during this phase. In addition to TBI, the ABS has been used with patients with anoxia and stroke (Corrigan & Bogner, 1994).

Item description

The ABS comprises 14 items, which cover the range of behaviours seen in agitated patients after TBI, including cognitive (e.g., short attention span), emotional (e.g., sudden changes in mood), physical (e.g., wandering) and verbal (e.g., rapid talking) impairments.

Scale development

Although agitation occurs frequently in the early stages of recovery from severe TBI, Corrigan (1989) observed that there was no validated, quantitative instrument available that adequately addressed the types of behaviours seen in this clinical group. A thorough and systematic approach was adopted in the development of the ABS to ensure content validity. The first stage involved a literature review to develop a pool of potential items. Second, multidisciplinary staff members working in a TBI rehabilitation unit were asked to list all behaviours observed in agitated patients. They then participated in structured and unstructured procedures of item elicitation, following which expert judges reviewed the lists. This produced a preliminary scale of 39 items that were rated on a 4-point scale for degree of the behaviour (either severity or frequency). The scale was trialled for an 8-week period on 14 patients with TBI by two nursing staff. The resulting 67 observations were then subjected to a series of analyses to reduce the items. Consideration was given to inter-rater reliability of items, differentiation of agitation and frequency of occurrence. In the final stages a principal components analysis was used to identify items that significantly contributed to the latent factor. The resulting 14-item scale was then validated on an independent sample of 35 people with TBI.

Administration procedures, response format and scoring

The ABS is designed to be completed after a period of observation of the patient, but specific details regarding such observation are not provided. In the validation studies, nurses or therapists completed the ABS at the end of their shift. Completion of the ABS is quick and easy.

Items are rated on a 4-point scale: 1 (absent), 2 (present to a slight degree), 3 (present to a moderate degree), 4 (present to an extreme degree). The total score ranges from 14 to 56, with higher scores indicating greater degrees of agitation. Corrigan and Bogner (1994) suggested the use of a cut-off score of 21/22 (mean score for TBI group) to indicate a clinically significant degree of agitation, with levels of agitation being defined in multiples of 7 (the standard deviation). Thus, scores from 22 to 28 are classified as low agitation, from 29 to 35 as moderate agitation, and > 35 as high agitation.

Psychometric properties

Corrigan (1989) provided information on psychometric properties of the ABS during its development, using a sample of 35 patients with TBI (descriptive data shown in Data box 5.1) who were consecutive admissions over a 7-month period recruited from an inpatient TBI rehabilitation unit in the USA. This yielded 98 observations, and inter-rater reliability was examined with four clinicians (two nurses, an occupational therapist and a

Data box 5.1 Descriptive data from the standardization sample (Corrigan, 1989)

	Age Mean	Education Median	ABS *M* (*SD*)	Cut-off score	Sensitivity / Specificity
TBI rehabilitation inpatients (*n* = 35):	28.2	12		21/22	No information
Nurse 1 (*n* = 98 observations)			20.90 (7.34)		
Nurse 2 (*n* = 135)			21.13 (7.37)		
Occupational Therapist (*n* = 166)			20.09 (6.56)		
Physical Therapist (*n* = 170)			19.95 (5.50)		

physiotherapist) who completed ratings on the same day.

There were no validated measures suitable for examining concurrent validity. Corrigan therefore constructed two 10-point global scores, from 1 (not agitated) to 10 (extremely agitated), for which ratings were made, first comparing the patient to "other patients" (COP) and then comparing the patient's current day to "other days" (COD). The Braintree Agitation Scale (BAS), completed by a medical resident, was also used as a validation measure, although Corrigan noted that it did not have published normative, reliability or validity data. A later study (Corrigan, Mysiw, Gribble, & Chock, 1992) made repeated examinations of 20 rehabilitation inpatients with TBI during their acute phase of recovery (over $M = 6.5$ weeks). Measures were taken of cognitive status using the Orientation Group Monitoring System (OGMS), and simple and choice reaction times (SRT and CRT respectively).

The study of Azouvi, Jokic, Attal, Denys, Markab, and Bussel (1999) provided evidence for responsiveness, as well as discriminative validity. Ten patients with TBI showing agitation on the ABS ($M = 32.7$, $SD = 8.2$) participated in an 8-week trial of carbamazepine. A significant decrease on ABS occurred, but there was no change on the Mini-Mental State Examination (MMSE). The factor structure of the ABS was studied in 212 patients mainly with TBI, who were randomized to three samples for the purpose of conducting confirmatory factor analysis (Corrigan & Bogner, 1994). A three-factor model produced the best fit ($rho = .77–.85$ in the samples), with factors labelled Disinhibition, Aggression, and Lability. The factors were intercorrelated (range $r = .60–.85$) and the authors suggested the three factors represented different facets of a general construct of agitation. Findings from Corrigan (1989), except where otherwise stated, are shown in Box 5.1.

Box 5.1

Validity:	Criterion: *Concurrent*: with BAS: $r = .42–.71$ – with average COP: $r = .67–.78$ – with average COD: $r = .63–.72$
	Corrigan et al.: with OGMS: $r = .70$ – with SRT: $r = .70$ – with CRT: $r = .63$
	Construct: *Internal consistency:* Cronbach alpha: 2 nurses: .91–.92, 2 therapy staff: .84–.87
	Factor analysis: Corrigan & Bogner: 3 factors: Disinhibition (7 items), Aggression (4 items) and Lability (3 items)
Reliability:	Inter-rater: $r_s = .28–.67$ (with $r_s < .6$ for 11/14 items between 2 nurses); – using gamma, coefficients were higher: $\gamma = .54–.94$ ($\gamma > .8$ for 6/14, $\gamma < .6$ for 1/14 items)
	Test–retest: No information available
Responsiveness:	Azouvi et al.: Post-treatment change from pre-treatment: ABS: 8.3 ($p = .02$, $d = 1.0$; but MMSE: 1.0, $p > .05$, $d = .12$) – Pre-treatment ABS $M = 32.7$ ($SD = 8.2$) vs Time 4 $M = 24.4$ ($SD = 9.0$), $d = 1.01$

Comment

The ABS is a carefully developed instrument and generally has sound psychometric properties: it has high internal consistency and there is evidence of responsiveness with a large effect size, along with content, concurrent and construct validity. Information on temporal stability is lacking, however, and inter-rater reliability at the item level was variable. Inter-rater reliability was probably underestimated in this study, because the raters did not make their ratings on the same sample of behaviour. Rather, ratings were made at the end of the shift regarding behaviours that different clinicians had observed during the course of the day, and Corrigan commented on the adverse influence of "environmental factors" (the one-to-one structure of a therapy session compared with the "looser supervision on the nursing floor"). Additionally, some items showed a low frequency of occurrence (e.g., item 14, self-abusive behaviour), but were retained because of their clinical salience. Notwithstanding these points, the ABS is a sensitive and valid measure for assessing agitated behaviour in the early stages of TBI.

Key references

Azouvi, P., Jokic, C., Attal, N., Denys, P., Markab, S., & Bussel, B. (1999). Carbamazepine in agitation and aggressive behaviour following severe closed-head injury: Results of an open trial. *Brain Injury*, *13*(10), 797–804.

Corrigan, J. D. (1989). Development of a scale for assessment of agitation following traumatic brain injury. *Journal of Clinical and Experimental Neuropsychology*, *11*(2), 261–277.

Corrigan, J. D., & Bogner, J. A. (1994). Factor structure of the Agitated Behavior Scale. *Journal of Clinical and Experimental Neuropsychology*, *16*(3), 386–392.

Corrigan, J. D., Mysiw, W. J., Gribble, M. W., & Chock, S. K. L. (1992). Agitation, cognition and attention during post-traumatic amnesia. *Brain Injury*, *6*(2), 155–160.

Agitated Behavior Scale

Corrigan (1989)

Name:	**Administered by:**	**Date:**

Instructions: At the end of the observation period indicate whether each behaviour was present and, if so, to what degree: slight, moderate or extreme. The degree can be based on either frequency of the behaviour or severity of a given incident. Use the following numerical values for every behaviour listed. DO NOT LEAVE BLANKS.

Response key:
1 = Absent
2 = Present to a slight degree
3 = Present to a moderate degree
4 = Present to an extreme degree

	RESPONSE
1. Short attention span, easy distractibility, inability to concentrate	______
2. Impulsive, impatient, low tolerance for pain or frustration	______
3. Uncooperative, resistant to care, demanding	______
4. Violent and/or threatening violence towards people or property	______
5. Explosive and/or unpredictable anger	______
6. Rocking, rubbing, moaning, or other self-stimulating behaviour	______
7. Pulling at tubes, restraints, etc.	______
8. Wandering from treatment areas	______
9. Restlessness, pacing, excessive movement	______
10. Repetitive behaviours, motor and/or verbal	______
11. Rapid, loud or excessive talking	______
12. Sudden changes of mood	______
13. Easily initiated or excessive crying and/or laughter	______
14. Self-abusiveness, physical and/or verbal	______
TOTAL SCORE	______

Acknowledgement: From Corrigan, J. D. (1989). Development of a scale for assessment of agitation following traumatic brain injury. *Journal of Clinical and Experimental Neuropsychology*, *11*(2), 261–277, Fig. 1, p. 265, reprinted by permission of Taylor & Francis.

Apathy Evaluation Scale (AES)

Marin, Biedrzycki, and Firinciogullari (1991)

Source

Items of the AES are available in Marin et al. (1991), which also contains detailed administration guidelines in an appendix. Additionally, the AES is available on the website of the Center for Outcome Measurement in Brain Injury (http://www.tbims.org/combi/aes/index.html), and is also reproduced below.

Purpose

The AES is a rating scale using clinician, informant and/or self-ratings. It was designed for clinicians to identify apathy states, discriminate between apathy and depression, and distinguish severity levels of apathy in different diagnostic groups. The AES was developed primarily for people with apathy of neurological aetiology. The original validation studies were conducted with people with Alzheimer's disease (AD), stroke, and major depression (MD). The AES has been studied subsequently with other neurological groups including hypoxia (Andersson, Krogstad, & Finset, 1999), Parkinson's disease (PD; Starkstein, Mayberg, Preziosi, Andrezejewski, Leiguarda, & Robinson, 1992) and traumatic brain injury (TBI; Kant, Duffy, & Pivovarnik, 1998).

Item description

The AES contains 18 items, mainly assessing cognitive (8 items), behavioural (5 items) and emotional (2 items) aspects of apathy; the remaining three items assessing other aspects. There are three versions of the AES, each with identical items, formatted for informant, self and clinician administration. The clinician version administers the AES in the context of a semi-structured interview.

Scale development

The developmental process of the AES described by Marin et al. (1991) was systematic. The authors defined apathy in terms of lack of motivation – "a state characterized by simultaneous diminution in the overt behavioral, cognitive, and emotional concomitants of goal-directed behaviour" (p. 145). Item development used three sources: pertinent literature, consultation with colleagues, and the authors' clinical experience with patients demonstrating apathy. They reported that "several hundred" potential items were reduced to 56 items and trialled with 40 patients, aged 55 to 85 years, with a diagnosis of depression or dementia. Twenty-seven items with item-total correlation coefficients in excess of .4 were subject to "rational and statistical criteria for reaching the 18-item scale" (p. 146). For example, seven items that were *not* significantly correlated with items of the Hamilton Rating Scale for Depression (HRSD; also known as the Hamilton Depression Rating Scale, HDRS) were retained because they would contribute to discriminating between apathy and depression.

Administration procedures, response format and scoring

The AES does not require any special equipment, but some training is required for administration – in the validation process, the less experienced clinician was given detailed training with 30 pilot participants. The clinician version uses a semi-structured interview (also see Marin, 1990, for guidelines regarding the clinical evaluation of apathy in general), followed by administration of the 18 core items; informant and self versions simply use the 18-item rating scale, with instructions to indicate the most appropriate response categories that applied over the preceding 4 weeks. The appendix contains administrative guidelines, which include criteria for those items (1, 2, 4, 5, 12) that require coding.

Items are rated on a 4-point scale: 1 (not at all characteristic), 2 (slightly characteristic – trivial, questionable, minimal), 3 (somewhat characteristic – moderate, definite), 4 (very characteristic – a great deal, strongly; verbal or non-verbal evidence of intensity is required). "Characteristic" is operationally defined as "the level

Data box 5.2 Descriptive data from the standardization sample (Marin et al., 1991)

	Age M (SD)	Education M*	AES M (SD)	Cut-off score	Sensitivity / Specificity
Healthy controls (n = 31):	68.3 (5.7)	3.8		Older people: normal vs apathy AES > 38 & HDRS/HRSD < 11	No information
Clinician			26.0 (6.2)		
Informant			26.3 (7.5)		
Left hemisphere (n = 19):	66.2 (6.6)	2.6			
Clinician			31.9 (9.6)		
Informant			28.1 (6.9)		
Right hemisphere (n = 22):	70.1 (5.0)	2.1			
Clinician			34.7 (7.3)		
Informant			35.4 (10.9)		
Alzheimer's disease (n = 21):	70.8 (7.6)	3.1			
Clinician			44.4 (11.1)		
Informant			49.1 (9.9)		
Major depression (n = 30):	71.6 (5.7)	2.3			
Clinician			40.5 (9.7)		
Informant			41.7 (15.0)		

*Education: 1 = ≤ 12 years, 2 = completed high school, 3 = > 12 years, 4 = college graduate, 5 = some graduate training.

obtained by normal individuals". In scoring the AES, the coding of all positively worded items (i.e., all items except 6, 10 and 11) is inverted (i.e., 4 = 1, 3 = 2 etc.), so that higher scores indicate greater apathy. The total score ranges from 18 to 72. Various cut-off scores have been suggested: based on clinical experience with the AES and HRSD (HDRS), Marin, Firinciogullari, and Biedrzychki (1993) diagnose an apathy syndrome in older people when apathy scores are elevated relative to depression scores (viz. AES > 38 and HRSD/HDRS < 11); Kant et al. (1998) used a cut-off score of 33/34 for younger people with TBI.

Psychometric properties

Marin et al. (1991) examined the AES in a sample of 123 people recruited from community and clinical centres in Pittsburgh, USA, using a multitrait-multimethod matrix to examine convergent and divergent validity for apathy, depression and anxiety. There were four clinical groups, as shown in Data box 5.2, and a sample of healthy older people. Ratings were provided by four respondents: two clinicians, an informant-relative and self-rating. The factor structure of the AES was examined through a series of principal components analyses using data from the two clinicians, informant and self-ratings. Three similar components were extracted, accounting for 50% to 65% of the variance: General apathy, Curiosity/novelty seeking, and Insight/concern/dependence on others. This study also provided other psychometric information on the AES. Strong evidence for the convergent and divergent validity of the AES in relation to apathy and depression was also provided by Andersson et al. (1999), who examined a mixed neurological sample (n = 72, age M = 38.6 years, range 16–60 years; M = 12.6 months post-onset, SD = 10.9). Patterns of hypothesized correlations with the three factors of the Montgomery and Asberg Depression Rating Scale (MADRS; Depressed Mood, Somatic Symptoms, and Negative Symptoms) were examined.

In the course of their study of the application of the AES to people with TBI, Kant et al. (1998) standardized the AES on n = 108 healthy younger people (aged 20–65 years). The AES score was M = 24.4 (SD = 4.5), and a cut-off score was established at 33/34, representing 2 SD above the mean (although Glenn, Burke, O'Neil-Pirozzi, Goldstein, Jacob, & Kettell (2002) have questioned this cut-off score, their own study did not identify a cut-off score). Kant et al. applied cut-off scores for apathy and depression using the Beck Depression Inventory (BDI > 11) to 83 people with (mostly mild) TBI (age M = 38 years, range 14–64) recruited from a neuropsychiatric clinic: 60% experienced both apathy and depression, 11% had apathy but not depression, 11% had depression but not apathy, and 18% had neither. Andersson et al. (1999) also demonstrated such patterns of apathy and depression in their sample. Psychometric details from Marin et al. (1991), except where otherwise stated, are shown in Box 5.2.

Box 5.2

Validity:	Criterion: *Concurrent:* Clinician AES with HDRS (HRSD)-Depression: $r = .39$ – with HDRS (HRSD)-Anxiety: $r = .35$
	Construct: *Internal consistency:* Cronbach alpha: .90 (Clinician: .90, Informant: .94, Self: .86)
	Factor structure: 3 factors with Clinician 1: General apathy (9 items), Curiosity/novelty seeking (5 items), Insight/concern/dependence on others (4 items)
	Convergent/divergent: Andersson et al.: higher correlation with similar constructs (with MADRS Negative Symptoms $r = .62$); lower correlation with dissimilar constructs (with MADRS Depressed Mood $r = .17$)
	Comparable findings reported by Marin et al. (1993)
	Discriminant: Clinician ratings: significant group differences ($F = 17.20$, $p < .001$); post hoc analyses – control group significantly different from AD, MD and RH; no differences between RH and LH groups (descriptive data shown in Data box 5.2 above)
Reliability:	Inter-rater: ICC = .94, $k = .58$
	Test–retest: 25 days: Clinician: $r = .88$, Informant: $r = .94$, Self: $r = .76$
Responsiveness:	Kant (cited in Kant & Smith-Seemiller): using stimulant treatments – pre-treatment $M = 46.6$ ($SD = 15.5$) vs after 12 weeks of treatment $M = 34.76$ ($SD = 9.0$); $p < .004$, $d = .76$

Comment

The AES is an exceptionally well-designed instrument and it is a major achievement to produce a scale that is able to make differential diagnosis between apathy and depression, conditions that share overlapping symptomatology. Moreover, the AES is easy to administer, score and interpret. The authors have thoroughly examined its psychometric properties with excellent results in all the major domains. Results from independent samples with a variety of neurological and age groups have replicated its strong measurement characteristics. The main drawback, however, is the limited normative data set. Nonetheless, the AES is a welcome addition to the field and fills a major gap in providing a specific instrument that is pertinent to both clinical evaluation and research studies.

Key references

Andersson, S., Krogstad, J. M., & Finset, A. (1999). Apathy and depressed mood in acquired brain damage: Relationship to lesion localization and psychophysiological reactivity. *Psychological Medicine*, *29*(2), 447–456.

Glenn, M. B., Burke, D. T., O'Neil-Pirozzi, T., Goldstein, R., Jacob, L., & Kettell, J. (2002). Cutoff score on the Apathy Evaluation Scale in subjects with traumatic brain injury. *Brain Injury*, *16*(6), 509–516.

Kant, R., Duffy, J. D., & Pivovarnik, A. (1998). Prevalence of apathy following head injury. *Brain Injury*, *12*(1), 87–92.

Kant, R., & Smith-Seemiller, L. (2002). Assessment and treatment of apathy syndrome following head injury. *NeuroRehabilitation*, *17*(4), 325–331.

Marin, R. S. (1990). Differential diagnosis and classification of apathy. *The American Journal of Psychiatry*, *147*(1), 22–30.

Marin, R. S., Biedrzycki, R. C., & Firinciogullari, S. (1991). Reliability and validity of the Apathy Evaluation Scale. *Psychiatry Research*, *38*(2), 143–162.

Marin, R. S., Firinciogullari, S., & Biedrzycki, R. C. (1993). The sources of convergence between measures of apathy and depression. *Journal of Affective Disorders*, *28*(1), 7–14.

Starkstein, S. E., Mayberg, H. S., Preziosi, T. J., Andrezejewski, P., Leiguarda, R., & Robinson, R. G. (1992). Reliability, validity and clinical correlates of apathy in Parkinson's disease. *Journal of Neuropsychiatry and Clinical Neurosciences*, *4*, 134–139.

Apathy Evaluation Scale

Marin, Biedrzycki, and Firinciogullari (1991)

Clinician administration instructions

Name:	**Administered by:**	**Date:**

Clinician instructions to patient: "I am going to ask you a series of questions about your thoughts, feelings, and activities. Base your answers on the last 4 weeks. To begin, tell me about your current interests. Tell me about anything that is of interest to you. For example, hobbies or work; activities you are involved in or that you would like to do; interests within the home or outside; with other people or alone; interests that you may be unable to pursue, but which are of interest to you – for example, swimming even though it's winter."

Interviewer then notes:

1. number of interests reported, 2. degree of details reported for each interest, 3. affective aspects of expression (verbal and non-verbal)

Interviewer then states: "Now I'd like you to tell me about your average day. Start from the time you wake up and go to the time you go to sleep."

How the patient deals with this (and all other) questions is assumed to provide information about how other activities are dealt with (e.g., with initiative, exuberance and energy). Therefore, prompting is indicated only if the patient seems not to understand what information is being sought or has forgotten the question.

Interviewer then notes:

1. number of activities, 2. degree of detail, intensity and duration of involvement, 3. affect associated with presentation of data.

Instructions for rating scale: Each item is now presented using the wording of the item itself. Additional information may be requested to clarify responses. Item 15 (accurate understanding of problems) is rated by appraising the patient's awareness and understanding of personal or, if present, clinical problems. Simple bridges between items may be used to preserve a conversational quality to the interview. Items are rated as they are presented using all the information acquired. The response recorded is the clinician's assessment of the patient's response. Thus, if a patient states "a lot" but the clinician judges "somewhat", the latter is used. The only exceptions are the self-evaluation (SE) items (#3, #8, #13, #16). For these items, the patient specifies which response code to use (e.g., Not at all, Slightly); the clinician rater's appraisal is not considered for SE items.

Criteria for applying codes to items #1, #2, #4, #5, and #12: 1 = Not at all (0 items); 2 = Slightly (1–2 items); 3 = Somewhat (2–3 items); 4 = Very (3 or more items).

When there is difficulty in choosing between ratings, the following guidelines are used:

1. In general, rate towards the more apathetic score
2. Consider the degree of differentiation of responses. For example, rate "interest in things" as Slightly if a patient simply specified "reading and television" as interests, but Somewhat if specific books or television programmes can be specified. Similarly, if a patient is interested "only" in reading, but provides multiple examples of reading materials, rate Somewhat or Very, based on the number of examples given.
3. Consider the presence of verbal and non-verbal evidence of affect. For example, rate toward lower apathy if subject uses phrases such as "very much" or "tremendously" or uses facial expression, gesture, or vocal intonation to suggest affect.
4. If still in doubt, ask the patient whether, for example, "Somewhat" or "Very" is the more appropriate descriptor.

Scoring: All positively phrased items (all items except #6, #10 and #11) are reverse scored.

Apathy Evaluation Scale

Marin, Biedrzycki, and Firinciogullari (1991)

Name:	**Administered by:**	**Date:**

Instructions: For each question, write in the number that best decribes your (his/her) thoughts, feelings and actions during the past 4 weeks.

Response key:

1 = Not at all characteristic
2 = Slightly characteristic (trivial, questionable, minimal)
3 = Somewhat characteristic (moderate, definite)
4 = Very characteristic (a great deal, strongly);
requires verbal or non-verbal evidence of intensity

Note: very characteristic is the level obtained by normal individuals

	RESPONSE
1. S/he is interested in things	______
2. S/he gets things done during the day	______
3. Getting things started on his/her own is important to him/her	______
4. S/he is interested in having new experiences	______
5. S/he is interested in learning new things	______
6. S/he puts little effort into anything	______
7. S/he approaches life with intensity	______
8. Seeing a job though to the end is important to her/him	______
9. S/he spends time doing things that interest her/him	______
10. Someone has to tell him/her what to do each day	______
11. S/he is less concerned about her/his problems than s/he should be	______
12. S/he has friends	______
13. Getting together with friends is important to her/him	______
14. When something good happens, s/he gets excited	______
15. S/he has an accurate understanding of her/his problems	______
16. Getting things done during the day is important to her/him	______
17. S/he has initiative	______
18. S/he has motivation	______
TOTAL SCORE	______

Acknowledgement: From Marin, R. S. et al. (1991). Reliability and validity of the Apathy Evaluation Scale. *Psychiatry Research*, *38*(2), 143–162, pp. 150–152 and Appendix, pp. 161–162, reproduced with permission from Elsevier Ireland Ltd.

Behavioral Dyscontrol Scale (BDS)

Grigsby and Kaye (1990/1996)

Source

Items from the BDS are described in general terms in Kaye, Grigsby, Robbins, and Korzun (1990), as well as Grigsby, Kaye, and Robbins (1992) and are produced below. A detailed test manual (Grigsby & Kaye, 1990/1996) is available from Dr Grigsby (Center for Health Services Research, University of Colorado Health Sciences Centre, 1355 South Colorado Boulevard, #306, Denver, Colorado 80222, USA; email: jim.grigsby@uchsc.edu).

Purpose

The BDS is an objective, clinician-administered test, which examines one aspect of executive abilities: behavioural self-regulation. The BDS was initially developed for older adults to predict the person's capacity to independently regulate his or her behaviour. Subsequently it has been used to diagnose dysexecutive disorders (Grigsby & Kaye, 1996). The BDS has been used in large-scale population surveys and neurological groups, including Alzheimer's disease (AD), mild cognitive impairment (MCI; Belanger, Wilder-Willis, Malloy, Salloway, Hamman, & Grigsby, 2005), multiple sclerosis (MS; Grigsby, Kravcisin, Ayarbe, & Busenbark, 1993), stroke (Grigsby, Kaye, Kowalsky, & Kramer, 2002a), and traumatic brain injury (TBI; Leahy, Suchy, Sweet, & Lam, 2003).

Item description

The 9-item BDS includes a range of "primarily novel and/or repetitive motor tasks adapted from Luria's studies of patients with frontal lobe lesions" (Kaye et al., 1990, p. 1305). Seven items examine voluntary control of motor activity (e.g., alternating tapping sequences, learning of simple motor sequences), one item examines working memory and capacity to flexibly shift attention, and the final item assesses insight.

Scale development

The BDS has its theoretical underpinnings in Luria's model of frontal lobe functioning, but Grigsby and Kaye (1996) emphasized that the BDS "was not developed as a 'frontal lobe measure'" (p. 4). Rather, the "goal was to construct a valid and reliable theory-based test that will predict the capacity to engage independently in purposeful activity such as ADLs [activities of daily living]" (Kaye et al., 1990, p. 1305). Thus, Grigsby et al. (1992) had commented that the BDS is "unusual among neuropsychological tests in that we began by establishing its ecological validity" (p. 883). Limited information is available regarding the item selection process, but the authors incorporated those cognitive and motor tasks described by Luria (1980) that had been shown previously to distinguish between frontal and non-frontal lesion groups (Malloy, Webster, & Russell, 1985). The authors reported that the BDS underwent "several modifications", from its initial 20-item set, with results of analyses indicating that reduction of items had a "negligible effect" on the sensitivity and specificity of the test.

Administration procedures, response format and scoring

Detailed administration and scoring instructions are provided in the manual (Grigsby & Kaye, 1996) and some training is recommended for administration of the BDS: examiners need to be "thoroughly familiar with the rationale, administration, scoring, interpretation and limitations of the scale" (p. 2). Supervised experienced and/or structured training during the first few administrations of the test is advised, and a training video is available from the authors. Administration time is 10 to 12 minutes. No equipment is required.

Each item is scored according to level of performance. In the standard scoring method, the first eight items are scored on a 3-point scale, each of which is operationalized for the individual item: 0 (equivalent of failure – inability to complete the task), 1 (equivalent of impaired performance), 2 (equivalent of adequately smooth and accurate performance and adequate learning). The final insight item uses a 4-point scale, with each point operationalized: 0 (equivalent of complete lack of insight into accuracy of performance), 1 (equivalent of partial/occasional awareness of errors), 2 (equivalent of limited understanding of significance of errors), 3 (equivalent of congruence between perception and actual performance). The total score ranges from 0 to 19, with higher scores indicating better performance. The cut-off score is 14/15 (Grigsby, Kaye, Shetterly, Baxter, Morgenstern, & Hamman, 2002b). Scores for levels of impairment subgroups, which were derived from "research and clinical work with geriatric patients" (Grigsby & Kaye, 1996), are as follows: scores from 11 to 14 are classified as mild impairment, 7 to 10 as moderate, and 0 to 6 as severe impairment.

Because the BDS shows ceiling effects and skewed distribution of scores, Grigsby and Kaye (1996) suggested an alternative scoring system to distinguish between "adequate and excellent performances". All items are rated on a 4-point scale, the extra point being given for "quick learning and rapid performance with no errors" (p. 478). This scoring method is referred to as BDS-2, with the total score thus ranging from 0 to 27. Leahy et al. (2003) examined a sample of 49 people with TBI and confirmed the slight advantage using the extended score range. Results of receiver operating characteristic (ROC) analyses indicated the optimal cut-off score to identify frontal dysfunction using the BDS-2 scoring was 15/16, with 86.7% sensitivity and 87.5% specificity. The authors made a qualification regarding the small sample size on which these analyses were conducted, noting that different sensitivity/specificity rates may be found in different samples.

It is also noted that higher cut-off scores were suggested by Belanger et al. (2005) who examined ROC curves to differentiate AD from other groups. The optimal cut-off score to differentiate AD from the elderly control group was 17 (sensitivity 83%; specificity 73%; positive and negative predictive values 65% and 81% respectively), and AD from MCI was 16 (sensitivity 81%; specificity 70%).

Normative data for the BDS for older people are provided in Grigsby et al. (2002b). The sample comprised 1313 adults living in two rural counties in Southern Colorado, USA who were 60 years of age or older and living in the community or nursing homes. Non-impaired scores (> 14/19) were obtained by 66% of the sample ($n = 867$): scores of 17% were in the mild range, 9% moderate, and 8% severe. The BDS score was significantly correlated with age ($r = -.36$) and education ($r = .52$). Impaired scores were obtained by 7% of those in their 60s, 16% of those in their 70s, 32% of those in their 80s, and 45% of those in their 90s.

Psychometric properties

Measurement properties of the BDS were first reported by Grigsby et al. (1992). A series of samples of older people (all > 60 years) was used, mainly recruited from a Geriatric Clinic in Denver, Colorado, USA. Inter-rater reliability was examined in 19 outpatients, examined by one rater but observed by two raters who separately scored the BDS responses. Temporal stability was examined in 13 participants in an independent research project who were examined 8 weeks and 6 months after initial assessment. A sample of 229 adults (descriptive data shown in Data box 5.3) was used to determine internal consistency and examine the factor structure of the BDS. A principal components analysis extracted three factors, relabelled by Suchy, Blint, and Osmon (1997) as Motor programming (38% of variance), Fluid intelligence (37% of variance) and Environmental independence (26% of variance). A confirmatory factor analysis with 441 people referred for neuropsychological assessment (age $M = 61.89$ years, $SD = 18.87$) provided "qualified support" for this three-factor solution (Ecklund-Johnson, Miller, & Sweet, 2004).

Various aspects of validity have been examined in many samples, including the following. Concurrent validity, using the Mini-Mental State Examination (MMSE), Barthel Index (BI) and other measures, was examined in 246 patients with stroke examined within 3 days of discharge from rehabilitation (Grigsby et al., 2002a). Suchy et al. (1997) reported on the capacity of BDS scores from 46 patients collected during rehabilitation admission to predict independence in living situation and Functional Independence Measure (FIM)

Data box 5.3 Descriptive data from the standardization sample (Grigsby et al., 1992)

	Age *M* (*SD*)	**Education** *M* (*SD*)	**BDS** *M* (*SD*)	**Cut-off score**	**Sensitivity / Specificity**
Total elderly: $n = 229$	79.8 (8.4) (range: 63–102)	10.6 (3.6)	10.5 (5.0)	14/15	No information
Cognitively normal subset: $n = 141$		No information	12.8 (3.9)		
Young healthy adults: $n = 47$	30.1 (range: 21–52)	No information	17.5 (1.4)		

scores 3 months after discharge. Results from Kaye et al. (1990), who examined 50 male outpatients (age $M = 80.1$ years, range 63–105), provided information on patterns of correlations with similar and dissimilar constructs (MMSE and Geriatric Depression Scale (GDS) respectively). Evidence for discriminant validity was provided by Grigsby et al. (1993), who compared 23 people with MS with a matched control group ($n = 23$). Scalability of the BDS items was examined by Diesfeldt (2004) using Mokken's procedures, finding that the first eight items met criteria for forming a hierarchy of increasing difficulty. Results from Grigsby et al. (1992), except where otherwise stated, are shown in Box 5.3.

Box 5.3

Validity:	Criterion *Concurrent:* Grigsby et al. (2002a): with BI: $r = .42$ – with MMSE: $r = .67$ *Predictive:* Suchy et al.: correlation with follow-up living situation: $r = .49$ – with FIM: $r = .44$ Construct: *Internal consistency:* Cronbach alpha: .87 *Factor analysis:* Three factors: Motor programming (4 items), Fluid intelligence (3 items), Environmental independence (2 items) *Convergent/divergent:* Kaye et al.: higher correlation with similar constructs (with MMSE: $r = .60$); lower correlation with dissimilar constructs (with GDS: $r = -.13$) *Discriminant:* Grigsby et al. (1993): MS $M = 13.3$ ($SD = 4.4$) vs controls $M = 17.3$ ($SD = 1.6$); $F = 16.2$, $p < .001$; no significant differences with MMSE ($M = 27.8$, $SD = 1.9$ vs $M = 28.4$, $SD = 1.5$ respectively)
Reliability:	Inter-rater: ICC = .98 Test–retest: 8 weeks: $r = .89$ *Practice effects:* improvement of 1.3 points between test occasions – 6 months: $r = .93$ *Practice effects:* improvement of 1.2 points between test occasions
Responsiveness:	No information available

Comment

The BDS is one of the few instruments to provide an objective, performance-based test of behavioural regulation. This feature alone makes the BDS a welcome addition to an area that is dominated by rating scales. Admittedly, Luria's items used as the basis for the BDS have been available for 40 years, along with their reincarnation in batteries such as the Luria-Nebraska Neuropsychological Battery. Yet, it is the metric and stand-alone aspect of the BDS that is advantageous. In general, the BDS has very good psychometric properties, with high internal consistency, excellent inter-rater reliability and temporal stability, good scalability and evidence of concurrent and construct validity. Further, the BDS is an ecologically valid instrument, with demonstrated capacity to predict functional ADL and living situation. It has been validated with a range of neurological groups, including younger populations. In addition to its psychometric strengths, advocates of the BDS have enumerated many other practical advantages, including it being well tolerated by patients, brief, easy to administer and score, and no need for equipment. The provision of normative data and cut-off scores makes the BDS useful for diagnostic purposes, although its ceiling effects indicate that the BDS could almost be used as a criterion-referenced test. In this respect, further examination of the BDS-2 scoring system would be helpful.

Key references

Belanger, H. G., Wilder-Willis, K., Malloy, P., Salloway, S., Hamman, R. F., & Grigsby, J. (2005). Assessing motor and cognitive regulation in AD, MCI and controls using the Behavioral Dyscontrol Scale. *Archives of Clinical Neuropsychology*, *20*(2), 183–189.

Diesfeldt, H. F. A. (2004). Executive functioning in psychogeriatric patients: Scalability and construct validity of the Behavioral Dyscontrol Scale (BDS). *International Journal of Geriatric Psychiatry*, *19*(11), 1065–1073.

Ecklund-Johnson, E., Miller, S. A., & Sweet, J. J. (2004). Confirmatory factor analysis of the Behavioral Dyscontrol Scale in a mixed clinical sample. *The Clinical Neuropsychologist*, *18*(3), 395–410.

Grigsby, J., & Kaye, K. (1996). *Behavioral Dyscontrol Scale: Manual* (2nd ed.). Denver, CO: University of Colorado Health Sciences Center. (1st ed. published 1990)

Grigsby, J., Kaye, K., Kowalsky, J., & Kramer, A. M. (2002a). Association of behavioral self-regulation with concurrent functional capacity among stroke rehabilitation patients. *Journal of Clinical Geropsychology*, *8*(1), 25–33.

Grigsby, J., Kaye, K., & Robbins, L. J. (1992). Reliabilities, norms and factor structure of the Behavioral Dyscontrol Scale. *Perceptual and Motor Skills*, *74*(3), 883–892.

Grigsby, J., Kaye, K., Shetterly, S. M., Baxter, J., Morgenstern, N. E., & Hamman, R. F. (2002b). Prevalence of disorders of executive cognitive functioning among the elderly: Findings from the San Luis Valley Health and Aging Study. *Neuro-epidemiology*, *21*(5), 213–220.

Grigsby, J., Kravcisin, N., Ayarbe, S. D., & Busenbark, D. (1993). Prediction of deficits in behavioral self-regulation among persons with multiple sclerosis. *Archives of Physical Medicine and Rehabilitation*, *74*(12), 1350–1353.

Head, H. (1920). *Studies in neurology* (Vol. 2). London: Oxford Medical Publishers.

Kaye, K., Grigsby, J., Robbins, L. J., & Korzun, B. (1990). Prediction of independent functioning and behavior problems in geriatric patients. *Journal of the American Geriatrics Society*, *38*(12), 1304–1310.

Leahy, B., Suchy, Y., Sweet, J. J., & Lam, C. S. (2003). Behavioral Dyscontrol Scale deficits among traumatic brain injury patients, Part 1: Validation with nongeriatric patients. *The Clinical Neuropsychologist*, *17*(4), 474–491.

Luria, A. R. (1980). *Higher cortical functions in man* (2nd ed.). New York: Basic Books.

Malloy, P. F., Webster, J. S., & Russell, W. (1985). Tests of Luria's Frontal Lobe Syndromes. *The International Journal of Clinical Neuropsychology*, *7*(22), 88–95.

Suchy, Y., Blint, A., & Osmon, D. C. (1997). Behavioral Dyscontrol Scale: Criterion and predictive validity in an inpatient rehabilitation unit population. *The Clinical Neuropsychologist*, *11*(3), 258–265.

Items from the Behavioral Dyscontrol Scale

Grigsby, Kaye, and Robbins (1992)

1. Tap twice with the dominant hand and once with the non-dominant hand, repetitively
2. Tap twice with the non-dominant hand and once with the dominant hand, repetitively
3. Patient squeezes examiner's hand when examiner says "red" and does nothing when examiner says "green"
4. If examiner taps twice, patient taps once. If examiner taps once, patient taps twice
5. Alternate between touching the thumb and each finger of dominant hand, in succession, to table top
6. Place dominant hand in the sequence of positions: fist–edge–palm
7. Adaptation of Head's test (Head, 1920: facing the examiner, the patient is asked to duplicate the position of the examiner's hands, using the same hand as the examiner – i.e., without mirroring)
8. Alternate counting with recitation of the alphabet through the letter "L" (i.e., 1a2b . . .)
9. Examiner rating of patient insight into performance

Acknowledgement: From Grigsby, J. et al. (1992). Reliabilities, norms and factor structure of the Behavioral Dyscontrol Scale. *Perceptual and Motor Skills*, *74*(3), 883–892, reprinted by permission of Ammos/Perceptual and Motor Skills.

Behavioral Pathology in Alzheimer's Disease Rating Scale (BEHAVE-AD)

Reisberg (1986)

Source

An appendix to Reisberg, Borenstein, Salob, Ferris, Franssen, and Georgotas (1987) contains the items and response format for the BEHAVE-AD, and they are reproduced below. The empirical observation version (Auer, Monteiro, & Reisberg, 1996) and frequency-weighted version (Monteiro, Boksay, Auer, Torossian, Ferris & Reisberg, 2001) are also briefly described below.

Purpose

The BEHAVE-AD is a clinician rating scale based on information provided by informants. The scale was developed to assess common behavioural symptomatology (as opposed to cognitive features) associated with Alzheimer's disease (AD). It has also been used with other dementia groups, including frontotemporal dementia (FTD; Mendez, Perryman, Miller, & Cummings, 1998) and vascular dementia (Brodaty et al., 2003).

Item description

The BEHAVE-AD comprises two parts. Part 1 examines 25 symptoms in seven categories: paranoid and delusional ideation (7 items), hallucinations (5 items), activity disturbances (3 items), aggressiveness (3 items), diurnal rhythm disturbances (1 item), affective disturbance (2 items), and anxieties and phobias (4 items). Part 2 contains a single item, which provides an overall rating of the magnitude of the symptoms.

Scale development

Development of the BEHAVE-AD was "motivated in part because of the lack of a scale to measure behavioral disturbance in dementia separately from cognitive and functional disturbances associated with the disorder" (Reisberg, Auer, & Monteiro, 1996, p. 302). The authors also wanted a specific scale to facilitate evaluation of treatment efficacy of psychological and pharmacotherapies. A precursor to the BEHAVE-AD was the nine-item Symptoms of Psychosis in Alzheimer's Disease rating scale (SPAD; Reisberg & Ferris, 1985). Item development for the BEHAVE-AD was based on a medical chart review of 57 outpatients with AD who had Global Deterioration Scores (GDS) ≥ 4, Reisberg et al. (1987) noting that scores ≥ 4 were associated with negative outcomes. Documentation was made of any behavioural symptoms recorded for each patient visit or telephone contact. Thirty-three (58%) outpatients had significant behavioural symptomatology, totalling 23 separate symptoms, which were developed into the BEHAVE-AD.

Administration procedures, response format and scoring

The BEHAVE-AD is designed to be completed by a clinician, based on caregiver reports of symptoms occurring over the previous 2 weeks (Reisberg et al., 1996). De Deyn and Wirshing (2001, p. 20) describe the BEHAVE-AD as "a relatively simple scale that can be completed in a short period of time".

Items for Part 1 are rated on a 4-point scale, with behavioural descriptors tailored to the response option for each item, ranging from 0 (not present) to 3. The total score for Part 1 ranges from 0 to 75. For the single Part 2 item the scores range from 0 (not at all troubling to the caregiver or dangerous to the patient) to 3 (severely troubling or intolerable to the caregiver or dangerous to the patient). Higher scores for both parts indicate greater severity of behavioural symptomatology.

Psychometric properties

Limited information on the psychometric properties of the BEHAVE-AD is available from the early publications, but its measurement characteristics have been examined subsequently. Sclan, Saillon, Franssen, Hugonot-Diener, Saillon, and Reisberg (1996) examined inter-rater reliability in caregivers of 18 patients with AD enrolled in the Aging and Dementia Research Centre, in New York, USA. Two physician-raters were

Data box 5.4 Descriptive data from the validation sample (Sclan et al., 1996)

	Age M (SD)	Education	BEHAVE-AD M (SD)	Cut-off score	Sensitivity / Specificity
Alzheimer's disease (n = 142):	73.4 (9.1)	No information		No information	No information
GDS Level 4 (n = 40)			5.12 (5.80)		
GDS Level 5 (n = 40)			9.67 (5.83)		
GDS Level 6 (n = 40)			11.17 (8.38)		
GDS Level 7 (n = 22)			2.64 (3.26)		

Note: GDS = Global Deterioration Scale.

used, one of whom interviewed the informant while the other observed. Ratings were made independently and the interviewer/observer alternated. These investigators also examined discriminant validity of the BEHAVE-AD in distinguishing among dementia severity levels in 142 people with AD (descriptive data shown in Data box 5.4). This study confirmed the curvilinear relationship between dementia severity and behaviour disturbance, using the GDS staging system. The highest frequency of behaviour pathology occurred in people with dementia severity which was moderate (GDS5, $n = 40$, $M = 9.67$, $SD = 5.83$) or moderately severe (GDS6, $n = 40$, $M = 11.17$, $SD = 8.38$). Low levels of disturbance were found in both mild (GDS4, $n = 40$, $M = 5.12$, $SD = 5.80$) and severe dementia (GDS7, $n = 22$, $M = 2.64$, $SD = 3.26$) dementia. Discriminant validity was also supported by the study of Mendez et al. (1998) who examined two groups of community dwelling people meeting established criteria for FTD ($n = 29$) or AD ($n = 29$).

Information on responsiveness of the BEHAVE-AD is available from the results of clinical trials. Brodaty et al. (2003) conducted a 12-week trial of risperidone in the treatment of behavioural symptomatology in 345 residents of nursing homes with DSM-IV diagnosis of AD and/or vascular dementia. The factor structure of the BEHAVE-AD was examined by Harwood, Ownby, Barker, and Duara (1998) in 151 people with AD (age $M = 80.2$ years, range 65–97) living in the community. Using 19 of the 25 items that had > 10% response, a five-factor model was extracted receiving significant loadings from 15 out of 19 items and accounting for 40% of the variance. Schreinzer et al. (2005) also conducted a factor analysis, using the seven categories (rather than items) in a consecutive series of 145 chronic inpatients of a geriatric hospital (age $M = 86.7$ years, range 61–100). Principal components analysis extracted three components accounting for 71.9% of the variance. This study also compared the BEHAVE-AD with the Clinical Dementia Rating scale (CDR), and although the association was statistically significant, the coefficients were generally low ($r = .25$, category range $r = -.20$ to $r = .45$). Results of these studies are shown in Box 5.4.

Box 5.4

Validity:	Construct: *Factor structure:* Harwood et al.: 5 factors: Agitation/anxiety (3 items), Psychosis (3 items), Aggression (4 items), Depression (2 items), Activity disturbance (2 items)
	Schreinzer et al.: 3 factors: Agitation-aggressiveness (2 categories), Affectivity (2 categories), Day/night disturbances/delusions (2 categories)
	Discriminant: Sclan et al.: GDS 4 (mild) $M = 5.12$ ($SD = 5.80$) vs GDS 5 (moderate) $M = 9.67$ ($SD = 5.83$); $p < .05$ – GDS 6 (moderately severe) $M = 11.17$ ($SD = 8.38$) vs GDS 7 (severe) $M = 2.64$ ($SD = 3.26$); $p < .05$
	Mendez et al.: Global score FTD $M = 46$ vs AD $M = 10$; ANCOVA = 8.55, $p < .01$ – Verbal outbursts FTD $M = 16$ vs AD $M = 6$; ANCOVA = 4.16, $p < .05$
Reliability:	Inter-rater: Sclan et al.: ICC = .96 (category range: ICC = .65–.91)
	Test–retest: No information available
Responsiveness:	Brodaty et al.: mean change in BEHAVE-AD scores between baseline and post-treatment for placebo (–2.3) vs risperidone groups (–6.8); difference: –4.5; ANCOVA $p < .001$

Derivatives of the BEHAVE-AD: (1) Empirical observation version (E-BEHAVE-AD); Auer, Monteiro, and Reisberg (1996)

The authors have produced two derivatives of the BEHAVE-AD. In recognition that informant report of patient behaviours can be biased (either over- or under-reporting), Auer et al. (1996) developed a 12-item clinician observation version of this scale. Six of the seven categories of Part 1 of the BEHAVE-AD were retained (Diurnal rhythm disturbance was not included), along with the Part 2 global severity item. The E-BEHAVE-AD is based on a 20-minute interview with the patient without his or her caregivers present. The clinical interview concerns the patient's condition and daily activities, as well as "informal dialogue" about current events, interests, and so forth. During the course of the interview, the examiner observes the patient's behavioural responses. Items are rated on a 4-point scale, from 0 (not observed) to 3, with individual behavioural descriptors attached to the response options for each category. The total score ranges from 0 to 36, with higher scores indicating more severe pathology. Comparison of the standard BEHAVE-AD and the E-BEHAVE-AD with 49 patients who were part of a larger study on ageing and dementia was $r = .51$. Inter-rater reliability (using 20 interviews) was excellent (ICC = .97; item range: ICC = .76–1.00). Items are available in an appendix to Auer et al.

(2) Frequency-weighted version (BEHAVE-AD-FW); Monteiro, Boksay, Auer, Torossian, Ferris and Reisberg (2001)

In this second derivative of the BEHAVE-AD, Monteiro et al. (2001) added a frequency rating to each item of the traditional scale. For 24 of the 25 items the rating is as follows: 1 (once in the past 2 weeks), 2 (every several days), 3 (daily), 4 (more than once daily). Item 19 (Diurnal rhythm disturbance) is rated on a 3-point scale (the 4th response option not being applicable). Response to each item of the BEHAVE-AD as traditionally rated (i.e., the severity rating) is then multiplied by the frequency score to obtain a "frequency-weighted" score. Inter-rater reliability, with two raters and 28 interviews, for the severity score was excellent (ICC = .90, category range: ICC = .75–.97), as it was for the frequency score (ICC = .96, category range: ICC = .86–.97), and the frequency-weighted score (ICC = .91, category range: ICC = .69–.98). Items for the BEHAVE-AD-FW are available in the appendix to Monteiro et al.

Comment

The BEHAVE-AD is one of the most widely used instruments for the evaluation of behavioural symptomatology associated with dementia (Schreinzer et al., 2005). It captures a range of typical behaviours from psychotic symptoms through to activity disturbances and affective changes, although "deficiencies in behaviour" (e.g., social withdrawal, loss of interest, motor retardation) are not well represented (Mack & Patterson, 1994). Strengths of the BEHAVE-AD are its sensitivity, along with its derivative versions (observation-based clinical ratings and frequency-weighted version), which enhance its clinical and research applications. Limited information is available for some measurement properties, but it does have excellent inter-rater reliability, support for construct validity and evidence of responsiveness. Item content focuses on pathological behaviours, none of which is expected in normal people, thereby obviating the need for comparative data in order to interpret scores.

Key references

Auer, S. R., Monteiro, I. M., & Reisberg, B. (1996). The Empirical Behavioral Pathology in Alzheimer's Disease (E-BEHAVE-AD) rating scale. *International Psychogeriatrics*, *8*(2), 247–264.

Brodaty, H., Ames, D., Snowdon, J., Woodward, M., Kirwan, J., Clarnette, R., et al. (2003). A randomized placebo-controlled trial of risperidone for the treatment of aggression, agitation and psychosis of dementia. *Journal of Clinical Psychiatry*, *64*(2), 134–143.

De Deyn, P. P., & Wirshing, W. C. (2001). Scales to assess efficacy and safety of pharmacologic agents in the treatment of behavioral and psychological symptoms of dementia. *Journal of Clinical Psychiatry*, *62*(S21), 19–22.

Harwood, D. G., Ownby, R. L., Barker, W. W., & Duara, R. (1998). The Behavioral Pathology in Alzheimer's Disease Scale (BEHAVE-AD): Factor structure among community dwelling Alzhemier's disease patients. *International Journal of Geriatric Psychiatry*, *13*, 793–800.

Mack, J. L., & Patterson, M. B. (1994). The evaluation of behavioral disturbances in Alzheimer's disease: The utility of three rating scales. *Journal of Geriatic Psychiatry and Neurology*, *7*, 99–115.

Mendez, M. F., Perryman, K. M., Miller, B. L., & Cummings, J. L. (1998). Behavioural differences between frontotemporal dementia and Alzheimer's disease: A comparison on the BEHAVE-AD Rating Scale. *International Psychogeriatrics*, *10*(2), 155–162.

Monteiro, I. M., Boksay, I., Auer, S. R., Torossian, C., Ferris, S. H., & Reisberg, B. (2001). Addition of a frequency-weighted score to the Behavioral Pathology in Alzheimer's Disease Rating Scale: the BEHAVE-AD-FW: Methodology and reliability. *European Psychiatry*, *16*(S1), S5–S24.

Reisberg, B. (1986). The Behavioral Pathology in Alzheimer's Disease Rating Scale (BEHAVE-AD). In B. Reisberg, J. Borenstein, S. P. Salob, S. H. Ferris, E. Franssen, & A. Georgotas (1987). Behavioral symptoms in Alzheimer's disease: Phenomenology and treatment. *Journal of Clinical Psychiatry*, *48*(5 Suppl), 9–15.

Reisberg, B., Auer, S. R., & Monteiro, I. M. (1996). Behavioral Pathology in Alzheimer's Disease (BEHAVE-AD) Rating Scale. *International Psychogeriatrics*, *8*(S3), 301–308.

Reisberg, B., Borenstein, J., Salob, S. P., Ferris, S. H., Franssen, E., & Georgotas, A. (1987). Behavioral symptoms in Alzheimer's disease: Phenomenology and treatment. *Journal of Clinical Psychiatry*, *48*(5 Suppl), 9–15.

Reisberg, B., & Ferris, S. H. (1985). A clinical rating scale for symptoms of psychosis in Alzheimer's disease. *Psychopharmacology Bulletin*, *21*(1), 101–104.

Schreinzer, D., Ballaban, T., Brannath, W., Lang, T., Hilger, E., Fasching, P., et al. (2005). Components of behavioural pathology in dementia. *International Journal of Geriatric Psychiatry*, *20*, 137–145.

Sclan, S. G., Saillon, A., Franssen, E., Hugonot-Diener, L., Saillon, A., & Reisberg, B. (1996). The Behavior Pathology in Alzheimer's Disease Rating Scale (BEHAVE-AD): Reliability and analysis of symptom category scores. *International Journal of Geriatric Psychiatry*, *11*(9), 819–830.

Behavioral Pathology in Alzheimer's Disease Rating Scale (BEHAVE-AD)

Reisberg (1986)

Name: **Administered by:** **Date:**

PART 1: SYMPTOMATOLOGY

A. PARANOID AND DELUSIONAL IDEATION

1. "People are stealing things" delusion
   - 0 Not present
   - 1 Delusion that people are hiding objects
   - 2 Delusion that people are coming into the home and hiding objects or stealing objects
   - 3 Talking and listening to people coming into the home
2. "One's house is not one's home" delusion
   - 0 Not present
   - 1 Conviction that the place in which one is residing is not one's home (e.g., packing to go home; complaints, while at home, of "take me home")
   - 2 Attempt to leave domiciliary to go home
   - 3 Violence in response to attempts to forcibly restrict exit
3. "Spouse (or other caregiver) is an impostor" delusion
   - 0 Not present
   - 1 Conviction that spouse (or other caregiver) is an impostor
   - 2 Anger towards spouse (or other caregiver) for being an impostor
   - 3 Violence toward spouse (or other caregiver) for being an impostor
4. "Delusion of abandonment" (e.g., to an institution)
   - 0 Not present
   - 1 Suspicion of caregiver plotting abandonment or institutionalization (e.g., on the telephone)
   - 2 Accusation of a conspiracy to abandon or institutionalize
   - 3 Accusation of impending or immediate desertion or institutionalization
5. "Delusion of infidelity"
   - 0 Not present
   - 1 Conviction that spouse and/or children and/or other caregivers are unfaithful
   - 2 Anger towards spouse, relative, or other caregiver for infidelity
   - 3 Violence toward spouse, relative, or other caregiver for supposed infidelity
6. "Suspiciousness/paranoia" (other than above)
   - 0 Not present
   - 1 Suspicious (e.g., hiding objects that he/she later may be unable to locate)
   - 2 Paranoia (i.e., fixed conviction with respect to suspicions and/or anger as a result of suspicions)
   - 3 Violence as a result of suspicions

   Unspecified? ______________________________

   Describe ______________________________

   ____

   ____
7. Delusions (other than above)
   - 0 Not present
   - 1 Delusional
   - 2 Verbal or emotional manifestations as a result of delusions
   - 3 Physical actions or violence as a result of delusions

   Unspecified? ______________________________

   Describe ______________________________

   ____

   ____

   ____

   ____

B. HALLUCINATIONS

8. Visual hallucinations
   - 0 Not present
   - 1 Vague: not clearly defined
   - 2 Clearly defined hallucinations of objects or persons (e.g., sees other people at the table)
   - 3 Verbal or physical actions or emotional responses to the hallucinations
9. Auditory hallucinations
   - 0 Not present
   - 1 Vague: not clearly defined
   - 2 Clearly defined hallucinations of words or phrases
   - 3 Verbal or physical actions or emotional response to the hallucinations
10. Olfactory hallucinations
    - 0 Not present
    - 1 Vague: not clearly defined
    - 2 Clearly defined
    - 3 Verbal or physical actions or emotional response to the hallucinations
11. Haptic hallucinations
    - 0 Not present
    - 1 Vague: not clearly defined
    - 2 Clearly defined
    - 3 Verbal or physical actions or emotional responses to the hallucinations
12. Other hallucinations
    - 0 Not present
    - 1 Vague: not clearly defined
    - 2 Clearly defined
    - 3 Verbal or physical actions or emotional responses to the hallucinations

    Unspecified? ______________________________

    Describe ______________________________

    ____

    ____

    ____

    ____

    ____

BEHAVE-AD page 2 of 2

C. ACTIVITY DISTURBANCES

13. Wandering: Away from home or caregiver
    - 0 Not present
    - 1 Somewhat, but not sufficient to necessitate restraint
    - 2 Sufficient to require restraint
    - 3 Verbal or physical actions or emotional responses to attempts to prevent wandering
14. Purposeless activity (cognitive abulia)
    - 0 Not present
    - 1 Repetitive, purposeless activity (e.g., opening and closing pocketbook, packing and unpacking clothing, repeatedly putting on and removing clothing, opening and closing drawers, insistent repeating of demands or questions)
    - 2 Pacing or other purposeless activity sufficient to require restraint
    - 3 Abrasions or physical harm from purposeless activity
15. Inappropriate activity
    - 0 Not present
    - 1 Inappropriate activities (e.g., storing and hiding objects in inappropriate places, such as throwing clothing in wastebasket or putting empty plates in the oven; inappropriate sexual behaviour, such as inappropriate exposure)
    - 2 Present and sufficient to require restraint
    - 3 Present, sufficient to require restraint, and accompanied by anger or violence when restraint is used

D. AGGRESSIVENESS

16. Verbal outbursts
    - 0 Not present
    - 1 Present (including unaccustomed use of foul or abusive language)
    - 2 Present and accompanied by anger
    - 3 Present, accompanied by anger, and clearly directed at other persons
17. Physical threats and/or violence
    - 0 Not present
    - 1 Threatening behaviour
    - 2 Physical violence
    - 3 Physical violence accompanied by vehemence
18. Agitation (other than above)
    - 0 Not present
    - 1 Present
    - 2 Present with emotional component
    - 3 Present with emotional and physical component

Unspecified? ____________________

Describe ____________________

____

____

____

E. DIURNAL RHYTHM DISTURBANCES

19. Day/night disturbance
    - 0 Not present
    - 1 Repetitive wakenings during the night
    - 2 50% to 75% of former sleep cycle at night
    - 3 Complete disturbance of diurnal rhythm (i.e., less than 50% of former sleep cycle at night)

F. AFFECTIVE DISTURBANCE

20. Tearfulness
    - 0 Not present
    - 1 Present
    - 2 Present and accompanied by clear affective component
    - 3 Present and accompanied by affective and physical component (e.g., "wrings hands" and other gestures)
21. Depressed mood: Other
    - 0 Not present
    - 1 Present (e.g., occasional statement "I wish I were dead," without clear affective concomitants)
    - 2 Present with clear concomitants (e.g., thoughts of death)
    - 3 Present with emotional and physical concomitants (e.g., suicide gestures)

Unspecified? ____________________

Describe ____________________

____

G. ANXIETIES AND PHOBIAS

22. Anxiety regarding upcoming events (Godot syndrome)
    - 0 Not present
    - 1 Present: Repeated queries and/or other activities regarding upcoming appointments and/or events
    - 2 Present and disturbing to caregivers
    - 3 Present and intolerable to caregivers
23. Other anxieties
    - 0 Not present
    - 1 Present
    - 2 Present and disturbing to caregivers
    - 3 Present and intolerable to caregivers

Unspecified? ____________________

Describe ____________________

____

24. Fear of being left alone
    - 0 Not present
    - 1 Present: Vocalized fear of being alone
    - 2 Vocalized and sufficient to require specific action on part of caregiver
    - 3 Vocalized and sufficient to require patient to be accompanied at all times
25. Other phobias
    - 0 Not present
    - 1 Present
    - 2 Present and of sufficient magnitude to require specific action on part of the caregiver
    - 3 Present and sufficient to prevent patient activities

Unspecified? ____________________

Describe ____________________

____

PART 2: GLOBAL RATING

With respect to the above symptoms, they are of sufficient magnitude as to be:

- 0 Not at all troubling to the caregiver or dangerous to the patient
- 1 Mildly troubling to the caregiver or dangerous to the patient
- 2 Moderately troubling to the caregiver or dangerous to the patient
- 3 Severely troubling or intolerable to the caregiver or dangerous to the patient

Acknowledgement: From Reisberg, B. et al. (1987). Behavioral symptoms in Alzheimer's disease: Phenomenology and treatment. *Journal of Clinical Psychiatry*, *48*(5, Suppl), 9–15, reprinted by permission of the author.

Behavior Rating Inventory of Executive Function (BRIEF)

Gioia, Isquith, Guy, and Kenworthy (1996)

Source

The school version of the BRIEF (Gioia et al., 1996), along with the preschool version (Gioia, Espy, & Isquith, 2003), adolescent version (Guy, Isquith, & Gioia, 2004), and adult version (Roth, Isquith, & Gioia, 2005), are commercially available from Psychological Assessment Resources (http://www.parinc.com).

Purpose

The BRIEF is an informant rating scale that aims "to assess executive function behaviors in the home and school environment" (Gioia et al., 1996, p. 1). The school version was designed for children aged between 5 and 18 years. The BRIEF has been used with a number of clinical groups with executive impairment, including attention deficit hyperactivity disorder (ADHD; Jarratt, Riccio, & Siekierski, 2005), phenylketonuria, hydrocephalus (Anderson, Anderson, Northam, Jacobs, & Mikiewicz, 2002), autism spectrum disorder (ASD), affective disorder, learning disorder, seizure disorder, Tourette syndrome (Gioia, Isquith, Retzlaff, & Espy, 2002) and traumatic brain injury (TBI; Mangeot, Armstrong, Colvin, Yeates, & Taylor, 2002).

Item description

The BRIEF has two forms, Parent and Teacher (with almost, but not complete, item overlap – the phrasing of 18 of the items reflect the different settings, home vs school respectively). It contains 86 items, with 73 items on the Parent scale (and 74 on the Teacher scale) contributing to two indexes (Behavioral regulation, BRI and Metacognition, MI), eight clinical scales, and two validity scales. The remaining items are not included in the clinical scales, but are regarded as "additional items of interest" (Gioia et al., 1996, p. 21) that are relevant to specific clinical populations (e.g., TBI) and may assist in formulating remediation programmes. An overall score can be obtained (Global Executive Composite, GEC).

The BRI contains three scales: Inhibit (10 items in both Parent and Teacher versions, e.g., "Interrupts others"), Shift (8–10 items, e.g., "Becomes upset with new situations") and Emotional control (9–10 items, e.g., "Has explosive, angry outbursts"). The MI contains five scales: Initiate (7–8 items, e.g., "Is not a self-starter"), Working memory (10 items, e.g., "Has a short attention span"), Planning/organizing (10–12 items, e.g., "Has good ideas but cannot get them on paper"), Organization of materials (6–7 items, e.g., "Leaves playroom a mess"), and Monitor (8–10 items, e.g., "Makes careless errors"). The two validity scales are Inconsistency of response (10 pairs of comparable items, e.g., "Mood changes frequently" vs "Has outbursts for little reason") and Negativity (9 items, which if frequently endorsed suggest "an unusually negative manner [of response] relative to the clinical samples" Gioia et al., 1996, p. 14).

Scale development

Development of the BRIEF commenced with a literature review of executive function as these abilities develop in children. Neuropsychology colleagues were also asked to describe domains of functioning encompassed by executive skills. Nine domains were identified for initial inclusion, which were reduced to two "meta-domains": Metacognition and Behavioural regulation. The authors drew on their previous interview notes from their clinical neuropsychology caseloads to develop item content; additionally, existing rating scales were surveyed to ensure completeness. These methods yielded an initial item pool of 180 items. Approximately 50 redundant items were removed. Sentence length and word complexity were assessed at a 4.75 grade reading level. A 129-item Parent form and 127-item Teacher form were trialled with 212 parents and 120 teachers of clinical patients and 120 healthy controls. A series of psychometric analyses was conducted, including reliability and factor analyses, and as a result a final pool of 86 items was confirmed.

Administration procedures, response format and scoring

The manual advises that although no specialist qualifications are required for administration of the BRIEF, interpretation of resulting scores and profiles requires graduate training in branches of psychology, medicine or closely related fields, as well as relevant accredited training in interpretation of psychological tests. Detailed instructions for administering and scoring the BRIEF are provided in the manual. Administration time is 10 to 15 minutes.

Items are rated on a 3-point scale according to whether there has been a problem in the previous 6 months: never (N; score = 1), sometimes (S; score = 2), often (O; score = 3). A scoring sheet is used to facilitate the calculation of raw scores for each of the scales, which are summed, and then converted to T scores ($M = 50$, $SD = 10$) and percentiles using the normative data tables. Scores greater than $T = 65$ are clinically significant.

Normative data are provided in the manual (Gioia et al., 1996). Participants were recruited from 25 schools throughout urban and rural areas of the state of Maryland, USA, resulting in 1419 Parent and 720 Teacher responses. Parent and Teacher samples were weighted to reflect the 1999 USA Census distributions for sex and ethnicity. Normative tables were constructed separately for Parent and Teacher forms, stratified by the child's sex and age group (5–7 years, 8–10 years, 11–13 years, and 14–18 years).

Psychometric properties

The standardization sample was used to establish the psychometric properties. Temporal stability was examined in a subset of the normative samples for the Parent and Teacher forms ($n = 54$ and $n = 41$ respectively), as well as for 40 Parent forms in the clinical sample when the BRIEF was readministered on average 2 to 3.5 weeks later. Gioia, Isquith, Kenworthy, and Barton (2002) identified different BRIEF profiles in a number of diagnostic groups: ADHD ($n = 53$), ASD ($n = 54$), TBI ($n = 67$) and reading disorders (RD, $n = 34$), using data from the normative sample ($n = 208$). Nadebaum, Anderson, and Catroppa (2007) studied 45 children with TBI sustained between 1 and 7 years of age, who were followed up at 5 years post-trauma. Subsets with mild ($n = 17$), moderate ($n = 24$) and severe ($n = 18$) injuries were compared with an uninjured group ($n = 17$). Significant differences were found between the control and severe TBI group, but not between any other TBI subgroups.

Vriezen and Pigott (2002) examined concurrent validity of the BRIEF Index scores (BRI, MI and GEC) in 48 children with TBI (age $M = 8.3$ years, $SD = 3.7$ at injury) who were followed up almost 3 years post-trauma. Validating instruments included the Wechsler Intelligence Scale for Children-III (WISC-III) and performance-based executive measures, including the Wisconsin Card Sorting Test (WCST), Trail Making Test (TMT) and verbal generativity. Concurrent validity was not established, however, in that the coefficients were of small magnitude (range $r = .08$ to $r = -.30$) and with one exception were not statistically significant. A summary of the findings for the BRIEF, derived from Gioia et al. (1996), except where otherwise indicated, is shown in Box 5.5.

Box 5.5

Validity:	Criterion: *Concurrent:* Vriezen & Pigott: with WISC-III highest coefficients with the verbal scale: BRI: $r = -.22$, MI: $r = -.30$, GEC: $r = -.28$ – with executive tests: BRI: range $r = -.03$ (TMT) to $r = -.19$ (animal generativity), MI: range $r = -.12$ (WCST) to $r = -.26$ (letter generativity), GEC: range $r = .08$ (TMT) to $r = -.23$ (letter generativity)
	Construct: *Internal consistency:* Cronbach alpha: *Normal samples*: Parent – range for indexes: .94–.97, clinical scales: .80–.91 – Teacher – range for indexes: .97–.98, clinical scales: .90–.96 – *Clinical samples*: Parent – range for indexes: .96–.98, clinical scales: .82–.94 – Teacher – range for indexes: .96–.98, clinical scales: .84–.95
	Factor analysis: Using normative sample, 2 factors extracted (74% of the variance): Metacognition and Behavioural regulation; clinical sample extracted the same 2 factors (76% of the variance)
	Convergent/divergent: higher correlation with similar constructs (e.g., BRIEF-Inhibit with Child Behavior Checklist (CBCL) Aggressive Behavior scale: $r = .73$); lower correlation with dissimilar constructs (e.g., BRIEF-Inhibit with CBCL Somatic scale: $r = .11$)

	Discriminant: significant differences between severe TBI ($n = 34$) vs Controls ($n = 35$) on all Behaviour Regulation Index scales and some Metacognition scales (Initiative, Plan/organize, and Working memory)
	Nadebaum et al.: significant differences between control (and severe TBI (but not mild or moderate groups) – data presented in graphical format
Reliability:	Inter-rater: No information available
	Test–retest: *Normal samples*: Parent: 2 weeks – range for indexes: $r = .84–.88$, clinical scales: Mean $r = .81$ (range $r = .76–.85$) – Teacher: 3.5 weeks – range for indexes: $r = .90–.92$, clinical scales: Mean $r = 0.87$ (range $r = .83–.92$) – *Clinical samples:* 3 weeks: Parent – range for indexes: $r = .80–.83$, clinical scales: Mean $r = .79$ (range $r = .72–.84$)
Responsiveness:	No information available

Derivatives of the BRIEF: (1) Preschool version (BRIEF-P); Gioia, Espy, and Isquith (2003)

The preschool version of the BRIEF is designed for ages 2 years to 5 years 11 months. It has a similar structure to the BRIEF, but contains 63 items and five clinical scales: Inhibit, Emotional control, Shift, Working memory, and Plan/organize. The clinical scales contribute to three indexes: Inhibitory self-control (containing the Inhibit and Emotional control scales with 16 and 10 items respectively), Flexibility index (containing the Shift and Emotional control scales, 10 items in each), and Emergent metacognition (comprising the Working memory and Plan/organize scales, 17 and 10 items respectively), along with an overall composite score, the Global Executive Composite. There is considerable item overlap between the BRIEF and BRIEF-P. Development of the BRIEF-P initially used the original BRIEF, with items being scrutinized for their application to the preschool group. Pertinent literature was reviewed, clinical neuropsychology colleagues consulted, items from the BRIEF were rewritten as appropriate, additional items generated from the authors' clinical interview notes, and item content of existing instruments surveyed. An initial pool of 140 items was reduced to 97 items that were field tested with 327 parents and 201 teachers, and following a series of statistical analyses, resulted in the 63 item BRIEF-P. Normative data for the BRIEF-P are available in the manual (460 Parent and 320 Teacher forms), stratified by the child's sex and age group (2–3 years and 4–5 years).

(2) Adult version (BRIEF-A); Roth, Isquith, and Gioia (2005)

As with development of the BRIEF-P, the BRIEF-A used the previously developed BRIEF scales as a starting point for item development. Initially, the 86 items of the BRIEF were revised to reflect age-appropriate behaviours for an adult population. The item pool was broadened and contents of other measures consulted to ensure completeness of item content. These procedures generated a pool of 160 items. Redundant or unsuitable items were eliminated, resulting in a reduced pool of 146 items, which were piloted on a sample of 313 people comprising both healthy adults and clinical populations. On the basis of results from reliability and factor analytic studies, item content was further reduced, resulting in a 75-item scale (70 clinical items and 5 validity items from the Infrequency validity scale). The items represent nine clinical scales: Inhibit (8 items), Shift (6 items), Emotional control (10 items), Self-monitor (6 items), Initiate (8 items), Working memory (8 items), Plan/organize (10 items), Task monitor (6 items) and Organization of materials (8 items). Reading analyses indicated a 4th-grade reading level was required. Like the BRIEF, the clinical scales of the BRIEF-A comprise two indexes (Behavioural regulation and Metacognition) and an overall score (Global Executive Composite). The BRIEF-A has both Self-report and Informant-report forms. Normative data for the BRIEF-A were collected from a sample designed to be representative of demographic distributions of the 2002 USA Census. The manual provides normative tables for 1050 Self-report and 1200 Informant-report forms. Data are stratified by age, using seven age bands in decades from 18 to 90 years. Psychometric data are also provided in the manual, including its application in (very) small samples ($n = 7–23$) of neurological groups (Alzhimer's disease, epilepsy, mild cognitive impairment, multiple sclerosis and TBI).

Comment

Development of the BRIEF scales in each case was careful and systematic, and psychometric properties have been examined, generally with very good results, especially for the indexes, indicating that the scales are reliable and valid. The availability of a large normative data base, stratified by sex and age groups, enables meaningful interpretation of scores. As Malloy and Grace (2005) note in their review, the BRIEF has not yet been examined with respect to specificity of lesion site in neurological populations. Nonetheless, the BRIEF is reputed as being able to "measure something that is not routinely captured by other existing instruments" (Donders, 2002, p. 230) and provides pertinent information on the important behavioural and cognitive domains contributing to executive functioning. At this stage concurrent validity has not been extensively examined, and there was insufficient evidence in the study of Vriezen and Pigott (2002). They concluded that the BRIEF assesses different functions to those measured by performance-based executive tests and for this reason, further examination of criterion validity with a comparable instrument would be helpful.

Key references

Anderson, V. A., Anderson, P., Northam, E., Jacobs, R., & Mikiewicz, O. (2002). Relationships between cognitive and behavioral measures of executive function in children with brain disease. *Child Neuropsychology*, *8*(4), 231–240.

Donders, J. (2002). The Behavior Rating Inventory of Executive Function: Introduction. *Child Neuropsychology*, *8*(4), 229–230.

Gioia, G. A., Espy, K. A., & Isquith, P. K. (2003). *BRIEF-P: Behavior Rating Inventory of Executive Function – Preschool version. Professional manual.* Lutz, FL: Psychological Assessment Resources, Inc.

Gioia, G. A., Isquith, P. K., Guy, S. C., & Kenworthy, L. (1996). *BRIEF: Behavior Rating Inventory of Executive Function. Professional manual*: Odessa, FL: Psychological Assessment Resources, Inc.

Gioia, G. A., Isquith, P. K., Kenworthy, L., & Barton, R. M. (2002). Profiles of everyday executive function in acquired and developmental disorders. *Child Neuropsychology*, *8*(2), 121–137.

Gioia, G. A., Isquith, P. K., Retzlaff, P. D., & Espy, K. A. (2002). Confirmatory factor analysis of the Behavior Rating Inventory of Executive Function (BRIEF) in a clinical sample. *Child Neuropsychology*, *8*(4), 249–257.

Guy, S. C., Isquith, P. K., & Gioia, G. A. (2004). *Behavior Rating Inventory of Executive Function – Self-report version.* Lutz, FL: Psychological Assessment Resources, Inc.

Jarratt, K. P., Riccio, C. A., & Siekierski, B. M. (2005). Assessment of attention deficit hyperactivity disorder (ADHD) using the BASC and BRIEF. *Applied Neuropsychology*, *12*(2), 83–93.

Malloy, P., & Grace, J. (2005). A review of rating scales for measuring behaviour change due to frontal systems damage. *Cognitive and Behavioural Neurology*, *18*(1), 18–27.

Mangeot, S., Armstrong, K., Colvin, A. N., Yeates, K. O., & Taylor, H. G. (2002). Long-term executive function deficits in children with traumatic brain injuries: Assessment using the Behavior Rating Inventory of Executive Function (BRIEF). *Child Neuropsychology*, *8*(4), 271–284.

Nadebaum, C., Anderson, V., & Catroppa, C. (2007). Executive function outcomes following traumatic brain injury in young children: A five year follow-up. *Developmental Neuropsychology*, *32*(2), 703–728.

Roth, R. M., Isquith, P. K., & Gioia, G. A. (2005). *BRIEF-A: Behavior Rating Inventory of Executive Function – Adult version.* Lutz, FL: Psychological Assessment Resources, Inc.

Vriezen, E. R., & Pigott, S. E. (2002). The relationship between parental report on the BRIEF and performance-based measures of executive function in children with moderate to severe traumatic brain injury. *Child Neuropsychology*, *8*(4), 296–303.

Cohen-Mansfield Agitation Inventory (CMAI)

Cohen-Mansfield, Marx, and Rosenthal (1989a)

Source

Items for the CMAI are available in Cohen-Mansfield and Libin (2004). A 37-item community form was developed by Cohen-Mansfield, Werner, Watson, and Pasis (1995), and an observational form, the Agitation Behavior Mapping Instrument (Cohen-Mansfield, Werner, & Marx, 1989b), was derived from the CMAI.

Purpose

The CMAI is a clinician rating scale, initially designed for nurses to measure the frequency of a wide range of "agitated-related behaviors, disruptive behaviors, and care-related problems occurring in elderly people with dementia" (Rabinowitz, Davidson, De Deyn, Katz, Brodaty, & Cohen-Mansfield, 2005, p. 992). It was originally developed for research purposes for use with older people in nursing homes and in community-dwelling people with dementia. The CMAI is also used clinically, including as a guide to treatment decisions (Cohen-Mansfield, 1996).

Item description

The CMAI contains 29 items including 14 aggression items, both physical (e.g., spitting) and verbal (e.g., cursing), and 15 non-aggressive behaviours, both physical (e.g., pacing) and verbal (e.g., repeated requests for help).

Scale development

A literature review on agitated behaviours in older people was published by Cohen-Mansfield and Billig (1986), in which a conceptual framework for its assessment was proposed. They defined agitation as "inappropriate verbal, vocal, or motor activity that is not explained by needs or confusion per se" (p. 712). Part II of the report (Cohen-Mansfield, 1986) presented results of a survey of 66 nursing home residents. In that study, 13 areas of agitated behaviours were enumerated (corresponding to 15 of the 29 CMAI items), which were rated on a 7-point scale. Average inter-rater reliability was reported as .88. The first reference to the CMAI as a scale, however, is the study of 408 nursing home residents (Cohen-Mansfield et al., 1989a), which reported on the use of the 29-item CMAI, making reference back to the instrument used by Cohen-Mansfield (1986). Cohen-Mansfield et al. stated that items for the CMAI were identified by questioning nursing home staff members and reviewing the literature, but no further information is available regarding the item selection or development process.

Administration procedures, response format and scoring

Cohen-Mansfield (1996) advises that a manual is available providing operational definitions of the behaviours and instructions for administration. The CMAI can be administered by a clinician as part of an interview, or independently completed by caregivers, if they have been appropriately instructed in the scale. Ratings are made of the frequency of the 29 behaviours over the previous 2 weeks. De Deyn and Wirshing (2001) report that administration time is approximately 10 to 15 minutes.

Items are rated on a 7-point scale: 1 (never), 2 (less than once a week), 3 (once or twice a week), 4 (several times a week), 5 (once or twice a day), 6 (several times a day), 7 (several times an hour). Cohen-Mansfield and Libin (2004) also include a 5-point "disruptiveness" scale for each item, from "not at all" to "extremely". No explicit information is provided regarding scoring procedures for the CMAI. In their paper, Cohen-Mansfield et al. (1989a) reported averaged ratings for each item, thus anchoring the scale back to the 7-point rating scale, which aids interpretation. Other investigators have used summed scores to obtain a total (Finkel, Lyons, & Anderson, 1992), or subscale scores (e.g., aggression using 14 items and non-aggression using 15 items; Brodaty et al., 2003). In an early publication (Cohen-Mansfield, 1986), participants were defined as agitated if they exhibited both (i) at least one behaviour several times per day, and (ii) another behaviour once or twice per week; non-agitated participants were defined as exhibiting behaviours less than once per week. Number of agitated behaviours has also been used (Cohen-Mansfield et al., 1989a).

Psychometric properties

Measurement characteristics of the CMAI were not fully explored in the early publications. A comprehensive psychometric study was reported by Finkel et al. (1992) who examined 232 residents of nursing homes, aged $M = 86$ years (range 65–102). Nurses on day, evening and night shifts were interviewed by a psychiatrist with the CMAI and data were used to examine internal consistency. Nurses also completed the CMAI and the Behavioral Pathology in Alzheimer's Disease (BEHAVE-AD) in a subset of 40 randomly selected residents, and independent ratings from two nurses were used to examine inter-rater reliability in another random sample ($n = 20$). Weiner et al. (1998) compared a 38-item version of the CMAI and the Behaviour Rating Scale for Dementia (BRSD) in 206 community dwelling people with probable Alzheimer's disease (age $M = 72.3$ years, $SD = 9.01$). Patterns of correlations between similar and dissimilar constructs were explored, and 1 month test–retest reliability was examined in a subset ($n = 114$). Evidence for responsiveness is available from the pooled data of three clinical trials of risperidone in 1150 nursing home residents (Rabinowitz, Katz, De Deyn, Brodaty, Greenspan, & Davidson, 2004). Brodaty et al. (2003) had previously examined total aggression score in a subset ($n = 153$) of the above study.

Factor analysis and confirmatory factor analysis were conducted on data from three large multinational clinical trials ($n = 1265$) in residents of nursing homes who exhibited behavioural and psychological symptoms of dementia (Rabinowitz et al., 2005). A four-factor solution was identified in two samples (accounting for 46.1% and 49.4% of the variance) and confirmed in the third sample: Aggressive behaviour, Physical non-aggressive behaviour, Verbally agitated behaviour, and Hiding and hoarding. Five items did not have significant loadings on any factor. The factors are similar to those identified by Cohen-Mansfield et al. (1989a), although they found some variation in factor structure for different nursing shifts. Findings from the above studies are shown in Box 5.6.

Box 5.6

Validity:	Criterion: *Concurrent:* Finkel et al.: with BEHAVE-AD day shift ratings: $r = .43$, evening: $r = .28$, night: $r = .21$ Weiner et al.: with BRSD: $r = .76$ Construct: *Internal consistency:* Cronbach alpha: Finkel et al.: .86, .91 and .87 for day, evening and night shifts respectively *Factor analysis:* Rabinowitz et al. (2005): Aggressive behaviour (12 items), Physical non-aggressive behaviour (6 items), Verbally agitated behaviour (4 items), and Hiding and hoarding (2 items) *Convergent/divergent:* Weiner et al.: higher correlations with similar constructs (with BRSD behavioural dysregulation factor: $r = .71$); lower correlation with dissimilar constructs (with BRSD inertia factor: $r = .23$, $p > .05$)
Reliability:	Inter-rater: Finkel et al.: Total score ICC = .41 (subtypes: physical aggression: ICC = .66, verbal agitation: ICC = .61, physical non-aggression: ICC = .26) Test–retest: Finkel et al.: between shifts: day/evening: ICC = .51, day/night: ICC = .55, evening/night: ICC = .41 Weiner et al.: 1 month: $r = .83$
Responsiveness:	Rabinowitz et al. (2004): Significant post-treatment changes on 10/20 items Brodaty et al.: post-treatment change from baseline: risperidone group $M = -7.5$ vs placebo group $M = -3.1$ ($p < .001$)

Comment

The CMAI is very widely used in published research studies of older people. Its psychometric properties as reported in different studies show high internal consistency, good evidence for responsiveness, concurrent and construct validity. Reliability, however, is more variable, with fair temporal stability and inter-rater reliability. Unfortunately, little direction and few data are provided to facilitate the interpretation of scores for clinical application of the instrument. Item content of the CMAI is designed to focus on behavioural excesses (e.g., restlessness, hitting, screaming) and does not consider the deficiencies in behaviour (e.g., apathy, inactivity, withdrawal). Within the behavioural excesses, however, item content is comprehensive, in that the CMAI measures both aggressive and non-aggressive, verbal and physical behaviours.

Key references

Brodaty, H., Ames, D., Snowdon, J., Woodward, M., Kirwan, J., Clarnette, R., et al. (2003). A randomized placebo-controlled trial of risperidone for the treatment of aggression, agitation and psychosis of dementia. *Journal of Clinical Psychiatry*, *64*(2), 134–143.

Cohen-Mansfield, J. (1986). Agitated behaviors in the elderly II: Preliminary results in the cognitively deteriorated. *Journal of the American Geriatrics Society*, *34*(10), 722–727.

Cohen-Mansfield, J. (1996). Conceptualization of agitation: Results based on the Cohen-Mansfield Agitation Inventory and the Agitation Behavior Mapping Instrument. *International Psychogeriatrics*, *8* (Suppl. 3), 309–315.

Cohen-Mansfield, J., & Billig, N. (1986). Agitated behaviors in the elderly I: A conceptual review. *Journal of the American Geriatrics Society*, *34*(10), 711–721.

Cohen-Mansfield, J., & Libin, A. (2004). Assessment of agitation in elderly patients with dementia: Correlations between informant rating and direct observation. *International Journal of Geriatric Psychiatry*, *19*(9), 881–891.

Cohen-Mansfield, J., Marx, M. S., & Rosenthal, A. S. (1989a). A description of agitation in a nursing home. *Journal of Gerontology*, *44*(3), M77–84.

Cohen-Mansfield, J., Werner, P., & Marx, M. S. (1989b). An observational study of agitation in agitated nursing home residents. *International Psychogeriatrics*, *1*(2), 153–165.

Cohen-Mansfield, J., Werner, P., Watson, V., & Pasis, S. (1995). Agitation among elderly persons at adult day-care centers: The experiences of relatives and staff members. *International Psychogeriatrics*, *7*(3), 447–458.

De Deyn, P. P., & Wirshing, W. C. (2001). Scales to assess efficacy and safety of pharmacologic agents in the treatment of behavioral and psychological symptoms of dementia. *Journal of Clinical Psychiatry*, *62* (Suppl. 21), 19–22.

Finkel, S. I., Lyons, J. S., & Anderson, R. L. (1992). Reliability and validity of the Cohen-Mansfield Agitation Inventory in institutionalized elderly. *International Journal of Geriatric Psychiatry*, *7*(7), 487–490.

Rabinowitz, J., Davidson, M., De Deyn, P. P., Katz, I., Brodaty, H., & Cohen-Mansfield, J. (2005). Factor analysis of the Cohen-Mansfield Agitation Inventory in three large samples of nursing home patients with dementia and behavioral disturbance. *The American Journal of Geriatric Psychiatry*, *13*(11), 991–998.

Rabinowitz, J., Katz, I. R., De Deyn, P. P., Brodaty, H., Greenspan, A., & Davidson, M. (2004). Behavioral and psychological symptoms in patients with dementia as a target for pharmacotherapy with risperidone. *Journal of Clinical Psychiatry*, *65*(10), 1329–1334.

Weiner, M. F., Koss, E., Patterson, M., Jin, S., Teri, L., Thomas, R., et al. (1998). A comparison of the Cohen-Mansfield Agitation Inventory with the CERAD Behavioral Rating Scale for dementia in community-dwelling persons with Alzheimer's disease. *Journal of Psychiatric Research*, *32*(6), 347–351.

Fatigue Impact Scale (FIS)

Fisk, Ritvo, Ross, Haase, Marrie, and Schlech (1994)

Source

Items for the FIS are available in an appendix to Fisk et al. (1994) and are reproduced below. An adapted eight-item version, suitable for daily administration (D-FIS; see below), was published by Fisk and Doble (2002) and items are available in an appendix to that paper and are also reproduced below.

Purpose

The FIS is a self-rating scale, designed to measure the respondent's experience of fatigue in terms of the disability associated with fatigue, not the severity of the symptoms. It was developed with people with multiple sclerosis (MS). A 68-item version was used by LaChapelle and Finlayson (1998) in a mixed neurological sample including aneurysm, stroke, cerebral infections and traumatic brain injury.

Item description

The 40-item FIS is a multidimensional fatigue scale and examines the impact of fatigue in cognitive (10 items), physical (10 items) and psychosocial (20 items) domains. The five-item version used by Chwastiak et al. (2005) contains those items that correlate most strongly with the total score: less alert, unable to do things away from home, maintaining physical effort, able to complete tasks, trouble concentrating.

Scale development

Development of the FIS arose in response to the limited sampling of fatigue items that was available from generic health-related quality of life scales. The perspective that Fisk et al. (1994) adopted was previously recommended by researchers into fatigue; namely, examining the effects of fatigue on everyday functioning was more sensitive than ratings of fatigue severity. Development of the FIS was thorough. Item selection drew on existing instruments, along with interviews of 30 people with MS regarding the ways in which fatigue had affected their lives. Audio-recordings of the interviews were transcribed and responses were grouped thematically into cognitive, physical, and psychosocial domains. On the basis of computer analysis of the readability levels of the items, early versions were modified to ensure readability was less than the grade 8 level.

Administration procedures, response format and scoring

The FIS was designed for self-administration and is easy to complete. Items are rated from the perspective of the respondent's experiences during the preceding month.

Responses to each item are made using a 5-point scale: 0 (no problem), 1 (small problem), 2 (moderate problem), 3 (big problem), 4 (extreme problem). Total scores range from 0 to 160, with higher scores representing greater difficulty.

Data box 5.5 Descriptive data from the validity study of Chipchase et al. (2003)

	Age *M* (*SD*)	**Education**	**FIS Median**	**Cut-off score**	**Sensitivity / Specificity**
Control ($n = 20$)	47.0 (9.33)	No information		No information	No information
Cognitive			3.0		
Physical			2.0		
Psychosocial			6.0		
Multiple sclerosis ($n = 40$)	45.0 (8.3)				
Cognitive			12.0		
Physical			21.5		
Psychosocial			29.0		

Psychometric properties

The initial psychometric study (Fisk et al., 1994) recruited 145 patients from Halifax, Canada being investigated for chronic fatigue (ChF, age $M = 37.8$ years, $SD = 10.8$), along with a comparison group of 105 patients with probable or definite MS (age $M = 42.5$ years, $SD = 11.6$), and a control group of 34 patients with mild hypertension (age $M = 47.1$ years, $SD = 9.0$) who were not expected to experience problems with fatigue. The FIS was validated against the Sickness Impact Profile (SIP), using an adjusted version that excluded two SIP categories sensitive to fatigue-type symptoms. Data on discriminant validity are available from Chipchase, Lincoln, and Radford (2003) who compared 40 patients with MS and 20 healthy controls (descriptive data shown in Data box 5.5). Results from Fisk et al. (1994), except where otherwise stated, are shown in Box 5.7.

Box 5.7

Validity:	Criterion: *Concurrent:* with adjusted SIP score: ChF: $r = .57$, MS: $r = .53$, Control: $r = .55$
	Construct: *Internal consistency:* Cronbach alpha: total sample ($n = 284$): .98
	Discriminant: Significant differences between ChF, MS and Control groups; $F = 63.7$, $p < .001$ – post hoc pairwise comparisons on total score distinguished between all groups; $t > 5.3$, $p < .001$ for all comparisons, – as did scores from the cognitive, physical and psychosocial subscales; $t > 3.8$, $p < .001$
	Chipchase et al.: Cognitive: MS median = 12.0 vs Control median = 3.0; $p < .001$ – Physical MS median = 21.5 vs Control median = 2.0; $p < .001$ – Psychosocial MS median = 29.0 vs Control median = 6.0; $p < .001$
Reliability:	Inter-rater: Not applicable
	Test–retest: No information
Responsiveness:	No information, but see D-FIS below

Derivatives of the FIS: Fatigue Impact Scale – Daily Administration (D-FIS); Fisk and Doble (2002)

The D-FIS was developed because the FIS uses a time-frame of the preceding month and so is not suitable for determining changes in fatigue over the short term. The D-FIS is administered with respect to the previous 24 hours. Rasch analysis was used for initial item reduction to produce a preliminary scale, which was then applied to a sample of 93 people with flu-like symptoms and item content was further refined. The resulting eight items showed goodness-of-fit with the Rasch measurement model and high internal consistency (Cronbach alpha .91). Responsiveness of the D-FIS was examined in a sample of 26 people with acute onset of flu-like symptoms (in which fatigue is a common accompaniment), recruited from employees of a health sciences centre or ambulatory patients attending walk-in clinics. The D-FIS was completed on Days 1 to 5 when fatigue symptoms were expected to be at their peak and compared with Days 10 and 21 when improvement/resolution was expected. Significant differences were found among days ($F = 23.73$, $p < .001$), with post hoc analyses showing differences between Days 10/21 and all other days ($t > 4.0$, $p < .001$), as well as between Days 2 and 3, and between Days 4 and 5 ($t > 3.5$ $p < .01$). No differences were found between the very acute days (Days 1 vs 2) or the end days (Days 10 vs 21).

Comment

The FIS provides a comprehensive measure of the impact of fatigue on everyday functioning. It was carefully developed and its multidimensional structure, incorporating cognitive, physical and psychosocial items, samples each of the function, activity and participation components of the ICF. It also affords analysis of the components of fatigue, not possible with shorter scales, and the shorter D-FIS is useful for tracking fatigue levels over time. Although, at 40 items, the FIS appears lengthy, Chipchase et al. (2003) reported that in their sample of patients with MS it was practical to administer, which is probably ensured because of the readability analyses conducted in the developmental stages. The FIS shows excellent internal consistency and evidence of concurrent and construct validity. Temporal stability has not been examined specifically, although the responsiveness study of the D-FIS may provide some evidence in this regard. No differences in scores were found in the very acute (Days 1 vs 2) or end (Days 10 vs 21) stages of recovery from symptoms of flu. The D-FIS appears to be a suitable instrument to measure responsiveness in both clinical trials as well as clinical practice.

Key references

Chipchase, S. Y., Lincoln, N. B., & Radford, K. A. (2003). Measuring fatigue in people with multiple sclerosis. *Disability and Rehabilitation*, *25*(14), 778–784.

Chwastiak, L. A., Gibbons, L. E., Ehde, D. M., Sullivan, M., Bowen, J. D., Bombardier, C. H., et al. (2005). Fatigue and psychiatric illness in a large community sample of persons with multiple sclerosis. *Journal of Psychosomatic Research*, *59*, 291–298.

Fisk, J. D., & Doble, S. E. (2002). Construction and validation of a fatigue impact scale for daily administration (D-FIS). *Quality of Life Research*, *11*(3), 263–272.

Fisk, J. D., Ritvo, P. G., Ross, L., Haase, D. A., Marrie, T. J., & Schlech, W. F. (1994). Measuring the functional impact of fatigue: Initial validation of the Fatigue Impact Scale. *Clinical Infectious Diseases*, *18* (Suppl. 1), S79–S83.

LaChapelle, D. L., & Finlayson, M. A. J. (1998). An evaluation of subjective and objective measures of fatigue in patients with brain injury and healthy controls. *Brain Injury*, *12*(8), 649–659.

Fatigue Impact Scale

Fisk, Ritvo, Ross, Haase, Marrie, and Schlech (1994)

Name: **Administered by:** **Date:**

Instructions: Please read through each of the statements below and rate how much of problem fatigue has caused you during the past month, including today.

Response key:
0 = No problem
1 = Small problem
2 = Moderate problem
3 = Big problem
4 = Extreme problem

	RESPONSE
1. I feel less alert	______
2. I feel that I am more isolated from social contact	______
3. I have to reduce my workload or responsibilities	______
4. I am more moody	______
5. I have difficulty paying attention for a long period	______
6. I feel like I cannot think clearly	______
7. I work less effectively (this applies to work inside or outside the home)	______
8. I have to rely more on others to help me or do things for me	______
9. I have difficulty planning activities ahead of time	______
10. I am more clumsy and uncoordinated	______
11. I find that I am more forgetful	______
12. I am more irritable and more easily angered	______
13. I have to be careful about pacing my physical activities	______
14. I am less motivated to do anything that requires physical effort	______
15. I am less motivated to engage in social activities	______
16. My ability to travel outside my home is limited	______
17. I have trouble maintaining physical effort for long periods	______
18. I find it difficult to make decisions	______
19. I have few social contacts outside of my own home	______
20. Normal day-to-day events are stressful for me	______
21. I am less motivated to do anything that requires thinking	______

Response key:
0 = No problem
1 = Small problem
2 = Moderate problem
3 = Big problem
4 = Extreme problem

	RESPONSE
22. I avoid situations that are stressful for me	______
23. My muscles feel much weaker than they should	______
24. My physical discomfort is increased	______
25. I have difficulty dealing with anything new	______
26. I am less able to finish tasks that require thinking	______
27. I feel unable to meet demands that people place on me	______
28. I am less able to provide financial support for myself and my family	______
29. I engage in less sexual activity	______
30. I find it difficult to organize my thoughts when I am doing things at home or at work	______
31. I am less able to complete tasks that require physical effort	______
32. I worry about how I look to other people	______
33. I am less able to deal with emotional issues	______
34. I feel slowed down in my thinking	______
35. I find it hard to concentrate	______
36. I have difficulty participating fully in family activities	______
37. I have to limit my physical activities	______
38. I require more frequent or longer periods of rest	______
39. I am not able to provide as much emotional support to my family as I should	______
40. Minor difficulties seem like major difficulties	______

TOTAL SCORE: ______

Acknowledgement: From Fisk, J. D. et al. (1994). Measuring the functional impact of fatigue: Initial validation of the Fatigue Impact Scale. *Clinical Infectious Diseases*, *18* (Suppl. 1), S79–S83, Appendix, pp. S82–S83, used by permission of University of Chicago Press.

Daily Fatigue Impact Scale

Fisk and Doble (2002)

Name:	**Administered by:**	**Date:**

Fatigue is a feeling of physical tiredness and lack of energy that many people experience from time to time. In certain medical conditions, feelings of fatigue can be more frequent and more of a problem than usual. The following questionnaire has been designed to help us understand how you experience fatigue and how it has affected your life. Below is a list of statements that describe how fatigue may cause a problem in people's lives.

Instructions: Please read each of the statements carefully and rate **how much of a problem fatigue has been for you today**. Do not skip any items

Response key:
0 = No problem
1 = Small problem
2 = Moderate problem
3 = Big problem
4 = Extreme problem

	RESPONSE
1. Because of fatigue, I feel less alert	________
2. Because of fatigue, I have to reduce my workload or responsibilities	________
3. Because of fatigue, I am less motivated to do anything that requires physical effort	________
4. Because of fatigue, I have trouble maintaining physical effort for long periods	________
5. Because of fatigue, I find it difficult to make decisions	________
6. Because of fatigue, I am less able to finish tasks that require thinking	________
7. Because of fatigue, I feel slowed down in my thinking	________
8. Because of fatigue, I have to limit my physical activities	________
TOTAL SCORE:	________

Acknowledgement: From Fisk, J. D., & Doble, S. E. (2002). Construction and validation of a fatigue impact scale for daily administration (D-FIS). *Quality of Life Research*, *11*(3), 263–272, Appendix A, p. 271, reproduced by permission of Springer.Com.

Fatigue Severity Scale (FSS)

Krupp, LaRocca, Muir-Nash, and Steinberg (1989)

Source

Items of the FSS are available in Krupp et al. (1989) and are also reproduced below. An expanded version, the Fatigue Assessment Instrument (FAI; see below), was described by Schwartz, Jandorf, and Krupp (1993).

Purpose

The FSS is a self-rating scale, described as a fatigue-function measure. It is designed to measure the consequences of fatigue in everyday life and was developed with patients diagnosed with multiple sclerosis (MS) and systemic lupus erythematosus (SLE). The FSS has also been used with other neurological groups, including Parkinson's disease (PD; Herlofson & Larsen, 2002) and traumatic brain injury (TBI; Ziino & Ponsford, 2005).

Item description

The nine-item FSS samples the effects of fatigue on motivation (e.g., "my motivation is lower when I am fatigued"), activity levels (e.g., "my fatigue prevents sustained physical functioning"), and social participation (e.g., "fatigue interferes with carrying out certain duties and responsibilities").

Scale development

Limited details are available in Krupp et al. (1989) regarding the item development and selection process for the FSS. The authors report that a 28-item fatigue questionnaire was administered to patients with MS, SLE, and healthy volunteers. The nine-item FSS was derived from this questionnaire "using factor analysis, item analysis, and theoretical considerations" (p. 1121). It was intended that the items would be consistent with the features of fatigue experienced by people with MS and SLE. Clinical and control samples were then used to examine the psychometric properties of the FSS (see below).

Administration procedures, response format and scoring

The FSS is designed for self-completion. There is no suggested time-frame within which to rate the fatigue. The scale is very brief and easy to administer and score.

Items are rated on a 7-point scale with two anchor points: 1 (strongly disagree) and 7 (strongly agree). A mean total score is used (range 1–7), with higher scores indicating greater fatigue. A cut-off score of 3/4 is used, with scores of 4 or higher indicating significant fatigue.

Psychometric properties

Krupp et al. (1989) examined the psychometric properties of the FSS in three groups: people with MS, SLE and healthy controls (descriptive data shown in Data box 5.6). The clinical patients were recruited from an MS research centre in New York and an outpatient unit in Bethesda, Maryland, USA.

Concurrent validity was examined with a 100 mm visual analogue scale (VAS) of fatigue. Temporal stability of the FSS was examined with 11 patients with SLE ($n = 5$) or MS ($n = 6$) who were given no treatment

Data box 5.6 Descriptive data from the standardization sample (Krupp et al., 1989)

	Age *M* (*SD*)	**Education**	**FSS** *M* (*SD*)	**Cut-off score**	**Sensitivity / Specificity**
Control ($n = 20$)	39.7 (9.0)	No information	2.3 (0.7)	3/4	No information
Multiple sclerosis ($n = 25$)	44.8 (10.0)		4.6 (1.3)		
Systemic lupus erythematosus ($n = 29$)	35.6 (8.9)		4.7 (1.5)		

for fatigue over a 10-week period. Examination of responsiveness was conducted with eight patients with Lyme disease ($n = 6$) or MS ($n = 2$) who were treated with antibiotic therapy and pemoline (central nervous system stimulant) respectively, and re-tested with the FSS an average 16.9 weeks ($SD = 9.3$) later. Discriminant validity was examined by Pepper, Krupp, Friedberg, Doscher, and Coyle (1993), comparing 69 people with chronic fatigue syndrome, 65 with MS, and 20 with a diagnosis of major depression using criteria of the *Diagnostic and Statistical Manual of Mental Disorders* 3rd ed. – Revised (DSM-III-R). Performance of the FSS in other neurological groups has been examined by Herlofson and Larsen (2002) in 66 patients with PD and 131 matched controls and by Ziino and Ponsford (2005) in 49 people with TBI and 49 healthy controls. Results of Krupp et al. (1989), except where otherwise stated, are shown in Box 5.8.

Box 5.8

Validity:	Criterion: *Concurrent:* with VAS and total score: $r = .68$ (SLE: $r = .81$, MS: $r = .47$, healthy volunteers: $r = .50$)
	Ziino & Ponsford: with VAS: $r = .46$
	Construct: *Internal consistency:* Cronbach alpha: all samples: .88; SLE: .89, MS: .81, Controls: .88
	Ziino and Ponsford: Cronbach alpha: .90
	Convergent/divergent: Controls: higher correlation with similar constructs (with VAS: $r = .50$); lower correlation with dissimilar constructs (with depression: $r = .20$) – a similar but attenuated pattern in MS group (with VAS: $r = .47$ vs with depression: $r = .26$) and SLE group (with VAS: $r = .81$ vs with depression: $r = .46$)
	Discriminant: MS $M = 4.8$ ($SD = 1.3$) vs Controls $M = 2.3$ ($SD = 0.7$); $p < .001$ – SLE $M = 4.7$ ($SD = 1.5$) vs Controls $M = 2.3$ ($SD = 0.7$); $p < .001$
	Pepper et al.: CFS $M = 6.0$ ($SD = 0.7$) vs depression group $M = 4.6$ ($SD = 1.5$); $t = 6.0, p < .001$
	Ziino & Ponsford: TBI $M = 4.36$ ($SD = 1.52$) vs Controls $M = 3.55$ ($SD = 1.11$); $p < .01$
	Herlofson & Larsen: PD $M = 4.1$ ($SD = 1.4$) vs Controls $M = 2.9$ ($SD = 1.6$); $p < .01$
Reliability:	Inter-rater: Not applicable
	Test–retest: 10 weeks: $r = .84$
Responsiveness:	Pre-treatment: $M = 5.7$ ($SD = 0.8$) vs post-treatment: $M = 3.6$ ($SD = 1.2$); $t = 2.16$, $p < .01$, $d = 2.6$

Derivatives of the FSS: Fatigue Assessment Instrument (FAI); Schwartz, Jandorf, and Krupp (1993)

The 29-item FAI incorporates the nine-item FSS. It was designed to capture both the quantitative and qualitative aspects of fatigue, and examines fatigue, over the preceding 2 weeks, using the same 7-point rating scale as the FSS. The authors generated the items on the basis of their clinical experience, along with open-ended interviews with 25 patients regarding their experience with fatigue. Psychometric properties were examined in 198 patients from six diagnostic categories (including MS, $n = 40$), and a healthy control group ($n = 37$). Four factors were extracted (Severity, Situation-specificity, Consequences of fatigue, and Responds to sleep/rest). Cronbach alpha coefficients for the factors were .92, .77, .70 and .85 respectively. Two-week temporal stability was examined in an independent sample of 61 patients with MS, but coefficients were variable: $r = .69$, .51, .62 and .39 for the four respective factors.

Comment

The FSS affords a very brief yet sensitive rating of the functional effects of fatigue. The most important measurement properties of the scale have been examined, with excellent results. The FSS shows high internal consistency, good temporal stability, sensitivity to real changes occurring in the patient with a large effect size, and evidence of concurrent and construct validity. The important study by Pepper et al. (1993) provides additional evidence, showing that the FSS can discriminate between the overlapping symptoms of fatigue and depression. Its measurement properties also stand up well in other neurological groups, such as TBI and PD. A challenge for fatigue scales has been to establish cut-off scores to determine clinically significant levels of fatigue, which other scales have not reported. The score of 3/4 for the FSS was suggested (Krupp et al.,

1989). Although only 5% of their own control group were misclassified, Herlofson and Larsen (2002) found a much higher proportion in their (older) control group (25%), which they suggested could be either a problem of specificity of the scale or of the prevalence of fatigue in elderly people.

Key references

Herlofson, K., & Larsen, J. P. (2002). Measuring fatigue in patients with Parkinson's disease – the Fatigue Severity Scale. *European Journal of Neurology*, *9*(6), 595–600.

Krupp, L. B., LaRocca, N. G., Muir-Nash, J., & Steinberg, A. D. (1989). The Fatigue Severity Scale: Application to patients with multiple sclerosis and systemic lupus erythematosus. *Archives of Neurology*, *46*(10), 1121–1123.

Pepper, C. M., Krupp, L. B., Friedberg, F., Doscher, C., & Coyle, P. K. (1993). A comparison of neuropsychiatric characteristics in chronic fatigue syndrome, multiple sclerosis, and major depression. *The Journal of Neuropsychiatry and Clinical Neurosciences*, *5*(3), 200–205.

Schwartz, J. E., Jandorf, L., & Krupp, L. B. (1993). The measurement of fatigue: A new instrument. *Journal of Psychosomatic Research*, *37*(7), 735–762.

Ziino, C., & Ponsford, J. (2005). Measurement and prediction of subjective fatigue following traumatic brain injury. *Journal of the International Neuropsychological Society*, *11*(4), 416–425.

Fatigue Severity Scale

Krupp, LaRocca, Muir-Nash, and Steinberg (1989)

Name:	**Administered by:**	**Date:**

Instructions: Choose a number from 1 to 7 that indicates your degree of agreement with each statement, where 1 indicates Strongly Disagree and 7 indicates Strongly Agree

1	2	3	4	5	6	7
Strongly disagree						Strongly agree

	RESPONSE
1. My motivation is lower when I'm fatigued	______
2. Exercise brings on my fatigue	______
3. I am easily fatigued	______
4. Fatigue interferes with my physical functioning	______
5. Fatigue causes frequent problems for me	______
6. My fatigue prevents sustained physical functioning	______
7. Fatigue interferes with carrying out certain duties and responsibilities	______
8. Fatigue is among my three most disabling symptoms	______
9. Fatigue interferes with my work, family or social life	______
TOTAL SCORE:	______

Acknowledgement: From Krupp, L. B. et al. (1989). The Fatigue Severity Scale: Application to patients with multiple sclerosis and systemic lupus erythematosus. *Archives of Neurology*, *46*(10), 1121–1123, p. 1122 reproduced with permission of the American Medical Association.

Frontal Behavioral Inventory (FBI)

Kertesz, Davidson, and Fox (1997)

Source

Items for the FBI are available in the appendix to Kertesz et al. (1997) and are also reproduced below.

Purpose

The FBI is a clinician rating scale administered in the context of an interview. It was designed to assess behavioural features associated with the frontal lobe dementias (FLD, now termed frontotemporal dementia, including Pick's disease, and later stages of primary progressive aphasia, PPA). It also aims to assist in differential diagnosis of FLD from depression, as well as Alzheimer's disease (AD) and other types of dementias.

Item description

The FBI contains 24 items encompassing both "positive behaviours" (excesses) and "negative behaviours" (deficiencies). The 12 positive behaviours include impairments such as perseveration, excessive/childish jocularity, aggression, utilization behaviour. The 12 negative behaviours include indifference, concreteness, personal neglect, disorganization. Each item has a specifically scripted question.

Scale development

Development of the FBI was based partly on the Lund–Manchester consensus statement of the core features of frontotemporal dementia (Brun et al., 1994), as well as the authors' clinical experience with 12 patients with FLD. The frequency of 32 symptoms, derived from the clinical histories of the patients with FLD, was generated. Infrequently occurring symptoms (in less than 20% of patients) were eliminated from further consideration, except if their occurrence was highly specific to FLD (e.g., utilization behaviour, jocularity). Items with poor specificity were also eliminated (e.g., forgetfulness, rambling speech) and other symptoms were subsumed within similar behaviours to reduce item redundancy. A final set of 24 items was trialled with the 12 FLD patients, 16 patients with probable AD, and 11 patients with depressive disorder (DD). Results yielded a highly specific scale, with very little overlap between the patients with FLD versus DD, and no overlap with those with AD. Using the scattergram of individual patient scores for the FLD, DD and AD groups, a cut-off score of 27 included all FLD, but also one false positive, and the authors recommended the more conservative cut-off score of 29/30, which eliminated all false positives.

Administration procedures, response format and scoring

Although the FBI is a rating scale drawing on information provided by a caregiver, the authors advise that it should be administered in the context of a face-to-face interview with the informant, in order "to elicit accurate and complete details of the target behaviours and to note other symptoms that may be recounted. That is why it was decided not to have the care-giver fill out the form and score it alone" (Kertesz et al., 1997, p. 34). It is suggested that interviewers emphasize that the focus of the scale is on a change in the patient's behaviour and personality since illness onset, not life-long characteristic traits. Minimal training of the clinician is required, although experience with clinical interview technique is advantageous: "the caregiver may have a tendency to discuss behaviours that are not related to the questions asked. Although flexibility is desirable, and extra information may be useful, caregivers should be reoriented towards the item" (Kertesz, Nadkarni, Davidson, & Thomas, 2000, p. 466). Administration time is variable: Kertesz et al. (1997) initially reported 10 to 15 minutes depending on the informant and the extent of behavioural impairments in the patient, but later indicated a slightly longer time-frame of 15 to 30 minutes (Kertesz et al., 2000).

Items are rated on a 4-point scale: 0 (none), 1 (mild/occasional), 2 (moderate), 3 (severe/most of the time). The total score ranges from 0 to 72, with higher scores indicating greater impairment in behaviour and a cut-off score is set at 29/30.

Data box 5.7 Descriptive data from the standardization sample (Kertesz et al., 1997)

	Age M (SD)	Education	FBI M (SD)	Cut-off score	Sensitivity /Specificity*
		No information		29/30	FLD vs non-FLD: 94% / 90%
Frontal lobe dementia (n = 12)	57.3 (10.1)		38.8 (6.9)		
Alzheimer's disease (n = 16)	70.9 (5.9)		9.5 (6.3)		
Depressive dementia (n = 11)	59.4 (13.4)		11.2 (9.6)		

* Using data from Kertesz et al. (2000).

Psychometric properties

The initial validation study (Kertesz et al., 1997) was conduced with 39 people recruited from the Cognitive Neurology Clinic of St Joseph's Health Centre, London, Ontario, Canada, with descriptive data shown in Data box 5.7. A subsequent study using a larger sample size (n = 108) was reported by Kertesz et al. in 2000. New clinical groups were included (vascular dementia n = 16, PPA n = 11), and sample sizes of the other clinical groups were increased (AD n = 38, FLD n = 26, DD n = 17). The patient groups were used to examine discriminant validity, with Kertesz et al. (2000) replicating the earlier results of Kertesz et al. (1997). Using data from 14 patients, Kertesz et al. (2000) also examined internal consistency and inter-rater reliability using four raters who made independent ratings from videotapes of the patients. Data on responsiveness are available from the longitudinal study of Marczinski, Davidson, and Kertesz (2004) who examined 12 patients with frontotemporal dementia and 14 with PPA on three occasions at 12-month intervals over 3 consecutive years. Results from Kertesz et al. (2000), unless otherwise stated, are summarized in Box 5.9.

Box 5.9

Validity:	Construct: *Internal consistency:* Cronbach alpha: .89 *Discriminant:* Kertesz et al. (1997): FLD M = 38.8 (SD = 6.9) vs AD M = 9.5 (SD = 6.3) vs DD M = 11.2 (SD = 9.6); F = 59.8, $p < .001$ Differential diagnosis between FLD and non-FLD using a cut-off score of 29/30: sensitivity 94%, specificity 90%
Reliability:	Inter-rater: k = .90 (range: r_s = .78–.97 between pairs of raters) Test–retest: No information available
Responsiveness:	Marczinski et al.: significant deterioration over 3 years (F = 25.12, $p < .001$); at the item level significant deterioration was found on 2/24 items in the frontotemporal dementia group, and on 11/24 items in the PPA group

Comment

The FBI is a well-designed instrument with item content that is consistent with established criteria for frontotemporal dementia. Initial psychometric studies indicate that it has good inter-rater reliability, and evidence of construct validity and responsiveness. Information on its temporal stability is needed. One of the aims of the FBI was to enable the differential diagnosis among dementia subtypes. Although it discriminates FLD very well from AD, DD and PPA, a subsequent study showed that a significant proportion of false positive errors occurred with the vascular dementia group (almost 20%; Kertesz et al., 2000). The authors recommend that historical data (e.g., sudden onset, history of stroke, focal deficit) may be useful in the differentiation of vascular dementia from FLD. More generally, the authors suggest that the combination of the FBI with other investigations including neuroimaging, language and cognitive assessment, will assist to confirm diagnosis and quantify severity (Kertesz, Davidson, McCabe, & Munoz, 2003). The FBI is an important addition to the literature; as a screening tool its strengths are, as noted by the authors, "its brevity, specificity and its ability to discriminate FLD from AD and DD" (Kertesz et al., 1997, p. 34).

Key references

Brun, A., Englund, B., Gustafson, L., Passant, U., Mann, D. M. A., Neary, D., et al. (1994). Clinical and neuropathological criteria for frontotemporal dementia. *Journal of Neurology, Neurosurgery, and Psychiatry*, *57*(4), 416–418.

Kertesz, A., Davidson, W., & Fox, H. (1997). Frontal Behavioral Inventory: Diagnostic criteria for frontal lobe dementia. *Canadian Journal of Neurological Sciences*, *24*(1), 29–36.

Kertesz, A., Davidson, W., McCabe, P., & Munoz, D. (2003). Behavioral quantitation is more sensitive than cognitive testing in frontotemporal dementia. *Alzheimer Disease and Associated Disorders*, *17*(4), 223–229.

Kertesz, A., Nadkarni, N., Davidson, W., & Thomas, A. W. (2000). The Frontal Behavioral Inventory in the differential diagnosis of frontotemporal dementia. *Journal of the International Neuropsychological Society*, *6*(4), 460–468.

Marczinski, C. A., Davidson, W., & Kertesz, A. (2004). A longitudinal study of behavior in frontotemporal dementia and primary progressive aphasia. *Cognitive and Behavioural Neurology*, *17*(4), 185–190.

Frontal Behavioral Inventory

Kertesz, Davidson, and Fox (1997)

Name:	Administered by:	Date:

Instructions for the clinician: Explain to the caregiver that you are looking for a change in behaviour and personality. Ask the caregiver these questions in the absence of the patient. Elaborate if necessary. At the end of each question, ask about the extent of behavioural change, and then score it according the following:

Response key:
0 = None
1 = Mild/occasional
2 = Moderate
3 = Severe/most of the time

RESPONSE

1. Apathy: Has s/he lost interest in friends or daily activities? ______
2. Aspontaneity: Does s/he start things on his/her own, or does s/he have to be asked? ______
3. Indifference, emotional flatness: Does s/he respond to occasions of joy or sadness as much as ever, or has s/he lost emotional responsiveness? ______
4. Inflexibility: Can s/he change his/her mind with reason or does s/he appear stubborn or rigid in thinking lately? ______
5. Concreteness: Does s/he interpret what is being said appropriately or does s/he choose only the concrete meanings of what is being said? ______
6. Personal neglect: Does s/he take as much care of his/her personal hygiene and appearance as usual? ______
7. Disorganization: Can s/he plan and organize complex activity or is s/he easily distractible, impersistent, or unable to complete a job? ______
8. Inattention: Does s/he pay attention to what is going on or does s/he seem to lose track or not follow at all? ______
9. Loss of insight: Is s/he aware of any problems or changes, or does s/he seem unaware of them or deny them when discussed? ______
10. Logopenia: Is s/he as talkative as before or has the amount of speech significantly decreased? ______
11. Verbal apraxia: Has s/he been talking clearly or has s/he been making errors in speech? Is there slurring or hesitation? ______
12. Perseveration: Does s/he repeat or perseverate actions or remarks? ______
13. Irritability: Has s/he been irritable, short-tempered, or is s/he reactive to stress or frustration as s/he always had? ______
14. Excessive jocularity: Has s/he been making jokes excessively or offensively or at the wrong time? ______
15. Poor judgement: Has s/he been using good judgement in decisions or in driving, or has s/he acted irresponsibly, neglectfully or in poor judgement? ______
16. Inappropriateness: Has s/he kept social rules or has s/he said or done things outside what is acceptable? Has s/he been rude, or childish? ______
17. Impulsivity: He s/he has acted or spoken without thinking about consequences, on the spur of the moment? ______

RESPONSE

18. Restlessness: Has s/he been restless or hyperactive, or is the activity level normal?

19. Aggression: Has s/he shown aggression, or shouted at anyone, or hurt them physically?

20. Hyperorality: Has s/he been drinking more than usual, eating excessively anything in sight, or even putting objects in his/her mouth?

21. Hypersexuality: Has sexual behaviour been unusual or excessive?

22. Utilization behaviour: Does s/he seem to need to touch, feel, examine, or pick up objects within reach and sight?

23. Incontinence: Has s/he wet or soiled him or herself? (excluding physical illness, such as urinary infection or immobility)

24. Alien hand: Does s/he have any problems using a hand, and does it interfere with the other hand? (excluding arthritis, trauma, paralysis, etc.)

TOTAL SCORE:

Acknowledgement: From Kertesz, A. et al. (1997). Frontal Behavioral Inventory: Diagnostic criteria for frontal lobe dementia. *Canadian Journal of Neurological Sciences*, *24*(1), 29–36, Appendix 1, pp. 35–36, reprinted by permission of the *Canadian Journal of Neurological Sciences*.

Frontal Systems Behavior Scale (FrSBe)

Grace and Malloy (2001)

Source

The FrSBe (formerly entitled the Frontal Lobe Personality Scale, FLOPS; Grace, Stout, & Malloy, 1999) is now commercially available from Psychological Assessment Resources (http://www.parinc.com).

Purpose

The FrSBe is a rating scale, completed by an informant or by the person with brain impairment. It is designed to measure changes in behaviour as a consequence of frontal systems dysfunction, including cortical (Alzheimer's disease) and subcortical (Huntington's disease, Parkinson's disease) dementias. It has also been used with multiple sclerosis (Chiaravalloti & De Luca, 2003).

Item description

The FrSBe is a 46-item rating scale, with three subscales: Apathy (14 items), Disinhibition (15 items) and Executive dysfunction (17 items). Item content of the Apathy scale samples "problems with initiation, psychomotor retardation, spontaneity, drive, persistence, loss of energy and interest, lack of concern about self-care, and/or blunted affective expression" (Grace and Malloy, 2001, p. 16). The Disinhibition subscale items assess problems with inhibitory control of actions and emotions, including impulsivity, hyerpactivity, social inappropriateness, emotional lability, explosiveness, irritability. Problem areas addressed in the Executive dysfunction subscale include "sustained attention, working memory, organization, planning, future orientation, sequencing, problem solving, insight, mental flexibility, self-monitoring of ongoing behaviour, and/or the ability to benefit from feedback or modify behaviour following errors" (p. 17). The FrSBe has Self-rating and Family forms, with identical items but phrased as appropriate.

Scale development

Item selection for the FrSBe was developed in a number of stages. First, the literature on clinical descriptions of frontal systems dysfunction was examined, in which three distinct behavioural symptom clusters have been identified (cognitive dysfunction, frontal disinhibition, and frontal abulia or apathy). A pool of 60 items describing pertinent features was generated. Item review by a group of neuropsychologists eliminated 14 items considered redundant, poorly written or difficult to rate. Items were assigned to subscales and a content validation study, using Q-sort procedure, was conducted. Using the normative sample ($n = 436$), most item-total correlation coefficients ranged between .2 to .6 (44/46 for Family and 40/46 for Self). Items with low coefficients were retained because of their clinical relevance.

Administration procedures, response format and scoring

The manual for the FrSBe (Grace & Malloy, 2001) provides instructions for administration. The FrSBe is completed by either an informant who has good knowledge of the person both premorbidly and currently and/or person with brain impairment. FrSBe items are completed twice, first from the premorbid perspective (BEFORE) and then in terms of current level of functioning (AFTER). Administration time is approximately 10 minutes.

Formal training in neuropsychology or related fields is not necessary for administration and scoring of the FrSBe, but in such situations the manual advises that it should be done under supervision. The Self form of the FrSBe is not recommended for people with severe dementia (e.g., Mini-Mental Status Examination scores 0–10) because the ratings are likely to be unreliable; people with moderate and mild degrees of dementia will still require guidance in completion. The manual also advises examiners to be vigilant in the selection of informants, particularly those over age of 80 years, given the high level of cognitive impairment in older people.

Items are rated on a 5-point scale: 1 (almost never), 2 (seldom), 3 (sometimes), 4 (frequently), 5 (almost always). Profile forms are required to score the FrSBe in which raw scores are converted to T scores ($M = 50$, $SD = 10$) using normative data. Four scores are obtained: Total, Apathy, Disinhibition and Executive. Scores greater than $T = 65$ are considered clinically significant. Interpretation of FrSBe scores and profiles requires relevant professional training.

Normative data are available in the manual (Grace & Malloy, 2001). The FrSBe was standardized on 436 healthy English-speaking, Caucasian people, age $M = 48.1$ years (range 18–95), education $M = 14.2$ years ($SD = 2.4$). Normative data are stratified by sex, age and years of education. Comparison data for nine different neurological conditions are also provided in the manual, although sample sizes for seven of the groups are small ($n < 40$).

Psychometric properties

The standardization sample was recruited from community and volunteer organizations in the New England states of the USA (Grace & Malloy, 2001). FrSBe AFTER ratings (i.e., assessing current level of functioning) were used. This sample was also used to determine the internal consistency of the FrSBe. Stout, Ready, Grace, Malloy, and Paulsen (2003) examined the factor structure of the FrSBe (Family ratings) in a mixed neurological sample ($n = 324$) covering eight diagnostic groups. Data from a number of the participants were drawn from previous studies of the FrSBe. Principal components analysis, specifying a three-factor solution, extracted three components accounting for 41% of the variance: Executive dysfunction, Disinhibition and Apathy. Using the FLOPS (Family ratings), discriminant validity was examined by Grace et al. (1999) with 24 patients with frontal lesions from a range of neurological disorders, 15 patients with stroke resulting in nonfrontal lesions verified neuroradiologically, and 48 healthy controls.

Data on concurrent and construct validity and temporal stability are available from Velligan, Ritch, Sui, DiCocco, and Huntzinger (2002) who assessed 131 people with schizophrenia twice in a 3-month period; a comparison group of 51 healthy controls was also assessed. Validating instruments were cognitive tests, including Verbal Fluency (VF), and Trail Making Test – Part B for time (TMT-Btime) and errors (TMT-Berrors). Patterns of hypothesized correlations with similar and dissimilar constructs were examined. It is noted however, that in their sample of 26 patients with multiple sclerosis Chiaravalloti and De Luca (2003) did not find the striking patterns reported by Velligan et al. Results of the above studies are shown in Box 5.10.

Box 5.10

Validity:	Content: Formally established with Q-sort procedure
	Criterion: *Concurrent:* Velligan et al.: Executive with VF: $r = -.43$ – with TMT-Btime: $r = .48$
	Construct: *Internal consistency:* Grace & Malloy: Normative group: Cronbach alpha: Family form – Total: .92 (Apathy: .78, Disinhibition: .80, Executive: .97) – Self form – Total: .88 (Apathy: .72, Disinhibition: .75, Executive: .79)
	Factor structure: Stout et al.: Executive dysfunction (14 items), Disinhibition (9 items), Apathy (10 items)
	Convergent/divergent: Velligan et al.: higher correlation with similar constructs (FrSBe Apathy with VF: $r = -.47$, FrSBe Disinhibition with TMT-Berrors: $r = .42$); lower correlation with dissimilar constructs (FrSBe Apathy with TMT-Berrors: $r = .17$; FrSBe Disinhibition with VF: $r = -.16$)
	Discriminant: Grace et al.: AFTER ratings frontal group $M = 123.23$ ($SD = 26.98$) vs non-frontal group $M = 97.16$ ($SD = 37.21$) vs controls $M = 69.80$ ($SD = 16.94$); $F = 39.65$, $p < .001$ – Post hoc analyses: significant differences: frontal > non-frontal > controls
Reliability:	Inter-rater: Velligan et al.: assessed $n = 10$ with 6 raters, reporting Cronbach alpha coefficients of .83–.89 for the total score and .79–.92 for subscales
	Test–retest: Velligan et al.: 3 months – Total: $r = .78$ (Apathy: $r = 0.68$, Disinhibition: $r = .65$, Executive: $r = .65$)
Responsiveness:	No information available

Comment

The FrSBe has many areas of strength. It is a well-developed instrument with item content providing a comprehensive sampling of behavioural excesses and deficiencies, as well as cognitive features commonly associated with frontal systems dysfunction. The psychometric properties that have been examined demonstrate mostly good internal consistency for the Family ratings, along with evidence of content, concurrent and construct validity. Further data on reliability are needed, however, particularly given that temporal stability data are only currently available for a schizophrenia sample and the coefficients over a 3-month period were not high. The FrSBe is appropriate for adults of all ages, as well as for people with progressive and non-progressive neurological conditions. A particular asset is the availability of normative data from a relatively large sample. The standardization sample is, however, a relatively well-educated group and also composed of English-speaking, Caucasian individuals. Hence application of the FrSBe to groups who are non-English speaking, have limited formal education, or different cultural backgrounds is as yet untested. Another good feature of the FrSBe is the administration format, in which separate ratings are made of the premorbid and current level of functioning.

Key references

Chiaravalloti, N. D., & De Luca, J. (2003). Assessing the behavioral consequences of multiple sclerosis: An application of the Frontal Systems Behavior Scale (FrSBe). *Cognitive and Behavioural Neurology*, *16*(1), 54–67.

Grace, J., & Malloy, P. F. (2001). *FrSBe. Frontal Systems Behavior Scale: Professional manual*. Lutz: FL: Psychological Assessment Resources, Inc.

Grace, J., Stout, J. C., & Malloy, P. F. (1999). Assessing frontal lobe behavioral syndromes with the Frontal Lobe Personality Scale. *Assessment*, *6*(3), 269–284.

Stout, J. C., Ready, R. E., Grace, J., Malloy, P. F., & Paulsen, J. S. (2003). Factor analysis of the Frontal Systems Behavior Scale (FrSBe). *Assessment*, *10*(1), 79–85.

Velligan, D. I., Ritch, J. L., Sui, D., DiCocco, M., & Huntzinger, C. D. (2002). Frontal Systems Behavior Scale in schizophrenia: Relationships with psychiatric symptomatology, cognition and adaptive function. *Psychiatry Research*, *113*(3), 227–236.

Harmful Behaviours Scale (HBS)

Draper, Brodaty, Low, Richards, Paton, and Lie (2002b)

Source

Items comprising the HBS factors are described in Draper, Brodaty, Low, and Richards (2003) and are reproduced below.

Purpose

The HBS is an observational rating scale that aims to measure self-destructive behaviours. It was designed for residents of nursing homes, who are generally elderly and many of whom have dementia.

Item description

The HBS contains 20 items selected to represent direct (e.g., self-cutting) and indirect (e.g., refusal to eat or drink) self-destructive behaviours. Items are grouped into five scales, derived from factor analysis: Uncooperativeness (5 items), Active self-harm (5 items), Risk-taking (4 items), Passive self-harm (4 items) and Disorganized behaviour (2 items).

Scale development

Draper and colleagues (2002b) developed the HBS to meet the need for an instrument to assess behaviours that affect the person's own health and quality of life, as opposed to those behaviours that affect staff and other residents, these already being the focus of many scales. Item development drew on direct and indirect self-destructive behaviours described in the literature and 23 items were selected for the HBS. Initial validation of the HBS was conducted with 610 residents of nursing homes (Draper et al., 2002b, see below). Items with low inter-rater reliability were excluded, resulting in the 20-item scale (Draper, Brodaty, & Low, 2002a).

Administration procedures, response format and scoring

The HBS is clinician-rated, based on behaviours observed over the previous 2-week period. Completion of the scale itself is quick. In the initial validation studies the registered nursing staff member who was most familiar with the resident completed the HBS.

Items are rated on a 5-point scale: 0 (never), 1 (less than once per week), 2 (about once per week), 3 (several times per week), 4 (once or more per day). The total score ranges from 0 to 80. Higher scores indicate more frequent self-destructive behaviours. Draper et al. (2003) also use scores from the five factors.

Psychometric properties

Draper et al. (2002b) examined the psychometric properties of the preliminary 23-item version of the HBS in 610 residents from 22 out of 25 nursing homes in

Data box 5.8 Descriptive data from the predictive validity study (Draper et al., 2003)

	Age ***M (SD)***	**Education**	**HBS Mean**	**Cut-off score**	**Sensitivity / Specificity**
Nursing home residents alive 2.3 years later (*n* = 297/593):	82.0 (10.4)	No information		No information	No information
Total score:			6.45		
Uncooperativeness			2.90		
Active self-harm			0.45		
Risk-taking			1.10		
Passive self-harm			1.08		
Disorganized behaviour			0.15		

the eastern area of Sydney, Australia, 59% of whom had a diagnosis of dementia. "Indirect" behaviours occurred in 61% of residents and "direct" behaviours in 14%. Inter-rater reliability was examined in a subset ($n = 41$). Temporal stability was not specifically addressed in the study, but some information is suggested by the correlation coefficient provided between the morning and evening shifts ($n = 600$) – although this probably represents an underestimate of temporal stability because diurnal stability was not expected, Draper et al. (2002b) commenting that "certain behaviours tended to occur only at particular times" (p. 355). Concurrent validity was examined with the BEHAVE-AD and other instruments. The factor structure of the HBS was examined by Draper et al. (2003) in 647 residents of nursing homes. Five factors, accounting for 60.3% of the variance were extracted: Uncooperativeness, Active self-harm, Risk-taking, Passive self-harm, and Disorganized behaviour. Predictive validity was also examined from this sample (descriptive data for those alive at follow-up are shown in Data box 5.8). The residents had been recruited in 1996/1997 for a clinical trial and mortality data were obtained in 1999 (2 years 3 months later, during which time 50% had died). Cox proportional hazards modelling was used with the five HBS factors. Details from Draper et al. (2002b), except where otherwise stated, are shown in Box 5.11.

Comment

The HBS takes a unique perspective in examining changes in behaviour commonly associated with dementia, focusing on behaviours that affect the individual with dementia, as opposed to other people. The psychometric studies conducted to date suggest that the HBS has sound measurement properties, with good internal consistency and excellent inter-rater reliability for the total score. It also shows evidence of concurrent validity with the BEHAVE-AD, yet there is not complete overlap, indicating that the HBS measures slightly different constructs from the BEHAVE-AD. The HBS is sensitive to group differences (e.g., people with vs without dementia). The HBS is easily completed and can be used to guide the clinical management of residents, patients or other clinical groups who are vulnerable to self-destructive behaviours.

Box 5.11

Validity:	Criterion: *Concurrent:* with BEHAVE-AD: $r = .68$ Draper et al. (2003): BEHAVE-AD with 5 HBS factors: range $r = .26–.66$ *Predictive:* Draper et al. (2003): One factor (Passive self-harm) had a "weak but significant effect" on prediction of mortality. Construct: *Internal consistency:* Cronbach alpha: morning ratings: .86, evening ratings: .85 *Factor structure:* Draper et al. (2003): 5 factors extracted: Uncooperativeness (5 items), Active self-harm (5 items), Risk-taking (4 items), Passive self-harm (4 items), Disorganized behaviour (2 items) *Discriminant:* residents with a diagnosis of dementia had significantly higher HBS scores than those without dementia ($t = -4.77$, $p < .001$ – descriptive data not provided) Draper et al. (2003): those who died had higher scores ($M = 8.69$) than those alive ($M = 6.45$); $t = 2.88$, $p = .004$
Reliability:	Inter-rater: Total score: ICC = .90; item range: $k = .28–.60$ (k for individual items not reported, but $k \geq .37$ for 22/23 items) Test–retest: ~12 hours: correlation between morning ratings and evening ratings: $r = .63$
Responsiveness:	No information available

Key references

Draper, B., Brodaty, H., & Low, L.-F. (2002a). Types of nursing home residents with self-destructive behaviours: Analysis of the Harmful Behaviours Scale. *International Journal of Geriatric Psychiatry*, *17*(7), 670–675.

Draper, B., Brodaty, H., Low, L.-F., & Richards, V. (2003). Prediction of mortality in nursing home residents: Impact of passive self-harm behaviours. *International Psychogeriatrics*, *15*(2), 187–196.

Draper, B., Brodaty, H., Low, L.-F., Richards, V., Paton, H., & Lie, D. (2002b). Self-destructive behaviors in nursing home residents. *Journal of the American Geriatrics Society*, *50*(2), 354–358.

Harmful Behaviours Scale

Draper, Brodaty, Low, Richards, Paton, and Lie (2002)

Name:	Administered by:	Date:

Instructions: Please indicate how often the following self-injuries occurred in the past month.

Response key:
0 = Never
1 = Occasionally, less than once per week
2 = Often, about once per week
3 = Frequently, several times per week but less than every day
4 = Very frequently, once or more per day

		RESPONSE
1	Cutting self with sharp object	________
2	Burning or scalding	________
3	Hitting walls, doors, etc.	________
4	Scratching excessively	________
5	Falls	________
6	Removing catheters, tubes, dressings	________
7	Verbal suicide expression	________
8	Eats foreign objects, drinks toxic liquids	________
9	Refuses to eat or drink	________
10	Not eating/drinking on own when capable	________
11	Refuses to take medication	________
12	Takes unauthorized medication	________
13	Refuses to follow staff requests	________
14	Verbal abuse	________
15	Alienates staff, provokes rejection	________
16	Tries to walk unassisted against advice	________
17	Tries to abscond from nursing home	________
18	Exposes self to hazards	________
19	Physical abuse of staff/residents	________
20	Resists activities of daily living assistance	________

TOTAL SCORE: ________

Acknowledgement: Adapted from Draper, B. et al. (2003) Prediction of mortality in nursing home residents: Impact of possible self-harm behaviours. *International Psychogeriatrics*, *15*(2), 187–196, Table 1, p. 191, with permission of Cambridge University Press. Item order provided by Dr Draper.

Katz Adjustment Scale – Form R1 (KAS-R1)

Katz and Lyerly (1963)

Source

In 1963, Katz and Lyerly published a set of five inventories of adjustment and social behaviour, collectively referred to as the Katz Adjustment Scales (KAS). This entry describes the most commonly used scale in relation to the subject matter of this chapter, Form R1. Items for all the scales are available in Katz and Lyerly along with a detailed appendix of instructions. Items for Form R1 are also reproduced below.

Purpose

The KAS set of five rating scales was originally developed for the psychiatric population "for objectively assessing the adjustment and social behaviour" (Katz & Lyerly, 1963, p. 503). Form R1 of the KAS uses relatives' ratings of patient symptoms and social behaviour (the other four scales address aspects of "socially expected" and free-time activities). Form R1 has been used with neurological groups, including cerebrovascular disorders (Baird et al., 1987), but most frequently with traumatic brain injury (TBI; Fabiano & Goran, 1992; Goran & Fabiano, 1993; Jackson, Hopewell, Glass, Warburg, Dewey, & Ghadiali, 1992; Stambrook, Moore, & Peters, 1990).

Item description

The KAS-R1 comprises 127 items spanning a broad range of behaviours. The 12 clusters originally identified by Katz and Lyerly (1963) comprised 77 items: Belligerence (4 items), Verbal expansiveness (5 items), Negativism (9 items), Helplessness (4 items), Suspiciousness (4 items), Anxiety (6 items), Withdrawal and retardation (6 items), General psychopathology (e.g., social obstreperousness; 24 items), Nervousness (4 items), Confusion (3 items), Bizarreness (e.g., strange behaviours, delusions; 5 items), and Hyperactivity (3 items); an additional cluster of adaptive behaviours, Stability, contains nine items. No information is provided on the remaining 41 out of the 127 items that do not fit into the clusters.

Scale development

In developing the KAS-R1, Katz and Lyerly (1963) aimed to construct a scale consistent with theoretical conceptualizations of adjustment and mental health. In particular, they were critical of the "common practice [of limiting] the criteria to negative considerations, i.e., the absence of psychopathology" (p. 507). The 127 items drew on operationally defined criteria of adjustment and social behaviour; "the intention [was] to sample all psychiatric symptoms, minor and major, as comprehensively as possible" (p. 511). A cluster analysis was conducted on data from 100 people recruited from Spring Grove State Hospital, USA, who were "newly admitted, predominantly schizophrenic in character". Twelve clusters were identified, as described above.

Administration procedures, response format, and scoring

The KAS-R1 is designed to be completed by an informant who knows the person well. Judgements are based on the person's behaviours and mood during "the past few weeks". No information is available regarding administration time.

Responses are made using on a 4-point scale: 1 (almost never), 2 (sometimes), 3 (often), 4 (almost always). Reverse scoring is required for 14 of the 127 items (46, 54, 57, 58, 62, 63, 65, 66, 69, 70, 75, 87, 89, 96). Scores can be calculated for the individual clusters and compared with the normative data, as was done by Stambrook et al. (1990) for their TBI sample. Total scores for each of the clusters vary as a consequence of the variable numbers of items contained in the clusters. Higher scores indicate greater behavioural maladjustment.

Normative and comparison data for the KAS-R1 are available for the clusters (Hogarty & Katz, 1971). Four hundred and fifty people were systematically sampled from 3% of the households in a metropolitan county of Maryland, USA. Norms are stratified separately for sex, age group (six bands from 15–19 years through to ≥ 60 years), marital status and social class status. In addition, comparison data are provided from a "typical psychiatric patient sample", representing 133 consecutive admissions to a psychiatric day hospital.

Psychometric properties

Data on the psychometric properties in Katz and Lyerly (1963) focused on construct validity. Principal components analysis was conducted on 11 of the clusters from 404 people with acute schizophrenia recruited from nine hospitals. Three components were extracted, accounting for 57% of the variance: Social obstreperousness, Acute psychoticism and Withdrawn depression. Results of other psychometric studies addressing the reliability and validity of the KAS-R1 with psychiatric populations have been reviewed by Clopton and Greene (1994). In a schizophrenia sample ($n = 24$), Parker and Johnston (1989, cited in Clopton & Greene) had both parents make ratings at hospital admission. Evidence for the responsiveness of the KAS-R1 is provided by the study of Azouvi, Jokic, Attal, Denys, Markab, and Bussel (1999), who treated 10 patients with TBI showing agitation in an 8-week trial of carbamazepine.

Standardization of the KAS-R1 in the TBI group has focused on construct validity, yet all studies examining the factor structure have been problematic in one way or another. Fabiano and Goran (1992) had an unacceptable sample size for the analysis (subject:variable ratio, 88:127; i.e., < 1:1). Thus, their 10-component model was probably very unreliable and requires replication, and the subsequent reduction of KAS-R1 item content to 79 items (Goran & Fabiano, 1993) was premature. Baker, Schmidt, Heinemann, Langley, and Miranti (1998) aimed to validate the Fabiano and Goran factor structure, but their sample size was also small relative to the number of variables (105:127; i.e., < 1:1). The study of Jackson et al. (1992) was the most reliable, although combined spinal and brain-injured samples ($n = 463$) were used, and the subject:variable ratio was still low (< 4:1). Items were grouped into three broad domains (psychosocial/emotional, physical/intellectual and psychiatric) and separate analyses conducted. Thirty factors were extracted and subjected to a second factor analysis, which extracted seven second-order factors. Results from Katz and Lyerly (1963), except where otherwise indicated, are shown in Box 5.12.

Box 5.12

Validity:	Construct: *Internal consistency:* Kuder-Richardson formula for 12 clusters: original sample ($n = 242$ from 9 sites) range: .41–.81 *Factor analysis:* 3 components: Social obstreperousness (4 clusters – Belligerence, Negativism, Verbal expansiveness, General psychopathology), Acute psychosis (3 clusters – Anxiety, Bizarreness, Hyperactivity), Withdrawn depression (2 clusters – Withdrawal and retardation, Helplessness) Jackson et al.: 30 first-order and 7 second-order factors – Social maladjustment, Functional dependency, Withdrawal, Problem-focused behaviour, Reactive depression, Frustration/resistance, Asocial behaviour
Reliability:	Inter-rater: Parker & Johnston (1989, cited in Clopton & Greene): Admission range: $r = .3–.6$ – 1 month post-discharge range: $r = .15–.98$ – 9 months post-discharge: $r = .25–.83$ Test–retest: No information available
Responsiveness:	Azouvi et al.: Significant decrease in the number of items with a score of "frequent" from pre-treatment ($n = 219$ items) to post-treatment ($n = 131$ items); $p < .01$

Comment

For many years, the KAS-R1 was one of the few instruments to provide a comprehensive overview of adjustment and social behaviour, focusing on the regulatory aspects of behaviour, thought and emotions. It was developed for people with psychiatric disorders and consequently there are limitations in its application to neurological groups. A number of research groups have examined the factor structure of the KAS-R1 within the context of TBI. Jackson et al. (1992), for example, conclude that their studies produced "factors which appear clinically relevant and correspond more closely to those 'syndromes' frequently identified in the trauma populations" (pp. 123–124). Apart from examination of construct validity, other psychometric data on the KAS-R1 with neurological groups are lacking, and even for the psychiatric group for which it was developed reviewers have been critical of its item content, reliability and validity. Clopton and Greene (1994) conclude that most of the inter-rater reliability coefficients "are so low that they raise serious concerns about the reliability of the R1 subscales" (p. 359). Moreover, the normative data are now outdated. Currently, there are available a number of recently developed, condition-specific instruments for various neurological groups with good psychometric properties that are described elsewhere in this chapter, and these probably afford a more pertinent evaluation of regulatory aspects of behaviour, thought and emotions in neurological populations.

Key references

Azouvi, P., Jokic, C., Attal, N., Denys, P., Markab, S., & Bussel, B. (1999). Carbamazepine in agitation and aggressive behaviour following severe closed-head injury: Results of an open trial. *Brain Injury*, *13*(10), 797–804.

Baird, A. D., Brown, G. G., Adams, K. M., Shatz, M. W., McSweeny, A. J., Ausman, J. I., et al. (1987). Neuropsychological deficits and real-world dysfunction in cerebral revascularization candidates. *Journal of Clinical and Experimental Neuropsychology*, *9*(4), 407–422.

Baker, K. A., Schmidt, M. F., Heinemann, A. W., Langley, M., & Miranti, S. V. (1998). The validity of the Katz Adjustment Scale among people with traumatic brain injury. *Rehabilitation Psychology*, *43*(1), 30–40.

Clopton, J. R., & Greene, R. L. (1994). Katz Adjustment Scales. In M. E. Maruish (Ed.), *The use of psychological testing for treatment planning and outcome assessment* (pp. 352–370). Hillsdale, NJ: Lawrence Erlbaum Associates, Inc.

Fabiano, R. J., & Goran, D. A. (1992). A principal component analysis of the Katz Adjustment Scale in a traumatic brain injury rehabilitation sample. *Rehabilitation Psychology*, *37*(2), 75–85.

Goran, D. A., & Fabiano, R. J. (1993). The scaling of the Katz Adjustment Scale in a traumatic brain injury rehabilitation sample. *Brain Injury*, *7*(3), 219–229.

Hogarty, G. E., & Katz, M. M. (1971). Norms of adjustment and social behavior. *Archives of General Psychiatry*, *25*(5), 470–480.

Jackson, H. F., Hopewell, C. A., Glass, C. A., Warburg, R., Dewey, M., & Ghadiali, E. (1992). The Katz Adjustment Scale: Modification for use with victims of traumatic brain and spinal injury. *Brain Injury*, *6*(2), 109–127.

Katz, M. M., & Lyerly, S. B. (1963). Methods for measuring adjustment and social behavior in the community: I. Rationale, description, discriminative validity and scale development. *Psychological Reports*, *13*(2), 503–535.

Stambrook, M., Moore, A. D., & Peters, L. C. (1990). Social behaviour and adjustment to moderate and severe traumatic brain injury: Comparison to normative and psychiatric samples. *Cognitive Rehabilitation*, *8*(1), 26–30.

Katz Adjustment Scale – Form R1

Katz and Lyerly (1963)

Name:	**Administered by:**	**Date:**

Instructions: This form is designed to give us some idea of how your relative is from day to day, his or her behaviour, and how he or she gets along with other people. It will give us some idea of what he or she has been doing. There are a number of statements on this list that describe different kinds of behaviour and mood. These include symptoms that people who have been in hospital sometimes show. Would you go through them and indicate how he or she has looked to you during the past few weeks on these things. Do not spend too much time on any one question but make sure that you check every question.

Response key:
1 = Almost never
2 = Sometimes
3 = Often
4 = Almost always

	RESPONSE
1 Has trouble sleeping	
2 Gets very self critical, starts to blame her/himself for things	
3 Cries easily	
4 Feels lonely	
5 Acts as if s/he has no interest in things	
6 Is restless	
7 Has periods where s/he can't stop moving or doing something	
8 Just sits	
9 Acts as if s/he doesn't have much energy	
10 Looks worn out	
11 Feelings get hurt easily	
12 Feels that people don't care about her/him	
13 Does the same thing over and over again without reason	
14 Passes out	
15 Gets very sad, blue	
16 Tries too hard	
17 Needs to do things very slowly to do them right	
18 Has strange fears	
19 Afraid something terrible is going to happen	
20 Gets nervous easily	
21 Jittery	
22 Worries or frets	
23 Gets sudden fright for no reason	
24 Has bad dreams	
25 Acts as if s/he sees people or things that aren't there	
26 Does strange things without reason	
27 Attempts suicide	
28 Gets angry and breaks things	
29 Talks to her/himself	
30 Acts as if s/he had no control over his emotions	

	RESPONSE
31 Laughs or cries at strange times	
32 Has mood changes without reason	
33 Has temper tantrums	
34 Gets very excited for no reason	
35 Gets very happy for no reason	
36 Acts as if s/he doesn't care about other people's feelings	
37 Thinks only of her/himself	
38 Shows her/his feelings	
39 Generous	
40 Thinks people are talking about her/him	
41 Complains of headaches, stomach trouble, other physical ailments	
42 Bossy	
43 Acts as if s/he's suspicious of people	
44 Argues	
45 Gets into fights with people	
46 Is cooperative	
47 Does the opposite of what s/he is asked	
48 Stubborn	
49 Answers when talked to	
50 Curses at people	
51 Deliberately upsets routine	
52 Resentful	
53 Envious of other people	
54 Friendly	
55 Gets annoyed easily	
56 Critical of other people	
57 Pleasant	
58 Gets along well with people	
59 Lies	
60 Gets into trouble with the law	
61 Gets drunk	
62 Is dependable	
63 Is responsible	
64 Doesn't argue (talk) back	
65 Obedient	

KATZ – Form R1 page 2 of 2

	RESPONSE
66 Shows good judgement	
67 Stays away from people	
68 Takes drugs other than recommended by hospital or clinic	
69 Shy	
70 Quiet	
71 Prefers to be alone	
72 Needs a lot of attention	
73 Behaviour is childish	
74 Acts helpless	
75 Is independent	
76 Moves about very slowly	
77 Moves about in a hurried way	
78 Clumsy; keeps bumping into things or dropping things	
79 Very quick to react to something you say or do	
80 Very slow to react	
81 Gets into peculiar positions	
82 Makes peculiar movements	
83 Hands tremble	
84 Will stay in one position for a long period	
85 Loses track of day, month or year	
86 Forgets her/his address or other places s/he knows well	
87 Remembers the names of people s/he knows well	
88 Acts as if s/he doesn't know where s/he is	
89 Remembers important things	
90 Acts as if s/he's confused about things; in a daze	
91 Acts as if s/he can't get certain things out of her/his mind	
92 Acts as if s/he can't concentrate on one thing	
93 Acts as if s/he can't make decisions	
94 Talks without making sense	
95 Hard to understand her/his words	
96 Speaks clearly	
97 Refuses to speak at all for periods of time	
98 Speaks so low you cannot hear her/him	

	RESPONSE
99 Speaks very loudly	
100 Shouts or yells for no reason	
101 Speaks very fast	
102 Speaks very slowly	
103 Acts as if s/he wants to speak but can't	
104 Keeps repeating the same idea	
105 Keeps changing from one subject to another for no reason	
106 Talks too much	
107 Says that people are talking about her/him	
108 Says that people are trying to make her/him do or think things s/he doesn't want to	
109 Talks as if s/he committed the worst sins	
110 Talks about how angry s/he is at certain people	
111 Talks about people or things s/he is very afraid of	
112 Threatens to injure certain people	
113 Threatens to tell people off	
114 Says s/he is afraid that s/he will injure somebody	
115 Says that s/he is afraid that s/he will not be able to control her/himself	
116 Talks about strange things that are going on inside her/his body	
117 Says how bad or useless s/he is	
118 Brags about how good s/he is	
119 Says the same thing over and over again	
120 Complains about people and things in general	
121 Talks about big plans s/he has for the future	
122 Says or acts as if people are after her/him	
123 Says something terrible is going to happen	
124 Believes in strange things	
125 Talks about suicide	
126 Talks about strange sexual ideas	
127 Gives advice without being asked	

Acknowledgement: From Katz, M. M., & Lyerly, S. B. (1963). Methods for measuring adjustment and social behavior in the community: I. Rationale, description, discrimination, validity, and scale development. *Psychological Reports*, *13*(2), 503–535 (Monogr. Suppl. 4-V13).

Katz Adjustment Scale – Form R1

Katz and Lyerly (1963)

Scoring procedures

Reverse scoring: required for the following items:
46, 54, 57, 58, 62, 63, 65, 66, 69, 70, 75, 87, 89, 96

Score summary

Total: _______

1 Belligerence: _______
Items:
28:
45:
50:
113:

2 Verbal expansiveness: _______
Items:
99:
100:
105:
106:
118:

3 Negativism: _______
Items:
36:
37:
46:
47:
48:
51:
56:
59:
60:

4 Helplessness: _______
Items:
3:
74:
92:
93:

5 Suspiciousness: _______
Items:
40:
43:
107:
108:

6 Anxiety: _______
Items:
18:
19:
23:
111:
122:
125:

7 Withdrawal and retardation: _______
Items:
8:
17:
70:
76:
80:
84:

8 General psychopathology: _______
Items:
5:
12:
30:
31:
32:
33:
34:
42:
44:
52:
55:
67:
71:
73:
79:
90:
91:
94:
97:
98:
110:
119:
121:
127;

9 Nervousness: _______
Items:
20:
21:
22:
38:

10 Confusion: _______
Items:
85:
86:
88:

11 Bizarreness: _______
Items:
24:
25:
26:
116:
124:

12. Hyperactivity: _______
Items:
6:
7:
13:

Neuropsychiatric Inventory (NPI)

Cummings, Mega, Gray, Rosenberg-Thompson, Carusi, and Gornbein (1994)

Source

The NPI is available from Dr Cummings (Neurobehavior Unit, Psychiatry Service (116AF), West Los Angeles VAMC, 11301 Wilshire Boulevard, Los Angeles, CA, 90073, USA; email: jcummings@mednet.ucla.edu). A brief questionnaire version of the NPI (NPI-Q) is also available (Kaufer et al., 2000) and is briefly described below.

Purpose

The NPI is a clinician rating scale based on interview with an informant. It aims to provide a quick assessment of a wide range of commonly occurring behaviours in different types of dementias, measuring both their severity and their frequency. The NPI is very widely used, particularly in Alzheimer's disease (AD) and frontotemporal dementia groups. It has been used with other neurological conditions also, including Huntington's disease (Paulsen, Ready, Hamilton, Mega, & Cummings, 2001), multiple sclerosis (Diaz-Olavarrieta, Cummings, Velazquez, & Garcia de la Cadena, 1999), Parkinson's disease (Aarsland, Cummings, & Larsen, 2001), stroke (Angelelli et al., 2004), and traumatic brain injury (Masanic, Bayley, vanReekum, & Simard, 2001).

Item description

A clinical interview with an informant using scripted questions forms the basis for rating 10 behavioural subscales: Delusions, Hallucinations, Agitation/aggression, Dysphoria, Anxiety, Euphoria, Apathy, Disinhibition, Irritability/lability and Aberrant motor activity. Later versions of the NPI (Cummings, 1997) included another two subscales: Night-time disturbances and Eating/appetite, making 12 subscales in total. Each subscale has a screening question and, if it is endorsed, then the area is explored in further detail with seven or eight supplementary questions. An example of a question for delusions is as follows: "Does the patient believe that others are stealing from her or him?"

Scale development

Development of the NPI was thorough. The selected behavioural domains were based on a comprehensive literature review, identifying representative behaviours that occur commonly in dementia. Items included also had the potential to distinguish among behavioural profiles that characterize different types of dementias, particularly AD, vascular dementia and frontotemporal dementia. Content validity was examined with a Delphi panel of 10 experts who rated scale items in terms of covering the essential elements of the behaviours. Results for 9 of the 10 subscales indicated high content validity and the remaining category was reformulated (Aberrant motor activity). The two neuro-vegetative symptoms (night-time and eating/appetite disturbances) were added because of their occurrence in patients with dementia, but Perrault, Oremus, Demers, Vida, and Wolfson (2000) reported that they are seldom used.

Administration procedures, response format and scoring

The NPI is administered in the context of an interview to an informant who has detailed knowledge of the client; that is, contact on at least a daily basis. It is also recommended that if the clinician is aware of information that contradicts the informant's ratings, then the NPI is invalid and should be discarded. In the original psychometric studies of the NPI, raters were trained by observing experienced clinicians administering several interviews and familiarizing themselves with administration instructions. This procedure is advisable for inexperienced clinicians. Administration time when all screening questions are passed is 7 to 10 minutes, but more time is required when it is necessary to ask the supplementary questions.

During the course of the interview, the informant rates severity and frequency of behaviours over the preceding month: severity on a 3-point scale: 1 (mild), 2 (moderate), 3 (severe); frequency on a 4-point scale: 1 (occasionally, less than once per week), 2 (often, about once per week), 3 (frequently, several times per week but

Data box 5.9 Descriptive data from the validation sample (Cummings et al., 1994)

	Age *M*	**Education**	**NPI** *M (SD)* **Freqency**	**NPI** *M (SD)* **Severity**	**Cut-off score**	**Sensitivity / Specificity**
Dementia (*n* = 40):	75.7 years	No information			No information	No information
Delusions			0.48 (1.11)	0.28 (0.60)		
Hallucinations			0.25 (0.71)	0.15 (0.36)		
Agitation/aggression			1.28 (1.52)	0.70 (0.82)		
Dysphoria			1.35 (1.56)	0.70 (0.82)		
Anxiety			1.40 (1.71)	0.68 (0.86)		
Euphoria			0.13 (0.52)	0.08 (0.27)		
Apathy			2.83 (1.55)	1.35 (0.83)		
Disinhibition			0.65 (1.23)	0.35 (0.00)		
Irritability/lability			1.28 (1.58)	0.58 (0.81)		
Aberrant motor behaviour			1.25 (1.8)	0.41 (0.64)		

less than every day), 4 (very frequent, once or more per day/continuously). A number of scores can be derived for each subscale, with higher scores indicating greater problems: severity (range 1–3), frequency (range 1–4) and a total score, obtained by multiplying the severity and frequency scores (range 0–12). A global score can also be obtained by summing the total scores for each subscale (range 0–144 or 0–120 for the 10-domain version), although the authors caution that this score represents the amalgamation of very disparate behaviours and therefore should only be regarded as "an imprecise guide".

Psychometric properties

An overview of the psychometric properties of the NPI is available in Cummings (1997) and a critical review is provided by Perrault et al. (2000). The initial measurement characteristics of the NPI were examined in two samples (Cummings et al., 1994). A control group comprised 40 residents of a retirement community in Southern California, USA. Family members of 40 people with a broad range of severity of different dementia subtypes (including AD, vascular and frontotemporal dementias; age range 56–90 years) completed the NPI (descriptive data shown in Data box 5.9).

The patient group was recruited from either dementia clinics or ongoing clinical trials. A subset of 20 informants was retested 3 weeks later. Inter-rater reliability ($n = 45$) was established using seven raters who formed pairs, with one member conducting the interview. A factor analysis was reported by Cummings et al. (2006) using the baseline data from 275 patients with dementia recruited for their clinical trial of donepezil. A five-factor solution was optimal (percentage of variance was not reported): Factor 1: Delusions, hallucinations and sleep abnormalities; Factor 2: Agitation, irritability and aberrant motor behaviour; Factor 3: Depression, anxiety and apathy; Factor 4: Euphoria and disinhibition; Factor 5: Appetite and eating disorders. Responsiveness of the NPI has been demonstrated in clinical trials. Cummings et al. (2006) reported on 120 patients participating in the above trial. NPI scores showed a significant improvement after 20 weeks of treatment. Results from Cummings et al. (1994), except where otherwise indicated, are shown in Box 5.13.

Derivates of the NPI: Neuropsychiatric Inventory – Questionnaire version (NPI-Q; Kaufer et al., 2000)

The NPI-Q was developed to facilitate administration in everyday clinical practice settings. Administration time for the NPI-Q is 5 minutes or less. It comprises 12 items (covering the 10 NPI domains and 2 additional items: night-time behavioural disturbance and appetite/eating disturbances). Item wording uses the screening questions of the NPI, which are written onto a two-page self-administered questionnaire. Informants circle "yes" or "no" to each item, and a severity rating is made to the endorsed items: 1 (mild), 2 (moderate), 3 (severe). Total NPI-Q scores range from 0 to 36, with higher scores indicating greater symptom severity. Additionally, for each item a caregiver distress rating is made from 0 (none) to 5. Total NPI-Q distress scores range from 0 to 60, with higher scores indicating greater caregiver distress. Informants of a consecutive series of 60 people with AD were administered the standard NPI and the NPI-Q. There was a high degree of association between the NPI (total score) and NPI-Q ($r = .91$), as well as significant correlation between the Mini-Mental State Examination and the NPI-Q ($r = -.41$). Caregiver distress on the NPI-Q and the total (severity) score on the NPI-Q were highly correlated ($r = .93$). A subset ($n = 15$) was also asked to complete another NPI-Q later the same day (~ 7 hours later), with $r = .80$.

Box 5.13

Validity:	Content: Formally established with Delphi panel Criterion: *Concurrent:* with BEHAVE-AD: Severity: $r = .71$, Frequency: $r = .66$, Total: $r = .66$ – NPI Dysphoria Scale with Hamilton Depression Rating Scale (Hamilton Rating Scale for Depression): Severity: $r = .59$, Frequency: $r = .70$, Total: $r = .62$ Construct: *Internal consistency:* Cronbach alpha: Overall: .88, Severity: .87, Frequency: .88 *Factor analysis:* Cummings et al. (2006): Factor 1: Delusions, hallucinations and sleep abnormalities; Factor 2: Agitation, irritability and aberrant motor behaviour; Factor 3: Depression, anxiety and apathy; Factor 4: Euphoria and disinhibition; Factor 5: Appetite and eating disorders
Reliability:	Inter-rater: Percentage agreement: Severity: range 89.4–100%, Frequency: range 93.6–100% Test–retest: 3 weeks: Severity: Overall: $r = .86$ (range: $r = .51$–1.00), Frequency: Overall: $r = .79$ (range: $r = .51$–.98)
Responsiveness:	Cummings et al. (2006): Baseline $M = 31.4$ ($SD = 15.9$), post-treatment change from baseline: $M = -8.2$ ($p < .001$), effect size $d = .52$ – effect sizes for 3/5 factors were $d = .34$ (Factors 1 and 2) to $d = .39$ (Factor 3)

Comment

The NPI is a well-respected instrument and is widely accepted as eminently suitable for examining personality and behavioural changes associated with progressive brain disorders. The developmental process of the NPI was thorough, lending support to its content validity. Perrault et al. (2000) conducted a careful review of the literature on the NPI in AD and concluded that although reports of the measurement characteristics of the NPI are satisfactory, there are some limitations in the methods used and further work is warranted. Nonetheless, testimony to the success of the NPI is its widespread use, translations into and validations for many languages, and inclusion in clinical trials to measure treatment efficacy.

Key references

Aarsland, D., Cummings, J. L., & Larsen, J. P. (2001). Neuropsychiatric differences between Parkinson's disease with dementia and Alzheimer's disease. *International Journal of Geriatric Psychiatry*, *16*, 184–191.

Angelelli, P., Paolucci, S., Bivona, U., Piccardi, L., Ciurli, P., Cantagallo, A., et al. (2004). Development of neuropsychiatric symptoms in post-stroke patients: A cross-sectional study. *Acta Psychiatrica Scandinavica*, *110*, 55–63.

Cummings, J. L. (1997). The Neuropsychiatric Inventory: Assessing psychopathology in dementia patients. *Neurology*, *48*(5, Suppl. 6), S10–S16.

Cummings, J. L., McRae, T., Zhang, R., & The Donepezil-Sertraline Study Group. (2006). Effects of donepezil on neuropsychiatric symptoms in patients with dementia and severe behavioral disorders. *American Journal of Geriatric Psychiatry*, *14*(7), 605–612.

Cummings, J. L., Mega, M., Gray, K., Rosenberg-Thompson, S., Carusi, D. A., & Gornbein, J. (1994). The Neuropsychiatric Inventory: Comprehensive assessment of psychopathology in dementia. *Neurology*, *44*(12), 2308–2314.

Diaz-Olavarrieta, C., Cummings, J. L., Velazquez, J., & Garcia de la Cadena, C. (1999). Neuropsychiatric manifestations of multiple sclerosis. *Journal of Neuropsychiatry and Clinicial Neurosciences*, *11*(1), 51–57.

Kaufer, D. I., Cummings, J. L., Ketchel, P., Smith, V., MacMillan, A., Shelley, T., et al. (2000). Validation of the NPI-Q, a brief clinical form of the Neuropsychiatric Inventory. *Journal of Neuropsychiatry and Clinical Neurosciences*, *12*(2), 233–239.

Masanic, C. A., Bayley, M. T., vanReekum, R., & Simard, M. (2001). Open-label study of donepezil in traumatic brain injury. *Archives of Physical Medical Rehabilitation*, *82*, 896–901.

Paulsen, J. S., Ready, R. E., Hamilton, J. M., Mega, M. S., & Cummings, J. L. (2001). Neuropsychiatric aspects of Huntington's disease. *Journal of Neurology, Neurosurgery, and psychiatry*, *71*, 310–314.

Perrault, A., Oremus, M., Demers, L., Vida, S., & Wolfson, C. (2000). Review of outcome measurement instruments in Alzheimer's disease drug trials: Psychometric properties of behaviour and mood scales. *Journal of Geriatric Psychiatry and Neurology*, *13*, 181–196.

Neuropsychology Behavior and Affect Profile (NBAP)

Nelson, Satz, and D'Elia (1994)

Source

The NBAP is commercially produced and available from Mind Garden Press (http://www.mindgarden.com).

Purpose

The NBAP is a rating scale, completed by an informant or by the person with brain impairment. It was developed specifically to measure personality and affective changes after brain impairment. The NBAP was originally designed for people with dementia (Nelson et al., 1989), and was subsequently validated with other neurological populations, including stroke (Nelson et al., 1993a; Nelson, Mitrushina, Satz, Sowa, & Cohen, 1993b) and traumatic brain injury (TBI; Nelson, Debring, Satz, & Uchiyama, 1998).

Item description

The NBAP comprises 106 randomly ordered items, with 91 items contributing to five clinical scales: Inappropriateness (14 items, e.g., "My relative has habits that seem odd and different"), Indifference (15 items, e.g., "My relative seems unusually unaware of any existing health problem"), Depression (16 items, e.g., "My relative often seems unhappy"), Pragnosia (i.e., defective social/pragmatic communication; 19 items, e.g., "My relative often seems to 'miss the point' of the discussion"), and Mania (27 items, e.g., "My relative is excessively talkative"). In addition, a set of 15 "Neutral" items (e.g., "My relative enjoys gardening") is included to guard against response set. The NBAP comprises two subscales (Before and Now) and two forms (Form O for an "other" informant and Form S for self-rating).

Scale development

Development of the NBAP arose in response to the dearth of available measures to examine non-cognitive changes in behaviour and affect resulting from acquired brain impairment. A systematic and thorough approach was used in its construction. Item development occurred over a 2-year period with a team of six members representing neuropsychology and neurolinguistics. A set of 106 items met consensual agreement and was subjected to further study. Content relevance was investigated using six raters who blind-sorted items into five fixed categories. A total of 66 items had agreement from five of the six judges. Although empirical and psychometric support was provided for this 66-item version in the initial validation study (Nelson et al., 1989), the internal

Data box 5.10 Descriptive data from the standardization sample (Nelson et al., 1989)

	Age *M* (*SD*)	**Education** *M* (*SD*)	**NBAP** *M* (*SD*) **"Before"**	**NBAP** *M* (*SD*) **"Now"**	**Cut-off score**	**Sensitivity / Specificity**
Control (*n* = 88):	70.7 (5.37)	14.1(2.86)			No information	No information
Indifference			10.3 (17.8)	11.5 (18.8)		
Inappropriateness			11.0 (17.9)	11.8 (19.5)		
Pragnosia			13.7 (16.0)	14.9 (17.1)		
Depression			10.9 (14.5)	14.3 (17.4)		
Mania			13.8 (13.4)	14.4 (12.6)		
Dementia clinic referrals (*n* = 61):	73.3 (12.2)	12.98 (8.2)				
Indifference			11.6 (15.8)	41.0 (28.1)		
Inappropriateness			14.0 (20.4)	40.5 (25.4)		
Pragnosia			15.5 (15.7)	47.6 (24.2)		
Depression			17.4 (20.7)	51.9 (28.0)		
Mania			14.4 (17.6)	12.8 (12.1)		

consistencies of a number of scales were appreciably higher with the original item pool. This was replicated in a stroke sample (Nelson et al., 1993b) and the authors consequently recommended the larger item pool be used when deriving scale scores. Studies in three clinical populations raised issues about the Mania scale, in which a relatively high number of items were poor discriminators, and the authors considered that additional research on that scale was warranted (Nelson et al., 1998).

Administration procedures, response format and scoring

The NBAP is designed either for self-completion or for completion by an informant who knew the person premorbidly. Items were written to be understood by people with less than 6th grade education. The NBAP is completed twice – once rating the person as he or she was before the onset of the neurological condition (Before version) and then in terms of his or her current functioning (Now version). The manual advises that administration time is within 20 minutes for most people.

Items are endorsed ("yes") if they are true; that is, occur typically or often. The number of endorsed items is summed for each scale (the five Before and five Now scales) and then converted to either percentages or T scores ($M = 50$, $SD = 10$) using data from the manual. Some authors have also used a mean percentage score of the five scales to derive a Full Scale NBAP score (e.g., Groom, Shaw, O'Connor, Howard, & Pickens, 1998; Mathias & Coats, 1999).

Normative and comparative data are provided in the manual, stratified by neurological group: dementia (61 patients and 88 controls), stroke (42 patients and 42 controls) and TBI ($n = 42$).

Psychometric properties

The initial standardization sample consisted of the relatives of 61 people referred to a dementia or neurobehavioural clinic in Los Angeles, California, USA for investigation of symptoms of dementia (Nelson et al., 1989 – descriptive data shown in Data box 5.10). Discriminant validity was examined, comparing the clinical group with 88 healthy control participants recruited from a retirement centre at Camarillo, California. Internal consistency of the NBAP was evaluated and temporal stability over a 1-month period examined in a subset ($n = 39$). Groom et al. (1998) studied relatives of 153 people with TBI, recruited mainly from local brain injury support groups in the Midwestern states, USA, who were $M = 4.2$ years post-trauma (range: 1 month to 40 years), 80% of whom had sustained moderate or severe injuries. A small comparison group comprising relatives of 27 healthy college students was also examined, and the General Functioning Scale of the Family Assessment Device (FAD) and Perceived Stress Scale (PSS) were administered in addition to the NBAP.

Box 5.14

Validity:	Criterion: *Concurrent:* Groom et al.: with TBI, Total NBAP score with FAD: $r = .54$ (scale range $r = .29 - .44$)
	Construct: *Internal consistency:* Cronbach alpha: Nelson et al. (1989): *Before* (66-item set) ratings: Pragnosia: .49, Inappropriateness: .59, Indifference: .72, Mania: .74, Depression: .78 – using 91 items increased coefficients by about 2 points for Pragnosia, Inappropriateness and Depression scales – *Now* ratings: Inappropriateness: .68, Mania: .70, Pragnosia: .75, Depression: .78, Indifference: .82, – using 91 items increased coefficients for Inappropriateness: .81, Depression: .81, and Pragnosia: .80 scales
	– Groom et al.: Cronbach alpha: *Now-Informant* (66-item set): Total: .92 (scale range: .79–.81)
	Discriminant: Nelson et al. (1989): *Now* scores: statistically significant differences between dementia and control groups on all scales except Mania: Indifference $F = 51.52$, Inappropriateness $F = 49.85$, Depression $F = 107.48$, Pragnosia $F = 93.86$, all $p < .001$)
	Groom et al.: Total score: TBI $M = 39$ ($SD = 20$) vs controls $M = 16$ ($SD = 11$; $t = 8.6, p < .01$. Similar results for all scales except Mania
Reliability:	Inter-rater: No information available
	Test–retest: Nelson et al. (1989) 1 month, using 66-item set: *Before* range: ICC: .97–.99; *Now* range: ICC: .92–.97
Responsiveness:	No information available

Correlation coefficients with the PSS were low (Total $r = .28$, scale range $r = .12 - .29$). Results of the above studies are shown in Box 5.14.

Comment

At the time the NBAP was developed, assessment of non-cognitive changes after ABI was a relatively neglected area. The NBAP was one of the first standardized rating scales specifically constructed for this purpose, thus filling a major gap. It remains one of the few measures that has been standardized for a stroke population. The NBAP has a number of psychometric strengths, and particularly noteworthy is its excellent temporal stability, and evidence for content and construct validity. At 106 items, the NBAP is lengthy, but attempts to reduce item content using the 66 items identified in the content validity study compromised its internal stability. The report of Groom et al. with a TBI sample however, showed high internal consistency using the 66-item set. Features of the NBAP that make it particularly attractive are its item content and format. The initial item selection process was carefully conducted and the five scales provide a comprehensive selection of commonly occurring patterns of behavioural and affective changes. In particular, the inclusion of the Depression scale assists in differential diagnosis from apathy (see the Indifference scale) within a single instrument, as well as examination of the interplay between emotional and organic factors. Additionally, the model of comparing measures representing two time points (premorbid vs post-onset) was an important innovation – the premorbid ratings providing the essential comparison standard against which changes in behaviour, affect and personality need to be measured, at least in the early to mid stages after onset.

Key references

Groom, K. N., Shaw, T. G., O'Connor, M. E., Howard, N. I., & Pickens, A. (1998). Neurobehavioral symptoms and family functioning in traumatically brain-injured adults. *Archives of Clinical Neuropsychology*, *13*(8), 695–711.

Mathias, J. L., & Coats, J. L. (1999). Emotional and cognitive sequelae to mild traumatic brain injury. *Journal of Clinical and Experimental Neuropsychology*, *21*(2), 200–215.

Nelson, L. D., Cicchetti, D., Satz, P., Stern, S., Sowa, M., Cohen, S., et al. (1993a). Emotional sequelae of stroke. *Neuropsychology*, *7*(4), 553–560.

Nelson, L. D., Drebing, C., Satz, P., & Uchiyama, C. (1998). Personality change in head trauma: A validity study of the Neuropsychology Behavior and Affect Profile. *Archives of Clinical Neuropsychology*, *13*(6), 549–560.

Nelson, L. D., Mitrushina, M., Satz, P., Sowa, M., & Cohen, S. (1993b). Cross-validation of the Neuropsychology Behavior and Affect Profile in stroke patients. *Psychological Assessment*, *5*(3), 374–376.

Nelson, L., Satz, P., & D'Elia, L. F. (1994). *Neuropsychology Behavior and Affect Profile (Manual)*. Menlo Park, CA: Mind Garden Press.

Nelson, L. D., Satz, P., Mitrushina, M., Van Gorp, W., Cicchetti, D., Lewis, R., et al. (1989). Development and validation of the Neuropsychology Behavior and Affect Profile. *Psychological Assessment*, *1*(4), 266–272.

Overt Aggression Scale – Modified for Neurorehabilitation (OAS-MNR)

Alderman, Knight, and Morgan (1997)

Source

The OAS-MNR is presented in an appendix to Alderman et al. (1997). It includes instructions and operational description of severity levels, which are reproduced below.

Purpose

This observational rating scale is designed to assess the type, severity and frequency of aggressive behaviour in people with acquired brain impairment (ABI), as well as the antecedents and interventions surrounding the aggressive acts. It is also intended to facilitate a functional behavioural analysis of aggressive behaviours necessary for designing a rehabilitation programme. Alderman et al. (1997) have used the OAS-MNR in a variety of neurological conditions, including hypoxia, stroke and traumatic brain injury.

Item description

Aggressive behaviours are classified using one of four categories that are hierarchically arranged from least to most aggressive as follows: Verbal aggression, Aggression against objects, Aggression against self, and Aggression against others. Within each category there are four levels of severity, organized from low to high. Verbal aggression, for example, ranges from "shouts angrily, but not directed to another person" to "makes clear threats of violence". Additionally, the OAS-MNR documents the antecedents to the aggressive behaviour (18 categories, which are recorded by codes), along with the interventions that were implemented (one of 14 possible types).

Scale development

Development of the OAS-MNR is based on the original OAS devised by Yudofsky, Silver, Jackson, Endicott, and Williams (1986) for use with adults and children in inpatient psychiatric settings. Those investigators were critical of existing instruments (self-report questionnaires or clinician rating scales such as the Brief Psychiatric Rating Scale), which contained items to rate aggression, but did not assess the frequency, type or severity of aggressive behaviours. Moreover, Alderman et al. (1997) point out that it is the configuration of these components that requires analysis – a simple frequency count of aggressive behaviours is insufficient. Thus, there is a need to distinguish between those behaviours that are low in frequency but serious in consequence, and conversely those high in frequency but without substantial impact. Further, interventions may differentially affect the severity and frequency components. The refinements made by Alderman and colleagues to adapt the OAS for people with ABI in a rehabilitation setting included increasing the categories of antecedent behaviours preceding the aggressive act (e.g., given a direct verbal prompt to comply with an instruction) and expanding the range of interventions to manage aggressive behaviour (e.g., physical distraction).

Administration procedures, response format and scoring

The OAS-MNR is completed following direct observation of an aggressive act. Yudofsky and colleagues (1986) highlighted the need for initial staff training, monitoring of and feedback about their ratings in order to ensure reliability and validity. Alderman, Davies, Jones, and McDonnel (1999) developed a staff training programme, which is described in their paper. In cases where aggression is frequent, the authors advise the use of a second clinician for recording purposes. Administration time varies according to the method used; for example the time-sampling procedures to document aggressive behaviours for the reliability study involved minimum observation periods of 30 minutes, with each participant having more than 20 hours of observation. Completion time for the actual recording form is, however, brief.

Scoring the behaviours for the OAS-MNR adopted the method of weighted ratings developed by Kay, Wolkenfield, and Murrill (1988). The four categories of aggressive behaviour were ranked in terms of their severity and given weights, as follows: Verbal aggression was judged the least severe category and was assigned a weight of 1 (score range 1–4, relating to the four levels within each category); Aggression against objects was considered next most severe and levels were multiplied by 2 (range 2–8); then Aggression against self, with ratings multiplied by 3 (range 3–12); and finally Aggression against others was considered to be the most severe and levels were multiplied by 4 (range 4–16). Thus the score for any single behaviour, depending on the type and severity, can range between 1 and 16. For clinical purposes, a total score is not calculated.

Psychometric properties

Inter-rater reliability of the original OAS had been established (ICC = .87; Yudofsky et al., 1986). In relation to ABI, Alderman et al. (1997) reported on an initial psychometric study with 18 people with very severe brain injury who demonstrated "challenging behaviours of sufficient severity to prevent rehabilitation in conventional settings" (p. 507) and were resident in two high dependency hospital wards, in Northhampton, UK. Validity was established by using data from the interventions consequent on the aggression. Prior to the study, 20 clinicians from the hospital were asked to rank order the interventions from the least to most intrusive. Severity of OAS-MNR ratings was then correlated with intrusiveness of the interventions. Examination of inter-rater reliability used two trained raters who observed the people simultaneously and then completed the OAS-MNR independently. Information is only reported on summary scores for overall severity, type and so forth, rather than at the individual category level. Results of this study are shown in Box 5.15.

Box 5.15

Validity:	Criterion *Concurrent:* Severity with intrusiveness of the intervention: $r = .64$
Reliability:	Inter-rater: Severity ratings: $k = .94$, type of aggression: $k = 1.00$, antecedents: $k = .74$, interventions: $k = .75$ Test–retest: No information available
Responsiveness:	No information available

Comment

The OAS-MNR is a more complex instrument than the standard rating scale, but this is in part a function of producing an instrument that measures contextual factors surrounding the aggression act (antecedents and interventions), in addition to the frequency and type of aggression. This feature makes the OAS-MNR a superior instrument. Consequently, the information yielded is sufficiently detailed to provide the basis for an individually tailored therapeutic programme. Because it is an observational tool, administration time to collect data is a lengthy process, as it generally is for all observational scales. Moreover, training is required to use the OAS-MNR. The training programme developed by Alderman and colleagues (1999) is described in detail in their paper. It is clearly effective, given the excellent inter-rater reliability those investigators were able to achieve, at least at the summary score level. Further information on other psychometric properties, however, is needed. One of the strengths of the OAS-MNR is its application in a clinical setting to standardize observations and plan remediation programmes. Alderman, Knight, and Henman (2002) have also used the OAS-MNR for clinical audit purposes, where they note that the OAS-MNR "may be helpful in highlighting resource needs within a service, and where such resources should be distributed . . . [and] to help set boundaries regarding the type and severity of challenging behaviour a service can safely manage" (p. 487).

Key references

Alderman, N., Davies, J. A., Jones, C., & McDonnel, P. (1999). Reduction of severe aggressive behaviour in acquired brain injury: Case studies illustrating clinical use of the OAS-MNR in the management of challenging behaviours. *Brain Injury*, *13*(9), 669–704.

Alderman, N., Knight, C., & Henman, C. (2002). Aggressive behaviour observed within a neurobehavioral rehabilitation service: Utility of the OAS-MNR in clinical audit and applied research. *Brain Injury*, *16*(6), 469–489.

Alderman, N., Knight, C., & Morgan, C. (1997). Use of a modified version of the Overt Aggression Scale in the measurement and assessment of aggressive behaviours following brain injury. *Brain Injury*, *11*(7), 503–523.

Kay, S. R., Wolkenfield, F., & Murrill, L. M. (1988). Profiles of aggression among psychiatric patients: II. Covariates and predictors. *Journal of Nervous and Mental Disease*, *176*, 547–557.

Yudofsky, S. C., Silver, J. M., Jackson, W., Endicott, J., & Williams, D. (1986). The Overt Aggression Scale for the objective rating of verbal and physical aggression. *The American Journal of Psychiatry*, *143*(1), 35–39.

Overt Aggression Scale – Modified for Neurorehabilitation

Alderman, Knight, and Morgan (1997)

Instructions

Instructions for using the recording form:

The OAS-MNR consists of three parts. Parts 1 and 2 are for reference; Part 3 is the recording form itself. Part 1 defines the four acts of aggression (verbal, physical against objects, physical against self and physical against others), and provides the anchor points for the rating of severity (1–4). Part 2 defines the codes used on the recording form to specify antecedents and interventions used. Part 3 is the recording form on which the rating/codes pertaining to any act of aggression are entered.

More detailed information concerning the three parts of the scale follows.

Part 1 (Reference Form 1): Categories of aggression:

There are four categories of behaviour:

1. Verbal aggression.
2. Physical aggression against objects.
3. Physical aggression against self.
4. Physical aggression against others.

The four categories are ranked in order of level of severity. "Physical aggression against others" is the category of behaviour rated as most severe.

Each category has four levels, ranked in order from the least severe to the most severe behaviour within that category. Therefore, the severity of behaviours has been numbered on a level system from 1 to 4, with 1 being the least severe behaviour of that category, and 4 the most severe. For example, if a patient should kick and push someone, the code for this would be "Physical aggression against other people (PP), level 2."

Part 2 (Reference Form 2): Codes for antecedents and interventions:

At present there are 18 antecedents all numbered (coded) from 1 to 25. There are two sets. The first set (numbered 1–3) are not obvious triggers of verbal/physical aggression in their own right. However, they may be a contributing factor in the event of any aggression. The second set of antecedents (numbered 11–25) are objective and overt antecedents that are directly observed to precede aggression.

At present there are 14 categories for recording possible interventions made following any act of aggression. Each intervention has been coded with a letter; therefore, intervention codes range from A to N. For example, the code for "time-out-on-the-spot" (TOOTS) is A.

Part 3: Instructions for completing the recording form:

Date/time: For each event/episode the date and the time when the aggressive behaviour was observed will be recorded.

1. Recording the behaviour(s):

a) Each episode of behaviour is to be recorded on the form. An episode of behaviour may be one or more behaviours. Each event/episode of behaviour(s) is to be recoded on one row of the table. Therefore, a new row must be started for each subsequent event/episode.

b) The behaviour should be recorded by first finding the appropriate box; for example, if someone bangs their head the box for this will be "Physical aggression against self, level 2".

c) This behaviour is then indicated by writing in the appropriate box the codes for the antecedent(s) observed, and the intervention(s) used.

d) If there are two behaviours, but only one method of intervention, then the most severe behaviour should be recorded. For example, if a patient made directed verbal threats toward another person ("Verbal aggression, level 3") and at the same time made a threatening gesture toward the person ("Physical aggression against other people, level 1"), only the latter would be recorded on the form as physical aggression against other people is ranked as more severe than verbal aggression. Remember, the rank order for the four categories of aggression is as indicated in Reference Form 1 (Verbal aggression, Physical aggression against objects, Physical aggression against self, Physical aggression against other people).

2. Recording the antecedent(s):

a) Antecedents are to be recorded by placing the code in the box indicating the behaviour. If for example the antecedent observed before throwing a chair was a direct verbal prompt to attend a session, then the code for this would be 11, and 11 would be marked in box headed "Physical aggression, level 4".

b) At least one of the antecedents from the second set will always be recorded (numbered 11–25). In addition, one or more of the first set of antecedents (numbered 1–3) may also be recorded. For example, if a patient was obviously agitated (23, second set) and at the same time there was another client constantly screaming and shouting in the background (2, first set), this would be recorded as 2, 23. Codes from the first set of antecedents (if applicable) should always be recorded first. Where possible, codes should be recorded to reflect the order of antecedents leading up to the act of aggression. For example, codes entered as follows 1, 2, 11 indicates that the act of aggression occurred during a structured activity (1), the environment was noisy (2), and that immediately preceding the aggressive act the client had been given a direct verbal prompt to comply with an instruction (11).

c) Particular attention should be given to the antecedent coded 1; that is, whether the patient was engaged in some structured activity when the act of aggression was observed. On each occasion of recording the antecedent, if the code 1 has not been marked in the box, then this will be an indication the behaviour occurred in unstructured time.

d) Where there may be one or more antecedents these should be recorded in the order in which they occurred (see b above).

e) Antecedents not specified on the coding sheet should be recorded as 25 in the appropriate box, and a description should be written on the back of the record form.

3. Recording the intervention(s)

a) The intervention is recorded using the same principle as the antecedents; that is, record in the appropriate box the type(s) of intervention used. For example, if a verbal threat directed toward a member of staff was managed using "time-out-on-the-spot" (TOOTS), then A would be recorded under "Verbal aggression, level 3".

b) Where there are multiple (consecutive) interventions, record them in the order in which they were used. For example, A, B, D indicates that the act of aggression was initially "timed-out-on-the-spot" (A), then the patient was spoken to (B), and finally the patient was physically restrained by staff (D).

c) Where the person may be on an additional special behaviour modification programme, record the code L for "special programmes".

Overt Aggression Scale – Modified for Neurorehabilitation

Alderman, Knight, and Morgan (1997)

Reference Forms

Note: Remember the "2-second rule" – if at least 2 seconds separates aggressive acts then each of these needs to be recorded separately; if several acts occur simultaneously, rate the most severe (as in the order indicated below).

REFERENCE FORM 1: BEHAVIOURS

	Verbal aggression (VA; ranked in severity by content and direction at some other person)
1	Makes loud noises, shouts angrily, is clearly not directed at some other person (e.g., "Bloody hell!")
2	Makes mild personal insults clearly directed at some other person but does not include swearing/offensive sexual comments (e.g., "You are stupid!", "idiot")
3	Swearing, use of foul language, moderate threats directed at others or self (e.g., "Fuck off you bastard!")
4	Makes clear threats of violence directed towards others or self (e.g., "I'm going to kill you!") or requests help to control self (i.e., expresses anxieties that they will engage in aggressive act beyond own control unless staff make some immediate intervention)

	Physical aggression against objects (PO)
1	Slams doors, scatters clothing, makes a mess in clear response to some antecedent
2	Throws objects down (without some other person(s) at risk of being hit, regardless of intention, by the object(s) thrown), kicks furniture without breaking it, marks the wall
3	Breaks objects, smashes windows
4	Sets fire, throws objects dangerously (i.e., some other person(s) is at risk of being hit, regardless of intention, by the objects(s) thrown but is not actually hit – if the object thrown down comes into contact, code using PP2, PP3 or PP4 depending on the outcome)

	Physical aggression against self (PS)
1	Picks and scratches skin, hits self, pulls hair (with no or minor injury only)
2	Bangs head, hits fist into objects, throws self onto floor or into objects (hurts self without serious injury)
3	Inflicts small cuts or bruises, minor burns to self
4	Mutilates self, causes deep cuts, bites that bleed, internal injury, fracture, loss of consciousness, loss of teeth

	Physical aggression against other people (PP)
1	Makes threatening gesture that is clearly directed towards some other person, swings at people, grabs at clothes
2	Strikes, kicks, pushes, pulls hair (without significant injury to person(s) aggression directed at)
3	Attacks others, causing mild to moderate physical injury (bruises, sprains, welts) to person(s) aggression directed at
4	Causes severe physical injury (broken bones, deep lacerations, internal injury) to person(s) aggression directed at

REFERENCE FORM 2: (i) ANTECEDENTS

Set 1 (coded 1–3): Contributing factors

1. Structured activity (i.e., formal rehabilitation session [including hygiene programme], meal times, toileting)
2. Noisy environment
3. Has had an epileptic fit within the last 24 hours

Set 2 (coded 11–25): Observed directly before aggression

11. Given direct verbal prompt to comply with instruction (e.g., "Your task is to . . .")
12. Given verbal guidance/advice to assist completion of task/activity
13. Given verbal/visual feedback about performance (e.g., token system, special programmes)
14. Direct response to other client's verbal behaviour (this may or may not be specifically directed at the client for whom the recording has been made)
15. Request explicitly denied by another person (i.e., told "no")
16. Any other verbal interactions (e.g., general conversation)
17. Physical guidance/facilitation (including TOOTS-assist) to complete a task
18. Direct response to other client's physically aggressive behaviour when this is directed at them
19. Direct response to other client's physically aggressive behaviour when this is directed at another person
20. During restraint/while being assisted to seclusion
21. Given item (e.g., food, therapy materials)
22. Purposeful behaviour is "TOOTS" by person(s) at whom it is directed
23. Obviously agitated/distressed
24. No obvious antecedent
25. Other (specify on back of individual record form)

REFERENCE FORM 2: (ii) INTERVENTIONS

A. Aggression, ignored, includes use of time-out-on-the-spot (TOOTS)
B. Talking to patient (e.g., prompted to "stop being aggressive" or used verbal distraction)
C. Closer observation
D. Holding patient (physical restraint)
E. Immediate medication given by mouth
F. Immediate medication given by injection
G. Isolation without seclusion (time out)
H. Seclusion
I. Use of other restraints
J. Injury requires immediate medical treatment for patients
K. Injury requires immediate treatment for other person
L. Special programme
M. Physical distraction (leading the patient away from the situation)
N. Other (record on the back of form)

Acknowledgement: From Alderman, N. et al. (1997). Use of a modified version of the Overt Aggression Scale in the measurement and assessment of aggressive behaviours following brain injury. *Brain Injury*, *11*(7), 503–523, table and text reproduced with permission of Taylor & Francis, http://www.tandf.co.uk/journals/titles/10799893.asp.

Overt Aggression Scale – Modified for Neurorehabilitation

Alderman, Knight, and Morgan (1997)

Record Form

Name:	**Administered by:**

AGGRESSION		VERBAL AGGRESSION **VA**				PHYSICAL AGGRESSION AGAINST OBJECTS **PO**				PHYSICAL AGGRESSION AGAINST SELF **PS**				PHYSICAL AGGRESSION AGAINST OTHER PEOPLE **PP**			
LEVELS		1	2	3	4	1	2	3	4	1	2	3	4	1	2	3	4
DATE/TIME	ANT./INTER.																
	A																
	I																
	A																
	I																
	A																
	I																
	A																
	I																
	A																
	I																

Note: A = antecendent; I = intervention

Description of antecedents/interventions where not specified on coding sheet

Date/Time	Behaviour				Description of antecedent and/or intervention
	VA	PO	PS	PP	

Note: Under the behaviour heading, select the correct column and indicate this by filling in the level number.

Overt Behaviour Scale (OBS)

Kelly, Todd, Simpson, Kremer, and Martin (2006)

Source

The OBS rating scale and manual are available from Dr Kelly (Diverge Consulting Inc., PO Box 243, Seddon West, Victoria 3011, Australia; http://www.diverge.org.au). The structure of the rating scale is reproduced below.

Purpose

The OBS is primarily a clinician rating scale, although it can also be used as an observational instrument. It was designed to measure common challenging behaviours, suitable for people with acquired brain impairment (ABI) living in the community. In the validation studies, the OBS was mainly used with people with traumatic brain injury (TBI), but people with hypoxia, stroke and other neurological conditions were also included.

Item description

The OBS contains nine categories, within eight of which contain three to six hierarchical levels (making a total of 34 levels across the scale): Verbal aggression (4 levels), Aggression against objects (4 levels), Aggression against self (4 levels), Aggression against people (4 levels), Inappropriate sexual behaviour (6 levels), Perseveration/repetition (3 levels), Wandering/absconding (3 levels), Inappropriate social behaviour (5 levels). The final category, Lack of initiative, contains a single level. The hierarchy of levels within the categories represent increasing severity. For example, the five levels of the Inappropriate social behaviour scale are as follows: socially awkward, nuisance/annoyance, non-compliant/oppositional, unlawful behaviour, presents a danger/risk to self/others.

Scale development

The OBS is an extension of the Overt Aggression Scale (Yudofsky, Silver, Jackson, Endicott, & Williams, 1986) and its modification for people with ABI participating in neurorehabilitation, the OAS-MNR (Alderman, Knight, & Morgan, 1997; also described in this chapter). The OBS retained the four aggression categories of the OAS/OAS-MNR and developed an additional five categories, using a multi-stage procedure. Initially, a review was conducted on 543 referrals over a 5-year period to the ABI Behaviour Consultancy, in Melbourne, Australia. All of the overt and challenging behaviours exhibited by the clients were classified into the four aggression categories of the OAS/OAS-MNR, as well as an additional five categories, which, in total, accounted for approximately 90% of the behaviours. Experienced clinicians were used as judges to rank order the behaviours in terms of their severity. This was successfully achieved for all categories except Lack of initiative (examining *absence* of overt behaviours) and a dichotomous classification was thus developed for that category (presence/absence of the behaviour). The nine categories and severity level items were then reviewed by eight clinicians experienced in ABI case management. Only one of the categories (Socially inappropriate behaviour) was considered problematic and further developmental work was conducted on that category. Data reduction procedures resulted in a total of 34 severity levels for the nine categories of the OBS. This final set was rated by a new group of 20 clinicians previously unfamiliar with the OBS. Agreement was high and the overall kappa coefficient was excellent ($k = .94$).

Administration procedures, response format and scoring

Instructions for administering and scoring the OBS are provided in the manual. No specific recommendation is made regarding training in use of the scale. The OBS categories are designed to be administered in a set order so that "double-counting" of behaviours that may fit multiple categories is avoided (e.g., sexual behaviours are rated in the specific Sexually inappropriate behaviour category, rather than in the more general Socially inappropriate behaviour category to which they may also apply). The manual suggests that a rating timeframe as long as the preceding 3 months can be used. Within each category, a screening question is first asked,

Data box 5.11 Descriptive data from the standardization sample (Kelly et al., 2006)

	Age M (SD)	Education	OBS M (SD)	Cut-off score	Sensitivity / Specificity
TBI (n = 30):	31.5 (13.2)	No information		No information	No information
Cluster			4.87 (1.59)		
Total Levels			9.53 (4.49)		
Total Clinical Weighted Severity*			19.93 (9.79)		

Note: * Total Clinical Weighted Severity score uses the original 0–77 scale.

and if the behaviour is endorsed as problematic, the rater then completes the more specific 1 to 6 severity level items within that category, first endorsing those behaviours that occur, then rating their frequency (from 1 = less than once per month to 5 = multiple times daily), and their impact on other people (from 1 = no impact to 5 = extreme impact). Administration time is reported as 5 to 10 minutes.

Scoring uses three key indices: Cluster score, which refers to the number of categories where the behaviour occurs (range 0–9), Total Levels score, which refers to the number of levels that are endorsed (range 0–34), and Total Clinical Weighted Severity score, which is a summation of severity scores assigned to each of the levels – severity scores vary among the categories and range from 1 to a maximum of 5. The Total Clinical Weighted Severity score ranges from 0 to 84 (revised from 0–77 in the original publication; personal communication, G. Kelly, 4 February 2008). The frequency and impact scores do not contribute to the scoring, but rather are included for clinical purposes.

Psychometric properties

Kelly et al. (2006) report a reliability and validity study, in which 30 clients (descriptive data shown in Data box 5.11) were recruited from a community TBI rehabilitation service in Sydney, Australia. Two clinician-raters independently rated the OBS based on information provided by treating staff during an interview with one rater while the other observed. Temporal stability was examined 1 week later, using one rater to re-interview the staff-informants. For both inter-rater and test–retest reliability, data are only provided for the summary statistics (Clusters and Levels) and no information is reported for the individual categories. This sample was also administered additional measures to examine the concurrent validity of the OBS: Neurobehavioural Rating Scale – Revised (NRS-R), Mayo-Portland Adaptability Inventory (MPAI – version 3) and Current Behaviour Scale (CBS). Divergent validity was examined using scales that did *not* examine overt behaviour, including the MPAI Cognitive, Everyday Behaviours and Physical/Medical scales. A second sample consisted of clients of the Melbourne-based ABI Behaviour Consultancy Service. Data on responsiveness were available on 28 clients who received behaviour management interventions. OBS ratings were made on two occasions, prior to the intervention and 4 months later. A summary of the findings is shown in Box 5.16.

Box 5.16

Validity:	Criterion: *Concurrent:* NRS-R Total Score with Cluster: r_s = .40, Levels: r_s = .37, Weights: r_s = .42 – MPAI Total Score with Levels: r_s = .43, Weights: r_s = .45 – CBS-Loss of Emotional Control Factor with Cluster: r_s = .51, Levels: r_s = .66, Weights: r_s = .63 Construct: *Convergent/divergent:* higher correlation with similar constructs (e.g., Weights with MPAI-Behaviour: r = .56, with MPAI-Emotion: r = .59); no statistically significant correlation with dissimilar constructs (e.g., with MPAI-Physical/Medical, MPAI-Everyday Activities – coefficients not reported)
Reliability:	Inter-rater: Cluster: r_s = .99, Levels: r_s = .97 Test–retest: 1 week: Cluster: r_s = .72, Levels: r_s = .77
Responsiveness:	Significant improvement in behaviour after 4 months of treatment (Weights: Time 1 Median = 11.0 vs Time 2 Median = 7.5; z = −2.24, p = .025)

Comment

Psychometric properties examined to date indicate that the summary statistics (Clusters and Levels) have excellent inter-rater reliability, adequate temporal stability, are sensitive to real changes occurring as a result of therapeutic interventions, and show evidence of content, concurrent and construct validity. More detailed information regarding the reliability of the individual categories would be helpful, especially for clinical practitioners. The OBS is, however, quite a complex instrument. The scoring format is initially difficult to grasp, with scores for clusters, levels, total clinical weighted severity levels, frequency and impact. These difficulties are offset by a well-designed and easy to follow recording form. The OBS has a number of strengths in addition to its psychometric properties. As Kelly et al. (2006) note, its routine use in clinical practice will facilitate the use of a common language to describe challenging behaviours, as well as provide a clear focus for clinical management; the comprehensiveness of the OBS and its application in community settings means that it will indeed "fill a niche".

Key references

Alderman, N., Knight, C., & Morgan, C. (1997). Use of a modified version of the Overt Aggression Scale in the measurement and assessment of aggressive behaviours following brain injury. *Brain Injury*, *11*(7), 503–523.

Kelly, G., Todd, J., Simpson, G., Kremer, P., & Martin, C. (2006). The Overt Behaviour Scale (OBS): A tool for measuring challenging behaviours following ABI in community settings. *Brain Injury*, *20*(3), 307–319.

Yudofsky, S. C., Silver, J. M., Jackson, W., Endicott, J., & Williams, D. (1986). The Overt Aggression Scale for the objective rating of verbal and physical aggression. *The American Journal of Psychiatry*, *143*(1), 35–39.

Items from the Overt Behaviour Scale

Kelly, Todd, Simpson, Kremer, and Martin (2006)

1. VERBAL AGGRESSION

1	Makes loud noises, shouts angrily
2	Makes mild personal insults . . .
3	Swearing, use of foul language . . .
4	Makes clear threats of violence . . .

2. PHYSICAL AGGRESSION AGAINST OBJECTS

1	Slams doors, scatters clothing . . .
2	Throws objects down . . .
3	Inflicts small cuts or bruises . . .
4	Sets fire, throws objects dangerously . . .

3. PHYSICAL AGGRESSION AGAINST SELF

1	Picks or scratches skin . . .
2	Bangs head . . .
3	Inflicts small cuts or bruises . . .
4	Mutilates self, causes deep cuts . . .

4. PHYSICAL AGGRESSION AGAINST OTHER PEOPLE

1	Makes threatening gesture . . .
2	Strikes, kicks, pushes . . .
3	Attacks others . . .
4	Causes severe physical injury . . .

5. INAPPROPRIATE SEXUAL BEHAVIOUR

1	a Sexual talk
	b Touching (non-genital)
2	a Exhibitionism
	b Masturbation
3	Touching (genital)
4	Coercive sexual behaviour, rape

6. PERSEVERATION/REPETITION

Prolonged repetition of behaviour resulting

1	in no physical harm (e.g., questions)
2	in minor physical harm
3	in serious physical harm

7. WANDERING/ABSCONDING

1	Goes into prohibited areas (e.g., staff office)
2	Leaves the familiar, "safe" environment . . .
3	Escapes secure premises

8. INAPPROPRIATE SOCIAL BEHAVIOUR

1	Socially awkward
2	Nuisance/annoyance
3	Non-compliant/oppositional
4	a Petty crime/unlawful behaviour
	b Presents a danger or risk to self/others

9. LACK OF INITIATIVE

1	Present vs absent

Acknowledgement: From Kelly, G.et al. (2006). The Overt Behaviour Scale (OBS): A tool for measuring challenging behaviours following ABI in community settings. *Brain Injury*, *20*(3), 307–319, Table 1, p. 310, with permission of Taylor & Francis, www.tandf.co.uk/journals.

6 Scales of sensory, ingestion and motor functions

Ian D. Cameron

Instruments presented in Chapter 6 map to the components, domains and categories of the *International Classification of Functioning, Disability and Health* (ICF; WHO, 2001) as depicted in Figure 6.1.

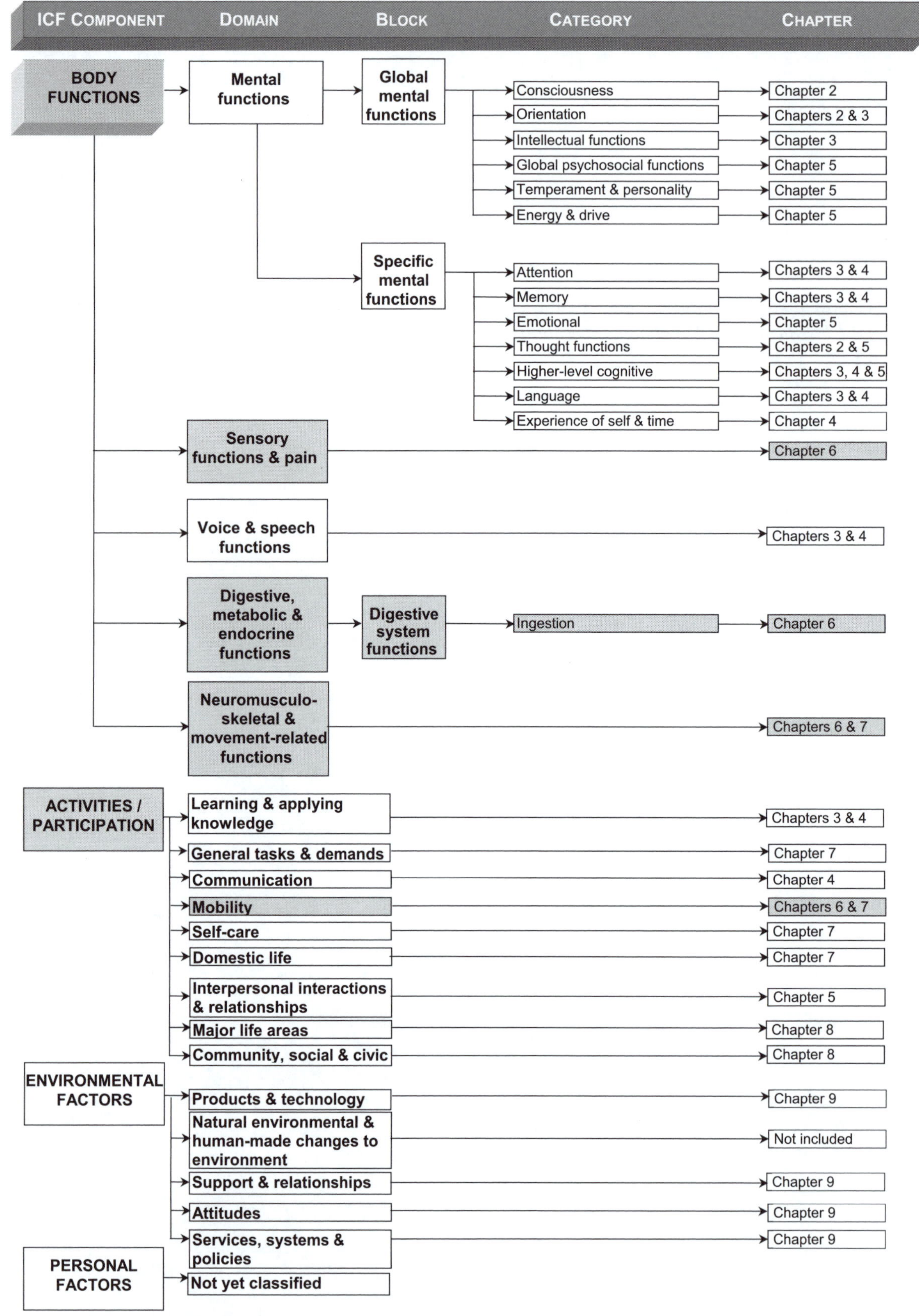

Figure 6.1 Instruments included in the compendium in relation to the ICF taxonomy – the highlighted components, domains and category appear in this chapter. *Note:* the Figure presents a partial listing of five out of the eight Body Function domains and does not include any of the Body Structure domains. Categories for Mental functions also represent a partial listing and categories for the remaining domains are not listed. Refer to Appendix C for further detail on the ICF taxonomy.

Introduction

This chapter provides a broad selection of scales that are relevant to the assessment of body functions other than the Mental functions. These functions are seeing, hearing, smell, touch, pain, ingestion, muscle power and muscle tone, and movement. The scales have been chosen to provide an overview of instruments relevant to people with acquired brain impairment (ABI). Of necessity a limited number of scales are presented and these sample the breadth of assessment in these widely divergent areas. The criteria for inclusion of scales are prevalence of the issue for people with ABI, the extent of clinical use of the scale and psychometric factors. In a number of areas there are variants of assessment scales for an area of functioning and these are grouped. For example, there are a large number of scales that assess movement functions by timing gait and these are included as a single entry.

As discussed in the introductory chapter of this book, decisions were made regarding the presentation of scales in categories that will be relevant to clinical considerations rather than exclusively following the ICF taxonomy. In this chapter this particularly applies to movement functions. There is inevitably overlap with activities and participation that are correlated with movement-related functions. All tests and scales that primarily assess movement functions, as distinct from multiple Activities/Participation domains including Mobility, are included in this chapter.

The assessment scales presented here have a varied provenance. Those assessing seeing, hearing, smell, touch, pain, and muscle power functions have developed over long periods within specific areas of (mainly) medical practice. The conceptual approaches to these scales vary greatly and there is no unifying principle except for striving to develop psychometrically valid methods for the assessment of core human functions. By contrast scales assessing movement functions were developed initially in the context of stroke and were later broadened to other areas of clinical practice.

Summaries of a larger number of assessment scales for movement and pain (and some other functions and activities) are presented in Cole, Finch, Gowland, and Mayo (1995). The authors have not identified other compendia addressing the range of body functions presented in this chapter.

Scales in this chapter are included if they require no, or minimal, equipment for assessment, and can be applied by a health professional with minimal specific training in the use of the assessment. In a few cases this is not feasible and the reader is directed to other sources of more detailed information about assessment of these functions.

References

Cole, B., Finch, E., Gowland, C., & Mayo, N. (1995). *Physical rehabilitation outcome measures*. Baltimore: Williams & Wilkins.

World Health Organization (2001). *International classification of functioning, disability and health*. Geneva: World Health Organization.

SECTION 1
Scales assessing sensory functions

1.1 Seeing functions

Snellen Chart

Snellen (1864)

Source

Snellen published the initial chart in 1864. It was subsequently adopted internationally, although variants have been suggested and debated (Bennett, 1965). Charts are now available readily from the internet (e.g., http://www.i-see.org/block_letter_eye_chart.pdf, accessed 19 January 2010).

Purpose

The Snellen Chart is an objective test of visual acuity, which is the smallest detail that can be seen. This is measured through the ability to identify small letters (or numbers) presented at high contrast from the background at a specified distance.

Item description

The original Snellen Chart (Snellen's optotypes) had seven lines of type that were designed to be viewed at a distance of 6 metres. The lines approximate a geometric progression in size, in which the eye detects the details of letters that, in their smallest dimension, subtend 1 minute of arc in the eye.

Scale development

Snellen used letters of a particular typeface that was constructed to be 5 units in height and either 5 or 6 units in width, with the thickness of the limbs being 1 unit (which is the minimum detail to be discerned). The second edition, in English, was published in 1864 (Bennett, 1965). The measurement of visual acuity has been hotly debated for well over a century and Bennett provides a review of other methods of assessment of visual acuity up to the 1960s.

Variants of the Snellen Chart

A number of alternative forms of the Snellen Chart are available. These make it possible to assess people with very limited or no literacy, including children and people with cognitive impairment. The version of the chart for these people is generally termed the "tumbling E chart", which has the letter "E" shown in different orientations. The Snellen Chart is also available in versions suitable for administration at a variety of distances.

The logMAR charts (logarithm of the minimum angle of resolution) have been developed and these are an improvement psychometrically on the Snellen Chart because legibility of a letter is impaired if contours (such as other letters) are placed in close proximity (McGraw, Winn, & Whitaker, 1995). Most obviously the number of letters on each line is the same in these charts, and a different method of scoring is used. LogMAR charts are more commonly used in research settings but their use in clinical practice is feasible (Laidlaw, Abbott, & Rosser, 2003).

Administration procedures, response format and scoring

An appropriately constructed Snellen Chart is required. An example of this rating scale is included below, but a chart of the correct type and size should be obtained for clinical use.

The chart must be attached at the correct distance and the standard is 6 metres. Charts are available for other distances. In addition, it is essential that the chart is brightly illuminated.

The respondent has one eye covered and reads the letters on the chart line by line. The visual acuity is the line with the smallest letters in which the respondent is able to read more than half of the letters. Visual acuity is recorded for each eye, and both eyes.

Successful recognition of the smallest letters on the last line of most charts is a visual acuity of 6/6. If it is possible to read only the top line of the chart the visual acuity is 6/60 which means that the person can read at 6 metres what a person with "normal" visual acuity can read at 60 metres.

Visual acuity decreases substantially with increasing age. Most people over the age of 40 to 50 years have a reduction in visual acuity termed presbyopia which causes restriction of seeing near objects. Also, some young adults have a visual acuity of better than 6/6.

The definition of severe reduction of visual acuity (and the criterion set for "blindness" in many countries) is 6/60. Restriction of seeing to an acuity of worse than 6/12 is abnormal.

If visual acuity screening is conducted using a Snellen Chart a significant number of people will have "false positive" results because of refractive problems. These can be reduced by more than 50% by having participants read the chart through a pinhole (Loewenstein, Palmberg, Connett, & Wentworth, 1985).

Psychometric properties

Snellen did not provide details of the derivation of the chart. It is likely to have been guided by clinical experimentation and progressive development. Philp, Lowles, Armstrong, and Whitehead (2002) studied 50 older people (aged $M = 79$ years) attending a day rehabilitation unit with assessments by nurses (see Box 6.1).

Box 6.1

Validity	No information available
Reliability:	Inter-rater: Blackhurst & Maguire: in a research setting, found differences of less than one Snellen Chart line in 87% of examinations Test–retest: Philp et al.: in older people with disability over 1 or 2 weeks: $k = .51$
Responsiveness:	Not applicable

Comment

The prevalence of visual impairments in the context of acquired brain impairment is high. The Snellen Chart has fair reliability if carefully used. It is not a sufficient assessment of visual functioning, but it has an established role as an initial screening test. Other important aspects of visual function are not assessed with this test, such as overall visual function, or specific visual impairments such as restriction in visual fields or disorders of ocular motility.

Key references

Bennett, A. G. (1965). Ophthalmic test types. A review of previous work and discussions on some controversial questions. *The British Journal of Physiological Optics*, *22*(4), 238–271.

Blackhurst, D. W., & Maguire, M. G. (1989). Reproducibility of refraction and visual acuity measurement under a standard protocol. The Macular Photocoagulation Study Group. *Retina*, *9*(3), 163–169.

Laidlaw, D. A., Abbott, A., & Rosser, D. A. (2003). Development of a clinically feasible logMAR alternative to the Snellen chart: Performance of the "compact reduced logMAR" visual acuity chart in amblyopic children. *The British Journal of Ophthalmology*, *87*(10), 1232–1234.

Loewenstein, J. I., Palmberg, P. F., Connett, J. E., & Wentworth, D. N. (1985). Effectiveness of a pinhole method for visual acuity screening. *Archives of Ophthalmology*, *103*(2), 222–223.

McGraw, P., Winn, B., & Whitaker, D. (1995). Reliability of the Snellen chart. *British Medical Journal*, *310*(6993), 1481–1482.

Philp, I., Lowles, R. V., Armstrong, G. K., & Whitehead, C. (2002). Repeatability of standardized tests of functional impairment and well-being in older people in a rehabilitation setting. *Disability and Rehabilitation*, *24*(5), 243–249.

Snellen, H. (1864). *On methods of determining the acuity of vision* (2nd, English, ed.). Utrecht: PW van der Weijer.

Snellen Chart

Snellen (1864)

Near Vision Test Card

Hold at a distance of 16 inches (40.6 centimeters).

160 in.	E O P Z T L C D F	4.0 m
80 in.	T D P C F Z O E L	2.0 m
56 in.	D Z E L C F O T P	1.4 m
48 in.	F E P C T L O Z D	1.2 m
40 in.	P T L F C Z D E O	1.0 m
32 in.	E L Z T C O F P D	80 cm
24 in.	D Z E C L P T O F	60 cm
20 in.	L O P F Z E D C T	50 cm
16 in.	Z L T C F P D O E	40 cm

NOTE: This is provided as an example. For clinical use a chart of the correct size, should be used at a specified distance with correct illumination. A chart can be obtained from http://www.i-see.org/block_letter_eye_chart.pdf

1.2 Hearing functions

Whispered Voice Test (WVT)

Uhlmann, Rees, Psaty, and Duckert (1989)

Source

This assessment has been in clinical use for a long time. It was systematized in the 1980s and this probably occurred independently in a number of settings. A readily accessed source of this assessment is Pirozzo, Papinczak, and Glasziou (2003) and this is used here.

Purpose

This objective test was developed to assess impairment of hearing functioning.

Item description

Items of the WVT comprise a combination of three numbers or letters (e.g., 4–K–2) that are whispered by the examiner. Two of these sequences are used in each test.

Scale development

Uhlmann et al. (1989) and others (including Pirozzo et al., 2003) reviewed a number of frequently described methods of testing hearing impairment. These had been described in textbooks of physical examination for health professionals. They concluded that the WVT was superior (Ulmann et al., 1989). It was validated in adults and children (Pirozzo et al., 2003) and standardized instructions for its administration were developed.

Administration procedures, response format and scoring

The following description is taken from Pirozzo et al. (2003). The examiner stands arm's length (0.6 m) behind the seated patient and whispers a combination of three numbers and letters (for example, 4–K–2) and then asks the patient to repeat the sequence. The examiner determines the sequence. The examiner should quietly exhale before whispering to ensure as quiet a voice as possible. If the patient responds correctly, hearing is considered normal; if the patient responds incorrectly, the test is repeated using a different number/letter combination. The examiner always stands behind the patient to prevent lip reading. Each ear is tested separately, starting with the ear with better hearing, and during testing the non-test ear is masked by gently occluding the auditory canal with a finger and rubbing the tragus in a circular motion. The other ear is assessed similarly with a different combination of numbers and letters. Slightly different instructions are given in other descriptions, for example Uhlmann et al. (1989).

The patient is considered to have passed the screening test if they repeat at least three out of a possible six individual numbers or letters correctly.

The person being assessed should be able to hear the whispered voice (see below). This is a screening test and should be followed by an audiometric assessment if the screening test is failed.

Box 6.2

Validity:	Criterion: *Predictive:* Bagai et al.: an inability to perceive a whispered voice has a likelihood ratio of 6.1 (95% CI, 4.5–8.4) while normal perception has a likelihood ratio of 0.03 (95% CI, 0–0.24); – Self-reported hearing impairment had a likelihood ratio of 2.5 (95% CI, 1.7–3.6) with no response having a likelihood ratio of 0.13 (95% CI, 0.09–0.19)
Reliability:	Inter-rater: Uhlmann et al.: between an otolaryngologist and an audiologist, people without dementia ICC = .67, people with dementia ICC = .78 – Eekhof et al.: between seven examiners, k = .16 to 1.0 Test–retest: Philp et al.: 1–2 weeks: k = .41
Responsiveness:	No information available

Psychometric properties

Uhlmann et al. (1989) studied 65 older people with and without dementia. A total of 11.7% of 130 ears failed the whispered voice test (the number of patients failing is not stated). Philp, Lowles, Armstrong, and Whitehead (2002) studied 50 older people (aged $M = 79$ years) attending a day rehabilitation unit with assessments by nurses. Bagai, Thavendiranathan, and Detsky (2006) conducted a systematic review and meta-analysis (see Box 6.2).

Comment

The WVT is a good choice as a screening test for impairment of hearing function. Most of its validity data come from older populations. This test should be carefully applied using standard methods to achieve adequate reliability. When the test is failed, or if the patient reports impairment of hearing, audiometric assessment should be undertaken.

Key references

Bagai, A., Thavendiranathan, P., & Detsky, A. S. (2006). Does this patient have hearing impairment? *Journal of the American Medical Association*, *295*(4), 416–428.

Eekhof, J. A., de Bock, G. H., de Laat, J. A., Dap, R., Schaapveld, K., & Springer, M. P. (1996). The whispered voice: The best test for screening for hearing impairment in general practice? *British Journal of General Practice*, *46*(409), 473–474.

Philp, I., Lowles, R. V., Armstrong, G. K., & Whitehead, C. (2002). Repeatability of standardized tests of functional impairment and well-being in older people in a rehabilitation setting. *Disability and Rehabilitation*, *24*(5), 243–249.

Pirozzo, S., Papinczak, T., & Glasziou, P. (2003). Whispered voice test for screening for hearing impairment in adults and children: Systematic review. *British Medical Journal*, *327*(7421), 967.

Uhlmann, R. F., Rees, T. S., Psaty, B. M., & Duckert, L. G. (1989). Validity and reliability of auditory screening tests in demented and non-demented older adults. *Journal of General Internal Medicine*, *4*(2), 90–96.

1.3 Smell functions

San Diego Odor Identification Test (SOIT)

Murphy, Anderson, and Markison (1994)

Source

This test is as presented by Murphy et al. (1994) in a conference proceedings document. It is not specifically named in the document but subsequently has been termed the San Diego Odor Identification test (Eibenstein, Fioretti, Lena, Rosati, Amabile, & Fusetti, 2005).

Purpose

The SOIT is an objective screening test of olfactory functioning and specifically assesses odour identification. Odour threshold is usually assessed using dilutions of *N*-butyl alcohol and this method of assessment is outside the scope of this chapter.

Item description

Murphy et al. (1994) describe a Children's and an Adults' test. The Children's test includes eight substances: baby powder, bubble gum, cinnamon, chocolate, coffee, mustard, peanut butter and Play-Doh. The Adults' test utilizes 10 substances: ammonia, baby powder, chocolate, cinnamon, coffee, Ivory soap, mothballs, peanut butter, Vicks (an ointment containing camphor) and wintergreen.

Scale development

The prime motivation of Murphy and colleagues was to develop a children's odour identification test because they found that the available adult batteries did not perform adequately with children. The Adult test was a byproduct from the children's scale development and was used with adults with Down syndrome, cystic fibrosis patients and control healthy children.

Administration procedures, response format and scoring

The test odours are presented in opaque jars. First, the participants are shown a cue sheet containing both the odour names and distractors. The number of distractors for the adult test is not stated but for the children's test it was approximately the same number as the test substances. Participants in the test are first shown the cue sheet and identify the items. The examiner clarifies these items if needed. The participant uses a blindfold and the tester holds the odourant under the nostril for 5 seconds and instructs the examinee to sniff.

In the Children's test (described in the same chapter) each item is rated correct or incorrect and the percentage of items correct is presented. It is presumed that the Adults' test is scored in the same way.

Psychometric properties

Murphy et al. (1994) reported data from 92 children and 22 adults with Down syndrome (age $M = 31$ years) who attended a University Hospital Medical Centre Nasal Dysfunction Clinic. No adult data are presented but for normal children 25 out of 28 of the sample scored 75% or greater correct. All data in Box 6.3 are from Murphy et al.

Box 6.3

Validity:	Construct: *Discriminative:* Children identified 76% of items in the Children's test compared with 39% of items in the Adults' test. Patients with cystic fibrosis had lower mean correct score than controls (66% versus 88%).
Reliability:	Inter-rater: No information available
	Test–retest: Children: $M = 5.4$ days: $r = .86$
Responsiveness:	No information available

Doty, McKeown, Lee, & Shaman (1995) have shown that a number of the commercially available tests of smell functioning have adequate reliability (e.g., University of Pennsylvania Smell Identification Test, test–retest $r = .90$), but this is dependent on test length and the specific test used.

Comment

Adequate reliability data for the SOIT of smell function are not available. It could be used as a screening test but its sensitivity and specificity are unknown. There are validated short tests of smell functioning that are commercially available. These are University of Pennsylvania Smell Identification Test (Doty, Shaman, Kimmelman, & Dann, 1984), and the Sniffin' Sticks Test that is widely used in Europe and elsewhere (Kobal, Hummel, Sekinger, Barz, Roscher, & Wolf, 1996). Both these tests are available in screening versions and population norms are available (Mackay-Sim, Grant, Owen, Chant, & Silburn, 2004). Given that detection of impairment of smell functioning is important in the context of traumatic brain injury and some types of acquired brain impairment, for example Alzheimer's disease and Parkinson's disease, clinicians should strongly consider the purchase of commercially available testing kits. These kits have single use components or a limited shelf life. Assessment of smell function using universally available materials is not feasible.

Key references

Doty, R. L., McKeown, D. A., Lee, W. W., & Shaman, P. (1995). A study of the test–retest reliability of ten olfactory tests. *Chemical Senses*, *20*(6), 645–656.

Doty, R. L., Shaman, P., Kimmelman, C. P., & Dann, M. S. (1984). University of Pennsylvania Smell Identification Test: A rapid quantitative olfactory function test for the clinic. *Laryngoscope*, *94*(2), 176–178.

Eibenstein, A., Fioretti, A. B., Lena, C., Rosati, N., Amabile, G., & Fusetti, M. (2005). Modern psychophysical tests to assess olfactory function. *Neurological Sciences*, *26*(3), 147–155.

Kobal, G., Hummel, T., Sekinger, B., Barz, S., Roscher, S., & Wolf, S. (1996). "Sniffin' sticks": Screening of olfactory performance. *Rhinology*, *34*(4), 222–226.

Mackay-Sim, A., Grant, L., Owen, C., Chant, D., & Silburn, P. (2004). Australian norms for a quantitative olfactory function test. *Journal of Clinical Neuroscience*, *11*(8), 874–879.

Murphy, C., Anderson, J., & Markison, S. (1994). Psychophysical assessment of chemosensory disorders in clinical populations. In K. Kurihara, N. Suzuchi & H. Ogawa (Eds.), *Olfaction and taste XI* (pp. 609–613). New York: Springer-Verlag.

1.4 Touch functions

Semmes Weinstein Monofilament (SWM)

Bell-Krotoski, Weinstein, and Weinstein (1993)

Source

This method of assessment follows the description of Bell-Krotoski et al. (1993). Semmes and Weinstein had previously described the use of nylon monofilaments and the procedures were gradually refined. A monofilament is a single strand of untwisted nylon fibre that has a standard diameter and properties. This method of assessment of touch functioning uses equipment that is found in most medical settings, but it is acknowledged these materials may not be universally available.

Purpose

These nylon monofilaments were developed to objectively assess touch functioning in the context of peripheral neuropathy. If significant abnormalities of touch functioning are present there is the risk of ulceration in the lower extremities. These methods were originally developed in Hansen's disease but now have international use in diabetes mellitus.

Item description

Monofilaments are provided in a range of diameters and are attached at a right angle to a holder. Six filaments are generally presented in a kit but a single filament of an appropriate diameter (number 2.83) can be used as a screening test.

Scale development

Weinstein designed the filaments to produce a constant pressure against the skin. Multiple studies were performed that established there was a spectrum of loss of touch functioning, which if greater than a certain amount is associated with risk of skin ulceration. Mawdsley et al. (2004) provide a review of these studies and the scale development. The different diameter monofilaments are manufactured to exert standardized forces across a gradient from normal sensation, to reduced light touch and eventually to loss of protective sensation.

Administration procedures, response format and scoring

Generally, six 38 mm long monofilaments are provided in a testing pack, although other combinations are available. These have been manufactured to careful specifications. The filaments are designed to apply a constant force to the skin despite vibration of testers' hands. Progressive increases in force occur when the diameters of the filaments increase. The filaments are applied perpendicular to the skin with a force sufficient to maintain a bent position against the skin. All parts of the body can be tested, but generally it is the extremities that are assessed.

Ascending and descending testing methods and a combination of the two methods have been described. In the ascending method, the lightest filament is applied first and then the larger diameter filaments are applied in the ascending order of their forces until one is detected. This method is preferred as it is easier for the patient and reduces assessment time.

The filament should be held in place for 1 to 2 seconds, and then removed. The stimulus should be applied up to three times in the same location to elicit a response. If the participant does not indicate a positive response, the next largest filament is used until a response occurs, or until all of the filaments are used.

The aim of the assessment is to define a touch pressure threshold. The force exerted by the filaments increases logarithmically. If the participant does not respond to the largest filament the threshold is not established, although it is clearly established that the person has abnormal touch function.

Filament number 2.83 is the upper limit of the normal range; number 3.61 is at the top of the range of diminished light touch; number 4.31 is at the limit of the range of diminished protective sensation; and number 6.65 is at the upper limit of loss of protective sensation (Mawdsley et al., 2004). While normal touch function is an ability to identify the 2.83 filament, on the sole of the foot the threshold is higher and is said to be the 3.61 filament.

Psychometric properties

Mawdsley et al. (2004) studied 22 people (16 female) with diabetes who had the age range of 47 to 95 years. All data in Box 6.4 are from Mawdsley et al. (2004) unless otherwise stated.

Box 6.4

Validity:	Criterion: *Concurrent:* Rosen, Dahlin, & Lundborg: $r = .59$ for patients' estimated impact on activities of daily living
Reliability:	Inter-rater: for nine sites on feet: $r = .46–.88$ Test–retest: during "one session": for nine sites on feet: $r = 0.49–0.86$ – Klenerman, McCabe, Cogley, Crerand, Laing, & White: absence of protective sensation recorded on two occasions at variable intervals for 85% of the patients on the left foot and for 88% of the patients on the right foot
Responsiveness:	Large effect size reported by Rosen & Lundborg after nerve injury

Comment

This assessment method is in widespread clinical use in the context of peripheral neuropathy. In diabetes and peripheral nerve injury this method has adequate psychometric properties. The appropriateness and ability of this test to assess central sensory changes in acquired brain impairment are not known. Although there are other methods of assessment of touch functioning, such as two-point discrimination, this monofilament method has the widest use and best established validity and reliability.

Key references

Bell-Krotoski, J., Weinstein, S., & Weinstein, C. (1993). Testing sensibility, including touch-pressure, two-point discrimination, point localization, and vibration. *Journal of Hand Therapy*, *6*(2), 114–123.

Klenerman, L., McCabe, C., Cogley, D., Crerand, S., Laing, P., & White, M. (1996). Screening for patients at risk of diabetic foot ulceration in a general diabetic outpatient clinic. *Diabetic Medicine*, *13*(6), 561–563.

Mawdsley, R. H., Behm-Pugh, A. T., Campbell, J. D., Carroll, C. R., Chernikovich, K. A., Mowbray, M. K., et al. (2004). Reliability of measurements with Semmes-Weinstein monofilaments in individuals with diabetes. *Physical and Occupational Therapy in Geriatrics*, *22*, 19–36.

Rosen, B., Dahlin, L. B., & Lundborg, G. (2000). Assessment of functional outcome after nerve repair in a longitudinal cohort. *Scandinavian Journal of Plastic and Reconstructive Surgery and Hand Surgery*, *34*(1), 71–78.

Rosen, B., & Lundborg, G. (2000). A model instrument for the documentation of outcome after nerve repair. *Journal of Hand Surgery*, *25*(3), 535–543.

1.5 Pain functions

Multidimensional pain scales

Visual Analogue Scale (VAS) For Pain, Numeric Rating Scales (NRS), and other pain scales

Huskisson (1974)

Source

The 10 centimetre VAS for pain and the Numeric Rating Scale can be drawn with a ruler. For the VAS a 10 cm horizontal line is drawn and the words "No pain" are placed at the left end and "Worst pain imaginable" or "Pain as bad as it can be" at the right end. The Numeric Rating Scale is similar in concept and each point is labelled from 0 to 10 (see Jensen, Karoly, & Braver, 1986, below).

Purpose

These rating scales assess pain intensity. Variants of them can be used to measure affective dimensions of pain (Jensen, Karoly, O'Riordan, Bland, & Burns, 1989), but this review is limited to evaluation of pain intensity (see entry on the McGill Pain Questionnaire, page 362, for information about affective dimensions of pain).

Item description

The Visual Analogue Scale for pain is a 10 centimetre horizontal line with the left end labelled "No pain" and the right end labelled "The most intense pain sensation imaginable" (Price, Bush, Long, & Harkins, 1994). The descriptor at the severe end of the scale is variable between studies and has included "unbearable pain" (Seymour, 1982) and "worst pain imaginable" (Thomas & Griffiths, 1982).

Scale development

Visual analogue scales were consistently applied in pain assessment and research in the 1970s. They were described by a number of authors who acknowledge the development of VAS in the context of psychological research in the 1920s (Huskisson, 1974; Joyce, Zutshi, Hrubes, & Mason, 1975; Scott & Huskisson, 1976).

Related assessment scales

The VAS for pain is itself a derivative of other unidimensional pain scales. There are NRS for pain, which are described below, verbal rating scales, and picture pain rating scales. For people who are unable to directly provide information to allow an assessment of pain, observational pain scales have also been developed.

Numeric rating scales continue to be widely used and provide a valid measurement of pain (Farrar, Young, LaMoreaux, Werth, & Poole, 2001; Seymour, 1982). These scales have the numerals 0 to 10 presented in a row, with the ends labelled with the same descriptors as the VAS for pain.

Verbal rating scales have been used extensively (Jensen et al., 1989) but now have less currency than the two methods described above. These are 4- or 5-point scales with the descriptors "No pain at all, Some pain, Considerable pain, Pain that could not be more severe" (Joyce et al., 1975) or "None, Mild, Moderate, Severe, Very severe" (Frank, Moll, & Hort, 1982).

Picture or face pain scales that illustrate facial expressions of people experiencing different levels of pain have been developed (Frank et al., 1982). They have had most use for children (Keck, Gerkensmeyer, Joyce, & Schade, 1996) and for older people (Stuppy, 1998).

Observation methods are particularly applicable to young children and people with central nervous system abnormalities, particularly acquired brain impairment. Observational methods can be global, or based on non-language vocalization, on facial expressions, or on bodily activity other than facial expression. The Facial Action Coding System (Ekman and Friesen, 1978) has been the gold standard for developing scales based on facial expression because it is anatomically based and reliable. However, it requires extensive training and slow motion video recording and is not eligible as a scale for this publication.

Keefe and Block (1982) developed an observation method based on bodily activity in people with back pain, and ratings based on the occurrence of defined behaviours (guarding, bracing, rubbing, grimacing, and sighing). Hadjistavropoulos, LaChapelle, MacLeod, Snider, and Craig (2000) have studied self-report and observational methods in cognitively impaired older people and concluded that self-report and observational methods should both be used as they assess different aspects of pain.

Administration procedures, response format and scoring

The VAS for pain (and NRS) are readily drawn but are generally pre-printed. For the VAS a 10 cm horizontal line is conventionally used and the appropriate labels should be shown adjacent to each end of the scale. The patient is instructed to place a mark, usually a vertical line, on the point on the scale that describes their current pain.

The interval from the zero point of the scale to the mark is measured with a ruler and the pain intensity is reported as the number of centimetres to one decimal place, or the number of millimetres.

Generally, NRS for pain are labelled zero to 10 (an 11-point scale) and the patient is asked to circle the number that best describes his or her pain. The whole number is reported as the pain intensity. A change of 2 points, or a reduction of 30%, has been reported as a clinically significant difference using this scale (Farrar et al., 2001).

Psychometric properties

Many of the standardization and validation studies do not report actual pain scores. Farrar et al. (2001) reported a meta-analysis of data from 10 studies of chronic pain with a variety of neurological and musculoskeletal conditions. The baseline pain (mean (SD)) ranged from 6.2 (1.4) to 7.0 (1.3) with mean age ranging from 48 to 72 years and percentage female ranging from 39 to 91%.

The non-completion rate for the VAS appears to be higher than the other scales in some groups (Jensen et al., 1986; Kremer, Atkinson, & Ignelzi, 1981). VAS is a ratio scale, providing accurate estimates of ratios of pain intensity and percentage changes in pain (Price et al., 1994) (see Box 6.5).

Box 6.5

Validity:	Criterion: *Concurrent:* Seymour (1982): VAS: $r = .95$ for effect of analgesic after dental extraction
	Construct: *Factor analysis:* Jensen et al. (1986); Jensen et al. (1989): Single factor: Pain
	Convergent/divergent: Price, McGrath, Rafii, & Buckingham: VAS pain intensity is a logarithmic function of the temperature of a thermal stimulus
	Jensen et al. (1989): pain intensity not highly correlated with behaviour or affect
	Discriminant: Farrar et al.: NRS: sensitivity 78%, specificity 75% for improvement on global perceived effect change in pain rating
Reliability:	Inter-rater: not applicable
	Test–retest: patients with traumatic brain injury: Leung, Moseley, Fereday, Jones, Fairbairn, & Wyndham: ICC for NRS .50–1.00
	Love, Leboeuf, & Crisp: "some days": current pain: $r = .77$
	Price et al. (1983): (interval not reported) thermal stimulus: $r = .97$
Responsiveness:	Bolton & Wilkinson: VAS for pain, NRS and verbal rating scale all responsive to chiropractic treatment of painful conditions (effect sizes $d = .77$, .86, .76 respectively)
	Farrar et al.: reduction of 2 points on a NRS or 30% is a clinically important difference

Comment

Unidimensional scales for the assessment of pain intensity are in universal use and appear valid in most populations. For people with acquired brain impairment and markedly restricted cognitive functioning, observational pain scales are available but there are fewer data related to their psychometric properties. In most situations a VAS for pain, or 11-point NRS for pain, will provide an accurate assessment method for pain intensity. The latter are more appropriate for people with significant acquired brain impairment.

Key references

Bolton, J. E., & Wilkinson, R. C. (1998). Responsiveness of pain scales: A comparison of three pain intensity measures in chiropractic patients. *Journal of Manipulative and Physiological Therapeutics*, *21*(1), 1–7.

Ekman, P., & Friesen, W. V. (1978). *Facial Action Coding System: A technique for the measurement of facial movement*. Palo Alto, CA: Consulting Psychologists Press.

Farrar, J. T., Young, J. P. J., LaMoreaux, L., Werth, J. L., & Poole, R. M. (2001). Clinical importance of changes in chronic pain intensity measured on an 11-point numerical pain rating scale. *Pain*, *94*(2), 149–158.

Frank, A. J., Moll, J. M., & Hort, J. F. (1982). A comparison of three ways of measuring pain. *Rheumatology and Rehabilitation*, *21*(4), 211–217.

Hadjistavropoulos, T., LaChapelle, D. L., MacLeod, F. K., Snider, B., & Craig, K. D. (2000). Measuring movement-exacerbated pain in cognitively impaired frail elders. *Clinical Journal of Pain*, *16*(1), 54–63.

Huskisson, E. C. (1974). Measurement of pain. *The Lancet*, *9*(2), 1127–1131.

Jensen, M. P., Karoly, P., & Braver, S. (1986). The measurement of clinical pain intensity: A comparison of six methods. *Pain*, *27*(1), 117–126.

Jensen, M. P., Karoly, P., O'Riordan, E. F., Bland, F. J., & Burns, R. S. (1989). The subjective experience of acute pain. An assessment of the utility of 10 indices. *Clinical Journal of Pain*, *5*(2), 153–159.

Joyce, C. R. B., Zutshi, D. W., Hrubes, V., & Mason, R. M. (1975). Comparison of fixed interval and visual analogue scales for rating chronic pain. *European Journal of Clinical Pharmacology*, *8*(6), 415–420.

Keck, J. F., Gerkensmeyer, J. E., Joyce, B. A., & Schade, J. G. (1996). Reliability and validity of the Faces and Word Descriptor Scales to measure procedural pain. *Journal of Pediatric Nursing*, *11*(6), 368–374.

Keefe, F. J., & Block, A. R. (1982). Development of an observation method for assessing pain behavior in chronic low back pain patients. *Behavior Therapy*, *13*, 363–375.

Kremer, E., Atkinson J. H., & Ignelzi R. J. (1981). Measurement of pain: Patient preference does not confound pain measurement. *Pain*, *10*, 241–248.

Leung, J., Moseley, A., Fereday, S., Jones, T., Fairbairn, T., & Wyndham, S. (2007). The prevalence and characteristics of shoulder pain after traumatic brain injury. *Clinical Rehabilitation*, *21*(2), 171–181.

Love, A., Leboeuf, C., & Crisp, T. C. (1989). Chiropractic chronic low back pain sufferers and self-report assessment methods. Part I. A reliability study of the Visual Analogue Scale, the Pain Drawing and the McGill Pain Questionnaire. *Journal of Manipulative and Physiological Therapeutics*, *12*(2), 21–25.

Price, D. D., Bush, F. M., Long, S., & Harkins, S. W. (1994). A comparison of pain measurement characteristics of mechanical visual analogue and simple numeric rating scales. *Pain*, *56*, 217–226.

Price, D. D., McGrath, P. A., Rafii, A., & Buckingham, B. (1983). The validation of visual analogue scales as ratio scale measures for chronic and experimental pain. *Pain*, *17*(1), 45–56.

Scott, J., & Huskisson, E. C. (1976). Graphic representation of pain. *Pain*, *2*(2), 175–184.

Seymour, R. A. (1982). The use of pain scales in assessing the efficacy of analgesics in post-operative dental pain. *European Journal of Clinical Pharmacology*, *23*(5), 441–444.

Stuppy, D. J. (1998). The Faces Pain Scale: Reliability and validity with mature adults. *Applied Nursing Research*, *11*(2), 84–89.

Thomas, A., & Griffiths, M. J. (1982). A pain slide rule. *Anaesthesia*, *37*, 960–961.

Visual Analogue Scale For Pain, Numeric Rating Scales, and other pain scales

Jensen, Karoly, and Braver (1986)

The Ten Centimetre Visual Analogue Scale.

No pain |————————————————| Pain as bad as it could be

The 101-point Numerical Rating Scale (NRS-101).

Please indicate on the line below the number between 0 and 100 that best describes your pain. A zero (0) would mean "no pain", and a one hundred (100) would mean "pain as bad as it could be." Please write only one number.

______

The 11-point Box Scale (BS-11).

If a zero (0) means "no pain", and a ten (10) means "pain as bad as it could be", on this scale of 0 to 10, what is your level of pain? Put an "X" through that number.

0	1	2	3	4	5	6	7	8	9	10

The 6-point Behavioral Rating Scale (BRS-6).

( ) No pain
( ) Pain present, but can easily be ignored
( ) Pain present, cannot be ignored, but does not interfere with everyday activities
( ) Pain present, cannot be ignored, interferes with concentration
( ) Pain present, cannot be ignored, interferes with all tasks except taking care of basic needs such as toileting and eating
( ) Pain present, cannot be ignored, rest or bedrest required

The 4-point Verbal Rating Scale (VRS-4).

( ) No pain
( ) Some pain
( ) Considerable pain
( ) Pain which could not be more severe

The 5-point Verbal Rating Scale (VRS-5).

( ) Mild
( ) Discomforting
( ) Distressing
( ) Horrible
( ) Excrutiating

Acknowledgement: From Jensen, M. P. et al. (1986). The measurement of clinical pain intensity: A comparison of six methods. *Pain*, *27*(1), 117–126, Figure 1, p. 119, used with permission of Elsevier.

Multidimensional pain scales

McGill Pain Questionnaire (MPQ)

Melzack (1975, 1987)

Source

The original MPQ was published in 1975 (Melzak, 1975). A "Short-Form" (SF-MPQ) was developed by Melzack in 1987 and is described below.

Purpose

The MPQ is a rating scale designed to assess multiple dimensions of the experience of pain. Melzack (1975) defined relevant domains as sensory-discriminative, motivational-affective and cognitive-evaluative. The aim was to develop an examination that could improve on unidimensional pain scales such as verbal or numeric rating scales, or visual analogue scales, by providing specific information about the nature of the pain experience.

For the development of the short form of the MPQ "the strategy was to select a small representative set of words from the sensory and affective categories of the standard form, and to use the present pain intensity and visual analogue scale to provide indices of overall intensity" (Melzack, 1987, p. 192).

Item description

In the first component of the SF-MPQ there are 15 words. Eleven words address sensory experiences "throbbing, shooting, stabbing, sharp, cramping, gnawing, hot-burning, aching, heavy, tender, splitting", and the remaining four words address affective components: "tiring-exhausting, sickening, fearful and punishing-cruel". These are rated as described below. Two other items of the SF-MPQ are a Visual Analogue Scale (VAS) for pain and the Present Pain Intensity (PPI), which is a six-level verbal rating scale.

Scale development

Melzack and co-workers had physicians and other university graduates classify words that are relevant to the description of pain and were derived from the clinical literature. The classification was into the three domains noted above – sensory-discriminative, motivational-affective and cognitive-evaluative (the latter domain is only used in the MPQ, not in the short form). The words were then classified on the basis of intensity within the three classes. As a result of a preliminary study (Melzack, 1975), words forming an additional fourth "miscellaneous" class were added. Also included was the PPI, which is a six-category verbal graphic rating scale ("no pain" to "excruciating") and line drawings of the body on which the location of pain was recorded.

The SF-MPQ was developed "for some types of research (such as pharmacological studies) which require more rapid acquisition of data than the standard MPQ" (Melzack, 1987, p. 192). Melzack stated "the strategy was to select a small, representative set of words from the sensory and affective categories of the standard form, and to use the PPI and visual analogue scale (VAS) to provide indices of overall intensity." The basis of item reduction was to select descriptors chosen by more than 33% of patients with a wide variety of painful conditions and the addition of the word "splitting" because it had been identified as a discriminative word in dental pain.

Administration procedures, response format and scoring

In the SF-MPQ each of the 15 words is rated on a four-category verbal graphic scale ("none, mild, moderate, severe"). These descriptors are allocated a score of 0, 1, 2, and 3, respectively.

The SF-MPQ is scored by summing the values within the sensory and affective dimensions. These can be added to give a pain rating index total (PRI-T) score and the PPI and VAS are also reported.

Psychometric properties

Melzack (1987) studied patients in a variety of wards and outpatient departments of a Canadian hospital. For the SF-MPQ the mean (*SD*) PRI-T scores as measured before and after a therapeutic intervention were: post-surgical pain 15.4 (9.6) to 9.1 (9.7); musculoskeletal pain 15.7 (11.9) to 4.7 (2.9) (see Box 6.6).

Box 6.6

Validity:	Construct: Reading, Everitt, & Sledmere: replicated the scale's derivation and found that the grouping of descriptors was acceptable, but the intensity of pain associated with descriptors was questionable.
Reliability:	Inter-rater: Not applicable
	Test–retest: Melzack (1987): $r = .68–.88$ for sensory dimension and $r = .69–.94$ for the affective dimension for SF-MPQ and MPQ
	Love, Leboeuf, & Crisp: MPQ over "several days" $r = .83$
Responsiveness:	Melzack (1987): acute pain (post-surgical, labour, musculoskeletal) large reductions ($p < .001$)

Comment

This scale is very widely used and is available in at least 20 languages other than English (Melzack & Katz, 2001). The scale is accepted as the "gold standard" of multi-dimensional pain scales. The short form is also well validated and accepted, and used very widely. It should be considered first as a multidimensional pain assessment method.

Key references

Love, A., Leboeuf, C., & Crisp, T. C. (1989). Chiropractic chronic low back pain sufferers and self-report assessment methods. Part I. A reliability study of the Visual Analogue Scale, the Pain Drawing and the McGill Pain Questionnaire. *Journal of Manipulative and Physiological Therapeutics*, *12*(2), 21–25.

Melzack, R. (1975). The McGill Pain Questionnaire: Major properties and scoring methods. *Pain*, *1*(3), 277–299.

Melzack, R. (1987). The Short-Form McGill Pain Questionnaire. *Pain*, *30*(2), 191–197.

Melzack, R., & Katz, J. (2001). The McGill Pain Questionnaire: Appraisal and current status. In D. C. Turk & R. Melzack (Eds.), *Handbook of pain assessment*. New York: Guilford Press.

Reading, A. E., Everitt, B. S., & Sledmere, C. M. (1982). The McGill Pain Questionnaire: A replication of its construction. *British Journal of Clinical Psychology*, *21*(Pt 4), 339–349.

Short-Form McGill Pain Questionnaire

Melzack (1987)

Name: **Administered by:** **Date:**

Response key:
0 = None
1 = Mild
2 = Moderate
3 = Severe

	None	Mild	Moderate	Severe
1. Throbbing	______	______	______	______
2. Shooting	______	______	______	______
3. Stabbing	______	______	______	______
4. Sharp	______	______	______	______
5. Cramping	______	______	______	______
6. Gnawing	______	______	______	______
7. Hot-burning	______	______	______	______
8. Aching	______	______	______	______
9. Heavy	______	______	______	______
10. Tender	______	______	______	______
11. Splitting	______	______	______	______

SENSORY TOTAL: ______

12. Tiring-exhausting	______	______	______	______
13. Sickening	______	______	______	______
14. Fearful	______	______	______	______
15. Punishing-cruel	______	______	______	______

AFFECTIVE TOTAL: ______

TOTAL: PAIN RATING INDEX (Sensory + Affective): ______

Overall Pain Intensity:

No pain |————————————————————| Worst possible pain

Present pain intensity:

0	No pain
1	Mild
2	Discomforting
3	Distressing
4	Horrible
5	Excruciating

Acknowledgement: From Melzack, R. (1987). The Short-Form McGill Pain Questionnaire. *Pain*, *30*(2), 191–197, Figure 1, p. 193, reprinted by permission of Elsevier.

SECTION 2
Scales assessing ingestion functions

Bedside Swallowing Assessment (BSA)

Smithard et al. (1998)

Source

The BSA as reported by Smithard et al. (1998) appears below.

Purpose

The BSA is a performance-based test. Smithard et al. (1997) set out to "examine the changes in swallowing ability following stroke" (p. 188), and "the patient was considered to have a compromised swallow, if after the bedside assessment, they were considered to be at risk of aspirating" (p. 189) which was termed "unsafe swallowing" (Smithard et al., 1998).

Item description

The patient ingests a small amount of water, followed by a larger amount, if their level of consciousness is adequate. The rater assesses voice quality and whether the ingestion provokes a cough.

Scale development

A number of short tests of swallowing function have been reported. The first published was by DePippo, Holas, and Reding (1992). This was further developed, probably independently, by Smithard and colleagues (1998). Further variants have been reported by Ellul and Barer (1996), Perry (2001) and others.

It appears that swallowing of water was considered first (DePippo et al., 1992). Ellul and Barer (1996) described assessment of swallowing in three stages – general assessment (level of consciousness and postural control), sipping water from a spoon and, if safe, drinking water from a glass. Specific signs are observed (voice quality and coughing) and an overall judgement of safety is made.

The method of Smithard et al. (1998) is reported here as it has been progressively developed, has been evaluated between health disciplines (medicine and speech and language therapy) and has been compared to videofluoroscopy. It should be noted that videofluoroscopy is not necessarily a "gold standard" because of its variable interpretation by different raters (Smithard et al., 1998; Perry, 2001).

Administration procedures, response format and scoring

If the patient has a significant reduction in level of consciousness (Glasgow Coma Score < 10) they are not assessed. In the 1998 publication Smithard et al. provide explicit criteria for scoring the assessment:

> the medical bedside assessment was divided into two stages. If the patient was unable to swallow a 5 ml spoonful of water (coughing and/or choking on more than one occasion out of three attempts and or a wet voice (indicating weak laryngeal function), then stage two (swallowing with 60 ml of water within 2 min) is not attempted. Failure to go on to stage 2; coughing and/or choking during stage 2; or the presence of a wet voice indicated an unsafe swallow. (p. 100)

DePippo et al. (1992) described the Water Swallow Test, which is similar to the above. Patients with suspected dysphagia are asked to drink 90 ml of water from a cup "without interruption". It is implied that the patient is seated in an upright position. Coughing during or for 1 minute after completion, or the presence of a post-swallow wet-hoarse voice quality were scored as abnormal.

Psychometric properties

In conscious patients with recent stroke (median age 79 years, 58% female) Smithard et al. (1997) reported the percentage of people with swallowing impairment at 3, 7, 28 and 180 days post-onset as 31%, 33%, 3%, and 3% respectively. However, assessing the validity of the swallowing assessment is difficult because of limited reliability of reporting of videofluoroscopy (Smithard

Box 6.7

Validity:	Criterion: *Predictive:* Smithard et al. (1996) with significant ($p < .001$) univariate association with poor nutritional state and death ($p = .001$) and chest infection ($p = .05$)
	Construct: *Discriminant:* DePippo et al.: 90 ml of water method had 76% sensitivity and 59% specificity with use of the modified barium swallow as the standard to detect aspiration. The sensitivity and specificity for aspiration of large amounts were 94% and 26% respectively.
Reliability:	Inter-rater: Perry: $k = .88$ with "summative clinical judgement of swallow function"
	Smithard et al. (1997): $k = .48$ with speech and language therapist assessment
	Smithard et al. (1996): greater agreement between speech and language therapists ($k = .79$) than medical practitioners ($k = .5$)
	Test–retest: No information available
Responsiveness:	Smithard et al. (1996): decreased prevalence of "compromised swallow" at 7, 28 & 180 days after onset of stroke (see above)

et al., 1998). Kappa for rating of videofluoroscopy by a second radiologist was $k = .48$. Because of this it is difficult to establish the gold standard for comparison. Some studies set explicit criteria for assessment of videofluoroscopic data. This is probably a proxy for the important outcome of clinically significant aspiration which causes restriction of respiratory function (see Box 6.7).

Comment

The Bedside Swallowing Assessment is a brief and practical assessment that has marginal validity and reliability in the context of stroke. Its utility in other types of acquired brain impairment has not been studied. It can be used as a screening test in the context of acquired brain impairment (particularly stroke), where it has been shown to have fair sensitivity in detecting aspiration. Although its specificity is poor this is acceptable for a screening test as other more specific diagnostic tests will be applied as second line assessments.

Key references

DePippo, K. L., Holas, M. A., & Reding, M. J. (1992). Validation of the 3-oz water swallow test for aspiration following stroke. *Archives of Neurology*, *49*(12), 1259–1261.

Ellul, J., & Barer, D., on behalf of ESDB/COSTAR Collaborative (1996). Abstract interobserver reliability of a standardized bedside swallowing assessment (SSA). *Cerebrovascular Diseases*, *6*(S2), 152–153.

Perry, L. (2001). Screening swallowing function of patients with acute stroke. Part one: Identification, implementation and initial evaluation of a screening tool for use by nurses. *Journal of Clinical Nursing*, *10*(4), 463–473.

Smithard, D. G., O'Neill, P. A., England, R. E., Park, C. L., Wyatt, R., Martin, D. F., et al. (1997). The natural history of dysphagia following a stroke. *Dysphagia*, *12*(4), 188–193.

Smithard, D. G., O'Neill, P. A., Park, C., England, R., Renwick, D. S., Wyatt, R., et al. (1998). Can bedside assessment reliably exclude aspiration following acute stroke? *Age and Ageing*, *27*(2), 99–106.

Smithard, D. G., O'Neill, P. A., Park, C., Morris, J., Wyatt, R., England, R., et al. (1996). Complications and outcome after acute stroke. Does dysphagia matter? *Stroke*, *27*(7), 1200–1204.

Bedside Swallowing Assessment

Smithard et al.

for the North West Dysphagia Group (1998)

Name:	**Administered by:**	**Date:**

1. CONSCIOUS LEVEL

1 Alert
2 Drowsy but rousable
3 Response but no eye opening to speech
4 Responds to pain

2. HEAD AND TRUNK CONTROL

1 Normal sitting balance
2 Sitting balance not maintained
3 Head control only
4 No head control

3. BREATHING PATTERN

1 Normal
2 Abnormal

4. LIP CLOSURE

1 Normal
2 Abnormal

5. PALATE MOVEMENT

1 Symmetrical
2 Asymmetrical
3 Minimal/absent

6. LARYNGEAL FUNCTION (aah/ee)

1 Normal
2 Weak
3 Absent

7. GAG

1 Present
2 Absent

8. VOLUNTARY COUGH

1 Normal
2 Weak
3 Absent

Instructions
Items 9–14 – Stage 1: give a teaspoon (5 ml) of water three times

9. DRIBBLES WATER

1 None/once
2 > Once

10. LARYNGEAL MOVEMENT ON ATTEMPTED SWALLOW

1 Yes
2 No

11. "REPEATED MOVEMENTS" FELT?

1 None/once
2 > Once

12. COUGH ON SWALLOWING

1 None/once
2 > Once

13. STRIDULOUS ON SWALLOWING

1 No
2 Yes

14. LARYNGEAL FUNCTION AFTER SWALLOWING

1 Normal
2 Weak/wet
3 Absent

Instructions
Items 15–19 – Stage 2: if the swallow is normal in stage 1 (two out of three attempts), try 60 ml of water in a beaker

15. ABLE TO FINISH?

1 Yes
2 No

Time taken to finish (secs)?______

Number of sips:________________

16. COUGH DURING OR AFTER SWALLOWING

1 No
2 Yes

17. STRIDOR DURING OR AFTER SWALLOWING

1 No
2 Yes

18. LARYNGEAL FUNCTION AFTER SWALLOWING

1 Normal
2 Weak/wet
3 Absent

19. DO YOU FEEL ASPIRATION IS PRESENT?

1 No
2 Possible
3 Yes

TOTAL SCORE:________

Acknowledgement: From Smithard, D. G. et al. (1998). Can bedside assessment reliably exclude aspiration following acute stroke? *Age and Ageing*, *27*(2), 99–106, Appendix, pp. 105–106, by permission of Oxford University Press.

SECTION 3
Scales assessing motor functions

3.1 Muscle power functions

Medical Research Council Motor Scale (MRC-MS)

Medical Research Council (1943)

Source

This method of assessing muscle power function was described in a monograph under the imprint of the United Kingdom Medical Research Council in 1943. It has been very widely adopted into routine medical practice and it also has been incorporated into other assessment scales, for example the Motricity Index (see page 394). It is often referred to by the abbreviation, MMT (manual muscle testing).

Purpose

The MRC Motor Scale is a performance-based measurement of muscle functioning through an assessment of muscle power. The original aim of the scale was to monitor recovery from injuries to peripheral nerves.

Item description

The clinician assesses the patient's muscle power by determining the function of specific muscles as shown in the MRC monograph, or of muscle groups producing movement in specific directions at each joint.

Scale development

No details of the development of the scale are available. It seems likely that the group of clinicians listed in the monograph, who treated patients with muscle weakness as a result of peripheral nerve injuries, developed the scale by consensus.

Administration procedures, response format and scoring

The scale assesses muscle power function by examining movement at specific joints. Responses are classified into six grades as follows: 0 (no contraction), 1 (flicker or trace of contraction), 2 (active movement with gravity eliminated), 3 (active movement against gravity), 4 (active movement against gravity and resistance), and 5 (normal muscle power, as subjectively evaluated by the examiner) (MRC, 1943).

Conventionally, the muscle power is reported as a numerical grade (from 0 to 5). The grade is specified for each muscle, or muscle group, that is tested.

Psychometric properties

In this assessment higher grades include wide ranges of muscle power. Clinically, it is well recognized that precision is more difficult to achieve at grades 4 and 5. Bohannon (2005) studied 107 consecutive patients with mixed diagnoses (60% with stroke) in an acute rehabilitation unit (see Box 6.8).

Box 6.8

Validity:	Construct: *Discriminant:* Bohannon: sensitivity 72%, specificity 77% for 30% difference in muscle power as measured by dynamometry
Reliability:	Inter-rater: Jepsen, Laursen, Larsen, & Hagert (2004): mixed diagnoses, for selected upper extremity muscles: *k* = .54
	Test–retest: Great Lakes ALS Study Group: 6 months: motor neurone disease: Mean power of 34 muscles: *r* = .67
Responsiveness:	Not applicable

Comment

This assessment scale is in universal use and is a component of a routine neurological examination. Although its psychometric properties are limited, it remains a quick and readily understood method of assessment of muscle power. It was developed in the context of peripheral nerve injuries but has been applied very widely in acquired brain impairment and has fair validity in this setting. An alternative is electronic manual muscle testing, but this requires specialized equipment and is difficult to use for large muscle groups.

Key references

Bohannon, R. W. (2005). Manual muscle testing: Does it meet the standards of an adequate screening test? *Clinical Rehabilitation*, *19*(6), 662–667.

Great Lakes ALS Study Group. (2003). A comparison of muscle strength testing techniques in amyotrophic lateral sclerosis. *Neurology*, *61*(11), 1503–1507.

Jepsen, J. R., Laursen, L. H., Larsen, A. I., & Hagert, C. G. (2004). Manual strength testing in 14 upper limb muscles: A study of inter-rater reliability. *Acta Orthopaedica Scandinavica*, *75*(4), 442–448.

Medical Research Council. (1943). *Aids to the investigation of peripheral nerve injuries* (Revised 2nd ed.). London: War Memorandum No. 7.

3.2 Muscle tone functions

Ashworth Scale (AS)

Ashworth (1964)

Source

Ashworth described a 5-level categorical scale in 1964 to measure spasticity in multiple sclerosis. The modified version (MAS; 6-level categorical scale) of Bohannon and Smith (1987) is reproduced below.

Purpose

This performance-based scale aims to measure spasticity.

Item description

The examiner grades muscle tone while the limb is being passively moved at the joint where the spasticity is being assessed.

Scale development

No specific details are given in the initial publication. Ashworth (1964) appears to have developed the scale based on clinical experience.

Administration procedures, response format and scoring

The rating of spasticity is made after the clinician tests the resistance to passive motion of a joint. The assessor perceives the resistance while moving the joint through a full range of movement (with the exception of grade 4). A score is then allocated.

Ashworth (1964) stated that the patient should be lying in a relaxed position. It is suggested that the velocity of movement should be kept low, less than 80° per second, the patient's positioning is standardized, the starting angle is specified and the presence of pain is noted (Pandyan, Johnson, Price, Curless, Barnes, & Rodgers, 1999). However, in patients with impairment of consciousness Mehrholz et al. (2005b) found that the velocity of movement did not influence reliability. The assessment can be performed very quickly – within a minute. Specific training has been suggested (two 45 minute sessions) (Mehrholz et al., 2005b).

The original scale had the following categories: 0 (no increase in muscle tone), 1 (slight increase in tone giving a catch when the limb was moved in flexion or extension), 2 (more marked increase in tone but limb easily flexed), 3 (considerable increase in tone, passive movement difficult), 4 (affected parts rigid in flexion or extension) (Ashworth, 1964, p. 541).

Psychometric properties

Ashworth (1964) studied 24 patients, aged 25 to 61 years, with substantial disability as a result of multiple sclerosis. Psychometric properties of the scale appear to vary in different muscle groups, for example Sloan, Sinclair, Thompson, Taylor, and Pentland (1992) demonstrated greater reliability in the upper extremity than in the lower extremity (see Box 6.9).

Derivative of the Ashworth Scale: Modified Ashworth Scale (MAS); Bohannon and Smith (1987)

Bohannon and Smith (1987) modified the Ashworth scale by adding a sixth category. They added a category 1+ (slight increase in muscle tone, manifested by a catch followed by minimal resistance through the remainder), with the aim of increasing the sensitivity of the scale. Mehrholz et al. (2005a) and colleagues criticize the MAS because the terms "catch" and "release" in the added category (1+) are not defined.

Comment

The AS and MAS are widely used in acquired brain impairment. Validity is not clearly established and inter-rater reliability is variable. This may be caused by the lack of recognition that soft tissue contracture, as well as spasticity, limits movement at a joint. In spite of their widespread use, these scales are not recommended methods for assessment of spasticity in the clinical or research settings. The Tardieu Scale (see page 373) could be used clinically, and laboratory methods should be considered for use in research studies.

Box 6.9

Validity:	Criterion: *Concurrent:* Patrick & Ada: laboratory measure: $k = .24$ (upper extremity), $k = .25$ (lower extremity) *Convergent/divergent:* Pandyan et al. (2003): questioned validity because r = .51 between modified Ashworth score and resistance to passive movement suggests it measures stiffness of soft tissues rather than spasticity per se
Reliability:	Inter-rater: Bohannon & Smith: at elbow 87% agreement (MAS) Allison, Abraham, & Petersen: at ankle in TBI, $k = .40$ Mehrholz et al. (2005b): multiple muscle groups: $k \sim 0.5$ (MAS) Mehrholz, Major, Meissner, Sandi-Gahun, Koch, & Pohl: $k = .16–.42$ (MAS) Test–retest: Allison et al.: 24 hours: $r = .82$ (plantar flexors) Mehrholz et al. (2005b): 24 hours: $k = .74$ (upper & lower extremities)
Responsiveness:	Ashworth: 16/24 improved with medication

Key references

Allison, S. C., Abraham, L. D., & Petersen, C. L. (1996). Reliability of the Modified Ashworth Scale in the assessment of plantarflexor muscle spasticity in patients with traumatic brain injury. *International Journal of Rehabilitation Research*, *19*(1), 67–78.

Ashworth, B. (1964). Preliminary trial of carisoprodal in multiple sclerosis. *The Practitioner*, *192*, 540–542.

Bohannon, R. W., & Smith, M. B. (1987). Interrater reliability of a Modified Ashworth Scale of muscle spasticity. *Physical Therapy*, *67*(2), 206–207.

Mehrholz, J., Major, Y., Meissner, D., Sandi-Gahun, S., Koch, R., & Pohl, M. (2005a). The influence of contractures and variation in measurement stretching velocity on the reliability of the Modified Ashworth Scale in patients with severe brain injury. *Clinical Rehabilitation*, *19*(1), 63–72.

Mehrholz, J., Wagner, K., Meissner, D., Grundmann, K., Zange, C., Koch, R., et al. (2005b). Reliability of the Modified Tardieu Scale and the Modified Ashworth Scale in adult patients with severe brain injury: A comparison study. *Clinical Rehabilitation*, *19*(7), 751–759.

Pandyan, A. D., Johnson, G. R., Price, C. I. M., Curless, R. H., Barnes, M. P., & Rodgers, H. (1999). A review of the properties and limitations of the Ashworth and modified Ashworth Scales as measures of spasticity. *Clinical Rehabilitation*, *37*, 373–383.

Pandyan, A. D., Price, C. I. M., Barnes, M. P., & Johnson, G. R. (2003). A biomechanical investigation into the validity of the modified Ashworth Scale as a measure of elbow spasticity. *Clinical Rehabilitation*, *17*(3), 290–293.

Patrick, E., & Ada, L. (2006). The Tardieu Scale differentiates contracture from spasticity whereas the Ashworth Scale is confounded by it. *Clinical Rehabilitation*, *20*(2), 173–182.

Sloan, R. L., Sinclair, E., Thompson, J., Taylor, S., & Pentland, B. (1992). Inter-rater reliability of the modified Ashworth Scale for spasticity in hemiplegic patients. *International Journal of Rehabilitation Research*, *15*(2), 158–161.

Modified Ashworth Scale

Bohannon and Smith (1987)

Instructions (adapted from Mehrholz et al., 2005b):

Assess the person lying supine on his or her back, with the upper limbs as parallel as possible to the trunk, elbows extended and wrists in a neutral position, the lower limbs parallel to one another.

Move the limb through its full range of motion at a stretching velocity standardized by timing the movement of the limb (counting "one thousand and one . . ." as the time to complete the movement). Keep repeated movement cycles at a minimum.

Extend the patient's limb first from a position of maximal possible flexion to maximal possible extension (the point at which the first soft resistance is met). Next, assess spasticity while moving from extension to flexion. Exceptions are for shoulder extensors (moving from extension to 90° of flexion), shoulder internal rotators (moving from neutral to maximum external rotation) and ankle plantar flexors (moving from extension to flexion first with knee extended and second with knee flexed).

Score a grade (as below) at each joint, and in each direction of movement, for which a rating is required.

Grade	Description
0	No increase in muscle tone
1	Slight increase in muscle tone, manifested by a catch and release or by minimal resistance at the end of the range of motion when the affected part(s) is moved in flexion or extension
1+	Slight increase in muscle tone, manifested by a catch, followed by minimal resistance throughout the remainder (less than half) of the range of motion
2	More marked increase in muscle tone through most of the range of motion, but affected part(s) easily moved
3	Considerable increase in muscle tone, passive movement difficult
4	Affected part(s) rigid in flexion or extension

Acknowledgement: Adapted from Merholz, J., Wagner, K., Meissner, D., Grundmann, K., Zange, C., Koch, R., et al. (2005b). Reliability of the Modified Tardieu Scale and the Modified Ashworth Scale in adult patients with severe brain injury: a comparison study. *Clinical Rehabilitation*, *19* (7), 751–759.

Tardieu Scale (TS)

Gracies, Marosszeky, Renton, Sandanam, Gandevia, and Burke (2000)

Source

Gracies et al.'s (2000) description of the TS is the source.

Purpose

The TS is an objective test that aims to measure spasticity, defined as a velocity dependent increase in muscle tone.

Item description

The scale rates spasticity as the difference between the reactions of a muscle to stretch at a slow and a fast speed. The slow velocity of the first stretch remains below the threshold for any significant stretch reflex and provides the clinician with an assessment of the passive range of motion. In contrast, the stretch at a fast velocity maximizes the involvement of the stretch reflex. If any spasticity is present, during this fast stretch, there is a sensation of catch-and-release, or of clonus, fatigable or not, depending on the amount of spasticity. The key parameter of the scale is the spasticity angle, which is the difference between the angle of arrest at slow speed and the angle of catch at fast speed (Gracies et al., 2000).

Scale development

Tardieu and colleagues described a clinical method of assessing spasticity muscle by muscle at several predefined velocities in the 1960s and 1970s. The method was simplified by Held and Pierrot-Deseilligny. These publications were in French. Tardieu's method was simplified by Gracies and colleagues (2000) and named the Tardieu Scale.

Administration procedures, response format and scoring

Three stretching velocities are described. V1 is as slow as possible and measures the passive range of motion. V2 is the speed that the limb segment falls under gravity, and V3 is as fast as possible (faster than with gravity). There is some concern at causing injury by stretching at a fast velocity and the recent reliability study of Mehrholz et al. (2005) was conducted at V2 to minimize the risk of injury. The assessment can be performed very quickly – within a minute. Specific training (two 45 minute sessions) has been suggested (Mehrholz et al., 2005).

The quality of the muscle reaction is reported, as well as the angle at which the catch occurs. This angle is measured with a goniometer. Ideally, assessments should be performed at a specific time during the day, with the patient in the same position.

Psychometric properties

Recent studies have been performed using semi-standardized conditions (Gracies et al., 2000; Mehrholz et al., 2005). In patients with stroke the percentage of exact agreement between assessors and a standard electromechanical method of assessment of spasticity at elbow flexors and ankle plantarflexors was 100%. Reliability varies with the joint and stretching direction without a clear pattern evident (Mehrholz et al., 2005). Gracies et al. (2000) studied a convenience sample of 16 patients, with hemiparesis and upper limb spasticity as a result of chronic stroke (see Box 6.10).

Box 6.10

Validity:	Criterion:
	Concurrent: Patrick & Ada: laboratory measure: $k = .86$ (elbow flexors), $k = .62$ (ankle plantar flexors)
Reliability:	Inter-rater: Mehrholz et al.: $k = .29–.53$
	Test–retest: Mehrholz et al.: 24 hours: $k = .53–.87$
Responsiveness:	No information available

Comment

The TS is used in acquired brain impairment (stroke and other conditions). It should be considered if spasticity is to be assessed in clinical practice. To optimize reliability, careful attention should be given to standardization of its administration. Because inter-rater reliability is poor to fair and temporal stability is in general fair, laboratory methods of evaluation of spasticity (such as stretch-induced electromyographic activity) should be considered for use in research studies.

Key references

Gracies, J. M., Marosszeky, J. E., Renton, R., Sandanam, J., Gandevia, S. C., & Burke, D. (2000). Short-term effects of dynamic lycra splints on upper limb in hemiplegic patients. *Archives of Physical Medical and Rehabilitation*, *81*(12), 1547–1555.

Mehrholz, J., Wagner, K., Meissner, D., Grundmann, K., Zange, C., Koch, R., et al. (2005). Reliability of the Modified Tardieu Scale and the Modified Ashworth Scale in adult patients with severe brain injury: A comparison study. *Clinical Rehabilitation*, *19*(7), 751–759.

Patrick, E., & Ada, L. (2006). The Tardieu Scale differentiates contracture from spasticity whereas the Ashworth Scale is confounded by it. *Clinical Rehabilitation*, *20*(2), 173–182.

Tardieu Scale

Gracies, Marosszeky, Renton, Sandanam, Gandevia, and Burke (2000)

Instructions

Grading is always performed at the same time of the day, in a constant position of the body for a given limb. Other joints, particularly the neck, must also remain in a constant position throughout the test and between tests. For each muscle group, reaction to stretch is rated at a specified stretch velocity (V) with 2 parameters, quality of muscle reaction (X; see table below) and angle of muscle reaction (Y). The angle of muscle reaction is measured relative to the position of minimal stretch of the muscle (corresponding to angle 0°) for all joints except hip, where it is relative to the resting anatomic position.

The rater moves the joint first with a very slow stretching velocity (described as V1) through its full range of motion. The full passive range of motion is measured with a goniometer.

Next the joint is moved by the rater "as fast as possible" in the same direction and through the same full movement arc. To avoid possible injury to the measured joints, use a stretching velocity chosen to simulate the limb segment falling under the influence of gravity (V2) instead of a maximum stretching velocity (V3), for elbow, wrist and knee extensor muscles.
The Tardieu Scale is then rated at the fastest stretching velocity (either V2 or V3) and scores range from 0 to 4 (tabulated below). If quality of muscle reaction score is 2 or higher, the angle of the first spasticity provoked point of "catch" (i.e., quality of muscle reaction), is measured with the goniometer.

Velocity of stretch (V)
V1: As slow as possible (minimizing stretch reflex).
V2: Speed of the limb segment falling under gravity.
V3: As fast as possible (faster than the rate of the natural drop of the limb segment under gravity).

V1 is used to measure the passive range of motion (PROM). Only V2 or V3 are used to rate spasticity

Quality of muscle reaction (X)

0	No resistance throughout the course of the passive movement
1	Slight resistance throughout the course of the passive movement, with no clear catch at a precise angle
2	Clear catch at a precise angle, interrupting the passive movement, followed by release
3	Fatigable clonus (< 10 seconds when maintaining pressure) occurring at a precise angle
4	Infatigable clonus (≥ 10 seconds when maintaining pressure) occurring at a precise angle

Measurement
Spasticity is present if X ≥ 2 at V2 or V3
(as defined by Patrick & Ada, 2006)

Acknowledgement: Adapted from Gracies, J. M. et al. (2000). Short-term effects of dynamic lycra splints on upper limb in hemiplegic patients. *Archives of Physical Medicine and Rehabilitation*, *81*(12), 1547–1555, Appendix 1, p. 1555, with permission from American Congress of Rehabilitation Medicine and the American Academy of Physical Medicine and Rehabilitation and Elsevier.

3.3 Movement functions

Berg Balance Scale (BBS)

Berg, Wood-Dauphinee, Williams, and Gayton (1989)

Source

Items for the BBS are available in Berg et al. (1989) and detailed administration and scoring procedures are available on a number of websites, including the University of Missouri (http://www.missouri.edu), and are reproduced below.

Purpose

The BBS is a performance-based test. It is designed to assess balance and risk of falls in community dwelling older people. Specifically it was developed with the intention of providing a means to determine change in balance ability over time. Although the BBS was initially developed to assess balance, it is often used to assess movement functions more broadly and to predict outcome in rehabilitation programmes (Feld, Rabadi, Blau, & Jordan, 2001; Wee, Bagg, & Palepu, 1999; Wee, Wong, & Palepu, 2003). The BBS has been used widely in other clinical populations and there are some reports in traumatic brain injury (TBI; e.g., Bateman, Culpan, Pickering, Powell, Scott, & Greenwood, 2001; Newstead, Hinman, & Tomberlin, 2005).

Item description

The BBS comprises 14 items including sitting, transferring, turning and reaching. Items are arranged in order from less difficult to more difficult.

Scale development

The BBS was developed through interviews with health professionals, and people with balance problems, to generate a 38-item pool. Through a review of perceived usefulness, clarity, internal consistency and reliability the pool was reduced to a final list of 14 items.

Administration procedures, response format and scoring

The BBS was designed for clinical use and can be completed in 20 minutes. A step, a stopwatch, a ruler and two chairs (one with arms and the other without) are the equipment that is required.

The 14 items are each scored on a 5-point ordinal scale (0–4), with higher scores indicating better functioning. The score on each item is summed to give a total score, ranging from 0 to 56. Specific criteria are listed for the scoring of each item.

Psychometric properties

Substantial psychometric data are available both in the initial report (Berg et al., 1989) and subsequently (see Box 6.11). The initial report included 38 older patients and 32 health professionals from a variety of disciplines. At admission to an inpatient stroke rehabilitation programme, English, Hillier, Stiller, and Warden-Flood (2006) reported a mean BBS of 30.3 ($SD = 6.8$). The sample size was 70, mean age 65 years, but time since onset of stroke was not reported. For a similar clinical group ($n = 246$, mean age 74.9 years), mean BBS, at admission to a stroke rehabilitation ward, was 25.4 ($SE = 0.9$) for stroke patients who returned home (Wee et al., 1999).

Derivatives of the Berg Balance Scale

Short forms of the BBS have been developed and the 7-item short form has similar psychometric properties to the full BBS and is easier and faster to complete (Chou, Chien, Hsueh, Sheu, Wang, & Hsieh, 2006).

A modification of the scoring procedures of the BBS was proposed by Wang, Hsueh, Sheu, Yao, and Hseih (2004). The three middle levels of the scale are collapsed, so that each item is scored 0, 2, 4. It is reported to have similar psychometric properties to the original scale.

Comment

The BBS was carefully developed and is a very useful clinical tool. Although it was developed as a balance test for older people, it has had wide use with other populations including people with acquired brain impairment. It can be conceptualized as a scale that assesses "balance" as well as movement functions more broadly.

Box 6.11

Validity	Criterion: *Concurrent:* Feld et al. (2001) with Functional Independence Measure in patients with ABI, $r = .86$ *Predictive:* Wee et al. (1999), for length of stay in stroke: $r = -.6$ Construct: *Internal consistency:* Berg et al. (1989): Cronbach alpha .96
Reliability:	Inter-rater: Berg et al. (1992): Total score: $r = .98$ Sackley, Richardson, McDonnell, Ratib, Dewey, & Hill: Total score: $r = .74–1.00$ Test–retest: Sackley et al.: 1 week: $k = .37$ Newstead et al.: within 1 week: ICC = .99 Bateman et al.: no significant change over time in TBI in intervention study
Responsiveness:	English et al. & Wee et al. (2003): excellent sensitivity for inpatient stroke rehabilitation Stevenson: minimum detectable change: +/– 6 points

Key references

Bateman, A., Culpan, F. J., Pickering, A. D., Powell, J. H., Scott, O. M., & Greenwood, R. J. (2001). The effect of aerobic training on rehabilitation outcomes after recent severe brain injury: A randomized controlled evaluation. *Archives of Physical Medical and Rehabilitation*, *82*(2), 174–182.

Berg, K., Wood-Dauphinee, S. L., Williams, J. I., & Gayton, D. (1989). Measuring balance in the elderly: Preliminary development of an instrument. *Physiotherapy Canada*, *41*, 304–311.

Berg, K. O., Wood-Dauphinee, S. L., Williams, J. I., & Maki, B. (1992). Measuring balance in the elderly: Validation of an instrument. *Canadian Journal of Public Health*, *83*(S2), S7–S11.

Chou, C. Y., Chien, C. W., Hsueh, I. P., Sheu, C. F., Wang, C. H., & Hsieh, C. L. (2006). Developing a short form of the Berg Balance Scale for people with stroke. *Physical Therapy*, *86*(2), 195–204.

English, C. K., Hillier, S. L., Stiller, K., & Warden-Flood, A. (2006). The sensitivity of three commonly used outcome measures to detect change amongst patients receiving inpatient rehabilitation following stroke. *Clinical Rehabilitation*, *20*(1), 52–55.

Feld, J. A., Rabadi, M. H., Blau, A. D., & Jordan, B. D. (2001). Berg Balance Scale and outcome measures in acquired brain injury. *Neurorehabilitation and Neural Repair*, *15*(3), 239–244.

Newstead, A. H., Hinman, M. R., & Tomberlin, J. A. (2005). Reliability of the Berg Balance Scale and balance master limits of stability tests for individuals with brain injury. *Journal of Neurological Physical Therapy*, *29*(1), 18–23.

Sackley, C., Richardson, P., McDonnell, K., Ratib, S., Dewey, M., & Hill, H. J. (2005). The reliability of balance, mobility and self-care measures in a population of adults with a learning disability known to a physiotherapy service. *Clinical Rehabilitation*, *19*(2), 216–223.

Stevenson, T. J. (2001). Detecting change in patients with stroke using the Berg Balance Scale. *Australian Journal of Physiotherapy*, *47*(1), 29–38.

Wang, C. H., Hsueh, I. P., Sheu, C. F., Yao, G., & Hsieh, C. L. (2004). Psychometric properties of 2 simplified 3-level balance scales used for patients with stroke. *Physical Therapy*, *84*(5), 430–438.

Wee, J. Y., Bagg, S. D., & Palepu, A. (1999). The Berg Balance Scale as a predictor of length of stay and discharge destination in an acute stroke rehabilitation setting. *Archives of Physical Medical and Rehabilitation*, *80*(4), 448–452.

Wee, J. Y., Wong H., & Palepu, A. (2003). Validation of the Berg Balance Scale as a predictor of length of stay and discharge destination in stroke rehabilitation. *Archives of Physical Medical and Rehabilitation*, *84*(5), 731–735.

Berg Balance Scale

Berg, Wood-Dauphinee, Williams, and Gayton (1989)

Name: **Administered by:** **Date:**

Summary score sheet (see below for response format):

	Score
1. Sitting unsupported	______
2. Change of position: sitting to standing	______
3. Change of position: standing to sitting	______
4. Transfers	______
5. Standing unsupported	______
6. Standing with eyes closed	______
7. Standing with feet together	______
8. Tandem standing	______
9. Standing on one leg	______
10. Turning trunk (fixed feet)	______
11. Retrieving objects from floor	______
12. Turning 360 degrees	______
13. Stool stepping	______
14. Reaching forward while standing	______

TOTAL SCORE: ______

Response format:

1. SITTING TO STANDING

Instructions: Please stand up. Try not to use your hands for support.

4 Able to stand without using hands and stabilize independently
3 Able to stand independently using hands
2 Able to stand using hands after several tries
1 Needs minimal aid to stand or to stablize
0 Needs moderate or maximal assist to stand

2. STANDING UNSUPPORTED

Instructions: Please stand for 2 minutes without holding.

4 Able to stand safely for 2 minutes
3 Able to stand 2 minutes with supervision
2 Able to stand 30 seconds unsupported
1 Needs several tries to stand 30 seconds unsupported
0 Unable to stand 30 seconds unassisted

If patient is able to stand 2 minutes unsupported, score full points for sitting unsupported. Proceed to item # 4 (standing to sitting)

3. SITTING WITH BACK UNSUPPORTED BUT FOOT SUPPORTED ON FLOOR OR ON A STOOL

Instructions: Please sit with arms folded for 2 minutes.

4 Able to sit safely and securely 2 minutes
3 Able to sit 2 minutes under supervision
2 Able to sit 30 seconds
1 Able to sit 10 seconds
0 Unable to sit without support 10 seconds

4. STANDING TO SITTING

Instructions: Please sit down.

4 Sits safely with minimal use of hands
3 Controls descent by using hands
2 Uses back of legs against chair to control descent
1 Sits independently but has uncontrolled descent
0 Needs assistance to sit

5. TRANSFERS

Instructions: Arrange chairs for a pivot transfer. Ask patient to transfer one way towards a seat with armrests and one way toward a seat without armrests. You may use two chairs (one with and one without armrests) or a bed and a chair.

4 Able to transfer safely with minor use of hands
3 Able to transfer safely definite need of hands
2 Able to transfer with verbal cueing and / or supervision
1 Needs one person to assist
0 Needs two people to assist or supervise to be safe

6. STANDING UNSUPPORTED WTH EYES CLOSED

Instructions: Please close your eyes and stand still for 10 seconds.

4 Able to stand 10 seconds safely
3 Able to stand 10 seconds with supervision
2 Able to stand 3 seconds
1 Unable to keep eyes closed 3 seconds but stays steady
0 Needs help to keep from falling

7. STANDING UNSUPPORTED WTH FEET TOGETHER

Instructions: Place your feet together and stand without holding.

4 Able to place feet together independently and stand 1 minute safely
3 Able to place feet together independently and stand for 1 minute with supervision
2 Able to place feet together independently and to hold for 30 seconds
1 Needs help to attain position but able to stand 15 seconds feet together
0 Needs help to attain position and unable to hold for 15 seconds

8. REACHING FORWARD WITH OUTSTRETCHED ARM WHILE STANDING

Instructions: Lift arm to 90 degrees. Stretch out your fingers and reach forward as far as you can. Examiner places a ruler at end of fingertips when arm is at 90 degrees, Fingers should not touch the ruler while reaching forward. The recorded measure is the distance forward that the finger reaches while the patient is in the most forward lean position. When possible, ask patient to use both arms when reaching to avoid rotation of the trunk.

4 Can reach forward confidently > 25 cm (10 inches)
3 Can reach forward > 12.5 cm safely (5 inches)
2 Can reach forward > 5 cm safely (2 inches)
1 Reaches forward but needs supervision
0 Loses balance while trying/requires external support

9. PICK UP OBJECT FROM THE FLOOR FROM A STANDING POSITION

Instructions: Pick up the shoe/slipper that is placed in front of your feet.

4 Able to pick up slipper safely and easily
3 Able to pick up slipper but needs supervision.
2 Unable to pick up but reaches 2–5 cm (1–2 inches) from slipper and keeps balance independently
1 Unable to pick up and needs supervision while trying
0 Unable to try/needs assist to keep from losing balance or falling

10. TURNING TO LOOK BEHIND OVER LEFT AND RIGHT SHOULDER WHILE STANDING

Instructions: Turn to look **directly** behind you over toward left shoulder. Repeat to the right. Examiner may pick an object to look at directly behind the patient to encourage a better twist turn.

4 Looks behind from both sides and weight shifts well
3 Looks behind one side only, other side shows less weight shift
2 Turns sideways only but maintains balance
1 Needs supervision when turning
0 Needs assist to keep from losing balance or falling

11. TURN 360 DEGREES

Instructions: Turn completely around in a full circle. Pause. Then turn a full circle in the other direction.

4 Able to turn 360 degrees safely in 4 seconds or less
3 Able to turn 360 degrees safely one side only in 4 seconds or less
2 Able to turn 360 degrees safely but slowly
1 Needs close supervision or verbal cueing
0 Needs assistance while turning

12. PLACING ALTERNATE FEET ON STEP OR STOOL WHILE STANDING UNSUPPORTED

Instructions: Place each foot alternately on the step/stool. Continue until each foot has touched the step / stool four times.

4 Able to stand independently and safely complete 8 steps in 20 seconds
3 Able to stand independently and complete 8 steps in > 20 seconds
2 Able to complete 4 steps without aid, with supervision
1 Able to complete > 2 steps, needs minimal assist
0 Needs assistance to keep from falling/unable to try

13. STANDING UNSUPPORTED ONE FOOT IN FRONT

Instructions: Demonstrate to patient: Place one foot directly in front of the other. If you feel that you cannot place your foot directly in front, try to step far enough ahead that the heel of your forward foot is ahead of the toes on the other foot.
Scoring: for 3 points, the length of the step should exceed the length of the other foot and the width of the stance should approximate the patient's normal stride width.

4 Able to place foot tandem independently and hold 30 seconds
3 Able to place foot ahead of other independently and hold 30 seconds
2 Able to take small step independently and hold 30 seconds
1 Needs help to step but can hold 15 seconds
0 Loses balance while stepping or standing

14. STANDING ON ONE LEG

Instructions: Stand on one leg as long as you can without holding.

4 Able to lift leg independently and hold > 10 seconds
3 Able to lift leg independently and hold 5–10 seconds
2 Able to lift leg independently and hold ≥ 3 seconds
1 Tries to lift leg, unable to hold 3 seconds but remains standing independently
0 Unable to try or needs assistance to prevent fall

TOTAL SCORE: ________ / 56

Fugl-Meyer Assessment (FMA)

Fugl-Meyer, Jaasko, Leyman, Olsson, and Steglind (1975)

Source

The items and scoring procedures for the FMA are available in Fugl-Meyer et al. (1975) and are reproduced below.

Purpose

The FMA is a performance-based test. Fugl-Meyer and colleagues (1975, p. 13) describe the FMA as a "system for assessment of the development of motor function and balance" in patients who have had a stroke. Its aim is "to assess motor performance of the upper and lower limb as well as control of sitting and standing balance" (Kwakkel, Kollen, & Twisk, 2006, p. 2349). Use of the FMA has largely been in people with stroke.

Item description

The FMA "comprises three different but interdependent parts: I Motor function and balance; II Some sensation qualities; III Passive range of motion and occurrence of joint pain" (Fugl-Meyer et al., 1975, p. 13). Motor function is assessed in the upper extremity in three regions – Shoulder/elbow forearm "A"; Wrist "B"; Hand "C"; and then with reference to Coordination/speed "D". Motor function in the lower extremity is assessed in three categories – Hip/knee/ankle "E"; Coordination/speed "F"; and Balance "G". Finally Sensation "H" and Joint motion and Joint pain "J" are assessed. In total there are 49 items.

Scale development

The FMA was developed to evaluate changes in motor function after stroke in the areas of balance, lower and upper extremity motor function and coordination, joint range of motion and pain (Fugl-Meyer et al., 1975). The test assumes that motor recovery occurs in a set sequence in which reflexes return, then there is stereotyped movement, followed by some control and lastly normal movement.

Administration procedures, response format and scoring

Equipment is required to administer the FMA: a plinth or mat, a ball, a small jar, paper, a reflex hammer, a cotton ball, a goniometer and a stopwatch. Administration time is 30 to 45 minutes and training is required. Duncan, Propst, and Nelson (1983) provided 1 to 2 hours training for physical therapists for their reliability study.

Scoring is detailed and varies among items. Generally there are three response categories for each item (0, 1, 2), which contain specific descriptors. The score for each item is summed. The maximum total motor score is 100 (66 points for Upper extremity and 34 points for Lower extremity), while the maximum scores for the other components are Balance ("G") 14, Sensation ("H") 24, Joint motion and Joint pain ("J") 44 for each. Higher scores indicate better functioning.

Psychometric properties

See Box 6.12 for details.

Box 6.12

Validity:	Criterion: *Concurrent:* Poole & Whitney: with Motor Assessment Scale: $r = .88$
Reliability	Test–retest: Duncan et al. (1983): 3 weeks: Total score: $r = .98$
Responsiveness:	Duncan et al. (1998): adequate responsiveness in a clinical trial – Kwakkel et al.: adequate responsiveness in prognostic study.

Comment

This scale of motor recovery is reliable and responsive. It is largely an impairment-based scale with upper and lower extremity items. It has been used as a "gold standard" in research but is likely to have limited application clinically because of its complexity and lengthy administration time.

Key references

Duncan, P. W., Propst, M., & Nelson, S. G. (1983). Reliability of the Fugl-Meyer assessment of sensorimotor recovery following cerebrovascular accident. *Physical Therapy*, *63*(10), 1606–1610.

Duncan, P., Richards, L., Wallace, D., Stoker-Yates, J., Pohl, P., Luchies, C., et al. (1998). A randomized, controlled pilot study of a home-based exercise program for individuals with mild and moderate stroke. *Stroke*, *29*(10), 2055–2060.

Fugl-Meyer, A. R., Jaasko, L., Leyman, I., Olsson, S., & Steglind, S. (1975). The post-stroke hemiplegic patient. 1. A method for evaluation of physical performance. *Scandinavian Journal of Rehabilitation Medicine*, *7*(1), 13–31.

Kwakkel, G., Kollen, B., & Twisk, J. (2006). Impact of time on improvement of outcome after stroke. *Stroke*, *37*(9), 2348–2353.

Poole, J. L., & Whitney, S. L. (1988). Motor assessment scale for stroke patients: Concurrent validity and interrater reliability. *Archives of Physical Medical and Rehabilitation*, *69*(3 Pt 1), 195–197.

Items from the Fugl-Meyer Assessment

Fugl-Meyer, Jaasko, Leyman, Olsson, and Steglind (1975)

UPPER EXTREMITY

A. SHOULDER/ELBOW/FOREARM

I	Reflex activity	Flexors
		Extensors
IIa	Shoulder	Retraction
		Elevation
		Abduction
		Outward rotation
	Elbow	Flexion
	Forearm	Supination
IIb	Shoulder	Add-/inward rotation
	Elbow	Extension
	Forearm	Pronation
III	Hand to lumbar spine	
	Shoulder	Flexion 0°–90°
	Elbow 90°	Pro-/supination
IV	Shoulder	Abduction 0°–90°
		Flexion 90°–180°
	Elbow 0°	Pro/supination
V	Normal reflex activity	

B. WRIST

Elbow 90°	Wrist stability
Elbow 90°	Wrist flexion/extension
Elbow 0°	Wrist stability
Elbow 0°	Wrist flexion/extension
Circumduction	

C. HAND

Fingers mass flexion
Fingers mass extension
Grasp a
Grasp b
Grasp c
Grasp d
Grasp e

D. COORDINATION/SPEED

Tremor
Dysmetria
Time

LOWER EXTREMITY

E. HIP/KNEE/ANKLE

I	Reflex activity	Flexors
		Extensors
IIa	Hip	Flexion
	Knee	Flexion
	Ankle	Dorsiflexion
IIb	Hip	Extension
		Adduction
	Knee	Extension
	Ankle	Plantar flexion
III	Knee	Flexion
	Ankle	Dorsiflexion
IV	Knee	Flexion
	Ankle	Dorsiflexion
V	Normal reflex activity	

F. COORDINATION/SPEED

Tremor
Dysmetria
Time

G. BALANCE

Sit without support
Protective reaction non-affected side
Protective reaction affected side
Stand with support
Stand without support
Stand on non-affected leg
Stand on affected leg

H. SENSATION

a.	Light touch	Arm
		Vola
		Leg
		Plantar
b.	Position	Shoulder
		Elbow
		Wrist
		Thumb
		Hip
		Knee
		Ankle
		Toes

J. PASSIVE JOINT MOTION/JOINT PAIN

Shoulder	Flexion
	Abduction → 90°
	Outward rotation
	Inward rotation
Elbow	Flexion
	Extension
Forearm	Pronation
	Supination
Wrist	Flexion
	Extension
Fingers	Flexion
	Extension
Hip	Flexion
	Abduction
	Outward rotation
	Inward rotation
Knee	Flexion
	Extension
Ankle	Dorsiflexion
	Plantar flexion
Foot	Pronation
	Supination

Acknowledgement: Assessment test from Fugl-Meyer, A. R. et al. (1975). The post-stroke hemiplegic patient. 1. A method for evaluation of physical performance. *Scandinavian Journal of Rehabilitation Medicine*, *7*(1), 13–31, pp. 14–19 used by permission of Professor A. Fugl-Meyer.

High-level Mobility Assessment Tool (HiMAT)

Williams, Robertson, Greenwood, Goldie, and Morris (2005a)

Source

Items of the HiMAT are available from the website of the Center for Outcome Measurement in Brain Injury (http://www.tbims.org/combi/himat/index.html), and are also reproduced below.

Purpose

The HiMAT is a performance-based scale designed "to assess high-level mobility deficits following traumatic brain injury and quantify therapy outcomes" (Williams, Robertson, Greenwood, Goldie, & Morris, 2005b, p. 925).

Item description

The HiMAT comprises nine types of activity that generate 13 scores. These include a range of mobility and gait items, including more challenging tasks such as running and bounding.

Scale development

Existing mobility scales were reviewed to identify possible items for inclusion and experts were consulted. The *International Classification of Functioning Disability and Health* (WHO, 2001) informed the review and scale development. At the first expert meeting and telephone interviews, a pool of potential items was generated based on expert opinion and the literature review. A questionnaire was developed listing potential items and the experts commented on this. The authors adjudicated the suggested inclusions and a second meeting was held to confirm consensus. A total of 157 items or variations on items was generated from the group meeting (111 items) and telephone interviews (46 items). Twenty items were presented to the second group meeting. After this second meeting there was substitution of three items with others for reasons of practicability and support from the literature. Five of the 20 final items were generated by the experts. Reliability and validity studies were then conducted and the best 13 items were retained.

Administration procedures, response format and scoring

The HiMAT is suitable for people who can walk for more than 20 metres without assistance, and may use orthoses. The walking item is administered first. A flight of 14 stairs is required, as well as a house brick and a stopwatch. In many settings assessment will need to be conducted outdoors because a 20 metre distance is used for a number of items (including running).

Administration time is reported by the authors to be 5 to 10 minutes. Participants are permitted one practice trial for each item and are instructed to undertake each task at their maximum safe speed, except the bounding and stair items.

Each item is timed or measured. Most items require careful observation because non-compliance with requirements is scored as a fail on that item. The mean of three trials of bounding is used to calculate this item score. The total score is the sum of each item score and ranges from 0 to 54, with higher scores indicating greater mobility.

Comparison data

Performance data are presented for the standardization sample (Williams et al., 2005a). A small number of examples are provided on the COMBI website (Williams, 2006).

Psychometric properties

Williams and colleagues (2005a, 2006a, 2006b) provide detailed information on psychometric properties in the development of the scale, using a sample of 103 patients with traumatic brain injury (TBI; age median = 27 years, 80% male, median duration of post-traumatic amnesia = 43.5 days) who were patients at Epworth Hospital, Melbourne, Australia. Three physiotherapists were the raters for the reliability studies with a test–retest interval of 2 days (see Box 6.13).

Box 6.13

Validity:	Criterion: *Concurrent:* Williams (2006): with Rivermead Mobility Assessment: $r = .87$
	Construct: *Internal consistency:* Williams et al. (2006a): Cronbach alpha .97
	Factor analysis: Williams et al. (2005a): 1 factor "high level mobility"
Reliability:	Inter-rater: Williams et al. (2006a): ICC = .99
	Test–retest: Williams et al. (2006a): 2 days: ICC = .99
Responsiveness:	Williams et al. (2006b): Mean change in 3 months for 14 people median 3 months after TBI was 12.1 points. Assessed using three methods and judged "highly responsive"

Comment

The HiMAT is a new and carefully developed instrument that has sound psychometric properties. It is appropriate for use with people with high level restriction in gait and mobility and has been developed and validated with people with TBI.

Key references

Williams, G. (2006). *The High Level Mobility Assessment Tool. The Center for Outcome Measurement in Brain Injury*. Retrieved 9 March 2007, from http://www.tbims.org/combi/himat

Williams, G. P., Greenwood, K. M., Robertson, V. J., Goldie, P. A., & Morris, M. E. (2006a). High-Level Mobility Assessment Tool (HiMAT): Interrater reliability, retest reliability, and internal consistency. *Physical Therapy*, *86*(3), 395–400.

Williams, G. P., Robertson, V., Greenwood, K. M., Goldie, P. A., & Morris, M. E. (2005a). The High-level Mobility Assessment Tool (HiMAT) for traumatic brain injury. Part 2: Content validity and discriminability. *Brain Injury*, *19*(10), 833–843.

Williams, G., Robertson, V., Greenwood, K., Goldie, P., & Morris, M. E. (2005b). The High-level Mobility Assessment Tool (HiMAT) for traumatic brain injury. Part 1: Item generation. *Brain Injury*, *19*(11), 925–932.

Williams, G., Robertson, V., Greenwood, K., Goldie, P., & Morris, M. E. (2006b). The concurrent validity and responsiveness of the High-level Mobility Assessment Tool for measuring the mobility limitations of people with traumatic brain injury. *Archives of Physical Medical and Rehabilitation*, *87*(3), 437–442.

World Health Organization (2001). *International classification of functioning, disability and health*. Geneva: World Health Organization.

High-level Mobility Assessment Tool

Williams, Robertson, Greenwood, Goldie, and Morris (2005a)

Instructions

General instructions: Patient suitability: The HiMAT is appropriate for assessing people with high-level balance and mobility problems. The minimal mobility requirement for testing is independent walking over 20 m without gait aids. Orthoses are permitted.

Testing takes 5–10 minutes. Patients are allowed 1 practice trial for each item.

Patients are instructed to perform at their maximum safe speed, except for the bounding and stair items.

Scoring: All times and distances are recorded in the "performance" column of the score sheet. The corresponding score for each item is then circled and each column is then subtotalled. Subtotals are then added to calculate the HiMAT score.

1. Walking	The middle 10 m of a 20 m trial is timed.
2. Walking backward	As for walking.
3. Walk on toes	As for walking. Any heel contact during the middle 10 m is recorded as a fail.
4. Walk over obstacle	As for walking. A house brick is placed across the walkway at the midpoint. Patients must step over the brick without contacting it. A fail is recorded if patients step around the brick or make contact with the brick.
5. Run	The middle 10 m of a 20 m trial is timed. A fail is recorded if patients fail to have a consistent flight phase during the trial.
6. Skipping	The middle 10 m of a 20 m trial is timed. A fail is recorded if patients fail to have a consistent flight phase during the trial.
7. Hop forward	Patients stand on their more affected leg and hop forward. The time to hop 10 metres is recorded.
8. Bound (affected)	A bound is a jump from one leg to the other with a flight phase. Patients stand behind a line on their less affected leg, hands on hips, and jump forward *landing on their more affected* leg. Each bound is measured from the line to the heel of the landing leg. The average of three trials is recorded.
9. Bound (less affected)	Patients stand behind a line on their more affected leg, hands on hips, and jump forward *landing on their less affected* leg. The average of three trials is recorded.
10. Up stairs	Patients are asked to walk up a flight of 14 stairs as they normally would and at their normal speed. The trial is recorded from when the patient starts until both feet are at the top. Patients who use a rail or a non-reciprocal pattern are scored on *Up Stairs Dependent*. Patients who ascend the stairs reciprocally without a rail are scored on *Up Stairs Independent* and get an additional 5 points in the last column of Up Stairs Dependent.
11. Down stairs	As for Up stairs.

High-level Mobility Assessment Tool

Williams, Robertson, Greenwood, Goldie, and Morris (2005a)

Score sheet

Name:	**Administered by:**	**Date:**

AFFECTED SIDE: LEFT/RIGHT

ITEM	PERFORMANCE	0	1	2	3	4	5
WALK	_______ sec	X	>6.6	5.4–6.6	4.3–5.3	<4.3	X
WALK BACKWARD	_______ sec		>13.3	8.1–13.3	5.8–8.0	<5.8	X
WALK ON TOES	_______ sec		>8.9	7.0–8.9	5.4–6.9	<5.4	X
WALK OVER OBSTACLE	_______ sec		>7.1	5.4–7.1	4.5–5.3	<4.5	X
RUN	_______ sec		>2.7	2.0–2.7	1.7–1.9	<1.7	X
SKIP	_______ sec		>4.0	3.5–4.0	3.0–3.4	<3.0	X
HOP FORWARD (AFFECTED)	_______ sec		>7.0	5.3–7.0	4.1–5.2	<4.1	X
BOUND (AFFECTED)	1) _______ cm 2) _______ cm 3) _______ cm		<80	80–103	104–132	>132	X
BOUND (LESS AFFECTED)	1) _______ cm 2) _______ cm 3) _______ cm		<82	82–105	106–129	>129	X
UP STAIRS DEPENDENT (Rail OR not reciprocal: if not, score 5 and rate below)	_______ sec		>22.8	14.6–22.8	12.3–14.5	<12.3	X
UP STAIRS INDEPENDENT (No rail AND not reciprocal: if not, score 0 and rate above)	_______ sec		>9.1	7.6–9.1	6.8–7.5	<6.8	X
DOWN STAIRS DEPENDENT (Rail OR not reciprocal: if not, score 5 and rate below)	_______ sec		>24.3	17.6–24.3	12.8–17.5	<12.8	X
DOWN STAIRS INDEPENDENT (No rail AND reciprocal: if not, score 0 and rate above)	_______ sec		>8.4	6.6–8.4	5.8–6.5	<5.8	X
	SUBTOTAL						

TOTAL HiMAT SCORE: _______ /54

Acknowledgement: From Williams, G. P. et al. (2005a). The High-level Mobility Assessment Tool (HiMAT) for traumatic brain injury. Part 2: Content validity and discriminability. *Brain Injury*, *19*(10), 833–843, Appendix, pp. 842–843, reproduced by permission of Taylor & Francis Ltd, www.tandf.co.uk/journals.

Motor Assessment Scale (MAS)

Carr, Shepherd, Nordholm, and Lynne (1985)

Source

Carr and colleagues published the initial description of the MAS in 1985. This version is reproduced in the present chapter because it is in regular current use. However, the muscle tone item of the MAS is not in current use (see below; Loewen & Anderson, 1988).

Purpose

The MAS is a performance-based test "designed to measure the progress of stroke patients" (Carr et al., 1985, p. 175).

Item description

The MAS measures eight different motor function (both lower and upper extremities) and, in addition, tone on the affected side. The eight motor items are supine to side lying onto intact side, supine to sitting over side of bed, balanced sitting, sitting to standing, walking, upper arm function, hand movements and advanced hand activities.

Scale development

The scale "was developed . . . over many years, after examining forms of assessment published in the literature" (Carr et al., 1985, p. 175). It was designed to be brief and easily administered, have good reliability, not use expensive equipment, be clearly written, be responsive, not duplicate other information, measure "everyday motor activities" and "measure the patient's best performance" (Carr et al., 1985, p. 175).

Administration procedures, response format and scoring

There is a specific descriptor for scoring each category on the nine items. The scoring sheets must be used to utilize the correct criteria. The scores for each item can be displayed on a grid (Carr et al., 1985) or summed to give a total score.

Equipment required to administer the MAS comprises a plinth or mat, a chair, 10 m space, a table, a cylinder, a 14 cm ball, a Styrofoam cup, a pen cap and pen/paper, eight jelly beans, two tea cups, a toothbrush, and a spoon. Administration time is 15 to 30 minutes and training is required. Carr et al. (1985) comment that high reliability was achieved with a minimum of practice by physiotherapists and final year physiotherapy students. However, Loewen and Anderson (1988) noted that 4 hours training on average was undertaken by raters in their study.

Each item is scored a 7-point ordinal scale, from 0 (the equivalent of unable to perform any aspect of the task) to 6 (the equivalent of optimal motor behaviour). The scores are presented for each category or summed (with the tone item excluded, the scores range from 0–48), with higher scores indicating a better level of functioning.

A recommendation was made to drop tone as a category in the Modified Motor Assessment Scale (Loewen & Anderson, 1988; Poole & Whitney, 1988) because of poor reliability. A change to the hierarchy of advanced hand activities was also recommended because the spoon and comb items are often easier than the drawing task.

Psychometric properties

Carr et al. (1985) provided initial validation data based on research with 15 stroke patients (aged $M = 70$ years). Loewen and Anderson (1988) stated that assessment of tone was unreliable (on clinical grounds) while Poole and Whitney (1988) demonstrated $r = .29$ for the tone item (see Box 6.14).

Comment

The MAS is a widely used and adequately validated evaluation of lower and upper extremity motor functioning. It is relatively brief to administer, and uses multiple items of equipment that are readily available. It is reliable in clinical and research settings with the tone item omitted. Training is required to achieve good reliability.

Box 6.14

Validity:	Criterion: *Concurrent:* Poole & Whitney: with Fugl-Meyer Assessment (Total score): $r = .88$
Reliability:	Inter-rater: Carr et al.: $r = .95$ Poole & Whitney: $r = .99$ (except tone) Test–retest: Carr et al.: 4 weeks: $r = .98$
Responsiveness:	English, Hillier, Stiller, & Warden-Flood: walking item most responsive in patients with stroke, between admission and discharge from inpatient rehabilitation, and arm items less responsive Dean & Mackey: demonstrated responsiveness in a similar patient group.

Key References

Carr, J. H., Shepherd, R. B., Nordholm, L., & Lynne, D. (1985). Investigation of a new motor assessment scale for stroke patients. *Physical Therapy*, *65*(2), 175–180.

Dean, C., & Mackey, F. (1992). Motor Assessment Scale scores as a measure of rehabilitation outcome following stroke. *Australian Journal of Physiotherapy*, *38*, 31–35.

English, C. K., Hillier, S. L., Stiller, K., & Warden-Flood, A. (2006). The sensitivity of three commonly used outcome measures to detect change amongst patients receiving inpatient rehabilitation following stroke. *Clinical Rehabilitation*, *20*(1), 52–55.

Loewen, S. C., & Anderson, B. A. (1988). Reliability of the Modified Motor Assessment Scale and the Barthel Index. *Physical Therapy*, *68*(7), 1077–1081.

Poole, J. L., & Whitney, S. L. (1988). Motor Assessment Scale for stroke patients: Concurrent validity and interrater reliability. *Archives of Physical Medical and Rehabilitation*, *69*(3 Pt 1), 195–197.

Motor Assessment Scale

Carr, Shepherd, Nordholm, and Lynne (1985)

General Instructions

1. The test should preferably be carried out in a quiet private room or curtained-off area.
2. The test should be carried out when patient is maximally alert. For example, not when s/he is under the influence of hypnotic or sedative drugs. Record should be made if patient is under the influence of one of these drugs.
3. Patient should be dressed in suitable street clothes with sleeves rolled up and without shoes and socks. Items 1 to 3 inclusive may be scored if necessary with patient in her/his night clothes.
4. Each item is recorded on a scale of 0 to 6.
5. All items are to be performed independently by the patient unless otherwise stated. "Stand-by help" means that the physical therapist stands by and may steady the patient but must not actively assist.
6. Items 1 to 8 are recorded according to the patient's responses to specific instructions. General tonus, item 9, is scored from continuous observations and handling throughout the assessment.
7. Patients should be scored on their best performance. Repeat three times unless other specific instructions are stated.
8. Because the scale is designed to score the patient's best performance, the physical therapist should give general encouragement but should not give specific feedback on whether the response is correct or incorrect. Sensitivity to the patient is necessary to enable her/him to produce her/his best performance.
9. Instructions should be repeated and demonstrations given to the patient if necessary.
10. The order of administration of items 1 to 9 can be varied according to convenience.
11. If the patient becomes emotionally labile at any stage during scoring, the physical therapist should wait 15 seconds before attempting to follow procedures:
    1) ask the patient to close her/his mouth and take a deep breath;
    2) hold patient's jaw closed and ask the patient to stop crying.

    If patient is unable to control behaviour, the examiner should cease testing her/him, and rescore this item and any other items unscored at a more suitable time.
12. If performance is scored differently on left and right side, the physical therapist may indicate this with a L in one box and R in another box.
13. The patient should be informed when s/he is being timed.
14. You will need the following equipment: a low wide plinth, a stopwatch, a polystyrene cup, eight jellybeans, two teacups, a rubber ball approximately 14 cm (5 in) in diameter, a stool, a comb, a top of a pen, a table, a dessert spoon and water, a pen, a prepared sheet for drawing lines, and a cylindrical object such as a jar.

Motor Assessment Scale

Carr, Shepherd, Nordholm, and Lynne (1985)

Name:	**Administered by:**	**Date:**

1. SUPINE TO SIDE LYING ONTO INTACT SIDE

Starting position must be supine lying, not knees flexed. Patient pulls her/himself into side lying with intact arm, moves affected leg with intact leg. For levels 2–6, arm is left behind.

0 Unable to perform
1 Pulls her/himself into side lying
2 Moves leg across actively and the lower half of the body follows
3 Arm is lifted across body with other arm. Leg is moved actively and body follows in a block
4 Moves arm across body actively and the rest of the body follows in a block
5 Moves arm and leg and rolls to side but overbalances (Shoulder protracts and arm flexes forward)
6 Rolls to side in 3 seconds (Must not use hands)

2. SUPINE TO SITTING OVER SIDE OF BED

For levels 4–6, must be able to perform with no stand-by help

0 Unable to perform
1 Side lying, lifts head sideways but cannot sit up (Patient assisted to side lying)
2 Side lying to sitting over side of bed (Therapist assists patient with movement. Patient controls head position throughout)
3 Side lying to sitting over side of bed (Therapist gives stand-by help [see instructions above] by assisting legs over side of bed)
4 Side lying to sitting over side of bed (with no stand-by help)
5 Supine to sitting over side of bed (with no stand-by help)
6 Supine to sitting over side of bed within 10 seconds (with no stand-by help)

3. BALANCED SITTING

0 Unable to perform
1 Sits only with support (Therapist should assist patient into sitting)
2 Sits unsupported for 10 seconds (Without holding on, knees and feet together, feet can be supported on floor)
3 Sits unsupported with weight well forward and evenly distributed (Weight should be well forward at the hips, head and thoracic spine extended, weight evenly distributed on both sides)
4 Sits unsupported, turns head and trunk to look behind (Feet supported and together on floor. Do not allow legs to abduct or feet to move. Have hands resting on thighs, do not allow hands to move onto plinth)
5 Sits unsupported, reaches forward to touch floor, and returns to starting position (Feet supported on floor. Do not allow patient to hold on. Do not allow legs and feet to move, support affected arm if necessary. Hand must touch the floor at least 10 cm (4 in) in front of feet)
6 Sits on stool unsupported, reaches sideways to touch floor, and returns to starting position (Feet supported on floor. Do not allow patient to hold on. Do not allow legs and feet to move, support affected arm if necessary. Patient must reach sideways not forward)

4. SITTING TO STANDING

For levels 3–6 do not allow uneven weight distribution

0 Unable to perform
1 Gets to standing with help from therapist (any method)
2 Gets to standing with stand-by help (Weight unevenly distributed, uses hands for support)
3 Gets to standing (Do not allow help from hands)
4 Gets to standing and stands for 5 seconds with hips and knees extended
5 Sitting to standing to sitting with no stand-by help (Full extension of hips and knees)
6 Sitting to standing to sitting with no stand-by help three times in 10 seconds

MAS page 3 of 3

5. WALKING

0 Unable to perform
1 Stands on affected leg and steps forward with the other leg (Weight-bearing hip must be extended. Therapist may give stand-by help)
2 Walks with stand-by help from one person
3 Walks 3 metres (10 ft) alone or uses any aid but no stand-by help
4 Walks 5 metres (16 ft) with no aid in 15 seconds
5 Walks 10 metres (33 ft) with no aid, turns around, picks up a small sandbag from floor, and walks back in 25 seconds (May use either hand)
6 Walks up and down four steps with or without an aid but without holding on to the rail three times in 35 seconds

6. UPPER-ARM FUNCTION

0 Unable to perform
1 Lying, protract shoulder girdle with arm in elevation (Therapist places arm in position and supports it with elbow in extension)
2 Lying, hold extended arm in elevation for 2 seconds (Physical therapist should place arm in position and patient must maintain position with some external rotation. Elbow must be held within 20° of full extension)
3 Flexion and extension of elbow to take palm to forehead with arm as in 2 (Therapist may assist supination of forearm)
4 Sitting, hold extended arm in forward flexion at 90° to body for 2 seconds (Therapist should place arm in position and patient must maintain position with some external rotation and elbow extension. Do not allow excess shoulder elevation)
5 Sitting, patient lifts arm to above position, holds it there for 10 seconds, and then lowers it (Patient must maintain position with some external rotation. Do not allow pronation)
6 Standing, hand against wall. Maintain arm position while turning body toward wall (Have arm abducted to 90° with palm flat against the wall)

7. HAND MOVEMENTS

Therapist should have patient sitting at a table with forearm resting on the table. Therapist places cylindrical object in palm of patient's hand. Patient is asked to lift object off the table by extending the wrist. Do not allow elbow flexion.

0 Unable to perform
1 Sitting, extension of wrist
2 Sitting, radial deviation of wrist (Therapist should place forearm in midpronation-supination, i.e., resting on ulnar side, thumb in line with forearm and wrist in extension, fingers around a cylindrical object. Patient is asked to lift hand off table. Do not allow elbow flexion or pronation)
3 Sitting, elbow into side, pronation and supination (Elbow unsupported and at a right angle. Three-quarter range is acceptable)
4 Reach forward, pick up large ball of 14 cm (15 in) diameter with both hands and put it down (Ball should be on table so far in front of patient that he has to extend arms fully to reach it. Shoulders must be protracted, elbows extended, wrist neutral or extended. Palms should be kept in contact with the ball)
5 Pick up a polystyrene cup from table and put it on table across other side of body (Do not allow alteration in shape of cup)
6 Continuous opposition of thumb and each finger more than 14 times in 10 seconds (Each finger in turns taps the thumb, starting with index finger. Do not allow thumb to slide from one finger to the other, or to go backwards)

8. ADVANCED HAND ACTIVITIES

0 Unable to perform
1 Picking up the top of a pen and putting it down again (Patient stretches arm forward, picks up pen top, releases it on table close to body)
2 Picking up one jellybean from a cup and placing it in another cup (Teacup contains eight jellybeans. Both cups must be at arm's length. Left hand takes jellybean from cup on right and releases it in cup on left)
3 Drawing horizontal lines to stop at a vertical line 10 times in 20 seconds (At least five lines must touch and stop at a vertical line)
4 Holding a pencil, making rapid consecutive dots on a sheet of paper (Patient must do at least 2 dots a second for 5 seconds. Patient picks pencil up and positions it without assistance. Patient must hold pen as for writing. Patient must make a dot not a stroke)
5 Taking a dessert spoon of liquid to the mouth (Do not allow head to lower towards spoon. Do not allow liquid to spill)
6 Holding a comb and combing hair at back of head

9. GENERAL TONUS

1 Flaccid, limp, no resistance when body parts are handled
2 Some response felt as body parts are moved
3 Variable, sometimes flaccid, sometimes good tone, sometimes hypertonic
4 Consistently normal response
5 Hypertonic 50% of the time
6 Hypertonic at all times

Motor Assessment Scale

Carr, Shepherd, Nordholm, and Lynne (1985)

Summary score sheet

Name:	**Administered by:**	**Date:**

	0	1	2	3	4	5	6
1. Supine to side lying							
2. Supine to sitting over side of bed							
3. Balanced sitting							
4. Sitting to standing							
5. Walking							
6. Upper-arm function							
7. Hand movements							
8. Advanced hand activities							
9. General tonus							

Comments (if applicable):

Acknowledgement: From Carr, J. H. et al. (1985). Investigation of a new motor assessment scale for stroke patients. *Physical Therapy*, *65*(2), 175–180, Figure 1 p. 176, Appendix 1 pp. 178–179, and clinical instructions, p. 180, by permission of the American Physical Therapy Association.

Motricity Index (MI)

Demeurisse, Demol, and Robaye (1980)

Source

Demeurisse et al. first described the Motricity Index (MI) in 1980. Collin and Wade (1990) validated guidelines for the administration of the MI and their description is used for this entry.

Purpose

The MI is a performance-based test that aims to give an overall indication of a patient's limb impairment using methods that can be quickly administered (Collin & Wade, 1990). Its role is "to measure strength in [the] upper and lower paretic extremity" (Kwakkel, Kollen, & Twisk, 2006). It was developed for patients with stroke.

Item description

The MI contains six items to evaluate three movements in both the upper and lower extremities (Collin & Wade, 1990; Demeurisse et al., 1980). Movements assessed are elbow flexion, shoulder abduction, pinch grip, ankle dorsiflexion, knee extension and hip flexion. Positioning of the patient for each item was standardized by Collin and Wade (1990). It is assumed that the patient has a hemiparesis and therefore the affected side of the body is rated.

Scale development

The MI was originally developed as a longer scale. Thirty-one movements at the joints of the upper and lower extremities were measured, and the motor function for each movement were classified using the Medical Research Council (MRC) muscle strength grades (MRC, 1943). Using principal components analysis, the number of movements were reduced to one at each joint that represented the general strength of the movement of the joint using the MRC muscle strength grades.

Administration procedures, response format and scoring

Equipment required for the MI comprises a chair, a bed or mat, and a 2.5 cm cube. Administration time is approximately 5 minutes. No special training is specified, although familiarity with the Medical Research Council motor power grading system is required (Collin & Wade, 1990).

The six-category MI scale has weighted scores allocated to each of its six items that range from 0 (no movement) to 33 (normal power). Intermediate categories are 9 (palpable contraction but no movement), 14 (visible movement, but not full range of movement against gravity), 19 (full range of movement against gravity but not against resistance), and 25 (full range of movement against resistance, but weaker than the other side). Pinch is tested using a 2.5 cm cube and there are slightly different descriptors for each category of this item. The total Arm score is the sum of the upper extremity items and the total Leg score is the sum of the lower extremity items. One point is added to each to give a total of 100 for each of the upper and lower extremities. A "side score" can also be calculated by adding the arm and leg scores and dividing the result by 2.

Psychometric properties

Collin and Wade (1990) studied 26 people with hemiplegia (age $M = 60$ years) (see Box 6.15).

Comment

The MI provides a quick measure of motor power function in people with hemiparesis. It has acceptable reliability and validity and it has been widely used with reference to stroke.

Key references

Cameron, D., & Bohannon, R. W. (2000). Criterion validity of lower extremity Motricity Index scores. *Clinical Rehabilitation*, *14*(2), 208–211.

Collen, F. M., Wade, D. T., & Bradshaw, C. M. (1990). Mobility after stroke: Reliability of measures of impairment and disability. *International Disability Studies*, *12*(1), 6–9.

Collin, C., & Wade, D. (1990). Assessing motor impairment after stroke: A pilot reliability study. *Journal of Neurology, Neurosurgery and Psychiatry*, *53*(7), 576–579.

Box 6.15

Validity:	Criterion: *Concurrent:* Collin & Wade: with Rivermead Motor Assessment: $r = .73–.81$ Cameron & Bohannon: with dynamometer (for lower extremity): $r = .90$ Construct: *Internal consistency:* Cameron & Bohannon: lower extremity score: Cronbach alpha .77
Reliability:	Inter-rater: Collin & Wade: Arm score: $r = .88$; Leg score: $r = .88$ Test–retest: Collen, Wade, & Bradshaw: 5 weeks: lower extremity scale 95% of paired readings being within 25 points, 2 years after stroke with residual disability
Responsiveness:	Kwakkel et al.: adequate responsiveness in prognostic study.

Demeurisse, G., Demol, O., & Robaye, E. (1980). Motor evaluation in vascular hemiplegia. *European Neurology*, *19*(6), 382–389.

Kwakkel, G., Kollen, B., & Twisk, J. (2006). Impact of time on improvement of outcome after stroke. *Stroke*, *37*(9), 2348–2353.

Medical Research Council. (1943). *Aids to the investigation of peripheral nerve injuries* (Revised 2nd ed.). London: War Memorandum No. 7.

Motricity Index

Demeurisse, Demol, and Robaye (1980)
with instructions from Collin and Wade (1990)

Name:	**Administered by:**	**Date:**

General instructions: The patient should be sitting in a chair or on the edge of the bed, but can be tested lying supine if necessary. In the arm the three movements tested are pinch grip, elbow flexion, and shoulder abduction. In the leg the three movements tested are ankle dorsiflexion, knee extension, and hip flexion.

MOTRICITY INDEX				
ARM	RIGHT		LEFT	
	MRC	MOT	MRC	MOT
1. Pinch grip				
2. Elbow flexion (from 90°)				
3. Shoulder abduction				
LEG				
4. Ankle dorsiflexion				
5. Knee extension				
6. Hip flexion				
ARM SCORE [1 + 2 + 3] + 1				
LEG SCORE [4 + 5 + 6] + 1				
SIDE SCORE [Arm and leg] / 2				

SCORING				
MRC GRADES		MOTRICITY SCORES		
		MRC	Test 1 (pinch grip)	Test 2–6
0	No movement	0	0	0
1	Palpable flicker	1	11	9
2	Movement without gravity	2	19	14
3	Movement against gravity	3	22	19
4	Movement against resistance	4	26	25
5	Normal	5	33	33

ARM

1. Pinch grip

Instructions: Assessed by asking the patient to grip a 2.5 cm cube between the thumb and forefinger. The object should be on a flat surface (e.g., a book).

Scoring for item 1

0 = No movement
11 = Beginnings of prehension (any movement of finger or thumb)
19 = Able to grip the cube, but not hold it against gravity (examiner may need to lift wrist)
22 = Able to grip and hold the cube against gravity, but not against a weak pull
26 = Able to grip and hold the cube against a weak pull, but weaker than the other side
33 = Normal pinch grip

Scoring for items 2 to 6

0 = No movement
9 = Palpable contraction in muscle, but no movement
14 = Visible movement, but not full range and not against gravity
19 = Full range of movement against gravity but not against resistance
25 = Full movement against resistance, but weaker than other side
33 = Normal power

2. Elbow flexion

Instructions: The elbow is tested with elbow flexed to 90°, forearm horizontal and upper arm vertical. The patient is asked to bend the elbow so that the hand touches the shoulder. The examiner resists with a hand on the wrist, and monitors the *biceps*.

If there is no movement, the examiner may hold the elbow out so that the arm is horizontal, and give a score of 14 if movement is then seen.

3. Shoulder abduction

Instructions: The elbow is fully flexed and against the chest and the patient asked to abduct the arm. The examiner monitors contraction of the *deltoid* (movement of shoulder girdle does not count – there must be movement of the humerus in relation to the scapula).

A score of 19 is given when the shoulder is abducted to more than 90° beyond the horizontal against gravity but not against resistance.

LEG

4. Ankle dorsiflexion

Instructions: Tested with the foot relaxed in a plantar flexed position. The patient is asked to dorsiflex the foot ("As if standing on your heels") and the examiner monitors the *tibialis anterior*.

A score of 14 is given when there is less than a full range of dorsiflexion.

5. Knee extension

Instructions: Tested with the foot unsupported and the knee at 90°. The patient is asked to extend the knee to touch the examiner's hand level with the knee, and the examiner monitors contraction of the *quadriceps*.

A score of 14 is given for less than 50% of full extension (i.e., 45° only), and a score of 19 when the knee is fully extended, but easily pushed down.

6. Hip flexion

Instructions: Tested with the hip bent at 90°. The patient is asked to lift the knee towards the chin and the examiner checks for the associated (trick) movement of leaning back by placing the hand behind the back and asking the patient not to lean back. The examiner then monitors contraction of *ilio-psoas/rectus femoris* (anterior thigh).

A score of 14 is given for less than a full range of possible flexion (check passive movement), and a score of 19 when the hip is fully flexed, but easily pushed down.

Acknowledgement: From Collin, C., & Wade, D. (1990). Assessing motor impairment after stroke: A pilot reliability study. *Journal of Neurology, Neurosurgery and Psychiatry*, *53*(7), 576–579, Table 1, p. 578, by permission of British Medical Journal and Rightslink.

Rivermead Mobility Index (RMI)

Collen, Wade, Robb, and Bradshaw (1991)

Source

The Rivermead Mobility Index was developed by Collen et al. (1991) to improve on existing scales and was termed "a further development of the Rivermead Motor Assessment" (Lincoln & Leadbitter, 1979).

Purpose

The RMI is (mainly) a clinician rating scale, which aims to quickly assess a range of mobility functions in people with stroke or brain injury (Collen et al., 1991).

Item description

The RMI comprises 15 items, ranging from turning over in bed to running 10 metres. The items are ordered in increasing difficulty from bed mobility, to standing, transferring, walking and eventually to running.

Scale development

In the initial development items were selected for the mobility tasks in two categories: those that are essential for basic functioning (Fundamental) and others that are "Elective". The actual functioning in these mobility tasks was ascertained by questioning the patient and caregivers, and one observation (standing for 10 seconds) was added to confirm their self-reports. Items were selected from the Rivermead Mobility Assessment Gross Function subscale (RMA-GF), the Barthel Index, the Nottingham Extended ADL Index (NEADL) and the Frenchay Activities Index.

Collen et al. (1991) noted that the developers had already established that the RMA-GF could be assessed reliably by questioning (and observation of the tasks was not required). The first version of the RMI Fundamental derived most of its items from the RMA-GF, while the initial version of the RMI Elective derived most of its items from the NEADL. The RMI Elective was not sufficiently reliable in an initial validation study. The RMI Fundamental was then subjected to a second validation study and demonstrated reasonable validity.

The RMI, as initially published in 1991, is the RMI Fundamental and is described by the authors as a development of the RMA-GF because nine of the 15 items came from that scale.

Administration procedures, response format and scoring

No equipment or training is required for the RMI and administration is quick and easy, being less than 5 minutes. The authors suggest that a note is made in the comment section of the scale when a task cannot be achieved. They also suggest that all questions are asked, even though the scale is probably hierarchical.

Modifications to increase the number of response categories have been proposed and validated, but a 4-level response category was not found to be any more discriminative than the 2-category version (Rossier & Wade, 2001).

The 15 items in the RMI are scored 1 ("yes") or 0 ("no"). To score 1 most items require the person to achieve the task without help.

Psychometric properties

Collen et al. (1991) developed the RMI with 23 people (13 of whom had a head injury) with mean age 43.5 years (*SD* 19.5). Their RMI ranged from 0 to 14 with mean 11 (*SD* 3.8) (see Box 6.16).

Comment

The RMI is a very brief measure of motor function. It has excellent concurrent validity with similar measures and is responsive. If a brief rating scale for mobility is required in acquired brain impairment, the RMI is a good choice.

Box 6.16

Validity:	Criterion: *Concurrent:* Collen et al.: with Barthel Index: $r = .91$ – with 10 m gait velocity: $r = .82$ Construct: *Factor analysis:* Antonucci, Aprile, & Paolucci: unidimensional scale with easy to hard hierarchy of items (Rasch analysis)
Reliability:	Inter-rater: Collen et al.: $r = .94$ Sackley, Richardson, McDonnell, Ratib, Dewey, & Hill: $r = .9$ Test–retest: Green, Forster, & Young: 1 week: $k > .63$ for all items except one Sackley et al.: 1 week: $k = .7$
Responsiveness:	Forlander & Bohannon: adequately responsive Hseih, Hsueh, & Mao: 76% of subjects increased by > 3 points during inpatient rehabilitation with stroke

Key references

Antonucci, G., Aprile, T., & Paolucci, S. (2002). Rasch analysis of the Rivermead Mobility Index: A study using mobility measures of first-stroke inpatients. *Archives of Physical Medical and Rehabilitation, 83*(10), 1442–1449.

Collen, F. M., Wade, D. T., Robb, G. F., & Bradshaw, C. M. (1991). The Rivermead Mobility Index: A further development of the Rivermead Motor Assessment. *International Disability Studies, 13*(2), 50–54.

Forlander, D. A., & Bohannon, R. W. (1999). Rivermead Mobility Index: A brief review of research to date. *Clinical Rehabilitation, 13*(2), 97–100.

Green, J., Forster, A., & Young, J. (2001). A test–retest reliability study of the Barthel Index, the Rivermead Mobility Index, the Nottingham Extended Activities of Daily Living Scale and the Frenchay Activities Index in stroke patients. *Disability and Rehabilitation, 23*(15), 670–676.

Hsieh, C. L., Hsueh, I. P., & Mao, H. F. (2000). Validity and responsiveness of the Rivermead Mobility Index in stroke patients. *Scandinavian Journal of Rehabilitation Medicine, 32*(3), 140–142.

Lincoln, N., & Leadbitter, D. (1979). Assessment of motor function in stroke patients. *Physiotherapy, 65*(2), 48–51.

Rossier, P., & Wade, D. T. (2001). Validity and reliability comparison of 4 mobility measures in patients presenting with neurologic impairment. *Archives of Physical Medical and Rehabilitation, 82*(1), 9–13.

Sackley, C., Richardson, P., McDonnell, K., Ratib, S., Dewey, M., & Hill, H. J. (2005). The reliability of balance, mobility and self-care measures in a population of adults with a learning disability known to a physiotherapy service. *Clinical Rehabilitation, 19*(2), 216–223.

Rivermead Mobility Index

Collen, Wade, Robb, and Bradshaw (1991)

Name:	**Administered by:**	**Date:**

<u>Instructions</u>: The patient is asked the following 15 questions, and observed (for item 5). A score of 1 is given for each "yes" answer. Note that most require independence from personal help, but method is otherwise unimportant.

<u>Response key:</u>
1 = Yes
0 = No

	RESPONSE
1. **Turning over in bed** Do you turn over from your back to your side without help?	______
2. **Lying to sitting** From lying in bed, do you get up to sit on the edge of the bed on your own?	______
3. **Sitting balance** Do you sit on the edge of the bed without holding on for 10 seconds?	______
4. **Sitting to standing** Do you stand up (from any chair) in less than 15 seconds and stand there for 15 seconds (using hands and with an aid if necessary)?	______
5. **Standing unsupported** Observe standing for 10 seconds without any aid or support	______
6. **Transfer** Do you manage to move (e.g., from bed to chair and back) without any help?	______
7. **Walking inside, with an aid if needed** Do you walk 10 m, with an aid or furniture if necessary, but with no standby help?	______
8. **Stairs** Do you manage a flight of stairs without help?	______
9. **Walking outside (even ground)** Do you walk around outside, on pavements without help?	______
10. **Walking inside, with no aid** Do you walk 10 metres inside, with no calliper, splint, aid or use of furniture, and no standby help?	______
11. **Picking off the floor** If you drop something on the floor, do you manage to walk 5 m, pick it up and then walk back?	______
12. **Walking outside (uneven ground)** Do you walk over uneven ground (grass, gravel, dirt, snow, ice, etc.) without help?	______
13. **Bathing** Do you get into/out of a bath or shower unsupervised and wash self?	______
14. **Up and down four steps** Do you manage to go up and down four steps with no rail and without help, but using an aid if necessary?	______
15. **Running** Do you run 10 metres without limping in 4 seconds? (fast walk is acceptable)	______
TOTAL SCORE:	______

Acknowledgement: From Collen, F. M. et al (1991). The Rivermead Mobility Index: A further development of the Rivermead Motor Assessment. *International Disability Studies*, *13*(2), 50–54, p. 53 used by permission of Informa Healthcare.

Timed Gait Pattern Function Tests

Various authors (see below)

Source

There is a large group of tests that provide an assessment of gait pattern functions. The term "timed gait pattern tests" is used to match the terminology of the *International Classification of Functioning Disability and Health* (WHO, 2001): a specific movement function is b770 "Gait pattern function". Indirectly, these tests also provide assessments of other functions, including cardiovascular and respiratory system functions, muscle functions, joint and bone functions, and movement functions other than gait.

Purpose

These assessments examine gait function by recording the time taken to walk a set distance. They were originally developed as a method of assessing cardiovascular or respiratory functioning (Cooper, 1968; McGavin, Gupta, & McHardy, 1976). The 12-minute walk test remains one of the standard durations (McGavin et al., 1976) but many other durations (Butland, Pang, Gross, Woodcock, & Geddes, 1982) and distances (Guralnik, Ferrucci, Simonsick, Salive, & Wallace, 1995) have been described. A variant that was developed to assess movement functions in addition to gait and is the Timed Up and Go Test (Podsiadlo & Richardson, 1991).

Scale development and item description

The initial test developed by Cooper (1968) was a 12-minute run. This test is highly correlated with maximal oxygen consumption as measured in the laboratory ($r = .897$). For populations with chronic disease this was unsatisfactory and a walking test of the same duration was described (McGavin et al., 1976). Subsequently walking for shorter periods was described (2 and 6 mins) and it was established that the gait velocity selected by people is largely constant. Both comfortable and fast walking speeds can be measured (Bohannon, 1997; Steffen, Hacker, & Mollinger, 2002).

The Timed Up and Go Test (Podsiadlo & Richardson, 1991) was derived from the Get-up and Go Test (Mathias, Nayak, & Isaacs, 1986). The subject rises from chair with seat height of approximately 46 cm and arm height of approximately 64 cm, walks 3 metres, turns and returns to sit in the chair. The Get-up and Go Test rates performance on a 5-category ordinal scale, whereas the Timed Up and Go records the time taken to complete this task.

Administration procedures, response format and scoring

The person is asked to walk over a standard distance and is given several metres to accelerate and decelerate before and after the test distance. Standard instructions and encouragement should be given. If being assessed at comfortable walking speed, people are asked to walk at their normal pace. If the study is at maximum speed, they are asked to walk as fast as they can safely without running (Bohannon, 1997). A practice walk is suggested and two trials are generally conducted with the average speed reported (Steffen et al., 2002). The time is recorded with a stopwatch.

Psychometric properties

Bohannon (1997) has established comfortable and maximum walking speeds for adults aged from 20 to 80 years. For males this speed declined from approximately 1.40 m/s in the third decade to 1.33 m/s in the eighth decade. For females these data were approximately 1.40 m/s to 1.27 m/s. At admission to an inpatient stroke rehabilitation programme, English, Hillier, Stiller, and Warden-Flood (2006) reported a gait speed of 0.4 m/s ($SD = 0.42$).

Podsiadlo and Richardson (1991) recorded a mean time of 8.5 seconds for the Timed Up and Go in 10 normal elderly volunteers. In other groups they found that older people completing the assessment in < 20 seconds were relatively independent in personal activities of daily living, while people completing the test in > 30 seconds generally required assistance with these activities and were housebound.

There are extensive psychometric data for gait pattern function tests and a sample are presented in Box 6.17.

Box 6.17

Validity:	Criterion: *Concurrent:* Podsiadlo & Richardson: Timed Up and Go with Berg Balance Scale: $r = -.81$ – with gait speed: $r = -.61$ – with Barthel Index: $r = -.78$
	Dean, Richards, & Malouin: patients with stroke: walking speed over a short distance overestimates gait velocity over a longer distance
	Predictive: Guralnik et al., Lan, Melzer, Tom, & Guralnik, Melzer, Lan, & Guralnik: gait speed is highly correlated with disability and is a predictor of future disability and mortality
	Lord, McPherson, McNaughton, Rochester, & Weatherall: gait velocity is predictive of community ambulation after stroke
Reliability:	Inter-rater: van Loo, Moseley, Bosman, de Bie, & Hassett (2003): ICC = .998
	Test–retest: van Loo et al. (2004): 1 week: ICC = .98 (people with traumatic brain injury for comfortable walking speed)
	Jette, Jette, Ng, Plotkin, & Bach: (interval not specified) 8-foot (2.4-metre) walk (older people): ICC = .79
	Steffen et al.: (interval not specified) gait speed (10 metre walkway): ICC = .96
Responsiveness:	Flansbjer, Holmback, Downham, Patten, & Lexell: people with hemiparesis after stroke: smallest clinically significant differences are 13% for 6-minute walk, 22% for gait at comfortable speed, 23% for Timed Up and Go
	English et al.: gait speed is responsive to change after stroke

Comment

These tests provide reliable assessments of gait functioning that have established predictive validity and responsiveness. Although other body functions potentially influence performance using these procedures, they are very useful methods of assessment in the context of acquired brain impairment.

Key references

Bohannon, R. W. (1997). Comfortable and maximum walking speed of adults aged 20–79 years: Reference values and determinants. *Age and Ageing*, *26*(1), 15–19.

Butland, R. J., Pang, J., Gross, E. R., Woodcock, A. A., & Geddes, D. M. (1982). Two-, six-, and 12-minute walking tests in respiratory disease. *British Medical Journal*, *284*(6329), 1607–1608.

Cooper, K. H. (1968). A means of assessing maximal oxygen intake. Correlation between field and treadmill testing. *Journal of the American Medical Association*, *203*(3), 135–138.

Dean, C. M., Richards, C. L., & Malouin, F. (2001). Walking speed over 10 metres overestimates locomotor capacity after stroke. *Clinical Rehabilitation*, *15*(4), 415–421.

English, C. K., Hillier, S. L., Stiller, K., & Warden-Flood, A. (2006). The sensitivity of three commonly used outcome measures to detect change amongst patients receiving inpatient rehabilitation following stroke. *Clinical Rehabilitation*, *20*(1), 52–55.

Flansbjer, U. B., Holmback, A. M., Downham, D., Patten, C., & Lexell, J. (2005). Reliability of gait performance tests in men and women with hemiparesis after stroke. *Journal of Rehabilitation Medicine*, *37*(2), 75–82.

Guralnik, J. M., Ferrucci, L., Simonsick, E. M., Salive, M. E., & Wallace, R. B. (1995). Lower-extremity function in persons over the age of 70 years as a predictor of subsequent disability. *The New England Journal of Medicine*, *332*(9), 556–561.

Jette, A. M., Jette, D. U., Ng, J., Plotkin, D. J., Bach, M. A., & Musculoskeletal Impairment (MSI) Study Group (1999). Are performance-based measures sufficiently reliable for use in multicenter trials? *Journal of Gerontology*, *54*(1), M3–M6.

Lan, T. Y., Melzer, D., Tom, B. D., & Guralnik, J. M. (2002). Performance tests and disability: Developing an objective index of mobility-related limitation in older populations. *Journal of Gerontology*, *57*(5), M294–M301.

Lord, S. E., McPherson, K., McNaughton, H. K., Rochester, L., & Weatherall, M. (2004). Community ambulation after stroke: How important and obtainable is it and what measures appear predictive? *Archives of Physical Medical and Rehabilitation*, *85*(2), 234–239.

McGavin, C. R., Gupta, S. P., & McHardy, G. J. R. (1976). Twelve-minute walking test for assessing disability in chronic bronchitis. *British Medical Journal*, *1*(6013), 822–823.

Mathias, S., Nayak, U. S. L., & Isaacs, B. (1986). Balance in elderly patients: The "Get-up and Go" Test. *Archives of Physical Medical and Rehabilitation*, *67*(6), 387–389.

Melzer, D., Lan, T. Y., & Guralnik, J. M. (2003). The predictive validity for mortality of the index of mobility-related limitation: Results from the EPESE study. *Age and Ageing*, *32*(6), 619–625.

Podsiadlo, D., & Richardson, S. (1991). The Timed "Up & Go": A test of basic functional mobility for frail elderly persons. *Journal of the American Geriatric Society*, *39*(2), 142–148.

Steffen, T. M., Hacker, T. A., & Mollinger, L. (2002). Age- and gender-related test performance in community-dwelling elderly people: Six-Minute Walk Test, Berg Balance Scale, Timed Up & Go Test, and gait speeds. *Physical Therapy*, *82*(2), 128–137.

van Loo, M. A., Moseley, A. M., Bosman, J. M., de Bie, R. A., & Hassett, L. (2003). Inter-rater reliability and concurrent validity of walking speed measurement after traumatic brain injury. *Clinical Rehabilitation*, *17*(7), 775–779.

van Loo, M. A., Moseley, A. M., Bosman, J. M., de Bie, R. A., & Hassett, L. (2004). Test–re-test reliability of walking speed, step length and step width measurement after traumatic brain injury: A pilot study. *Brain Injury*, *18*(10), 1041–1048.

World Health Organization (2001). *International classification of functioning, disability and health*. Geneva: World Health Organization.

Part B

Activities and Participation

Part B of this compendium includes two chapters describing scales addressing the Activities and Participation component of the World Health Organization (WHO) *International Classification of Functioning, Disability and Health* (ICF; WHO, 2001). Activities and Participation were previously labelled Disabilities and Handicap respectively in the original 1980 WHO model. As described in Chapter 1, Activity is defined as the execution of a task or action by an individual, whereas Participation refers to involvement in a life situation. There are nine domains of Activities/Participation in the ICF (see Appendix C and Figure 7.1), five of which are included in Part B (General Tasks and Demands; Self-care; Domestic Life; Major Life Areas; and Community, Social and Civic Life). Scales representing the remaining four Activities/Participation domains can be found in Part A of the compendium (Scales of Body Functions): Learning and Applying Knowledge (Chapters 3 and 4), Communication (Chapter 4), Mobility (Chapter 6) and Interpersonal Interactions and Relationships (Chapter 5). The reason that scales assessing these domains are not included in Part B is largely because of their item overlap with scales of Body Functions. In the interests of providing a coherent structure to the book, those instruments assessing conceptually similar constructs (e.g., intellectual functions/specific mental functions/learning and applying knowledge; language/speech/communication; movement-related/mobility; global psychosocial functions/interpersonal interactions and relationships) are placed together.

In the original classification (WHO, 1980), impairments, disabilities and handicaps were described as "distinct and independent classifications, each relating to a different plane of experience consequent upon disease" (p. 13). Accordingly, there was a clear demarcation between Disabilities, defined as "any restriction or lack (resulting from an impairment) of ability to perform an activity in the manner or within the range considered normal for a human being" (p. 143) versus Handicaps, defined as "a disadvantage for a given individual, resulting from an impairment or a disability, that limits or prevents the fulfilment of a role that is normal (depending on age, sex, and social and cultural factors) for that individual" (p. 183). Disabilities and Handicaps contained mutually exclusive sets of eight and six specific dimensions respectively. By contrast, the ICF has resisted specifying a particular partitioning between Activities and Participation, and instead lists a common set of nine domains. One of the arguments for *not* partitioning the Activities/Participation component is that any function can have both "activity" and "participation" aspects. For instance, although there is unanimous agreement that categories within the Mobility domain should be classified as Activities, the Australian Institute of Health and Welfare (AIHW, 2003) has noted that some people would also argue that Mobility categories are integral to Participation, asking "how can you participate in your society if you can't move around in it?" (p. 37).

Other authors, however, have provided empirical data in support of separate and distinct listing of items for Activities and Participation (Jette, Haley, & Kooyoomijian, 2003). Indeed, at definitional and conceptual levels there are distinctions. The *ICF Australian User Guide* (AIHW, 2003, pp. 35–36) provides a set of "draft criteria" that enumerate at least five ways in which Activities can be distinguished from Participation, as shown in Data box B.1.

Data box B.1

Activities **Execution of a task or action by an individual**	**Participation** **Involvement in a life situation**
1. focuses on the person's individual functioning	1. emphasizes the person's involvement in society
2. completely externally observable	2. refers to the lived experience
3. can relate to test (see capacity) and real (see performance) environments with or without equipment	3. has little meaning without consideration of the physical and social environment; "involvement in society" relates to societal roles
4. fine-grained	4. broad-brushed
5. about action or process	5. relates to overall goal or sets of actions

Data compiled from the text of AIHW (2003), pp. 35–36.

Not only does the ICF not specify a particular partitioning of the nine domains of Activities/ Participation, but in fact it suggests any of four methods for this purpose (see Annex 3; WHO, 2001). In this compendium, Chapters 7 and 8, for Activities and Participation respectively, adopt a division for five of the domains (see Figure 7.1): scales assessing General Tasks and Demands, Self-care, and/or Domestic Life are presented in Chapter 7 (Scales Assessing Activities of Daily Living), and those addressing Major Life Areas and/or Community, Social and Civic Life are featured in Chapter 8 (Scales Assessing Participation and Social Role). This division is arbitrary and approximate and is driven by the item content of existing scales rather than by a conceptual demarcation suggested in the ICF. Even so, within some scales there is often considerable item overlap between Chapters 7 and 8, and in particular scales of instrumental activities of daily living, which have been placed in Chapter 7 because of their emphasis on Domestic Life, often include items on social functioning and leisure, which clearly fall within the Community, Social and Civic Life domain. Additionally, multidimensional scales that include items from different ICF components often provide a sampling of items representing the Activities/Participation component, and these instruments are featured in Chapter 10. Interested readers may also consult Appendices D and E. Appendix D provides a checklist of the number of items featured in scales from Chapters 7, 8 and 10 vis-à-vis the ICF Activities/Participation domains. Appendix E provides a comparative checklist of the item content of scales assessing specific functional activities of daily living from a clinical perspective.

7 Scales assessing activities of daily living

Instruments presented in Chapter 7 map to the components and domains of the *International Classification of Functioning, Disability and Health* (ICF; WHO, 2001) as depicted in Figure 7.1.

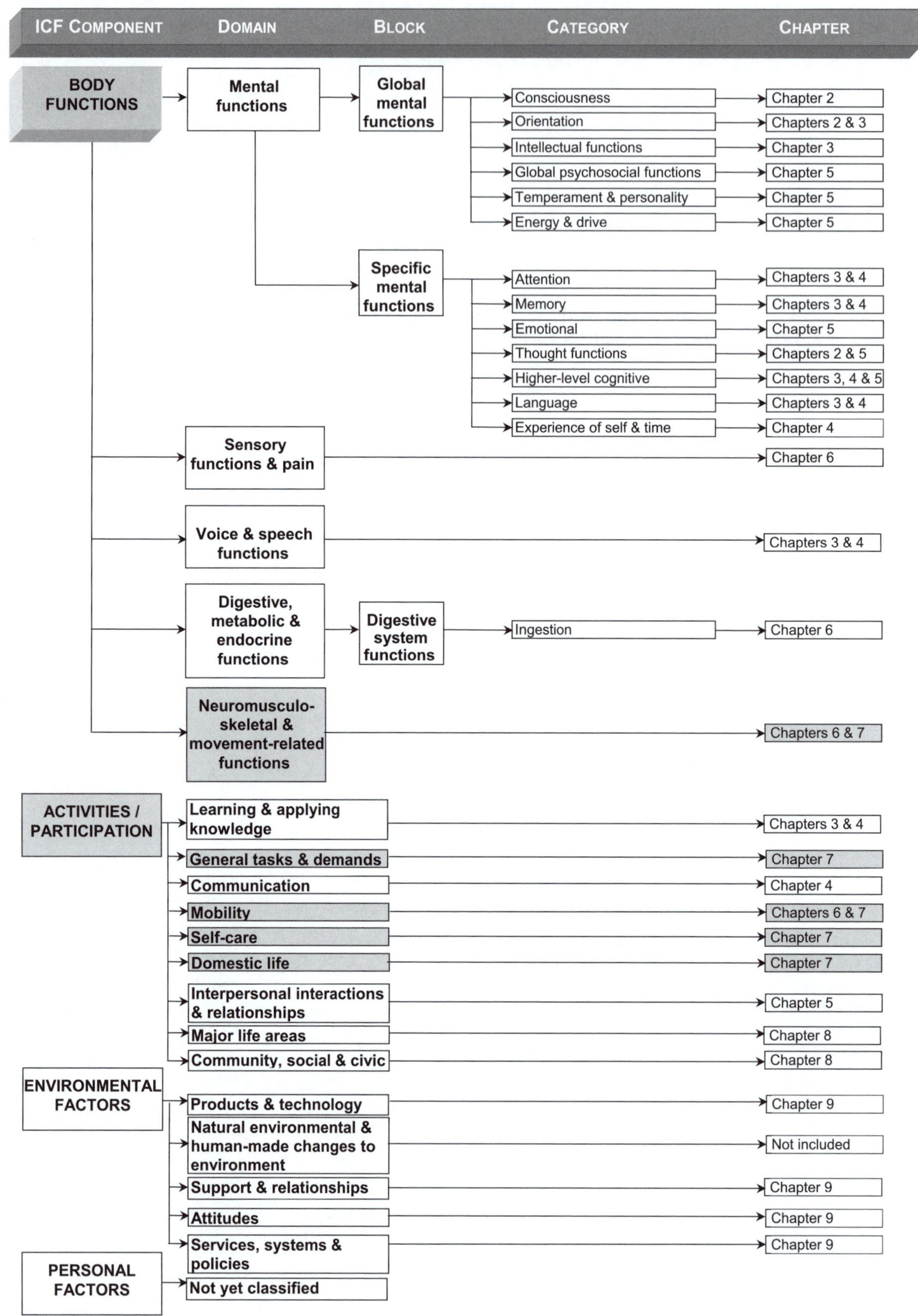

Figure 7.1 Instruments included in the compendium in relation to the ICF taxonomy – the highlighted components and domains appear in this chapter. *Note:* the Figure presents a partial listing of five out of the eight Body Function domains and does not include any of the Body Structure domains. Categories for Mental functions also represent a partial listing and categories for the remaining domains are not listed. Refer to Appendix C for further detail on the ICF taxonomy.

Introduction

From a clinical perspective, many scales of Activities/Participation used with the acquired brain impairment (ABI) population fall into three clusters according to their item content. There is also a distinct historical trend to the development of instruments in this area. Standardized instruments were originally developed in the 1950s and 1960s to assess functional independence in older adults, and the item content of these scales focused exclusively on so-called basic activities of daily living (ADL); namely, self-care tasks and mobility. Subsequent investigators were critical of their limited item content, which only partially assessed independence. Consequently the 1970s and 1980s saw the development of scales of extended activities of daily living (EADL), also known as instrumental activities of daily living (IADL), these terms being used predominantly in the UK and North America respectively, with the latter term now used more widely. Most items in these IADL scales focused on domestic activities, although some scales included items sampling work and leisure (see the domains of Major life areas; Community, social and civic life). For some neurological groups where functional disability in self-care, mobility and domestic ADL is less common (e.g., traumatic brain injury), these scales were seen as not able to elicit the characteristic type of disablement commonly experienced. Consequently, in the 1980s and 1990s instruments were developed that focused on resumption of the previous lifestyle in terms of "involvement in life situations"; namely, participation in major life areas, along with community, social and civic life.

The present chapter focuses on the first two types of ADL scales, addressing an admixture of self-care, mobility and domestic tasks. (Instruments assessing mobility in isolation from other functions are described in Chapter 6.) These scales map to four ICF domains in the Activities/Participation component: General tasks and demands, Mobility, Self-care, and Domestic life. All but the first of these domains is self-explanatory from the label. As depicted in Appendix C, the domain of General tasks and demands contains four categories: undertaking a single task, undertaking multiple tasks, carrying out daily routines, and handling stress and other psychological demands. ADL and IADL scales are generally used to measure level of functional independence, but Bucks, Ashworth, Wilcock, and Siegfried (1996) also highlight their role in the diagnosis of dementia. Diagnostic criteria for dementia (see introduction to Chapter 3) are not restricted to cognitive impairment alone, but such impairment has to be of sufficient magnitude to interfere with everyday living. In these instances, use of ADL/IADL scales assists in standardizing the evaluation for diagnostic purposes.

Traditionally, there have been two approaches to the development of ADL scales. Some scales use a range of items that are individually rated and the scores summed to obtain a total and/or subscale scores. The advantage of these types of scales is that level of independence in a range of functional areas (e.g., dressing vs walking) can be directly compared. A number of criticisms have been levelled against them, however. Ebrahim, Nouri, and Barer (1985) question the procedure by which "qualitatively different activities, such as dressing ability and walking, are combined into a single score, [because] no indication is given of the pattern of disability or even the amount of help required" (p. 86). More specifically, Barer and Murphy (1993) comment that the same score can reflect different patterns of disability, and in functional terms a higher score does not necessarily indicate a different degree of disability from a slightly lower score. Further, summing items and subscales transgresses statistical assumptions regarding the treatment of ordinal-level data that are usually used in rating scales (see Chapter 1; Domholdt, 2005). Occasionally, the latter problem has been addressed by some researchers who have applied scaling procedures such as Rasch analysis to convert such scales to an interval level of measurement. An example of the problems of treating ordinal data as if they were interval data comes from the work of Linacre, Heinemann, Wright, Granger, and Hamilton (1994) using Rasch analysis on the Functional Independence Measure (FIM). At the extremes of the FIM score ranges, a change of 10 raw score points represents four times the amount of change on a linear scale as a change of 10 raw score points represents at the mid ranges.

The other approach in developing ADL scales uses a set of items that are ordered hierarchically, often using Guttman scaling procedures. There are many advantages to a hierarchical scale, in which items are ordered in terms of their level of difficulty. A single score is obtained, and that score conveys information about the severity of disability as well as about the actual items that have been passed and failed. As Lincoln and Edmans (1990) observe, this makes it possible to describe abilities on the basis of the total score alone. For example, a score of 4 on the Nottingham ADL Scale (NADLS; Ebrahim et al., 1985) not only means that the patient can successfully transfer from the bed to the chair (i.e., score 4), it also means the patient can successfully complete tasks lower in the hierarchy (drink from a cup, eat, wash face and hands), but generally cannot complete items higher in the hierarchy (e.g., item 5, walk/use wheelchair, etc.). The hierarchical scale also allows the assessment to be conducted efficiently and has the advantage of not unduly overstressing and discouraging the patient. On the NADLS, Barer (1989) notes that if the patient is unable to successfully complete items 3 and 4, then it is very unlikely that he or she can complete items 7 to 10, and in such cases these items do not need to be administered.

Instruments representing both types of procedures (i.e., hierarchical structure vs summed items) are included in this chapter. In studies where Guttman procedures are used to test the hierarchical structure of a scale, adequacy of the result is measured with coefficients of reproducibility (CR, i.e., accuracy of prediction regarding items passed/failed) and scalability (CS, i.e., as for CR, but with corrections made for the relative frequency of passing/failing). Critical values of CR > 0.9 and CS > 0.6 have been recommended (Barer & Murphy, 1993). When Rasch analysis is used to examine unidimensionality, one test of the adequacy of the observed ratings (items and/or persons) in conforming to a Rasch model is the "fit" of items. The statistic usually reported is fit mean-square and, depending on the sample size, mean-squares in the range 0.7 to 1.3 are generally considered acceptable (Tesio, 2003); but see also Bond and Fox (2007) for detailed consideration of the issues involved in interpreting fit statistics.

Twenty years ago, Barer and Nouri (1989) commented on the "bewildering number" of ADL scales, which generally included "the same basic set of activities with variations in the assessment criteria and methods of scoring" (p. 179). In spite of the large number of existing ADL scales, newly developed scales continue to appear in the literature. Although a number of review papers on ADL scales are available (e.g., Christiansen, 2005; Cohen & Marino, 2000), there is no consensus for use of a single scale. The present chapter includes a selection of 15 instruments, some of which are established and commonly used and others that were published more recently. Many ADL instruments are simple rating scales, completed on the basis of the clinician's knowledge of the patient or informant/self-report. Detailed instruments that provide an observational, performance-based examination (e.g., Assessment of Motor and Process Skills, AMPS; Fisher, 2004) are available, but these are generally time-consuming, often require specialist training and are thus beyond the scope of this compendium. A small number of brief instruments that have the facility for observational performance-based evaluation are described in this chapter.

References

Australian Institute of Health and Welfare. (2003). *ICF Australian user guide. Version 1.0*. Canberra: Australian Institute of Health and Welfare.

Barer, D., & Nouri, F. (1989). Measurement of activities of daily living. *Clinical Rehabilitation*, *3*(3), 179–187.

Barer, D. H. (1989). Use of the Nottingham ADL scale in stroke: Relationship between functional recovery and length of stay in hospital. *Journal of the Royal College of Physicians of London*, *23*(4), 242–247.

Barer, D. H., & Murphy, J. J. (1993). Scaling the Barthel: A 10-point hierarchical version of the Activities of Daily Living Index for use with stroke patients. *Clinical Rehabilitation*, *7*(4), 271–277.

Bond, T. G., & Fox, C. M. (2007). *Applying the Rasch model. Fundamental measurement in the human sciences* (2nd ed.). Mahwah, NJ: Lawrence Erlbaum Associates, Inc.

Bucks, R. S., Ashworth, D. L., Wilcock, G. K., & Siegfried, K. (1996). Assessment of activities of daily living in dementia: Development of the Bristol Activities of Daily Living Scale. *Age and Ageing*, *25*, 113–120.

Christiansen, C. H. (2005). Principles of evaluation and management of self-care and other activities of daily living. In J. A. DeLisa, B. M. Gans, N. E. Walsh, W. L. Bockenek, W. R. Frontera, S. R. Geiringer, et al. (Eds.), *Physical medicine and rehabilitation: Principles and practice* (pp. 975–1003). Philadelphia: Lippincott, Williams & Wilkins.

Cohen, M., & Marino, R. J. (2000). The tools of disability outcomes research functional status measures. *Archives of Physical Medical and Rehabilitation*, *81*(2), S21–S29.

Domholdt, E. (2005). *Rehabilitation research. Principles and applications* (3rd ed.). Philadelphia: Elsevier Saunders.

Ebrahim, S., Nouri, F., & Barer, D. (1985). Measuring disability after a stroke. *Journal of Epidemiology and Community Health*, *39*(1), 86–89.

Fisher, A. G. (2004). *AMPS. Assessment of Motor and Process Skills* (5th ed.). Fort Collins, CO: Three Star Press, Inc.

Jette, A. M., Haley, S. M., & Kooyoomijian, J. T. (2003). Are the ICF and participation dimensions distinct? *Journal of Rehabilitation Medicine*, *35*(3), 145–149.

Linacre, J. M., Heinemann, A. W., Wright, B. D., Granger, C. V., & Hamilton, B. B. (1994). The structure and stability of the Functional Independence Measure. *Archives of Physical Medicine and Rehabilitation*, *75*(2), 127–132.

Lincoln, N. B., & Edmans, J. A. (1990). A re-validation of the Rivermead ADL scale for elderly patients with stroke. *Age and Ageing*, *19*(1), 19–24.

Tesio, L. (2003). Measuring behaviours and perceptions: Rasch analysis as a tool for rehabilitation research. *Journal of Rehabilitation Medicine*, *35*(3), 105–115.

World Health Organization. (1980). *International classification of impairments, disabilities and handicaps*. Geneva: World Health Organization.

World Health Organization. (2001). *International classification of functioning, disability and health*. Geneva: World Health Organization.

Activities of Daily Living Questionnaire (ADLQ)

Johnson, Barion, Rademaker, Rehkemper, and Weintraub (2004)

Source

Items for the ADLQ appear in an appendix to Johnson et al. (2004) and are reproduced below.

Purpose

The ADLQ is an informant rating scale that is designed for administration in an outpatient clinic setting. It was developed for people with Alzheimer's disease (AD), as well as other forms of dementia, including frontotemporal dementia (FTD) and primary progressive aphasia (PPA) (Wicklund, Johnson, Rademaker, Weitner, & Weintraub, 2007). A specific aim of the ADLQ is to track changes in functional status over time.

Item description

The 28-item ADLQ consists of six subscales: Self-care (6 items), Household care (6 items), Employment and recreation (4 items), Shopping and money (3 items), Travel (4 items), and Communication (5 items).

Scale development

Johnson and colleagues (2004) observed that many scales of activities of daily living developed for older people focused on basic activities of self-care that were performed "daily, habitually and universally". Yet, in people with dementia, physical abilities can remain well preserved for extended periods of time. By contrast, cognitive abilities, which are fundamental to performance of instrumental activities of daily living (such as shopping, use of transport), and which require competent planning and organizational abilities, typically decline early. Other more representative scales were observation-based or lengthy, thereby having limited application in a busy clinical setting. Hence the ADLQ was developed to meet the need for a brief yet sensitive instrument. Items were selected based on the authors' clinical experience of patients with dementia and knowledge of the areas of functional decline that may affect everyday activities.

Administration procedures, response format and scoring

The ADLQ is completed by an informant, the primary caregiver. Respondents are instructed to "score each item according to the patient's current level of ability relative to his/her customary performance prior to the onset of dementia symptoms" (Johnson et al., 2004, p. 224). Administration time is 5 to 10 minutes, and the authors report that in the standardization sample the respondents did not experience any difficulty understanding the instructions.

Each item is rated on a 4-point scale, with individually scripted responses specific to each item: 0 (equivalent of no problem) to 3 (no longer capable of performing the activity). An additional "not applicable" response category (score = 9) is provided for "don't know"/ "never did the activity" responses, and such items are not included in calculation of the final scores. ADLQ scores are calculated for each subscale separately, using the following procedure. Scores for endorsed items (i.e., all items except those coded with 9) are summed and divided by the sum of the maximum score of the items within each section for which an applicable response is made. This result is then multiplied by 100, which thus provides a percentage score of the degree of impairment. For example, if responses to the five items in the Communication subscale are A = not applicable (= 9), B = 2, C = 1, D = 3, E = 1, then the sum of the scores for that scale is 7, which is divided by the sum of the maximum score (i.e., 3) of the 4 items for which an applicable response is made (items B, C, D, E = 12). Hence, 7/12 = 0.58, which is multiplied by 100 = 58% impairment. A total ADLQ score can be obtained by summing each subscale score and dividing by 6. Retaining the six subscales as separate scores, however, facilitates interpretation of areas of differential impairment. Total percentage scores ranging from 0 to 33 are classified as no/mild impairment, 34 to 66 as moderate impairment, and > 66 as severe impairment.

Psychometric properties

The standardization sample was used to establish basic psychometric properties of the ADLQ (Johnson et al., 2004). Data on the ADLQ from 140 people with dementia were retrieved from the Northwestern Alzheimer's Disease Center Clinical Core Registry, Chicago, Illinois, USA, and additional participants were recruited to examine other psychometric properties of the ADLQ. The first sample ($n = 140$) was diagnosed with a range of dementias, including probable/possible AD ($n = 65$), vascular/mixed dementia ($n = 28$), and FTD/PPA ($n = 44$). Concurrent validity was examined with the Mini-Mental State Examination (MMSE) and Clinical Dementia Rating (CDR) scale and responsiveness determined by examining the sample 12 months later. Test–retest reliability was examined in 28 people with probable AD, with a 2 to 8 week retest interval ($M = 25.6$ days, $SD = 12.2$). Convergent and divergent validity, using the Record of Independent Living (RIL), was assessed in a group of 29 people with mixed dementia diagnoses. Patterns of hypothesized correlations with similar and dissimilar constructs were examined.

Information on discriminant validity is available from the study of Wicklund et al. (2007) who compared three groups in the early stages of dementia: probable AD ($n = 100$), FTD ($n = 57$) and PPA ($n = 61$). As hypothesized, impairment scores on the Communication subscale were higher in the PPA group than either the AD or FTD groups; conversely impairment scores on the Self-care subscale were higher in the AD (but not FTD) group in comparison with the PPA group. Results from Johnson et al., unless otherwise indicated, are shown in Box 7.1.

Box 7.1

Validity:	Criterion: *Concurrent:* with MMSE: $r = -.42$ – with CDR: $r = .50$
	Construct: *Convergent/divergent*: higher correlation with similar constructs (e.g., ADLQ Self-care with RIL Activities: $r = .75$); lower correlation with dissimilar constructs (e.g., ADLQ Self-care with RIL Behaviour: $r = .32$)
	Discriminant: Wicklund et al.: Adjusted means: Communication: PPA $M = 39$ ($SE = .03$) vs AD $M = 29$ ($SE = .02$); $p < .01$
	– Self-care: AD $M = 14$ ($SE = .02$) vs PPA $M = 5$ ($SE = .01$); $p < .001$, FTD $M = 11$ ($SE = .02$) vs PPA $M = 5$ ($SE = .01$); $p = .001$
Reliability:	Inter-rater: No information available
	Test–retest: 2–8 weeks: Total score: $r = .96$ (range $r = .87$–$.95$ for 5/6 subscales; employment scale $r = .65$)
Responsiveness:	12 month retest: significant increase in impairment: Time 1 $M = 33.6$ ($SD = 20.0$) vs Time 2 $M = 43.5$ ($SD = 21.0$); $F = 73.1$, $p < .001$, $d = .50$

Comment

The ADLQ fulfils the authors' aim of developing a brief instrument that is sensitive and has the capacity to detect real changes occurring over time. The scoring procedures for the ADLQ are a little more complex than most ADL scales, but this is offset by three distinct advantages: (i) ensuring that items are relevant to the person's situation, thus bypassing sex-role differences that can occur in activities of daily living (e.g., males may not have had responsibility for doing laundry; females may not have engaged in home repairs), (ii) having a readily interpretable result in terms of percent impairment relative to the person's premorbid level, thereby overcoming the need for normative data, and (iii) each of the six subscales having a common metric and thus being directly comparable. Psychometric properties examined to date are strong, indicating that the ADLQ is a reliable and responsive instrument, with evidence of concurrent and construct validity. The availability of the ADLQ as a single, brief, sensitive instrument that spans both basic and instrumental everyday activities is a welcome addition to the field.

Key references

Johnson, N., Barion, A., Rademaker, A., Rehkemper, G., & Weintraub, S. (2004). The Activities of Daily Living Questionnaire: A validation study in patients with dementia. *Alzheimer Disease and Associated Disorders*, *18*(4), 223–230.

Wicklund, A. H., Johnson, N., Rademaker, A., Weitner, B. B., and Weintraub, S. (2007). Profiles of decline in activities of daily living in non-Alzheimer dementia. *Alzheimer Disease and Associated Disorders*, *21*(1), 8–13.

Activities of Daily Living Questionnaire
Johnson, Barion, Rademaker, Rehkemper, and Weintraub (2004)

Name:	**Administered by:**	**Date:**

Instructions: Circle one number for each item

SELF-CARE ACTIVITIES

1. **Eating**
   - 0 No problem
   - 1 Independent, but slow or some spills
   - 2 Needs help to cut or pour; spills often
   - 3 Must be fed most foods
   - 9 Don't know
2. **Dressing**
   - 0 No problem
   - 1 Independent, but slow or clumsy
   - 2 Wrong sequence, forgets items
   - 3 Needs help with dressing
   - 9 Don't know
3. **Bathing**
   - 0 No problem
   - 1 Bathes self, but needs to be reminded
   - 2 Bathes self with assistance
   - 3 Must be bathed by others
   - 9 Don't know
4. **Elimination**
   - 0 Goes to the bathroom independently
   - 1 Goes to the bathroom when reminded; some accidents
   - 2 Needs assistance for elimination
   - 3 Has no control over either bowel or bladder
   - 9 Don't know
5. **Taking pills or medicine**
   - 0 Remembers without help
   - 1 Remembers if dose is kept in a special place
   - 2 Needs spoken or written reminders
   - 3 Must be given medicine by others
   - 9 Does not take regular pills or medicine **OR** Don't know
6. **Interest in personal appearance**
   - 0 Same as always
   - 1 Interested if going out, but not at home
   - 2 Allows self to be groomed, or does so on request only
   - 3 Resists efforts of caretaker to clean and groom
   - 9 Don't know

HOUSEHOLD CARE

7. **Preparing meals, cooking**
   - 0 Plans and prepares meals without difficulty
   - 1 Some cooking, but less than usual, or less variety
   - 2 Gets food only if it has already been prepared
   - 3 Does nothing to prepare meals
   - 9 Never did this activity **OR** Don't know
8. **Setting the table**
   - 0 No problem
   - 1 Independent, but slow or clumsy
   - 2 Forgets items or puts them in the wrong place
   - 3 No longer does this activity
   - 9 Never does this activity **OR** Don't know
9. **Housekeeping**
   - 0 Keeps house as usual
   - 1 Does at least half of his/her job
   - 2 Occasional dusting or small jobs
   - 3 No longer keeps house
   - 9 Never did this activity **OR** Don't know
10. **Home maintenance**
    - 0 Does all tasks usual for him/her
    - 1 Does at least half of usual tasks
    - 2 Occasionally rakes or some other minor job
    - 3 No longer does any maintenance
    - 9 Never did this activity **OR** Don't know
11. **Home repairs**
    - 0 Does all the usual repairs
    - 1 Does at least half of usual repairs
    - 2 Occasionally does minor repairs
    - 3 No longer does any repairs
    - 9 Never did this activity **OR** Don't know
12. **Laundry**
    - 0 Does laundry as usual (same schedule, routine)
    - 1 Does laundry less frequently
    - 2 Does laundry only if reminded; leaves out detergent, steps
    - 3 No longer does laundry
    - 9 Never did this activity **OR** Don't know

EMPLOYMENT AND RECREATION

13. **Employment**
    - 0 Continues to work as usual
    - 1 Some mild problems with routine responsibilities
    - 2 Works at an easier job or part-time; threatened with loss of job
    - 3 No longer works
    - 9 Never worked **OR** Retired before illness **OR** Don't know

14. Recreation
0 Same as usual
1 Engages in recreational activities less frequently
2 Has lost some skills necessary for recreational activities (e.g., bridge, golfing); needs coaxing to participate
3 No longer pursues recreational activities
9 Never engages in recreational activities **OR** Don't know

15. Organizations
0 Attends meetings, takes responsibilities as usual
1 Attends less frequently
2 Attends occasionally; has no major responsibilities
3 No longer attends
9 Never participated in organizations **OR** Don't know

16. Travel
0 Same as usual
1 Gets out if someone else drives
2 Gets out in wheelchair
3 Home- or hospital-bound
9 Don't know

SHOPPING AND MONEY

17. Food shopping
0 No problem
1 Forgets items or buys unnecessary items
2 Needs to be accompanied while shopping
3 No longer does the shopping
9 Never had responsibility in this activity **OR** Don't know

18. Handling cash
0 No problem
1 Has difficulty paying the proper amount, counting
2 Loses or misplaces money
3 No longer handles money
9 Never had responsibility for the activity **OR** Don't know

19. Managing finances
0 No problems paying bills, banking
1 Pays bills late; some trouble writing cheques
2 Forgets to pay bills; has trouble balancing chequebook; needs help from others
3 No longer manages finances
9 Never had responsibility for this activity **OR** Don't know

---

TRAVEL

20. Public transportation
0 Uses public transportation as usual
1 Uses public transportation less frequently
2 Has got lost using public transportation
3 No longer uses public transportation
9 Never used public transportation regularly **OR** Don't know

21. Driving
0 Drives as usual
1 Drives more cautiously
2 Drives less carefully; has got lost while driving
3 No longer drives
9 Never drove **OR** Don't know

22. Mobility around the neighbourhood
0 Same as usual
1 Goes out less frequently
2 Has gotten lost in the immediate neighbourhood
3 No longer goes out unaccompanied
9 This activity has been restricted in the past **OR** Don't know

23. Travel outside familiar environment
0 Same as usual
1 Occasionally gets disorientated in strange surroundings
2 Gets very disorientated but is able to manage if accompanied
3 No longer able to travel
9 Never did this activity **OR** Don't know

COMMUNICATION

24. Using the telephone
0 Same as usual
1 Calls a few familiar numbers
2 Will only answer telephone (won't make calls)
3 Does not use the telephone at all
9 Never had a telephone OR Don't know

25. Talking
0 Same as usual
1 Less talkative; has trouble thinking of words or names
2 Makes occasional errors in speech
3 Speech is almost unintelligible
9 Don't know

26. Understanding
0 Understands everything that is said as usual
1 Asks for repetition
2 Has trouble understanding conversations or specific words occasionally
3 Does not understand what people are saying most of the time
9 Don't know

27. Reading
0 Same as usual
1 Reads less frequently
2 Has trouble understanding or remembering what he/she has read
3 Has given up reading
9 Never read much **OR** Don't know

28. Writing
0 Same as usual
1 Writes less often; makes occasional spelling errors
2 Signs name but no other writing
3 Never writes
9 Never wrote much **OR** Don't know

Activities of Daily Living Questionnaire
Scoring instructions
Johnson, Barion, Rademaker, Rehkemper, and Weintraub (2004)

Name:	**Administered by:**	**Date:**

For each section (e.g., self-care, household care etc.), count the total number of questions answered (i.e., questions that are NOT rated as "9", Don't know). Multiply the total number of questions answered by 3. This equals the total points possible for that section. Add up the actual total score (i.e., the sum of the responses) for that section and divide by the total points possible. Multiply by 100 to get the percent impairment.

	Number of questions answered	**Total points possible (number of questions answered × 3)**	**Actual total score**	**Percent impairment (actual score/total points possible × 100)**
Self-care Activities				
Household Care				
Employment and Recreation				
Shopping and Money				
Travel				
Communication				
TOTAL:				

Acknowledgement: Adapted from Johnson, N. et al. (2004). The Activities of Daily Living Questionnaire: A validation study in patients with dementia. *Alzheimer Disease and Associated Disorders*, *18*(4), 223–230, Appendix, pp. 228–229, used with permission of Lippincott Williams & Wilkins, and Wolters Kluwer.

Assessment of Living Skills and Resources (ALSAR)

Drinka, Williams, Schram, Farrell-Holtan, and Euhardy (2000)

Source

The ALSAR instrument was originally published in 1991 (Williams, Drinka, Greenberg, Farrell-Holtan, Euhardy, & Schram) and the current revised format appeared in Drinka et al. (2000). It is available from the Madison Geriatric Research Education and Clinical Center, William S. Middleton Veterans Hospital, 2500 Overlook Terrace, Madison WI, 53705, USA, and is also reproduced below.

Purpose

The ALSAR is a clinician rating scale, developed for older people living in the community. It focuses on instrumental activities of daily living (IADL) and aims to assess maintenance of independent life in the community, identify needs, assess risk, prioritize treatment goals, and promote interdisciplinary problem solving. The ALSAR has also been used with people with traumatic brain injury (TBI; Simpson, Secheny, Lane-Brown, Strettles, Ferry, & Phillips, 2004).

Item description

The 11 items of the ALSAR comprise the following: telephoning, reading, leisure activity, medication management, money management, transportation, shopping, meal preparation, laundering, housekeeping, and home maintenance.

Scale development

The ALSAR, which was developed "through the collaborative efforts" of a multidisciplinary group of health professionals, varies from many other scales of IADL. It draws on the structure of those IADL scales that take into account both functional status and environmental resources. Williams et al. (1991) argue that "assessment of IADL skills is meaningful only when each skill deficit is linked to an assessment of resources for mitigating the adverse effects of the skill impairment" (p. 85). Skill is defined as the accomplishment of a task, whereas Resource refers to a support for the task to be accomplished, which may be human or technical, formal or informal. The integration of Skill and Resource provides an index of Risk (i.e., "the likelihood that the individual will be unable to accomplish a task given current skills and resources" p. 84). It is expected that Risk predicts negative outcome.

In developing the ALSAR, basic self-care and mobility items were excluded intentionally. The 11 items were considered to be "complex self-maintenance tasks essential for a safe, satisfying, and independent life-style" (Williams et al., 1991, p. 85) for older people. The authors noted that one difficulty with IADL scales is a sex-role bias (e.g., males and females often taking responsibility for managing finances and meal preparation respectively). Consequently a number of IADL items are traditionally scored "not applicable". Williams et al. overcame this difficulty by use of the concept of "procurement"; that is, the task was accomplished by another person, which "can substitute for independent performance only if the *patient* takes responsibility for procurement" (p. 85). Content validity of the ALSAR was formally examined using five clinicians with backgrounds in occupational therapy, physiotherapy and social work. Each skill/resource dyad was reviewed to determine (a) the validity of the descriptors for skill and resource to measure the task and (b) whether the levels were mutually exclusive. Disagreements were resolved by consensus. Williams et al. (1991) had 13 clinicians from the clinical team complete a questionnaire to evaluate the experience of using the ALSAR.

Administration procedures, response format and scoring

A clinician completes the ALSAR based on knowledge of the client or the client/an informant is interviewed. For each of the 11 tasks (e.g., meal preparation) current status of both Skill level and Resource level is rated. Four or five scripted questions tailored to each task are used (e.g., for Skill: who does the cooking in your home? vs for Resource: do you have help getting meals?) in order to facilitate the ratings (or interviews, if these are conducted). Risk scores are also calculated (see below). Administration time is approximately 20 to 30 minutes; a training video is available (personal communication, T. Drinka, 7 February 2007), as are revised scoring criteria (Kuo et al., 2006).

Scoring the ALSAR is a little more involved than for other scales. Two 3-point rating scales are used for assessing the Skill and Resources components of each item. Ratings for Skill are 0 (independent and consistent performance or procurement if they take responsibility), 1 (partially independent), 2 (dependent and no responsibility is taken for task performance or procurement). The total Skill score thus ranges from 0 to 22. Resource is also rated on a 3-point scale: 0 (adequate resources to accomplish the task and that are consistently available), 1 (resources are inconsistently available), 2 (resources are insufficient for task accomplishment or available resources are not used). The total Resource score also ranges from 0 to 22. The Risk score is calculated by summing the scores for Skill and Resources. For each item, the Risk score thus ranges from 0 (low risk) to 4 (high risk); a score of 0 or 1 represents low risk, 2 is moderate risk, and 3 or 4 is high risk. The total Risk score ranges from 0 to 44. The authors advise against the use of cut-off scores, in preference to a clinical understanding of the areas of risk and need.

Psychometric properties

Standardization and examination of the psychometric properties of the ALSAR were conducted with 75 people, aged 51 to 94 years, recruited from the William S. Middleton Memorial Veterans Hospital, Madison, Wisconsin, USA. The ALSAR was validated against the Barthel Index (BI) and Mini-Mental State Examination (MMSE). Predictive validity was examined by following participants over 6 months and examining adverse changes in living arrangements and mortality. Inter-rater reliability was assessed using two trained clinicians who conducted separate interviews with a subset of the sample ($n = 32$). The interviews were conducted 1 to 5 days apart, however, which in effect was a measure of temporal stability rather than inter-rater reliability. Two inter-rater reliability studies have been conducted by Kuo et al. (2006). The first study used seven raters who were trained in use of the ALSAR. They made independent ratings on 10 patients, aged ≥ 65 years who were recruited from a geriatric and rehabilitation unit of a large hospital. Although the reliability for the total Risk score was excellent (ICC = .77), reliabilities for individual items were variable (range $k = .36–.73$, with $k \geq .6$ for 4 out of the 11 items and $k < .4$ for 2 of the 11 items). Inter-rater reliability improved substantially with revised scoring criteria, using an independent sample of 10 patients (see Box 4.17).

Box 7.2

Validity:	Content: Formally assessed (see Scale development section)
	Criterion: *Concurrent:* with BI: $r = -.58$ – with MMSE: $r = -.26$
	Simpson et al.: with BICRO subtests (e.g., Self-organization: $r = -.67$; Mobility: $r = -.70$) – with SPRS: $r = -.61$
	Predictive: Mortality: initial Risk score significantly higher in those who died ($n = 11$, Time 1 $M = 16.0$, $SD = 5.5$) vs those who did not die ($n = 64$, $M = 11.6$, $SD = 7.2$); $t = 1.94$, $p < .05$ – Structured living arrangements: initial Risk score significantly higher in those who did ($n = 9$, $M = 17.3$, $SD = 3.5$) vs. those who did not require structured living ($n = 51$, $M = 10.7$, $SD = 7.2$); $t = 4.33$, $p < .001$
	Construct: *Internal consistency*: Cronbach alpha .91
	Conner-Spady et al.: Cronbach alpha .85
Reliability:	Inter-rater: Kuo et al.: Total Risk score: ICC = .895 (range ICC = .67–.90); Skill: ICC = .54–.77 (with ICC ≥ .6 for 9/11 items); Resource: ICC = .61–.89
	Test–retest: 1–5 days: Skill: $k = .53–.90$ (with $k \geq .6$ for 8/11 items); Resource: $k = .27–1.0$ (with $k \geq .6$ for 9/11 items; $k < .4$ for 2/11 items – telephone, money)
Responsiveness:	Simpson et al.: Risk score: Admission $M = 17.20$ ($SD = 7.18$) vs Discharge $M = 9.66$ ($SD = 7.56$); $z = -5.77$, $d = 1.05$
	Conner-Spady et al.: Risk score – males: Admission $M = 19.48$ ($SD = 5.19$) vs Discharge $M = 16.10$ ($SD = 4.88$), $d = .65$ – females: Admission $M = 14.83$ ($SD = 5.67$) vs Discharge $M = 10.45$ ($SD = 6.91$); overall $F = 37.2$, $p < .001$, $d = .77$

Responsiveness of the ALSAR was examined in the course of evaluating the effect of a transitional living programme for 50 people with TBI (Simpson et al., 2004). Ratings were made at admission and discharge (interval $M = 7$ weeks). The ALSAR was correlated with other measures, including the Brain Injury Community Rehabilitation Outcomes (BICRO) and Sydney Psychosocial Reintegration Scale (SPRS), providing evidence for its concurrent validity in the TBI group. Conner-Spady, Slaughter, and MacLean (1999) examined responsiveness in 63 patients (aged 60–92 years) attending a geriatric assessment and treatment programme 2 days per week for approximately 3 weeks. Results from Williams et al., except where otherwise stated, are shown in Box 7.2.

Comment

The ALSAR has special features that set it aside from other IADL scales. It is, as the authors intended, a multidimensional instrument, and in that sense it crosses the ICF components of Activities/Participation and Environmental Factors. Additionally, the combination of personal skill (cf., Activities/Participation) and resource (cf., Environmental Factors), and the translation of this into a numerical score representing Risk, makes the ALSAR very useful for clinical practice and assists in targeting therapeutic interventions. The ALSAR also bypasses sex-role bias to which IADL scales can be subject. Its psychometric properties with the older adult group are good, with high internal consistency, good temporal stability, and evidence of content, concurrent and predictive validity. With revised scoring criteria developed by Kuo et al. (2006), inter-rater reliability is excellent. The ALSAR has also shown both concurrent validity and responsiveness in a younger TBI population with a large effect size. Finally, Williams et al. (1991) report that the ALSAR is well received by clinicians, who find it useful not only for treatment planning and monitoring patient progress but also in identifying areas of caregiver stress and needs.

Key references

Conner-Spady, B. L., Slaughter, S., & MacLean, S. L. (1999). Assessing the usefulness of the Assessment of Living Skills and Resources (ALSAR) in a geriatric day hospital. *Canadian Journal of Rehabilitation*, *12*(4), 265–272.

Drinka, T. J. K., Williams, J., Schram, M., Farrell-Holtan, J., & Euhardy, M. (2000). Assessment of Living Skills and Resources (ALSAR), an instrumental activities of daily living assessment instrument. In D. Osterweil, K. Brummel-Smith, & J. Beck (Eds.), *Comprehensive geriatric assessment*. (pp. 726–729). New York: McGraw-Hill.

Kuo, J., Fleming, J., Dermer, B., Cullen, C., Jack, C., Bacon, E., et al. (2006). Reliability of the original and revised versions of the Assessment of Living Skills and Resources. *Australian Occupational Therapy Journal*, *53*(1), 1–8.

Simpson, G., Secheny, T., Lane-Brown, A., Strettles, B., Ferry, K., & Phillips, J. (2004). Post-acute rehabilitation for people with traumatic brain injury: A model description and evaluation of the Liverpool Hospital Transitional Living Program. *Brain Impairment*, *5*(1), 67–80.

Williams, J. H., Drinka, T. J. K., Greenberg, J. R., Farrell-Holtan, J., Euhardy, R., & Schram, M. (1991). Development and testing of the Assessment of Living Skills and Resources (ALSAR) in elderly community-dwelling veterans. *The Gerontologist*, *31*(1), 84–91.

Assessment of Living Skills and Resources
Drinka, Williams, Schram, Farrell-Holtan, and Euhardy (2000)

ALSAR TASKS	SKILLS (Individual accomplishes or procures task) Independent - **0**; Partially Independent - **1**; Dependent - **2**. Record SKILL level		TASK RISK SCORE Combined Skill + Resource Level. 3 or 4 = High; 2 = Moderate; 0 or 1 = Low		RESOURCES (Support for task completion extrinsic to individual) **0** - Consistently Available; **1** - Inconsistently Available; **2** - Not Available or in Use. Record RESOURCE level
Telephoning	Locates phone numbers, dials, sends and receives information				Resources for telephoning
Reading	Reads and uses written information				Resources for reading
Leisure	Plans and performs satisfying leisure activities				Resources for satisfying leisure activities
Medication Management	Procures and takes medicine as ordered				Resources for managing medications
Money Management	Manages finances or procures financial services				Resources for managing finances
Transportation	Walks, drives or procures rides				Resources for transportation
Shopping	Lists, selects, buys, orders, stores goods				Resources for shopping
Meal Preparation	Performs all aspects of meal preparation or procures meals				Resources for meal preparation
Laundering	Performs or procures all aspects of doing laundering				Resources for laundering
Housekeeping	Cleans own living space or procures housekeeping service				Resources for housekeeping
Home Maintenance	Performs or procures home maintenance				Resources for home maintenance

"R" SCORE ( ) (sum of 11 TASK RISK SCORES)

Name: ______________________ Interviewer: ______________________

Date: ______________________ Information Source: ______________________

Assessment of Living Skills and Resources
Drinka, Williams, Schram, Farrell-Holtan, and Euhardy (2000)
Suggested questions

Suggested Skills questions | **TASKS** | **Suggested Resources questions**

TELEPHONING (Using the phone to send and receive information)

Skills:
- How often do you use the phone?
- Do you make calls or only use the phone if someone calls you?
- Can you hear the phone ringing?
- Can you hear what is being said?
- What number would you dial for an emergency?

Resources:
- How many phones do you have? (location)
- Can you get to the phone if its ringing?
- Any special devices on your phone? Amplified headset? Large scale numbers on phone?
- Are emergency numbers listed by each phone?

READING (Using written information)

Skills:
- Do you have any difficulty reading?
- What do you usually read?
- Can you read newspaper size print, mail, medicine bottles?
- Can you read dials on the TV, thermostat, appliances?

Resources:
- Do you wear glasses? Last vision test?
- Do you have any low vision aids? Magnifier? Large print materials? Talking books?
- Does someone read things for you?

LEISURE (Using time not spent for work, sleep, or self-care)

Skills:
- What do you do in your spare time (for fun)?
- Do you have any hobbies/pastimes?
- Are you active in any clubs or organizations?
- Are there any activities that you have given up recently?

Resources:
- Is there a senior centre near you?
- How do you keep in touch with friends and family?
- How often do you see them? Talk to them?
- Are there any activities you would like to begin?

MEDICATION MANAGEMENT (Taking medicine as ordered)

Skills:
- Do you take any medications? How many? How often?
- What are they for?
- How often do you forget to take your medications?
- How do you renew your prescriptions?

Resources:
- Does anyone help you take your medicine or reorder medicine?
- Do you have a system for taking medication?
- Do you have insurance to cover medications?
- Any medications you don't take because you can't pay for them?

MONEY MANAGEMENT (Managing finances)

Skills:
- How do you manage your finances? Pay the bills?
- Do you use a checking account?
- How do you do your taxes?
- Can you live within your income?

Resources:
- Does anyone help you with finances?
- Do you bank in person or by mail?
- Do you have a power of attorney?

TRANSPORTATION (Walking, driving, and using public transit)

Skills:
- Do you drive? At night?
- Do you drive out of town, or only in town?
- Are there restrictions on your licence?
- Do you use public transportation?
- Do you arrange for your own transportation?

Resources:
- How do you get around?
- Do you have a person drive you?
- Are your methods of transportation reliable?

SHOPPING (Listing, selecting, carrying, and storing items)

Skills:
- Do you do your own shopping?
- Do you carry your purchases?
- How often do you go shopping?
- Do you ever shop by mail or phone?

Resources:
- Does someone shop for you?
- Is that person available when you need them?
- Are there stores located near you?
- Do you use anything to carry your purchases?

MEAL PREPARATION (Food planning, storage, cooking, and serving)

Skills:
- Do you cook your meals?
- Do you prepare your own snacks, breakfast or lunch?
- What do you do when your regular system for meals is not available?

Resources:
- Are there restaurants or meal sites that you use?
- Does someone cook for you?
- Are your kitchen appliances adequate?

LAUNDRY (Carrying, washing, drying, and putting away clothing)

Skills:
- Do you do your laundry?
- Do you do sorting? Carrying? Folding? Putting away?
- How often is laundry done?
- Do you arrange for a laundry service?

Resources:
- Does someone do the laundry?
- Where is the washer/dryer located?
- What do you use to carry the laundry?
- Are the laundry facilities adequate?

HOUSEKEEPING (Keeping dishes washed, pathways clear, rooms clean)

Skills:
- Do you do the housekeeping?
- Do you do light work such as dishwashing, dusting, vacuuming?
- How often do you do the housekeeping?
- Do you arrange for housekeeping services?

Resources:
- Does someone do your housekeeping? How often?
- Are these services adequate?
- Could you afford housekeeping services?

HOME MAINTENANCE (Controlling temperature, clearing paths, and mowing lawn)

Skills:
- What type of house do you live in?
- How do you do the outdoor work? Lawn? Paths? Windows?
- How do you do major (e.g., fix leaking tap) or minor (e.g., change lightbulb) repairs?
- How do you control the temperature of your home?

Resources:
- Does someone maintain your home for you?
- What equipment do you have for home upkeep (e.g., tools, ladder, lawnmower)?
- Are maintenance supports readily available and reliable?

Acknowledgement: Reproduced by permission of Theresa Drinka © Dr Theresa Drinka.

Barthel Index (BI)

Mahoney and Barthel (1965)

Source

Items and scoring procedures for the BI are detailed in Mahoney and Barthel (1965) and other publications. Collin, Wade, Davies, and Horne (1988) describe a commonly used version that is produced below. Scale items are also available from the Internet Stroke Center website (http://www.strokecenter.org).

Purpose

The BI is a clinician rating scale that aims to (i) assess level of independence in mobility and self-care tasks and (ii) chart improvement over time. It was developed for people undergoing rehabilitation for neuromuscular and musculoskeletal disorders. The BI is very widely used with older people and people after stroke. It has also been used with patients with other neurological conditions, including multiple sclerosis (MS; Einarsson, Gottberg, Fredrikson, Bergendal, von Koch, & Holmqvist, 2003) and traumatic brain injury (TBI; Collin et al., 1988).

Item description

The BI comprises 10 items, assessing mobility (3 items), feeding (1 item), continence and toileting (3 items), bathing (2 items), and dressing (1 item).

Scale development

Apart from reporting that the BI was in use since 1955, Mahoney and Barthel (1965) did not provide any details about its development. The original scoring procedures, whereby weights were assigned "based on the time and amount of actual physical assistance required" (p. 61), appear to have been arbitrarily derived based on the authors' clinical experience, rather than being determined empirically. Subsequently, a number of modifications have been proposed: a 15-item version was used by Granger, Albrecht, and Hamilton (1979) and Collin et al. (1988) suggested scoring modifications, with increments of 1 point rather than the original 5-point increments, Wade and Collin (1988) arguing that the latter gave "a spurious feeling of accuracy" (p. 65). Other scoring modifications have been suggested to increase the sensitivity of the BI (e.g., Shah, Vanclay, & Cooper, 1989). Barer and Murphy (1993) examined the "hierarchical tendency" of the BI items to meet requirements for a Guttman scale, comparing the Collin et al. 20-point version and a simplified 10-point version using dichotomous scoring. The 20-point version did not meet statistical criteria for a hierarchical scale, but the 10-point version did, with coefficient of reproducibility of .95 and coefficient of scalability of .82.

Administration procedures, response format and scoring

The BI is intended to be administered at admission to rehabilitation and at regular intervals thereafter. A clinician usually completes the BI based on their knowledge of the patient's current functional status. Completion time is 2 to 5 minutes. Collin et al. (1988) provide guidelines specifying detailed operational definitions of the items and behaviours that are expected for varying degrees of independence. The original emphasis on physical disablement as a reason for non-completion of tasks was emended by Collin et al. who recognized that cognitive impairment in some patients with acquired brain impairment necessitates set-up and supervision time to perform physical activity tasks. They stipulated that if supervision is needed then the person is *not* independent.

Various scoring procedures are available for the BI,*

* Mahoney and Barthel (1965) originally assigned scores of 0, 5 or 10 to the items according to the patient's level of independence. Usually (with some exceptions), 5 was assigned if the patient required assistance and 10 if the patient was independent. The total score ranged from 0 to 100, with higher scores indicating greater independence. An alternative scoring system was developed by Shah et al. (1989), using a 5-point scale: 1 (equivalent of unable to perform the task), 2 (attempts task but unsafe), 3 (moderate assistance/supervision required), 4 (minimal assistance/supervision required), 5 (fully independent). Different weights were applied to the response categories for different items, resulting in a total score range from 0 to 100.

and that developed by Collin et al. (1988) is widely used and is described in this entry. Score ranges for each item are variable, from 0 (equivalent of unable to do) to a maximum of 1 (e.g., bathing item), 2 (e.g., dressing item) or 3 (e.g., mobility item). The total score ranges from 0 to 20, with higher scores indicating greater independence. On the basis of their temporal stability study, Green, Forster, and Young (2001) suggested that a change in score > 2/20 points represents real change occurring in the patient.

Psychometric properties

Mahoney and Barthel (1965) did not provide any psychometric data on the BI, but subsequently it has been researched extensively. A comprehensive study was conducted by Hsueh, Lee, and Hsieh (2001), with 121 patients (age $M = 69.2$ years, $SD = 11.2$) with stroke recruited from a university hospital in Taiwan. They were assessed at 14, 30, 90 and 180 days post-stroke. Validating instruments were the Fugl-Meyer Motor Assessment (FM) and Berg Balance Scale (BBS). Predictive validity of the BI was examined against the Frenchay Activities Index (FAI), which was administered at 180 days post-stroke. Responsiveness was examined by comparing BI scores at the four data collection time-points. Inter-rater reliability was assessed with two occupational therapists who made independent assessments in randomized order. Assessments were not simultaneous, however, but occurred within a 24-hour period. Collin et al. (1988) compared four sources of data collection (self-report, nurse who worked with the patient for at least one shift, a trained nurse and independent testing by an occupational therapist), examining 25 people mainly with stroke and TBI participating in inpatient rehabilitation. Data on test–retest reliability are available from Green et al. (2001) who examined 22 people ($M = 15$ months post-stroke) using the 20-point BI. Other data on responsiveness of the BI are available from Donkervoort, Dekker, Stehmann-Saris, and Deelman (2001) who examined the effectiveness of 8 weeks of strategy training compared to usual practice in improving functional independence in 93 patients with apraxia after stroke.

The factor structure of the BI was examined by Laake, Laake, Hylen Ranhoff, Sveen, Wyller, and Bautz-Holter (1995) in groups of patients with various diagnoses, including a stroke group ($n = 87$). They used linear structural equations to take account of the ordinal scales, with the items having 2 to 4 levels. Two items (toileting and bathing) were excluded because of multicollinearity. A single factor was extracted. Information on convergent and divergent validity is available from the study of Hobart et al. (2001), who assessed 149 rehabilitation inpatients mainly with stroke and MS.

Box 7.3

Validity:	Criterion: *Concurrent:* at 4 different time points post-stroke with FIM: $r = .78–.81$ – with BBS: $r = .89–.94$
	Predictive: with FAI at 180 days, using BI at 14 days ($r = .59$), 30 days ($r = .66$), and 90 days ($r = .63$)
	Construct: *Internal consistency:* Cronbach alpha: .89–.92 at 4 different time points
	Factor structure: Laake et al.: a unidimensional scale in the stroke group using 8/10 items
	Convergent/divergent: Hobart et al.: higher correlation with similar constructs (with OPCS: $r = .84$); lower correlation with dissimilar constructs (with LHS: $r = .33$, GHQ: $r = .14$, SF36-Physical: $r = .30$, SF36-Mental: $r = .11$)
Reliability:	Inter-rater: Total score: ICC = .92 (item range $k = .53–.94$, Median = 0.71); but note that data were not collected simultaneously (see text)
	– Collin et al.: Kendall's coefficient of concordance among 4 raters = .93
	Test–retest: Green et al.: 1 week: $k \geq .6$ for 6/8 items*, $k < .4$ for 2/8 items (bladder, walking). *Note: kappa not calculated for 2/10 items with perfect agreement
Responsiveness:	Effect size for change in scores between 14–180 days post-stroke: Baseline $M = 7.6$ ($SD = 6.1$), change from baseline $M = 7.0$ (reported $d = 1.27$); – also between 14–30 days ($M = 2.61$, reported $d = .56$) – between 30–90 days ($M = 3.56$, reported $d = .53$)
	Donkervoort et al.: Baseline: Strategy group $M = 10.7$ ($SD = 4.9$) vs Control group $M = 11.2$ ($SD = 5.0$); post-treatment change from baseline: Strategy group = 2.44, Control group = 1.15 ($F = 7.31$, $p < .01$, $d = .47$ in favour of the Strategy group)

They examined patterns of correlations with similar constructs using a disability measure, the Office of Population Censuses and Surveys Disability Scales (OPCS), and with dissimilar constructs of participation (London Handicap Scale, LHS), psychological well-being (General Health Questionnaire, GHQ) and physical and mental health status (Short-Form Health Survey, SF-36). Results of Hsueh et al. (2001), except where otherwise indicated, are shown in Box 7.3.

Comment

The BI continues to be very widely used and is described by Hobart et al. (2001) as remaining "a cornerstone of disability measurement" (p. 639). Wade and Collin (1988) pointed to the proliferation of scales of activities of daily living (ADL) and, on the basis of its psychometric properties, proposed that the BI be adopted as the standard index for clinical and research purposes. It shows good reliability and responsiveness and is valid for the purpose for which it was developed, showing evidence of concurrent, predictive and construct validity. Mahoney and Barthel (1965) intended the BI to be a simple and brief scale and they acknowledged the limitations in content sampling – even if the patient obtains the maximum score "this does not mean that he is able to live alone" (p. 62). For this reason, the BI is often used in conjunction with an instrumental ADL scale, commonly the Nottingham Extended ADL Scale (NEADL; see entry in this chapter), the brevity of administration of both instruments (each a matter of minutes) making this very feasible. Moreover, the hierarchical structure of both scales affords even more efficiency of administration, and, as suggested by Barer and Murphy (1993), indicates that functional recovery after stroke follows a consistent pattern with relatively few exceptions. Similarly, Hsueh, Wang, Sheu, and Hsieh (2004) have examined a Rasch-based composite of the BI and Frenchay Activities Index.

Key references

Barer, D. H., & Murphy, J. J. (1993). Scaling the Barthel: A 10-point hierarchical version of the activities of daily living index for use with stroke patients. *Clinical Rehabilitation*, *7*(4), 271–277.

Collin, C., Wade, D. T., Davies, S., & Horne, V. (1988). The Barthel ADL Index: A reliability study. *International Disability Studies*, *10*(2), 61–63.

Donkervoort, M., Dekker, J., Stehmann-Saris, F. C., & Deelman, B. G. (2001). Efficacy of strategy training in left hemisphere stroke patients with apraxia: A randomised clinical trial. *Neuropsychological Rehabilitation*, *11*(5), 549–566.

Einarsson, U., Gottberg, K., Fredrikson, S., Bergendal, G., von Koch, L., & Holmqvist, L. W. (2003). Multiple sclerosis in Stockholm County. A pilot study exploring the feasibility of assessment of impairment, disability and handicap by home visits. *Clinical Rehabilitation*, *17*, 294–303.

Granger, C. V., Albrecht, G. L., & Hamilton, B. B. (1979). Outcome of comprehensive medical rehabilitation: Measurement by PULSES profile and the Barthel Index. *Archives of Physical Medical and Rehabilitation*, *60*(4), 145–154.

Green, J., Forster, A., & Young, J. (2001). A test–retest reliability study of the Barthel Index, the Rivermead Mobility Index, the Nottingham Extended Activities of Daily Living Scale and the Frenchay Activities Index in stroke patients. *Disability and Rehabilitation*, *23*(15), 670–676.

Hobart, J. C., Lamping, D. L., Freeman, J. A., Langdon, D. W., McLellan, D. L., Greenwood, R. J., et al. (2001). Evidence-based measurement: Which disability scale for neurologic rehabilitation? *Neurology*, *57*(4), 639–644.

Hsueh, I.-P., Lee, M.-M., & Hsieh, C.-L. (2001). Psychometric characteristics of the Barthel Activities of Daily Living Index in stroke patients. *Journal of the Formosan Medical Association*, *100*(8), 526–532.

Hsueh, I.-P., Wang, W.-C., Sheu, C.-F., & Hsieh, C.-L. (2004). Rasch analysis of combining two indices to assess comprehensive ADL function in stroke patients. *Stroke*, *35*(3), 721–726.

Laake, K., Laake, P., Hylen Ranhoff, A., Sveen, U., Wyller, T. B., & Bautz-Holter, E. (1995). The Barthel ADL Index: Factor structure depends upon the category of patient. *Age and Ageing*, *24*(5), 393–397.

Mahoney, F. I., & Barthel, D. W. (1965). Functional evaluation: The Barthel Index. *Maryland State Medical Journal*, *Feb*(14), 61–65.

Shah, S., Vanclay, F., & Cooper, B. (1989). Improving the sensitivity of the Barthel Index for stroke rehabilitation. *Journal of Clinical Epidemiology*, *42*(8), 703–709.

Wade, D. T., & Collin, C. (1988). The Barthel ADL Index: A standard measure of physical disability? *International Disability Studies*, *10*(2), 64–67.

Barthel ADL Index

Mahoney and Barthel (1965)

Using scoring procedures from Collin, Wade, Davies, and Horne (1988)

Name:	**Administered by:**	**Date:**

1. Bowels
- 0 Incontinent (or needs to be given enemata)
- 1 Occasional accident (once/week)
- 2 Continent

2. Bladder
- 0 Incontinent, or catheterized and unable to manage
- 1 Occasional accident (maximum once per 24 hours)
- 2 Continent (for over 7 days)

3. Grooming
- 0 Needs help with personal care
- 1 Independent face/hair/teeth/shaving (implements provided)

4. Toilet use
- 0 Dependent
- 1 Needs some help, but can do something alone
- 2 Independent (on and off, dressing, wiping)

5. Feeding
- 0 Unable
- 1 Needs help cutting, spreading butter, etc.
- 2 Independent (food provided in reach)

6. Transfer
- 0 Unable – no sitting balance
- 1 Major help (one or two people, physical) can sit
- 2 Minor help (verbal or physical)
- 3 Independent

7. Mobility
- 0 Immobile
- 1 Wheelchair independent including corners, etc.
- 2 Walks with help from one person (verbal or physical)
- 3 Independent (but may use any aid, e.g., stick)

8. Dressing
- 0 Dependent
- 1 Needs help, but can do about half unaided
- 2 Independent (including buttons, zips, laces, etc.)

9. Stairs
- 0 Unable
- 1 Needs help (verbal, physical, carrying aid)
- 2 Independent up and down

10. Bathing
- 0 Dependent
- 1 Independent (or in shower)

TOTAL SCORE:__________

Barthel ADL Index

Mahoney and Barthel (1965)

Scoring procedures from Collin, Wade, Davies, and Horne (1988)

General

- The Index should be used as a record of *what a patient does*, NOT as a record of *what a patient could do.*
- The main aim is to establish *degree of independence from any help*, physical or verbal, however minor and for whatever reason.
- The need for *supervision* renders the patient, NOT *independent*.
- A patient's performance should be established *using the best available evidence*. Asking the patient, friends/relatives and nurses will be the usual source, but direct observation and common sense are also important. However, *direct testing is not needed*.
- Usually the performance over the *preceding 24–48* hours is important, but occasionally longer periods will be relevant.
- *Unconscious patients should score "0"* throughout, even if not yet incontinent.
- Middle categories imply that patient supplies *over 50% of the effort*.
- *Use of aids* to be independent is *allowed*.

1. Bowels (preceding week)

- If needs enema from nurse, then "incontinent".
- Occasional = once a week.

2. Bladder (preceding week)

- Occasional = less than once a day.
- A catheterized patient who can completely manage the catheter alone is registered as "continent".

3. Grooming (preceding 24–48 hours)

- Refers to personal hygiene: doing teeth, fitting false teeth, doing hair, shaving, washing face.
- Implements can be provided by helper.

4. Toilet use

- Should be able to reach toilet/commode, undress sufficiently, clean self, dress and leave.
- With help = can wipe self, and do some other of above.

5. Feeding

- Able to eat any normal food (not only soft food). Food cooked and served by others. But not cut up.
- Help = food cut up, patient feeds self.

6. Transfer

- From bed to chair and back.
- Dependent = NO sitting balance (unable to sit); two people to lift.
- Major help = one strong/skilled, or two normal people. Can sit up.
- Minor help = one person easily, OR needs any supervision for safety.

7. Mobility

- Refers to mobility about house or ward, indoors. May use aid. If in wheelchair, must negotiate corners/doors unaided.
- Help = by one, untrained person, including supervision/moral support.

8. Dressing

- Should be able to select and put on all clothes, which may be adapted.
- Half = help with buttons, zips, etc. (check!), but can put on some garments alone.

9. Stairs

- Must carry any walking aid used to be independent.

10. Bathing

- Usually the most difficult activity.
- Must get in and out unsupervised, and wash self.
- Independent in shower = "independent" if unsupervised/unaided.

Acknowledgement: From Colin, C., Wade, D. T., Davies, S., & Horne, V. (1988). The Barthel Activities of Daily Living Index: A reliability study?. *International Disability Studies*, *10*(2), 61–63, Barthel Scale used by permission of Informa Healthcare.

Bristol Activities of Daily Living Scale (BADLS)

Bucks, Ashworth, Wilcock, and Siegfried (1996)

Source

Items for the BADLS are available in the appendix to Bucks et al. (1996) and are reproduced below.

Purpose

The BADLS is an informant rating scale specifically designed for use in the community as "a short assessment of functional ability" (Bucks et al., 1996, p. 114). It was developed for people with dementia, primarily to provide a baseline assessment and identify changes over time.

Item description

The BADLS comprises 20 items in four domains: Self-care (9 items), Mobility (2 items), Orientation (2 items), and Instrumental Activities of Daily Living (IADL, 7 items).

Scale development

The BADLS was developed to meet the needs of the dementia group. Bucks et al. (1996) enumerated limitations of current measures, many of which were developed to assess functional status either in normal older people or in those with physical disabilities and hence were not sensitive to changes experienced by people with dementia. A three-phase approach was adopted in the development of the BADLS. First, a review of six widely used functional scales identified a pool of 22 items that were used in two or more of the scales. These items were trialled in a postal survey with 50 caregivers of people with dementia living in the community, who rated the items on a 3-point scale (independent, requires assistance or dependent). Additionally, they were asked to comment on the items and the type of assistance required, and to identify five functions they would most like to see improved or maintained. In the second phase, a draft version of the BADLS was constructed using the caregiver responses to devise severity statements and was administered to caregivers on two occasions by (independent) nurses. Additionally, a preliminary validation was conducted using direct observation of functional performance of the person with dementia on a series of ADL tasks that corresponded as closely as possible to the BADLS items. Item content was revised on the basis of caregiver feedback, and psychometric properties were further examined in the third phase (see below).

Administration procedures, response format and scoring

The BADLS is completed by an informant using the reference of typical level of functional performance in the preceding 2 weeks. Administration time is short and the authors report that the caregivers found the BADLS easy to complete.

Each item is rated on a 4-point scale, with individually tailored responses for each item: 0 (equivalent of independent) to 3 (dependent on others to do the task). An additional "not applicable" response category is used when the respondent is unable to provide a response or the item is not applicable to the person, and such responses are scored zero. Bucks et al. (1996) noted that in their standardization studies missing data occurred infrequently (2.4%) and thus minimal distortion was introduced by "giving ratings of independence on a task when the 'not applicable' option was chosen" (p. 117). The total score ranges from 0 to 60, with higher scores indicating greater dependency. A decrease of >3 points is suggested to represent a clinically meaningful improvement; conversely, an increase of > 1 point a clinically meaningful deterioration (Byrne, Wilson, Bucks, Hughes, and Wilcock, 2000), these criteria being determined empirically.

Psychometric properties

The standardization sample in Phase 3 of the development of the BADLS (Bucks et al., 1996) comprised 59 caregivers of people with dementia living in the community who were recruited from the Bristol Memory Disorders Clinic, Bristol, UK. They were aged $M = 73$

years ($SD = 7.4$) and 35 of the 59 had probable Alzheimer's disease (AD), diagnosed with established criteria. A nurse administered the BADLS, along with the Mini-Mental State Examination (MMSE). In Phase 2, 27 people with dementia (22/27 with probable AD) had been administered the BADLS and direct observation of their functional performance was also assessed. Test–retest reliability was evaluated approximately 1 week later. Principal components analysis extracted four components, accounting for 65% of the variance, which largely correspond to the domains of the scale. Some evidence for responsiveness is provided by the results of the AD2000 Collaborative Group (2004). Community-dwelling people with mild to moderate AD ($n = 565$) participated in a clinical trial of donezepil and were assessed after 12 weeks of treatment and at multiple follow-ups from 24 weeks to 2 years. It is noted, however, that although improvement was statistically significant, the magnitude was not as large as suggested by Byrne et al. (2000) to meet criterion for a clinically meaningful change. Discriminant validity was examined in the study of McKeith et al. (2006) who hypothesized that patients with dementia with Lewy bodies (DLB, $n = 41$) would have lower BADLS scores than patients with AD ($n = 42$), because of the extrapyramidal motor symptoms characteristic of DLB. Results of Bucks et al., except where otherwise stated, are shown in Box 7.4.

Comment

Development of the BADLS was careful and thorough, with caregivers participating in the developmental process in order to increase the relevance of structure, item content and response format. The authors recognized the limitations of the BADLS being an informant-based rating scale, as opposed to the method of direct observation; conversely, the format "has the advantage of allowing patients to be evaluated over the full range of their abilities" (Bucks et al., 1996, p. 114). The authors have, however, demonstrated that the BADLS has evidence of concurrent validity with direct observation of functional ability. The scoring system takes into account items that are not applicable given people's different circumstances (e.g., handling finances, food preparation). The "not applicable" response was, however, rarely used (2.4% of responses). The practical strengths of the BADLS include its efficient sampling of a comprehensive coverage of self-care and IADL items and the quick and easy administration and scoring format. Measurement characteristics available to date are positive, especially the data indicating that the BADLS is stable and valid.

Box 7.4

Validity:	Criterion: *Concurrent:* with direct observation of functional ability: $r = .65$ – with MMSE: $r = -.67$
	Construct: *Factor analysis*: 4 components: IADL (7 items), Self-care (6 items), Orientation (5 items), Mobility (2 items)
	Discriminant: McKeith et al.: DLB $M = 18.2$ ($SD = 9.8$) vs AD $M = 12.3$ ($SD = 9.1$); $t = -2.8$, $p = .006$. Significant differences also occurred for 6/20 items (eating, cleaning teeth, bath, toilet, transfers, mobility)
Reliability:	Inter-rater: No information available
	Test–retest: $M = 8.6$ days: Total score: $r = .95$ (item range $k = .27 - .94$; with $k \geq .6$ for 14/22 items; $k < .4$ for 3/20 items – time, space, transfers)
Responsiveness:	AD2000 Collaborative Group: Donezepil group improved by an average of 1 point at each assessment occasion (0.5–1.6, $p < .0001$) over the 2-year treatment period

Key references

AD2000 Collaborative Group. (2004). Long-term donepezil treatment in 565 patients with Alzheimer's disease (AD2000): Randomised double-blind trial. *The Lancet*, *364*(9427), 2105–2115.

Bucks, R. S., Ashworth, D. L., Wilcock, G. K., & Siegfried, K. (1996). Assessment of activities of daily living in dementia: Development of the Bristol Activities of Daily Living Scale. *Age and Ageing*, *25*, 113–120.

Byrne, L. M., Wilson, P. M. A., Bucks, R. S., Hughes, A. O., & Wilcock, G. K. (2000). The sensitivity to change over time of the Bristol Activities of Daily Living Scale in Alzheimer's disease. *International Journal of Geriatric Psychiatry*, *15*(7), 656–661.

McKeith, I. G., Rowan, E., Askew, K., Naidu, A., Allan, L., Barnett, N., et al. (2006). More severe functional impairment in dementia with Lewy bodies than Alzheimer disease is related to extrapyramidal motor dysfunction. *American Journal of Geriatric Psychiatry*, *14*(7), 582–588.

Bristol Activities of Daily Living Scale (BADLS)

Bucks, Ashworth, Wilcock, and Siegfried (1996)

Name:	**Administered by:**	**Date:**

Instructions: This questionnaire is designed to reveal the everyday ability of people who have memory difficulties of one form or another. For each activity (items 1–20), statements 0 to 3 refer to a different level of ability. Thinking of the last 2 weeks, tick the box that best represents your relative's/friend's ability. Only one box should be ticked for each activity. (If in doubt about which box to tick, chose the level of ability that represents his/her average performance over the last 2 weeks.)

1. Food
- 0 ☐ Selects and prepares food as required
- 1 ☐ Able to prepare food if ingredients set out
- 2 ☐ Can prepare food if prompted step by step
- 3 ☐ Unable to prepare food even with prompting and supervision
- 0 ☐ Not applicable

2. Eating
- 0 ☐ Eats appropriately using correct cutlery
- 1 ☐ Eats appropriately if food made manageable and/or uses spoon
- 2 ☐ Uses fingers to eat food
- 3 ☐ Needs to be fed
- 0 ☐ Not applicable

3. Drink
- 0 ☐ Selects and prepares drinks as required
- 1 ☐ Can prepare drinks if ingredients left available
- 2 ☐ Can prepare drinks if prompted step by step
- 3 ☐ Unable to make a drink even with prompting and supervision
- 0 ☐ Not applicable

4. Drinking
- 0 ☐ Drinks appropriately
- 1 ☐ Drinks appropriately with aids, beaker/ straw, etc.
- 2 ☐ Does not drink appropriately even with aids but attempts to
- 3 ☐ Has to have drinks administered (fed)
- 0 ☐ Not applicable

5. Dressing
- 0 ☐ Selects appropriate clothing and dresses self
- 1 ☐ Puts clothes on in wrong order and/or back to front and/or dirty clothing
- 2 ☐ Unable to dress self but moves limbs to assist
- 3 ☐ Unable to assist and requires total dressing
- 0 ☐ Not applicable

6. Hygiene
- 0 ☐ Washes regularly and independently
- 1 ☐ Can wash self if given soap, flannel, towel, etc.
- 2 ☐ Can wash self if prompted and supervised
- 3 ☐ Unable to wash self and needs full assistance
- 0 ☐ Not applicable

7. Teeth
- 0 ☐ Cleans own teeth/dentures regularly and independently
- 1 ☐ Cleans teeth/dentures if given appropriate items
- 2 ☐ Requires some assistance, toothpaste on brush, brush to mouth, etc.
- 3 ☐ Full assistance given
- 0 ☐ Not applicable

8. Bath/shower
- 0 ☐ Bathes regularly and independently
- 1 ☐ Needs bath to be drawn/shower turned on but washes independently
- 2 ☐ Needs supervision and prompting to wash
- 3 ☐ Totally dependent, needs full assistance
- 0 ☐ Not applicable

9. Toilet/commode
- 0 ☐ Uses toilet appropriately when required
- 1 ☐ Needs to be taken to the toilet and given assistance
- 2 ☐ Incontinent of urine or faeces
- 3 ☐ Incontinent of urine and faeces
- 0 ☐ Not applicable

10. Transfers
- 0 ☐ Can get in/out of chair unaided
- 1 ☐ Can get into chair but needs help to get out
- 2 ☐ Needs help getting in and out of chair
- 3 ☐ Totally dependent on being put into and lifted from chair
- 0 ☐ Not applicable

11. Mobility
- 0 ☐ Walks independently
- 1 ☐ Walks with assistance, i.e., furniture, arm for support
- 2 ☐ Uses aides to mobilize, i.e., frame, sticks, etc.
- 3 ☐ Unable to walk
- 0 ☐ Not applicable

12. Orientation – Time
- 0 ☐ Fully orientated to time/day/date, etc.
- 1 ☐ Unaware of time/day etc. but seems unconcerned
- 2 ☐ Repeatedly asks the time/day/date
- 3 ☐ Mixes up night and day
- 0 ☐ Not applicable

13. Orientation – Space

0	☐	Fully orientated to surroundings
1	☐	Orientated to familiar surroundings only
2	☐	Gets lost in home, needs reminding where bathroom is, etc.
3	☐	Does not recognize home as own and attempts to leave
0	☐	Not applicable

14. Communication

0	☐	Able to hold appropriate conversation
1	☐	Shows understanding and attempts to respond verbally with gestures
2	☐	Can make self understood but difficulty understanding others
3	☐	Does not respond to or communicate with others
0	☐	Not applicable

15. Telephone

0	☐	Uses telephone appropriately, including obtaining correct number
1	☐	Uses telephone if number given verbally/ visually or predialled
2	☐	Answers telephone but does not make calls
3	☐	Unable/unwilling to use telephone at all
0	☐	Not applicable

16. Housework/gardening

0	☐	Able to do housework/gardening to previous standard
1	☐	Able to do housework/gardening but not to previous standard
2	☐	Limited participation even with a lot of supervision
3	☐	Unwilling/unable to participate in previous activities
0	☐	Not applicable

17. Shopping

0	☐	Shops to previous standard
1	☐	Only able to shop for 1 or 2 items with or without a list
2	☐	Unable to shop alone, but participates when accompanied
3	☐	Unable to participate in shopping even when accompanied
0	☐	Not applicable

18. Finances

0	☐	Responsible for own finances at previous level
1	☐	Unable to write cheque but can sign name and recognizes money values
2	☐	Can sign name but unable to recognize money values
3	☐	Unable to sign name or recognize money values
0	☐	Not applicable

19. Games/hobbies

0	☐	Participates in pastimes/activities to previous standard
1	☐	Participates but needs instruction/ supervision
2	☐	Reluctant to join in, very slow, needs coaxing
3	☐	No longer able or willing to join in
0	☐	Not applicable

20. Transport

0	☐	Able to drive, cycle or use public transport independently
1	☐	Unable to drive but uses public transport or bike, etc.
2	☐	Unable to use public transport alone
3	☐	Unable/unwilling to use transport even when accompanied
0	☐	Not applicable

Thank you for taking the time to complete this questionnaire

TOTAL SCORE: ___

Acknowledgement: From Bucks, R. S. et al. (1996). Assessment of activities of daily living in dementia: Development of the Bristol Activities of Daily Living Scale. *Age and Ageing*, *25*(2), 113–120, Appendix, pp. 118–119, by permission of Oxford University Press.

Frenchay Activities Index (FAI)

Holbrook and Skilbeck (1983)

Source

Items and response categories for the FAI appear in an appendix to Holbrook and Skilbeck (1983) and are reproduced below.

Purpose

The FAI is primarily a self/informant rating scale, designed to measure "the broader everyday activities of normal living" (Holbrook & Skilbeck, 1983, p. 166). It was developed for people with stroke and has also been used with older adults (Bond, Clark, Smith, & Harris, 1995).

Item description

The 15 items of the FAI sample three statistically derived domains of instrumental activities of daily living (ADL): Domestic/chores (5 items), Leisure/work (4 items) and Outdoor activity (6 items).

Scale development

Holbrook and Skilbeck (1983) were critical of ADL scales of the day, which were restricted in focus to the capacity for self-care and basic mobility. They developed the FAI as a scale that would encompass a broader perspective of the person's lifestyle with an unspecified number of items "selected intuitively to cover a wide range of positive activities (excluding passive interests such as watching television)" (p. 167). The scale was developed with a sample of 122 patients with stroke (and their spouses) recruited from the Frenchay Hospital, Bristol, UK who answered a series of questions about their premorbid lifestyle 6 weeks prior to their stroke. As many as possible were also followed up 12 months post-stroke. Highly inter-correlated items were excluded, resulting in a final pool of 15 items. Factor analysis on the items yielded three main factors, accounting for 52% of the variance: Domestic chores, Leisure/work and Outdoor activities, but a number of items were complex, loading on two factors.

Administration procedures, response format and scoring

Administration of the FAI was originally conducted by interview, but the standardized questionnaire lends itself to self/informant completion, which takes less than 5 minutes. In their sample of 96 people with stroke, Schuling, de Haan, Limburg, and Groenier (1993) noted that communication difficulties did not impede administration. In an effort to maximize inter-rater reliability, Piercy, Carter, Mant, and Wade (2000) developed detailed guidelines providing operational definitions of the activities, and these are available in an appendix to their paper.

Responses are made in terms of frequency of occurrence over the preceding 3 or 6 months. Scoring the FAI uses a 4-point scale with response categories tailored to groups of items, ranging from 1 (never/none) to 4 (maximum frequency, which varies according to the item, e.g., most days, > 30 hours/week). A complicated scoring system was used by Holbrook and Skilbeck (1983), whereby item loadings from the factor analysis were applied and then converted to Sten scores ($M = 5.5$, $SD = 2.0$), conversion tables being available from the authors. Wade, Legh-Smith, and Langton Hewer (1985) proposed a less sophisticated but more practical approach, which has since been adopted widely (though not universally). Items are rated on a 4-point scale of 0 (never/none) to 3 (most days/at least weekly/over 30 hours per week, etc., depending on the item), with the total score ranging from 0 to 45, and higher scores indicating greater frequency of activities.

Normative data have been reported by Schuling et al. (1993), who mailed the FAI to 322 people recruited from four general practitioners in Groningen, the Netherlands who were older than 65 years of age and living in the community (no information was provided on their health status, although they had not had stroke). Response rate was 65% ($n = 216$) and mean age was 74 years (range 65–91 years). They used the original scoring system (scores ranging from 1–4 per item), but simply summed the scores so that the total score ranged from 15 to 60, with higher scores indicating greater frequency of activities. The mean FAI score ($M = 40.86$, $SD = 9.37$) indicated that "impairment of functional status was quite common": 14% had scores between 15 and 30, 48% between 31 and 45, and only 38% had scores > 45.

Psychometric properties

The original sample of people with stroke with whom the FAI was developed (Holbrook & Skilbeck, 1983) was used to refine item content and examine construct validity, but no other measurement characteristics of the FAI were reported in that study. Psychometric properties of the FAI have been evaluated subsequently by other investigators. Information on concurrent validity of the FAI is available from Schuling et al. (1993) who examined 96 people with stroke at 26 weeks post-onset using the Barthel Index (BI) and Sickness Impact Profile (SIP). A principal components analysis identified a two-factor structure, accounting for 52% of the variance. Convergent and divergent validity was explored with patterns of expected correlations with SIP subscales measuring similar (e.g., Home management) versus dissimilar (e.g., Emotional behaviour) constructs. Temporal stability of the FAI was assessed by Green, Forster, and Young (2001), who examined 22 people with stroke ($M = 15$ months post-onset) or their caregivers on two occasions 1 week apart. Information on inter-rater reliability is available from Wade et al. (1985) in a sample of 14 people from a larger study of approximately 500 people with stroke. The investigators had also administered the BI to the larger sample. Results of the above studies are shown in Box 7.5.

Comment

The FAI is widely used, particularly in the UK. Some reviews have been critical of the item content and psychometric properties of the FAI in comparison with basic ADL scales (Bond et al., 1995; Green et al., 2001). As occurs for other instrumental ADL scales, however, reliability in the assessment of more complex activities generally cannot match the level achieved for simpler tasks of self-care and mobility. The tighter operational definitions of the items provided by Piercy et al. (2000) assist in maximizing inter-rater reliability. Tooth, McKenna, Smith, and O'Rourke (2003) advise caution in using informants for the FAI because of the poor patient-proxy agreement on a significant number of items (using a 13-item version of the FAI, $k_w < .4$ on 5/13 items). The FAI is commonly used in conjunction with self-care and mobility scales (frequently the BI), to obtain a more representative evaluation of everyday functioning. Hsueh, Wang, Sheu, and Hsieh (2004) used a Rasch-based 23-item composite BI/FAI that demonstrated a unidimensional ADL function. Relative to their brevity, the combined scales thus provide a comprehensive sampling of everyday activities.

Box 7.5

Validity:	Criterion: *Concurrent:* Schuling et al.: with BI: $r = .66$
	Wade et al.: with BI at 6 months post-stroke ($n = 482$): $r = .61$ – with BI at 12 months ($n = 444$): $r = .65$
	Construct: *Internal consistency:* Schuling et al.: Cronbach alpha: Stroke .87, Controls .83
	Factor analysis: Holbrook & Skilbeck: 3 factors: Domestic (5 items), Work/leisure (4 items), Outdoor activity (6 items)
	Schuling et al.: 2 components: Domestic activities (4 items), Outdoor activities (9 items)
	Convergent/divergent: Schuling et al.: higher correlation with similar constructs (eg., with SIP Home Management: $r = -.73$, with SIP Recreation and Pastimes: $r = -.47$); lower correlation with dissimilar constructs (eg., with SIP Emotional Behaviour: $r = -.15$, with SIP Alertness Behaviour: $r = -0.14$)
Reliability:	Inter-rater: Wade et al.: Total score: $r = .80$ ($r > .80$ for 5/15 items; $r = .48$–$.56$ for 4/15 items; no information provided on the remaining 6/15 items)
	Test–retest: Green et al.: 1 week: $k \geq .6$ for 10/14* items; $k < .4$ for 1/14 (heavy housework). *Note: kappa not calculated for 1/15 items with perfect agreement
Responsiveness:	No information available

Key references

Bond, M. J., Clark, M. S., Smith, D. S., & Harris, R. D. (1995). Lifestyle activities of the elderly: Composition and determinants. *Disability and Rehabilitation, 17*(2), 63–69.

Green, J., Forster, A., & Young, J. (2001). A test–retest

reliability study of the Barthel Index, the Rivermead Mobility Index, the Nottingham Extended Activities of Daily Living Scale and the Frenchay Activities Index in stroke patients. *Disability and Rehabilitation*, *23*(15), 670–676.

Holbrook, M., & Skilbeck, C. E. (1983). An activities index for use with stroke patients. *Age and Ageing*, *12*(2), 166–170.

Hsueh, I.-P., Wang, W.-C., Sheu, C.-F., & Hsieh, C.-L. (2004). Rasch analysis of combining two indices to assess comprehensive ADL function in stroke patients. *Stroke*, *35*(3), 721–726.

Piercy, M., Carter, J., Mant, J., & Wade, D. T. (2000). Inter-rater reliability of the Frenchay activities index in patients with stroke and their carers. *Clinical Rehabilitation*, *14*(4), 433–440.

Schuling, J., de Haan, R., Limburg, M., & Groenier, K. H. (1993). The Frenchay Activities Index. Assessment of functional status in stroke patients. *Stroke*, *24*(8), 1173–1177.

Tooth, L. R., McKenna, K. T., Smith, M., & O'Rourke, P. (2003). Further evidence for the agreement between patients with stroke and their proxies on the Frenchay Activities Index. *Clinical Rehabilitation*, *17*, 656–665.

Wade, D. T., Legh-Smith, J., & Langton Hewer, R. (1985). Social activities after stroke: Measurement and natural history using the Frenchay Activities Index. *International Rehabilitation Medicine*, *7*(4), 176–181.

Frenchay Activities Index

Holbrook and Skilbeck (1983)

Name:	**Administered by:**	**Date:**

During previous 3 months:

1. **Preparing main meals**
   1 = Never
   2 = Less than once weekly
   3 = 1–2 times a week
   4 = Most days
2. **Washing-up**
   1 = Never
   2 = Less than once weekly
   3 = 1–2 times a week
   4 = Most days
3. **Washing clothes**
   1 = Never
   2 = 1–2 times in 3 months
   3 = 3–12 times in 3 months
   4 = At least weekly
4. **Light housework**
   1 = Never
   2 = 1–2 times in 3 months
   3 = 3–12 times in 3 months
   4 = At least weekly
5. **Heavy housework**
   1 = Never
   2 = 1–2 times in 3 months
   3 = 3–12 times in 3 months
   4 = At least weekly
6. **Local shopping**
   1 = Never
   2 = 1–2 times in 3 months
   3 = 3–12 times in 3 months
   4 = At least weekly
7. **Social outings**
   1 = Never
   2 = 1–2 times in 3 months
   3 = 3–12 times in 3 months
   4 = At least weekly
8. **Walking outdoors over 15 minutes**
   1 = Never
   2 = 1–2 times in 3 months
   3 = 3–12 times in 3 months
   4 = At least weekly
9. **Pursuing active interest in hobby**
   1 = Never
   2 = 1–2 times in 3 months
   3 = 3–12 times in 3 months
   4 = At least weekly
10. **Driving a car/travel on bus**
   1 = Never
   2 = 1–2 times in 3 months
   3 = 3–12 times in 3 months
   4 = At least weekly

During previous 6 months:

11. **Outings/car rides**
   1 = Never
   2 = 1–2 times in 6 months
   3 = 3–12 times in 6 months
   4 = At least weekly
12. **Gardening**
   1 = None
   2 = Light
   3 = Moderate
   4 = All necessary
13. **Household and/or car maintenance**
   1 = None
   2 = Light
   3 = Moderate
   4 = All necessary
14. **Reading books**
   1 = None
   2 = 1 in 6 months
   3 = Less than 1 a fortnight
   4 = More than 1 a fortnight
15. **Gainful work**
   1 = None
   2 = Up to 10 hours/week
   3 = 10–30 hours/week
   4 = More than 30 hours/week

TOTAL SCORE: ________________

Acknowledgement: From Holbrook, M., & Skilbeck, C. E. (1983). An activities index for use with stroke patients. *Age and Ageing*, *12*(2), 166–170, p. 170, 1 scale, by permission of Oxford University Press.

Functional Independence Measure (FIM)

Granger, Hamilton, Keith, Zielezny, and Sherwin (1986)

Source

The FIM is officially available from the Uniform Data System for Medical Rehabilitation (http://www.udsmr.org). General information on the FIM, and its two derivatives also described in this chapter (Functional Independence Measure for Children, WeeFIM, and Functional Assessment Measure, FAM), can be accessed through the Center for Outcome Measurement in Brain Injury (COMBI) website (http://www.tbims.org/combi/FIM/index.html).

Purpose

The FIM is a clinician rating scale, described as a measure of functional disability, designed to measure "burden of care". It is a generic instrument, intended to be suitable for a range of clinical groups accessing medical rehabilitation, both neurological (e.g., stroke, spinal cord injury) and non-neurological (e.g., cancer, orthopaedic). The FIM is used extensively with these and other neurological groups, including multiple sclerosis (MS; Brosseau & Wolfson, 1994; Granger, Cotter, Hamilton, Fieldler, & Hens, 1990) and traumatic brain injury (TBI; Corrigan, Smith-Knapp, & Granger, 1997).

Item description

The FIM comprises 18 items that are grouped into two scales. The Motor scale contains 13 items in 4 subscales: Self-care (6 items: eating, grooming, bathing, dressing upper and lower body, toileting), Sphincter control (2 items: bladder and bowel management), Transfers (3 items: to/from bed, toilet and bath), and Locomotion (2 items: walking/wheelchair and stairs). The Cognitive scale contains 5 items in 2 subscales: Communication (2 items: language comprehension and expression) and Social cognition (3 items: social interaction, problem solving and memory).

Scale development

The FIM was developed in the 1980s in response to political and health care financing policies in the USA (Granger et al., 1986). In 1983, the American Congress of Rehabilitation Medicine and the American Academy of Physical Medicine and Rehabilitation established a task force to develop a uniform national data system for medical rehabilitation to document outcomes and costs of care. A range of multidisciplinary health professional organizations also participated in the development of the system. The framework within which the FIM was designed was the WHO (1980) tripartite model of impairment, disability and handicap; the rehabilitation process having special emphasis on "life functions" (i.e., activity and social role). The FIM was developed as the measure of disability for the national data system. Stipulated requirements for the instrument included its applicability (i) across the lifespan, (ii) in multiple settings, and (iii) to all clinical groups accessing medical rehabilitation, along with use by health professionals with different backgrounds, "as well as nonclinicians, family members, and patients when they have had sufficient orientation" (Hamilton, Granger, Sherwin, Zielezny, & Tashman, 1987, p. 141).

Some background information on the item development process is provided by Granger et al. (1986). The task-force reviewed 36 published and unpublished functional assessment scales in order to "select the most common and useful functional assessment items" (p. 65). Granger et al. (1990) commented that the FIM "incorporates items of the BI [Barthel Index] but is more sensitive and inclusive" (p. 870). The FIM was trialled over a 3-year period from 1985. During the initial pilot and trial phases, feedback was sought from many hundreds of clinicians from some 25 facilities regarding their use of the FIM, and a major revision was to increase the number of response categories from four to seven.

Administration procedures, response format and scoring

Ratings are made by a clinician who has knowledge of the patient's level of functioning or through an objective assessment. Interview administration of the FIM items is referred to as a "phone-FIM". The COMBI website advises that the FIM can be completed in approximately 20 to 30 minutes, although other investigators have documented a broader time range depending on the functional status of the patient (e.g., Brosseau & Wolfson, 1994, reported 10–45 mins). For clinical purposes, it is recommended that the FIM be administered within 72 hours of admission to rehabilitation and prior to discharge, as well as follow-up if indicated. Great efforts have been made to ensure consistency in administration and scoring of the FIM. A training manual is provided, which has clear scoring guidelines, facilitated by presentation of decision trees. Training courses are also provided, comprising didactic instruction and proficiency tests (requiring > 80% accuracy).

Responses to FIM items are made on a 7-point scale, with descriptors attached to response categories tailored to the individual items: 1 (equivalent of total assistance – patient expends < 25% of effort or unable to do the task), 2 (maximal assistance – 25–49% of effort), 3 (moderate assistance – 50–74% of effort), 4 (minimal assistance – ≥ 75% of effort), 5 (supervision or set-up), 6 (modified independence – use of a device/aid, safety or time issues), or 7 (complete independence, without modification, aid or device, and performed in a safe and timely manner).

As shown in the FIM diagram, this scale recognizes two broad levels of functioning (independence and dependence), the crucial difference being whether another person is required to help with the task. Help can take the form of physical assistance, set-up or supervision. Each of the two levels is further subdivided. For the independence level, there are two subcategories: complete and modified, which are differentiated in terms of time taken to complete the activity, use of aids and/or safety issues. The five subcategories of dependence range from set-up/supervision (including cueing, coaxing or prompting) to physical dependency. The latter dependency categories are distinguished on the basis of the time and effort required by another person to complete the task, from the patient performing ≥ 75% of the task to the patient performing < 25% of the task. The FIM total score ranges from 18 to 126 (Motor scale: 13–91, Cognitive scale: 5–35), with higher scores indicating greater independence.

Psychometric properties

Limited published data on the measurement characteristics of the FIM were available when it was first

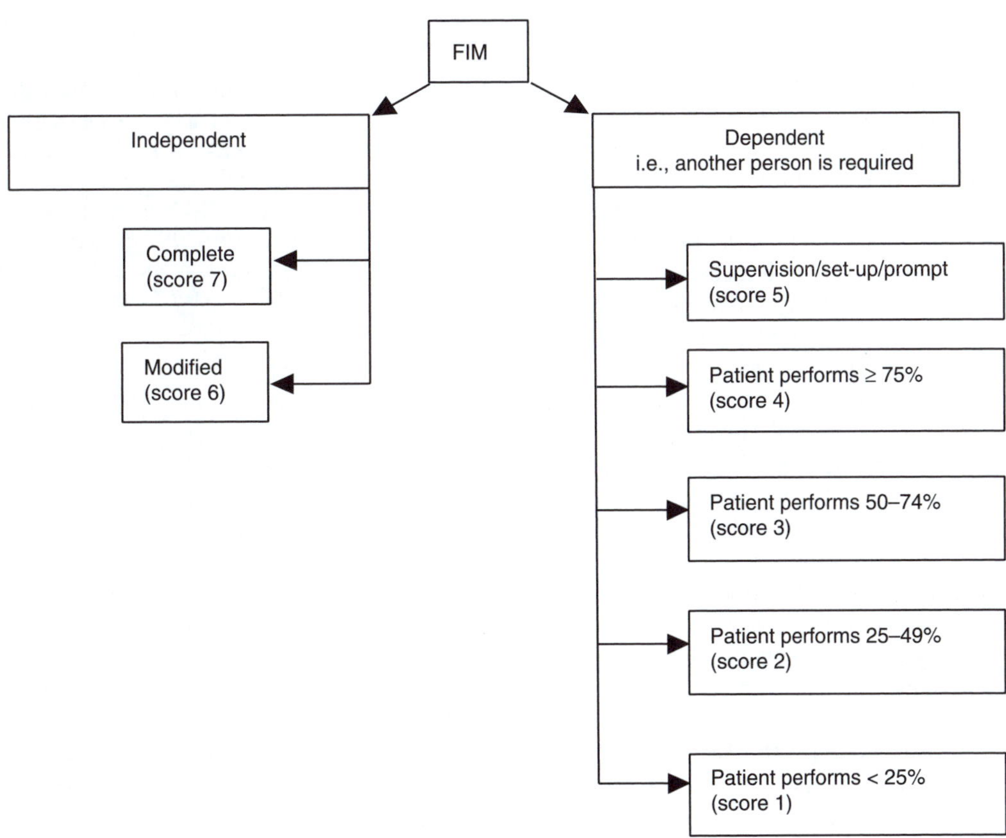

introduced, but many psychometric studies were published in the subsequent decade. As a measure of "burden of care", Heinemann et al. (1997) studied 129 rehabilitation inpatients with TBI and examined the correlation between minutes of nursing contact time during two 24-hour periods in the first and final weeks of hospitalization with FIM admission and discharge scores. A similar study had been reported by Granger et al. (1990) with 24 community-dwelling people with MS who kept a "Help at Home Journal" over a 7-day period. A complementary study was reported by Corrigan et al. (1997) who included the need for supervision, as well as minutes of direct assistance. They analysed data from a range of measures, including the Neurobehavioral Rating Scale (NBRS), on 95 people with TBI at 6 to 59 months after discharge. Heinemann, Linacre, Wright, Hamilton, and Granger (1994) analysed data from 27,669 rehabilitation inpatients from 72 rehabilitation facilities (approximately 10,000 with stroke or other ABI) to determine predictive validity of the FIM regarding length of stay.

The FIM has been subject to Rasch analysis in a number of studies. Linacre, Heinemann, Wright, Granger, and Hamilton (1994) used data from 14,799 medical rehabilitation patients, including 6412 with stroke. When the 18 items were combined into a single measure there was misfit (values < 0.7 or > 1.3 – bladder, stairs, comprehension and expression). When the data were reanalysed for the Motor and Cognitive items separately, 4 Motor items showed serious misfit (eating, bladder, bowel, stairs), but values for the Cognitive items were acceptable. In all analyses, eating was the easiest Motor item and stairs the most difficult; comprehension was the easiest Cognitive item and problem solving the most difficult. The study of Lundgren-Nilsson et al. (2005), using 2546 rehabilitation inpatients with stroke recruited from 31 rehabilitation facilities in six European countries, indicated that the Rasch measurement model showed cross-cultural variability. Items had different levels of difficulty across countries, with adjustments required to enable comparison of data.

Ottenbacher, Hsu, Granger, and Fieldler (1996) analysed data from 11 studies of (mainly, 81%) inter-rater reliability, resulting in a pool of 1568 patients. A standard inter-rater reliability study is reported by Brosseau and Wolfson (1994), where two physiotherapists trained in FIM procedures rated 81 people with MS. These investigators also examined concurrent validity of the FIM against the Expanded Disability Status Scale (EDSS). A comprehensive psychometric study on the FIM and other instruments was reported by Hobart et al. (2001), who assessed 149 rehabilitation inpatients (age $M = 46.2$ years, $SD = 14.8$, range 16–77) mainly with stroke (30%) and MS (43%) recruited from two hospitals in London and Southampton, UK. Responsiveness was examined by comparing admission and discharge scores, and test–retest reliability was assessed in a subset ($n = 56$), although the time frame was not specified. The FIM was validated against measures of disability (Office of Population Censuses and Surveys Disability Scales, OPCS) and cognition (Wechsler Adult Intelligence Scale-Revised-Verbal IQ, WAIS-R-VIQ). Convergent and divergent validity were explored with patterns of expected correlations, using additional measures of participation (London Handicap Scale, LHS), psychological well-being (General Health Questionnaire, GHQ) and physical and mental health status (Short-Form Health Survey, SF-36). Results of the foregoing studies are shown in Box 7.6.

Box 7.6

Validity:	Criterion: *Concurrent:* Brosseau & Wolfson: with EDSS: $r = -.91$ Hobart et al.: Total score with OPCS: $r = .82$ (Motor $r = .84$, Cognitive $r = .43$) – with WAIS-R-VIQ: $r = .35$ (Motor $r = .27$, Cognitive $r = .51$) Heinemann et al. (1997): FIM Motor with minutes of nursing care at admission ($r = -.54$) and discharge ($r = -.51$) – FIM Cognitive: $r = -.35$ and $r = -.47$ respectively Corrigan et al.: FIM Motor was the best predictor of need for physical assistance: sensitivity 79%, specificity 86% – FIM Motor, FIM Cognitive and NBRS-Somatic/Anxiety factor were the best predictors of need for supervision: sensitivity 82%, specificity 82% *Predictive:* Heinemann et al. (1994): FIM Motor admission score was the strongest predictor of length of stay Construct: *Internal consistency:* Hobart et al.: Cronbach alpha: Total score .95 (Motor .95, Cognitive .89) *Convergent/divergent:* Hobart et al.: Total score: higher correlation with similar constructs (with OPCS: $r = .82$); lower correlation with dissimilar constructs (with LHS: $r = .32$, GHQ: $r = .13$, SF36-Physical: $r = .26$, SF36-Mental: $r = .10$)

Reliability:	Inter-rater: Ottenbacher et al.: median reliability coefficients: Total score: .95 (Motor .97, Cognitive .93), but greater variability within Cognitive subscales (.78 for Social cognition; .87 for Communication) than Motor subscales (range: .91 for Sphincter control to .95 for Self-care) Brosseau & Wolfson: Total score: ICC = .83; for items $k = .14–.70$ (with $k \geq .6$ for 8/13 Motor items, 0/5 Cognitive items; $k < .4$ for 1/13 Motor items – walking/wheelchair and 4/5 Cognitive items – comprehension, social interaction, problem solving, memory) Test–retest: Hobart et al.: (interval not reported) Total score: ICC = 0.98 (Motor 0.98, Cognitive 0.95)
Responsiveness:	Hobart et al.: medium effect sizes for change in scores between admission and discharge for Total ($d = .48$) and Motor ($d = .54$), but small effect size for Cognitive ($d = .17$) – descriptive data not reported

Comment

The FIM is used extensively, both for clinical and research purposes. A number of the research studies have used very large sample sizes (many thousands of subjects) and consequently the derived statistics and coefficients from such samples are very reliable. The FIM was intentionally developed as a generic instrument and, as such, it has the advantage of use across a broad spectrum of conditions. The disadvantage is that it shows inevitable limitations in its application to specific groups, including people with acquired brain impairment (ABI). The authors of the FIM recognized that the items represented "a selected *minimum* number of key activities" (Hamilton et al., 1987, p. 141), but even so, item content has been criticized. FIM items have a distinct physical bias (72% of items relate to motor functioning), and this necessitated development of complementary items to address the cognitive and psychosocial disability characteristic of people with ABI. Augmenting the FIM items has not completely solved the problem, however (see entry on the FAM). Additionally, ceiling effects are problematic for the ABI group – rehabilitation discharge scores were at ceiling for 53% of a stroke group (Linn, Blair, Granger, Harper, O'Hara, & Maciura, 1999) and 49% of a TBI group (Hall, Mann, High, Wright, Kreutzer, & Wood, 1996). Rehabilitation *admission* scores, however, are not subject to ceiling effects (e.g., Hobart et al., 2001). One of the undoubted strengths of the FIM is its standardized training, administration and scoring procedures, thereby maximizing reliability of the instrument and comparability of data sets among institutions. The detailed operational definitions for the seven response levels also potentially enhance its reliability and sensitivity. Although the motor items have good psychometric properties the cognitive items are more variable, with some studies showing poor inter-rater reliability and responsiveness. Linacre et al. (1994) emphasized that "the motor and cognitive items do not work together in a homogenous way to measure disability" (p. 129). The strength of the FIM thus appears to be in the Motor scale, which provides a reliable and valid screening instrument for the clinical rating of basic mobility and self-care functions.

Key references

Brosseau, L., & Wolfson, C. (1994). The inter-rater reliability and construct validity of the Functional Independence Measure for multiple sclerosis subjects. *Clinical Rehabilitation*, *8*(2), 107–115.

Corrigan, J. D., Smith-Knapp, K., & Granger, C. V. (1997). Validity of the Functional Independence Measure for persons with traumatic brain injury. *Archives of Physical Medicine and Rehabilitation*, *78*(8), 828–834.

Granger, C. V., Cotter, A. C., Hamilton, B. B., Fieldler, R. C., & Hens, M. M. (1990). Functional assessment scales: A study of persons with multiple sclerosis. *Archives of Physical Medicine and Rehabilitation*, *71*(11), 870–875.

Granger, C. V., Hamilton, B. B., Keith, R. A., Zielezny, M., & Sherwin, F. S. (1986). Advances in functional assessment for medical rehabilitation. *Topics in Geriatric Rehabilitation*, *1*(3), 59–74.

Hall, K. M., Mann, N., High, W. M., Wright, J., Kreutzer, J. S., & Wood, D. (1996). Functional measures after traumatic brain injury: Ceiling effects of FIM, FIM + FAM, DRS, and CIQ. *Journal of Head Trauma Rehabilitation*, *11*(5), 27–39.

Hamilton, B. B., Granger, C. V., Sherwin, F. S., Zielezny, M., & Tashman, J. S. (1987). A uniform national data system for medical rehabilitation. In M. J. Fuhrer (Ed.), *Rehabilitation outcomes: Analysis and measurement* (pp. 137–147). Baltimore: Paul H. Brookes Publishing Co.

Heinemann, A. W., Kirk, P., Hastie, B. A., Semik, P., Hamilton, B. B., Linacre, J. M., et al. (1997). Relationships between disability measures and nursing effort during medical rehabilitation for patients with traumatic brain and spinal cord injury. *Archives of Physical Medicine and Rehabilitation*, *78*(2), 143–149.

Heinemann, A. W., Linacre, J. M., Wright, B. D., Hamilton, B. B., & Granger, C. (1994). Prediction of rehabilitation outcomes with disability measures. *Archives of Physical Medicine and Rehabilitation*, *75*(2), 133–143.

Hobart, J. C., Lamping, D. L., Freeman, J. A., Langdon, D. W., McLellan, D. L., Greenwood, R. J., et al. (2001). Evidence-based measurement: Which disability scale for neurologic rehabilitation? *Neurology*, *57*(4), 639–644.

Linacre, J. M., Heinemann, A. W., Wright, B. D., Granger, C. V., & Hamilton, B. B. (1994). The structure and stability of the Functional Independence Measure. *Archives of Physical Medicine and Rehabilitation*, *75*(2), 127–132.

Linn, R. T., Blair, R. S., Granger, C. V., Harper, D. W., O'Hara, P. A., & Maciura, E. (1999). Does the Functional Assessment Measure (FAM) extend the Functional Independence Measure (FIM) instrument? A Rasch analysis of stroke inpatients. *Journal of Outcome Measurement*, *3*(4), 339–359.

Lundgren-Nilsson, A., Grimby, G., Ring, H., Tesio, L., Lawton, G., Slade, A., et al. (2005). Cross-cultural validity of Functional Independence Measure items in stroke: A study using Rasch analysis. *Journal of Rehabilitation Medicine*, *37*(1), 23–31.

Ottenbacher, K. J., Hsu, Y., Granger, C. V., & Fieldler, R. C. (1996). The reliability of the Functional Independence Measure: A quantitative review. *Archives of Physical Medicine and Rehabilitation*, *77*(12), 1226–1232.

World Health Organization. (1980). *International classification of impairments, disabilities, and handicaps*. Geneva: World Health Organization.

Functional Independence Measure and Functional Assessment Measure (FIM+FAM)

Hall, Hamilton, Gordon, and Zasler (1993)

This entry should be read in conjunction with the Functional Independence Measure (FIM; page 434–438).

Source

The FAM items are not intended to be used as a stand-alone scale, but rather as an adjunct to the FIM, such that the 30-item composite scale is referred to as the FIM+FAM. Items comprising the FIM+FAM appear in Hall et al. (1993) and are reproduced below. General information on the FIM+FAM is available from the Center for Outcome Measurement in Brain Injury (COMBI) website (http://www.tbims.org/combi/FAM/index.html).

Purpose

The FIM+FAM is a clinician rating scale of functional disability. The FAM items were added to the FIM to cater to the type of disablement experienced after acquired brain impairment, which often has major cognitive and psychosocial components. Consequently, the FAM is most commonly used with people for whom it was developed – those with stroke and traumatic brain injury (TBI).

Item description

The FAM consists of 12 items. The three motor items are swallowing, car transfer, and community access. The nine cognitive/psychosocial items are reading, writing, speech intelligibility, emotional status, adjustment to limitations, employability, orientation, attention span, and safety judgement. These items are added to the FIM 13-item Motor scale and 5-item Cognitive scale, resulting in two FIM+FAM scales: Motor (16 items) and Cognitive (14 items).

Scale development

The FAM was first described by Hall in 1992. It was developed to further extend the FIM for adults with ABI. Hall et al. (1993) observed that the FIM "has a relative dearth of cognitive-behavioral, communication, and community-related functional items relevant to assessing persons with TBI" (p. 71). Rehabilitation professionals from representative disciplines suggested items, with the final set of 12 items (3 for the Motor scale and 9 for the Cognitive scale) emphasizing the cognitive and psychosocial aspects of disability.

Administration procedures, response format and scoring

Training procedures for the FAM use two vignettes that are available from the COMBI website. The website also contains operational definitions of the FAM items. Additionally, Turner-Stokes, Nyein, Turner-Stokes, and Gatehouse (1999), identified "troublesome" items in terms of their subjective nature and difficulty in scoring, and they constructed detailed operational definitions for these items. The authors termed this version the UK FIM+FAM.* Administration time for the FIM+FAM is reported to be approximately 35 minutes (Hall et al., 1993). It can be considerably shorter, however, using completion of the FIM+FAM within a case conference context when team members have completed rating items relevant to their area of expertise prior to the team meeting (~10–18 mins; Donaghy & Wass, 1998), but longer if raters need to familiarize themselves with the patient. McPherson, Pentland, Cudmore, and Prescott (1996) reported the assessment for each patient took 1 to 1.5 hours, which included observation of the patient in the ward environment and interviews with the patient, primary nurse and therapists.

The FAM items use the same 7-point rating scale as for the FIM, ranging from 1 (equivalent of total assistance) to 7 (complete independence). Scores <6 indicate another person is required for physical assistance, set-up or supervision. The FIM+FAM total

* A manual for the UK FIM+FAM version is available from Dr Turner-Stokes, Regional Rehabilitation Unit, Northwick Park Hospital, Watford Road, Harrow, Middlesex HAI 3UJ, UK; lynne.turner-stokes@dial.pipex.com.

score ranges from 30 to 210 (Motor subscale 16–112; Cognitive subscale 14–98), with higher scores indicating greater independence.

Psychometric properties

Hall et al. (1993) compared the FIM+FAM with the FIM and Disability Rating Scale (DRS) using data from 332 patients recorded in the national database of the TBI model systems, USA. Psychometric properties of the FIM+FAM were reported by Hawley, Taylor, Hellawell, and Pentland (1999), who analysed data from 10 clinical sites in the UK relating to 965 patients participating in rehabilitation after TBI. Principal components analysis extracted two components accounting for 84% of the variance, but a number of items were complex, having loadings on both components. Rasch analysis revealed that although person separation and item separation were high for the scale as a whole and each subscale, infit and/or outfit values were beyond acceptable limits for 4 of the 15 physical items, 3 of the 15 cognitive items and 5 of the 30 items for the scale as a whole, indicating the scale was an imperfect fit to a Rasch model. The authors considered that the result may be partly attributable to the TBI group being "notoriously heterogeneous in the range and extent of their disabilities" (p. 753). They recommended the scale *not* be modified on the basis of their results, however. In their Rasch analysis on an independent sample ($n = 60$ with TBI), Tesio and Cantagallo (1998) also found misfit with a number of FIM+FAM items.

McPherson et al. (1996) examined inter-rater reliability of the FIM+FAM in 30 inpatients on a neurorehabilitation ward, with two raters (physician and nurse) who independently rated patients on the same day. In their inter-rater reliability study, using data from 53 patients with TBI, Donaghy and Wass (1998) used the procedure of having clinicians with different backgrounds make ratings only on those FIM+FAM items pertinent to their contact with the patient (thereby approximating the type of consensus-based FIM+FAM rating commonly used in clinical practice during case conference). That is, specific subsets of the 30 items were rated by different pairs of clinicians. The comprehensive psychometric study of Hobart et al. (2001), who examined 149 people (age $M = 46.2$ years, $SD = 14.8$) mainly with stroke and multiple sclerosis described in the FIM entry, also examined the same properties for the FIM+FAM. Validation instruments included measures of disability (Office of Population Census and Surveys, OPCS), cognition (Wechsler Adult Intelligence Scale-Revised-Verbal IQ, WAIS-R-VIQ), handicap (London Handicap Scale, LHS), psychological well-being (General Health Questionnaire, GHQ-28), and quality of life (SF36-Physical and SF36-Mental). A subset ($n = 56$) was reassessed on a second occasion (interval unspecified). Results of the above studies are shown in Box 7.7.

Box 7.7

Validity:	Criterion *Concurrent:* Hall et al. (1993): FIM+FAM Motor with FIM Motor: $r = .99$ – with DRS $r = .68$ FIM+FAM Cognitive with FIM Cognitive: $r = .95$ – with DRS $r = .75$
	Hobart et al.: with OPCS: Total score: $r = .77$ (Motor $r = .84$, Cognitive $r = .50$) – with WAIS-R-VIQ: Total score: $r = .42$ (Motor $r = .29$, Cognitive $r = .54$)
	Construct: *Internal consistency:* Hobart et al.: Cronbach alpha: Total score .96 (Motor .96, Cognitive .91)
	Factor analysis: Hawley et al.: 2 components: Physical functioning (16 items), Cognitive, language and psychosocial functioning (14 items)
	Convergent/divergent: Hobart et al.: Total FIM+FAM: higher correlation with similar constructs (with OPCS: $r = .77$), lower correlation with dissimilar constructs (with LHS: $r = .32$, GHQ-28: $r = .13$, SF36-Physical: $r = .24$, SF36-Mental: $r = .12$)
Reliability:	Inter-rater: McPherson et al.: $k \geq .6$ for 15/15 Motor items, 6/15 Cognitive items; $k < .4$ for 1 item (adjustment to limitations: $k = .35$)
	Donaghy & Wass: Total score: ICC = .83 (Motor ICC = .91, Cognitive ICC = .74)
	Test–retest: Hobart et al.: (interval not reported) Total score: ICC = .98 (Motor ICC = .98, Cognitive ICC = .97)
Responsiveness:	Hobart et al.: effect sizes for change in scores between admission and discharge were medium for Total score ($d = .42$) and Motor ($d = .52$), but small for Cognitive ($d = .19$) – descriptive data not reported

Comment

The FIM+FAM shows very similar psychometric properties to the FIM (Hobart et al., 2001). Although the FIM+FAM does ameliorate to some extent the ceiling effects that operate with the FIM when used with some neurological groups, Hall, Mann, High, Wright, Kreutzer, and Wood (1996) still found that 34% of patients with TBI scored at ceiling at discharge on the FIM+FAM, compared with 49% on the FIM alone. Hall et al. (1993) considered that the addition of the FAM items may increase the sensitivity of post-acute functional assessment, but even so the FIM+FAM Cognitive scale does not show the responsiveness of the Motor scale (Hobart et al.). As with the FIM, inter-rater reliability coefficients of the Cognitive items of the FIM+FAM are lower than for the Motor items. This has been attributed partly to their "abstract" nature, being less amendable to direct observation (Alcott, Dixon, & Swann, 1997; Hall et al., 1993). Additionally, Turner-Stokes et al. (1999) commented on the response format for rating levels of dependency (scores 1–4), noting the "problems in extrapolating this concept of an individual performing 25%, 50% and 75% of the task, when the 'task' is an area of psychosocial function" (pp. 278–279). A number of investigators have concluded that for the TBI population the FIM+FAM does not appreciably add to the FIM (Gurka, Felmingham, Baguley, Schotte, Crooks, & Marosszeky, 1999; Linn, Blair, Granger, Harper, O'Hara, & Maciura, 1999; Tesio & Cantagallo, 1998), a possibility that Hall et al. (1993, 1996) themselves considered.

Key references

Alcott, D., Dixon, K., & Swann, R. (1997). The reliability of the items of the Functional Assessment Measure (FAM): Differences in abstractness between FAM items. *Disability and Rehabilitation*, *19*(9), 355–358.

Donaghy, S., & Wass, P. J. (1998). Interrater reliability of the Functional Assessment Measure in a brain injury rehabilitation program. *Archives of Physical Medical and Rehabilitation*, *79*(10), 1231–1236.

Gurka, J. A., Felmingham, K. L., Baguley, I. J., Schotte, D. E., Crooks, J., & Marosszeky, J. E. (1999). Utility of the Functional Assessment Measure after discharge from inpatient rehabilitation. *Journal of Head Trauma Rehabilitation*, *14*(3), 247–256.

Hall, K. M. (1992). Overview of functional assessment scales in brain injury rehabilitation. *NeuroRehabilitation*, *2*(4), 98–113.

Hall, K. M., Hamilton, B. B., Gordon, W. A., & Zasler, N. D. (1993). Characteristics and comparisons of functional assessment indices: Disability Rating Scale, Functional Independence Measure, and Functional Assessment Measure. *Journal of Head Trauma Rehabilitation*, *8*(2), 60–74.

Hall, K. M., Mann, N., High, W. M., Wright, J., Kreutzer, J. S., & Wood, D. (1996). Functional measures after traumatic brain injury: Ceiling effects of FIM, FIM + FAM, DRS, and CIQ. *Journal of Head Trauma Rehabilitation*, *11*(5), 27–39.

Hawley, C. A., Taylor, R., Hellawell, D. J., & Pentland, B. (1999). Use of the functional assessment measure (FIM+FAM) in head injury rehabilitation: A psychometric analysis. *Journal of Neurology, Neurosurgery and Psychiatry*, *67*(6), 749–754.

Hobart, J. C., Lamping, D. L., Freeman, J. A., Langdon, D. W., McLellan, D. L., Greenwood, R. J., et al. (2001). Evidence-based measurement: Which disability scale for neurologic rehabilitation? *Neurology*, *57*(4), 639–644.

Linn, R. T., Blair, R. S., Granger, C. V., Harper, D. W., O'Hara, P. A., & Maciura, E. (1999). Does the Functional Assessment Measure (FAM) extend the Functional Independence Measure (FIM) instrument? A Rasch analysis of stroke patients. *Journal of Outcome Measurement*, *3*(4), 339–359.

McPherson, K. M., Pentland, B., Cudmore, S. F., & Prescott, R. J. (1996). An inter-rater reliability study of the Functional Assessment Measure (FIM + FAM). *Disability and Rehabilitation*, *18*(7), 341–347.

Tesio, L., & Cantagallo, A. (1998). The Functional Assessment Measure (FAM) in closed traumatic brain injury outpatients: A Rasch-based psychometric study. *Journal of Outcome Measurement*, *2*(2), 79–96.

Turner-Stokes, L., Nyein, K., Turner-Stokes, T., & Gatehouse, C. (1999). The UK FIM+FAM: Development and evaluation. *Clinical Rehabilitation*, *13*(4), 277–287.

Items of the Functional Independence Measure (FIM) and Hall, Hamilton, Gordon, and Zasler (1993) Functional Assessment Measure (FAM)

MOTOR ITEMS:

Self-care

- Eating
- Grooming
- Bathing
- Dressing upper body
- Dressing lower body
- Toileting
- Swallowing *

Sphincter control

- Bladder management
- Bowel management

Mobility

- Bed/chair/wheelchair transfer
- Toilet transfer
- Tub/shower transfer
- Car transfer *
- Walking/wheelchair locomotion
- Stairs
- Community mobility *

COGNITION ITEMS:

Communication

- Comprehension
- Expression
- Reading *
- Writing *
- Speech intelligibility *

Psychosocial adjustment

- Social interaction
- Emotional status *
- Adjustment to limitations *
- Employability *

Cognitive function

- Problem solving
- Memory
- Orientation *
- Attention *
- Safety judgement *

---

* FAM items denoted by asterisk

Acknowledgement: From Hall, K. M. et al. (1993). Characteristics and comparisons of functional assessment indices: Disability Rating Scale, Functional Independence Measure, and Functional Assessment Measure. *Journal of Head Trauma Rehabilitation*, *8*(2), 60–74, Box figure 1, p. 64, used with permission of Lippincott Williams & Wilkins/Wolters Kluwer.

Functional Independence Measure for Children (WeeFIM)

Braun and Granger (1991)

This entry should be read in conjunction with the Functional Independence Measure (FIM; page 434–438).

Source

Items for the WeeFIM are the same as those for the FIM and are officially available from the Uniform Data System for Medical Rehabilitation (www.udsmr.org).

Purpose

The WeeFIM is a clinician rating scale, described as measuring "functional abilities in a developmental context" (Braun & Granger, 1991, p. 47). It is a direct adaptation of the FIM, and hence is a generic screening test, containing "a minimum number of items meant to give clinicians an overall view of the child" (p. 47), suitable for a range of neurological and non-neurological groups accessing medical rehabilitation. The WeeFIM is intended for children aged between 6 months and 7 years (with corresponding age-appropriate expectations for the items). In children with disabilities the WeeFIM can be used in older age groups.

Item description

The WeeFIM comprises the 18 FIM items. The 13 items of the Motor scale are arranged in four subscales: Self-care (6 items: eating, grooming, bathing, dressing upper and lower body, toileting), Sphincter control (2 items: bladder and bowel management), Transfers (3 items: to/from bed, toilet and bath), and Locomotion (2 items: walking/wheelchair and stairs). The five items of the Cognitive scale are categorized into 2 subscales: Communication (2 items: language comprehension and expression) and Social cognition (3 items: social interaction, problem solving and memory).

Scale development

The applicability of the FIM to children was examined by Braun and Granger (1991): "Each item was considered in relation to chronological age, developmental norms and realistic expectations for children aged 6 months to 7 years" (p. 47). The instrument was piloted with 111 healthy children aged from 6 months to 7 years recruited from the Ambulatory Pediatric Clinic of The Children's Hospital of Buffalo, New York, USA. Moderate to high correlation coefficients between age and scores on all WeeFIM items were found, ranging from .50 (locomotor) to .83 (comprehension, memory). Content validity was formally examined by McCabe and Granger (1990). A three-phase process was used with eight clinicians from five disciplines. Although agreement for the first two phases (relevance of items to the six subscales and placement of items into the subscales) was good, results for the third phase were poor. None of the six subscales was rated as adequately represented conceptually by the items. The authors considered that this reflected:

> the bias of the experts' specialities. That is, each expert believed that the items in the subdomains [subscales] associated with his or her specialty did not fully cover the meaning of the concept represented by the subdomain. For example, the occupational therapist judged the subdomain of feeding as not conceptually adequate, whereas experts from other disciplines judged it to be conceptually adequate. (McCabe & Granger, 1990, p. 121)

Administration procedures, response format and scoring

Like the FIM, the WeeFIM is not a discipline-specific instrument. A standard training programme for the WeeFIM is available. Interview administration of the WeeFIM is reported as taking 15 to 20 minutes (Msall, DiGaudio, Duffy, LaForest, Braun, & Granger, 1994).

The same 7-point rating scale used by the FIM is also used for the WeeFIM, ranging from 1 (equivalent of total assistance) to 7 (complete independence). Scores < 6 indicate that another person is required for physical assistance, set-up or supervision. The WeeFIM total score ranges from 18 to 126 (Motor scale: 13–91; Cognitive scale: 5–35), with higher scores indicating greater independence.

Normative data are required to interpret WeeFIM data. Msall et al. (1994) examined 417 healthy children aged from 6 months to 8 years. Children were fairly evenly represented in four groups (6–21 months, 22–45 months, 46–62 months and 63–100 months). Msall et al. found a high correlation ($r = .80$) between the total score and age groups from 2 to 5 years. They suggested that although the WeeFIM provides a concise evaluation of independence across the ages 6 months to 8 years, it is most useful for the group aged between 2 and 5 years. The WeeFIM normative data are shown in Data box 7.1, and show the total score, along with the corresponding level of assistance that is required for the various ages.

Data box 7.1

Age (years)	WeeFIM total score Mean (*SD*)	Score equivalence in functional terms
1	20 (5)	1 – total assistance
1.5	38 (9)	2 – maximal assistance
2	54 (13)	3 – moderate assistance
3	84 (12)	4 – minimal assistance
3.5	91 (12)	5 – supervision
> 4	> 100	Some parental supervision, but no direct help
5	110 (11)	6 – modified independence
7	120 (4)	7 – complete independence

Psychometric properties

Concurrent validity was assessed by Sperle, Ottenbacher, Braun, Lane, and Nochajski (1997) who compared FIM administration using direct observation versus informant report (mainly via telephone) in 30 children with developmental disabilities (aged 19–71 months). The direct observation took the form of observation for "1 to 2 hours during his or her typical school day" (p. 37), and consequently two items (bathing and transfer to bath/shower) were not observed consistently. There was an interval of up to 14 days between test occasions for 27 of the 30 participants. Predictive validity was examined by DeNise-Annunziata and Scharf (1998) in 59 children hospitalized for a variety of neurological and non-neurological conditions. Admission WeeFIM scores were obtained from chart review and inter-rater reliability was established on a subset of the sample ($n = 7$), although the results are reported in general terms and suggest considerable item variability. Rasch analysis of the motor items found that item order varied across age groups (Chen, Bode, Granger, & Heinemann, 2005). Ottenbacher et al. (1996) examined 2-week temporal stability of the WeeFIM in 67 children (12–76 months of age), with ($n = 30$) and without ($n = 37$) developmental motor disabilities. The group was reassessed 14 days later to determine temporal stability. Discriminant validity was evaluated by comparing WeeFIM scores in the disabled and non-disabled groups. Results of the above studies are shown in Box 7.8.

Box 7.8

Validity:	Content: Formally assessed, but with mixed results (see Scale development section) Criterion: *Concurrent:* Sperle et al.: FIM direct observation vs informant report: Total score: ICC = .93 (Motor ICC = .93, Cognitive ICC = .75) – range for Motor items: ICC = .50–.98, with ICC ≥ .6 in 8/11 tested items – range for Cognitive items ICC = .41–.68, with ICC ≥ .6 in 1/5 items (comprehension) *Predictive:* DeNise-Annunziata & Scharf: with length of hospitalization: $r = -.29$ Construct: *Internal consistency:* DeNise-Annunziata & Scharf: Cronbach alpha: Total score .94 *Discriminant:* Ottenbacher et al.: Total score: Disabled group $M = 63.90$ ($SD = 29.64$) vs Non-disabled group $M = 79.90$ ($SD = 31.16$); $p < .05$ – Significant differences also on Motor and Cognitive scales ($p < .05$), and all subscales except Sphincter control
Reliability:	Inter-rater: DeNise-Annunziata & Scharf: Overall $k = .68$, range 43% agreement (problem solving) to 100% (bladder management) Test–retest: Ottenbacher et al.: 14 days: Disabled group: Total score ICC = .97 (Motor ICC = .98, Cognitive ICC = .96); subscale range: ICC = .94–.97; item range: ICC = .90–.99
Responsiveness:	No information available

Comment

The FIM/WeeFIM is one of the very few instruments that has application across the lifespan. Psychometric properties of the WeeFIM have not been as extensively studied as the FIM, and a formal content validity study did not fully endorse the adequacy of the items to conceptually represent the six domains. A normative data set ($n = 417$ from 6 months to 8 years of age) is available, enabling interpretation of scores in relation to expected developmental stages. The normative data available are limited, however, in that they are restricted to total scores, and for clinical purposes it would be helpful to have a detailed breakdown at the subscale and item level. Like the FIM, the WeeFIM is best regarded as a screening instrument that samples selected key areas of disablement, with Braun and Granger (1991) commenting that the "WeeFIM is not meant to replace assessment tools that analyse individual component tasks of activities of daily living" (p. 47).

Key references

Braun, S. L., & Granger, C. V. (1991). A practical approach to functional assessment in pediatrics. *Occupational Therapy Practice*, *2*(2), 46–51.

Chen, C. C., Bode, R. K., Granger, C. V., & Heinemann, A. W. (2005). Psychometric properties and developmental differences in children's ADL item hierarchy. *American Journal of Physical Medicine and Rehabilitation*, *84*(9), 671–679.

DeNise-Annunziata, D., & Scharf, A. A. (1998). Functional status as an important predictor of length of stay in a pediatric rehabilitation hospital. *Journal of Rehabilitation Outcomes Measurement*, *2*(2), 12–21.

McCabe, M. A., & Granger, C. V. (1990). Content validity of a pediatric functional independence measure. *Applied Nursing Research*, *3*(3), 120–122.

Msall, M. E., DiGaudio, K., Duffy, L. C., LaForest, S., Braun, S., & Granger, C. V. (1994). WeeFIM. Normative sample of an instrument for tracking functional independence in children. *Clinical Pediatrics*, *33*(7), 431–438.

Ottenbacher, K. J., Taylor, E. T., Msall, M. E., Braun, S., Lane, S. J., Granger, C. V., et al. (1996). The stability and equivalence reliability of the functional independence measure for children (WeeFIM). *Developmental Medicine and Child Neurology*, *38*(10), 907–916.

Sperle, P. A., Ottenbacher, K. J., Braun, S. L., Lane, S. J., & Nochajski, S. (1997). Equivalence reliability of the Functional Independence Measure for Children (WeeFIM) administration methods. *The American Journal of Occupational Therapy*, *51*(1), 35–41.

Index of Activities of Daily Living also known as the Katz Index of Activities of Daily Living (KIADL)

Staff of Benjamin Rose Hospital (1959)

Source

Items for the KIADL are described and operationalized in the 1959 publication, as well as in Katz, Ford, Moskowitz, Jackson, and Jaffe (1963), and are reproduced below.

Purpose

The KIADL is an observational rating scale of basic self-care activities, in which the person is classified into a hierarchical level of recovery. It was developed for older people and those with chronic illness. The standardization samples included people with hip fracture (Staff of Benjamin Rose Hospital, 1959), as well as neurological conditions such as multiple sclerosis and stroke. It has also been used with people with Alzheimer's disease (AD; Andrieu et al., 2002). The original aims of the scale were to measure treatment effects and prognosis.

Item description

The six items of the KIADL comprise bathing, dressing, toileting, transferring, continence and feeding.

Scale development

The KIADL was developed from observations of many activities performed by patients with hip fracture who were admitted to the Benjamin Rose Hospital, Cleveland, USA. The activities of interest were those basic everyday activities performed "habitually and universally". In addition to the *types* of activities, the authors aimed to identify *patterns* of recovery of these basic ADL functions. They hypothesized that recovery of functional activities would be consistent with the developmental sequence of competencies in childhood, and empirical data were gathered from 45 patients with hip fracture (Staff of Benjamin Rose Hospital, 1959). Using a "Guttman-type approach" (Katz & Akpom, 1976, p. 495), seven patterns or "classes" were identified, which accounted for 105 out of 106 observations of the 45 patients. Katz et al. (1963) subsequently studied 1001 people from a range of facilities (e.g., homes for the aged, hospitals, outpatient clinics) with a variety of medical conditions, including hip fracture ($n = 250$), stroke ($n = 239$), multiple sclerosis ($n = 138$), arthritis ($n = 60$). The participants were requested to show the examiner the bathroom and another specified room, which provided the opportunity for the examiner to directly observe functional ability in transfers, locomotion and communication. A "basic pattern" of recovery was confirmed in 86%, involving three sequential stages: (i) early recovery of independence in feeding and continence, (ii) followed by transfers and toileting, (iii) and finally bathing and dressing. Katz, Hedrick, and Henderson (1979) later reported that items were "empirically derived through the application of Guttman scaling techniques to data on several samples of patients" (p. 4), but no coefficients were reported on the results of the statistical procedures.

Administration procedures, response format and scoring

The KIADL was originally developed as an observational tool: "By means of a series of questions and observations, the observer forms a mental picture of the patient's ADL status as it existed during a 2-week period preceding the evaluation" (Katz, Downs, Cash, & Grotz, 1970, p. 20). More frequently, the KIADL is used as a rating scale, drawing on information provided by the clinician, an informant or self-report. As a rating scale, it is easy and quick to administer, with Hartig, Engle, and Graney (1997) reporting administration time of 1.2 minutes (range 0.2–14.4) following 2 weeks of nursing observations.

Responses are made using either a 2-category scale (independent vs dependent) or a 3-category scale (independent, assistance, dependence), with levels of response for each item being operationally defined. In converting the 3-category scale to the 2-category format, Katz et al. (1963) note that "the intermediate description is classified as dependent for certain functions (e.g., transfers) and independent for others (e.g., feeding)" (p. 915). Results from the 2-category scale are then converted to one of seven grades, in terms of the number and type of areas of independence, as shown in Data box 7.2.

Results from the KIADL are often used descriptively (Grades A–G). Assignment of numerical scores is necessary for any statistical computation, however, but there is no agreed method. Katz et al. (1963) used trichotomized grades, distinguishing among Grades A (independent), B to C (partial independence), and D to G as well as Other (dependence). Åsberg and Nydevik (1991) distinguished between Grades A to C versus D to G and Ruscin and Semla (1996) dichotomized Grade A (no physical dependency, score = 0) and Grades B to G (physical dependency, score = 1). Other investigators have summed the number of deficiencies (scores 0–6; Chin et al., 1999) or assigned scores (1 = independent, 2 = assistance, 3 = dependent) to each of the six items, which are then summed to provide a score range 6 to 18, with higher scores indicating greater dependency (Hartig et al., 1997).

Psychometric properties

The original samples with which the KIADL was developed (Staff of Benjamin Rose Hospital, 1959; Katz et al., 1963) were used to refine item content, establish construct validity in terms of sequences of recovery, and discriminant validity regarding patterns of recovery. Discriminant validity of the KIADL was further examined by Ruscin and Semla (1996) with respect to the medication management abilities of 59 older adults living in the community, 54% of whom had cognitive impairment. There is substantial evidence for the predictive validity of the KIADL. Katz et al. (1970) reported data from 300 consecutive discharges from a hospital for chronically ill patients and their mobility and house-confinement 2 years later. Andrieu et al. (2002) examined the predictive validity of the KIADL in the course of their longitudinal study of 134 patients in the early to middle stages of AD who were living in the community. Åsberg and Nydevik (1991) examined length of hospitalization of 230 people with stroke who were assessed with the KIADL 5 to 7 days post-stroke. Chin et al. (1999) also examined the predictive capacity of the number of deficiencies on the KIADL in 983 older people admitted to an emergency department and their health-related quality of life 3 months post-discharge. Information on the concurrent validity of the KIADL is provided by the study of Rockwood, Stolee, and Fox (1993) who administered the Barthel Index (BI), Functional Independence Measure (FIM) and Physical Self-Maintenance Scale (PSMS), along with the KIADL, to 50 frail, older adults requiring rehabilitation (47% of whom had dementia). Hartig et al. (1997)

Data box 7.2

Grades	Katz et al. (1963)	Åsberg & Nydevik (1991)	Ruscin & Semla (1996)	Description of grades
A	Independent vs	Assistance 1–2 times/day	No physical dependency vs	Independent in all 6 functional areas
B }	Partial dependence	↓	Physical dependency	Independent in 5/6 functional areas
C }	vs	vs	↓	Independent in 4/6 areas, with the non-independent areas being bathing and one other function
D	Dependence	Assistance day and night	↓	Independent in 3/6 areas, with the non-independent areas being bathing, dressing and one other function
E	↓	↓	↓	Independent in 2/6 areas, with the non-independent areas being bathing, dressing, toileting, and one other function
F	↓	↓	↓	Independent in 1/6 areas, with the non-independent areas being bathing, dressing, toileting, transferring and one other function
G	↓	↓	↓	Dependent in all 6 areas
Other				Dependent in at least 2 areas, but not classifiable as C, D, E, or F

conducted an inter-rater reliability study with 96 older people resident in nursing homes, where the KIADL was completed by a nurse aide and nurse practitioner based on a minimum of 2 weeks of direct observation. Summary results of the above studies are shown in Box 7.9.

Box 7.9

Validity:	Criterion: *Concurrent:* Rockwood et al.: with BI: $r = .78$ – with FIM: $r = .68$ – with PSMS: $r = -.74$
	Predictive: Katz et al. (1970): 2 years later: with mobility: $r = .50$ – with house-confinement: $r = .39$
	Andrieu et al.: significant differences on 3/6 items (bathing, toileting, eating) in AD patients who did vs did not have an acute hospital admission over a 12-month period
	Åsberg & Nydevik: 95% with Grades A–C at 5–7 days post-stroke were discharged home within 1 month vs 6% with Grades D–G
	Chin et al.: number of KIADL deficiencies at admission was a significant predictor of health-related quality of life 3 months after discharge
	Construct: *Internal consistency:* Hartig et al.: Cronbach alpha for 2 raters: .88–.89
	Discriminant: Katz et al. (1963): 79% of Grade D–G patients required external attendant care vs 45% of patients with Grade B–C ($p < .002$), and none at Grade A
	Ruscin & Semla: with medication management: 66% with Grade A could perform all 5 medication tasks vs 15% with Grades B+
Reliability:	Inter-rater: Hartig et al.: Total score $r_s = .84$ (range $r_s = .73–.90$)
	Test–retest: No information available
Responsiveness:	No direct evidence

Comment

The KIADL is widely regarded as one of the classic ADL scales. Its development was based on the natural observations of more than a thousand patients with a range of neurological and non-neurological conditions. On the basis of these observations, the authors identified six basic ADL functions that are hierarchically ordered. As an observational tool, the KIADL affords a direct and objective assessment of the patient's level of function. There is substantial evidence for the predictive validity of the KIADL, which was one aim in its development, but less evidence is available in support of the other aim, namely responsiveness. Efforts towards a more comprehensive examination of the psychometric properties of the KIADL may have been hampered by use of alphabetical notation in preference to numerals. This has made the scale unsuitable for any kind of statistical analysis and researchers have generally resorted to their own preferred numerical system. If numerical scores are to be used for the purpose of statistical analysis, however, it would be beneficial if a standardized method of scoring the KIADL were adopted.

Key references

Andrieu, S., Reynish, E., Nourhashemi, F., Shakespeare, A., Moulias, S, Ousset, P. J., et al. (2002). Predictive factors of acute hospitalisation in 134 patients with Alzheimer's disease: A one year prospective study. *International Journal of Geriatric Psychiatry*, *17*(5), 422–426.

Åsberg, K. H., & Nydevik, I. (1991). Early prognosis of stroke outcome by means of Katz Index of Activities of Daily Living. *Scandinavian Journal of Rehabilitation Medicine*, *23*(4), 187–191.

Chin, M. H., Jin, L., Karrison, T. G., Mulliken, R., Hayley, D. C., Walter, J., et al. (1999). Older patients' health-related quality of life around an episode of emergency illness. *Annals of Emergency Medicine*, *34*(5), 595–603.

Hartig, M. T., Engle, V. F., & Graney, M. J. (1997). Accuracy of nurses aides' functional health assessments of nursing home residents. *Journal of Gerontology*, *52A*(3), M142–M148.

Katz, S., & Akpom, C. A. (1976). A measure of primary sociobiological functions. *International Journal of Health Services*, *6*(3), 493–507.

Katz, S., Downs, T. D., Cash, H. R., & Grotz, R. C. (1970). Progress in development of the index of ADL. *The Gerontologist*, *10*(1), 20–30.

Katz, S., Ford, A. B., Moskowitz, R. W., Jackson, B. A., & Jaffe, M. W. (1963). Studies of illness in the aged: The index of ADL. A standardized measure of biological and psychosocial function. *Journal of the American Medical Association*, *185*(2), 914–919.

Katz, S., Hedrick, S. C., & Henderson, N. S. (1979). The measurement of long-term care needs and impact. *Health and Medical Care Services Review*, *2*(1), 1–21.

Rockwood, K., Stolee, P., & Fox, R. A. (1993). Use of goal attainment scaling in measuring clinically important change in the frail elderly. *Journal of Clinical Epidemiology*, *46*(10), 1113–1118.

Ruscin, J. M., & Semla, T. P. (1996). Assessment of medication management skills in older outpatients. *The Annals of Pharmacotherapy*, *30*(10), 1083–1088.

The Staff of the Benjamin Rose Hospital (1959). Multidisciplinary studies of illness in aged persons. II A new classification of functional status in activities of daily living. *Journal of Chronic Disease*, *9*(1), 55–62.

Katz Index of Activities of Daily Living

Katz, Ford, Moskowitz, Jackson, and Jaffe (1963)

Name:	**Administered by:**	**Date:**

Instructions: For each area of functioning listed below, check description that applies. (The word "assistance" means supervision, direction of personal assistance.)

1. Bathing – either sponge bath, tub bath or shower

☐	☐	☐
Receives no assistance (gets in and out of tub by self if tub is usual means of bathing)	Receives assistance in bathing only one part of the body (such as the back or a leg)	Receives assistance in bathing more than one part of the body (or not bathed)

2. Dressing – gets clothes from closets and drawers – including underclothes, outer garments, and using fasteners (including braces if worn)

☐	☐	☐
Gets clothes and gets completely dressed without assistance	Gets clothes and gets dressed without assistance except for assistance in tying shoes	Receives assistance in getting clothes or in getting dressed, or stays partly or completely undressed

3. Toileting – going to the "toilet room" for bowel and urine elimination; cleaning self after elimination, and arranging clothes

☐	☐	☐
Goes to "toilet room", cleans self, and arranges clothes without assistance (may use object for support such as cane walker, or wheelchair and may manage night bedpan or commode, emptying same in morning)	Receives assistance in going to "toilet room" or in cleansing self or in arranging clothes after elimination or in use of night bedpan or commode	Doesn't go to room termed "toilet" for the elimination process

4. Transfer

☐	☐	☐
Moves in and out of bed as well as in and out of chair without assistance (may be using object for support such as cane or walker)	Moves in or out of bed or chair with assistance	Doesn't get out of bed

5. Continence

☐	☐	☐
Controls urination and bowel movement completely by self	Has occasional "accidents"	Supervision helps keep urine or bowel control; catheter is used, or is incontinent

6. Feeding

☐	☐	☐
Feeds self without assistance	Feeds self except for getting assistance in cutting meat or buttering bread	Receives assistance in feeding or is fed partly or completely by using tubes or intravenous fluids

Katz Index of Activities of Daily Living

Katz, Ford, Moskowitz, Jackson, and Jaffe (1963)

Scoring instructions

The Index of Independence in Activities of Daily Living is based on an evaluation of the functional independence or dependence of patients in bathing, dressing, going to the toilet, transferring, continence, and feeding. Specific definitions of functional independence and dependence appear below the index.

A: Independent in feeding, continence, transferring, going to toilet, dressing, and bathing

B: Independent in all but one of these functions

C: Independent in all but bathing and one additional function

D: Independent in all but bathing, dressing and one additional function

E: Independent in all but bathing, dressing, going to the toilet, and one additional function

F: Independent in all but bathing, dressing, going to the toilet, transferring and one additional function

G: Dependent in all six functions

Other: Dependent in at least two functions, but not classifiable as C, D, E, or F.

Independence means without supervision, direction, or active personal assistance, except as specifically noted below. This is based on actual status and not on ability. A patient who refuses to perform a function is considered as not performing the function, even though he is deemed able.

1. **Bathing** (sponge, shower or tub)
   - Independent: assistance only in bathing a single part (such as back, or disabled extremity), or bathes self completely
   - Dependent: assistance in bathing more than one part of body; assistance in getting in or out of tub; or does not bathe self
2. **Dressing**
   - Independent: gets clothes from closets and drawers; puts on clothes, outer garments, braces; manages fasteners; act of tying shoes is excluded
   - Dependent: does not dress self or remains partly undressed
3. **Going to toilet**
   - Independent: gets to toilet; gets on and off toilet; arranges clothes; cleans organs of excretion (may manage own bedpan used at night only and may or may not be using mechanical supports)
   - Dependent: uses bedpan or commode or receives assistance in getting to and using toilet
4. **Transfer**
   - Independent: moves in and out of bed independently and moves in and out of chair independently (may or may not be using mechanical supports)
   - Dependent: assistance in moving in or out of bed and/or chair; does not perform one or more transfers
5. **Continence**
   - Independent: urination and defecation entirely self-controlled
   - Dependent: partial or total incontinence in urination or defecation; partial or total control by enemas, catheters or regulated use of urinals and/or bed pans
6. **Feeding**
   - Independent: gets food from plate or its equivalent into mouth (precutting of meat and preparation of food, such as buttering bread, are excluded from evaluation)
   - Dependent: assistance in act of feeding (see above); does not eat at all or parenteral feeding

---

Acknowledgement: From Katz, S. et al. (1963). Studies of illness in the aged: The index of ADL. A standardized measure of biological and psychosocial function. *Journal of the American Medical Association*, *185*(2), 914–919, p. 915. © American Medical Association, by permission of the Association.

Instrumental Activities of Daily Living Scale (IADLS) and Physical Self-Maintenance Scale (PSMS)

Lawton and Brody (1969)

Source

Items for the IADLS and PSMS are tabulated in Lawton and Brody (1969) and are reproduced below.

Purpose

These two clinician rating scales, assessing self-care (PSMS) and everyday activities at home and in the community (IADLS), were developed for older people living in a range of settings, both community and institutional. The IADLS, in particular, was probably the earliest such scale to be developed that is still widely used, particularly for older adults and people with dementia.

Item description

The PSMS contains six self-care and mobility items (toileting, feeding, dressing, grooming, physical ambulation and bathing). The IADLS contains eight items (telephone use, shopping, food preparation, housekeeping, laundry, transport, medication use, and finance management).

Scale development

Lawton and Brody (1969) were the first to use the term "instrumental activities of daily living", which relates to "everyday functional competence" (p. 179). The conceptual underpinnings of both the PSMS and IADLS were described in terms of a "schema of competence". In this schema, physical self-maintenance was regarded as a less complex level of functional health than "instrumental self-maintenance". The PSMS drew on the Langley-Porter scale developed by Lowenthal (1964), with content adapted to improve its application to people living in the community or residential care settings. Lawton and Brody pointed to previous "noble, though unsatisfying attempts" to develop a scale to assess everyday functional competence, and their IADLS measured "the maintenance of earlier life levels of adequacy" in everyday tasks. They recognized the sex-role bias in these types of tasks, and that fewer such activities applied to men. Having drawn up items and a corresponding hierarchical response format, the scales were tested with a sample of 265 older adults, using Guttman scaling to confirm the ordering of the response levels. The coefficient of reproducibility (CR) was acceptable for both PSMS and IADLS (CR > .9; no information was provided on the coefficient of scalability).

Administration procedures, response format and scoring

The PSMS and IADLS are designed to be completed by a clinician, using information gathered from a variety of sources including the caregiver. Using this method, the scales are quick and easy to complete and score. In interview format with patients, however, Edwards (1990) reported that the combined scales took 20 to 30 minutes. In that study, the second observer received training in the use of the scales.

Each item of the PSMS has five response categories, with individually scripted responses appropriate to the item, ranging from the equivalent of independent through to the equivalent of dependent on other people. The scoring system, however, is dichotomous, with a score of 1 allocated to the independent response, and all levels of assistance/dependency allocated 0. The total score thus ranges from 0 to 6, with higher scores indicating greater independence.

The IADLS has a similar structure. Each item contains three to five individually scripted response levels, ranging from the equivalent of independent through to the equivalent of unable to do the activity. A dichotomous scoring system is also used, but three items (food preparation, housekeeping and laundry) are not scored for males. In contrast to the PSMS, however, the score of 1 is allocated not only to the most independent response, but also to lesser levels of competence. For example, the 4-level responses for telephone use award the score of 1 for the highest level ("able to operate telephone on own initiative"), as well as two lesser levels of competence ("dials a few well-known numbers" and "answers telephone but does not dial"). Only the lowest level response category ("does not use telephone at all") is scored 0. For scoring each item, however, a dichotomous score is used; thus the total score ranges from 0 to 8 for females and 0 to 5 for males, with higher scores indicating greater independence.

Psychometric properties

Lawton and Brody (1969) validated the scales in a sample of 180 older adults recruited from the Philadelphia Geriatric Center, Philadelphia, USA. Validating instruments comprised the Physical Classification (PC), a rating scale of functional health, Mental Status Questionnaire (MSQ) examining orientation and memory, and a Behaviour and Adjustment Rating Scale (BARS). Inter-rater reliability was examined by the authors in a number of specific studies. The PSMS used pairs of nurses rating 36 patients, and subsequently two research assistants rated another 14 impaired and non-impaired patients; for the IADLS two social workers rated 12 patients. Inter-rater reliability among five multidisciplinary clinicians was also examined by Hokoishi et al. (2001) in 25 patients with probable Alzheimer's disease (AD), using Japanese versions of the scales. Rockwood, Stolee, and Fox (1993) administered the Barthel Index (BI), Functional Independence Measure (FIM) and Katz Index of ADL (KIADL), along with the PSMS, to 50 frail older adults requiring rehabilitation. Evidence for predictive validity of the IADLS is available from Andrieu et al. (2002) in the course of their longitudinal study of 134 patients in the early to middle stages of AD and who were living in the community. A comprehensive psychometric study was reported by Edwards (1990) who examined 30 patients from two geriatric hospital wards with a range of measures, including the Functional Independence Measure (FIM). Interview with the patient was also compared with direct observation of two ADL tasks (feeding and ambulation) and two IADL tasks (telephone use and finance management). Interviews were repeated 3 to 5 days later and inter-rater reliability was examined with two raters who simultaneously observed, but independently rated the patients. Results of Lawton and Brody, except where otherwise indicated, are shown in Box 7.10.

Comment

Lawton and Brody were pioneers in the development and assessment of IADL and their instruments were among the earliest standardized scales that are still in common use today. In particular, their conceptual framework underpinning the IADLS has had an enduring effect on the structure of all subsequent IADL scales. The PSMS and IADLS are stand-alone scales

Box 7.10

Validity:	Criterion: *Concurrent:* PSMS with PC: $r = .62$ – IADLS with MSQ: $r = .48$ – IADLS with BARS: $r = .36$ – PSMS with IADLS: $r = .61$ Rockwood et al.: PSMS with BI: $r = -.87$ – with KIADL: $r = -.74$ – with FIM: $r = -.80$ Edwards: PSMS with FIM: $r = .70$ – IADLS with FIM: $r = .33$ – with direct observation: PSMS: $r = .65$, IADLS: $r = .76$ (but at the item level coefficients are reported as poor: $r = .17–.45$) *Predictive*: Andrieu et al.: IADLS distinguished between AD patients who did ($M = 3.03$, $SD = 1.98$) vs did not ($M = 4.02$, $SD = 1.82$) have an acute hospital admission over a 12-month period ($p = .012$) Construct: *Internal consistency:* Guttman scaling: CR for PSMS .96, for IADLS males .96, females .93 *Discriminant:* Edwards: significant differences between the group that could be discharged home ($n = 18$) vs the group that was institutionalized ($n = 12$), both for PSMS ($F = 5.41$, $p = .03$) and IADLS ($F = 4.72$, $p = .04$)
Reliability:	Inter-rater: PSMS: nurses: $r = .87$, research assistants: $r = .91$ – IADLS: social workers: $r = .85$ Edwards: PSMS: ICC = .96, IADLS: ICC = .99 Hokoishi et al.: 5 multidisciplinary raters, PSMS: ICC = .82–.96, IADLS: ICC = .90–.95 Test–retest: Edwards: 3–5 days: PSMS: ICC = .56, IADLS: ICC = .93
Responsiveness:	No information available

that provide a brief sampling of the main features of self-care/mobility and domestic life respectively, with the IADLS more widely used than the PSMS. Basic psychometric properties are adequate, both being reliable and discriminative scales.

Key references

Andrieu, S., Reynish, E., Nourhashemi, F., Shakespeare, A., Moulias, S, Ousset, P. J., et al. (2002). Predictive factors of acute hospitalisation in 134 patients with Alzheimer's disease: A one year prospective study. *International Journal of Geriatric Psychiatry*, *17*(5), 422–426.

Edwards, M. M. (1990). The reliability and validity of self-report activities of daily living scales. *Canadian Journal of Occupational Therapy*, *57*(5), 273–278.

Hokoishi, K., Ikeda, M., Maki, N., Nomura, M., Torikawa, S., Fujimoto, N., et al. (2001). Interrater reliability of the Physical Self-Maintenance Scale and the Instrumental Activities of Daily Living Scale in a variety of health professional representatives. *Aging and Mental Health*, *5*(1), 38–40.

Lawton, M. P., & Brody, E. M. (1969). Assessment of older people: Self-maintaining and instrumental activities of daily living. *The Gerontologist*, *9*(3), 179–186.

Lowenthal, M. F. (1964). *Lives in distress. The paths of the elderly to the psychiatric ward.* New York: Basic Books.

Rockwood, K., Stolee, P., & Fox, R. A. (1993). Use of goal attainment scaling in measuring clinically important change in the frail elderly. *Journal of Clinical Epidemiology*, *46*(10), 1113–1118.

Physical Self-Maintenance Scale

Lawton and Brody (1969)

Name: **Administered by:** **Date:**

	SCORE
1. Toilet	
• Cares for self at toilet completely, no incontinence	1
• Needs to be reminded, or needs help in cleaning self, or has rare (weekly at most) accidents	0
• Soiling or wetting while asleep more than once a week	0
• Soiling or wetting while awake more than once a week	0
• No control of bowels or bladder	0
2. Feeding	
• Eats without assistance	1
• Eats with minor assistance at meal times and/or with special preparation of food, or help in cleaning up after meals	0
• Feeds self with moderate assistance and is untidy	0
• Requires extensive assistance for all meals	0
• Does not feed self at all and resists efforts of others to feed him/her	0
3. Dressing	
• Dresses, undresses, and selects clothes from own wardrobe	1
• Dresses and undresses self, with minor assistance	0
• Needs moderate assistance in dressing or selection of clothes	0
• Needs major assistance in dressing, but cooperates with efforts of others to help	0
• Completely unable to dress self and resists efforts of others to help	0
4. Grooming (neatness, hair, nails, hands, face, clothing)	
• Always neatly dressed, well groomed, without assistance	1
• Grooms self adequately with occasional minor assistance, e.g., shaving	0
• Needs moderate and regular assistance or supervision in grooming	0
• Needs total grooming care, but can remain well-groomed after help from others	0
• Actively negates all efforts of others to maintain grooming	0
5. Physical ambulation	
• Goes about grounds or city	1
• Ambulates within residence or about one block distant	0
• Ambulates with assistance of (check one): ( ) another person, ( ) railing, ( ) cane, ( ) walker, ( ) wheelchair	0
1____ Gets in and out without help	
2____ Needs help in getting in and out	
• Sits unsupported in chair or wheelchair, but cannot propel self without help	0
• Bedridden more than half of the time	0
6. Bathing	
• Bathes self (tub, shower, sponge bath) without help	1
• Bathes self with help getting in and out of tub	0
• Washes face and hands only, but cannot bathe rest of body	0
• Does not wash self but is cooperative with those who bathe him/her	0
• Does not try to wash self and resists efforts to keep him/her clean	0
TOTAL SCORE:	______

Acknowledgement: From Lawton, M. P., & Brody, E. M. (1969). Assessment of older people: Self-maintaining and instrumental activities of daily living. *The Gerontologist*, *9*(3), 179–186, Table 1, p. 180; also from *Psychopharmacology Bulletin*, 1988, *24*(4), reproduced by permission of Medworks Media and Psychological Assessment Resources.

Instrumental Activities of Daily Living Scale

Lawton and Brody (1969)

Name: **Administered by:** **Date:**

	SCORE	
	MALES	**FEMALES**
1. Ability to use telephone		
• Operates telephone on own initiative – looks up and dials numbers, etc.	1	1
• Dials a few well-known numbers	1	1
• Answers telephone but does not dial	1	1
• Does not use telephone at all	0	0
2. Shopping		
• Takes care of all shopping needs independently	1	1
• Shops independently for small purchases	0	0
• Needs to be accompanied on any shopping trip	0	0
• Completely unable to shop	0	0
3. Food preparation		
• Plans, prepares and serves adequate meals independently	N/A	1
• Prepares adequate meals if supplied with ingredients		0
• Heats and serves prepared meals, or prepares meals but does not maintain adequate diet		0
• Needs to have meals prepared and served		0
4. Housekeeping		
• Maintains house alone or with occasional assistance (e.g., “heavy work-domestic help”)	N/A	1
• Performs light daily tasks such as dishwashing, bedmaking		1
• Performs light daily tasks but cannot maintain acceptable level of cleanliness		1
• Needs help with all home maintenance tasks		1
• Does not participate in any housekeeping tasks		0
5. Laundry		
• Does personal laundry completely	N/A	1
• Launders small items – rinses socks, stockings, etc.		1
• All laundry must be done by others		0
6. Mode of transportation		
• Travels independently on public transportation or drives own car	1	1
• Arranges own travel via taxi, but does not otherwise use public transportation	1	1
• Travels on public transportation when assisted or accompanied by another	0	1
• Travel limited to taxi or automobile with assistance of another	0	0
• Does not travel at all	0	0
7. Responsibility for own medication		
• Is responsible for taking medication in correct dosages at correct time	1	1
• Takes responsibility if medication is prepared in advance in separate dosages	0	0
• Is not capable of dispensing own medication	0	0
8. Ability to handle finances		
• Manages financial matters independently (budgets, writes cheques, pays rent, bills, goes to bank), collects and keeps track of income	1	1
• Manages day-to-day purchases, but needs help with banking, major purchases, etc.	1	1
• Incapable of handling money	0	0
TOTAL SCORE:	______	______

Acknowledgement: From Lawton, M. P., & Brody, E. M. (1969). Assessment of older people: Self-maintaining and instrumental activities of daily living. *The Gerontologist*, *9*(3), 179–186, Table 2, p. 181; also from *Psychopharmacology Bulletin*, 1988, *24*(4), reproduced by permission of Medworks Media and Psychological Assessment Resources.

Northwick Park Dependency Score (NPDS)

Turner-Stokes, Tonge, Nyein, Hunter, Nielson, and Robinson (1998)

Source

Items for the NPDS are available in an appendix to Turner-Stokes et al. (1998) and the scale and instruction manual are available from Dr Turner-Stokes (Regional Rehabilitation Unit, Northwick Park Hospital, Watford Road, Harrow, Middlesex HA1 3UJ, UK; email: lynne.turner-stokes@dial.pipex.com). The NPDS is reproduced below.

Purpose

The NPDS is a clinician rating scale that aims to measure nursing dependency in an inpatient rehabilitation setting. It was developed for people with stroke and traumatic brain injury (TBI) and designed "to evaluate the full range of dependency, and in particular to be sensitive to small changes at the 'heavy' end of the scale" (Turner-Stokes et al., 1998, p. 305). A complementary measure, the Northwick Park Care Needs Assessment (NPCNA), is described in Chapter 9.

Item description

The NPDS contains two sections. The Basic Care Needs (BCN) section is described as having 12 items, but a number of items have multiple components. Items are organized into 5 domains: mobility and transfers (2 items); continence and toileting (4 items); washing, bathing, and dressing (3 items); feeding (3 items); safety, communication and behaviour (4 items). The Special Nursing Needs (SNN) section contains seven items that are either specific to a hospital/therapeutic environment (e.g., acute medical/surgical intervention) or require skilled/trained help (e.g., tracheostomy management). The third section of the NPDS recording form (see below) pertains to the NPCNA (see Chapter 9).

Scale development

Turner-Stokes et al. (1998) observed that although scales of functional independence, such as the Barthel Index (BI) and Functional Independence Measure (FIM) show significant correlation with a patient's care needs, they do not provide a direct measure of such needs in terms of the amount of time taken or number of staff required to attend to the patient's needs. The NPDS was developed for this purpose and it was intended that it would be useful in measuring changes in patients who scored at the floor on instruments such as the BI and FIM. In collaboration with nursing staff, items for the NPDS were selected from existing instruments based on the time required by nurses to assist and supervise patients in the course of their day. Items included, but were not limited to, basic self-care tasks and mobility. Each item was described in terms of a hierarchy of levels representing increasing intensity of involvement from nursing staff. The order of the hierarchy was determined in consultation with senior rehabilitation nurses from the unit. Preliminary versions of the NPDS were trialled and refined over a 2-year period, with version 6 being the most recent.

Administration procedures, response format and scoring

The NPDS is accompanied by an instruction manual. It is completed by a nurse or other clinician based on his or her knowledge of the patient's needs and can be completed very quickly, in approximately 3 to 5 minutes. Hatfield, Hunt, and Wade (2003) reported $M = 4$ minutes 42 seconds by a medical doctor (range 2 mins 24 s to 7 mins 31 s) and $M = 5$ minutes 15 seconds by a senior nurse. In the study of Post, Visser-Meily, and Gispen (2002) completion time was not longer than 10 minutes for any patient. Turner-Stokes et al. (1998) suggest completing the NPDS on a fortnightly basis.

Responses for the items of the BCN section use a variable scale from 0 (the equivalent of independent) to 3, 4 or 5 (e.g., for item 6, bathing/showering: needs help from two people and takes more than 30 mins). The total score for this section ranges from 0 to 65, with higher scores indicating greater dependency. Turner-Stokes, Paul, and Williams (2006) have described scores as follows: < 10 = low dependency, 10–24 = medium dependency, and > 24 = high dependency. The seven items in the SNN section are scored dichotomously, either 0 (not required) or 5 (required). These weightings are given because of the "substantial workload" that is involved. The score range is 0 to 35, although the authors note that it is rare for more than a couple of items from this section to occur simultaneously. The total score for the combined sections ranges from 0 to 100, with higher scores indicating greater dependency.

Psychometric properties

Psychometric properties of versions 5 and 6 of the NPDS are reported by Turner-Stokes et al. (1998) in patients participating in rehabilitation mainly following stroke or TBI who were recruited from Northwick Park Hospital, Harrow, UK. Concurrent validity of version 5 was established with the BI. Inter-rater reliability was assessed in 23 patients for version 5 and 21 patients for version 6 (shown in Box 7.11), using independent ratings from nurses. Temporal stability was examined by comparing ratings made 2 days later. Post et al. (2002) examined concurrent validity of the NPDS as well as the BCN and SSN sections with the BI, drawing on data provided by 31 people with stroke participating in neurorehabilitation. Re-evaluations on multiple occasions during admission provided information on responsiveness of the NPDS. Hatfield et al. (2003) examined inter-rater reliability of the BCN section in 22 patients (mainly stroke and TBI) undergoing inpatient neurorehabilitation. There was, however, up to a 7-day interval between assessments, which is a test of temporal stability, rather than inter-rater reliability. Additionally, they documented minutes of nursing care ($M = 214$ per 24 hours, range 35–499), and administered the BI and Short Orientation, Memory and Concentration Test (SOMCT). Svensson, Sonn, and Sunnerhagen (2005) examined inter-rater reliability of a Swedish version of the NPDS using members of the same (nursing) and different (occupational therapy, OT) disciplines. Data were derived from 40 patients mainly with stroke and TBI participating in inpatient neurorehabilitation, and temporal stability was examined 5 days later. Results of Turner-Stokes et al., except where otherwise indicated, are shown in Box 7.11.

Comment

The NPDS takes the novel approach of assessing "what does it take to accomplish the task?", as opposed to "can the task be completed?" It provides a comprehensive evaluation of the amount and type of support because it recognizes the range of care needs during the course of the patient's day, not only physically oriented but also non-physical dependency. In a direct comparison between the BI and NPDS, Post et al. (2002) found that their nurses "judged the NPDS to provide better, more precise and complete information about the actual need for care of the patients" (p. 182). The important psychometric properties of the NPDS have

Box 7.11

Validity:	Criterion: *Concurrent:* with BI: $r_s = -.91$ Hatfield et al.: NPDS with BI: $r_s = -.89$ – with minutes of nursing time: $r = .87$ – with SOMCT: $r_s = .34$ – BCN with BI: $r_s = -.95$ – BCN with mins of nursing time: $r_s = .88$ Post et al.: mean scores over multiple assessments: NPDS with BI: $r = -.92$ – BCN with BI: $r = -.93$ – SSN with BI: $r = -.34$
Reliability:	Inter-rater: NPDS: $r_s = .90$ – BCN: $r_s = .91$ (item range: $r_s = .38$–1.00, with $r > .8$ for 8/16 items, $r < .6$ for 4/16 items – toilet/bladder, urinary incontinence, washing/grooming, behaviour) – SNN: $r_s = .68$ Svensson et al.: 16 BCN items using 2 nurses: $k = .63$–1.00, but greater variability between disciplines: $k = .28$–.80 (with $k \geq .6$ for 11/16 items, $k < .4$ for 2/16 items – drinking, bathing/showering) Test–retest: 2 days: NPDS: $r_s = .93$, BCN: $r_s = .95$, SNN: $r_s = .81$ – Time 1 $M = 21.58$ vs Time 2 $M = 21.76$ Svensson et al.: 5 days: nurse 1: $k = .77$–1.00, nurse 2: $k = .53$–1.00, OT: $k = .74$–1.00
Responsiveness:	Post et al.: NPDS Admission $M = 15.4$ ($SD = 8.2$) vs 4 weeks later $M = 10.5$ ($SD = 8.7$); $z = -3.62$, $p < .001$, $d = .58$ – Admission $M = 15.4$ ($SD = 8.2$) vs Discharge $M = 4.8$ ($SD = 8.1$); $z = -4.06$, $p < .001$, $d = 1.3$

been assessed. There is evidence of content validity, inter-rater reliability for the NPDS (and BCN section) is high, and it shows excellent temporal stability, yet is responsive to real change occurring in the patient, with medium to large effect sizes between admission and discharge. The SNN section, however, shows relatively poorer inter-rater reliability. Concurrent validity between the NPDS and BCN section with the BI is very high (approximately $r = .90$ in independent samples), suggesting significant redundancy between measures. Hatfield et al. (2003) suggest that the BI is probably as accurate a measure of dependency as the NPDS, but the latter arguably yields a richer set of clinically relevant information for very little expenditure of time.

Key references

Hatfield, A., Hunt, S., & Wade, D. T. (2003). The Northwick Park Dependency Score and its relationship to nursing hours in neurological rehabilitation. *Journal of Rehabilitation Medicine*, *35*(3), 116–120.

Post, M. W. M., Visser-Meily, J. M. A., & Gispen, L. S. F. (2002). Measuring nursing needs of stroke patients in clinical rehabilitation: A comparison of validity and sensitivity to change between the Northwick Park Dependency Score and the Barthel Index. *Clinical Rehabilitation*, *16*(2), 182–189.

Svensson, S., Sonn, U., & Sunnerhagen, K. S. (2005). Reliability and validity of the Northwick Park Dependency Score (NPDS) Swedish version 6.0. *Clinical Rehabilitation*, *19*(4), 419–425.

Turner-Stokes, L., Tonge, P., Nyein, K., Hunter, M., Nielson, S., & Robinson, I. (1998). The Northwick Park Depedency Score (NPDS): A measure of nursing dependency in rehabilitation. *Clinical Rehabilitation*, *12*(4), 304–318.

Turner-Stokes, L., Paul, S., & Williams, H. (2006). Efficiency of specialist rehabilitation in reducing dependency and costs of continuing care for adults with complex acquired brain injuries. *Journal of Neurology, Neurosurgery, and Psychiatry*, *77*, 634–639.

Northwick Park Dependency Score

Turner-Stokes, Tonge, Nyein, Hunter, Nielson, and Robinson (1998)

PATIENT DETAILS: Surname: .... Forename(s): ....

Hosp No: .... Sex: Male/Female Date of birth: ....

Diagnosis:..

OCCASION: Admission/Fortnightly review /Discharge

Date of assessment ...../...../..... SCORER:.....................................

FOR EACH ITEM, CIRCLE THE HIGHEST SCORE THAT APPLIES
And answer any additional questions

SECTION 1. BASIC CARE NEEDS

1. MOBILITY
(Give most usual method of mobility around bay (hospital) or indoors (home))

Description	Dependency
a) Walks fully independently	0
b) Independent in electric/self-propelled chair	1
c) Walks with assistance/supervision of one	2
d) Uses attendant-operated wheelchair	3
e) Bed-bound (unable to sit in wheelchair)	4

2. BED TRANSFERS

Description	Dependency
a) Fully independent	0
b) Requires help from one person	1
c) Requires help from two people	2
d) Requires hoisting by 1, and takes < 1/2 hr **or**	3
e) Requires hoisting by 2, and takes < 1/4 hr	3

3. TOILETING BLADDER
3.1. MODE OF EMPTYING

Which of the following does the patient use to empty their bladder?

By DAY		By NIGHT
☐	Toilet	☐
☐	Commode	☐
☐	Bottles	☐
☐	Catheter/convene	☐
☐	Bed-pan	☐
☐	Pads	☐

3.2. NEED FOR ASSISTANCE
(Includes getting there, transferring onto toilet, cleaning themselves, adjusting clothing, and washing hands afterwards.
IF USING BOTTLE: includes reaching for it, positioning and replacing it unspilt)

Description	Dependency
a) Able to empty their bladder independently	0
b) Set-up only (e.g., copes if bottles left within reach) **or**	1
c) Has indwelling catheter/ convene	1
d) Needs help/supervision from 1, and takes < 1/4 hr	2
e) Needs help from 1, and takes more than 1/4 hr	3
f) Needs help from 2, and takes < 1/4 hr	4

3.3. FREQUENCY OF EMPTYING BLADDER
If he/she needs help to pass urine

How many times do they pass urine during the day?
up to 4 times 5–6 times > 6 times

How many times do they pass urine during the night?
0 1 2 > 2

3.4. URINARY INCONTINENCE

Description	Dependency
a) No accidents or leakage from catheter/convene	0
b) Continent if toiletted regularly. Occasional accidents	1
c) 1–2 episodes of incontinence/leakage in 24 hrs	2
d) >2 episodes of incontinence/leakage in 24 hrs	3

If scored 1: How many times per week? 1 2 3 4 5 6

If scored 3: How many times in 24 hrs? 1 2 3 4 5 6

4. TOILETING BOWELS

4.1. NEED FOR ASSISTANCE

(Includes getting to and transferring onto toilet, cleaning themselves, adjusting clothing, and washing hands afterwards. IF HAS COLOSTOMY, includes emptying/changing bag hygienically)

Description	Dependency
a) Able to empty their bowels independently	0
b) Set-up only (e.g., giving suppositories/enema)	1
c) Needs help/supervision from 1, and takes < 1/4 hr	2
d) Needs help from 1, and takes more than 1/4 hr	3
e) Needs help from 2, and takes < 1/4 hr	4
f) Needs help from 2, and takes more than 1/4 hr	5

4.2. FREQUENCY OF OPENING BOWELS (or emptying colostomy bag)

☐ 2–3 times per week ☐ 4–5 times per week
☐ Once a day ☐ Twice a day ☐ > twice a day
(Do not include faecal incontinence here)

What times of day do they normally open their bowels?
☐ Morning ☐ Midmorning ☐ Midday ☐ Afternoon ☐ Evening ☐ Bedtime

Do they need to open their bowels during the night?

0 1 2 > 2

4.3. FAECAL INCONTINENCE

Description	Dependency
a) No faecal accidents	0
b) Requires regular bowel regimen – suppositories/enemas in order to remain continent ***Enter Section 3: Care Needs Assessment Item No. 4a***	1
c) Occasional faecal accidents (less than daily)	2
d) Regular incontinence of faeces	3

If scored 2: How many times per week? 1 2 3 4 5 6

If scored 3: How many times in 24 hrs? 1 2 3 4 5 6

5. WASHING AND GROOMING

(Includes washing hands and face, cleaning teeth, brushing hair, and shaving or make-up)

NB. This item does not include bathing/showering

Description	Dependency
a) Able to wash and groom independently	0
b) Needs help to set up only (e.g., laying out things, filling bowl with water)	1
c) Needs help from 1, and takes < 1/2 hr	2
d) Needs help from 1, and takes more than 1/2 hr	3
e) Needs help from 2, and takes < 1/2 hr	4
f) Needs help from 2, and takes more than 1/2 hr	5

Note: It is very rare to need help from 2 to wash unless patient requires restraint

6. BATHING/SHOWERING
(Includes getting to bath/shower-room, transferring in and out, washing and drying)
NB. If unable to bath or shower: Complete as for THOROUGH STRIPWASH

Description	Dependency
a) Able to have bath/shower independently	0
b) Needs help to set up only (e.g., running bath soaping flannel etc.)	1
c) Needs help from 1, and takes < 1/2 hr	2
d) Needs help from 1, and takes more than 1/2 hr	3
e) Needs help from 2, and takes < 1/2 hr	4
f) Needs help from 2, and takes more than 1/2 hr	5

7. DRESSING
(Includes putting on shoes, socks, tying laces, putting on splint or prosthesis)

Description	Dependency
a) Able to dress independently	0
b) Needs help to set up only (e.g., laying out clothes) **or** c) Needs incidental help from 1 (e.g., just with shoes)	1 1
d) Needs help from 1, and takes < 1/2 hr	2
e) Needs help from 1, and takes more than 1/2 hr	3
f) Needs help from 2, and takes < 1/2 hr	4
g) Needs help from 2, and takes more than 1/2 hr	5

8.1. EATING

Description	Dependency
a) Entirely gastrostomy/nasogastric fed	0
b) Able to eat independently	0
c) Needs help to set up only (e.g., opening packs or passing special cutlery)	1
d) Needs help from 1, and takes < 1/2 hr	2
e) Needs help from 1, and takes more than 1/2 hr	3

8.2. DRINKING

Description	Dependency
a) Entirely gastrostomy/nasogastric fed	0
b) Able to pour own drink and drink it independently	0
c) Able to drink independently if left within reach	1
d) Needs help or supervision, and takes < 1/2 hr	2
e) Needs help/supervision, and takes more than 1/2 hr	3

8.3. ENTERAL FEEDING (GASTROSTOMY or NASOGASTRIC TUBE)

Description	Dependency
a) No enteral feeding/manage feeds independently	0
b) Needs help to set up feed just once a day	1
c) Needs help to set up feed twice a day	2
d) Needs help to set up feed three times a day	3
e) Needs extra flushes during the day	4
f) Needs extra flushes during the day and night	4

9. SKIN PRESSURE RELIEF

Description	Dependency
a) Skin intact, able to relieve pressure independently	0
b) Needs prompting only to relieve pressure	1
c) Skin intact, needs help from 1 to turn (4 hrly)	2
d) Skin intact, needs help from 2 to turn (4 hrly)	3
e) Skin marked or broken, needs 1 to turn (2 hrly)	4
f) Skin marked or broken, needs 2 to turn (2 hrly)	5

10. SAFETY AWARENESS

Description	Dependency
a) Fully orientated, aware of personal safety	**0**
b) Requires some help with safety and orientation but Safe to be left for more than 2 hrs + could summon help in emergency	**1**
c) Requires help to maintain safety Could not be left for 2 hrs + could not summon help in an emergency	**2**
d) Requires constant supervision	**3**

11. COMMUNICATION

Description	Dependency
a) Able to communicate all needs	**0**
b) Able to communicate basic needs without help	**1**
c) Able to communicate basic needs with a little help or by using a communication aid or chart	**2**
d) Able to respond to direct questions about basic needs	**3**
e) Responds only to gestures and contextual cues	**4**
f) No effective means of communication	**5**

12. BEHAVIOUR

Description	Dependency
a) Compliant and socially appropriate	**0**
b) Needs verbal /physical prompting for daily activities	**1**
c) Needs persuasion to comply with rehab or care	**2**
d) Needs structured behavioural modification programme	**3**
e) Disruptive, inclined to aggression	**4**
f) Inclined to wander off ward/out of house	**5**

SECTION 2: SPECIAL NURSING NEEDS

ADD 5 FOR EACH OF THE BELOW	Dependency
1. Tracheostomy	**5**
2. Open pressure sore/wound requiring dressings	**5**
3. > 2 interventions required at night	**5**
4. Pt or relatives need substantial psychological support	**5**
5. MRSA screening/isolation	**5**
6. Intercurrent medical/surgical problem	**5**
7. Needs one-to-one “specializing”	**5**

	TOTAL SCORES
SECTION 1: BASIC CARE NEEDS	....
SECTION 2: SPECIAL NURSING NEEDS	....
NPDS NURSING DEPENDENCY SCORE	....

SECTION 3: CARE NEEDS ASSESSMENT

1. STAIRS		
a) Do they need help or supervision to negotiate stairs:		
In the morning	☐ Yes	☐ No
At bed-time	☐ Yes	☐ No

2. MAKING A SNACK/MEAL	
a) Not applicable as entirely gastrostomy fed	0
b) Able to make a snack and drink at home independently	**0**
c) Able to help themselves if a snack is left out in the kitchen	**1**
d) Needs meals or drinks put in front of them	**2**

3. MEDICATION (Including remembering to take it, opening bottles etc.)	
a) Not applicable (e.g., on no medication)	**0**
b) Able to take all medication independently	**0**
c) Able to help themselves if tablets left out in the morning	**1**
d) Requires help for medication to be given	**2**

If requires help, which times does medication need to be given? (Tick all that apply)

☐ Morning ☐ Midmorning ☐ Midday ☐ Afternoon ☐ Evening ☐ Bedtime

4. Do they require skilled help from a NURSE or TRAINED CARER for any of the following tasks?		
a) Suppositories/Enema	☐ Yes	☐ No
b) Stoma Care (Tracheostomy, gastrostomy etc.)	☐ Yes	☐ No
c) Pressure Sore/wound dressing	☐ Yes	☐ No
d) Special medication (e.g., insulin injections)	☐ Yes	☐ No
e) Other..................................		

If skilled help is required

How many times a week?		Who provides that help?		
	Times per week	Family	Home Care	Nurse
for a)	....	☐	☐	☐
b)	....	☐	☐	☐
c)	....	☐	☐	☐
d)	....	☐	☐	☐

5. Do they require help for DOMESTIC DUTIES		
a) Light housework	☐ Yes	☐ No
b) Heavy housework	☐ Yes	☐ No
c) Shopping	☐ Yes	☐ No
d) Laundry	☐ Yes	☐ No

Acknowledgement: From Turner-Stokes, L. et al. (1998). The Northwick Park Dependency Score: A measure of nursing dependency in rehabilitation. *Clinical Rehabilitation*, *12*(4), 304–318, Appendix, pp. 315–318, used by permission of Sage Publications; format provided by Dr Turner-Stokes.

Nottingham Activities of Daily Living Scale (NADLS)

Ebrahim, Nouri, and Barer (1985)

Source

Items for the NADLS, also known as the Nottingham 10-point, are tabulated in Ebrahim et al. (1985) and operational definitions of the requirements for each item are provided in Barer (1989). The items appear below.

Purpose

The NADLS is a rating scale of basic activities of daily living (ADL), designed with the facility of being either an observational tool or a clinician/informant/self-rating scale. It was designed for people with stroke, particularly during the early stage of recovery in the first few weeks post-onset.

Item description

Two domains are sampled: Self-care (8 items covering feeding, toileting, washing, dressing, and making a hot drink) and Mobility (2 items). Items are arranged hierarchically in terms of level of difficulty.

Scale development

Item selection for the NADLS was determined empirically (Ebrahim et al., 1985). Initially, 19 relevant items were taken from ADL scales used in other centres in the UK. Occupational therapists (OT) rated the functional ability of 78 rehabilitation inpatients who were at various stages of recovery after stroke. Data from the 19 items were analysed in order to determine those items that would form an acceptable Guttman scale. Ten items were selected, which represented a range of tasks necessary for self-care and were considered to be easy to test. Guttman scaling was used to rank the items, with results indicating a valid and unidimensional scale. A second sample of patients ($n = 107$) was used to refine item order on the basis of further Guttman scaling and to establish the psychometric properties of the instrument.

Administration procedures, response format and scoring

The NADLS is designed to be rated by a clinician who has observed or has knowledge of the patient's level of functioning. Additionally, it was also intended to be suitable for completion by the patient or an informant in a postal version. The scale is reported to be quick and easy to complete.

A dichotomous response format is used, with items endorsed if the task can be completed independently. Items so completed are scored 1. The patient is assigned the score that represents the most difficult item in the hierarchy that is passed. The total score ranges from 0 to 10, with higher scores representing greater independence.

Psychometric properties

The standardization samples consisted of two groups of people with stroke, recruited from hospitals in Nottingham, UK (Ebrahim et al., 1985). The first sample, used to identify suitable items, comprised 78 people currently participating in inpatient rehabilitation; they had been rated by their OT using standard procedures. Guttman scaling yielded an acceptable coefficient of reproducibility (CR) and coefficient of scalability (CS), in excess of the recommended levels of .9 and .6 respectively. The second sample (a consecutive series of $n = 107$) was assessed 1 month post-onset, 59 were still hospitalized and 48 had been discharged home. A subset of the hospitalized group (32/59) had an independent full OT evaluation of each of the NADLS items. In the same week as an "informal" procedure collated information from reports of nursing and rehabilitation staff regarding the patient's requirements for assistance in self-care tasks and was used as the basis to complete the NADLS. Disagreements occurred in 20 of the 320 (6%) items assessed, with a difference of $M = 0.5$ scale points, which Ebrahim and colleagues described as being "of no statistical or practical significance" (p. 88). A subset of the discharged group (22/48) returned a postal questionnaire prior to a direct home-assessment of seven ADL items. Again, there were few disagreements (8/154 items, 5%). Barer (1989) used the NADLS in a clinical trial of beta-blockade in the treatment of 302 people with acute stroke. Guttman scaling properties were replicated (CR .95; CS .88). These coefficients were also replicated in another clinical trial of nimodine in 1870 assessments from 730 patients at 1 week ($n = 702$), 3 weeks ($n = 524$) and 24 weeks ($n = 524$) after stroke: CR .97; CS .87 (Barer & Murphy, 1993). Results from Ebrahim et al., except where otherwise stated, are shown in Box 7.12.

Box 7.12

Validity:	Criterion: *Concurrent:* Barer: NADLS Discharge score with length of stay: $r_s = -.54$ Barer & Murphy: with neurological scores at 1, 3 and 24 weeks: $r = .83–.84$ *Predictive:* 15/18 (83%) patients still in hospital at 6 months had a NADLS score < 4 at 1 month post-onset; 16/24 (67%) patients who had died between 1 and 6 months had a NADLS score < 4 at 1 month post-onset Barer & Murphy: NADLS scores at 1 week with status at 6 months: $r = .67$ Construct: *Internal consistency*: Guttman scaling confirmed a valid, unidimensional scale: CR .95, CS .87
Reliability:	Inter-rater: No direct information: but few disagreements (6% inpatients, 5% outpatients) between objective OT assessment and NADLS scores Test–retest: No information available
Responsiveness:	No information available

Comment

The NADLS is a valid, quick and easily completed scale, which can be used in a clinical setting to evaluate a patient's level of functioning. It is also versatile in that it can be used as either an observational instrument or a clinician/informant/self-rating scale, although specific information on inter-rater reliability and temporal stability is lacking. Barer (1989) points to the efficiency of the Guttman scaling procedure – if a patient cannot achieve items 3 and 4 in the NADLS hierarchy, then it is unlikely that he or she can achieve items 7 to 10, and these items thus do not need to be assessed. The use of the ranking procedure enables a score to be directly interpreted as "an easily identified step on the road back to full independence" (Ebrahim et al., 1985, p. 86). The scale shows good agreement with objective clinician assessment and it is therefore particularly well suited for research studies which require an indication of level of independence in mobility and self-care tasks. The hierarchical structure of the NADLS makes it less suitable, however, in situations where a detailed evaluation of components of mobility and self-care tasks is required.

Key references

Barer, D. H. (1989). Use of the Nottingham ADL scale in stroke: Relationship between functional recovery and length of stay in hospital. *Journal of the Royal College of Physicians of London*, *23*(4), 242–247.

Barer, D. H., & Murphy, J. J. (1993). Scaling the Barthel: A 10-point hierarchical version of the activities of daily living index for use with stroke patients. *Clinical Rehabilitation*, *7*(4), 271–277.

Ebrahim, S., Nouri, F., & Barer, D. (1985). Measuring disability after a stroke. *Journal of Epidemiology and Community Health*, *39*(1), 86–89.

Nottingham 10-point ADL Scale

Ebrahim, Nouri, and Barer (1985)

Name:	**Administered by:**	**Date:**

1. ☐ Drink from a cup
2. ☐ Eat
3. ☐ Wash face and hands
4. ☐ Transfer from bed to chair
5. ☐ Walk (or use wheelchair) indoors
6. ☐ Toilet
7. ☐ Undress
8. ☐ Dress
9. ☐ Make a hot drink
10. ☐ Get in and out of bath

SCORE: _______

Acknowledgement: From Ebrahim, S. et al. (1985). Measuring disability after a stroke. *Journal of Epidemiology and Community Health*, *39*(1), 86–89, Table 1, p. 87, by permission of BMJ and Rightslink.

Nottingham Extended Activities of Daily Living (NEADL)

Nouri and Lincoln (1987)

Source

Items for the NEADL (also known as the Daily Living Activities Questionnaire) are available in the appendix to Nouri and Lincoln (1987) and are reproduced below.

Purpose

The NEADL is an informant rating scale, originally designed for postal survey to assess level of independence in daily living in people who have been discharged from hospital after stroke.

Item description

The 22-item NEADL has four subsections: Mobility (6 items), Kitchen (5 items), Domestic (5 items) and Leisure (6 items). Guttman scaling was used to arrange items hierarchically within subsections, in order of their difficulty level.

Scale development

A pool of 22 items "thought to be important for daily living at home" was compiled (Nouri & Lincoln, 1987, p. 302). The scale was posted to people with stroke who were 12 months post-discharge and living at home, with responses received from 52 out of 80. Data from a 4-point scale were dichotomized: independent (done on own/with difficulty) versus dependent (done with help/not done). Guttman scaling was then used to rank items within each subsection in order of difficulty. Coefficients of reproducibility (CR) and scalability (CS) were acceptable for three of the four subsections (CR for the Mobility domain was .85, less than the recommended criterion of .90). The results were used to reorder and retest the scale. The revised version of the NEADL was then posted to another 20 patients at least 6 months post-stroke and living at home. Lincoln and Gladman (1992) subsequently examined the feasibility of the 22 NEADL items forming an unidimensional, hierarchical scale, thus allowing the use of a total score. Two samples of stroke patients were used ($n = 49$ and $n = 303$) but in both samples the CR (.86 and .85 respectively) was slightly lower than the recommended criterion. CS was acceptable (> .6) in both samples (.81 and .75 respectively). There was, however, support for a combined Household subsection, being an amalgamation of Kitchen and Domestic (CR: .88–.92; CS: .79–.81).

Administration procedures, response format and scoring

The NEADL is designed to be self-administered or completed by an informant. Item length and response format make the NEADL quick and easy to administer.

Responses are made on a 4-point scale, focusing on whether the person actually does (as opposed to "can do") the activity: done on own, done with difficulty, done with help, not done. Scoring is dichotomous, with responses from the 4-point scale re-scored: 1 (independent: "done on own" or "done with difficulty") or 0 (dependent: "done with help" or "not done"). Each subsection (Mobility, Kitchen, Domestic and Leisure) is separately scored, with higher scores indicating a greater level of independence.

It is noted that some investigators use a total NEADL score, and although this was not supported by the results of Guttman scaling, Lincoln and Gladman (1992) suggest that because the CR was only marginally lower than the usual criterion that use of a total score could be "sufficiently robust for use with groups of patients . . . though it must be recognized that, with individual patients, the scaling properties are not perfect and therefore subsection, rather than overall, totals should be considered when evaluating a patient's progress" (p. 42).

Psychometric properties

The standardization sample for the NEADL comprised postal data from a consecutive series of 52 out of 80 people with stroke admitted to hospitals in Nottingham, UK and discharged home (Nouri & Lincoln, 1987). Temporal stability over a 2-week interval was examined with 12 people with stroke who were more than 6 months post-onset and living at home. Green, Forster, and Young (2001) also examined test–retest reliability over a 1-week period in 22 people with stroke who were $M = 15$ months post-stroke. Gompertz, Pound, and Ebrahim (1994) examined the natural history of recovery after stroke, recruiting 361 patients and following them up at 6 months ($n = 191$) and 12 months ($n = 159$) post-onset with the NEADL and Barthel Index (BI). Information on responsiveness is available from Gompertz et al., as well as from a meta-analysis of eight randomized controlled trials ($n = 1143$) for community occupational therapy after stroke (Walker et al., 2004). Results of Nouri and Lincoln (1987), except where otherwise indicated, are shown in Box 7.13.

Box 7.13

Validity:	Criterion: *Concurrent:* Gompertz et al.: with BI at 6 and 12 months post-stroke: $r = .83–.84$ Construct: *Internal consistency:* Guttman scaling: CR for Mobility .85, Kitchen .95, Domestic .93, Leisure .92 – CS for Mobility .69, Kitchen .88, Domestic .90, Leisure .87
Reliability:	Inter-rater: No information available Test–retest: 2 weeks: Mobility: $k = .83–1.0$, Kitchen: $k = .62–1.0$, Domestic $k = .29–.84$ (with $k \geq .6$ for 3/5 items; $k < .4$ for 1/5 items – housework), Leisure: $k = .76–1.0$ Green et al.: 1 week: Mobility: $k = .30–.89$ (with $k \geq .6$ for 4/6 items, $k < .4$ in 1/6 items – walking outside), Kitchen: $k = .48–.80$ (with $k \geq .6$ for 3/5 items), Domestic $k = .61–.88$, Leisure: $k = .14–.86$ (with $k \geq .6$ in 2/6 items, $k < .4$ for 4/6 items – reading, telephone, going out socially, garden)
Responsiveness:	Gompertz et al.: effect size between 1 and 6 months post-stroke: $d = .6$ Walker et al.: meta-analysis: weighted mean difference 1.3 points higher at the end of trial compared with groups randomized to usual care; for treatments specific to ADL tasks, weighted mean difference = 1.6 points

Comment

The NEADL is an established IADL scale, and has been used to validate other scales, such as the London Handicap Scale. An advantage is the hierarchical ranking of items using Guttman scaling procedures, which makes scores readily interpretable in terms of the patient's level of functioning. Although the CR was slightly lower than recommended levels, Lincoln and Gladman (1992) argued that the limits are "based on judgement, and therefore there is no firm criterion level on which scales are based" (p. 42). Green et al. (2001) were critical of the reliability of the NEADL (5/22 items showing poor temporal stability) in comparison with self-care and mobility scales, but the likely reason is the greater complexity of the IADL construct. For example, the study of Gompertz et al. (1994) demonstrated that in addition to the BI score, a range of demographic variables were predictors of NEADL subcategories. This also highlights the need for normative data and they "emphasize the importance of standardizing for cultural, gender and social class differences" (p. 279). Nouri and Lincoln (1987) suggest that the NEADL could also be used to chart a patient's progress over time, and in spite of the dichotomous scoring for individual items, evidence from Gompertz et al. indicates that the scale is responsive, showing a moderate effect size between 1 and 6 months post-stroke.

Key references

Gompertz, P., Pound, P., & Ebrahim, S. (1994). Validity of the extended activities of daily living scale. *Clinical Rehabilitation*, *8*(4), 275–280.

Green, J., Forster, A., & Young, J. (2001). A test–retest reliability study of the Barthel Index, the Rivermead Mobility Index, the Nottingham extended Activities of Daily Living Scale and the Frenchay Activities Index in stroke patients. *Disability and Rehabilitation*, *23*(15), 670–676.

Lincoln, N. B., & Gladman, J. R. F. (1992). The Extended Activities of Daily Living Scale: A further validation. *Disability and Rehabilitation*, *14*(1), 41–43.

Nouri, F. M., & Lincoln, N. B. (1987). An extended activities of daily living scale for stroke patients. *Clinical Rehabilitation*, *1*, 301–305.

Walker, M. F., Leonardi-Bee, J., Bath, P., Langhorne, P., Dewey, M., Corr, S., et al. (2004). Individual patient data meta-analysis of randomized controlled trials of community occupational therapy for stroke patients. *Stroke*, *35*(9), 2226–2232.

Nottingham Extended Activities of Daily Living (NEADL)

Nouri and Lincoln (1987)

Name: **Administered by:** **Date:**

Instructions: Please answer the following questions. Read them through carefully before answering. Use a tick (√) in the appropriate box to mark your answer. Only tick one box for each question

	On my own	On my own with difficulty	With help	No
MOBILITY				
1. Do you walk around outside?	☐	☐	☐	☐
2. Do you climb stairs?	☐	☐	☐	☐
3. Do you get in and out of the car?	☐	☐	☐	☐
4. Do you walk over uneven ground?	☐	☐	☐	☐
5. Do you cross roads?	☐	☐	☐	☐
6. Do you travel on public transport?	☐	☐	☐	☐
IN THE KITCHEN				
7. Do you manage to feed yourself?	☐	☐	☐	☐
8. Do you manage to make yourself a hot drink?	☐	☐	☐	☐
9. Do you take hot drinks from one room to another?	☐	☐	☐	☐
10. Do you do the washing up?	☐	☐	☐	☐
11. Do you make yourself a hot snack?	☐	☐	☐	☐
DOMESTIC TASKS				
12. Do you manage your own money when you are out?	☐	☐	☐	☐
13. Do you wash small items of clothing?	☐	☐	☐	☐
14. Do you do your own housework?	☐	☐	☐	☐
15. Do you do your own shopping?	☐	☐	☐	☐
16. Do you do a full clothes wash?	☐	☐	☐	☐
LEISURE ACTIVITIES				
17. Do you read newspapers or books?	☐	☐	☐	☐
18. Do you use the telephone?	☐	☐	☐	☐
19. Do you write letters?	☐	☐	☐	☐
20. Do you go out socially?	☐	☐	☐	☐
21. Do you manage your own garden?	☐	☐	☐	☐
22. Do you drive a car?	☐	☐	☐	☐

Coding: On my own = 1; On my own with difficulty = 1; With help = 0; No = 0

Acknowledgement: From Nouri, F. and Lincoln, N. B. (1987). An extended activities of daily living index for stroke patients. *Clinical Rehabilitation*, *1*, 301–305, Scale p. 305, reproduced by permission of Sage Publications Ltd.

Rivermead Activities of Daily Living (RADL)

Whiting and Lincoln (1980)

Source

The RADL items, administration instructions and recording form are provided in an appendix to Whiting and Lincoln (1980). A slightly revised version of item ordering and scoring format was published by Lincoln and Edmans (1990) and is reproduced below.

Purpose

The RADL is a hierarchically based, observational rating scale of basic and instrumental activities of daily living (ADL), designed for both clinical and research use. It was developed for people with stroke, and specifically for those with hemiplegia. In the process of standardization, the RADL was also tested with patients with traumatic brain injury (TBI).

Item description

The revised item ordering of the 31-item RADL consists of two subscales: Self-care (16 items) and Household (15 items).

Scale development

Item selection for the RADL drew on ADL items recommended for use by the British Association of Occupational Therapists, as well as content of ADL scales in clinical use. Two groups of items were generated: "self-care items, thought to be necessary for all patients, and household items which would not be applicable to all" (Whiting & Lincoln, 1980, p. 44). The conceptual underpinning of the RADL was that items would form a hierarchy, representing an order of recovery. The original scale (Whiting & Lincoln) had three subscales: Self-care (16 items), Household 1 (9 items – assessing cooking and shopping), and Household 2 (6 items – assessing laundry and cleaning). A subsequent revalidation of the RADL for use with a broader age range refined the item order and the two household subscales were collapsed into a single 15-item Household subscale (Lincoln & Edmans, 1990). Various scoring procedures were trialled, including use of a 5-point scale, but this was impractical and inter-rater reliability was difficult to achieve. Two independent samples of 50 patients were used to validate the hierarchical order of the RADL subscales.

Administration procedures, response format and scoring

Detailed and explicit administration instructions are provided in the appendix to Whiting and Lincoln (1980). No information is provided regarding training, although in the standardization studies the RADL was administered by an occupational therapist. RADL items are administered until the occurrence of three consecutive dependency scores (see below). Administration time varies according to the number of items administered and the level of disablement of the individual, but the hierarchical ordering of items in terms of difficulty maximizes administration efficiency.

In the 1990 revision, each item is scored 1 (independent, with or without aids) or 0/0v (dependent/ needs verbal supervision respectively). The 0v notation is used to furnish additional clinical information but does not contribute to the score. The total score ranges from 0 to 16 for the Self-care section and 0 to 15 for the Household section, with higher scores indicating greater independence.

Psychometric properties

The RADL was initially standardized on two independent samples of 50 patients with right or left hemiplegia from stroke recruited from the Rivermead Rehabilitation Centre, Oxford, UK and who were generally younger than 65 years and were more than 1 month post-stroke (Whiting & Lincoln, 1980). The first sample was used to establish the scalability of the RADL, using Guttman scaling procedures. The second sample was used for cross-validation. In both samples the coefficient of reproducibility (CR) was above the recommended level of .9, and the coefficient of scalability (CS) above the recommended level of .6. The Self-care section was also tested with 50 TBI patients aged 16 to 62 years (CR .90; CS .73). Inter-rater reliability of the Self-care and Household sections was assessed with 15 patients more than 2 months post-stroke using observations from three occupational therapists. Ten patients more than 6 months post-stroke who were considered stable in their recovery were tested on the Self-care section on two occasions 4 weeks apart. The RADL was subsequently revalidated with 150 stroke patients, recruited from hospitals in Nottingham, UK with a broader age range than the original samples (39–89 years; Lincoln & Edmans, 1990). Responsiveness of the RADL has been demonstrated in a number of clinical trials. Drummond, Miller, Colquohoun, and Logan (1996) conducted a randomized controlled trial in which 176 patients were treated on a specialized stroke unit and 139 patients received rehabilitation on a conventional hospital ward. They were followed up 3, 6 and 12 months after randomization. Walker, Drummond, and Lincoln (1996) used a randomized cross-over study to treat dressing ability in 32 patients with stroke. Results of the above studies are shown in Box 7.14.

Comment

The RADL has many areas of strength. It provides a standardized, objective method of assessment using direct observation of patient performance in a range of self-care and IADL areas. Although administration time is of necessity longer than occurs with a rating scale, the distinct advantage is that the results are not subject to the limitations of informant or self-report. Moreover, the hierarchical ordering of the items streamlines the assessment process. Many rating scales of ADL and IADL functioning are available, but there is a relative paucity of performance scales, such as the RADL. Inter-rater reliability and temporal stability of the RADL are excellent, and it is responsive to real changes occurring in the patient. No study, however, has provided data on a direct comparison of the RADL with other activity scales, and information on its concurrent validity would clarify the advantages and disadvantages of the RADL relative to informant-based ADL and IADL instruments.

Box 7.14

Validity:	Construct: *Internal consistency:* Guttman scaling: Whiting & Lincoln: in sample 2, Self-care: CR .91, CS .79; Household 1: CR .92, CS .68; Household 2: CR .94, CS .92 Lincoln & Edmans: Self-care: CR .99, CS .97; Household: CR .93, CS .90
Reliability:	Inter-rater: Whiting & Lincoln: Kendall coefficients of concordance: Self-care: .89; Household 1: .84; Household 2: .87 Test–retest: 4 weeks for Self-care: $r = .95$ Time 1 $M = 10.1$ vs Time 2 $M = 9.4$
Responsiveness:	Drummond et al.: significant differences 3 months after treatment. Self-care $p = .03$ (specifically 4 items – cleaning teeth, eating, undressing, dressing), Household $p < .001$ (specifically 5 items – cope with money, prepare hot drink, car entry/exit, prepare snack, prepare meal). Differences also occurred at other time periods (6 and 12 months) Walker et al.: Post-treatment change compared with control phase: median change 2.0; $z = 2.62$, $p = .008$

Key references

Drummond, A. E. R., Miller, N., Colquohoun, M., & Logan, P. C. (1996). The effects of a stroke on activities of daily living. *Clinical Rehabilitation*, *10*(1), 12–22.

Lincoln, N. B., & Edmans, J. A. (1990). A re-validation of the Rivermead ADL Scale for elderly patients with stroke. *Age and Ageing*, *19*(1), 19–24.

Walker, M. F., Drummond, A. E. R., & Lincoln, N. B. (1996). Evaluation of dressing practice for stroke patients after discharge from hospital: A crossover design study. *Clinical Rehabilitation*, *10*(1), 23–31.

Whiting, S., & Lincoln, N. (1980). An ADL assessment for stroke patients. *Occupational Therapy*, *Feb*, 44–46.

Rivermead Activities of Daily Living Assessment – Revised

Whiting and Lincoln (1980); Lincoln and Edmans (1990)

Administration instructions

General:

- All aids supplied or recommended to be stated on the form.
- Decide where to start. If patient can do that item, go back three to make sure patient can do these well, and forward until three consecutive failures – then stop. This applies to each section.
- Instructions should be strictly followed.

SELF-CARE

1. **Drinking:** A full cup of hot liquid, not spilling more than one-eighth of the contents
2. **Comb hair:** To be presentable on completion
3. **Wash face and hands:** At basin (not with bowl), including putting in plug and managing taps and patient drying self (all materials to hand)
4. **Make up or shave:** Shaving to be done by patient's preferred method
5. **Clean teeth:** Unscrewing toothpaste – putting toothpaste on brush. Managing tap
6. **Eating:** A slice of cheese on toast eaten with knife and fork (this was chosen as being reasonably tough to cut and an easy snack to prepare)
7. **Undress:** Dressing gown, pyjamas, socks and shoes to be taken off
8. **Bed to chair:** From lying covered, to chair with arms within reach
9. **Lavatory:** Mobility to toilet (less than 10 metres). To include managing pants and trousers, cleaning self and transferring
10. **Indoor mobility:** Moving from one room to another – turns must be to left. Distance of 10 metres
11. **Dressing:** Does not involve fetching clothes. Clothes to be within reach in a pile but not in any specific order. All essential fastenings to be done up by patient
12. **Wash in bath:** Showing movements, i.e., ability to wash all over body. Ability to manage taps and plugs
13. **Overall wash:** Not in bath – at basin (not with bowl). Patient must be able to wash good arm, stand up, and touch toes from sitting, in order to be able to wash overall
14. **Floor to chair:** From lying, to upholstered chair without arms, seat 15 inches high
15. **Outdoor mobility:** To cover a distance of 50 metres and to include going up a ramp and through a door
16. **In and out of bath:** A dry bath

HOUSEHOLD

17. **Cope with money:** Match coins to packet of sugar, cornflakes and margarine. Ask from change of 34p from 50p (16p); 72.5p from £1 (27.5p); £3.21 from £5 (£1.79)
18. **Preparation of hot drink:** Fill electric kettle, everything to be ready on working surface
19. **Washing:** Handwash smalls at sink
20. **Get in and out of car:** Front seat of any car except sports model
21. **Preparation of snack:** Making a sandwich – materials to be easily reached. Washing and clearing work surface to be done afterwards
22. **Light cleaning:** Cleaning the tidying surfaces – height 13–37 inches
23. **Preparation of a meal:** Peel a potato, fry sausage. Frozen vegetable from fridge. Open tin
24. **Bedmaking:** Putting on sheet and blanket, straightening and tucking in. Bed 21 inches high
25. **Ironing:** Not with steam iron. Organize ironing surface (board or table)
26. **Carrying shopping:** ½ lb butter, 14 oz tin and money
27. **Hang out washing:** On rail indoors, away from sink, no pegs
28. **Crossing roads:** Cross at traffic lights with kerbs – no pedestrian crossing
29. **Transport self to shop and back** – distance of ½ mile
30. **Heavy cleaning:** Vacuum, sweep and dustpan/brush in 11 ft square room, moving dining-room chairs only
31. **Public transport:** Travel on bus (not Park and Ride). Distance at least 1 mile with minimum three stops before destination

Scoring

1 = Independent, with or without aid. All aids should be listed on each page.
0v = Verbal assistance only.
0 = Dependent (if not assessable, if patient medically unfit, if not safe to try, or too soon to try, if time taken is beyond practical bounds).

Rivermead Activities of Daily Living Assessment – Revised

Whiting and Lincoln (1980); Lincoln and Edmans (1990)

Name:	**Administered by:**	**Date:**

Response key:
1 = Independent with or without aids
0v = Needs verbal supervision
0 = Dependent

SELF-CARE	**Comment on aids or other relevant issues**	**RESPONSE**
1. Drinking		______
2. Comb hair		______
3. Wash face/hands		______
4. Make up or shave		______
5. Clean teeth		______
6. Eating		______
7. Undress		______
8. Bed to chair		______
9. Lavatory		______
10. Indoor mobility		______
11. Dressing		______
12. Wash in bath		______
13. Overall wash		______
14. Floor to chair		______
15. Outdoor mobility		______
16. In/out of bath		______

SELF-CARE SCORE: ______

HOUSEHOLD		
17. Cope with money		______
18. Preparation of hot drink		______
19. Washing		______
20. Get in/out of car		______
21. Prepare snack		______
22. Light cleaning		______
23. Prepare meal		______
24. Bedmaking		______
25. Ironing		______
26. Carry shopping		______
27. Hang out washing		______
28. Crossing roads		______
29. Transport self to shop		______
30. Heavy cleaning		______
31. Public transport		______

HOUSEHOLD SCORE: ______

Acknowledgement: From Lincoln, N. B., & Edmans, J. A. (1990). A re-validation of the Rivermead ADL Scale for elderly patients with stroke. *Age and Ageing*, *19*(1), 19–24, Appendix, pp. 22–23, reproduced by permission of Oxford University Press and the authors.

Systeme de Mesure de l'Autonomie Fonctionnelle (SMAF)* (known in English as the Functional Autonomy Measurement System)

Hébert, Carrier, and Bilodeau (1980/1988)

Source

The SMAF was developed in 1980 (Hébert et al., 1980) and published in English in 1988 by Hébert et al. The items and scoring procedures are detailed in the original article, and a revised version was developed in 1993 with a description and validation of this version published in 1995 (Desrosiers, Bravo, Hébert, & Dubuc).

Purpose

The purpose of the SMAF "is to evaluate the needs of individuals by measuring the disabilities and handicaps with which they are afflicted" (Hébert et al. 1988, p. 293). Also included in the scale is "an appraisal of the available material and social resources which partially or totally make up for the disabilities" (p. 294). It was developed specifically for older people with a variety of health conditions, in order to "help allocate community services or chronic care beds". It has been in use since the mid-1980s in residential care, hospital and community settings, as well as in epidemiological studies. It has been used with people with acquired brain impairment, including stroke and traumatic brain injury.

Item description

The 29 items of the SMAF are grouped into 5 subscales that focus on activities of daily living (7 items), mobility (6 items), communication (3 items), mental functions (5 items), and instrumental activities of daily living (8 items). These subscales are based on the *International Classification of Impairments, Disabilities, and Handicap* (ICIDH; WHO, 1980) classification. Each item includes a description of resources that are scored to provide a handicap score. Stability is rated for each item on a 3-point scale.

In addition, a six-item social subscale for the SMAF has been developed and validated (Pinsonnault, Desrosiers, Dubuc, Kalfat, Colvez, & Delli-Colli, 2003). The SMAF is available in English, French and a number of other languages.

Scale development

The SMAF is explicitly based on the concepts of disability and handicap as embodied in the ICIDH. It evaluates disabilities over 29 functions that were defined from literature reviews and with reference to items from the ICIDH that are relevant to older people (Hébert et al., 1988). Limited more specific information is available in English on the procedures used in item selection and development of the SMAF.

Administration procedures, response format and scoring

The SMAF can be administered at any time that a measurement of disability is required. It is designed to be used by a health professional and specific training is not required (Hébert et al., 1988). The clinician completes the SMAF based on questioning the patient or informants, or by observing or testing the patient. The initial validation studies appear to have used a combination of these methods based on the comments in the papers and the administration time recorded ($M = 42$ mins, $SD = 17$) (Hébert et al., 1988). No comparison of different methods of administration methods (including self-report) is available.

In the original version of the SMAF, response for each item was made on a 4-point scale according to the patient's level of independence: 0 (complete autonomy), 1 (requires surveillance or stimulation), 2 (requires help), 3 (total dependence). The modified SMAF includes an intermediate level (generally 0.5) that "describes a subject who performs the activity independently but with difficulty" (Desrosiers et al., 1995, p. 402). This version of the scale is used currently. It is noted that in some publications the scores are expressed as negatives to reflect reduced autonomy. Scores are summed, with the total score ranging from 0 to 87. Higher scores indicate greater dependency.

* This entry was prepared by Ian Cameron.

Psychometric properties

Reliability of the SMAF was reported by Desrosiers et al. (1995). They studied 90 older people in residential settings ranging from home to long-term care facilities on two occasions within 2 weeks. Inter-rater reliability was examined with two nurse assessors who concurrently assessed but independently completed the SMAF. Test–retest reliability was examined 2 weeks later in half of the sample. In a subsequent validation study in a stroke population, Desrosiers, Rochette, Noreau, Bravo, Hébert, and Boutin (2003) recruited 132 people at admission to rehabilitation and at discharge, and two subsequent times (2 weeks and 6 months after discharge). Validating instruments included the Functional Independence Measure (FIM). The underlying factor structure of the SMAF in a stroke population was explored by Mercier, Audet, Hébert, Rochette, and Dubois (2001). They used data from 100 older people with stroke and four factors were extracted that the authors reported accounted for 93% of the variance. Results of the above studies are shown in Box 7.15.

Box 7.15

Validity	Criterion: *Concurrent:* Desrosiers et al. (2003): with FIM in patients with stroke: $r = .93$
	Predictive: Hébert, Guilbault, Desrosiers, & Dubuc (2001): with minutes of nursing care time: $R^2 = .85$
	Construct: *Factor structure:* Mercier et al.: 4 factors: Perceptual, Cognitive, Motor (balance) and Motor (upper extremities). Number of items per factor not reported
Reliability:	Inter-rater: Hébert et al. (1988): $k = .75$ (range: $K_w = .53–.76$)
	Desrosiers et al. (1995): ICC = .96
	Test–retest: Desrosiers et al. (1995): 2 weeks: ICC = .95
Responsiveness:	Hébert, Spiegelhalter, & Brayne (1997): 12-month retest: significant increase in impairment: mean change 2.45 (*SD* = 7.57); $p < .001$
	The minimal detectable change is 5 points (Hébert et al., 1997)

Comment

This scale has been carefully developed and validated. While it was initially developed with older people, it has been applied to people with acquired brain impairment. It has the advantage of including instrumental activities of daily living as well as personal activities of daily living in the one instrument. In addition it has five mental function items, and specifically assesses communication. It also assesses contextual factors. Because of its comprehensive coverage its administration time is relatively long (approximately 40 minutes). It is a good choice if evaluation of a wide range of functioning is required.

Key references

Desrosiers, J., Bravo, G., Hébert, R., & Dubuc, N. (1995). Reliability of the revised functional autonomy measurement system (SMAF) for epidemiological research. *Age and Ageing*, *24*(5), 402–406.

Desrosiers, J., Rochette, A., Noreau, L., Bravo, G., Hébert, R., & Boutin, C. (2003). Comparison of two functional independence scales with a participation measure in post-stroke rehabilitation. *Archives of Gerontology and Geriatrics*, *37*(2), 157–172.

Hébert, R., Carrier, R., & Bilodeau, A. (1980). L'elaboration d'un instrument de mesure des handicaps: Le systeme de mesure de l'autonomie fonctionnelle (SMAF). In C. Tilquin (Ed.), *Editions sciences des systemes*. Montreal: Systed 83.

Hébert, R., Carrier, R., & Bilodeau, A. (1988). The Functional Autonomy Measurement System (SMAF): Description and validation of an instrument for the measurement of handicaps. *Age and Ageing*, *17*(5), 293–302.

Hébert, R., Guilbault, J., Desrosiers, J., & Dubuc, N. (2001). The Functional Autonomy Measurement System (SMAF): A clinical-based instrument for measuring disabilities and handicaps in older people. *Geriatrics Today*, *4*, 141–147.

Hébert, R., Spiegelhalter, D. J., & Brayne, C. (1997). Setting the minimal metrically detectable change on disability rating scales. *Archives of Physical Medicine and Rehabilitation*, *78*(12), 1305–1308.

Mercier, L., Audet, T., Hébert, R., Rochette, A., & Dubois, M.-F. (2001). Impact of motor, cognitive and perceptual disorders on ability to perform activities of daily living after stroke. *Stroke*, *32*(11), 2602–2608.

Pinsonnault, E., Desrosiers, J., Dubuc, N., Kalfat, H., Colvez, A., & Delli-Colli, N. (2003). Functional autonomy measurement system: Development of a social subscale. *Archives of Gerontology and Geriatrics*, *37*(3), 223–233.

World Health Organization. (1980). *International classification of impairments, disabilities, and handicaps*. Geneva: World Health Organization.

Systeme de Mesure de l'Autonomie Fonctionnelle

Hébert, Carrier, and Bilodeau (1980/1988)

Example of item structure

DISABILITIES	RESOURCES 1. Family 3. Employee 5. Nurse 2. Neighbour 4. Aids 6. Volunteer	HANDICAP	STABILITY*
B. MOBILITY 6. NEGOTIATING STAIRS [0] Goes up and down stairs alone [-1] Requires cueing, supervision or guidance to negotiate OR does not safely negotiate stairs [-2] Needs help to go up and down stairs [-3] Unable to negotiate stairs	The client's actual residence ☐ Does not have stairs ☐ Has stairs that must be negotiated ↓ Does the client presently have the resources (help and/or supervision) necessary to overcome this handicap? ☐ yes ☐ no Description ☐☐☐	[0] [-1] [-2] [-3]	[−] [+] [•]

*STABILITY: In future weeks, is it foreseeable that these resources will [−] lessen, [+] increase,
[•] remain stable or does not apply.

Acknowledgement: From Hébert, R. et al. (1988). The Functional Autonomy Measurement System (SMAF): Description and validation of an instrument for the measurement of handicaps. *Age and Ageing*, *17*(5), 293–302, Fig. 1, p. 296, reprinted by permission of Oxford University Press.

8 Scales assessing participation and social role

Instruments presented in Chapter 8 map to the component and domains of the *International Classification of Functioning, Disability and Health* (ICF; WHO, 2001) as depicted in Figure 8.1.

ICF Component	Domain	Block	Category	Chapter
BODY FUNCTIONS	Mental functions	Global mental functions	Consciousness	Chapter 2
			Orientation	Chapters 2 & 3
			Intellectual functions	Chapter 3
			Global psychosocial functions	Chapter 5
			Temperament & personality	Chapter 5
			Energy & drive	Chapter 5
		Specific mental functions	Attention	Chapters 3 & 4
			Memory	Chapters 3 & 4
			Emotional	Chapter 5
			Thought functions	Chapters 2 & 5
			Higher-level cognitive	Chapters 3, 4 & 5
			Language	Chapters 3 & 4
			Experience of self & time	Chapter 4
	Sensory functions & pain			Chapter 6
	Voice & speech functions			Chapters 3 & 4
	Digestive, metabolic & endocrine functions	Digestive system functions	Ingestion	Chapter 6
	Neuromusculo-skeletal & movement-related functions			Chapters 6 & 7
ACTIVITIES / PARTICIPATION	Learning & applying knowledge			Chapters 3 & 4
	General tasks & demands			Chapter 7
	Communication			Chapter 4
	Mobility			Chapters 6 & 7
	Self-care			Chapter 7
	Domestic life			Chapter 7
	Interpersonal interactions & relationships			Chapter 5
	Major life areas			Chapter 8
	Community, social & civic			Chapter 8
ENVIRONMENTAL FACTORS	Products & technology			Chapter 9
	Natural environmental & human-made changes to environment			Not included
	Support & relationships			Chapter 9
	Attitudes			Chapter 9
	Services, systems & policies			Chapter 9
PERSONAL FACTORS	Not yet classified			

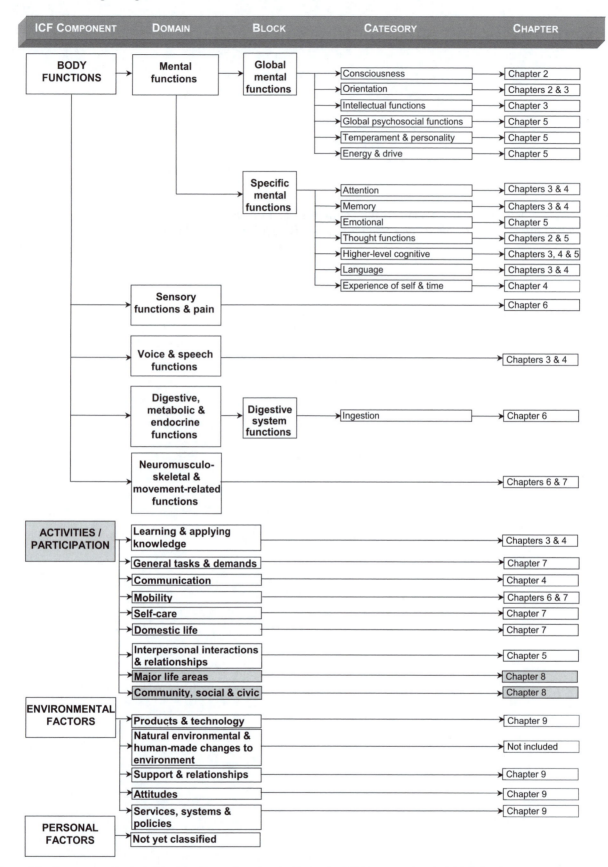

Figure 8.1 Instruments included in the compendium in relation to the ICF taxonomy – the highlighted component and domains appear in this chapter. *Note:* the Figure presents a partial listing of five out of the eight Body Function domains and does not include any of the Body Structure domains. Categories for Mental functions also represent a partial listing and categories for the remaining domains are not listed. Refer to Appendix C for further detail on the ICF taxonomy.

Introduction

This chapter complements Chapters 7, 9 and 10. It brings together scales focusing on two domains of the Activities/Participation component of the ICF: Major life areas, along with Community, social and civic life. As depicted in Appendix C, Major life areas contains three blocks (Education, Work/Employment, and Economic life), which are further subdivided into a total of 12 specific categories; the domain of Community, social and civic life contains five specific categories (Community life, Recreation and leisure, Religion and spirituality, Human rights, and Political life and citizenship). In comparison with most other domains of the Activities/Participation component, these two domains are undisputedly about participation; that is, involvement in a life situation. After acquired brain impairment (ABI) or other health condition, many people experience restriction in their participation, or handicap, to use the older terminology of the *International Classification of Impairments, Disabilities and Handicaps* (ICIDH; WHO, 1980). Participation restriction is modulated by environmental factors (see Chapter 9) and affects quality of life (see Chapter 10).

As noted in Chapters 1 and 7, there is no recommended partitioning between domains of the Activities/Participation component of the ICF. Rather, the list of domains can be used "in different ways" – as a single set, or using any of four options to distinguish between Activities and Participation. Some authors contend that the domains can be differentially partitioned into Activities or Participation, with Jette, Haley, and Kooyoomijian (2003) providing empirical support for this view. Others argue that the domains share features of both Activities and Participation (see Australian Institute of Health and Welfare; AIHW, 2003, for discussion of these issues). Jette et al. (p. 145) assert that the "differentiation [between Activities and Participation] is essential if the ICF is to achieve acceptance by individuals, organizations and associations as an international classification of human functioning and disability". Furthermore, while there remains uncertainty about the position of the WHO regarding the recommended method to partition Activities and Participation, then it is impossible for test developers to produce scales of activity or participation with any confidence that such a scale will meet standards for content validity.

On the other hand, it needs to be recognized that the concept of participation vis-à-vis the ICF comes with a history and a legacy, and this may be part of the reason that to date the WHO has shied away from making a definitive ruling on the partitioning between Activities and Participation. The handicap dimension of the original ICIDH was subject to controversy and criticism, much of it centred on difficulties in operationalizing and measuring the construct of handicap. The same issues apply to participation. Yet it is not only about *what* constitutes participation (which has implications for item content of instruments purporting to measure participation), it is also about *how* it should be measured, and *who* should measure it. Cardol, de Haan, van den Bos, de Jong, and de Groot (1999) observed that "functional skills and capacities considered to be essential by the professional may be differently valued by the individual concerned" (p. 412). So who should call the shots regarding assessment of a person's involvement in a life situation? Is the "gold standard" to be the perspective of the professional or should it be that of the person themselves?

Like handicap, participation is essentially an ideographic construct, but it is not uncommonly treated from a nomothetic perspective. Stewart, Kidd, and Thompson (1995) highlight the validity problems that occur when social roles, inherent in the construct of handicap (and participation), are evaluated from a socioeconomic perspective. In recognition of the importance of "who does the assessing" a number of researchers have been critical of extant instruments of handicap/participation, "which do not reflect an individual's perception and needs, but are normative and focus on general abilities, tasks and roles" (Cardol, de Haan, de Jong, van den Bos, & de Groot, 2001, p. 210). These and other researchers have adopted a client- or patient-centred approach to assessing participation, and a number of such scales are featured in this chapter. Yet, while not diminishing the importance and relevance of the patient-centred perspective, people with ABI often have major impairments in memory, judgement and/or awareness, which can compromise the reliability and validity of their response. Arguably, patient-centred scales alone are insufficient to provide the complete picture of a person's participation and they need to be complemented with objective data.

Wade and Halligan (2003) suggest that the ICF can be readily adapted to accommodate both the subjective/internal view, along with an external/objective perspective. In terms of participation restriction, the respective aspects are role satisfaction ("person's judgement (valuation) of their own role performance (what and how well)") and handicap/participation ("judgement (valuation) of important others (local culture) on role performance (what and how well)", p. 352). Although role satisfaction is generally considered to be aligned to the construct of quality of life, which is not covered in the ICF, the overlap between role satisfaction/quality of life and participation is obvious. A small number of scales developed for the ABI population do provide a dual view of participation, incorporating both societal and client-centred perspectives of participation (e.g.,

Brown, Dijkers, Gordon, Ashman, Charatz, & Cheng, 2004; Cardol et al., 2001).

The forgeoing presents some of the challenges in measuring participation. Perhaps it was for such reasons that Wade (2003) said that measures of participation are curently less developed than measures of more basic activities. And further, that participation "is rarely the focus of rehabilitation research trials, and it is rarely measured" (p. S28). Clearly, this is a problem that needs to be redressed. Nonetheless, reliable and valid scales of participation do exist and this chapter presents an array of instruments that profess to do the job of assessing participation and social role; the difficult decisions are those of selecting the instrument that best measures what needs to be measured for a given purpose and determining who is the best person to measure it.

References

Australian Institute of Health and Welfare. (2003). *ICF Australia user guide. Version 1.0*. Canberra: Australian Institute of Health and Welfare.

Brown, M., Dijkers, M. P. J. M., Gordon, W. A., Ashman, T., Charatz, H., & Cheng, Z. (2004). Participation Objective, Participation Subjective: A measure of participation combining outsider and insider perspectives. *Journal of Head Trauma Rehabilitation*, *19*(6), 459–481.

Cardol, M., de Haan, R. J., de Jong, B. A., van den Bos, G. A., & de Groot, I. J. M. (2001). Psychometric properties of the Impact on Participation and Autonomy Questionnaire. *Archives of Physical Medicine and Rehabilitation*, *82*(2), 210–216.

Cardol, M., de Haan, R. J., van den Bos, G. A. M., de Jong, B. A., & de Groot, I. J. M. (1999). The development of a handicap assessment questionnaire: The Impact on Participation and Autonomy (IPA). *Clinical Rehabilitation*, *13*(5), 411–419.

Jette, A. M., Haley, S. M., & Kooyoomijian, J. T. (2003). Are the ICF and participation dimensions distinct? *Journal of Rehabilitation Medicine*, *35*(3), 145–149.

Stewart, G., Kidd, D., & Thompson, A. J. (1995). The assessment of handicap: An evaluation of the Environmental Status Scale. *Disability and Rehabilitation*, *17*(6), 312–316.

Wade, D. T. (2003). Outcome measures for clinical rehabilitation trials: Impairment, function, quality of life or value. *American Journal of Physical Medicine and Rehabilitation*, *82*(10), S26–S31.

Wade, D. T., & Halligan, P. (2003). New wine in old bottles: The WHO ICF as an explanatory model of human behaviour. *Clinical Rehabilitation*, *17*(4), 349–354.

World Health Organization. (1980). *International classification of impairments, disabilities and handicaps*. Geneva: World Health Organization.

World Health Organization. (2001). *International classification of functioning, disability and health*. Geneva: World Health Organization.

Child and Adolescent Scale of Participation (CASP)

Bedell (2004)

Source

Items for the CASP appear in an appendix to Bedell (2004) and are also reproduced below.

Purpose

The CASP, which is Section 2 of the Child and Family Follow-up Survey (CFFS), is an informant rating scale that measures participation in home, school and community at an age-appropriate level in children and adolescents with acquired brain impairment (ABI). It is one of the very few instruments that targets participation which is suitable for this age and clinical group. In the standardization study, the children and young people (aged between 4 months and 21 years) had a variety of neurological conditions, most commonly brain infection, brain tumour, seizure disorder, stroke and traumatic brain injury.

Item description

The CASP contains 20 items arranged in four domains: Home participation (6 items), Neighbourhood/community participation (4 items), School participation (5 items) and Home and community living activities (5 items).

Scale development

Bedell (2004) observed that, unlike the situation for adults, there was no instrument in common and widespread use to survey or monitor outcomes after ABI that was suitable for children and adolescents. The CFFS was developed to meet this need. The CFFS consists of five sections, with Sections 2 and 3 containing stand-alone scales. The CASP (Section 2), the focus of this entry, addresses participation. Section 3 contains two other instruments, (Child and Adolescent Factors Inventory, along with the Child and Adolescent Scale of Environment), but measurement properties of these scales have not been published and hence they were not considered for inclusion in this book. The remaining sections of the CFFS contain various questions addressing a wide range of areas, including six questions about health, hospitalizations and so forth (Section 1); six questions about current educational placement, service need, satisfaction and quality of life (Section 4); and two questions about ways in which services could be improved (Section 5). Development of the CFFS (including the CASP) was guided by information derived from a number of sources to ensure items and content domains were relevant and applicable to a wide range of age groups and sociocultural contexts: the *International Classification of Functioning, Disability and Health* (World Health Organization, 2001), national government policy, existing literature and instruments, as well as feedback from service providers, administrators and families of children with ABI.

Development and trialling of the CFFS were undertaken with young people with ABI (and their families) discharged from the Franciscan Children's Hospital and Rehabilitation Center, Boston, Massachusetts, USA. A random sample of 50 families was invited to participate in development of the CFFS; 21 consented and were administered the initial version of the instrument by telephone. The CFFS was revised on the basis of the results, along with feedback from the participants, other service recipients, service providers and two experts in measurement and paediatric rehabilitation. The revised (Phase 2) CFFS was posted to 168 families, and 60 were returned. Psychometric properties were examined and reported for the CASP (see below), and some "minor revisions" were made, resulting in the Phase 3 version.

Administration procedures, response format and scoring

The CASP is designed to be completed by a family member or caregiver, not the child/young person with ABI. It can be administered in person, by telephone or completed by the informant independently. Administration time for the full CFFS was reported as 45 minutes (range 30–60 mins), but the 20-item CASP will require less time.

Responses are made on a 4-point rating scale: 1

(unable), 2 (very limited), 3 (somewhat limited), 4 (age-expected). A "not applicable" option is also available. Scores are summed, divided by the maximum possible score (i.e., using the items that have *not* been endorsed as "not applicable"), and then multiplied by 100. The total score ranges from 25 to 100, with higher scores indicating a greater extent of age-appropriate participation.

Psychometric properties

The CASP was validated with the 60 family respondents used in the Phase 2 development (Bedell, 2004), with results shown in Box 8.1. The children and young people were aged from 4 months to 21 years, and time post-onset ranged from 4 months to 6.5 years. Scores on the children and adolescent's archived discharge data on the Pediatric Evaluation of Disability Inventory (PEDI) were compared with CASP scores. Internal consistency was examined on the sample, with missing data for the "not applicable" items filled with the mean scores. The underlying factor structure was explored with principal components analysis, and two components were extracted (Movement-related and Social-based), accounting for 78% of the variance. Bedell noted, however, that 16 of the 20 items had significant loadings (> 0.4) on both components. On the basis of the high internal consistency and the results of the factor analysis, suggesting that the CASP may be unidimensional, a preliminary Rasch analysis was conducted. Three items showed significant infit and/or outfit statistics (< 0.7 > 1.3), indicating that the CASP showed measurement imprecision in relation to a Rasch model with this sample. Additional descriptive data on this sample are reported in Bedell and Dumas (2004), which included information on temporal stability (interval not specified) in a subset ($n = 33$).

Comment

The CASP is a newly developed instrument that has excellent internal consistency and shows evidence of content validity. It shows moderately high correlation with PEDI, length of hospitalization and service provision, along with excellent temporal stability (time-frame unspecified). The measure itself is brief, pertinent

Box 8.1

Validity:	Criterion: *Concurrent*: with Discharge PEDI-Self-care: $r = .72$ – with PEDI-Social: $r = .65$ – with PEDI-Mobility: $r = .51$
	Bedell & Dumas: with length of hospitalization: $r = -.57$ – with number of services received: $r = -.59$
	Construct: *Internal consistency:* Cronbach alpha .95
	Factor analysis: 2 factors: Movement-related (6 items with "higher or more distinct loadings"), Social-based (4 "distinct" items)
Reliability:	Inter-rater: No information available
	Test–retest: (interval not specified): Bedell & Dumas: ICC = .94
Responsiveness:	No information available

and easy to complete and score. As the author acknowledges, further psychometric studies are required, and in particular, the reliability of the CASP needs to be examined. At this stage, the CASP is an instrument that shows promise and has the potential to fill a major gap.

Key references

Bedell, G. M. (2004). Developing a follow-up survey focused on participation of children and youth with acquired brain injuries after discharge from inpatient rehabilitation. *NeuroRehabilitation*, *19*(3), 191–205.

Bedell, G. M., & Dumas, H. M. (2004). Social participation of children and youth with acquired brain injuries discharged from inpatient rehabilitation: A follow-up study. *Brain Injury*, *18*(1), 65–82.

World Health Organization. (2001). *International classification of functioning, disability and health*. Geneva: World Health Organization.

Child and Adolescent Scale of Participation

Bedell (2004)

Name:	**Administered by:**	**Date:**

Response key:
1 = Unable
2 = Very limited
3 = Somewhat limited
4 = Age expected
NA = Not applicable

HOME PARTICIPATION	**RESPONSE**
1. Social, play, or leisure activities with family members at home (e.g., games, hobbies, "hanging out")	______
2. Social play, or leisure activities with friends at home (can include conversations on the phone or internet)	______
3. Family chores, responsibilities, and decisions at home (for younger children this may be getting things or putting things away when asked, or helping with small parts of household chores; for older children this may be more involvement in household chores and decisions about family activities and plans)	______
4. Self-care activities (e.g., eating, dressing, bathing, combing or brushing hair, using the toilet)	______
5. Moving about in and around the home	______
6. Communicating with other children and adults at home	______
NEIGHBOURHOOD AND COMMUNITY PARTICIPATION	
7. Social, play or leisure activities with friends in the neighbourhood and community (e.g., casual games, "hanging out", going to public places such as a movie theatre, park or restaurant)	______
8. Structured events and activities in the neighbourhood and community (e.g., team sports, clubs, holiday or religious events, concerts, parades and fairs)	______
9. Moving around the neighbourhood and community (e.g., public buildings, parks, restaurants, movies) – please consider your child's primary way of moving around, NOT his or her use of transportation	______
10. Communicating with other children and adults in the neighbourhood and community	______
SCHOOL PARTICIPATION	
11. Educational (academic) activities with other children in the classroom	______
12. Social, play, and recreational activities with other children at school (e.g., "hanging out", sports, clubs, hobbies, creative arts, lunchtime or recess activities)	______
13. Moving around at school (e.g., getting to and using the bathroom, playground, cafeteria, library or other rooms and services that are available to other children his or her age)	______
14. Using educational materials and equipment available to other children in his or her classroom, or using materials and equipment that have been modified for your child (e.g., books, computers, chairs, and desks)	______
15. Communicating with other children and adults at school	______
HOME AND COMMUNITY LIVING ACTIVITIES	
16. Household activities (e.g., preparing some meals, doing laundry, washing dishes)	______
17. Shopping and managing money (e.g., shopping at stores, working out correct change)	______
18. Managing daily schedule (e.g., doing and completing daily activities on time; organizing and adjusting time and schedule when needed)	______
19. Using transportation to get around in the community (e.g., to and from school, work, social or leisure activities). Driving vehicle or using public transportation are both applicable	______
20. Work activities and responsibilities (e.g., task completion, punctuality, attendance, and getting along with supervisors and co-workers)	______
TOTAL SCORE:	______

Acknowledgement: From Bedell, G. M. (2004). Developing a follow-up survey focused on participation of children and youth with acquired brain injuries after discharge from inpatient rehabilitation. *NeuroRehabilitation*, *19*(3), 191–205, Appendix A, pp. 202–203, reproduced with permission of IOS Press.

Community Integration Measure (CIM)

McColl, Davies, Carlson, Johnston, and Minnes (2001)

Source

Items for the CIM are available in the appendix to McColl et al. (2001) and are also reproduced below.

Purpose

The CIM is a self-rating scale developed for people with acquired brain impairment (ABI). It is one of the very small number of client-centred measures, focusing on the underlying subjective "experience of belonging and participating" (McColl et al., 2001, p. 433).

Item description

The CIM comprises 10 items, using the language of the participants. The items cover four factors capturing the clients' experience of community integration: Assimilation (acceptance, conformity and orientation; 4 items), Social support (2 items), Occupation (both productive and leisure; 2 items), and Independent living (2 items).

Scale development

Early revisions of the World Health Organization (WHO) construct of participation (WHO, 2001) informed the development of the CIM, as did the personal perspectives of community integration by people with ABI. McColl et al. (1998) conducted monthly interviews with a group of 18 people with ABI during the first year after discharge from rehabilitation units in Canada. This study, using qualitative methodology, was the basis for item development. The authors noted that a special feature of the CIM was that it did not make assumptions about the quality of independence or relationships. Thus McColl and colleagues (2001) wanted their scale to measure successful (as opposed to independent) community living, arguing that "independent participation is (not) a sign of greater integration than is supported or mutual coparticipation" (p. 430).

Administration procedures, response format and scoring

The CIM is designed to be administered to the client either in face-to-face interview or by telephone. It is also appropriate for self-administration and only basic literacy skills are required. Administration time is 3 to 5 minutes.

Responses are made on a 5-point rating scale: 1 (always disagree), 2 (sometimes disagree), 3 (neutral), 4 (sometimes agree), 5 (always agree). A total score is used (range: 10–50), with higher scores indicating better community integration.

Psychometric properties

McColl et al. (2001) reported results of a validity study on the CIM. Three samples were used: 41 people with moderately-severe ABI (age $M = 35.4$ years, $SD = 10.7$), 15 family members (age $M = 55.2$ years, $SD = 13.3$) and 36 college students (age $M = 22.9$ years, $SD = 4.1$). Evaluation of concurrent validity was made difficult by the absence of a suitable "gold standard", but was explored with the Community Integration Questionnaire (CIQ) and Interpersonal Support Evaluation List (ISEL). Construct validity was established by examining group differences and the underlying structure of the scale. An initial principal components analysis (PCA) on the combined samples ($n = 92$) yielded a one-component solution; other factor solutions were examined, and the authors considered the two-factor solution (Belonging and Independent participation), accounting for 58% of the variance, to be "readily interpretable". The factor structure of Reistetter, Spencer, Trujillo, and Abreu (2005) in their study of 51 adults with ABI (mainly traumatic) and a control group ($n = 40$) differed from that of McColl et al. Three components were extracted, accounting for 64% of the variance: Support, Occupation, Independence. Items from the last two components had complete overlap with the Independent participation component of McColl et al. Reistetter et al. also examined concurrent validity using a revised version of the CIQ (CIQ-R) and the Satisfaction with Life Scale

(SWLS). Results from McColl et al., except where otherwise stated, are summarized in Box 8.2.

Box 8.2

Validity:	Criterion: *Concurrent*: with CIQ: $r = .34$ – with ISEL: $r = .43$
	Reistetter et al.: with CIQ-R: $r = .34$ – with SWLS: $r = .52$
	Construct: *Internal consistency:* Cronbach alpha: .87 (self: .83, family .92, students .78)
	Factor analysis: 2 factors: Belonging (5 items), Independent participation (5 items)
	Reistetter et al.: 3 factors: Support (5 items), Occupation (3 items), Independence (2 items)
	Convergent/divergent: Reistetter et al.: higher correlation with similar constructs (with CIQ-R-Social: $r = .58$); lower correlation with dissimilar constructs (with CIQ-R-Home: $r = .10$, CIQ-R-Productive: $r = .11$)
	Discriminant: ABI $M = 28.8$ ($SD = 7.7$) vs family $M = 32.0$ ($SD = 8.4$) vs students $M = 33.9$ ($SD = 4.4$); $F = 5.5, p < .006$
	Reistetter et al.: ABI $M = 42.65$ ($SD = 7.65$) vs controls $M = 45.65$ ($SD = 7.26$); $t = 2.30, p = .02$
Reliability:	Inter-rater: Not applicable
	Test–retest: No information available
Responsiveness:	No information available

Comment

Client-centred measures are increasingly recognized as providing an essential perspective of community integration, and the CIM is an important contributor to this new generation of instruments. A great deal of attention was paid to its development resulting in an appealing instrument that has successfully achieved the difficult task of quantifying a qualitative construct. It provides a valid and comprehensive yet brief evaluation of community integration from the client's perspective, using an easy administration and scoring format. The quantitative score derived from the CIM makes it potentially very useful for both research and programme evaluation, although in this respect information on temporal stability and responsiveness are required. Content and construct validity of the CIM are well established. Correlation coefficients with objective measures, such as the CIQ have been lower than with instruments taking client-centred approaches, such as measures of satisfaction. This suggests the commonality between the CIM and instruments measuring the more objective, factual aspects of community integration is limited (only 12% with CIQ) indicating the need for both types of measures in order to obtain a comprehensive picture of a client's community integration.

Key references

McColl, M. A., Carlson, P., Johnston, J., Minnes, P., Shue, K., Davies, D., et al. (1998). The definition of community integration: Perspectives of people with brain injuries. *Brain Injury*, *12*(1), 15–30.

McColl, M. A., Davies, D., Carlson, P., Johnston, J., & Minnes, P. (2001). The Community Integration Measure: Development and preliminary validation. *Archives of Physical Medicine and Rehabilitation*, *82*(4), 429–434.

Reistetter, T. A., Spencer, J. C., Trujillo, L., & Abreu, B. C. (2005). Examining the Community Integration Measure (CIM): A replication study with life satisfaction. *NeuroRehabilitation*, *20*(2), 139–148.

World Health Organization. (2001). *International classification of functioning, disability and health*. Geneva: World Health Organization.

Community Integration Measure

McColl, Davies, Carlson, Johnston, and Minnes (2001)

Name: **Administered by:** **Date:**

Instructions: For each of the following statements, please indicate whether you agree or disagree

1. I feel like part of this community, like I belong here
☐ Always agree ☐ Sometimes agree ☐ Neutral ☐ Sometimes disagree ☐ Always disagree

2. I know my way around this community
☐ Always agree ☐ Sometimes agree ☐ Neutral ☐ Sometimes disagree ☐ Always disagree

3. I know the rules in this community and I can fit in with them
☐ Always agree ☐ Sometimes agree ☐ Neutral ☐ Sometimes disagree ☐ Always disagree

4. I feel that I am accepted in this community
☐ Always agree ☐ Sometimes agree ☐ Neutral ☐ Sometimes disagree ☐ Always disagree

5. I can be independent in this community
☐ Always agree ☐ Sometimes agree ☐ Neutral ☐ Sometimes disagree ☐ Always disagree

6. I like where I'm living now
☐ Always agree ☐ Sometimes agree ☐ Neutral ☐ Sometimes disagree ☐ Always disagree

7. There are people I feel close to in this community
☐ Always agree ☐ Sometimes agree ☐ Neutral ☐ Sometimes disagree ☐ Always disagree

8. I know a number of people in this community well enough to say hello and have them say hello back
☐ Always agree ☐ Sometimes agree ☐ Neutral ☐ Sometimes disagree ☐ Always disagree

9. There are things that I can do in this community for fun in my free time
☐ Always agree ☐ Sometimes agree ☐ Neutral ☐ Sometimes disagree ☐ Always disagree

10. I have something to do in this community during the main part of my day that is useful and productive
☐ Always agree ☐ Sometimes agree ☐ Neutral ☐ Sometimes disagree ☐ Always disagree

TOTAL SCORE:_______

Coding: 5 = Always agree; 4 = Sometimes agree; 3 = Neutral; 2 = Sometimes disagree; 1 = Always disagree

Acknowledgement: From McColl, M. A. et al. (2001). The Community Integration Measure: Development and preliminary validation. *Archives of Physical Medicine and Rehabilitation*, *82*(4), 429–434, reprinted with permission of the American Congress of Rehabilitation Medicine and the American Academy of Physical Medicine and Rehabilitation and Elsevier.

Community Integration Questionnaire (CIQ)

Willer, Rosenthal, Kreutzer, Gordon, and Rempel (1993)

Source

Items for the CIQ are reproduced in Willer, Ottenbacher, and Coad (1994b) and appear below. The items, along with other information including scoring procedures and psychometric properties, are also available from the website of the Center for Outcome Measurement in Brain Injury (http://www.tbims.org/combi/ciq/index.html).

Purpose

The CIQ was designed as a self-rating scale developed to measure community integration, "the converse of handicap" (Willer et al., 1993, p. 76). It was originally developed for people with traumatic brain injury (TBI) for use in the USA TBI Model Systems (TBIMS) data set.

Item description

The CIQ comprises 15 items in three subscales: Home integration (5 items), Social integration (6 items) and Productive activities (4 items). The focus of the items is on objective, quantifiable information (e.g., hours of work, frequency of contact with friends).

Scale development

Development of the CIQ arose from a 2-day consensus conference in 1990 of a group of 14 people including rehabilitation clinicians, researchers and consumers (Willer, Linn, & Allen, 1994a). An initial pool of 47 items was generated in three domains (home integration, social roles and productive activity). The items were piloted with a group of 49 people with TBI (aged 16–79 years) living in the community. Principal component analysis was used to reduce the item pool to 15 items in the three domains described in Willer et al. (1994a). Dijkers (1997) raised concerns about the small sample size and statistical procedures used in development of the item content. In response to this, Sander, Fuchs, High, Hall, Kreutzer, and Rosenthal (1999) re-examined the factor structure of the CIQ in a sample of 312 patients with TBI using a 14-item version (omitting the child-care item). On the basis of the results, two items were moved to different subscales (finances from Social to Home, travel from Productive to Social). Additionally, it was recommended that one item (shopping frequency) be excluded, thereby resulting in a 13-item CIQ.

Administration procedures, response format and scoring

The CIQ was designed to be completed by people with TBI, with assistance from an interviewer/informant if necessary. Telephone administration is also common. Additionally, a computerized version of the CIQ is available. Administration time is reported as less than 15 minutes.

Responses are coded, with scoring for most items using a 3-point scale from 0 (corresponding to the poorest response) to 2 (corresponding to the best response). Using the original CIQ, the total score ranges from 0 to 29, with higher scores indicating better community integration. Subscale score ranges are as follows: Home: 0 to 10; Social: 0 to 12; Productive: 0 to 7. In the revised 13-item CIQ of Sander et al. (1999), the corresponding maximum scores for the subscales are Home (10), Social (10) and Productive (5), with the maximum score being 25.

Normative and comparative data are available in Willer et al. (1993). Normative data were derived from a convenience sample of 237 (aged 18–91 years) recruited from a county fair in New York State, USA. Comparison data are also provided for 352 people with TBI living in the community who were recruited from a head injury association in Ontario, Canada, along with 94 people from the TBIMS.

Psychometric properties

The measurement properties of the CIQ have been examined in various samples (see Dijkers, 1997 for a review). The initial report on the CIQ provided data from a sample of 16 people with moderate to severe TBI and their family members (Willer et al., 1993). The participants completed the CIQ on two occasions approximately 10 days apart (type of reliability coefficients were not specified in this report). Evidence was provided for hypothesized patterns of similar and dissimilar constructs between the CIQ and the Craig Handicap Assessment and Reporting Technique (CHART). In a sample of 59 patients discharged from the TBIMS, information was provided on the correspondence between patient and family member. Data on discriminant validity are available from Willer et al. (1994b) who compared CIQ scores of 310 people with TBI (age $M = 35.1$ years, range 18–74) recruited from the Ontario Head Injury Association, Canada, and a subset ($n = 211$) of the normative group (age $M = 34.29$ years, range 18–91). Additionally, a subset of the TBI group ($n = 304$) was divided into those who lived independently ($n = 57$), in supported accommodation ($n = 207$) or in an institution ($n = 40$). Corrigan and Deming (1995) used the CIQ in a study of 46 people with TBI and 171 people with other neurological and non-neurological disabilities. Retrospective premorbid ratings on the CIQ were made, as well as prospective assessments at follow-up 3 to 6 months post-trauma, the latter set of data being reported below. The factor analysis conducted by Sander et al. (1999) with 312 people with TBI described earlier, yielded three factors accounting for 51% of the variance. One item (frequency of shopping) loaded on two factors, the remaining 13 items clearly loading on specific factors. Sander et al. additionally examined concurrent validity with the Functional Independence Measure (FIM), Functional Assessment Measure (FAM), and Disability Rating Scale (DRS). Data on responsiveness are available from Cicerone, Mott, Azulay, and Friel (2004), who compared an intensive therapy programme with standard treatment in 56 people with TBI. Results from Willer et al. (1993), except where otherwise stated, are shown in Box 8.3.

Box 8.3

Validity	Criterion: *Concurrent:* with CHART-Total: Family: Total score: .70 (subscale range: .51–.58); TBI: Total score: .62 (subscale range: .42–.50)
	Sander et al.: with DRS: Total score: $r = -.47$ (subscale range: $r = -.25$ to $r = -.46$)
	Construct: *Internal consistency:* Corrigan and Deming: Cronbach alpha: TBI: Total score .84 (subscale range: .26–.95; alpha < .8 for 2/3 subscales – Social, Productive) – Other disabilities: Total score .90 (subscale range: .58–.90; alpha < .8 for 2/3 subscales – Social, Productive)
	Factor analysis: Sander et al.: 3 factors: Home (5 items), Social (5 items), Productive (3 items)
	Convergent/divergent: higher correlation with similar constructs (CIQ-Productive with CHART-Occupation: .72); lower correlation with dissimilar constructs (CIQ-Home with CHART-Social: .01); but some hypotheses did not hold up (e.g., CIQ-Social with CHART-Social: .25)
	Discriminant: Willer et al. (1994b): TBI $M = 13.02$ ($SD = 6.02$) vs Controls $M = 20.71$ ($SD = 3.21$); $p < .001$. TBI group also scored lower on all CIQ subscales ($p < .001$)
	Willer et al. (1994b): TBI-Living Independently $M = 20.51$ ($SD = 4.63$) vs Supported $M = 13.29$ ($SD = 4.89$) vs Institution $M = 10.35$ ($SD = 6.55$); Kruskal Wallis ANOVA = 108.35, $p < .001$
Reliability:	Inter-rater: No information available
	Test–retest: 10 days: Family: Total score: .97 (range .90–.97); TBI: Total score: .91 (range .83–.93)
Responsiveness:	Cicerone et al.: Intensive group: Pre-treatment $M = 11.6$ ($SD = 4.6$) vs Post-treatment $M = 16.8$ ($SD = 4.2$), $d = 1.13$ – Standard group: Pre-treatment $M = 13.7$ ($SD = 4.4$) vs Post-treatment $M = 16.1$ ($SD = 5.4$), $d = 0.55$ – main effect for time ($F = 40.49$, $p < .001$) and significant interaction effect ($F = 5.66$, $p = .02$)

Comment

The CIQ is very widely used, particularly in the USA where it was developed for use in the TBIMS data set. The strengths of the scale are that it samples the commonly measured domains of functioning relevant to community integration after TBI, it is relatively brief, and it can be administered either as an in-person interview or by telephone. Its psychometric properties are also acceptable, demonstrating good internal consistency for the total score, moderate correlations with similar measures and evidence of construct validity. It shows temporal stability, yet is responsive to real changes occurring in the patient with a large effect size. Nonetheless, a number of reviews have been critical about features of the CIQ (Dijkers, 1997; Hall, Mann, High, Wright, Kreutzer, & Wood, 1996), including item content. Additionally, the quantitative focus of the items in the Occupational and Social subscales (e.g., hours of work, frequency of activity) may not capture qualitative changes in functioning (e.g., type of work, quality of social relationships). Efforts have been made to improve the measurement characteristics of the CIQ (e.g., 13-item CIQ of Sander et al., 1999). More recently, Johnston, Goverover, and Dijkers (2005) have reverted to the original 47-item version used in the scale development process, which they labelled CIQ–2, and using data from 162 people it was a good fit to a Rasch model, providing empirical support for two dimensions (Functional/instrumental and Social/recreational).

Key references

Cicerone, K. D., Mott, T., Azulay, J., & Friel, J. C. (2004). Community integration and satisfaction with functioning after intensive cognitive rehabilitation for traumatic brain injury. *Archives of Physical Medicine and Rehabilitation*, *85*, 943–950.

Corrigan, J. D., & Deming, R. (1995). Psychometric characteristics of the Community Integration Questionnaire: Replication and extension. *Journal of Head Trauma Rehabilitation*, *10*(4), 41–53.

Dijkers, M. (1997). Measuring the long-term outcomes of traumatic brain injury: A review of the Community Integration Questionnaire. *Journal of Head Trauma Rehabilitation*, *12*(6), 74–91.

Hall, K. M., Mann, N., High, W. M., Wright, J., Kreutzer, J. S., & Wood, D. (1996). Functional measures after traumatic brain injury: Ceiling effects of FIM, FIM + FAM, DRS, and CIQ. *Journal of Head Trauma Rehabilitation*, *11*(5), 27–39.

Johnston, M. V., Goverover, Y., & Dijkers, M. (2005). Community activities and individuals' satisfaction with them: Quality of life in the first year after traumatic brain injury. *Archives of Physical Medicine and Rehabilitation*, *86*, 735–745.

Sander, A. M., Fuchs, K. L., High, W. M., Hall, K. M., Kreutzer, J. S., & Rosenthal, M. (1999). The Community Integration Questionnaire revisited: An assessment of factor structure and validity. *Archives of Physical Medicine and Rehabilitation*, *80*, 1303–1308.

Willer, B., Linn, R., & Allen, K. (1994a). Community integration and barriers to integration for individuals with brain injury. In M. A. J. Finlayson & S. H. Garner (Eds.), *Brain injury rehabilitation: Clinical considerations*. Baltimore: Williams & Wilkins.

Willer, B., Ottenbacher, K. J., & Coad, M. L. (1994b). The Community Integration Questionnaire: A comparative examination. *American Journal of Physical Medicine and Rehabilitation*, *73*(2), 103–111.

Willer, B., Rosenthal, M., Kreutzer, J. S., Gordon, W. A., & Rempel, R. (1993). Assessment of community integration following rehabilitation for traumatic brain injury. *Journal of Head Trauma Rehabilitation*, *8*(2), 75–87.

Community Integration Questionnaire

Willer, Rosenthal, Kreutzer, Gordon, and Rempel (1993)

Name: **Administered by:** **Date:**

HOME INTEGRATION	**RESPONSE**	**SCORE**
1. Who usually does shopping for groceries or other necessities in your household?	______	______
2. Who usually prepares meals in your household?	______	______
3. In your home who usually does normal everyday housework?	______	______
4. Who usually cares for the children in your home?	______	______
5. Who usually plans social arrangements such as get togethers with family and friends?	______	______
	HOME INTEGRATION:	______

SOCIAL INTEGRATION

6. Who usually looks after your personal finances, such as banking and paying bills?	______	______
Can you tell me approximately how many times **a month** you now usually participate in the following activities *outside your home*?		
7. Shopping	______	______
8. Leisure activities such as movies, sports, restaurants, etc.	______	______
9. Visiting friends or relatives	______	______
10. When you participate in leisure activities do you usually do this alone or with others?	______	______
11. Do you have a best friend with whom you confide?	______	______
	SOCIAL INTEGRATION:	______

INTEGRATION INTO PRODUCTIVE ACTIVITIES

12. How often do you travel outside the home? ______ ______
13. Please choose the answer below that best corresponds to your current (during the past month) work situation:
    - ☐ Full time employment (more than 20 hrs per week)
    - ☐ Part time employment (20 hrs per week or less)
    - ☐ Not working, but actively looking for work
    - ☐ Not working, not looking for work
    - ☐ Not applicable, retired due to age
    - ☐ Volunteer job in the community ______
14. Please choose the answer below that best corresponds to your current (during the past month) school or training programme situation:
    - ☐ Full time
    - ☐ Part time
    - ☐ Not attending school or training programme ______
15. In the past month, how often did you engage in volunteer activities? ______ ______

PRODUCTIVE ACTIVITIES: ______

TOTAL SCORE: ______

Acknowledgement: From Willer, B. et al. (1994). The Community Integration Questionnaire: A comparative examination. *American Journal of Physical Medicine and Rehabilitation*, *73*(2), 103–111, p. 110, by permission of the author.

Community Integration Questionnaire – Scoring Instructions

Willer, Rosenthal, Kreutzer, Gordon, and Rempel (1993)

<table>
<tr><th>HOME INTEGRATION</th><th>SOCIAL INTEGRATION</th><th>PRODUCTIVITY</th></tr>
<tr><td>Item 1: Shopping
Score: 2 = yourself alone
1 = yourself and someone else
0 = someone else</td><td>Item 6: Finances
Score: 2 = yourself alone
1 = yourself and someone else
0 = someone else</td><td>Item 12: Travel outside the home
Score: 2 = almost every day
1 = almost every week
0 = seldom/never (< once per week)</td></tr>
<tr><td>Item 2: Meal preparation
Score: 2 = yourself alone
1 = yourself and someone else
0 = someone else</td><td>Item 7: Shopping – times per month
Score: 2 = 5 or more times
1 = 1 to 4 times
0 = never</td><td rowspan="4">Items 13 to 15, although collected individually, are combined to form one variable, Job/School:
Score: 5 = works full-time (> 20 hours/ week)AND attends school part-time
OR
attends school full-time AND works part-time (< 20 hours per week)
4 = attends school full-time
OR
works full-time (> 20 hours/ week)
3 = attends school part-time
OR
works part-time (< 20 hours per week
2 = actively looking for work
AND/OR
volunteers 5 or more times per month
1 = volunteers 1 to 4 times per month
AND
not working, not looking for work, not in school
0 = not working, not looking for work, not going to school, no volunteer activities</td></tr>
<tr><td>Item 3: Housework
Score: 2 = yourself alone
1 = yourself and someone else
0 = someone else</td><td>Item 8: Leisure activities – times per month
Score: 2 = 5 or more times
1 = 1 to 4 times
0 = never</td></tr>
<tr><td>Item 4: Care of the children
Score: 2 = yourself alone
1 = yourself and someone else
0 = someone else
* = not applicable/no children under 17 years of age in the home (score the average of items 1, 2, 3 and 5)</td><td>Item 9: Visiting friends or relatives – times per month
Score: 2 = 5 or more times
1 = 1 to 4 times
0 = never</td></tr>
<tr><td rowspan="2">Item 5: Plans social arrangements
Score: 2 = yourself alone
1 = yourself and someone else
0 = someone else</td><td>Item 10: Participating in leisure
Score: 2 = combination of family and friends
2 = mostly friends without head injury
1 = mostly with family members
1 = mostly with friends with head injury
0 = mostly alone</td></tr>
<tr><td>Item 11: Best friend
Score: 2 = yes
0 = no</td><td>If retired because of age, the Job/ School variable is based on Item 15 (volunteer activities) only.
Score: 4 = 5 or more times in the past month
2 = 1 to 4 times in the past month
0 = never</td></tr>
<tr><td>Total for Home Integration: ____</td><td>Total for Social Integration: ____</td><td>Total for Productivity: _______</td></tr>
<tr><td colspan="3">Total for CIQ (Home + Social + Productivity): _______</td></tr>
</table>

Acknowledgement: Scoring format adapted from Dijkers, M. (2000). *The Community Integration Questionnaire*. The Center for Outcome Measurement in Brain Injury, http//www.tbims.org/combi/ciq, accessed 10 November 2008.*

* This citation is for the COMBI web material. Dr Dijkers is not the scale author for the CIQ.

Community Outcome Scale (COS)

Stilwell, Stilwell, Hawley, and Davies (1998)

Source

An appendix to Stilwell et al. (1998) provides the COS dimensions and response categories, which are reproduced below. The interview from which ratings are derived, however, is only described in general terms in the paper.

Purpose

The COS is a clinician rating scale, derived from results of an interview, which was developed to measure handicap in people with traumatic brain injury (TBI). It is client-centred in that it is "a measure that focuses on the flexibility of the community in minimising barriers, and the impact of particular problems in particular circumstances, rather than on the objective severity of individual problems" (Stilwell et al., 1998, p. 527). The COS has three aims: (i) to measure the impact of an individual's problems on their community participation, (ii) to be sensitive to community response, and (iii) to discriminate between impairments/activities versus handicap.

Item description

The COS represents a summary rating of four "dimensions" using information obtained from a semi-structured interview. Three of the six original handicap domains from the *International Classification of Impairments, Disabilities and Handicaps* (World Health Organization, 1980) are included: Mobility, Occupation, and Social integration. A fourth dimension, Engagement, was added to capture "the extent to which an individual is enabled to become a valued member of the community" (Stilwell et al., 1998, p. 523). Each dimension commences with an operational definition, followed by detailed descriptions for each response category.

Scale development

Development of the COS was based on semi-structured interviews administered to 563 people with TBI and their families recruited from 10 community-based rehabilitation services in England, UK (Stilwell et al., 1998). The interviews, which were recorded in free text, focused on current problems and strengths, drawing on the WHO (1980) model of handicap. Interviews were described as being of "a funnel design; that is, they were initially semi-structured, with more structured questions asked as the interview progressed" (Stilwell, Stilwell, Hawley, & Davies, 1999, p. 282). Resulting data were processed via a specially designed computer program that streamlined the procedures: sorting responses into problem areas; classifying problems as impairments, disabilities and other problems; coding the impairments/disabilities; identifying handicap dimensions. The four dimensions of the COS were developed on the basis of the problems reported.

Administration procedures, response format and scoring

In the original study, COS ratings were based on a semi-structured interview with clients and their families, in which they were asked "to describe their current problems and strengths" (Stilwell et al., 1998, p. 523). Information derived from the interview is then used to make ratings on the COS dimensions.

Each dimension contains a 7-point rating scale, ranging from 0 (no problem, or problem fully compensated) to 6 (no longer living in the community). Each point has individually scripted responses, pertinent to the dimension, thereby assisting in translating the data gathered from the semi-structured interview to the rating scale. The COS uses the four scores separately (one for each dimension), rather than a total score. Higher scores represent poorer accessibility to the community.

Psychometric properties

Limited psychometric data are available on the COS. The only published psychometric study is that of Stilwell et al. (1998) for which information is shown in Box 8.4. Their study provided data on concurrent validity in a large sample (initially $n = 563$) with TBI (aged 16–65 years) representing the range of injury severity (6.5% mild, 25% moderate, and 68% severe) who were followed prospectively and interviewed at 3, 18 and 36 months post-trauma. Comparison measures were the Functional Independence Measure and Functional Assessment Measure (FIM+FAM) and the Hospital Anxiety and Depression Scale (HADS).

Box 8.4

Validity:	Criterion: *Concurrent*: with FIM+FAM at 18 months ($n = 325$): Motor scale: Mobility: $r = -.62$, Social: $r = -.52$, Occupation: $r = -.57$, Engagement: $r = -.55$ – Cognitive scale: Mobility: $r = -.62$, Social: $r = -.64$, Occupation: $r = -.66$, Engagement: $r = -.67$ Engagement with HADS Anxiety: $r = .45$, with HADS Depression: $r = .55$
Reliability:	Inter-rater: No information available Test–retest: No information available
Responsiveness:	No information available

Comment

The COS adopts a client-centred perspective, which is evident from the response categories that "were designed to measure the failure of communities to remain accessible, rather than the failure of individuals to access them" (Stilwell et al., 1999, p. 289). Client-centred measures are still relatively few in number, and thus the COS is a potentially useful measure. An appealing feature is the use of clinicians' classification and rating of patients' responses rather than merely recording the person's perceptions on a simple rating scale. This approach has two advantages – it allows the clinician to synthesize the information into a clinically meaningful result and it bypasses possible problems when self-rating scales are used, such as impairments in insight and awareness affecting reliability and validity of the response. As the authors acknowledge, however, further work on its psychometric properties is required. Indeed, at this stage information is only available on concurrent validity and the COS requires a more complete psychometric work-up. Moreover, the original study used the semi-structured interview to derive the COS dimensions, and it is not made clear how the scale is to be used – whether the semi-structured interview is administered from which ratings are made or whether it lends itself to being completed by a clinician who has knowledge of the patient.

Key references

Stilwell, P., Stilwell, J., Hawley, C., & Davies, C. (1998). Measuring outcome in community-based rehabilitation services for people who have suffered traumatic brain injury: The Community Outcome Scale. *Clinical Rehabilitation*, *12*(6), 521–531.

Stilwell, P., Stilwell, J., Hawley, C., & Davies, C. (1999). The National Traumatic Brain Injury Study: Assessing outcomes across settings. *Neuropsychological Rehabilitation*, *9*(3/4), 277–293.

World Health Organization. (1980). *International classification of impairments, disabilities and handicaps*. Geneva: World Health Organization.

Community Outcome Scale

Stilwell, Stilwell, Hawley, and Davies (1998)

Name:	**Administered by:**	**Date:**

MOBILITY

Definition: The mobility dimension reflects the response of the client's customary communities, new communities or local services to restrictions on the client's movement within a familiar environment following head injury.

0 No problem, or problem fully compensated

1 Strategies or services are in place that enable the client to move freely within his or her customary environment, although not quite in the same way as previously

2 Restrictions on mobility mean that customary communities are more difficult to access, although they continue to be accessible

3 The client's customary environment is noisy or busy or otherwise threatening to the extent that his or her mobility is limited, and there are constraints on the choice of transport

4 A number of modes of transport are unavailable to the client, for whatever reason, and he or she avoids certain environments, with the result that some customary communities or activities are no longer accessible

5 The client's customary communities or activities are almost totally inaccessible, because no stratagems have been offered that make the local environment less hostile

6 No longer living in the community

OCCUPATION

Definition: Occupation is the degree of receptivity at the client's workplace, or the degree to which he or she is enabled to learn new and valued skills, and to make a meaningful contribution to the life of his or her community, without experiencing undue stress or being forced to sacrifice other valued roles and activities.

0 No problem, or problem fully compensated

1 Client continues to follow his or her premorbid occupation or studies, but the demands of these may impose some stress or tiredness, or impinge on other customary roles and activities

2 On the whole the client is able meaningfully to occupy his or her time but some adjustments need to be made in the work environment to reduce stress levels, and the client may experience periods of inactivity

3 It is difficult to match the client's level of skill with his or her premorbid work environment but there is not sufficient flexibility in his or her customary communities to accommodate this, so that the client is unable to exercise remaining skills or learn new ones, or is subject to undue stress

4 The client's premorbid occupation or activities are no longer suited to his or her changed circumstances, and are no longer open to him or her, but no suitable alternatives have been found, so that the client is largely unoccupied during the day. Or the pressure of continuing to fulfil responsibilities incurred prior to the accident is causing unacceptable strain and fatigue and threatening other roles

5 The client either has nothing to do, or continues at great cost to fulfil premorbid responsibilities that are no longer suited to his or her skills or capabilities

6 The client is not currently living in the community

SOCIAL INTEGRATION

Definition: Social integration is relevant to a scale ranging from complete acceptance by family, friends, work colleagues and the wider community, to complete isolation.

0 No problem, or problem fully compensated

1 Friends and social contacts may be a little less welcoming, but the client still sees them regularly and feels confident in their company. Loss of sporting or work skills may result in some restriction on social activities

2 Accessing customary communities presents difficulties, so that social contacts are less frequent

3 A number of factors combine to make the client's customary communities less accessible or less welcoming, and the resulting loss of social contact has not been adequately compensated

4 Opportunities for leisure activities or for making new friends are strictly limited, while old friends have largely dropped away. Relationships within the family may be under strain

5 No provision has been made to address the client's difficulties so that customary communities are virtually inaccessible, or perceived as threatening and unwelcoming

6 The client is not currently living in the community

ENGAGEMENT

Definition: Engagement is the degree of receptivity of the client's customary communities, or the degree to which he or she is enabled to access new communities that allow him or her to achieve status, recognition and self-fulfilment.

0 No problem, or problem fully compensated

1 Reflects a less welcoming attitude on the part of the client's customary communities, which is enough to affect his or her self-esteem and confidence to some degree, although they continue to be accessible

2 Customary communities may be unwilling to accommodate changed roles, resulting in stress and tension at work, disruptions in family dynamics, and marital stress

3 The client experiences feelings of rejection by customary communities, and grief for uncompensated loss of skills

4 The client finds previous work, social and family communities increasingly inaccessible, and has no confidence that they will become more accepting in the future

5 Previous communities now appear so threatening or unwelcoming that no attempt is made to access them

6 The client is not currently living in the community

Acknowledgement: From Stilwell, P. et al. (1998). Measuring outcome in community-based rehabilitation services for people who have suffered traumatic brain injury: The Community Outcomes Scale. *Clinical Rehabilitation*, *12*(6), 521–531, pp. 529–531, by permission of Sage Publications Ltd.

Craig Handicap Assessment and Reporting Technique (CHART)

Whiteneck, Charlifue, Gerhart, Overholser, and Richardson (1992)

Source

The recording form, manual and other information on the CHART are available from the website of the Center for Outcome Measurement in Brain Injury (http://www.tbims.org/combi/chart/index.html). Items are available in an appendix to Whiteneck et al. (1992) and, for the Cognitive independence dimension in Mellick, Walker, Brooks, and Whiteneck (1999). The CHART items are reproduced below. A 19-item short form of the CHART is also available.

Purpose

The CHART is a clinician rating scale, developed as a "simple, objective measure" of handicap in the community setting. It was originally designed for people with spinal cord injury (SCI), but has been validated in groups with multiple sclerosis (MS), stroke and traumatic brain injury (TBI; Mellick et al., 1999).

Item description

The most recent version of the CHART contains 32 items, in six dimensions: Physical independence (3 items), Cognitive independence (5 items), Mobility (9 items), Occupation (7 items), Social integration (6 items), and Economic self-sufficiency (2 items). Items sample objective, quantifiable information (e.g., number of hours, occasions, contacts) or other factual information (e.g., cost, access), and responses are recorded for later coding.

Scale development

The dimensions of the CHART were developed in accordance with the World Health Organization model of handicap (WHO, 1980). Originally, five of the six WHO handicap dimensions were covered (27 items): physical independence, mobility, occupation, social integration and economic self-sufficiency. The subsequent development of the CHART Cognitive independence dimension (5 items) was designed to address the final handicap dimension of the WHO model (Mellick et al., 1999). Although this sixth WHO dimension is labelled "orientation", it actually refers to a broad set of constructs "including the planes of seeing, listening, touching, speaking, and assimilation of these functions by the mind" (WHO, 1980, p. 185). The 19-item short form of the CHART was derived using a multidimensional analysis.

The item development process followed a literature review that did not identify any standardized, quantifiable measure examining all pertinent handicap domains (Whiteneck et al., 1988/1992). A team of rehabilitation and research professionals met regularly and discussed suitable items for inclusion in the scale. The aim was to construct items that "identified the degree to which respondents fulfilled the roles typically expected of able-bodied members of their society" (Whiteneck et al., 1992, p. 520), focusing on objectively observable criteria.

Weights were developed for scoring purposes, based on estimates of values that society places on aspects of social roles. For example, for occupation, "it was concluded that society values work, school, homemaking, and home maintenance substantially more than volunteer work, recreation, or other self-improvement activities. Therefore, the first four items were given twice the weight of the last three items" (Whiteneck et al., 1992, p. 520). Pilot testing was conducted with people with SCI, as well as people without disabilities, to calibrate scoring procedures. One hundred people with SCI nominated an age- and sex-matched peer who did not have disability, resulting in 88 people (20 females and 68 males). These people were administered the CHART and weights were applied to their scores, adjusted to ensure that the majority of the sample scored 100 points for each dimension. An independent study of 135 people with SCI investigated various item weightings but there was little difference in scores and they were "highly intercorrelated" suggesting "the choice of item weights was not a critical issue" (Whiteneck et al., 1992, p. 522).

The Cognitive independence dimension (Mellick et al., 1999) was developed after the original version of the CHART was first published in 1992. A group of clinicians, researchers and consumers initially generated a preliminary set of items. These were piloted in a series of studies, the largest with 298 people (88 of whom had brain injury), including examination of temporal stability. A set of seven items was then subjected to further testing with 1110 people with a range of conditions, both neurological and non-neurological and patient-proxy agreement was examined in that sample (Mellick et al., 1999). Five items were retained, forming the Cognitive independence dimension.

Administration procedures, response format and scoring

The CHART is designed as an interview, administered either face-to-face or via the telephone. The authors also refer to a mailed-out version, but note that information likely to be elicited via prompts from an interviewer may be lost. Administration time is approximately 15 minutes.

Scoring requires the transformation of raw score responses into weighted scores. This procedure is less straightforward than the scoring procedures of many other scales, but clear scoring guidelines are provided in the manual. Score range for each dimension is 0 to 100, with higher scores indicating less handicap or higher social and community participation. These procedures mean that normative data are not required to interpret CHART scores, which represent the discrepancy from the level achieved by the majority of the normative group.

Psychometric properties

Whiteneck et al. (1992) reported results of the initial reliability and validity studies for 135 people with SCI, aged 16 to 74 years, 2 to 35 years post-trauma and living in the community, who were recruited from regional spinal injury centres in the USA. Discriminant validity was examined by having clinicians rate level of handicap as high ($n = 65$) or low ($n = 70$). Temporal stability was examined over a 1-week period (type of coefficient was not specified). Results of Rasch analysis suggest a well-calibrated scale, with good fit of both items and persons to the model.

Because the CHART was developed with people without acquired brain impairment (ABI), a number of investigators have validated it with people with ABI. A large study was conducted by Walker, Mellick, Brooks, and Whiteneck (2003) who examined 1100 people, 713 of whom had ABI (MS $n = 223$, stroke $n = 248$, TBI $n = 242$). Temporal stability was examined 2 weeks later. Segal and Schall (1995) examined 40 people with stroke and their informants. Inter-rater reliability was examined in a subset of the sample ($n = 8$) whose responses were videotaped and later scored by an independent rater. Concurrent validity was examined with the Functional Independence Measure (FIM), and patterns of correlations with similar and dissimilar constructs assessed convergent and divergent validity. In the course of their study on patient-proxy agreement with approximately 200 people with TBI and their informants, Cusick, Gerhart, and Mellick (2000) also examined 2-week temporal stability. Results from the above studies are shown in Box 8.5.

Box 8.5.

Validity:	Criterion: *Concurrent:* Segal & Schall: with FIM: $r = .41$
	Construct: *Convergent/divergent:* Segal & Schall.: higher correlation with similar constructs (CHART-Physical with FIM: $r = .63$); lower correlation with dissimilar constructs (CHART-Economic with FIM: $r = .05$)
	Walker et al.: Physical independence scores significantly lower in SCI ($M = 84.48$) than TBI ($M = 94.15$); but Cognitive independence scores significantly lower in TBI ($M = 77.44$) than SCI ($M = 93.62$); significant differences across impairment groups ($p < .001$ on total and all dimensions)
	Discriminant: Whiteneck et al. (1992): High handicap – CHART $M = 333$ vs low handicap – CHART $M = 438$; $t = 6.36, p < .001$
Reliability:	Inter-rater: Segal & Schall: ICC = .97
	Test–retest: Whiteneck et al. (1992): 1 week: .93 (dimension range: .80–.95)
	Cusick et al.: 2 week: ICC = .83 (dimension range ICC = .60–.83)
	Walker et al.: 2 week: MS ICC = .92 (dimension range ICC = .75–.89) – stroke ICC = .95 (range ICC = .74–.91) – TBI ICC = .92 (range ICC = .77–.83)
Responsiveness:	No information available

Comment

The CHART was developed for people with SCI, who are predominantly a young group, without brain impairment. Because it was one of the first standardized measures of handicap, its application to people with ABI was examined. Investigators have reported favourably on it for the TBI population (Ponsford, Olver, Nelms, Curran, & Ponsford, 1999), particularly with the inclusion of the Cognitive independence dimension. Some concerns have been voiced by researchers using it with the stroke population, however. Segal and Schall (1995) found that older people were disadvantaged on the Occupational dimension. This was primarily because of the weights, whereby the activities of gainful employment, school and house maintenance receive twice the weights of voluntary work, recreation, and self-improvement activities. They suggested the use of norms for this dimension for older people, but an alternative is the application of weights to reflect the occupational "roles typically expected of able-bodied" *older* people. Additionally, while the focus of the CHART on objective, observable criteria guards against subjective interpretations, this is done at the expense of measuring qualitative factors. Occupation, for example, is examined exclusively from the perspective of number of hours of work activity; social contacts are measured in terms of number of contacts per month. This approach runs the risk of not detecting qualitative changes in the *type* of occupational activity or the *nature* of interpersonal relationships that may have occurred consequent on the ABI. In spite of the foregoing issues encountered in validating an instrument in populations for which it was not developed, the psychometric properties of the CHART are very good, both in the original sample of people with SCI, as well as ABI groups.

Key references

Cusick, C. P., Gerhart, K. A., & Mellick, D. C. (2000). Participant-proxy reliability in traumatic brain injury outcome research. *Journal of Head Trauma Rehabilitation, 15*(1), 739–749.

Mellick, D., Walker, N., Brooks, C. A., & Whiteneck, G. (1999). Incorporating the cognitive independence domain into CHART. *Journal of Rehabilitation Outcomes Measurement, 3*(3), 12–21.

Ponsford, J., Olver, J., Nelms, R., Curran, C., & Ponsford, M. (1999). Outcome measurement in an inpatient and outpatient traumatic brain injury rehabilitation programme. *Neuropsychological Rehabilitation, 9*(3/4), 517–534.

Segal, M. E., & Schall, R. R. (1995). Assessing handicap of stroke survivors. A validation study of the Craig Handicap Assessment and Reporting Technique. *American Journal of Physical Medicine and Rehabilitation, 74*(4), 276–286.

Walker, N., Mellick, D., Brooks, C. A., & Whiteneck, G. G. (2003). Measuring participation across impairment groups using the Craig Handicap Assessment Reporting Technique. *American Journal of Physical Medicine and Rehabilitation, 82*(12), 936–941.

Whiteneck, G. G., Brooks, C. A., Charlifue, S., Gerhart, K. A., Mellick, D., Overholser, D., et al. (1988/1992). *Craig Handicap Assessment and Reporting Technique*. Englewood, CO: Craig Hospital.

Whiteneck, G. G., Charlifue, S. W., Gerhart, K. A., Overholser, J. D., & Richardson, G. N. (1992). Quantifying handicap: A new measure of long-term rehabilitation outcomes. *Archives of Physical Medicine and Rehabilitation, 73*(6), 519–526.

World Health Organization. (1980). *International classification of impairments, disabilities and handicaps*. Geneva: World Health Organization.

Craig Handicap Assessment and Reporting Technique

Whiteneck, Charlifue, Gerhart, Overholser, and Richardson (1992)
and Mellick, Walker, Brooks, and Whiteneck (1999)

Name: **Administered by:** **Date:**

PHYSICAL INDEPENDENCE **SCORE**

1. How many hours in a typical 24-hour day do you have someone with you to provide for personal care activities, such as eating, bathing, dressing, toileting and mobility? (hours paid _______ / hours unpaid _______) _______
2. Not including any regular care as reported above, how many hours in a typical month do you occasionally have assistance with such things as grocery shopping, laundry, housekeeping, or infrequent medical needs because of the disability? _______ _______
3. Who takes responsibility for instructing and directing your attendants and/or caregivers? _______

   _______ Self _______ Someone else _______ Not applicable, does not use attendant care

PHYSICAL DIMENSION SCORE: _______

COGNITIVE INDEPENDENCE

4. How much time is someone with you in your home to assist you with activities that require remembering, decision-making and judgement? _______
   [ ] someone else is always with me to observe or supervise
   [ ] someone else is always around, but they only check on me now and then
   [ ] sometimes I am left alone for an hour or two
   [ ] sometimes I am left alone for most of the day
   [ ] I have been left alone all day and all night, but someone checks in on me
   [ ] I am left alone without anyone checking on me
5. How much of the time is someone with you to help you with remembering, decision-making or judgement when you go away from your home? _______
   [ ] I am restricted in leaving, even with someone else
   [ ] someone is always with me to help with remembering, decision-making or judgement when I go anywhere
   [ ] I go places on my own as long as they are familiar
   [ ] I do not need help going anywhere
6. How often do you have difficulty communicating with other people? _______
   [ ] I almost always have difficulty
   [ ] I sometimes have difficulty
   [ ] I almost never have difficulty
7. How often do you have difficulty remembering important things that you must do? _______
   [ ] I almost always have difficulty
   [ ] I sometimes have difficulty
   [ ] I almost never have difficulty
8. How much of your money do you control? _______
   [ ] none, someone makes all money decisions for me
   [ ] a small amount of spending money is given to me periodically
   [ ] most of my money, but someone does help me make major decisions
   [ ] I make all my own money decisions (or if married, in joint participation with my partner)

COGNITIVE DIMENSION SCORE: _______

MOBILITY **SCORE**

9. On a typical *day* how many hours are you out of bed? _______ _______

10. In a typical *week*, how many days do you get out of your house and go somewhere? _______ _______

11. In the last *year*, how many nights have you spent away from your home (excluding hospitalizations)? _______
    [ ] none
    [ ] 1–2
    [ ] 3–4
    [ ] 5 or more

12. Can you enter and exit your home without any assistance from someone? _______
    [ ] yes
    [ ] no

13. In your home, do you have independent access to your sleeping area, kitchen, bathroom, telephone, and TV (or radio)? _______
    [ ] yes
    [ ] no

14. Can you use your transportation independently? _______
    [ ] yes
    [ ] no

15. Does your transportation allow you to get to all the places you would like to go? _______
    [ ] yes
    [ ] no

16. Does your transportation let you get out whenever you want? _______
    [ ] yes
    [ ] no

17. Can you use your transportation with little or no advance notice? _______
    [ ] yes
    [ ] no

MOBILITY DIMENSION SCORE: _______

OCCUPATION

18. How many hours per week do you spend working in a job for which you get paid? _______ _______

19. How many hours per week do you spend in school working toward a degree or in an accredited technical training programme? (Hours in class and studying) _______ _______

20. How many hours per week do you spend in active homemaking, including parenting, housekeeping and food preparation? _______ _______

21. How many hours per week do you spend in home maintenance activities such as gardening, house repairs, or home improvement? _______ _______

22. How many hours per week do you spend in ongoing volunteer work for an organization? _______ _______

23. How many hours per week do you spend in recreational activities such as sports, exercise, playing cards or going to the movies? Please do not include time spent watching TV or listening to the radio. _______ _______

24. How many hours per week do you spend in other self-improvement activities such as hobbies or leisure reading? Please do not include time spent watching TV or listening to the radio. _______ _______

OCCUPATIONAL DIMENSION SCORE: _______

SOCIAL INTEGRATION **SCORE**

25. Do you live: _______
    - ☐ alone

      OR
    - ☐ (a) with a spouse or significant other
    - ☐ (b) with children (how many) _______
    - ☐ (c) with other relatives (how many) _______
    - ☐ (d) with roommate (how many) _______
    - ☐ (e) with attendant (how many)? _______

26. If you don't live with a spouse, or significant other, are you involved in a romantic relationship? _______
    [ ] yes
    [ ] no

27. How many relatives (not in your household) do you visit, phone or write to at least once a month? _______ _______

28. How many business or organizational associates do you visit, phone, or write to at least once a month? _______ _______

29. How many friends (non-relatives contacted outside business or organizational settings) do you visit, phone or write to at least once a month? _______ _______

30. With how many strangers have you initiated a conversation in the last month (e.g., to ask information or place an order)? _______
    [ ] none
    [ ] 1–2
    [ ] 3–5
    [ ] 6 or more

SOCIAL DIMENSION SCORE: _______

ECONOMIC SELF-SUFFICIENCY

31. Approximately what was the combined annual income in the last year of **all family members in your household?** (Consider all sources, including wages and earnings, disability benefits, pensions and retirement income, income from court settlements, investments and trust funds, child support and alimony, contributions from relatives, and any other source) _______ _______

32. Approximately how much did you pay last year for medical care expenses? (Consider any amounts paid by yourself or the family members of the household and not reimbursed by insurance or benefits) _______ _______

ECONOMIC SELF-SUFFICIENCY DIMENSION SCORE: _______

Acknowledgement: From Whiteneck, G. G. et al. (1992). Quantifying handicap: A new measure of long-term rehabilitation outcomes. *Archives of Physical Medicine and Rehabilitation*, *73*(6), 519–526, pp. 525–526, reprinted with permission of the American Congress of Rehabilitation Medicine and the American Academy of Physical Medicine and Rehabilitation and Elsevier, and David Mellick and Craig Hospital.

Craig Handicap Assessment and Reporting Technique (CHART) – Scoring Instructions

Whiteneck, Brooks, Charlifue, Gerhart, Mellick, Overholser, et al. (1988/1992)

PHYSICAL INDEPENDENCE		COGNITIVE INDEPENDENCE		MOBILITY	
Item 1: Daily care Score: Total the hours of paid and unpaid care	***A*** _____	*(NB: Assign points to responses in items 4 to 8 as follows: Response #1 = 0 points; Response #2 = 1 point; Response #3 = 2 points; Response #4 = 3 points; Response #5 = 4 points; Response #6 = 5 points)*		Item 9: Hours out of bed Score: Multiply number of hours by 2	***A*** ____ × 2 = _____
		Item 4: Score: Assign points for responses 1–6 as above and multiply score by 8	***A*** ____ × 8 = _____		
Item 2: Occasional care Score: Divide the number of hours of occasional care by 30	***B*** ____ / 30 = _____	Item 5: Score: Assign points for responses 1–4 as above and multiply score by 8	***B*** ____ × 8 = _____	Item 10: Days out of house Score: Multiply number of days by 5	***B*** ____ × 5 = _____
	C A + B = _____	Item 6: Score: Assign points for responses 1–3 as above and multiply score by 6	***C*** ____ × 6 = _____	Item 11: Nights away from home Score: No nights out = 0; 1–2 nights out = 10; 3–4 nights out = 15; 5 or more nights out = 20	***C*** ____ × 2 = _____
Item 3: Care directives Score: If respondent directs own caregiver, multiply C by 3. If other directs caregivers, multiply C by 4.	***D*** ____ × 3 or ____ × 4 = _____	Item 7: Score: Assign points for responses 1–3 as above and multiply score by 6	***D*** ____ × 6 = _____	Items 12–17: Score: Assign 5 points for each "yes" response and 0 points for each "no" response.	***D*** #12 + #13 + ... + #17 = _____
TOTAL: Subtract D from 100	***TOTAL*** 100 – D = _____	Item 8: Score: Assign points for responses 1–4 as above and multiply score by 4	***E*** ____ × 4 = _____	TOTAL: Add the sums from "A", "B", "C", and "D". If the total sum is greater than 100, enter 100.	***TOTAL*** A+B+C+D = _____
		TOTAL: Add scores A, B, C, D, and E	***TOTAL*** A+B+C+D+E = _____		
Total for Physical Independence: ____	☐	**Total for Cognitive Independence:** ____	☐	**Total for Mobility Independence:** ____	☐

OCCUPATION		**SOCIAL INTEGRATION**		**ECONOMIC SELF-SUFFICIENCY**	
Item 18: Hours working Score: Multiply the number of hours working by 2	***A*** ______	Item 25: Living alone Score: Assign 30 points if living with spouse/ partner OR assign 20 points if living with unrelated roommate and/or attendant.	***A*** ______	Calculate family size by adding respondent, partner, number of children and relatives in household.	***A*** 1 + #25a + #25b + #25c = ______
Item 19: Hours studying Score: Multiply the number of hours studying by 2	***B*** ______	Item 26: Romantic relationship Score: Assign 20 points if in a romantic relationship, unless points are assigned in “A”. If in a romantic r/ship and points are assigned in “A”, then “B” equals 30 – “A”.	***B*** ______	Item 31: Annual income Score: Combined annual income in the last year of all household.	______
Item 20: Hours parenting/homemaking Score: Multiply the number of hours by 2	***C*** ______	Item 27: Relatives Score: Add the number of children and other relatives in household (25b and 25c) to number of relatives contacted monthly and multiply by 5.	***C*** 5 × (#25b + #25c + #27) = ______ (max of 25)	Item 32: Medical expenses Score: Medical expenses for household in the last year.	______
Item 21: Hours home maintenance Score: Multiply the number of hours by 2	***D*** ______	Item 28: Business associates Score: If living with more than one attendant, add extra attendants to the response to item #28 and multiply by 2.	***D*** 2 × (#25e + #28) = ______ (max of 20)	Subtract the unreimbursed medical expenses from the annual income.	***B*** #31 – #32 = ______
Items 22–24: Hours recreation Score: Add hours for items #22, #23, & #24	***E*** #22 + #23 + #24 = ______	Item 29: Friends Score: If living with more than one roommate, add extra roommate to the response to item #29 and multiply by 10.	***E*** 10 × (#25d + #29) = ______ (max of 50)	Poverty level is determined from family size.	***C*** A = ______
TOTAL: Add scores A, B, C, D, and E. If greater than 100, enter 100	***TOTAL*** A+B+C+D+E = ______	Item 30: Strangers Score: Assign as follows: none = 0 points; 1–2 = 10 points; 3–5 = 15 points; 6 or more = 20 points.	***F*** ______	Divide the value from “B” by the poverty level from “C”.	***D*** B / C = ______
		TOTAL: Add scores A, B, C, D, E, and F. If greater than 100, enter 100	***TOTAL*** A+B+C+D+E+F = ______	TOTAL: Determine points as follows: If sum from D is: 0.0 to < 0.5 = 0 points 0.5 to < 1.0 = 25 points 1.0 to < 1.5 = 50 points 1.5 to < 2.0 = 75 points 2.0 or greater = 100 points	***TOTAL*** ______
Total for Occupation: ____	[ ]	**Total for Social Integration**: ____	[ ]	**Total for Economic Self-Sufficiency**: ____	[ ]

Acknowledgement: Adapted from Whiteneck, G. G. et al. (1988/1992). *Craig Handicap Assessment and Reporting Technique*. Englewood, CO: Craig Hospital.

Impact on Participation and Autonomy (IPA) Questionnaire

Cardol, de Haan, de Jong, van den Bos, and de Groot (2001)

Source

The IPA was originally published as a 23-item scale (Cardol, de Haan, van den Bos, de Jong, & de Groot, 1999b). Items of a revised 39-item version are available in an appendix to the report of Cardol et al. (2001) and are reproduced below. The most recent 41-item version is available from the authors' website (http://www.nivel.nl).

Purpose

The IPA is a self-rating scale, designed for people with chronic disabilities, including stroke and traumatic brain injury (TBI). It is a client-centred measure and as such focuses on autonomy and participation as opposed to ability or capacity. Suggested uses include constructing profiles of disease severity, conducting needs assessment, and outcome evaluation.

Item description

In the published 39-item version of the IPA, the first 32 items address "perceived participation" in five domains: Autonomy indoors (7 items), Family role (7 items), Autonomy outdoors (5 items), Social relations (6 items), and Work and educational opportunities (6 items). The final domain ("perceived problems") comprises eight items.

Scale development

Cardol et al. (1999b) drew the distinction between handicap or participation restriction that is assessed from the societal perspective (e.g., loss of occupational capacity) versus the person's own perceptions of their situation, saying that "functional skills and capacities considered to be essential by the professional may be differently valued by the individual concerned" (p. 412). In a previous study they had demonstrated that handicap questionnaires available at that time, were not suitable to assess "person-perceived handicap" (Cardol, Brandsma, de Groot, van den Bos, de Haan, & de Jong, 1999a). Item derivation for the IPA was based on the participation component of the then-available draft version of the *International Classification of Functioning, Disability and Health* (World Health Organization, 2001), as well as the authors' clinical experience, and a "small qualitative pilot study". An original pool of 41 items was reviewed by experts from health fields, as well as by consumers. The items were tested with a reference sample of 100 people with a range of disabling conditions (mainly neuromuscular disease) from a rehabilitation department in the Netherlands (Cardol, et al. 1999b). An item reduction process was used whereby items that were not relevant to 75% of the sample were deleted, as were items found to be unclear, and those that did not contribute to the homogeneity of the scale, resulting in a 23-item instrument. The initial psychometric study reported a number of statistical analyses, but the scale had some difficulties in that items pertaining to work were omitted because they "proved to be unclear and need to be rephrased" (p. 413). This limited the comprehensiveness of the IPA as a measure of participation. The revised 39-item version of the IPA was reviewed for item content and phrasing, and included the "perceived problems" domain (Cardol et al., 2001). The IPA has been validated in English (Sibley, Kersten, Ward, White, Mehta, & George, 2006).

Administration procedures, response format and scoring

The IPA is designed for self-administration. Cardol et al. (1999b) reported that administration time for the initial pool of 41 items was 30 minutes ($SD = 15$).

Items in the five "perceived participation" domains are rated on a 5-point scale: 1 (very good), 2 (good), 3 (fair), 4 (poor), 5 (very poor). The website 41-item version uses a score range 0 to 4. Items for the final "perceived problems" domain are rated on a 3-point scale: 0 (no problem), 1 (minor problems), 2 (severe problems). Scores are summed for each of the domains separately, with higher scores indicating greater restrictions in participation.

Psychometric properties

The psychometric properties of the 39-item version of the IPA were examined in a mail-out questionnaire received from 126 respondents (49% response rate) with a range of medical conditions, including stroke (21%) recruited from a number of rehabilitation centres and departments in the Netherlands (Cardol et al., 2001). Four of the five domains for "perceived participation" (Autonomy indoors, Family role, Autonomy outdoors and Social relations) were examined for validity, using measures including the London Handicap Scale (LHS) and Medical Outcomes Study Health Survey – Short Form (SF-36). Hypothesized patterns of expected correlations with the LHS were examined for convergent and divergent validity. Factor analysis was conducted on 25 of the 31 items from these four domains (the 6 work items were excluded because of the small number of people to whom these items applied; $n = 19$). Four factors were extracted (Autonomy indoors, Family role, Autonomy outdoors, Social relations), accounting for 67% of the variance, and item loadings showed very close correspondence with the scale structure. Temporal stability ($M = 15$ days) was examined in a randomly selected subset of the sample ($n = 72$). Data on responsiveness are available from Cardol, Beelen, van den Bos, de Jong, de Groot, and de Haan (2002) who assessed 49 people with "various diagnoses" participating in a rehabilitation programme, who were assessed at baseline and three months later. The authors report "small improvement in 3 of 5 domains", but the effect sizes were small. Results from Cardol et al. (2001), except where otherwise stated, are shown in Box 8.6.

Comment

The IPA is one of the growing number of scales adopting a client-centred focus to measure participation. As such, its emphasis is on the individual's perceptions, a commonly ignored area of assessment in rehabilitation, particularly in the arena of ABI. The IPA has sound psychometric properties, although effect sizes for its responsiveness are small. But in other respects it demonstrates good to excellent internal consistency for each of the domains, as well as temporal stability, and shows evidence of construct validity, both in terms of the underlying structure of the scale, as well as hypothesized patterns of associations and dissociations. There is good correspondence with quality of life measures, such as the SF-36, as well as the traditionally oriented (objective) measures of participation, such as the LHS. Yet there is not complete correspondence, indicating that the measures assess different constructs. As Cardol et al. (2001) acknowledge, further testing of the scale including the Work/educational opportunities domain is

Box 8.6

Validity:	Criterion: *Concurrent:* SF-36-Physical with Autonomy indoors: $r = -.43$, with Family role: $r = -.49$, with Autonomy outdoors: $r = -.51$, with Social relations: $r = -.26$
	– SF-36-Mental with above domains: $r = -.43, -.50, -.49, -.47$ respectively
	Construct: *Internal consistency:* Cronbach alpha: Autonomy indoors .91, Family role .90, Autonomy outdoors .81, Social relations .86, Work/education .91
	Factor analysis: 4 factors: Autonomy indoors (7 items), Family role (7 items), Autonomy outdoors (5 items), Social relations (5 items)
	Convergent/divergent: higher correlation with similar constructs (IPA-Autonomy outdoors with LHS-Mobility: $r = -.55$, IPA-Social relations with LHS-Social: $r = -.51$); lower correlation with dissimilar constructs (IPA-Autonomy indoors with LHS-Economic: $r = -.01$)
Reliability:	Inter-rater: Not applicable
	Test–retest: 15 days: ICC = .83–.91 for domains (item range $k_w = .56$–$.90$; for 4/5 domains $k \geq .6$ for all items). "Perceived problems": item range $k = .59$–$.87$ (with $k \geq .62$ for 6/7 items)
Responsiveness:	Cardol et al. (2002): "small improvement" from Baseline to 3 months: Family role: Baseline $M = 21.0$ ($SD = 6.6$) vs 3 months $M = 20.0$ ($SD = 7.0$), $d = .17$; Autonomy outdoors: Baseline $M = 14.7$ ($SD = 4.6$) vs 3 months $M = 14.2$ ($SD = 5.3$), $d = .1$; Work and education: Baseline $M = 16.4$ ($SD = 5.2$) vs 3 months $M = 15.9$ ($SD = 5.9$), $d < .01$

required with a larger sample of people engaging in work/education. A special feature of the IPA is its item content and phrasing, for example, respondents are asked about whether they can do *what* they want, *when* they want, the *way* they want. Although at some 40 items the IPA is a relatively lengthy instrument, requiring about 30 minutes for completion, on the other hand it provides a detailed picture of the person's perceptions on a wide range of issues relevant to participation that are rarely addressed, even in the more objectively focused scales.

Key references

Cardol, M., Beelen, A., van den Bos, G. A., de Jong, B. A., de Groot, I. J., & de Haan, R. J. (2002). Responsiveness of the Impact on Participation and Autonomy Questionnaire. *Archives of Physical Medicine and Rehabilitation*, *83*(11), 1524–1529.

Cardol, M., Brandsma, J. W., de Groot, I. J. M., van den Bos, G. A. M., de Haan, R. J., & de Jong, B. A. (1999a). Handicap questionnaires: What do they assess? *Disability and Rehabilitation*, *21*(3), 97–105.

Cardol, M., de Haan, R. J., de Jong, B. A., van den Bos, G. A. M., & de Groot, I. J. M. (2001). Psychometric properties of the Impact on Participation and Autonomy Questionnaire. *Archives of Physical Medicine and Rehabilitation*, *82*(2), 210–216.

Cardol, M., de Haan, R. J., van den Bos, G. A. M., de Jong, B. A., & de Groot, I. J. M. (1999b). The development of a handicap assessment questionnaire: The Impact on Participation and Autonomy (IPA). *Clinical Rehabilitation*, *13*(5), 411–419.

Sibley, A., Kersten, P., Ward, C. D., White, B., Mehta, R., & George, S. (2006). Measuring autonomy in disabled people: Validation of a new scale in a UK population. *Clinical Rehabilitation*, *20*(9), 793–803.

World Health Organization. (2001). *International classification of functioning, disability and health*. Geneva: World Health Organization.

Impact on Participation and Autonomy Questionnaire

Cardol, de Haan, de Jong, van den Bos, and de Groot (2001)

Name: **Administered by:** **Date:**

PART 1: PARTICIPATION

Response key:
1 = Very good
2 = Good
3 = Fair
4 = Poor
5 = Very poor

AUTONOMY INDOORS **RESPONSE**

In the context of illness or disability . . .

1. My chances of getting around in my house *where* I want to are . . . ________
2. My chances of getting around in my house *when* I want to are . . . ________
3. My chances of washing, bathing or showering and dressing, *the way* I wish, either by myself or with help are . . . ________
4. My chances of having a bath and dressing *when* I want to, either by myself or with help are . . . ________
5. My chances of getting up and going to bed *when* I want to are . . . ________
6. My chances of going to the toilet *when* I need to are . . . ________
7. My chances of eating and drinking *when* I want to are . . . ________

AUTONOMY INDOORS SCORE: ________

FAMILY ROLE

In the context of illness or disability . . .

8. My chances of contributing to looking after my home *the way* I want to are . . . ________
9. My chances of getting minor housework jobs done, either by myself or by someone else *the way* I want them done are . . . ________
10. My chances of getting major housework jobs done, either by myself or by others, *the way* I want them done are . . . ________
11. My chances of getting housework done, either by myself or by others, *when* I want them done are . . . ________
12. My chances of getting minor repairs and maintenance work done in my house, either by myself or by others, *the way* I want them done are . . . ________
13. My chances of fulfilling my role at home as I would like are . . . ________
14. My chances of spending my own money as I wish are . . . ________

FAMILY ROLE SCORE: ________

AUTONOMY OUTDOORS

In the context or illness or disability . . .

15. My chances of visiting relatives and friends *when* I want to are . . . ________
16. My chances of going on the sort of trips and holidays I want to go on are . . . ________
17. My chances of seeing people as often as I want are . . . ________
18. My chances of living life the way I want are . . . ________
19. My chances of spending leisure time the way I want to are . . . ________

AUTONOMY OUTDOORS SCORE: ________

IPA page 2 of 2

Response key:
1 = Very good
2 = Good
3 = Fair
4 = Poor
5 = Very poor

SOCIAL RELATIONS **RESPONSE**

In the context of illness or disability . . .

20. My chances of talking to people close to me on equal terms are . . . ________
21. The quality of my relationship with people who are close to me is . . . ________
22. The respect I receive from people who are close to me is . . . ________
23. My chances of having an intimate relationship are . . . ________
24. My relationships with acquaintances are . . . ________
25. The respect I receive from acquaintances is . . . ________

SOCIAL RELATIONS SCORE: ________

PAID WORK AND EDUCATION

In the context of illness or disability . . .

26. My chances of doing the paid work I want to do are . . . ________
27. My chances of doing my job *the way* I want to are . . . ________
28. My contacts with people I work with are . . . ________
29. My chances of maintaining or changing my working role as I would wish are . . . ________
30. My chances of getting a different job are . . . ________
31. My chances of getting the training or education I want are . . . ________

WORK AND EDUCATION SCORE: ________

PART 2: PROBLEM EXPERIENCE

Response key:
0 = No problems
1 = Minor problems
2 = Severe problems

---

1. With regard to your mobility, to what extent does your health or disability cause problems? ________
2. With regard to your self-care, to what extent does your health or disability cause problems? ________
3. With regard to your family role, to what extent does your health or disability cause problems? ________
4. With regard to controlling your finances, does your health or disability cause problems? ________
5. With regard to your leisure time, to what extent does your health or disability cause problems? ________
6. With regard to your relationships, to what extent does your health or disability cause problems? ________
7. With regard to paid work, to what extent does your health or disability cause problems? ________

8 With regard to your education, to what extent does your health or disability cause problems? ________

PROBLEM EXPERIENCE SCORE: ________

Acknowledgement: From Cardol, M. et al. (2001). Psychometric properties of the Impact on Participation and Autonomy Questionnaire. *Archives of Physical Medicine and Rehabilitation*, *82*(2), 210–216, pp. 215–216, with permission from the American Congress of Rehabilitation Medicine and the American Academy of Physical Medicine and Rehabilitation and Elsevier.

Leeds Assessment Scale of Handicap (LASH)

Geddes, Tennant, and Chamberlain (2000)

Source

Scale items and response categories for the LASH are available in an appendix to Geddes et al. (2000) and are reproduced below.

Purpose

The LASH is a clinician rating scale that was developed specifically to assess handicap in an inpatient rehabilitation setting. The target population was adults with acquired brain impairment, the standardization sample mainly comprising people with stroke (69%) and traumatic brain injury (TBI; 13%).

Item description

The LASH examines nine hierarchical levels of functioning in four domains: Physical independence, Mobility, Orientation and Social integration. Physical independence ranges from the lowest level, constant attendance day and night, to the highest level, no help needed for any activity; Mobility ranges from bedfast through to the ability to go anywhere; Orientation ranges from unconscious through to no problems with sensory, memory and communication functions; and Social integration ranges from socially isolated through to full participation in social relationships. Each domain commences with an operational definition, followed by detailed response categories.

Scale development

Development of the LASH was based on the conceptual framework of the *International Classification of Impairments, Disabilities and Handicaps* (ICIDH; World Health Organization [WHO], 1980). Two of the six WHO handicap dimensions were excluded (Occupation and Economic self-sufficiency), the remaining four dimensions comprising Physical independence, Mobility, Orientation and Social integration. The authors argued that "for practical reasons . . . it is only these four items that are of immediate relevance and . . . can be readily measured in an inpatient setting" (Geddes et al., 2000, p. 529). Using descriptions in the WHO manual, operational definitions were developed for each of the four items, along with the response categories of the rating scale. The scale was piloted and refined over a 6-month period. Members of a multidisciplinary team further tested the instrument on patients discussed at case conference using the intended procedure of completion, "a collaborative effort" approach, whereby clinicians pool their knowledge from different situations (e.g., rating the mobility item using observations of functioning on the ward by nurses and in therapy by physiotherapists).

Administration procedures, response format and scoring

The recommended method of completing the LASH is at a multidisciplinary case conference using the clinicians' collective knowledge and observations of the patient to classify level of functioning on the four items. Completion time is quick.

Each item is rated on a 9-point scale, with each level of response for each item having a detailed, individually scripted, operational definition. Scores for each item range from 0 (comparable to no problem) to 8 (comparable to total dependence), with the total score ranging from 0 to 32. Higher scores indicate greater degrees of handicap (participation restriction).

Psychometric properties

Geddes et al. (2000) examined the measurement characteristics of the LASH in a sample of 242 people admitted to the Rehabilitation Unit of the Leeds National Demonstration Centre in Rehabilitation, Chapel Allerton Hospital, Leeds, UK. Concurrent validity was examined with the Barthel Index (BI), a mental status test described as the "Mayo" and clinical ratings of behaviour. Predictive validity was established using admission LASH scores and examining length of rehabilitation admission and discharge destination. Responsiveness was determined by examining the change in LASH scores between admission and discharge. Inter-rater reliability was studied in two samples; kappa statistics were reported for results from two raters using data from a community sample of 60 patients with TBI. These patients were part of a larger study (Bowen, Neumann, Conner, Tennant, & Chamberlain, 1998) in which cognitive tests and the Sickness Impact Profile were administered and the resulting data used to classify the patients on the LASH. Results are shown in Box 8.7.

Comment

The LASH draws on some of the dimensions of the original ICIDH, and maps to six of the nine ICF domains of Activities/Participation. The authors' aim was to produce a scale for use at an inpatient level and for this reason the original Occupational and Economic Self-sufficiency dimensions of the ICIDH model were excluded intentionally. Yet, for a scale of handicap (participation), exclusion of the Occupation domain, in particular, raises issues of content validity and serves to restrict the application of the LASH beyond the in-patient setting should it be desired to track the patient's functioning following discharge. A distinctive feature of the LASH is its method of completion (multidisciplinary team at case conference). This has obvious advantages, but will be a limitation in settings that do not function in this manner (e.g., a single clinician). At a psychometric level, the LASH shows evidence of concurrent validity with other measures of physical, cognitive and behavioural functioning. It is predictive of length of stay in rehabilitation and patient discharge destination, and is responsive to real changes occurring in the patient between admission and discharge, with a medium effect size. Kappa statistics for inter-rater reliability are good, although the authors noted that complete agreement between raters for each item was variable (range 72–90%); additionally, temporal stability is unknown. Given the emphasis that is placed on measuring impairments and activity during inpatient rehabilitation admission, however, the LASH could be used to advantage to provide a complementary perspective of the patient's level of "overall competency".

Box 8.7

Validity:	Criterion: *Concurrent:* BI with LASH Physical: $r = -.74$, with LASH Mobility: $r = -.77$ – Mental status exam (Mayo) with LASH Orientation: $r = .72$ – clinical ratings of behaviour with LASH Social: $\chi^2 = 23.28$
	Predictive: admission LASH score with length of admission: $r = .58$
	Construct: *Discriminant:* LASH admission scores of those discharged home (Median = 19) were significantly lower than those discharged to residential/nursing home (Median = 24); $p < .001$
Reliability:	Inter-rater: Mobility: $k = .82$, Physical independence: $k = .74$, Orientation: $k = .76$, Social integration: $k = .69$
	Test–retest: No information available
Responsiveness:	Admission vs discharge: Effect size: $d = .57$ (descriptive data not provided)

Key references

Bowen, A., Neumann, V., Conner, M., Tennant, A., & Chamberlain, M. A. (1998). Mood disorders following traumatic brain injury: Identifying the extent of the problem and the people at risk. *Brain Injury*, *12*(3), 177–190.

Geddes, J. M. L., Tennant, A., & Chamberlain, M. A. (2000). The Leeds Assessment Scale of Handicap: Its operationalization, reliability, validity and responsiveness in in-patient rehabilitation. *Disability and Rehabilitation*, *22*(12), 529–538.

World Health Organization. (1980). *International classification of impairments, disabilities and handicaps*. Geneva: World Health Organization.

Leeds Assessment Scale of Handicap

Geddes, Tennant, and Chamberlain (2000)

Name: **Administered by:** **Date:**

PHYSICAL INDEPENDENCE

Concerned with sustaining a customarily effective independent existence
Meals, heating, lighting, etc. are all provided to in-patients, therefore these factors will NOT be taken into account when categorizing patients. Categorization will be based on the frequency of assistance (physical or verbal) needed by patients.

Score	Handicap	Definition
0	Fully independent	Fully independent. No help for any activity*
1	Aided independence	Fully independent with aids/appliances, e.g., prosthesis*
2	Adapted independence	Fully independent with environmental adaptations, e.g., stair lift, wheelchair*
3	Situational dependence	Needs help infrequently, e.g., shopping, collecting pension, housework*
4	Long interval dependence	Needs help once or twice a day for, e.g., bathing, putting on/removing stockings
5	Short interval dependence	Needs help every few hours during the day. Needs are PREDICTABLE
6	Critical interval dependence	Needs help at least every few hours during the day. Needs are NOT predictable
7	Special care	Includes those in categories 5 and 6 who also require the presence of another at night, although actual assistance is not ALWAYS needed
8	Intensive	Constant attendance needed day and night. Includes those in categories 5, 6 and 7 who consistently require assistance at night. Also includes those with severe behavioural problems that manifest themselves day and night

* Not likely to be applicable to in-patients but possible, e.g., if patient admitted from home or returning from weekend leave and has demonstrated ability.

MOBILITY

Concerned with how far the person can go on his or her own, with bed as the starting point
Can use aids and adaptations such as hoists and wheelchairs. Categories will depend on observation. It is unlikely that in-patients will be able to achieve scores of 3 or less unless they have been admitted from home and their mobility in the community is known.

Score	Handicap	Definition
0	Fully mobile	Can go anywhere*
1	Variable restriction	Has problems with mobility now and then, e.g., because of asthma or decreased exercise tolerance in winter*
2	Impaired mobility	Impaired because takes longer. However, does not stop the person being fully mobile, just slower. Able to cope with public transport*
3	Reduced mobility	Experiences difficulty in getting around. May be able to get beyond immediate neighbourhood but not in all circumstances. Cannot always cope with public transport*
4	Neighbourhood restriction	Mobility limited to immediate neighbourhood of dwelling. Can get out of hospital into garden and grounds, but not beyond on own
5	Dwelling restriction	Confined to hospital. Can move between ward and department but cannot get out of dwelling on own
6	Room restriction	Confined to ward. Can get out of bed on own and move round ward but no further
7	Chair restriction	Confined to chair. Can get out of bed on own into chair, but can go no further on own
8	Bed fast	Cannot get out of bed on own

* Not likely to be applicable to in-patients as performance outside hospital is usually unknown.

ORIENTATION

Concerned with reception of signals from the environment, the processing of this information and the production of an appropriate response
Orientation includes seeing, hearing, understanding, remembering and communicating. Do not forget other aspects such as taste, smell and body awareness. It is determined by the number and severity of disabilities and impairments experienced by the person.

Score	Handicap	Definition
0	Fully orientated	No problems with any of the above
1	Fully compensated	Any of the above problems that patient may have are fully compensated, e.g., by spectacles, hearing aids, use of medication to control fits
2	Intermittent disturbance	Occasional difficulty with impairments, e.g., epilepsy, episodes of dizziness
3	Partially compensated	Person is vulnerable only in certain circumstances, e.g., noisy room if hearing affected OR dimly lit room if eyesight is poor OR if neglect causes occasional problems
4A	Moderate sensory/motor impediment	Score on this level if the person has ONE of the following: • Poor hearing (not compensated by aid), OR • Poor eyesight/visual impairment (not compensated by glasses)/hemianopia, OR • Slight/moderate expressive problems, e.g., dysarthria, OR • Neglect causing problems most of the time
4B	Moderate cognitive impediment	• Slight to moderate confusion, OR • Slight to moderate memory problems, OR • Slight to moderate dementia, OR • Slight to moderate receptive AND expressive communication problems
5A	Severe sensory/motor impediment	More severe categories of above impairments/disabilities. Person has one of the following: • Blindness, OR • Total deafness, OR • Severe dysarthria (so that person is unintelligible)
5B	Severe cognitive impediment	• Severe confusion/severe memory deficit/severe dementia, OR • Severe communication problem, both expressive AND receptive
6	Orientation deprivation	Any combination of impairments/disabilities in both categories 4 and 5. Any two or more impairments/disabilities in category 5
7	Disorientated	Person unable to orient him/her self because of number and severity of impairments/disabilities
8	Unconscious/coma	

SOCIAL INTEGRATION

Concerned with how well the person gets on with and socializes with others around him or her on the ward. Scoring will depend on observation by staff

Score	Handicap	Definition
0	Fully socially integrated	Full participation in social relationships with staff, other patients, family and visitors
1	Inhibited social integration	Observed to be inhibited in social relationships but this is because of shyness, embarrassment, etc. and unconnected with reasons for disability
2	Restricted social integration	Fully socializes with family and visitors and shows some degree of socialization with staff and other patients
3	Diminished social integration	Confines socialization to family and own visitors
4	Impoverished social integration	Does not fully socialize even with family and visitors. Also include those with mild behavioural disorders that adversely affect social relationships. Also consider here those patients whose communication difficulties preclude "normal" social interaction
5	Reduced social integration	Only fully relates socially to one other, e.g., spouse. Also include here those with moderate behavioural disorders
6	Disturbed social integration	Difficulty in relating effectively to significant others. Also include here those with severe behavioural disorders
7	Alienated	Unable to relate to others. Behavioural problems prevent coexistence. Cannot develop social relationships because of disability/impairment
8	Socially isolated	This category includes those whose social integration is "indeterminable because of their isolated situation" (see ICIDH). Examples given are those admitted to institutional care because of lack of support in home or community (e.g., children in orphanage, residents in old people's home)

Acknowledgement: From Geddes, J. M. et al. (2000). The Leeds Assessment Scale of Handicap: Its operationalization, reliability, validity and responsiveness in in-patient rehabilitation. *Disability and Rehabilitation*, *22*(12), 529–538, Appendix, pp. 536–537, with permission of Taylor & Francis, www.tandf.co.uk/journals.

London Handicap Scale (LHS)

Harwood, Gompertz, and Ebrahim (1994a)

Source

The LHS items and response categories are available in an appendix to Harwood et al. (1994a) and also appear below. A manual for the LHS (Harwood & Ebrahim, 1995) is available from Dr Harwood (Department of Health Care of the Elderly, University Hospital, Nottingham, NG7 2UH, UK).

Purpose

The LHS is an informant and/or self-rating scale, described more specifically by the authors as a "classification questionnaire". It was developed primarily for population studies and postal surveys to evaluate outcome in health care interventions and services, rather than for individual patient assessment and therapy programming. The LHS was designed for older people, especially those with multiple and chronic health conditions, including people with stroke. It has also been used with people with multiple sclerosis (Thompson, 1999) and younger people with traumatic brain injury (Tate, Hodgkinson, Veerabangsa, & Maggiotto, 1999).

Item description

The LHS evaluates hierarchical levels of functioning in six dimensions: Mobility, Physical independence, Occupation, Social integration, Orientation and Economic self-sufficiency. Mobility ranges from the lowest level, being confined to bed, to the highest level, being able to go anywhere; Physical independence ranges from needing help or constant attention with everything, through to being able to look after oneself; Occupation ranges from sitting all day doing nothing, through to doing everything the person wants to; Social integration ranges from not being able to get along with anyone, through to getting along well with people and seeing them when wanted; Orientation ranges from unconsciousness through to having functional sensory and cognitive processes; Economic self-sufficiency ranges from having no money, through to being able to afford everything that is needed.

Scale development

The six dimensions of handicap, as enumerated in the World Health Organization (WHO, 1980) *International Classification of Impairments, Disabilities and Handicaps* (ICIDH; orientation, physical independence, mobility, occupation, social integration and economic self-sufficiency), were formulated into items for the LHS. Item description underwent rigorous pilot testing with professional and lay people "to ensure simplicity and clarity and to avoid jargon and ambiguity while remaining faithful to the classification categories laid down by the ICIDH" (Harwood, Rogers, Dickinson, & Ebrahim, 1994b, pp. 11–12). In order to ensure an interval level of measurement, weighted scores were developed. Data for the weights were derived from interviews with 79 out of 101 consenting people drawn from a larger random sample of 240 people from two general practices in London, UK, aged between 55 and 74 years and living in the community. Judges (n = 240) made valuations of disadvantage associated with the levels (referred to as utility measurements) and the technique of conjoint analysis was applied (Harwood et al., 1994b).

Administration procedures, response format and scoring

The LHS is designed to be self-administered, or completed by an informant. It can also be used in (and was designed for) postal surveys. Thompson (1999) advises that administration time is brief, a maximum of 10 minutes. A manual is available (Harwood & Ebrahim, 1995), detailing scoring procedures and interpretation guidelines.

Responses are made in terms of functioning during the previous week. Each dimension contains a hierarchy of response levels, which form a 6-point scale: 1 (not at all), 2 (very slightly), 3 (quite a lot), 4 (very much), 5 (almost completely), 6 (completely). Behavioural descriptors tailored to the individual items are attached to each level. Weighted scores are applied to the responses, providing a valid basis for combining the scores from the individual items into a total score. A constant is added and the weights are summed, with the total score ranging from 0 (maximum handicap) to 1 (no handicap). A score range of 0 to 100 has also been used, thereby avoiding the use of decimal points that occurred with the original scoring system (Harwood & Ebrahim, 2000). Normative data are not required given that the LHS has already been calibrated using weighted scores.

The use of weights makes scoring the LHS somewhat cumbersome, and Jenkinson, Mant, Carter, Wade, and Winner (2000) provided empirical evidence to advocate against the use of weights, finding very high correlation ($r = .98$) between standard and "unweighted" versions of the LHS in 303 people with stroke. They reported "a striking similarity" between the pattern of correlations using standard and unweighted LHS scores with instruments such as the Barthel Index (BI; $r = .73$ vs $r = .78$ respectively) and Frenchay Activities Index ($r = .76$ vs $r = .81$ respectively). In the unweighted version a 6-point rating scale (0 = extreme disability/handicap to 5 = no disability/handicap) was used for each dimension, with the ratings summed to obtain a total score (range 0–30), with higher scores indicating less handicap.

Box 8.8

Validity:	Criterion: *Concurrent*: with BI: $r = .56$ – with NEADL: $r = .69$ (scale range $r = .52–.66$) – with NHP (total score from Part 1): $r = –.42$
	Construct: *Internal consistency:* Harwood & Ebrahim (1995): Cronbach alpha: stroke sample ($n = 293$) .88
	Factor analysis: Harwood & Ebrahim (1995): stroke sample ($n = 293$): 1 factor, labelled Handicap
Reliability:	Inter-rater: Good (see text)
	Test–retest: 2 weeks: $r = .91$
Responsiveness:	Harwood & Ebrahim (2000): 3 months post-surgery: significant decrease in handicap: (Pre-surgery $M = 67$ ($SD = 11$), M change +7 ($SD = 5.9$), $d = .62$

Psychometric properties

The LHS was validated on 89 people with stroke living in the community in two health districts in London, UK (Harwood et al., 1994a). Temporal stability was examined in a subset of the sample ($n = 37$) in which the LHS was completed 2 weeks later. Validation instruments included the BI, Nottingham Extended Activities of Daily Living (NEADL) and Nottingham Health Profile (NHP). Responsiveness of the LHS was examined by Harwood and Ebrahim (2000) in 81 patients before and after hip replacement, with assessments taken after 3 months ($n = 74$) and 6 to 12 months ($n = 57$). The test manual (Harwood & Ebrahim, 1995) reports results from several psychometric studies. This included examination of internal consistency in 293 people with stroke. The factor structure was also examined in that sample, with the extraction of a single factor, accounting for 62% of the variance. The manual also reports results from "an indirect assessment" of inter-rater reliability, in which one interviewer examined a random sample of 225 out of 644 participants and other interviewers examined the remaining 419 participants: "Since the assignment of subjects was random, the handicap scores can be compared between these two groups" (p. 44). The mean difference was 0.4/100, "representing almost perfect agreement". Results of Harwood et al. (1994a), except where otherwise indicated, are shown in Box 8.8.

Comment

The development process of the LHS has resulted in an elegant and user-friendly instrument and it is one of the very few rating scales of participation designed to have interval-level measurement. The interval-level measurement, however, requires the application of weights, which Jenkinson et al. (2000) have argued is limiting and "adds little to the validity of the summary measure". They provide empirical data supporting the simple summation of scores. Basic psychometric properties of the LHS have been established, providing sound evidence of content and concurrent validity, as well as temporal stability, yet being responsive to real changes occurring in the patient with a moderate effect size. The rationale and conceptual underpinning of the LHS derived from the ICIDH and the question thus arises as to the extent to which the LHS is portable to its revision, the *International Classification of Functioning, Disability and Health* (ICF; WHO, 2001). Although the LHS does not map as directly to the nine ICF Activities/Participation domains as it did to the six Handicap dimensions of the ICIDH, all LHS items tap into eight of the nine domains and at least some of the categories. In their comparative review, Perenboom and Chorus (2003) identified the LHS as one of two measures that exclusively addressed the participation construct of the ICF. As designed, the LHS is sufficiently brief and user friendly for postal format, making it ideal for research purposes. Harwood et al. (1994b) advise caution, however, in its application in clinical assessment to measure changes in individual patients. The main reason they cite is that, by definition, handicap is a construct that only the person themselves can rate, whereas the score weights for the LHS were derived from the general population.

Key references

Harwood, R. H., & Ebrahim, S. (1995). *Manual of the London Handicap Scale*. Nottingham, UK: Department of Health Care of the Elderly, University of Nottingham.

Harwood, R. H., & Ebrahim, S. (2000). A comparison of the responsiveness of the Nottingham Extended Activities of Daily Living Scale, London Handicap Scale and SF-36. *Disability and Rehabilitation*, *22*(17), 786–793.

Harwood, R. H., Gompertz, P., & Ebrahim, S. (1994a). Handicap one year after a stroke: Validity of a new scale. *Journal of Neurology, Neurosurgery, and Psychiatry*, *57*(7), 825–829.

Harwood, R. H., Rogers, A., Dickinson, E., & Ebrahim, S. (1994b). Measuring handicap: The London Handicap Scale, a new outcome measure for chronic disease. *Quality in Health Care*, *3*(1), 11–16.

Jenkinson, C., Mant, J., Carter, J., Wade, D., & Winner, S. (2000). The London Handicap Scale: A re-evalutation of its validity using standard scoring and simple summation. *Journal of Neurology, Neurosurgery, and Psychiatry*, *68*(3), 365–367.

Perenboom, R. J. M., & Chorus, A. M. J. (2003). Measuring participation according to the *International Classification of Functioning, Disability and Health* (ICF). *Disability and Rehabilitation*, *25(11/12)*, 577–587.

Tate, R., Hodgkinson, A., Veerabangsa, A., & Maggiotto, S. (1999). Measuring psychosocial recovery after traumatic brain injury. Psychometric properties of a new scale. *Journal of Head Trauma Rehabilitation*, *14(6)*, 543–557.

Thompson, A. J. (1999). Measuring handicap in multiple sclerosis. *Multiple Sclerosis*, *5*(4), 260–262.

World Health Organization. (1980). *International classification of impairments, disabilities and handicaps*. Geneva: World Health Organization.

World Health Organization. (2001). *International classification of functioning, disability and health*. Geneva: World Health Organization.

London Handicap Scale

Harwood, Gompertz, and Ebrahim (1994)

Name:	**Administered by:**	**Date:**

YOUR HEALTH AND YOUR LIFE

Instructions:

This questionnaire asks six questions about your everyday life. Please answer each question. Circle the response next to the sentence that describes you best. Think about the things you have done over the last week. Compare what you can do with what someone like you who is in good health can do.

1. GETTING AROUND (MOBILITY):

Think about how you get from one place to another, using any help, aids or means of transport that you normally have available.

Does your health stop you from getting around?

1 Not at all: You go everywhere you want to, no matter how far away
2 Very slightly: You go most places you want to, but not all
3 Quite a lot: You get out of the house, but not far away from it
4 Very much: You don't go outside, but you can move around from room to room indoors
5 Almost completely: You are confined to a single room, but can move around in it
6 Completely: You are confined to a bed or a chair. You cannot move around at all. There is no one to move you

2. LOOKING AFTER YOURSELF (PHYSICAL INDEPENDENCE):

Think about the things like housework, shopping, looking after money, cooking, laundry, getting dressed, washing, shaving and using the toilet.

Does your health stop you looking after yourself?

1 Not at all: You can do everything yourself
2 Very slightly: Now and again you need a little help
3 Quite a lot: You need help with some tasks (such as heavy housework or shopping), but no more than once a day
4 Very much: You can do things but need help more than once a day. You can be left alone safely for a few hours
5 Almost completely: You need help to be available all the time. You cannot be left alone safely
6 Completely: You need help with everything: You need constant attention, day and night

3. WORK AND LEISURE (OCCUPATION):

Think about things like work (paid or not), housework, gardening, sports, hobbies, going out with friends, travelling, reading, looking after children, watching television and going on holiday.

Does you health limit your work or leisure activities?

1 Not at all: You can do everything you want to do
2 Very slightly: You can do almost all the things you want to do
3 Quite a lot: You find something to do almost all the time, but cannot do some things for as long as you would like
4 Very much: You are unable to do a lot of things, but can find something to do most of the time
5 Almost completely: You are unable to do most things, but can find something to do some of the time
6 Completely: You sit all day doing nothing. You cannot keep yourself busy or take part in any activities

4. GETTING ON WITH PEOPLE (SOCIAL INTEGRATION):

Think about family, friends and people you might meet during a normal day.

Does your health stop you getting on with people?

1 Not at all: You get on well with people, see everyone you want to see and meet new people
2 Very slightly: You get on well with people, but your social life is slightly limited
3 Quite a lot: You are fine with people you know well, but you feel uncomfortable with strangers
4 Very much: You are fine with people you know well, but you have few friends and little contact with neighbours. Dealing with strangers is very hard
5 Almost completely: Apart from the person who looks after you, you see no one. You have no friends and no visitors
6 Completely: You don't get on with anyone, not even people who look after you

---

5. AWARENESS OF YOUR SURROUNDINGS (ORIENTATION):

Think about taking in and understanding the world around you, and finding your way around in it.

Does your health stop you understanding the world around you?

1 Not at all: You fully understand the world around you. You see, hear, speak and think clearly, and your memory is good
2 Very slightly: You have a problem with hearing, speaking, seeing or your memory, but these do not stop you doing most things
3 Quite a lot: You have problems with hearing, speaking, seeing, or your memory, which make life difficult a lot of the time. But you understand what is going on
4 Very much: You have great difficulty understanding what is going on
5 Almost completely: You are unable to tell where you are or what day it is. You cannot look after yourself at all
6 Completely: You are unconscious, completely unaware of anything going on around you

---

6. AFFORDING THE THINGS YOU NEED (ECONOMIC SELF-SUFFICIENCY):

Think about whether health problems have led to any extra expenses, or have caused you to earn less than you would if you were healthy.

Are you able to afford the things you need?

1 Yes, easily: You can afford everything you need. You have easily enough money to buy modern labour-saving devices, and anything you may need because of ill-health
2 Fairly easily: You have just about enough money. It is fairly easy to cope with expenses caused by ill-health
3 Just about: You are less well-off than other people like you; however, with sacrifices you can get by without help
4 Not really: You only have enough money to meet your basic needs. You are dependent on state benefits for any extra expenses you have because of ill-health
5 No: You are dependent on state benefits, or money from other people or charities. You cannot afford the things you need
6 Absolutely not: You have no money at all and no state benefits. You are totally dependent on charity for most of your basic needs

---

Acknowledgement: From Harwood, R. et al. (1994). Handicap one year after a stroke: Validity of a new scale. *Journal of Neurology, Neurosurgery, and Psychiatry*, *57*(7), 825–829, Scale, pp. 828–829, by permission of BMJ and Rightslink.

Nottingham Leisure Questionnaire (NLQ)

Drummond and Walker (1994)

Source

The revised set of items for the NLQ is available in Drummond, Parker, Gladman, and Logan (2001) and is reproduced below.

Purpose

The NLQ is a self-rating scale, designed to measure leisure activity. It was originally developed for people with stroke.

Item description

The NLQ contains 30 items in the revised set, as well as an "other" item to take account of additional leisure activities not included in the set. Items are not grouped under specific domains, but rather comprise a single listing of leisure activities: solitary and social activities, physically active and physically passive, indoor and outdoor.

Scale development

Drummond (1990) previously defined leisure as "an activity chosen primarily for its own sake after the practical necessities of life have been attended to" (p. 157). She investigated a set of 37 recreational activities engaged in by people before and after stroke. The list was derived from the contents of previous studies that fitted the operational definition of leisure. These items were then examined to determine inter-rater reliability and temporal stability (Drummond & Walker, 1994). Subsequently the NLQ was modified slightly to facilitate self-administration and use in postal surveys and clinical trials (Drummond et al., 2001). Three items that did not reflect positive leisure activities were excluded (viz., just sitting, daydreaming, meditation/relaxation), as was one item with low endorsement (attending classes). Three items (swimming, bicycling, fishing) were grouped with "sporting activities". These changes resulted in the 30-item scale. Drummond et al. also reduced response categories from five to three. Data from the Drummond and Walker study using the original NLQ were reanalysed with the shortened version and the same results were found.

Administration procedures, response format and scoring

The 30-item version of the NLQ is designed for self-completion, however the scale has not been validated in people with major communication problems. Drummond et al. (2001) reported that in their clinical trial involving hundreds of participants, 36% received help from a caregiver to complete the questionnaires.

Responses are made with respect to activities occurring in the previous few weeks. In the 30-item version, responses are made on a 3-point scale: 0 (never), 1 (occasionally), 2 (regularly). The total score ranges from 0 to 60, with higher scores indicating a greater number of and more frequent engagement in leisure activities.

Psychometric properties

Drummond and Walker (1994) reported results of two reliability studies. Inter-rater reliability was examined with 20 people more than 1 year after stroke who were recruited from the Nottingham Stroke Register, Nottingham, UK. Two raters were present at an interview in which the NLQ was administered by one of the raters (one rater conducted half of the interviews and then alternated with the other rater) and independent recordings of responses were made. Two-week temporal stability was examined with 21 of the 50 people who returned the posted questionnaires on both occasions. They were at least 1 year post-stroke, living in the community, and did not have major communication problems. The 30-item NLQ was examined by Drummond et al. (2001) in the course of a clinical trial with a large sample. Data were collected on the Nottingham Extended Activities of Daily Living (NEADL), Barthel Index, and General Health Questionnaire (GHQ-12), with NLQ data received from $n = 374$ at the 6-month follow-up and $n = 331$ at 12 months. Two-week temporal stability was examined in a consecutive series of 137 patients, with data received on the test and retest occasions by approximately $n = 70$. Data on discriminant validity and responsiveness of the NLQ are available from a number of other clinical trials on the effect of day activity and leisure programmes. Drummond and Walker (1995) compared groups randomized to leisure rehabilitation ($n = 21$), conventional occupational therapy ($n = 21$) or control ($n = 23$) conditions. Assessments were conducted at baseline and 3 and 6 months later. The leisure group improved between baseline and 6 months, but the other two groups obtained lower scores at 6 months in comparison with baseline. Corr, Phillips, and Walker (2004) used a cross-over design, in 26 people after stroke; compliance was problematic and intention-to-treat analyses were used, thereby providing a rigorous test of the treatment effect. Results from these studies are shown in Box 8.9.

Comment

There is a dearth of detailed measures addressing leisure and recreation activities that have been developed for or standardized on people with acquired brain impairment. This paucity is all the more surprising given that, for many people, return to work after a brain injury is not possible because of the effects of neurophysical and/or neuropsychological impairments. For such people, activities traditionally regarded as leisure and recreation become a way by which they incorporate meaningful occupation into their day. The NLQ thus fills an important gap. It has good inter-rater reliability and temporal stability is adequate for most items. There is some evidence for construct validity and responsiveness. Given the likely wide variation in leisure activities engaged in by the general population, however, normative data are necessary for clinical application. Item content may also be an issue, not only with respect to the update of leisure activities (e.g., Drummond et al., 2001, commented on computer use, which is not one of the items), but also demographic and cultural differences with respect to leisure activities. Drummond et al. caution about the application of the NLQ to other countries, cultures and age groups, given that it was developed with older adults living in the UK in the 1990s, but clearly its standardization on other groups would be advantageous.

Box 8.9

Validity:	Criterion: *Concurrent:* Drummond et al.: Using regression analyses, factors associated with NLQ score at 6 months were 3/4 NEADL subtests and GHQ-12 score, accounting for 54% of the variance
	Construct: *Discriminant:* Drummond & Walker (1995): higher post-treatment scores in the leisure rehabilitation group $M = 48.50$ ($SD = 11.12$) vs 2 control groups $M = 32.20$ ($SD = 11.12$) and $M = 33.15$ ($SD = 10.66$); Kruskal-Wallis ANOVA = 19.95, $p < .001$
Reliability:	Inter-rater: Drummond & Walker (1994): item range: $k = .65$–1.00 ($k > .75$ for 36/37 items)
	Test–retest: Drummond & Walker (1994): 2 weeks: item range: $k = .0$–1.0 (with $k \geq .6$ for 22/33 items with data, $k < .4$ for 6 items – watching TV, visiting family/friends, swimming, just sitting, going to plays/museums/cinema, activities at clubs/centres)
	Drummond et al.: consecutive series: 2 weeks: item range: $k = .44$–.94 ($k \geq .6$ on 21/30 items) – clinical trial sample: correlation between scores at 6 and 12 months: $r_s = .86$
Responsiveness:	Corr et al.: number of activities: Group A (Experimental): Pre-treatment Median = 11.5 (range 4–24) vs Post-treatment Median = 15.0 (range 8–23); $z = -1.70$, $p = .085$
	– Group B (Wait-list, after cross-over): Pre-treatment Median = 10.0 (range 6–26) vs Post-treatment Median = 16.0 (range 8–29); $z = -2.19$, $p = .023$

Key references

Corr, S., Phillips, C. J., & Walker, M. (2004). Evaluation of a pilot service designed to provide support following stroke: A randomized cross-over design study. *Clinical Rehabilitation*, *18*(1), 69–75.

Drummond, A. (1990). Leisure activity after stroke. *International Disability Studies*, *12*(4), 157–160.

Drummond, A. E. R., Parker, C. J., Gladman, J. R. F., & Logan, P. A. (2001). Development and validation of the Nottingham Leisure Questionnaire (NLQ). *Clinical Rehabilitation*, *15*(6), 647–656.

Drummond, A. E. R., & Walker, M. F. (1994). The Nottingham Leisure Questionnaire for stroke patients. *British Journal of Occupational Therapy*, *57*(11), 414–418.

Drummond, A. E. R., & Walker, M. F. (1995). A randomized controlled trial of leisure rehabilitation after stroke. *Clinical Rehabilitation*, *9*(4), 283–290.

Nottingham Leisure Questionnaire

Drummond and Walker (1994); Drummond, Parker, Gladman, and Logan (2001)

Name:	**Administered by:**	**Date:**

Instructions: These are questions about things you may do in your free time. Please record how often you have done each activity IN THE LAST FEW WEEKS. You should put the number that corresponds to each activity.

Response key:
0 = Never
1 = Occasionally
2 = Regularly

How often do you do the following:	**RESPONSE**
1. Watching TV	______
2. Listening to radio/music	______
3. Visiting family/friends	______
4. Reading books	______
5. Singing	______
6. Gardening	______
7. Crafts, e.g., knitting/sewing	______
8. Attending sports events	______
9. Collecting things	______
10. Shopping for pleasure	______
11. Cooking for pleasure	______
12. Reading newspapers/magazines	______
13. Walking	______
14. Volunteer work	______
15. Indoor games/cards/bingo/dominoes	______
16. Dancing	______
17. Looking after/exercising pets	______
18. Eating out	______
19. Going to pubs	______
20. Going to plays/museums/cinemas	______
21. Photography	______
22. Exercise/fitness	______
23. Attendance at day centres and clubs	______
24. Going to parties	______
25. Entertaining at home	______
26. Church activities	______
27. Driving	______
28. DIY ("do it yourself" activities)	______
29. Sporting activities, e.g., tennis/bowling/bicycling/fishing/swimming	______
30. Holidays	______
31. Any other activities not already mentioned: please specify	

____

____

____

TOTAL SCORE ______

Acknowledgement: From Drummond, A. E. R. et al. (2001). Development and validation of the Nottingham Leisure Questionnaire (NLQ). *Clinical Rehabilitation*, *15*(6), 647–656, Appendix, p. 655, by permission of Sage Publications Ltd.

Participation Objective, Participation Subjective (POPS)

Brown, Dijkers, Gordon, Ashman, Charatz, and Cheng (2004)

Source

An appendix to Brown et al. (2004) enumerates the POPS items, which are reproduced below. Information on the POPS, including the recording form and scoring algorithm, is also available through the Center for Outcome Measurement in Brain Injury (COMBI) website (http://www.tbims.org/combi/pops/index.html).

Purpose

The POPS is a rating scale, designed to be administered in the context of an interview to measure both objective (societal/normative) and subjective (the person's perspective) components of participation. It was developed for people with traumatic brain injury (TBI).

Item description

The POPS comprises 26 items (described as "activities"), which are organized into five subscales: Domestic life (8 items), Interpersonal interactions and relationships (8 items), Major life areas (3 items), Transportation (2 items), and Community, recreational and civic life (5 items). For the Participation Objective (PO) component of the POPS, factual information is sought on the frequency of/involvement in activities; for the Participation Subjective (PS) component information is sought on the perceived importance of the activity and the desire to change the current level of functioning.

Scale development

Brown et al. (2004) argued that with the introduction of the *International Classification of Functioning, Disability and Health* (ICF; World Health Organization, 2001) measures of participation needed to incorporate "the perspective of the disability insider, whose life it is" (Brown et al., 2004, p. 460). In developing the POPS to be consistent with ICF philosophy, they questioned the "more is better" principle commonly encountered in traditional measures of community integration (e.g., more friends, higher income). The POPS had its origins in an instrument that the authors had developed for previous research studies, which drew on items appearing in other well-known instruments of community integration. These items were "pared down" to the 26 items for the POPS, each representing commonly occurring activities that are "part of expected social role functioning for a large segment of adults" (Brown et al., 2004, p. 463). No information is provided on the process by which item reduction occurred. The items map to five of the nine domains of the Activities/Participation component of the ICF, and indeed four of the subscales use virtually the same labels as the ICF nomenclature. The structure of the PS component of the POPS was adapted from the work of Flanagan (1978, 1982) on quality of life.

Administration procedures, response format and scoring

The POPS is designed to be administered to the person with TBI within the context of an interview. The recording form is available from the COMBI website, which also advises that administration time is 10 to 20 minutes.

POPS items are rated three times: once for the PO component and twice for the PS component. The PO component rates the *current activity level* and response alternatives vary with each subscale. Domestic life items are rated on a 4-point scale: 0 (none), 1 (some), 2 (most), 3 (all). Items from the Major life areas and Transportation subscales record the number of hours per day/week/month, as appropriate. The final two subscales, Interpersonal interactions and relationships, along with Community, recreational and civic life, also use a frequency scale to rate items in terms of the number of occasions per day/week/month, as appropriate.

For the PS component, first the respondent is asked whether they would like a *change* in the frequency of functioning. Items are rated using the same 3-point scale for all items: 1 (more), 2 (less), 3 (same). (Responses are subsequently converted to a dichotomous scale for scoring, i.e., –1 for both the "more" and "less" response categories; +1 for the "same" response category.) Then the person is asked how important their life satisfaction is regarding his or her level of functioning in each activity item. These *importance* ratings use the same 5-point scale for each item: 0 (not important), 1 (a little bit important), 2 (moderately important), 3 (very important), 4 (one of the most important).

In order to convert PO responses into scores, the Statistical Package for the Social Sciences (SPSS) is required to run a scoring program (syntax for the program is available on the COMBI website). In brief, the steps involve the following: (1) responses to items in all subscales except Domestic life are converted to a standard frequency per month; (2) z scores are calculated with reference to the means and standard deviations of the combined TBI and Control groups, and a fixed range of z scores is set (from −3 to +3) in order to deal with outliers who are allocated the extreme z score; (3) the z score is then weighted by the mean importance rating of the combined TBI and Control groups. These scores are then combined to form subscale and total scores, with higher scores indicating better participation.

Scoring the PS component is somewhat simpler: the Importance score (range 0–4) is multiplied by the Change score (−1 or +1), such that the items range from +4 (a most important area of life and the person is engaging in it to a satisfactory level) to −4 (a most important area of life that the person wants to do either more or less of). The total PS score is the mean of the 26 items, range −4 to +4, with higher scores indicating higher subjective satisfaction in relation to their importance for the person.

Psychometric properties

Brown et al. (2004) reported data on the POPS and other validating instruments for 454 people with TBI (age $M = 38.2$ years, $SD = 17.9$) living in the community who were recruited from patient lists of Mount Sinai School of Medicine, New York, USA, along with a control group of 120 healthy individuals. The TBI group was heterogeneous with respect to age (range 21–93 years), time post-trauma (1 month to 54 years), and injury severity (mild to severe). Temporal stability over a 1- to 3-week period was examined in a subset ($n = 65$) of the TBI group. Validating instruments included the Beck Depression Inventory (BDI) and Flanagan's Quality of Life Questionnaire. As the authors expected, given results of previous research, correlation between the PO and PS components was "very weak" ($r = .23$ and $r = .21$ for the mild and moderate/severe TBI groups respectively). Discriminant validity was examined by comparing TBI subgroups with mild versus moderate/severe degrees of injury. Results are shown in Box 8.10.

Box 8.10

Validity:	Criterion: *Concurrent:* PO: with BDI: $r = -.21$ & $-.19$ (for mild & moderate/severe injury subgroups respectively) – with Flanagan unmet needs: $r = -.23$ & $-.10$ respectively
	PS: with BDI: $r = -.43$ & $-.39$ (for mild & moderate/severe injury subgroups respectively) – with Flanagan unmet needs: $r = -.37$ & $-.33$ respectively
	Construct: *Internal consistency:* subscale-total correlations: PO: range .35–.63; PS: range .60–.73
	Discriminant: PS: mild: $M = -0.40$ ($SD = 0.98$) vs moderate/severe $M = -0.11$ ($SD = 1.00$); $F = 6.52$, $p = .01$; significant differences on 2/5 PS subscales (Domestic life and Transportation); no differences for PO total or subscales
Reliability:	Inter-rater: No information available
	Test–retest: 1–3 weeks: PO: Total score: ICC = .75 (subscale range: ICC = .28–.89; ICC ≥ .6 for 3/5 subscales, ICC < .4 for 2/5 subscales – Transportation; Community, recreation and civic life)
	PS: Total score: ICC = .80 (subscale range: ICC = .42–.68; ICC ≥ .6 for 1/5 subscales)
Responsiveness:	No information available

Comment

The admirable feature of the POPS is the synthesis of objective (societal, normative) and subjective (personal, ideographic) aspects of community integration into a single measure. Additionally, item content is sufficiently detailed to enable a comprehensive overview of functioning in the commonly recognized arenas of domestic and community life. Psychometrically, the POPS requires further examination. In particular, given that the PO component measures participation from an external/objective perspective, concurrent validity needs to be established with a comparable instrument, rather than scales that are more akin to the PS construct (e.g., BDI). In the Brown et al. (2004) study, the PS component performed better than PO. Group differences between TBI subgroups with mild versus moderate/severe degrees of injury were found for PS subscales, but no PO subscale; temporal stability, while excellent for both the summary PO and PS components, was poor for two of the five PO subscales. A possible drawback of the POPS is the scoring format for the PO component, which is complex and involved, and the need for a statistical program to calculate scores may limit the feasibility of using the POPS in clinical settings.

Key references

Brown, M., Dijkers, M. P. J. M., Gordon, W. A., Ashman, T., Charatz, H., & Cheng, Z. (2004). Participation Objective, Participation Subjective: A measure of participation combining outsider and insider perspectives. *Journal of Head Trauma Rehabilitation*, *19*(6), 459–481.

Flanagan, J. C. (1978). A research approach to improving our quality of life. *American Psychologist*, *33*(2), 138–147.

Flanagan, J. C. (1982). Measurement of the quality of life: Current state of the art. *Archives of Physical Medical and Rehabilitation*, *63*(2), 56–59.

World Health Organization. (2001). *International classification of functioning, disability and health*. Geneva: World Health Organization.

Participation Objective Participation Subjective (subscales and activities)

Brown, Dijkers, Gordon, Ashman, Charatz, and Cheng (2004)

DOMESTIC LIFE (proportion of what occurs in a household performed by the person)

1. Shopping for groceries, drugs, other necessities
2. Preparing meals, cooking
3. Cleaning the house
4. Caring for and supervising children and dependent adults
5. Making social arrangements such as get-togethers and parties
6. Paying bills, balancing the chequebook, banking
7. Doing home repairs
8. Doing garden work

INTERPERSONAL INTERACTIONS AND RELATIONSHIPS (frequency per day/week/month)

9. Socialize with friends, by phone or at home
10. Socialize with relatives, by phone or at home
11. Socialize with schoolmates, co-workers and the like by phone or at work/school
12. Go out to visit friends or family, social events and occasions
13. Engage in sex
14. Go to places where you might meet new people
15. Speak with your neighbours
16. Start a conversation or speak with strangers (e.g., order a meal or ask for directions)

MAJOR LIFE AREAS (hours per day/week/month)

17. Work for pay
18. Go to school, training programme, study
19. Do volunteer work

TRANSPORTATION (hours per day/week/month)

20. Drive or ride in a car
21. Ride in buses, taxis or other public transport

COMMUNITY RECREATION AND CIVIC LIFE (frequency per day/week/month)

22. Go to the movies
23. Eat in restaurants
24. Go shopping
25. Attend religious services or church social events
26. Attend sports events as a spectator

Acknowledgement: From Brown, M. et al. (2004). Participation Objective, Participation Subjective: A measure of participation combining outsider and insider perspectives. *Journal of Head Trauma Rehabilitation*, *19*(6), 459–481, Appendix, p. 481, with permission of Lippincott Williams & Wilkins and Wolters Kluwer.

Reintegration to Normal Living (RNL) Index

Wood-Dauphinee and Williams (1987)

Source

Items of the RNL are described in Wood-Dauphinee and Williams (1987) and are reproduced below. An adapted version, suitable for postal administration, is available (Daneski, Coshall, Tilling, & Wolfe, 2003) and is also briefly described below.

Purpose

The RNL is described as a visual analogue self-rating scale, in that the respondent chooses "a point within a bar" (Wood-Dauphinee, Opzoomer, Williams, Marchand, & Spitzer, 1988, p. 585). It was developed for clinical and research purposes for patients with incapacitating illness or severe trauma. A specific aim of the instrument was that it would be sensitive to real changes occurring in the patient. The RNL has been also used with patients with acquired brain impairment (ABI), including cerebral aneurysms (Chung, Carter, Norbash, Budzik, Putnam, & Ogilvy, 2000), stroke (Béthoux, Calmels, & Gautheron, 1999; Daneski et al., 2003) and traumatic brain injury (Chen, Rodger, & Polatajko, 2002).

Item description

The RNL comprises 11 items, addressing mobility (3 items), self-care (1 item), occupation (2 items), social role and relationships (4 items) and coping skills (1 item). A second version of the RNL, suitable for people who use aids, adaptive devices or another person for assistance, is also available.

Scale development

Wood-Dauphinee and Williams (1987) and Wood-Dauphinee et al. (1988) describe in detail the systematic process that was used in the construction of the RNL, which was developed concurrently in English and French. Following an extensive literature review, a multidisciplinary group used their clinical experience to create a clinical vignette, "to set the tone for the respondents" (Wood-Dauphinee & Williams, 1987, p. 494). Two questionnaires were constructed, focusing on the activities, roles and relationships to be resumed, as well as difficulties to be overcome before the person considered himself or herself reintegrated. Experts examined the questionnaires for completeness, clarity and applicability. A series of three advisory panels was established from 42 matched triplets of professionals, patients and lay people recruited from a variety of institutions. They completed the questionnaires and their responses suggested the construct of reintegration was "the ability to function, to do what one wants to do or feels one has to do, not that one must be free of symptoms or even disability" (Wood-Dauphinee et al., 1988, p. 585). This information was used to develop the items of the RNL that, along with a range of response formats, were trialled.

Administration procedures, response format and scoring

Responses are made by choosing a point within a 10cm bar that contains extreme anchor points: "does not describe my situation" to "fully describes my situation". Each item is scored from 1 (minimal reintegration) to 10 (complete reintegration) and summed, the total score ranging from 11 to 110. Scores are then proportionally converted to a 100-point system, with higher scores indicating better integration.

Psychometric properties

Two samples were used to initially establish the validity of the RNL (Wood-Dauphinee & Williams, 1987, with results reported in detail in Wood-Dauphinee et al., 1988). Sample 1 (a mixed diagnostic group of 109 people with cancer, cardiac, orthopaedic and neurological conditions) was used to determine the internal consistency of the RNL. Sample 2 ($n = 70$ newly diagnosed people with cardiac and cancer conditions) was used to examine concurrent and construct validity with the Quality of Life Index (QLI). This sample was also used to examine the factor structure of the RNL. In the patient data two factors were extracted (percentage of the variance not reported), but informant data yielded a single factor (accounting for 49% of the variance). Responsiveness was studied with patients from Sample 2 who were followed up 3 months later. A third sample was reported by Wood-Dauphinee et al., comprising 250 people newly diagnosed with cancer and who were followed for 18 months. Patterns of hypothesized correlations with similar and dissimilar constructs were examined. Responsiveness of the RNL was examined by following patients over a 3-month period. Further data were provided by Chen et al. (2002), who reported on a mixed neurological case series ($n = 12$) participating in a 4-week occupational therapy (OT) intervention. Raw data were provided in the report and statistical analysis was conducted on these by the author. Results from Wood-Dauphine et al., except where otherwise stated, are shown in Box 8.11.

Box 8.11

Validity:	Content See text
	Criterion: *Concurrent*: with QLI: $r = .72$
	Construct: *Internal consistency:* Cronbach alpha: patients .90, informants .92, clinicians .95
	Factor analysis: Patient data: 2 factors: Daily functioning (8 items) and Perceptions of self (3 items) – Informant data: 1 factor
	Convergent/divergent: Wood-Dauphine & Williams: higher correlation with similar constructs (RNL-Daily functioning with QLI-Activity and daily living scale: $r = .67$); lower correlation with dissimilar constructs (RNL-Daily functioning with QLI-Support and outlook: $r = .07$)
Reliability:	Inter-rater: Not applicable
	Test–retest: No information available (but see RNLI-P version below)
Responsiveness:	3-month retest: Time 1: $M = 83.9$ ($SD = 14.7$) vs Time 2 $M = 90.4$ ($SD = 13.1$); $t = 3.28$, $d = .44$
	Chen et al.: Pre-treatment: $M = 48.25$ ($SD = 15.11$) vs Post-treatment $M = 69.50$ (SD = 7.28); $t = 7.62$, $p < .001$, $d = 1.41$

Derivatives of the RNL: Postal version of the Return to Normal Living Index (RNLI-P); Daneski, Coshall, Tilling, and Wolfe (2003)

Patients with ABI, particularly those with stroke, can have visual field defects (specifically, hemianopia) and unilateral spatial neglect, which may interfere with the completion of visual analogue scales. Daneski and colleagues adapted the RNL, primarily for use in postal surveys, by simplifying item wording and using a dichotomous response format (agree/disagree). Psychometric properties were very good. Two-week temporal stability was examined in 26 patients who were 3 to 12 months post-stroke (with $k \geq .6$ for 7/11 items, $k < .4$ for 1/11 – embarrassed when with others). Concurrent validity was examined with an independent sample of 76 patients with stroke who completed the Barthel index (BI, $r = .42$), Frenchay Activities Index ($r = .69$), Medical Outcomes Study Health Survey – Short Form-36 ($r = .74$), and the Hospital Anxiety and Depression Scale (Anxiety $r = -.38$, Depression $r = -.61$). Internal consistency was good (Cronbach alpha .84). Convergent and divergent validity was shown with the two RNL factors and the BI, with significant correlation ($r = .48$) with the Daily function factor and non-significant correlation with the Perceptions of self factor ($r = .06$).

Comment

The RNL index is a carefully developed instrument, ensuring content validity. It was intentionally developed as a client-centred instrument: "extensive efforts were made to solicit and incorporate the opinions and judgements of patients and those close to them" (Wood-Dauphinee et al., 1988, p. 585). It achieves this aim well, showing high correlation with quality of life measures, as well as being responsive to the changing states of patients. Other psychometric properties are acceptable, although no information is available regarding its temporal stability. The RNL was developed for a general disability population, but item content is well suited to people with ABI. There are relatively few instruments that use a visual response format and this was intentionally adopted for the RNL as the preferred method following feedback, after trialling 3- and 5-point rating scales. This format can present difficulties for people with ABI who have visual field defects and/or unilateral spatial neglect, however. The dichotomous-response, postal version of the RNL (Daneski et al., 2003) also has good psychometric properties and could be considered an alternative for use with such patients. As with other client-centred instruments, the focus of the RNL is to measure the patient's perspectives and perceptions, which may not accord with actual functioning, which thus needs assessment in its own right.

Key references

Béthoux, F., Calmels, P., & Gautheron, V. (1999). Changes in the quality of life of hemiplegic stroke patients with time: A preliminary report. *American Journal of Physical Medicine and Rehabilitation*, *78*(1), 19–23.

Chen, Y.-H., Rodger, S., & Polatajko, H. (2002). Experiences with the COPM and client-centred practice in adult neurorehabilitation in Taiwan. *Occupational Therapy International*, *9*(3), 167–184.

Chung, R. Y., Carter, B. S., Norbash, A., Budzik, R., Putnam, C., & Ogilvy, C. S. (2000). Management outcomes for ruptured and unruptured aneurysms in the elderly. *Neurosurgery*, *47*(4), 827–833.

Daneski, K., Coshall, C., Tilling, K., & Wolfe, C. D. A. (2003). Reliability and validity of a postal version of the Reintegration to Normal Living Index, modified for use with stroke patients. *Clinical Rehabilitation*, *17*(8), 835–839.

Wood-Dauphinee, S. L., Opzoomer, A., Williams, J. I., Marchand, B., & Spitzer, W. O. (1988). Assessment of global function: The Reintegration to Normal Living Index. *Archives of Physical Medical and Rehabilitation*, *69*(8), 583–590.

Wood-Dauphinee, S., & Williams, J. I. (1987). Reintegration to normal living as a proxy to quality of life. *Journal of Chronic Disease*, *40*(6), 491–499.

Items for the Reintegration to Normal Living Index

Wood-Dauphinee and Williams (1987)

1. I move around my living quarters as I feel necessary (wheelchairs, other equipment and resources may be used)
2. I move around my community as I feel is necessary (wheelchairs, other equipment and resources may be used)
3. I am able to take trips out of town as I feel necessary (wheelchairs, other equipment and resources may be used)
4. I am comfortable with how my self-care needs (dressing, feeding, toileting, bathing) are met (adaptive equipment, supervision and/or assistance may be used)
5. I spend most of my days occupied in work activity that is necessary or important to me (work activity could be paid employment, housework, volunteer work, school, etc. Adaptive equipment, supervision and/or assistance may be used)
6. I am able to participate in recreational activities (hobbies, crafts, sports, reading, television, games, computers, etc.) as I want to (adaptive equipment, supervision, and/or assistance may be used)
7. I participate in social activities with family, friends and/or business acquaintances as is necessary or desirable to me (adaptive equipment, supervision and/or assistance may be used)
8. I assume a role in my family which meets my needs and those of other family members (family means people with whom you live and/or relatives with whom you don't live but see on a regular basis. Adaptive equipment, supervision and/or assistance may be used)
9. In general, I am comfortable with my personal relationships
10. In general, I am comfortable with myself when I am in the company of others
11. I feel that I can deal with life events as they happen

Acknowledgement: From Wood-Dauphinee and Williams. 1987. *Journal of Chronic Disease*, 40(6), Figure 2 p.495 by permission of Wiley-Blackwell Publishers

Sydney Psychosocial Reintegration Scale (SPRS)

Tate, Hodgkinson, Veerabangsa, and Maggiotto (1996/1999)

Source

Items for the SPRS are described in Tate et al. (1999). Recording forms for version 2 of the SPRS (SPRS-2) and the manual can be downloaded from the website of the Rehabilitation Studies Unit (http://www.rehab.med.usyd.edu.au). Scale items are also reproduced below.

Purpose

The SPRS is primarily a clinician rating scale, designed to measure psychosocial functioning in people with traumatic brain injury (TBI). It was designed as both a research tool and a clinical instrument.

Item description

The SPRS comprises 12 items in three domains: Occupational activity (4 items), Interpersonal relationships (4 items), and Independent living skills (4 items). Factual background data regarding occupational, interpersonal and living status are obtained using an additional 15-item background interview, but this contextual information is not scored. This standard version of the SPRS (Form A) measures "change since the injury"; a complementary version (Form B), using the same set of 12 items measures "current competency" (Tate, Pfaff, Veerabangsa, & Hodgkinson, 2004). For each version there are separate forms for Clinician, Self and Informant ratings. Each form has identical items, with variations in phrasing as appropriate.

Scale development

Development of the SPRS is described in Tate et al. (1999). It had its origins in a categorical scale that was developed for use in a research study (Tate, Lulham, Broe, Strettles, & Pfaff, 1989). The scale drew on the World Health Organization (WHO, 1980) construct of handicap and the psychosocial investigations of McKinlay, Brooks, Bond, Martinage, and Marshall (1981). This nascent version of the SPRS used a semi-structured interview, focusing on three domains of functioning (occupational activity, interpersonal relationships and independent living skills). Interview data were classified into one of three levels of functioning (good, limited, poor) for each of the three domains, using consensus ratings. A subsequent study with a TBI sample ($n = 92$), described in Tate et al. (1996), revealed good 6-week temporal stability ($r_s = .87$), but inter-rater reliability was only moderate ($r_s = .76$). The scale was therefore revised to improve inter-rater reliability. The three domains were retained and a pool of 25 structured items was developed, trialled and refined, resulting in the final set of 12 items. The scale was further revised in order to improve its feasibility in a clinical setting – an on-line version was developed and the rating scale reduced from a 7-point scale to a 5-point scale (referred to as SPRS-2). The data from previous studies were reanalysed with the 5-point scale, and the pattern of psychometric properties remained the same, including responsiveness and lack of ceiling or floor effects.

Administration procedures, response format and scoring

The SPRS can be administered by a clinician to an informant/patient in a face-to-face interview, or clinicians can make ratings based on their knowledge of the patient. It can also be independently completed by informants or patients, although it is not suitable for people with significant degrees of cognitive impairment affecting memory, judgement or awareness. Additionally, the SPRS can be completed on-line by clinicians, informants or patients. The interview format takes approximately 15 to 20 minutes, whereas clinician ratings based on their knowledge require less than 5 minutes.

For SPRS-2, responses on Form A are made on a 5-point scale in terms of the amount of change since the injury: 0 (equivalent of extreme change), 1 (a lot), 2 (moderate), 3 (a little), 4 (not at all, including "better than before"). Specific behavioural descriptors are attached to response categories 0 to 3 for each item. The total score ranges from 0 to 48 (0–16 for each domain), with higher scores representing better levels of psychosocial reintegration (on the original 7-point scale the total score ranged from 0 to 72 and each of the domains from 0 to 24). Some investigators (e.g., Kervick & Kaemingk, 2005) have used mean scores for domains, thereby anchoring the score back to the original descriptors, which makes it readily interpretable in terms of the response categories. For Form B, responses are made on a comparable 5-point scale in terms of current level of competency: 0 (equivalent of extremely poor), 1 (a lot of difficulty), 2 (definite difficulty), 3 (a little difficulty), 4 (very good). Form B also uses specific behavioural descriptors attached to response categories 0 to 3 for each item.

Box 8.12

Validity:	Criterion: *Concurrent:* with LHS: $r_s = -.85$
	Tate et al. (2004): Form B: with LHS: $r_s = -.71$ – Form A with Form B: $r_s = .97$
	Kuipers et al.: with CIQ: $r_s = .60$ (CIQ-Productive vs SPRS-Occupation: $r = .41$, CIQ-Social vs SPRS-Relationships: $r_s = .49$, CIQ-Home vs SPRS-Living skills: $r_s = .57$)
	Draper et al.: Informant with GOSE $r = 0.68$ (domain range 0.61 to 0.68)
	Construct: *Internal consistency:* Cronbach alpha: Total score .90 (domain range: .69–.89; with < .8 for 2/3 domains – Relationships, Living skills)
	Tate et al. (2004): Form B Cronbach alpha: Total score .93 (domain range: .82–.86)
	Factor analysis: Kuipers et al.: 2 dimensions: Productivity/personal life and Independent/dependent
	Convergent/divergent: Higher correlation with similar constructs (SPRS-Work with SIP-Work + Recreation: $r = -.72$, SPRS-Relationships with SIP-Psychosocial: $r = -.76$); lower correlation with dissimilar constructs (SPRS-Work with SIP-Relationships: $r = -.45$, SPRS-Relationships with SIP-Work + Recreation: $r = -.41$)
	Discriminant: GOS-Good $M = 52.68$ ($SD = 9.21$) vs GOS-Moderate $M = 30.13$ ($SD = 11.68$) vs GOS-Severe $M = 18.36$ ($SD = 12.39$); Kruskal-Wallis ANOVA = 35.66, $p < .001$
Reliability:	Inter-rater: ICC = .95 (domain range: ICC = .86–.94)
	Tate et al. (2004): Form B: ICC = .84 (domain range: ICC = .63–.82)
	Test–retest: 1 month: ICC = .90 (domain range: ICC = .77–.93)
	Tate et al. (2004): Form B: 1 week: ICC = .90 (range: ICC = .76–.93)
Responsiveness:	Significant improvement between admission $M = 4.00$ ($SD = 6.84$) vs discharge $M = 30.80$ ($SD = 18.13$); $z = -3.82$, $p < .001$, $d = 3.9$
	Simpson et al.: Significant improvement after intervention: Pre-treatment $M = 32.45$ ($SD = 9.48$) vs Post-treatment: $M = 41.26$ ($SD = 12.36$); $z = -5.87$, $p < .013$, $d = .93$

Psychometric properties

Psychometric properties of the SPRS (using the original 7-point rating scale) were reported by Tate et al. (1999) for Form A (change since injury) and by Tate et al. (2004) for Form B (current competency). For Form A, data from 40 people with TBI living in the community were used to examine inter-rater reliability, 1-month temporal stability ($n = 34$) and validity. Concurrent and discriminant validity were examined with the London Handicap Scale (LHS) and the Glasgow Outcome Scale (GOS) respectively. Convergent and divergent validity was examined with hypothesized correlations between similar and dissimilar constructs using the Sickness Impact Profile (SIP). Responsiveness was examined in 20 rehabilitation inpatients. Kuipers, Kendall, Fleming, and Tate (2004) examined the factor structure of the SPRS (Form A) using multidimensional scaling and compared the SPRS with the Community Integration Questionnaire (CIQ) in a community sample ($n = 91$ people with acquired brain impairment and $n = 121$ proxy respondents). Draper, Ponsford and Schönberger (2007) examined 53 people with TBI ranging from mild

(20%) to severe (67%) at ten years post-trauma and compared to the SPRS with the GOS-Extended (GOSE). Data on responsiveness of Form A are available from the case series of Simpson, Secheny, Lane-Brown, Strettles, Ferry, and Phillips (2004) who treated 50 people with TBI in a transitional living programme. For Form B, inter-rater reliability was examined using independent ratings from two clinicians on 66 people with TBI at discharge from inpatient rehabilitation, a subset ($n = 46$) was rated again 1 week later, and a small group of informants ($n = 21$) completed the LHS. Results from Tate et al. (1999) using Form A, unless otherwise stated, are shown in Box 8.12.

Comment

A particular area of strength of the SPRS is the availability of two complementary forms measuring different perspectives of psychosocial integration ("change from the pre-injury level" vs "current competency") using comparable item content and scoring format. This makes the SPRS a versatile instrument. Additionally, the response categories enable it to capture qualitative changes in the individual's level of functioning, as well as quantitative changes. Both versions, A (change from injury) and B (current competency), of the SPRS have sound psychometric properties, with excellent internal consistency for the total score, very good inter-rater reliability and temporal stability, and evidence of concurrent validity with established instruments. For Form A there is also evidence of construct validity and it is sensitive to real changes occurring in the patient with large effect sizes. Psychometric properties, however, have only been established for the original 7-point rating scale, and have yet to be examined with the 5-point scale used in SPRS-2.

Key references

Draper, K., Ponsford, J., & Schönberger, M. (2007). Psychosocial and emotional outcomes 10 years following traumatic brain injury. *Journal of Head Trauma Rehabilitation*, *22*(5), 278–287.

Kervick, R. B., & Kaemingk, K. L. (2005). Cognitive appraisal accuracy moderates the relationship between injury severity and psychosocial outcomes in traumatic brain injury. *Brain Injury*, *19*(11), 881–889.

Kuipers, P., Kendall, M., Fleming, J., & Tate, R. (2004). Comparison of the Sydney Psychosocial Reintegration Scale (SPRS) with the Community Integration Questionnaire (CIQ): Administration and psychometric properties of two outcome measures. *Brain Injury*, *18*(2), 161–177.

McKinlay, W. W., Brooks, D. N., Bond, M. R., Martinage, D. P., & Marshall, M. M. (1981). The short-term outcome of severe blunt head injury as reported by the relatives of the injured person. *Journal of Neurology, Neurosurgery, and Psychiatry*, *44*, 527–533.

Simpson, G., Secheny, T., Lane-Brown, A., Strettles, B., Ferry, K., & Phillips, J. (2004). Post-acute rehabilitation for people with traumatic brain injury: A model description and evaluation of the Liverpool Hospital Transitional Living Program. *Brain Impairment*, *5*(1), 67–80.

Tate, R. L., Hodgkinson, A. E., Veerabangsa, A., & Maggiotto, S. (1996). Measuring psychosocial outcome after traumatic brain injury. Reliability and validity of a new scale. In J. Ponsford, P. Snow, & V. Anderson (Eds.), *International perspectives in traumatic brain injury* (pp. 415–419). Queensland, Australia: Australian Academic Press, ASSBI.

Tate, R., Hodgkinson, A., Veerabangsa, A., & Maggiotto, S. (1999). Measuring psychosocial recovery after traumatic brain injury. Psychometric properties of a new scale. *Journal of Head Trauma Rehabilitation*, *14*(6), 543–557.

Tate, R. L., Lulham, J. M., Broe, G. A., Strettles, B., & Pfaff, A. (1989). Psychosocial outcome for the survivors of severe blunt head injury: The results from a consecutive series of 100 patients. *Journal of Neurology, Neurosurgery, and Psychiatry*, *52*, 1128–1134.

Tate, R. L., Pfaff, A., Veerabangsa, A., & Hodgkinson, A. E. (2004). Measuring psychosocial recovery after brain injury: Change versus competency. *Archives of Physical Medicine and Rehabilitation*, *85*, 538–545.

World Health Organization. (1980). *International classification of impairments, disabilities and handicaps*. Geneva: World Health Organization.

Sydney Psychosocial Reintegration Scale-2
Form A: Change since injury (Relative version)
Tate, Hodgkinson, Veerabangsa, and Maggiotto (1996, 1999)

Name: **Administered by:** **Date:**

BACKGROUND INTERVIEW

1. What is your relative's current occupation?
2. What are his/her work duties at present?
3. What was your relative's job at the time of the injury?
4. What were his/her work duties in that job?
5. How many jobs has he/she had since the injury (not including work trials or voluntary work)?

6 & 7. What are/were your relative's leisure interests, recreation, hobbies, and club membership, at present and at time of injury?

6. AT TIME OF INJURY	7. AT PRESENT
•	• ....
•	• ....
•	• ....
•	• ....

8 & 9. What is/was your relative's weekly programme of work, leisure/recreational activities at present and at time of injury?

8. AT TIME OF INJURY	9. AT PRESENT
•	• ....
•	• ....
•	• ....
•	• ....

10. What was your relative's marital status at time of injury?
11. What is it at present?
12. Who was in his/her circle of close friends at time of the injury?
13. Who is in his/her circle of close friends at present?
14. Who did your relative live with at time of injury?
15. Who does he/she live with at present?

OCCUPATIONAL ACTIVITY

1. Current work: Have the hours of work (or study), or the type of work (or study) changed because of the injury?

Note: If your relative is a student, answer the questions in this section in terms of changes in his/her studies

4 Not at all: Same or better

3 A little: Now works fewer hours per week
OR work duties (study) have changed to easier/lighter ones

2 Moderately: Works casually
OR has some help from others in doing some work (study)

1 A lot: Now unemployed
OR in rehabilitation
OR in a supported work programme
OR does volunteer work
OR receives remedial assistance in studies

0 Extreme: Is almost unable to (or is unable to) work (study) at present

NA Unable to assess: Did not work before the injury and still does not work

2. Work skills: Have the work (or study) skills changed because of the injury?

4 Not at all: Same or better

3 A little: Not quite as good; e.g., has to put in a lot of effort to get the same result, gets tired easily, loses concentration

2 Moderately: Definitely not as good; e.g., sometimes makes mistakes

1 A lot: Much worse; e.g., he or she is slower

0 Extreme: Very much worse; e.g., makes many mistakes, is very slow, work is of poor quality, needs constant supervision and/or reminders at present

3. Leisure: Has there been any change in the number or type of leisure activities or interests because of the injury?

4 Not at all: Same or more, and done as often or more

3 A little: Has most of the same activities and interests,
OR has the same activities and interests but does them less often

2 Moderately: Definitely less, but may have developed new activities and interests

1 A lot: Only has some of the leisure activities and interests and has not developed new ones

0 Extreme: Almost none (or no) leisure activities at present

NA Unable to assess: Did not have leisure activities before the injury and still does not have leisure activities

4. Organizing activities: Has there been any change in the way your relative organizes work and leisure activities because of the injury?

4 Not at all: Same or better

3 A little: Needs prompts or supports from others

2 Moderately: More dependent on other people to organize activities; e.g., others suggest what to do and how to go about it

1 A lot: Needs other people to do the organizing; e.g., making arrangements, providing transport

0 Extreme: Almost completely (or completely) dependent on other people to suggest and organize activities at present

OCCUPATIONAL ACTIVITIES SCORE: ________

INTERPERSONAL RELATIONSHIPS

5. Spouse or partner: Did your relative have a partner or spouse at the time of the injury? If NO, go to part b)

a) If YES, has the relationship changed because of the injury?

4 Not at all: Same or better

3 A little: Not quite the same due to the effects of the injury, but he/she still has the skills to form and maintain such relationships

2 Moderately: Definitely not the same due to the effects of the injury but he/she probably has the skills to form and maintain such relationships

1 A lot: A lot of changes, but he/she might have the skills to form a new relationship

0 Extreme: Nature of the relationship has changed in a major way (e.g., partner takes on most responsibilities or is the primary caregiver
OR has broken down and he/she probably does not have the skills to form a new relationship

b) How much change is there in his/her ability to form and maintain such a relationship compared to before the injury?

4 Not at all: Same or better

3 A little: Not quite the same, but he/she still has the skills to form and maintain such relationships

2 Moderately: Definitely not the same, but he/she probably has the skills to form and maintain such relationships

1 A lot: A lot of changes, but he/she might have the skills to form a new relationship

0 Extreme: Probably does not (or does not) have the skills to form a new relationship

6. Family: Have your relative's relationships with other family members changed because of the injury?

4 Not at all: Same or better

3 A little: Not quite the same

2 Moderately: Definitely not the same

1 A lot: A lot of changes in relationships with some family members

0 Extreme: Changed in a major way
OR a breakdown of relationships with some family members because of the effects of the injury

NA Unable to assess: Did not have contact with family before the injury

7. Friends and other people: Have your relative's relationships with other people outside family (such as close friends, work mates, neighbours) changed because of the injury?

4 Not at all: Same or better

3 A little: Not quite the same, but still sees some friends weekly or more, makes new friends, and gets along with others (e.g., work mates, neighbours)

2 Moderately: Definitely not the same, but still sees some friends once a month or more and can make new friends

1 A lot: Only sees a few friends (or other people outside family), and does not make new friends easily

0 Extreme: Sees hardly any friends (or no friends at all), or other people outside family

8. Communication: Have your relative's communication skills (i.e., talk with other people and understand what others say) changed because of the injury?

4 Not at all: Same or better

3 A little: Some changes; e.g., rambles and gets off the point, talk is sometimes inappropriate, has some trouble finding the words to express himself or herself

2 Moderately: Definite changes; e.g., difficulty in thinking of things to say, joining in talk with groups of people, only talks about himself or herself

1 A lot: A lot of changes; e.g., having trouble understanding what people say

0 Extreme: Major changes, but can communicate basic needs
OR uses aids for communication
OR communication is almost impossible

INTERPERSONAL RELATIONSHIPS SCORE: ________

LIVING SKILLS

9. Social skills: Have your relative's social skills and behaviour in public changed because of the injury?

4 Not at all: Same or better
3 A little: Some changes; e.g., is awkward with other people, does not worry about what other people think or want
2 Moderately: Definite changes; e.g., can act in a silly way, is not as tactful or sensitive to other people's needs
1 A lot: A lot of changes; e.g., is more dependent on other people, is socially withdrawn
0 Extreme: Major changes; e.g., has difficulty interacting appropriately with other people, behaviour is unpredictable, temper outbursts in public, requires supervision when with other people

10. Personal habits: Have your relative's personal habits (e.g., his/her care in cleanliness, dressing and tidiness) changed because of the injury?

4 Not at all: Same or better
3 A little: Does not take as much care as before
2 Moderately: Attends to own hygiene, dress and tidiness, but has definitely changed in this area; needs supervision
1 A lot: Needs prompts, reminders or advice from others, but responds to these
OR needs stand-by assistance
0 Extreme: Needs prompts, reminders or advice from others, but responds to these only after repeated requests
OR needs hands-on assistance
OR is totally dependent for assistance

11. Community travel: Have your relative's use of transport and travel around the community changed because of the injury?

Note: Do not include the driver of transport, or other passengers using such transport, in rating whether a person can travel "alone" or "by himself/herself"

4 Not at all: Same or better
3 A little: Unable to use some forms of transport (e.g., driving a car) but can still get around in the community by using other forms of transport without help
2 Moderately: Definite changes in use of transport, but after training can travel around the community on his/her own
1 A lot: Needs assistance to plan use of transport, but with such help can travel around the community on his/her own
0 Extreme: Very restricted in use of transport, but with supervision can make short, familiar journeys around the community on his/her own (e.g., going out to the local shop)
OR is unable to go out into the community alone

12. Accommodation: Has your relative's living situation changed because of the injury?

4 Not at all: Same or better
3 A little: Lives in the community, but with emotional or social supports provided by other people, such as family, friends or neighbours. Could not be left alone without supports for a 2-week period
2 Moderately: Definite changes and could not be left alone for a weekend unless someone was available to check that everything was OK
1 A lot: Lives in the community, but in supported accommodation, such as a group home, boarding house, transitional living unit
OR in family home but requires daily supervision or assistance
0 Extreme: Almost unable to live in the community, even with daily supervision or assistance
OR needs care, which may be at home requiring extensive, daily supervision or other care
OR is in an institution, such as a nursing home, residential service, rehabilitation unit

LIVING SKILLS SCORE: _______

TOTAL SPRS SCORE (OA + IR + LS): _______

Acknowledgement: Scale items from Tate, R. et al. (1999). Measuring psychosocial recovery after traumatic brain injury. Psychometric properties of a new scale. *Journal of Head Trauma Rehabilitation*, *14*(6), 543–557, pp. 543–547 and Appendix, p. 557, reprinted with permission of Lippincott Williams & Wilkins and Wolters Kluwer. Format provided by Dr Tate.

World Health Organization Disability Assessment Schedule II (WHODAS II)

World Health Organization (WHO, 2000)

Source

The WHO website (http://www.who.int/icidh/whodas/index.html) provides general information on the WHODAS II, along with items for versions of different lengths and a training manual.

Purpose

The WHODAS II is a self-rating scale that examines everyday activities. It was designed as a generic instrument, suitable for use with different health conditions, and in different countries and cultures. The WHO website advises that information from the WHODAS II can be used to identify needs, match patients to interventions, track functioning over time, and measure clinical outcomes and treatment effectiveness. As yet, few studies of the WHODAS II have been published using an acquired brain impairment (ABI) sample; a population survey of people with disabilities including persons with epilepsy, multiple sclerosis and stroke was reported by Gallagher and Mulvany (2004) and Soberg, Bautz-Holter, Roise, and Finset (2007) examined a trauma sample, including patients with head and neck injuries. Pösel, Cieza, and Stucki (2007) studied the psychometric properties of the WHODAS II in a multicentre study with rehabilitation patients, including patients with stroke.

Item description

The WHODAS II is a 36-item instrument (32 items for respondents who do not work) that covers six activity domains, as well as overall disability. The six domains and their items directly map to the *International Classification of Functioning, Disability and Health* (ICF; WHO, 2001) Activities/Participation component: Understanding and communication (6 items, which also include the cognitive areas of concentration, learning, memory and problem solving), Getting around (5 items), Self-care (4 items), Getting along with other people (5 items), Life activities (which address domestic, 4 items, as well as school/employment areas, 4 items), and Participation in society (8 items). For each endorsed item, one or two follow-up questions are asked regarding the extent to which difficulties interfere with life, and the frequency of activities/difficulties over the past month. Self, informant and interviewer-administered versions are available, as well as shorter forms (12-item, 12-item screen +24 additional items, and 6-item).

Scale development

At the time of writing, no published document is available on the development of the WHODAS II, and the following information was obtained from the WHO website (http://www.who.int/icidh/whodas/index.html, last accessed 5 June, 2009). The WHODAS II is a revision of the WHO Disability Assessment Schedule (WHODAS; WHO, 1988), which aimed to evaluate social adjustment and behavioural disturbances in people with mental disorders. In contrast to the WHODAS, the WHODAS II was not designed solely for people with mental health disorders, or necessarily to be clinician-rated. Rather, it "represents a complete revision", incorporating the different conceptual underpinnings of the ICF. The WHODAS II was cross-culturally developed so that it would be appropriate "across the spectrum of cultural and educational backgrounds". A series of field trials was conducted with early versions of the WHODAS II in 1998 (89-item version tested across 21 sites in 19 countries) and 1999. Content was reduced to 36 items, based on results of these trials and psychometric analyses, but no details are provided regarding the item reduction process. Reliability and validity of the WHODAS II were examined in further trials (16 sites in 14 countries), but no details are provided regarding these psychometric properties.

Administration procedures, response format and scoring

The WHODAS II can be administered by an interviewer, or completed by an informant or the person themselves. The interviewer-administered, 36-item version is recommended by the WHO and a training manual is available from the WHO website. Administration time for the 36-item version is 20 minutes; the 12-item version takes 5 minutes.

Responses are made from the perspective of difficulties experienced in the past 30 days. A 5-point scale is used: 1 (equivalent of no difficulties), 2 (mild), 3 (moderate), 4 (severe), to 5 (extreme/cannot do). Separate scores are used for the supplementary questions regarding frequency, using either DAY CODES (ratings on a 5-point ordinal scale) or DAYS (actual number of days). For the 36-item version, scores are available for each of the six domains and an overall score.

The WHO website advises that scoring uses averaged responses that are then transformed into a standard scale for a total score, and each subscale, ranging from 0 to 100. Higher scores reflect greater difficulties in functioning. The WHO website further advises that at this stage, scoring procedures for the WHODAS II are only available to registered users and the Statistical Package for the Social Sciences (SPSS) is required to run syntax that converts the responses into scores.

Psychometric properties

Published information on the psychometric properties of the WHODAS II is gradually starting to accumulate, although data with ABI groups remains sparse. Pösel et al. (2007) studied the German version of the WHODAS II in 904 rehabilitation patients from 19 participating centres. Patients had a range of medical conditions, including stroke ($n = 116$, 13% of the sample). The Medical Outcomes Study Health Survey – Short Form 36 (SF-36) scales were used to examine convergent and divergent validity with hypothesized correlations between similar and dissimilar constructs. The WHODAS II was administered twice, before and after a rehabilitation intervention, thereby providing information on responsiveness. The factor structure was examined in patients with musculoskeletal conditions ($n = 296$) because of the larger sample size than the stroke sample. Six factors were extracted, accounting for 64% of the variance. Because of multiple cross-loadings, the authors concluded that the structure of the original scale could not be replicated. A comprehensive psychometric study of the (32-item) WHODAS II with 380 older adults with hearing loss was reported by Chisholm, Abrams, McArdle, Wilson, and Doyle (2005). Validating instruments included the SF36-Veteran's Version (SF-36V) and Abbreviated Profile of Hearing Aid Benefit (APHAB). Temporal stability was examined with a subset of the sample ($n = 189$) assessed on two occasions at 2 and 10 weeks after baseline.

Information on other psychometric properties is available from other clinical groups. A schizophrenia sample ($n = 54$) was studied by McKibbin, Patterson, and Jeste (2004), along with 22 healthy controls. Discriminant validity was examined and 12-week temporal stability was assessed in a subset of the sample ($n = 18$). The WHODAS II was compared with other instruments, including Quality of Well-Being (QWB). Responsiveness was examined by Soberg et al. (2007), who assessed 105 people admitted to a Level 1 trauma centre with severe trauma (unspecified type, but included 38% with head/neck injuries). Patients were assessed 6 weeks post-discharge (approximately 20 weeks post-trauma), and at 1 and 2 years post-trauma. Cankurtaran, Ulug, Saygi, Tiryaki, and Akalan (2005) examined 22 patients with mesial temporal lobe epilepsy pre-surgery, and 3 and 6 months post-operatively. Results of these studies are shown in Box 8.13.

Comment

The WHODAS II is an important instrument, if for no other reason than it is the disability measure both developed and endorsed by the WHO. Additionally, it has been trialled cross-culturally and is a generic instrument, with the aim of treating "all disorders at parity when determining level of functioning". It is, however, difficult to access specific information on the developmental procedures or psychometric properties of the WHODAS II. The psychometric information that is starting to appear in the literature is limited and has been largely restricted to non-ABI populations. There are, however, promising reliability, validity and responsiveness data from other clinical groups, as detailed above and elsewhere. Surprisingly, there is little evidence to suggest that the WHODAS II has widespread use in ABI populations, either as a research tool or in clinical practice, but this may change with increased efforts to introduce minimum sets of core instruments to enable comparison across health conditions and clinical settings. Scoring procedures for the WHODAS II appear to be somewhat cumbersome and the need for a computerized scoring program written for SPSS may be a disadvantage that may exert an adverse effect on the widespread application of the WHODAS II in clinical practice.

Box 8.13

Validity:	Criterion: *Concurrent:* Pösel et al. (stroke sample): Total score with SF-36-Physical component: $r = -.62$ – with SF-36-Mental component: $r = -.50$ Chisholm et al.: with SF-36V-Physical component: $r = -.55$ (domain range: $r = -.25$ to $-.58$) – with SF-36-Mental component: $r = -.64$ (domain range: $r = -.36$ to $-.64$) McKibbin et al.: with QWB: $r = .63$ Construct: *Internal consistency:* Pösel et al. (stroke sample): Cronbach alpha: domain range: .84–.97 Chisholm et al.: Total score .94 (domain range .68–.91; with < .8 for 1/6 domains – Getting along) *Factor structure:* Pösel et al. (musculoskeletal sample): 6 factors, but these did not match the structure of the original scale *Convergent/divergent:* Pösel et al. (stroke sample): higher correlation with similar constructs (WHODAS II-Self-care with SF-36-Physical functioning: $r = -.62$, WHODAS-II-Getting along with SF-36-Social functioning: $r = -.44$); lower correlation with dissimilar constructs (WHODAS II-Self-care with SF-36-Social functioning: $r = -.25$, WHODAS II-Getting along with SF-36-Physical functioning: $r = -.37$) Chisholm et al.: higher correlation with similar constructs (WHODAS II-Understanding and communication with APHAB-Global: $r = .43$, WHODAS-II-Getting around with SF-36V-Physical: $r = -.69$); lower correlation with dissimilar constructs (WHODAS II-Understanding and communication with SF-36V-Physical: $r = -.27$, WHODAS II-Getting around with APHAB-Global: $r = .19$) *Discriminant:* McKibbin et al.: Clinical sample $M = 24.8$ ($SD = 14.2$) vs Controls $M = 3.1$ ($SD = 5.6$); $t = 9.6$, $p < .001$
Reliability:	Inter-rater: No information available Test–retest: Chisholm et al.: 2 weeks: ICC = .93 (domain range: ICC = .81–.91) – 10 weeks: ICC = .87 (domain range: ICC = .71–.79) McKibbin et al.: 12 weeks: ICC = .89
Responsiveness:	Pösel et al. (stroke sample): Total score reflects slight increase in difficulties: baseline $M = 38.7$ ($SD = 24.8$) vs after rehabilitation intervention $M = 42.8$ ($SD = 24.7$); domain range: $d = .01–.20$ Cankurtaran et al.: significant improvement in Participation domain: pre-operative $M = 29.3$ ($SD = 13.2$) vs 6 months post-operative $M = 14.8$ ($SD = 13.6$), $d = 1.10$; no other domain showed significant change Soberg et al.: 1 and 2 year retests: significant decrease in disability: 6 weeks post-discharge $M = 40.77$ ($SD = 15.86$) vs 1 year $M = 28.31$ ($SD = 19.11$); $p < .001$, $d = .79$, but not between 1 year vs 2 year $M = 27.27$ ($SD = 19.19$); $d = .05$, $p > .05$

Key references

Cankurtaran, E. S., Ulug, B., Saygi, S., Tiryaki, A., & Akalan, N. (2005). Psychiatric morbidity, quality of life, and disability in mesial temporal lobe epilepsy patients before and after anterior temporal lobectomy. *Epilepsy and Behavior*, *7*(1), 116–122.

Chisholm, T. H., Abrams, H. B., McArdle, R., Wilson, R. H., & Doyle, P. J. (2005). The WHO-DAS II: Psychometric properties in the measurement of functional health status in adults with acquired hearing loss. *Trends in Amplification*, *9*(3), 111–126.

Gallagher, P., & Mulvany, F. (2004). Levels of ability and functioning: Using the WHODAS II in an Irish context. *Disability and Rehabilitation*, *26*(9), 506–517.

McKibbin, C., Patterson, T. L., & Jeste, D. V. (2004). Assessing disability in older patients with schizophrenia: Results from the WHODAS-II. *Journal of Nervous and Mental Disease*, *192*(6), 405–413.

Pösel, M., Cieza, A., & Stucki, G. (2007). Psychometric properties of the WHODAS II in rehabilitation patients. *Quality of Life Research*, *16*, 1521–1531.

Soberg, H. L., Bautz-Holter, E., Roise, O., & Finset, A. (2007). Long-term multidimensional functional consequences of severe multiple injuries two years after trauma: A prospective longitudinal cohort study. *Journal of Trauma*, *62*(2), 461–470.

World Health Organization. (1988). *WHO Psychiatric Disability Assessment Schedule (WHO/DAS)*. Geneva: World Health Organization.

World Health Organization. (2000). *Disability Assessment Schedule. WHODAS II*. Available at http://www.who.int/icidh/whodas/index.html.

World Health Organization. (2001). *International classification of functioning, disability and health*. Geneva: World Health Organization.

World Health Organization – Disability Assessment Schedule II

World Health Organization (2004)

Name:	**Administered by:**	**Date:**

Instructions: This interview is about difficulties people have because of health condition. By health conditions I mean diseases or illnesses, other health problems that may be short or long lasting, injuries, mental or emotional problems and problems with alcohol or drugs.

I remind you to keep all of your health problems in mind as you answer the questions. When I ask you about difficulties in doing an activity think about:

- Increased effort
- Discomfort or pain
- Slowness
- Changes in the way you do an activity.

When answering, I'd like you to think back over the last 30 days. I would also like you to answer these questions thinking about how much difficulty you have, on average over the past 30 days, while doing the activity as you usually do it.

Response key:	Day codes:
1 = None	A = 1 day
2 = Mild	B = up to 1 week (2 to 7 days)
3 = Moderate	C = up to 2 weeks (8 to 14 days)
4 = Severe	D = more than 2 weeks (15 to 29 days)
5 = Extreme/cannot do	E = all days (30 days)

UNDERSTANDING AND COMMUNICATING

"I am going to ask some questions about understanding and communicating."
In the questions below, for responses greater than None (1), ask: "How many days was this difficulty present?" Record codes for days (A–E)

In the last 30 days, how much difficulty did you have in:	**RESPONSE**	**DAY CODE**
1. (D1.1) Concentrating on doing something for 10 minutes?	______	______
2. (D1.2) Remembering to do important things?	______	______
3. (D1.3) Analysing and finding solutions to problems in day-to-day life?	______	______
4. (D1.4) Learning a new task, for example, learning how to get to a new place?	______	______
5. (D1.5) Generally understanding what people say?	______	______
6. (D1.6) Starting and maintaining conversation?	______	______

Probe: If any of D1.1–1.6 are rated greater than None (1), ask:

P1.1 How much did these difficulties interfere with your life? ______

Response key:	Day codes:
1 = None	A = 1 day
2 = Mild	B = up to 1 week (2 to 7 days)
3 = Moderate	C = up to 2 weeks (8 to 14 days)
4 = Severe	D = more than 2 weeks (15 to 29 days)
5 = Extreme/cannot do	E = all days (30 days)

GETTING AROUND

"I am now going to ask you about difficulties in getting around."
In the questions below, for responses greater than None (1), ask: "How many days was this difficulty present?" Record codes for days (A–E)

In the last 30 days, how much difficulty did you have in:	**RESPONSE**	**DAY CODE**
7. (D2.1) Standing for long periods such as 30 minutes?	______	______
8. (D2.2) Standing up from sitting down?	______	______
9. (D2.3) Moving around inside your home?	______	______
10. (D2.4) Getting out of your home?	______	______
11. (D2.5) Walking a long distance such as a kilometre (or equivalent)?	______	______

Probe: If any of D2.1–2.5 are rated greater than None (1), ask:

P2.1 How much did these difficulties interfere with your life? ______

SELF-CARE

"I am now going to ask you about difficulties in taking care of yourself."
In the questions below, for responses greater than None (1), ask: "How many days was this difficulty present?" Record codes for days (A–E)

In the last 30 days, how much difficulty did you have in:	**RESPONSE**	**DAY CODE**
12. (D3.1) Washing your whole body?	______	______
13. (D3.2) Getting dressed?	______	______
14. (D3.3) Eating?	______	______
15. (D3.4) Staying by yourself for a few days?	______	______

Probe: If any of D3.1–3.4 are rated greater than None (1), ask:

P3.1 How much did these difficulties interfere with your life? ______

GETTING ALONG WITH PEOPLE

"I am now going to ask you about difficulties in getting along with people. Please remember that I am asking only about difficulties that are a result of health problems. By this I mean diseases or illnesses, injuries, mental or emotional problems and problems with alcohol or drugs."

In the questions below, for responses greater than None (1), ask: "How many days was this difficulty present?" Record codes for days (A–E)

In the last 30 days, how much difficulty did you have in:	**RESPONSE**	**DAY CODE**
16. (D4.1) Dealing with people you do not know?	______	______
17. (D4.2) Maintaining a friendship?	______	______
18. (D4.3) Getting along with people who are close to you?	______	______
19. (D4.4) Making new friends?	______	______
20. (D4.5) Sexual activities?	______	______

Probe: If any of D4.1–4.5 are rated greater than None (1), ask:

P4.1 How much did these difficulties interfere with your life? ______

Response key:	Day codes:
1 = None	A = 1 day
2 = Mild	B = up to 1 week (2 to 7 days)
4 = Severe	D = more than 2 weeks (15 to 29 days)
5 = Extreme/cannot do	E = all days (30 days)

LIFE ACTIVITIES

a) Household activities: "The following questions are about activities involved in maintaining your household, and in caring for people with whom you live or those close to you. These activities include cooking, cleaning, shopping, caring for others and caring for your belongings."

D5.1 How many hours do you spend in these activities in a typical week? ________

In the questions below, for responses greater than None (1), ask: "How many days was this difficulty present?" Record codes for days (A–E)

Because of your health condition, in the last 30 days, how much difficulty did you have in:	**RESPONSE**	**DAY CODE**
21. (D5.2) Taking care of your household responsibilities?	________	________
22. (D5.3) Doing your most important household tasks well?	________	________
23. (D5.4) Getting all the household work done that you needed to do?	________	________
24. (D5.5) Getting your household work done as quickly as needed?	________	________
	________	________

Probe: If any of D5.2–5.5 are rated greater than None (1), ask:

P5.1 How much did these difficulties interfere with your life?

		No. of days
D5.6 In the last 30 days, on how many days did you reduce or completely miss household work because of your health condition?	________	________

b) If respondent works (paid, non-paid, self-employed) or goes to school, complete questions D5.7–D5.13. Otherwise, skip to D6.1. "Now I will ask some questions about your work or school."

D5.7 How many hours do you spend in work (which includes school) in a typical work week? ________

In the questions below, for responses greater than None (1), ask: "How many days was this difficulty present?" Record codes for days (A–E)

Because of your health condition, in the last 30 days how much difficulty did you have in:	**RESPONSE**	**DAY CODE**
25. (D5.8) Your day-to-day work?	________	________
26. (D5.9) Doing your most important work tasks well?	________	________
27. (D5.10) Getting all the work done that you needed to do?	________	________
28. (D5.11) Getting your work done as quickly as needed?	________	________
D5.12 Have you had to work at a lower level because of a health condition?	No: 1 Yes: 2	
D5.13 Did you earn less money as the result of a health condition?	No: 1 Yes: 2	

Probe: If any of D5.8–5.13 are rated greater than None (1), ask:

P5.2 How much did these difficulties interfere with your life?	________	
D5.14 In the last 30 days, on how many days did you miss work for half a day or more because of your health condition?		________

Response key:	Day codes:
1 = None	A = 1 day
2 = Mild	B = up to 1 week (2 to 7 days)
3 = Moderate	C = up to 2 weeks (8 to 14 days)
4 = Severe	D = more than 2 weeks (15 to 29 days)
5 = Extreme/cannot do	E = all days (30 days)

PARTICIPATION IN SOCIETY

"Now, I am going to ask you about your participation in society and the impact of your health problems on you and your family. Some of these questions may involve problems that go beyond the last 30 days, however in answering, please focus on the last 30 days. Again, I remind you to answer these questions while thinking about health problems: physical, mental or emotional, alcohol or drug related."
Note that the number of days for each question in this domain is not requested.

In the last 30 days:	RESPONSE	DAY CODE
29. (D6.1) How much of a problem did you have joining in community activities (e.g., festivities, religious or other activities) in the same way as everyone else can?	______	
30. (D6.2) How much of a problem did you have because of barriers or hindrances in the world around you?	______	
31. (D6.3) How much of a problem did you have living with dignity because of the attitudes and actions of others?	______	
32. (D6.4) How much time did you spend on your health condition, or its consequences?	______	
33. (D6.5) How much have you been emotionally affected by your health condition?	______	
34. (D6.6) How much has your health been a drain on financial resources of you or your family?	______	
In the last 30 days:		
35. (D6.7) How much of a problem did your family have because of your health problems?	______	
36. (D6.8) How much of a problem did you have in doing things by yourself for relaxation or pleasure?	______	

Probe: If any of D6.1–6.8 are rated greater than None (1), ask:

P6.1 How much did these difficulties interfere with your life?	______	
P6.2 In the last 30 days' for how many days did you have these difficulties?		______
H3 Overall, in the past 30 days, how many days did you experience any of the difficulties that we have discussed during this interview?		______

This concludes our interview, thank you for participating.

Acknowledgement: Adapted from WHO website: http://www.who.int/icidh/index.html1 Last accessed 15 October 2009.

Part C

Contextual Factors

The undisputed strength of the *International Classification of Functioning, Disability and Health* (ICF; WHO, 2001) is the introduction of Contextual Factors, both environmental and personal, which contributed to the change of focus of the original classification (WHO, 1980) from a medical model of illness to a biopsychosocial model of health. In the ICF, Contextual Factors have two components: Environmental Factors and Personal Factors (see Appendix C). As described in Chapter 1, the Personal Factors component contains a broad constellation of factors ranging from simple demographics (e.g., race, age, education) through to complex psychosocial constructs (e.g., upbringing, coping styles, psychological assets). The Personal Factors component has not yet been classified within the ICF. Environmental Factors refer to "the physical, social and attitudinal environments in which people live and conduct their lives" (WHO, 2001, p. 10), and are the subject of the present chapter.

9 Scales of environmental factors

Instruments presented in Chapter 9 map to the component and domains of the *International Classification of Functioning, Disability and Health* (ICF; WHO, 2001) as depicted in Figure 9.1.

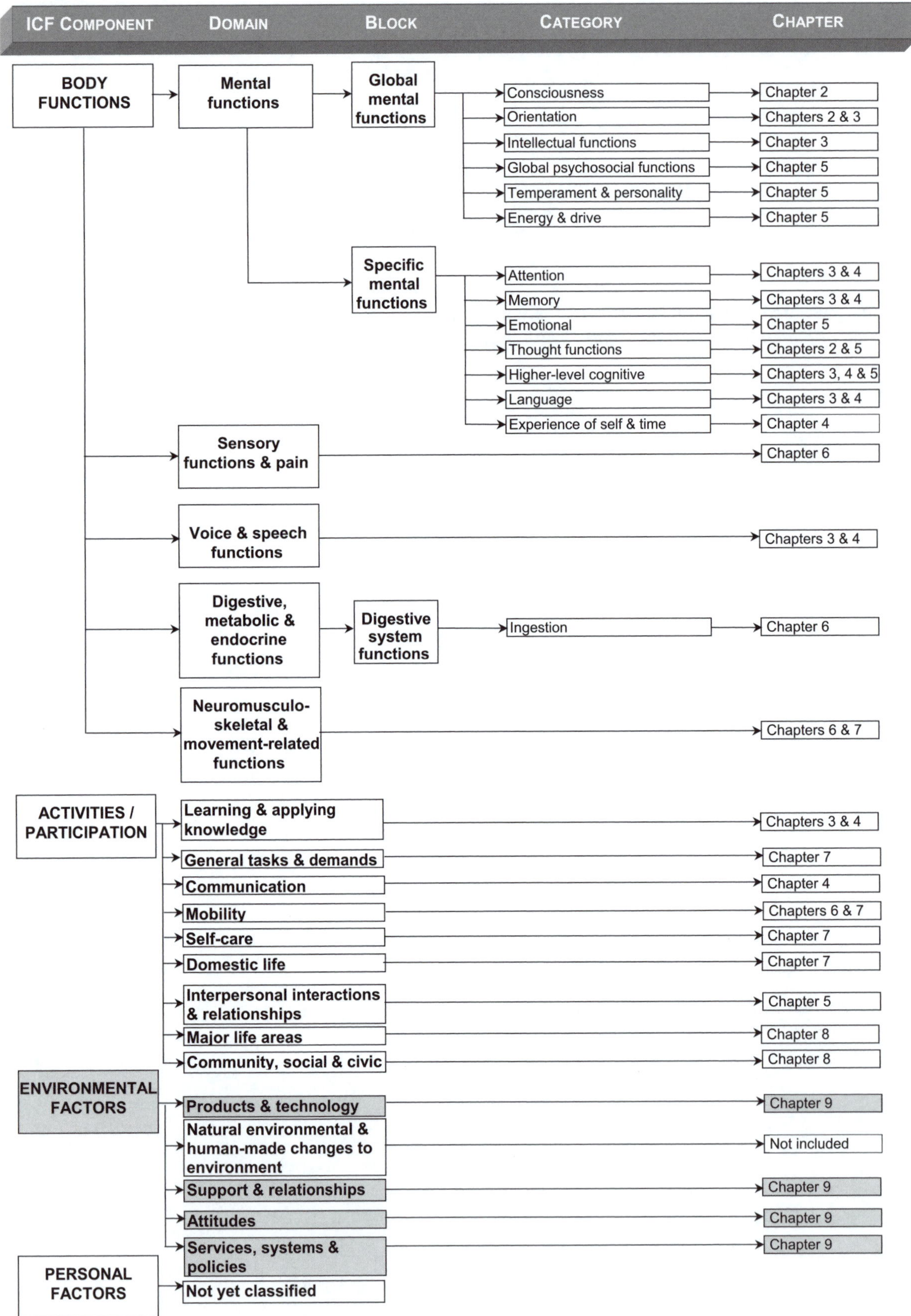

Figure 9.1 Instruments included in the compendium in relation to the ICF taxonomy – the highlighted component and domains appear in this chapter. *Note:* the Figure presents a partial listing of five out of the eight Body Function domains and does not include any of the Body Structure domains. Categories for Mental functions also represent a partial listing and categories for the remaining domains are not listed. Refer to Appendix C for further detail on the ICF taxonomy.

Introduction

The significance of environmental factors is highlighted by Whiteneck, Harrison-Felix, Mellick, Brooks, Charlifue, and Gerhart (2004, p. 1324):

> physical, attitudinal, and policy barriers in the environment are viewed as having as great an impact, or greater, than the underlying organ system impairments in determining a person's activity limitations, participation restrictions, and the development of many secondary conditions.

Moreover, Fougeyrollas (1995, p. 150) observes that:

> without an evaluation of environmental factors there can be no ecological approach to handicaps, no social change, no transformation of what we call in anthropology the social normative context. The significance of impairments and disabilities can, depending on the circumstances, lead to stigma and exclusion.

The Environmental Factors component of the ICF contains five domains (see Figure 9.1 and Appendix C). In the past, there were few systematic and standardized instruments to measure some of these domains, such as products and technologies; attitudes; and services, systems and policies. Even now, there exists only a limited array of standardized measures suitable for the acquired brain impairment (ABI) group, but a selection of scales with established psychometric properties is presented in this chapter (see also the Assessment of Living Skills and Resources, ALSAR, published by Williams and colleagues in 1991 and described in Chapter 7, which provides a risk evaluation pertinent to environmental factors). Excluded are those instruments that do not have scaling characteristics, such as lists and catalogues of products and technologies that are used as equipment, assistive devices and aids for everyday living. For information in these areas, the interested reader is referred to the broader rehabilitation literature (e.g., DeLisa et al., 2005; McInnes, Hailey, & Cowley, 1995; Sohlberg & Mateer, 2001; Wielandt & Strong, 2000). Additionally, some investigators have developed checklists to document service utilization by people with ABI (e.g., Corrigan, 2001; Heinemann, Sokol, Garvin, & Bode, 2002; High et al., 1995; Hodgkinson, Veerabangsa, Drane, & McCluskey, 2000), but with the exception of the scale of Heinemann et al., psychometric properties of other scales remain to be investigated.

In contrast to the foregoing domains, the supports and relationships domain of Environmental Factors has a history of using standardized instruments with established psychometric properties. Many of these scales were developed for the older population, and have had limited exposure and application in the area of ABI. It is expected that with the integration of the ICF into clinical and research practice, the use of such instruments will increase. A small number of scales measuring social supports from the perspectives of structure (i.e., social networks) and function (i.e., people on whom one can rely for support) is presented in this chapter.

In delineating the domain of supports and relationships, the ICF explicitly states that this domain "does not encompass the attitudes of the persons or people that are providing the support" (WHO, 2001, p. 187). This is unfortunate for a number of reasons. It is well recognized that family members and significant others provide substantial (and not uncommonly, the only) support and/or care for people with ABI. By convention, care and support provided by family members or significant others is referred to as "informal support", possibly to distinguish it from support provided by formal institutions and systems, including paid care. The term "informal support", however, has connotations of it being less important than "formal support", less demanding, and even an optional extra. Yet, the provision of such "informal support" can come at huge cost to the support-provider – financially, physically, socially and psychologically. The plethora of scales addressing caregiver burden, caregiver strain, parental stress, family functioning and so forth is testimony to the toll of providing "informal support" (see Visser-Meily, Post, Riphagen, & Lindeman, 2004; Vitaliano, Young, & Russo, 1991 for a review of scales in stroke and dementia respectively). This is not to imply that provision of informal support is inevitably a burden or that there are no positive aspects to it (see Cafferata & Stone, 1989; Lawton, Kleban, Moss, Rovine, & Glicksman, 1989; Machamer, Temkin, & Dikmen, 2002; Roff, Burgio, Gitlin, Nichols, Chaplin, & Hardin, 2004), but the reality is that in many situations, at many times, caregiving and support provision cause strain.

From a clinical perspective, it is also well recognized that if the support-provider is no longer able to fill that role because of the burden/stress/strain, then not only will the support-recipient certainly need the "formal" services, but also he or she will be at risk of further limitations in everyday living and restrictions in community participation (Whiteneck et al., 2004). Arguably, if one is interested in measuring the social network and social support of a person with ABI, one should also be interested in measuring the stability and viability of that social support, which can be jeopardized if the support-provider is under strain. Because the ICF does not incorporate the perspective of the caregiver, scales addressing caregiver strain and quality of family relationships have not been included in this compendium.

References

Cafferata, G. L., & Stone, R. (1989). The caregiving role: Dimensions of burden and benefits. *Comprehensive Gerontology. Suppl. Issue A*+B, *3*, 57–64.

Corrigan, J. D. (2001). Conducting statewide needs assessments for persons with traumatic brain injury. *Journal of Head Trauma Rehabilitation*, *16*, 1–19.

DeLisa, J. A., Gans, B. M., Walsh, N. E., Bockenek, W. L., Frontera, W. R. Geiringer, S. R., et al. (Eds.). (2005). *Physical medicine and rehabilitation: Principles and practice* (4th ed.). Philadelphia: Lippincott, Williams and Wilkins.

Fougeyrollas, P. (1995). Documenting environmental factors for preventing the handicap creation process: Québec contributions relating to ICIDH and social participation of people with functional differences. *Disability and Rehabilitation*, *17*(3/4), 145–153.

Heinemann, A. W., Sokol, K., Garvin, L., & Bode, R. K. (2002). Measuring unmet needs and services among persons with traumatic brain injury. *Archives of Physical Medicine and Rehabilitation*, *83*, 1052–1059.

High, W. M., Gordon, W. A., Lehmkuhl, L. D., Newton, C. N., Vandergoot, D., Thoi, L., et al. (1995). Productivity and service utilization following traumatic brain injury: Results of a survey by the RSA regional TBI centers. *Journal of Head Trauma Rehabilitation*, *10*(4), 64–80.

Hodgkinson, A. E., Veerabangsa, A., Drane, D., & McCluskey, A. (2000). Service utilisation following traumatic brain injury. *Journal of Head Trauma Rehabilitation*, *15*, 1208–1226.

Lawton, M. P., Kleban, M. H., Moss, M., Rovine, M., & Glicksman, A. (1989). Measuring caregiving appraisal. *Journal of Gerontology*, *44*(3), P61–P71.

Machamer, J., Temkin, N., & Dikmen, S. (2002). Significant other burden and factors related to it in traumatic brain injury. *Journal of Clinical and Experimental Neuropsychology*, *24*(4), 420–433.

McInnes, P., Hailey, D., & Cowley, D. (1995). *Assistive devices for people with disabilities: An information paper*. Australian Institute of Health and Welfare. Canberra: Australian Government Publishing Service.

Roff, L. L., Burgio, L. D., Gitlin, L., Nichols, L., Chaplin, W., & Hardin, J. M. (2004). Positive aspects of Alzheimer's caregiving: The role of race. *Journal of Gerontology*, *59B*(4), 185–190.

Sohlberg, M. M., & Mateer, C. A. (2001). *Cognitive rehabilitation. An integrative neuropsychological approach*. New York: Guildford.

Visser-Meily, J. M. A., Post, M. W. M., Riphagen, I. I., & Lindeman, E. (2004). Measures used to assess burden among caregivers of stroke patients: A review. *Clinical Rehabilitation*, *18*, 601–623.

Vitaliano, P. P., Young, H. M., & Russo, J. (1991). Burden: A review of measures used among caregivers of individuals with dementia. *The Gerontologist*, *31*(1), 67–75.

Whiteneck, G. G., Harrison-Felix, C. L., Mellick, D. C., Brooks, C. A., Charlifue, S. B., & Gerhart, K. A. (2004). Quantifying environmental factors: A measure of physical, attitudinal, service, productivity, and policy barriers. *Archives of Physical Medicine and Rehabilitation*, *85*, 1324–1335.

Wielandt, T., & Strong, J. (2000). Compliance with prescribed adaptive equipment: A literature review. *British Journal of Occupational Therapy*, *63*(2), 65–75.

Williams, J. H., Drinka, T. J. K., Greenberg, J. R., Farrell-Holtan, J., Euhardy, R., & Schram, M. (1991). Development and testing of the Assessment of Living Skills and Resources (ALSAR) in elderly community-dwelling veterans. *The Gerontologist*, *31*(1), 84–91.

World Health Organization. (1980). *International classification of impairments, disabilities and handicaps*. Geneva: World Health Organization.

World Health Organization. (2001). *International classification of functioning, disability and health*. Geneva: World Health Organization.

Care and Needs Scale (CANS)

Tate (2003)

Source

A description of the CANS Support Levels, along with the checklist of items used to determine the levels, appears in an appendix to Tate (2004). The recording form and manual are available from the website of the Rehabilitation Studies Unit, University of Sydney (http://www.rehab.med.usyd.edu.au), and the recording form is reproduced below.

Purpose

The CANS is a clinician rating scale, designed to amalgamate information obtained from a range of sources and use it to document support needs required for everyday functional activities and community living. It was developed for people with traumatic brain injury (TBI) and aims to capture the gamut of support needs, from very high to minimal requirements.

Item description

The CANS contains two sections: the Needs Checklist documents *type* of support and Support Levels documents the *extent* of support, as indexed by the length of time the person can be left alone. The 24-item Needs Checklist is categorized into four groups that are hierarchically organized according to intensity of need. Group A (special needs) contains nine items covering very high level needs, such as tracheostomy management, harmful behaviours; Group B (basic activities of daily living, ADL) has three items covering personal hygiene, dressing, food preparation; Group C (instrumental activities of daily living, IADL, and psychosocial) contains 10 items addressing shopping, transport, relationships, work and so forth; and Group D contains two items, informational (e.g., information, knowledge, advice) and emotional supports. The second section contains eight Support Levels that are also hierarchically arranged: 0 (equivalent of does not need contact), 1 (needs intermittent contact, less than weekly), 2 (needs weekly contact), 3 (needs contact every few days), 4 (needs daily contact), 5 (can be left alone during the day, but not at night), 6 (can be left alone for a few hours), 7 (cannot be left alone).

Scale development

The impetus to develop the CANS arose from the need to document support needs of people who were living in the community many years after a TBI (Tate, 2004). Existing scales expressed the minimum need required as a portion of a 24-hour day, but clinically it was well known that a significant proportion of people with TBI have support needs on less than a daily basis, the candidate group being those described by Boake (1996) as needing "supervision from afar". The Needs Checklist and Support Levels were derived from the author's clinical and research experience, along with the literature on published scales of disability and outcome. The conceptual framework within which the CANS was developed was the *International Classification of Functioning, Disability and Health* (ICF; WHO, 2001), with items from the Needs Checklist mapping to eight of the nine domains of the Activities/Participation component of the ICF (all except d1: Learning and applying knowledge) and three of the five Environmental Factors (e1: Products and technology, e3: Supports and relationships, and e5: Services, systems and policies) pertinent to Support Levels. Various configurations of Support Levels were trialled with a group of 67 people with TBI, the final version of eight levels being the most clinically informative.

Administration procedures, response format, and scoring

The CANS can be completed by a clinician based on current knowledge of the person with TBI or using information provided by an informant. The method of the clinician-completed CANS is quick and easy, although interview format with an informant generally takes somewhat longer (10–15 mins). Training is advised in order to maintain high inter-rater reliability and a 2-hour workshop was developed for this purpose.

Each of the 24 items from the Needs Checklist from Groups A to D is endorsed if the person has a need in that area irrespective of its nature or extent. This information is then used to classify the needs into one of the eight Support Levels, using prepared conversion procedures. In brief, the Support Level allocated is that which corresponds to the highest group (A–D) of endorsed checklist items. Some degree of clinical judgement is used in synthesising the information from the Needs Checklist and converting it to a Support Level, and also taking account of current contextual factors in the individual's life that may have bearing on the level of support required. Training in this decision-making process is covered in the workshop and general principles are described in the manual. The Support Level allocated ranges from 0 to 7 (revised from Tate, 2004, which ranged from 1 to 8), with higher scores indicating greater intensity of support need.

Psychometric properties

The measurement characteristics of the CANS have been examined in three independent samples recruited from TBI rehabilitation units in Sydney, Australia. Tate (2004) examined the validity of the CANS in a consecutive series of 67 people with TBI who were 20 to 26 years post-trauma, most of whom (95.5%) were living in the community. Validating instruments included the Supervision Rating Scale (SRS), Craig Handicap Assessment and Reporting Technique (CHART), and the original categorical version of the Sydney Psychosocial Rating Scale (SPRS). Reliability of the CANS was examined in two samples (Soo et al., 2007). Inter-rater reliability (3 raters; 2 occupational therapists and a case manager) and 1-week temporal stability were examined in 30 people with TBI (Median = 42 months post-trauma, range 5–209) who were living in the community. Sample 3 ($n = 40$, Median = 31 months post-trauma, range 5–356) examined agreement among researcher, clinician, informants and patients. Additionally, data from sample 3 address responsiveness, concurrent and predictive validity (Soo et al., in press). Results of the above studies are shown in Box 9.1.

Comment

There are two main approaches to measuring support requirements of an individual: support received versus support need. The CANS adopts the latter approach. Measuring support need, however, involves subjective judgement in contrast to documenting support received, thus raising issues of reliability. In this respect the CANS fares very well, with excellent inter-rater reliability and 1-week temporal stability. There is also evidence for concurrent validity with similar measures and it discriminates among groups with different degrees of disability. The CANS is a summary measure and as such it provides a convenient format to synthesise information obtained from a disparate array of measures. Of note, the CANS does not evaluate impairment of body function per se (e.g., cognitive and motor-sensory impairments); rather, the focus is on the functional consequences of such impairments (as evident in activity limitation and participation restriction). A particular strength of the CANS is that it has three intermediate response categories between full independence (Level 0) and needing support for part of each day (Level 4), thereby enabling it to capture support requirements of people whose needs are less than daily. A paediatric version of the CANS (PCANS; Soo, Tate, Williams, Waddingham, & Waugh, 2008) for children and adolescents from ages 5 to 18 years is currently under development.

Box 9.1

Validity:	Criterion: *Concurrent:* Tate: with SRS: $r_s = .75$ – with CHART: Physical: $r_s = -.80$, Mobility: $r_s = -.62$, Cognitive: $r_s = -.76$, Occupational: $r_s = -.66$, Social: $r_s = -.46$ – with categorical SPRS Total score: $r_s = -.79$
	Soo et al. (in press): with SRS: $r_s = .68$ – with Disability Rating Scale: $r_s = .64$
	Predictive: Soo et al. (in press): CANS at inpatient rehabilitation discharge vs 6 month follow-up on SRS ($r_s = .43$), Disability Rating Scale ($r_s = .42$)
	Construct: *Discriminant:* Tate: SPRS-Good Median = 1.0 vs SPRS-Limited Median = 2.0 vs SPRS-Poor Median = 5.0; Kruskal-Wallis ANOVA $\chi^2 = 44.6$ ($p < .001$) – significant differences between SPRS-Good vs SPRS-Limited ($p < .001$); SPRS-Limited vs SPRS-Poor ($p < .001$)
Reliability:	Inter-rater: Soo et al. (2007): 3 clinician-raters: ICC = .93–.96
	Test-retest: Soo et al. (2007): 1 week: ICC = .98
Responsiveness:	significant decrease in support needs: Discharge $M = 5.10$ ($SD = 1.69$) vs 6-month follow-up $M = 3.45$ ($SD = 1.78$), $d = .98$ (Soo et al., in press)

Key references

Boake, C. (1996). Supervision Rating Scale: a measure of functional outcome from brain injury. *Archives of Physical Medicine and Rehabilitation*, *77*, 765–772.

Soo, C.A., Tate, R., Aird, A., Browne, S., Carr, B., Coulston, C., et al. (in press). Validity and responsiveness of the Care and Needs Scale (CANS) for assessing support needs following traumatic brain injury. *Archives of Physical Medicine and Rehabilitation.*

Soo, C. A., Tate, R. L., Hopman, K., Forman, M., Secheny, T., Aird, V., et al. (2007). Reliability of the Care and Needs Scale (CANS) for assessing support needs after traumatic brain injury. *Journal of Head Trauma Rehabilitation*, *22*(5), 288–295.

Soo, C., Tate, R. L., Williams, L., Waddingham, S., & Waugh, M.-C. (2008). Development and validation of the Paediatric Care and Needs Scale (PCANS) for assessing support needs of children and young people with acquired brain injury. *Developmental Neurorehabilitation*, *11*(3), 204–214.

Tate, R. L. (2003). The Care and Needs Scale. In R. L. Tate (2004). Assessing support needs for people with traumatic brain injury: The Care and Needs Scale (CANS). *Brain Injury*, *18*(5), 445–460.

Tate, R.L. (2004). Assessing support needs for people with traumatic brain injury: The Care and Needs Scale (CANS). *Brain Injury*, *18*(5), 445–460.

World Health Organization. (2001). *International classification of functioning, disability and health*. Geneva: World Health Organization.

Care and Needs Scale

Tate (2003)

Name:	**Administered by:**	**Date:**

Instructions: Tick any of the care and support needs that apply (Section 1), then circle the number that corresponds to length of time that the person concerned can be left alone (Section 2)

Section 1: Type of care and support need		Section 2: Length of time that can be left alone
Group A: CANS Levels 7, 6, 5 or 4: Requires nursing care, surveillance for severe behavioural/cognitive disabilities, and/or assistance with or supervision for very basic ADLs: ☐ tracheostomy management ☐ nasogastric/PEG feeding ☐ bed mobility (e.g., turning) ☐ wanders/gets lost ☐ exhibits behaviours that have the potential to cause harm to self or others ☐ has difficulty in communicating basic needs because of language impairments ☐ continence ☐ feeding ☐ transfers/mobility (including stairs and indoor surfaces) ☐ other: ______	7 6 5 4	Cannot be left alone – Needs nursing care, assistance and/or surveillance 24 hours per day Can be left alone for a few hours – Needs nursing care, assistance and/or surveillance 20–23 hours per day Can be left alone for part of the day, but not overnight – Needs nursing care, assistance, supervision and/or direction 12–19 hours per day Can be left alone for part of the day and overnight – Needs a person each day (up to 11 hours) for assistance, supervision, direction and/or cueing for occupational activities, interpersonal relationships and/or living skills
Group B: CANS Level 4: Requires assistance, supervision, direction and/or cueing for basic ADLs: ☐ personal hygiene/toileting ☐ bathing/dressing ☐ simple food preparation ☐ other: ______	4	Can be left alone for part of the day and overnight – Needs a person each day (up to 11 hours) for assistance, supervision, direction and/or cueing for occupational activities, interpersonal relationships and/or living skills
Group C: CANS Levels 4, 3, 2 or 1: Requires assistance, supervision, direction and/or cueing for instrumental ADLs and/or social participation: ☐ shopping ☐ housework/home maintenance ☐ medication use ☐ money management ☐ everyday devices (e.g., telephone, television) ☐ transport and outdoor surfaces ☐ parenting skills ☐ interpersonal relationships ☐ leisure and recreation/play ☐ employment/school ☐ other: ______	4 3 2 1	Can be left alone for part of the day and overnight – Needs a person each day (up to 11 hours) for assistance, supervision, direction and/or cueing for occupational activities, interpersonal relationships and/or living skills Can be left alone for a few days a week – Needs contact for occupational activities, interpersonal relationships, living skills or emotional support a few days a week Can be left alone for almost all week – Needs contact for occupational activities, interpersonal relationships, living skills or emotional support at least once a week Can live alone, but needs intermittent (i.e., less than weekly) contact for occupational activities, interpersonal relationships, living skills or emotional support
Group D: CANS Levels 3, 2 or 1: Requires supports: ☐ informational supports (e.g., advice) ☐ emotional supports ☐ other: ______	3 2 1	Can be left alone for a few days a week – Needs contact for occupational activities, interpersonal relationships, living skills or emotional support a few days a week Can be left alone for almost all week – Needs contact for occupational activities, interpersonal relationships, living skills or emotional support at least once a week Can live alone, but needs intermittent (i.e., less than weekly) contact for occupational activities, interpersonal relationships, living skills or emotional support
Group E: CANS Level 0: Fully independent: ○ Lives fully independently, with or without physical or other aids (e.g., hand rails, diary notebooks), and allowing for the usual kinds of informational and emotional supports the average person uses in everyday living	0	Can live in the community, totally independently – Does not need contact © R. L. Tate, 2003/2007

Acknowledgement: From Tate, R. L. (2004). Assessing support needs for people with traumatic brain injury: The Care and Needs Scale (CANS). *Brain Injury*, *18*(5), 445–460, reprinted by permission of the author.

Craig Hospital Inventory of Environmental Factors (CHIEF)

Craig Hospital Research Department (2001)

Source

Information on the CHIEF was first published by Whiteneck, Harrison-Felix, Mellick, Brooks, Charlifue, and Gerhart (2004b). Background information, including the items and a 12-item short form, is available from the website of the Center for Outcome Measurement in Brain Injury (http://www.tbims.org/combi/chief/index.hmtl). Items appear in an appendix to Whiteneck et al. (2004b) and are also reproduced below.

Purpose

The CHIEF is a self-rating scale with the aim of measuring perceived negative environmental influences; that is, the barriers "that keep people with disabilities from functioning within the household and community and from doing what they need or want to do" (Whiteneck, Meade, Dijkers, Tate, Bushnik, & Forchheimer, 2004c, pp. 1795–1796). It was designed "for the general population as well as for persons representing the full range of possible disabilities" (Whiteneck et al., 2004b, p. 1326). In terms of the latter group, people with acquired brain impairment, primarily multiple sclerosis (MS) and traumatic brain injury (TBI), were also included in the development of the scale. Intended purposes for the CHIEF are population-based research, as well as surveillance systems and individually focused investigations.

Item description

The 25-item CHIEF contains five statistically derived subscales representing environmental barriers: (i) Physical and structural (6 items), (ii) Attitudes and support (5 items), (iii) Services and assistance (7 items), (iv) Policy (4 items), and (v) Work and school (3 items). A 12-item short form retains two to three items from each of the subscales.

Scale development

Development of the CHIEF, described in Whiteneck et al. (2004b), was systematic and thorough. A group of 32 people with expertise in four areas of disability (mobility, self-care, learning, and communication) was assembled and met for four 2-day meetings. Members represented a broad range of backgrounds, including people with disabilities, family members of people with developmental disabilities and TBI, disability researchers from pertinent fields (e.g., public health, economics, sociology), advocacy groups, governmental agencies and clinicians. They were divided into four representative panels, with the task of identifying environmental factors during the course of their meetings. Each panel independently produced a draft instrument, and the "surprising consistency" enabled a single instrument to be formed "by synthesising the vital elements". Two response formats to capture facilitators and barriers were pilot tested with 97 people, 50 of whom had disabilities. Results indicated that the preferred response categories addressed frequency of barriers (rather than facilitators) and this format was adopted; additionally, some adaptations were incorporated in order to capture "magnitude" aspects of environmental barriers. A short form was developed by retaining those items from each subscale that had "the greatest conceptual clarity and discriminant validity" (Whiteneck et al., 2004c, p. 1796). Inter-correlations between the long and short forms for the total and subscale scores ranged from .79 to .96.

Administration procedures, response format and scoring

The CHIEF is designed as a self-report instrument, completed from the perspective of the previous 12 months. Administration time is reported as 10 to 15 minutes for the 25-item version.

Item response uses a two-step procedure. First, each item is rated for frequency of occurrence on a 5-point scale: 0 (never), 1 (less than monthly), 2 (monthly), 3 (weekly), 4 (daily). Those items endorsed with a frequency from 1 to 4 are then rated dichotomously in terms of magnitude (1 = a little problem; 2 = a big problem). In order to circumvent items that are rated "not applicable", the total score uses the mean score of

Data box 9.1 Descriptive data from the standardization samples (Whiteneck et al., 2004b)

	Age *M*	Total *M* (*SD*)	Physical and structural	Attitudes and support	Services and assistance	Policy	Work and school
Population survey:	44 y						
Not disabled: *n* = 1788		0.41 (0.53)	0.39 (0.60)	0.39 (0.66)	0.33 (0.64)	0.39 (0.60)	0.62 (1.08)
Disabled: *n* = 481		0.69 (0.87)	0.78 (1.22)	0.72 (1.39)	0.58 (0.93)	0.78 (1.22)	0.89 (1.34)
Disability sample:							
TBI: *n* = 120	41 y	0.89 (1.19)	1.05 (1.30)	0.88 (1.44)	0.75 (1.18)	1.05 (1.30)	0.63 (1.36)

endorsed items. The "frequency–magnitude product" results in a possible item score range from 0 to 8, with higher scores representing greater perceived environmental barriers. Subscale scores can also be calculated, using the above procedure.

Psychometric properties

The measurement characteristics of the CHIEF were initially examined in three samples (Whiteneck et al., 2004b). Construct validity drew on data collected as part of a population-based, telephone survey in Colorado, USA, in which the CHIEF was added to the survey measure. Data were collected from 2269 people, 481 of whom identified themselves as disabled. Descriptive data are shown in Data box 9.1. Principal components analysis of the CHIEF data extracted five components accounting for 48% of the variance, which were labelled as follows: (i) Physical and structural, (ii) Attitudinal and support, (iii) Services and assistance, (iv) Policy, and (v) Work and school. The population data were also used to examine discriminant validity and internal consistency.

Two independent samples were used to further evaluate discriminant validity and establish reliability. The first sample, referred to as the disability sample to distinguish it from the population survey, comprised 409 people previously treated at Craig Hospital, Colorado, which included 120 people with TBI. Temporal stability was assessed in a subset of 103 of the 409 people, who completed the CHIEF a second time, 2 weeks later. Preliminary evidence for convergent and divergent validity was suggested from comparisons within the disability sample, with respect to hypothesized differences between the spinal cord injury (SCI) and TBI groups. The authors noted there were numerical discrepancies between the Physical/structural subscale, where more barriers were reported in the SCI samples than in the TBI samples (SCI $M = 1.80$, $SD = 1.34$ vs TBI $M = 1.05$, $SD = 1.30$), but conversely on the Attitudes/support subscale fewer barriers were reported in the SCI samples than in the TBI samples (SCI $M = 0.78$, $SD = 1.25$ vs TBI $M = 0.88$, $SD = 1.44$). Statistical verification was not provided, however.

Box 9.2

Validity:	Criterion: *Concurrent:* Whiteneck et al. (2004a): with CHART: $r = -.38$ – with SWLS: $r = -.39$
	Construct: *Internal consistency*: Disability sample: Cronbach alpha: total .93 (subscale range: .76–.81; 4/5 subscales < .80) – Population survey: total .86 (subscale range .62–.74)
	Factor analysis: 5 factors: Physical and structural (6 items), Attitudes and support (5 items), Services and assistance (7 items), Policy (4 items), Work and school (3 items)
	Convergent & divergent: Whiteneck et al. (2004a): higher correlation between similar constructs (e.g., CHIEF Physical/structural with CHART Mobility: $r = -.33$); lower correlation between dissimilar constructs (e.g., CHIEF Work/school with CHART Mobility: $r = -.18$)
	Discriminant: Population survey: significant differences between disabled vs non-disabled groups for the total score and all subscales (see Data box 9.1)
Reliability:	Inter-rater: Not applicable
	Test–retest: 2 week: ICC = .93 (subscale range: ICC = .77–.89; item range: ICC = .33–.88, with ICC ≥ .6 for 17/25 items, ICC < .4 for 1/25 items – employment/education policies)
Responsiveness:	No information available

Statistical evidence for convergent and divergent validity is available from the study of Whiteneck, Gerhart, and Cuisick (2004a). They examined concurrent validity of the CHIEF in 73 adults with TBI who were at least 12 months post-trauma using the Craig Handicap Assessment and Reporting Technique (CHART) and the Satisfaction with Life Scale (SWLS). Results from Whiteneck et al. (2004b), except where otherwise stated, are shown in Box 9.2.

Comment

The CHIEF is one of the emerging set of new instruments to measure environmental factors, and it has many features to recommend it. At a conceptual level, it was developed within a framework that is compatible with the *International Classification of Functioning, Disability and Health* (WHO, 2001), as well as current disability policy and legislation in the USA. The item development process was conducted with a large and representative group of relevant experts, including consumers and family members. In general, the CHIEF also has good psychometric properties, with evidence of concurrent and construct validity, and excellent temporal stability (for the total and subscales). Similarly, internal consistency for the total score is excellent. A large normative data set is available from the general population. The authors are also candid about limitations of the CHIEF. For example, it only addresses those environmental factors that are potential barriers and it does not include facilitators, items in the work/school subscale are not completed by people who do not work/attend school, and responses reflect the person's perceptions of environmental factors without account being taken of the objective situation. Indeed, Whiteneck et al. (2004a) comment on their counterintuitive findings that those with mild TBI reported more environmental barriers than people with severe TBI. Yet Whiteneck et al. (2004b) do not recommend that the CHIEF be completed by proxy respondents because participant–proxy agreement was not always high (subscale range k = .46–.66).

Key references

Craig Hospital Research Department. (2001). *Craig Hospital Inventory of Environmental Factors*. http://www.craighospital.org

Whiteneck, G. G., Gerhart, K. A., Cusick, C. P. (2004a). Identifying environmental factors that influence the outcomes of people with traumatic brain injury. *Journal of Head Trauma Rehabilitation*, *19*(3), 191–204.

Whiteneck, G. G., Harrison-Felix, C. L., Mellick, D. C., Brooks, C. A., Charlifue, S. B., & Gerhart, K. A. (2004b). Quantifying environmental factors: A measure of physical, attitudinal, service, productivity, and policy barriers. *Archives of Physical Medicine and Rehabilitation*, *85*, 1324–1335.

Whiteneck, G., Meade, M. A., Dijkers, M., Tate, D. G., Bushnik, T., & Forchheimer, M. B. (2004c). Environmental factors and their role in participation and life satisfaction after spinal cord injury. *Archives of Physical Medicine and Rehabilitation*, *85*, 1793–1803.

World Health Organization. (2001). *International classification of functioning, disability and health*. Geneva: World Health Organization.

Craig Hospital Inventory of Environmental Factors

Craig Hospital Research Department (2001)

Name:	**Administered by:**	**Date:**

Instructions: Being an active, productive member of society includes participating in such things as working, going to school, taking care of your home, and being involved with family and friends in social, recreational and civic activities in the community. Many factors can help or improve a person's participation in these activities, while other factors can act as barriers or limit participation.

First of all, do **you** think you have had the same opportunities as other people to participate in and take advantage of:

Education:	☐ Yes	☐ No
Employment:	☐ Yes	☐ No
Recreation/Leisure:	☐ Yes	☐ No

First, please tell me how often each of the following has been a barrier to your own participation in the activities that matter to you. Think about the past year, and tell me whether each item on the list below has been a problem **daily, weekly, monthly, less than monthly**, or **never**. If the item occurs, then answer the question as to how big a problem the item is in regard to your participation in the activities that matter to you. (Note: If a question asks specifically about school or work and you neither work nor attend school, check "not applicable".)

In the past 12 months, how often . . .	**Daily**	**Weekly**	**Monthly**	**Less than monthly**	**Never**	**N/A**	**Big Problem**	**Little Problem**
1. Has the availability of transportation been a problem for you?	☐	☐	☐	☐	☐			
When this problem occurs has it been a big problem or a little problem?							☐	☐
2. Has the design and layout of your home made it difficult to do what you want or need to do?	☐	☐	☐	☐	☐			
When this problem occurs has it been a big problem or a little problem?							☐	☐
3. Has the design and layout of buildings and places you use at school or at work made it difficult to do what you want or need to do?	☐	☐	☐	☐	☐	☐		
When this problem occurs has it been a big problem or a little problem?							☐	☐
4. Has the design and layout of buildings and places you use in your community made it difficult to do what you want or need to do?	☐	☐	☐	☐	☐			
When this problem occurs has it been a big problem or a little problem?							☐	☐
5. Has the natural environment – temperature, terrain, climate – made it difficult to do what you want or need to do?	☐	☐	☐	☐	☐			
When this problem occurs has it been a big problem or a little problem?							☐	☐
6. Have other aspects of your surroundings – lighting, noise, crowds, etc. – made it difficult to do what you want or need to do?	☐	☐	☐	☐	☐			
When this problem occurs has it been a big problem or a little problem?							☐	☐

	Daily	Weekly	Monthly	Less than monthly	Never	N/A	Big Problem	Little Problem
7. Has the information you wanted or needed not been available in a format that you can use or understand?	☐	☐	☐	☐	☐			
When this problem occurs has it been a big problem or a little problem?							☐	☐
8. Has the availability of the education and training you needed been a problem for you?	☐	☐	☐	☐	☐			
When this problem occurs has it been a big problem or a little problem?							☐	☐
9. Has the availability of health care services and medical care been a problem for you?	☐	☐	☐	☐	☐			
When this problem occurs has it been a big problem or a little problem?							☐	☐
10. Has the lack of personal equipment and special adapted devices been a problem for you? (Examples might include hearing aids, eyeglasses or wheelchairs.)	☐	☐	☐	☐	☐			
When this problem occurs has it been a big problem or a little problem?							☐	☐
11. Has the lack of computer technology been a problem for you?	☐	☐	☐	☐	☐			
When this problem occurs has it been a big problem or a little problem?							☐	☐
12. Did you need someone else's help in your home and could not get it easily?	☐	☐	☐	☐	☐			
When this problem occurs has it been a big problem or a little problem?							☐	☐
13. Did you need someone else's help at school or at work and could not get it easily?	☐	☐	☐	☐	☐	☐		
When this problem occurs has it been a big problem or a little problem?							☐	☐
14. Did you need someone else's help in your community and could not get it easily?	☐	☐	☐	☐	☐			
When this problem occurs has it been a big problem or a little problem?							☐	☐
15. Have other people's attitudes toward you been a problem at home?	☐	☐	☐	☐	☐			
When this problem occurs has it been a big problem or a little problem?							☐	☐
16. Have other people's attitudes toward you been a problem at school or at work?	☐	☐	☐	☐	☐	☐		
When this problem occurs has it been a big problem or a little problem?							☐	☐
17. Have other people's attitudes toward you been a problem in the community?	☐	☐	☐	☐	☐			
When this problem occurs has it been a big problem or a little problem?							☐	☐

CHIEF page 3 of 3

In the past 12 months, how often . . .	Daily	Weekly	Monthly	Less than monthly	Never	N/A	Big Problem	Little Problem
18. Has a lack of support and encouragement from others in your home been a problem?	☐	☐	☐	☐	☐			
When this problem occurs has it been a big problem or a little problem?							☐	☐
19. Has a lack of support and encouragement from others at school or at work been a problem?	☐	☐	☐	☐	☐	☐		
When this problem occurs has it been a big problem or a little problem?							☐	☐
20. Has a lack of support and encouragement from others in your community been a problem?	☐	☐	☐	☐	☐			
When this problem occurs has it been a big problem or a little problem?							☐	☐
21. Did you experience prejudice or discrimination?	☐	☐	☐	☐	☐			
When this problem occurs has it been a big problem or a little problem?							☐	☐
22. Has the lack of programmes and services in the community been a problem?	☐	☐	☐	☐	☐			
When this problem occurs has it been a big problem or a little problem?							☐	☐
23. Did the policies and rules of business and organizations make problems for you?	☐	☐	☐	☐	☐			
When this problem occurs has it been a big problem or a little problem?							☐	☐
24. Did education and employment programmes and policies make it difficult to do what you want or need to do?	☐	☐	☐	☐	☐	☐		
When this problem occurs has it been a big problem or a little problem?							☐	☐
25. Did government programmes and policies make it difficult to do what you want or need to do?	☐	☐	☐	☐	☐			
When this problem occurs has it been a big problem or a little problem?							☐	☐

Coding: 0 = Daily, 1 = Weekly, 2 = Monthly, 3 = Less than monthly, 4 = Never; 1 = Little problem, 2 = Big problem

Acknowledgement: From Whiteneck, G. C. et al. (2004). Quantifying environmental factors: A measure of physical, attitudinal, service, productivity, and policy barriers. *Archives of Physical Medicine and Rehabilitation*, *85*, 1324–1335, reprinted by permission of Elsevier.

Home and Community Environment (HACE) Instrument

Keysor, Jette, and Haley (2005)

Source

Items for the HACE Instrument are available in an appendix to Keysor et al. (2005) and are also reproduced below.

Purpose

The HACE Instrument is a self-rating scale, designed to provide a characterization of positive and negative features in the home and community environments that may influence level of participation. It was developed mainly with older people living in the community who had "a variety of functional mobility limitations" (Keysor et al., 2005, p. 42).

Item description

The HACE Instrument contains 36 items in six domains: Home mobility (9 items), Community mobility (5 items), Basic mobility devices (9 items), Communication devices (4 items), Transportation (5 items), and Attitudes (4 items).

Scale development

In designing the HACE Instrument, Keysor et al. (2005) argued the need for an objective measure: "The environment assessment needs to identify the extent to which various factors are present, i.e., 'does the environment have . . .', rather than identifying whether an individual perceives that aspects of his or her environment restrict participation in daily life" (p. 38). They also aimed to produce an instrument that could be used as "an independent, self-report assessment" rather than a time-consuming, observational tool. Following a review of the pertinent literature and communication with other researchers working in the area, the authors adopted the conceptual framework and domains covered by the Craig Hospital Inventory of Environmental Factors (CHIEF): physical and architectural environment, supports and services, political and attitudinal aspects of home and community environments. Items assessing *social* supports were intentionally excluded "because existing measures capture this domain" (p. 39). The authors then generated descriptive characteristics of each domain. The initial instrument contained 44 items, which were reviewed by two experts regarding their representation of the above domains. The prototype HACE Instrument, incorporating reviewer suggestions, was tested psychometrically with 62 older people (see below). Based on results of that study, eight items (including all political items) were removed, mainly because of missing data from >20% of respondents or low test–retest reliability.

Administration procedures, response format and scoring

The HACE Instrument is designed for self-completion, with an administration time of approximately 10 minutes.

Response format and scoring the HACE Instrument varies among items and domains, from items that use a dichotomous format (e.g., some items from the Transportation domain) to those rated on a 5-point scale (e.g., Attitudes domain); responses to other items are coded (e.g., item for number of steps at entrance to the home: "0", "1 or 2", "several", "10 or more"). For two domains (Home mobility, Community mobility) higher scores indicate greater obstacles, whereas for another two domains (Transportation, Attitudes) higher scores indicate absence of barriers (opportunities for transportation and absence of negative attitudes respectively). For the remaining two domains (Basic mobility devices, Communication devices), higher scores indicate the greater availability of assistive devices (i.e., facilitators). Six domain scores are thus calculated, rather than a total score. Score ranges are as follows: Home mobility 0 to 10, Community mobility 0 to 5, Basic mobility devices 0 to 9, Communication devices 0 to 4, Transportation 0 to 5, and Attitudes 0 to 4.

Psychometric properties

The HACE Instrument was standardized with 62 older people (age $M = 70$ years, range 32–94) recruited from community organizations and outpatient rehabilitation centres in Boston, Massachusetts, USA (Keysor et al., 2005). A randomly selected subset of the sample ($n = 24$) completed the HACE Instrument on a second occasion 1 to 3 weeks later. Discriminant validity was examined with hypothesized subsets of the sample. For example, it was anticipated that people who lived in private homes would report more Home obstacles than those who lived in multi-unit dwellings. Results from the above study are shown in Box 9.3.

Box 9.3

Validity:	Construct: *Discriminant:* Home mobility obstacles: private homes (100%) vs multi-unit dwellings (26%); $\chi^2 = 29.99$, $p < .001$
Reliability:	Inter-rater: No information available
	Test–retest: 1–3 weeks: domain range: $k = .47$–1.00 (with $k \geq .6$ for 4/5 domains) – item range: $k = .00$–1.00 (with $k \geq .6$ for 19/36 items, $k < .4$ for 6/36 items – chairlift in main living area, places to sit and rest, curbs with curb-cuts, communication aids, voice output aids, disabled people's parking)
Responsiveness:	No information available

Comment

Given the dearth of instruments addressing environmental factors, the HACE Instrument is a promising tool, although as the authors acknowledge, much additional work, including psychometric examination, is required. A distinct advantage of the HACE Instrument is its provision of an objective measure of environmental factors, without the need for a time-consuming observational assessment. In so doing, it allows the respondent to describe discrete characteristics of the home and community environment without requiring a value judgement. Moreover, some items and domains address facilitators (e.g., aids, assistive devices, opportunities), in addition to features that may cause barriers or obstacles. Item content of the HACE Instrument, however, has a pronounced physical bias, and the four attitude items are very general statements that are at odds with the specificity of the remaining 32 items. A problematic aspect of the HACE Instrument as it currently stands is the scoring format. The variable directional scoring system (higher scores are better for some domains and worse for others) is cumbersome, and revision of scoring procedures would make the HACE Instrument a more user-friendly instrument.

Key reference

Keysor, J. J., Jette, A. M., & Haley, S. M. (2005). Development of the Home and Community Environment (HACE) Instrument. *Journal of Rehabilitation Medicine*, *37*, 37–44.

Home and Community Environment Instrument

Keysor, Jette, and Haley (2005)

Name: **Administered by:** **Date:**

HOME MOBILITY

1. What type of home do you live in?
   - ☐ single family, multi-family, apartment building or condominium complex
   - ☐ congregate housing, assisted living
   - ☐ nursing/rest home
   - ☐ other: ____________________
2. How many steps are at the main entrance of your home?
   ☐ none ☐ 1 or 2 steps ☐ several steps ☐ 10 or more steps
3. Is there a railing at the steps?
   ☐ yes ☐ no
4. Is there a ramp at the main entrance?
   ☐ yes ☐ no
5. Does the door at the main entrance open electronically or is someone available to open the door?
   ☐ yes ☐ no
6. How many steps are there from the main entrance of your building to your main living areas?
   ☐ none ☐ 1 or 2 steps ☐ several steps ☐ 10 or more steps
7. How many steps are there inside your main living area?
   ☐ none ☐ 1 or 2 steps ☐ several steps ☐ 10 or more steps
8. Is there a chairlift or elevator inside your main living area?
   ☐ yes ☐ no
9. Is there a chairlift or elevator inside your building?
   ☐ yes ☐ no

COMMUNITY MOBILITY

To what extent does your local community have:

10. Uneven sidewalks or other walking areas?
    ☐ a lot ☐ some ☐ not at all ☐ don't know
11. Parks and walking areas that are easy to get to and easy to use?
    ☐ a lot ☐ some ☐ not at all ☐ don't know
12. Safe parks and walking areas?
    ☐ a lot ☐ some ☐ not at all ☐ don't know
13. Places to sit and rest at bus stops, in parks, or in other places where people walk?
    ☐ a lot ☐ some ☐ not at all ☐ don't know
14. Curbs with curb-cuts?
    ☐ a lot ☐ some ☐ not at all ☐ don't know

BASIC MOBILITY DEVICES

Do you have:

15. Manual wheelchair? ☐ yes ☐ no
16. Electric wheelchair or electric scooter? ☐ yes ☐ no
17. Walker? ☐ yes ☐ no
18. Cane or crutch? ☐ yes ☐ no
19. Bedside commode, raised toilet seat or grab bars near toilet? ☐ yes ☐ no
20. Grab bars or bench in tub or shower? ☐ yes ☐ no
21. Reachers? ☐ yes ☐ no
22. Dressing aids such as button adapters or zipper pulls? ☐ yes ☐ no
23. Eating aids such as built-up silverware, or kitchen aids such as cutting boards that hold food, or utensils that are designed to be used with one hand? ☐ yes ☐ no

COMMUNICATION DEVICES

Do you have:

24. Aids to help you communicate with people such as boards or papers with pictures, or telephones with big dials or hearing devices? ☐ yes ☐ no
25. Voice-output communication aids, such as voice generating computers? ☐ yes ☐ no
26. A computer? ☐ yes ☐ no
27. Access to the internet? ☐ yes ☐ no

TRANSPORTATION FACTORS

28. Do you have a car available to you at your home? ☐ yes ☐ no
29. Do you drive? ☐ yes ☐ no

To what extent does your local community have:

30. Public transportation that is close to your home?
    ☐ a lot ☐ some ☐ not at all ☐ don't know
31. Public transportation with adaptations for people who are limited in their daily activities, such as buses that lower to the ground and chairlifts for wheelchairs?
    ☐ a lot ☐ some ☐ not at all ☐ don't know
32. Adequate disabled people's parking?
    ☐ a lot ☐ some ☐ not at all ☐ don't know

ATTITUDES

33. People in your building have negative attitudes toward persons with limitations in daily activities
    ☐ strongly agree ☐ agree ☐ neither agree nor disagree ☐ disagree ☐ strongly disagree
34. People in your building are willing to help persons with limitations in daily activities
    ☐ strongly agree ☐ agree ☐ neither agree nor disagree ☐ disagree ☐ strongly disagree
35. People in your community have negative attitudes toward persons with limitations in daily activities
    ☐ strongly agree ☐ agree ☐ neither agree nor disagree ☐ disagree ☐ strongly disagree
36. People in your community are willing to help persons with limitations in daily activities
    ☐ strongly agree ☐ agree ☐ neither agree nor disagree ☐ disagree ☐ strongly disagree

---

Acknowledgement: From Keysor, J. J. et al. (2005). Development of the Home and Community Environment (HACE) Instrument. *Journal of Rehabilitation Medicine*, *37*, 37–44, Appendix A, p. 44, by permission of Journal of Rehabilitation Medicine Society.

Home and Community Environment Instrument

Keysor, Jette, and Haley (2005)

Scoring procedures

The *home mobility* domain consists of 3 items that describe the main entrance to a person's home, the main living area and the area between the main entrance and the main living area. To characterize the main entrance to a person's home, a score is calculated that includes the number of steps at the main entrance, whether a ramp is present, whether a railing is present, or whether mechanical or human assistance is available to help open the door. Number of steps at the main entrance is scored as: 0 = no steps; 1 = 1 or 2 steps; 2 = several steps; or 3 = 10 or more steps. The entrance ramp item is scored as: 0 = no ramp, 1 = ramp present. If a ramp is present the step score of the front entrance is set to 0. If a railing is present at the entrance to the home 1 point is subtracted from the number of steps score. If the participant indicated that assistance was not present at the main door, the score on the computed stair variable is increased by 1 point. The score for this variable ranges from 0 to 4 obstacles. Variable scores describing obstacles from the main entrance to the main living area and inside the main living area are created in the same manner. The 3 home mobility variables are summed to represent a total score ranging from 0 to 10 points, with higher scores indicating more obstacles for home mobility.

In the *community mobility* domain each item is scored to reflect the presence or absence of a factor and summed across the 5 items. Scores range from 0 to 5, with higher scores indicating more obstacles.

To compute *basic mobility* devices, 9 items are scored to record the number of available mobility assistive technologies, ranging from 0 to 9 assistive devices. In a similar fashion, a *communication devices* score consists of the sum of 4 communication items, with higher scores indicating more communication technologies available to the subject.

The *transportation* variable includes 2 items pertaining to driving, 2 items pertaining to public transportation and 1 pertaining to disabled people's parking. Scores range from 0 transportation opportunities available to 5, with higher scores indicating more transportation opportunities available.

To calculate an *attitudes* variable, responses for each of the 4 attitudinal items are scored as 1 for the absence of a negative community attitude towards persons with limitations in daily activities. Scores are summed and range from 0 to 4 negative community attitudes toward persons with limitations present.

Acknowledgement: From Keysor, J. J. et al. (2005). Development of the Home and Community Environment (HACE) Instrument. *Journal of Rehabilitation Medicine*, *37*, 37–44, column 2, p. 39, by permission of Journal of Rehabilitation Medicine Society.

Interpersonal Support Evaluation List (ISEL)

Cohen and Hoberman (1983)

Source

Items for the 48-item college student version of the ISEL are available in an appendix to Cohen and Hoberman (1983). Items for the 40-item version, suitable for the general population, originally appeared in an appendix to Cohen, Mermelstein, Kamarck, and Hoberman (1985). The 40-item general population version that is currently used varies slightly from the original. It is available from the following website (http://www.psy.cmu.edu/~scohen/ISEL.html) and is reproduced below.

Purpose

The ISEL is a self-rating scale. Cohen et al. (1985) report that the ISEL was "designed to assess the perceived availability of four separate functions of social support" (p. 75; see below). The ISEL was developed for the general population, and has been used with people with traumatic brain injury (TBI; McColl, Davies, Carlson, Johnston, & Minnes, 2001) and their caregivers (Benn & McColl, 2004; Chronister & Chan, 2005).

Item description

The general population version of the ISEL contains 40 items that are grouped into four dimensions, each with 10 items: Tangible support (items 2, 9, 14, 16, 18, 23, 29, 33, 35, 39), Appraisal support (items 1, 6, 11, 17, 19, 22, 26, 30, 36, 38), Self-esteem support (items 3, 4, 8, 13, 20, 24, 28, 32, 37, 40), and Belonging support (items 5, 7, 10, 12, 15, 21, 25, 27, 31, 34). The 48-item college student version of the ISEL contains 12 items per dimension. Items are evenly divided in terms of positive and negative phrasing in order to minimize response bias.

Scale development

Developmental procedures for the ISEL are described in Cohen et al. (1985). It was developed within the context of the literature on stress, appraisal and coping, wherein the authors were particularly interested in the buffering effects of social supports and their protective role against stress. In constructing the ISEL, the authors first defined social supports as the resources that are provided by other people. Then they developed a typology of functions served by interpersonal relationships, based on their related work (Cohen & McKay, 1984). The focus was on ways in which other people could influence the person's response to stressful events. Four categories were proposed: tangible support (i.e., material aid), appraisal support (someone to talk to about one's problems), self-esteem support (availability of a positive comparison in relation to others) and belonging support (people available with whom to do things). Items were developed "on theoretical grounds to cover the domain of supportive social resources that could potentially facilitate coping with stressful events" (Cohen et al., 1985, p. 75). The authors opted to measure the person's perceptions of social support, rather than the objective existence of such supports. Drawing on the work of Lazarus (1977), they argued that the buffering effect of social support is a cognitively mediated construct in which appraisal of the situation is more relevant than the objective availability.

Administration procedures, response format and scoring

The ISEL is designed for self-report and is easily completed.

Responses were originally made in terms of whether the item is "probably true" or "probably false". Other researchers modified the response format in order to increase the variance. For example, McColl and Skinner (1995) used a 4-point scale (always, sometimes, seldom, never). The current version of the ISEL (website last accessed 4 May 2009) uses a 4-point scale: definitely true, probably true, probably false, definitely false. Half of the items (3, 6, 9, 10, 11, 13, 14, 15, 17, 24, 25, 27, 28, 29, 30, 34, 35, 36, 39, 40) require reverse scoring. The score range is 0 to 120, with higher scores indicating greater perceived social support.

Psychometric properties

Cohen et al. (1985) summarized the results of 12 psychometric studies on the ISEL, using the original dichotomous scoring format, five of which were conducted with the general population. The authors conducted a validity study of 216 people from the general population (demographic details were not reported), in which the ISEL was compared with the Family Environment Scale (FES), the number of close friends and relatives, as well as depression using the Center for Epidemiological Study of Depression Scale (CES-D). Jacobi (undated, cited in Cohen et al.) examined 31 females from the general population and correlated the ISEL with the Rosenberg Self-Esteem Scale (RSES). Evidence supporting the construct validity of the ISEL was provided by Cohen and Hoberman (1983) who found that in a college student sample, social support (on all ISEL dimensions except Tangible support) was beneficial to people under high (but not low) levels of stress. Mermelstein, Cohen, and Lichtenstein (1983; cited in Cohen et al.) examined temporal stability with 64 people who were participating in a smoking cessation programme (type of reliability coefficient was not specified).

Brookings and Bolton (1988) conducted a confirmatory factor analysis on ISEL data from 131 college students, using LISREL. The 4-factor model was a reasonable fit to the data, and additionally there was support for a second-order general social support factor. Comparable findings were reported by McColl and Skinner (1995) who used an amended version of the ISEL with a spinal cord injury group. They reorganized ISEL items to fit three dimensions previously described by House (cited in McColl & Skinner): Instrumental (similar to ISEL-Tangible), Informational (similar to ISEL-Appraisal), and Emotional (similar to ISEL-Belonging and self-esteem, omitting "items representing purely self-esteem" p. 28). Confirmatory factor analysis yielded the above three factors, using 25 items. McColl et al. (2001) used this adapted version of the ISEL and the Community Integration Questionnaire (CIQ) to validate the Community Integration Measure (CIM) in people with TBI. Results of the above studies are shown in Box 9.4.

Box 9.4

Validity:	Criterion: *Concurrent:* Cohen et al.: with FES: $r = .30$ – with number of close friends: $r = .46$ – with number of close relatives: $r = .42$ – with CES-D: $r = -.52$
	Jacobi (in Cohen et al.): with non-overlapping items of the RSES: $r = .58$
	McColl et al.: adapted ISEL with CIM: $r = .43$ – with CIQ: $r = .34$
	Construct: *Internal consistency:* Cohen et al. cite studies from the general population: Cronbach alpha: Total .88–.90 (Appraisal .70–.82, Self-esteem .62–.73, Belonging .73–.78, Tangible .73–.81)
	Factor analysis: Brookings & Bolton: confirmatory factor analysis: 4 factors, as in original, and a second order factor (general social support)
	Discriminant: Cohen & Hoberman: e.g., high stress groups: depressive symptomatology: Low Appraisal support $M = 21.80$ vs High Appraisal support $M = 14.15$; $F = 5.33, p < .02$
Reliability:	Inter-rater: Not applicable
	Test–retest: Mermelstein et al. (in Cohen et al.): 6 week: .70 (dimension range: .63–.69)
	– 6 month: .74 (dimension range: .49–.68)
Responsiveness:	No information available

Comment

Cohen et al. (1985) conclude that "the most important contribution of the scale is its ability to indicate the type of resources that operate to improve health and well-being in any particular situation" (p. 89). This statement resonates with and is particularly apposite for people with acquired brain impairment (ABI), whose social network often undergoes radical alteration as a consequence of their functional impairments in everyday life. Although the ISEL is widely used, including with other medical groups, it has had limited exposure for people with ABI. Psychometrically, the ISEL demonstrates adequate temporal stability, criterion and construct validity, as well as internal consistency for the total score. The psychometric properties of the ISEL need to be more fully examined in the ABI population, however, but based on the work of McColl and colleagues using an adapted version, its conceptual underpinnings suggest that it could be a helpful measure to throw new light on social functioning after ABI, both in terms of clinical practice and research application.

Key references

Benn, K. M., & McColl, M. A. (2004). Parental coping following childhood acquired brain injury. *Brain Injury*, *18*(3), 239–255.

Brookings, J. B., & Bolton, B. (1988). Confirmatory factor analysis of the Interpersonal Support Evaluation List. *American Journal of Community Psychology*, *16*(1), 137–147.

Chronister, J., & Chan, F. (2005). A stress process model of caregiving for individuals with traumatic brain injury. *Rehabilitation Psychology*, *51*(3), 190–201.

Cohen, S., & Hoberman, H. M. (1983). Positive events and social supports as buffers of life change stress. *Journal of Applied Social Psychology*, *13*(2), 99–125.

Cohen, S., & McKay, G. (1984). Interpersonal relationships as buffers of the impact of psychological stress on health. In A. Baum, J. E. Singer, & S. E. Taylor (Eds.), *Handbook of psychology and health* (pp. 253–267). Hillsdale, NJ: Lawrence Erlbaum Associates, Inc.

Cohen, S., Mermelstein, R., Kamarck, T., & Hoberman, H. M. (1985). Measuring the functional components of social support. In I. G. Sarason & B. R. Sarason (Eds.), *Social support: Theory, research and application* (pp. 73–94). Dordrecht: Martinus Nijhoff.

Lazarus, R. S. (1977). Psychological stress and coping in adaptation and illness. In Z. J. Lipowski, D. R. Lipsitt, & P. C. Whybrow (Eds.), *Psychosomatic medicine: Current trends*. New York: Oxford University Press.

McColl, M. A., Davies, D., Carlson, P., Johnston, J., & Minnes, P. (2001). The Community Integration Measure: Development and preliminary validation. *Archives of Physical Medicine and Rehabilitation*, *82*, 429–434.

McColl, M. A., & Skinner, H. (1995). Assessing inter- and intrapersonal resources: Social support and coping among adults with a disability. *Disability and Rehabilitation*, *17*(1), 24–34.

Interpersonal Support Evaluation List – adult version

Cohen, Mermelstein, Kamarck, and Hoberman (1985)

Name:	Administered by:	Date:

Instructions: This scale is made up of a list of statements each of which may or may not be true about you. For each statement write in the numbers corresponding to "definitely true" if you are sure it is true about you and "probably true" if you think it is true but are not absolutely certain. Similarly, you should write in the numbers corresponding to "definitely false" if you are sure the statement is false and "probably false" if you think it is false but are not absolutely certain.

Response key:
0 = Definitely false
1 = Probably false
2 = Probably true
3 = Definitely true

	RESPONSE
1. There are several people that I trust to help solve my problems	________
2. If I needed help fixing an appliance or repairing my car, there is someone who would help me	________
3. Most of my friends are more interesting than I am	________
4. There is someone who takes pride in my accomplishments	________
5. When I feel lonely, there are several people I can talk to	________
6. There is no one that I feel comfortable talking to about intimate personal problems	________
7. I often meet or talk with family and friends	________
8. Most people I know think highly of me	________
9. If I needed a ride to the airport very early in the morning, I would have a hard time finding someone to take me	________
10. I feel like I'm not always included by my circle of friends	________
11. There really is no one who can give me an objective view of how I'm handling my problems	________
12. There are several different people I enjoy spending time with	________
13. I think that my friends feel that I'm not very good at helping them solve their problems	________
14. If I were sick and needed someone (friend, family member, or acquaintance) to take me to the doctor, I would have trouble finding someone	________
15. If I wanted to go on a trip for a day (e.g., to the mountains, beach, or country), I would have a hard time finding someone to go with me	________
16. If I needed a place to stay for a week because of an emergency (e.g., example, water or electricity out in my apartment or house), I could easily find someone who would put me up	________
17. I feel that there is no one I can share my most private worries and fears with	________
18. If I were sick, I could easily find someone to help me with my daily chores	________
19. There is someone I can turn to for advice about handling problems with my family	________
20. I am as good at doing things as most other people are	________

ISEL page 2 of 2

Response key:

0 = Definitely false
1 = Probably false
2 = Probably true
3 = Definitely true

	RESPONSE
21. If I decide one afternoon that I would like to go to a movie that evening, I could easily find someone to go with me	________
22. When I need suggestions on how to deal with a personal problem, I know someone I can turn to	________
23. If I needed an emergency loan of $100, there is someone (friend, relative, or acquaintance) I could get it from	________
24. In general, people do not have much confidence in me	________
25. Most people I know do not enjoy the same things that I do	________
26. There is someone I could turn to for advice about making career plans or changing my job	________
27. I don't often get invited to do things with others	________
28. Most of my friends are more successful at making changes in their lives than I am	________
29. If I had to go out of town for a few weeks, it would be difficult to find someone who would look after my house or apartment (the plants, pets, garden, etc.)	________
30. There really is no one I can trust to give me good financial advice	________
31. If I wanted to have lunch with someone, I could easily find someone to join me	________
32. I am more satisfied with my life than most people are with theirs	________
33. If I was stranded 10 miles from home, there is someone I could call who would come and get me	________
34. No one I know would throw a birthday party for me	________
35. It would be difficult to find someone who would lend me their car for a few hours	________
36. If a family crisis arose, it would be difficult to find someone who could give me good advice about how to handle it	________
37. I am closer to my friends than most other people are to theirs	________
38. There is at least one person I know whose advice I really trust	________
39. If I needed some help in moving to a new house or apartment, I would have a hard time finding someone to help me	________
40. I have a hard time keeping pace with my friends	________

Acknowledgement: From Cohen, S., & Hoberman, H. (1983). Positive events and social supports as buffers to life change stress. *Journal of Applied Social Psychology*, *13*(2), 99–125, and Cohen, S. et al. (1985). Measuring the functional components of social support. In I. G. Sarason & B. R. Sarason (Eds.), *Social support: Theory, research, and application* (pp. 73–94). The Hague: Martinus Nijhoff, reprinted by kind permission of Springer Science and Business Media.

Lubben Social Network Scale (LSNS)

Lubben and Gironda (2004)

Source

Items for the original 10-item LSNS appear in an appendix to Lubben (1988). The 12-item revised version of the LSNS (Lubben & Gironda, 2004), along with 18-item and 6-item versions, appear on the website of the Graduate School of Social Work, Boston College, USA (http://www2.bc.edu/~norstraj/default.html). The 18-item revised version (LSNS-R) is reproduced below.

Purpose

The LSNS (and LSNS-R) is a self-rating scale, designed to measure structural social support systems (i.e., social contacts). It was originally developed for older people, but has been used with people with acquired brain impairment (ABI), including stroke (Boynton de Sepulveda, & Chang, 1994) and traumatic brain injury (TBI; MacMillan, Hart, Martelli, & Zasler, 2002), as well as caregivers of people with dementia (Colantonio, Cohen, & Pon, 2001).

Item description

The 12-item LSNS-R focuses on the social networks of family (6 items) and friendships (6 items); the 18-item version is similar to the 12-item version but it includes a subscale on neighbours (6 items). Number of people in the social network is measured, along with frequency of contact and closeness. The 6-item abbreviated version (referred to by Lubben & Gironda, 2000, as LSNS-A or LSNS-6) contains three items from each of the family and friendships subscales, with the latter subscale encompassing both friends and neighbours.

Scale development

Lubben (1988) described the LSNS as refinement of the Berkman-Syme Social Network Index (SNI; Berkman & Syme, 1979), developed to assess social networks in the general population. The SNI examined social contacts in four categories (marriage, close friends and relatives, church membership, and informal and formal group associations). The scoring system applied weights to take account of the relative importance of different types of contacts. Lubben reduced item content and, in particular, items were excluded that dealt "with secondary social relationships (viz., group and church membership) because these organizational participation items showed limited variance when used with older populations" (Lubben & Gironda, 2004, p. 25). The scoring procedures were also substantially revised and simplified. Lubben and Gironda reported on subsequent refinement of the LSNS, which was conducted using "four guiding principles": (i) to improve the distinction between family and friend networks, (ii) to replace items with limited response variance, (iii) to disaggregate double-barrelled items, and (iv) to produce an instrument that was suitable for both research and practice settings by ensuring the scale was short and efficient. These procedures resulted in the revised 12-item scale.

Administration procedures, response format and scoring

Designed for self-completion, the LSNS (and LSNS-R) is quick and easy, taking 5 to 10 minutes.

Responses are made on a 6-point scale, with response descriptors varying in accordance with item content. Some items (e.g., number of family contacts per month) are coded from 0 (no contacts) to 5 (9 or more contacts), other subjective items (e.g., "How often is one of your relatives available for you to talk to when you have an important decision to make?") use a rating scale 0 (never) to 5 (always). The total score for the 18-item LSNS-R ranges from 0 to 90 (for the original 10-item LSNS the range is from 0 to 50, for the 12-item LSNS-R it is from 0 to 60, and for the 6-item version it is 0 to 30), with higher scores indicating larger social networks and/or more frequent social contact.

Normative data from the standardization sample (Lubben, 1988). For the LSNS (score range 0–50) the mean score was $M = 25.1$ ($SD = 9.6$), and Lubben suggested a cut-off score of 19/20 "for screening those elderly who are apt to be at greater risk of extremely limited social networks" (p. 48). In their study of 45 adults with TBI using the LSNS, MacMillan et al. (2002) used tripartite splits to create cut-off scores, which were labelled Low (scores 0–23), Medium (scores 24–27) and High (scores 28–50). No cut-off scores have been reported for the LSNS-R.

Psychometric properties

Lubben (1988) examined the psychometric properties of the LSNS as part of another study involving a random sample of 1037 older adults (age $M = 77.2$ years) living in the community in eight representative areas in California, USA. Validating instruments were the Life Satisfaction Index (LSI), ≥ 6 days hospitalization in previous 12 months, and "Alameda 7" – a checklist of seven health practices. All correlation coefficients with LSNS were statistically significant at $p < .001$, but their magnitudes were low to very low ($r = .10 - .21$), raising the question as to whether they did provide evidence for concurrent validity. As part of another study, Rutledge, Matthews, Lui, Stone, and Cauley (2003) followed a group of 7524 women aged ≥ 65 years over a 6-year period. Using LSNS quartiles, they found that a significantly lower age-adjusted mortality occurred for each quartile in comparison with the lowest LSNS quartile. Evidence for discriminant validity is available from a study by Tremethick (2001), who compared the living situations of 160 older adults who did not have dementia but required assistance with at least one activity of daily living. Half of the sample ($n = 80$) lived in their own homes and received assistance in their homes, and the remaining 80 people lived in assisted accommodation. Lubben and Gironda (2004) reported on the underlying factor structure of the 12-item LSNS-R in 201 older people who were selected from a Los Angeles County survey using a series of multistage random samplings. Three factors were extracted: one "single, clean family factor" and two friend factors (percentage of variance was not reported). No clear conceptual distinction occurred between the two "friend" factors, with both factors containing number/frequency of contact and closeness items. Results of these studies are shown in Box 9.5.

Comment

In contrast to the area of functional social supports (i.e., quality of social contacts), few standardized scales are available to measure structural social supports (i.e., quantity/frequency of social contacts). Arguably, both types of scales are needed to adequately capture an individual's social support system and Lubben and Gironda (2000) suggest a composite scale comprising the 6-item LSNS-R and three items from the Social Support Survey (Sherbourne & Stewart, 1991). The psychometric properties of the LSNS in the initial standardization study were problematic in that concurrent validity was, in fact, not established because the magnitudes of the coefficients were very low (range $r = .10–.20$), albeit statistically significant because of the large sample size. On the positive side, however, the LSNS was predictive of mortality and discriminated between older adults in different living situations. Administrative advantages of the LSNS (and LSNS-R) are ease of completion, brevity and simplicity of scoring. In its application to people with ABI, however, the LSNS-R needs a thorough psychometric workup in terms of both its reliability and its validity.

Box 9.5

Validity:	Criterion: *Concurrent:* Lubben: with LSI: $r = .21$ – with hospitalization: $r = .10$ – with Alameda 7: $r = .13$
	Predictive: Rutledge et al.: low LSNS scores predicted mortality: in comparison with the 1st quartile, the risk ratio (95% confidence interval) for the 2nd quartile was .84 (.73–.97), 3rd quartile .74 (.64–.86), 4th quartile .67 (.57–.78)
	Construct: *Internal consistency:* Lubben: Cronbach alpha LSNS: .70
	Rutledge et al.: Cronbach alpha LSNS: .55, item-total correlations $r \geq .4$ for 9/10 items
	Lubben & Gironda (2004): Cronbach alpha LSNS .66, 12-item LSNS-R .78
	Factor structure: Lubben & Gironda (2004): 12-item LSNS-R: 3 factors: Family (6 items), Friend A (3 items), Friend B (3 items)
	Discriminant: Tremethick: LSNS: Home health $M = 28.30$ ($SD = 7.77$) vs Assisted living $M = 25.44$ ($SD = 9.47$); $t = 2.09$, $p < .05$
Reliability:	Inter-rater: no information available
	Test–retest: no information available
Responsiveness:	No information available

Key references

Berkman, L. F., & Syme, S. L. (1979). Social networks, host resistance, and mortality: A nine-year follow-up study of Alameda county residents. *American Journal of Epidemiology*, *109*(2), 186–204.

Boynton de Sepulveda, L. I., & Chang, B. (1994). Effective coping with stroke disability in a community setting: The development of a causal model. *Journal of Neuroscience Nursing*, *26*(4), 193–203.

Colantonio, A., Cohen, C., & Pon, M. (2001). Assessing support needs of caregivers of persons with dementia: Who wants what? *Community Mental Health Journal*, *37*(3), 231–243.

Lubben, J. E. (1988). Assessing social networks among elderly people. *Family and Community Health*, *11*(3), 42–52.

Lubben, J., & Gironda, M. (2000). Social support networks. In D. Osterweil, K. Brummel-Smith, & J. C. Beck (Eds.), *Comprehensive geriatric assessment* (pp. 121–137). New York: McGraw-Hill.

Lubben, J., & Gironda, M. (2004). Measuring social networks and assessing their benefits. In C. Phillipson, G. Allan, & D. Ashgate (Eds.), *Social networks and social exclusion: Sociology and policy perspectives* (pp. 20–34). Aldershot, UK: Ashgate.

MacMillan, P. J., Hart, R. P., Martelli, M. F., & Zasler, N. D. (2002). Pre-injury status and adaptation following traumatic brain injury. *Brain Injury*, *16*(1), 41–49.

Rutledge, T., Matthews, K., Lui, L.-Y., Stone, K. L., & Cauley, J. A. (2003). Social networks and marital status predict mortality in older women: Prospective evidence from the study of osteoporotic fractures (SOF). *Psychosomatic Medicine*, *65*, 688–694.

Sherbourne, C. D., & Stewart, A. L. (1991). The MOS Social Support Survey. *Social Science in Medicine*, *32*(6), 705–714.

Tremethick, M. J. (2001). Alone in a crowd. A study of social networks in home health and assisted living. *Journal of Gerontological Nursing*, *27*(5), 42–57.

Lubben Social Network Scale – Revised

Lubben and Gironda (2004)

Name:	**Administered by:**	**Date:**

FAMILY

Considering the people to whom you are related either by birth or marriage . . .

1. How many relatives do you see or hear from at least once per month?
   0 = none
   1 = one
   2 = two
   3 = three or four
   4 = five to eight
   5 = nine or more
2. How often do you see or hear from the relative with whom you have the most contact?
   0 = never
   1 = seldom
   2 = sometimes
   3 = often
   4 = very often
   5 = always
3. How many relatives do you feel at ease with so that you can talk about private matters?
   0 = none
   1 = one
   2 = two
   3 = three or four
   4 = five to eight
   5 = nine or more
4. How many relatives do you feel close to such that you could call on them for help?
   0 = none
   1 = one
   2 = two
   3 = three or four
   4 = five to eight
   5 = nine or more
5. When one of your relatives has an important decision to make, how often do they talk to you about it?
   0 = never
   1 = seldom
   2 = sometimes
   3 = often
   4 = very often
   5 = always
6. How often is one of your relatives available for you to talk to when you have an important decision to make?
   0 = never
   1 = seldom
   2 = sometimes
   3 = often
   4 = very often
   5 = always

NEIGHBOURS

Considering those people who live in your neighbourhood . . .

7. How many of your neighbours do you see or hear from a least once a month?
   0 = none
   1 = one
   2 = two
   3 = three or four
   4 = five to eight
   5 = nine or more
8. How often do you see or hear from the neighbour with whom you have the most contact?
   0 = never
   1 = seldom
   2 = sometimes
   3 = often
   4 = very often
   5 = always
9. How many neighbours do you feel at ease with so that you can talk about private matters?
   0 = none
   1 = one
   2 = two
   3 = three or four
   4 = five to eight
   5 = nine or more
10. How many neighbours do you feel close to such that you could call on them for help?
   0 = none
   1 = one
   2 = two
   3 = three or four
   4 = five to eight
   5 = nine or more
11. When one of your neighbours has an important decision to make, how often do they talk to you about it?
   0 = never
   1 = seldom
   2 = sometimes
   3 = often
   4 = very often
   5 = always
12. How often is one of your neighbours available for you to talk to when you have an important decision to make?
   0 = never
   1 = seldom
   2 = sometimes
   3 = often
   4 = very often
   5 = always

FRIENDSHIPS

Considering your friends who do not live in your neighbourhood . . .

13. How many of your friends do you see or hear from at least once a month?
   0 = none
   1 = one
   2 = two
   3 = three or four
   4 = five to eight
   5 = nine or more
14. How often do you see or hear from the friend with whom you have the most contact?
   0 = never
   1 = seldom
   2 = sometimes
   3 = often
   4 = very often
   5 = always
15. How many friends do you feel at ease with so that you can talk about private matters?
   0 = none
   1 = one
   2 = two
   3 = three or four
   4 = five to eight
   5 = nine or more
16. How many friends do you feel close to such that you could call on them for help?
   0 = none
   1 = one
   2 = two
   3 = three or four
   4 = five to eight
   5 = nine or more
17. When one of your friends has an important decision to make, how often do they talk to you about it?
   0 = never
   1 = seldom
   2 = sometimes
   3 = often
   4 = very often
   5 = always
18. How often is one of your friends available for you to talk to when you have an important decision to make?
   0 = never
   1 = seldom
   2 = sometimes
   3 = often
   4 = very often
   5 = always

TOTAL SCORE: _______

Acknowledgement: 18-item Scale LSNS available from the website: http://www2.bc.edu/~norstraj, by permission of Professor J. E. Lubben.

Measure of Quality of the Environment (MQE)

Fougeyrollas, Noreau, and St-Michel (1997)

Source

The initial description of the MQE was in French (Noreau & Fougeyrollas, 1996). The English version was published by Fougeyrollas et al. (1997), and version 2.0 by Fougeyrollas, Noreau, St-Michel, and Boschen (1999). The MQE is available from Dr Fougeyrollas (The Rehabilitation Institute of Québec City, 525 Boulevard Hamel, Québec, QC, CANADA, GIM 2S8).

Purpose

The MQE is a self-rating scale, designed to assess the perceived influence of physical and social environmental factors (both positive and negative) on participation. It is a generic tool that has been used with older people (Levasseur, Desrosiers, & Noreau, 2004) and people with acquired brain impairment (ABI) after stroke (Rochette, Desrosiers, & Noreau, 2001).

Item description

Version 2.0 of the MQE comprises 109 items in six categories: support and attitudes of family and friends (14 items), income, job and income security (15 items), governmental and public services (27 items), equal opportunity and political orientation (10 items), physical environment and accessibility (38 items), and technology (5 items). The first four categories are described as encompassing the social environment and the last two categories relate to the physical environment.

Scale development

The MQE was developed within the conceptual framework of the Disability Creation Process (DCP) and its measurement (Fougeyrollas, Noreau, Bergeron, Cloutier, Dion, & St-Michel, 1998; Fougeyrollas, Noreau, & Boschen, 2002). This model was developed by the Québec Committee (QC) of the *International Classification of Impairments, Disabilities and Handicaps* (ICIDH; WHO, 1980). The QC was formed to improve an understanding of the disablement process, and it had proposed that a new concept, environmental factors, be introduced to the ICIDH, defined as "all social, cultural and physical dimensions that determine the organization and context of a society. These factors can either become obstacles or supports to individual functioning." (Fougeyrollas, 1995, p. 147). In constructing the MQE, Fougeyrollas and colleagues generated an initial list of 84 situations and factors to cover most environmental categories of their DCP model and grouped the items into six themes. The rating scale constructs were operationally defined: Barrier: "an environmental factor that impedes the accomplishment of daily activities or social roles (social participation)"; Facilitator: "a factor that supports such accomplishment" (Noreau, Fougeyrollas, & Boschen, 2002, p. 59). A metric was applied, content validity formally examined with a group of clinicians and researchers, and temporal stability examined in a group of young adults with cerebral palsy who did not have cognitive impairment.

Administration procedures, response format and scoring

The MQE is self-administered. For each item, a general question is posed: "Indicate to what extent the following factors or situations influence your daily activities and social roles, taking into account your abilities and personal limits". No information is available on administration time; although the instrument is lengthy, only those items that apply to the respondent's situation are rated.

Responses are made on a 7-point rating scale, ranging from −3 to +3 and including zero. Negative responses indicate barriers (from −3 = major barrier to −1 = minor barrier), and conversely, positive responses indicate faciltators (from +1 = minor facilitator to +3 = major facilitator). The zero response is made when an item (environmental factor) does not influence social participation for the respondent. Situations that are not relevant to the respondent or where the respondent is unable to make a response are marked "not applicable"/ "do not know". Scores are summed separately for barriers and facilitators. A higher absolute numerical value indicates greater facilitators if the score is positive, or greater barriers if the score is negative. Frequency scores are also used at the item level (Noreau et al., 2002), for example, the percentage (and type) of items that represent barriers and/or facilitators, along with percentages at major, moderate and minor levels. Mean scores (maximum +3 for facilitators and –3 for barriers) have been used by Rochette et al. (2001), which have the advantage of anchoring the score back to the original rating scale, thereby making the result more easily interpretable.

Psychometric properties

Limited information about the psychometric properties of the MQE is available in English. A pertinent validation study was conducted with a stroke sample by Rochette et al. (2001), using a handicap measure developed by their research group, LIFE-H. They examined 51 people, who did not have aphasia or cognitive impairment, 6 months after discharge from rehabilitation. Boschen, Noreau, and Fougeyrollas (1998) initially provided information on temporal stability of the MQE in 28 people with cerebral palsy (who did not experience cognitive or sensory impairment), aged 17 to 25 years and randomly selected from a client database in Québec City, Canada. A parallel English version of the MQE was also administered to 30 people (clinical condition not specified) from Toronto, Canada. Results of these studies are shown in Box 9.6.

Box 9.6

Validity:	<u>Criterion:</u> *Concurrent:* Rochette et al.: with LIFE-H: $r = .42$ for barriers (but $r = -.08$ for facilitators)
	<u>Construct:</u> *Convergent/divergent:* Rochette et al.: higher correlations with similar constructs (e.g., MQE-Physical environment/ Accessibility with LIFE-H-Residence: $r = .46$); lower correlations with dissimilar constructs (MQE-Physical environment/Accessibility with LIFE-H-Communication: $r = .23$)
Reliability:	<u>Inter-rater:</u> Not applicable
	<u>Test–retest</u>: Boschen et al.: Québec sample: 2 week: $k \geq .6$ for 37/84 items (44%) (kappa range not provided)
Responsiveness:	No information available

Comment

The MQE was constructed within the context of the authors' influential theoretical model, and the developmental process supports the content validity of the scale. An additional important strength of the MQE is the inclusion of facilitators as well as barriers. At 109 items for version 2.0 of the MQE, it is certainly comprehensive, yet the length will exert an impact on the feasibility of the MQE in various applications. The MQE is designed as a generic instrument, and hence not all responses apply to every individual. Boschen et al. (1998) noted that "numerous items were identified by the 17–25-year-old respondents as being not applicable to their present stage of life" (p. 185). In their temporal stability study, 42% of items were not analysed from the English sample, because they were identified by more than 20% as "not applicable". There are advantages and disadvantages to this structure – on the one hand, the population of relevant items is included and comparisons across clinical conditions can be made; conversely, the instrument is time-consuming and adjustments to scoring processes are necessary, thereby limiting the statistical analyses that can be applied. In this respect, further examination of the psychometric properties of the MQE, particularly with an ABI population, will be helpful.

Key references

Boschen, K. A., Noreau, L., & Fougeyrollas, P. (1998). Reliability studies of the Measure of the Quality of the Environment (MQE). *Canadian Journal of Rehabilitation, 11*(4), 184–185.

Fougeyrollas, P. (1995). Documenting environmental factors for preventing the handicap creation process: Québec contributions relating to ICIDH and social participation of people with functional differences. *Disability and Rehabilitation, 17*(3/4), 145–153.

Fougeyrollas, P., Noreau, L., Bergeron, H., Cloutier, R., Dion, S.-A., & St-Michel, G. (1998). Social consequences of long term impairments and disabilities: Conceptual approach and assessment of handicap. *International Journal of Rehabilitation Research, 21*, 127–141.

Fougeyrollas, P., Noreau, L., & Boschen, K. A. (2002). Interaction of environment with individual characteristics and social participation: Theoretical perspectives and applications in persons with spinal cord injury. *Topics in Spinal Cord Injury Rehabilitation, 7*(3), 1–16.

Fougeyrollas, P., Noreau, L., & St-Michel, G. (1997). The Measure of the Quality of Environment. *ICIDH and Environmental Factors International Network, 9*, 32–39.

Fougeyrollas, P., Noreau, L., St-Michel, G., & Boschen, K. (1999). *Measure of the quality of the environment, Version 2.0.* International Network of the Disability Creation Process. Lac St-Charles, Québec.

Levasseur, M., Desrosiers, J., & Noreau, L. (2004). Relationships between environment and quality of life of older adults with physical disabilities. *Physical and Occupational Therapy in Geriatrics*, *22*(3), 37–53.

Noreau, L., & Fougeyrollas, P. (1996). L'Évaluation des situations de handicap: La "Mesure des habitudes de vie" appliqué aux personnes ayant une lesion de la moelle épinère. *Revue Canadienne de Réadaption*, *10*, 81–97.

Noreau, L., Fougeyrollas, P., & Boschen, K. A. (2002). Perceived influence of the environment on social participation among individuals with spinal cord injury. *Topics in Spinal Cord Injury Rehabilitation*, *7*(3), 56–72.

Rochette, A., Desrosiers, J., & Noreau, L. (2001). Association between personal and environmental factors and the occurrence of handicap situations following a stroke. *Disability and Rehabilitation*, *23*(13), 559–569.

World Health Organization. (1980). *International classification of impairments, disabilities and handicaps*. Geneva: World Health Organization.

Northwick Park Care Needs Assessment (NPCNA)

Turner-Stokes, Nyein, and Halliwell (1999)

This entry should be read in conjunction with the Northwick Park Dependency Score (NPDS; see Chapter 7).

Source

Two appendices in Turner-Stokes et al. (1999) contain the additional NPCNA items to be added to the NPDS (Turner-Stokes, Tonge, Nyein, Hunter, Nielson, & Robinson, 1998), along with a detailed description for the rules for transfer of information from the NPDS to the NPCNA. A manual and simple computer program for entry of NPDS data and automatic calculation of NPCNA outputs are available, free of charge, from Dr Turner-Stokes (Regional Rehabilitation Unit, Northwick Park Hospital, Watford Road, Harrow, Middlesex HA1 3UJ, UK; email: lynne.turner-stokes@dial.pipex.com). The NPDS recording form (see Chapter 7) is required to complete the NPCNA.

Purpose

The NPCNA, which is derived from the NPDS, is a clinician rating scale to which a computerized algorithm is applied to provide a directly costable measure of care needs across a wide range of dependency. It was designed for people living in the community with acquired brain impairment, and has been used with people with stroke and traumatic brain injury, as well as with older people in care settings.

Item description

The NPCNA adds five additional items (stairs, snack/meal preparation, medication, special nursing needs and domestic duties) to the NPDS in order to translate the information into an assessment of care needs. It then applies an algorithm based on a validated set of assumptions to derive a timetable of care needs in the community. From this it calculates the total care hours required, the category of care package (including needs for basic care, skilled nursing and domestic assistance using one of 14 care packages), and an estimate of the approximate weekly cost of care.

Scale development

The NPCNA shares the conceptual underpinnings of the NPDS, described in Chapter 7. In brief, these complementary scales were developed to meet the need for a standardized method of measuring the amount of time and number of people required to meet a patient's needs. Whereas the NPDS quantifies dependency, the NPCNA uses that information (and the five additional NPCNA items) to estimate number of hours of care and costs of that care. Having constructed the NPDS, Turner-Stokes et al. (1999) developed a set of assumptions for each NPDS item to determine the number of hours required to meet that need (e.g., "help for dressing would be provided twice a day – to dress in the morning and to undress at bedtime" p. 255). This process was conducted in consultation with a panel of care providers and community health care planners who had direct experience in brain injury. The number of people required to meet an individual patient's specific need/s, the time required, and the frequency of help are multiplied to provide the total number of hours of care per week. Account was taken of the fact that "if help is required for several tasks in one visit, these will be taken simultaneously and the total care time reduced" (p. 255), which the authors refer to as "restricted hours" (versus total hours). Fourteen care packages, which are flexible and can be used in combination to meet the needs of the individual patient, were developed and costed.

Administration procedures, response format and scoring

A manual is available for the NPCNA. First the clinician rates the items of the NPDS and the five additional NPCNA items, using his or her knowledge of the patient to inform the response. The authors advise that this takes approximately 5 minutes.

As noted in the NPDS entry in Chapter 7, items on

the NPDS are rated using a variable format, with the total score ranging from 0 to 100. NPCNA items are rated similarly, using a variable format. Following completion of the NPDS (and additional items), data are then entered into a computer program based on Microsoft Excel to derive the NPCNA (the procedure can also be performed manually if necessary). Translation of the NPDS data to the NPCNA requires an additional 5 minutes (10 mins in total). The elements of the care packages (from least to most intensive) are as follows: (i) domestic, (ii) 1 hour of daily care, (iii) 2 hours, (iv) 3 hours, (v) 4 hours, (vi) 5 hours of daily care, (vii) a live-in caregiver, (viii) a live-in caregiver and 4 hours of cover daily, as well as second caregivers for (ix) 1 to 2 hours per day, (x) 3 to 4 hours, (xi) 5 hours a day, (xii) a second live-in caregiver, along with (xiii) waking care and finally, (xiv) skilled nursing care/trained caregiver. As noted, combination packages are also possible. Costings are also available, but these relate to the London, UK prices, and Turner-Stokes et al. (1999) advise that the costings will not necessarily be applicable to other communities. A worked example of using both the NPDS and NPCNA is provided in Turner-Stokes (1999) and appears below.

Psychometric properties

Turner-Stokes et al. (1999) compared the NPCNA with the usual method of determining care needs, a 40- to 60-minute detailed structured interview conducted by an independent assessor with the patient and a nurse of the patient's choice. Thirty-five patients from the neurorehabilitation unit, Northwick Park Hospital, UK, mainly with stroke (80%) were assessed. Williams, Harris, and Turner-Stokes (2007a, 2007b) examined the capacity of the NPCNA to estimate hours of nursing care in two different samples admitted to an inpatient neurorehabilitation ward. In the 2007a sample ($n = 59$) moderate correlation ($r = .31$) was found, and in the 2007b sample ($n = 28$) the NPCNA overestimated care hours (median = 330 mins) compared with actual hours (median = 103 mins). Data on responsiveness are available from Nyein, Turner-Stokes, and Robinson (1999) who assessed 39 patients with the NPCNA, along with the Functional Independence Measure (FIM), in the first and last weeks of the admission to an inpatient neurorehabilitation unit. They also compared the NPCNA in hospital and home settings in 28 patients who reached discharge during the course of the study, hypothesizing that more hours would be required in the home setting because hospitals are especially adapted to meet the needs of patients with disability. Results of these studies using the variable, NPCNA "restricted hours", unless otherwise stated, are shown in Box 9.7.

Box 9.7

Validity:	Criterion: *Concurrent:* Turner-Stokes et al. (1999): with structured interview: $r_s = .90$ – NPCNA care package with structured interview: $r_s = .73$
	Nyein et al.: with FIM Admission: $r = -.77$ – with FIM Discharge: $r = -.84$
	Construct: *Discriminant:* Nyein et al.: Home Median = 22 hrs/week vs Hospital discharge Median = 15 hrs/week; $z = -2.73$, $p = .02$
Reliability:	Inter-rater: No information available (but see below)
	Test–retest: No information available (but see below)
Responsiveness:	Nyein et al.: Admission Median = 37 hrs/week vs Discharge Median = 15 hrs/week; $z = -5.38$, $p < .001$

Comment

Turner-Stokes et al. (1999) emphasize that the NPCNA "is not intended to provide an exhaustive estimate of socioeconomic or opportunity costs. Instead emphasis was placed on simplicity and practicality for routine use in a busy clinical setting" (p. 260). The NPCNA provides a method to translate levels of dependency into corresponding levels of required care, along with the costs of that care. Psychometrically, there is evidence that the NPCNA method is valid and responsive, but at this stage other psychometric properties, including inter-rater reliability and temporal stability are unknown. Such data are available for the NPDS, however, Turner-Stokes et al. (1998) reporting excellent inter-rater reliability ($r_s = .90$) and 2-day test–retest reliability ($r_s = .93$), which suggests that the NPCNA may have similar characteristics. The fact that the intercorrelation between the structured interview and the clinician's rating using the NPCNA was so high ($r = .90$), indicates that the clinician attending the patient is optimally placed to make an evaluation of needs, representing considerable savings in time. Williams et al. (2007a, 2007b) observe that the NPCNA was designed to assess direct care needs in community settings, but other applications (e.g., nursing hours in inpatient rehabilitation settings) will require further development of the algorithm. Further work by Turner-Stokes (2007) and

Turner-Stokes, Paul, and Williams (2006) indicates that NPCNA shows promise as a tool to demonstrate cost-efficiencies in rehabilitation practice.

Key references

Nyein, K., Turner-Stokes, L., & Robinson, I. (1999). The Northwick Park Care Needs Assessment (NPCNA): A measure of community care needs: sensitivity to change during rehabilitation. *Clinical Rehabilitation*, *13*(6), 482–491.

Turner-Stokes, L. (1999). Outcome measures for inpatient neurorehabilitation settings. *Neuropsychological Rehabilitation*, *9*(3/4), 329–343.

Turner-Stokes, L. (2007). Cost-efficiency of longer stay rehabilitation programmes: Can they provide value for money? *Brain Injury*, *21*(10), 1015–1021.

Turner-Stokes, L., Nyein, K., & Halliwell, D. (1999). The Northwick Park Care Needs Assessment (NPCNA): A directly costable outcome measure in rehabilitation. *Clinical Rehabilitation*, *13*(3), 253–267.

Turner-Stokes, L., Paul, S., & Williams, H. (2006). Efficiency of specialist rehabilitation in reducing dependency and costs of continuing care for adults with complex acquired brain injuries. *Journal of Neurology, Neurosurgery, and Psychiatry*, *77*, 634–639.

Turner-Stokes, L., Tonge, P., Nyein, K., Hunter, M., Nielson, S., & Robinson, I. (1998). The Northwick Park Dependency Score (NPDS): A measure of nursing dependency in rehabilitation. *Clinical Rehabilitation*, *12*(4), 304–318.

Williams, H., Harris, R., & Turner-Stokes, L. (2007a). Can the Northwick Park Care Needs Assessment be used to estimate nursing staff requirements in an inpatient rehabilitation setting? *Clinical Rehabilitation*, *21*, 535–544.

Williams, H., Harris, R., & Turner-Stokes, L. (2007b). Northwick Park Care Needs Assessment: Adaptation for inpatient neurological rehabilitation settings. *Journal of Advanced Nursing*, *59*(6), 612–622.

Northwick Park Care Needs Assessment (NPCNA)
WORKED EXAMPLE

	Morning	Mid-morning	Mid-day	Mid-afternoon	Evening	Bed-time	Night-time	2nd helper
SELF CARE								
Transfers	0.25					0.25		
Stairs								
Toileting: Bladder	0.25	0.25	0.25	0.00	0.25	0.25	>2	
Toileting: Bowels	0.50							
Washing & Grooming	0.50					0.50		
Bathing/Showering	0.50							0.50
Dressing	1.00					1.00		
SELF CARE TOTAL	**3.00**	**0.25**	**0.25**	**0.00**	**0.25**	**2.00**	**>2**	**0.50**
Second Helper	0.50							
FEEDING								
Making a snack/meal	0.25		0.25		0.25			
Eating	0.25		0.25		0.25			
Drinking	0.25		0.25		0.25			
Enteral feeding								
FEEDING TOTAL	**0.75**		**0.75**		**0.75**			
OTHER DAILY CARE								
Skin care	0.25		0.25			0.25		
Safety awareness	0.25		0.25			0.25		
Medication								
OTHER DAILY CARE TOTAL	**0.50**		**0.50**		**0.00**	**0.50**		
Second Helper								
DAILY CARE								Total/day
TOTAL CARE HOURS	**4.25**	**0.25**	**1.50**	**0.00**	**1.00**	**2.50**		**9.50**
Second helper	**0.50**							**0.50**
RESTRICTED CARE HOURS	**2.00**	**0.50**	**1.00**	**0.00**	**1.00**	**1.00**	**>2**	**5.50**

ADDITIONAL WEEKLY CARE

Urinary incontinence	**None**
Faecal incontinence	**None**

Night time care	**Waking**
CONSTANT SUPERVISION	**None**
SKILLED CARE TOTAL	**4**
Domestic help	**4**

TOTALS PER WEEK

Total Care Hours	**66.50**	per week
Restricted Care Hours	**38.50**	per week
Approximate Cost	**£1,836**	per week
Care Package Category		**Live-in carer + 2nd carer 1–2 hours + waking night care + Skilled care 4 hrs per week**

Acknowledgement: From Turner-Stokes, L. et al. (1999). The Northwick Park Care Needs Assessment (NPCNA): a directly costable outcome measure in rehabilitation. *Clinical Rehabilitation. 13*(3), pp.253—267, Figure 2, p. 259. Used by permission of Sage Publications, format provided by Dr Turner-Stokes.

Social Support Survey (SSS)

Sherbourne and Stewart (1991)

Source

Items for the Medical Outcomes Study (MOS) SSS are available in an appendix to Sherbourne and Stewart (1991), and are reproduced below.

Purpose

The SSS is a self-rating scale, designed to measure the perceived availability of functional social supports. It was initially developed for use in a longitudinal research study of patients with "chronic conditions", and has also been used with people with stroke (Hilari & Northcott, 2006).

Item description

The main focus of the SSS is the 19 items representing five dimensions of functional social support: (i) Emotional support (4 items, e.g., empathic understanding from other people), (ii) Informational support (4 items, e.g., offering of advice), (iii) Tangible support (4 items, e.g., provision of material aid), (iv) Affectionate support (3 items, e.g., expression of love), and (v) Positive social interactions (4 items, e.g., availability of other people for recreation). An additional two items (marital status and number of people in whom the person can confide) provide contextual background.

Scale development

Sherbourne and Stewart (1991) distinguished between functional and structural approaches to measuring social support. Structural social support refers to the social network – "the existence and quantity of social relationships" (p. 705), whereas the SSS draws on functional social support, defined as (p. 705):

> the degree to which interpersonal relationships serve particular functions. The functions most often cited are (1) emotional support which involves caring, love and empathy, (2) instrumental support (referred to by many as tangible support), (3) information, guidance or feedback that can provide a solution to a problem, (4) appraisal support which involves information relevant to self-evaluation and, (5) social companionship, which involves spending time with others in leisure and recreational activities.

Following a review of existing measures, the authors generated a pool of 50 items that were intended to be distinct from related constructs, such as mental health, family functioning and so forth. Initial validity testing used six judges (behavioural scientists) who allocated items to categories. Thirteen items that proved difficult to classify were eliminated. The 37-item scale, along with (unspecified) validating instruments, was then piloted with patients recruited from a rural health clinic. This process resulted in a further 18 items being excluded because they were not internally consistent with hypothesized dimensions or did not discriminate between social support and other health-related behaviours. Two items were included that tapped into structural social support in order to understand how this type of social support may be related to functional social support.

Administration procedures, response format and scoring

The SSS is an easily completed, self-administered scale.

The structural support items (marital status and number of people in whom the person can confide) are not scored. Responses for the 19 functional items are made on a 5-point scale: 1 (none of the time), 2 (a little of the time), 3 (some of the time), 4 (most of the time), 5 (all of the time). In addition to using mean scores, Sherbourne and Stewart (1991) report descriptive data whereby scores on the scales are transformed (range 0–100), but no information is provided regarding procedures to be used for transforming the raw scores. In their study of people with aphasia, Hilari and Northcott (2006) used mean scores alone, thereby anchoring the score back to the five response categories, resulting in an easily interpreted metric.

Psychometric properties

Sherbourne and Stewart (1991) examined the measurement characteristics of the SSS in a large sample ($n = 2987$) drawn from the MOS, a population study recruiting from three sites in the USA (Boston, Chicago and Los Angeles). Participants were aged 18 to 98 years ($M = 55$ years) and 46% had completed high school ($M = 13.3$ years education). The study intentionally included people "who appeared to have one or more of four chronic diseases (hypertension, diabetes, coronary heart disease, and depression)" (p. 706). Fourteen measures of health and well-being specifically developed for the MOS, 11 of which showed acceptable internal consistency (Cronbach alpha > .8), were used to validate the SSS. The SSS was readministered 1 year later. As expected there were low to moderate correlation coefficients between structural social support (number of close friends/relatives) and the functional support items of the SSS, both for the total score ($r = .23$) and for the dimensions (range: $r = .18$–$.24$). Correlation coefficients between marital status and functional social support were somewhat higher (range: $r = .20$–$.33$). The intercorrelation matrix showed considerable item overlap between the Emotional support and Information support items, and these were grouped into a single Emotional/Informational scale. One Positive social interaction item did not discriminate well and was excluded from factor analysis. Confirmatory factor analysis of the SSS produced the same four factors. Additionally, principal components analysis (PCA) produced a single factor, with loadings from each of the items ranging between .67 and .88, supporting the use of an overall index (percentage of variance not reported). A higher order factor analysis, using the four SSS factors and 12 other physical, mental and social support measures, extracted three factors: social support (the four SSS factors), physical health (seven measures), and mental health (four measures). Yu, Lee, and Woo (2004) examined the psychometric properties of a Chinese version of the SSS in a sample of 110 cardiac patients. Results from Sherbourne and Stewart, except where otherwise stated, are shown in Box 9.8.

Box 9.8

Validity:	Criterion: *Concurrent:* Total score with loneliness: $r = -.67$ (dimension range: $r = -.53$ to $-.69$) – with family functioning: $r = .53$ (dimension range: $r = .38$–$.56$) – with marital functioning: $r = .56$ (dimension range: $r = .44$–$.57$) – with mental health: $r = .45$ (dimension range: $r = .36$–$.57$)
	Yu et al.: Hospital Anxiety and Depression Scale: $r = -.58$ (dimension range: $r = -.53$ to $-.60$)
	Construct: *Internal consistency*: Cronbach alpha .97 (dimension range: .91–.96)
	Yu et al.: Cronbach alpha .98 (dimension range: .93–.96)
	Factor analysis: Confirmatory factor analysis: 4 factors: Tangible support (4 items), Affectionate support (3 items), Positive social interactions (3 items), and Emotional/ Informational support (8 items). PCA extracted a single factor
	Yu et al.: Confirmatory factor analysis: 4 factors (as above)
	Convergent/ divergent: Higher correlation between hypothesized similar constructs (e.g., total score with loneliness: $r = -.67$, with family functioning: $r = .53$); lower correlation with hypothesized dissimilar constructs (e.g., total score with physical functioning: $r = .11$, with pain severity: $r = -.19$)
Reliability:	Inter-rater: Not applicable
	Test–retest: 1 year: $r = .78$ (dimension range: $r = .72$–$.76$)
	Yu et al.: 2 weeks: ICC = .84
Responsiveness:	No information available

Comment

The SSS is a good choice of instrument to provide an evaluation of perceived functional social supports. It was carefully developed and intentionally designed to minimize the administrative burden on its intended respondents with chronic illness, yet at the same time the items afford representation of different components of social support (e.g., access to people who can advise, share recreational activities, show understanding). It is unclear from Sherbourne and Stewart (1991), however, how the SSS is to be scored, but using the mean score, both for the dimensions as well as the total, makes the SSS readily interpretable. The SSS has good psychometric properties with excellent temporal stability over a

2-week period and internal consistency, both for the dimensions and the combined total score, as well as showing evidence for convergent and divergent validity. The SSS has had limited exposure in the acquired brain impairment population, however, and further work is needed to establish its psychometric properties with different neurological groups.

Key references

Hilari, K., & Northcott, S. (2006). Social support in people with chronic aphasia. *Aphasiology*, *20*(1), 17–36.

Sherbourne, C. D., & Stewart, A. L. (1991). The MOS Social Support Survey. *Social Science in Medicine*, *32*(6), 705–714.

Yu, D. S. F., Lee, D. T. F., & Woo, J. (2004). Psychometric testing of the Chinese version of the Medical Outcomes Study Social Support Survey (MOS-SSS-C). *Research in Nursing and Health*, *27*, 135–143.

Social Support Survey

Sherbourne and Stewart (1991)

Name:	**Administered by:**	**Date:**

Instructions: These are some questions about the support that is available to you.

1. About how many close friends and close relatives do you have (people you feel at ease with and can talk to about what is on your mind)?

Write in number of close friends and close relatives: ____________

Instructions: People sometimes look to others for companionship, assistance, or other types of support. How often is each of the following kinds of support available to you if you need it?

Response key:
1 = None of the time
2 = A little of the time
3 = Some of the time
4 = Most of the time
5 = All of the time

	RESPONSE
2. Someone to help you if you were confined to bed	________
3. Someone you can count on to listen to you when you need to talk	________
4. Someone to give you good advice about a crisis	________
5. Someone to take you to a doctor if you needed it	________
6. Someone who shows you love and affection	________
7. Someone to have a good time with	________
8. Someone to give you information to help you understand a situation	________
9. Someone to confide in or talk to about yourself or your problems	________
10. Someone who hugs you	________
11. Someone to get together with for relaxation	________
12. Someone to prepare your meals if you were unable to do it yourself	________
13. Someone whose advice you really want	________
14. Someone to do things with to help you get your mind off things	________
15. Someone to help with daily chores if you were sick	________
16. Someone to share your most private worries and fears with	________
17. Someone to turn to for suggestions about how to deal with a personal problem	________
18. Someone to do something enjoyable with	________
19. Someone who understands your problems	________
20. Someone to love and make you feel wanted	________

Acknowledgement: From Sherbourne, C. D., & Stewart, A. L. (1991). The MOS Social Support Survey. *Social Science in Medicine*, *32*(6), 705–714, Appendix, pp. 713–714, reprinted with permission of Elsevier.

Supervision Rating Scale (SRS)

Boake (1996)

Source

Response categories for the SRS are available in an appendix to Boake (1996) and also appear below. Information regarding the SRS and the recording form are available on the website of the Center on Outcome Measurement in Brain Injury (http://www.tbims.org/combi/srs/index.html).

Purpose

The SRS is a clinician rating scale designed to provide an overall index of the level of supervision received by a person after brain injury. Supervision is defined broadly to encompass "all forms of help that require the caregiver to be in the physical vicinity of the patient . . . nursing care, physical assistance, verbal cues, and even the presence of another person on the same premises to ensure the patient's safety" (Boake, 1996, p. 765). The SRS was developed for people with traumatic brain injury (TBI).

Item description

There are no items for the SRS per se. Rather the patient is classified into one of 13 hierarchical categories that can be collapsed into five levels, also hierarchically organized. Overnight supervision, along with varying degrees of daytime supervision, is required for four of the five levels. Levels are as follows: Level 1: independent (2 categories; (i) complete independence and (ii) unsupervised overnight); Level 2: overnight supervision (1 category); Level 3: part-time supervision (4 categories); Level 4: full-time indirect supervision (2 categories); Level 5: full-time direct supervision (4 categories).

Scale development

Boake (1996) observed that there are many types and methods of measuring outcomes after brain injury. Level of supervision is one type of outcome, which is rated highly by caregivers and payors alike. He argued for an overall index "because a patient's level of supervision should reflect the cumulative impact of all of the patient's impairments and disabilities" (p. 765). Boake emphasized the distinction between the level of supervision actually received versus the amount of supervision needed. He argued that a disadvantage of the latter approach is that subjective judgements can lead to under- or over-estimation of a patient's needs; hence rendering a scale unreliable. It was therefore intended that the SRS should measure the actual frequency and intensity of supervision received. Definitions for the five levels of the SRS were based on the design of existing scales of supervision described in the literature.

Administration procedures, response format and scoring

The SRS is designed to be completed by a clinician, based on interviews with the patient and an informant who has direct knowledge of the supervision provided.

No actual administration or scoring is required; rather the patient is assigned to one of 13 categories (referred to as points) that most closely represents his or her level of supervision received. Detailed operational definitions are provided for each of the 13 categories. If using categories, the score ranges from 1 (patient lives alone or independently) to 13 (patient is in physical restraints). Alternatively, if using levels, the score ranges from 1 (independent) to 5 (full-time direct supervision).

Psychometric properties

Measurement characteristics of the SRS were initially examined in a sample 114 of people with TBI living in the community or non-hospital facility (e.g., nursing home) who were referred for neuropsychological evaluation at a rehabilitation hospital in the USA (Boake, 1996). Most participants (80%) sustained severe injuries, and the group was on average 3.8 years post-trauma (range: 3.5 months to 13.3 years). Validating instruments included the Disability Rating Scale (DRS) and the 5-category Glasgow Outcome Scale (GOS), along with ratings of five self-care items and six instrumental activities of daily living (IADL). Inter-rater reliability was assessed in a subset of the sample ($n = 19$) using the author and one of 10 other raters, who simultaneously observed the interviews (for 17/19 participants) but independently rated the SRS. Data on responsiveness of the SRS were reported for 112 people admitted to inpatient rehabilitation after TBI (High, Roebuck-Spencer, Sander, Struchen, & Sherer, 2006). The subgroup that was admitted earlier than 6 months post-trauma showed a significant reduction in SRS scores between admission and discharge ($p < .001$), as well as between discharge and follow-up at 1.5 years post-trauma ($p < .001$); those who were admitted later post-trauma (6–12 months or > 12 months post-trauma) also showed significant reduction between admission and discharge ($p = .001$ and $p = .002$ respectively), but not between discharge and follow-up.

The SRS was examined in detail in a large multicentre study ($n = 563$) that provided information on demographic and injury predictors of supervision received at 12 months post-trauma (Hart, Millis, Novack, Englander, Fidler-Sheppard, & Bell, 2003). Three SRS groups were formed: independent (SRS 1–2 points), moderate supervision (SRS 3–5 points), and heavy supervision (SRS 6–13 points) and discriminant validity was examined in relation to injury severity (using duration of post-traumatic amnesia, PTA). Hart et al. also reported on neuropsychological functioning using standard measures in a subset without physical disability ($n = 452$ with scores ≥ 6 on all motor items of the Functional Independence Measure, FIM) at 12 months post-trauma. Results of Boake, except where otherwise indicated, are shown in Box 9.9.

Comment

The SRS is widely used in clinical settings in the USA, being included in the Traumatic Brain Injury Model Systems (TBIMS) data collection protocol in 1997 (Hart et al., 2003). It is most suited for the inpatient rehabilitation setting, where it is responsive to patients' improved level of recovery (High et al., 2006), but has more limited application in community settings, where ceiling effects between 69% and 73% have been consistently reported in independent samples from different countries (Hall, Bushnik, Lakisic-Kazazic, Wright, & Cantagallo, 2001; Hart et al., 2003; Tate, 2004; Wood & Rutherford, 2006). In 11 of the 13 categories, the patient is supervised overnight, with varying levels of supervision during the day and thus the scale is focused on the more intense levels of supervision. Boake (1996) recognized that the SRS may be insensitive at the lesser levels of disability because it only considers supervision "when it is provided in the patient's physical vicinity, and ignores any monitoring or guidance received from persons who are not physically present" (p. 770) and he identified the need for a measure for those who require "supervision from afar". Psychometrically, although there is no information on its temporal stability, the SRS shows good to excellent inter-rater reliability, is responsive, and shows concurrent validity with other measures of functional ability, as well as discriminant validity in being able to distinguish among various groups.

Box 9.9

Validity:	Criterion: *Concurrent:* 13-point SRS with GOS: Kendall tau = .73 – with DRS: tau = .65 – 5-level SRS with GOS: tau = .63 – 5-level SRS with DRS: tau = .64
	Hart et al.: with FIM: $r_s = -.45$
	Construct: *Discriminant:* Significant group differences on the 13-point SRS and living situation: independent ($n = 10$) vs with support ($n = 95$) vs facility ($n = 9$); $\chi^2 = 32.0$, $p < .001$ – 5-level SRS: significant group differences with respect to percentage independence in self-care ($\chi^2 = 50.2$, $p < .001$) and IADL; $\chi^2 = 61.1$, $p < .001$
	Hart et al.: Significant differences duration between SRS-Independent vs SRS-moderate supervision on PTA duration ($p < .001$) – on 15/16 neuropsychological tests ($p < .003$)
Reliability:	Inter-rater: 13-point SRS: ICC = .86 – 5-level SRS: $k = .64$
	Test–retest: no information available
Responsiveness:	High et al.: significant reduction in SRS scores between admission and discharge to rehabilitation ($p < .001$ – descriptive data only presented in graphical form)

Key references

Boake, C. (1996). Supervision Rating Scale: A measure of functional outcome from brain injury. *Archives of Physical Medicine and Rehabilitation*, *77*, 765–772.

Hall, K. M., Bushnik, T., Lakisic-Kazazic, B., Wright, J., & Cantagallo, A. (2001). Assessing traumatic brain injury outcome measures for long-term follow-up of community-based individuals. *Archives of Physical Medicine and Rehabilitation*, *82*, 367–374.

Hart, T., Millis, S., Novack, T., Englander, J., Fidler-Sheppard, R., & Bell, K. R. (2003). The relationship between neuropsychologic function and level of caregiver supervision at 1 year after traumatic brain injury. *Archives of Physical Medicine and Rehabilitation*, *84*, 221–230.

High, W. M., Roebuck-Spencer, T., Sander, A. M., Struchen, M. A., & Sherer, M. (2006). Early versus later admission to postacute rehabilitation: Impact on functional outcome after traumatic brain injury. *Archives of Physical Medicine and Rehabilitation*, *87*, 334–342.

Tate, R. L. (2004). Assessing support needs for people with traumatic brain injury: The Care and Needs Scale (CANS). *Brain Injury*, *18*(5), 445–460.

Wood, R. L., & Rutherford, N. A. (2006). Psychosocial adjustment 17 years after severe brain injury. *Journal of Neurology, Neurosurgery, and Psychiatry*, *77*, 71–73.

Supervision Rating Scale

Boake (1996)

Name:	**Administered by:**	**Date:**

Instructions: Circle the rating (numbers 1 through 13) that is closest to the amount of supervision that the patient actually receives. "Supervision" means that someone is responsible for being with the patient.

LEVEL 1: INDEPENDENT

1. Patient lives alone or independently. Other persons can live with the patient, but they cannot take responsibility for supervision (e.g., a child or an elderly person)
2. The patient is unsupervised overnight. The patient lives with one or more persons who could be responsible for supervision (e.g., a spouse or roommate), but they are all sometimes absent overnight

LEVEL 2: OVERNIGHT SUPERVISION

3. The patient is only supervised overnight. One or more supervising persons are always present overnight but they are all sometimes absent for the rest of the day

LEVEL 3: PART-TIME SUPERVISION

4. The patient is supervised overnight and part-time during waking hours, but is allowed on independent outings. One or more supervising persons are always present overnight and are also present during part of the waking hours every day. However, the patient is sometimes allowed to leave the residence without being accompanied by someone who is responsible for supervision
5. The patient is supervised overnight and part-time during waking hours, but is unsupervised during working hours. Supervising persons are all sometimes absent for enough time for them to work full-time outside the home
6. The patient is supervised overnight and during most waking hours. Supervising persons are all sometimes absent for periods longer than 1 hour, but less than the time needed to hold a full-time job away from home
7. The patient is supervised overnight and during almost all waking hours. Supervising persons are all sometimes absent for periods shorter than 1 hour

LEVEL 4: FULL-TIME INDIRECT SUPERVISION

8. The patient is under full-time indirect supervision. At least one supervising person is always present, but the supervising person does not check on the patient more than once every 30 minutes
9. Same as no.8 plus requires overnight safety precautions (e.g., a deadbolt on the outside door)

LEVEL 5: FULL-TIME DIRECT SUPERVISION

10. The patient is under full-time supervision. At least one supervising person is always present and the supervising person checks on the patient more than once every 30 minutes
11. The patient lives in a setting in which the exits are physically controlled by others (e.g., a locked ward)
12. Same as no.11 plus a supervising person is designated to provide full-time line-of-sight supervision (e.g., an escape watch or suicide watch)
13. The patient is in physical restraints

Acknowledgement: From Boake, C. (1996). Supervision Rating Scale: A measure of functional outcome from brain injury. *Archives of Physical Medicine and Rehabilitation*, *77*, 765–772, Appendix, pp. 771–772, reprinted with permission of American Congress of Rehabilitation Medicine and American Academy of Physical Medicine and Rehabilitation and Elsevier.

Survey of Unmet Needs and Service Use (SUNSU)

Heinemann, Sokol, Garvin, and Bode (2002)

Source

Items listed in the survey of unmet needs and service use (abbreviated to SUNSU for ease of reference) are tabulated in Heinemann et al. (2002) and are reproduced below.

Purpose

The SUNSU, which is part of a larger needs assessment survey, is primarily a self-rating scale. Heinemann et al. (2002) recognized the importance of having "a reliable means of measuring unmet and service needs that is specifically designed for the TBI [traumatic brain injury] population" (p. 1052).

Item description

The SUNSU comprises 27 items, representing a broad spectrum of needs. Items address areas of impairment (e.g., improving memory, solving problems), basic activities of daily living (e.g., obtaining personal care attendant/personal assistant services), instrumental activities of daily living (e.g., managing money, paying bills), occupational activities (e.g., improving job skills), psychological needs (e.g., fulfilling needs for intimacy), community access (e.g., finding places and opportunities to socialize with others). The set of items is used to create two scales: (i) Unmet Service Need and (ii) Services Received.

Scale development

Heinemann and colleagues (2002) argued that "effective service planning requires an appreciation of how individuals with TBI use services, what their unmet needs are, and what subgroups are most vulnerable to service deprivation" (p. 1052). In developing their survey, Heinemann et al. drew on the work of Patrick and Peach (1989) in distinguishing between felt needs (perceived wants of services) and unfelt needs (service needs of which the person is unaware); as well as expressed needs (actual requests for services), unmet needs (needs not satisfied by current service provision) and undermet needs (needs that are only partially met). The aim was to address unmet needs, "rather than focusing on nuances of undermet or unfelt needs" (p. 1053). Heinemann et al. developed the listing of needs within the context of a state-wide consumer needs assessment survey conducted in Illinois, USA. Existing needs assessments were reviewed and a comprehensive list of service needs relevant to TBI was generated. A range of groups contributed to development of the survey, including the state department, three consumer groups, and an advisory committee. The survey was trialled and distributed to 14 facilities and organizations, who posted it to 5915 of their members/service recipients. Responses were received from 1045 individuals, of which 895 related to people with TBI and were suitable for analysis. Rasch analysis was conducted on the SUNSU data to examine construct validity (see below).

Administration procedures, response format and scoring

The survey, including the SUNSU items, was designed for self-completion, as well as postal survey. Informants can also complete the survey if necessary, and in the report of Heinemann et al. (2002), 44% of surveys were completed either by an informant on behalf of the person with TBI (26%) or by the person with TBI who received some help (18%). In order to obtain information on the two SUNSU subscales, the set of items is completed twice, first in terms of reporting services that are currently used (or help that is received now) and then in terms of reporting services (or help) that are needed or wanted.

The response format is not specified in Heinemann et al. (2002), but it is implied that items are endorsed if the person with TBI indicates that he or she has a need in that area. Unmet need is determined by calculating the need for a service that is not currently received. Following the Rasch analysis, scaling procedures were used by Heinemann et al., whereby scores were converted to a scale ranging from 0 to 100, with higher scores indicating (i) fewer unmet needs for the Unmet Service

Need scale and (ii) fewer services received for the Services Received scale.

Psychometric properties

Rasch analysis was used to determine the scaling characteristics of the SUNSU items (Heinemann et al., 2002), using the data from the 895 respondents. In applying Rasch analysis to the SUNSU, difficulty referred to the frequency with which needs were endorsed, and ability referred to the amount of the underlying construct (viz. service need) the person possessed. Person separation reliability for the Unmet Service Needs scale identified three strata (low < 4 unmet service needs, middle $M = 12$ unmet service needs, high $M = 23$ unmet service needs). Reliability for both the Unmet Service Needs scale and the Services Received scale was above the recommended level of .8 and fit statistics were between the accepted limits of 0.7 to 1.3. Results are shown in Box 9.10.

Comment

Advantages of the SUNSU include its development with consumer representation, thereby ensuring its relevance and providing evidence for content validity. It has also been subjected to Rasch analysis, with evidence to support its internal reliability and hence its use as a unidimensional scale. Other psychometric information is pertinent, however, particularly for inter-rater reliability and temporal stability, given that almost half of the people with TBI in the Heinemann et al. (2002) study received assistance in completing the survey.

Box 9.10

Validity:	Construct: Internal reliability: Unmet Service Needs scale: person reliability .83; fit statistics for all items between 0.85–1.15 – Services Received scale: person reliability .82; fit statistics for all items between 0.83–1.21
Reliability:	Inter-rater: No information available Test–retest: No information available
Responsiveness:	No information available

Nonetheless, having a listing of needs and services with good scaling characteristics is an important development and, as Heinemann et al. note, will provide "a consistent language to describe needs and services, thus making it easier to examine trends or differences across groups" (p. 1058).

Key references

Heinemann, A. W., Sokol, K., Garvin, L., & Bode, R. K. (2002). Measuring unmet needs and services among persons with traumatic brain injury. *Archives of Physical Medicine and Rehabilitation*, *83*, 1052–1059.

Patrick, D., & Peach, H. (1989). *Disablement in the community*. Oxford: Oxford University Press.

Survey of Unmet Needs and Service Use

Heinemann, Sokol, Garvin, and Bode (2002)

Name: **Administered by:** **Date:**

Instructions: Below is a list of needs you may have. If you are currently (within the last 12 months) receiving help with this need, place a tick beside it in the **receive help now** column on the left. If you want help in this area, place a tick beside it in the **need/want help** column on the right.

Receive help now		**Need/want help**
______	travelling in my community	______
______	finding housing that is affordable and accessible	______
______	increasing my income	______
______	improving my job skills	______
______	finding paid employment	______
______	increasing my educational qualifications	______
______	coordinating the services I receive	______
______	managing my money, paying bills	______
______	increasing my independence in housekeeping, cooking, shopping	______
______	caring for my children	______
______	handling legal problems	______
______	feeling part of my community	______
______	finding places and opportunities to socialize with others	______
______	obtaining personal care attendance/personal assistant services	______
______	controlling alcohol and/or drug use	______
______	improving my memory, solving problems better	______
______	controlling my temper	______
______	improving my mood	______
______	managing stress, emotional upsets	______
______	expressing my needs, understanding others	______
______	fulfilling my needs for intimacy	______
______	obtaining equipment such as wheelchairs, computers, etc.	______
______	improving my health	______
______	increasing my independence in eating, dressing, bathing, toileting, etc.	______
______	increasing my independence in walking, lifting, balancing	______
______	participating in sports and recreation	______
______	participating in religious services or spiritual programmes	______
______	other needs (specify): 1.______________________	______
______	2.______________________	______
______	3.______________________	______

Acknowledgement: From Heinemann, A. W. et al. (2002). Measuring unmet needs and services among persons with traumatic brain injury. *Archives of Physical Medicine and Rehabilitation*, *83*, 1052–1059, Service Needs Table 1, p. 1054, with permission of American Congress of Rehabilitation Medicine and American Academy of Physical Medicine and Rehabilitation and Elsevier. Format provided by Dr Heinemann.

Part D

Multi-domain Scales

10 Global, multidimensional and quality of life scales

Introduction

This chapter contains those instruments that do not fall neatly into the components and domains of the World Health Organization (2001) *International Classification of Functioning, Disability and Health* (ICF) that characterize the preceding chapters. There are two types of such scales. Multidimensional scales contain a selection of items generally encompassing both the Body Functions and Activities/Participation components of the ICF. The second type of scale is the global rating scale that provides an overall rating of the level of functioning. The global rating scale generally contains a hierarchically ordered set of categories, and the person is classified into the level of "best fit". Often such scales are used to monitor changes over time. Some scales, referred to as staging scales, focus on decline, for use in conditions such as dementia; other scales monitor recovery, such as after stroke. Global rating scales have been presented in a number of preceding chapters, but in those cases the scales focused on specific domains of functioning that are addressed within the ICF, such as consciousness (e.g., Rancho Los Amigos Levels of Cognitive Functioning Scale, Chapter 2), self-care activities of daily living (e.g., Katz Index of Activities of Daily Living, Chapter 7), and so forth.

Multidimensional scales hold an interesting position vis-à-vis the ICF taxonomy. A number of them measure so-called quality of life (QOL), and specifically, in the present context, health-related quality of life. In their chapter, Whiteneck, Fougeyrollas, and Gerhart (1997) made a cogent argument for elaborating the model of disablement beyond the predominantly medical model of the original *International Classification of Impairments, Disabilities and Handicaps* (WHO, 1980). One area of need they identified was the inclusion of the subjective perceptions of people with disabilities (Whiteneck et al., 1997, p. 95):

> Although rehabilitationists can objectively quantify the degree of impairment, disability, and handicap by measuring organ system performance, ADL performance, and social role performance in comparison to people without disabilities, such objective assessments tell only half of the story. The subjective perceptions of people regarding their own impairments, disabilities, and handicaps are equally valid and merit equal attention . . . [These subjective perceptions] are closely related to quality of life.

The WHO (2001) manual describes uses of the ICF, one of which is as a research tool to measure inter alia QOL, but the QOL concept is not covered in the ICF taxonomy. Although QOL is nominated as one of the possible future directions for development of the ICF, the WHO heralds concerns regarding "concept compatibility" between "subjective well-being" and the "objective and exteriorized signs" of disease/disability (p. 251). There are, however, precedents within the ICF model where the subjective perspective is readily incorporated. For example, in the domain of supports and relationships in the Environmental Factors component (see Chapter 9) scales of functional social supports adopt an ideographic perspective – there is widespread agreement that social supports can only be meaningfully understood from the person's perspective. Moreover, the two seminal instruments that have been developed for, and specifically based on, the ICF construct of Environmental Factors in fact measure the person's perceptions of the environment (Fougeyrollas, Noreau, & St-Michel, 1997; Whiteneck, Harrison-Felix, Mellick, Brooks, Charlifue, & Gerhart, 2004). Similarly, scale developers in the area of Participation (see Chapter 8) have also recognized the importance of including the person's perceptions, and instruments have been specifically developed using this perspective (e.g., Brown, Dijkers, Gordon, Ashman, Charatz, & Cheng, 2004; Cardol, de Haan, de Jong, van den Bos, & de Groot, 2001; McColl, Davies, Carlson, Johnston, & Minnes, 2001; Wood-Dauphinee & Williams, 1987).

There is general agreement that QOL is an ill-defined and complex construct, and "the complexity increases dramatically when damage to the brain is involved" (Seibert et al., 2002). Dijkers (2003) provides a critical review of extant instruments: "many appear to measure nothing more than what in previous decades was called health status" (p. S3). How does one measure QOL? Ask the patient, say Fayers and Machin (2000), and they go on to observe that "there is general agreement that patients' opinions vary considerably from the expectations of both staff and relatives" (p. 15). Patient self-report, however, is a necessary but not sufficient criterion for a QOL measure. Item content needs to go beyond function and health status. In Dijkers' view (2003, p. S3):

> the essence of QOL [is] having one's individual needs and desires fulfilled, to a reasonable degree; a belief that life is offering or lacking the right balance of challenges and successes in those areas that are of personal salience; and happiness and satisfaction that life is delivering all or most of what is expected or desired. Quantifying only physical, cognitive, social, and emotional functioning fails to capture what most of us would consider the quality of our lives.

A small selection of some of the more common generic QOL measures in current use is presented in this chapter, but the degree to which their item content and measurement approach meets Dijkers' gold standard is variable.

References

Brown, M., Dijkers, M. P. J. M., Gordon, W. A., Ashman, T., Charatz, H., & Cheng, Z. (2004). Participation Objective, Participation Subjective: A measure of participation combining outsider and insider perspectives. *Journal of Head Trauma Rehabilitation*, *19*(6), 459–481.

Cardol, M., de Haan, R. J., de Jong, B. A., van den Bos, G. A. M., & de Groot, I. J. M. (2001). Psychometric properties of the Impact on Participation and Autonomy Questionnaire. *Archives of Physical Medicine and Rehabilitation*, *82*(2), 210–216.

Dijkers, M. P. (2003). Individualization in quality of life measurement: Instruments and approaches. *Archives of Physical Medicine and Rehabilitation*, *84*(Suppl. 2), S3–S14.

Fayers, P. M., & Machin, D. (2000). *Quality of life. Assessment, analysis and interpretation*. Chichester, UK: Wiley.

Fougeyrollas, P., Noreau, L., & St-Michel, G. (1997). The Measure of the Quality of Environment. *ICIDH and Environmental Factors International Network*, *9*, 32–39.

McColl, M. A., Davies, D., Carlson, P., Johnston, J., & Minnes, P. (2001). The Community Integration Measure: Development and preliminary validation. *Archives of Physical Medicine and Rehabilitation*, *82*(4), 429–434.

Seibert, P. S., Reedy, D. P., Hash, J., Webb, A., Stridh-Igo, P., Basom, J. et al. (2002). Brain injury: Quality of life's greatest challenge. *Brain Injury*, *16*(10), 837–848.

Whiteneck, G. G., Fougeyrollas, P., & Gerhart, K. A. (1997). Elaborating the model of disablement. In M. Fuher (Ed.), *Assessing medical rehabilitation practices: The promise of outcomes research* (pp. 91–102). Baltimore: Paul H. Brooks Publishing Co.

Whiteneck, G. G., Harrison-Felix, C. L., Mellick, D. C., Brooks, C. A., Charlifue, S. B., & Gerhart, K. A. (2004). Quantifying environmental factors: A measure of physical, attitudinal, service, productivity, and policy barriers. *Archives of Physical Medicine and Rehabilitation*, *85*, 1324–1335.

Wood-Dauphinee, S., & Williams, J. I. (1987). Reintegration to normal living as a proxy to quality of life. *Journal of Chronic Disease*, *40*(6), 491–499.

World Health Organization. (1980). *International classification of impairments, disabilities and handicaps*. Geneva: World Health Organization.

World Health Organization. (2001). *International classification of functioning, disability and health*. Geneva: World Health Organization.

SECTION 1
Global scales

Clinical Dementia Rating (CDR) Scale

Hughes, Berg, Danziger, Coben, and Martin (1982) and Berg (1984)

Source

Descriptions of the levels comprising the CDR appear in Hughes et al. (1982) and Berg (1984) and are reproduced below.

Purpose

The CDR is a clinician rating scale that aims to determine the degree of dementia severity. A global categorical classification (clinical staging) procedure is used that evaluates "the influence of cognitive loss on the ability to conduct everyday activities" (Morris et al., 1997, p. 1508). The CDR was originally developed for people with Alzheimer's disease and subsequently it has been widely used with all types of dementia.

Item description

The CDR rates level of functioning in six categories: Memory, Orientation, Judgement/problem solving, Home and hobbies, Community affairs, Personal care. Completion of the CDR requires availability of background information, and in the standardization study the authors used a semi-structured interview, the Initial Subject Protocol (ISP), along with a series of Likert rating scales. Instruments such as the Blessed Dementia Rating Scale (BDRS) are administered to an informant to determine level of functioning in cognition and activities of everyday living. The patient's cognitive functioning is also independently assessed with objective procedures, such as the 10-item Short Portable Mental Status Exam (SPMSE; also known as the Short Portable Mental Status Questionnaire, SPMSQ).

Scale development

Hughes et al. (1982) reviewed various methods used in the evaluation of patients with dementia. They considered that the available psychometric tests and behaviour rating scales were problematic in one way or another. Simplified psychometric tests, although "reasonably accurate" in diagnosing cognitive impairment, had floor effects in distinguishing among the more severe grades of dementia. Behaviour rating scales were unstandardized, thereby affecting their reliability. Hughes et al. (1982) thus argued that "a useful 'rating' of dementia can only be 'global', one which assesses both behavioural and psychometric data" (p. 566). Limited information is available on the development of the grades of the CDR. The authors reported that the CDR was similar to some previous, more detailed, scales and had been "used extensively" in a research programme from the Washington University, St Louis, Missouri, USA. Previous pilot testing with 35 patients had shown that inter-rater reliability was good ($r = .89$). The CDR was initially trialled psychometrically with 58 healthy control subjects and 59 patients with mild dementia or for whom the diagnosis of dementia was uncertain; a further 21 patients with moderate or severe dementia were also examined to test the full range of the scale (see below). The algorithms to obtain the global rating scale were originally reported in Hughes et al. (1982) and subsequently slightly modified and refined by Berg (1984) and Morris (1993, p. 2414) "as experience permitted resolution of ambiguities".

Administration procedures, response format and scoring

Hughes et al. (1982) advise that the CDR is suitable for administration by clinicians experienced in assessing cognitive functions of older people. Information from the semi-structured interview combined with other instruments (BDRS and SPMSE/SPMSQ) can be used as a basis to complete the CDR. Morris et al. (1997) developed a standardized training protocol (using worksheets and video recordings) that showed good levels of agreement with a "gold standard" rating, both for previously inexperienced raters (78–85%) and experienced raters (82–87%). Administration time of the CDR itself is quick, although collection of background information required for valid completion adds length to the completion time. Berg, Miller, Baty, Rubin, Morris, and Figiel

(1992) reported that the interview and other measures used to derive the CDR score in their study took 90 minutes.

Ratings in each of the six categories are made on a 5-point scale: 0 (no impairment), 0.5 (questionable impairment), 1 (mild impairment), 2 (moderate impairment), 3 (severe impairment). Category scores are then converted to a global rating (also using the above 5-point scale) by applying algorithms in which the Memory category is the primary category and other categories (viz. Orientation, Judgement/problem solving, Home and hobbies, Community affairs, and Personal care) are secondary. The algorithms are as follows. In brief:

- CDR = the Memory score, if the scores of ≥ 3/5 secondary categories are the same as the Memory score
- If the scores of ≥ 3/5 secondary categories are higher or lower than the Memory score, then (with one exception) the CDR = the score of the majority of the categories. Exception: if the scores of the secondary categories fall either side of the Memory score, then CDR = Memory score
- If the Memory score = 0.5, and if ≥ 3/4 or more specific secondary categories (viz. Orientation, Judgement/problem solving, Home and hobbies, Community affairs – i.e., not Personal care) have scores of 1 or higher, then CDR = 1
- If the Memory score = 0, then the CDR = 0, unless ≥ 2/5 secondary categories have scores of 1 or higher, in which case the CDR = 0.5 in persons who are neither clearly healthy nor clearly have dementia.

As noted, the global score ranges from 0 (no impairment) to 3 (severe impairment). An extended version, including ratings of 4 (profound impairment) and 5 (terminal stage), was published by Heyman and colleagues (1987) and independently validated by Dooneief, Marder, Tang, and Stern (1996).

An alternative, commonly used scoring method is referred to as "sum of boxes", which provides "a more detailed quantitative global measure". This is calculated by summing the impairment ratings (scores 1–3) in each of the six categories (boxes) from which the CDR is derived: maximum score is $6 \times 3 = 18$ (or for the extended CDR $6 \times 5 = 30$).

Psychometric properties

The initial psychometric study of the CDR (Hughes et al., 1982) used a range of validating instruments (BDRS, SPMSE/SPMSQ and the Face–Hand Test, FHT). Burke et al. (1988) reported on inter-rater reliability with five raters who were trained neurologists and psychiatrists and who independently completed the CDR from 25 videotaped interviews. Data on 1-month temporal stability from 62 patients are available from Marin et al. (2001) who adapted the CDR slightly for use in a chronic care facility. Diagnostic accuracy of the CDR against examination by a neurologist was examined in a population survey of 656 people aged 75 years or older from Helsinki, Finland (Juva, Sulkava, Erkinjuntti, Ylikoski, Valvanne, & Tilvis, 1995). They used a demarcation of CDR ≥ 1 to indicate presence of dementia. Data on responsiveness are available from Berg et al. (1988), who followed the standardization sample ($n = 58$ healthy controls, $n = 43$ patients with mild dementia, CDR = 1) longitudinally over 7 years. Results from Hughes et al., except where otherwise stated, are shown in Box 10.1.

Box 10.1

Validity:	Criterion: *Concurrent:* with BDRS: $r = .74$ – with SPMSE (SPMSQ): $r = .84$ – with FHT: $r = .57$
	Construct: *Discriminant:* Juva et al.: Differential diagnosis of dementia vs no dementia, using cut-off score of 0.5/1: sensitivity 95%, specificity 94%
Reliability:	Inter-rater: Burke et al.: $k_w = .87$ (category range: $k_w = .75–.94$) – sum of boxes: $k_w = .87$
	Marin et al.: ICC = 0.99 (category range: ICC = .95–.98)
	Test–retest: Marin et al.: 1 month: ICC = .92 (category range: ICC = .86–.93)
Responsiveness:	Berg et al. (1988): over 5.5 years, 7% controls developed questionable dementia (CDR = 0.5); 9% of controls had died vs 37% with CDR = 1; $\chi^2 = 12.53$, $p < .001$

Comment

The CDR is an established instrument for the staging of Alzheimer's disease, and is frequently used to validate other scales of dementia. It has been incorporated into the Consortium to Establish a Registry for Alzheimer's Disease (CERAD) battery (Morris, 1997). The CDR demonstrates excellent inter-rater reliability, both for the CDR and "sum of boxes", because of the clear guidelines provided for combining the six categories into the global rating. Temporal stability is also excellent, yet the CDR is responsive to real changes occurring in the patient; there is also substantial evidence for validity. Hughes et al. (1982) highlight a particular advantage of the CDR being the focus on "cognitive function, not on disability arising from other medical, social or emotional problems" (p. 571), with it having a special application for those people "who are neither clearly normal nor clearly demented".

Key references

Berg L. (1984). Clinical dementia rating. *British Journal of Psychiatry*, *145*, 339.

Berg, L., Miller, J. P., Baty, J., Rubin, E. H., Morris, J. C., & Figiel, G. (1992). Mild senile dementia of the Alzheimer type. 4. Evaluation of intervention. *Annals of Neurology*, *31*, 242–249.

Berg, L., Miller, J. P., Storandt, M., Duchek, J., Morris, J. C., Rubin, E. H., et al. (1988). Mild senile dementia of the Alzheimer type: 2. Longitudinal assessment. *Annals of Neurology*, *23*(5), 477–484.

Burke, W. J., Miller, J. P., Rubin, E. H., Morris, J. C., Cohen, L. A., Duchek, J., et al. (1988). Reliability of the Washington University Clinical Dementia Rating. *Archives of Neurology*, *45*(1), 31–32.

Dooneief, G., Marder, K., Tang, M., & Stern, Y. (1996). The Clinical Dementia Rating scale: Community-based validation of "profound" and "terminal" stages. *Neurology*, *46*(6), 1746–1749.

Heyman, A., Wilkinson, W. E., Hurwitz, B. J., Helms, M. J., Haynes, C. S., Utley, C. M., et al. (1987). Early-onset Alzheimer's disease: Clinical predictors of institutionalization and death. *Neurology*, *37*, 980–984.

Hughes, C. P., Berg, L., Danziger, W. L., Coben, L. A., & Martin, R. L. (1982). A new clinical scale for the staging of dementia. *British Journal of Psychiatry*, *140*, 566–572.

Juva, K., Sulkava, R., Erkinjuntti, T., Ylikoski, R., Valvanne, J., & Tilvis, R. (1995). Usefulness of the Clinical Dementia Rating scale in screening for dementia. *International Psychogeriatrics*, *7*(1), 17–24.

Marin, D. B., Flynn, S., Mare, M., Lantz, M., Hsu, M.-A., Laurans, M., et al. (2001). Reliability and validity of a chronic care facility adaptation of the Clinical Dementia Rating scale. *International Journal of Geriatric Psychiatry*, *16*, 745–750.

Morris, J. C. (1993). The Clinical Dementia Rating (CDR): Current version and scoring rules. *Neurology*, *43*(11), 2412–2414.

Morris, J. C. (1997). Clinical assessment of Alzheimer's disease. *Neurology*, *49*(S3), S7–S10.

Morris, J. C., Ernesto, C., Schafer, K., Coats, M., Leon, S., Sano, M., et al. (1997). Clinical Dementia Rating training and reliability in multicenter studies: The Alzheimer's Disease Cooperative Study experience. *Neurology*, *48*(6), 1508–1510.

Clinical Dementia Rating (CDR)

Hughes, Berg, Danziger, Coben, and Martin (1982); Berg (1984)

	Healthy CDR 0	Questionable CDR 0.5	Mild dementia CDR 1	Moderate dementia CDR 2	Severe dementia CDR 3
Memory	No memory loss or slight inconsistant forgetfulness	Mild consistent forgetfulness; partial recollection of events; "benign" forgetfulness	Moderate memory loss, more marked for recent events; defect interferes with everyday activities	Severe memory loss; only highly learned material retained; new material rapidly lost	Severe memory loss; only fragments remain
Orientation	Fully oriented	Fully oriented	Some difficulty with time relationships; oriented for place and person at examination but may have geographic disorientation	Usually disoriented in time, often to place	Orientation to person only
Judgement and Problem Solving	Solves everyday problems well; judgement good in relation to past performance	Only doubtful impairment in solving problems, similarities, differences	Moderate difficulty in handling complex problems; social judgement usually maintained	Severely impaired in handling problems, similarities, differences; social judgement usually impaired	Unable to make judgements or solve problems
Community Affairs	Independent function at usual level in job, shopping, business and financial affairs, volunteer and social groups	Only doubtful or mild impairment, if any, in these activities	Unable to function independently at these activities though may still be engaged in some; may still appear normal to casual inspection	No pretence of independent function outside home Appears well enough to be taken to functions outside a family home	No pretence of independent function outside home Appears too ill to be taken to functions outside a family home
Home and Hobbies	Life at home, hobbies, intellectual interests well maintained	Life at home, hobbies, intellectual interests slightly impaired	Mild but definite impairment of function at home; more difficult chores abandoned; more complicated hobbies and interests abandoned	Only simple chores preserved; very restricted interests, poorly sustained	No significant function in home outside of own room
Personal Care	Fully capable of self-care	Fully capable of self-care	Needs prompting	Requires assistance in dressing, hygiene, keeping of personal effects	Requires much help with personal care; often incontinent

Expanded Disability Status Scale (EDSS)

Kurtzke (1955, 1983)

Source

The original Disability Status Scale (DSS; reproduced below) is described in Kurtzke (1955), although the scale was used in a clinical trial published the previous year (Kurtzke & Berlin, 1954). The subsequently expanded DSS (EDSS) was presented in an appendix to Kurtzke (1983).

Purpose

The DSS/EDSS is a clinician rating scale that was developed for people with multiple sclerosis (MS). The scale has three goals: (i) to adequately describe the sum total of a patient's disabilities, (ii) to be responsive to changes in the patient's condition, and (iii) to be simple and manageable to use.

Item description

The original DSS contained 11 hierarchical categories from 0 (normal neurological examination) to 10 (death). Motor-sensory impairment and disablement were the focus of the scale, and no mention was made of cognitive impairments. The EDSS subdivides steps 1 to 10 of the DSS with a 0.5 rating, such that the total range remains between 0 and 10. It also makes use of seven Functional Systems (Pyramidal, Cerebellar, Brain stem, Sensory, Bowel and bladder, Visual [Optic] and Cerebral [Mental]), along with an Other category, to determine the EDSS level. Each Functional System (except the Other category) contains 5 to 6 grades with detailed behavioural descriptions that are used to enable classification into the category of "best fit".

Scale development

The DSS was developed in response to the need for "an objective and reproducible method" to document level of disability in people with MS. Kurtzke (1955) emphasized the "unpredictable course" of MS, and thence the need for a sensitive instrument to monitor changes in the patient. No specific information is available regarding developmental procedures, but a driving force was its use in people with MS participating in a clinical trial in New York, USA (Kurtzke & Berlin, 1954). The scale was used to chart the progress of 175 patients who were admitted to hospital following exacerbation of their symptoms in the previous 2 years. One-third of the patients improved on the DSS, one-sixth deteriorated and the remainder showed no change.

Administration procedures, response format and scoring

The clinician completes the DSS by classifying the patient into the status or level of "best fit". The score ranges from 0 to 10, with higher scores indicating greater disablement.

Psychometric properties

The original publications (Kurtzke, 1955, 1983) focused on a description of the DSS/EDSS and no psychometric data were reported. Hobart, Freeman, and Thompson (2000) reported a comprehensive study of the psychometric properties of the EDSS in 311 patients with MS undergoing rehabilitation at the National Hospital for Neurology and Neurosurgery, London, UK. Subsets of the sample were used to calculate inter-rater reliability with independent raters on 40 patients, temporal stability ($n = 125$), as well as validity and responsiveness ($n = 64$). Validating instruments included the Barthel Index (BI) and Functional Independence Measure (FIM). Convergent and divergent validity were examined with hypothesized associations between similar constructs (as assessed with the BI and FIM), and dissimilar constructs (e.g., quality of life measured with the Medical Outcomes Study Health Survey – Short-Form 36 – Mental Component Summary, SF-36-MCS, and psychological distress using the General Health Questionnaire, GHQ-28). Another comprehensive psychometric study was reported by Sharrack, Hughes, Soudain, and Dunn (1999), who examined 64 patients with MS and followed them for 9 months, with assessments at 3-monthly intervals. Subsets of patients for whom there was (independent) agreement between them and their neurologist regarding a subjective evaluation of change or no change in the condition since the previous assessment were used to examine responsiveness ($n = 25$) and temporal stability ($n = 35$) respectively. Inter-rater reliability was examined with three experienced clinicians, who were trained with the EDSS. They used similar validating instruments to Hobart et al., as well as the London Handicap Scale (LHS). Results from Hobart et al., except where otherwise stated, are shown in Box 10.2.

Comment

The DSS/EDSS has been described because, like a number of other instruments included in this compendium, it was one of the first standardized instruments developed for this purpose which continues to be very widely used. Sharrack et al. (1999) concluded that the EDSS was "reliable within 1.0 point (two 0.5 steps), valid as an impairment and disability scale, but not responsive" (p. 157). Hobart et al. (2000) recognized that the DSS/EDSS was developed more than 50 years ago, and for that time "Kurtzske demonstrated perception and insight. He recognized that the effectiveness of therapeutic interventions could be determined only if disease severity could be quantified accurately" (p. 1027). It represents "an important milestone in the history of measurement of disease severity in multiple sclerosis", although more recently developed instalments (e.g., Multiple Sclerosis Functional Composite; Cutter et al., 1999) show greater sensitivity.

Box 10.2

Validity:	Criterion: *Concurrent:* with BI: $r = -.89$ – with FIM: $r = -.84$
	Sharrack et al.: with BI: $r = -.74$ – with FIM: $r = -.87$ – with SF-36: $r = -.82$ – with LHS: $r = -.69$
	Construct: *Convergent/divergent:* higher correlation with similar constructs (e.g., with BI: $r = -.89$); lower correlation with dissimilar constructs (e.g., with GHQ-28: $r = -.06$, with SF-36-MCS: $r = -.22$)
Reliability:	Inter-rater: ICC = .78
	Sharrack et al.: $k = .65$, ICC = .99
	Test–retest: 2–3 days: rater 1: ICC = .94 – rater 2 (composite of 10 consecutive secondary raters): ICC = .61
	Sharrack et al.: approximately 9 months: $k = .7$, ICC = .99
Responsiveness:	Admission $M = 7.1$ ($SD = 1.0$) vs Discharge $M = 7.0$ ($SD = 1.1$), $d = .10$
	Sharrack et al.: 9 months in 25 patients with changed status: $d = .11$

Key references

Cutter, G. R., Baier, M. L., Rudick, R. A., Cookfair, D. L., Fischer, J. S., Petkau, J., et al. (1999). Development of Multiple Sclerosis Functional Composite as a clinical trial outcome measure. *Brain*, *122*(Pt 5), 871–882.

Hobart, J., Freeman, J., & Thompson, A. (2000). Kurtzke scales revisited: The application of psychometric methods to clinical intuition. *Brain*, *123*, 1027–1040.

Kurtzke, J. F. (1955). A new scale for evaluating disability in multiple sclerosis. *Neurology*, *5*(8), 580–583.

Kurtzke, J. F. (1983). Rating neurologic impairment in multiple sclerosis: An expanded disability status scale (EDSS). *Neurology*, *33*(11), 1444–1452.

Kurtzke, J. F., & Berlin, L. (1954). The effects of isoniazid on patients with multiple sclerosis; Preliminary report. *American Review of Tuberculosis*, *70*(4), 577–592.

Sharrack, B., Hughes, R. A. C., Soudain, S., & Dunn, G. (1999). The psychometric properties of clinical rating scales used in multiple sclerosis. *Brain*, *122*(Pt 1), 141–159.

Disability Status Scale
Kurtzke (1955)

0 Normal neurologic function

1 No dysfunction, minimal signs (Babinski, minimal finger to nose ataxia, diminished vibration sense)

2 Minimal dysfunction (slight weakness or stiffness, mild disturbance of gait, awkwardness, mild visuomotor disturbance)

3 Moderate dysfunction (monoparesis, mild hemiparesis, moderate ataxia, disturbing sensory loss, prominent urinary or eye symptoms, or combinations of lesser dysfunctions)

4 Relatively severe dysfunction not preventing ability to work or carry on normal activities of living, excluding sexual function. This includes the ability to be up and about 12 hours a day

5 Dysfunction severe enough to preclude working, with maximal motor function walking unaided up to several blocks.

6 Assistance required for walking (canes, crutches, braces)

7 Restricted to wheelchair (able to wheel self and enter and leave chair alone)

8 Restricted to bed but with effective use of arms

9 Totally helpless bed patient

10 Death resulting from multiple sclerosis

Acknowledgement: From Kurtzke, J. F. (1955). A new scale for evaluating disability in multiple sclerosis. *Neurology*, *5*(8), 580–583, extract from text p. 580, last paragraph, reproduced with permission of Lippincott Williams & Wilkins/Wolters Kluwer.

Glasgow Outcome Scale (GOS)

Jennett and Bond (1975)

Source

The original GOS (5-category classificatory scale) is described in Jennett and Bond (1975) and Jennett, Snoek, Bond, and Brooks (1981) and it is summarized below. Its expansion to eight categories is presented in Jennett et al. (1981). A structured interview was later developed to provide greater "objectivity and reliability" (Wilson, Pettigrew, & Teasdale, 1998). Items of this "extended" interview version, referred to as the GOSE, are available in Wilson et al. and are also described and reproduced below. Additionally, a children's version of the GOS, the King's Outcome Scale for Childhood Head Injury (KOSCHI; Couchman, Rossiter, Colaco, & Forsyth, 2001), is briefly described below.

Purpose

The GOS is a clinician rating scale. It was initially developed to evaluate the efficacy of different types of medical management on social outcome and quality of life after acquired brain impairment (ABI). The GOS is widely used, both in stroke and traumatic brain injury (TBI), as well other neurological groups, and is frequently employed in clinical trials.

Item description

The original GOS is a five-category, hierarchical scale: death, persistent vegetative state, severe disability, moderate disability, good recovery. The level of classification represents the sum total of the physical and mental sequelae of the injury and the effects of these on social functioning. Detailed descriptions of the clinical profiles in each of the levels of outcome are provided in Jennett and Bond (1975). Jennett et al. (1981) used an expanded version in their research project, in which the last three categories were subdivided into a better and worse level of functioning, resulting in an eight-category scale.

Scale development

From its inception, the GOS was intended to be "a practical scale". In their 1975 paper, Jennett and Bond graphically describe the poverty of assessment instruments to measure social outcome and quality of life after ABI, in which "persisting disability may remain concealed beneath a blanket of euphemisms" (p. 483). An aim of the GOS was to describe outcome using behavioural terms covering a range of levels of recovery. The original version of the GOS arose from clinical observation of and experience with patients with TBI from the authors' neurosurgical and psychological medicine units in Glasgow, UK.

Administration procedures, response format and scoring

For the original GOS (both 5-category and 8-category), no specific items are used; rather classification into the category of "best-fit" is made on the basis of the clinician's knowledge of the patient. Completion time is thus very quick.

Psychometric properties

The initial publication on the GOS (Jennett & Bond, 1975) focused on a description of the categories of the scale, but apart from some general data indicative of responsiveness, no information was presented on its psychometric properties. Jennett et al. (1981) later reported that inter-rater agreement between two raters on 150 patients was > 95%, but subsequent researchers reported lower agreement. Anderson, Housley, Jones, Slattery, and Miller (1993) examined inter-rater reliability with 58 patients with TBI using raters with different backgrounds (general practice medicine, psychology, clinical research). Criterion and construct validity of the GOS have been well established by many other researchers, and the GOS is often used to establish the validity of new instruments. McCauley et al. (2001) used the GOS to validate the Neurobehavioral Rating Scale-Revised (NRS-R) in 210 people with severe TBI, recruited from multiple centres in the USA and examined at 3 and 6 months post-trauma. Gouvier, Blanton, LaPorte, and Nepomuceno (1987) used a 10-category expansion of the GOS to validate the Disability Rating Scale (DRS) in 40 patients with TBI who were admitted to an acute rehabilitation centre. Results of these studies are shown in Box 10.3.

Box 10.3

Validity:	Criterion: *Concurrent:* McCauley et al.: with NRS-R: $r = .72$
	10 category GOS: Gouvier et al.: with DRS: $r = .85$
Reliability:	Inter-rater: Jennett et al.: agreement between 2 raters: > 95%
	Anderson et al.: psychologist vs clinical researcher: $k_w = .79$ – psychologist vs medical practitioner: $k_w = .45$
	Test–retest: No information available
Responsiveness	No information available

Derivatives of the GOS: (1) GOS-Extended (GOSE – Interview Version); Teasdale, Pettigrew, Wilson, Murray, and Jennett (1998); Wilson, Pettigrew, and Teasdale (1998)

The reason for development of the extended interview version (GOSE) was to obviate the "open-ended format [of the GOS which] encourages impressionistic use of the scale" (Wilson et al., 1998, p. 573). In this way, the GOSE could also address limitations of the GOS raised in the literature, in particular improving inter-rater reliability and operational definitions for the lesser levels of disability (Pettigrew, Wilson, & Teasdale, 1998). The development process of the structured interview version of the GOSE is described in Teasdale et al. (1998). Close attention was paid to following the original descriptions of the GOS by the authors with the aim of "identifying the key factors responsible for allocating a patient to one or other category" (Teasdale et al., 1998, p. 588). Pilot versions were subject to expert review, including with the original authors, and modifications made and pilot tested for inter-rater reliability and spread of score distribution.

While retaining the eight-category classification taxonomy, the GOSE adopts a different approach to assessment. It samples seven main areas (consciousness, independence in the home, independence outside the home (for shopping and travel), work, social and leisure activities, family and friends, and return to normal life). An additional three items enquire about related factors, such as epilepsy. Items addressing pre-injury level of functioning are a feature of the interview version. Administration is easy and straightforward. The procedure for conducting the interview is described in Wilson et al. (1998) and should be used as a guide for administration. Questions are organized hierarchically, with items indicative of maximum disability administered first. In this way, classification can progress in stages, such that if the person is unable to do activities lower in the hierarchy (e.g., independence in the home for self-care tasks), it is unlikely that they will be able to do activities higher in the hierarchy (e.g., work). No details are available regarding administration time for the interview version. Scoring the interview version is conducted hierarchically. First, responses to sections on independence inside and outside the home are used to determine whether patients are in the Severe Disability category. Then responses to work, social/leisure activities, and family/friends are used to distinguish Moderate Disability and Good Recovery.

Reliability of the GOSE has been examined in detail in a number of studies. Wilson et al. (1998) examined 50 patients with TBI recruited from a regional neurosurgical unit in Glasgow, UK. The patients were aged $M = 39.4$ years (range 18–76) and were 5 to 17 months post-trauma. They were interviewed by two independent raters on the same day ($k_w = .85$). Pettigrew, Wilson, and Teasdale (2003) reported data on temporal stability under a number of conditions, both different administration modes (in-person and telephone) and using different raters. In an initial study, a single rater examined 30 people with TBI on two occasions approximately 6 days apart. On the first occasion an in-person interview was conducted and the second occasion used telephone interview ($k_w = .92$). In the second study, 56 people with TBI were examined on two occasions 16 days apart, first with a nurse via the telephone and subsequently in an in-person interview with a psychologist ($k_w = .84$). Concurrent validity was examined by Wilson, Pettigrew, and Teasdale (2000) in 135 people with TBI (age 16–69 years) recruited from a neurosurgical unit who were 5 to 10 months post-trauma. Validating instruments included the DRS ($r = -.89$) and Barthel Index ($r = .46$), as well as duration of post-traumatic amnesia ($r = .52$). Other instruments examining mood (Beck Depression Inventory; $r = .64$), quality of life (Medical Outcomes Study Health Survey – Short-Form 36, subscale range: $r = .47$–$.71$), and neuropsychological tests (e.g., delayed Logical Memory: $r = .37$, verbal fluency: $r = .42$, Trail Making Test – Part B: $r = -.35$) were also administered.

(2) King's Outcome Scale for Childhood Head Injury (KOSCHI); Couchman, Rossiter, Colaco, and Forsyth (2001)

The target population for the KOSCHI is children aged between 2 and 16 years. The operational definitions for each category of the scale are described in Couchman et al. (2001) and are also reproduced below. Like the parent GOS, the KOSCHI is a classificatory scale comparable to the eight-point version of the GOS. Development of the KOSCHI was based on 200 children with TBI admitted to King's College Hospital in London, UK between 1990 and 1997. A 26-item checklist guided follow-up interviews with these children. This was supplemented with a detailed semi-structured interview with a small group of parents of the more severely injured children. These sources of information were used to adapt the GOS categories for the paediatric population. The descriptive classification does not require scoring. If statistical analysis is required, the scoring convention ranges from 1 to 8, with higher scores indicating a better outcome.

Inter-rater reliability of the KOSCHI was examined with six raters with specialist experience in paediatric TBI, using information available in clinical reports of the follow-up of 90 children. One of the six raters was an outlier, but even excluding those data, inter-rater agreement was only fair ($k = .58$). It also varied among outcome categories (highest for very severely disabled children, $k = .88$; lowest for moderate disability lower level, $k = .28$). Construct validity was examined in an independent sample of 80 children with TBI, again using information contained in clinical reports. One rater assigned a KOSCHI category and the other calculated "functional scores" based on a rating scale developed for the study sampling seven cognate areas. The KOSCHI categories were predicted by the functional component scores ($R^2 = .82$).

Comment

The visionary work of the Glasgow group in the 1970s led the way in setting a standard regarding an expectation for objective evaluation of the results of medical treatments and interventions. The resulting GOS was quickly taken up world-wide for research studies ranging from acute neurosurgical interventions, to rehabilitation programmes, to clinical trials. The continued development of the GOS into an interview version will address many of the previous criticisms of the GOS, with it now demonstrating excellent inter-rater reliability in various situations, as well as temporal stability. Even so, Wilson et al. (1998) note that the GOSE "is not intended to provide detailed information about the specific difficulties faced by individual patients, but to give a general index of overall outcome" (p. 574). The GOSE, however, is a very different instrument to the GOS – even though both scales use the same classification. There are undoubted advantages to having the interview version of the GOSE, but it is likely that the GOS will continue to be used in many situations because of its very quick completion time.

Key references

Anderson, S. I., Housley, A. M., Jones, P. A., Slattery, J., & Miller, J. D. (1993). Glasgow Outcome Scale: An inter-rater reliability study. *Brain Injury*, *7*(4), 309–317.

Couchman, M., Rossiter, L., Colaco, T., & Forsyth, R. (2001). A practical outcome scale for paediatric head injury. *Archives of Diseases in Childhood*, *84*, 120–124.

Gouvier, W. D., Blanton, P. D., LaPorte, K. K., & Nepomuceno, C. (1987). Reliability and validity of the Disability Rating Scale and the Levels of Cognitive Functioning Scale in monitoring recovery from severe head injury. *Archives of Physical Medicine and Rehabilitation*, *68*(2), 94–97.

Jennett, B., & Bond, M. (1975). Assessment of outcome after severe brain damage. A practical scale. *Lancet*, *i* (March 1), 480–484.

Jennett, B., Snoek, J., Bond, M. R., & Brooks, N. (1981). Disability after severe head injury: Observations on the use of the Glasgow Outcome Scale. *Journal of Neurology, Neurosurgery, and Psychiatry*, *44*, 285–293.

McCauley, S. R., Levin, H. S., Vanier, M., Mazaux, J. M., Boake, C., Goldfader, P. R., et al. (2001). The neurobehavioural rating scale-revised: Sensitivity and validity in closed head injury assessment. *Journal of Neurology, Neurosurgery, and Psychiatry*, *71*(5), 643–651.

Pettigrew, L. E. L., Wilson, J. T. L., & Teasdale, G. M. (1998). Assessing disability after head injury: Improved use of the Glasgow Outcome Scale. *Journal of Neurosurgery*, *89*, 939–943.

Pettigrew, L. E. L., Wilson, J. T. L., & Teasdale, G. M. (2003). Reliability of ratings on the Glasgow Outcome Scales from in-person and telephone structured interviews. *Journal of Head Trauma Rehabilitation*, *18*(3), 252–258.

Teasdale, G. M., Pettigrew, L. E. L., Wilson, J. T., Murray, G., & Jennett, B. (1998). Analyzing outcome of treatment of severe head injury: A review and update on advancing the use of the Glasgow Outcome Scale. *Journal of Neurotrauma*, *15*(8), 587–597.

Wilson, J. T. L., Pettigrew, L. E. L., & Teasdale, G. M. (1998). Structured interviews for the Glasgow Outcome Scale and the Extended Glasgow Outcome Scale: Guidelines for their use. *Journal of Neurotrauma*, *15*(8), 573–585.

Wilson, J. T. L., Pettigrew, L. E. L., & Teasdale, G. M. (2000). Emotional and cognitive consequences of head injury in relation to the Glasgow Outcome Scale. *Journal of Neurology, Neurosurgery, and Psychiatry*, *69*, 204–209.

Summary description of the Glasgow Outcome Scale categories
after Jennett and Bond (1975); Jennett, Snoek, Bond, and Brooks (1981)

Death

Vegetative State

Non-sentient, not obeying commands, no verbal response, no meaningful response; but may breathe spontaneously, have sleep–wake cycles, spontaneous eye opening and ability to follow moving objects with their eyes, may swallow food placed in the mouth, show reflex responses in their limbs.

Severe Disability – conscious but dependent

Needs the assistance of another person for some activities of daily living, which may range from total dependency (e.g., feeding, washing) to assistance for only one activity, such as dressing or going outside to a shop. May have little or no physical disability but are unable to organize their lives effectively; could not be left alone overnight.

Moderate Disability – independent but disabled

Independent in activities of daily life, for instance can travel by public transport; some previous activities (e.g., work or social life) are no longer possible, but resumption at a lower level may be possible.

Good Recovery

Capable of resuming normal occupational and social activities; may have minor physical or mental deficits or complaints.

Glasgow Outcome Scale – Extended

Wilson, Pettigrew, and Teasdale (1998)

Administration note: The procedure for conducting the interview is described in the above paper and should be used as a guide for administration. Reference details are as follows:

Wilson, J. T. L., Pettigrew, L. E. L., & Teasdale, G. M. (1998). Structured interviews for the Glasgow Outcome Scale and the Extended Glasgow Outcome Scale: Guidelines for their use. *Journal of Neurotrauma*, *15*(8), 573–585.

Patient's name:________________ Date of interview:________________

Date of Birth:________________ Date of injury________________ Gender: M / F

Age at injury:________________ Interval post-injury:________________

Respondent: Patient alone ________ Relative/ friend/ carer alone ________ Patient + relative/ friend/ carer ________

Interviewer:________________

CONSCIOUSNESS

1. Is the head injured person able to obey simple commands, or say any words? ☐ 1 = No (VS) 2 = Yes

Anyone who shows ability to obey even simple commands, or utter any word or communicate specifically in any other way is no longer considered to be in the vegetative state. Eye movements are not reliable evidence of meaningful responsiveness. Corroborate with nursing staff. Confirmation of VS requires full assessment as in the Royal College of Physician Guidelines.

INDEPENDENCE IN THE HOME

2a Is the assistance of another person at home essential every day for some activities of daily living? ☐ 1 = No 2 = Yes

If "No" go to question 3a.

For "No" answer they should be able to look after themselves at home for 24 hours if necessary, though they need not actually look after themselves. Independence includes the ability to plan for and carry out the following activities: getting washed, putting on clean clothes without prompting, preparing food for themselves, dealing with callers, and handling minor domestic crises. The person should be able to carry out activities without needing prompting or reminding, and should be capable of being left alone overnight.

2b Do they need frequent help or someone to be around at home most of the time? ☐ 1 = No (Upper SD) 2 = Yes (Lower SD)

For a "No" answer they should be able to look after themselves at home for up to 8 hours during the day if necessary, though they need not actually look after themselves.

2c Was assistance at home essential before the injury? ☐ 1 = No 2 = Yes

INDEPENDENCE OUTSIDE THE HOME

3a Are they able to shop without assistance? ☐ 1 = No (Upper SD) 2 = Yes

This includes being able to plan what to buy, take care of money themselves, and behave appropriately in public. They need not normally shop, but must be able to do so.

3b Were they able to shop without assistance before the injury? ☐ 1 = No 2 = Yes

4a Are they able to travel locally without assistance? ☐ 1 = No (Upper SD) 2 = Yes

They may drive or use public transport to get around. Ability to use a taxi is sufficient, provided the person can phone for it themselves and instruct the driver.

4b Were they able to travel without assistance before the injury? ☐ 1 = No 2 = Yes

WORK

5a Are they currently able to work to their previous capacity? ☐ 1 = No 2 = Yes

If they were working before, then their current capacity for work should be at the same level. If they were seeking work before, then the injury should not have adversely affected their chances of obtaining work or the level of work for which they are eligible. If the patient was a student before injury then their capacity for study should not have been adversely affected.

5b How restricted are they? ☐ 1 = a (Upper MD) 2 = b (Lower MD)
a) Reduced work capacity.
b) Able to work only in a sheltered workshop or non-competitive job, or currently unable to work.

5c Were they either working or seeking employment before the injury (answer "yes") or were they doing neither (answer "no")? ☐ 1 = No 2 = Yes

SOCIAL & LEISURE ACTIVITIES

6a Are they able to resume regular social and leisure activities outside home? ☐ 1 = No 2 = Yes

They need not have resumed all their previous leisure activities, but should not be prevented by physical or mental impairment. If they have stopped the majority of activities because of loss of interest or motivation then this is also considered a disability.

6b What is the extent of restriction on their social and leisure activities? ☐ 1 = a (Lower GR) 2 = b (Upper MD) 3 = c (Lower MD)
a) Participate a bit less: at least half as often as before injury.
b) Participate much less: less than half as often.
c) Unable to participate: rarely, if ever, take part.

6c Did they engage in regular social and leisure activities outside home before the injury? ☐ 1 = No 2 = Yes

FAMILY & FRIENDSHIPS

7a Have there been psychological problems that have resulted in ongoing family disruption or disruption to friendships? ☐ 1 = No 2 = Yes

Typical post-traumatic personality changes: quick temper, irritability, anxiety, insensitivity to others, mood swings, depression, and unreasonable or childish behaviour.

7b What has been the extent of disruption or strain? 1 = a (Lower GR) 2 = b (Upper MD) 3 = c (Lower MD)
a) Occasional – less than weekly
b) Frequent – once a week or more, but tolerable.
c) Constant – daily and intolerable.

7c Were there problems with family or friends before the injury? ☐ 1 = No 2 = Yes

If there were some problems before injury, but these have become markedly worse since injury then answer "No" to Q7c

RETURN TO NORMAL LIFE

8a Are there any other current problems relating to the injury that affect daily life? ☐ 1 = No (Upper GR) 2 = Yes (Lower GR)

Other typical problems reported after head injury: headaches, dizziness, tiredness, sensitivity to noise or light, slowness, memory failures, and concentration problems.

8b Were similar problems present before the injury? ☐ 1 = No 2 = Yes

If there were some problems before injury, but these have become markedly worse since injury then answer "No" to Q8b

Epilepsy:
Since the injury has the head injured person had any epileptic fits? No / Yes
Have they been told that they are currently at risk of developing epilepsy? No / Yes

What is the most important factor in outcome?
Effects of head injury _______ Effects of illness or injury to another part of the body _______ A mixture of these _______

Scoring: The patient's overall rating is based on the lowest outcome category indicated on the scale. Refer to Guidelines for further information concerning administration and scoring

---

1 Dead
2 Vegetative State (VS)
3 Lower Severe Disability (Lower SD)
4 Upper Severe Disability (Upper SD)
5 Lower Moderate Disability (Lower MD)
6 Upper Moderate Disability (Upper MD)
7 Lower Good Recovery (Lower GR)
8 Upper Good Recovery (Upper GR)

☐

Acknowledgement: Glasgow Outcome Scale Extended used by permission of the authors Drs. L. Wilson, L. Pettigrew and G. Teasdale, 1998.

King's Outcome Scale for Childhood Head Injury

Couchman, Rossiter, Colaco, and Forsyth (2001)

1 Death

2 Vegetative State

The child is breathing spontaneously and may have sleep/wake cycles. He/she may have non-purposeful or reflex movements of limbs or eyes. There is no evidence of ability to communicate verbally or non-verbally or to respond to commands.

3 Severe Disability

a) The child is at least intermittently able to move part of the body/eyes to command or make purposeful spontaneous movements; for example, confused child pulling at nasogastric tube, lashing out at carers, rolling over in bed. May be fully conscious and able to communicate but not yet able to carry out any self-care activities such as feeding.

b) Implies a continuing high level of dependency, but the child can assist in daily activities; for example, can feed self or walk with assistance or help to place items of clothing. Such a child is fully conscious but may still have a degree of post-traumatic amnesia.

4 Moderate Disability

a) The child is mostly independent but needs a degree of supervision/actual help for physical or behavioural problems. Such a child has overt problems; for example a 12-year-old with moderate hemiplegia and dyspraxia insecure on the stairs or needing help with dressing.

b) The child is age-appropriately independent but has residual problems with learning/behaviour or neurological sequelae affecting function. He/she probably should have special needs assistance but his/her special needs may not have been recognized/met. Children with symptoms of post-traumatic stress are likely to fall into this category.

5 Good Recovery

a) This should only be assigned if the head injury has resulted in a new condition that does not interfere with the child's well-being and/or functioning; for example:

- Minor headaches not interfering with social or school functioning
- Abnormalities on brain scan without any detectable new problem
- Prophylactic anticonvulsants in the absence of clinical seizures
- Unsightly scarring of face/head likely to need cosmetic surgery at some stage
- Mild neurological asymmetry but no evidence of effect on function of limb. Includes isolated change in hand dominance in young child

b) Implies that the information available is that the child has made a complete recovery with no detectable sequelae from the head injury.

Acknowledgement: From Couchman, M. et al. (2001). A practical outcome scale for paediatric head injury. *Archives of Diseases in Childhood*, *84*, 120–124, Table 2, p. 121, reproduced by permission of the BMJ Publishing Group Ltd.

Global Deterioration Scale (GDS)[1] and Functional Assessment Staging (FAST)[2]

[1]Reisberg, Ferris, de Leon, and Crook (1982) and [2]Reisberg et al. (1984)

Source

Stages of the GDS are described in Reisberg et al. (1982) and are also available from the Geriatric Resources website (http://www.geriatric-resources.com). Items for the FAST are available in an appendix to Reisberg (1988). The FAST maps onto the GDS and together these instruments have been referred to as the GDS/FAST staging system (Auer & Reisberg, 1997).

Purpose

The GDS and FAST are clinician rating scales, designed to monitor progression of deficits in degenerative dementias, such as Alzheimer's disease (AD).

Item description

The seven levels of the GDS, described in Reisberg et al. (1982), are briefly summarized as follows:

- Stage 1: no cognitive decline
- Stage 2: very mild cognitive decline – for example, complaints of forgetfulness, but no objective evidence of memory failure in either clinical interview or work and social situations
- Stage 3: mild cognitive decline – includes objective evidence of memory impairment; requires detailed interview by a trained professional, other people are aware of decreased performance in work and social situations, deficits documented on formal cognitive testing although brief mental status tests may be performed without error
- Stage 4: moderate cognitive decline – consistent with a confusional phase in which cognitive impairments are evident in many areas, there is difficulty performing everyday tasks accurately and efficiently, and errors are made on brief mental status tests
- Stage 5: moderately severe cognitive decline – the early phase of dementia, and patients require assistance for some aspects of daily living; deficits are readily apparent on brief mental status tests
- Stage 6: severe cognitive decline – corresponds to the middle stage of dementia; patients require substantial assistance with daily living tasks, cognitive impairments are marked (e.g., they "may occasionally forget the name of their spouses, on whom they depend entirely for survival" p. 1137), various personality and emotional changes become apparent
- Stage 7: very severe cognitive decline – late dementia in which all verbal abilities are lost, the patient is incontinent, requires assistance for eating and may be unable to walk.

The FAST contains 16 levels, each of which captures the essence of characteristic stages of decline in AD. The levels range from the highest (no difficulties, either subjectively or objectively) through to the lowest (unable to hold head up). In between the extremes, the levels range from the least impaired (complains of forgetting location of objects, subjective work difficulties) to the most impaired (unable to sit independently, smile, hold up head).

The 16 FAST levels are designed to be "optimally concordant" with the GDS. They are anchored to the seven GDS stages by using GDS notation for the FAST items. Hence, the first five GDS stages correspond to the first five FAST levels, GDS Stage 6 contains five FAST levels (which are thus denoted 6a to 6e), and GDS Stage 7 contains six FAST stages (denoted 7a to 7f), as shown in Data box 10.1.

Scale development

The GDS was developed to meet the need for a global scale that was able to accurately stage the gradual onset and decline of function in people with progressive dementias, such as AD. Development drew on the authors' previous work in characterizing the clinical presentation of dementia (Reisberg, 1981; Schneck, Reisberg, & Ferris, 1982). Limited details are provided regarding the developmental process of either the GDS or the FAST, but at the time of the original publication of the GDS the authors had used it for more than 5 years in "thousands" of interviews. Reisberg (1988)

Data box 10.1

GDS stage	FAST level	Description of FAST
Stage 1 – no decline	1	No difficulties, either subjectively or objectively
Stage 2 – very mild	2	Complains of forgetting location of objects; subjective work difficulties
Stage 3 – mild	3	Decreased job functioning evident to co-workers; difficulty in travelling to new locations
Stage 4 – moderate	4	Decreased ability to perform complex tasks (e.g., planning dinner for guests; handling finances; shopping)
Stage 5 – moderately severe	5	Requires assistance in choosing proper clothing
Stage 6 – severe	6 = 6a	Difficulty putting clothing on properly
	7 = 6b	Unable to bathe properly; may develop fear of bathing
	8 = 6c	Inability to handle mechanics of toileting (i.e., forgets to flush, doesn't wipe properly)
	9 = 6d	Urinary incontinence
	10 = 6e	Faecal incontinence
Stage 7 – very severe	11 = 7a	Limited ability to speak (1 to 5 words a day)
	12 = 7b	All intelligible vocabulary lost
	13 = 7c	Non-ambulatory
	14 = 7d	Unable to sit up independently
	15 = 7e	Unable to smile
	16 = 7f	Unable to hold head up

Acknowledgement: Adapted from Reisberg, B. et al. (1982). The Global Deterioration Scale for assessment of primary degenerative dementia. *American Journal of Psychiatry*, *139*(9), 1136–1139, and Reisberg, B. et al. (1984). Functional staging of dementia of the Alzheimer's type. *Annals of the New York Academy of Sciences*, *435*, 481–483, as appeared in *Psychopharmacology Bulletin* (1988). *24*(4), reproduced by permission of Medworks Media and Psychological Assessment Resources.

described the FAST as being derived from and representing a more detailed version of the 7-point Brief Cognitive Rating Scale (BCRS) developed by Reisberg, Schneck, Ferris, Schwartz, and de Leon (1983).

Administration procedures, response format and scoring

Both the GDS and the FAST are rated by the clinician, drawing on information obtained from patient and informant interview and patient assessment. Reisberg and colleagues (1982) emphasize the need for skilled diagnosticians to conduct the patient interview, particularly in the earlier stages (e.g., GDS Stage 3 – mild cognitive decline). The patient assessment component uses results from mental status testing, as well as more detailed neuropsychological evaluation.

Both the GDS and the FAST contain detailed operational definitions for each level/stage to guide the clinician to classify the patient accurately. These take account of clinical presentation, history of symptoms, functional capacity in everyday living, and cognitive profile. For clinical purposes, descriptive stages of the GDS (1 to 7) or levels of the FAST (1 to 7f) are used, and for both scales higher scores represent poorer levels of functioning.

Psychometric properties

The initial report on the GDS (Reisberg et al., 1982) focused on description and clinical application of the scale, but validation data were also reported. Patients ($n = 54$) with "very mild to moderately severe cognitive decline consistent with primary degenerative dementia" (p. 1138) were administered a range of cognitive tests, including the Buschke Verbal Learning (BVL), Perceptual Speed (PS) and Category Retrieval (CR) tasks. Computerized tomography (CT) and positron emission tomography (PET) were also conducted in 43 patients.

Initial validation for the FAST used 50 outpatients with normal ageing or AD (Reisberg et al., 1984). In another sample of 40 similar outpatients, the FAST was compared with results from the Mini-Mental State Examination (MMSE). The FAST was subject to Guttman scaling techniques in 50 patients, and the unidimensional and hierarchical ordering of the levels was confirmed, with the coefficient of reproducibility (CR) and coefficient of stability (CS) within recommended limits (> .9 and > .6 respectively). Shimada et al. (2004) examined the staging process of the FAST from a different perspective. They examined 24 patients with moderate to severe dementia with the Japanese version of the Binet Intelligence Scale, to identify a Binet Age (BA). Results of the above studies are shown in Box 10.4.

Box 10.4

Validity:	<u>Criterion:</u> *Concurrent:* GDS: Reisberg et al. (1982): with BVL: $r = -.54$ to $-.61$ for 5 trials, $-.64$ for delayed recall – with PS: $r = -.52$ – with CR easy: $r = -.43$, difficult: $r = -.39$ – with CT ventricular dilatation: $r = .62$ – with CT sulcal enlargement: $r = .53$ – with PET sites: $r = .69$–$.83$ FAST: Reisberg (1988): with 10 cognitive tests: $r = .59$–$.73$ – with clinical assessments: $r = .83$–$.94$ – with MMSE: $r = .87$ Shimada et al.: FAST with BA: $r = -.85$ <u>Construct:</u> *Internal consistency:* FAST: Reisberg (1988): Guttman scaling: CR = .99, CS = .98 *Discriminant:* FAST: Shimada et al.: FAST stage 5 BA $M = 4.2$ ($SD = 0.9$) vs FAST stage 6 $M = 2.3$ ($SD = 0.7$); $F = 10.2$, $p < .01$
Reliability:	<u>Inter-rater:</u> No information available <u>Test–retest:</u> No information available
Responsiveness:	No information available

Comment

Both the GDS and the FAST are widely used in research studies of people with AD. Reisberg (1988) highlighted the singular advantage of these instruments as being their applicability to all stages of dementia. Thus they are not subject to the floor or ceiling effects that affect cognitive tests – for no single test is suitable to examine both mild cognitive decline and severe dementia. Additionally, they take account of all clinical manifestations of the disease, not only cognitive impairments. Eisdorfer et al. (1992), however, were critical of the conceptual and methodological underpinnings of the GDS, and observed that the developers had not provided any empirical data in support of the "linearity, temporality and interdependencies of cognitive, functional, and behavioural impairment as well as neuroanatomical integrity" (p. 191). In this respect there is more empirical support for the validity of the FAST as a unidimensional staging scale, although both scales lack essential reliability data that are of critical importance for rating scales.

Key references

Auer, S., & Reisberg, B. (1997). The GDS/FAST staging system. *International Psychogeriatrics*, *9*(Suppl. 1), 167–171.

Eisdorfer, C., Cohen, D., Paveza, G. J., Ashford, J. W., Luchins, D. J., Gorelick, P. B., et al. (1992). An empirical evaluation of the Global Deterioration Scale for staging Alzheimer's disease. *American Journal of Psychiatry*, *149*(2), 190–194.

Reisberg, B. (1981). *Brain failure: An introduction to current concepts of senility*. New York: Free Press/Macmillan.

Reisberg, B. (1988). Functional assessment staging (FAST). *Psychopharmacology Bulletin*, *24*(4), 653–659.

Reisberg, B., Ferris, S. H., Anand, R., de Leon, M. J., Schneck, M. K., Buttinger, C., et al. (1984). Functional staging of dementia of the Alzheimer's type. *Annals of the New York Academy of Sciences*, *435*, 481–483.

Reisberg, B., Ferris, S. H., de Leon, M. J., & Crook, T. (1982). The Global Deterioration Scale for assessment of primary degenerative dementia. *American Journal of Psychiatry*, *139*(9), 1136–1139.

Reisberg, B., Schneck, M. K., Ferris, S. H., Schwartz, G. E., & de Leon, M. J. (1983). The Brief Cognitive Rating Scale (BCRS): Findings in primary degenerative dementia (PDD). *Psychopharmacology Bulletin*, *19*, 47–50.

Schneck, M. K., Reisberg, B., & Ferris, S. H. (1982). An overview of current concepts of Alzheimer's disease. *American Journal of Psychiatry*, *139*(2), 165–173.

Shimada, M., Hayat, J., Meguro, K., Oo, T., Jafri, S., Yamadori, A., et al. (2004). Correlation between functional assessment staging and the "Binet Age" by the Binet scale supports the retrogenesis model of Alzheimer's disease: A preliminary study. *Psychogeriatrics*, *3*(2), 82–87.

Modified Rankin Scale (mRS)

Rankin (1957)

Source

The items and scoring procedures for the scale are detailed in Rankin (1957), and a minor modification, referred to as the modified Rankin Scale (mRS; UK-TIA Study Group, 1988), is currently used. A further adaptation was introduced by Bamford et al. (1988), who renamed the scale the Oxford Handicap Scale (OHS). The original scale items, along with an interview version incorporating the UK-TIA items (Wilson, et al., 2002) is reproduced below.

Purpose

The mRS is a clinician rating scale, designed to classify "ultimate prognosis (functional recovery)" (Rankin, 1957, p. 210) after stroke. Subsequently it has been widely used as an outcome measure in clinical trials of treatments for stroke.

Item description

The original article (Rankin, 1957) provides short operational definitions of each of the fives grades of functional recovery: 1: No significant disability, 2: Slight disability, 3: Moderate disability, 4: Moderately severe disability, 5: Severe disability. The mRS adds a sixth grade: 0: No symptoms at all, and slightly rephrases the descriptors for Grades 1 and 2 (UK-TIA Study Group, 1988).

Scale development

No information is provided on the development of the Rankin Scale in the initial publication in which it was used (Rankin, 1957). The article examined prognostic factors for recovery after stroke and introduced the five-level categorical scale for classifying level of disability, reporting the outcome of a series of 192 patients with stroke using the scale.

Administration procedures, response format and scoring

There are no specific instructions for the administration of the Rankin Scale, but in the inter-rater reliability study of Wilson et al. (2005), novice raters performed assessments on 8 to 12 patients prior to the study. This group of investigators has also used a structured interview method (see below), which has improved inter-rater reliability (Wilson et al., 2002).

The descriptors of the mRS are clear, making classification relatively easy, although in their inter-rater reliability study, van Swieten, Koudstaal, Visser, Schouten, and van Gijn (1988) found most disagreement for the intermediate grades (2, 3 and 4). A 1-grade change is often deemed a clinically significant change, because of the large category sizes (Banks & Marotta, 2007; Kasner, 2006).

Psychometric properties

The original publication did not provide any details about the psychometric properties of the scale, and given the widespread use of the Rankin Scale and it derivatives, surprisingly few psychometric studies have been reported – New and Buchbinder's (2006) systematic review identified only a small number of studies specifically devoted to psychometric analysis, none of which provided a comprehensive evaluation; Banks and Marotta (2007) described the studies identified in their review as representing "a broad but fragmented literature" (p. 1091). Wilson et al. (2005) examined inter-rater reliability of the mRS using 15 raters from different disciplines, including medicine, nursing, occupational and physical therapies. Ratings were made both with ($n = 117$) and without ($n = 113$) the structured interview format in patients with stroke (age $M = 70$ years, range 30–92) who were $M = 13.3$ months post-onset. Temporal stability was examined with two raters who examined an independent sample of stroke patients ($n = 48$) on two occasions, with a median interval of 7 days (range 4–13). van Swieten et al. (1988) found similar coefficients in their inter-rater reliability study of 100 patients with stroke.

Concurrent validity of the mRS has been demonstrated by Kwon, Hartzema, Duncan, and Lai (2004), who analysed data from 1680 patients participating in the Kansas City Stroke Study. Validating instruments were the Barthel Index (BI) and the Motor scale from the Functional Independence Measure (FIM-M). They also found that both the BI and FIM-M were unable to distinguish among the upper levels of the mRS (levels 0, 1, and 2), thus showing ceiling effects relative to the mRS. Similar findings with respect to the BI and mRS were reported by Weimar et al. (2002). de Haan, Horn, Limburg, van der Meulen, and Bossuyt (1993) compared the mRS with five stroke-specific scales: Mathew Scale, Orgogozo, Scandinavian Stroke Scale, National Institutes of Health Scale, and the Canadian Neurological Scale. Schiemanck, Post, Witkamp, Kappelle, and Prevo (2005) examined lesion volumes with magnetic resonance imaging in 94 patients 1 week post-stroke. No difference was found for mRS scores between patients with small (0–30 ml; $n = 45$; mRS Median = 3.0) versus large (> 30 ml; $n = 49$; mRS Median = 4.0) lesion volumes. Data on responsiveness are available from Lai and Duncan (2001) who reported on changes between baseline and 3 months post-onset in 459 patients from the Kwon et al. sample, finding that 62% changed by at least 1 grade point. Results of these studies are shown in Box 10.5.

Box 10.5

Validity:	Concurrent: Kwon et al.: with BI: $r = -.89$ – with FIM-M: $r = -.89$
	de Haan et al.: with Mathew Scale: $r = -.71$ – with Orgogozo Scale: $r = -.64$ – with Scandinavian Stroke Scale: $r = -.66$ – with National Institutes of Health Scale: $r = .60$ – with Canadian Neurological Scale: $r = -.63$
	Schiemanck et al.: with lesion volume: $r = .45$
Reliability:	Inter-rater: Wilson et al. (2005): $k = .25$; $k_w = .71$ – with structured interview: $k = .74$; $k_w = .91$
	van Swieten et al.: $k = .56$; $k_w = .91$
	Test–retest: Wilson et al. (2005): 7 days, using 2 raters: $k = .84/.97$ and $k_w = .96/.99$
Responsiveness:	Lai & Duncan: 62% (284/459) changed mRS grade by ≥ 1 point between baseline and 3 months post-onset

Comment

The mRS is reported as being the most popular measure of global outcome in stroke (Wilson et al., 2005). These investigators consider that a particular strength is the capacity to encompass "the full spectrum of limitations in activity and participation after stroke" (p. 777). Systematic reviews, however, have been mixed, depending on the focus of the review. New and Buchbinder's (2006) review of the psychometric properties of the Rankin Scale and its two derivatives (mRS and OHS) was critical, and they concluded that "the appropriateness of using these scales as an outcome measure in their current form is questionable" (p. 13). By contrast, Kasner (2006) indicated that the mRS "offers an easy and rapid assessment in clinical practice" (p. 607), with the "probing questions" of the structured interview offering the potential to identify broader clinical issues that would benefit from intervention; although a drawback is its lack of specificity. The results of the Kwon et al. (2004) study indicate that relative to other commonly used instruments, the mRS has a better capacity to detect disability "in the higher ADL levels"; that is, grades 0 to 2.

Key references

Bamford, J. M., Vessey, M., Fowler, G., Molyneux, A., Hughes, T., Burn, J., et al. (1988). A prospective study of acute cerebrovascular disease in the community: The Oxfordshire Community Stroke Project 1981–1986. 1. Methodology, demographic and incident cases of first-ever stroke. *Journal of Neurology, Neurosurgery, and Psychiatry*, *51*, 1373–1380.

Banks, J. L., & Marotta, C. A. (2007). Outcomes validity and reliability of the Modified Rankin Scale: Implications for stroke clinical trials. *Stroke*, *38*, 1091–1096.

de Haan, R., Horn, J., Limburg, M., van der Meulen, J., & Bossuyt, P. (1993). A comparison of five stroke scales with measures of disability, handicap, and quality of life. *Stroke*, *24*, 1178–1181.

Kasner, S. E. (2006). Clinical interpretation and use of stroke scales. *The Lancet Neurology*, *5*, 603–612.

Kwon, S., Hartzema, A. G., Duncan, P. W., & Lai, S.-M. (2004). Disability measures in stroke: Relationship among the Barthel Index, the Functional Independence Measure, and the Modified Rankin Scale. *Stroke*, *35*, 918–923.

Lai, S.-M., & Duncan, P. W. (2001). Stroke recovery profile and the Modified Rankin Assessment. *Neuroepidemiology*, *20*, 26–30.

New, P. W., & Buchbinder, R. (2006). Critical appraisal and review of the Rankin Scale and its derivatives. *Neuroepidemiology*, *26*, 4–15.

Rankin, J. (1957). Cerebral vascular accidents in patients over the age of 60. II Prognosis. *Scottish Medical Journal*, *2*, 200–215.

Schiemanck, S. K., Post, M. W. M., Witkamp, Th. D., Kappelle, L. J., & Prevo, A. J. H. (2005). Relationship between ischemic lesion volume and functional status in the 2nd week after middle cerebral artery stroke. *Neurorehabilitation and Neural Repair*, *19*(2), 133–138.

UK-TIA Study Group. (1988). United Kingdom Transient Ischaemic Attack (UK-TIA) aspirin trial: Interim results. *British Medical Journal*, *296*, 316–320.

van Swieten, J. C., Koudstaal, P. J., Visser, M. C., Schouten, H. J. A., & van Gijn, J. (1988). Interobserver agreement for the assessment of handicap in stroke patients. *Stroke*, *19*(5), 604–607.

Weimar, C., Kurth, T., Kraywinkel, K., Wagner, M., Busse, O., Haberl, R. L., et al. (2002). Assessment of functioning and disability after ischaemic stroke. *Stroke*, *33*, 2053–2059.

Wilson, J. T. L., Hareendran, A., Grant, M., Baird, T., Schulz, U. G. R., Muir, K. W. et al. (2002). Improving the assessment of outcomes in stroke: Use of a structured interview to assign grades on the Modified Rankin Scale. *Stroke*, *33*, 2243–2246.

Wilson, J. T. L., Hareendran, A., Hendry, A., Potter, J., Bone, I., & Muir, K., W. (2005). Reliability of the modified Rankin Scale across multiple raters: Benefits of a structured interview. *Stroke*, *36*(4) 777–781.

Rankin Scale

Rankin (1957)

Grade	
I	*No significant disability*; able to carry out all usual duties and activities
II	*Slight disability*; unable to carry out some of previous activities but able to look after own affairs without assistance
III	*Moderate disability*; requiring some help, but able to walk without assistance
IV	*Moderately severe disability*; unable to walk without assistance and unable to attend to own bodily needs without assistance
V	*Severe disability*; bedridden, incontinent and requiring constant nursing care and attention
VI	*Dead*

Acknowledgement: From Rankin, J. (1957). Cerebral vascular accidents in patients over the age of 60. II Prognosis. *Scottish Medical Journal*, *2*, 200–215, p. 210, lines 12–26, reprinted by permission of the *Scottish Medical Journal*.

Modified Rankin Scale – structured interview

Wilson et al. (2002)

Name:	**Administered by:**	**Date:**

Modified Rankin Scale	**Structured Interview for the Modified Rankin Scale**
5 = Severe disability: bedridden, incontinent and requiring constant nursing care and attention.	*5* = Severe disability; someone needs to be available at all times; care may be provided by either a trained or an untrained caregiver. Question: Does the person require constant care?
4 = Moderately severe disability: unable to walk without assistance and unable to attend to own bodily needs without assistance.	*4* = Moderately severe disability; need for assistance with some basic activities of daily living (ADL) but not requiring constant care. Question: Is assistance essential for eating, using the toilet, daily hygiene, or walking?
3 = Moderate disability; requiring some help, but able to walk without assistance.	*3* = Moderate disability; need for assistance with some instrumental ADL but not basic ADL. Question: Is assistance essential for preparing a simple meal, doing household chores, looking after money, shopping, or travelling locally?
2 = Slight disability; unable to carry out some of previous activities but able to look after own affairs without assistance	*2* = Slight disability; limitations in participation in usual social roles, but independent for ADL. Questions: Has there been a change in the person's ability to work or look after others if these were roles before stroke? Has there been a change in the person's ability to participate in previous social and leisure activities? Has the person had problems with relationships or become isolated?
1 = No significant disability despite symptoms; able to carry out all usual duties and activities	*1* = No significant disability; symptoms present but not other limitations. Question: Does the person have difficulty reading or writing, difficulty speaking or finding the right word, problems with balance or coordination, visual problems, numbness (face, arms, legs, hands, feet), loss of movement (face, arms, legs, hands, feet), difficulty with swallowing, or other symptoms resulting from stroke?
0 = No symptoms at all	*0* = No symptoms at all; no limitations and no symptoms.

Acknowledgement: From Wilson, J. T. L. et al. (2002). Improving the assessment of outcomes in stroke: Use of a structured interview to assign grades on the Modified Rankin Scale. *Stroke*, *33*, 2243–2246, Table 1, p. 2244, reproduced by permission of Wolters Kluwer.

SECTION 2
Multidimensional and quality of life scales

Disability Rating Scale (DRS)

Rappaport, Hall, Hopkins, Belleza, and Cope (1982)

Source

Full details for the DRS items, definitions, scoring procedures and other information are available in Rappaport et al. (1982), as well as the website of the Center for Outcome Measurement in Brain Injury (http://www.tbims.org/combi.drs/index.html). The DRS items are also reproduced below.

Purpose

The DRS is a clinician rating scale. It was developed for people with traumatic brain injury (TBI) to monitor progress from the acute stages of recovery through to longer-term outcome. The DRS is widely used in the USA, where it is a core instrument in the TBI Model Systems database.

Item description

The DRS is an eight-item scale covering four domains. The arousal and awareness domain uses three items from the Glasgow Coma Scale (GCS; eye-opening, motor response and verbal response). The second domain, cognitive capacity for self-care tasks, uses three items (feeding, toileting and grooming). Rappaport et al. (1982) emphasize that this item does not rate physical ability to do the task, but rather cognition – knowing "how and when to perform [the] functions" (p. 119). The final two domains each contain a single item: physical dependency on other people (referred to as level of functioning) and employability in the work place (or home duties or schooling, as appropriate).

Scale development

Rappaport and colleagues (1982) highlighted the need for a scale that could chart the progress of patients with severe TBI "from coma to community, particularly through the midzone of the recovery spectrum, between early arousal from coma and early sentient functioning" (p. 118). In order to achieve this goal, such a scale needed to be able to document functioning across a disparate set of domains: arousal and awareness, self-care activities, physical dependence on other people, and "psychosocial adaptability" (operationalized as "the ability to do useful work as independently as possible in a socially relevant context"; p. 118). The authors were critical of existing scales, some of which "go into excessive detail that may be useful on a day-to-day or week-to-week programme evaluation effort but become too cumbersome, time consuming, and inefficient to track overall rehabilitation progress over periods of time that extend beyond the hospitalization episode" (p. 119). They therefore aimed to construct a brief scale that was easy to learn to use, sensitive, reliable, valid and an advance over existing instruments. Limited information was provided on the item selection process, but some of the items were taken directly from other instruments (such as the three items of the GCS) and some (such as the level of functioning item) were adapted from other instruments.

Administration procedures, response format and scoring

Rappaport et al. (1982) advise that the DRS is completed by a clinician using information based on their knowledge and observations of the patient and information obtained from other sources (e.g., nursing staff). They suggest that the scale can be completed in 5 to 15 minutes of observing and relating to a patient and, if necessary, obtaining pertinent information from relatives or staff.

Each of the items and response levels has detailed operational definitions. Items have a variable score range: the three items of the GCS are scored on the traditional 4 to 6 point scale of the GCS (but with the scoring direction reversed). The three self-care items are each rated on a 4-point scale from 0 (complete independence) to 3 (no independence), the level of functioning item on a 6-point scale from 0 (completely independent) to 5 (totally dependent), and "employability" on a 4-point scale from 0 (not restricted) to

3 (not employable). A total score is used for the DRS, ranging from 0 to 30, with higher scores indicating greater impairment/disability.

Scores can also be collapsed into eight broad categories as follows:

0–3	= none (0), mild (1), partial (2–3)
4–6	= moderate
7–11	= moderately severe
12–16	= severe
17–21	= extremely severe
22–24	= vegetative state
25–29	= extreme vegetative state
30	= death

Psychometric properties

Rappaport et al. (1982) initially reported on the psychometric properties of the DRS in a sample of 88 patients with severe TBI (descriptive data were not provided). Inter-rater reliability was assessed with four trained raters. Patients were assessed at admission to rehabilitation and approximately 12 months post-trauma. Cortical evoked potentials (EP) were also recorded at admission. Gouvier, Blanton, LaPorte, and Nepomuceno (1987) conducted a comprehensive psychometric evaluation in 40 patients with TBI (age $M = 24.8$ years, range 5–69) who were admitted to an acute rehabilitation centre. DRS scores were recorded 4 days per week until discharge. Inter-rater reliability was examined with one pair of raters who made ratings on the 4th day of every week, and test–retest reliability used the procedure of comparing scores of all the odd days with scores of all the even days. Validation instruments included the Stover-Zeiger (S-Z) scale and a 10-category expansion of the Glasgow Outcome Scale (EGOS). Zhang, Abreu, Gonzales, Seale, Masel, and Ottenbacher (2002) compared the DRS with other outcome measures, including the Craig Handicap Assessment and Reporting Technique (CHART) and Community Integration Questionnaire (CIQ). They examined 70 patients with TBI at admission to post-acute rehabilitation services. Results of a Rasch analysis with data from 266 patients were reported in general terms by Hall, Hamilton, Gordon, and Zasler (1993): the data appeared to fit a Rasch model, wherein items were described as showing "excellent" range of item difficulty. Gaps between items at the higher end of the scale (reflecting cognitive ability for self-care vs level of functioning vs employability) were "consistent with the observation of less sensitivity to change in the DRS in individuals functioning at high levels" (p. 67) – that is, with *lower* total scores. Results of Rappaport et al., except where otherwise stated, are shown in Box 10.6.

Box 10.6

Validity:	Criterion: *Concurrent:* with EP: $r = .78$ Gouvier et al.: with S-Z: $r_s = .81$ – with EGOS: $r_s = .85$ Zhang et al.: with CIQ: $r = -.43$ (Home: $r = -.49$, Social: $r = -.25$, Productive: $r = -.17$) – with CHART: $r = -.53$ (Physical: $r = -.52$, Motor: $r = -.41$, Social: $r = -.09$, Occupation: $r = -.36$) *Predictive:* admission DRS with 1-year DRS: $r = .53$ Gouvier et al.: admission DRS with discharge EGOS: $r_s = .73$ Construct: *Internal consistency:* Item-total correlation: range: $r = .54$–$.94$
Reliability:	Inter-rater: $r = .97$–$.98$ Gouvier et al.: $r_s = .98$ Test–retest: Gouvier et al.: 1 day: $r_s = .95$
Responsiveness:	Gouvier et al: Admission $M = 14.9$ ($SD = 7.8$) vs Discharge $M = 10.2$ ($SD = 7.0$); $d = .60$ Hall, Mann, High, Wright, Kreutzer, & Wood: Admission $M = 13.3$ ($SD = 5.0$) vs Discharge $M = 5.8$ ($SD = 2.9$); $d = 1.5$ – Discharge $M = 5.8$ ($SD = 2.9$) vs 1 year $M = 3.2$ ($SD = 2.9$); $d = .90$ – 1 year $M = 3.2$ ($SD = 2.9$) vs 2 year $M = 3.0$ ($SD = 3.5$); $d = .07$

Comment

The DRS is one of the most established outcome measures for TBI and it has the advantage of being quick and easy to administer. A singular strength is its application to all stages of the recovery and outcome process, although as Rappaport et al. (1982) initially observed, the DRS was not designed to detect subtle degrees of neuropsychological impairment. Subsequent research also found that it does not have the specificity of some other instruments (Hall et al., 1996). The DRS has been extensively researched and has commendable psychometric properties in independent samples, with excellent inter-rater reliability and temporal stability, and evidence of criterion and construct validity, as well as responsiveness with medium to large effect sizes up to 1 year post-trauma. The DRS is not without its limitations, however, but it does meet the authors' aim of providing an overview of functioning relevant to all stages of outcome. In this regard, the DRS continues to fill a niche that is not addressed as easily by other instruments. Hall et al. (1996) conclude that "One gives up depth in return for brevity and breadth, but the DRS consistently demonstrates good scale properties and has been shown to predict employment well" (p. 36).

Key references

Gouvier, W. D., Blanton, P. D., LaPorte, K. K., & Nepomuceno, C. (1987). Reliability and validity of the Disability Rating Scale and the Levels of Cognitive Functioning Scale in monitoring recovery from severe head injury. *Archives of Physical Medicine and Rehabilitation*, *68*(2), 94–97.

Hall, K. M., Hamilton, B. B., Gordon, W. A., & Zasler, N. D. (1993). Characteristics and comparisons of functional assessment indices: Disability Rating Scale, Functional Independence Measure, and Functional Assessment Measure. *Journal of Head Trauma Rehabilitation*, *8*(2), 60–74.

Hall, K. M., Mann, N., High, W. M., Wright, J., Kreutzer, J. S., & Wood, D. (1996). Functional measures after traumatic brain injury: Ceiling effects of FIM, FIM+FAM, DRS, and CIQ. *Journal of Head Trauma Rehabilitation*, *11*(5), 27–39.

Rappaport, M., Hall, K. M., Hopkins, K., Belleza, T., & Cope, D. N. (1982). Disability Rating Scale for severe head trauma: Coma to community. *Archives of Physical Medicine and Rehabilitation*, *63*(3), 118–123.

Zhang, L., Abreu, B. C., Gonzales, V., Seale, G., Masel, B., & Ottenbacher, K. J. (2002). Comparison of the Community Integration Questionnaire, the Craig Handicap Assessment and Reporting Technique, and the Disability Rating Scale in traumatic brain injury. *Journal of Head Trauma Rehabilitation*, *17*(6), 497–509.

Disability Rating Scale

Rappaport, Hall, Hopkins, Belleza, and Cope (1982)

Name:	**Administered by:**	**Date:**

			Score
AROUSABILITY	**Eye-opening**	Spontaneously To speech To pain None	0 1 2 3
	Verbalization	Oriented Confused Inappropriate Incomprehensible None	0 1 2 3 4
	Motor response	Obeying Localizing Withdrawing Flexing Extending None	0 1 2 3 4 5
COGNITIVE ABILITY FOR SELF-CARE ACTIVITIES (Does patient know how and when? Ignore motor disability)	**Feeding**	Complete Partial Minimal None	0 1 2 3
	Toileting	Complete Partial Minimal None	0 1 2 3
	Grooming	Complete Partial Minimal None	0 1 2 3
DEPENDENCE ON OTHERS	**Level of functioning**	Completely independent Independent (in special environment) Mildly dependent (needs limited assistance – non-resident helper) Moderately dependent (needs moderate assistance – person in home) Markedly dependent (needs assistance with all major activities at all times) Totally dependent (24 hour nursing care)	0 1 2 3 4 5
PSYCHOSOCIAL ADAPTABILITY	**Employability**	Not restricted Selected jobs – competitive Sheltered workshop – non-competitive Not employable	0 1 2 3
		TOTAL SCORE:	____

Acknowledgement: From Rappaport, M. et al. (1982). Disability Rating Scale for severe head trauma: Coma to community. *Archives of Physical Medicine and Rehabilitation*, *63*(3), 118–123, p. 119, reprinted by permission of the American Congress of Rehabilitation Medicine and the American Academy of Physical Medicine and Rehabilitation, and Elsevier.

European Brain Injury Questionnaire (EBIQ)

Teasdale et al. (1997)

Source

Teasdale et al. (1997) published data on the development of the EBIQ, although a preliminary French version was described the year before (Deloche et al., 1996). Items for the EBIQ are available in an appendix to Deloche, Dellatolas, and Christensen (2000), are on the author's website (http://teasdale.psy.ku.dk), and also appear below.

Purpose

The EBIQ is both an informant and a self-rating scale designed to measure the subjective experience of acquired brain impairment (ABI). The standardization sample included people with a range of ABI conditions, mainly stroke and traumatic brain injury (TBI), as well as cerebral infections, hypoxia and tumour.

Item description

The EBIQ contains 66 items; 63 relating to the person with ABI and 3 focusing on the effects of the injury on the relative. This is referred to as 63 + 3 items. The Danish version has slightly different item content, resulting in 62 + 3 items (see Svendsen, Teasdale, & Pinner, 2004), but Teasdale regards the 63 + 3 item version as the "standard" version (personal communication, T. Teasdale, 27 October 2008). Both versions result in the same nine scales.

The 63 + 3 item version contains 62 items in eight clinical scales: Somatic (8 items), Cognitive (13 items), Motivation (5 items), Impulsivity (13 items), Depression (9 items), Isolation (4 items), Physical (6 items), and Communication (4 items). The final item is a global rating. A ninth or "core scale" contains a subset of 34 of the 62 items, which can be used as a stand-alone measure of "general severity of restrictions in quality of life" (Teasdale et al., 1997, p. 547). Two versions of the EBIQ are available, one for relative/informant and the other for self-rating.

Scale development

Development of the EBIQ was a multinational collaboration of seven European countries, as well as Brazil, and it is therefore available in several European languages. It was initially intended that the EBIQ focus on emotionality, but was broadened out "in keeping with our generally holistic view of brain injury" (Teasdale, 1997, p. 547). Accordingly, the guiding framework for item selection was a biopsychosocial model (viz. sequelae of ABI and their effect on the person), but no specific information is available regarding the item selection process. Teasdale (personal communication) advises that items were partly adapted from the Katz Adjustment Scale and the Symptom Checklist-90, as well as a locally used questionnaire on activities of daily living. Item content was modified during a series of meetings and in response to clinical experience with the scale. The underlying structure of the scale was examined with data from 395 patients with ABI, using multidimensional scaling. Eight "quite readily interpretable" scales were identified, with the spatial representation of 34 items allowing construction of the ninth "core" scale.

Administration procedures, response format and scoring

Teasdale et al. (1997) report that completion of the EBIQ with people with ABI is usually conducted "in the presence of, and if necessary with the assistance of, a clinician" (p. 547). Informants usually complete the scale independently. The EBIQ is completed with reference to the preceding month. No information is available on administration time, but the EBIQ "was deliberately brief to avoid excessive exertion and tiring effects" for people with ABI (Teasdale et al., p. 547) and is estimated to take between 10 and 30 minutes.

Items are rated on a 3-point scale: 1 (not at all), 2 (a little), 3 (a lot). Mean scores are used for each of the scales, including the core scale. This procedure is advantageous in that it enables direct comparison among scales that contain a variable number of items.

Additionally, by using the mean score, the results can be directly interpreted in terms of the 3-point scale.

Normative and comparison data (Teasdale et al., 1997) for the summary scales of the EBIQ are available. The normative data come from 203 people (mainly hospital staff, their spouses and their contacts), aged between 19 and 74 years, from France and Brazil. Comparison data on 905 people with ABI (mainly stroke, 63%, and TBI, 29%), aged between 16 and 93 years, are also provided. Informant data for the ABI ($n = 869$) and control groups are also reported.

Psychometric properties

Validity data for the EBIQ were reported by Teasdale et al. (1997). Their multinational study contained 905 patients with ABI from seven European countries (Belgium, Denmark, Finland, France, Germany, Portugal and Spain), as well as Brazil, and 203 non-brain impaired control participants. Descriptive data are provided above. Group comparisons were conducted to explore construct validity. Further support for discriminant validity was provided by Santos, Farrajota, Castro-Caldas, and de Sousa (1999), who compared responses of 55 spouses of people with chronic aphasia with 37 spouses of people without physical or cognitive impairment. Additionally, group differences within a TBI sample reflecting different levels of injury severity (cranial fracture group, $n = 114$, vs cerebral lesion group, $n = 126$) were reported by Teasdale and Engberg (2005). Some evidence was provided for convergent and divergent validity in the Teasdale et al. sample by comparing different neurological conditions in which patterns of differences on EBIQ scales were expected given known characteristic clinical features of the groups (e.g., greater impairments in the communication domain for stroke vs TBI; by contrast, greater impairments in the behavioural regulation domain for TBI vs stroke).

Sopena, Dewar, Nannery, Teasdale, and Wilson (2007) examined 1-month temporal stability in 50 patients with ABI, 20 of their relatives and a control group ($n = 51$). Information on responsiveness is available from Schönberger, Humle, and Teasdale (2006) who administered the EBIQ on two occasions to 86 patients (mainly with stroke, 57%) prior to and following a holistic neuropsychological rehabilitation programme. Similarly, Coetzer and Rushe (2005) reported on 55 patients with TBI who participated in a neurorehabilitation programme. Moderate effect sizes were found for both self-ratings and informant report in the subgroup less than 2 years post-trauma ($n = 29$). Results from Teasdale et al. (1997), unless otherwise indicated, are shown in Box 10.7.

Box 10.7

Validity:	Construct: *Internal consistency:* Cronbach alpha: Core scale .92 (scale range: .54–.87; < .8 for 5/8 scales)
	Factor analysis: Multidimensional scaling identified 8 "quite readily identifiable" scales, but statistical results were not provided
	Convergent/divergent: For Communication: stroke group $M = 1.99$ ($SD = 0.51$) had higher scores than the TBI group $M = 1.92$ ($SD = 0.54$), $p < .05$; Conversely, for Impulsivity: TBI group $M = 1.83$ ($SD = 0.49$) had higher scores than stroke group $M = 1.68$, ($SD = 0.44$), $p < .002$
	Discriminant: Core: Self-ratings: Control $M = 1.45$ ($SD = 0.30$) vs TBI $M = 1.68$ ($SD = 0.36$); Informant ratings: Control $M = 1.43$ ($SD = 0.29$) vs TBI $M = 1.78$ ($SD = 0.38$); each $p < .01$
	Teasdale & Engberg: No scale was elevated in the Fracture group relative to the normative data, but the majority of scales were elevated in the Lesion group at $p < .05$
	Santos et al.: Core: Aphasia group: $M = 1.88$ vs Control group: $M = 1.56$; $t = 4.56$, $p < .001$
Reliability:	Inter-rater: no information available
	Test–retest: Sopena et al.: 1 month: Self-ratings: Core: $r = .88$ (scale range: $r = .61$–.88; $r > .8$ for 3/8 scales; other scales: Depression: $r = .79$, Motivation: $r = .71$, Physical consequences: $r = .67$, Isolation: $r = .64$, Communication: $r = .61$) – Relative ratings: Core: $r = .76$ (scale range: $r = .55$–.90; $r > .8$ for 4/8 scales; other scales: Impulsivity: $r = .76$; Communication: $r = .59$; Isolation: $r = .58$, Physical consequences: $r = .55$) – Controls ratings: Core: $r = .81$ (scale range: $r = .57$–.77)

Responsiveness:	Schönberger et al.: Core: Pre-treatment $M = 1.70$ ($SD = 0.34$) vs Post-treatment $M = 1.51$ ($SD = .27$); $p < .001$, $d = .56$ – all other scales also showed significant differences between pre- and post-treatment Coetzer & Rushe: Subgroup less than 2 years: Self-ratings: Pre-treatment $M = 113.2$ ($SD = 25.7$) vs Post-treatment $M = 100.9$ ($SD = 24.5$), $d = .49$ – Informant ratings: Pre-treatment $M = 114.5$ ($SD = 24.1$) vs Post-treatment $M = 102.0$ ($SD = 22.6$), $d = .54$

Comment

The EBIQ is one of the few instruments that was intentionally constructed to be applicable cross-culturally and was developed from a holistic rehabilitation perspective. Accordingly, the items sample a wide range of effects of ABI, including areas that are directly related to the injury in terms of impairments (e.g., Cognitive and Somatic scales) and activity limitations (e.g., Physical and Communication scales), as well as psychosocial consequences (e.g., Isolation and Depression scales). One of the strengths of the EBIQ is the normative data set, which provides an essential comparison standard for clinical interpretation of the scores – data on each of the nine scales indicated that the control group was not free of symptomatology (Self-ratings $M = 1.30$–1.61; Informant $M = 1.32$–1.63). In this regard, the provision of frequency data for the control group would be helpful in order to determine base rates. Currently, there is evidence for construct validity of the EBIQ and the Core scale shows excellent internal consistency, and good temporal stability over a 1-month period, yet is sensitive to changes occurring in the patient with moderate effect size following neurorehabilitation programmes.

Key references

Coetzer, R., & Rushe, R. (2005). Post-acute rehabilitation following traumatic brain injury: Are both early and later improved outcomes possible? *International Journal of Rehabilitation Research*, *28*, 361–363.

Deloche G., Dellatolas, G., & Christensen, A.-L. (2000). The European Brain Injury Questionnaire. Patients' and families' subjective evaluation of brain-injured patients' current and prior to injury difficulties. In: A.-L. Christensen & B. Uzzell (Eds.), *International handbook of neuropsychological rehabilitation*. (pp. 81–92). New York: Kluwer Academic.

Deloche, G., North, P., Dellatolas, G., Christensen, A.-L., Cremel, N., Passadori, A., et al. (1996). Le handicap des adultes cérébrolésés: Le point de vue des patients et de leur entourage. *Annales de Rédaption et de Médecine Physique*, *39*, 21–29.

Santos, M. E., Farrajota, M. L., Castro-Caldas, A., & de Sousa, L. (1999). Problems of patients with chronic aphasia: Different perspectives of husbands and wives? *Brain Injury*, *13*(1), 23–29.

Schönberger, M., Humle, F., & Teasdale, T. W. (2006). Subjective outcome of brain injury rehabilitation in relation to the therapeutic working alliance, client compliance and awareness. *Brain Injury*, *20*(12), 1271–1282.

Sopena, S., Dewar, B.-K., Nannery, R., Teasdale, T. W., & Wilson, B. A. (2007). The European Brain Injury Questionnaire (EBIQ) as a reliable outcome measure for use with people with brain injury. *Brain Injury*, *21*(10), 1063–1068.

Svendsen, H. A., Teasdale, T. W., & Pinner, M. (2004). Subjective experience in patients with brain injury and their close relatives before and after a rehabilitation programme. *Neuropsychological Rehabilitation*, *14*(5), 495–515.

Teasdale, T. W., Christensen, A.-L., Willmes, K., Deloche, G., Braga, L., Stachowiak, F., et al. (1997). Subjective experience in brain-injured patients and their close relatives: A European Brain Injury Questionnaire study. *Brain Injury*, *11*(8), 543–563.

Teasdale, T. W., & Engberg, A. W. (2005). Subjective well-being and quality of life following traumatic brain injury in adults: A long-term population-based follow-up. *Brain Injury*, *19*(12), 1041–1048.

European Brain Injury Questionnaire

Teasdale et al. (1997)

Relative version

Name: **Administered by:** **Date:**

Instructions: This questionnaire is concerned with a number of problems or difficulties that people sometimes experience in their lives. We would like to know how much you have experienced any of these **within the last month**. Please read each item in the questionnaire and respond by writing the number that corresponds with your response: "Not at all" or "A little" or "A lot". Do not spend too much time on any item. Just give your immediate response.

Response key:
1 = Not at all
2 = A little
3 = A lot

How much have you experienced the following:	**RESPONSE**
1. Headaches	______
2. Failing to get things done on time	______
3. Reacting too quickly to what others say or do	______
4. Trouble remembering things	______
5. Difficulty participating in conversations	______
6. Others do not understand your problems	______
7. Everything is an effort	______
8. Being unable to plan activities	______
9. Feeling hopeless about your future	______
10. Having temper outbursts	______
11. Being confused	______
12. Feeling lonely, even when together with other people	______
13. Mood swings without reason	______
14. Feeling critical of others	______
15. Having to do things slowly in order to be correct	______
16. Faintness or dizziness	______
17. Hiding your feelings from other people	______
18. Feeling sad	______
19. Being "bossy" or dominating	______
20. Needing to be reminded about personal hygiene	______
21. Difficulty managing your finances	______
22. Trouble concentrating	______
23. Failing to notice other people's moods	______
24. Feeling anger against other people	______
25. Having your feelings easily hurt	______
26. Feeling unable to get things done	______
27. Annoyance or irritation	______
28. Problems with household chores	______
29. Lack of interest in hobbies at home	______
30. Feeling lonely	______
31. Feeling inferior to other people	______
32. Sleep problems	______
33. Feeling uncomfortable in crowds	______
34. Shouting at people in anger	______
35. Difficulty in communicating what you want to say	______
36. Being unsure what to do in dangerous situations	______

EBIQ page 2 of 2

Response key:
1 = Not at all
2 = A little
3 = A lot

How much have you experienced the following: **RESPONSE**

37. Being obstinate ______
38. Lack of interest in your surroundings ______
39. Thinking only of yourself ______
40. Mistrusting other people ______
41. Crying easily ______
42. Difficulty in finding your way in new surroundings ______
43. Being inclined to eat too much ______
44. Getting into quarrels easily ______
45. Lack of energy or being slowed down ______
46. Forgetting the day of the week ______
47. Feeling of worthlessness ______
48. Lack of interest in hobbies outside the home ______
49. Needing help with personal hygiene ______
50. Restlessness ______
51. Feeling tense ______
52. Acting inappropriately in dangerous situations ______
53. Feeling life is not worth living ______
54. Forgetting appointments ______
55. Leaving others to take initiative in conversations ______
56. Loss of sexual interest or pleasure ______
57. Throwing things in anger ______
58. Preferring to be alone ______
59. Difficulty in making decisions ______
60. Losing contact with your friends ______
61. Lack of interest in current affairs ______
62. Behaving tactlessly ______
63. Having problems in general ______

Instructions: If you have a close relative who is also completing this questionnaire, then please answer the following questions about that person

64. Do you think that your relative's life has changed after you had the injury? ______
65. Do you think that your relative is having problems as a result of your present situation? ______
66. Do you think that your relative's mood has changed as a result of your present situation? ______

Any other comments? ______________________________

Acknowledgement: Reproduced with permission of Dr. T. Teasdale.

Functional Status Examination (FSE)

Dikmen, Machamer, Miller, Doctor, and Temkin (2001)

Source

The FSE, including a worked example, is described in Dikmen et al. (2001) and further information is available from Dr Dikmen (Department of Rehabilitation Medicine, University of Washington, Box 356490, Seattle, Washington, USA; email: dikmen@u.washington.edu).

Purpose

The FSE is a structured interview that aims to measure functional status in physical, social and psychological domains, as well as "the full spectrum of possible outcomes" (Dikmen et al., 2001, p. 129). It was designed for people with traumatic brain injury (TBI). The authors also considered the FSE would be appropriate for other conditions with abrupt onset and it has been used with people with subarachnoid haemorrhage (Kirkness et al., 2002).

Item description

The structured interview of the FSE measures functioning in 10 categories covering three broad domains: Physical (Personal care, Ambulation, Travel), Social (Work/School, Home management, Leisure and recreation, Social integration, Financial independence, Standard of living), and Psychological (Cognitive/Behavioural competencies). The FSE is a "tightly structured" interview with "each category assessed using a decision tree with carefully structured probes" (Hudak et al., 2005, p. 1320).

Scale development

Dikmen et al. (2001) developed the FSE based on their research experience with instruments used for outcome studies and clinical trials of people with TBI. They found that commonly used instruments were subject to one or more limitations: poor operational definitions, lack of sensitivity and ceiling effects, inability to evaluate patients with very low levels of functioning, restricted range of the spectrum of outcomes, assessment of a limited number of domains of functioning. The authors defined the domain of their interest being "a broad range of everyday activities within physical, social and psychological domains" (Dikmen et al., 2001, p. 129). They intentionally excluded other outcomes that may be related to the injury: perceptions of health, subjective symptoms (e.g., headache) or affective status (e.g., mood). The FSE was designed to cover the domains of the World Health Organization model and those included in other health outcome measures. Limited information is provided about the instrument development process, but the authors report that refinement and piloting of the instrument occurred over a number of years. Scoring procedures were "kept simple (four levels), anchored against important concepts of degree of change and dependence on others to help interpretability and improve reliability" (Dikmen et al., 2001, p. 138).

Administration procedures, response format and scoring

Dikmen et al. (2001) suggest that the structure and "interview tree" procedure of the FSE mean that an experienced clinician is not required, although inexperienced administrators "need practice to develop fluency and spontaneity" (p. 130). The interview is generally conducted with the patient and administration time is reported to be approximately 15 minutes.

Responses are made with reference to the premorbid level of functioning and are rated on a 4-point scale: 0 (no change from pre-injury), 1 (difficulty in performing the activity, but still total independence), 2 (dependence on others some of the time to perform the activities in that area/does activity substantially less often *or* has dropped some activities), 3 (completely dependent on others/does not perform the activity at all). Each of the response levels corresponds to one of the possible outcomes for each category. For example, in the Work category, the respondent is asked if they currently work, and if the answer is "no", this is scored 3 and the next interview question is posed. If the answer is "yes", the nature of the work is probed in a hierarchical manner: if it is non-competitive (also score 3), if less money (≥ 25%) is earned compared with previously (score 2), if there are difficulties on the job, such as fatigue, concentration, getting along with co-workers (score 1), if special aids are used to help with work (also score 1), or finally if work is the same as before (score 0).

The total FSE score ranges from 0 to 30 (score 31 is allocated to those who have died), with higher scores indicating poorer levels of functioning. It is noted that this score range is revised from the initial publication on the FSE (Dikmen et al., 2001). Temkin, Machamer, and Dikmen (2003) classified scores into three levels of outcome: Good (score 0), and at the other extreme, Poor (≥4/10 categories with at least score = 1 – i.e., difficulties in performing activities, which corresponded to a median score of 18, range 11–28). In between these categories is the Intermediate classification (with 1–3 categories endorsed as at least "difficult", which corresponded to a median score of 4, range 1–13).

Psychometric properties

Initial psychometric studies of the FSE, reported in Dikmen et al. (2001), examined a sample of 105 people with TBI (age $M = 33.15$ years, $SD = 13.92$) recruited from a level I trauma centre at Harborview Medical Center, Seattle, Washington, USA. The range of severity levels was represented, from mild (52%) to severe (21%). Validating instruments included the Sickness Impact Profile (SIP), Glasgow Outcome Scale (GOS), and the Medical Outcomes Study Health Survey – Short Form (SF-36). Initial assessment occurred at 6 months post-trauma, and a subset of the sample ($n = 39$) was reassessed 2 to 3 weeks later to examine temporal stability. A different interviewer was used on the subsequent occasions to guard against memory of the previous interview. Responsiveness was tested using a 6-month period. Further information on concurrent validity was provided by Temkin et al. (2003) in their sample of 209 patients with TBI. Validating instruments included GOS, SF-36, as well as cognitive tests (including Trail Making Test, TMT, and California Verbal Learning Test, CVLT), along with measures of mood (Center for Epidemiological Studies-Depression, CES-D), and symptomatology (Brief Symptom Inventory, BSI). Data on discriminant validity are available from Hudak et al. (2005), who examined 177 patients with TBI spanning all injury severity levels, from mild (38%) to severe (53%). Similar evidence was reported by Dikmen, Machamer, Powell, and Temkin (2003) using the modified Abbreviated Injury Scale. Results from Dikmen et al. (2001), except where otherwise stated, are shown in Box 10.8.

Box 10.8

Validity:	Criterion: *Concurrent:* Informant: with SIP: $r = .80$ – with GOS: $r_s = -.75$ – with injury severity data: Glasgow Coma Scale: $r_s = -.54$, duration of post-traumatic amnesia: $r_s = .76$
	Temkin et al.: with GOS: $r = -.65$ – with SF-36: Physical: $r = -.62$, Mental: $r = -.41$ – with cognitive tests: TMT-Part A: $r = .37$, TMT-Part B: $r = .40$, CVLT: $r = -.38$ – with psychological status: CES-D: $r = .55$ – with symptomatology: BSI: $r = .62$
	Construct: *Convergent/divergent:* higher correlation with similar constructs such as functional status (with SF-36 Physical: $r = -.64$); lower correlation with dissimilar constructs such as emotional functioning (with SF-36 Mental: $r = -.27$)
	Discriminant: Hudak et al.: mild injury $M = 10.1$ ($SD = 8.0$) vs moderate $M = 12.6$ ($SD = 8.6$) vs severe $M = 13.9$ ($SD = 8.9$); $p = .025$ – length of hospitalization: > 17 days $M = 16.3$ ($SD = 8.2$) vs ≤ 17 days $M = 8.8$ ($SD = 7.5$); $p < .001$
Reliability:	Inter-rater: No information available
	Test–retest: 2–3 weeks: $r_s = .80$
Responsiveness:	Significant improvement between 1 month post-trauma: Informant data: $M = 14.41$ ($SD = 5.2$) vs 6 months post-trauma $M = 7.74$ ($SD = 4.8$); $p < .001$, $d = 1.28$

Comment

The FSE is a well-designed instrument. It was developed specifically for people with TBI and therefore targets the characteristic types of functional difficulties experienced by that group, resulting in a comprehensive evaluation.

The "decision tree" format of the interview streamlines the interview process and provides an effective means of quantifying level of functioning across 10 domains. Dikmen et al. (2001) report that some patients have "complicated circumstances that are not easily classifiable" (p. 130) and in these circumstances scoring used consensus agreement. In addition to these features, psychometric properties of the FSE that have been reported to date provide evidence of an instrument that shows concurrent validity with similar outcome instruments, as well as injury severity indices, symptomatology, and cognitive test scores. There is evidence that it is a discriminating instrument with good temporal stability, yet is sensitive to changes over time, with a large effect size for recovery in the post-acute stages. No information is currently available on the internal consistency of the FSE or inter-rater reliability. With respect to the latter, Dikmen et al. (2001) argue that because different raters blind to previous results were used to assess temporal stability, this high result ($r_s = .80$) can be taken as "an underestimate" of inter-rater reliability.

Key references

Dikmen, S., Machamer, J., Miller, B., Doctor, J., & Temkin, N. (2001). Functional Status Examination: A new instrument for assessing outcome in traumatic brain injury. *Journal of Neurotrauma*, *18*(2), 127–140.

Dikmen, S. S., Machamer, J. E., Powell, J. M., & Temkin, N. R. (2003). Outcome 3 to 5 years after moderate to severe traumatic brain injury. *Archives of Physical Medicine and Rehabilitation*, *84*, 1449–1457.

Hudak, A. M., Caesar, R. R., Frol, A. B., Krueger, K., Harper, C. R., Temkin, N. R., et al. (2005). Functional outcome scales in traumatic brain injury: A comparison of the Glasgow Outcome Scale (Extended) and the Functional Status Examination. *Journal of Neurotrauma*, *22*(11), 1319–1326.

Kirkness, C. J., Thompson, J. M., Ricker, B. A., Buzaitis, A., Newell, D. W., Dikmen, S., et al. (2002). The impact of aneurysmal subarachnoid haemorrhage on functional outcome. *Journal of Neuroscience Nursing*, *34*(3), 134–141.

Temkin, N. R., Machamer, J. E., & Dikmen, S. S. (2003). Correlates of functional status 3–5 years after traumatic brain injury with CT abnormalities. *Journal of Neurotrauma*, *20*(3), 229–241.

Functional Status Examination

Dikmen, Machamer, Miller, Doctor, and Temkin (2001)

Example of item structure

Are you currently working?

NO
Not working because of the injury
Explain:
....
....
....

YES
Because of your injury, do you work in a special setting (e.g., sheltered workshop, supported employment, etc.)?

YES
Non-competitive work
Explain: ....
....
....
....

NO
Compared to your pre-injury work experiences are you currently earning less money (at least 25% less), or are you in a job that has less responsibility because of the injury? Have you received a demotion? Have you reduced your work hours by 25% or more? Is someone taking over any of your previous job duties?

YES
Explain: ....
....
....
....
....
....

NO
Are you having difficulty on the job now because of the injury? Is it taking you longer to accomplish things? Are problems with fatigue, concentration, memory, motivation or pain making your job harder? Are you having more trouble getting along with co-workers? Have you reduced your hours by < 25%, or are you taking more days off from work because of your health? Do any other physical, cognitive or emotional problems interfere with work?

YES
Are you now using any special aids or devices to help you do your job?
Explain: ....
....

NO
SAME AS BEFORE

YES
Explain: ....
....

NO

CODE 3 | CODE 3 | CODE 2 | CODE 1 | CODE 1 | CODE 0

Acknowledgement: From Dikmen, S. et al. (2001). Functional Status Examination: A new instrument for assessing outcome in traumatic brain injury. *Journal of Neurotrauma*, *18*(2), 127–140, used with permission of Mary Ann Liebert, Inc.

Health of the Nation Outcome Scales (HoNOS)

Wing, Curtis, and Beevor (1996)

Source

A detailed glossary of the HoNOS items appears in an appendix to Wing et al. (1996). Items are also tabulated in Wing, Beevor, Curtois, Park, Hadden, and Burns (1998). The HoNOS has been modified for various populations, including children and adolescents (HoN-OSCA; Gowers et al., 1999) and older people (HoNOS 65+; Burns et al., 1999). The adaptation for people with acquired brain impairment (HoNOS-ABI) is available from the Royal College of Psychiatrists' College Research Unit, 6th Floor, 83 Victoria Street, London SW1H 0HW, UK. Items for the HoNOS are reproduced below.

Purpose

The HoNOS is a clinician rating scale designed to measure mental health status. It is a generic instrument developed for routine clinical use, and hence was designed to be sufficiently brief yet covering the seminal domains. It has been used as a screening instrument, both in community and hospital settings. The HoNOS has been adapted for people with ABI and its reliability examined (Fleminger, Leigh, Eames, Langrell, Nagraj, & Logsdail, 2005).

Item description

The 12-item HoNOS targets a diverse range of functions and outcomes in four sections: Behavioural (3 items: Aggression and overactivity, Self-harm, Substance use), Impairment (2 items: Cognition, Physical health), Symptoms (3 items: Hallucinations and delusions, Depression, Other symptoms), and Social (4 items: Social relations, General functioning, Housing, Activities).

The HoNOS-ABI contains the same 12 items and response format as the HoNOS, but the glossary is more targeted to the typical manifestation characteristic of ABI as opposed to psychiatric disorders. The differences for Item 1 are shown in Data box 10.2.

Scale development

Development of the HoNOS is described in detail in the final report (Wing et al., 1996) and summarized elsewhere (Wing et al., 1998). It was constructed as part of a UK government strategy in the early 1990s to improve the health and social functioning of people with mental health conditions. To this end the Royal College of Psychiatrists' Research Unit undertook development. A literature search constituted the first phase, where no instrument was identified that met their five basic clinical requirements: a) short and simple for routine use, acceptable to nurses and psychiatrists, b) adequate coverage of clinical and social functions, c) sensitive to improvement, deterioration or lack of change over time, d) known reliability, and e) known relationship to more established scales. Therefore, a 20-item instrument was developed and pilot tested in nine sites. Following feedback, the scale was reduced to 12 items to avoid redundancy. Field trials of the revised version, referred to as HoNOS-3, were conducted in 25 participating sites, which each contributed up to 200 patients who were followed for a 3-month period (or to the end of the episode of contact). Some minor changes to the HoNOS were made, and the final version (HoNOS-4) was subjected to further reliability and validity testing.

Administration procedures, response format and scoring

A training guide and rater's pack are available as appendices to the main report (Wing et al., 1996). Each item is operationally defined with inclusion and exclusion criteria. The clinician makes a rating on each of the items and completion time is reported as 5 to 8 minutes (Bech, Bille, Schütze, Søndergaard, Waarst, & Wiese, 2003).

Responses are made within the time period of the preceding 2 weeks. Each response level for each item has an individually scripted response. Ratings are made on a 5-point scale: 0 (equivalent of no problem), 1 (equivalent of minor problem requiring no action), 2 (equivalent of mild problem that is definitely present), 3 (equivalent of moderately severe problem), or 4 (equivalent of

Data box 10.2

HoNOS	HoNOS-ABI
Item 1: Overactive, aggressive, disruptive or agitated behaviour – Include such behaviour resulting from any cause (e.g., drugs, alcohol, dementia, psychosis, depression, etc.) – Do not include bizarre behaviour rated at Scale 6	**Item 1: Active disturbance of social behaviour, e.g., overactive, aggressive, disruptive or agitated behaviour, uncooperative, resistive or disinhibited behaviour** – Include such behaviour resulting from any cause. This scale rates antisocial acts. Rate passive disturbance of social behaviour, e.g., social withdrawal, under scale 9 or 10 – Do *not* include bizarre but non-aggressive behaviour that is probably or definitely attributable to hallucinations or delusions, rated at Scale 6
0 = No problem of this kind during the rating period	0 = No problem of this kind during the rating period
1 = Irritability, quarrels, restlessness, etc. not requiring action	1 = Occasional irritability, quarrels, restlessness, etc. but generally calm and cooperative and not requiring any specific action
2 = Includes aggressive gestures, pushing or pestering others; threats or verbal aggression; lesser damage to property (e.g., broken cup, window); marked overactivity or agitation	2 = Includes aggressive gestures, e.g., pushing or pestering others and/or verbal threats or aggression; lesser damage to objects/property (e.g., broken cup, window); significant overactivity or agitation; intermittent restlessness and/or wandering (day or night); uncooperative at times, requiring encouragement and persuasion
3 = Physically aggressive to others or animals (short of rating 4); threatening manner; more serious overactivity or destruction of property	3 = Physically aggressive to others (short of rating 4); more serious damage to or destruction of property; frequent threatening manner; more serious and/or persistent overactivity or agitation; frequent restlessness and/or wandering (e.g., day and night); significant problems with cooperation, largely resistant to help/assistance. Mild sexually disinhibited talk.
4 = At least one serious physical attack on others or on animals; destruction of property (e.g., fire-setting); serious intimidation or obscene behaviour	4 = At least one serious physical attack on others (over and above rating on 3); major and/or persistent destructive activity (e.g., fire-setting); persistent and serious threatening behaviour; severe overactivity or agitation; sexually disinhibited or other inappropriate behaviour (e.g., deliberate inappropriate urination and/or defaecation); virtually constant restlessness and/or wandering; severe problems related to non-compliant/resistive behaviour

severe to very severe problem). The total score ranges from 0 to 48, with higher scores indicating more severe problems. Wing et al. (1998) advise that if information is not available on the final two items (Housing and Activities), then the first 10 items should be used, yielding a total score range of 0 to 40. Parabiaghi, Barbato, D'Avanzo, Erlicher, and Lora (2005) established a 2-stage algorithm for determining severity, building on the original definition of Lelliott (1999), as shown in the HoNOS diagram below.

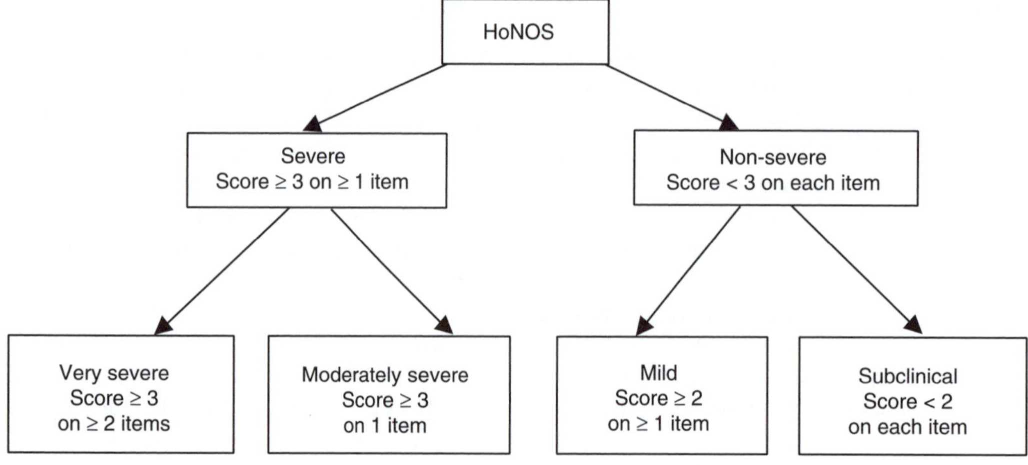

Based on data from 9417 people attending 10 community mental health services, Parabiaghi et al. (2005) also determined the reliable change index to indicate reliable and clinically significant change, using the method of Jacobson and Truax (1991). The reliable change index (i.e., that the observed change is real and not a result of measurement error of the test) was 8/9 points for the group as a whole. Using data from 4759 patients evaluated twice, they were then able to determine two cut-off points for deterioration versus remission (11/12 vs 5/6 respectively). Thus, a clinically significant change occurs when (a) there is a difference of more than 8 points, and (b) such a change in score also results in the patient crossing over one of the established cut-off scores for clinical significance: the cut-off score of 11/12 distinguished the very severe from the other groups and at the other extreme, the cut-off score of 5/6 distinguished the subclinical group from the other groups.

Psychometric properties

An overview of the psychometric properties of the HoNOS (and HoNOSCA) is provided in Pirkis, Burgess, Kirk, Dodson, Coombs, and Williamson (2005). The original psychometric studies for the final version (HoNOS-4) were conducted in Nottingham and Manchester, UK (Wing et al., 1996, 1998). Descriptive data available in Wing et al. (1996) indicate that the main ICD-10 diagnoses were psychosis (44%), affective disorders (33%) and dementia (12%). Sixty per cent were aged between 25 and 64 years, with 32% 65 years or older. Inter-rater reliability was examined with 100 patients from Nottingham who were rated by one trained assessor and the second rater was the patient's keyworker who was most knowledgeable about his or her condition. The results were largely replicated in the Manchester sample ($n = 97$). Concurrent validity was examined with a subset of 33 patients (Nottingham sample), with data reported on the Brief Psychiatric Rating Scale (BPRS) and Role Functioning Scale (RFS).

The internal structure of the HoNOS was examined with data from the field trials (using the very similar HoNOS-3). Given the disparate item content, internal consistency was not expected to be high and indeed the authors reported that of the 12 × 12 matrix only three coefficients were .3 or higher (the highest being .55 between items 10 and 11). A similar profile was found for the final testing of the HoNOS-4. Principal components analysis from the field trials data extracted a 5-factor solution for the Time 1 data ($n = 2702$), accounting for 62% of the variance, and a 4-factor solution (56%) of the variance for the Time 2 data ($n = 1669$).

Temporal stability and responsiveness were also examined in the field trials. Test–retest reliability was specifically examined in 212 pairs of ratings over a 35-day period in 52 patients who were predicted at Time 1 to show no change. Responsiveness was assessed over the approximately 3-month time period for the full field

Box 10.9

Validity:	Content: See Scale development section Criterion: *Concurrent:* with BPRS: $r = .84$ – with RFS: $r = .65$ HoNOS-ABI: Coetzer & du Toit: with PAI: $r = .75$ – with GMHP: $r = .45$ Construct: *Factor structure:* Field trials (HoNOS-3): Time 1: Social problems (3 items); Cognitive/physical/general functioning (3 items); Mood/other symptoms/personal relationships (4 items), Hallucinations/delusions (2 items), Self-harm/substance abuse (2 items) Time 2: General symptoms/aggression (4 items), Social problems/general functioning (4 items); Cognitive/physical impairment (3 items); Self-harm/substance abuse (2 items)
Reliability:	Inter-rater: Nottingham sample: Total score ICC = .86 (Behaviour: .89, Impairment: .87, Symptoms: .88, Social: .82; item range: .49–.97; ICC ≥ .75 in 9/12 items) HoNOS-ABI: Fleminger et al.: item range: $k_w = .43–.84$; ≥ .6 for 2/10 items Test–retest: Field trials (HoNOS-3): 35 days: ICC = .83 (range: .61–.88; ICC ≥ .75 in 10/12 items)
Responsiveness:	Field-trials (HoNOS-3) same-raters: Time 1 $M = 9.77$ vs Time 2 $M = 6.67$; $p < .001$ (*SD* not provided) Page et al.: Admission $M = 12.3$ ($SD = 5.0$) vs Discharge $M = 4.4$ ($SD = 3.8$); $d = 1.58$

trial, with the HoNOS showing a significant improvement, both using the same raters ($n = 871$) and different raters ($n = 798$). Other data on responsiveness are available in Page, Hooke, and Rutherford (2001) who examined a sample of 754 patients on admission to and discharge from a private psychiatric facility over a 2-year period in Perth, Australia. The majority (67%) had a DSM-IV diagnosis of mood disorder (mainly major depression), but much smaller percentages had psychotic or substance-abuse problems (approximately 3% each).

Comment

At this stage, psychometric data for the HoNOS-ABI are limited. Coetzer and du Toit (2001) validated the HoNOS-ABI against the Portland Adaptability Inventory (PAI) and Grafton Manor Study Hierarchy of Placements (GMHP) in 40 outpatients with brain injury. Fleminger et al. (2005) reported an inter-rater reliability study using 24 raters from a range of health professions (psychiatry, psychology and nursing) with 50 patients. Ratings were made independently in the course of routine clinical practice. Only 10 of the 12 items suitable for inpatients were rated. Results from Wing et al. (1996), unless otherwise stated, are shown in Box 10.9.

The authors have achieved their aim of developing a sensitive measure that captures the common mental health problem areas and yet is sufficiently brief to be feasible for routine clinical use. Inter-rater reliability of the HoNOS is excellent for the total scores, four sections, and most of the items. Test–retest reliability is also excellent, and it has demonstrated validity and responsiveness. These features have been ensured by the careful and extensive development phase of the HoNOS, which included rater training and the use of multiple centres with many raters and thousands of patients. The HoNOS-ABI has been validated and shows moderate to good inter-rater reliability at the item level in brain injury populations. The clinical relevance and brevity of the HoNOS is a particular advantage in the ABI arena for those situations where there is a need to screen for comorbidity.

Key references

Bech, P., Bille, J., Schütze, T., Søndergaard, S., Waarst, S., & Wiese, M. (2003). Health of the Nation Outcome Scales (HoNOS): Implementability, subscale structure and responsiveness in the daily psychiatric hospital routine over the first 18 months. *Nordic Journal of Psychiatry, 57*, 285–290.

Burns, A., Beevor, A., Lelliott, P., Wing, J., Blakey, A., Orrell, M., et al. (1999). Health of the Nation Outcome Scales for Elderly People (HoNOS 65+). *The British Journal of Psychiatry, 174*(5), 424–427.

Coetzer, R., & du Toit, P. L. (2001). HoNOS-ABI; a clinically useful outcome measure? *Psychiatric Bulletin, 25*, 421–422.

Fleminger, S., Leigh, E., Eames, P., Langrell, L., Nagraj, R., & Logsdail, S. (2005). HoNOS-ABI: A reliable outcome measure of neuropsychiatric sequelae to brain injury? *Psychiatric Bulletin, 29*, 53–55.

Gowers, S. G., Harrington, R. C., Whitton, A., Lelliott, P., Beevor, A., Wing, J., et al. (1999). Brief scale for measuring the outcomes of emotional and behavioural disorders in children: Health of the Nation Outcome Scales for Children and Adolescents (HoNOSCA). *British Journal of Psychiatry, 174*(5), 413–416.

Jacobson, N. S., & Truax, P. (1991). Clinical significance: A statistical approach to defining meaningful change in psychotherapy research. *Journal of Consulting and Clinical Psychology, 59*(1), 12–19.

Lelliott, P. (1999). Definition of severe mental illness. In P. Charlwood, A. Mason, M. Goldacre, R. Cleary, & E. Wilkinson (Eds.), *Health outcome indicators: Severe mental illness. Report of a working group to the Department of Health* (pp. 87–89). Oxford: National Centre for Health Outcomes Development.

Page, A. C., Hooke, G. R., & Rutherford, E. M. (2001). Measuring mental health outcomes in a private psychiatric clinic: Health of the National Outcome Scales and Medical Outcomes Short Form SF-36. *Australian and New Zealand Journal of Psychiatry, 35*(3), 377–381.

Parabiaghi, A., Barbato, A., D'Avanzo, B., Erlicher, A., & Lora, A. (2005). Assessing reliable and clinically significant change on Health of the Nation Outcome Scales: Method for displaying longitudinal data. *Australian and New Zealand Journal of Psychiatry, 39*, 719–725.

Pirkis, J. E., Burgess, P. M., Kirk, P. K., Dodson, S., Coombs, T. J., & Williamson, M. K. (2005). A review of the psychometric properties of the Health of the Nation Outcome Scales (HoNOS) family of measures. *Health and Quality of Life Outcomes, 3*, 76.

Wing, J. K., Beevor, A. S., Curtis, R. H., Park, S. B. G., Hadden, S., & Burns, A. (1998). Health of the Nation Outcome Scales (HoNOS). Research and development. *British Journal of Psychiatry, 172*, 11–18.

Wing, J. K., Curtis, R. H., & Beevor, A. S. (1996). *HoNOS. Health of the Nation Outcome Scales. Report on research and development.* London: Royal College of Psychiatrists, College Research Unit.

Health of the Nation Outcome Scales

Wing, Curtis, and Beevor (1996)

Name:	**Administered by:**	**Date:**

Instructions:

1) Rate each scale in order from 1 to 12
2) Do not include information rated in an earlier item except for item 10, which is an overall rating
3) Rate the MOST SEVERE problem that occurred during the period rated
4) All scales follow the format:
    0 = no problem
    1 = minor problem requiring no action
    2 = mild problem but definitely present
    3 = moderately severe problem
    4 = severe to very severe problem
    Rate 9 if not known

1. Overactive, aggressive, disruptive or agitated behaviour

- Include such behaviour resulting from any cause (e.g. drugs, alcohol, dementia, psychosis, depression, etc.)
- Do not include bizarre behaviour, rated at Scale 6

0 No problem of this kind during the period rated
1 Irritability, quarrels, restlessness, etc. not requiring action
2 Includes aggressive gestures, pushing or pestering others; threats or verbal aggression; lesser damage to property (e.g., broken cup, window); marked overactivity or agitation
3 Physically aggressive to others or animals (short of rating 4); threatening manner; more serious overactivity or destruction of property
4 At least one serious physical attack on others or on animals; destruction of property (e.g. fire-setting); serious intimidation or obscene behaviour

2. Non-accidental self-injury

- Do not include accidental self-injury (resulting from, e.g., dementia or severe learning disability); the cognitive problem is rated at Scale 4 and the injury at Scale 5
- Do not include illness or injury as a direct consequence of drug/alcohol use, rated at Scale 3 (e.g., cirrhosis of the liver or injury resulting from drink driving are rated at Scale 5)

0 No problem of this kind during the period rated
1 Fleeting thoughts about ending it all but little risk during the period rated; no self-harm
2 Mild risk during period rated; includes non-hazardous self-harm (e.g. wrist scratching)
3 Moderate to serious risk of deliberate self-harm during the period rated; includes preparatory acts (e.g., collecting tablets)
4 Serious suicidal attempt and/or serious deliberate self-injury during the period rated

3. Problem-drinking or drug-taking

- Do not include aggressive/destructive behaviour resulting from alcohol or drug use, rated at Scale 1
- Do not include physical illness or disability resulting from alcohol or drug use, rated at Scale 5

0 No problem of this kind during the period rated
1 Some over-indulgence but within social norm
2 Loss of control of drinking or drug-taking, but not seriously addicted
3 Marked craving or dependence on alcohol or drugs with frequent loss of control, risk taking under the influence
4 Incapacitated by alcohol/drug problem

4. Cognitive problems

- Include problems of memory, orientation and understanding associated with any disorder: learning disability, dementia, schizophrenia, etc.
- Do not include temporary problems (e.g., hangovers) resulting from drug/alcohol use, rated at Scale 3

0 No problem of this kind during the period rated
1 Minor problems with memory or understanding (e.g., forgets names occasionally)
2 Mild but definite problem (e.g., has lost the way in a familiar place or failed to recognize a familiar person); sometimes mixed up about simple decisions
3 Marked disorientation in time, place or person; bewildered by everyday events; speech is sometimes incoherent; mental slowing
4 Severe disorientation (e.g., unable to recognize relatives); at risk of accidents; speech incomprehensible; clouding or stupor

5. Physical illness or disability problems

- Include illness or disability from any cause that limits or prevents movement, or impairs sight or hearing, or otherwise interferes with personal functioning
- Include side-effects from medication; effects of drug/alcohol use; physical disabilities resulting from accidents or self-harm associated with cognitive problems, drink driving, etc.
- Do not include mental or behavioural problems, rated at Scale 4

0 No physical health problems during the period rated
1 Minor health problems during the period (e.g., cold, non-serious fall, etc.)
2 Physical health problem imposes mild restriction on mobility and activity
3 Moderate degree of restriction on activity resulting from physical health problem
4 Severe or complete incapacity resulting from physical health problem

6. Problems associated with hallucinations and delusions

- Include hallucinations and delusions irrespective of diagnosis
- Include odd and bizarre behaviour associated with hallucinations or delusions
- Do not include aggressive, destructive or overactive behaviours attributed to hallucinations or delusions, rated at Scale 1

0 No evidence of hallucinations or delusions during the time period rated
1 Somewhat odd or eccentric beliefs not in keeping with cultural norms
2 Delusions or hallucinations (e.g., voices, visions) are present, but there is little distress to patient or manifestation in bizarre behaviour, i.e., clinically present but mild
3 Marked preoccupation with delusions or hallucinations, causing much distress and/or manifested in obviously bizarre behaviour, i.e., moderately severe clinical problem
4 Mental state and behaviour are seriously and adversely affected by delusions or hallucinations, with severe impact on patient

7. Problems with depressed mood

- Do not include overactivity or agitation, rated at Scale 1
- Do not include suicidal ideation or attempts, rated at Scale 2
- Do not include delusions or hallucinations, rated at Scale 6

0 No problem associated with depressed mood during the period rated
1 Gloomy; or minor changes in mood
2 Mild but definite depression and distress (e.g., feelings of guilt; loss of self-esteem)
3 Depression with inappropriate self-blame; preoccupied with feelings of guilt
4 Severe or very severe depression, with guilt or self-accusation

8. Other mental and behavioural problems

- Rate only the most severe clinical problem not considered at items 6 or 7 as follows
- Specify the type of problem by entering the appropriate letter: A phobic; B anxiety; C obsessive-compulsive; D mental strain/tension; E dissociative; F somatoform; G eating; H sleep; I sexual; J other, specify

0 No evidence of any of these problems during the period rated
1 Minor problems only
2 A problem is clinically present at a mild level (e.g., patient has a degree of control)
3 Occasional severe attack or distress, with loss of control (e.g., has to avoid anxiety-provoking situations altogether, call in a neighbour to help, etc.), i.e., moderately severe level of problem
4 Severe problem dominates most activities

9. Problems with relationships

- Rate the patient's most severe problem associated with active or passive withdrawal from social relationships, and/or non-supportive, destructive or self-damaging relationships.

0 No significant problem during the period rated
1 Minor non-clinical problem
2 Definite problem in making or sustaining supportive relationships; patient complains and/or problems are evident to others
3 Persisting major problem resulting from active or passive withdrawal from social relationships and/or to relationships that provide little or no comfort or support
4 Severe and distressing social isolation resulting from an inability to communicate socially and/or withdrawal from social relationships

10. Problems with activities of daily living

- Rate the overall level of functioning in activities of daily living (ADL) (e.g., problems with basic activities of self-care such as eating, washing, dressing, toilet; also complex skills such as budgeting, organizing where to live, occupation and recreation, mobility and use of transport, shopping, self-development, etc.)
- Include any lack of motivation for using self-help opportunities, since this contributes to a lower overall level of functioning
- Do not include lack of opportunities for exercising, intact abilities and skills, rated at Scales 11–12

0 No problem during period rated; good ability to function in all areas
1 Minor problems only (e.g., untidy, disorganized)
2 Self-care adequate, but major lack of performance of one of more complex skills (see above)
3 Major problem in one or more area of self-care (eating, washing, dressing, toilet) as well as major inability to perform several complex skills
4 Severe disability or incapacity in all or nearly all areas of self-care and complex skills

11. Problems with living conditions

- Rate the overall severity of problems with the quality of living conditions and daily domestic routine
- Are the basic necessities met (heat, light, hygiene)? If so, is there help to cope with disabilities and a choice of opportunities to use skills and develop new ones?
- Do not rate the level of functional disability itself, rated at Scale 10
- NB: Rate patient's usual accommodation. If in acute ward, rate the home accommodation. If information not available, rate 9

0 Accommodation and living conditions are acceptable; helpful in keeping any disability rated at Scale 10 to the lowest level possible, and supportive of self-help
1 Accommodation is reasonably acceptable although there are minor or transient problems (e.g., not ideal location, not preferred option, doesn't like the food, etc.)
2 Significant problem with one or more aspects of the accommodation and/or regime (e.g., restricted choice; staff or household have little understanding of how to limit disability or how to help use or develop new or intact skills)
3 Distressing multiple problems with accommodation (e.g., some basic necessities absent); housing environment has minimal or no facilities to improve patient's independence
4 Accommodation is unacceptable (e.g., lack of basic necessities, patient is at risk of eviction, or "roofless", or living conditions are otherwise intolerable), making patient's problems worse

12. Problems with occupation and activities

- Rate the overall level of problems with quality of daytime environment. Is there help to cope with disabilities, and opportunities for maintaining or improving occupational and recreational skills and activities? Consider factors such as stigma, lack of qualified staff, access to supportive facilities (e.g., staffing and equipment of day centres, workshops, social clubs, etc.)
- Do not rate the level of functional disability itself, rated at Scale 10
- NB: Rate patient's usual situation. If in acute ward, rate activities during period before admission. If information not available, rate 9

0 Patient's daytime environment is acceptable: helpful in keeping any disability rated at Scale 10 to the lowest level possible, and supportive of self-help
1 Minor or temporary problems (e.g., late giro cheques): reasonable facilities available but not always at desired times, etc.
2 Limited choice of activities; lack of reasonable tolerance (e.g., unfairly refused entry to public library or baths, etc.); handicapped by lack of a permanent address; insufficient carer or professional support; helpful day setting available but for very limited hours
3 Marked deficiency in skilled services available to help minimize level of existing disability; no opportunities to use intact skills or add new ones; unskilled care difficult to access
4 Lack of any opportunity for daytime activities makes patient's problems worse

---

Acknowledgement: From Wing, J. K. et al. (1996). *Health of the Nation Outcome Scales. Report on research and development*. London: Royal College of Psychiatrists, College Research Unit.

Mayo-Portland Adaptability Inventory – 4 (MPAI-4)

Malec and Lezak (2003)

Source

The recording form and manual for the current MPAI-4 version (Malec & Lezak, 2003) are available from the website of the Center for Outcome Measurement in Brain Injury (http://www.tbims.org/combi/mpai/index.html). The manual was updated in January 2008 to include information on a paediatric adaptation (MPAI-P). MPAI items are shown below.

Purpose

The MPAI is a rating scale that can be completed using clinician, informant or self-ratings. It was designed for the clinical assessment of people with acquired brain impairment (ABI) in the post-acute period, and the evaluation of rehabilitation programmes. The MPAI standardization samples included people with hypoxia, stroke, traumatic brain injury (TBI) and tumour. Although designed for adults, it has also been used in a paediatric ABI population (Oddson, Rumney, Johnson, & Thomas-Stonell, 2006) – also see the updated MPAI manual (Malec & Lezak, 2003).

Item description

Item content of the MPAI-4 (described below) is similar to that of previous versions, although the scoring formats for previous versions differ, and hence the scales are not completely interchangeable (but see Malec, 2004). The MPAI-4 contains 29 core items and 6 additional items. The core items represent common sequelae of ABI in the physical, cognitive, emotional, behavioural and social domains. They are grouped into three subscales: Ability (12 items, focusing on sensory, motor and cognitive abilities), Adjustment (9 items, addressing mood, interpersonal interactions) and Participation (8 items, evaluating social contacts, initiation, money management). The outstanding items from previous MPAI versions have been retained, and added to, making a fourth subscale, Pre-existing and associated conditions, containing six items. These "non-core" items are not scored.

Scale development

The MPAI was derived from the 23-item Portland Adaptability Inventory (PAI), which was developed by Lezak (1987) to provide "meaningful documentation of the variety of behavioral and social challenges that face many persons with acquired brain injury" (Malec & Lezak, 2003, p. 48). Malec and Thompson (1994) expanded the PAI to 30 items, containing a 24-item Cognitive scale and 6-item Non-cognitive scale, using a 4-point rating scale (labelled Version I by Malec, Moessner, Kragness, & Lezak, 2000). A validity study was conducted with 50 people being assessed for an outpatient neuropsychological rehabilitation programme (see below). The underlying structure of the MPAI-Version I was examined (Bohac, Malec, & Moessner, 1997) and later refined with Rasch analysis and principal components analysis (Malec et al., 2000). Data from 305 people with ABI were analysed, and in order to improve its measurement characteristics, the best fitting 22 items were retained (labelled Version II, MPAI-22 in Malec et al., 2000). A subsequent version, referred to in the literature as MPAI-2.3, used the 22-item version, but introduced a 6-point rating scale to replace the 4-point scale (see Malec, Kragness, Evans, Finlay, Kent, & Lezak, 2003). Further Rasch analysis indicated that a 5-point rating scale provided better results. New items were added "to better represent the milder end of challenges for persons with ABI" (Malec et al., 2003, p. 480), and this was labelled MPAI-3. Malec and colleagues (2003) revisited the original 30-item version and conducted further Rasch analysis with data from 386 people. Eliminating one item and recoding of some other items increased the fit of items with the overall measure, resulting in the current 29-item MPAI-4, with three "rational groupings": Ability, Adjustment and Participation subscales.

Administration procedures, response format and scoring

Detailed item description and instructions for administration of the MPAI-4 are provided in the manual

(Malec & Lezak, 2003). Clinician ratings are often made by consensus of a multidisciplinary team following their individual assessments (Malec et al., 2000). All versions of the MPAI were also designed to be completed by informants, as well as by people with ABI, unless they experience severe cognitive impairment. The manual suggests that informants and people with ABI should be instructed in its completion by professional staff, and staff should also be available to answer questions that may arise during the course of completion.

Responses are made on a 5-point scale. The response descriptors are tailored to the individual items, generally along the lines of 0 (equivalent of no problem), 1 (equivalent of mild problem that does *not* interfere with activities; may use assistive device or medication), 2 (equivalent of mild problem that interferes with activities 5–24% of the time), 3 (equivalent of moderate problem; interferes with activities 25–75% of the time), 4 (equivalent of severe problem; interferes with activities more than 75% of the time).

The manual advises that scoring and interpretation of the MPAI-4 require professional training and experience. Scoring of a number of items (audition, pain and headache, communication, transportation, and employment) requires special procedures, described in the manual and summarized on the recording form. Three items in the Adjustment scale (family relationships, contacts with friends and others, and leisure/recreational activities) are also used to derive the Participation score; thus when calculating a total MPAI score they need to be subtracted to avoid double counting. The six items from the Pre-existing and associated conditions scale are not included in the MPAI score. Raw scores are calculated and can be transformed to *T*-scores ($M = 50$, $SD = 10$) for comparison with other ABI groups, using tables in the manual. Higher scores indicate more severe difficulties relative to other people with ABI.

Comparative data (Malec & Lezak, 2003) for the MPAI-4 are provided in the manual. This includes a national sample ($n = 386$), mainly TBI (88%), drawn from the south-east, mid-west, south-west/mountains and California regions of the USA. Data from a Mayo sample ($n = 134$), again mainly TBI (65%), are also provided. For each sample, data are provided from three groups: clinicians, informants, and people with ABI. Data are provided for the total scale and three subscales, but no data are reported for the Pre-existing and associated conditions scale.

Psychometric properties

Malec and Thompson (1994) reported results of an initial validation study of the MPAI-Version I with 50 people with ABI (age $M = 33.2$ years, range 18–59) recruited from the Mayo Brain Injury Outpatient Program, Rochester, Minnesota, USA. Concurrent validity was examined with the Disability Rating Scale (DRS). Data on convergent and divergent validity were available from patterns of correlations between cognitive tests and the MPAI-Version I Cognitive/Non-cognitive scales. Representative cognitive tests included the sum of trials on the Rey Auditory-Verbal Learning Test (RAVLT) and perseverative errors on the Wisconsin Card Sorting Test (WCST). Discriminant validity was examined by comparing scores on subgroups at Level 7 ($n = 18$) and Level 8 ($n = 20$) of the Rancho Los Amigos Levels of Cognitive Functioning Scale. Results from the most recent Rasch analysis on the MPAI-Version I using data from 386 people with ABI resulted in the MPAI-4 (Malec et al., 2003). That report also described results from a principal components analysis (PCA), in which seven (unlabelled) components were extracted (percentage of variance was not reported). Malec et al. (2003) drew attention to the similarity of this PCA to that reported by Bohac et al. (1997), which extracted eight components accounting for 64.4% of the variance. Data on responsiveness of the MPAI-22 are available from Malec (2001), who described data from 62 people with ABI completing a comprehensive outpatient brain injury rehabilitation programme (NB: Rasch standardized scores were used $M = 500$, $SD = 100$.) That report also investigated the predictive validity of the MPAI-22, examining discharge versus 1-year follow-up of living status and vocational outcome. Results of the above studies are shown in Box 10.10.

Comment

The MPAI has undergone extensive psychometric analysis with large samples, as well as a considerable number of revisions, in order to improve its measurement characteristics. This has resulted in a scale with a substantial body of psychometric data supporting its validity. It is a good fit to a Rasch model, correlates with similar measures and is discriminative. It is also responsive to real changes occurring in the patient as a result of therapeutic interventions, showing a large effect size. No information is available on temporal stability or inter-rater reliability – although information is available on patient-proxy agreement, this is not an index of inter-rater reliability per se. Malec (2004) studied patient–clinician–informant data in detail using both Rasch and traditional psychometric procedures, and on the basis of the results argued that each information source has inherent biases. He concluded that the MPAI "possesses sufficient reliability, regardless of rating source, to be completed by people with ABI and their SO [significant other] as well as by rehabilitation staff" (p. 573). A major strength of the MPAI is its item

Box 10.10

Validity:	Criterion: *Concurrent:* Malec & Thompson: MPAI-Version I: with DRS: $r_s = .81$ *Predictive:* Malec (2001): MPAI-22: discharge: with 1 year independent living: $r = -.64$ – with 1 year vocational outcome: $r = -.37$ Construct: *Internal consistency:* Malec et al. (2003): MPAI-3: Rasch analysis: Person separation (2.68), reliability (0.88); item separation (10.80), reliability (0.99) – Cronbach alpha .89 *Factor analysis:* Malec et al. (2003): 7 components: I (7 items), II (5 items), III (4 items), IV (3 items), V (4 items), VI (3 items), VII (3 items) *Convergent/divergent:* Malec & Thompson: MPAI-Version I: Higher correlation with similar constructs (Cognitive index with RAVLT: $r = -.55$, with WCST: $r = .56$); lower correlation with dissimilar constructs (Non-cognitive index with RAVLT: $r = -.22$, with WCST: $r = .29$) *Discriminant:* Malec & Thompson: MPAI-Version I: Rancho 7 Median = 32.5 (range 21–52) vs Rancho 8 Median = 16.5 (range 6–35); Kruskal-Wallis = 22.07, $p < .001$
Reliability:	Inter-rater: No information available Test–retest: No information available
Responsiveness:	Malec: (2001): MPAI-22: Pre-treatment $M = 546.3$ ($SD = 57.3$) vs Discharge $M = 448.3$ ($SD = 104.8$); $t = 8.35$, $p < .001$, $d = 1.71$

content and multidimensionality – "by including indicators of impairment and activity, the MPAI provides some information on the 'why' of limited participation" (Malec et al., 2000, p. 672).

Key references

Bohac, D. L., Malec, J. F., & Moessner, A. M. (1997). Factor analysis of the Mayo-Portland Adaptability Inventory: Structure and validity. *Brain Injury*, *11*(7), 469–482.

Lezak, M. D. (1987). Relationships between personality disorder, social disturbances and physical disability following traumatic brain injury. *Journal of Head Trauma Rehabilitation*, *2*, 57–69.

Malec, J. F. (2001). Impact of comprehensive day treatment on societal participation for persons with acquired brain injury. *Archives of Physical Medicine and Rehabilitation*, *82*, 885–895.

Malec, J. F. (2004). Comparability of Mayo-Portland Adaptability Inventory ratings by staff, significant others and people with acquired brain injury. *Brain Injury*, *18*(6), 563–575.

Malec, J. F., Kragness, M., Evans, R. W., Finlay, K. L., Kent, A., & Lezak, M. D. (2003). Further psychometric evaluation and revision of the Mayo-Portland Adaptability Inventory in a national sample. *Journal of Head Trauma Rehabilitation*, *18*(6), 479–492.

Malec, J. F., & Lezak, M. D. (2003, April). *Manual for the Mayo-Portland Adaptability Inventory (MPAI-4)* (1st ed.). Available from http://www.tbims.org/combi/mpai (accessed 28 August 2008).

Malec, J. F., Moessner, A. M., Kragness, M., & Lezak, M. D. (2000). Refining a measure of brain injury sequelae to predict postacute rehabilitation outcome: Rating scale analysis of the Mayo-Portland Adaptability Inventory. *Journal of Head Trauma Rehabilitation*, *15*(1), 670–682.

Malec, J. F., & Thompson, J. M. (1994). Relationship of the Mayo-Portland Adaptability Inventory to functional outcome and cognitive performance measures. *Journal of Head Trauma Rehabilitation*, *9*(4), 1–15.

Oddson, B., Rumney, P., Johnson, P., & Thomas-Stonell, N. (2006). Clinical use of the Mayo-Portland Adaptability Inventory in rehabilitation after paediatric acquired brain injury. *Developmental Medicine and Child Neurology*, *48*(11), 918–922.

Mayo-Portland Adaptability Inventory
Malec and Lezak (2003)
Item and subscale description

Ability	**Adjustment**	**Participation**
Mobility	Anxiety	*Initiation
Use of hands	Depression	*Social contact
Vision	Irritability, anger, aggression	*Leisure/recreational activities
Audition	Pain and headache	Self-care
Motor speech	Fatigue	Residence
Communication	Sensitivity to mild symptoms	Transportation
Attention-concentration	Inappropriate social interaction	Work/school
Memory	Family/significant relationships	Money management
Fund of information	Impaired self-awareness	
Novel problem-solving	Initiation*	
Visuospatial abilities	Social contact*	
Dizziness	Leisure/recreational activities*	

If a stand-alone Participation score is required, then the three asterisked items from the Adjustment Scale are included for that purpose.

Acknowledgement: From Malec, J. F. et al. (2003). Further psychometric evaluation and revision of the Mayo-Portland Adaptability Inventory in a national sample. *Journal of Head Trauma Rehabilitation*, *18*(6), 479–492.

Neurobehavioral Functioning Inventory (NFI)

Kreutzer, Seel, and Marwitz (1999)

Source

Items of the NFI initially appeared in a table in the original publication (Kreutzer, Marwitz, Seel, & Serio, 1996). The scale is now commercially available from the Psychological Corporation (http://www.psychcorp.com). Description of the scale is also available from the website of the Center for Outcome Measurement in Brain Injury (http://www.tbims.org/combi/nfi/index.html).

Purpose

The NFI is a self and informant rating scale, which evaluates the frequency of "a wide spectrum of post-injury behaviors and symptoms commonly encountered in daily life" (Kreutzer et al., 1996, p. 117). It was developed for adolescents and adults with traumatic brain injury (TBI), and the manual advises that it is also appropriate for other neurological conditions.

Item description

Seventy of the 76 NFI items contribute to six scales derived from factor analysis: Depression (13 items, e.g., "feel worthless"), Somatic (11 items, e.g., "nauseous"), Memory/attention (19 items, e.g., "forget if you have done things"), Communication (10 items, e.g., "trouble understanding conversations"), Aggression (9 items, e.g., "curse at others") and Motor (8 items, e.g., "move slowly"). The remaining six "critical items" are described as "data related to patient safety and community integration": blackout spells, seizures, threaten self-harm, cannot be left alone, miss or cannot attend work/school, double or blurred vision. These items are placed first in the scale, but do not contribute to the score. Two versions of the NFI are available, for self and informant rating, each with identical items, but phrased as appropriate. Reading level of the items is at the 6th grade and the "list format" of the items was intentional for ease of reading.

Scale development

In evaluating neurobehavioural functioning after TBI, Kreutzer and colleagues (1996) adopted the perspective that "an accurate impression of brain injury consequences requires blending information from several assessment methods" (p. 116). They observed that although significant advances had occurred with respect to standardized tests and clinical observations, there was little progress in methods using information collected from relatives and other informants. Despite known limitations, this source of information was considered important, in that relatives "often have a unique opportunity to observe day-to-day behaviours and symptoms in natural settings" (p. 117). Existing scales, which were mainly semi-structured interviews, checklists and questionnaires, did not lend themselves to numerical scoring procedures or psychometric evaluation.

Limited information is available regarding the developmental procedures of the NFI. It was initially described as a 105-item instrument with five categories (Somatic, Cognitive, Behaviour, Communication and Social problems), which was part of a larger questionnaire used by the authors, the General Health and History Questionnaire (Kreutzer et al., 1996). This 105-item version was later referred to as the Brain Injury Problem Checklist (Kreutzer et al., 1999). Initial psychometric studies of the scale used a sample of 520 outpatients (and families) referred to a regional Level 1 trauma centre in Richmond, USA, 80% of whom sustained their injuries in road traffic crashes. Confirmatory factor analysis was used to examine four models. The model using the original groupings from the 105-item scale "inadequately characterized the data" (p. 118) and principal components analysis was used to identify an alternative. This included an item reduction process whereby only items with factor loadings $>.4$ were retained, and 35 items were excluded at this stage. Confirmatory factor analysis for a 70-item, 6-factor scale yielded the best goodness of fit statistics, and this version was then validated (described below).

Administration procedures, response format and scoring

The NFI assesses "how the patient *currently* functions on a typical day" (Kreutzer et al., 1999, p. 26). It is designed to be self-administered, as well as completed by an informant. Both respondents should be included where possible, in order to obtain different perspectives. The informant chosen should be able to accurately describe the patient's functioning. The authors have also used mail-out versions of the NFI, with responses reviewed with the patient/informant at clinic appointment. Administration time is 20 to 40 minutes. The manual suggests that interpretation of the NFI should be done by a licensed mental health professional.

Items use a 5-point rating scale: 1 (never), 2 (rarely), 3 (sometimes), 4 (often), 5 (always). The recording form lends itself to easy computation of scores, which is done manually. The score for each item is transcribed to its respective scale. Raw scores for each scale are summed and then converted to *T*-scores ($M = 50$, $SD = 10$) and percentiles, using data provided in the manual. Separate tables are used for Family and Self ratings. Higher scores indicate more frequent occurrence of the problem.

Comparative data from the validation sample ($n = 520$) were used to develop tables from Family and Self ratings were used to develop tables and are provided in the manual. Data are stratified by four age groups (patient age at assessment: 17–24 years, 25–34 years, 35–44 years, ≥ 45 years) and three levels of injury severity (unconscious < 1 hour, 1 hour to 13 days, ≥ 14 days).

Psychometric properties

Kreutzer et al. (1996, 1999) reported results of a validation study of the NFI using informant ratings and subsets of the previously described sample of 520 outpatients with TBI. They were aged $M = 31.3$ years ($SD = 12.7$, range 16–82), had coma duration of $M = 14.6$ days ($SD = 33.1$, median = 0.25), and time post-trauma was 2.9 years ($SD = 4.1$, median = 1.3). Validation instruments included cognitive tests assessing attention, learning and memory (Rey Auditory-Verbal Learning Test, paragraph recall, subtests from the Wechsler Memory Scale), visuo-motor function (Symbol Digit Modalities Test, SDMT – oral version, Grooved Pegboard), and language and communication (Gray Oral Reading Test [Comprehension and Accuracy] and Controlled Word Association Test). Incomplete information is reported in the above publications – in spite of administering specific tests of memory, no correlation coefficients with the NFI Memory/attention scale are provided; only those for the NFI Communication scale are reported. Many of the inter-correlations reported between conceptually similar tests and NFI scales were of low magnitude, thereby raising the question as to whether in fact they provide evidence of concurrent validity. The Minnesota Multiphasic Personality Inventory (MMPI-2) was used to measure behaviour and personality, and coefficients were somewhat higher.

Box 10.11

Validity:	Criterion: *Concurrent:* NFI Communication scale with tests of language and communication: range: $r = -.20$ to $-.26$ – NFI Memory/attention scale with Symbol Digit Modalities Test: $r = -.18$ – with 5 MMPI scales: range of statistically significant coefficients: $r = .21$–$.65$
	Construct: *Internal consistency:* Cronbach alpha on factor scores: Total scale .97 (Depression .93, Somatic .86, Memory/attention .95, Communication .88, Aggression .89, Motor .89)
	Factor structure: 6 factors: Depression 13 items, Somatic 11 items, Memory/attention 19 items, Communication 10 items, Aggression 9 items, Motor 8 items
	Convergent/divergent: higher correlation with similar constructs (NFI Somatic with MMPI Scale 1 (Hypochondriasis): $r = .65$, NFI Depression with MMPI Scale 2 (Depression): $r = .47$); lower correlations with dissimilar constructs (NFI Somatic with MMPI Scale 8 (Schizophrenia): $r = -.35$, NFI Depression with MMPI Scale 3 (Hysteria): $r = .28$)
	Discriminant: Significant differences among injury severity subgroups on 4/6 scales: Somatic ($F = 41.5$), Memory/attention ($F = 5.45$), Communication ($F = 5.34$), Motor ($F = 11.62$); all $p < .01$
Reliability:	Inter-rater: No information available
	Test–retest: No information available
Responsiveness:	No information available

Discriminant validity was evaluated by examining injury severity levels, using length of unconsciousness (≤ 1 hour, > 1 hour to < 14 days, ≥ 14 days), and convergent and divergent validity using hypothesized patterns of correlations with the MMPI. Confirmatory factor analysis was performed on the six-scale NFI, yielding a Comparative Fit Index of .84. Wilson, Pettigrew, and Teasdale (2000) used an earlier version of the NFI (4-point rating scale) to validate the extended version of the Glasgow Outcome Scale (GOSE) in 106 people with TBI and their families ($n = 100$). Only graphed data that "illustrate consistent associations" (p. 208) were provided, however, and correlation coefficients were not reported. Results from Kreutzer et al. (1996) are shown in Box 10.11.

Comment

The NFI is best regarded as a multidimensional scale of body functions, encompassing motor, cognition and behaviour. Unlike the usual multidimensional scale, it does not contain items relating to Activities/Participation. This is not necessarily a weakness, however, and at 70 items, its value is in providing a comprehensive survey of impairments of body functions particularly pertinent to TBI. Kreutzer et al. (1999) note that the NFI was not intended to be a diagnostic tool and that neurological and neuropsychological tests are better suited for this purpose. Indeed, correlation coefficients between the NFI scales using informant ratings and objective cognitive tests were of low magnitude, indicating that informant ratings on the NFI should not be used in lieu of objective cognitive tests. There is evidence for construct validity of the NFI, but it would be helpful to have psychometric data regarding its reliability and responsiveness.

Key references

Kreutzer, J. S., Marwitz, J. H., Seel, R., & Serio, C. D. (1996). Validation of a Neurobehavioral Functioning Inventory for adults with traumatic brain injury. *Archives of Physical Medicine and Rehabilitation*, *77*, 116–124.

Kreutzer, J. S., Seel, R. T., & Marwitz, J. H. (1999). *Neurobehavioral Functioning Inventory*. San Antonio, TX: The Psychological Corporation.

Wilson, J. T. L., Pettigrew, L. E. L., & Teasdale, G. M. (2000). Emotional and cognitive consequences of head injury in relation to the Glasgow Outcome Scale. *Journal of Neurology, Neurosurgery, and Psychiatry*, *69*(2), 204–209.

Neurobehavioral Rating Scale – Revised (NRS-R)

Levin et al. (1987)

Source

Items for the original NRS are available in an appendix to Levin et al. (1987). Items for the revised (French) version (NRS-R; Levin et al., 1990) appear in English in an appendix to Vanier, Mazaux, Lambert, Dassa, and Levin (2000), and are reproduced below.

Purpose

The NRS/NRS-R is a clinician rating scale that draws on the results of objective cognitive tests and behavioural observations. It was one of the first rating scales to be developed for clinicians to document neurobehavioural consequences of traumatic brain injury (TBI), and was designed to sample the diversity of neurobehavioural sequelae occurring in all grades of severity. The reliability of the NRS has been examined in patients with dementia (Sultzer, Berisford, & Gunay, 1995) and used with patients with Alzheimer's disease (Harwood, Sultzer, Feil, Monserratt, Freedman, & Mandelkern, 2005), Parkinson's disease (Mathias, 2003), and focal cerebral lesions including arteriovenus malformations, infarction and tumour (Ettlin, Kischka, Beckson, Gaggiotti, Rauchfleisch, & Benson, 2000).

Item description

The NRS-R comprises 29 scales sampling commonly experienced neurobehavioural sequelae of TBI, covering eight domains: Attention, Orientation, Memory, Awareness, Language, Behaviour regulation, Post-concussion symptomatology and Emotional state. The short cognitive tests include the Galveston Orientation and Amnesia Test (see Chapter 2), serial sevens, explanation of proverbs, planning and mental flexibility tasks, and delayed recall of three objects presented at the beginning of the interview.

Scale development

Development of the NRS had its origins in an initial outcome study reported by Levin and Grossman (1978), in which they used the Brief Psychiatric Rating Scale (BPRS). Levin et al. (1987) retained 14 of the 16 BPRS items, and added other items that were more specific to the types of sequelae experienced by people with TBI. The NRS was standardized with 101 patients with TBI (42% mild, 12% moderate, 47% severe) who had been admitted to the neurosurgery service at the University of Texas Medical Branch, Galveston, USA, as well as two rehabilitation units in Houston and Galveston. A principal components analysis identified four factors, but there was not a lot of item correspondence between this factor structure and those subsequently reported by Vanier et al. (2000) and McCauley et al. (2001). Inter-rater reliability used a method whereby raters "first discussed their observations to verify they recorded the same data before independently assigning NRS ratings" (Levin et al., 1987, p. 185). This method yielded good reliability ($r = .88–.90$ between pairs of raters) in that study. Other investigators (Corrigan, Dickerson, Fisher, & Meyer, 1990; Vanier et al., 2000) did not find such high coefficients, however, and this provided an impetus for revision of the scale. The NRS-R has slight modification of item content, the main change being in scoring procedures.

Administration procedures, response format and scoring

Completion of the NRS-R uses a brief structured interview and cognitive tests (see above), along with clinical observations made during the course of the interview. Approximately one-third of the items are based solely on examiner observation (McCauley et al., 2001). Variable administration times have been reported: Vanier et al. (2000) advise that for patients who are "well enough to undergo the full extent of the evaluation, the interview and brief cognitive tests comprising the NRS/NRS-R can be completed within an hour" (p. 797); McCauley et al. report that administration time is typically 15 to 20 minutes. Corrigan et al. (1990) used an alternative administration procedure by having clinicians make ratings of their observations of the patient's behaviour during the preceding week. Training is required for reliable completion of the NRS-R. In their inter-rater reliability study, Vanier et al. used three training sessions for their raters who were experienced clinicians, which included videotape demonstrations of administration procedures, along with study of scoring procedures from a prepared manual and discussion. Additionally, the raters conducted practice administrations of the NRS-R with TBI patients.

In the revised version, Vanier et al. (2000) classified responses to the 29 scales on a 4-point scale as follows: 1 (absent), 2 (mild), 3 (moderate), 4 (severe), with higher scores indicating poorer levels of functioning. Operational definitions are provided for each level "based on the impact of the deficit on social skills and on occupational outcome" (p. 798). Specific information about how scores are used is not provided, but some authors sum scores and use a total score, as well as scores for individual factors (e.g., McCauley et al., 2001). Using the five factors, Vanier et al. calculated a mean score of the items comprising each factor. This procedure has the advantage of anchoring the score to the original rating scale, which facilitates interpretation of scores, and additionally allows comparison among the factors that contain variable numbers of items.

Box 10.12

Validity:	Criterion: *Concurrent:* at 6 months: Total score with GOS: $r = .72$ – with DRS: $r = .74$ – with neuropsychological test scores: range (absolute scores): $r = .46–.61$
	Construct: *Internal consistency:* Cronbach alpha on factor scores: Executive/cognitive .88, Positive symptoms .75, Negative symptoms .62, Mood/affect .72, Oral/motor .75
	Factor structure: 5 factors: Executive/cognitive (8 items), Positive symptoms (7 items), Negative symptoms (4 items), Mood/affect (5 items), Oral/motor (4 items)
	Vanier et al.: 5 factors: Intentional behaviour (8 items), Emotional state (3 items), Survival oriented behaviour/emotional state (8 items), Arousal state (4 items), Language (3 items)
	Convergent/divergent: higher correlation with similar constructs (Executive/cognition factor with neuropsychological test scores: range: $r = .51–.70$); lower correlations with dissimilar constructs (Positive symptoms factor with neuropsychological test scores: none statistically significant (coefficients not reported))
	Discriminant: GOS subgroups $F = 116.5$ ($p < .001$), with differences between each of three subgroups (only graphed data were provided)
Reliability:	Inter-rater: Vanier et al.: using 3 raters, median: $k = 0.40$ (range $k = 0.22–.77$) – raters 1 vs: $k \geq .6$ for 3/17 scales with sufficient variance to calculate kappa, $k < .4$ for 11/17 scales – raters 2 vs: $k \geq .6$ for 2/16 scales, $k < .4$ for 10/16 scales – raters 1 vs: $k \geq .6$ for 3/16, $k < .4$ for 3/16 scales
	Test–retest: No information available
Responsiveness:	For 105 patients who did not improve on GOS, significant improvement on 2/5 NRS-R factors and total score: 3 months $M = 43.33$ ($SD = 10.93$) vs 6 months $M = 42.06$ ($SD = 9.22$), $t = -1.86$, $p = .05$ ($\sim d = .12$)
	Levin et al. (1987) on NRS: significant improvement on 2/4 factors between initial hospitalization and 6 month follow-up: – original Factor 1 (Cognition/energy) Baseline $M = 14.8$ ($SD = 5.5$) vs Follow-up $M = 11.6$ ($SD = 3.8$); $F = 16.5$, $p < .007$, $d = .69$ – original Factor II (Metacognition) Baseline $M = 9.9$ ($SD = 2.7$) vs Follow-up $M = 8.4$ ($SD = 2.3$); $F = 15.7$, $p < .008$, $d = .56$

Psychometric properties

Two main psychometric studies have been reported on NRS-R (McCauley et al., 2001; Vanier et al., 2000), both reporting a similar pattern of results. The sample in the McCauley et al. study comprised 210 people (age $M = 29.5$ years, $SD = 11.0$) with severe TBI who were recruited from multiple participating centres in the national acute brain injury study in the USA and examined at 3 and 6 months post-trauma. They were also administered the Glasgow Outcome Scale (GOS) and Disability Rating Scale (DRS), and at 6 months post-trauma were administered a selection of neuropsychological tests sampling verbal and visual memory, flexibility, processing speed, manual dexterity and verbal fluency. The factor structure was very similar to that identified by Vanier et al. (2000). Five factors were extracted, which were reported to account for 93% of the variance: Executive/cognitive, Positive symptoms, Negative symptoms, Mood/affect, Oral/motor. Three items were complex and had significant loadings on two factors. A "stringent" test of responsiveness was reported for a subgroup of 105 patients at 3 and 6 months post-trauma who did *not* change GOS subgroups between 3 and 6 months. Effect sizes were small, however, and descriptive data were not reported for the larger series. The original study of Levin et al. (1987) reported responsiveness data in 20 patients evaluated during acute hospitalization and 1 month later, with a medium effect size. The results of the McCauley et al. study on the NRS-R, unless otherwise stated, are shown in Box 10.12.

Comment

The NRS and its revision (NRS-R) has set itself an ambitious goal – that, in the space of a brief interview, the clinician will be able to reliably and validly assess the range and extent of cognitive, behavioural, affective and neuropsychiatric symptomatology in people with TBI. Refinement and testing in independent samples have resulted in a scale with strong evidence of concurrent and construct validity, as well as responsiveness, with medium effect sizes. The NRS-R is not, however, a simple rating scale and its administration requires training and experience. Although the authors have gone to considerable lengths to improve inter-rater reliability and administrator burden, the results from Vanier et al. suggest that inter-rater reliability of many of the scales was poor ($k < .4$) and temporal stability is unknown. The previous method of Levin et al. (1987), whereby raters conferred about their observations prior to making their ratings, resulted in good inter-rater reliability ($r = .88$–$.90$), and it may be that consensus ratings provide a more reliable method of using the NRS-R.

Key references

Corrigan, J., D., Dickerson, J., Fisher, E., & Meyer, P. (1990). The Neurobehavioural Rating Scale: Replication in an acute, inpatient rehabilitation setting. *Brain Injury*, *4*(3), 215–222.

Ettlin, T. M., Kischka, U., Beckson, M., Gaggiotti, M., Rauchfleisch, U., & Benson, D. F. (2000). The Frontal Lobe Score: Part 1: Construction of a mental status of frontal systems. *Clinical Rehabilitation*, *14*(3), 260–271.

Harwood, D. G., Sultzer, D. L., Feil, D., Monserratt, L., Freedman, E., & Mandelkern, M. A. (2005). Frontal lobe hypometabolism and impaired insight in Alzheimer disease. *American Journal of Geriatric Psychiatry*, *13*(11), 934–941.

Levin, H. S., & Grossman, R. G. (1978). Behavioral sequelae of closed head injury. *Archives of Neurology*, *35*, 720–727.

Levin, H. S., High, W. M., Goethe, K. E., Sisson, R. A., Overall, J. E., Rhoades, H. M., et al. (1987). The Neurobehavioural Rating Scale: Assessment of the behavioural sequelae of head injury by the clinician. *Journal of Neurology, Neurosurgery, and Psychiatry*, *50*(2), 183–193.

Levin, H. S., Mazaux, J.-M., Vanier, M., Dartigues, J. F., Giroire, J. M., Daverat, P., et al. (1990). Evaluation des troubles neurophysiologiques et comportementaux des traumatisés cràniens par le clinicien: Proposition d'une èchelle neurocomportementale et premiers résultats de sa version française. *Annales de Réadaptation et de Médecine Physique*, *33*, 35–40.

Mathias, J. L. (2003). Neurobehavioral functioning of persons with Parkinson's disease. *Applied Neuropsychology*, *10*(2), 57–68.

McCauley, S. R., Levin, H. S., Vanier, M., Mazaux, J.-M., Boake, C., Goldfader, P. R., et al. (2001). The Neurobehavioural Rating Scale-Revised: Sensitivity and validity in closed head injury assessment. *Journal of Neurology, Neurosurgery, and Psychiatry*, *71*(5), 643–651.

Sultzer, D. L., Berisford, M. A., & Gunay, I. (1995). The Neurobehavioral Rating Scale: Reliability in patients with dementia. *Journal of Psychiatric Research*, *29*(3), 185–191.

Vanier, M., Mazaux, J.-M., Lambert, J., Dassa, C., & Levin, H. S. (2000). Assessment of neuropsychologic impairments after head injury: Interrater reliability and factorial and criterion validity of the Neurobehavioral Rating Scale – Revised. *Archives of Physical Medicine and Rehabilitation*, *81*(6), 796–806.

Neurobehavioral Rating Scale – Revised
Levin et al. (1990)

Name:	**Administered by:**	**Date:**

Response key:
1 = Absent
2 = Mild
3 = Moderate
4 = Severe

	RESPONSE
1. Reduced alertness	______
2. Hyperactivity and agitation	______
3. Disorientation	______
4. Attentional difficulties	______
5. Difficulties in articulation	______
6. Difficulties in oral expression	______
7. Difficulties in oral comprehension	______
8. Memory difficulties	______
9. Motor slowing	______
10. Exaggerated somatic concern	______
11. Self-appraisal difficulties	______
12. Hallucinations	______
13. Unusual thought content	______
14. Anxiety	______
15. Depressive mood	______
16. Guilt	______
17. Lability of mood	______
18. Blunted affect	______
19. Irritability	______
20. Disinhibition	______
21. Excitement	______
22. Hostility	______
23. Suspiciousness	______
24. Emotional withdrawal	______
25. Conceptual disorganization	______
26. Difficulty in mental flexibility	______
27. Difficulty in planning	______
28. Decreased initiative or motivation	______
29. Mental fatigability	______

Acknowledgement: From Vanier, M. et al. (2000). Assessment of neuropsychologic impairments after head injury: Interrater reliability and factorial and criterion validity of the Neurobehavioral Rating Scale – Revised. *Archives of Physical Medicine and Rehabilitation*, *81*(6), 796–806, Appendix 1, p. 805, reprinted with permission of American Congress of Rehabilitation Medicine and the American Academy of Physical Medicine and Rehabilitation and Elsevier.

Rivermead Post-Concussion Symptoms Questionnaire (RPQ)

King, Crawford, Wenden, Moss, and Wade (1995)

Source

Items for the RPQ are available in an appendix to King et al. (1995) and are reproduced below.

Purpose

The RPQ is a self-rating scale, designed to measure the severity of post-concussive symptomatology in people with traumatic brain injury (TBI).

Item description

The 16-item RPQ includes the physical symptoms (headaches, dizziness, nausea/vomiting, sleep disturbance, noise sensitivity, light sensitivity, blurred vision, double vision), cognitive symptoms (forgetfulness, poor concentration, slowed thinking), and behavioural symptoms (fatigue, irritability, tearfulness/depression, impatience, restlessness) characteristic of the post-concussion syndrome.

Scale development

Limited information is available regarding item development for the RPQ. King et al. (1995) cite the work of Mittenberg, DiGiulio, Perrin, and Bass (1992) regarding the "remarkably consistent" cluster of symptoms that commonly occur after milder degrees of TBI. Item content of the RPQ consisted of "the most commonly reported [symptoms] in the literature" (p. 588), and classified by the World Health Organization as the post-concussion syndrome. King and colleagues were critical of the dichotomous checklist approach to documenting the presence of post-concussive symptomatology because it failed to assess the impact of the symptoms on psychosocial functioning, and for this reason they opted to measure severity of symptomatology.

Administration procedures, response format and scoring

The RPQ is designed for self-completion, which is quick and easy.

Responses are made from the perspective of symptoms experienced in the preceding 24 hours. Ratings are made on a 5-point scale: 0 (not experienced at all), 1 (no more of a problem), 2 (a mild problem), 3 (a moderate problem), 4 (a severe problem). A total score is calculated using all scores except score 1 (which corresponds to resolution of a previous symptom). The total score ranges from 0 to 64, with higher scores indicating more severe symptomatology. Some authors (e.g., Ingebrigsten, Waterloo, Marup-Jensen, Attner, & Romner, 1998) use the RPQ to diagnose the post-concussion syndrome when three or more symptoms are present.

Normative data are available from Chan (2001) who administered the RPQ to 85 community-dwelling people (age $M = 33.9$ years, $SD = 10.4$) without TBI or neurological/psychiatric history who were participating in another study. The RPQ total score was $M = 9.45$ ($SD = 8.08$, median = 8, range 0–31), and presence of symptoms ranged from 65.9% (slower thinking) to 2.4% (sensitivity to noise). Only 5 out of 16 symptoms were experienced by less than 33% of this normal sample (tearfulness/depression 31.8%, dizziness 31.8%, double vision 13%, nausea/vomiting 13%, noise sensitivity 2.4%).

Psychometric properties

King et al. (1995) examined administration mode and temporal stability of the RPQ in two samples. Sample 1 comprised a consecutive series of 41 consenting people registered with the Head Injury Service in Oxford, UK. Median duration of post-traumatic amnesia (PTA) was 1 hour. At 7 days post-trauma they received the RPQ and were requested to complete it and return it by post. Approximately 24 hours later they were visited by a researcher and completed another RPQ. In Sample 2, 46 consenting people who were consecutive registrants to the same head injury service were interviewed with the RPQ at 6 months post-trauma. They were then reinterviewed by a second interviewer approximately 9 days later (range 3–34), with the two researchers alternating the order of interviews. The authors reported this procedure as an examination of inter-rater reliability, but given the 9-day time interval it is more indicative of temporal stability. In their cross-validation study, King, Crawford, Wenden, Caldwell, and Wade (1999) interviewed 57 people with mild TBI (PTA duration <24 hours) at 7 to 10 days post-trauma with the RPQ and other measures, including the Impact of Events Scale (IES) and Hospital Anxiety and Depression Scale (HADS). The RPQ was readministered at 6 months post-injury.

Construct validity, using Rasch analysis, was examined by Eyres, Carey, Gilworth, Neumann, and Tennant (2005) on the data from 309 of 1689 consecutive patients referred for skull X-ray following a TBI 3 to 6 months previously. The RPQ was readministered to a subset of the sample ($n = 93$) 2 weeks later. Initial Rasch analysis indicated that three items (headaches, dizziness and nausea) misfitted the model, and when they were removed, the remaining 13 items were a good fit (item fit $M = -0.28$, $SD = 1.40$, $\chi^2 = 83.73$, $p = .058$; item separation .95). When analysed separately, the three deleted items also showed good fit to the model (item fit $M = -0.13$, $SD = 1.96$, $\chi^2 = 19.96$, $p = .068$; item separation .81). The authors thus recommended that two scores should be derived for the RPQ (RPQ-13 and RPQ-3). Data on responsiveness may be available from a clinical trial (Wade, King, Wenden, Crawford, & Caldwell, 1998) in which 132 patients receiving an early intervention service were compared with 86 receiving standard treatment at 6 months post-trauma. Although significant between-group differences were found at follow-up, baseline data were not reported, thereby limiting interpretation. Results of the above studies are shown in Box 10.13.

Comment

One of the strengths of the RPQ is that it examines severity of symptomatology, thereby avoiding the base rate problems well demonstrated by the data of Chan (2001). In that non-injured sample, more than 33% endorsed presence of symptomatology on 11 out of 16 items in the previous 24 hours. Thus a simple documentation of the *presence* of post-concussive symptoms has poor diagnostic specificity. Using the RPQ with its severity rating, however, Chan demonstrated that the base rate for *severity* of post-concussive symptomatology was, in fact, low ($M = 9.45$, range 0–31). The RPQ is quick and easy to complete and it shows good temporal stability. There is also evidence for concurrent and predictive validity. King et al. (1995) cautioned about measuring the severity of individual symptoms because of their lower coefficients than the total score, yet on the other hand Eyres et al. (2005) argued that the RPQ in its original form is not a unidimensional instrument. They were able to obtain a better fit to a Rasch model by using 13-item and 3-item RPQ subscales and they suggested using a total score on the two separate subscales.

Box 10.13

Validity:	Criterion: *Concurrent:* King et al. (1999): with HADS Anxiety: $r = .45$, HADS Depression: $r = .32$ – with IES Intrusions: $r = .33$, IES Avoidance: $r = .37$
	Predictive: King et al. (1999): RPQ at 7–10 days post-trauma with 6 month scores on RPQ: $r = .37$ – with HADS Anxiety: $r = .61$, HADS Depression: $r = .61$ – IES Intrusions: $r = .33$, IES Avoidance: $r = .50$
	Construct: *Internal consistency*: Eyres et al.: Rasch analysis initially showed poor fit, but use of 2 subscales (RPQ-13 and RPQ-3) achieved unidimensionality (see text)
Reliability:	Inter-rater: No information available
	Test–retest: King et al. (1995): 24-hour: Total score: $r_s = .90$ (range $r_s = .50$–.91; with $r_s > .8$ for 8/15 items)
	– alternating interviewers (9 days apart): Total score: $r_s = .87$ (range $r_s = .47$–1.0; with $r_s > .8$ for 4/15 items – 1 item endorsed by too few people)
	Eyres et al.: 2 week: RPQ-13: $r = .89$ (item range $r = .62$–.85); RPQ-3: $r = .72$ (item range: $r = .59$–.69)
Responsiveness:	No definitive information available

References

Chan, R. C. K. (2001). Base rate of post-concussion symptoms among normal people and its neuropsychological correlates. *Clinical Rehabilitation*, *15*(3), 266–273.

Eyres, S., Carey, A., Gilworth, G., Neumann, V., & Tennant, A. (2005). Construct validity and reliability of the Rivermead Post-Concussion Symptoms Questionnaire. *Clinical Rehabilitation*, *19*(8), 878–887.

Ingebrigsten, T., Waterloo, K., Marup-Jensen, S., Attner, E., & Romner, B. (1998). Quantification of post-concussion symptoms 3 months after minor head injury in 100 consecutive patients. *Journal of Neurology*, *245*(9), 609–612.

King, N. S., Crawford, S., Wenden, F. J., Caldwell, F. E., & Wade, D. T. (1999). Early prediction of persisting post-concussion symptoms following mild and moderate head injuries. *British Journal of Clinical Psychology*, *38*(1), 15–25.

King, N. S., Crawford, S., Wenden, F. J., Moss, N. E. G., & Wade, D. T. (1995). The Rivermead Post Concussion Symptoms Questionnaire: A measure of symptoms commonly experienced after head injury and its reliability. *Journal of Neurology*, *242*(9), 587–592.

Mittenberg, W., DiGiulio, D. V., Perrin, S., & Bass, A. E. (1992). Symptoms following mild head injury: Expectation as aetiology. *Journal of Neurology, Neurosurgery, and Psychiatry*, *55*(3), 200–204.

Wade, D. T., King, N. S., Wenden, F. J., Crawford, S., & Caldwell, F. E. (1998). Routine follow up after head injury: A second randomised controlled trial. *Journal of Neurology, Neurosurgery, and Psychiatry*, *65*(2), 177–183.

Rivermead Post-concussion Symptoms Questionnaire
King, Crawford, Wenden, Moss, and Wade (1995)

Name: **Administered by:** **Date:**

Instructions: After a head injury or accident some people experience symptoms that can cause worry or nuisance. We would like to know if you now suffer any of the symptoms given below. As many of these symptoms occur normally, we would like you to compare yourself now with before the accident. For each item please write in the number closest to your answer.

Response key:
0 = Not experienced at all
1 = No more of a problem
2 = A mild problem
3 = A moderate problem
4 = A severe problem

Compared with before the accident, do you now (i.e., over the last 24 hours) suffer from:

	RESPONSE
1. Headaches	________
2. Feelings of dizziness	________
3. Nausea and/or vomiting	________
4. Noise sensitivity, easily upset by loud noise	________
5. Sleep disturbance	________
6. Fatigue, tiring more easily	________
7. Being irritable, easily angered	________
8. Feeling depressed or tearful	________
9. Feeling frustrated or impatient	________
10. Forgetfulness, poor memory	________
11. Poor concentration	________
12. Taking longer to think	________
13. Blurred vision	________
14. Light sensitivity, easily upset by bright light	________
15. Double vision	________
16. Restlessness	________
17. Are you experiencing any other difficulties?	________
Please specify, and rate as above	________
1 ______________________;	________
2 ______________________	________

Acknowledgement: From King, N. S. et al. (1995). The Rivermead Post Concussion Symptoms Questionnaire: A measure of symptoms commonly experienced after head injury and its reliability. *Journal of Neurology*, *242*(9), 587–592, Appendix 1, p. 591, reproduced by permission of Springer.com.

Satisfaction with Life Scale (SWLS)

Diener, Emmons, Larsen, and Griffin (1985)

Source

Items for the SWLS are described in Diener et al. (1985) and are reproduced below. They also appear on the website of the Center for Outcome Measurement in Brain Injury (http://www.tbims.org/combi/swls/index.html).

Purpose

The SWLS is a self-rating scale that aims to measure "global life satisfaction". It was designed as a generic instrument and has been commonly used with the traumatic brain injury (TBI) group (e.g., Corrigan, Bogner, Mysiw, Clinchot, & Fugate, 2001; Johnston, Goverover, & Dijkers, 2005).

Item description

Five items are used in the SWLS, each focused on providing a rating of life satisfaction as a whole. For example, Item 1: "In most ways my life is close to ideal". Items are intentionally global, rather than specific, which enables an overall judgement.

Scale development

In developing the SWLS, Diener et al. (1985) highlighted two conceptual criteria. First, that evaluation of life satisfaction involved a "cognitive-judgemental process" in which "judgements of satisfaction are dependent upon a comparison of one's circumstances with what is thought to be an appropriate standard" (p. 71). This recognizes that an individual may place different value on a particular construct (e.g., health, energy) than the researcher/clinician/other individuals. It also follows that such a standard is set by the individual and is not externally imposed. Second, that the judgement is holistic or global, rather than a summation of satisfaction with specific components of life. Details regarding the initial developmental phase of the SWLS are described in general terms by Diener et al. (1985). A list of 48 items was generated and factor analysis (on an unspecified sample) yielded three factors: positive affect, negative affect and satisfaction. Only the 10 items from the third factor were retained. A further five items with high semantic similarity were omitted, leaving the final set of five items comprising the scale. This set was examined in a sample of 176 undergraduate university students (details below).

Administration procedures, response format and scoring

The SWLS is a very short scale, which is easily completed within a few minutes.

Ratings are made on a 7-point scale: 1 (strongly disagree), 2 (disagree), 3 (slightly disagree), 4 (neither agree nor disagree), 5 (slightly agree), 6 (agree), 7 (strongly agree). The total score ranges from 5 to 35, with higher scores indicating greater satisfaction. Pavot and Diener (1993) suggest interpretation of various score ranges, which correspond to the following: 5 to 9 is extremely dissatisfied, 10 to 14 dissatisfied, 15 to 19 slightly dissatisfied, 20 is the neutral point in the scale, 21–25 slightly satisfied, 26 to 30 satisfied, 31 to 35 extremely satisfied. They report that most groups fall in the range 23 to 28 (slightly satisfied to satisfied).

Normative and comparative data for various student and non-student samples are reported in Pavot and Diener (1993). Comparative data from people with TBI at 1 year ($n = 170$) and 2 years ($n = 160$) post-trauma are reported in Corrigan et al. (2001): 1 year: $M = 20.32$ ($SD = 8.13$); 2 years: $M = 20.80$ ($SD = 8.42$).

Psychometric properties

An overview of results from early studies on the SWLS is reported by Pavot and Diener (1993). Measurement properties of the SWLS were initially examined in a sample of undergraduate students ($n = 176$) from the University of Illinois, USA (Diener et al., 1985). Temporal stability was examined in a subset ($n = 76$) 2 months later. The SWLS was validated in the above sample as well as an independent sample comprising 163 students, using a range of measures of subjective well-being, and the patterns of correlation coefficients showed close correspondence between samples. A third sample of older people ($n = 53$, age $M = 79$ years) from a range of living situations, including nursing homes, was also examined. Following an hour interview with the participants, interviewers made a global rating of the participants' life satisfaction (LS) on a 7-point scale. Factor analysis with data from the student sample revealed a single factor, accounting for 66% of the variance. Pavot, Diener, Colvin, and Sandvik (1991) subsequently replicated the factor structure in a sample of 39 older people (age $M = 74$ years, range 53 to 92 years). The SWLS has been examined in clinical samples of people with TBI. Reistetter, Spencer, Trujillo, and Abreu (2005) studied 91 people with ($n = 51$) and without ($n = 40$) TBI, administering the client-centred Community Integration Measure (CIM) and Community Integration Questionnaire (CIQ), along with the SWLS. Results from Diener et al. (1985), except where otherwise stated, are shown in Box 10.14.

Box 10.14

Validity:	Criterion: *Concurrent:* Sample 1 (student): range: $r = -.37$ (with Affect Balance Scale – Negative score) to $r = .75$ (with Semantic Differential Scale) – Sample 3 (older people): with interviewer global LS rating: $r = .46$
	Reistetter et al.: with CIM: $r = .52$ – with CIQ: $r = .33$
	Construct: *Internal consistency:* Cronbach coefficient alpha .87
	Factor analysis: a single factor
Reliability:	Inter-rater: Not applicable
	Test–retest: 2 months: $r = .82$
Responsiveness:	No information available

Comment

Alfonso, Allison, Rader, and Gorman (1996) consider that one of the strengths of the SWLS is that it measures the cognitive component of subjective well-being and is not confounded by the affective components. Other advantages include an emphasis on the person's own standards of evaluation and a focus on those domains that the person finds relevant in judging life satisfaction. Yet these advantages are also its disadvantages – using "whatever standard she or he deems to be appropriate . . . means we do not know to what standard the person has compared the conditions of his or her life" (Pavot & Diener, 1993, p. 170). By virtue of its global orientation, the SWLS does not afford a multidimensional analysis, and this may be a drawback for some applications. An interesting perspective on the issue of global versus specific ratings of life satisfaction is furnished by the study of Johnston et al. (2005) who found very low correlation coefficients (median $r = .06$) in their TBI sample between report of satisfaction in global terms versus 49 specific activities. Use of the SWLS with the TBI group has increased considerably since its addition to the USA TBI Model Systems database in 1998, and it would be useful to have more specific psychometric information on its application in neurological populations.

Key references

Alfonso, V. C., Allison, D. B., Rader, D. E., & Gorman, B. S. (1996). The Extended Satisfaction with Life Scale: Development and psychometric properties. *Social Indicators Research*, *38*, 275–301.

Corrigan, J. D., Bogner, J. A., Mysiw, W. J., Clinchot, D., & Fugate, L. (2001). Life satisfaction after traumatic brain injury. *Journal of Head Trauma Rehabilitation*, *16*(6), 543–555.

Diener, E., Emmons, R. A., Larsen, R. J., & Griffin, S. (1985). The Satisfaction with Life Scale. *Journal of Personality Assessment*, *49*(1), 71–75.

Johnston, M. V., Goverover, Y., & Dijkers, M. (2005). Community activities and individuals' satisfaction with them: Quality of life in the first year after traumatic brain injury. *Archives of Physical Medicine and Rehabilitation*, *86*, 735–745.

Pavot, W., & Diener, E. (1993). Review of the Satisfaction with Life Scale. *Psychological Assessment*, *5*(2), 164–172.

Pavot, W., Diener, E., Colvin, C. R., & Sandvik, E. (1991). Further validation of the Satisfaction with Life Scale: Evidence for the cross-method convergence of well-being measures. *Journal of Personality Assessment*, *57*(1), 149–161.

Reistetter, T. A., Spencer, J. C., Trujillo, L., & Abreu, B. C. (2005). Examining the Community Integration Measure (CIM): A replication study with life satisfaction. *NeuroRehabilitation*, *20*, 139–148.

Satisfaction with Life Scale

Diener, Emmons, Larsen, and Griffin (1985)

Name:	**Administered by:**	**Date:**

Instructions: Below are five statements with which you may agree or disagree. Using the 1–7 scale below, indicate your agreement with each item by placing the appropriate number on the line next to that item. Please be open and honest in your responding.

Response key:
1 = Strongly disagree
2 = Disagree
3 = Slightly disagree
4 = Neither agree nor disagree
5 = Slightly agree
6 = Agree
7 = Strongly agree

	RESPONSE
1. In most ways my life is close to ideal	______
2. The conditions of my life are excellent	______
3. I am satisfied with my life	______
4. So far I have got the important things I want in life	______
5. If I could live my life over, I would change almost nothing	______
TOTAL SCORE:	______

Acknowledgement: From Diener, E. et al. (1985). The Satisfaction with Life Scale. *Journal of Personality Assessment*, *49*(1), 71–75, Table 1, p. 72, used by permission of Informa Healthcare.

Short-Form 36 Health Survey (SF-36)

Ware, Kosinski, and Dewey (2000a)

Source

Items for the Medical Outcomes Study 36-item Short-Form Health Survey (SF-36) are available in an appendix to an early report on development of the scale (Ware & Sherbourne, 1992). Detailed information on the SF-36 is available from the original manual (Ware, Kosinski, & Gandek, 2000b) and website (http://www.sf36.org). Version 2 of the SF-36 (SF-36v2) is available in Ware, Kosinski, and Dewey (2000a) and is reproduced below. Also available are 8-item and 12-item versions. Licensing arrangements for use of the SF-36v2 can be made through the following website: http://www.qualitymetric.com.

Purpose

The SF-36 is a self-rating scale, designed to measure the patient's perspective of his or her health. It is a generic scale, with the aim of yielding "a profile of scores that would be useful in understanding population differences in physical and mental health status, the health burden of chronic disease and other medical conditions, and the effects of treatment of general health status" (Ware et al., 2000b, p. 3:10). The SF-36 is very widely used in population studies and many medical conditions. It has also been used, although less commonly, in acquired brain impairment (ABI) groups, including neurological populations such as multiple sclerosis (MS; Nortvedt, Riise, Myhr, & Nyland, 2000; Riazi et al., 2003), Parkinson's disease (PD; Riazi et al., 2003), stroke (Lai, Perera, Duncan, & Bode, 2003) and traumatic brain injury (TBI; Findler, Cantor, Haddad, Gordon, & Ashman, 2001; MacKenzie et al., 2002).

Item description

As the name suggests, the SF-36 contains 36 items. These cover eight health concepts, which are grouped into two components: physical and mental. The Physical component contains 21 items from four scales: Physical functioning (10 items), Role-physical (4 items), Bodily pain (2 items), and General health perceptions (5 items). The Mental component contains 14 items from four scales: Vitality (4 items), Social functioning (2 items), Role-emotional (3 items), and Mental health (5 items). The final item, Reported health transition, provides a comparison with status 1 year previously.

Scale development

The SF-36 was one of the instruments spawned by the Medical Outcomes Study (MOS). Overall, the MOS surveys assessed 40 physical and health concepts, of which the eight concepts considered to be of the greatest importance were formulated into the SF-36 (Ware et al., 2000b). There was an identified need for a brief instrument that would minimize refusal of study participants to complete lengthy survey instruments, yet which would still afford a multidimensional evaluation of health concepts. Developmental phases of the instrument saw 18-item and 20-item versions. These were replaced by the 36-item version (Ware & Sherbourne, 1992) designed to obtain the best "trade-offs between breadth of concepts represented and the depth of measurement for each concept" (Ware et al., 2000b, p. 3:2).

The SF-36 aimed to measure concepts within each component of physical and mental health: (i) behavioural functioning, (ii) perceived well-being, (iii) social and role disability and (iv) personal evaluations of health in general. Item selection drew on previously published instruments that had been reviewed by Ware and his colleagues in the 1970s and 1980s, focusing on those items that measured limitations in physical, social and role functioning. Rationale for selection of each of the items is provided in Ware et al. (2000b). Use of the SF-36 in the UK included "minor modifications to the wording of six items" and changes to scoring procedures of two dichotomous items which were replaced with 5-point rating scales (Jenkinson, Stewart-Brown, Petersen, & Paice, 1999). These changes were adopted by the authors, resulting in version 2 (the "international version"), which Ware et al. (2000a) recommend for use over the "standard version".

Administration procedures, response format and scoring

Ware et al. (2000b) provide specific guidelines and instructions for administrating the SF-36. Importantly, it is requested that the SF-36 be completed prior to any other health data forms or the patient's consultation with a health professional. Administrators can read or repeat questions, but should not interpret or explain questions. Additionally, the scale is to be completed by the patients themselves, and they should not receive help from family members or other people. For SF-36v2, the scale can be completed with reference to functioning in the preceding 4 weeks (standard) or 1 week (acute). Ware and Sherbourne (1992) report that administration time is 5 to 10 minutes.

A variable response format accompanies the items for the SF-36v2: the formats of rating scales include 5-point and 3-point scales. Some items are rated in terms of quality of functioning ("excellent" to "poor"), others in terms of frequency ("all of the time" to "none of the time").

Scoring algorithms are provided in Ware et al. (2000a) for calculating SF-36v2 scores and are necessary to interpret the obtained data against normative data. Computer software is also available for this purpose and a test database is available against which users can compare their results (info@QualityMetric.com). A number of steps is involved in the scoring process, including reverse scoring for specified items, procedures to deal with missing data where this occurs, transforming raw scores to a 0 to 100 scale, and transforming those scores to norm-based *T* scores ($M = 50$, $SD = 10$). Higher scores indicate better perceived health state.

Normative data for SF-36v2 (both 4-week and 1-week) are available for the eight scales based on 1998 general USA population ($n = 6742$), stratified by age and sex. Normative data, also using SF-36v2 for a UK random sample of the population (8889 respondents from 13,800 people contacted), aged 18 to 64 years, are available in Jenkinson et al. (1999), stratified by sex, social class and illness chronicity. Australian data for approximately 18,000 adults participating in a national health survey are available from the Australian Bureau of Statistics (1995).

Psychometric properties

Direct comparison of the measurement characteristics of the SF-36 and SF-36v2 is reported in Ware et al. (2000a). Using a large general USA population study, participants were randomized to receive either the SF-36 standard version ($n = 2031$) or version 2 ($n = 5038$). Version 2 showed better internal consistency and less susceptibility to floor and ceiling effects. Internal consistency was also reported for the UK population study by Jenkinson et al. (1999). The underlying structure of the eight scales was also examined in this sample using principal components analysis. Two components were extracted (Physical and Mental), accounting for 74% of the variance. Brazier et al. (1992), also using the SF-36v2, examined a random sample of approximately 1500 patients attending two general practices in Sheffield, UK. Evidence for convergent and divergent validity was provided by comparison of similar and dissimilar constructs with the Nottingham Health Profile (NHP). They also reported on 2-week temporal stability in a subset of 187 patients.

Some studies have examined the validity of the SF-36 in ABI samples. Findler et al. (2001) reported findings from 597 people, 326 of whom sustained mild ($n = 98$) or moderate to severe ($n = 228$) TBI, the remaining 369 having no injury. Validating instruments were a 67-item symptom checklist (SCL), a health problems list (HPL), and the Beck Depression Inventory II (BDI-II). Analyses were conducted controlling for age, sex and income. Significant differences between the control and the two TBI groups were found on all scales, with the TBI group having lower scores. Within the TBI group, however, the mild injury group had lower scores than the moderate–severe group on seven scales (no differences on the Physical scale). Similarly, MacKenzie et al. (2002) assessed 1197 patients with TBI previously admitted to trauma centres. Injury severity ranged from mild ($n = 977$) to severe ($n = 155$) and results were compared with population norms. Although six of the scales showed significant differences from the population norms (the exceptions being Mental health and Vitality), subgroup comparisons by injury severity revealed no differences on any scale. Other data on discriminant validity and responsiveness in a TBI population are available from Lippert-Grüner, Maegele, Haverkamp, Klug, and Wedekind (2007) who analysed SF-36 data taken at 6 and 12 months post-trauma from 49 people with severe injury, 28 of whom had polytrauma. No differences were found between those with and without polytrauma. Significant improvement in scores occurred on seven scales, but most effect sizes were small. Results from Ware et al. (2000a) for the SF-36v2, except where otherwise stated, are shown in Box 10.15.

Comment

The SF-36 has a number of areas of strength. It has been developed, trialled and refined over many years, and has good psychometric properties in general populations, along with large normative databases. It is widely used, and its generic nature has thereby yielded information enabling comparison among different clinical conditions and geographical areas. There are,

Box 10.15

Validity:	Criterion: *Concurrent:* Brazier et al.: SF-36 with similar constructs from NHP: – Physical with NHP Physical morbidity: $r = -.52$ – Social with NHP Social isolation: $r = -.41$ – Pain with NHP Pain: $r = -.55$ – Mental with NHP Emotional reactions: $r = -.67$ – Vitality with NHP Energy: $r = -.68$ Findler et al.: In mild/moderate–severe TBI respectively, SF-36 with similar constructs: – Physical with SCL Physical: $r = -.63$ / $-.41$ – Mental with SCL Cognitive: $r = -.61$ / $-.37$ – Emotional with SCL Affective: $r = -.44$ / $-.53$ – General health with HPL: $r = -.75$ / $-.54$ – Emotional with BDI-II: $r = -.61$ / $-.60$ Construct: *Internal consistency*: Cronbach alpha .83–.95 Jenkinson et al. (1999): Cronbach alpha .80–.95 Findler et al.: Cronbach alpha for mild TBI: .83–.91 – for moderate–severe TBI: .79–.92 *Factor structure:* 2 components: Physical (4 scales) and Mental (4 scales) *Convergent/divergent:* Brazier et al.: higher correlation with similar constructs (SF-36-Physical with NHP-Physical morbidity: $r = -.52$; SF-36-Mental with NHP-Emotional reactions: $r = -.68$); lower correlation with dissimilar constructs (SF-36-Physical with NHP-Emotional reactions: $r = -.18$; SF-36-Mental with NHP-Physical morbidity: $r = -.19$)
Reliability:	Inter-rater: Not applicable Test–retest: Brazier et al.: 2 weeks: $r = .60$–$.81$ (5 dimensions $r < .8$)
Responsiveness:	Lippert-Grüner et al.: significant improvement between 6 and 12 months post-trauma on 7 scales, but effect sizes were $d < .5$: from Physical: Time 1 $M = 69$ ($SD = 31.2$) vs Time 2 $M = 77$ ($SD = 28.6$), $d = -.26$, to Pain: Time 1 $M = 61$ ($SD = 28.71$) vs Time 2 $M = 74$ ($SD = 26.7$), $d = -.45$

however, some limitations that have a bearing on content and construct validity. As Ware and Sherbourne (1992) recognized, it does not cover a number of important health concepts, including cognitive, sexual and family functioning, health distress and sleep disorder; the first of these having particular relevance for people with ABI. Moreover, Dijkers (2003) notes that, like other health-related quality of life instruments, the SF-36 does not consider the broader (non-health) domains that contribute to and may be especially salient for an individual's quality of life (e.g., finances, environment). In terms of its application to people with ABI, empirical data accumulated to date raise some questions. In some ABI conditions, such as PD, it failed to measure constructs (cognition, communication and perceived social stigma) identified by the condition-specific Parkinson's Disease Questionnaire (Jenkinson, Peto, Fitzpatrick, Greenhall, & Hyman, 1995), and for the TBI group it lacked discriminative ability within subgroups in terms of failure to distinguish between those with and without polytrauma (Lippert-Grüner et al., 2007) or various levels of injury severity (MacKenzie et al., 2002). Nortvedt et al. (2000) and Riazi et al. (2003) both concluded that although their MS groups performed more poorly than the general population on the SF-36, it appeared to underestimate the mental health problems experienced by people with MS. The counterintuitive findings of Findler et al. (2001) that people with mild TBI had poorer SF-36 scores than the more severely injured led to their conclusion that the SF-36 may be less sensitive in people with moderate to severe TBI.

Key references

Australian Bureau of Statistics. (1995). *National Health Survey. SF-36 population norms*. Canberra: Australian Bureau of Statistics.

Brazier, J. E., Harper, R., Jones, N. M. B., O'Cathain, A., Thomas, K. J., Usherwood, T., et al. (1992). Validating the SF-36 health survey questionnaire: New outcome measure for primary care. *British Medical Journal, 305*(6846), 160–164.

Dijkers, M. P. (2003). Individualization in quality of life measurement: Instruments and approaches. *Archives of*

Physical Medicine and Rehabilitation, *84*(Suppl. 2), S3–S14.

Findler, M., Cantor, J., Haddad, L., Gordon, W., & Ashman, T. (2001). The reliability and validity of the SF-36 health survey questionnaire for use with individuals with traumatic brain injury. *Brain Injury*, *15*(8), 715–723.

Jenkinson, C., Peto, V., Fitzpatrick, R., Greenhall, R., & Hyman, N. (1995). Self-reported functioning and well-being in patients with Parkinson's disease: Comparison of the short-form health survey (SF-36) and the Parkinson's Disease Questionnaire (PDQ-39). *Age and Ageing*, *24*(6), 505–510.

Jenkinson, C., Stewart-Brown, S., Petersen, S., & Paice, C. (1999). Assessment of the SF-36 version 2 in the United Kingdom. *Journal of Epidemiology and Community Health*, *53*(1), 46–50.

Lai, S.-M., Perera, S., Duncan, P. W., & Bode, R. (2003). Physical and social functioning after stroke. Comparison of the Stroke Impact Scale and the Short Form-36. *Stroke*, *34*, 488–493.

Lippert-Grüner, M., Maegele, M., Haverkamp, H., Klug, N., & Wedekind, C. (2007). Health-related quality of life during the first year after severe brain trauma with and without polytrauma. *Brain Injury*, *21*(5), 451–455.

MacKenzie, E. J., McCarthy, M. L., Ditunno, J. F., Forrester-Staz, C., Gruen, G. S., Marion, D. W., et al. (2002). Using the SF-36 for characterizing outcome after multiple trauma involving head injury. *Journal of Trauma*, *52*(3), 527–534.

Nortvedt, M. W., Riise, T., Myhr, K.-M., & Nyland, H. I. (2000). Performance of the SF-36, SF-12, and RAND-36 summary scales in a multiple sclerosis population. *Medical Care*, *38*(10), 1022–1028.

Riazi, A., Hobart, J. C., Lamping, D. L., Fitzpatrick, R., Freeman, J. A., Jenkinson, C., et al. (2003). Using the SF-36 measure to compare the health impact of multiple sclerosis and Parkinson's disease with normal population health profiles. *Journal of Neurology, Neurosurgery, and Psychiatry*, *74*, 710–714.

Ware, J. E., Kosinski, M., & Dewey, J. E. (2000a). *How to score Version 2 of the SF-36 ® Health Survey*. Lincoln, RI: QualityMetric Incorporated.

Ware, J. E., Kosinski, M., & Gandek, B. (2000b). *SF-36 ® Health Survey: Manual and interpretation guide*. Lincoln, RI: QualityMetric Incorporated.

Ware, J. E., & Sherbourne, C. D. (1992). The MOS 36-item Short Form Health Survey (SF-36). I. Conceptual framework and item selection. *Medical Care*, *30*(6), 473–483.

Items from the MOS Health Survey Short-Form 36

Ware, Kosinski, and Dewey (2000)

A. Standard Self Report for Your Health and Well Being (FOUR WEEK RECALL)

Your Health in General

Please answer every question. Some questions may look like others, but each one is different. Please take the time to read and answer each question carefully, and mark an ☒ in the box that best describes your answer. *Thank you for completing this survey!*

1. In general, would you say your health is:

2. Compared to one year ago, how would you rate your health in general now?

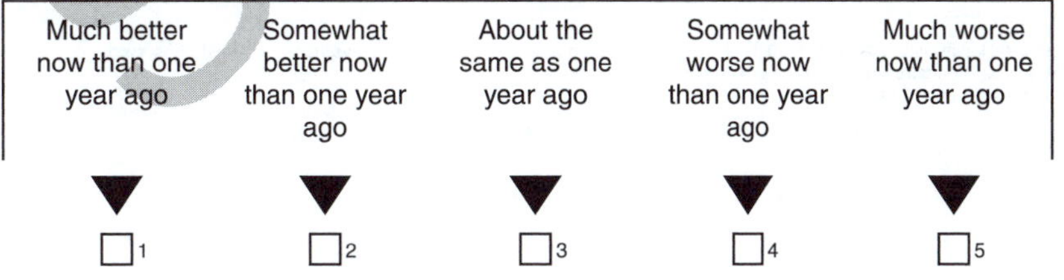

3. The following questions are about activities you might do during a typical day. Does your health now limit you in these activities? If so, how much?

	Yes, limited a lot	Yes, limited a little	No, not limited at all
a Vigorous Activities, such as running, lifting heavy objects, participating in strenuous sports	☐ 1	☐ 2	☐ 3
b Moderate Activities, such as moving a table, pushing a vacuum cleaner, bowling, or playing golf	☐ 1	☐ 2	☐ 3
c Lifting or carrying groceries	☐ 1	☐ 2	☐ 3
d Climbing several flights of stairs	☐ 1	☐ 2	☐ 3
e Climbing one flight of stairs	☐ 1	☐ 2	☐ 3
f Bending, kneeling, or stooping	☐ 1	☐ 2	☐ 3
g Walking more than a mile	☐ 1	☐ 2	☐ 3
h Walking several hundred yards	☐ 1	☐ 2	☐ 3
i Walking one hundred yards	☐ 1	☐ 2	☐ 3
j Bathing or dressing yourself	☐ 1	☐ 2	☐ 3

4. During the <u>past 4 weeks</u>, how much of the time have you had any of the following problems with your work or other regular daily activities <u>as a result of your physical health</u>?

	All of the time	Most of the time	Some of the time	A little of the time	None of the time
a Cut down on the amount of time you spent on work or other activities	☐ 1	☐ 2	☐ 3	☐ 4	☐ 5
b Accomplished less than you would like	☐ 1	☐ 2	☐ 3	☐ 4	☐ 5
c Were limited in the kind of work or other activities	☐ 1	☐ 2	☐ 3	☐ 4	☐ 5
d Had difficulty performing the work or other activities (for example, it took extra effort)	☐ 1	☐ 2	☐ 3	☐ 4	☐ 5

5. During the <u>past 4 weeks</u>, how much of the time have you had any of the following problems with your work or other regular daily activities <u>as a result of any emotional problems</u> (such as feeling depressed or anxious)?

	All of the time	Most of the time	Some of the time	A little of the time	None of the time
a Cut down on the amount of time you spent on work or other activities	☐ 1	☐ 2	☐ 3	☐ 4	☐ 5
b Accomplished less than you would like	☐ 1	☐ 2	☐ 3	☐ 4	☐ 5
c Did work or other activities less carefully than usual	☐ 1	☐ 2	☐ 3	☐ 4	☐ 5

6. 6) During the past 4 weeks, to what extent has your physical health or emotional problems interfered with your normal social activities with family, friends, neighbors, or groups?

Not at all	Slightly	Moderately	Quite a bit	Extremely
☐ 1	☐ 2	☐ 3	☐ 4	☐ 5

7. How much bodily pain have you had during the past 4 weeks?

None	Very mild	Mild	Moderate	Severe	Very Severe
☐ 1	☐ 2	☐ 3	☐ 4	☐ 5	☐ 6

8. During the past 4 weeks, how much did pain interfere with your normal work (including both work outside the home and housework)?

Not at all	A little bit	Moderately	Quite a bit	Extremely
☐ 1	☐ 2	☐ 3	☐ 4	☐ 5

9. These questions are about how you feel and how things have been with you during the past 4 weeks. For each question, please give the one answer that comes closest to the way you have been feeling. How much of the time during the past 4 weeks...

	All of the time	Most of the time	Some of the time	A little of the time	None of the time
a Did you feel full of life?	☐1	☐2	☐3	☐4	☐5
b Have you been very nervous?	☐1	☐2	☐3	☐4	☐5
c Have you felt so down in the dumps that nothing could cheer you up?	☐1	☐2	☐3	☐4	☐5
d Have you felt calm and peaceful?	☐1	☐2	☐3	☐4	☐5
e Did you have a lot of energy?	☐1	☐2	☐3	☐4	☐5
f Have you felt downhearted and depressed?	☐1	☐2	☐3	☐4	☐5
g Did you feel worn out?	☐1	☐2	☐3	☐4	☐5
h Have you been happy?	☐1	☐2	☐3	☐4	☐5
i Did you feel tired?	☐1	☐2	☐3	☐4	☐5

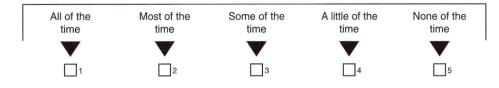

10. During the past 4 weeks, how much of the time has your physical health or emotional problems interfered with your social activities (like visiting friends, relatives, etc.)?

All of the time	Most of the time	Some of the time	A little of the time	None of the time
☐1	☐2	☐3	☐4	☐5

11. How TRUE or FALSE is each of the following statements for you?

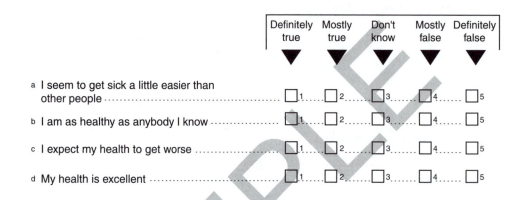

	Definitely true	Mostly true	Don't know	Mostly false	Definitely false
a I seem to get sick a little easier than other people	☐1	☐2	☐3	☐4	☐5
b I am as healthy as anybody I know	☐1	☐2	☐3	☐4	☐5
c I expect my health to get worse	☐1	☐2	☐3	☐4	☐5
d My health is excellent	☐1	☐2	☐3	☐4	☐5

THANK YOU FOR COMPLETING THESE QUESTIONS!

Acknowledgement: From Ware, J. E. et al. (2000). *How to score Version 2 of the SF-36 Health Survey*. Lincoln, RI: QualityMetric Incorporated, Appendix A, pp. 105–110, reproduced by permission of QualityMetric. Copyright © 2000, 2002 by the Medical Outcomes Trust and QualityMetric Incorporated. SF-36 is a registered trademark of the Medical Outcomes Trust, used under licence to QualityMetric Incorporated.

QM licenses the SF-36 and other health surveys to a wide range of users, and any clinician or researcher who wishes to administer the Survey needs to contact QM at http://www.qualitymetric.com/contact/.

World Health Organization Quality of Life (WHOQOL)

World Health Organization (1998)

Source

The WHOQOL-100, and the short form, WHOQOL-BREF, are available from the WHO website (http://www.who.int/mental_health/evidence/who_qol_user_manual_98.pdf). The standard 100-item version is reproduced below.

Purpose

The WHOQOL-100 is a self-rating scale designed to measure quality of life. It is a generic instrument that aims to be applicable cross-culturally, and a large number of reports have been published from different countries and cultures. The WHOQOL-100 has been used frequently in non-clinical samples, including older people. In clinical samples, it has been used commonly in mental and other health conditions, but has had more limited application in the acquired brain impairment population. Meldolesi et al. (2006) report on its use in temporal lobe epilepsy and Chiu et al. (2006) used the WHOQOL-BREF in traumatic brain injury.

Item description

The WHOQOL-100 contains 100 items that are classified into six domains, each domain containing a variable number of "facets" or subscales: Physical (3 facets: pain and discomfort; energy and fatigue; sleep and rest), Psychological (5 facets: positive feelings; negative feelings; thinking, learning, memory and concentration; self-esteem; body image), Independence (4 facets: mobility; activities of daily living; medication, working capacity), Social (3 facets: personal relations; practical and social support; sexual activity), Environment (8 facets: physical safety and security; home; financial resources; access to health and social care; information and skills; recreation and leisure; physical environment; transport), and Spiritual (1 facet: spirituality, religion and personal beliefs). Each of these facets contains four items, totalling 96 items. An additional 4 items provide a global perspective on quality of life and general health.

The WHOQOL-BREF (The WHOQOL Group, 1998b) is a shortened 26-item version of the standard WHOQOL, which uses 24 items for scoring purposes. The 24 items correspond to the facets of the standard version, which are grouped into four domains (Physical, 7 items, containing the 7 facets from the Physical and Independence domains), Psychological (6 items, containing the 6 facets from the Psychological and Spiritual domains), Social (3 items), and Environment (8 items).

Scale development

The WHOQOL is a carefully developed instrument and information on the detailed developmental process is available from a number of sources (The WHOQOL Group, 1994a, 1994b, 1995, 1998a). In order to achieve an instrument that would be applicable cross-culturally, it was developed simultaneously in different cultures and languages, rather than merely using translations once a base instrument had been developed. The WHO initiated the project to develop the WHOQOL. As a first step, "concept clarification" involved defining quality of life by international expert review:

> individuals' perception of their position in life in the context of the culture and value system in which they live and in relation to their goals, expectations, standards and concerns. It is a broad ranging concept affected in a complex way by the persons' physical health, psychological state, level of independence, social relationships and their relationship to salient features of their environment.
>
> (The WHOQOL Group, 1995, p. 1405)

The components of this definition were analysed and then operationalized. Separate focus groups were held comprising healthy people, people with health conditions, and health personnel. The focus groups generated suggestions for aspects of quality of life that were subjected to scrutiny and refined in a series of procedures, ultimately resulting in a set of 29 facets. Eleven field centres, including expert and lay people, participated in question-writing panels. This resulted in some 1800 items, which were reduced to approximately 1000 after semantically similar items were excluded.

These items were then rank-ordered for each of the facets by the chief field investigators in terms of their relevance to quality of life in their culture. A set of 236 items in six domains and covering 29 facets was then selected for piloting in 15 field centres. Each centre, working in its own national language, provided a sample of approximately 300 people, 250 of whom had a health condition, resulting in a total sample size of 4802. Results of frequency analyses and internal reliability of the items, along with a multi-trait analysis, identified five facets as problematic. These were excluded, resulting in 24 specific factors and four general items. Four items were selected from each facet, this being the minimum number recommended for reliability analysis. This resulted in the 100-item scale, which was subjected to psychometric examination (see below).

Administration procedures, response format and scoring

The WHOQOL-100 is designed to be self-administered. It is, however, acceptable for items to be read out by an interviewer if the person is unable to do this for themselves. Administration time for the 100-item version was 10 to 20 minutes for a small sample of university employees (Bonomi, Patrick, Bushnell, & Martin, 2000).

Items are answered from the perspective of the preceding 2 weeks. Responses use a 5-point scale which varies in accordance with item content: some items are rated in terms of extent of difficulty (1 = not at all, 2 = a little, 3 = a moderate amount, 4 = very much, 5 = an extreme amount), others in terms of satisfaction (1 = very dissatisfied, 2 = dissatisfied, 3 = neither satisfied not dissatisfied, 4 = satisfied, 5 = very satisfied), frequency (1 = never, 2 = seldom, 3 = quite often, 4 = very often, 5 = always) and so forth. A number of items require reverse scoring and SPSS syntax is available from the website for scoring purposes. Scores are summed within each of the 24 facets, with the total score for each facet ranging from 4 to 20. These scores are then transformed to a 0 to 100 scale, with higher scores indicating better quality of life. For the WHOQOL-BREF, the mean score for each domain is calculated and then multiplied by 4, resulting in a score range of 4 to 20 for each of the domains, which are then transformed to the 0 to 100 scale.

Normative data for the WHOQOL-100 are available from the initial psychometric study reported in the WHOQOL Group (1998a), $n = 4802$, stratified by 15 world centres, age and sex.

Psychometric properties

The initial psychometric study on the WHOQOL-100 was reported by the WHOQOL Group (1998a) and

Box 10.16

Validity:	Content: See Scale development section
	Criterion: *Concurrent:* Bonomi et al.: WHOQOL-Global with SF-36 subscales: r = .15–.60 – predicted that 45/56 possible correlation coefficients between WHOQOL and SF-36 subscales would be significant; magnitude of 13/45 coefficients $r > .5$ – with SQLP predicted that 22/28 possible correlation coefficients between WHOQOL and SQLP subscales would be significant; magnitude of 6/22 coefficients $r > .5$
	Construct: *Internal consistency:* Cronbach alpha: facet range .65–.93; with < .8 for 8/24 facets (pain, positive feelings, thinking, body image, relationships, safety, leisure, environment)
	Bonomi et al.: healthy sample ($n = 128$): domain scores: Physical .83, Psychological .86, Independence .86, Social .82, Environment .91, Spiritual .87 – childbearing sample ($n = 64$): domain scores: Physical .85, Psychological .92, Independence .92, Social .85, Environment .94, Spiritual .90
	Factor structure: 4 factors: Physical (8 facets), Environment (8 facets), Psychological and Spiritual (4 facets), Social (4 facets)
	Convergent/divergent: Bonomi et al.: higher correlation with similar constructs (WHOQOL-Independence with SQLP-Functional: $r = .66$; WHOQOL-Social with SQLP-Social: $r = .66$); lower correlation with dissimilar constructs (WHOQOL-Independence with SQLP-Social: $r = .22$; WHOQOL-Social with SQLP-Independence: $r = .39$)
	Discriminant: significant differences between sick and healthy groups on all domains (each $p < .0001$) and 22/24 facets (each $p < .001$)

Reliability:	Inter-rater: Not applicable
	Test–retest: Bonomi et al.: 2 week: Global ICC = .83 (domains: Physical ICC = .83, Psychological ICC = .84, Independence ICC = .96, Social ICC = .88, Environment ICC = .92, Spiritual ICC = .86)
Responsiveness:	Bonomi et al.: large effect size for domains hypothesized to show improvement following childbirth: Independence $d = .91$, Physical $d = .86$, but effect sizes for remaining domains were small ($d = .1–.22$)

those for the WHOQOL-BREF by the WHOQOL Group (1998b) and Skevington, Lotfy, and O'Connell (2004). For the WHOQOL-100, the 15 field centres contributed data from 4802 people. A sampling quota was imposed to ensure that in each centre there was an even distribution of people older and younger than 45 years, an even sex distribution, and an over-representation of people with "disease or impairment" (83%). Principal components analysis (PCA) was used to examine the underlying factor structure using a split half random sample ($n = 2056$). Four factors were extracted, accounting for 58% of the variance. Confirmatory factor analysis was used to compare the fit of a single factor, the four factors identified in the PCA and the six domain structure of the scale. The four-factor solution had better comparative fit index than the other models, although it was still less than the recommended value of .9, which the authors suggested was probably compromised by the heterogeneity and size of the sample. Discriminant validity was examined by comparing the results from the "sick" ($n = 3889$) versus "healthy" ($n = 913$) subgroups.

A comprehensive psychometric study is reported by Bonomi et al. (2000), who administered the WHOQOL-100 to a number of samples, including 128 healthy adults, 64 of whom (age $M = 48.7$ years, $SD = 15.7$) completed the WHOQOL-100 on a second occasion 2 weeks later. Validating instruments were the Health Survey Short-Form 36 (SF-36) and Subjective Quality of Life Profile (SQLP). Responsiveness was examined in a sample of 64 women (age $M = 29.8$ years, $SD = 6.2$), who were assessed on two occasions 1 month before and 8 weeks following childbirth. It was hypothesized that quality of life, particularly in terms of independence and physical well-being (and to a lesser extent in the psychological, social, environmental and spiritual domains) would improve following childbirth. Results on the WHOQOL-100 from the WHOQOL Group (1998a), except where otherwise indicated, are shown in Box 10.16.

Comment

The WHOQOL is an instrument that can boast a laudable development process, within (and hence is applicable to) cross-cultural contexts. It has good psychometric properties, being internally consistent at the domain level, with evidence of content and construct validity, excellent temporal stability, and responsiveness. Concurrent validity is mixed, but this may be a function of the difficulty in having an adequate comparison measure – for example, the SF-36 is often used as a validating measure, but Huang, Wu, and Frangakis (2006) concluded that the SF-36 and WHOQOL measure different constructs (health-related quality of life versus global quality of life respectively). The availability of a 26-item short form (WHOQOL-BREF) is a distinct advantage because of the administrative burden of lengthy instruments on people who are frail, sick or impaired. At this stage, however, there is very limited information available about its application to people with ABI, and given the problems in establishing discriminant validity in ABI samples with other generic quality of life instruments, it is critical that the psychometric properties of the WHOQOL be comprehensively examined with ABI groups.

Key references

Bonomi, A. E., Patrick, D. L., Bushnell, D. M., & Martin, M. (2000). Validation of the United States' version of the World Health Organization Quality of Life (WHOQOL) instrument. *Journal of Clinical Epidemiology*, *53*, 1–12.

Chiu, W.-T., Huang, S.-J., Hwang, H.-F., Tsauo, J.-Y., Chen, C.-F., Tsai, S.-H., et al. (2006). Use of the WHOQOL-BREF for evaluating persons with traumatic brain injury. *Journal of Neurotrauma*, *23*(11), 1609–1620.

Huang, I. C., Wu, A. W., & Frangakis, C. (2006). Do the SF-36 and the WHOQOL-BREF measure the same constructs? Evidence from the Taiwan population. *Quality of Life Research*, *15*(1), 15–24.

Meldolesi, G. N., Picardi, A., Quarato, P. P., Grammaldo, L. G., Esposito, V., Mascia, A., et al. (2006). Factors associated with generic and disease-specific quality of life in temporal lobe epilepsy. *Epilepsy Research*, *69*(2), 135–146.

Skevington, S. M., Lofty, M., & O'Connell, K. A. (2004). The World Health Organization's WHOQOL-BREF quality of life assessment: Psychometric properties and results of the international field trial. A report from the WHOQOL group. *Quality of Life Research*, *13*(2), 299–310.

The WHOQOL Group. (1994a). Development of the WHOQOL: Rationale and current status. *International Journal of Mental Health*, *23*(3), 24–56.

The WHOQOL Group. (1994b). The development of the World Health Organization Quality of Life Assessment Instrument (the WHOQOL). In J. Orley & W. Kuyken (Eds.), *Quality of life assessment: International perspectives* (pp. 41–57). Berlin: Springer-Verlag.

The WHOQOL Group. (1995). The World Health Organization Quality of Life Assessment (WHOQOL): Position paper from the World Health Organization. *Social Science in Medicine*, *41*(10), 1403–1409.

The WHOQOL Group. (1998b). Development of the World Health Organization WHOQOL-BREF Quality of Life Assessment. *Psychological Medicine*, *28*, 551–558.

The WHOQOL Group. (1998a). The World Health Organization Quality of Life Assessment (WHOQOL): Development and general psychometric properties. *Social Science and Medicine*, *46*(12), 1569–1585.

World Health Organization. (1998). *WHOQOL user manual.* Available at http://www.who.int/mental_health/evidence/who_qol_user_manual_98.pdf.

WHO Quality of Life Assessment
World Health Organization (1998)

Name:	**Administered by:**	**Date:**

Instructions: This questionnaire asks how you feel about your quality of life, health, and other areas of your life.

Please answer all the questions. If you are unsure about which response to give to a question, please choose the one that appears most appropriate. This can often be your first response.

Please keep in mind your standards, hopes, pleasures and concerns.

The following set of questions ask about **how much** you have experienced certain things in the last 2 weeks, for example, positive feelings such as happiness or contentment. If you have experienced these things an extreme amount write in the number 5 in the far right **RESPONSE** column. If you have not experienced these things at all, write in the number 1 in the far right **RESPONSE** column. You should write a number in between if you wish to indicate your answer lies somewhere between "Not at all" and "Extremely". Questions refer to the last 2 weeks.

Using the following response key:

1	2	3	4	5
Not at all	A little / Slightly	A moderate amount / Moderately	Very much / Very	An extreme amount / Extremely

		RESPONSE
F1.2	Do you worry about your pain or discomfort?	______
F1.3	How difficult is it for you to handle any pain or discomfort?	______
F1.4	To what extent do you feel that (physical) pain prevents you from doing what you need to do?	______
F2.2	How easily do you get tired?	______
F2.4	How much are you bothered by fatigue?	______
F3.2	Do you have any difficulties with sleeping?	______
F3.4	How much do any sleep problems worry you?	______
F4.1	How much do you enjoy life?	______
F4.3	How positive do you feel about the future?	______
F4.4	How much do you experience positive feelings in your life?	______
F5.3	How well are you able to concentrate?	______
F6.1	How much do you value yourself?	______
F6.2	How much confidence do you have in yourself?	______
F7.2	Do you feel inhibited by your looks?	______
F7.3	Is there any part of your appearance that makes you feel uncomfortable?	______
F8.2	How worried do you feel?	______
F8.3	How much do any feelings of sadness or depression interfere with your everyday functioning?	______
F8.4	How much do any feelings of depression bother you?	______
F10.4	How much are you bothered by any limitations in performing everyday living activities?	______
F11.2	How much do you need any medication to function in your daily life?	______
F11.3	How much do you need any medical treatment to function in your daily life?	______
F11.4	To what extent does your quality of life depend on the use of medical substances or medical aids?	______
F13.1	How alone do you feel in your life?	______
F15.2	How well are your sexual needs fulfilled?	______
F15.4	Are you bothered by any difficulties in your sex life?	______
F16.1	How safe do you feel in your daily life?	______
F16.2	Do you feel you are living in a safe and secure environment?	______
F16.3	How much do you worry about your safety and security?	______
F17.1	How comfortable is the place where you live?	______

	1 Not at all	2 A little / Slightly	3 A moderate amount / Moderately	4 Very much / Very	5 An extreme amount / Extremely	**RESPONSE**
F17.4	How much do you like it where you live?					______
F18.2	Do you have financial difficulties?					______
F18.4	How much do you worry about money?					______
F19.1	How easily are you able to get good medical care?					______
F21.3	How much do you enjoy your free time?					______
F22.1	How healthy is your physical environment?					______
F22.2	How concerned are you with the noise in the area you live in?					______
F23.2	To what extent do you have problems with transport?					______
F23.4	How much do difficulties with transport restrict your life?					______

The following questions ask about **how completely** you experience or were able to do certain things in the last 2 weeks, for example, activities of daily living such as washing, dressing or eating. If you have been able to do these things completely write in the number 5 in the **RESPONSE** column. If you have not been able to do these things at all, write in the number 1 in the **RESPONSE** column. You should write in a number in between if you wish to indicate your answer lies somewhere between "Not at all" and "Completely". Questions refer to the last 2 weeks.

Using the following response key:

	1 Not at all	2 A little	3 Moderately	4 Mostly	5 Completely	**RESPONSE**
F2.1	Do you have enough energy for everyday life?					______
F7.1	Are you able to accept your bodily appearance?					______
F10.1	To what extent are you able to carry out your daily activities?					______
F10.2	To what extent do you have difficulty in performing your routine activities?					______
F11.1	How dependent are you on medications?					______
F14.1	Do you get the kind of support from others that you need?					______
F14.2	To what extent can you count on your friends when you need them?					______
F17.2	To what degree does the quality of your home meet your needs?					______
F18.1	Have you enough money to meet your needs?					______
F20.1	How available to you is the information that you need in your day-to-day life?					______
F20.2	To what extent do you have opportunities for acquiring the information that you feel you need?					______
F21.1	To what extent do you have the opportunity for leisure activities?					______
F21.2	How much are you able to relax and enjoy yourself?					______
F23.1	To what extent do you have adequate means of transport?					______

The following questions ask you to say how **satisfied, happy or good** you have felt about various aspects of your life over the last 2 weeks. For example, about your family life or the energy that you have. Decide how satisfied you are with each aspect of your life and write in the number in the far right **RESPONSE** column that best fits with how you feel about this. Questions refer to the last 2 weeks.

	1 Very dissatisfied	2 Dissatisfied	3 Neither satisfied nor dissatisfied	4 Satisfied	5 Very satisfied	**RESPONSE**
G2	How satisfied are you with the quality of your life?					______
G3	In general, how satisfied are you with your life?					______
G4	How satisfied are you with your health?					______
F2.3	How satisfied are you with the energy that you have?					______
F3.3	How satisfied are you with your sleep?					______
F5.2	How satisfied are you with your ability to learn new information?					______
F5.4	How satisfied are you with your ability to make decisions?					______

	1 Very dissatisfied	2 Dissatisfied	3 Neither satisfied nor dissatisfied	4 Satisfied	5 Very satisfied	**RESPONSE**
F6.3	How satisfied are you with yourself?					________
F6.4	How satisfied are you with your abilities?					________
F7.4	How satisfied are you with the way your body looks?					________
F10.3	How satisfied are you with your ability to perform your daily living activities?					________
F13.3	How satisfied are you with your personal relationships?					________
F15.3	How satisfied are you with your sex life?					________
F14.3	How satisfied are you with the support you get from your family?					________
F14.4	How satisfied are you with the support you get from your friends?					________
F13.4	How satisfied are you with your ability to provide for or support others?					________
F16.4	How satisfied are you with your physical safety and security?					________
F17.3	How satisfied are you with the conditions of your living place?					________
F18.3	How satisfied are you with your financial situation?					________
F19.3	How satisfied are you with your access to health services?					________
F19.4	How satisfied are you with the social care services?					________
F20.3	How satisfied are you with your opportunities for acquiring new skills?					________
F20.4	How satisfied are you with your opportunities to learn new information?					________
F21.4	How satisfied are you with the way you spend your spare time?					________
F22.3	How satisfied are you with your physical environment (e.g., pollution, climate, noise, attractiveness)?					________
F22.4	How satisfied are you with the climate of the place where you live?					________
F23.3	How satisfied are you with your transport?					________

13.2	Do you feel happy about your relationship with your family members?					________
	1 Very unhappy	2 Unhappy	3 Neither happy nor unhappy	4 Happy	5 Very happy	________

Using the following response key, please respond to the following five questions:

	1 Very poor	2 Poor	3 Neither poor nor good	4 Good	5 Very good	**RESPONSE**
G1	How would you rate your quality of life?					________
F15.1	How would you rate your sex life?					________
F3.1	How well do you sleep?					________
F5.1	How would you rate your memory?					________
F19.2	How would you rate the quality of social services available to you?					________

The following questions refer to **how often** you have felt or experienced certain things, for example the support of your family or friends or negative experiences such as feeling unsafe. If you have not experienced these things at all in the past two weeks, write in the number corresponding to "Never" (1). If you have experienced these things, decide how often and write in the appropriate number. So for example if you have experienced pain all the time in the last two weeks write in the number corresponding to "Always" (5). Questions refer to the last 2 weeks.

	1 Never	2 Seldom	3 Quite often	4 Very often	5 Always	**RESPONSE**
F1.1	How often do you suffer (physical) pain?					________
F4.2	Do you generally feel content?					________
F8.1	How often do you have negative feelings, such as blue mood, despair, anxiety, depression?					________

The following questions refer to **"work"** that you do. Work here means any major activity that you do. This includes voluntary work, studying full-time, taking care of the home, taking care of children, paid work or unpaid work. So work, as it is used here, means the activities you feel take up a major part of your time and energy. Questions refer to the last 2 weeks.

	1	2	3	4	5	
	Not at all	A little	Moderately	Mostly	Completely	**RESPONSE**
F12.1	Are you able to work?					________
F12.2	Do you feel able to carry out your duties?					________

Using the following response key, please respond to the question below:

	1	2	3	4	5	
	Very dissatisfied	Dissatisfied	Neither satisfied nor dissatisfied	Satisfied	Very satisfied	**RESPONSE**
F12.4	How satisfied are you with your capacity for work?					________

Using the following response key, please respond to the question below:

	1	2	3	4	5	
	Very poor	Poor	Neither poor nor good	Good	Very good	**RESPONSE**
F12.3	How would you rate your ability to work?					________

The next few questions ask about **how well you were able to move around,** in the last 2 weeks. This refers to your physical ability to move your body in such a way as to allow you to move about and do the things you would like to do, as well as the things that you need to do. Once again these questions refer to the last 2 weeks.

	1	2	3	4	5	
	Very poor	Poor	Neither poor nor good	Good	Very good	**RESPONSE**
F9.1	How well are you able to get around?					________

Using the following response key, please respond to the question below:

	1	2	3	4	5	
	Not at all	A little	Moderately	Mostly	Completely	**RESPONSE**
F9.3	How much do any difficulties in mobility bother you?					________
F9.4	To what extent do any difficulties in movement affect your way of life?					________

Using the following response key, please respond to the question below:

	1	2	3	4	5	
	Very dissatisfied	Dissatisfied	Neither satisfied nor dissatisfied	Satisfied	Very satisfied	**RESPONSE**
F9.2	How satisfied are you with your ability to move around?					________

The following few questions are concerned with **your personal beliefs,** and how these affect your quality of life. These questions refer to religion, spirituality and any other beliefs you may hold. Once again these questions refer to the last 2 weeks.

	1	2	3	4	5	
	Not at all	A little	A moderate amount	Very much	An extreme amount	**RESPONSE**
F24.1	Do your personal beliefs give meaning to your life?					________
F24.2	To what extent do you feel your life to be meaningful?					________
F24.3	To what extent do your personal beliefs give you the strength to face difficulties?					________
F24.4	To what extent do your personal beliefs help you to understand difficulties in life?					________

Acknowledgement: Adapted from the WHOQOL website: http://www.who.int/mental_health/evidence/who_qol_user_manual_98.pdf (last accessed 16 October 2008), reproduced with permission from the World Health Organization. Users of the WHOQOL must obtain permission from WHO to use the instrument in their studies or to translate in a language in which it is currently not available, though they can download and print the instrument for their perusal.

Appendices

Appendix A: Clinical populations for which scales were originally designed (indicated with *) and with which they have been used

Clinical population	*Scale*	*Chapter*
Acquired brain impairment (ABI):		
Dementia – specific groups (including Alzheimer's, Parkinson's, Huntington's diseases; fronto-temporal, vascular dementias)	Activities of Daily Living Questionnaire (ADLQ) *	7
	Addenbrooke's Cognitive Examination – Revised (ACE-R) *	3
	Apathy Evaluation Scale (AES)	5
	Behavioral Dyscontrol Scale (BDS)	5
	Behavioral Pathology in Alzheimer's Disease Rating Scale (BEHAVE-AD) *	5
	Behavior Rating Inventory of Executive Function (BRIEF)	5
	Blessed Information-Memory-Concentration Test (BIMCT)	3
	Bristol Activities of Daily Living Scale (BADLS)	7
	Capacity to Consent to Treatment Instrument (CCTI) *	3
	Clinical Dementia Rating (CDR) Scale *	10
	Dysexecutive Questionnaire (DEX)	4
	Everyday Memory Questionnaire (EMQ)	4
	Executive Interview (EXIT25)	4
	Fatigue Severity Scale (FSS)	5
	Frontal Assessment Battery (FAB)	4
	Frontal Behavioral Inventory (FBI) *	5
	Frontal Systems Behavior Scale (FrSBe) *	5
	Global Deterioration Scale (GDS) and Functional Assessment Staging (FAST) *	10
	Informant Questionnaire on Cognitive Decline in the Elderly (IQCODE)	3
	Instrumental Activities of Daily Living Scale (IADLS) and Physical Self-Maintenance Scale (PSMS)	7
	Katz Index of Activities of Daily Living (KIADL)	7
	Memory Compensation Questionnaire (MCQ)	4
	Memory Functioning Questionnaire (MFQ)	4
	Memory Impairment Screen (MIS) *	4
	Mini-Mental State Examination (MMSE)	3
	Montreal Cognitive Assessment (MoCA) *	3
	Neurobehavioral Rating Scale – Revised (NRS-R)	10
	Neuropsychiatric Inventory (NPI)	5
	Prospective and Retrospective Memory Questionnaire (PRMQ) *	4
	Rowland Universal Dementia Assessment Scale (RUDAS) *	3
	Severe Mini-Mental State Examination (SMMSE) *	3
	Short-Form 36 Health Survey (SF-36)	10
	Test for Severe Impairment (TSI)	3
Dementia – unspecified (including dementia screening)	Activities of Daily Living Questionnaire (ADLQ) *	7
	Blessed Information-Memory-Concentration Test (BIMCT) *	3
	Bristol Activities of Daily Living Scale (BADLS) *	7
	Clifton Assessment Procedures for the Elderly (CAPE) *	3
	Cognitive Abilities Screening Instrument (CASI) *	3
	Cohen-Mansfield Agitation Inventory (CMAI) *	5
	Dysexecutive Questionnaire (DEX) *	4
	Executive Interview (EXIT25) *	4
	Frontal Assessment Battery (FAB) *	4
	Frontal Systems Behavior Scale (FrSBe)	5
	General Practitioner Assessment of Cognition (GPCOG) *	3

Clinical population	*Scale*	*Chapter*
	Global Deterioration Scale (GDS) and Functional Assessment Staging (FAST)	10
	Harmful Behaviours Scale (HBS) *	5
	Hopkins Competency Assessment Test (HCAT)	3
	Informant Questionnaire on Cognitive Decline in the Elderly (IQCODE) *	3
	Instrumental Activities of Daily Living Scale (IADLS) and Physical Self-Maintenance Scale (PSMS)	7
	Memory Impairment Screen (MIS) *	4
	Mini-Cog *	3
	Mini-Mental State Examination (MMSE) *	3
	Mississippi Aphasia Screening Test (MAST)	4
	Montreal Cognitive Assessment (MoCA)	3
	Neurobehavioral Rating Scale – Revised (NRS-R)	10
	Neuropsychiatric Inventory (NPI) *	5
	Neuropsychology Behavior and Affect Profile (NBAP) *	5
	Rowland Universal Dementia Assessment Scale (RUDAS) *	3
	Severe Mini-Mental State Examination (SMMSE) *	3
	Telephone Interview for Cognitive Status (TICS) *	3
	Test for Severe Impairment (TSI) *	3
Hypoxia/anoxia	Agitated Behavior Scale (ABS)	5
	Apathy Evaluation Scale (AES)	5
	Awareness Questionnaire (AQ)	4
	Cognitive Log (Cog-Log)	3
	Comprehensive Levels of Consciousness Scale (CLOCS)	2
	European Brain Injury Questionnaire (EBIQ)	10
	JFK Coma Recovery Scale – Revised (CRS-R)	2
	Mayo-Portland Adaptability Inventory – 4 (MPAI-4)	10
	Mini-Mental State Examination (MMSE)	3
	Orientation Log (O-Log) *	2
	Overt Aggression Scale – Modified for Neurorehabilitation (OAS-MNR)	5
	Overt Behaviour Scale (OBS)	5
	Self-Awareness of Deficits Interview (SADI)	4
Multiple sclerosis	Ashworth Scale (AS) *	6
	Barthel Index (BI)	7
	Behavioral Dyscontrol Scale (BDS)	5
	Behavior Rating Inventory of Executive Function (BRIEF)	5
	Blessed Information-Memory-Concentration Test (BIMCT)	3
	Craig Handicap Assessment and Reporting Technique (CHART)	8
	Craig Hospital Inventory of Environmental Factors (CHIEF)	9
	Dysexecutive Questionnaire (DEX)	4
	Expanded Disability Status Scale (EDSS) *	10
	Everyday Memory Questionnaire (EMQ)	4
	Fatigue Impact Scale (FIS) *	5
	Fatigue Severity Scale (FSS) *	5
	Frontal Systems Behavior Scale (FrSBe)	5
	Functional Independence Measure (FIM)	7
	Katz Index of Activities of Daily Living (KIADL)	7
	London Handicap Scale (LHS)	8
	Memory Functioning Questionnaire (MFQ)	4
	Mini-Mental State Examination (MMSE)	3
	Neuropsychiatric Inventory (NPI)	5
	Short-Form 36 Health Survey (SF-36)	10
	World Health Organization Disability Assessment Schedule II (WHODAS II)	8
Stroke (including cerebrovascular)	Agitated Behavior Scale (ABS)	5
	Apathy Evaluation Scale (AES)	5
	Awareness Questionnaire (AQ)	4
	Barthel Index (BI)	7
	Bedside Swallowing Assessment (BSA) *	6
	Behavioral Dyscontrol Scale (BDS)	5

Clinical population	*Scale*	*Chapter*
	Berg Balance Scale (BBS)	6
	Blessed Information-Memory-Concentration Test (BIMCT)	3
	Cognitive Log (Cog-Log)	3
	Communicative Effectiveness Index (CETI) *	4
	Comprehensive Levels of Consciousness Scale (CLOCS)	2
	Craig Handicap Assessment and Reporting Technique (CHART)	8
	Dysexecutive Questionnaire (DEX) *	4
	European Brain Injury Questionnaire (EBIQ)	10
	Everyday Memory Questionnaire (EMQ)	4
	Fatigue Impact Scale (FIS)	5
	Frenchay Activities Index (FAI) *	7
	Frenchay Aphasia Screening Test (FAST) *	4
	Frontal Systems Behavior Scale (FrSBe)	5
	Fugl-Meyer Assessment (FMA) *	6
	Functional Independence Measure (FIM) *	7
	Functional Independence Measure and Functional Assessment Measure (FIM+FAM) *	7
	Functional Status Examination (FSE)	10
	Glasgow Coma Scale (GCS)	2
	Glasgow Outcome Scale (GOS)	10
	Impact on Participation and Autonomy (IPA) Questionnaire *	8
	JFK Coma Recovery Scale – Revised (CRS-R)	2
	Katz Adjustment Scale – Form R1 (KAS-R1)	5
	Katz Index of Activities of Daily Living (KIADL)	7
	Leeds Assessment Scale of Handicap (LASH) *	8
	London Handicap Scale (LHS) *	8
	Lubben Social Network Scale (LSNS)	9
	Mayo-Portland Adaptability Inventory – 4 (MPAI-4)	10
	Measure of Quality of the Environment (MQE)	9
	Medical Research Council Motor Scale (MRC-MS)	6
	Memory Impairment Screen (MIS)	4
	Mini-Mental State Examination (MMSE)	3
	Mississippi Aphasia Screening Test (MAST)	4
	Modified Rankin Scale (mRS) *	10
	Motor Assessment Scale (MAS) *	6
	Motricity Index (MI) *	6
	Neurobehavioral Rating Scale – Revised (NRS-R)	10
	Neuropsychiatric Inventory (NPI)	5
	Neuropsychology Behavior and Affect Profile (NBAP)	5
	Northwick Park Care Needs Assessment (NPCNA)	9
	Northwick Park Dependency Score (NPDS) *	7
	Nottingham Activities of Daily Living Scale (NADLS) *	7
	Nottingham Extended Activities of Daily Living (NEADL) *	7
	Nottingham Leisure Questionnaire (NLQ) *	8
	Orientation Log (O-Log) *	2
	Overt Aggression Scale – Modified for Neurorehabilitation (OAS-MNR)	5
	Overt Behaviour Scale (OBS)	5
	Patient Competency Rating Scale (PCRS)	4
	Problem Solving Inventory (PSI)	4
	Reintegration to Normal Living Index (RNL) Index *	8
	Rivermead Activities of Daily Living (RADL) *	7
	Rivermead Mobility Index (RMI) *	6
	Self-Awareness of Deficits Interview (SADI)	4
	Short-Form 36 Health Survey (SF-36)	10
	Social Support Survey (SSS)	9
	Systeme de Mesure de l'Autonomie Fonctionnelle (SMAF; English version: Functional Autonomy Measurement System)	7
	Tardieu Scale (TS)	6
	Telephone Interview for Cognitive Status (TICS)	3
	Timed Gait Pattern Function Tests	6
	Wessex Head Injury Matrix (WHIM)	2
	World Health Organization Disability Assessment Schedule II (WHODAS II)	8

Clinical population	*Scale*	*Chapter*
Traumatic brain injury	Agitated Behavior Scale (ABS) *	5
	Apathy Evaluation Scale (AES)	5
	Ashworth Scale (AS)	6
	Assessment of Living Skills and Resources (ALSAR)	7
	Awareness Questionnaire (AQ) *	4
	Barthel Index (BI)	7
	Behavioral Dyscontrol Scale (BDS)	5
	Behavior Rating Inventory of Executive Function (BRIEF)	5
	Berg Balance Scale (BBS)	6
	Blessed Information-Memory-Concentration Test (BIMCT)	3
	Care and Needs Scale (CANS) *	9
	Cognitive Failures Questionnaire (CFQ)	3
	Cognitive Log (Cog-Log)	3
	Cognitive Test for Delirium (CTD)	2
	Coma/Near Coma (C/NC) Scale	2
	Community Integration Measure (CIM)	8
	Community Integration Questionnaire (CIQ) *	8
	Community Outcome Scale (COS) *	8
	Comprehensive Assessment of Prospective Memory (CAPM)	4
	Comprehensive Levels of Consciousness Scale (CLOCS)	2
	Confusion Assessment Protocol (CAP) *	2
	Craig Handicap Assessment and Reporting Technique (CHART)	8
	Craig Hospital Inventory of Environmental Factors (CHIEF)	9
	Disability Rating Scale (DRS) *	10
	Dysexecutive Questionnaire (DEX) *	4
	European Brain Injury Questionnaire (EBIQ)	10
	Everyday Memory Questionnaire (EMQ) *	4
	Fatigue Impact Scale (FIS)	5
	Fatigue Severity Scale (FSS)	5
	Frenchay Aphasia Screening Test (FAST)	4
	Frontal Systems Behavior Scale (FrSBe)	5
	Functional Independence Measure (FIM)	7
	Functional Independence Measure and Functional Assessment Measure (FIM+FAM) *	7
	Functional Status Examination (FSE) *	10
	Galveston Orientation and Amnesia Test (GOAT) *	2
	Glasgow Coma Scale (GCS)	2
	Glasgow Outcome Scale (GOS)	10
	High-level Mobility Assessment Tool (HiMAT) *	6
	Impact on Participation and Autonomy (IPA) Questionnaire *	8
	Interpersonal Support Evaluation List (ISEL)	9
	JFK Coma Recovery Scale – Revised (CRS-R)	2
	Katz Adjustment Scale – Form R1 (KAS-R1)	5
	La Trobe Communication Questionnaire (LCQ) *	4
	Leeds Assessment Scale of Handicap (LASH) *	8
	London Handicap Scale (LHS)	8
	Lubben Social Network Scale (LSNS)	9
	Mayo-Portland Adaptability Inventory – 4 (MPAI-4)	10
	Memory Functioning Questionnaire (MFQ)	4
	Mini-Mental State Examination (MMSE)	3
	Mississippi Aphasia Screening Test (MAST)	4
	Moss Attention Rating Scale (MARS) *	4
	Neurobehavioral Functioning Inventory (NFI) *	10
	Neurobehavioral Rating Scale – Revised (NRS-R) *	10
	Neuropsychiatric Inventory (NPI)	5
	Neuropsychology Behavior and Affect Profile (NBAP)	5
	Northwick Park Care Needs Assessment (NPCNA) *	9
	Northwick Park Dependency Scale (NPDS) *	7
	Orientation Group Monitoring System (OGMS) *	2
	Orientation Log (O-Log) *	2
	Overt Aggression Scale – Modified for Neurorehabilitation (OAS-MNR)	5
	Overt Behaviour Scale (OBS)	5
	Participation Objective, Participation Subjective (POPS) *	8

Clinical population	*Scale*	*Chapter*
	Patient Competency Rating Scale (PCRS) *	4
	Post-traumatic Amnesia Questionnaire (PTAQ) *	2
	Problem Solving Inventory (PSI)	4
	Rancho Los Amigos Levels of Cognitive Functioning Scale (LCFS) *	2
	Rating Scale of Attentional Behaviour (RSAB) *	4
	Reintegration to Normal Living (RNL) Index	8
	Rivermead Activities of Daily Living (RADL)	7
	Rivermead Mobility Index (RMI)	6
	Rivermead Post Concussion Symptoms Questionnaire (RPQ) *	10
	Satisfaction with Life Scale (SWLS)	10
	Self-Awareness of Deficits Interview (SADI) *	4
	Short-Form 36 Health Survey (SF-36)	10
	Supervision Rating Scale (SRS) *	9
	Survey of Unmet Needs and Service Use (SUNSU) *	9
	Sydney Psychosocial Reintegration Scale (SPRS) *	8
	Systeme de Mesure de l'Autonomie Fonctionnelle (SMAF; English version: Functional Autonomy Measurement System)	7
	Telephone Interview for Cognitive Status (TICS)	3
	Timed Gait Pattern Function Tests	6
	Visual Analogue Scale (VAS) for Pain	6
	Wessex Head Injury Matrix (WHIM) *	2
	Western Neuro Sensory Stimulation Profile (WNSSP) *	2
	Westmead Post-traumatic Amnesia Scale (WPTAS) *	2
	World Health Organization Disability Assessment Schedule II (WHODAS II)	8
	World Health Organization Quality of Life (WHOQOL)	10
Other ABI (including impairment, rather than neurological, groups; e.g., aphasia, delirium, executive dysfunction)	Apathy Evaluation Scale (AES) *	5
	Ashworth Scale (AS) *	6
	Barthel Index (BI) *	7
	Berg Balance Scale (BBS)	6
	Clinical Dementia Rating (CDR) Scale	10
	Cognitive Log (Cog-Log) *	3
	Cognitive Test for Delirium (CTD) *	2
	Coma/Near Coma (C/NC) Scale *	2
	Communicative Effectiveness Index (CETI)	4
	Community Integration Measure (CIM)	8
	Comprehensive Levels of Consciousness Scale (CLOCS) *	2
	Confusion Assessment Method (CAM) *	2
	Delirium Rating Scale – Revised – 98 (DRS-R-98)	2
	Dysexecutive Questionnaire (DEX) *	4
	Executive Interview (EXIT25)	4
	Frenchay Aphasia Screening Test (FAST) *	4
	Frontal Assessment Battery (FAB) *	4
	Glasgow Coma Scale (GCS) *	2
	Glasgow Outcome Scale (GOS)	10
	Health of the Nation Outcome Scales (HoNOS)	10
	Hopkins Competency Assessment Test (HCAT) *	3
	JFK Coma Recovery Scale – Revised (CRS-R) *	2
	Leeds Assessment Scale of Handicap (LASH) *	8
	Mayo-Portland Adaptability Inventory – 4 (MPAI-4) *	10
	Memorial Delirium Assessment Scale (MDAS)	2
	Memory Compensation Questionnaire (MCQ)	4
	Mini-Mental State Examination (MMSE)	3
	Mississippi Aphasia Screening Test (MAST) *	4
	Overt Aggression Scale – Modified for Neurorehabilitation (OAS-MNR) *	5
	Overt Behaviour Scale (OBS) *	5
	Problem Solving Inventory (PSI)	4
	Rivermead Mobility Index (RMI)	6
	Tardieu Scale (TS)	6

Clinical population	*Scale*	*Chapter*
Other populations:		
Older people	Assessment of Living Skills and Resources (ALSAR) *	7
	Barthel Index (BI)	7
	Behavioral Dyscontrol Scale (BDS) *	5
	Berg Balance Scale (BBS) *	6
	Clifton Assessment Procedures for the Elderly (CAPE) *	3
	Cognitive Failures Questionnaire (CFQ)	3
	Cohen-Mansfield Agitation Inventory (CMAI) *	5
	Comprehensive Assessment of Prospective Memory (CAPM)*	4
	Dysexecutive Questionnaire (DEX)	4
	Executive Interview (EXIT25)	4
	Frenchay Activities Index (FAI)	7
	Harmful Behaviours Scale (HBS) *	5
	Home and Community Environment (HACE) Instrument *	9
	Informant Questionnaire on Cognitive Decline in the Elderly (IQCODE) *	3
	Instrumental Activities of Daily Living Scale (IADLS) and Physical Self-Maintenance Scale (PSMS) *	7
	Katz Index of Activities of Daily Living (KIADL) *	7
	London Handicap Scale (LHS) *	8
	Lubben Social Network Scale (LSNS)	9
	Measure of Quality of the Environment (MQE)	9
	Memory Compensation Questionnaire (MCQ) *	4
	Memory Functioning Questionnaire (MFQ)	4
	Mini-Mental State Examination (MMSE)	3
	Montreal Cognitive Assessment (MoCA)	3
	Northwick Park Care Needs Assessment (NPCNA)	9
	Prospective and Retrospective Memory Questionnaire (PRMQ) *	4
	Systeme de Mesure de l'Autonomie Fonctionnelle (SMAF; English version: Functional Autonomy Measurement System)	7
	Telephone Interview for Cognitive Status (TICS)	3
	Timed Gait Pattern Function Tests	6
	Whispered Voice Test (WVT)	6
	World Health Organization Quality of Life (WHOQOL)	10
Youth and children	Behavior Rating Inventory of Executive Function (BRIEF) *	5
	Child and Adolescent Scale of Participation (CASP) *	8
	Children's Memory Questionnaire (CMQ) * – see derivative of Everyday Memory Questionnaire (EMQ)	4
	Children's Orientation and Amnesia Test (COAT) * – see derivative of Galveston Orientation and Amnesia Test (GOAT)	2
	Functional Independence Measure for Children (WeeFIM) *	7
	Health of the Nation Outcome Scales for Children and Adolescents (HoNOSCA) * – see Health of the Nation Outcome Scales (HoNOS)	10
	Interpersonal Support Evaluation List (ISEL)	9
	King's Outcome Scale for Child Head Injury (KOSCHI) * – see derivative of Glasgow Outcome Scale (GOS)	10
	Mayo-Portland Adaptability Inventory – 4 (MPAI-4)	10
	Paediatric Glasgow Coma Scale (PGCS) * – see derivative of Glasgow Coma Scale (GCS)	2
	Westmead Post-traumatic Amnesia Scale – Child version (WPTAS-C) * – see derivative of Westmead Post-traumatic Amnesia Scale (WPTAS)	2
Generic scales used with the ABI population:		
General population	Cognitive Failures Questionnaire (CFQ) *	3
	Craig Hospital Inventory of Environmental Factors (CHIEF) *	9
	Interpersonal Support Evaluation List (ISEL) *	9
	Measure of Quality of the Environment (MQE) *	9
	Memory Functioning Questionnaire (MFQ) *	4
	Problem Solving Inventory (PSI) *	4
	San Diego Odor Identification Test (SOIT) *	6
	Satisfaction with Life Scale (SWLS) *	10

Clinical population	*Scale*	*Chapter*
	Short-Form 36 Health Survey (SF-36) *	10
	Snellen Chart *	6
	Whispered Voice Test (WVT) *	6
	World Health Organization Quality of Life (WHOQOL)	10
General medical conditions	Barthel Index (BI)	7
	Cognitive Test for Delirium (CTD) *	2
	Confusion Assessment Method (CAM) *	2
	Craig Handicap Assessment and Reporting Technique (CHART) *	8
	Craig Hospital Inventory of Environmental Factors (CHIEF) *	9
	Delirium Rating Scale – Revised – 98 (DRS-R-98) *	2
	Executive Interview (EXIT25)	4
	Functional Independence Measure (FIM) *	7
	Glasgow Coma Scale (GCS) *	2
	Home and Community Environment (HACE) Instrument *	9
	Impact on Participation and Autonomy (IPA) Questionnaire	8
	Katz Index of Activities of Daily Living (KIADL) *	7
	London Handicap Scale (LHS)	8
	McGill Pain Questionnaire (MPQ) *	6
	Medical Research Council Motor Scale (MRC-MS) *	6
	Memorial Delirium Assessment Scale (MDAS) *	2
	Orientation Log (O-Log) *	2
	Reintegration to Normal Living (RNL) Index	8
	Semmes Weinstein Monofilament (SWM) *	6
	Social Support Survey (SSS) *	9
	Systeme de Mesure de l'Autonomie Fonctionnelle (SMAF; English version: Functional Autonomy Measurement System)	7
	Timed Gait Pattern Function Tests *	6
	Visual Analogue Scale (VAS) for Pain *	6
	World Health Organization Disability Assessment Schedule II (WHODAS II) *	8
Mental health	Health of the Nation Outcome Scales (HoNOS) *	10
	Katz Adjustment Scale – Form R1 (KAS-R1) *	5

Appendix B: List of abbreviations

ABI	acquired brain impairment
ABS	Agitated Behavior Scale
ACE; ACE-R	Addenbrooke's Cognitive Examination; ~ Revised
AD	Alzheimer's disease
ADARDS	Alzheimer's Disease and Related Dementias Society
ADAS-Cog	Alzheimer Disease Assessment Scale
ADHD	attention deficit hyperactivity disorder
ADL	activities of daily living
ADLQ	Activities of Daily Living Questionnaire
ADRDA	Alzheimer's Disease and Related Disorders Association
AES	Apathy Evaluation Scale
AIHW	Australian Institute of Health and Welfare
AIREN	Association Internationale pour la Recherche et l'Enseignement en Neurosciences
ALSAR	Assessment of Living Skills and Resources
AMPS	Assessment of Motor and Process Skills
AMTS	Abbreviated Mental Test Score
APHAB	Abbreviated Profile of Hearing Aid Benefit
AQ	Awareness Questionnaire
AS	Ashworth Scale
ASD	autism spectrum disorder
BA	Binet Age
BADL	Basic Activities of Daily Living
BADLS	Bristol Activities of Daily Living Scale
BADS	Behavioural Assessment of the Dysexecutive Syndrome
BARS	Behaviour and Adjustment Rating Scale
BAS	Braintree Agitation Scale
BBS	Berg Balance Scale
BCN	Basic Care Needs
BCRS	Brief Cognitive Rating Scale
BDI	Beck Depression Inventory
BDRS	Blessed Dementia Rating Scale
BDS	Behavioral Dyscontrol Scale
BEHAVE-AD; BEHAVE-AD-FW	Behavioral Pathology in Alzheimer's Disease Rating Scale; ~ Frequency-weighted version
BI	Barthel Index
BICRO	Brain Injury Community Rehabilitation Outcomes
BIMCT	Blessed Information-Memory-Concentration Test
BNI	Barrow Neurological Institute
BNT	Boston Naming Test
BPRS	Brief Psychiatric Rating Scale
BRI	Behaviour Regulation Index
BRIEF; BRIEF-A; BRIEF-P	Behavior Rating Inventory of Executive Function (School version); ~ Adult version; ~ Preschool version
BRS	Behaviour Rating Scale
BRSD	Behaviour Rating Scale for Dementia
BSA	Bedside Swallowing Assessment
BSI	Brief Symptom Inventory
BVL	Buschke Verbal Learning
CAMCOG	Cambridge Cognitive Examination
CAMDEX	Cambridge Mental Disorder of the Elderly Examination

CAM; CAM-ICU	Confusion Assessment Method; ~ Intensive Care Unit
CANS	Care and Needs Scale
CAP	Confusion Assessment Protocol
CAPE	Clifton Assessment Procedures for the Elderly
CAPM	Comprehensive Assessment of Prospective Memory
CAS	Cognitive Assessment Scale
CASI	Cognitive Abilities Screening Instrument
CASP	Child and Adolescent Scale of Participation
CAST-R	Cognitive Assessment Screening Test – Revised
CBS	Current Behaviour Scale
CBCL	Child Behavior Checklist
CCTI	Capacity to Consent to Treatment Instrument
CDR	Clinical Dementia Rating Scale
CDT	Clock-Drawing Task
CERAD	Consortium to Establish a Registry for Alzheimer's Disease
CES-D	Center for Epidemiological Study of Depression Scale
CETI	Communicative Effectiveness Index
CFA	confirmatory factor analysis
CFFS	Child and Family Follow-up Survey
CFQ	Cognitive Failures Questionnaire
CHART	Craig Handicap Assessment and Reporting Technique
ChF	chronic fatigue
CHIEF	Craig Hospital Inventory of Environmental Factors
CIM	Community Integration Measure
CIQ	Community Integration Questionnaire
CLOCS	Comprehensive Levels of Consciousness Scale
CMAI	Cohen-Mansfield Agitation Inventory
CMQ	Children's Memory Questionnaire
C/NC	Coma/Near Coma Scale
CNS	central nervous system
COAT	Children's Orientation and Amnesia Test
COD	compared to other days
Cog-Log	Cognitive Log
COMBI	Center for Outcome Measurement in Brain Injury
COP	compared to other patients
COS	Community Outcome Scale
COWAT	Controlled Word Association Test
CR	Category Retrieval
CR	coefficient of reproducibility
CRS; CRS-R	Coma Recovery Scale; ~ Revised
CRT	choice reaction time
CS	coefficient of stability
CT	computerized tomography
CTD	Cognitive Test for Delirium
CVLT	California Verbal Learning Test
d	effect size
DCP	Disability Creation Process
DD	Depressive Disorder
DEX	Dysexecutive Questionnaire
DFA	discriminant function analysis
D-FIS	Fatigue Impact Scale – Daily Administration
DLB	dementia with Lewy bodies
DMT	Double Memory Test
DRS	Disability Rating Scale
DRS; DRS-R-98	Delirium Rating Scale; ~ Revised – 98
DS; DSB	Digit Span; ~ Backwards
DSM; DSM-III-R; DSM-IV	Diagnostic and Statistical Manual for Mental Disorders; ~ Third Edition – Revised; ~ Fourth Edition
DSS	Disability Status Scale
EADL	Extended Activities of Daily Living
E-BEHAVE-AD	Behavioural Pathology in Alzheimer's Disease Rating Scale – Empirical observation
EBIQ	European Brain Injury Questionnaire
EDSS	Expanded Disability Status Scale
EEG	electroencephalography
E-GOS	Expansion of the Glasgow Outcome Scale
EMQ	Everyday Memory Questionnaire

EP; EPR	evoked potential; evoked potential responses
EXIT25	Executive Interview
FAB	Frontal Assessment Battery
FAD	Family Assessment Device
FAI	Fatigue Assessment Instrument
FAI	Frenchay Activities Index
FAM	Functional Assessment Measure
FAST	Frenchay Aphasia Screening Test
FAST	Functional Assessment Staging
FBI	Frontal Behavioral Inventory
FCP	Functional Communication Profile
FCSRT	Free and Cued Recall Selective Reminding Test
FES	Family Environment Scale
FHT	Face–Hand Test
FIM; FIMM	Functional Independence Measure; ~ Motor
FIM+FAM	Functional Independence Measure and Functional Assessment Measure
FIS; FIS-D	Fatigue Impact Scale; ~ Daily Administration
FLD	frontal lobe dementia
FLOPS	Frontal Lobe Personality Scale
FM; FMA	Fugl-Meyer Assessment
FOUR	Full Outline of UnResponsiveness
FrSBe	Frontal Systems Behavior Scale
FSE	Functional Status Examination
FSS	Fatigue Severity Scale
FTD	Frontotemporal dementia
GCS; GCS-E	Glasgow Coma Scale; ~ Extended
GDS	Geriatric Depression Scale
GDS	Global Deterioration Scale
GEC	General Executive Composite
GHQ; GHQ-12; GHQ-28	General Health Questionnaire; ~ 12-item version; ~ 28-item version
GMHP	Grafton Manor Study Hierarchy of Placements
GOAT	Galveston Orientation and Amnesia Test
GOS; GOSE	Glasgow Outcome Scale; ~ Extended (interview) version
GPCOG	General Practitioner Assessment of Cognition
GPs	general practitioners
HACE	Home and Community Environment Instrument
HADS	Hospital Anxiety and Depression Scale
HBS	Harmful Behaviours Scale
HCAT	Hopkins Competency Assessment Test
HDRS; HRSD	Hamilton Depression Rating Scale; also known as Hamilton Rating Scale for Depression
HiMAT	High-level Mobility Assessment Tool
HoNOS; HoNOS-ABI; HoNOSCA; HoNOS 65+	Health of the Nation Outcome Scales; ~ for Acquired Brain Impairment; ~ for Children and Adolescents; ~ for older people (65+ years of age)
HPL	Health Problems List
HRSD	Hamilton Rating Scale for Depression (also see HDRS)
IADL	Instrumental Activities of Daily Living
IADLS	Instrumental Activities of Daily Living Scale
ICC	intra-class correlation coefficient
ICD-10	International Statistical Classification of Diseases and Health Related States, Tenth Revision
ICF	International Classification of Functioning, Disability and Health
ICIDH	International Classification of Impairments, Disabilities and Handicaps
IES	Impact of Events Scale
I/O	Information/Orientation
IPA	Impact on Participation and Autonomy Questionnaire
IQCODE	Informant Questionnaire on Cognitive Decline in the Elderly
ISEL	Interpersonal Support Evaluation List
ISP	Initial Subject Protocol
JFSPTAS	Julia Farr Services Post-traumatic Amnesia Scale
KAS; KAS-R1	Katz Adjustment Scale; ~ Form R1 for relatives
KIADL	Katz Index of Activities of Daily Living
KOSCHI	King's Outcome Scale for Childhood Head Injury
LASH	Leeds Assessment Scale of Handicap
LCFAS	Levels of Cognitive Functioning Assessment Scale
LCFS	(Rancho Los Amigos) Levels of Cognitive Functioning Scale
LCQ	La Trobe Communication Questionnaire
LHS	London Handicap Scale

logMAR	logarithm of the minimum angle of resolution
LS	legal standards
LS	Life Satisfaction
LSNS; LSNS-R	Lubben Social Network Scale; ~ Revised
M	mean score
MADRS	Montgomery and Asberg Depression Rating Scale
MARS	Moss Attention Rating Scale
MAS	Modified Ashworth Scale
MAS	Motor Assessment Scale
MAST	Mississippi Aphasia Screening Test
MCI	mild cognitive impairment
MCQ	Memory Compensation Questionnaire
MCS	minimally conscious state
MD	Major Depression
MDAS	Memorial Delirium Assessment Scale
MDRS	Mattis Dementia Rating Scale
MFQ	Memory Functioning Questionnaire
MI	Metacognition Index
MI	Motricity Index
MIA	Metamemory in Adulthood
mins	minutes
MIS	Memory Impairment Screen
MMPI	Minnesota Multiphasic Personality Inventory
MMSE	Mini-Mental State Examination
MMT	Manual Muscle Testing
MoCA	Montreal Cognitive Assessment
MOPTAS	Modified Oxford PTA Scale
MOS	Medical Outcomes Study
MPAI; MPAI-4; MPAI-P	Mayo-Portland Adaptability Inventory; ~ version 4; ~ Paediatric version
MPQ	McGill Pain Questionnaire
MQ	Metamemory Questionnaire
MQE	Measure of Quality of the Environment
MRC	Medical Research Council
MRI	magnetic resonance imaging
mRS	Modified Rankin Scale
MS	multiple sclerosis
MSQ	Mental Status Questionnaire
MTDDA	Minnesota Test for the Differential Diagnosis of Aphasia
mTSI	Modified Test for Severe Impairment
n	sample size
NADLS	Nottingham Activities of Daily Living Scale
NBAP	Neuropsychology Behavior and Affect Profile
NEADL	Nottingham Extended Activities of Daily Living Scale
NFI	Neurobehavioral Functioning Inventory
NHBPS	Nursing Home Behavior Problem Scale
NHP	Nottingham Health Profile
NINCDS	National Institutes of Neurological and Communicable Disorders and Stroke
NINDS	National Institute of Neurological Disorders and Stroke
NLQ	Nottingham Leisure Questionnaire
NP	neuropsychologist
NPCNA	Northwick Park Care Needs Assessment
NPDS	Northwick Park Dependency Score
NPI; NPI-Q	Neuropsychiatric Inventory; ~ Questionnaire version
NRS	Numeric Rating Scale
NRS; NRS-R	Neurobehavioral Rating Scale; ~ Revised
OARS	Older Americans Resources Scale
OAS; OAS-MNR	Overt Aggression Scale; ~ Modified for Neurorehabilitation
OBS	Overt Behaviour Scale
OGMS	Orientation Group Monitoring System
OHS	Oxford Handicap Scale
O-Log	Orientation Log
OPCS	Office of Population Censuses and Surveys Disability Scales
OT	occupational therapist theory
PAI	Portland Adaptability Inventory
PASAT	Paced Auditory Serial Addition Test
PC	Physical Classification

PCA	principal components analysis
PCRS; PCRS-NR	Patient Competency Rating Scale; ~ for Neurorehabilitation
PD	Parkinson's disease
PD	physical disability
PEDI	Pediatric Evaluation of Disability Inventory
PET	positron emission tomography
PGCS	Paediatric Glasgow Coma Scale
PO	Participation Objective
POPS	Participation Objective, Participation Subjective
PPA	primary progressive aphasia
PPI	Present Pain Intensity
PRI-T	Pain Rating Index – Total
PRMQ	Prospective and Retrospective Memory Questionnaire
PS	Participation Subjective
PS	Perceptual Speed
PSI	Problem Solving Inventory
PSMS	Physical Self-Maintenance Scale
PSQ	Problem Solving Questionnaire
PSS	Perceived Stress Scale
PT	physical therapists
PTA	post-traumatic amnesia
PTAQ	Post-traumatic Amnesia Questionnaire
PTCS	Post-traumatic Confusional State
QC	Québec Committee
QLI	Quality of Life Index
QOL	quality of life
QWB	quality of well-being
RADL	Rivermead Activities of Daily Living
RAVLT	Rey Auditory-Verbal Learning Test
RBMT; RBMT-PM	Rivermead Behavioural Memory Test; ~ Prospective Memory
RD	reading disorder
RFS	Role Functioning Scale
RIL	Record of Independent Living
RMA-GF	Rivermead Mobility Assessment – Gross Function subscale
RMI	Rivermead Mobility Index
RNL; RNLI-P	Reintegration to Normal Living Index; ~ Postal version
ROC	receiver operating characteristic
RPQ	Rivermead Post Concussion Symptoms Questionnaire
r_s	Spearman correlation
RSAB	Rating Scale of Attentional Behaviour
RSES	Rosenberg Self-Esteem Scale
RT	reaction time
RUDAS	Rowland Universal Dementia Assessment Scale
rWPTAS	Westmead Post-traumatic Amnesia Scale – Revised
SADI	Self-Awareness of Deficits Interview
SAT	Serial Addition Test
SCI	spinal cord injury
SCL	symptom checklist
SD	standard deviation
SDMT	Symbol Digit Modalities Test
SE	Standard Error
SET	Six Elements Test
SF-36; SF-36-v; SF-12; SF-36-MCS	Short-Form 36 Health Survey; ~ Veteran's version; ~ 12-item version; ~ Mental Component Summary
SIP	Sickness Impact Profile
SIS	Six-Item Screener
SLE	systemic lupus erythematosus
SMAF	Systeme de Mesure de l'Autonomie Fonctionnelle
SMMSE	Severe Mini-Mental State Examination
SMQ	Subjective Memory Questionnaire
SNN	Special Nursing Needs
SOIT	San Diego Odor Identification Test
SOMCT	Short Orientation-Memory-Concentration Test
SOPT	Self-Ordered Pointing Test
SP	speech pathologist
SPAD	Symptoms of Psychosis in Alzheimer's Disease Rating Scale

SPMSE; SPMSQ	Short Portable Mental Status Exam; also known as Short Portable Mental Status Questionnaire
SPMSQ	Short Portable Mental Status Questionnaire (also see SPMSE)
SPRS	Sydney Psychosocial Reintegration Scale
SPSS	Statistical Package for the Social Sciences
SQ	Speech Questionnaire
SQLP	Subjective Quality of Life Profile
SRS	Supervision Rating Scale
SRT	Selective Reminding Test
SRT	simple reaction time
SSS	Social Support Survey
SUNSU	Survey of Unmet Needs and Service Use
SWLS	Satisfaction with Life Scale
SWM	Semmes Weinstein Monofilament
SZS	Stover-Zeiger Scale
TBI	traumatic brain injury
TBIMS	TBI Model Systems
TIA	transient ischaemic attack
TICS; TICSm	Telephone Interview for Cognitive Status; ~ modified version
TMT; TMT-B	Trail Making Test; ~ Part B
TOTART	Toronto Test of Acute Recovery from TBI
TS	Tardieu Scale
TSI	Test for Severe Impairment
TT	Token Test
UK	United Kingdom
UPSIT	University of Pennsylvania Smell Identification Test
USA	United States of America
VAPS	Visual analogue pain scale
VAS	Visual Analogue Scale
VASC	Visual Analogue Scale for Confusion
VF	Verbal Fluency
VLOM	Verbal Fluency plus Language versus Orientation plus Memory
VS	vegetative state
WAB	Western Aphasia Battery
WAIS; WAIS-R-VIQ	Wechsler Adult Intelligence Scale; ~ Revised-Verbal IQ
WCST; WCST-PE	Wisconsin Card Sorting Test; ~ Perseverative errors
WeeFIM	Functional Independence Measure for Children
WHIM	Wessex Head Injury Matrix
WHO	World Health Organization
WHODAS II	World Health Organization Disability Assessment Schedule II
WHOQOL	World Health Organization Quality of Life
WMS-R	Wechsler Memory Scale – Revised
WNSSP	Western Neuro Sensory Stimulation Profile
WPTAS	Westmead Post-traumatic Amnesia Scale
WVT	Whispered Voice Test

Appendix C: Listing of ICF categories and codes pertinent to instruments included in the compendium

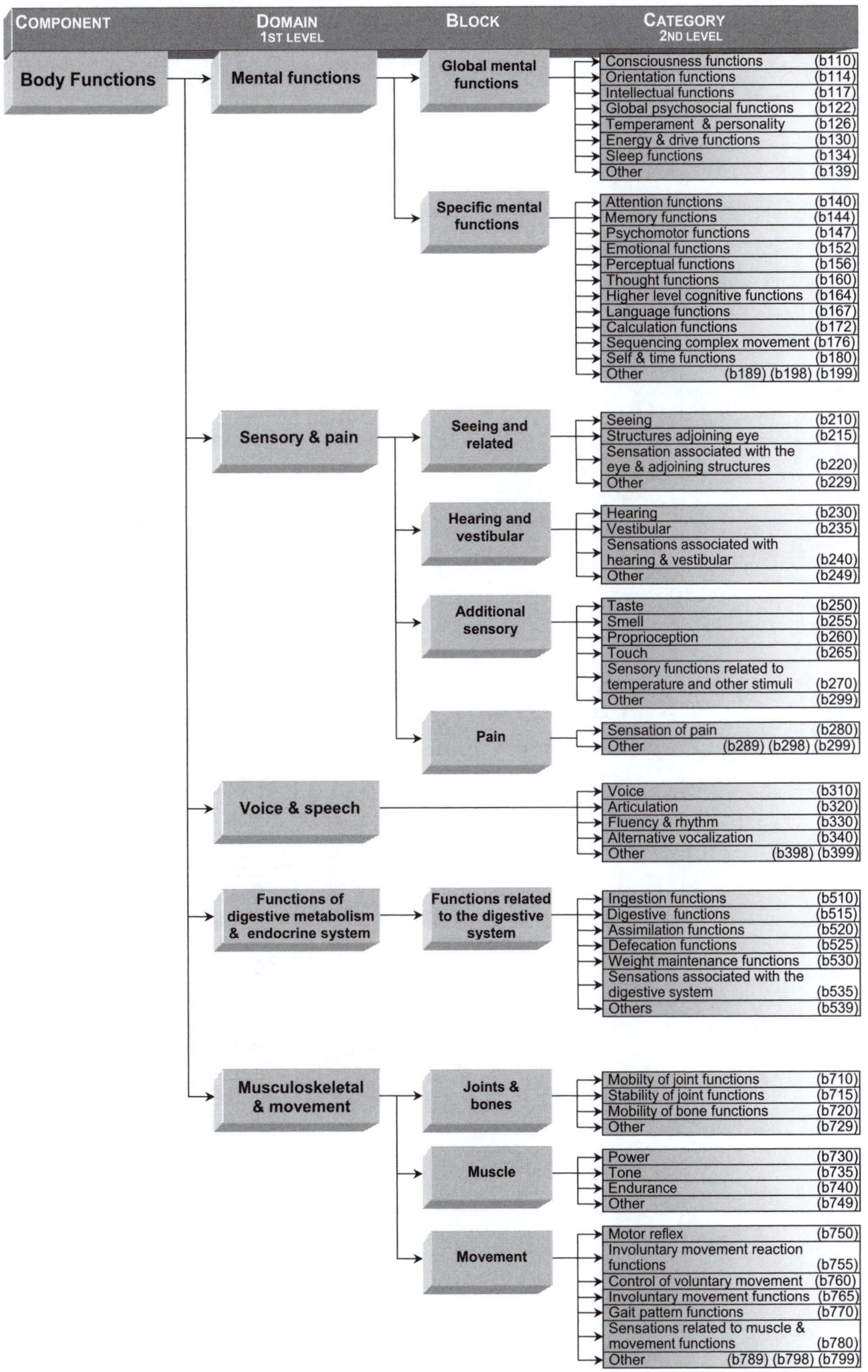

Note: Refer to the *International Classification of Functioning, Disability and Health* (WHO, 2001) for a complete listing of ICF components, domains, categories and codes.

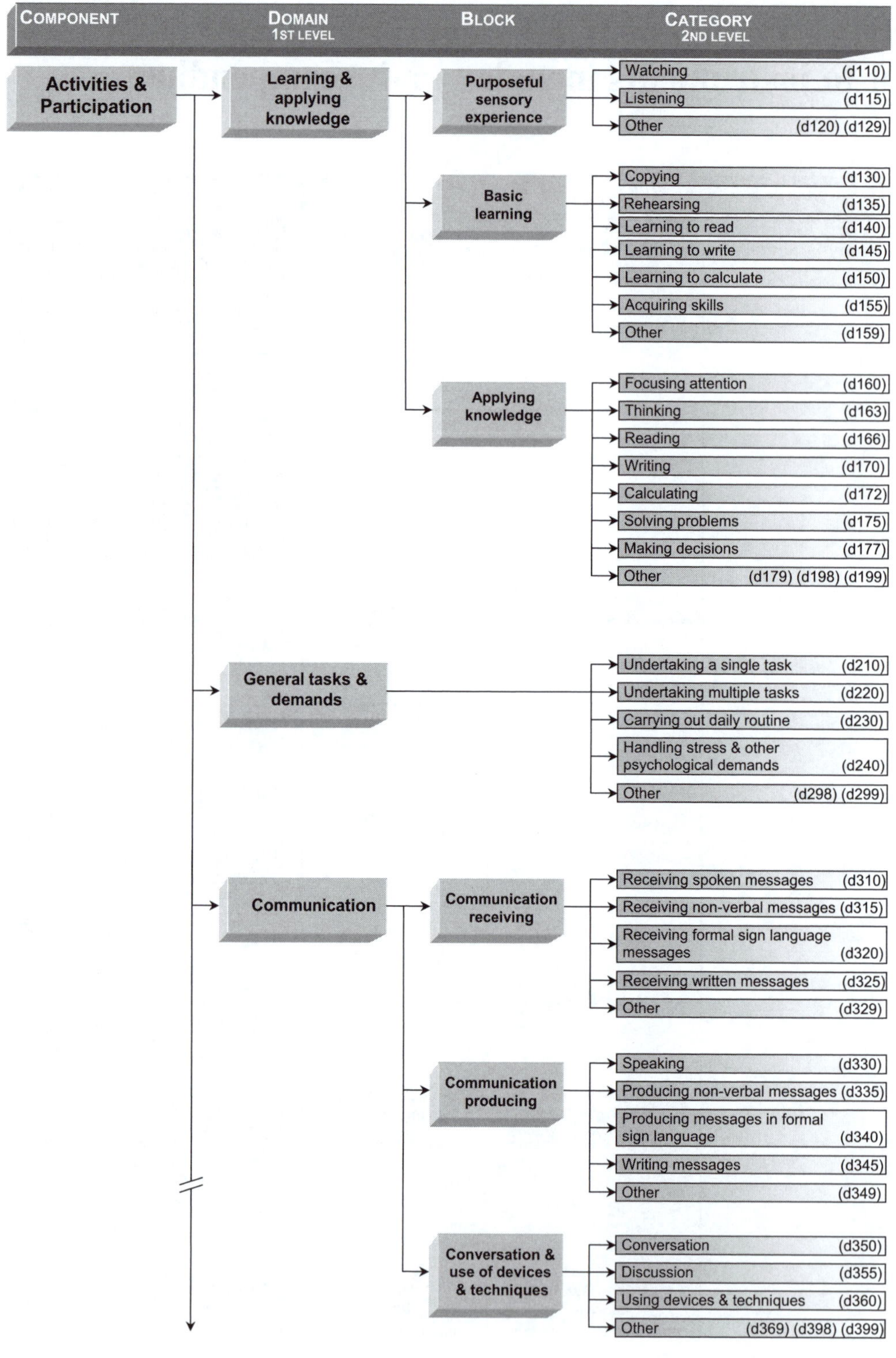
COMPONENT
DOMAIN 1ST LEVEL
BLOCK
CATEGORY 2ND LEVEL
Activities & Participation
Learning & applying knowledge
Purposeful sensory experience
Watching (d110)
Listening (d115)
Other (d120) (d129)
Basic learning
Copying (d130)
Rehearsing (d135)
Learning to read (d140)
Learning to write (d145)
Learning to calculate (d150)
Acquiring skills (d155)
Other (d159)
Applying knowledge
Focusing attention (d160)
Thinking (d163)
Reading (d166)
Writing (d170)
Calculating (d172)
Solving problems (d175)
Making decisions (d177)
Other (d179) (d198) (d199)
General tasks & demands
Undertaking a single task (d210)
Undertaking multiple tasks (d220)
Carrying out daily routine (d230)
Handling stress & other psychological demands (d240)
Other (d298) (d299)
Communication
Communication receiving
Receiving spoken messages (d310)
Receiving non-verbal messages (d315)
Receiving formal sign language messages (d320)
Receiving written messages (d325)
Other (d329)
Communication producing
Speaking (d330)
Producing non-verbal messages (d335)
Producing messages in formal sign language (d340)
Writing messages (d345)
Other (d349)
Conversation & use of devices & techniques
Conversation (d350)
Discussion (d355)
Using devices & techniques (d360)
Other (d369) (d398) (d399)

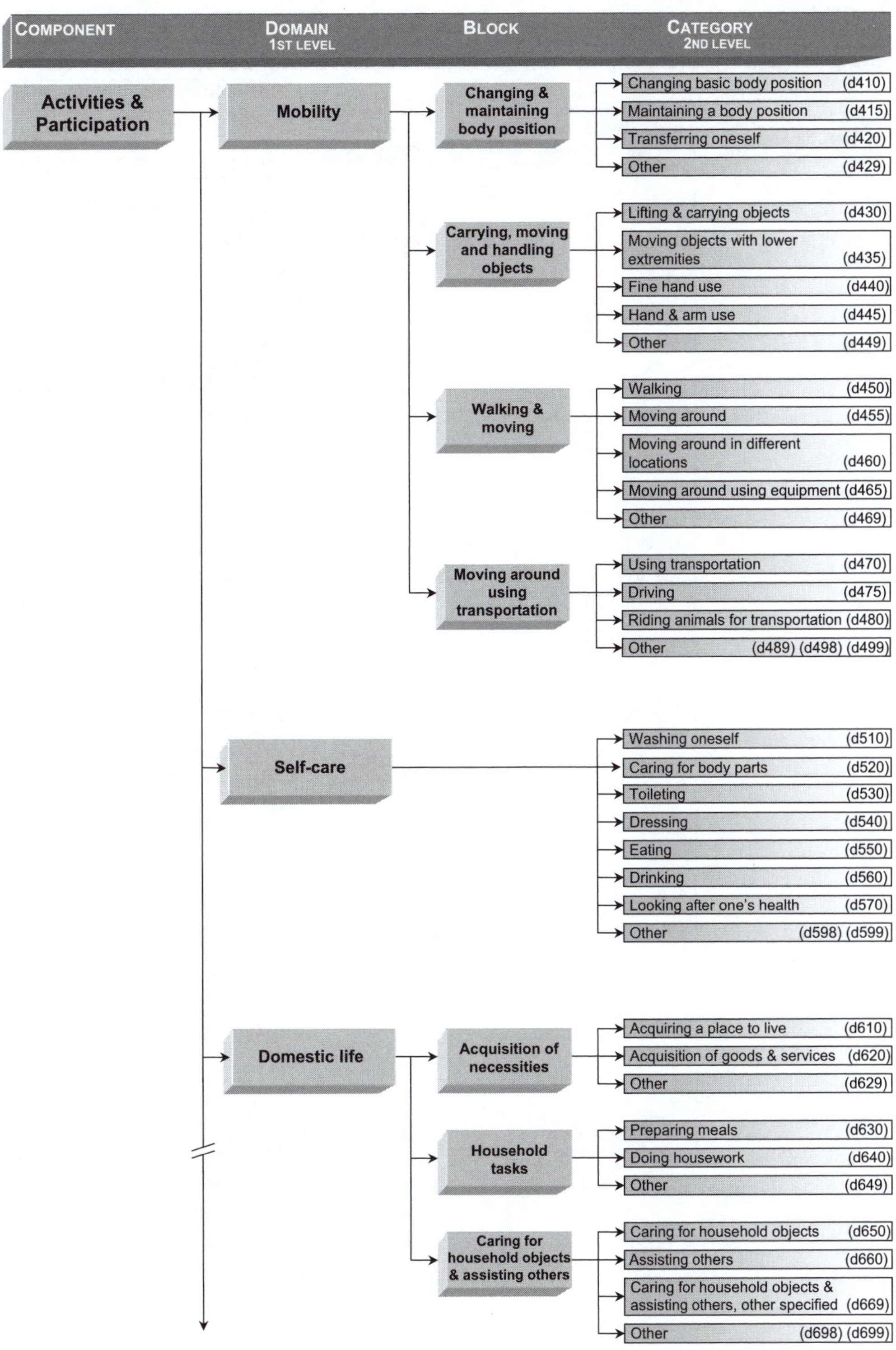
COMPONENT
DOMAIN 1ST LEVEL
BLOCK
CATEGORY 2ND LEVEL
Activities & Participation
Mobility
Changing & maintaining body position
Changing basic body position (d410)
Maintaining a body position (d415)
Transferring oneself (d420)
Other (d429)
Carrying, moving and handling objects
Lifting & carrying objects (d430)
Moving objects with lower extremities (d435)
Fine hand use (d440)
Hand & arm use (d445)
Other (d449)
Walking & moving
Walking (d450)
Moving around (d455)
Moving around in different locations (d460)
Moving around using equipment (d465)
Other (d469)
Moving around using transportation
Using transportation (d470)
Driving (d475)
Riding animals for transportation (d480)
Other (d489) (d498) (d499)
Self-care
Washing oneself (d510)
Caring for body parts (d520)
Toileting (d530)
Dressing (d540)
Eating (d550)
Drinking (d560)
Looking after one's health (d570)
Other (d598) (d599)
Domestic life
Acquisition of necessities
Acquiring a place to live (d610)
Acquisition of goods & services (d620)
Other (d629)
Household tasks
Preparing meals (d630)
Doing housework (d640)
Other (d649)
Caring for household objects & assisting others
Caring for household objects (d650)
Assisting others (d660)
Caring for household objects & assisting others, other specified (d669)
Other (d698) (d699)

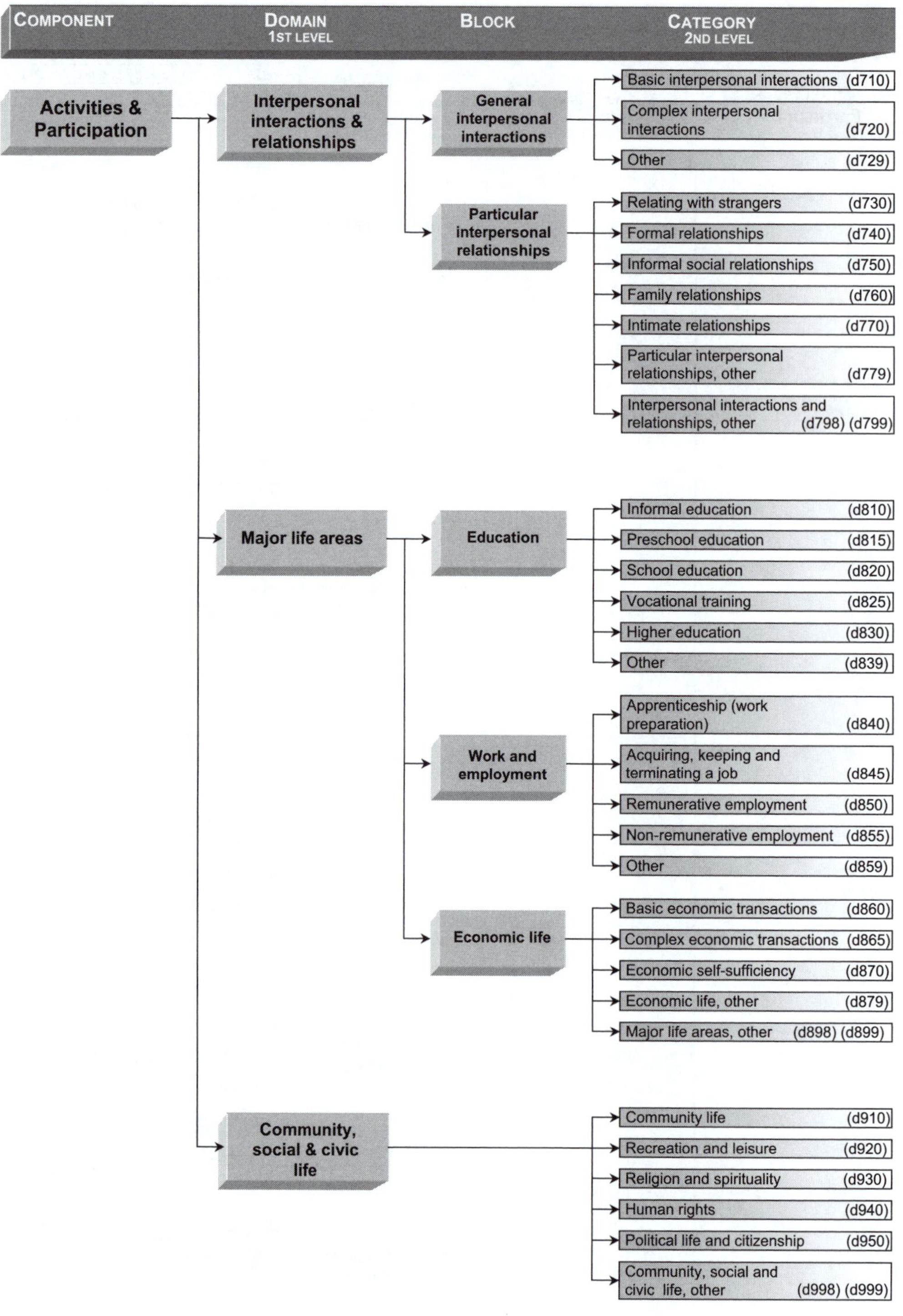
COMPONENT
DOMAIN 1ST LEVEL
BLOCK
CATEGORY 2ND LEVEL
Activities & Participation
Interpersonal interactions & relationships
General interpersonal interactions
Basic interpersonal interactions (d710)
Complex interpersonal interactions (d720)
Other (d729)
Particular interpersonal relationships
Relating with strangers (d730)
Formal relationships (d740)
Informal social relationships (d750)
Family relationships (d760)
Intimate relationships (d770)
Particular interpersonal relationships, other (d779)
Interpersonal interactions and relationships, other (d798) (d799)
Major life areas
Education
Informal education (d810)
Preschool education (d815)
School education (d820)
Vocational training (d825)
Higher education (d830)
Other (d839)
Work and employment
Apprenticeship (work preparation) (d840)
Acquiring, keeping and terminating a job (d845)
Remunerative employment (d850)
Non-remunerative employment (d855)
Other (d859)
Economic life
Basic economic transactions (d860)
Complex economic transactions (d865)
Economic self-sufficiency (d870)
Economic life, other (d879)
Major life areas, other (d898) (d899)
Community, social & civic life
Community life (d910)
Recreation and leisure (d920)
Religion and spirituality (d930)
Human rights (d940)
Political life and citizenship (d950)
Community, social and civic life, other (d998) (d999)

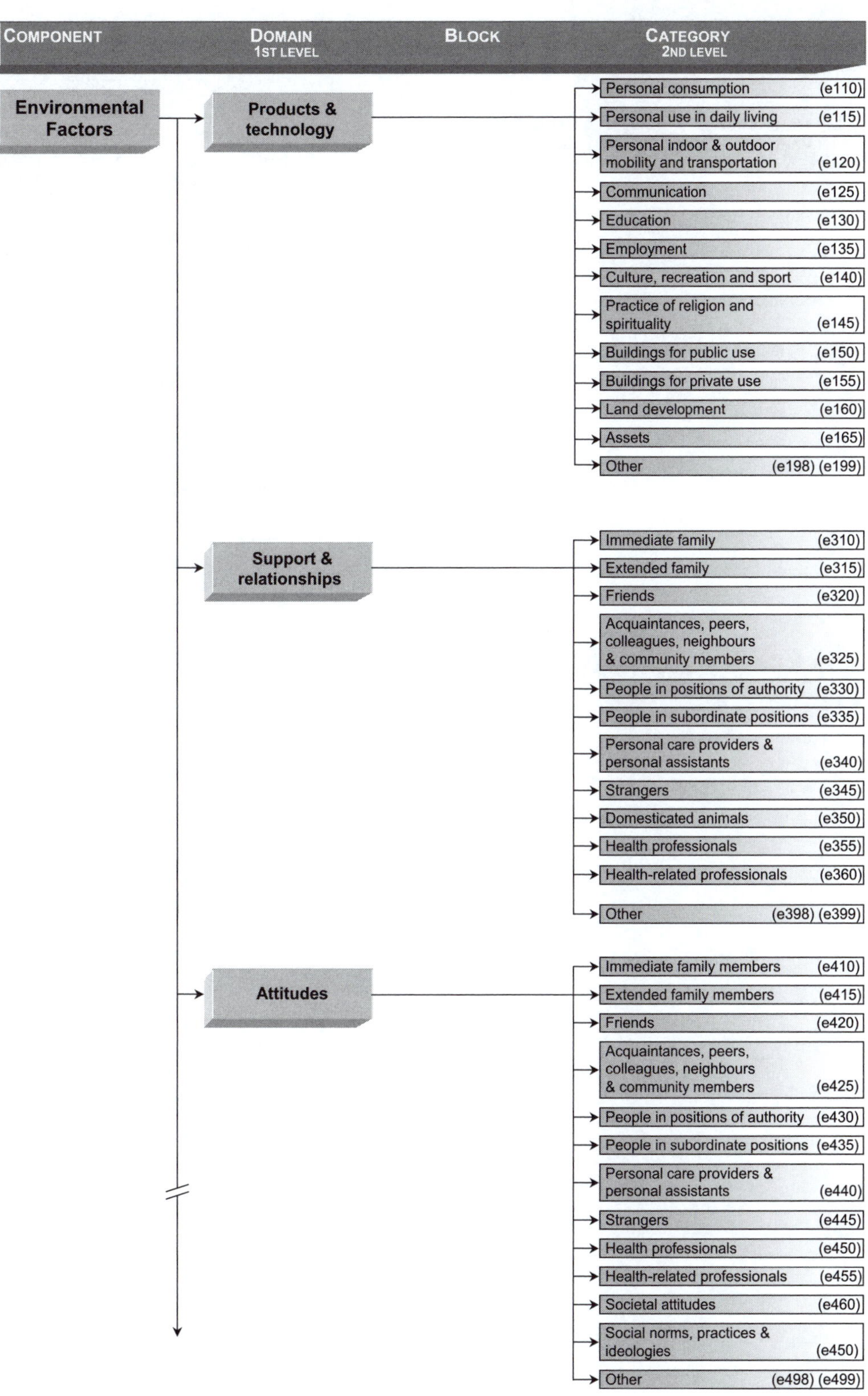
COMPONENT
DOMAIN 1ST LEVEL
BLOCK
CATEGORY 2ND LEVEL
Environmental Factors
Products & technology
Personal consumption (e110)
Personal use in daily living (e115)
Personal indoor & outdoor mobility and transportation (e120)
Communication (e125)
Education (e130)
Employment (e135)
Culture, recreation and sport (e140)
Practice of religion and spirituality (e145)
Buildings for public use (e150)
Buildings for private use (e155)
Land development (e160)
Assets (e165)
Other (e198) (e199)
Support & relationships
Immediate family (e310)
Extended family (e315)
Friends (e320)
Acquaintances, peers, colleagues, neighbours & community members (e325)
People in positions of authority (e330)
People in subordinate positions (e335)
Personal care providers & personal assistants (e340)
Strangers (e345)
Domesticated animals (e350)
Health professionals (e355)
Health-related professionals (e360)
Other (e398) (e399)
Attitudes
Immediate family members (e410)
Extended family members (e415)
Friends (e420)
Acquaintances, peers, colleagues, neighbours & community members (e425)
People in positions of authority (e430)
People in subordinate positions (e435)
Personal care providers & personal assistants (e440)
Strangers (e445)
Health professionals (e450)
Health-related professionals (e455)
Societal attitudes (e460)
Social norms, practices & ideologies (e450)
Other (e498) (e499)

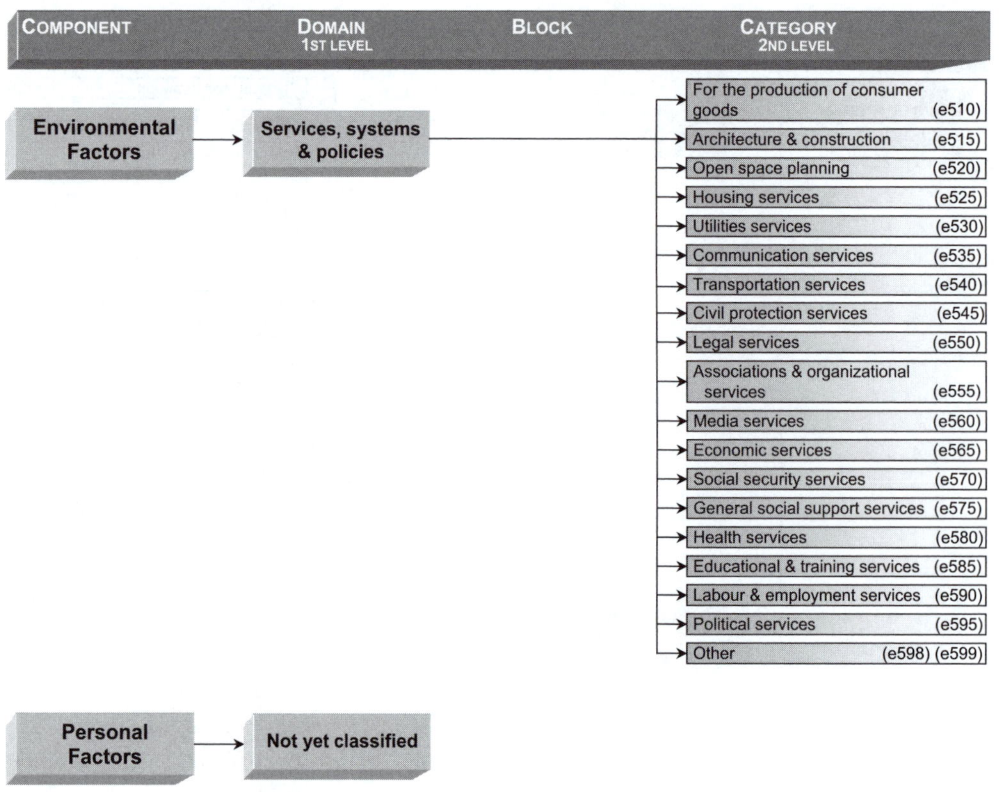

COMPONENT
DOMAIN 1ST LEVEL
BLOCK
CATEGORY 2ND LEVEL
Environmental Factors
Services, systems & policies
For the production of consumer goods (e510)
Architecture & construction (e515)
Open space planning (e520)
Housing services (e525)
Utilities services (e530)
Communication services (e535)
Transportation services (e540)
Civil protection services (e545)
Legal services (e550)
Associations & organizational services (e555)
Media services (e560)
Economic services (e565)
Social security services (e570)
General social support services (e575)
Health services (e580)
Educational & training services (e585)
Labour & employment services (e590)
Political services (e595)
Other (e598) (e599)
Personal Factors
Not yet classified

Appendix D: Items from scales of Activity/ Participation mapped to ICF domains

Scale			Body Function					Activities and Participation									Contextual Factors				Other
	Chapter	*Number of items*	*Mental functions*	*Sensory & pain*	*Voice & speech*	*Digestive, metabolic & endocrine*	*Musculoskeletal & movement*	*Learning & applying knowledge*	*General tasks & demands*	*Communication*	*Mobility*	*Self-care*	*Domestic life*	*Interpersonal interactions*	*Major life areas*	*Community, social & civic*	*Products & technology*	*Support & relationships*	*Attitudes*	*Services, systems, policies*	
ADLQ	7	28	–	–	–	–	–	2	1	3	5	6	6	–	3	2	–	–	–	–	–
ALSAR	7	11	–	–	–	–	–	1	–	1	1	1	5	–	1	1	–	–	–	–	–
BADLS	7	20	2	–	–	–	–	–	–	2	3	8	3	–	1	1	–	–	–	–	–
BI	7	10	–	–	–	–	–	–	–	–	3	7	–	–	–	–	–	–	–	–	–
CASP	8	20	–	–	–	–	–	–	1	3	4	1	2+ 0.5		3+ 0.5	5	–	–	–	–	–
CHART	8	32	–	–	–	–	–	3	–	1	9+ 0.5	0.5	3	5	4	2	–	–	–	–	4
CIM	8	10	–	–	–	–	–	–	–	–	0.33	0.33	1+ 0.33	3	1	3	–	–	–	–	1
CIQ	8	15	–	–	–	–	–	–	–	–	1	–	5	1	4	3	–	–	–	–	1
COS	8	4	–	–	–	–	–	–	–	–	1	–	–	1	1	–	–	–	1	–	4
DRS	10	8	1	1	–	–	1	–	3	–	0.33	0.33	0.33	–	1	–	–	–	–	–	–
EBIQ	10	63 (+3)	27	2	–	–	–	5	3	3	–	4	1	13	1	2	–	–	–	–	2
FAI	7	15	–	–	–	–	–	–	–	–	3	–	8	–	1	3	–	–	–	–	–
FIM / WeeFIM	7	18	–	–	–	–	–	2	–	2	5	8	–	1	–	–	–	–	–	–	–
FIM + FAM	7	30	2	–	1	1	–	5	–	2	7	9	–	1	1	–	–	–	–	–	1
FSE	10	10	–	–	–	–	–	0.2	0.2	–	2	1+ 0.2	1+ 0.2	1	1+ 0.2	1	–	–	–	–	2
GOSE	10	10	1+ 0.2	0.2	0.2	0.2	0.2	–	0.33	–	1	0.33	2× 0.33	1+ 0.5+ 0.33	1+ 0.33	0.5	–	–	–	–	–
IPA	8	39	–	–	–	–	–	–	–	–	4	5	5	10	9	3	–	–	2	–	1
KIADL	7	6	–	–	–	–	–	–	–	–	1	5	–	–	–	–	–	–	–	–	–
LASH	8	4	–	0.33	–	–	–	0.33	–	0.33	1	0.5	0.5	1	–	–	–	–	–	–	–
Lawton & Brody IADLS	7	8	–	–	–	–	–	–	–	1	1	1	4	–	1	–	–	–	–	–	–
Lawton & Brody PSMS	7	6	–	–	–	–	–	–	–	–	1	5	–	–	–	–	–	–	–	–	–
LHS	8	6	–	0.33	–	–	–	0.33	–	0.33	1	0.33	2× 0.33	1	2× 0.33	0.33	–	–	–	–	1
MPAI	10	29 (+6)	10	4	1	–	1	–	–	1	2	1	1	4	2	1	–	–	–	–	1
NADLS	7	10	–	–	–	–	–	–	–	–	3	6	1	–	–	–	–	–	–	–	–
NEADL	7	22	–	–	–	–	–	–	1	1	7	1	8	1	1	2	–	–	–	–	–
NLQ	8	30	–	–	–	–	–	2	–	–	2	–	2	1	1	22	–	–	–	–	–
NPDS	7	12	–	–	–	–	–	–	–	1	2	8	–	1	–	–	–	–	–	–	–
POPS	8	26	–	–	–	–	–	–	–	–	2	–	7	3	4	10	–	–	–	–	–
RADL	7	31	–	–	–	–	–	–	–	–	9	11	10	–	1	–	–	–	–	–	–
RNL	8	11	–	–	–	–	–	–	–	–	3	1	–	4	1	1	–	–	–	–	1
SMAF	7	29	1	2	–	–	–	2	–	3	6	9	4	1	1	–	–	–	–	–	–
SPRS	8	12	–	–	–	–	–	–	1	1	1	1	1	4	2	1	–	–	–	–	–
WHODAS II	8	36	–	–	–	–	–	4	1	2	5	3	4	5	4	2	0.25	0.25	1+ 0.25	0.25	4

Notes:

Numbers in cells refer to the number of items in a particular domain. In cases where a single item from a scale covered two, three (or more) domains, the notation 0.5, 0.33 respectively (etc.) is used. In cases of two such items, the notation "2×0.5" is used. The "Other" column refers to the number of items that address concepts not covered by the ICF.

ADLQ = Activities of Daily Living Questionnaire, *ALSAR* = Assessment of Living Skills and Resources, *BADLS* = Bristol Activities of Daily Living Scale, *BI* = Barthel Index, *CASP* = Child and Adolescent Scale of Participation, *CHART* = Craig Handicap Assessment and Reporting Technique, *CIM* = Community Integration Measure, *CIQ* = Community Integration Questionnaire, *COS* = Community Outcome Scale, *DRS* = Disability Rating Scale, *EBIQ* = European Brain Injury Questionnaire, *FAI* = Frenchay Activities Index, *FAM* = Functional Assessment Measure, *FIM* = Functional Independence Measure, *WeeFIM* = Functional Independence Measure for Children, *FSE* = Functional Status Examination, GOSE = Glasgow Outcome Scale – Extended, *IPA* = Impact on Participation and Autonomy Questionnaire, *KIADL* = Katz Index of Activities of Daily Living, *LASH* = Leeds Assessment Scale of Handicap, *Lawton & Brody IADLS* = Instrumental Activities of Daily Living Scale, *Lawton & Brody PSMS* = Physical Self-Maintenance Scale, *LHS* = London Handicap Scale, *MPAI* = Mayo-Portland Adaptability Inventory, *NADLS* = Nottingham Activities of Daily Living Scale, *NEADL* = Nottingham Extended Activities of Daily Living, *NLQ* = Nottingham Leisure Questionnaire, *NPDS* = Northwick Park Dependency Score, *POPS* = Participation Objective, Participation Subjective, *RADL* = Rivermead Activities of Daily Living, *RNL* = Reintegration to Normal Living Index, *SMAF* = Systeme de Mesure de l'Autonomie Fonctionnelle, *SPRS* = Sydney Psychosocial Reintegration Scale, *WHODAS II* = WHO Disability Assessment Schedule II

Appendix E: Item content of scales of Activity/Participation *

Scale	Chapter	# items	Feeding [1]	Bathing	Dressing [2]	Grooming [3]	Toileting / continence	Global self-care	Transfers [4]	Mobility [5]	Stairs	Transport / travel [6]	Prepare snack / drink	Prepare meal	Shopping	Housework / chores cleaning	Laundry	House/car maintenance [7]	Telephone	Medications	Money management	Family role / parenting	Global IADL	Communication	Reading / writing	Leisure / hobbies [8]	Social / behaviour [9]	Work / education [10]	Other [11]
ADLQ	7	28	1	1	1	1	1	–	–	1	–	4	–	1	1	2	1	2	1	1	2	–	–	2	2	1	1	1	–
ALSAR	7	11	–	–	–	–	–	–	–	–	–	1	–	1	1	1	1	1	1	1	1	–	–	–	1	1	–	–	–
BADLS	7	20	2	2	1	1	1	–	1	1	–	1	1	1	1	0.5	–	0.5	1	–	1	–	–	1	–	1	–	–	2
BI	7	10	1	1	1	1	3	–	1	1	1	–	–	–	–	–	–	–	–	–	–	–	–	–	–	–	–	–	–
CASP	8	20	–	–	–	–	–	1	–	3	–	1	–	–	0.5	1	–	–	–	–	0.5	–	1	3	–	1 + 0.5×4	0.5×4	3	1
CHART	8	32	–	–	–	–	–	1	–	4	–	5	–	–	–	–	–	1	–	–	2	–	1	1	–	2	6	3	6
CIM	8	10	–	–	–	–	–	0.5	–	–	–	–	–	–	–	–	–	–	–	–	–	–	0.5	–	–	1	2	1	5
CIQ	8	15	–	–	–	–	–	–	–	–	–	1	–	1	2	1	–	–	–	–	1	1	–	–	–	1	4	3	–
COS	8	4	–	–	–	–	–	–	–	1	–	–	–	–	–	–	–	–	–	–	–	–	–	–	–	–	1	1	1
DRS	10	8	1	–	–	1	1	–	–	–	–	–	–	–	–	–	–	–	–	–	–	–	–	–	–	–	–	1	4
EBIQ	10	63 (+3)	–	–	–	2	–	–	–	–	–	–	–	–	–	1	–	–	–	–	1	–	–	3	–	2	7	–	47
FAI	7	15	–	–	–	–	–	–	–	1	–	2	–	1	1	3	1	1	–	–	–	–	–	–	1	2	1	1	–
FIM / WeeFIM	7	18	1	1	2	1	3	1	3	1	1	–	–	–	–	–	–	–	–	–	–	–	–	2	–	–	1	–	2
FIM + FAM	7	30	2	1	2	1	3	–	4	1	1	1	–	–	–	–	–	–	–	–	–	–	–	3	2	–	1	1	7
FSE	10	10	–	–	–	–	–	1	–	1	–	1	–	–	–	–	–	–	–	–	–	–	1	–	–	1	1	1	3
GOSE	10	8	–	–	–	–	–	1	–	–	–	1	–	–	–	–	–	–	–	–	–	–	1	–	–	0.5	1+0.5	1	2
IPA	8	39	1	0.5×2	0.5×2	–	1	1	–	3	–	–	–	–	–	3	–	1	–	–	2	2	1	–	–	3	8	7	4
KIADL	7	6	1	1	1	–	2	–	1	–	–	–	–	–	–	–	–	–	–	–	–	–	–	–	–	–	–	–	–
LASH	8	4	–	–	–	–	–	0.5	–	0.5	–	0.5	–	–	–	–	–	–	–	–	–	–	0.5	–	–	–	1	–	1
Lawton & Brody IADLS	7	8	–	–	–	–	–	–	–	–	–	1	–	1	1	1	1	–	1	1	1	–	–	–	–	–	–	–	–
Lawton & Brody PSMS	7	6	1	1	1	1	1	–	–	1	–	–	–	–	–	–	–	–	–	–	–	–	–	–	–	–	–	–	–
LHS	8	6	–	–	–	–	–	0.5	–	0.5	–	0.5	–	–	–	–	–	–	–	–	–	–	0.5	–	–	0.5	1	0.5	2

Scale	Chapter	# items	Feeding [1]	Bathing	Dressing [2]	Grooming [3]	Toileting / continence	Global self-care	Transfers [4]	Mobility [5]	Stairs	Transport / travel [6]	Prepare snack / drink	Prepare meal	Shopping	Housework / chores cleaning	Laundry	House/car maintenance [7]	Telephone	Medications	Money management	Family role / parenting	Global IADL	Communication	Reading / writing	Leisure / hobbies [8]	Social / behaviour [9]	Work / education [10]	Other [11]
MPAI	10	29 (+6)	–	–	–	–	–	1	–	1	–	1	–	–	–	–	–	–	–	–	1	–	–	2	–	1	4	1	17
NADLS	7	10	2	–	2	1	1	–	2	1	–	–	1	–	–	–	–	–	–	–	–	–	–	–	–	–	–	–	–
NEADL	7	22	1	–	–	–	–	–	1	4	1	2	2	–	1	2	2	–	1	–	1	–	–	–	2	1	1	–	–
NLQ	8	30	–	–	–	–	–	–	–	1	–	1	–	1	1	–	–	–	–	–	–	–	–	–	2	16	7	1	–
NPDS	7	12	1	1	1	1	2	–	1	1	–	–	–	–	–	–	–	–	–	–	–	–	–	1	–	–	1	–	2
POPS	8	26	–	–	–	–	–	–	–	–	–	2	–	1	2	1	–	2	–	–	1	1	–	–	–	2	11	3	–
RADL	7	31	2	2	2	4	1	–	4	4	–	1	2	1	1	4	2	–	–	–	1	–	–	–	–	–	–	–	–
RNL	8	11	–	–	–	–	–	1	–	2	–	–	–	–	–	–	–	–	–	–	–	1	–	–	–	2	3	1	1
SMAF	7	29	1	1	2	1	3	–	1	3	1	1	–	1	1	1	1	–	1	1	1	–	–	2	–	–	1	–	5
SPRS	8	12	–	–	–	1	–	–	–	–	–	1	–	–	–	–	–	–	–	–	–	–	–	1	–	1	4	2	2
WHODAS II	8	36	1	1	1	–	–	–	1	3	–	–	–	–	–	–	–	–	–	–	–	1	4	2	–	1	6	4	11

Notes:
* Numbers in cells refer to the number of items in a particular functional category. In cases where a single item from a scale covered two functional categories, the notation 0.5 is used. In cases of two such items, the notation "2×0.5" is used. In cases where a single item from a scale covered more than two functional areas, the item was classified as "global self-care" or "global IADL", as necessary.

ADLQ = Activities of Daily Living Questionnaire, *ALSAR* = Assessment of Living Skills and Resources, *BADLS* = Bristol Activities of Daily Living Scale, *BI* = Barthel Index, *CASP* = Child and Adolescent Scale of Participation, *CHART* = Craig Handicap Assessment and Reporting Technique, *CIM* = Community Integration Measure, *CIQ* = Community Integration Questionnaire, *COS* = Community Outcome Scale, *DRS* = Disability Rating Scale, *EBIQ* = European Brain Injury Questionnaire, *FAI* = Frenchay Activities Index, *FAM* = Functional Assessment Measure, *FIM* = Functional Independence Measure, *WeeFIM* = Functional Independence Measure for Children, *FSE* = Functional Status Examination, *GOSE* = Glasgow Outcome Scale – Extended, *IPA* = Impact on Participation and Autonomy Questionnaire, *KIADL* = Katz Index of Activities of Daily Living, *LASH* = Leeds Assessment Scale of Handicap, *Lawton & Brody IADLS* = Instrumental Activities of Daily Living Scale, *Lawton & Brody PSMS* = Physical Self-Maintenance Scale, *LHS* = London Handicap Scale, *MPAI* = Mayo-Portland Adaptability Inventory, *NADLS* = Nottingham Activities of Daily Living Scale, *NEADL* = Nottingham Extended Activities of Daily Living, *NLQ* = Nottingham Leisure Questionnaire, *NPDS* = Northwick Park Dependency Score, *POPS* = Participation Objective, Participation Subjective, *RADL* = Rivermead Activities of Daily Living, *RNL* = Reintegration to Normal Living Index, *SMAF* = Systeme de Mesure de l'Autonomie Fonctionnelle, *SPRS* = Sydney Psychosocial Reintegration Scale, *WHODAS II* = WHO Disability Assessment Schedule II.

[1] Feeding: includes eating, drinking, swallowing
[2] Dressing: includes putting on/taking off prostheses
[3] Grooming: caring for body parts, including teeth, hair, nails, skin, washing face and hands (but not other body parts)
[4] Transfers: includes getting in and out of bed, bath, wheelchair, car
[5] Mobility: includes walking indoors (but not stairs), outdoors and community mobility (e.g., crossing roads; excludes transport/travel)
[6] Transport / travel: includes using public transport, driving a car, travel to and from unfamiliar places
[7] House/car maintenance: includes gardening (unless specified as a hobby and thus classified as Leisure)
[8] Leisure/hobbies: includes travelling on holidays
[9] Social/behaviour: includes social contacts, social interactions, sexual relations, challenging behaviours
[10] Work/education: includes paid and unpaid work, school, vocational training
[11] Other: items not usually classified as functional everyday activities, including cognition (with the exception of communication), emotional functioning, respect, belongingness, organizational skills, general health

Alphabetical list of scales

Indexes

Scale index

Author index

Subject index